The Americans

The History of
a People and a Nation

WINTHROP D. JORDAN
MIRIAM GREENBLATT
JOHN S. BOWES

McDougal, Littell & Company

EVANSTON, ILLINOIS
New York   Dallas   Sacramento

The Authors

Winthrop D. Jordan is a professor of history and Afro-American studies at the University of Mississippi. He holds a B.A. from Harvard, an M.A. from Clark University, and a Ph.D from Brown University. Formerly an instructor of history at Phillips Exeter Academy, Professor Jordan began teaching at the University of Mississippi in 1982. Prior to that he taught early American history for eighteen years at the University of California, Berkeley. He is the author of several books, including the highly acclaimed *White Over Black*, a study of American attitudes toward blacks from 1550 to 1812. The book won four national awards, one of which was the National Book Award.

Miriam Greenblatt is a teacher, an editor, and a nationally recognized educational consultant. A graduate of Hunter College and the University of Chicago, she has written for or contributed to more than twenty-five elementary, junior high, and high school social studies programs. She is a member of the National Council for the Social Studies, the Illinois Council for the Social Studies, and the Asia Society, and is an officer of the Committee on History in the Classroom of the American Historical Association.

John S. Bowes has taught United States history in junior and senior high schools in Boston and New York. He chaired the Social Studies Department at Bayport High School. He holds graduate degrees in American History and in Education from Boston University. He is the author of *Avenues to America's Past, Discovering Our Past: A History of the United States,* and articles in *Social Education* and *Social Studies.* He has edited and contributed to a number of social studies texts.

Special Contributors

Susan Dye Lee has taught United States history in senior high schools in Michigan and Illinois. She holds a Ph.D. in History from Northwestern University, where she also has taught United States history. An author and consultant for many educational publications, she is a member of the National Council for the Social Studies, the American Historical Association, the Organization of American Historians, and Women Historians of the Midwest.

Frances L. Hagemann is chairperson of the Social Studies Department at Corliss High School in Chicago. She holds an M.A. in History from Chicago State University. She is editor of the *Councilor,* a professional journal for Illinois social studies teachers, and has served as president of both the Illinois and Chicago Councils for the Social Studies. She also has been a member of the National Council for the Social Studies board of directors, and a member of the Curriculum Council of the Illinois State Board of Education.

Consultants

The authors and publisher wish to thank the educators who critically reviewed this book in manuscript and tested the work in their classrooms.

ETHEL CALLOWAY
Social Studies Chairperson
John Tyler High School
Tyler, Texas

CONSTANCE CASON
Edward H. White Senior High School
Jacksonville, Florida

E. EDWARD DUCKWORTH
Supervisor Social Studies
Hampton City Schools
Hampton, Virginia

ALFRED EGER
Social Studies Chairperson
and MATTHEW MANN
J. W. Sexton High School
Lansing, Michigan

DR. LYNDA C. FALKENSTEIN
School of Education
Portland State University
Portland, Oregon

JAMES HENSON
C. E. Donart High School
Stillwater, Oklahoma

DR. ARTHUR D. KALEDIN
Massachusetts Institute of Technology
Cambridge, Massachusetts

GAYLE KERNICH and
MARY THERESA MARELICH
Rio Americano High School
Sacramento, California

DOUGLAS MILLER and
MICHAEL MULVIHILL
Fremont High School
Sunnyvale, California

MARJORIE OSTENDORF
Glenbard North High School
Carol Stream, Illinois

FRANCES D. TILL
Edinburgh High School
Edinburgh, Texas

ISBN 0-86609-291-9

Acknowledgments: See page 861

Copyright © 1985 by McDougal, Littell & Company
Box 1667, Evanston, Illinois 60204
All rights reserved. Printed in the United States of America.   1985 Printing

CONTENTS

List of Maps

List of Charts and Graphs

Metric Conversion Table

Length and Distance

inches × 25 = millimeters
inches × 2.5 = centimeters
feet × 30 = centimeters
feet × 0.3 = meters
yards × 0.9 = meters
miles × 1.6 = kilometers
millimeters × 0.04 = inches
centimeters × 0.4 = inches
centimeters × 0.033 = feet
meters × 3.3 = feet
meters × 1.1 = yards
kilometers × 0.62 = miles

Surface and Area

square inches × 6.5 = square centimeters
square feet × 0.09 = square meters
square yards × 0.84 = square meters
acres × 0.4 = hectares
square miles × 2.6 = square kilometers
square centimeters × 0.16 = square inches
square meters × 11 = square feet
square meters × 1.2 = square yards
hectares × 2.5 = acres
square kilometers × 0.4 = square miles

Special Features of *The Americans*

Strong organization and a lively writing style unite in *The Americans* to form a powerful approach to the study of history. Each chapter features special elements that appeal to both students and teachers. These distinctive characteristics include the following:

1. Readable, Teachable Chapters. Each chapter follows a clear pattern:

■ THE OPENING PAGE provides (1) an overview, *Linking Past to Present*, that points out the relevance of history for today; and (2) an introduction to the *People in the Chapter* that describes significant individuals featured in the text.

■ SEVERAL LESSONS comprise each chapter, and all rely on fast-paced accounts to deepen students' understanding of our nation's history. These chronological narrative pages make history come alive by recounting stories of real people.

■ THE CHAPTER REVIEW PAGE consists of a Chapter Summary and questions especially designed to (1) promote critical thinking; (2) apply reading and social studies skills; and (3) evaluate information.

2. Consistent Unit Organization. The text comprises ten units. Each unit follows a regular pattern:

■ THE OPENING PAGES feature a large illustration that reflects the mood and spirit of that era.

■ A GLOBAL TIME LINE displays important events in American history in relation to events in other parts of the world.

■ SEVERAL CHAPTERS follow the unit opening pages and develop the main ideas of the unit.

■ THE UNIT REVIEW uses a regular questioning strategy to promote an understanding of history:

—Understanding Social Studies Concepts identifies important ideas in history, geography, economics, and government.

—Extending Map, Chart, Picture Skills provides practice in reading and analyzing maps and charts, and also encourages class discussion based on unit visuals.

—Understanding Current Events includes questions that help students relate current happenings to the past.

—Developing Effective Citizenship helps students recognize qualities important for citizens living in a democracy.

3. Unique Focus Features. Each chapter concludes with a special Focus Feature that highlights an important social studies topic in one of four areas: *American Heritage, Geography, Government, Free Enterprise.* Focus Features emphasize both present and past, and promote in-depth discussions of key subjects such as business cycles, foreign policy, justice, and world leadership. Together, narrative pages and Focus Features provide both readable history and significant detail. This powerful combination enables students to master important social studies concepts and skills.

4. Helpful Teaching Aids. These materials support the text:

■ VOCABULARY lists begin each lesson to identify special words defined in context.

■ THE GLOSSARY in the back of the text helps students understand important social studies terms.

■ CRITICAL THINKING QUESTIONS follow chronological pages, Focus Features, chapters, and units to stress comprehension and analysis.

■ MAP SKILLS appear often to emphasize geography.

■ SIGNIFICANT ILLUSTRATIONS introduce America's finest artists to promote interest and discussion.

■ THE CONSTITUTION section presents both the document and helpful annotations. This section emphasizes the living character of the Constitution by (1) identifying obsolete portions; (2) including all amendments; and (3) examining selected court cases.

5. Teacher's Resource Book. A complete range of support materials are available to supplement the text. All are part of the innovative Teacher's Resource Book, which includes:

■ A TEACHER'S MANUAL that provides specific lesson objectives and teaching suggestions.

■ STUDENT ACTIVITY SHEETS that reinforce concepts and skills for each chapter and section.

■ CHAPTER AND UNIT TESTS that help to evaluate students' mastery of basic concepts and skills.

■ COMPLETE ANSWER KEYS for all text questions and chapter and unit tests.

GLOBAL TIME LINE
to 1700

THE AMERICAS

THE OLD WORLD

1492 Columbus reaches West Indies.

1607 Jamestown founded.

1520 Spain completes conquest of Mexico.

1440 Montezuma I becomes Aztec ruler.

1535 Cartier explores St. Lawrence River.

1565 Spain founds St. Augustine.

— **1450** — **1500** — **1550** — **1600** —

1400s Renaissance in Europe leads to Age of Exploration.

1519–1522 Magellan sails around the world.

1588 England defeats Spanish Armada.

UNIT 1

Colonial Times

1620 Pilgrims land at Plymouth.

1664 England takes over New Amsterdam.

1675 King Philip's War.

1650 ——— **1700** ———

1618–1648 Thirty Years' War in Europe.

1688 Glorious Revolution in England.

1660 Monarchy restored in England.

CHAPTER 1

Migrants to a New Land

to 1600

Linking Past to Present

Scientists disagree about where the human race began. Some believe the first humans made their appearance somewhere in the Middle East. Others are equally certain that it was in Central Asia. A majority of scientists believe that humankind began somewhere in Africa. But almost all scientists agree on one thing—the human race did not begin in the Americas.

For millions of years the human family increased in numbers, perfected survival skills, and, in time, began spreading out over larger areas of the world. But although the American continents teemed with animal and plant life, no human voice was heard. No human foot trod its rich soil. America was like a vast stage waiting for the actors to appear. And then one day they did.

They came from Asia through the mountain passes of Alaska and Canada, and over thousands of years migration followed migration. Wars were waged and empires rose and fell. But the details, one historian noted, are "lost in the silence of centuries." We do, however, know, what happened to the descendants of those first immigrants. As a result of European invasions, they died by the millions and their civilizations were swept away. But in that destruction the seeds of a new and great nation were planted.

1 THE FIRST IMMIGRANTS ARRIVE

VOCABULARY   *Beringia   mastodon*

If you look at a map of the world, you will see that a narrow stretch of water separates North America from the Siberian part of the Soviet Union. This water is called the Bering Strait. It is only fifty-six miles wide, and there are two islands in it. If you sailed across, you would never be out of sight of land. The widest stretch of open sea is only twenty-six miles.

But scientists believe that when the first Americans arrived, the strait did not exist. Instead, the two continents were connected by a land bridge sometimes called Beringia. The first arrivals walked from Asia to America.

In that far distant past, the climate was quite different from what it is today. For millions of years large portions of North America were covered periodically by a series of glaciers, or ice caps, that crept south from the North Pole and then moved back to the north again. Each movement created an Ice Age that lasted for thousands of years. Each time, water was drawn up into the sky from the sea. But instead of falling back as rain, it fell onto the glaciers as snow which remained unmelted. This caused the level of the sea to drop. During those times, the land bridge of Beringia was exposed. Even now the strait is so shallow that

"We Were Here. Remember Us." That may be the message left by a pre-Columbian artist on a cliff wall in New Mexico. The human figure is surrounded by animals, which provided food and clothing. The cliff is fifteen miles outside of Taos, N.M.

First Migrations to the Americas

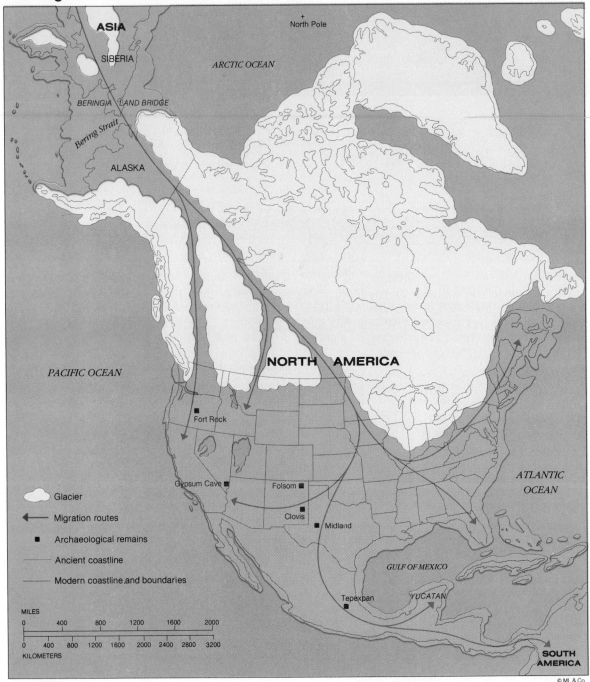

Map Skills *These routes are believed to have been followed by the first migrants to America. From what continent did the migrants come? What evidence of them has been found?*

if 120 feet of water were drawn off, the land bridge would reappear.

Scientists believe that during the latest Ice Age, the first Americans crossed the land bridge. They aren't sure quite when but it was sometime between 20,000 and 40,000 years ago.

As the glaciers retreated northward, a strip of ice-free land developed which ran from Siberia across to Alaska, along the Yukon and MacKenzie River valleys, and south into the present United

16

States. On either side of this wide corridor there loomed high glacier ice, but inside the corridor there was vegetation, fish and game. And what game!

There were giant mammoths, bison, and mastodon (a sort of shaggy elephant), as well as horses and camels. Except for the bison, these species died out in America, but the horse was brought back much later by the Spanish. These beasts provided a wealth of food and clothing, and as they wandered southward feeding on the thick vegetation, they were followed by the first human immigrants to American soil.

What They Were Like

Trying to understand people so far back in our past is like trying to see the bottom of a well with a candle. But from what evidence we now have, these early Americans were hunters and gatherers. They probably ate wild rye, choke cherries, gooseberries, and currants. They wore hides and furs, had fire, and cooked their food. But they did not have dogs. Apparently they had not domesticated the animal. Nor did they have bows and arrows. Their weapons were wooden spears tipped with sharpened stones.

As more and more people from Asia arrived, they pushed farther south. Of course this took thousands of years. Still, they fanned out into all parts of North America, and some even reached the tip of South America. The last to come over from Asia, scientists believe, were the Eskimos who today remain closest to the land bridge which now lies underwater.

When They Came

For a time scientists could only guess at the age of the few remains they found of ancient people. Then in the 1940s an accurate method of dating, using carbon 14, was discovered. Carbon is found in the air, and all living animals and plants absorb carbon 14 into their system. When they die, the carbon 14 leaves at a slow, steady, and known rate. An organism will lose about half its carbon in 6000 years. It will lose half of the rest in another 6000 years, and so on. By measuring the amount of carbon remaining in a bone, for example, scientists can get a good idea of how old the bone is. While there may be errors of a few hundred years more or less, the carbon 14 method is reasonably accurate.

Clues They Left

In 1925, near Folsom, New Mexico, a cowboy found some beautifully carved stones sharpened into points. They lay among some bleached bison bones in a dry creek bed. When scientists tested the bones with carbon 14, they learned that the Folsom points were about 9000 years old.

In 1932, near Clovis, New Mexico, fluted spear points of stone sticking in mammoth bones were found. They were dated as being about 11,000 years old. In 1952, at Fort Rock, Oregon, about a dozen spear points were found that also dated back about 11,000 years. In Gypsum Cave, Nevada, scientists found stone darts and the charcoal of a campfire that had gone out about 8500 B.C.

Although some twenty such stone and animal findings have been made in both South America and North America, there have been few findings of human remains. A possible reason is because the early Americans buried their dead on raised platforms where the bodies disintegrated into the air. In any event, in 1951 in a cave near the tip of South America scientists found some human remains which the carbon test put at about 6700 B.C. In 1949 the skeleton of a sixty-year old man was found under an old lake bed near Tepexpan, Mexico. He was named Tepexpan Man and is believed to have died about 9000 B.C. In 1953, in a sand pit near Midland, Texas, the bones of a woman about thirty years old were found. It seems that she was buried between 13,000 B.C. and 17,000 B.C., which makes her the oldest human thus far discovered in the United States.

The signs of a hunt that took place 8000 years ago near Folsom, N.M.—a spear point lying among bison bones.

The Empire Builders

While the new immigrants moved into all parts of the Western Hemisphere, those living between about latitude 25° north and latitude 15° south developed, over thousands of years, the first great civilizations in the New World. In the Old World, civilizations first developed in the warm river valleys of the Nile in Egypt, the Euphrates and Tigris in what is now Iraq, and along the Indus River valley in present-day Pakistan. In the New World, the great civilizations developed in the valley of central Mexico, in Central America, and in Peru.

In these warm, moist, and fertile lands, people no longer had to hunt and gather seeds for a living. They could settle down and farm. After a while, they built cities with huge palaces and spacious squares. They erected flat-topped pyramids that matched those of ancient Egypt and, like those in Egypt, can still be seen. On top of the pyramids they placed stone temples to their gods. Some of their roads were better constructed and more extensive than those of the Roman Empire.

Some of these societies had systems of counting and writing figures up to over a billion. Their mathematicians were the first to develop the concept of zero. Their astronomers worked out a calendar of 365 days. They could predict eclipses and chart the course of some planets.

The best known of these peoples are the Aztecs of central Mexico and the Incas of Peru. This is because they were unfortunate enough to be in the way when the Spanish explorers landed on their shores. As a result, their entire civilizations were wiped out.

Section 1 Review

COMPREHENSION   Developing Vocabulary

1. Explain these terms: Beringia, Tepexpan Man, mastodon.

COMPREHENSION   Mastering Facts

1. About when did the first immigrants reach America?
2. What sort of animals did they find in America?
3. Which group of the early immigrants came to America last?
4. What sort of weapons did the first immigrants have?

The ruins of the great Aztec city of Teotihuacan, north of Mexico City, show the remains of the main square and the temples of the sun and moon. The temples are pyramid in shape.

Some Early Groups of American Indians

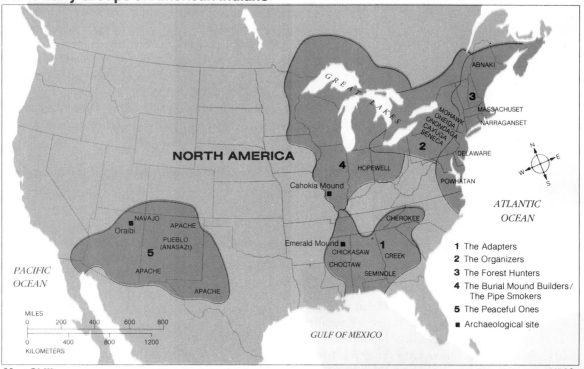

NORTH AMERICA

G R E A T   L A K E S

ABNAKI

MOHAWK
ONEIDA
ONONDAGA
CAYUGA
SENECA

MASSACHUSET

NARRAGANSET

DELAWARE

HOPEWELL

POWHATAN

Cahokia Mound ■

ATLANTIC OCEAN

NAVAJO

Oraibi ■   APACHE

PUEBLO
(ANASAZI)

CHEROKEE

5

APACHE

PACIFIC OCEAN

Emerald Mound ■

CHICKASAW   CREEK

CHOCTAW

1

SEMINOLE

APACHE

MILES
0   200   400   600   800

0   400   800   1200
KILOMETERS

GULF OF MEXICO

1 The Adapters
2 The Organizers
3 The Forest Hunters
4 The Burial Mound Builders/
   The Pipe Smokers
5 The Peaceful Ones
■ Archaeological site

© ML & Co.

Map Skills *What five principal groups of American Indians are shown? Which of the tribes was farthest north? Which archaeological site is nearest where you live?*

2 NATIVE AMERICANS SETTLE NORTH OF MEXICO

VOCABULARY   *adapted   matriarchal society   sachems   arbitrate   ratify   Anasazi   pueblos*

By about 1500 there were hundreds of tribes in the area now known as the United States and Canada. The latest population estimates range from 900,000 to 1.5 million. Some of their languages were as different from one another as English is from Chinese. For lack of a better name we will call these people Indians just as Columbus did when he thought he had reached the East Indies.

The Indian groups did not develop in total isolation. Just as the first civilizations of the Old World spread across Europe and Asia, so did the mighty Indian civilizations in Mexico, Central America, and South America influence the life of Indians thousands of miles to the north. We will describe the life of some of those tribes, particularly those whose later history was so affected by the Europeans.

The Adapters

Some of the people most influenced by the Aztec and Mayan civilizations were those in the southeastern part of the United States. They included the Cherokees, Chickasaws, Choctaws, Creeks, and Seminoles. They *adapted,* or put to their own particular use, ideas from Mexico and South America. It was easy for people and ideas to travel north from the Gulf of Mexico region. Although the people in the region lacked iron tools, they made seagoing canoes by hollowing out trees with fire and seashells and adding sails of palm leaf matting. Such boats could easily sail along the coasts of Central America and Mexico north to what is now Mississippi, Louisiana, and Florida.

The people in the Southeast built towns with open squares much like those of the Aztecs and Mayas. They did not have the same engineering ability nor as good materials. They did not erect their pyramids of stone, but of mud. Their temples on the pyramids were not of stone either, but of poles and thatch. But they did contain carved images of various gods of which the Sun was supreme just as it was for the Aztecs. Some of the Adapters'

19

This watercolor of Carolina Indians fishing was done by John White of the 1585 Roanoke Expedition.

pyramids can still be seen. One of them, which after all these centuries looks like a mound, is called Emerald Mound. Located in Mississippi, it is thirty-five feet high and covers seven acres. Inside were found pottery and drawings much like those farther south.

The people lived along the many creeks of southern rivers, which is how the Creeks got their English name. They used wooden bowls and stools and slept on platform beds—all customs that originated in the Caribbean region. They also used a Caribbean-type loom, not an upright one as used in Europe but a horizontal one staked out a few inches above the ground. On these looms they wove fibers of nettle and silk grass into what the Spanish, who were the first foreigners to see them, called as good as any thread made in Europe.

Each town was a city-state with a king, nobles, and administrative officials. The king was not a hereditary ruler but an elected one. The officials were often retired warriors with distinguished records. Some city councils met with the king every day to deal with business.

The Indians lived partly by farming. Explorer Jacques Le Moyne, writing in 1564, described their technique.

> [They] till the soil very diligently, using a kind of hoe made from fish bone fitted to wooden handles. Since the soil is light, these serve well enough to cultivate it. After the ground has been broken up and leveled, the planting is done by the women, some making holes with sticks, into which others drop seeds of beans and maize (corn).

The Southeastern Indians also lived from hunting and trading. The rivers that emptied into the Gulf were easy to navigate, so traffic from the sea into the interior, and vice versa, was common.

The Southeastern Indians had a type of *matriarchal society*—that is, one in which the women hold political, economic, and social power but usually behind the scenes. For example, Southeastern Indians counted descent through the mother. All those in a tribe who supposedly descended from

The influence of the architecture that produced the Mayan temple on the left is seen in the drawing of a reconstructed temple found in the lower Mississippi Valley.

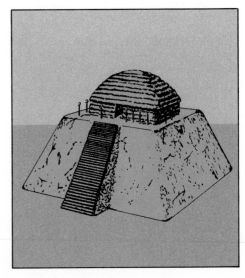

the same mother formed a clan. They were considered relatives and it was forbidden for them to marry each other. Each clan was named after some local animal such as a bear, bird, deer, or fox.

Marriages were arranged by the maternal relatives on both sides. The father had little to say about the upbringing of the children because they belonged to the mother's clan, not his. The women owned the houses and the land but they were not considered the heads of families. That position belonged to the wife's brother, who would come over to discipline his sister's children just as her husband would discipline his sister's family.

The Organizers

The Indians who are usually considered to have had the strongest, most efficient government north of Mexico were the Iroquois, or those tribes making up the League of Five Nations: the Cayuga, Mohawk, Oneida, Onondaga, and Seneca. They were also called the Iroquois Confederation. They lived in villages along rivers and lakes in what is now New York State. Their villages were protected by high log fences. Outside, the forest was cleared to make space for gardens. Inside the fence were large rectangular longhouses made of elm bark fastened on a wooden frame. The houses were partitioned to give each family a living space. Several hundred people lived in the villages, which were ruled by councils. The League itself was governed by a council of *sachems*, or chiefs. Membership on this fifty-man council was hereditary. Only males

Typical longhouses in an Iroquois village near Lake Ontario as they appeared in the early 1600s.

from certain clans in the various tribes were eligible.

The Iroquois had an even stronger matriarchal society than tribes in the Southeast. The head woman of each clan assembled all the women of the tribe and they selected the male who would succeed to the empty seat on the council of sachems. Not only did the women choose the council member; they could also depose him if they disapproved of his actions.

Property and goods were inherited through the female line. The women owned the longhouses, the garden plots, and the garden tools. Finally, in warfare, it was the women who decided which prisoners would live and which would die.

The League council had a constitution that was handed down orally from generation to generation. The League could not levy taxes and it lacked a police force. Nor could it interfere in the affairs of individual tribes. But in case of a quarrel between members of different tribes, the League would *arbitrate*, or act as judge. The tribes were pledged never to fight each other and never to commit the League to action unless there was unanimous consent by council members. But when they did go to war, the Iroquois was the most powerful and feared group in the Northeast.

The Forest Hunters

This Indian group and those with a similar language—such as the Abnaki, Delaware, the Powhatan, Narragansett, and Massachusett—were called the Algonquin because they all spoke the Algonquin language. These were the people who first came in contact with European settlers along the eastern seaboard. They introduced the settlers to corn, squash, beans, wild rice, succotash, hominy, popcorn, and persimmon bread. They also left their names on our maps with such words as Connecticut, Allegheny, and Illinois. Indeed, one historian has observed that if all Algonquin words were removed from our maps, there would be many blank spaces.

The Algonquin were also famous for *wampum*. Originally this was a string of clam and conch shell beads—usually blue or white—the Algonquin made. It had a sacred significance. But when the Europeans came with steel tools, the shell beads could be made more smooth and formed into different designs. In early colonial trade so many strings or inches of wampum were used as money.

The Algonquin birch bark canoes were so light they could be carried by one person. On the left a man fixes a leak with tree gum. On the right a family uses a canoe for shelter.

The Algonquin lived in villages of up to a hundred *wigwams* and *tepees*. The former were made of a wicker frame (interlaced small tree branches) covered with mattings of birchbark, grass, and bullrushes. Men prepared the poles and framework while women attached the mattings. Tepees were fashioned by erecting a frame of nine poles and covering it with birchbark. The door was made of tanned moosehide.

The Algonquin economy was one of forest hunters. Deer provided the main meat and fine skins for clothing. The Algonquin traveled widely in search of game, and they developed a light but sturdy canoe (often made of birchbark) for this purpose. It could be picked up easily and *portaged*, or carried, around rapids and from stream to stream.

Unlike the Iroquois, however, the Algonquin tribes were unable to unite their military efforts against a common enemy for any long period of time. Tribal frictions kept them from realizing their common danger. That is one of the reasons why they were conquered, tribe by tribe, by the European invaders.

The Burial Mound Builders

Some 2000 years ago a distinctive culture developed around the Great Lakes and between the Ohio and Mississippi Rivers. The culture is called Hopewell after the man on whose farm in Ohio some of its largest remains have been found.

The Hopewell people were characterized by the burial mounds they built and by their widespread trading empire. The mounds, which were made of earth, rose atop one another to heights of seventy and sometimes one hundred feet. Huge earthen walls were built around them. One such wall found in Ohio enclosed an area of four square miles. The mounds themselves were often shaped like serpents or birds.

Inside the burial mounds were objects that showed what an active and far-flung trade the Hopewell people had. There were ornaments made of copper from the Lake Superior region. There were knives made of *obsidian*, or black stone, from the Rocky Mountains, and alligator teeth and shells from the Gulf coast.

The Pipe Smokers

About the year 500, the Hopewell society died out, probably because of invasions from the east. These invading Algonquin-speaking people were called the Calumet. The word refers to a ceremonial pipe they used. Its bowl was usually made of red stone and its stem was ornamented with feathers. Since it was smoked to *ratify* (approve) agreements between groups, it became known as the peace pipe. It also served as a passport. Travelers who showed a peace pipe were safe from attack. One European reported, "You can march fearlessly amid enemies who even in the heat of battle lay down their arms when it is shown."

The Calumet lived around the Great Lakes and throughout much of Wisconsin and Illinois. Those near the Lakes lived by hunting and fishing. The prairie dwellers lived primarily by agriculture. To cope with the huge winter snowfalls, the Calumet invented the snowshoe. Like the Hopewell people before them, they too conducted active trade with areas as far away as the Gulf coast.

The Peaceful Ones

Some 3000 years ago, people in the southwestern part of what is now the United States were raising corn, pumpkins, and squash. They were the first people north of Mexico to do so. They lived quietly and peacefully, tending their plots of ground and adding to their diet by hunting desert deer. Some of them were called the Basketmakers because of the elaborate baskets they made from straw and reeds. Many were water-tight and were used as cooking vessels. You filled a basket with water and vegetables, and then dropped in hot rocks until the mush boiled.

Not only were the people peaceful, they were also extremely democratic. The houses of the chiefs and the religious leaders were rarely larger than anyone else's. There was no division of society into classes. There were no ambitious military or political leaders. In each settlement, four men were chosen by the inhabitants to be the ruling council. The person considered to be the best and wisest was chosen as principal leader.

An air view of the Great Serpent Mound in southern Ohio. Other mounds look like hills on which people built homes unaware of the archaeological treasures beneath them.

The life of these farmers was quite different from those farther east. There were few forests in this dry, sun-drenched land. Water had to be brought in by an elaborate system of irrigation. One irrigation network stretched about 150 miles, and parts of it can still be seen. Houses were not made of trees and bark, but earth and rock. The first homes were pit houses, dug into the ground and covered with soil. Later houses were built above ground, made of dried clay or adobe.

These people were called the *Anasazi* (ahn-eh-*sah*-zee). The name comes from the Navajo word for "the ancient ones." About the year 700 they began joining their houses together in a single building of many rooms and stories. The pit houses remained religious centers for the men. When the Spanish first saw the dwellings or apartment houses of the Anasazi, they called them *pueblos*, the Spanish word for people or town. The descendants of the Anasazi are known as the Pueblo Indians.

The best known of these giant community houses is Pueblo Bonito. It was five stories high with terraces and had more than 800 rooms, in which some 1000 people may have lived. Some of the pueblos were built right into the sides of cliffs.

When or why many of these buildings were abandoned is not known. It may have been because of a severe drought that lasted several years. Or the people may have tried to escape strangers, such as the Navaho and Apache, who were beginning to come into the area. The word *Apache* means enemy or stranger. Some pueblos were not abandoned. The pueblo of Oraibi (or-*eye*-bee), in Arizona, is said to be the oldest continually inhabited town in the United States. People have been living there since about 1300.

Section 2 Review

COMPREHENSION Developing Vocabulary

1. Explain these terms: adapted, matriarchal society, sachems, arbitrate, portaged, obsidian, ratify, Anasazi, pueblos.

COMPREHENSION Mastering Facts

1. Who owned property among the Adapters?
2. Why were the Iroquois the most powerful group in the Northeast?
3. What was found inside the burial mounds of the Hopewell people?
4. Why are the Indians in the Southwest called Pueblo Indians?

In Chaco Canyon, N.M., hundreds of great houses lined a flowing stream—now dry. In the foreground: ruins of a ''kiva'', a ceremonial room for important occasions.

VOCABULARY *Tierra Tenochtitlan conquistadors*

Who were the first Europeans to step onto American soil? And where and when did they do so? We will probably never know. The first persons who landed in America probably came by accident and almost certainly did not know where they were.

Early Visits

Fishermen from Ireland or from Scandinavia—Norwegians, Swedes, and Danes—may have been blown off course and later returned home to tell how they hovered off a "strange coast" for a day or two. They may even have spent time on shore exploring or looking for food and water. But such events apparently made little impression either on the voyagers or the people they told about it, for they never entered recorded history. Later, some landings became historical facts.

If you look at a map, you can see a series of island stepping-stones from northern Europe to Newfoundland and Labrador. The waters around these islands are cold and stormy. But that did not stop the Norsemen, who were hardy sailors. The Norwegian Eric the Red established two colonies on Greenland about 985.

Eric's son, Leif, voyaged farther west to a place he called Vineland because of its abundant grapes. Historians now believe that present-day Newfoundland is Leif Erikson's Vineland. In 1962, a half-burned timbered house of Norse design was found there; it was estimated to have caught fire about the year 1000. There is other scientific evidence that there may have been several landings by the Norsemen about that time in Newfoundland. But discovering a new land did not hold the same attraction it would later on. People were not interested in settling new continents. Who would want to go there? And why?

The Age of Discovery Begins

By the 1400s things were quite different. Europe was no longer what it had been in the year 1000. New ideas and habits had taken hold. There was a growing curiosity about the world outside Europe. From 1096 until 1272, thousands of European men and some women had traveled to the Middle East to help fight the Crusades. They had brought back wondrous tales of luxury items, such as spices, perfumes, drugs, silks, china, and glassware. Then Marco Polo wrote about his voyages (1271 to 1295) to the court of the Great Khan in China, where such luxuries were almost commonplace. People began to desire these items, particularly certain spices—cinnamon, cloves, and nutmeg. Spices were used especially to improve the taste of meat which, in the absence of refrigeration, was often partially spoiled when eaten.

It was not easy to bring goods from Asia to Europe. Trade routes were slow, expensive, and dangerous. The goods had to travel overland through Asia or by sea to India or the Middle East. Then they had to be transferred from ships to land transportation. Taxes and bribes had to be paid to townspeople and local rulers before the goods were allowed to pass. Handling charges had to be paid to shift them from ship to shore and again onto a caravan heading west. Consequently, Western merchants and rulers began to search for a faster and easier route to the treasures of the Far East.

The Portuguese. Portugal, at the west end of Europe and facing the Atlantic, did more than all other European countries combined to enlarge Europe's knowledge of the world. From the harbor of Lisbon, ships sailed to places never heard of—or even imagined—by Europeans.

Prince Henry of Portugal was so fascinated by exploration that he became known as "the Navigator." He established schools of seamanship and navigation throughout Portugal. The Portuguese invented a vessel with a sail that permitted ships to go against the wind. They also developed celestial navigation, which enabled them to tell their latitude by measuring the height of the sun and the North Star from the horizon. Between 1451 and 1470, Henry's captains discovered all the islands of the Azores. Some Portuguese may have sailed to Newfoundland and in 1500 a group of Portuguese fishermen made a northern landfall. The one who saw it first was a former farmer (*lavrador* in Portuguese), so, the land was named Tierra de Lavrador. It is still known in English as the land of Labrador.

By the time of Prince Henry's death, his ships had opened up the west coast of Africa with trade in gold, slaves, pepper, and ivory. And his captains were gaining world glory.

Early World Voyages of Discovery and Exploration   1271–1580

AUSTRALIA

MOLUCCAS

PHILIPPINES

Guam

30°S

0°

180°

150°E

120°E

90°E

60°E

30°E

DRAKE (1577-80)

INDIAN OCEAN

30°N

JAPAN

CHINA

Calicut

INDIA

POLO

(1271-95)

60°N

ASIA

150°W

North Pole

PACIFIC OCEAN

EUROPE

Venice

ENGLAND

Plymouth

AFRICA

30°E

60°N

NORTH AMERICA

PORTUGAL

Lisbon

SPAIN

Sanlúcar

Cape of
Good Hope

120°W

AZORES

DÍAZ (1487)

CAPE VERDE IS.

DA GAMA (1497-98)

ATLANTIC

0° Equator

Callao

SOUTH AMERICA

Rio de Janeiro

OCEAN

0°

30°N

MAGELLAN (1519-21)

Valparaiso

30°S

Rio de la Plata

San Julián

90°W

Strait of Magellan

Cape Horn

60°S

60°W

30°W

Polo (1271-95)
Díaz (1487)
Da Gama (1497-98)
Magellan (1519-21)
Drake (1577-80)

© ML & Co

Map Skills *Europeans were looking for ways to bring back the riches of Asia. Which expeditions went around the world? Which ones left from England? Spain? Portugal? Italy?*

26

Bartholomew Diaz rounded the cape of Africa in 1488, and Vasco da Gama reached India in 1498. Now the Portuguese could sail directly to the Far East. Since they no longer had to shift cargoes from land to water, as other countries did, Portuguese costs fell and their profits rose. Other countries could not compete with Portugal. The influence of ports along the old trade routes, such as Venice and Constantinople, began to decline. Power within Europe shifted westward.

Christopher Columbus. When Diaz sailed triumphantly into the port of Lisbon, one of the many people waiting to see him was Christopher Columbus, an Italian in the service of Spain. It was his view that an even faster way to the East was to sail in the opposite direction.

Columbus had spent years trying to find backers who believed that the closest route to the Indies could be found by sailing directly west from Spain's Canary Islands. The actual distance by air from the Canaries westward to, say, Japan is about 13,000 miles. But Columbus thought the globe was much smaller and that the distance to Japan was only about 3000 miles. And of course neither he nor anyone else had any idea that a continent or two—and the Pacific Ocean—lay between Europe and the Far East.

In 1492, Columbus finally found a backer. Queen Isabella of Castille helped him get three ships: the *Santa Maria*, the *Nina*, and the *Pinta*. Once he got to Asia, his task was to make contact with the Great Khan and establish trading posts.

Crewed by local men and boys, the expedition set out from Palos, Spain. First, Columbus stopped at the Canary Islands. Then on September 6, 1492, the ships headed west on one of the world's most important voyages of discovery. A month and some twenty-six hundred miles later, the sailors began complaining. They were bored and sometimes frightened. In their time, many people still believed in sea monsters. Some people still insisted that the world was flat and that it was possible to sail over the edge. But Columbus assured his men that the journey was nearly over and that God was guiding them accurately.

At two o'clock on the morning of October 12, the lookout of the *Pinta* saw a white cliff shining in the moonlight. He shouted *"Tierra!"* (land). It was the island now called San Salvador, in the Bahamas. Later Columbus set up trading posts in Hispaniola (Haiti) and Cuba. He was convinced these islands lay just off the coast of Asia.

The Spanish court backed Columbus in three additional expeditions, during which he explored the Caribbean area. He found no bejeweled officials of the Great Khan, and little gold or silver. In 1504 he returned to Spain; in 1506 he died.

In the meantime, so hot had the competition in discovery become, that Portugal and Spain appealed to the pope. By the Treaty of Tordesillas (tor-day-*see*-us) in 1494, he divided the world. All land found more than 370 leagues (about 1000 miles) west of the Cape Verde Islands would belong to Spain. All new-found land east of the dividing line would belong to Portugal. (That is how Portugal acquired Brazil.) Other European coun-

This scene, painted long after the event, reflects the importance of Columbus's achievement. He takes possession of the land in the name of the crown of Castille.

Early Voyages to the Americas 1000–1610

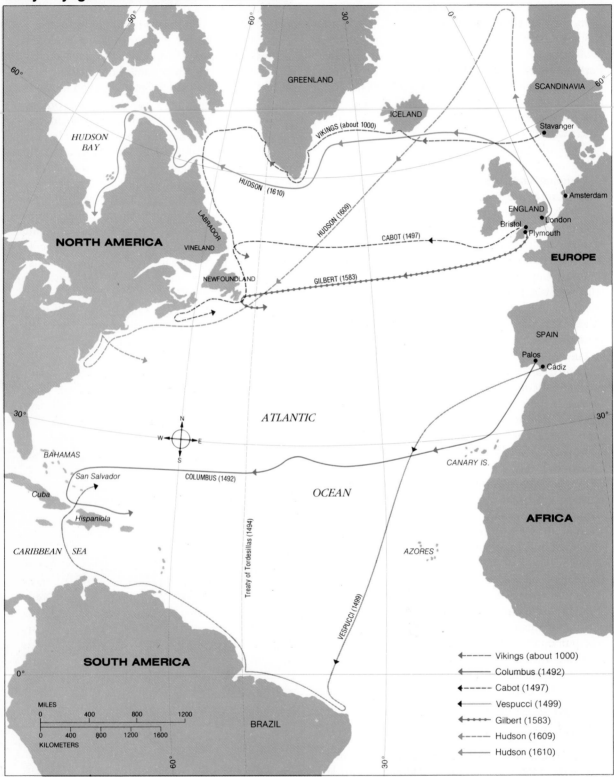

Vikings (about 1000)
Columbus (1492)
Cabot (1497)
Vespucci (1499)
Gilbert (1583)
Hudson (1609)
Hudson (1610)

Map Skills   *Which of the voyages shown reached present U.S. territory? The territory of what modern country was reached by Columbus in 1492? About how far was it from Spain?*

tries paid little attention to the pope's division, however, and began taking over whatever land they thought they could hold.

Ferdinand Magellan.

Ferdinand Magellan. Some eighteen years after Columbus's voyages, another Portuguese navigator proved what some people suspected. It was not possible to sail directly west from Europe to the treasures of the Far East.

In 1519 Ferdinand Magellan set out with 280 men and five ships to sail around the world. He sailed west and south through the South Atlantic Ocean, around the tip of South America through a strait that still bears his name, then north and west across the Pacific. In the Philippine Islands he was killed in a fight helping one local prince against another. Four of his ships were destroyed in storms, and most of his men died from disease and accidents. But miraculously, later, on September 8, 1522, the bedraggled *Victoria*, the only remaining ship, bearing 31 survivors of the original 280 men, sailed into the harbor of Sanlucar de Barrameda from which they had sailed three years before.

Europeans now knew that a huge land mass lay to the west between Europe and Asia. To get to China, people would have to go around it, as Magellan had done, or find a way across it. Perhaps there was a water passage from the Atlantic northwest to the Pacific. So began the dream of the Northwest Passage.

Surprisingly, the new world was not named for Columbus. It was named for another Italian, a geographer and banker from Florence called Amerigo Vespucci (ves-*poo*-chee). In 1499 he made a voyage along the coast of Brazil, following it with a second voyage in 1501. When he returned to Europe, he voiced the opinion that he had been looking, not at the Far East, but at a new continent which "it is proper to call a new world." A German publisher was so excited by the phrase that when he put out a world map in 1507, he labeled the continent America.

The Spanish: Exploring and Exploiting

Columbus died before his great discoveries were recognized for what they were. But it was not long before Spain was energetically exploring, colonizing, and plundering the New World.

The Conquests of Mexico and Peru. In 1519 the Spanish governor of Cuba wanted to establish a trading post on the Mexican coast. The local Mexican authorities seemed reluctant, so Hernando Cortes (kor-*tes*) landed in Mexico near Vera Cruz with 533 men and sixteen horses. They fought their way up 7300 feet to the Valley of Mexico. There, on an island in a large lake, they came upon the Aztec capital of Tenochtitlan (tay-nahch-tee-*tlahn*), now known as Mexico City. They defeated the Emperor Montezuma and sacked his city. Within a year Spain was the supreme ruler of Mexico.

One reason the Spanish were so successful was that they had guns while the Indians had none. Another reason was that Indians died from diseases the explorers brought with them. The Indians had no experience with smallpox or such childhood diseases as measles and whooping cough. When the Spanish brought Old World germs to the New World, Indians died by the millions. Fifty years after the Spanish invasion, the population of Mexico was reduced to one-tenth of what it had been.

Even so, the energy, greed, and sheer physical strength of these *conquistadors* (conquerors) of Spain was astounding. By 1533 Francisco Pizarro (fran-*sis*-ko pe-*zah*-ro) had invaded Peru, scaled the mighty Andes, and conquered the Inca empire and its great silver mines. New Granada (present-day Colombia) was also taken.

Expeditions Northward. In quick succession, expeditions in search of treasure were dispatched north from Mexico. In 1528 Panfilo de Narvaez (pan-*feel*-oh de nar-*vah*-es) led a party from Florida west along the Gulf coast. Most of his men were lost in a storm off Texas. The survivors—Cabeza de Vaca (ka-*bay*-sah de *va*-ka), two other Spaniards, and a black man named Esteban—spent about seven years wandering around New Mexico, Arizona, Texas, and possibly California. They were the objects of great curiosity, particularly Esteban, whose dark skin amazed many of the people they met. Eventually they found their way back to Mexico with wild tales about "hunchback cows" (buffalo) and people who lived in multistoried buildings. Perhaps it was the brown cliff houses of the Pueblo Indians that gave rise to the legend about the seven cities of gold called Cibola (see-*boh*-lah). In 1539 Hernando de Soto, formerly a captain under Pizarro, landed at Tampa Bay and

Spanish Exploration of North America 1513–1605

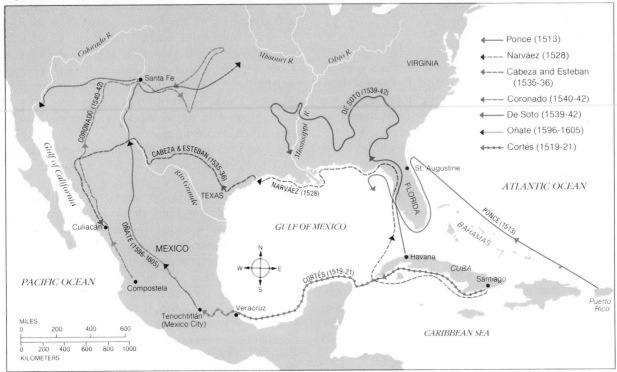

Legend:
- Ponce (1513)
- Narváez (1528)
- Cabeza and Esteban (1535-36)
- Coronado (1540-42)
- De Soto (1539-42)
- Oñate (1596-1605)
- Cortés (1519-21)

Map Skills *Which expedition crossed the Mississippi River? Which modern U.S. city was reached by Oñate? What part of present U.S. territory was reached by Cortés?*

© ML & Co.

marched all the way to the Mississippi River searching for gold. Because de Soto was considered a god by the Indians, his death in 1541 caused a problem for his men. Gods do not die. So the Spaniards buried their captain secretly in the Mississippi River.

To the east, Spanish explorers were not idle. In 1565 the fort of Saint Augustine was established in Florida. It became the oldest continuing European settlement in North America.

Perhaps the most destructive meeting between the Indians north of Mexico and the Spanish was the one between Francisco Vasquez Coronado (fran-*sis*-ko *vas*-kes kor-ah-*nah*-do) and the Pueblos. Coronado tried to convert the Indians to Christianity, but he also robbed or killed them. It is said the Indians still speak of that terrible time.

But the event that changed Pueblo life the most was the arrival of Juan de Onate (whan de oh-*nah*-tay) in 1598. He brought 128 colonists and their families with him and set up a provincial capital at Santa Fe. From then on, the Pueblo were subject to Spain.

De Vaca and his men rest somewhere along the Gulf of Mexico in this later drawing by A. Russell.

Spain Supreme.   By 1580 Spain was a giant that stood astride the world. Philip II of Spain had also become the ruler of Portugal and all its possessions. His empire stretched from Manila in the Philippines (named for him) around the world to Mexico and to most of the southwestern United States. Looking at a map of Spanish explorations and possessions, few people would have doubted that the New World would become Spanish. In a relatively short time, Spain had built one of the greatest empires in history.

Philip lived much of his time in the gloomy monastery of Escorial, outside Madrid. A sign of the king's piety could be seen in his quarters. His bedroom was next to the chapel so Philip had a door cut into his wall. This allowed him to observe Mass from his bed in case he was ill. He believed that God had given Spain the duty and honor of converting all people of the world to Christianity. That is why priests always accompanied the soldiers and explorers on their trips to the New World.

The French: Preaching and Trading

In the early 1600s, Spain feared France far more than England as a competitor in the New World. While the Spanish had come to save souls and find treasure, the French had come to save souls and establish a fur trade. As early as 1524, Francis I of France sent the Florentine navigator Giovanni da Verrazano (gee-oh-*vah*-ni da vehr-ah-*zah*-no), along the coast of North America searching for a passage through America. In 1535 Jacques Cartier (kar-ti-*yay*) explored the St. Lawrence River. Near the Indian village of Hochelaga was a mountain which Cartier named Mount Royal, the site of present-day Montreal. But there he also met the first rapids in the river and realized he was nowhere near China. Still he named the place La Chine (China, in French). The first permanent French settlement, in Quebec, was founded in 1608 by another French explorer, Samuel de Champlain.

After the establishment of Quebec, the French penetrated into the central part of the North

Two views of Quebec City, on the St. Lawrence River, at the beginning of the 1700s. In the "upper town" are found the government buildings, the houses of the religious orders, and the fortress. The "lower town", or more commercial section, is located at the foot of the cliffs.

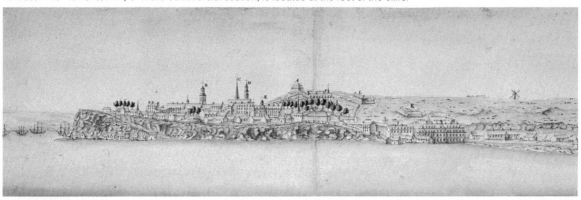

French Exploration of North America 1524–1682

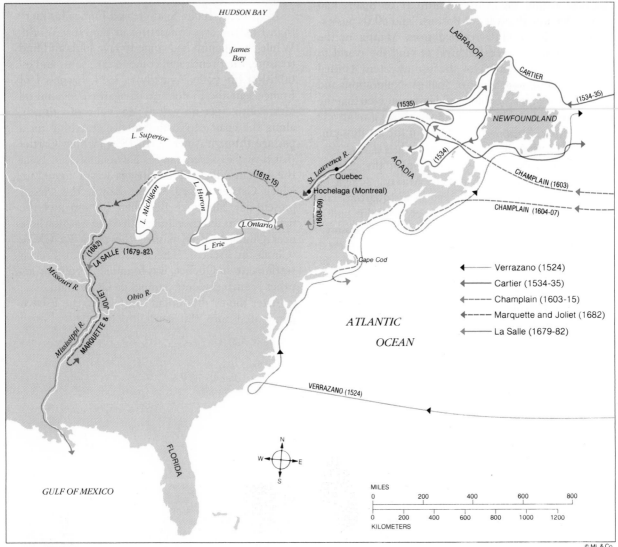

Map Skills *Which expedition went up the Great Lakes and down the Mississippi River? Which one went north of Newfoundland? past Cape Cod? What were the years of Champlain's voyages?*

© ML & Co

American continent. French priest Jacques Marquette and trader Louis Joliet explored the Great Lakes and the Upper Mississippi. Robert Cavelier, Sieur de La Salle, explored the lower Mississippi in 1682 and claimed the entire river valley, which he named Louisiana, for Louis XIV of France. New Orleans was founded by the French, as was Biloxi, on the Gulf of Mexico.

Most French settlements were a combination of forts, in which soldiers were quartered, and trading stations for French fur traders. Many traders married Indian women and adopted Indian ways. And, as did the Indians and the Spanish, the French left marks of their passage by geographical names, such

as Sault Ste. Marie, Michigan; Coeur d'Alene, Idaho; Des Moines, Iowa; Butte, Montana; St. Louis, Missouri; Baton Rouge, Louisiana; and Detroit, Michigan.

French priests and trappers were now spread across the northern part of North America and had come dangerously close, so the Spanish thought, to Spanish land in the Gulf of Mexico area.

The English: Lagging Behind

The northern and central parts of the North American continent had become, in effect, territories of France. The southern and southwestern parts of the continent were certainly under the rule of Spain. Year after year, the Spanish ships carried gold and silver from Mexico (and also Peru) home to Spain. How could England compete? It didn't at first.

Early Failures. In 1497 King Henry VII of England sent an Italian explorer, Giovanni Caboto (gee-oh-*vah*-ni ka-*boh*-toe), to search for new lands and to set up trading posts. John Cabot, as he was called in English, landed on an island that he named New Founde Lande. He thought it lay off the coast of Asia. On his second voyage Cabot was lost at sea, as were four of his five ships.

Almost one hundred years lapsed before Sir Humphrey Gilbert sailed across the Atlantic in 1583, hoping to found a settlement on Newfoundland. However, on the return trip Gilbert and his entire party were also lost at sea.

A year later Queen Elizabeth I gave Sir Walter Raleigh permission to settle anywhere north of the Spanish holdings along the Atlantic coast. Raleigh, in gratitude, named the place where he landed for the virgin queen.

Raleigh's first attempt to establish a colony on Roanoke Island failed. Two years later, in 1586, he sent out a second group of colonists. They also tried to settle on Roanoke Island, but again the effort failed. In 1588 an expedition sent to bring new supplies to the colony found the site deserted. The only clue was the word "Croatoan"—which resembled the name of the local Indian tribe, Croatan—carved on a post. No one knows what became of the lost colony. Probably some of its members starved to death, while others may have been killed by Indians who perhaps adopted the surviving children.

This was a poor beginning. Few people would have thought that England, coming so late and starting off in such a stumbling way, would end up the ruling power in North America. How did it happen?

Reasons for Final Success. France had entered a long civil war. Apart from Quebec, France had neither the interest nor the ability to support North American colonies. Spain had been thoroughly humiliated by the defeat of the great

This is one of the first maps of Roanoke Island. Drawn by John White in 1585, it shows two Indian towns and wrecks of earlier expeditions.

Armada it had sent against England in 1588. In fact, Spain could not even stop English raids on its treasure ships. Queen Elizabeth I of England herself knighted Francis Drake on the decks of the very ship, the *Golden Hind*, in which he had sailed around the world plundering Spanish galleons.

Spain had not used the gold and silver it obtained from the New World to build industries to manufacture goods. Instead Spain simply bought goods that it needed from other nations. But now that the gold and silver streams were drying up, or rather being diverted by the English, Spain could neither buy nor produce what was needed. Its decline was slow but sure.

But the crucial reason why English colonies succeeded, as you will read in chapter 2, was that the English settlements were made up mostly of people who looked on the New World as their home. By contrast, the Spanish and French hoped to make a quick fortune and then return to Europe. So, although Spain and France both controlled large areas of North America, it was the English who established hundreds of separate communities, brought over their families, and succeeded in building new lives for themselves and their descendants.

Section 3 Review

COMPREHENSION   Developing Vocabulary

1. Explain these terms: lavrador, Tierra, conquistadors, Tenochtitlan, Louisiana, Northwest Passage.

COMPREHENSION   Mastering Facts

1. The Treaty of Tordesillas divided the world between what two countries?
2. Who led the expedition that eventually made the first trip around the world?
3. Who first used the phrase "the new world"?
4. Where was the first English settlement in what is now the United States?

CHAPTER 1   Review

Chapter Summary

The first immigrants arrived in North America between twenty thousand and forty thousand years ago. As in the Old World, the first great civilizations in the New World developed in the warmer, more fertile areas. By 1500, many Indian cultures were represented in what was to become the United States. Various Indian groups had settled in the Northwest, Southeast, and Southwest. After Columbus arrived in 1492, Europeans continued their conquest of the Americas during the sixteenth century. The Spanish took an early lead but were soon followed by the French and English.

Questions for Critical Thinking

COMPREHENSION   Summarizing Main Ideas

1. In what ways was the council of the Iroquois Confederation an effective form of government? What were its weaknesses?
2. Explain how each of the following Indian groups coped with a particular problem:
   a. Creeks and the lack of iron tools
   b. Algonquin and the need to travel widely in search of game
   c. Calumet and huge winter snowfalls
   d. Pueblo and a shortage of water.
3. Based on your answers to the above, do you think the Indians did or did not make effective use of their environment?
4. What caused Europeans to develop new attitudes toward exploration during the period from 1000 to 1400?
5. What did Spain want from the New World? What did France want? What was England interested in the most?

COMPREHENSION   Interpreting Events

1. How did the Aztec and Mayan civilizations influence Indian groups in what is now the United States?
2. How did the burial mounds of the Hopewell people enable archaeologists to learn about the extent of Hopewell trade?
3. Why did Portugal and Spain take the lead in the Age of Discovery?

4. Why was the New World named for Vespucci? What other names might it have received? Which would you choose? Why?
5. Why was the defeat of the Spanish Armada significant for the future history of the United States?

APPLICATION   Using Skills To Evaluate Sources

One of the first and most important skills people need is the ability to acquire information. Here is a list of some well-known reference works:
   a. *Historical Statistics of the United States*
   b. *The New Columbia Encyclopedia*
   c. *Original Narratives of Early American History*
   d. *Who's Who in America*
   e. *Reader's Guide to Periodical Literature*
   f. William Prescott's *Conquest of Mexico*
   g. *American Heritage History of the Indians*
   h. *Webster's Seventh New Collegiate Dictionary*

Which of the above work or works would you use to locate material about each of the following?

1. The correct pronunciation of Panfilo de Narvaez
2. The Indian population of the Americas before the arrival of Columbus
3. The conquistadores' impressions of Aztec civilization
4. The religion of the Inca
5. Recent archaeological discoveries in the southwestern part of the United States
6. The life of Giovanni de Verrazano

EVALUATION   Comparing Past to Present

1. Compare the way in which the Calumet Indians ratified agreements with the way in which the United States ratifies agreements today. What might be a present-day equivalent of the peace pipe?
2. Compare the motives for exploration that western Europeans had in the fifteenth and sixteenth centuries with present-day motives for space exploration.

Opportunity

No migration in human history has ever equalled the movement of peoples to the Western Hemisphere. First on foot and later by ship, untold millions have made their way to America. Why did so many leave home to put down roots in an unknown land?

From the very beginning, newcomers have viewed America as a "Land of Opportunity," a place to stake out a better future. When the first Americans trudged across the ancient land bridge from Asia, they viewed what would come to be called America as a vast new hunting ground for food and clothing. They saw opportunity as a chance to improve their lives. Since that time, many have viewed America as the opportunity of a lifetime—a chance to get rich, a chance to live peacefully, a chance to erase the past and start anew. Right up through the present, America offers hope and promise.

Opportunity is a creation of dreamers who question the way things are. Dreamers imagine different realities and act on their imaginations to produce change. Christopher Columbus, for example, believed that he could reach the riches of the east by sailing west. So strongly did he believe in this idea that he succeeded in convincing Queen Isabella of its possibility. That interaction of people and ideas created a unique opportunity.

Risks and Rewards. Making use of an opportunity requires certain qualities of character—qualities such as confidence, conviction, and a willingness to gamble. But not everyone can tolerate the uncertainty of an unpredictable situation. Three European monarchs refused to back Columbus before he finally convinced the Spanish queen that the chances for gain far outweighed the risks. Queen Isabella gambled and put her money on an individual determined to create opportunity, a dreamer with the courage to confront an uncertain outcome. Her decision paid off handsomely; it won her lasting fame, and it opened the door to new opportunities.

Immigrants who came after Columbus shared his openness to change. They wanted to improve their lives and hoped that taking a chance on America would bring better circumstances. In America, opportunity was not reserved for a privileged few. From the time settlers planted colonies, some pioneers chose to venture westward in search of cheap land. By the time of the American Revolution, a majority of Americans owned their own land.

Success Stories. The American experience abounds with stories of people who have used opportunities successfully. In 1850 Levi Strauss, a German immigrant, came to California to seek his fortune during the gold rush. Strauss, however, did not plan to search for gold. Working first as a peddler, he eventually patented the use of rivets at stress points to make durable workpants for western miners. Like so many successful business people and inventors, Strauss took full advantage of an opportunity when he saw it. Today, the Levi's that Strauss invented are worn by people around the world.

Using opportunities successfully does not always mean becoming rich. Fat Yuen Lowe, a Chinese immigrant, came to the United States during the late 1800s. Working from dawn to nine at night seven days a week, Lowe sewed, ran errands, made deliveries, and swept floors in a clothing shop. Eventually Lowe and two brothers saved enough money to open their own garment shop. But the store was completely destroyed in the devastating San Francisco earthquake of 1906. Never one to give up, Lowe found a job in a dry goods store. Eventually he bought that business. His hard work enabled him and his wife to raise six children. Today his descendants revere Fat Yuen Lowe for the way he made use of opportunities in America.

Unequal Opportunity. It must be remembered, of course, that equal opportunity has not

What opportunities do these Cuban refugees hope for as they arrive in Florida?

been a consistent part of the American experience for all individuals. For most blacks until 1865, America was a land of slavery, a land of harsh limits rather than opportunity. Slaves could not enjoy the same opportunities that others took for granted: the chance to own land, to move around, to obtain an education, and to reap the fruits of their own labor. Virtually every ethnic and religious minority group—Germans, Poles, Chinese, Mexicans, Catholics, Jews—has endured discrimination. What was considered an "opportunity" for free land by European settlers was experienced as outright theft by native Americans already here.

Nonetheless, even deprived Americans have been able to overcome the limits of their opportunities. Frederick Douglass, for example, was born a slave. He learned to read from children in the streets; he taught himself to write by copying signs. The more he learned, the more he imagined other opportunities. He began to dream what freedom would be like. Eventually Douglass chose to take a serious risk in order to gain personal freedom. The risk succeeded, and after escaping north, Douglass spent the rest of his life trying to improve opportunities for others. He believed that his personal opportunities meant little unless all Americans shared the same freedoms he did.

From Dreams to Action. The meaning of opportunity in America has undergone many changes over the years. Since the Declaration of Independence, however, this nation has committed itself to the ideal that everyone in American society deserves a fair chance. Sometimes the nation falls far short of

the ideal—but the ideal nevertheless still remains. It is reflected in our family structure, our educational institutions, and our system of government. It is expressed in the values we hold, and it is exemplified by the leaders we admire. The heroes of our nation—Benjamin Franklin, Susan B. Anthony, John F. Kennedy, Jane Addams, Martin Luther King, Jr., and countless others—have all been individuals who acted on their ideas to create opportunities.

Are you a person who can translate dreams into action? Dreamers built America, and dreamers will continue to define the American experience by creating new opportunities.

Understanding Our Heritage

1. What past evidence shows that America is a land of opportunity?
2. Do you think that the United States today offers greater opportunities than other nations? Support your opinion with facts.
3. What remains for the United States to do in order to insure equal opportunity for all Americans?
4. What opportunities do you expect to use to improve your life? What barriers may stand in the way? How can you work to realize your dreams despite the barriers?

CHAPTER 2

Arrival of the English

1600–1700

People in the Chapter

John Smith—*the ex-soldier who saves the Jamestown settlement.*

Wahunsonacock—*the Algonquin chief, also called Powhatan, who welcomes the Jamestown settlers.*

Pocahontas—*the chief's daughter who marries John Rolfe and goes to live in England.*

James I—*the king of England (1603–1625).*

William Bradford—*the governor of Plymouth Colony.*

John Calvin—*the father of Puritanism.*

William Penn—*the Quaker founder of Pennsylvania.*

Linking Past to Present

Between 1607 and 1627 the French, the Dutch, the Swedes, and the Finns had established colonies along the Atlantic seaboard, north of the Spanish territory. But the most successful colonies, and the most numerous, were those established by the English. One reason for this success was the manner in which the English colonies were governed. In the other colonies people were ruled by the will of the European prince or his representative. But the English colonies in North America, like the British people in Britain, were self-governing. As John Smith of the Jamestown settlement told officials in London: "No one will go from [here] to have less freedom there than here." The first settlers, therefore, were governed by English common law, and they soon had a representative assembly.

Despite these personal freedoms, life was hard and dangerous in the two earliest colonies–Jamestown and Plymouth. There were times when the settlements were on the verge of failure. But Virginia's success was assured by a valuable crop—tobacco. The settlements in Massachusetts succeeded because they were supported by a steady stream of immigrants. Many of these settlers were deeply religious, hardworking Puritans who were determined to build a new world on the rocky shores of New England.

Chapter Outline

1 BEGINNINGS OF THE VIRGINIA COLONY
2 THE VIRGINIA COLONY FINALLY SUCCEEDS
3 THE PURITANS ARRIVE IN MASSACHUSETTS
4 DIFFERENT SETTLEMENTS BEGIN

1 BEGINNINGS OF THE VIRGINIA COLONY

VOCABULARY   *joint-stock companies   charter   artifacts*

England did not use the state treasury to finance its early settlements. The English used *joint-stock companies*. A group of people would each put up a certain amount of money in return for a stated number of shares. If there were 100 shares and a person bought ten shares, that person would get 10 percent of the profits from the settlement. On the other hand, if there were a loss, the person would be responsible for only 10 percent of it. So, in 1606 a group of "merchants and adventurers" from London, Bristol, Exeter, and Plymouth asked James I for permission to form a joint-stock company. They requested he grant them a *charter*, or official permit, to found a colony in Virginia.

The Virginia Company Expedition

These men saw several possibilities for profit. They hoped to discover a northwest passage so they could trade directly with Asia. They also hoped to trade with the Indians. Then, too, there might be gold and silver in Virginia. Even if there weren't, the men thought valuable products—such as silk, wine, and oranges—might be produced there.

The English king was interested. After all, the expedition would cost him nothing and might bring him a profit. According to custom, on such ventures the ruler got one-fifth of all gold and silver that was found. So James quickly granted the charter and wished the businessmen good luck.

A Charter of Rights.   The charter was the nearest thing to a written constitution the colony had. It gave the Virginia Company of London permission to settle along the mid-Atlantic coast of North America. It also gave the company a monopoly. In other words, no one else could trade with Virginia without the company's permission. In addition, the company had the right to rule Virginia as it thought best. However, the charter specifically declared that colonists would have the same rights and privileges that English people had in England. These included trial by jury and the right to own land.

Departure for Virginia.   In 1606 the company sent out, under the command of Captain Christopher Newport, 140 men and 4 boys in three tiny vessels—the *Discovery*, the *Goodspeed*, and the *Susan Constant*. They were well supplied with food, water, and beer. Beer was included because it did not go bad as fast as water did.

The ships sailed from London on December 20, 1606, but contrary winds slowed their progress. The men and boys were crammed tight, shoulder to shoulder, when they lay down to sleep. At times they were terrified by howling winds and mountainous seas. Many were seasick.

The voyagers had plenty of time to think about their grand adventure, for the voyage took three months. The ships first sailed to the island of Nevis in the West Indies where they got fresh provisions and then sailed northwest. Finally, around four o'clock in the morning of April 26, 1607, they could see, low on the horizon, the coast of Virginia.

Landfall.   You can imagine the joy and excitement the voyagers felt after so many weeks on board ship. As the land came more clearly into view, they must have gazed at it with the same awe

39

and wonderment that astronauts in the 1960s felt when they looked on the surface of the moon.

The Virginia countryside was flat, green, and heavily forested. The men could see vines tangling among the trees. As they sniffed the air, they smelled not the salt sea but the perfume of pine trees. It was a land smell they had not known in England, where there were no pines.

The ships dropped anchor, and some of the men set off in a small rowboat. One of them later wrote that they found "fair meadows and goodly tall trees with such fresh waters running through the woods [that] I was almost [overcome] at the sight thereof."And later, "We came into a little plot of ground full of fine and beautiful strawberries, four times bigger and better than ours in England."

The First Days

The English knew there were people who might be unfriendly in the forest. So instead of settling directly on the coast, they got back on board ship and sailed up a wide and beautiful river looking for a good spot to build a fort.

On April 29 they saw some Algonquin on the shore. The English again got into their small boat and rowed toward them. At first the Algonquin were frightened, as well they might have been at the sight of those white, round-eyed, bearded men in such heavy, outlandish clothes. But the English captain called out "and laid his hand on his heart." Then the Algonquin put down their bows and arrows and came boldly to meet the strangers. Later, the Algonquin gave the English a banquet.

The Founding of Jamestown

The English sailed slowly up the river and finally found a site that suited them on a little peninsula. They tied the ships to tall trees at the water's edge. They named the place Jamestown and the river the James, in honor of their king.

Jamestown was a good choice for defense purposes. The land was flat and nearly surrounded by water. But in other ways it was disastrous. Much of the land was swampy, and there were swarms of mosquitoes. At that time no one knew that mosquitoes carried deadly malaria. Because the land was flat, there was little drainage. No one knew that placing outdoor toilets near sources of drinking water could cause other diseases, particularly typhoid fever.

Following Instructions. The settlers opened up a sealed box from the directors of the Virginia Company. The names of the seven men who were to be the governing council were read out. The instructions of the directors said:

> When it shall please God to send you on the coast of Virginia, find a safe port. It should be at the entrance of some river. Choose one that runs farthest into the land. If you find two that do, choose the one that bendeth most toward the northwest. That way, you shall soonest find the other sea.

They were still looking for a northwest passage.

> Set your houses even and in line. Make your streets wide. Have your marketplace in a square. Every street should lead to it. In this way, you can command every street with a few guns.

And finally, the instructions warned:

> No one should write any letter that may discourage others from coming.

The site picked for Jamestown followed the company's directions fairly well. The men set to work and soon constructed a small, triangular fort at the water's edge. The walls were made of oak and walnut planks and posts. Then a problem arose. Most of the men were "gentlemen," and in England gentlemen did not work with their hands. That was done by the lower classes. The Jamestown settlers were more interested in finding gold or silver than in such dreary tasks as digging, shoveling, and clearing land. As a result, they ignored the basic rules for survival: they did not plan, plough, or build. If the Algonquin had wished, they could have easily wiped out the settlement. As it was they did not need to. Nature nearly did that for them.

Early Miseries. On June 22, two of the ships sailed back for England, leaving 104 people at Jamestown. As the ships disappeared, the settlers must have had pangs of homesickness. They were all alone with an unknown continent before them and the sea at their back. Things went bad quickly.

As the summer deepened, people fell ill. In his diary, one man wrote, "There died John Asbie of a bloody flux [hemorrhage]. The ninth day died George Flower of the swelling." Then, day after terrible day, the writer noted down the deaths:

William Brewster, Francis Midwinter, Edward Morris . . . and so on. Within thirty days, twenty-four men lay dead. In seven months all but thirty-two were dead. The diarist noted, "There was never Englishmen left in a foreign country in such misery as we were. . . . Our food was but a small can of barley [soaked] in water to five men each day . . . our men, night and day, groaning in every corner of the fort." Some nights, three or four died, then "in the morning, their bodies [were] trailed out of their cabins like dogs to be buried." The Indians saved those who were left. "It pleased God to move the Indians to bring us corn . . . when we rather expected they would destroy us." They also brought bread, fish, and meat in great quantity.

John Smith Takes Charge

In addition to their other difficulties, the men often quarreled over leadership. After a year of drifting, a forceful ex-soldier named John Smith, twenty-seven years old, simply took charge. By sheer force of strength and personality, he got the men to work. They complained about sore backs and blisters on their hands—but they worked. Smith also tried to improve their manners. Each time a man cursed, his punishment was to have a can of cold water poured up his sleeve.

Smith explored and mapped the surrounding area. Most important, he dealt directly with the chief of a powerful group of nearby Algonquin tribes. Smith flattered Powhatan, whose Indian name was Wahunsonacock (wa-hoon-*son*-a-kok), by saying how impressed he was with the chief's wide lands, rich crops, and handsome people. Wahunsonacock wanted to know why the English were there. Smith quickly replied that they had landed to repair a leak in their little boat. They were now waiting, he said, for a larger ship to come and lead them back across the sea.

Smith Meets Pocahontas. How much Wahunsonacock believed of all this is unknown, but the Algonquin were no fools. It is likely they had met other Europeans, or certainly had heard of them, because there had been landings at several places all along the Atlantic coast. The chief's daughter was a twelve- or thirteen-year-old girl, with black hair braided down her back, named Pocahontas. She probably spoke for the Algonquin when she said, "Many do inform me that your coming is not for trade but to invade my people and possess my country." From time to time there were small clashes between the Algonquin and the English, with dead and wounded on both sides. But for the most part, relations between the two peoples were peaceful.

Whether Pocahontas saved John Smith's life one day when her people were prepared to kill him is not really known. John Smith *said* that is what happened. But he was quite a talker, and he may have said that to astonish his friends when he went back to England. What *is* known, however, is that they did have a long friendship with one another. Pocahontas eventually married a settler named John Rolfe, and they had a son, Thomas. Later she went to England, where she was introduced to the king and given the name Rebecca.

In 1608, seventy more settlers arrived. Among them were two women: Anne Burrows, and her maid. Anne Burrows married John Laydon, a carpenter who had come over on the first voyage. Later, ships came with young women and widows who married the settlers and started families.

The Starving Time. In 1609 Smith was injured in a gunpowder explosion, and he soon left the colony for good. By then more supplies and some 400 additional settlers had arrived. Still, conditions in the colony went from bad to worse. During the winter of 1609–1610, there was famine and even cannibalism. This was the so-called "starving time." Smith later described the infant colony as a "miserie, a ruin, a death, a hell." People lived on roots and rats, and one man even murdered his wife and salted her away like salt pork.

By spring only sixty people remained alive. They decided to abandon the colony and return to England. They were actually sailing down the James River when they met an incoming ship from England. Aboard was the new governor, Lord de la Ware (from whom Delaware gets its name), with more settlers and supplies. Reluctantly, the colonists returned to Jamestown. The first permanent English colony in America had narrowly missed being abandoned.

Wolstenholme Towne

As settlers came into Jamestown, many others settled on land along the James River. One group of about 200 men, women, and children founded a town called Wolstenholme, some ten miles down-

Early Jamestown   1607–1622

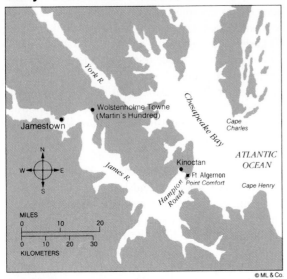

Map Skills   *How wide was the James River at Jamestown? What direction from Point Comfort was Jamestown?*

stream from Jamestown. It was on a grant of land called Martins Hundred. A "hundred" in medieval days meant enough land to support 100 families. The land was named for Richard Martin, a stockholder in the Virginia Company. The town was es-

tablished by 1620 and apparently flourished until 1622 when most of the people were massacred or captured by Indians. But in 1979 archaeologists discovered the remains of Wolstenholme Towne. The *artifacts*—pots, dishes, armor, and the like— give a fresh and vivid view of the day to day life of the settlers. Since the site of Jamestown has been washed away over the centuries by the James River, the finds of Wolstenholme provide some of the best evidence we have of what an early colonial village in Virginia was like.

Section 1 Review

COMPREHENSION   Developing Vocabulary

1. Explain these terms: joint-stock companies, charter, artifacts.

COMPREHENSION   Mastering Facts

1. When the Jamestown settlers first met Indians, what did the English captain do to persuade the Indians that the settlers came in peace?
2. To what large Indian group did the tribes on the east coast belong?
3. What two diseases were common in Jamestown?
4. Why were the settlers advised to build houses in a line and have every street lead to a central square?

An artist's reconstruction of part of Wolstenholme. From left: gardens, a barn, company compound and storehouse. Behind is the fort, a refuge from Indian attacks.

2 THE VIRGINIA COLONY FINALLY SUCCEEDS

VOCABULARY   *head right system   indentured servants   burgesses*

At home in England, the backers of the Virginia Company were secure and comfortable by their firesides. But they were worried by the gloomy reports from their American colony. No gold or silver had been discovered, and there were no signs of a northwest passage to China.

Renewed Efforts

Still, the directors had hope, and they redoubled their efforts to raise money for food, tools, and weapons to send to the struggling settlement. Again the colonists were urged to search for some product that would sell in London.

Encouraging Settlers.   Unlike the Spaniards, the English welcomed foreigners into their colonies almost from the beginning. In 1608 four Poles came to Jamestown to start production of tar, pitch, and turpentine for the British navy. Over the next few years another forty-five Poles arrived

to help make masts for British ships. Sawmill workers were brought from Hamburg in Germany, and expert lumbermen came from Scandinavia. To encourage the growing of different crops, grapevines and olive trees were imported from France, as well as experts in the art of producing wine and olives. Unfortunately, vineyards and olive trees did not flourish in colonial Virginia. ·

The Head Right System.   Then the company did a wise thing that would have great importance in coming years. It announced that any man who paid his way to Virginia would get fifty acres for himself and another fifty acres for every person he brought with him, whether a family member or a servant. So a man with a wife and eight children would be guaranteed an initial homesite of 500 acres. This was called the *head right system,* and it lasted throughout the 1600s. This lure of free land brought thousands from crowded Europe to Virginia.

Supply List for Newcomers to the Virginia Colony

Apparel for one man	li.	s.	d.*
1 Monmouth cap	00	01	10
3 shirts		07	06
1 waistcoat		02	02
1 canvas suit		07	06
1 cloth suit		10	00
3 pairs of Irish stockings		04	00
4 pairs of shoes		08	08
1 pair of garters			10
1 pair of canvas sheets		08	00
9 yards of canvas to make a bed and bolsters (to be filled in Virginia)		08	00
1 rug for a bed			
7 yards of coarse canvas to make a bed (straw-filled for sea voyage)		05	00
1 coarse rug (for sea voyage)			

Food supplies for one man for one year	li.	s.	d.
8 bushels of meal	02	00	00
2 bushels of peas		06	00
2 bushels of oatmeal		09	00
1 gallon of brandy		02	06
2 gallons of vinegar		02	00
1 gallon of oil		03	06

Arms for one man (if half the men have armor, all will need only swords and muskets)	li.	s.	d.
1 complete suit of light armor		17	00
1 5½ foot musket	01	02	00
1 ammunition belt		01	00
1 sword		05	00
20 pounds of powder		18	00
60 pounds of lead shot		05	00

Tools for a family of six	li.	s.	d.
5 broad hoes at 2 s. apiece		10	00
5 narrow hoes at 16 d. apiece		06	08
2 broad axes at 3 s. 8 d. apiece		07	04
2 cutting axes at 18 d. apiece		07	06
2 steel hand saws at 16 d. apiece		02	08
2 two-hand saws at 5 s. apiece		10	00
1 well-filed whip saw and file		10	00
2 hammers at 12 d. apiece		2	00
3 shovels at 18 d. apiece		04	06
2 spades at 18 d. apiece		03	00
2 large hand-drills at 6 d. apiece		01	00
6 chisels at 6 d. apiece		03	00
3 small hand-drills at 2 d. apiece	00	06	

	li.	s.	d.
2 hatchets at 21 d. apiece		03	06
2 cleavers for splitting wood at 18 d.		3	00
2 pruning tools at 20 d. apiece		03	04
1 grindstone at 4 s.		04	00
a variety of nails	02	00	00
2 pickaxes		03	00

Household implements for a family of six	li.	s.	d.
1 iron pot		07	00
1 kettle		06	00
1 large frying pan		02	06
1 gridiron		01	06
2 skillets		05	00
1 spit		02	00
platters, dishes, spoons (wooden)		04	00

Sugar, spices, and fruit for 6 at sea	li.	s.	d.
		12	06
Passage for each person is		06	00
Freight for the provisions of one man (which will be about half a ton)		01	10

*The symbols at the top of each column mean: li. = pounds, s. = shillings, d. = pence.

The first blacks arrive in Jamestown. Some historians believe that the early blacks were freed when they were baptized. But by 1671 blacks were slaves for life, baptized or not.

Indentured Servants. Some who could not pay came as *indentured servants.* This meant that in return for their passage they agreed to work for someone for a specified number of years, usually seven, after which they were free.

Most immigrants came as indentured servants. Between 1635 and 1680 about 1300 came every year. This eased unemployment in England. It also cleared English jails. Judges sent political prisoners and debtors to Virginia as indentured servants. They were often mistreated as you will read in chapter 3.

Two Important Events. In 1619 two things happened that had great impact on the future of the English colonies. On July 30, in the little church in Jamestown, Governor Yeardley and his council of twenty-two *burgesses,* or representatives—two from each of the eleven settlements scattered along the James River—met to make laws for the colony. Statutes were enacted based on English common law. From this time forward, Virginians jealously guarded the privilege of holding their own legislative assembly. And when Polish workers demanded that they be given the same rights as English colonists, their wishes were granted.

The second event was the arrival of a Dutch ship. In its hold were "twenty Negars" who were "sold" to the English settlers. They were listed as servants, and some historians believe they were treated as indentured servants who happened to be black. After a time they received land and their freedom. Other historians are not certain about the degree of freedom they received. You will learn more about the development of slavery when you read the next chapter.

The Human Cost of Jamestown. Over the years more settlers arrived. They were truly heroic to endure what had to be borne. Women in particular had difficult jobs. They had to maintain homes under the most primitive conditions, bear children and raise them, cook for the family, and, at times, work in the fields. Small wonder most of them died early of malnutrition and disease.

Then there was always the danger from Indians. In 1622 a relative of Wahunsonacock led the Algonquin forces in a major effort to wipe out the expanding English settlements. Before the fight ended, many warriors and one-third of the colonists lay dead.

By 1624 some 6000 English people had gone to Virginia, but the total English population there was only 1200. Almost five out of six had either gone home or lay under the forests of Virginia.

Saved by Smoke

What finally got the colony off to economic health was something as insubstantial as smoke. At first there was no intention of growing tobacco. It was an American plant, unknown in Europe before Columbus. Also, the kind of tobacco the Algonquin grew and smoked tasted bitter to Europeans.

But in 1612 John Rolfe, Pocahontas's husband, introduced into the Virginia colony a different type of tobacco from the Caribbean islands. It was much milder and suited European tastes. The plants grew well in Virginia, and cultivation did not require skilled labor. Soon, settlers were busily cultivating the "noxious weed," as nonsmoking Englishmen called it.

At first tobacco was valued in Europe as a medicine for curing all sorts of diseases. However, more and more people discovered that smoking the stuff in a pipe gave pleasure. (Cigarettes were unknown before the 1900s.) King James I opposed tobacco on the grounds that it was unhealthy and even wrote a "counter-blaste," in which he called it a "stinking weed." But tobacco became so popular in Europe that he permitted it to be brought into England, where it was handsomely taxed. The Virginia colonists had at last found a profitable crop—profitable for themselves and for their king.

Virginia Becomes a Royal Colony

Despite the discovery of tobacco, the company officials quarelled among themselves and the com-pany was not as efficient as it could have been. Finally, in 1624 King James lost patience with the company officials. He disbanded the Virginia Company and assumed direct control over the colony. From then on, the Crown would appoint a royal governor who would reside in the colony as the direct agent of royal power. However, the House of Burgesses, as Virginia's legislative assembly had come to be called, remained in existence. The settlers continued their practice of obeying laws and paying taxes only if their elected representatives authorized it.

Section 2 Review

COMPREHENSION   Developing Vocabulary

1. Explain these terms: head right system, indentured servants, burgesses.

COMPREHENSION   Mastering Facts

1. Name two nationalities other than English that helped build the Jamestown settlement.
2. Why did people become indentured servants?
3. What two significant events occurred in 1619?
4. What finally saved the Jamestown settlement from economic ruin?

3   THE PURITANS ARRIVE IN MASSACHUSETTS

VOCABULARY   *predestination   Separatists   compact*

It was a cold, snowy day that November 15, 1620, when five men and a dog were out hunting along the sandy shores of Cape Cod near the site of modern Provincetown. Suddenly, in the distance, they saw an extraordinary sight: a group of sixteen bearded white men. They wore heavy clothes, and some were covered in what looked like glistening metal. The white men made strange cries, while the one who seemed to be their leader waved.

The Indians had heard of these people who came from across the sea. They also knew about the long sticks some of them carried over their shoulders. The sticks shot flame and smoke, and made the loudest noise ever heard except for thunder and waterfalls. The Indians also knew that the bite of the stick was as deadly as a snake's. As the white men lumbered nearer, the Indians understandably took to their heels. This was the first encounter between Native Americans and the men, led by Miles Standish, of the *Mayflower* who had landed four days earlier at the northernmost point of Cape Cod. It was also the first known encounter between the people of the New World and the Puritans. What were the Puritans like?

Puritan Beliefs

The Puritans were people who wanted to purify, or make simpler, the elaborate religious ceremonies that had developed in the Anglican or state Church of England. The long ceremonies and the rich robes of bishops troubled them. It seemed too much like the Roman Catholic service, which King Henry VIII and later Elizabeth I had abolished in England. To the Puritans it appeared that the old ways were creeping back into Protestant services.

In general, Puritans followed the teachings of John Calvin. Calvin, a Frenchman who lived in Geneva, Switzerland, is considered to be the father of Calvinism—or Puritanism as it was known in England. Here are some of Calvin's and the Puritans' most important beliefs.

A painting of the 1800s shows the Mayflower, *covered with ice, in Plymouth harbor. Pilgrims set off in a small boat to explore the shore.*

Original Sin. The first book of the Bible tells about the sin of Adam and Eve, the parents of all humankind, who disobeyed God by eating the forbidden fruit. The Puritans believed that all humans inherited the same sinful character. Sinful people *deserved* to be damned to hell. So it was a sign of God's mercy that He had decided to save anyone at all.

Predestination. Puritans believed that God had decided the fate of all men and women before they were born. Each person was going either to heaven or hell. Nothing they did could alter that fact. Their fate, or destiny, had already been decided. That is the meaning of *predestination.*

Strict Moral Behavior. If everyone was predestined to be saved in heaven or damned in hell, why, you may wonder, did it matter how people behaved? Why bother to lead a good moral life when God had already decided your fate?

Puritans believed that each person—damned or saved—was nevertheless responsible for leading a moral life. They also believed that good behavior might be a sign that an individual was headed for salvation. Good behavior could not earn salvation, but it was an indication that a person already had God's favor.

Careful Watch of Self and Others. Puritans believed they should watch for signs of God's pleasure toward them. In this way, a person might even gain some assurance that he or she had been saved. The problem was that a person could never be absolutely certain about the matter. In daily life, therefore, Puritans were constantly examining themselves for clues to their eternal life.

Puritans thought they had to be vigilant about

the behavior of everyone in their communities. God required good behavior of everyone, so bad behavior had to be punished. As believers in original sin, the Puritans expected to find wickedness in their communities. They watched their neighbors and kept a sharp eye out for such sins as drunkenness, swearing, theft, assault, and idleness. When they discovered such sins, they punished the sinners severely.

Virtue of Hard Work. It may seem strange that the Puritans included "idleness" in their catalog of sins. But they believed that God required everyone to be busy. God "called" men and women to their jobs. The job might be that of a minister, farmer, mother, servant, or carpenter. Whatever the job one was called to, God required men and women to work long and hard at it.

Virtues of the Bible and Ministers. The Puritans believed in the importance of the Bible, which they regarded as the Word of God. All men and women had to know how to read so they could consult the Bible themselves. Puritans also believed that ministers should interpret the Bible to their congregations. Thus, the minister's most important job was to preach about the meaning of Biblical passages. Puritan ministers were highly educated men, with great reputations and influence. But they did not rule their churches the way bishops of the Anglican church did. They were hired—and could be fired—by the individual church congregations.

From Plymouth to Plymouth

The Puritans knew what was wrong with the Church of England, but they disagreed on what should be done about it. Some thought they should remain in the church and try to reform it from the inside. Others did not think that could be done, and they wanted to separate from the Anglican, or state, church completely and set up their own church. They were called Separatist Puritans, or Separatists.

The Separatists cut themselves off from the Anglican church. They formed small, independent congregations with their own ministers. They had to meet in secret because King James I was determined to punish those who would not follow the state church ceremonies and rituals.

British authorities tried to find out where the secret meetings were held and who went to them. When the king learned that Separatists would not obey their bishops, he was furious. "No bishops, no king," he declared, meaning that it was only a step from disobeying bishops to disobeying the king.

Flight to Holland. One congregation of Separatists decided to flee from England to Holland, where Dutch authorities were more tolerant in religious matters. They settled in the town of Leyden. But after several years they became discouraged. They were well liked by the Dutch, but had a hard time finding work. Their children were speaking Dutch and, in fact, were becoming more Dutch than English. Worst of all, some of the young people were drifting away from the Puritan faith. So the Separatists decided to risk migrating to America. There, they felt, Separatists could live successfully as an independent religious congregation. After several years they obtained financial backing and a grant of land in the northern part of Virginia.

The Mayflower Sails. Late in the summer of 1620, a small group of families finally set sail in two small ships from the English port of Plymouth. Almost immediately, one of the ships, the *Speedwell*, began leaking so badly that the tiny expedition had to turn back. The group then crowded aboard the more sturdy *Mayflower* and once again raised anchor.

These people called themselves Pilgrims, from the story in the Bible in which Abraham and the Hebrews are sent by God "as strangers and Pilgrims" into a strange country so as to better worship the Lord. Not all Pilgrims were Separatists, and some were not even Puritans. They were adventurers eager to improve their lives by settling in a new world.

The little ship *Mayflower* aimed for the northern coast of Virginia. It missed badly. Nine weeks later, when the ship's people first sighted land, they saw rolling sand dunes with a few tall waving blades of grass. We know now they were looking at Cape Cod and thus were off the coast that had earlier been named New England by Captain John Smith. They debated about sailing south, but decided to search the coast in front of them for a safe harbor and place for settlement. They found a spot on the inner shore of Cape Cod Bay and promptly named it for the town from which they had sailed—Plymouth.

Plymouth and Massachusetts Bay Colonies

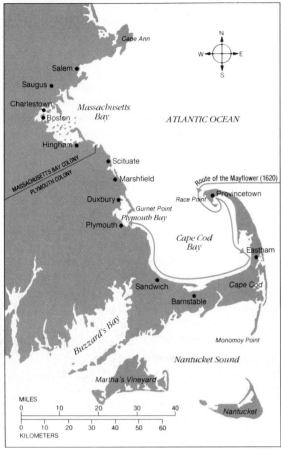

Map Skills The Mayflower *first put in at the site of what town? How far was it from the site of Plymouth?*

© ML & Co.

The Mayflower *Compact.* New England lay outside the authority of the Virginia government. So the Pilgrims had to decide what kind of government they wanted. While still on board the *Mayflower,* forty-one men gathered in the main cabin and signed their names to a *compact,* or agreement, about the kind of government they would set up. They agreed that laws approved by the majority would be binding on Puritans and non-Puritans alike.

❝ As the compact read in part:

> [We do] combine ourselves together into a civil body politic, for our better ordering and preservation and . . . do enact, constitute, and frame such just and equal laws, ordinances, acts, constitutions, and offices, from time to time, as shall be thought most meet and convenient for the general good of the colony. ❞

These few lines suggest that political authority rests on the will of the people. This compact of 1620 and the Virginia Assembly of 1619, which established the principle of representative government, are two important landmarks in the development of the American system of government.

The signers of the compact were the colony's free men. Neither women nor indentured servants could vote. The men chose the governor and made the laws. They also decided which newcomers could join the colony and which could not. First they chose John Carver as governor. But when he died a few months later, they chose William Bradford and reelected him nearly every year from 1621 until his death in 1657.

From Hardship to Success. The Pilgrims' prospects were not encouraging. The soil at Plymouth appeared sandy and unpromising. Worse, December had arrived, and the Pilgrims felt the first bite of a New England winter, which was far worse than any English winter. Women and children remained aboard the *Mayflower,* staring grimly at the shore. Their leader, William Bradford, sadly described their situation. "What could they see," he wrote, "but a hideous and desolate wilderness . . . what could now sustain them but the spirit of God and His grace?" Bradford's own wife disappeared overboard. Probably she was so homesick that she took her own life.

What happened in Jamestown was repeated in Plymouth. That winter Bradford wrote, "In two or three month's time, half of their company died, being the depth of winter and wanting houses and other comforts . . . being infected with scurvy and other diseases."

A plague, probably smallpox, had recently wiped out many Indians in the area. The plague had been brought by European fishermen. At Plymouth the Pilgrims found abandoned cornfields. And in the spring they took advantage of these fields for planting squash and beans. The Indians they met were cautious but not unfriendly.

Help from the Indians. One day when a group of men were unloading the *Mayflower,* an Indian came up and dumbfounded them by speaking in English. He said his name was Samoset. He had learned the language from some English fishermen who had come to the coast near his home. He also introduced them to his friend Tisquantum, or Squanto—as the Pilgrims called him—and to the local chief, Massasoit (mass-a-*soy*-it).

Squanto had actually spent several years in England, and he spoke English very well. He became the Pilgrims' guide and interpreter. Characteristically, Bradford described Squanto as "a special instrument sent by God for their good." Indeed, the Indians' aid saved the settlers' lives in New England just as it had saved them in Virginia. Squanto and his friends showed the Pilgrims what corn was and how to grow and cook it. (Corn was unknown in Europe at that time.) The Indians also taught the settlers how to gather and cook clams and where and how to catch the fattest fish.

Thanksgiving. In November 1621, one year after their arrival, the Pilgrims gathered their first harvest. Then they invited Massasoit and some ninety of his braves to a three-day feast, which included squash, beans, corn, wild turkeys, ducks, geese, and four deer the Indians brought. It was a time of Thanksgiving to God.

By 1642 the Pilgrims were able to repay their financial backers in London with shipments of lumber and furs. Gradually, their tiny settlement expanded. New Pilgrim towns sprang up on Cape Cod.

To meet the problems of government, the Pilgrims set up a system whereby the men of each town elected representatives to pass laws for the entire colony. Only males who were church members were allowed to vote. Even with this restriction, a far higher proportion of men could vote in the Plymouth colony than in England.

A New Colony on the Bay

Meanwhile, other English Puritans were turning their thoughts toward New England. They were not Separatists; they regarded themselves as loyal members of the Anglican church. But they believed that the church was corrupt, and they were becoming discouraged about reforming it from within. They could not get sufficient support in England. So they began to think about setting up a holy community of their own in America.

An Independent Government. One of the ablest of these Puritans was a well-to-do lawyer named John Winthrop. Some of his Puritan friends went about quietly getting a charter to settle in New England. This charter set forth the rules for a new joint-stock enterprise, the Massachusetts Bay Company. But there was an important omission in the charter: it failed to say where the company's headquarters should be. Winthrop and his friends took advantage of this omission and boldly transferred the charter itself and the company's headquarters to New England. The charter included a land grant and provisions for a form of government. So when Winthrop and other Puritans migrated, they took with them the authority for an independent government. Of course they would still owe loyalty to the king. But the king was 3000 miles away and was having enough difficulty with the Puritans who remained in England.

A Prosperous Start. The year 1630 saw the first really well-planned and sizable migration of English people to America. Winthrop had been named governing officer of the Massachusetts Bay Company. He and other devout Puritan leaders recruited other Puritans for the expedition. Few of the migrants were wealthy, but they were by no means as poor as the men and women who had gone to Virginia and to Plymouth. They had little difficulty in buying adequate supplies and a small fleet of ships. All in all, about a thousand men, women, and children set forth in 1630 for Massachusetts.

There was no "starving time" in the Massachusetts Bay Colony. During the next ten years, supplies kept coming. So did nearly 20,000 people, most of whom survived. The port town of Boston became the colony's thriving capital. The settlers established other towns nearby and eventually incorporated the Plymouth Colony into the Massachusetts Bay Colony.

Section 3 Review

COMPREHENSION Developing Vocabulary

1. Explain these terms: predestination, Separatists, compact.

COMPREHENSION Mastering Facts

1. What does "Puritan" mean?
2. According to the Puritans, what was the most important job for a minister?
3. What did King James I mean when he said "no bishops, no king"?
4. Why did the Puritans leave Holland?

VOCABULARY *heresy   theology   proprietors   absolute monarch   staple crop   unicameral*

The Puritans were a stern, honest, hardworking, and God-fearing people. They endured many hardships to reach a land where they could worship God as they wished. They thought their way was best, and they wanted all other people to worship as they did. They were, in fact, intolerant. If they did not like someone, they asked that person to leave the settlement. Others were publicly whipped or left sitting in the *stocks*. Stocks were heavy wooden fence-like structures with holes through which a person's feet and sometimes arms were pulled and securely fastened. Such punishments were for those who broke laws which forbade playing cards, dancing in public, or simply being idle.

In the first decade of settlement, Massachusetts authorities were challenged by two very different but able individuals.

Roger Williams Is Banished

Roger Williams was a Separatist minister who arrived in 1631. Everyone liked and respected him. Yet two of his opinions seemed especially threatening to the Massachusetts leaders. Williams declared that the English settlers had no rightful claim to the land unless they purchased it from the Indians. He also declared that government officials should devote themselves only to government business and should leave religious matters alone. To the Puritans, the first idea was ridiculous and the second was *heresy* (a belief rejected by the majority). They were thoroughly shocked, and in 1636 they banished Williams from the holy community of Massachusetts.

In the dead of winter, Williams tramped southward through the snow to the headwaters of Narragansett Bay. For a time he lived with the Narragansett Indians and took the trouble to learn their language. Soon he was joined by sympathizers from Massachusetts. He established the town of Providence, which became the center of a new colony, Rhode Island. In 1644 Williams went back to England and got a charter for his colony.

The charter of Rhode Island provided for a government similar to that of Massachusetts. But it contained some unusual provisions that reflected Williams's views. All Christian groups were allowed to worship, and there was a separation of

Colonists who disobeyed the strict Puritan rules were either run out of town or put in the stocks.

church and state. For many years Rhode Island was the freest colony in New England. Even men who were not members of any church were permitted to vote. In these matters, Rhode Island remained unique among the colonies for many years.

Anne Hutchinson Is Banished

Anne Hutchinson was a sharp-witted woman with a forceful personality. She was also an amateur *theologian* who took a keen interest in religious doctrines. The word *theology* comes from two Greek terms meaning "God" and "study of." She discussed Sunday sermons with an ever-widening circle of admirers. She differed with most New England ministers on important religious issues and she said so—loudly! She believed that if a person was truly inspired by God, she or he could judge right from wrong. There was no need for a minister to explain it.

The court banished Anne Hutchinson from Massachusetts. She and her family and some of her followers walked to Rhode Island. Later she moved farther west where she was killed by Indians. When news of her death reached Massachusetts, several Puritans unkindly interpreted it as another example of God's good work in the world.

New Hampshire and Connecticut Are Founded

In the meantime, Puritan settlers were venturing far from the cluster of towns around Boston. Some went north to settle on land that was claimed both by Massachusetts and by several wealthy individuals in England. After much confusion, this land, called New Hampshire, became a separate colony with a royal governor. The district of Maine remained part of Massachusetts.

In 1635 Reverend Thomas Hooker and his entire congregation in Newtown decided to move west from Massachusetts to the southern part of the fertile Connecticut River valley. There they established several towns, including Hartford, outside the limits of Massachusetts. Still another group of Puritans arrived directly from England to found the town of New Haven. In 1662 these towns were drawn together as the single colony of Connecticut. They obtained a charter which provided for a government similar to that of Massachusetts.

Despite all these settlements in New England, much of the Atlantic coast remained open for European colonization.

Anne Hutchinson was banned from Boston for leading religious discussions such as this one in her home.

The Dutch Wedge

While English Puritans were establishing colonies in New England, the Dutch were founding one a short distance to the south. As early as 1609, Henry Hudson—an Englishman employed by the Dutch—explored the New England coast and went up the Hudson River as far as Albany. Shortly afterwards, Dutch merchants sent traders to Manhattan Island, at the mouth of the Hudson, to engage in fur trade with the Indians. In 1624 the Dutch bought Manhattan from the Indians for trade goods worth about 24 dollars and built a little town there which they named New Amsterdam, after the most important city in Holland.

No one knew it at the time, but the location was an exceedingly important one. A glance at a

New Netherland and New Sweden 1624–1664

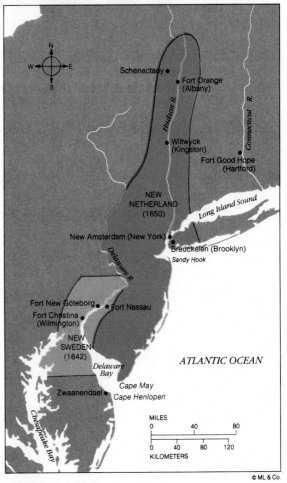

Map Skills *What modern city is on the site of Fort Orange? On what river was New Sweden?*

New Amsterdam about 1655. The town had a windmill, a church and one broad way or road through it. It gives no sign of its future greatness as New York City.

map shows why. The Hudson and its branch, the Mohawk River, cut through the great chain of the Appalachian Mountains. A series of lakes at the heads of these rivers complete the connection between the Atlantic coast and the St. Lawrence River valley to the north and the Great Lakes to the west. The site of New Amsterdam was the key to a vital lowland route into the interior of the North American continent.

Soon, Dutch traders founded Fort Orange (later named Albany) at the junction of the Hudson and Mohawk rivers. From there they made friendly contact with the Iroquois to the west and began trading with them for valuable furs.

By the 1630s the Dutch had built a number of enormous estates along both sides of the Hudson River. Dutch explorers also pushed east to the Connecticut River and ventured as far south as the Delaware River, where they took over a tiny colony of Swedish and Finnish settlers. But the Dutch never migrated in great numbers to their American colony, as the English did to theirs. Also, the Dutch lost a series of sea battles with the English in the middle of the century and were unable

to defend their holdings in North America. In 1664 New Amsterdam was taken over by the English, who renamed it New York for the king's younger brother, James, Duke of York. In fact, they named the entire Dutch area New York. The duke later gave a portion to two of his friends and it was named New Jersey for the British island of Jersey.

There are still Dutch place names all along the Hudson River, such as Tappan Zee, Stuyvesant, and Staatsburg. The Bowery, a part of New York City, comes from the Dutch word for farm (*bouwerie*). Harlem is named for the Dutch town of Haarlem.

The capture of New York was of the greatest importance. It was a crucial step in the English occupation of the entire seaboard between New France and Spanish Florida.

Maryland: A Proprietary Colony

Most of the early English colonies had been founded by joint-stock companies. Rhode Island and Connecticut were exceptions. A different method of organizing settlement was also tried in Maryland.

When King James died, his son, King Charles I, married a Roman Catholic. One of the major figures at his court, Sir George Calvert, was also a Catholic. Calvert had ambitions to found a colony in America. He hoped to profit financially from such a venture, and he also wanted to establish a haven for English Catholics, who were an unhappy minority in Protestant England.

Calvert's friend, the king, was well aware that the settlements around Jamestown did not occupy all the land of Virginia. So Charles I was happy to respond to Calvert's request for a land grant by giving him the part of Virginia that surrounded Chesapeake Bay. The gift was personal, and the royal charter provided that the Calvert family would be the *proprietors*, or owners, of the new colony. They could collect rents from everyone who settled there. The charter also gave Calvert broad powers of government in the colony. However, it provided for a representative assembly. It was, indeed, a magnificent gift. Calvert and his son gratefully named their colony Maryland—in honor of Charles's Catholic queen, Henrietta Maria.

George Calvert died while the charter was still being processed by royal bureaucrats. His son, Lord Baltimore, organized the expedition that left for Chesapeake Bay in 1633. There was no "starving time," because the Maryland settlers had learned from the sad experiences at Jamestown. They brought plenty of carefully selected provisions with them and soon discovered tobacco grew as well in Maryland as in Virginia.

The Calvert-Baltimore family had no desire to persecute Protestants in Maryland. And as large numbers of Protestants settled in the colony, Lord Baltimore began to fear that the Catholics might become victims of religious persecution themselves. In 1649 he requested that the Maryland legislature pass the Tolerance Act, which provided for freedom of worship.

The Carolinas: A Princely Gift

No other proprietary colony was established for thirty years. From 1642 to 1649 England was torn apart by its great civil war between loyalists to the king and those loyal to Parliament, many of whom were Puritans. The king tried to rule as an *absolute monarch*—that is, one with total power. He taxed people without the consent of Parliament. He declared that all who disagreed with the true (Anglican) church were an enemy of the kingdom. Finally, Charles dissolved Parliament and ruled without it. The armies of Parliament were victorious, and Charles was executed in 1649. For a

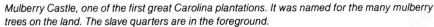

Mulberry Castle, one of the first great Carolina plantations. It was named for the many mulberry trees on the land. The slave quarters are in the foreground.

while, England became a commonwealth, or republic, headed first by General Oliver Cromwell, a Puritan, and then by his son. But the English grew weary of the rather grim and sober Puritan rule, and in 1660 Charles II was restored to the throne of his father. Charles owed political debts to his prominent supporters. So in 1663 he gave eight of them proprietary rights to Carolina (from the Latin for "land of Charles").

The first permanent settlement in Carolina was begun in 1670. Some of the settlers sailed directly from England, while others came from Barbados, an island in the West Indies. Slowly the colony grew. Charles Town, which later became Charleston, was the capital and chief port of the colony. There was much experimentation with a variety of crops. The weather proved too warm for tobacco but not for rice, which became Carolina's *staple crop*. Staple crops are those raw materials that have a fairly large and constant market.

Eventually the king made both South Carolina and North Carolina royal colonies. Both kept their representative assemblies. By this time such assemblies were regarded as normal and essential parts of English colonial governments.

Pennsylvania: The Holy Experiment

William Penn was the son of an admiral and was raised as a typical gentleman. He learned some Latin, law, and how to duel with a sword. In 1681 Charles II gave him a huge tract of land that ran north and west from the Delaware River and its bay. The king still owed Penn's late father, Admiral Penn, both gratitude and money for supporting his return to power. Charles repaid William handsomely with this land. It was named Pennsylvania, in honor of the admiral.

Quaker Beliefs. William Penn had become a Quaker. By doing so he had shocked and angered his father and many of his friends. He remained a

This sunny painting Penn's Treaty with the Indians by the Quaker Benjamin West reflects the artist's love of Indians. They taught him how to mix the red and yellow earths to make paint.

Types of American Colonies

Colony	Date	Leader	Type of Colony	Settlement
Virginia	1607	John Smith	Corporate (1607–1624) Royal (1624–1776)	Jamestown
Plymouth	1620	William Bradford	Corporate (1620–1691) Royal (1691–1776)	Plymouth
New Netherland (New York after 1663)	1626	Peter Minuit (for Dutch) Duke of York (for English)	Proprietary (1663–1685) Royal (1685–1776)	New Amsterdam (New York)
Massachusetts Bay	1630	John Winthrop	Corporate (1630–1691) Royal (1691–1776)	Boston
Maryland	1633	George Calvert	Proprietary (1632–1776)	St. Mary's
Rhode Island	1636	Roger Williams	Corporate (1643–1776)	Providence
Connecticut	1636	Thomas Hooker	Corporate (1643–1776)	Hartford
New Hampshire	1638	John Wheelwright	Proprietary (1639–1679) Royal (1679–1776)	Exeter
Delaware (Taken by Dutch from Swedish in 1655; taken by English from Dutch in 1664)	1638	Peter Minuit (who left Dutch West India Company and went into Swedish service)	Proprietary (1682–1776)	Wilmington
North Carolina: Albemarie Colony	1653	Group of eight proprietors	Proprietary (1663–1744) Royal (1744–1776)	Albemarie County
South Carolina	1663	Group of eight Proprietors	Proprietary (1663–1729) Royal (1729–1776)	Charleston
New Jersey	1664	Lord Berkeley Sir Carteret	Proprietary (1663–1702) Royal (1702–1776)	East Jersey — Carteret West Jersey — Salem
Pennsylvania	1682	William Penn,	Proprietary (1682–1776)	Philadelphia
Georgia	1732	James Oglethorpe	Proprietary (1732–1752) Royal (1752–1776)	Savannah

The colonies that developed on the eastern shore of what became the United States were proprietary, corporate, or royal colonies, depending on the kind of charter that was issued.

The Thirteen American Colonies 1750

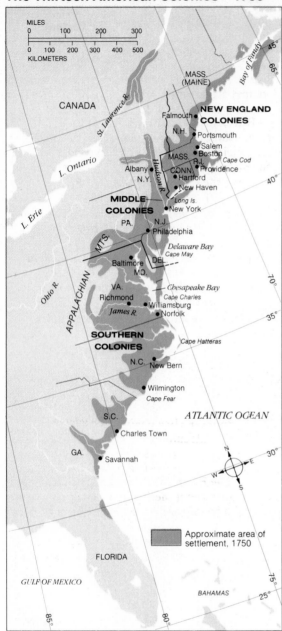

Map Skills *Which were the Middle Colonies? Did the area of settlement reach the Ohio River in 1750?* © ML & Co.

They gave aid and comfort to the poor and the distressed. They dressed plainly and refused to honor customary social distinctions. They would not raise their hats to nobles or even the king. They called everyone "thee" or "thou" in an age when most people used the plural "you" when speaking to people of high station. And, finally, Quakers were firm pacifists.

Penn's Policies. Penn provided a liberal plan of government for his colony. He gave the right to vote to all adult male landowners and taxpayers. All Christians were to have complete freedom of worship. And he helped plan the city of Philadelphia, which he called "the city of brotherly love."

In 1701 Penn approved the constitution that had been requested by the settlers in Pennsylvania. It provided for a *unicameral*, or single-house, legislature—the only one in the English colonies.

The constitution also provided for a separate assembly for the three southern counties along Delaware Bay. Delaware thereby gained a somewhat separate existence. However, it continued to have the same governor, whom Penn and his heirs appointed, as Pennsylvania.

A Successful Colony. Penn's colony was a great success. Early on, most of the settlers were English and Welsh Quakers who continued to dominate the government. But Penn's policies attracted many other groups who were drawn by promises of religious freedom and cheap land. More than any other proprietor, Penn was interested in establishing a good and fair society. He wanted it to be a "holy experiment" in living in the less corrupted, fresh environment of the New World. And, as things turned out, the experiment worked very well.

Section 4 Review

COMPREHENSION   Developing Vocabulary

1. Explain these terms: heresy, theology, proprietors, absolute monarch, staple crop, unicameral, stocks.

COMPREHENSION   Mastering Facts

1. What is a proprietary colony?
2. How did the English civil war (1642–1649) end?
3. What did the settlers in Carolina grow as their staple crop?
4. Where did Penn start his "holy experiment"?

courtly gentleman, but his Quaker ideas were regarded as foolish and dangerous.

The Quakers were a radical religious and social group of Protestant Christians. All Christians believed in good will toward others in principle. Quakers took this principle very seriously. They believed that a person's love of God could best be shown by brotherly love for every man and woman.

CHAPTER 2 Review

Chapter Summary

The first permanent English colony in the New World was Jamestown, established in 1607. Unlike Spain and France, England encouraged the growth and development of its colonial settlements by families. The English colonies were self-governing. This fact attracted increasing numbers of colonists, who also came because of economic opportunities and religious freedom. However, growing numbers of African slaves also came but worked unwillingly, mostly in the South. Between 1607 and 1732, thirteen English colonies were established.

Questions for Critical Thinking

COMPREHENSION   Summarizing Main Ideas

1. What were the advantages of the site on which Jamestown was established? What were the disadvantages of that location?
2. What were the three major difficulties that confronted English settlers in the Americas? How did the settlers manage to deal with each of these difficulties?

COMPREHENSION   Interpreting Events

1. Imagine that you had been an Algonquin at the time of the settlement at Jamestown. If you had been able to foresee the future, would you have given the English settlers food? Why or why not?
2. What effect did the head right system have on the settlement of Virginia?
3. How did the indenture system affect the unemployment problem in England? How did it affect the settlement of Virginia?
4. If you had been a member of the Virginia Company, what would you have done to encourage colonization in the New World?
5. If you had been living in the Massachusetts Bay Colony, would you have voted in favor of expelling Roger Williams? Anne Hutchinson? Why or why not?
6. If you had your choice, in which English colony would you have settled? Why?

APPLICATION   Using Skills To Evaluate Sources

Information can be obtained from many different sources. Since some sources are more reliable than others, it is important to evaluate them.

Below are several topics. Under each is a list of three sources which might provide information on that topic. For each topic, indicate which source is the most reliable, which source is second best, and which of the three is the least reliable.

1. The religious beliefs of the Puritans
   a. *The Scarlet Letter,* an American novel that deals with life in Puritan New England
   b. The collected sermons of John Calvin
   c. A contemporary account of the Massachusetts Bay Colony appearing in the official newsletter of the Anglican Church
2. The condition of indentured servants in Virginia
   a. A report by the Virginia Company to prospective settlers
   b. A letter from an indentured servant to a relative in England
   c. A letter by a member of the House of Burgesses to a relative in England
3. The events surrounding the adoption of the *Mayflower* Compact
   a. The diary of William Bradford
   b. *The Plymouth Adventure,* a motion picture about the Pilgrims
   c. A history of Plymouth written in 1700

EVALUATION   Comparing Past to Present

1. Compare the way in which the Pilgrims celebrated Thanksgiving in 1621 with the way in which your family celebrates it today.
2. What foods and other products did the Indians teach the English to use? Which of them do you use?
3. Identify any Puritan beliefs that are still held by people today.
4. Compare the techniques the Virginia Company used to encourage settlers to go to the New World with the techniques that states and cities in the United States use to encourage business firms to relocate from other parts of the country.

The Purpose of Colonies

In 1588 Spain's monopoly of the New World sank into the English Channel along with its Invincible Armada. After that victory, England entered the competition for New World colonies. The English started slowly, since the notion of making money from colonization was still a relatively new one. But during the next two centuries, England established and managed a highly profitable string of American colonies.

The primary purpose of the American colonies was to benefit the power and wealth of Great Britain. No one in the colonies or in England questioned it. That was the fundamental idea of *mercantilism,* the economic system followed eagerly by most European countries and their colonies from the 1500s to the 1700s.

Mercantilism refers, literally, to trading or other commercial activities. The theory of mercantilism held that the greater a nation's wealth, the greater its political and military power. Wealth was measured in terms of silver and gold in a nation's treasury.

The first and most obvious way of enriching a country was simply to get hold of large stores of gold and silver. The discovery in Central and South America of large deposits of gold and sil-

ver helped to make Spain, for a time, the most powerful nation in Europe. Between 1492 and 1600, more than 8,000,000 ounces of gold were mined in South America. As Spain paid for imports and for war debts in gold and silver, the precious metals streamed across Europe, allowing other countries to accumulate their own hoards.

But there were other ways of getting gold and silver. A major one was through trading. The rulers of France and England took control of their economies so as to stimulate manufacturing and trade. A ruler should control his or her country's commerce. After all, they reasoned, the head of a family manages the finances of the household, and the monarch is the father or mother of the nation. The goods created by manufacturing and trade could then be sold for gold and silver.

In directing the economic affairs of their kingdoms, mercantilist rulers kept one general principle in mind. For a nation to grow economically strong, it must maintain a favorable *balance of trade* with competitor countries. That meant that the nation should export more to those countries than it imports from them.

Mercantilist countries soon realized that, if they wanted an

ever-growing stock of gold and silver and a steady supply of raw materials for their manufacturing efforts, they could not rely simply on the resources of their own territory. Yet they did not wish to depend on other countries. The obvious solution was to acquire colonies rich with untapped resources. Governments therefore financed costly expeditions for explorers and conquerors who were to discover and subdue territories in Africa, the Far East, and the Americas. If those territories seemed promising, efforts were made to develop their resources and to encourage the emigration of permanent settlers. A population with roots in the land proved a more powerful defense for a colony than any army.

Colonization and the drive to accumulate wealth contributed significantly to the development of the black slave trade in the Western Hemisphere, particularly in South and Central America, the West Indies, and the American South. Early Spanish settlers used Indian slaves to do hard labor in mines and on plantations. The Indians were not used to such exhausting work. They became weak and caught diseases from the Spanish for which they had no resistance. The Indians died by the millions. Whole tribes were

Charleston about 1700. It has been called one of the loveliest colonial towns. Exports of rice and indigo to the British Empire enabled Charleston to prosper.

wiped out. Their numbers dwindled so rapidly that, in 1515, a Spanish bishop, Bartolomé de Las Casas, sought to protect the few survivors by suggesting the importation of Africans into the Americas. He argued that African slaves could better withstand the heat and drudgery of work in the colonies. As a result of this proposal (which the bishop soon regretted), millions of black slaves were sold to mine the gold, pick the cotton, and cut the sugar cane—the products that would strengthen the trading positions of European colonial powers.

What England wanted from its American colonies was a market for English produced goods and a source of the raw materials that it had been forced to import from other countries. At first, what England wanted fitted well with what the colonies wanted. North America was a huge continent with vast natural resources and a small population. The most profitable way of life for the settlers was to provide the raw materials, such as furs, iron, and lumber, for the English market. In England, there were comparatively few raw materials and a large population. Skilled English labor could turn the raw materials into fine furniture, clothes, and wrought iron. It was mutually advantageous for England to buy raw materials from the colonies and for the colonies to buy manufactured goods from England.

The British Empire in America was founded on strong commercial links between England and the colonies. Mercantilism, however, was based on the assumption that the economic dependence of the colonies would continue. It failed to take into account the growing spirit of free enterprise that existed in the colonies. The mercantile system could not reconcile two opposite goals: the enrichment of England and the enrichment of the colonies. This gap between the economic interests of England and its colonies was a major factor in the American struggle for independence.

Understanding Free Enterprise

1. How did the mercantilist idea of wealth differ from that of ours today?

2. Why was the mercantile system so beneficial to Britain and the colonies?

3. Why were settlers considered more important for colonial defense than an army from Britain?

CHAPTER 3

Colonial Life

1650–1700

People in the Chapter

Nathaniel Bacon—*the man who leads the frontier people of Virginia against the wealthy planters who run Virginia's government.*

William Berkeley—*the governor of Virginia and a bitter enemy of Bacon.*

Sarah Kemble Knight—*an early traveler through New England.*

West Africans—*people who come as slaves in increasing numbers to tend the tobacco fields of Virginia and the rice fields of South Carolina.*

Linking Past to Present

Not long after the English colonies were established, it became apparent that two very different life styles were developing in the northern and southern colonies. As early as 1611 the governor of Virginia complained to friends in England that his colonists were "so profane, so riotous and so full of mutiny that not many are Christians [except] in name."

But just a few years later the governor of Massachusetts Bay Colony praised his colonists by writing that "God had sifted a whole nation that he might send the choicest grain to the wilderness."

The differences between northern and southern colonies were due in part to climate, geography and the way the settlers made their living.

The South developed an agricultural society with a few very rich plantation owners and many poor people who were either slaves or indentured servants or small farmers. There was no large middle class and there were very few cities. The indentured servants were generally single people, mostly male, who did not have the stabilizing influence of spouses and families.

In the New England colonies, settlers came with their families. In fact, entire communities moved from England to the New World. People generally settled in towns. There were no great social differences. Life was more prosperous for the average person and society seemed more stable than in the South.

1 THE SOUTH: A DIVIDED AGRICULTURAL SOCIETY

VOCABULARY   *indigo   Tidewater   Piedmont*

Every colony had to find products to export. In the South these were agricultural crops, which were sold for cash to buy manufactured goods. Most southern colonies had one or two staple crops. These were raw materials which had a fairly large and constant market.

Some Characteristics of Southern Life

Virginia and Maryland had found a staple crop in tobacco. Colonists in South Carolina cultivated rice and later indigo (a blue-purple dye). North Carolina's principal exports were wood and wood by-products from its pine forests. Wood was used for staves, hoops, and barrelheads—which could be reassembled into barrels—while the sticky sap of the pine was used for filling cracks between the planks of sailing vessels. The colonies' lumber brought good prices in England and in the West Indies. Wood from tropical trees in the West Indies was too soft and crooked for making barrels. The island colonists needed the barrels to pack their sugar and molasses for shipment overseas.

Large Farms.   By 1650 Virginia had developed some of the characteristics that would mark its history. People were not settling in towns but on large farms or plantations scattered along the James River. Much land was needed to grow tobacco profitably. Tobacco quickly uses up the minerals in the soil so fields became exhausted and new land was needed.

These large plantations were located next to riv-

ers so there was very little reason for towns to develop. There was no need for city dock facilities because planters shipped their goods directly from the plantation to the northern colonies and to Europe. There was no need for city warehouses because goods could be stored on the plantation. And many of the goods which merchants might sell in a town were made on the plantation. So there was no great need for shops, bakeries, and markets.

Since there were few towns, there were few schools. People did not go from the surrounding areas into a central school. Children were taught to read and write at home.

This painting shows how a plantation was like a town with mills, storehouses, stables and a church.

Cheap Labor. Tobacco needed lots of workers and Virginia was getting them, as you know, in the form of indentured servants. Hundreds of young single men came over to seek their fortunes in Virginia.

Perhaps as many as one-third of all white settlers in the southern colonies came as indentured servants. During the servant's term of indenture, he or she could be bought and sold from one owner to another. At first servants were treated miserably, and some were almost worked to death. Masters had the legal right to whip their servants for any kind of disobedience, and they did so often. If a servant died as the result of this "reasonable correction," the master could not be tried for murder.

As the years went by, however, the treatment of servants improved. After all, the colonial assemblies did not want to discourage the flow of servants from England. They passed laws giving servants certain rights and protections. Laws required masters to equip their servants with clothes, tools, and, in some cases, free land at the end of their term.

So a single cash crop, large farms, cheap and plentiful labor, and a mild climate were beginning to produce a few wealthy tobacco planters who led a leisurely existence. And for some the road to riches was traveled swiftly. One colonist wrote to his friend Sir Didley Carleton, British ambassador to Holland.

66 Now that your Lordship may know that we are not the veriest (worst) beggars in the world, our cow keeper here of James City on Sunday goes accoutered (dressed) all in flesh flaming silk; and a wife of one that in England [had been a miner] wears her rough beaver hat with a fair pearl hat band, and a silken suit.99

The Causes of Bacon's Rebellion

The differences between the few rich and the many poor became especially important in Virginia. Some seventy years after the colony was founded, they helped cause a major conflict that also concerned treatment of Virginia's Indians.

This conflict in 1676 is usually known as Bacon's Rebellion after its leader Nathaniel Bacon. Its main causes had to do with social differences, the right to vote, the levying of taxes, and especially the treatment of Indians.

Tidewater Versus Frontier Farmers. As you know, under the head right system any person who paid his way to Virginia got fifty acres of land and an additional fifty acres for each person he brought with him. Thus, men who could afford to buy servants received more land than anyone else. More land and more servants meant that more tobacco could be raised. More tobacco brought in larger profits with which the planter bought even more servants, and for each one the planter received another fifty acres. Consequently, there emerged in Virginia a powerful and wealthy aristocracy of planters. Their plantations were generally located along the James, Potomac, Rappahannock, and York rivers in an area known as the *Tidewater*.

Tidewater Virginia is the stretch of land along the Atlantic coast that extends some seventy-five miles inland. It gets its name because these deep rivers are made slightly salty by the tides from the Atlantic Ocean. Beyond the Tidewater lies the *Piedmont*—a plateau of forests and rolling hills. To the west of the Piedmont are the Appalachian Mountains. (Refer to the map on page 63.)

When the good land in the Tidewater was all occupied, poorer people, ex-servants, and newly arrived immigrants moved westward into the Piedmont. The younger sons of Tidewater planters also had to move on because they did not inherit

Nathaniel Bacon leads a rebellion which drives Virginia Governor Berkeley from Jamestown.

any of their fathers' land. The soil of the Pidmont hills was less fertile than the land of the Tidewater. Further, farms were often smaller in the Piedmont. As a result of these two conditions, life in the Piedmont was much more difficult than in the Tidewater. The small farmers of the land in the western edge of the colonial settlements were very susceptible to economic hardships resulting from low prices. During the 1660s, the price of tobacco declined. This decline in price hurt the farmers in the Piedment seriously.

Unfair Taxes and Voting System. At the same time, by law, taxes fell most heavily on poor people. Some wealthy members of the governing council paid very few taxes. The Piedmont people bitterly resented this arrangement. Also, in Virginia only large landowners could vote. The small farmers of the backwoods areas had no vote. In fact, the colony's government was run by wealthy men largely for their own benefit. Large planters made all decisions about who could own what land. They passed tax laws that favored the rich and hurt the poor. Moreover, it seemed as if the situation would never change. In the northern colonies the governments were elected every year, thus giving people a chance to correct government abuses. But in Virginia the governor had not permitted an election in fourteen years. He kept the members of the House of Burgesses loyal to him by giving them opportunities to make money from their government position.

Disagreement over Indians. The greatest disagreement between the planter aristocracy and the hill farmers, however, was about the Indians. Virginia's long-time governor, crusty old William Berkeley, looked upon Indians as subjects of the king. Accordingly, he felt it was his duty to protect them against attack by settlers. The governor had another reason for treating the Indians with care: he and his wealthy friends had a profitable fur-trading arrangement with them. They did not want the trade disturbed.

But the poorer people of the backwoods lived much nearer to Indians and to Indian lands. They thought they did not have enough land of their own. They wanted more land from the Indians, and they preferred to fight for it rather than buy it. Bloody encounters broke out as Indians and settlers attacked each other. Many small farmers demanded that Governor Berkeley send soldiers for

Tidewater Virginia

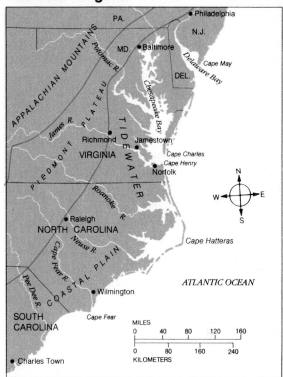

Map Skills *The Tidewater extends from Virginia into what other state? How wide is the Piedmont at the Potomac?*

their protection. The governor refused to do so and warned the backwoods settlers to respect the rights of Virginia's Indians.

In 1676 some settlers attacked a group of friendly Indians and drove them farther away from the white settlements. The attack was led by Nathaniel Bacon, a young man of some wealth and good social connections. In fact, Bacon was a cousin of Berkeley. But one of his overseers had been killed by the Indians, and he sympathized with the problems of the backwoods farmers.

The Rebellion Collapses

Anger at the Virginia government now boiled over. Bacon and his armed farmers and ex-indentured servants marched on Jamestown to demand that the government protect them against the Indians and to hear their other grievances. The governor did promise to call a new assembly, and the government declared it would make war on the Indians. But as time went by and nothing happened,

Bacon again went on the march. He burned Jamestown as Berkeley and his followers fled. Months of chaos followed. Indentured servants ran away from their masters. Probably about one hundred colonists died in the fighting. Bacon died of a fever.

The leaderless rebellion collapsed as quickly as it began. Eleven hundred troops arrived from England to restore order. Yet the British government sympathized with some of Bacon's complaints. The soldiers brought with them a royal pardon for the rebels. But Governor Berkeley was not a merciful man, and his pride had been stung when he was chased out of Jamestown. Before he was recalled to England, he had twenty-three rebel leaders hanged. Even King Charles was astounded. He remarked, "That old fool has hanged more men in that naked country than I have done for the murder of my father."

Bacon's Rebellion was the first popular uprising in the American colonies. It was a rebellion against a government that overtaxed the people yet tried to protect the Indians but did not serve their needs. The rebellion did not succeed. The established wealthy planters remained in control of political affairs. But they learned a lesson. Indentured servants had proven dangerous, especially because most of them owned guns. So the planters turned to a different kind of laborer—black slaves.

Section 1 Review

COMPREHENSION   **Developing Vocabulary**

1. Explain these terms: indigo, Tidewater, Piedmont, barrelheads.

COMPREHENSION   **Mastering Facts**

1. Why was North Carolina lumber needed in the West Indies?
2. What effect did indentured servants have on Virginia society?
3. What were three reasons for Bacon's Rebellion?

2   SLAVERY FLOURISHES IN THE SOUTH

VOCABULARY   *lineage   artisans   Gullah*

Slavery existed in *all* the English colonies, not just in the South. The Dutch in New Netherland owned slaves, and the English continued the practice after New Netherland became New York. The first African slaves came to Massachusetts from the West Indies in 1638. South Carolina settlers brought slaves with them from Barbados. Even the Quakers of Pennsylvania had slaves.

Slavery was different from indentured servitude in three important ways. First, the master of a slave did not own just the slave's labor, as was the case with an indentured servant. The master literally owned the slave as a living piece of property, the same way he might own a horse. Second, slavery was for life, not for a term of years. Third, the children of slaves automatically became slaves themselves.

An Unplanned Development

The English colonists did not plan to establish the institution of slavery. It developed gradually, but historians are not agreed on when it began.

We do know that in South Carolina, Indians were enslaved from the earliest days of the colony. Occasionally, English settlers enslaved Indian prisoners of war. More often, Indians sold captives from enemy tribes to the English. But most of them were difficult to control. Captive Indians had friends and relatives still living nearby. They knew the paths back to their own lands. They had far better knowledge of the fields and forests than the English had. They could slip away easily, and they were hard to find. English slavemasters knew about these difficulties, so they shipped many Indian slaves to the West Indies where they exchanged them for African slaves.

From the colonial point of view, Africans made much more satisfactory slaves. Once in the colonies, Africans were completely cut off from their homeland. Also, they were much more used to agriculture than to hunting. So eventually slavery in the colonies became Negro slavery, and most slaves were black Africans.

Slavery did not become popular in Virginia until after 1690. At that time there were an estimated 3000 blacks and 15,000 white servants out of a total population of 75,000. But a few blacks were free. They had been freed by their masters, sometimes for faithful service, sometimes because they became Christians, but most often because their masters were not used to the idea of slavery.

The African Slave Trade

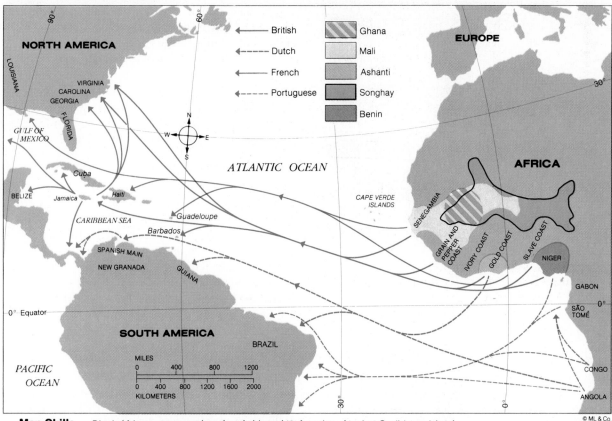

Map Skills *Black Africans were enslaved and shipped to America. At what Caribbean island did many stop on their way to the Southern colonies? What country brought slaves to Louisiana?*

African Immigration Begins

The first Africans who arrived in Virginia in 1619 were "sold" to the English settlers. At least a few of these Africans were freed after a term of servitude. Only a few more Africans arrived during the next forty years. By about 1660, however, at least some of them were serving for life. The Maryland and Virginia assemblies began passing laws that recognized the existence of this new status.

Africans arrived in the American colonies in massive numbers after 1700. Between 1720 and 1760 black people made up about 20 percent of the colonial population. (That was a higher proportion than today's figure of about 12 or 13 percent.) In the South at least 40 percent of the non–Indian population was black.

The African Homeland. African slaves came only from certain parts of Africa. In this respect they were like early European migrants to the New World. Both groups left from the western parts of

their continents. Most Africans came from West Africa and the western coast of central Africa. Although they lived near the coast, most Africans were not maritime peoples. Unlike so many of the English, they did not choose to venture far out to sea. They were basically land lovers. Yet among them were many skilled boatmen who operated enormous canoes on rivers and along the coastal waters.

The people of West Africa belonged to many different ethnic groups. They spoke more than one hundred distinct languages. Each language group had its own system of government and religion, and each was aware of being a distinct people. Except for a few Islamic Africans, the slaves who came to America were people of the spoken— rather than the written—word. Although their languages differed, they shared a common musical style—a similarity of beat and rhythm that served as an important means of communication on slave ships and in the New World.

65

The king of Benin leaves his palace preceded by musicians with pet tigers. Behind ride the nobles.

Lineage. There had been large empires in West Africa during the Middle Ages, but they had collapsed before the Western Europeans arrived in the 1400s. Most West Africans were living in tribal units somewhat similar to those of the American Indians. They felt that *lineage* was their most important social unit. A lineage consisted of people who were related to one another by blood and marriage. Often the lineage was thought to include all people descended from a single, mythical ancestor. The lineage included all those relatives who had died and all those yet to be born. For most Africans, one of the worst things about slavery was separation from one's lineage.

Slavery in Africa. Slavery existed in West Africa prior to the coming of Western Europeans. But in African societies, slavery was quite different than in colonial America. There was little plantation slavery in Africa. Slaves occupied a wide variety of positions, and most of them had legal rights. Some slaves were household workers, while others worked alongside their owner in the fields. Some were soldiers, often making up an elite unit. There were even slaves who served as governors of regions. People became slaves in Africa because they had been kidnapped, or were prisoners of war, or were poor people seeking a protective master. But unlike the American colonies, no one ever became a slave just because one happened to be black.

African rulers and merchants sold slaves to European slave traders. But as slavery became a growing business, African chiefs began to create more slaves. New crimes were invented so more criminals could be sold into slavery. Of course, some slaves were captured directly by European sailors. But such kidnapping was dangerous for Europeans because local African rulers were in good positions to take revenge. For the most part, European slave traders traded with the powerful chieftains of the coast. Europeans did not penetrate far inland and did not even settle on the African coast for long.

The Voyage. Conditions on the voyage to America were horribly brutal. Once purchased by a European trader, slaves were herded into the holds of slave ships. Men and women were packed into separate holds. They lay jammed side by side below deck, often without enough space to roll over. Many died, especially when disease swept the vessel. Some slaves spent months under such conditions. Storms on the Atlantic crossing meant closed hatches and air heavy with the smell of sweat, blood, vomit, and body wastes.

The survivors of this ordeal arrived in the American colonies in a state of shock, grief, horror, anger, and bewilderment. Many felt relieved to escape the terrible conditions aboard ship. But they found themselves in the hands of white men whose language and ways they could not understand.

Slavery in the Tobacco Colonies

In Virginia and Maryland, slaves were sold in small groups, often at the river landing place of a wealthy planter. They were sent off on foot to clearings in the woods. There, rows of plants were pointed out to them and familiar-looking hoes were thrust into their hands. Their new "home" was one of several single-room cabins standing at the edge of tobacco fields and cornfields. Usually they were many miles from their owner's house. Their work and their lives were directed by a white overseer, who slept in one of the cabins on the only mattress. By day he beat them when they did not understand his orders or pretended not to. They were almost completely isolated.

In Virginia there were few towns, so many of the jobs usually found in towns were done on the plantations. The slaves on these estates, most of whom were Virginia-born, were *artisans*. Artisans are people skilled in a trade—usually one in which they use their hands. There were blacksmiths, carpenters, and coopers who made barrels. They regarded their skills with pride and usually knew more about their work than the overseers did. Unlike the field laborers, most of whom were African-born, these artisans were not under constant supervision. They had considerable independence and mobility. A carpenter, for example, might be sent off more than twenty miles to build a cabin or an outhouse on one of the planter's smaller units.

There is no evidence that slave artisans envied the slaves who worked in the big plantation house. True, houseslaves did have the chance of getting leftovers from their master's dinner table, as well as castoff clothing from his family. But they were constantly under his critical eyes, and laziness, forgetfulness, or mistakes in housework were often severely punished.

Slavery in South Carolina

In South Carolina the slaves were concentrated in the coastal low country, where they outnumbered whites by as much as nine to one. This was rice country, and the rice planters were the wealthiest men in the colonies. They spent months at a time away from their plantations. They owned

Millions of Africans were taken to slavery on ships such as the one diagrammed below. It carried 454 people. Each man had a space of 6 × 1⅓ ft. Each woman had 5⅚ × 1⅓ ft.

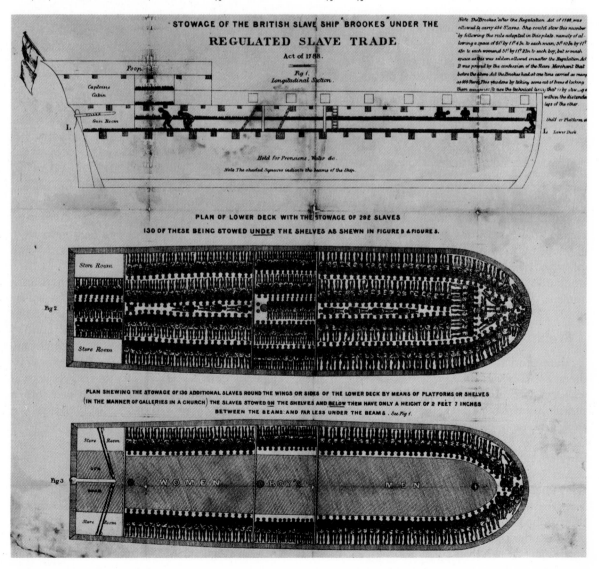

town houses in Charles Town, the only city in the colonial South. The life of their slaves was therefore somewhat different from the life of slaves in the tobacco colonies.

The slave artisan class in South Carolina was small because there were a number of skilled white craftsmen in Charles Town. The typical rice plantation was relatively large, with a minimum of thirty slaves. Rice-country slaves had less contact with whites and more with each other. The planters were wealthy enough to purchase them in large groups off the slave ships arriving in Charles Town. This meant that sizable numbers of slaves from the same ship, and even from the same African tribe, ended up living on the same plantation. So they remained more African in culture than slaves elsewhere in the colonies. They began to speak a language of their own, called *Gullah*. It was a mixture of English and various West African languages. White overseers had to learn it.

The technique of growing rice was complicated. Fields had to be flooded and then drained at precisely the right time. The English settlers were unfamiliar with rice-growing. In all probability they learned how to do it from African slaves who had cultivated rice in their homeland. This probably explains why the rice country had a unique pattern of work for slaves. Rather than being worked from dawn until dusk, slaves were assigned a task which was simply a certain amount of work to be done on a given day. When slaves finished their tasks, they could quit work. Many did so by mid-afternoon.

Section 2 Review

COMPREHENSION   Developing Vocabulary

1. Explain these terms: lineage, artisans, Gullah.

COMPREHENSION   Mastering Facts

1. How did slavery differ from the system of indentured servitude?
2. Why were Indians difficult to use as slaves?
3. From what area of Africa did blacks first come?
4. Since Africans spoke different languages, what method of communicating did they have?

3 THE NORTH DEVELOPS COMMERCE AND CITIES

VOCABULARY   *Middle Colonies   rumbullion*

Life in New England and in the Middle Colonies (those north of Virginia) developed differently because the economy was different. There was no single staple crop. Settlers in the northern colonies developed a wide variety of goods which could be sold at home and traded abroad. The story of New England's early experience shows this development.

Molasses and Rumbullion

Many Puritan migrants brought money with them. Previously established settlers were happy to sell corn, pigs, and other provisions to the newcomers to help them get established. In 1640 the great flow of migration was stopped by the outbreak of the English civil war. Immediately, New England suffered its first economic depression.

Yet very soon, as John Winthrop put it, "the Lord opened up a trade with the West Indies." The great sugar boom was just getting underway in the Caribbean islands. Slaves were beginning to pour into the West Indies, where they worked the sugarcane fields. New Englanders shipped salted meat, corn, butter, and other foods to the islands. Like settlers in North Carolina, they sold lumber and barrels, candles, and horses in the islands. And from the waters off New England and Newfoundland came fish that West Indian planters fed to their slaves.

In return, merchants received precious cash from wealthy sugar planters who had earned it by shipping molasses and sugar to England. Ships from Boston and other smaller ports also returned with sugar and its less expensive by-product, molasses. West Indian molasses became the usual sweetener for New England townspeople and farmers. Molasses could also be distilled into a throat-warming liquor known as *rumbullion*. We call it rum.

Shipping and Shipbuilding

Puritan sea captains guided their vessels into the rivers and harbors of other colonies. They sold such goods as guns, tools, nails, glass bottles, and kitchen utensils. At first they obtained these articles from England. As the years went by, artisans

Travel in America in the 1600s was not pleasant. Roads were merely paths hacked through the forest. Inns were rare, so all food and cooking equipment had to be taken along.

of New England began to manufacture some of these goods.

New England ships became important to the British Empire's merchant marine. They carried staples from southern colonies to England and southern Europe, and ventured to Africa for slaves. Shipbuilding became one of the most important industries in New England. Some of these ships were sold, along with their cargoes, when they reached London or some other English port.

Family Farming

Although numerous towns sprang up in the North, the great majority of people in the colonies were farmers.

Chores. Anyone who has ever lived on a family farm knows that such a life involves long hours and hard work for everyone. Children worked at least part time from the age when they could be shown how to shell peas, shuck corn, or fetch firewood. Women performed an unending round of tasks. They cooked in metal pots that were hung over the open fireplace. They baked in a hollow compartment in the chimney that served as an oven. They spun rough cloth and sewed it into clothing for the family. They washed clothes and bedding in wooden tubs with soap they made themselves.

Men did most of the heavy outdoor work. They cleared fields with a horse, ox, or mule, dragging away heavy stones, logs, underbrush, and tree stumps. They sowed the seed, prayed for rain, chopped the weeds, and prayed for clear skies at harvest time. After the harvest, they had time to build sheds, cut fence rails, mend the harnesses for the horses, trap raccoons, fix the chimneys, and help their womenfolk teach the children to behave, work, read, and pray.

Compensations. But there were compensations. There was very little paperwork or, indeed, paper of any kind. There were practically no bills to pay. Exchanges of goods and services were usually done on the spot between people who usually knew each other very well. Often no cash was involved. Credit normally depended on one's reputation with a peddler, an owner of a tiny general store, or a neighbor.

Taxes—whether imposed by the town, county, or colonial government—were a nuisance. But such taxes were easily understandable even when they seemed too large. Northern farmers knew exactly what they were paying for. Taxes would help support several widows and perhaps six or seven orphans in the town. They would pay the minister's salary. They would pay the travel costs of the town's two representatives to the colonial assembly. The farmers voted annually for these representatives and therefore had a sense of control over, or at least of participation in, the process of government.

Compared to farmers of the Old World, American farmers were quite prosperous. They had a far better chance of obtaining land of their own than did farmers in England. Because land was so easy to get, American farmers did not have to cultivate it so carefully. They could abandon farms when the soil wore out and move farther west.

Traveling Across Country

In the early 1700s, Sarah Kemble Knight took a trip from Boston to New York, staying at farms and country inns along the way. In a letter she described some of the people she met. When she arrived at one inn to spend the night, the innkeeper asked her a lot of impertinent questions.

" I told her she was quite rude to ask all those questions. Finally she led me to a parlor in a little shack in the back. It was almost filled with the bed. It was so high, I was forced to climb on a chair to get up to the wretched bed.

In the morning the woman brought me something to eat. It was like a twisted cable, but very white. Then she put it on a board and began to pull at it. When it began to spread, she served with it a dish of pork and cabbage. Over it she poured a purple sauce. She also gave me some Indian bread (cornbread). I was hungry but still had trouble eating this.

Next day I went to a merchant's house (store). In comes a tall country fellow. His mouth was full of tobacco. These people keep chewing and spitting as long as their eyes are open. The fellow went into the middle of the room. He nodded and spit quite a lot. These people generally stand around saying nothing when they first come into a store. I think they stand in awe of the merchant. **"**

Section 3 Review

COMPREHENSION   Developing Vocabulary
1. Explain these terms: rumbullion, Middle Colonies, provisions.

COMPREHENSION   Mastering Facts
1. What started the trading boom between New England and the West Indies?
2. Where was the oven in colonial houses?
3. What did colonial farmers tend to do when their land wore out?
4. How was tax money used in the northern colonies?

4   THE VARIETY OF COLONIAL LIFE

VOCABULARY   *pomanders   linsey-woolsey   militarism*

By 1700 only about 5 percent of the colonial population lived in cities. All the cities were seaports, because the sea was the highway to the larger world.

Several of these cities became especially important. Boston was the largest, with a population of about 17,000. But Philadelphia and New York would soon surpass it. Charles Town, South Carolina, and Newport, Rhode Island, were the fourth and fifth largest cities.

Prosperous Confusion

Many people from the country never saw a city in their entire lives. Those who did were astounded by the crowding and bustle. Many streets were actually paved with stones. Later, some of them were even lit by oil lamps.

Let's follow a visiting farmer's wagon, only one of many that creaks and rattles through the narrow streets. Most wagons are piled high with corn or wheat, vegetables, fruits, and boards or firewood. Now and then a brightly painted gentleman's carriage makes its way slowly through the traffic. Dogs yap and nip at the horses and oxen. Pigs and an occasional goat jostle for the garbage in the streets. Small herds of sheep and cattle move along their unknowing way to slaughterhouses. Hundreds of screaming seagulls circle overhead, waiting to feed on refuse from the slaughterhouses. More gulls circle the masts of the sailing vessels, tied up at the wharves or lying at anchor in the harbor. They await more stinking garbage from the ships or the arrival of a loaded fishing vessel.

Hundreds of doorways beckon the curious visitor. Our farming family can tell a good deal about what goes on behind these doors just by peering through the windows on either side. Or they can watch what sort of person goes in and out. Gentlemen wearing wigs and their well-dressed women visit at the silversmith's and the clock merchant's shops. Ship captains visit the *chandler's* shop to purchase clocks, telescopes, and ship fittings of all kinds. Weather-beaten mates clamber ashore from their longboats on their way to sail lofts and *rope walks* (the places where ropes are made). Sailmakers and ropemakers work in buildings that are far larger than the meetinghouse in the farmer's village.

There are many items to tempt our farm family. In the shops of grand merchant gentlemen, goods just off the ship from England are offered for sale. There are bells, buckles, brass buttons, books, copper kettles, music boxes, iron nails, and steel knives. There are heads for axes and heads for hoes. (Farmers make their own handles.) There are hinges, pulleys, hooks, and harness fittings. There are glass bottles filled with medicines and scents. There are *pomanders* (a cloth bag or clay globe containing a sweet-smelling spice), expensive oils, rolls of silks and satins, and rolls of the more humble cloth, *linsey-woolsey*—a mixture of wool and linen or cotton.

Everyone seems to be busy in the town—even the rich. The merchants work long hours. They supervise their account books, write out instructions

By about 1700 Philadelphia was the largest colonial city. Through this port flowed a world-wide trade.

for ship captains, and correspond with their agents in other colonies, the West Indies, and London.

Urban Problems

There were also urban problems that did not exist in the countryside. For example, by 1700 all the cities had exhausted their local supplies of firewood. This early energy crisis was met by bringing wood in from greater and greater distances. There was also the problem of crime. Cities had no regular police force, and part-time watchmen tried to keep the peace. Much of the crime was caused by the large temporary population of sailors that filled most towns.

There was little sanitation, but generally things were better than in parts of London and Paris. In Europe people in the narrow streets had to keep a sharp eye and ear out. When they heard the warning cry of "gardey loo!" they sprang out of the way to escape garbage descending from windows of houses that loomed up on each side. But gradually, sewers and pipes for drinking water were put under the ground of colonial cities.

Fires were a menace because the wooden houses were packed so tightly together. At one time or another every colonial city suffered a terrible fire that wiped out entire sections. Because there were no regular firefighters, citizens organized volunteer fire-fighting units. So great was the fire danger, that as early as 1646 the Massachusetts legislature banned smoking within five miles of any town.

A Flood of Human Resources

All immigrants had to pass through one of the colonial ports. This gave additional color, liveliness, and interest to the cities. During the 1600s most immigrants came from England, but later they were outnumbered by Africans and people from other European countries. Among the latter were the Germans and the Scotch-Irish.

The Germans. The first German immigrants arrived in the 1680s. They came from the western part of Germany. Most were attracted to Pennsylvania by William Penn's successful advertising campaign. Penn sent paid agents into the countryside of western Germany to attract settlers to his new colony. The agents stressed Penn's policy of complete religious freedom and free land.

Not surprisingly, the first group of German settlers were Quakers or members of religious groups with similar views. Soon other religious groups came, including Lutherans and Mennonites. These were hardworking, frugal, and pious people who were against *militarism* (war-like policies and attitudes) and left Europe to escape it.

Most of the Germans were peasants and very poor. Because they could not afford to pay their way across the Atlantic, they sold themselves into indentured servitude. Ship captains bought their labor on one side of the Atlantic and sold it on the other. Actually the ship captains sold only the survivors of the voyage because many passengers died at sea in the holds of the overcrowded vessels. Sometimes the survivors were forced into extra years of servitude in order to pay back the cost of passage of their dead relatives.

Many of the Germans took no active interest in Pennsylvania politics. They tended to keep to themselves and often did not even bother to learn English. They set up German language schools and newspapers. Partly because of their skillful use of fertilizer, they were the most productive farmers in colonial Pennsylvania. From German farms came great quantities of wheat, barley, rye, beef, and huge hams. German cattle produced a surplus of hides which became tanned leather goods or were exported raw to the European market.

The Scotch-Irish. By 1700 a much larger group of Scotch-Irish began arriving. They came to most of the colonies south of New England. But like the Germans, the great majority landed in Philadelphia.

The Scotch-Irish were themselves the descendants of migrants. Their ancestors had been moved by Queen Elizabeth I of England and her successor James I from lowland Scotland to the province of Ulster in northern Ireland. The monarchs wanted to drive out the native Catholic Irish and replace them with the Protestant Scots. Their religious beliefs were much like those of Puritans, but they were usually called Presbyterians. In Ulster the Scotch-Irish had prospered at the expense of the native Roman Catholic Irish. Conflict between the two groups left wounds that have still not healed. But economic depression struck Northern Ireland early in the 1700s. So tens of thousands set off for a better life in America. Many came as indentured servants.

In Pennsylvania most Scotch-Irish took up farming in frontier areas. There they soon got the reputation of being quick-tempered, particularly with the Indians. As their numbers grew, many Scotch-Irish, as well as some Germans, moved southward from Pennsylvania into the western parts of Maryland and Virginia. Later they moved still farther south into the backcountry of North and South Carolina. The Scotch-Irish were accepted more quickly by their neighbors than the Germans were, probably because they spoke English—though with a distinct accent.

A Variety of Peoples. Another large ethnic group were the descendants of the Dutch in New York and northern New Jersey. There were a number of smaller groups as well. French Calvinists fled persecution at home to settle in various American cities. A group of highland Scots as well as a few Irish Catholics settled in North Carolina. A small number of Jews, some from Portugal, settled in such cities as Newport and Philadelphia. Descendants of Swedes and Finns still lived along the banks of the Delaware River. All these different peoples, the forerunners of millions more who were to come, gave a rich and permanent character to American life. The variety of peoples and religious groups astounded European visitors to the American colonies. Only the New England colonies lacked this wide assortment of peoples.

Section 4 Review

COMPREHENSION   Developing Vocabulary

1. Explain these terms: pomanders, linsey-woolsey, militarism, Mennonites, Presbyterians, chandler, rope walks.

COMPREHENSION   Mastering Facts

1. What was the largest colonial city in 1700?
2. What were four problems that confronted colonial cities and towns?
3. Where did most German immigrants to America settle?
4. Where did most Scotch-Irish immigrants settle?

CHAPTER 3 Review

Chapter Summary

A *divided agricultural society developed in the South as both rich plantation owners and poorer frontier farmers sought land. The importation of slaves from Africa through the West Indies began in 1619. Although slavery existed in all of the English colonies, it became an especially important source of labor in the South. Meanwhile, commerce and trade began to flourish in the New England and Middle Colonies. The arrival of different ethnic groups brought much variety to colonial culture.*

Questions for Critical Thinking

COMPREHENSION   Summarizing Main Ideas

1. Compare slavery in Africa, the tobacco colonies, and the rice colonies. What two factors account for most of the differences in the way slaves in these three areas were treated?
2. Compare life on colonial farms with life in colonial cities. In which type of community would you have preferred to live? Give reasons for your choice.
3. Compare the northern and southern colonies with regard to the following: (a) economy; (b) importance of slavery; (c) importance of foreign trade; (d) number of cities; (e) social classes; (f) social mobility between classes; (g) form of government. Based on your comparisons, would you say that the two groups of colonies resembled each other, or not?

COMPREHENSION   Interpreting Events

1. Why were staple crops so important in the colonial economy?
2. What do you think might have been done to prevent Bacon's Rebellion?
3. What was the political significance of Bacon's Rebellion?
4. If Bacon's Rebellion had not taken place, do you think the slave trade with Africa would have increased? Why or why not?
5. Why did southern planters find it more advantageous to enslave blacks rather than Indians?
6. If you had been a farmer in Pennsylvania during the early 1700s, how do you think you would have reacted to the influx of German immigrants? Why?

7. Do you think that a wide variety of peoples was an advantage or a disadvantage to the colonies? Defend your opinion.

APPLICATION   Using Skills To Evaluate Sources

Sometimes, items of information from the same source may not be equally reliable. Below are two groups of statements that might have appeared in colonial newspapers in the late 1600s. For each group, indicate which of the three statements you consider the most reliable, and why.

1. The importation of slaves
   a. Charles Town port officials announced today that 50,000 blacks have been imported from West Africa this year, a drop of 5 percent from last year's figure.
   b. A source close to Charles Town Mayor Arvin Johnston said today that there has been a 15 percent increase in the importation of African slaves over the past twelve months.
   c. This reporter learned that Lawson Collins, supervisor of the port of Charles Town, will address the Chamber of Commerce tomorrow about his concerns over a reported 20 percent drop in the annual number of slaves being brought into South Carolina.
2. Reports on Bacon's Rebellion
   a. Official circles in the House of Burgesses have stated that Virginia will send an expedition against the Indians next month.
   b. Governor Berkeley said today that he has no intention of moving against Indians in the Piedmont area.
   c. Nathaniel Bacon told a cheering crowd of supporters that state officials have promised to send troops to help fight the Indians.

EVALUATION   Comparing Past to Present

1. Compare living conditions in colonial cities around 1700 with living conditions in American cities today. Which problems that existed in the past still exist? Have we changed the manner in which we try to handle any of these problems? Explain.
2. Do you think farmers in the United States today would be as amazed at urban life as farmers in 1700 were? Explain.

Family Life

Before churches and schools, before governments, even before the building of colonial towns, one institution had already been firmly established: the family. Since the earliest people populated the earth, families have played fundamental roles in the formations of cultures. Families were especially important in the settlement of the American colonies. One major feature which distinguished English pioneers from their French and Spanish counterparts was that families, not just individuals, settled in the English colonies.

Important Characteristics. Despite changing times, sizes, and functions, today's American family resembles the colonial family in several basic ways. Now, as then, a new family usually begins with a marriage ceremony that solemnizes a partnership between a man and a woman. This contract carries with it certain responsibilities which society generally recognizes. As a married couple, two people agree to share economic and social tasks and to provide mutual emotional support for the rest of their lives. Most married couples also choose to raise children. Parents and children compose what is commonly called a nuclear family.

Raising Children. These basic characteristics—marriage

ceremony, mutual economic obligations, a shared home, emotional support, and child-rearing—have remained quite constant despite the passage of time. Of these, perhaps most important is the function of raising children. In this process the family stands between society and the individual. In its role as transmitter of culture, the family serves as the institution through which children are socialized, that is, prepared to enter society as productive adults. In this respect, families are expected to provide children with the economic support, emotional attention, and educational training necessary for healthy development. But in a larger sense, the family continues the life and values of society itself. All the customs, attitudes, and values which together comprise our cultural heritage are passed on to us as children mainly through family members.

Colonial Families. Despite amazing endurance, the American family has had to adjust to changing times. Like other institutions of the colonial era, the family was once completely rooted in male authority. Men could legally treat women and children as their subordinates. Compare the colonial family of William and Hannah Penn, for example, with a modern family. Hannah and William did not

marry until her parents consented to the marriage. Together they had eight children, which was about average for many seventeenth-century families. Only five Penn babies survived infancy, however. While Hannah raised the children, William governed the colony of Pennsylvania. The couple remained married until William died in 1718. After his death, Hannah managed the colony, but only until one of their sons could succeed his father.

Colonial families also operated as an economic unit to a much greater degree than contemporary families. In this respect, large numbers of children enabled families to cooperate like a team. Its members were occupied with growing and producing the things needed for economic self-sufficiency. Home served as the workplace. Each person had responsibilities, usually divided by gender; men did the heavy labor, assisted by sons. For example, John Alden, a skilled laborer in the early Plymouth colony, made barrels and did other carpentry work. His wife Priscilla also produced goods. She wove cloth, made soap and candles, cured meat, pickled fruits and vegetables, managed the dairy, and prepared meals. Her daughters helped with these domestic chores and also cared for younger siblings (the Aldens had

Special customs and beliefs are passed on to children mainly by family members. Cooperation endures despite changing roles.

eleven children). Production required teamwork. Everyone worked at complementary tasks to help the family group survive.

Modern Families. During the nineteenth century, the family underwent fundamental changes as the United States became an urban, industrial society. Gradually, the modern family replaced the traditional, pre-Revolutionary family.

What are the characteristics of the contemporary family? To begin, most people today marry because of mutual affection, and parental approval is not the condition for marriage that it once was. In addition, family size has decreased greatly, and couples now usually have only two or three children. Along with smaller family size has come the recognition of childhood as a separate stage of life which requires careful nurturing. No longer are children expected to do adult work, nor do they have to, since an industrial age has replaced an agricultural economy.

Today, sex role divisions are not as strict as they once used to be. For example, child-rearing is likely to be shared between husband and wife, and often both work outside the home. In addition, women enjoy more legal rights than they did previously. Finally, the options of divorce, remarriage, single-parent families, and remaining single, though not unheard of in colonial times, are much more common in present-day society. Family living patterns will probably continue to change.

Families Will Endure. Over the years, the family has played a dynamic role in the development of our nation. It has both influenced and been influenced by the transformation of America from an agricultural to a complex, urban, industrial society. Nonetheless, certain family characteristics—chief among them a desire to love and to have children—continue to endure. Because of its importance as a transmitter of culture, the family seems likely to remain a significant part of American heritage.

Understanding Our Heritage

1. What characteristics define a family? Which have endured with the least number of changes?

2. Compare and contrast pre-industrial, traditional families with modern, urban families. Which does your family resemble?

3. What changes in the American family do you expect during your lifetime? What traits of family life do you expect to remain the same?

4. Do you consider family life to be personally important? Why?

CHAPTER 4

Conflict with Indians and England 1637–1700

People in the Chapter

King Philip—*the Algonquin, also known as Metacom, who leads a brave but futile war against the New England colonists.*

Sir Edmund Andros—*the unpopular governor of New England who is removed from office by the colonists when James II is overthrown in the Glorious Revolution of 1688.*

Jacob Leisler—*a New York merchant who leads a rebellion against Andros's deputy in New York City.*

Linking Past to Present

In general, the Indians first received the colonists on their shores with great curiosity, then with warm friendliness. Time and again, entire settlements such as Jamestown and Plymouth were saved from starvation by the Algonquins. If they had wished, they could have killed the colonists or forced them to flee back to their boats and the sea.

It was only after unmistakable signs of settlers intending to take over their land that the Indians became aroused to their danger. By then it was too late. Despite brief but bloody wars, the colonists had too many beachheads on the continent. They were backed up by seemingly unending supplies of people and material from Europe.

As the colonists' relationship with the Indians deteriorated, so did their relationship with England. During the civil war in England, the colonists had been left more or less on their own. They had developed trade habits that they found very profitable. But when the monarchy was restored, and Charles II tried to force the colonies into the old pattern of trade, they grew restless and angry. This first contest of wills between them and England cast a long shadow on the future.

1 THE INDIANS FIGHT FOR THEIR CULTURE

VOCABULARY   *medicine men   pacifists*

The clash of interests between Indians and settlers went on with unequal intensity all along the Atlantic seaboard. As we have already seen (chapter 3), there had been a sharp war with the Indians in Virginia as part of Bacon's Rebellion. In New Netherland, however, there was little difficulty. Few Indian tribes lived in the Hudson River valley, and the first Dutch traders had the good sense not to anger the powerful Iroquois League of Five Nations. In Maryland the tribes were small and poorly organized. It was in New England that the greatest trouble came.

Reasons for Conflict

Disputes between the Puritans and the Indians arose over two issues: land and Christianity. For every acre a colonial farmer needed to support life, an Indian hunter or fisher needed twenty. The more the settlers expanded their farms, the farther away they pushed the Indians.

Also the Indians did not have the same view about land that the settlers did. To the Indians, no one owned land. It was there for everyone to use. When they signed a land treaty they thought they were simply agreeing to let the white people share the land, not take it away from them. They also thought that the money, axes, kettles, or whatever they were given was a form of rent which they would receive again from time to time. This misunderstanding about land, ownership, and contracts caused a great deal of resentment between the Indians and the settlers, especially since most settlers thought it to their advantage not to explain matters clearly before the Indians signed.

In addition, the Puritans persisted with efforts to convert the Indians. Some became sincere and dedicated Christians, but most did not. Even so, the idea of the Christian God and the rules stated in the Bible were a threat to Indian society. In Indian life the chiefs and the medicine men (the priests and healers) were the authorities. They regulated the rules and customs of Indian life. The Christian religion, with its emphasis on the importance of the Bible, undermined the authority and position of the medicine men and chiefs, and they deeply feared and resented it.

The Pequot War

In 1637 the Pequot tribe decided to make a stand against the English. The colonists quickly formed an alliance with the Narragansetts, old enemies of the Pequots. The result of the Pequot War was the destruction of the Pequot nation. The end came at a Pequot fort on the Mystic River in Connecticut. The Puritans and their Narragansett allies surrounded the fort and set it afire. The Puritans knew that there were women and children as well as warriors in the fort. They shot them down as they tried to escape the flames. Only seven Pequots out of more than 400 survived. As William Bradford described the massacre, it "was a fearful sight to see them thus frying in the fire and the streams of blood quenching the same." Bradford also noted that the Puritans praised "God, who had . . . given them so speedy a victory over so proud and insulting an enemy."

The Puritans thought this kind of warfare was justifiable against a foreign and, in their eyes, heathen people. But their Narragansett allies were shocked by the slaughter. Like most other Indian

77

groups, the Narragansetts were accustomed to a different kind of warfare. They were used to taking some captives, including women and children. But they were not accustomed to killing large numbers of their enemies. As the Narragansetts said after the slaughter, the warfare of the English "is too furious and slays too many men."

There was no further major warfare between Puritans and Indians for forty years. But understandably, great tension existed between them, and a new war was probably inevitable.

King Philip's War

In 1675 the Wampanoag (wahm-pun-*no*-ag) Indians organized a last-ditch effort to wipe out the invaders. Two other Algonquin tribes, the Narragansetts and the Nipmucks, joined them. The alliance was led by the Wampanoag chief, Metacom, a son of Massasoit, who had welcomed the first Pilgrims to the New World. It is not clear why the English called Metacom, King Philip, but it may have had something to do with his manner when he visited Boston. There, dressed in fancy clothes, he liked to parade about town with a great deal of dignity.

Metacom's warriors began by attacking outlying Puritan towns. By March, Indians were attacking towns only twenty miles west of Boston! Many tribes had obtained guns, and some Indians were crack shots. Some Indian chiefs appeared in English armor—an iron helmet and a large rounded iron plate to protect the front of the body. Clearly, the Indians were learning to adopt some of the settlers' practices to good effect. King Philip's War went on for months.

The English were angered and frustrated by the guerrilla-type, hit-and-run tactics of the Indians. They responded by killing as many Indians as they could, even those of friendly tribes. The English burned the Indians' supply of corn as well.

Food shortages and disease helped stop the Indians' offensive. Finally, a force of 1000 men under General John Winslow exterminated almost 3000 Indians at Narragansett Bay. Metacom was killed by an Indian friendly to the whites, and Indian power in southeastern New England was gone forever. Metacom's head was exhibited at Plymouth for twenty years, and his wife and young son were sold as slaves in the West Indies.

But the Puritans had paid a high price for their victories. Of some ninety-two Puritan towns, fifty-two were attacked and sixteen were destroyed. The frontier of English settlement had been pushed back eastward. Relative to the size of the population, King Philip's War killed more people than were killed in the American Revolution or even the Civil War.

Deerfield, Mass. was the site of battles during King Philip's War. But the frontier remained uneasy. The Deerfield Massacre, shown here, occurred in 1704.

A Place of Peace

One colony was a distinct exception to this generally dismal pattern. William Penn was determined to treat the Indians in Pennsylvania fairly. He insisted that Indian lands be purchased and that treaties with the Indians be respected. Quaker principles required that the Indians, like all other peoples, be treated with brotherly love and consideration. The Quakers had another reason for dealing openly and fairly with the Delaware, Susquehannock, and other Pennsylvania tribes. Quakers were pacifists and had to avoid the possibility of war. They were successful in doing so for many years.

So long as Quakers remained in control of the colony, relations between the settlers and the Indians remained generally peaceful. For some seventy years after its founding, Pennsylvania continued to be an exception to the violent and sorrowful pattern that prevailed in some other colonies.

Section 1 Review

COMPREHENSION   Developing Vocabulary

1. Explain these terms: medicine men, pacifists, Narragansetts.

COMPREHENSION   Mastering Facts

1. What caused the disputes between the Puritans and the Indians?
2. What happened to the Pequots as a result of the Pequot War?
3. What happened to Metacom's wife and child?
4. What colony had the best relations with the Indians?

2   ENGLAND FASHIONS A COLONIAL EMPIRE

VOCABULARY   *mercantilism   naval stores   bureaucrats*

Within a period of seventy-five years (1607-1682) thirteen English colonies were established on the American continent. At first, England paid them little attention while the English civil war (1642-1649) produced further neglect. Nevertheless, people in both England and the colonies understood quite well that they each played a part in a mutually beneficial pattern of life. This relationship was based on an economic theory that had been followed by many European nations since the 1500s. This theory is called *mercantilism*.

The general principles of mercantilism and their application by the nations of western Europe to their colonies are explained in a Focus on Free Enterprise (see page 58). But the theory, as noted, received its most thorough application in the complex relationship that existed between England and its American colonies.

Mercantilism in Theory

The colonies, in theory, were to provide products, especially raw materials, that could not be found in the mother country. In fact, the main reason the English government permitted colonists to go to America was to aid this development. As early as the Jamestown settlement, settlers were urged to find or grow something not available in England. In this way, these products would not have to be purchased from another country. The raw materials were then to be sent to the mother country and there to be turned into finished or manufactured goods. These goods would then be sold back to the colonies and to other nations.

For the English, military power meant primarily naval power. The ships of His Majesty's navy were built in England, but trees for masts had to be imported because England had run out of suitable large trees. Northern pines were imported from Sweden and other Scandinavian countries. Yet such imports violated mercantilist principles in two ways. They cost money, and they made England dependent on foreign powers for a vital article of defense. In wartime, such dependence could be dangerous. So English authorities turned to the colonies. They reserved the largest pines in New England for the use of His Majesty's navy.

At that time, there was no clear dividing line between naval warships and civilian merchant ships. Many merchant ships were armed with cannon. In wartime, many of these ships were allowed to battle and seize enemy merchant vessels. For this reason, the English government encouraged the construction of ships of all sorts. According to mercantilist principles, this manufacturing should be done in England, not in the colonies. But in

Colonial Trade Routes

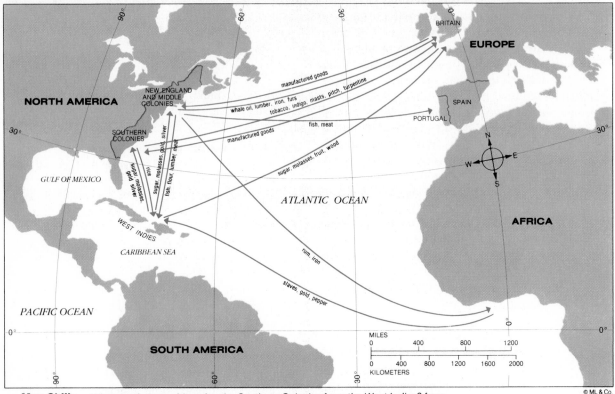

Map Skills *What goods were shipped to the Southern Colonies from the West Indies? from Britain? What goods were shipped from New England to the West Indies? to Britain?*

this case, the importance of defense overrode the economic principle. So the English government did encourage one kind of manufacturing in the colonies: shipbuilding.

Ships had to be manned by sailors. That was an additional reason why the government encouraged shipbuilding and a large merchant fleet. Skilled seamen on merchant vessels could be pressed into service aboard naval vessels during wartime emergencies. The government encouraged the fishing industry for the same reason. There men learned seamanship. The fishing ships, it was said, were "nurseries for seamen." The government even tried to retain the old Roman Catholic tradition of not eating meat on Fridays. By eating fish instead, the English people would help support England's maritime power.

The two principles of mercantilism—wealth and naval power—usually coincided. And in the 1600s and even later, these principles were in the best interests of the colonies. They did not have enough people to both farm and engage in large-scale man-

ufacturing. They produced raw materials which sold well in England. And in return they found that English manufacturers could supply them with a broad range of manufactured goods.

Mercantilism in Practice

Yet the fit between mercantilist principles and the interests of the colonies was not perfect. Left to themselves, the colonists might prefer to buy cloth from French manufacturers rather than English ones. They might prefer to sell masts, pitch, and tar to outfitters of Dutch ships rather than English ones. In order to work well, the mercantilist system required supervision by the home government. The English government never doubted that it had the right to undertake such supervision, nor did the colonists. But they sometimes found it convenient to evade regulations that hurt their economic interests. Obviously, the colonists had no desire to weaken English naval power or lessen England's wealth. But suppose the choice lay be-

80

tween filling colonial pockets or filling those of London merchants. The colonists would have been less than human if they had not chosen their own.

While the need for supervision was apparent, setting up an effective system of supervision was not easy. The colonies were 3000 miles and many weeks away from London. English government bureaucrats knew what sort of activity *ought* to be going on in the colonies. But often they found it difficult to discover what actually *was* going on. Sometimes the colonists were less than helpful in letting them know.

London Tightens Control

Attempts to supervise the mercantile system began in earnest after the restoration of King Charles II in 1660. Parliament passed a series of Navigation Acts to regulate the trade and shipping of the American colonies.

The Navigation Acts of 1660 and 1663. These acts set forth certain basic and strict regulations to safeguard the mercantile system. They remained until the American Revolution. In general, these were the rules stated by the acts:

1. No country could trade with the colonies unless the goods were shipped in colonial or English ships.

2. All vessels had to be manned by crews that were at least three-quarters English or colonial.

3. Certain colonial products, including sugar and tobacco, could be exported only to England or another English colony.

4. Almost all the goods traded between the colonies and any European country had to be shipped by way of England. This meant that goods had to be unloaded at an English port before continuing on their journey. This gave jobs to dockworkers, while the port duties fed the English treasury.

By and large, the colonies adjusted their trade to follow these acts. After all, they benefited too. Shipbuilding was stimulated, and the colonies got a monopoly of the English market in certain goods. As time went on, however, the system grew more complicated. The list of goods that could be sold only to England got longer. It included important colonial crops, such as rice and wood products known as "naval stores"—masts, smaller spars, pitch, tar, and turpentine. Indigo was added to the list because it was used to color sailors' uniforms.

Also, the government clamped down on certain colonial manufacturing enterprises that had developed in the early 1700s. These included woolen cloth, hats, and finished iron products.

Efforts to Enforce the Acts. Within the English government, a small group of *bureaucrats*, or officials, were responsible for colonial affairs. They were commonly known as the Lords of Trade. In 1664 they sent a royal commission to the colonies to find out what was going on and also to remind the colonists about their obligations under the new Navigation Acts.

The commissioners decided to investigate New England rather than the tobacco colonies. Virginia already had a royal governor, and Virginia and Maryland both seemed to be fitting very well into the mercantilist system by exporting large quantities of tobacco. New England, however, was not fitting into the mercantilist system so well. Except for exporting masts and spars, the New England colonies were not contributing to the wealth of old England. Exports of furs were falling off because of over-trapping, while Boston merchants were doing very nicely by trading with anyone they pleased, including the French and the Dutch.

When the commissioners arrived in Boston, Puritan leaders questioned their authority. After all, they had been used to having their own way for thirty-five years. Also, they did not take kindly to

Charles II was an easygoing monarch, but his officials kept a strict eye on colonial trade.

agents of a monarch who was persecuting their fellow Puritans in England. The people of Massachusetts valued the self-government that their original charter gave them.

The frustrated commissioners returned to London where they reported that Massachusetts was a nest of arrogant "independency." They recommended that the colony be compelled to observe the Navigation Acts. They also recommended that the Massachusetts charter be canceled.

Massachusetts Loses Its Charter. Nothing resulted from the commission's negative report. During the next twenty years, it was followed by more commissions and more reports. Massachusetts authorities and merchants went on as they had before. Yet they became increasingly disturbed by a young royal official named Edward Randolph. The Lords of Trade sent this able but disagreeable bureaucrat to the colonies several times. In each visit he collected damaging information about Massachusetts's violations of the Navigation Acts. Randolph also discovered that Massachusetts had been passing laws that were "contrary to the laws of England." For example, Massachusetts authorities punished people who did not attend church. The punishment was more severe than that allowed by English law. The original Massachusetts charter specifically forbade this.

Over the years, Randolph and other royal officials repeated the same recommendation: put an end to the Massachusetts charter. Finally, King Charles II was convinced. In 1684 Randolph presented his evidence to an English court, and the court nullified the Massachusetts charter. The most populous English colony in America no longer had any legal basis.

The Reign of Sir Edmund Andros

King Charles II died in 1685 and was succeeded by his brother, the Duke of York, who became King James II. He quickly took sweeping and drastic action to settle the Massachusetts problem. With a stroke of his pen, he created one vast colony called the Dominion of New England. This new administrative unit included all the New England colonies, New York, and East and West Jersey (which became New Jersey in 1702). This huge territory was to be administered from Boston by a royal governor, aided by a council appointed by

Sir Edmund Andros is shown being hustled out of town by an enraged group of Bostonians in 1688.

the crown. There were to be no representative assemblies in any part of the Dominion.

This sweeping reorganization sent a shudder throughout the colonies. What would government be like without the protection provided by elected colonial assemblies?

The man whom James appointed as governor of the Dominion of New England did nothing to calm these fears. Sir Edmund Andros was an able administrator. He was also arrogant and high-handed. Within a few weeks of arriving in Boston, he managed to make thousands of enemies.

Traditional political leaders found themselves out in the cold because the assemblies had been abolished. Andros and his royal councillors simply levied taxes on their own authority. Here was taxation without representation in its most naked form. Puritan leaders pointed out that such taxes violated their rights as freeborn Englishmen. Andros replied that such rights did not necessarily exist in the Dominion of New England.

Andros went further. He announced that the town governments established under the old Massachusetts charter were illegal. Therefore, he said, the land grants that the towns had made to individuals were also illegal. Landowners would have to reconfirm their land titles with Dominion authorities and pay rents to the Dominion as well. As if this were not enough, Andros even questioned the lawfulness of the Puritan churches. The proper church for English colonists, he said, was the established Church of England. He also made clear that the Navigation Acts would be enforced, and he brought in customs officers to do so.

The Massachusetts colonists were outraged. In 1687 they sent their most prominent minister, Increase Mather, to London. Mather's task was to get the old charter revived and to get Andros recalled. But just as Mather was putting his diplomatic skills to work, the entire political picture was changed by a bloodless revolution in England.

Section 2 Review

COMPREHENSION   Developing Vocabulary

1. Explain these terms: mercantilism, bureaucrats, naval stores, Dominion of New England.

COMPREHENSION   Mastering Facts

1. According to mercantilism, what were the two main sources of strength for a nation?
2. What manufacturing activity did England encourage in the colonies?
3. Why were the colonists worried when Charles II created the Dominion of New England?
4. What were the purposes of the Navigation Acts?

3   ADJUSTMENTS IN THE BRITISH EMPIRE

VOCABULARY   *dissenters   admiralty courts*

During his reign, James II managed to produce almost as much resentment in England as Andros did in Massachusetts. He was stubborn and tactless and had little idea of how much his subjects valued their Protestantism and their parliamentary rights. Himself a Roman Catholic, James appointed Catholics to high government positions. He also began tinkering with the organization of the army. Some English people wondered if he meant to use it at home against them rather than abroad. Then, worst of all, James fathered a son. England was faced with the possibility of a long line of Roman Catholic monarchs.

So in 1688 a group of parliamentary leaders boldly invited William of Orange to become their new king. William was Dutch, but he was a Protestant and was married to James's Protestant daughter Mary. William and his army landed in England without opposition. James fled abroad, and William and Mary were installed as joint monarchs. Parliament proceeded to pass a series of laws firmly limiting the power of the crown. An act of toleration gave religious freedom to all *dissenters*. These were the people who dissented from, or disagreed with, the Anglican Church of England. Ever afterwards, the English called these events the Glorious Revolution.

When news of the revolution crossed the Atlantic, there was an immediate reaction in New York and Massachusetts. Citizens in both colonies challenged James's colonial officials directly.

Revolt in Massachusetts

Upon learning that William had landed in England, a group of armed citizens of Massachusetts marched on Andros's house in Boston. They told him that he was finished as governor. Then they declared an end to the Dominion of New England. Andros and his royal councillors fled to an island fort in Boston harbor, and Massachusetts leaders settled back to await news of developments in England.

At first all the news was good. In London, Increase Mather succeeded in obtaining the official recall of Andros and the official abolition of the Dominion of New England. The northern colonies were thus returned to their previous status. However, Mather was unable to get the old Massachusetts charter restored. Instead, in 1691 a new charter was issued. In the new charter, the governor was appointed by the king. But the governor lacked the power to appoint members of his council, as was the case in other royal colonies. The governor's council would be elected by the lower house of assembly—a unique arrangement. The charter also provided for religious toleration in Massachusetts. The Puritans would no longer be able to persecute such groups as Quakers and

The Rulers of Britain During the Colonial Period

Elizabeth I	1558 – 1603	daughter of Henry VIII.
James I	1603 – 1625	son of Mary Queen of Scots and Elizabeth's cousin. He was James VI of Scotland, then called himself James I of Great Britain. The phrase "Great Britain" became official when Scotland and England were joined in the Act of Union in 1707.
Charles I	1625 – 1649	The English Civil War (1642 – 1649) abolished the monarchy. Charles I was beheaded. A new form of government called the Commonwealth was established.
The Commonwealth	1649 – 1660	The Commonwealth was headed by Oliver Cromwell and then by his son Richard. In 1660 the monarchy was restored.
Charles II	1660 – 1685	The ruler whose agents kept close watch on the colonies.
James II	1685 – 1688	James II was considered too strongly influenced by Catholics. This brought about the Glorious Revolution (1686 – 1688). James II fled to France and Parliament offered the crown to Mary, daughter of James II, and her husband William of Orange.
William III and Mary II	1688 – 1702	After Mary's death William ruled until 1702.
Anne	1702 – 1714	daughter of James II.
George I	1714 – 1727	Since Anne had no surviving children, at her death her cousin George of Hanover, Germany, was made king.
George II	1727 – 1760	The House of Hanover ruled until 1901.
George III	1760 – 1820	

members of the Church of England. Puritan leaders were not altogether happy with the new charter, but they could live with it.

Revolt in New York

New York also had a revolution. Andros's deputy in New York was Francis Nicholson, who shared Andros's contempt for popular rule. The overthrow of Andros and King James placed Nicholson in an awkward position because his authority was no longer clear. At the same time, New York City was filled with rumors that Anglicans and Catholics were conspiring to restore James to the throne and that Catholics were planning to invade the colony from Canada.

After months of confusion, a group of local militiamen seized control of New York City. They were led by Jacob Leisler, a successful German merchant who had lived in New York since the days of Dutch rule. Although he had grown rich in the fur, wine, and tobacco trade, he championed the cause of the middle class—the small merchants, artisans, and small farmers—against the large merchants and landowners. Leisler and his Protestant supporters believed the latter were too sympathetic to King James and Catholicism. Leisler sent Nicholson back to England. He then set himself up as the head of a revolutionary government and proclaimed William and Mary as the new sovereigns. As the defender of the Protestant faith and the champion of the common people, Leisler could have won widespread support. Unfortunately, he was arrogant and stubborn and soon offended even his own followers.

Finally, letters of instruction arrived from England. Unfortunately, they were vaguely worded, and Leisler interpreted them as giving him authority to continue his rule. His supporters even fired on a regiment of British troops, killing two and wounding seven. Meanwhile, Henry Slaughter, the officially appointed governor, arrived with clear instructions to take control of the colony. Leisler hesitated, insisting that his authority was legal and proper. Slaughter lost patience and accused Leisler of treason. There was a hasty trial, and Leisler and his son-in-law were hanged.

Later, officials in London pardoned Leisler's followers. Several years later they even reversed Leisler's sentence. But the entire confused and nasty set of events created much quarreling and hostility within the colony and poisoned the atmosphere of New York politics for years.

New Teeth in the Navigation Acts

In the early years of his reign, King William paid little attention to the colonies. His eyes were on France, with whom England was competing for control of Europe. As always when England was distracted with European problems, colonial affairs were left to drift by themselves. Colonial merchants violated the Navigation Acts with increasing frequency as they traded where they found the most profit, not where England told them to trade.

The ever-active Edward Randolph caught wind of these violations. Influential people in England listened to Randolph because he knew more about colonial trading practices than anyone else. So in 1696, Parliament decided to tighten up the imperial system again.

New Rules.   First, all colonial governors were required to swear an oath to uphold the Navigation Acts. If they refused to do so, they were removed from office. Second, customs officers were sent to each colony to enforce the customs laws. These officials had the power to inspect vessels and warehouses and even to break into them if it was suspected that they held smuggled goods. Third, people accused of smuggling were no longer to be tried in local courts before local and presumably sympathetic juries. They were to be tried in *admiralty courts,* which had no juries. Moreover, the judges were appointed by the crown. These new rules gave the English government great control over colonial trade.

Volunteers join Jacob Leisler's revolt against the royalist "aristocrats" of New York

New Board of Trade.   The king also acted in 1696 to strengthen the administration of the colonies. The old Lords of Trade were replaced by a new group of men known as the Board of Trade and Plantations. It had no power to make or enforce regulations for the colonies. Nor could it appoint royal governors or other officials. But the board could offer its advice on such matters. And its advice was often taken, because it was the only government agency that knew much about the colonies. Thus, while the board had no official powers, it did have considerable influence.

As an example of this influence, we may take the king's instructions to the royal governors. These instructions were issued to each governor when he was first appointed by the crown. They included detailed requirements about what the royal governor could and could not do in his colony. These instructions were issued by the king. But they were actually written by the active members of the Board of Trade.

The Role of Colonial Governors

After 1696 the royal governors served as the most important link in the chain of imperial control. Eight of the continental colonies had governors appointed by the crown. The governors of Maryland and Pennsylvania were appointed by the Baltimore and Penn family proprietors. Only Rhode Island and Connecticut elected their own.

The Power of Governors.   Most of the governors were men of high status. Most came from England. They accepted appointment in the colonies for various reasons. One was prestige. Another was money, for the governorships offered both a salary and the opportunity to keep various official fees. The governors varied greatly in ability. Some had the interests of the colonists at heart, while others looked to their own interests. For example, Governor William Shirley organized the Massachusetts militia for a successful expedition against the French in Canada. On the other hand, Governor Benjamin Fletcher allowed pirates to operate out of New York Harbor. But all governors enjoyed considerable prestige, for they directly represented the authority of the king.

The royal and proprietary governors had important legal powers. They called the meetings of the representative assemblies, and they could disband these assemblies at any time. They could also veto

How Britain Governed the Colonies

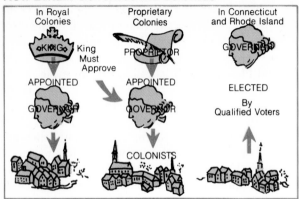

The Position of Colonial Governors

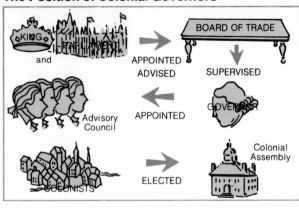

laws. Sometimes, however, the local pressure was so great that governors were pushed into approving laws they disliked or which directly violated their instructions. So, as a safety measure, authorities in London kept the right to veto any laws passed by a colonial assembly. They retained this right even though the king had lost his right to veto laws passed by Parliament.

In most colonies, the governor appointed the council. It consisted of wealthy, influential men who gave the governor advice. The council also served as the upper house of the colonial legislature and as the highest court of each colony.

The Weaknesses of Governors. In theory, the English government retained great power in the colonies. Yet this power was not nearly so great as it seemed on paper. Royal governors had to live and work with their council members and other appointees. Influential and wealthy colonists could dine and chat with the governor. They could tell him what a fine fellow he was, or they could describe popular resentment against him for doing such and such. These subtle pressures were often very effective.

The greatest weakness of the governor was that his salary was paid by the colonists and not by London. London might instruct the governor to raise a colonial army against the French, but the governor had to ask the colonial assembly for the necessary money. The money could only be raised by taxes passed by the assembly. Members of the assembly were, of course, patriotic men who had no more love for the French than the governor and His Majesty did. But, as some of the members hinted to the governor, before they raised taxes, perhaps the governor might be willing to approve certain laws without looking too closely at his instructions? Perhaps his own salary might be reduced a

trifle so that the people would not be over-burdened by taxes? These questioning hints were not lost on the governors.

The Imperial System in 1700

As the 1700s dawned on England and the colonies, the imperial system was working fairly well. The Glorious Revolution of 1688 had permanently established the supremacy of Parliament over the king. In theory, Parliament represented the people. So did the assemblies in the American colonies, and neither Parliament nor the king considered doing away with them. James II had done so briefly in New England, but he had been thrown out. The English on both sides of the Atlantic thought that, as a matter of course, colonists should be represented in legislatures.

Some imperial restrictions hurt the colonies, but not seriously. The Indians had been defeated—at least for the time being. The colonies enjoyed the protection of the nation that was becoming the most powerful on earth. Even so, the colonies were changing and acquiring a distinctive way of life.

Section 3 Review

COMPREHENSION Developing Vocabulary
1. Explain these terms: dissenters, admiralty courts.

COMPREHENSION Mastering Facts
1. Why were the Puritans unhappy at first with the Massachusetts charter of 1691?
2. Leisler's rebellion was directed against what groups in New York?
3. Which two colonies elected their governors?
4. What was the greatest hold any colony had on its royal governor?

CHAPTER 4   Review

Chapter Summary

As settlers sought more land, a clash of interests between Indians and colonists sometimes led to armed conflict. Meanwhile, using the concept of mercantilism, England began trying to fit the colonies into their place within the empire. To solve financial problems that developed after the English Civil War, Parliament passed a series of Navigation Acts. These and other imperial restrictions limited the colonies both politically and economically.

Questions for Critical Thinking

COMPREHENSION   Summarizing Main Ideas

1. Compare the attitude of the Indians toward land ownership with the attitude of the settlers. What are the economic advantages of each point of view? What are the social advantages? Can you think of any way in which the two views might have been reconciled?

2. What advantages did the settlers have in King Philip's War? What advantages belonged to the Indians?

COMPREHENSION   Interpreting Events

1. Do you think it might have been possible for settlers in all the colonies to follow the example of the Quakers in dealing with the Indians? Give reasons for your opinion.

2. Why were colonies an essential part of the mercantilist system?

3. What would your attitude toward mercantilism have been if you had been (a) the captain of a British merchant ship; (b) a New England producer of pitch and tar; (c) a tobacco grower in Virginia; (d) a Philadelphia manufacturer of nails and other iron products?

4. Do you think the British government was wise to pass the Navigation Acts of 1660 and 1663? Give reasons for your answer.

5. Would you have wanted to be a royal colonial governor in 1700? Why or why not?

APPLICATION   Using Skills To Distinguish Fact from Opinion

In evaluating information, it is essential to distinguish between facts and opinions or between facts and people's interpretation of them. For each of the statements below, indicate whether it is a fact or an opinion.

1. At first the Algonquin saved entire settlements from starvation.

2. If the Algonquins had wished, they could have killed the colonists or forced them to flee back to their boats and the sea.

3. The greatest trouble between the settlers and the Indians came in New England.

4. The Puritan massacre of the Pequots was justifiable.

5. The Narragansetts were shocked by the massacre of the Pequots.

6. The English defeated Metacom's warriors in 1675.

7. The English were able to defeat Metacom's warriors because food shortages and disease helped stop the Indians' offensive.

8. The English were able to defeat Metacom's warriors because they were better fighters.

9. Under the mercantilist theory, a nation's exports should be more valuable than its imports.

10. A nation should export more than it imports.

11. The main purpose of a colony is to produce raw materials for the mother country.

12. The English government encouraged shipbuilding in the colonies.

EVALUATION   Comparing Past to Present

1. Do you think people today who are interested in conservation might benefit by adopting the Indian attitude toward land? Explain.

2. According to the mercantilist theory, the two main sources of strength for a nation are wealth and military power. In your opinion, are these the main sources of strength for a nation today? If not, what are they? What means might a nation today use in order to become strong? Could nations use such means in 1700?

3. Compare the way in which control over the purse strings restricted the power of royal colonial governors with the way in which such control restricts the power of political officials today.

Environments of North America

Settling North America in the seventeenth century pitted people against nature in a contest for survival. Permanent settlement required courage, skill, and physical strength. Even after a century, the English occupied no more than a tiny fraction of the entire continent.

Despite the difficulties and dangers of settlement, colonists were often overwhelmed by the sheer magnificence of the North American continent. As pioneers pushed further westward, their impressions of abundance became a permanent theme. A French visitor once described America as "an immense booty." The treasures of the continent included rich soil, timber, furs, minerals, water, game, and so on. The history of the United States is a story of how Americans have discovered and utilized their abundant natural resources—and how this abundance has influenced the development of various economic, political, and social institutions.

Study the physical map on this page and note the different mountains, valleys, plains, rivers, and other bodies of water. As you can see, the land between the Atlantic and Pacific Oceans varies tremendously. As the earliest settlers soon discovered, the North American continent is a vast collection of many different environments.

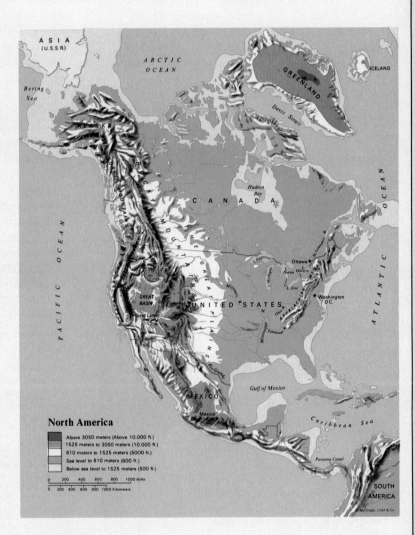

North America

- Above 3050 meters (Above 10,000 ft.)
- 1525 meters to 3050 meters (10,000 ft.)
- 610 meters to 1525 meters (5000 ft.)
- Sea level to 610 meters (600 ft.)
- Below sea level to 1525 meters (500 ft.)

0   200   400   600   800   1000 Miles
0   200   400   600   800 1000 Kilometers

McDougal, Littell & Co.

Understanding Geography

1. Which mountain ranges and bodies of water are identified on the map?

2. Name several different environmental regions of North America.

3. Why was the word *abundant* used when referring to settlement of the continent?

4. How does your physical environment influence your day-to-day life?

5. What word describes our continent's environment?

UNIT 1 Review

Understanding Social Studies Concepts

History

1. Arrange the following events in chronological order: (a) Columbus discovers the New World; (b) Norwegian colonies established on Greenland; (c) first permanent English colony established in the New World; (d) the Mound Builders inhabit the Great Lakes; (e) the Crusades were fought; (f) English defeat the Spanish Armada.
2. How did the religious conflicts of Europe affect the colonization of North and South America?
3. In what ways did the collapse of empires in West Africa contribute to the development of slavery in America?
4. By 1700, what differences existed between colonial patterns in towns and farms? Were there any similarities? Explain.
5. What were the major problems of colonial towns? Do any of these problems exist in American cities today? Explain.

Geography

1. Refer to the map on page 16. Describe which areas of the present United States were once covered by glaciers. To which regions of the present United States did early groups of people first migrate?
2. Refer to the map on page 80. What goods were imported and exported by the Southern Colonies? by the New England and Middle Colonies? Why is the trading pattern often described as the "Triangle of Trade"?
3. List several ways in which geography influenced European exploration and settlement of North America.

Economics

1. How did the economic law of supply and demand stimulate the Age of Discovery?
2. What economic benefits did Europeans expect to achieve through the discovery of new trade routes? Were they successful? Explain.

Government

1. Describe the type of government that was developed by early people called the Adapters, those who lived in the southeastern part of the present United States.
2. How were the colonies of Spain and France governed? How were the English colonies governed? Which system encouraged the most settlement? Why?

Extending Map, Chart, Picture Skills

1. Refer to maps in this unit to describe the general areas of the New World that were claimed by European nations during the 1600s. Which nation claimed the most land? the least?
2. Examine the supply list on page 43. Write a generalization about the kind of life a new settler could expect, based on the supply list.
3. Refer to the chart on page 55. By the mid-1700s, which English colonies were proprietary colonies? corporate? royal?

Understanding Current Events

1. How is space exploration today similar to exploration during the fifteenth and sixteenth centuries? In what ways is it different?
2. World trade has expanded greatly since the Age of Discovery. What are some products traded among nations in the 1600's that are still traded today?

Developing Effective Citizenship

1. What injustices were being protested by colonists who took part in Bacon's Rebellion? In what other ways could they have made their feelings known?
2. Which colony established the first law-making body? What was it called? Why is this an important part of our heritage?

THE COLONIES

THE WORLD

1704 First permanent colonial newspaper begun.

1718 French found New Orleans.

1732 Last English colony (Georgia) founded.

1740 "Great Awakening" begins in colonies.

1700 — 1710 — 1720 — 1730 — 1740 — 1750 —

1707 England and Scotland unite as Great Britain.

1727 George II begins 33-year reign in Britain.

1702–1713 War of the Spanish Succession (Queen Anne's War).

1744–1748 War of the Austrian Succession (King George's War).

UNIT 2

Revolutionary Times

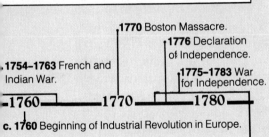

1770 Boston Massacre.

1776 Declaration of Independence.

1754–1763 French and Indian War.

1775–1783 War for Independence.

1760 — 1770 — 1780

c. 1760 Beginning of Industrial Revolution in Europe.

1783 Treaty of Paris ends fighting between England, France, Spain, and United States.

The Expansion of English America

1700–1760

People in the Chapter

George Whitefield—*a revivalist preacher who is the best-known person in America.*

Benjamin Franklin—*a man of genius in many fields.*

John Woolman—*a Quaker who points out the beginning of a prejudice against blacks.*

George Washington—*a twenty-two-year-old colonel who leads an expedition to test French strength in the Ohio country.*

Phillis Wheatley—*a poet who, in the 1700s, is perhaps the most famous American of African descent.*

Linking Past to Present

The 1700s are known in Europe as the Age of Enlightenment. To enlighten means to instruct or give insight. You know how a dark room can become gradually illuminated by people turning on more and more flashlights? In a way, that is what happened in Europe at this time. Europe was the dark room and flashlights were the new ideas. They involved new ways of looking at nature, human nature, and religion. People began questioning the laws and habits they had followed for generations. New theories often go well in a new country, and the English colonies welcomed them enthusiastically. Many colonists were confident that if they put the theories into practice, they could create an ideal society.

To create this world, however, a period of peace was needed. The American colonists feared their plans would be frustrated by their expansion-minded neighbors—the French in Canada, the Spanish in Florida. In 1732 Georgia was established as the thirteenth colony, partly to provide a home for the debtors of England and partly to be a buffer against the Spanish. In 1745 colonial militia won their first victory without any aid from Britain by capturing the French citadel of Louisbourg. This fort guarded the St. Lawrence River, which led to the heart of French Canada. The jubilant colonials now spoke of driving the French entirely out of North America.

1 THE COLONIES CONSIDER NEW IDEAS

VOCABULARY   *natural rights*

Today, the new ideas that developed during the Age of Enlightenment are taken for granted. But they were quite startling when they were first presented. An idea that seems reasonable in one age may seem peculiar in another.

Copernicus and the Movement of the Earth

As an example, consider the relationship between the earth and the sun. Everyday observation suggests that the sun goes around the earth. The sun rises in the morning, moves across the sky, and disappears on the other side of the earth at night. We cannot see or feel the earth rotate. But we can see the sun move. The obvious conclusion is that the sun moves around a stationary earth, and western Europeans believed this until the 1500s.

In 1543 a Polish clergyman, Nicolaus Copernicus (nik-oh-*la*-us ko-*per*-nik-oos) proposed a completely opposite view. He announced that the earth moves around the sun once a year. And he claimed that the earth itself did one full rotation every twenty-four hours. At first his theories shocked and even angered many people. But as time went on, they not only began to realize that Copernicus was correct but began to look critically at other aspects of the world around them. During the 1600s scientists who built on the work of Copernicus gathered evidence that the planets, like the earth, also revolved around the sun.

Newton and the Ordered Universe

In the 1700s an English scientist proposed another theory that was equally shocking to some and equally important in the development of science. Sir Isaac Newton declared that the world was governed not by chance or by miracles but by fixed mathematical laws.

Newton presented his idea in his famous *Principia Mathematica*, published in 1687. It is said that after observing how an apple fell to the ground from a tree—noting the speed and length of fall and the weight of the apple—he began to develop his theory of universal gravity.

Gravity, he said, is the force that attracts pieces of matter in the universe to each other. The earth, moon, planets, comets, the sun, and indeed the universe itself were held together and kept in motion by gravity. To many people, Newton's theory seemed to indicate that the universe was like a giant clock with one force—gravity—driving all the gears.

This engraving shows Isaac Newton analyzing a beam of light.

Newton's law seemed to bring order out of chaos. Everything apparently operated on a giant plan. Other scientists, encouraged by his theory, hoped to discover other laws of the natural world. By the 1700s a number of religious leaders were taking an active interest in scientific matters. They felt that by understanding the workings of God's universe, they would come closer to understanding God.

John Locke and Natural Rights

Once scientists began unlocking the secrets of the natural world by using human reason, it was inevitable that they would apply the same kind of logic to analyzing human society. If there was a law of nature, they reasoned, there must be laws for humans, for they are also part of nature.

One such thinker was the Englishman John Locke. In his work *An Essay Concerning Human Understanding*, published in 1690, Locke declared that God had indeed provided laws of *natural rights* to make the human world run as smoothly as the physical world. There were three such natural rights that God had given humanity: life, liberty, and property. And of the three, property was paramount. If a farmer plows and plants a piece of land, Locke argued, the work done in putting nature to use gives the farmer the right to own that land. Locke also argued that people have a right to life because of the work they do in order to feed and clothe themselves. A person's body is a form of property, and anyone who kills another person is stealing that person's property.

Locke believed that originally people lived without any sort of government in a state of nature, completely free of restraint. But the weak were often at the mercy of the strong. So in order to exercise their God-given rights without interference, people chose a ruler with whom they made an agreement. In exchange for the ruler's protection of their natural rights, the people agreed to obey the ruler. However, if the ruler or government became tyrannical and violated these rights, Locke maintained that the people no longer need obey; indeed, they had the right to overthrow the ruler.

In many parts of Europe poor peasants were locked into the tradition of their ancestors. They could not read or write and there was little opportunity for them to improve their condition. To them the new ideas of the Enlightenment meant

John Locke originated the contract theory of government between the people and the ruler.

little or nothing. But in the American colonies, where a new society was being created, where a new kind of government had been established—a government, moreover, which the people controlled—the ideas of the Enlightenment made good sense and were received with great enthusiasm.

Benjamin Franklin: An Enlightened American

It is not surprising that the person who became a living example of the ideas of the Enlightenment was an American, Benjamin Franklin.

Franklin was born in 1706 in Boston, where his father owned a small business. At age 12 he was apprenticed to his older brother as a printer's assistant. They did not get along together, so the younger Franklin left Boston for Philadelphia where he set himself up as a printer. By the age of forty, he had made a small fortune and was able to retire from active business affairs. Then he embarked on several careers, all of them distinguished. He was a scientist, inventor, writer, statesman, and diplomat.

Franklin invented many useful devices, including a metal stove which stood in the middle of a room so that the heat could radiate out from all sides. Franklin invented bifocal eyeglasses and an improved watering trough for horses. He showed ship captains how to shorten the voyage to Europe by taking advantage of the strong, swift current of

Franklin, by using charged pith balls, discovers two kinds of electricity: positive and negative.

ventions, explaining, "As we enjoy great advantages from the inventions of others, we should be glad of an opportunity to serve others by any invention of ours." Franklin thought that science should be useful to people. He felt the same way about government and the press. He kept his own newspaper open to a wide variety of opinions.

When he was an elderly man, Franklin became the American ambassador to France. At the extremely formal court of the French king, Franklin stood out because of his simple and sometimes eccentric clothes. He wore a long-haired wig, as all gentlemen did. But no one else walked the streets of Paris wearing a fur cap as well. He charmed the ladies and impressed the gentlemen by his direct manner. Explaining American ideas to Europeans, Franklin remarked that in America one did not say, "Who is he?" but, "What does he do?"

Section 1 Review

COMPREHENSION Developing Vocabulary

1. Explain these terms: natural rights, Age of Enlightenment.

COMPREHENSION Mastering Facts

1. How did Copernicus view the relationship between the sun and the earth?
2. What incident supposedly started Newton thinking about how, and why, planets move?
3. According to John Locke, what agreement did people originally make with their rulers?
4. Why didn't Benjamin Franklin take out patents on his inventions?

the Gulf Stream. He also charted the path of hurricanes and proved that those along the eastern coast moved in a northeasterly direction.

Franklin's most famous experiment showed that lightning and electricity are the same thing. One stormy day he flew a kite. At the end of his string he fastened a metal key. Lightning hit the kite, and immediately sparks flew from the key. Characteristically, Franklin gave his discovery a practical application. He invented the lightning rod, which ever since has protected many buildings.

Franklin did not take out any patents on his in-

2 SOCIAL INFLUENCES IN THE COLONIES

VOCABULARY   *Great Awakening   sects   libel*

As you have read, the Puritans fled to America to worship as they pleased. But, once in the New World, the Puritans were as intolerant of other religious beliefs as the Church of England had been.

But in the early 1700s, the grip of the Puritan church on the colonists began to weaken. Under the new Massachusetts Charter of 1691, the Puritans were forced to allow freedom of worship. The new charter also banned the Puritan practice of permitting only Puritan church members to vote.

Any religion that demands of its believers hard work, thrift, and healthy living is almost sure to have economic success. That is what happened to the Puritans. Business was good, and Puritan mer-

chants prospered. They became the leaders in New England, taking the place once held by such individuals as John Winthrop. The new upper class liked fine houses, stylish clothes, and good food and wine, and their interest in maintaining the strict Puritan code declined.

Revival of Religious Feelings

Material comfort was accompanied in the early decades of the 1700s by a decline in church membership. Many people seemed to be doing so nicely in this world that they paid less attention to the next. Many preachers seemed to lack spiritual warmth and enthusiasm. As a result, many people were ready for a revival of religious feelings.

Jonathan Edwards.

Certain ministers tried to promote such revivals in their churches by holding revival meetings. Among the best-known was the minister of the Congregational church in Northampton, Massachusetts.

Jonathan Edwards was one of the most influential thinkers ever to live in America. He was both a philosopher and a theologian.

Edwards declared that it did no good for people just to attend church, give money to the church, and pray regularly. Simply going through religious motions would not save them for eternal life. No, they had to do more. They had to face their own sinfulness. Edwards said that people must *feel* their sin. They must also *feel* the need for opening themselves to God's spirit. Conversion, for him, was a profound emotional experience of the heart rather than the head. In his sermons, Edwards described the dangers of sin and the torments that awaited sinners after they died. He roused such an emotional response in his audience that men and women fell to the floor in a faint or shrieked aloud and cried that they really did feel the power and love of God.

George Whitefield.

Another man stirred an even more widespread revival of religion. It began in 1740 and produced such general excitement that it soon became known as the *Great Awakening*. The man who sparked it was a young Englishman named George Whitefield. He was called the "great awakener." He was not a philosopher like Edwards, but he was an extremely effective preacher. It was not *what* but *how* Whitefield preached that drew the crowds. In a sense, he was a great actor.

Whitefield traveled from one colony to another. His sermons were shows. He awoke people to their religious shortcomings. First, he took the part of God; then he took the part of the devil. So frightful were his devilish faces and so vividly did he describe the wages of sin that his audiences were terrified. People screamed and some fainted. No building in any colony could hold the astonishing numbers of people who flocked to hear him. So he preached outdoors. In Philadelphia, Benjamin Franklin made a careful estimate and concluded that 30,000 people could hear him at the same time. (This sounds like an absurdly high number for a speaker without a microphone, but Franklin was not one to exaggerate.)

Whitefield's fame spread as newspapers reported his progress. At the end of 1740 he returned to England. In later years he made more trips to the colonies, but these failed to create the great stir of 1740. But as we look back on this cross-eyed preacher, we can see a significance the colonists could not. Whitefield was the first person to become known to almost everyone in every colony. He was one of the first celebrities in America.

George Whitefield even impressed skeptics. Benjamin Franklin went to hear him determined to give no collection. But afterwards Franklin said: "I emptied my pocket . . . gold and all."

Results of the Great Revival

Raging controversies developed in the wake of Whitefield's passage through the colonies. Many ministers saw his preaching as the work of God and tried to imitate his example. Some ministers, however, got carried away by their enthusiasm. One Connecticut minister, for instance, made a specialty of torchlit evening meetings at which he stripped to the waist and did imitations of the devil.

Conservative ministers considered this sort of behavior more the devil's work than God's. They were also disturbed that uneducated men who knew little of the Bible or church laws were wandering about preaching to anyone who would listen. They denounced these traveling upstarts. In turn, they found themselves denounced as cold, lifeless men of letters, totally lacking God's saving grace.

New Churches Formed. As these controversies mounted, church members began taking sides. Congregations split amid furious arguments over the proper qualifications of their minister. By 1742 the two largest Calvinist groups, the Congregationalists and the Presbyterians, were each divided into two camps: "New Lights" and "Old Lights." The Old Lights emphasized the need for learned preaching and a thoroughly educated ministry. The New Lights stressed the importance of emotional experience for both ministers and laity. As a result, many people left their churches, especially in New England, and founded independent churches of their own.

Over the course of the next generation, Baptists, Methodists, Mennonites, Presbyterians, and many other sects (religious groups) began organizing churches. This process has been a permanent feature of American religious life. If people did not like the church they were in, they set up another. But sometimes churches united. Splinter groups within the Presbyterians and the Congregationalists managed to reunite within fifteen years of coming apart. In general, New Light views were dominant.

Ministers Are Judged. In addition to forming new churches, people felt freer to judge their religious leaders. They even debated the question of whether particular ministers were saved or damned. A closely related development was the revival meeting. Usually these meetings were held outdoors to serve anyone who wanted to come. Intense religious feelings characterized these meetings. They afforded people an opportunity to hear and judge a popular preacher and also provided lonely rural people with the chance to exchange news and to meet each other. The revivalist tradition is still very much a part of American religious life.

Kindness Increases. The Great Awakening also led to a kindlier feeling toward less fortunate members of society. Jonathan Edwards defined virtue as "love of Being in general." By this he meant that there was a divine element in everyone that ought to be recognized out of love for God. The poor, orphans, Indians, and slaves shared in this Being, and for the first time their welfare became a concern to people.

Revivalists did not challenge slavery as an institution. But they did preach that everyone shared in the common brotherhood of the spirit and that God paid no attention to a person's color. Some blacks began attending revival meetings, and a few joined revival-minded churches. Several black men boldly began preaching to their fellow blacks. Indeed, the Great Awakening marked the beginning of the slow spread of Christian ideas and worship among American slaves.

John Woolman and the Quaker Revival

The Quakers did not join in the Great Awakening. Instead, they had their own form of revival in the mid-1750s. They went through a process of questioning whether they were living up to their own principles. In the process, a few of them concluded that it was wrong to enslave other people.

A leading antislavery Quaker was John Woolman of New Jersey. He spent most of his life gently urging his fellow Quakers to free their slaves. By the time of the American Revolution, they had done so. Thus, one American religious group established an important principle and example.

Woolman was a keen observer of human behavior. He was the first American to point out that whites were prejudiced against blacks simply because of their skin color. There had been slaves in all parts of the world for thousands of years. But in other periods slaves often had rights and even re-

John Woolman (right) made chilling conclusions about blacks and slavery.

spect. In ancient Rome, for example, Greek slaves were used as tutors because they were better educated than their owners. Slaves may have been unlucky because they were captured in war or sold for economic reasons, but there was no particular prejudice against them. In America, however, slavery and prejudice were closely connected because the only slaves were blacks. The enslavement of blacks by whites, Woolman said, "tends generally to fix a notion in the Mind, that they [blacks] are a sort of people below us in Nature." Woolman declared that the notion was false. He was the first to pinpoint, with sorrow and alarm, the beginning of a prejudice.

An End to Witchcraft

Up until the 1600s almost everyone in the colonies and Europe, including some ministers and scientists, believed in witchcraft and witches. In fact, people were burned as witches in Europe well into the 1700s. The belief in witchcraft faded more quickly in the colonies due in part to the Enlightenment, which discouraged superstition, and in part to the outbreak of witchcraft hysteria that swept Salem, Massachusetts, in 1692.

Two young girls jokingly accused a half-Indian, half-black female slave of being a witch. Her master beat her until she made a false confession and gave the names of two other women who, she said, were also witches. The girls, excited by all the at-

tention they were getting and at the same time growing terrified that they would be punished for making up such a story, stuck to their claim and accused still others of being witches. The episode snowballed. Those who were unjustly accused and afraid named other equally innocent people as witches. Hysteria gripped the town as more and more people were accused. There were official trials. The few sensible people who tried to stop the proceedings were themselves accused of being witches. People became too terrified to speak out. Still the accusations mounted, and the most prominent people in Boston were now being accused of witchcraft.

Finally, Increase Mather and other leading clergymen realized that the accusations were simply unbelievable and that masses of false evidence had been given by frightened people. The court where the trials took place was ordered closed. The witchcraft hysteria was over, but not before some 19 people had been hanged as witches, another had been killed by being crushed to death, 4 died in jail, and about 150 spent time in prison.

The Salem trials were the last witchcraft prosecutions in the colonies. As the scientific attitudes of the Age of Enlightenment spread, people began to doubt the reality of witches. William Penn dismissed a case against a woman charged with riding a broomstick. In doing so, he said, "There is no law in Pennsylvania against riding on broomsticks."

This old print clearly shows the terror and mass hysteria at the Salem witch trials.

Colonial Education

The American public was more *literate* than any other in the world. Literate means the ability to read and write. The proportion of people able to read was highest in New England, lower in the Middle Colonies, and lowest in the South.

Even more than most Protestants, the Puritans insisted that members of a godly community had to know how to read the Bible. The New England pattern of orderly settlement by towns made it possible to set up arrangements for formal schooling. From the 1640s on, Massachusetts law required all towns with more than fifty families to support a schoolmaster. In effect, all children were to be taught to read at public expense. In later years, other New England colonies passed similar laws. Often these laws were not observed, especially in small towns or in those exposed to attack by Indians. None of the townspeople liked the expense, but generally they subscribed to the ideal. By the 1720s many New England towns were maintaining schools that ran from the end of the harvest to spring planting time.

In the Middle Colonies no laws required public support of schools. Yet various Calvinist churches provided the same incentive that New England churches did for learning, and the Jewish population of these colonies had a high rate of literacy.

The situation in the southern colonies was more complicated. Because the life there was agricultural, there were few towns and, therefore, not many schools. What education most children received was given at home. In addition, more than 40 percent of the people were slaves, and hardly any of them knew how to read and write. The literacy rate among southern white males was probably about 50 percent. That was about the same percentage of adult males in England who knew how to read and write.

Education for Women. In all the colonies, fewer women than men learned to read and write. Women were not totally excluded from education but they were left behind. Many girls learned to read and write English, and a few learned French. But practically no girls were taught Latin and Greek. Sometimes, girls were taught fancy sewing rather than the fundamentals of arithmetic. No women attended college. However, the level of education among women was higher in the colonies than in England.

This is the only known copy of English artist William Burgis's view of Harvard College (1726).

American Colleges. The earliest American college was Harvard, in Massachusetts. It was founded in 1636 as a training ground for ministers. Students studied a wide variety of subjects, including Latin and Greek, mathematics, some sciences, and the philosophy of morals. But after about 1700 more than half the graduates of Harvard went into occupations other than the ministry.

By that time two other colleges had been established: William and Mary (1693) in Virginia, and Yale (1701) in Connecticut. Later, during a twenty-year period after the Great Awakening, five more colleges were founded: Princeton, Columbia, Pennsylvania, Brown, and Rutgers. Most were connected to some church group, but attendance was not restricted by church membership. Students usually came from well-to-do families. But there were bright farm boys at all colleges.

Life was not always easy at universities. Here are the rules and regulations a student at Harvard had to follow:

1. No student can enter the college unless he can speak and read Latin well.
2. The student must learn that the main purpose of his studies, and his life, is to learn the teachings of Jesus Christ.
3. The Bible should be read twice a day, and students should be able to discuss it sensibly.
4. There will be no swearing.
5. Students must attend classes faithfully and on time.

6. Students may not associate with people who lead an unfit life. Nor shall any student leave and go to any other town without the permission of his tutor.

7. Every student must be in his teacher's room at seven in the morning. He must also be there at five in the afternoon. He must explain what he has read during the day.

8. Any student who breaks any law of God or of the school may be punished.

The Written Word

The printing press served almost as an educational institution. A wide assortment of books was imported from England. Books were also printed in the northern colonies. Until about 1760 the most widely printed works were sermons. Also popular were annual almanacs filled with important dates and information about the stars and the weather. Benjamin Franklin's almanac, called *Poor Richard's Almanack*, offered bits of advice: "A penny saved is a penny earned. . . . The sleeping Fox catches no Poultry. . . . Keep thy Shop, and thy Shop will keep thee. . . . The second vice is Lying, the first is running into Debt."

Phillis Wheatley. Perhaps the best-known person of African descent was a former personal maid. Her name was Phillis Wheatley, and she wrote poems. She had been treated kindly by her owner and given a chance to learn to read. She studied history, geography, astronomy, and the Latin classics. And, of course, she often read the Bible. In fact, her first work was a poem entitled "On the Death of Reverend George Whitefield." She went to England and achieved a literary success there with other poems she composed. When she returned to the United States, one of her best-known poems was "His Excellency George Washington."

Most of her writings were not concerned with racial problems. They were, said one historian, "a method of escape" from the problems.

The Colonial Press. Newspapers served as the most important public tie between the colonies. Their circulations were tiny by modern standards, perhaps a few hundred. But they were widely read, being passed from hand to hand and read aloud at crossroad stores to those who were illiterate.

The first continuous colonial newspaper was the Boston *News-Letter*, founded in 1704. By 1760,

Phillis Wheatley enjoyed literary success both in colonial America and in England.

about twenty-five newspapers, all of them weeklies, were being published in the colonies. They contained four pages, the last two of which were mostly advertisements in small print. The only illustrations were a few small woodcuts showing the outline of a ship or a runaway. The ships appeared above listings of newly arrived ships and cargoes; the runaways appeared above advertisements describing indentured servants or slaves who had run away from their masters. There were no other drawings and, of course, no photographs.

News was called "latest advices" or "intelligence." Much of it was copied from English and other European newspapers and from newspapers published in other colonies. Sometimes the newspapers carried accounts about the latest activities of a colony's governor and assembly. Sometimes this led to ugly scenes between the papers and the authorities.

The Trial of John Peter Zenger

It was a hot, sticky day in August 1735. An eighty-year-old Philadelphia lawyer named Andrew Hamilton was delivering a speech in New York's city hall on behalf of a client. The client was John Peter Zenger, a German immigrant who ran a

This issue of August 2, 1742 is short of local news but full of European events.

printing press. Articles in a newspaper he printed had accused New York Governor William Cosby of rigging elections, accepting bribes, *confiscating* or taking land unlawfully, making money on a treaty with the Mohawk Indians, and being overly friendly with a notorious pirate.

At that time, British law held that anyone who criticized the government in writing was guilty of criminal *libel*. (Libel is a written or illustrated expression that results in injury to a person's reputation.) Hamilton suggested a different point of view. The issue was not whether Zenger had printed certain critical articles; he had. The issue was whether or not the articles were true. If they were true, then there was no libel.

Hamilton argued that people had a right to air grievances against their government.

❝ They have a right to oppose arbitrary power by speaking and writing truths. . . . The question before the court and you, gentlemen of the jury, is not of small or private concern. It is not the cause of a poor printer, nor of New York alone, which you are trying. No! It may, in its consequences, affect every freeman that lives under a British government, on the main [mainland] of America. It is the best cause; it is the cause of liberty. ❞

It took the jury ten minutes to decide that the articles about Cosby were true and that, therefore, Zenger was not guilty of libel. As a result, colonial newspapers were encouraged to speak out more boldly and to express differing political views. An example had been set for a basic American freedom: freedom of the press.

Section 2 Review

COMPREHENSION   Developing Vocabulary

1. Explain these terms: Great Awakening, libel, sects, literate, confiscating.

COMPREHENSION   Mastering Facts

1. Why was George Whitefield called the ''Great Awakener''?
2. Why did the Puritans insist that members of their communities learn to read?
3. What is the oldest college in the United States and why was it founded?
4. Why was the trial of John Peter Zenger important?

3   BRITAIN TRIUMPHS OVER FRANCE

VOCABULARY   *speculation*

As the colonies grew in population and wealth, the British government became increasingly concerned over the fact that they lay on a thin strip of land along the Atlantic. They stretched for over 1000 miles from Maine to Spanish Florida and were exposed to attack from the sea and from the interior of the continent. To the north, west, and south they were surrounded by England's traditional enemies and rivals—Spain and France. A move against the colonies by either power was a move against England.

The Founding of Georgia

It was partly to counter the power of Spain that the last and thirteenth colony was founded. The British government wished to establish a military outpost to protect the Carolinas from Spain. The government also had a second reason. It wanted a place of refuge for people who had been imprisoned because they could not pay their debts. In those days, if one did not pay a bill, one could—and probably would—end up in a debtor's prison.

In 1732 General James Oglethorpe and twenty other English gentlemen obtained a royal charter for a new colony to be located south of the Savannah River. The charter gave Oglethorpe and the other trustees the right to govern the colony for twenty-one years. Thereafter, it would be governed by the crown.

The Georgia trustees made certain rules which they hoped would advance both the military and the charitable aims of the colony. Landholdings were limited to 500 acres. People would not go there to become great landowners. Rum and brandy were banned because farmers and militia ought to be sober. Slavery was prohibited not because it was considered wrong, but because it would weaken the colony as a military outpost. But Georgia warmly welcomed all other groups, particularly German Lutheran and Jewish refugees.

Most of the hopeful plans for the new colony turned out badly. The trustees did support the settlement of some debtors from England. But these settlers were soon outnumbered by land-hungry men from South Carolina and other colonies. The trustees withdrew their ban on rum in the face of thirsty protesters. Planters from South Carolina bought up large tracts of land in the low country, brought in slaves, and began planting rice. By the time Georgia became a royal colony in 1752, it was a small copy of its northern neighbor.

Problems with France

Both the colonies and the British government felt that France was a greater danger than Spain. France and Britain were fighting each other all over the world as each tried to extend its empire at the expense of the other. From 1689 to 1763 the two countries went to war four times. The main battleground was in Europe, but each war caused reverberations in the New World. English settlers fought the French settlers and their Indian allies.

French Colonial Pressure. As you know, the French were installed in Canada. They had established forts along the St. Lawrence River, the southern Great Lakes, and the Mississippi River all the way to New Orleans. The French had also gained many of the Indian tribes as allies. The French attitude toward the Indians was different from that of the English. Because most French settlers were trappers, rather than farmers, they did not need vast amounts of Indian lands. They did not consider Indians barbarians, but a unique people with their own culture. French fur trappers often married Indian women and learned Indian languages.

The French government had tried to encourage farmers to settle in the New World, but without much success. Unlike the English colonists, the French had no religious or economic compulsion

---

Wars In Europe and Their Counterparts in the Colonies

Between 1689 and 1763 England was involved in a series of wars with France and Spain. Whenever England went to war, so did the colonies, but the wars were known by one name in Europe and by another name in the colonies.

The War Years	Name in Europe	Name in the Colonies
1689 – 1697	War of the League of Augsburg	King William's War
1702 – 1713	War of the Spanish Succession	Queen Anne's War
1744–1748	War of the Austrian Succession	King George's War
1756 – 1763	The Seven Years' War	The French and Indian War (began 1754)

to settle in far-away America. They were interested only in the fur trade. By 1760, therefore, there were only about 60,000 French people in all of Canada. English colonists numbered nearly 1.5 million. But this superior number was balanced by the friendship between the French and the Indians. Whenever there was a war between England and France, the French encouraged their Indian friends to attack English settlements.

New York became the most crucial battleground because it contained the only water-level break in the Appalachian mountain chain. Fortunately for the English, their friends, the Iroquois Confederacy, controlled the Mohawk River valley. The Iroquois preferred the English to the French. English blankets were warmer and lasted longer than the blankets that French traders sold, while British-made rum not only cost less than French brandy but also was more to the Iroquois' taste.

To the north and west of the Iroquois were the Hurons. The French had befriended the Hurons at an early date without knowing that they were traditional enemies of the Iroquois. Thus, the English were able to make alliances with the Iroquois against their common enemies, the Hurons and the French.

The Colonials Capture Louisbourg. Shortly after the founding of Georgia, war again broke out in Europe. From 1739 to 1748 Britain was fighting first with Spain and then with France. Until 1745 there was little action in the American colonies. But that year something astounding happened. Since 1713, the heavily armed fort of Louisbourg had stood on Cape Breton Island. It guarded the approaches to the St. Lawrence River, the gateway to New France. In 1745 Massachusetts and other New England colonies sent militiamen and sailors to assault Louisbourg. To almost everyone's surprise, the expedition succeeded. No British troops or sailors were involved.

The victory fired the imagination of colonials. They had proven their own strength. Colonial leaders, especially in Massachusetts, began to think in grander terms. Perhaps all of New France might be conquered. That would be a great triumph not only for England but for Protestantism as well.

A Brief Peace. Peace came three years later in 1748. The Treaty of Aix-la-Chapelle ended the conflict that was known in the colonies as King George's War. One of the treaty's provisions gave Louisbourg back to the French. Naturally, there was resentment in the colonies, especially in Massachusetts. It seemed that England did not appreciate the colonial war effort. But it was widely believed on all sides that the treaty was merely a temporary truce. King George's War had been a sideshow to the main conflict in Europe. Neither France nor England had really defeated the other. It was clear to people in London, Paris, and colonial capitals that a showdown was coming.

The expected war broke out in 1756. This time, North America became an important battleground in the worldwide conflict between Great Britain and France. In Europe the war was called the Seven Years' War. In America it was known as the French and Indian War and it began in 1754.

The French and Indian War

Before the ink was dry on the 1748 Treaty of Aix-la-Chapelle, both sides began to prepare for the expected showdown. The French refortified Louisbourg and also constructed a string of forts from Lake Erie southward to the "Forks of the Ohio." There, where the Allegheny and Monongahela rivers join to form the Ohio River, they built Fort Duquesne (du-*kane*) in 1753. (The site is now the city of Pittsburgh.) It stood on land claimed by both Pennsylvania and Virginia.

The Ohio Country. The British side was just as busy. In 1747 a group of wealthy Virginia planters formed the Ohio Company to obtain land beyond the Appalachians for purposes of *speculation.* Speculation is a form of gambling that the value of an item will go up or down. The Ohio Company speculators were gambling that the value of the land would rise. Two years later the Virginia government gave the company 200,000 acres west of the Monongahela. Authorities in London approved the grant in hopes of encouraging settlement in the area. In 1751 Robert Dinwiddie arrived in Virginia as the new royal governor. He promptly became a member of the Ohio Company. The interests of the British Empire and of private Virginia citizens were now locked together.

Both as a British patriot and as a land speculator, Dinwiddie took a keen interest in the Ohio country. He decided to find out what the French were doing in the area. In 1754 he sent out a group of Virginia militiamen under the command of a

The French and Indian War   1754–1763

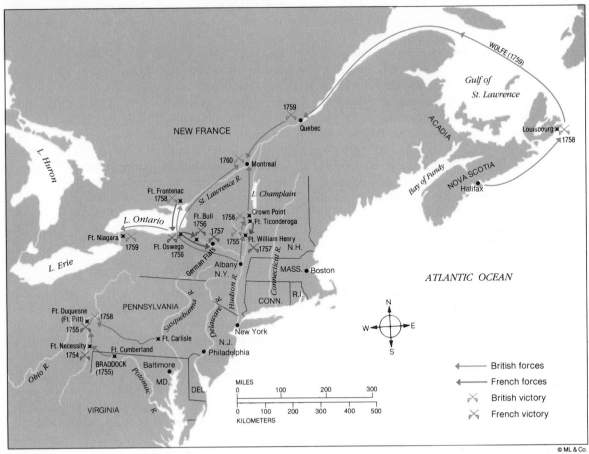

Map Skills   *The British and French fought this war for control of eastern North America. Who won the battle at Louisbourg? at German Flats? How far was Ft. Duquesne from Ft. Carlisle?*

twenty-two-year-old colonel named George Washington. The young man had good connections, since two of his brothers were members of the Ohio Company.

Washington led his small force toward the forks of the Ohio. He learned that a larger French force already occupied the site. Hoping for the best, Washington and his men erected a stockade some fifty miles south of the forks and aptly named it Fort Necessity. But the French attacked. Outnumbered by about 700 to 400, Washington's force surrendered. Since France and England were not yet officially at war, the French released the Virginians. They returned to Williamsburg with word that the Ohio country was firmly in the hands of France.

The skirmish at Fort Necessity was, in fact, the opening battle of the French and Indian War.

The Albany Congress.   While Washington was surrendering Fort Necessity, an important meeting took place in Albany, New York. The London government had summoned delegates from the colonies of New Hampshire, Massachusetts, New York, New Jersey, Pennsylvania, Maryland, and Virginia to meet with leaders of the Iroquois. All but two of these colonies—New Jersey and Virginia—sent delegates to the meeting. The English wanted Iroquois aid against the French. The purpose of the meeting was to draw up a treaty with the Indians that all the colonies would sign. Until then, each colony had made its own agreement or treaty with the Indians. For the first time, a uniform Indian policy was proposed.

The Iroquois leaders listened politely to the customary speeches of welcome and high regard. They gravely accepted the usual collection of gifts, which on this occasion were very generous. But the Iroquois would make no promises of support. They were well aware of growing French power in the west and had no desire to support a loser.

But there were other reasons why Indians were cool toward the English. Chief Hendrick of the Mohawks charged that dishonest land speculators had gotten "writings for all our lands" and intended to leave them only "the very spot we live upon and hardly that." He also accused the Albany traders of supplying the Mohawks' enemies with guns and powder in return for beaver pelts. In fact, even the governor of New York had himself been involved in this trading with the enemy. It was clear that the members of the Iroquois Confederacy were not enthusiastic about helping their old allies.

A Plan of Union.

After the Indians departed, a plan for joint colonial action was discussed. Before Benjamin Franklin left to attend the Albany Congress, he wrote in the Philadelphia *Gazette* for May 9 that the French were confident of victory over the English settlers because the colonies would never "agree to any speedy and effectual measures for our common defense." At the congress, therefore, Franklin proposed a "Plan of the Union" for the North American colonies. It was a plan to encourage cooperation by the setting up of a colonial council. The council would deal with the acquisition and settlement of western lands, joint defense, and relations with the Indians. And the council would raise taxes on its own for military purposes.

The Albany delegates sent the plan to the various colonies for their approval. In every colony, however, the plan was either rejected or ignored. The various assemblies had no wish to share their power of taxation with the government in London. Nor did they want a council with control over western lands. Each colony wanted to press its own claims to lands in the west. Authorities in London were relieved by the failure of the plan. They had no interest in seeing the colonies unite on a permanent basis.

British Defeat at Fort Duquesne.

After the defeat of Washington's militiamen, Virginia's Governor Dinwiddie and other colonial governors appealed for regular troops from Great Britain. The London government obliged by sending 1400 men under the command of Major General Edward Braddock, who had the reputation of being one of England's finest generals. The troops arrived in April 1755. Dinwiddie and Braddock planned a major expedition to level Fort Duquesne and drive the French from the Ohio country. Braddock's troops were joined by more than 1000 colonial militiamen. Only eight Indian guides could be found. The other Indians presumably had no desire to offend the French. Nevertheless, Braddock and his men, accompanied by George Washington as a member of Braddock's staff, marched off through western Maryland and then north into Pennsylvania toward the forks of the Ohio. It was the same route Washington had taken a year before.

The long march held no problems for the Americans. But Braddock was used to European warfare. He could not slip through the countryside. He had to stop, hack down trees, and put logs over swamps instead of going around them. In the words of an eyewitness, he spent time "leveling every molehill" that stood in his way.

Washington had warned Braddock of the dangers of an ambush. But Braddock bragged that the sight of his British redcoats would be enough to frighten away the French and the Indians. Sure enough, on July 8, about eight miles south of Fort Duquesne, the expedition was ambushed. The British soldiers, completely unused to frontier fighting, were bewildered and terrified by the deadly fire from men hidden in trees and bushes. They turned and fled. Braddock tried heroically to keep his men in line, but he was shot dead.

Washington, with his Virginia men, tried to cover the British retreat, but in vain. Two horses were shot from under him. Two bullets pierced his hat and four pierced his coat. Later he wrote to his mother about "the dastardly behavior" of the British soldiers. "They ran as sheep pursued by dogs and it was impossible to rally them." Nearly 1000 of them were killed or wounded.

This stunning defeat of some of Britain's supposedly best soldiers raised a question in colonial minds about the ability of British troops. It also badly weakened the prestige of the British among the Indians.

William Pitt Turns the Tide.

Discouraged and angry over the French gains in North America, George II in 1757 appointed William Pitt as one of two chief ministers in his government. Pitt was self-assured to the point of arrogance. But he brought new vigorous leadership and a new strategy to the war. He ignored the skyrocketing national debt and set about buying victory. On the European continent, he hired soldiers from his German allies and relied on them to do most of the fighting against the French. In the American colonies, he stopped begging for help from the assemblies. He simply told them that their wartime expenses would be covered by the British government. To get better leadership in the field he promoted able junior officers over the heads of senior ones.

The next year Pitt's policies began to pay off. George Washington finally had the pleasure of taking part in the capture of Fort Duquesne, which was renamed Fort Pitt and later Pittsburgh. A major British force recaptured Louisbourg, and news of the victory was celebrated with great bonfires in London and in various colonial capitals.

The Fall of Quebec. The next year, 1759, became known as the "Year of Victories." On sea and land, in India and Europe, British forces rolled up one triumph after another.

In America, British colonials and regulars moved northward across the lakes above Albany. Another British force sailed up the St. Lawrence River to Quebec.

Quebec was a walled city built high on cliffs overlooking the river. The British general in command, James Wolfe, was young, brilliant, and daring. One night he ordered his redcoats up some steep goat paths that led to the top of the cliffs. The next morning the French awoke to find a British army lined up for battle on the Plains of Abraham outside the city walls. The French troops under General Louis Joseph, Marquis de Montcalm marched out as the sun rose. In a brief but violent battle, both Wolfe and Montcalm were killed.

Wolfe died knowing that he had achieved a great victory. The rest of French Canada was now cut off from France. The next year British forces took Montreal, and French power in North America was at an end.

Section 3 Review

COMPREHENSION   Developing Vocabulary

1. Explain these terms: speculation, Fort Necessity, debtor's prison.

COMPREHENSION   Mastering Facts

1. What was the last English colony to be founded?
2. What was the French attitude toward the Indians?
3. What was the name given in North America to the Seven Years' War (1756–1763) between France and Britain?
4. What battle brought an end to French power in North America?

CHAPTER 5 Review

Chapter Summary

During the eighteenth century, the colonists embraced the ideas of the Enlightenment. Benjamin Franklin became a living example of enlightened thought in the colonies. In addition, religious and cultural revival led to the formation of new churches. Colonial education developed informed citizens ready to debate public issues. Then, as a result of the French and Indian War, the English took control of French Canada.

Questions for Critical Thinking

COMPREHENSION   Summarizing Main Ideas

1. According to John Locke, what three natural rights did God give to humanity?
2. What factors helped bring about the religious revival called the Great Awakening?
3. What three policies did William Pitt institute in England's struggle against France? Which of these policies were successful?

COMPREHENSION   Interpreting Events

1. To what kinds of problems did Copernicus and Newton apply human reason? To what did Locke apply it?
2. Why were American colonists especially receptive to the ideas of the Enlightenment?
3. Describe the relationship between the Puritans' religious beliefs and (a) their economic success; (b) their attitude toward education; (c) their attitude toward government.
4. According to John Woolman, how did slavery in America differ from slavery in ancient Rome? What effects did this difference have on the way American slaves were treated?
5. What were the political reasons for the founding of Georgia? What were the military reasons? How did the new colony attempt to achieve these goals? Was it successful? Explain your reasoning.
6. Why did most Indian tribes support the French rather than the English? Why were the Iroquois an exception at first? What made the Iroquois change their minds during the meeting of the Albany Congress?

APPLICATION   Using Skills To Evaluate Sources

Sources of historical information can be divided into two kinds. One kind consists of primary sources, such as the remains of buildings, tools and weapons, newspapers, autobiographies, tax records, and photographs. The second kind consists of secondary sources, such as textbooks, biographies, historical films and novels and paintings, and other works of art that deal with previous time periods.

For each of the following items, indicate whether it is a primary or a secondary source.

1. Isaac Newton's *Principia Mathematica*
2. *The Dictionary of American Biography*
3. *The New Columbia Encyclopedia*
4. A copy of *Poor Richard's Almanack*
5. A Franklin stove
6. Massachusetts Charter of 1691
7. The newspaper text of one of George Whitefield's sermons
8. A descriptive letter written by an individual who heard George Whitefield preach
9. The court record of one of the Salem witch trials
10. *The Crucible*, by Arthur Miller, a play that recreates the Salem witch trials
11. A bill of sale for Phillis Wheatley
12. Phillis Wheatley's poem "His Excellency George Washington"
13. A blanket used in the French fur trade with the Indians
14. Newspaper accounts of the Albany Congress
15. A musket used by a British regular at the Battle of Fort Duquesne
16. George Washington's diary

EVALUATION   Comparing Past to Present

1. Locke wrote that God had given humanity three rights. Which do most Americans still consider important? How are these rights protected?
2. Identify those Puritan beliefs that are held by many Americans today.
3. Compare the content of colonial newspapers with that of contemporary newspapers.

Adam Smith and the Wealth of Nations

The spirit of freedom and confidence expressed in the American colonies during the mid-1700s reflected a fresh, optimistic, and vigorous view of life held by an increasing number of people. Traders and manufacturers had grown impatient with the existing mercantilist system. Business operators felt frustrated and hindered by the direction and control of economic life exercised by the national government. They wanted more freedom to pursue their own personal advantage. Many people felt they were not getting the rewards to which their efforts entitled them. Instead they felt the rewards went to the state.

Such persons believed that by seeking their own advantage in business the entire nation would prosper. In other words, by helping oneself one helped the nation. This new feeling was best expressed by the Scottish economist and philosopher Adam Smith (1732–1790). His book *The Wealth of Nations*, published in 1776, captured the imagination of Europe and America and became, by far, the most influential work ever written by an economist. Smith's philosophy of freeing merchants and traders from restrictions was called *laissez faire* (literally, "allow them to do" or "leave alone"). It dominated economic thought for the next 150 years,

particularly in the young and ambitious colonies.

Adam Smith believed, along with the writers of the U.S. Constitution, that human behavior followed certain "laws of nature." (These were the same "Laws of Nature and of Nature's God" that Thomas Jefferson appealed to in the Declaration of Independence.) One of these laws was self-interest. Smith believed that people engaged in trade and manufacturing for their own profit—not for the sake of the nation or to benefit others.

Personally a charitable man, Smith nevertheless believed that the selfish foundation of business activity was actually a good thing. In a nation where everyone was allowed to seek his or her own personal advantage, everyone would automatically also contribute to the prosperity of the nation. The skilled worker who could command high wages, the manufacturer of cheap goods, and the trader who selected merchandise that would please customers—all were seeking their own profit. But they were also performing a useful service and benefiting society as a whole. It is as if an "invisible hand" were turning individual self-interest into the common good. A well-governed nation, Smith believed, would encourage the natural forces of self-interest, limiting them only

when they violated the principles of justice.

Mercantilism, the economic system which dominated Europe in Smith's day, represented the opposite of what he considered a natural system. In *The Wealth of Nations*, Smith blasts not only the mass of mercantilist controls over commerce but also the monopolies and privileges granted by governments to certain groups and individuals. These, he believed, only frustrated nature. Without the rivalry of other competitors, the privileged traders, producers, and merchants grew lazy and smug. This resulted in shoddy goods, lower profits, and finally a poorer nation.

Calling for an end to mercantilism, Adam Smith proposed a free choice of occupations. He urged the abolition of government apprenticeship rules and laws restricting settlements in certain parts of the country. He attacked duties, bounties, and the monopolies of chartered companies, such as those that operated in the British colonies in North America. However, even as he denounced these hindrances to trade, Smith realized that they played a crucial role in the British economy of his day. With this in mind, he advised that they should be lifted gradually whenever a quick repeal would cause serious unemployment. He also thought that it

Adam Smith, the Scottish economist, gave support to the idea of human progress through individual efforts.

was unrealistic to expect that a *completely* free trade or laissez-faire system would ever be established in Great Britain.

In Book V of *The Wealth of Nations*, Smith discusses the role of government in a laissez-faire society. He restricts the government to three functions: (1) national defense, (2) the enforcement of laws protecting life and property, and (3) the construction and maintenance of public works that might be highly useful but not profitable enough for private builders. Under this last heading, he included roads, bridges, canals, harbors, and, to some degree, schools.

It is clear that, for Smith, the government's participation in the affairs of the nation should be very much the exception rather than the rule. The simple system of "natural liberty" would, in his view, suffice in dealing with most of a country's problems.

As with the thoughts of many influential thinkers, Smith's ideas were used by some to suit their own purposes. For example, in the 1800s, manufacturers wanted no state interference in employer-employee disputes. Yet, some of these same manufacturers urged the state to pass tariff laws to block the importing of competing goods. They thus defended the policy of laissez faire only when it was convenient.

Despite these questionable uses of Adam Smith's theories, *The Wealth of Nations* stands as a groundbreaking work which almost alone established economics as a respected science. During the 1800s, Smith's ideas also served to spur the industrial development of such countries as England, France, and the United States.

Had Adam Smith published *The Wealth of Nations* earlier than 1776, it is quite possible that the American Revolution would never have taken place. Mercantilist measures, such as the Navigation Acts or the Molasses Act, angered American colonists and inspired thoughts of revolt. Smith, of course, called for the repeal of this type of interference in trade. "Great Britain," he wrote, "derives nothing but loss from the dominion she assumes over her colonies." Smith proposed a free trade association of independent countries in which Britain and the former colonies cooperate as "faithful, affectionate, and generous allies." But by the time these sensible proposals were published, the conflict between Great Britain and the American colonies had already begun.

Understanding Free Enterprise

1. If Adam Smith's *Wealth of Nations* had been published a few years earlier, do you think it might have changed the history of Britain and its colonies? Give reasons for your answer.

2. According to Smith, why was competition desirable?

3. Are there any U.S. government policies today that could be called mercantilist? Explain.

CHAPTER 6

Separating from Britain

1760–1775

Linking Past to Present

When the French and Indian War ended with the Treaty of Paris in 1763, the colonies and Britain had reason to be jubilant. All French Canada now belonged to Britain. The threat of a French attack on the colonies had disappeared, and Britain had decisively beaten its old rival. The British Empire had never been so large or seemingly so strong. But within twelve years, the thirteen American colonies were in rebellion. How did it happen?

With the establishment of peace, Britain felt that an enlarged empire needed firmer control from London. The government also felt that the colonies should pay a fair share of the costs of running the empire. This tightening of control over the empire collided with the growing self-interest of the colonies.

From 1763 to 1775 each side accumulated grievances caused partly by bad judgment and partly by genuine misunderstanding. Relations deteriorated rapidly as crisis followed crisis. Finally what seemed unthinkable just a few years earlier actually happened: the colonies and Britain went to war against each other.

Nova Scotia, Canada, and the British West Indies remained within the empire. From their point of view—and that of tens of thousands of loyal colonists who lived in the colonies—the rebels had treasonably abandoned their king and country.

1 BRITAIN TIGHTENS CONTROL OVER ITS COLONIES

VOCABULARY   *porphyria Proclamation of 1763*

George II died in October 1760, six weeks after the capture of Montreal. He was succeeded by his young grandson, George III, who reigned for the next sixty years. George's long life was an unhappy one. He lost one of the most important parts of his overseas empire. And at one point he startled his servants by climbing down from his carriage in a London park and opening up a conversation with an oak tree. Many historians believe he suffered from an inherited disease called *porphyria*. He eventually became so mentally unbalanced that a regent was appointed to rule in his place.

George III and the Treaty of Paris

In 1760 George III still showed no sign of insanity. He was neither stupid nor bright, but he was very much under the thumb of the Scottish Earl of Bute, who had been in charge of his upbringing. Bute had given him a sense of patriotism and a determination to rule as a strong, firm monarch. His mother always reminded him, "George, be a king!"

George III inherited William Pitt as chief minister. Pitt was popular both in the country at large and in the colonies. But he aroused dislike on the part of less able men who had to deal with him. He suffered from painful gout and was snappish even to the king. Pitt wanted to carry on the war against France in an aggressive fashion. But George III and Bute wanted peace. So the king dismissed his minister and relied on Bute to negotiate a peace settlement.

By the 1763 Treaty of Paris, millions of square miles of land changed hands. Britain took Florida from Spain because that country had supported France during the last years of the war. From France, Britain obtained Canada and all the land east of the Mississippi River except for the port of New Orleans. Britain could have gotten more, but Bute was not as interested in gaining more territory as he was in keeping a careful balance of power between Spain and France in Europe. So he returned Martinique and Guadalupe, in the West Indies, to France and persuaded that country, in a separate treaty, to give Spain the port of New Orleans and Louisiana. In those years, Louisiana included all the land drained by the western tributaries of the Mississippi River.

George III. The king's lack of tact and his stubborn will to punish the colonies helped lead to war.

111

Eastern North America After the French and Indian War

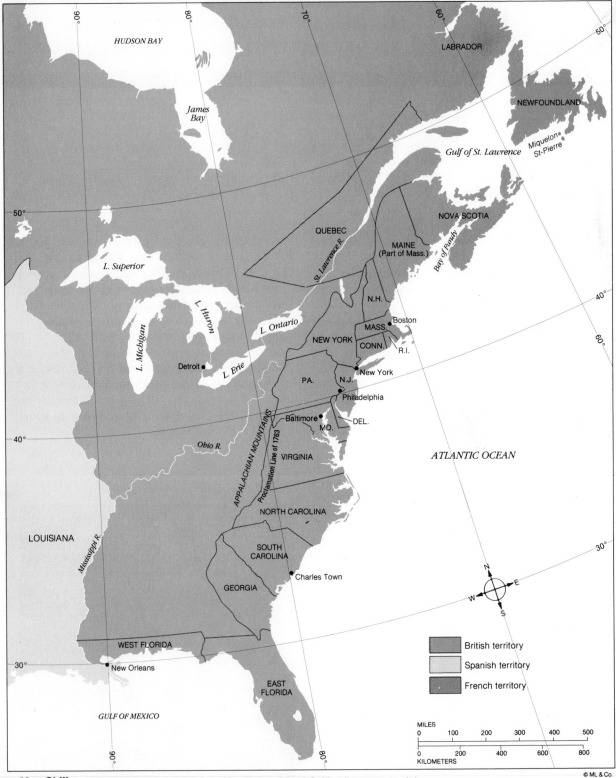

HUDSON BAY

James Bay

LABRADOR

NEWFOUNDLAND

Gulf of St. Lawrence

Miquelon·
St-Pierre

NOVA SCOTIA

Bay of Fundy

QUEBEC

St. Lawrence R.

MAINE
(Part of Mass.)

L. Superior

L. Huron

L. Michigan

L. Ontario

L. Erie

Detroit

N.H.

MASS. Boston

NEW YORK CONN.

R.I.

PA. N.J.

New York

Philadelphia

APPALACHIAN MOUNTAINS

Proclamation Line of 1763

Baltimore

DEL.

MD.

Ohio R.

VIRGINIA

ATLANTIC OCEAN

NORTH CAROLINA

LOUISIANA

Mississippi R.

SOUTH
CAROLINA

Charles Town

GEORGIA

N

E

W

S

WEST FLORIDA

New Orleans

EAST
FLORIDA

GULF OF MEXICO

British territory

Spanish territory

French territory

MILES
0   100   200   300   400   500

0   200   400   600   800
KILOMETERS

© ML & Co.

Map Skills   *The French defeat left them with what two islands? What line separated the British colonies from the Ohio valley? What city was near the mouth of the Mississippi?*

There was some reservation about the treaty in England. Some people feared that taking Canada would make the English colonists less dependent on the mother country for protection. The colonists in Canada, they said, might join forces with those farther south and create a union that might act independently of the Empire. But Benjamin Franklin, who was in London at the time, wrote a pamphlet ridiculing this argument. The English colonists had proved unable to unite against the French and Indians. Was it likely, asked Franklin, that they would unite against "their own nation" which "they love much more than they love one another"? A union between the colonies, Franklin wrote, "is not merely improbable, it is impossible." But he added, "When I say such a union is impossible, I mean without the most grievous tyranny and oppression."

The Earl of Bute resigned after signing the Treaty of Paris, and George III replaced him with George Grenville. Grenville was no expert on colonial affairs. But he soon found himself devoting most of his time and energy to events in America.

Regulating Indian-Colonial Affairs

The Indians in New France were alarmed by the fall of their French allies. They grew unhappier still as their old French trading partners were squeezed out by English fur traders. The English charged higher prices for their trade goods than the French did, which meant that the Indians had to trap more animals. Yet at the same time, English traders were unable to supply the Indians with powder and lead for hunting. Then, too, British traders often gave the Indians rum. Once the Indians were drunk, the British would cheat them out of their furs.

The Indians knew little about the land speculation that was going on in the Ohio country. But they could see that more and more English settlers were crossing the Appalachian Mountains. The Indians feared it would be only a matter of time before their land would be filled and their game driven away.

Pontiac Attacks. In the spring of 1763, the Ottawa chief Pontiac led his warriors in an attack against the small fort of Detroit. Other tribes joined in a general assault on British forts in the west. Within a few weeks, the Indians had captured seven of these outposts of British power.

British troops moved westward, and several battles followed with heavy losses on both sides. Although peace was restored by a number of treaties, everyone knew that the differences between the colonists and the Indians would not go away.

The Royal Proclamation of 1763. In the meantime, Grenville decided to try to stop the westward expansion of the colonists by drawing a line on a map. The royal Proclamation of 1763 forbade colonials from settling west of the Appalachian Mountains and ordered any colonists west of that line "forthwith to remove themselves." The hope was that restricting colonials to the seaboard would make governing them easier. Also, there would be less chance of trouble with the Indians.

But no paper fence could keep out speculators, traders, and farmers. The British government had intended the proclamation line as a holding operation. They hoped to buy time in order to work out a more permanent western policy. But they greatly underestimated the rate of colonial expansion. The fence leaked so badly that British agents found themselves in continuous negotiations with various Indian tribes.

The proclamation persuaded colonists of two things. First, that the British government was insensitive to their interests. Second, and more important, that the British government was unable to enforce its proclamations. There was general resentment and frustration over English policy. The public feeling was reflected in a poem that was popular in the colonies:

❝ We have an old Mother that peevish is grown.
She snubs us like children that scarce walk alone.
She forgets we've grown up and have Sense of our own. ❞

Imposing Troops and Taxes

Even before the end of the French and Indian War, a decision had been made to leave 10,000 British troops in the American colonies. The colonists suspected, but could not prove, that the presence of these troops was intended to keep them in line. There was a long-standing distrust in England of a large peacetime army. Since some British officials felt such an army was necessary, they came up with the idea of stationing it in the colonies instead of at home. As things turned out, however, colonial Americans had inherited the English people's historic distrust of a standing army in peacetime.

Grenville did not bother himself about such matters. He saw troops in terms of money. Since the colonies were prosperous, why shouldn't they pay for part of their own protection? After all, they had gained economically from the war. British soldiers and sailors had required housing, food, and equipment. Colonial shipbuilders, farmers, builders, rum distillers, leather workers—all these, and more, had prospered during the fighting.

The Sugar Act of 1764. When reviewing colonial finances, Grenville made a startling discovery. The American customs service was costing 8000 pounds a year and bringing in only 2000 pounds. Obviously, a great deal of smuggling was going on. Something had to be done.

Accordingly, Grenville pushed through Parliament an act that did three things. It halved the duty of sixpence a gallon on foreign-made molasses to threepence. It placed duties on certain imports that had not been taxed before. And it provided for enforcement of these duties.

The Sugar Act of 1764 alarmed many colonials. Merchants who had been smuggling cheap molasses from the French sugar islands in the Caribbean thought they would be ruined. Even though the new molasses duty was less, collection of the

As colonial unrest grew, British officials were often taken from home, then tarred and feathered.

duty would be enforced. And even three cents was more expensive than smuggling. And certainly no one liked the idea of higher prices for the newly taxed goods.

The British government also stated that violations of the Sugar Act would be tried only in admiralty courts. As you know, in such courts there were no juries, and the judges for the courts were sent over from England. Over the years, however, the colonists had been very resourceful about guiding smuggling cases into local courts with local judges and juries, where acquittals were easy to obtain. Now, instead of dealing with understanding colonists, violators would have to deal with unfriendly judges from England.

The Quartering Act of 1765. The next year Grenville came up with a means of getting the colonists to help support British troops. The Quartering Act required any colony where troops were stationed to provide them with living quarters. These colonies also had to provide certain supplies and traditional rations of cider, beer, or rum. Although English law allowed for the quartering of troops, the colonists resented the cost. New Yorkers were especially angry because most of the British troops were stationed there.

The Stamp Act of 1765. That same year, 1765, Grenville persuaded Parliament to pass the Stamp Act. It required that a tax stamp (ranging in value from a halfpenny to ten pounds) be purchased and placed on all legal documents, liquor and other licenses, college diplomas, newspapers, almanacs, playing cards, and dice. Further, the payment had to be made in British money, which was worth more than colonial money. The Stamp Act also provided that violators be tried in admiralty courts.

Grenville settled back to wait for his new revenue. But he never received any. No stamps were ever bought or used in the colonies. There was an outburst of protest and defiance the moment that word of the Stamp Act reached America.

No Taxation Without Representation. The colonial assemblies took the first steps. In Virginia, a fiery young planter and lawyer named Patrick Henry took the floor of the lower house to offer a set of seven resolutions. The house adopted five, which in general stated that Virginians could be taxed only by the Virginia assembly. The house rejected two resolutions that called for outright disobedience. Other assemblies soon passed similar resolutions, saying that Parliament had no right to tax the colonies since they were not represented in Parliament.

The assemblies took another important step. They decided on collective protest. In October, delegates from nine colonies met in New York City for what was called the Stamp Act Congress. (Four colonies had been prevented by their royal governors from selecting delegates.) The congress quickly agreed on a *Declaration of Rights and Grievances.* The declaration repeated the arguments presented in Virginia's resolutions and added that Parliament had no right to expand the jurisdiction of admiralty courts. As British subjects, the colonists were entitled to trial by jury. The declaration closed by demanding repeal of both the Sugar Act and the Stamp Act.

The colonists' position was clear and consistent. The colonial assemblies were the only bodies that represented the people of the colonies. Therefore, only the colonial legislatures could tax them.

This argument possessed one potential flaw. Even before the Stamp Act crisis, some people had suggested that the colonies elect representatives to sit in Parliament. Such a system would in fact have destroyed the colonists' position. But both sides realized that the Atlantic, which took from six to fifteen weeks to cross, was a real barrier to effective representation.

Section 1 Review

COMPREHENSION Developing Vocabulary

1. Explain these terms: Proclamation of 1763, porphyria, collective protest, Quartering Act.

COMPREHENSION Mastering Facts

1. What was the purpose of the Proclamation of 1763?
2. Why did colonists dislike admiralty courts?
3. What did the Sugar Act of 1764 try to prevent the colonists from doing?
4. Why did the colonists claim that the Stamp Act was illegal?

2 THE COLONIES ORGANIZE RESISTANCE TO BRITAIN

VOCABULARY   *non-importation   Townshend Acts*

By the time of the Stamp Act Congress, it was apparent that some colonials were willing to go considerably beyond the point of passing resolutions. That summer, citizens began to form secret organizations in most of the port cities. The Daughters of Liberty group urged people not to drink British tea. Instead, they gave out recipes for tea made from birchbark, sage, and rosemary. They spun thread and made clothes for their families instead of buying British-made clothes.

A group of men calling themselves Sons of Liberty was composed mostly of shopkeepers, artisans, and laborers. They were often led, however, by gentlemen of property and standing. They aimed at defending American liberties by making sure that no stamps were distributed. If it took mob action to do so, then mob action it would be.

The Use of Mob Action

In August a mob of men and women in Boston burned the records of the admiralty court and invaded the house of stamp distributor Andrew Oliver. The mob called for either his resignation or his head. Oliver had wisely removed himself before the mob arrived. However, the next day he read his resignation aloud to a jeering and cheering crowd. Similar mobs assembled in other cities and proved effective without killing anyone. By November 1, the day the Stamp Act was to go into effect, every stamp agent in the colonies had either resigned or promised not to issue any stamps.

Mobilizing large numbers of men and women outdoors was, of course, not new. George Whitefield had done the same thing for a different purpose. But the Stamp Act mobs brought a new dimension to American political life. They were well organized and were led by substantial citizens. And they proved very effective in gaining a specific political goal.

Repeal of the Stamp Act

Americans found another means of resistance in addition to mob action. Hundreds of merchants in the three major northern ports—Boston, New

This woodcut shows the women of Philadelphia making clothes instead of having to buy English goods.

York, and Philadelphia—signed agreements not to buy British goods until the Stamp Act was repealed. This boycott of British goods was called *non-importation*. The merchants guessed correctly that English manufacturers and merchants would be upset by it and would demand that Parliament repeal the Stamp Act.

For several weeks after November 1, trade was at a standstill. No legal cases were tried. No newspapers appeared. Then business perked up, cases began to clear the courts, and printers resumed publishing newspapers. And all without the required tax stamps! How did it happen? Judges and customs officials received threatening visits from members of the Sons of Liberty.

An argument prevented a showdown between England and the colonies. That summer George III dismissed Grenville, "his dearest friend," after the latter quarreled with George's mother. The king's new minister was the Marquess of Rockingham. Since English merchants were howling about their losses, Rockingham—with support from the king—got Parliament to repeal the Stamp Act in March 1766.

Yet few British leaders were willing to admit the truth of Pitt's statement that the Stamp Act had been a mistake, and that Parliament had no right to tax overseas English people who were not represented in Parliament. Therefore, on the same day Parliament repealed the Stamp Act, it passed the Declaratory Act. This asserted its full right to make laws "to bind the colonies and people of America . . . in all cases whatsoever." Parliament also renewed the Quartering Act.

When news of the repeal of the Stamp Act arrived in the colonies, there was an outburst of celebration and rejoicing. Bells rang everywhere, and the New York assembly even voted to put up statues of King George. Little attention was paid to the Declaratory Act and its ominous claims of parliamentary power.

The Townshend Acts

Four months after the repeal of the Stamp Act, Rockingham went the way of Grenville, and effective leadership fell into the hands of Charles Townshend, a man with much energy and little sense.

Townshend decided it was high time the colonies paid their fair share of taxes and learned that they must obey Parliament. A series of revenue laws were enacted that became known as the Townshend Acts. The new duties fell on certain manufactured goods imported into the colonies—glass, lead, paints, paper, and tea.

According to mercantilist theory, these duties made no sense at all. They were bound to discourage manufacturers in England and to encourage them in the colonies, just the opposite of what was supposed to happen under mercantilism. Nevertheless, Townshend intended to have the new duties enforced. He provided for admiralty-court jurisdiction over customs offenders. He also created a new Board of Customs Commissioners, which would reside in Boston. That city was notorious for smuggling and for the vigor of its tax resistance. In order to encourage the zeal of the new customs officials, the law provided that they would be paid from the fines imposed by the admiralty courts. The more convictions these officials obtained, the more they would receive!

The Townshend Acts also aimed at New York's failure to comply with the Quartering Act of 1766. The New York assembly had been providing only part of the money needed to house British troops. The act shut down the New York assembly until the full amount was appropriated.

American response to the Townshend Acts followed a different pattern than during the Stamp Act crisis. The new duties did not affect people in general the way the stamp tax had. This time the tax burden fell mostly on merchants. They revived the technique of boycotting imports from England. As with all boycotts, there was great difficulty in gaining unanimous cooperation. If merchants in one port agreed on non-importation, merchants in neighboring ports were tempted to continue business as usual.

The various Sons of Liberty groups made a two-pronged attack on this problem. They visited offending merchants and spoke persuasively about the rights of the colonists. They also pointed out the dangers of not going along with the Sons of Liberty.

Letters from a Farmer

While non-importation gradually grew more effective, some colonists grew busy with their pens. Pennsylvania's John Dickinson published a series of *Letters from a Farmer in Pennsylvania to the Inhabitants of the British Colonies*. These letters reached a wide audience in both the colonies and England.

Dickinson denounced the Townshend duties as a violation of the unwritten constitution of the British Empire. He agreed that Parliament had the right to use taxes to regulate trade. But taxes imposed for the purpose of raising money for the English treasury were another matter. They were no more acceptable in the form of import duties than in the form of stamps. "Let these truths be indelibly impressed on our minds, that we cannot be happy without being free—that we cannot be free without being secure in our property—that we cannot be secure in our property if without our consent others may as by right take it away."

Dickinson also pointed out that if Parliament could shut down the New York assembly, it could shut down others. In effect, he said, New York might merely be the first victim of "unlawful tyranny."

Section 2 Review

COMPREHENSION Developing Vocabulary

1. Explain these terms: non-importation, Townshend Acts, Sons of Liberty.

COMPREHENSION Mastering Facts

1. Why did stamp distributor Andrew Oliver resign?
2. What did the Declaratory Act say?
3. According to mercantilist theory, why did the Townshend Acts make no sense?
4. What arguments against Parliament were raised in *Letters from a Farmer?*

3 A TENSE SITUATION DEVELOPS IN MASSACHUSETTS

VOCABULARY   *massacre* *Whigs*

Dickinson's points were restated by the Massachusetts assembly in a letter to the other colonial assemblies. The actual author of this Massachusetts letter, which "condemned the Townshend Acts and called upon the other colonies to unite for the common defense," was Samuel Adams.

Adams was a Bostonian. After graduating from Harvard with a master's degree, he had gone into his father's brewery business. There "he did little good for lack of capacity, and little harm from lack of responsibility." But then he turned with great success to local politics. Using the Boston town meetings as his base of power, Adams was rapidly building a career as a popular agitator. He sniffed tyranny in every breeze. He pressed tirelessly for stronger measures.

Adams played his cards beautifully with the Massachusetts circular letter. Its tone angered the British ministry, which ordered all colonial governors to dissolve their assemblies if they attempted to endorse it. This was exactly what Adams hoped the ministry would do. By the time these orders were received in America, three other colonies had endorsed the Massachusetts letter, while Virginia's assembly had produced a letter of its own.

The ministry had given special instructions to the governor of Massachusetts. He was to dissolve the assembly if it failed to withdraw the letter. On June 30, 1768, the General Court voted ninety-two to seventeen against withdrawal. The next day the governor sent all the members packing.

The atmosphere in Boston was heated up by the activities of the newly arrived customs commissioners. They would have been resented no matter what they did. Neither smugglers nor legitimate merchants liked to pay taxes. Here were men who could line their own pockets by prosecutions in admiralty courts, which had no juries. And the customs officials proved to be far from saintly. The provisions of the Sugar Act and the Townshend duties furnished them with perfect tools for snaring the most innocent merchants in a trap of red tape. Shippers had to fill out complex forms concerning their cargoes and destinations. It was easy to file the wrong form or the right form in the wrong way. If you did that, you earned a "violation." And some violations were punishable by seizure of the ship and its entire cargo.

John Hancock's *Liberty*

Abuses by the customs officials were numerous. One incident became notorious.

A ship belonging to a wealthy merchant named John Hancock was tied up at a wharf in Boston. Word got out that there was a supply of Madeira wine aboard. Hancock thought he owed no duty on the wine, but several customs officials decided he did. The commissioners ordered the ship seized and towed out to anchor beside a British warship in the harbor. Menacing crowds assembled on the wharf and outside the commissioners' homes.

Although there was no real violence, the incident had important results. John Hancock's personal devotion to the cause of American liberty deepened considerably. He became something of a popular hero in Massachusetts. The commissioners of the customs were badly shaken. They removed themselves to Castle William on an island in Boston harbor. From there they wrote London requesting that troops be sent for their protection. The entire incident received considerable publicity. Its significance for Americans was underlined by the name of Hancock's ship—*Liberty*.

British Troops Arrive

Rumors about the possible arrival of British troops ran through Boston during that summer of 1768. Samuel Adams and other Sons of Liberty talked up the idea of active resistance. Two well-equipped British regiments did actually arrive in late September. As they marched up the wharves in impressive order, the townspeople watched with apprehension and resentment. But there was no violence. A Boston silversmith and engraver sat down to sketch the event. His name was Paul Revere.

In looking back, it is easy to see that the arrival of British soldiers in Boston was an important turning point in relations between the American colonies and their mother country. Many colonials thought so at the time. For more than a century, the English people in England and elsewhere had regarded a standing army in peacetime as a threat to their liberties.

Crispus Attucks and the Boston "Massacre"

British redcoats lived in Boston for eighteen months before a serious incident occurred. The cause of friction was competition for jobs between local laborers and the poorly paid redcoats who were looking for work in off-duty hours. On the afternoon of March 4, 1770, a fistfight broke out over this issue. That evening a mob gathered in front of the customshouse, which armed British soldiers were guarding. At first the crowd taunted the soldiers with cries of "Bloody Backs" and "Lobster Backs," referring to their red uniforms. Then the crowd began hurling firewood, stones, snowballs, and oyster shells at the soldiers. Among the colonials was a tall man named Crispus Attucks, well-known in the Boston dock area. Some said he was a runaway slave. Others said he came from the West Indies. A friend said of him that "his very looks were enough to terrify any person."

The frustrated soldiers stood their ground until, as an eyewitness later said, Attucks had the courage to grab a soldier's bayonet and throw the man down. The soldiers fired their muskets. Five men, including Attucks, were killed and three wounded. The bodies of the dead were carried to lie in state in Faneuil Hall, the site of Boston's town meetings.

To head off further clashes, Lieutenant Governor Thomas Hutchinson ordered the British troops to Castle William and to other islands in Boston harbor. There they remained for the next four years. Samuel Adams eagerly used this incident as propaganda against the British. The deaths of the men were tragic. But to most people, the affair was a brawl, not a "massacre" as Adams called it.

Lord North Calms Things Down

While anti-British feeling was being fanned in the colonies, events in England were moving in a more peaceful direction. Charles Townshend died, and George III finally found a chief minister he

The Boston Massacre was another in a long chain of events that led to the final outbreak of war.

could get along with. The ministry of Lord North began in January 1770 and lasted twelve years. King George and Lord North understood each other largely because they were rather alike. Both were hardworking English patriots. Both were moderately intelligent but without imagination.

Lord North realized that the Townshend Acts were costing more to enforce than they would ever bring in. English merchants were complaining loudly about the colonial boycott of their goods. So Lord North called upon Parliament to repeal all the taxes except the one on tea. He saw two obvious reasons for retaining this tax. Americans were drinking lots of tea and seemed willing to pay a good price for it. More important, continuation of this tax would maintain the principle of Parliament's power to tax the colonists. Parliament did what Lord North asked in April 1770. He also let the Quartering Act expire.

When word of this development reached the colonies, the non-importation movement collapsed. Business boomed, and the political atmosphere became more relaxed than at any time since word of the Sugar Act had arrived in 1764.

Friendly Voices in Parliament

There was a group of people in England who had watched events in the thirteen colonies with apprehension and sympathy. They wanted to limit royal power. How much they really cared about the colonial grievances, and how much they wanted to use these grievances to discredit the king and his ministers, it is almost impossible to say. But what is certain is that this political group, called *Whigs,* had one leader who spoke out with understanding and force in support of the colonists.

Edmund Burke was one of the greatest statesmen of his day. Time and again in parliamentary debate he warned that relations between nations should be as courteous as those between people. Human affairs, he said, cannot be twisted to fit into a "systematic imperial policy . . . it is not what a lawyer tells me I may do, but what humanity, reason and justice tell me I ought to do," that persuades people. He begged the British government to show a friendly and tolerant spirit toward the colonies.

Section 3 Review

COMPREHENSION Developing Vocabulary

1. Explain these terms: Whigs, Boston Massacre, Lobster Backs.

COMPREHENSION Mastering Facts

1. What did the circular letter written by Samuel Adams say?
2. What happened as a result of the *Liberty* incident?
3. What led to the first violence between the British soldiers and the people of Boston?
4. What was the only tax that Parliament retained in 1770?

From 1770 to 1773 there was a period of relative quiet. However, Samuel Adams and other agitators tried to take advantage of a few incidents. The most serious involved the *Gaspee*.

The *Gaspee* and Committees of Correspondence

For months the British customs schooner *Gaspee* had been boarding colonial vessels on Narragansett Bay, Rhode Island, to see if they were smuggling goods. Sailors from the *Gaspee* often went ashore, where they stole pigs and chickens and cut down fruit trees for firewood. So the ship and its crew were anything but popular.

On June 9, 1772, the *Gaspee* ran aground while pursuing a local vessel. That night eight boatloads of men rowed out from Providence to the stranded schooner. The men boarded the vessel, wounded its captain, removed its crew, and burned it to the waterline. Several of the attackers were prominent merchants, but their identities were not known to British authorities.

When word of this new outrage reached London, Lord North's ministry correctly concluded that no convictions could be obtained in local Rhode Island courts. So the king named a special commission to seek out the guilty and bring them back to England for trial.

Rhode Islanders successfully frustrated the commissioners. But the crown's plan to drag colonial Americans to England for trial aroused widespread alarm in the colonies. The assemblies of Massachusetts and Virginia set up *Committees of Correspondence* to communicate with other colonies about threats to American liberties. By 1774 most of the colonies had established such committees. They formed a network of communication in which all the colonies could be informed of what was happening and of each colony's reaction.

The Boston Tea Party

❝ "What are the Bostonians complaining about now?"
"They say the fish in their harbor all taste of tea." **❞**

(popular saying of the time)

Early in 1773 Lord North found a different colonial problem on his doorstep. The East India Company was a gigantic private business. The British government had given it responsibility for governing its colonies in India. The company was corrupt and mismanaged, and in 1773 was trembling on the brink of bankruptcy. But the company's warehouses bulged with 17 million pounds of India tea.

In order to save the company, Lord North pushed the Tea Act through Parliament. This act gave the company a monopoly on the sale of tea in

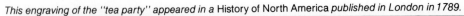

This engraving of the "tea party" appeared in a History of North America *published in London in 1789.*

the colonies. Previously, tea had been purchased at auction in London and then sold through a series of colonial middlemen. The new arrangement would provide cheaper tea for the colonists by eliminating the middlemen and having the tea sold by agents of the company directly to the American consumer. But there was a drawback: colonial merchants would be left out of the profitable trade.

Lord North thought that Americans liked tea more than they disliked monopolies. He was wrong. Mass meetings were held in most major colonial ports. Agents of the East India Company were persuaded to resign. In most cases, either the tea ships were turned back or the tea was unloaded and placed in warehouses unsold.

In Boston, however, Governor Thomas Hutchinson refused to let the tea ships leave without discharging their cargoes. On the evening of December 16, 1773, a well-organized group of colonials disguised themselves as Indians in blankets with greased faces. They boarded three ships, broke open the tea boxes so the tea would absorb water and sink, and threw 15,000 pounds of tea into the dark waters of Boston harbor. This incident is usually referred to as the Boston Tea Party.

Many colonial Americans thought the Boston men had gone too far. After all, they had destroyed private property, and Americans had been defending property rights for ten years. Also, they did not approve of violence. Their minds changed rapidly, however, when they learned of the British government's reaction to the Boston Tea Party.

The Intolerable and Other Acts

Pressed by a furious king and indignant editorials in the British press, Parliament in 1774 passed a series of measures that came to be known in the colonies as the Intolerable Acts. The Boston Port Act closed the city's harbor until the East India Company and the customs service were paid for their losses. Under the Administration of Justice Act, royal officials charged with a capital crime while putting down a riot or enforcing a law were to be tried in England rather than in the colonies.

The Massachusetts Government Act virtually tossed the Charter of 1691 out the window. The governor's council was now to be appointed by the crown rather than elected by the assembly. Many judges and sheriffs who had previously been elected by the people were now to be appointed by the governor. The same act aimed at the Massachusetts town meetings, which could now be held only when called by the governor.

Finally, a new Quartering Act authorized military commanders to house their soldiers in private homes as well as in taverns and vacant buildings. The troops stationed on islands in Boston harbor were reinforced and brought into the city itself. General Thomas Gage, commander in chief of all British troops in the colonies, was appointed the new governor of Massachusetts. In short, Boston was now under martial law. Parliament also passed the Quebec Act. This law had nothing to do with the situation in Boston. But its timing and provisions made it seem as intolerable to the colonists as the other acts.

Revolutionary War: Advantages and Disadvantages

	Strengths	Weaknesses
United States	1. familiarity of home ground 2. superior weapons and marksmen 3. experienced officers and soldiers trained in past colonial wars 4. leadership of George Washington 5. inspiring cause—independence	1. most soldiers untrained and undisciplined 2. shortage of food and ammunition 3. an infant navy 4. no central government capable of enforcing wartime policies
Great Britain	1. strong, well-trained army and navy 2. strong government with available money 3. support of Loyalists 4. Indian allies	1. distance of 3,000 miles separating Britain from battlefront 2. unfamiliar battlefronts 3. inability to use Loyalists effectively 4. weak military leaders

Delegates leaving a session of the First Continental Congress in 1774. Some feel revolution is now likely.

The Quebec Act set up a civilian government in Canada. Bowing to the traditions of the French inhabitants, the new government was to have no representative assembly, while court cases were to be tried by judges rather than juries. The Roman Catholic church was given a privileged position. These provisions seemed in London a generous and statesmanlike way of treating a conquered people. In the thirteen colonies, they appeared as an ominous new form of colonial government. Worse still, the Quebec Act enlarged that province to include all territory north of the Ohio River. It ignored the land claims of Virginia and other colonies in that area.

The First Continental Congress

The king and Lord North had hoped to isolate Massachusetts by singling out that unruly colony for special punishment and controls. Instead, their actions drove the colonies together.

People in other cities collected supplies to send to the suffering residents of Boston. The various Committees of Correspondence worked at keeping each other informed. And, most important, all the colonies except Georgia named delegates to the upcoming Continental Congress to be held in Philadelphia in September of 1774. The Congress was to decide what steps could be taken to defend the colonies against what was considered increasing tyranny.

The Suffolk Resolves. This First Continental Congress decided to endorse several resolutions known as the Suffolk Resolves. They had previously been adopted by a meeting of town delegates in Suffolk County, Massachusetts. The Suffolk Resolves denounced the Intolerable Acts and urged the colonies to form militias to resist enforcement of the acts. The Resolves also called on the colonies to suspend trade with the rest of the empire.

The Galloway Plan. Having adopted this show of support for Massachusetts, the delegates to the Continental Congress proceeded to consider a proposal by one of its most cautious and conservative members. He was Joseph Galloway of the colony of Pennsylvania. The Galloway Plan proposed a grand council of all the colonies which would share power with Parliament. Under this political arrangement, the council and Parliament would be able to veto the actions of the other concerning colonial matters.

Much of the opposition to the Galloway Plan came from New England delegates. They were the most sympathetic to Boston's difficulties and the firmest believers that Americans were being enslaved. They wanted no sharing of power with an unjust Parliament. The Galloway Plan was narrowly voted down.

Defeat of the Galloway Plan showed how far the thinking of many colonists had shifted since 1765. The colonists began by denying Parliament's right to tax them. Now a majority of the men at the Continental Congress denied that Parliament had the right to pass *any* laws for the colonies. The Congress did admit, however, that Parliament could regulate trade. In effect, its members asked that the clock be turned back to the good old days before 1763.

A New Boycott. The delegates set up the Continental Association to enforce a boycott of British imports and to block exports to Britain as well. The Continental Congress called upon every colony to set up local committees to publish the names of violators of this boycott as "enemies of American liberty." Within months, such committees were operating in most of the colonies.

Before adjourning on October 26, the Continental Congress agreed to meet again in May 1775 unless American grievances were fully met. The delegates knew that the countryside around Boston was becoming a powder keg that could explode at any moment.

The First Bloodshed

Encouraged by the actions of the Continental Congress, many towns in eastern New England stepped up military preparations. Special units of the colonial militia prepared to assemble at a minute's notice. These *minutemen* began stockpiling firearms and gunpowder. General Gage became increasingly aware of these activities and kept writing London for more troops. But military men in

England had a poor opinion of the colonials. Major General James Grant declared in the House of Commons that the Americans could not fight and that he could march from one end of the continent to the other with 5000 men.

On April 14, 1775, Gage received a letter (dated January 27) ordering him to attack the rebellious minutemen with the soldiers on hand. Gage immediately prepared to strike at Concord, twenty-one miles west of Boston, where informants told him there was a large collection of arms. General Gage realized he could not conceal his preparations. He had to bring in longboats from anchored warships in order to ferry his men across the Charles River.

On the night of April 18, 700 British soldiers set out for Concord. Paul Revere, William Dawes, and Samuel Prescott rode off to spread word of the troops' intended destination. The countryside rang with churchbells and gunshots. These were prearranged signals sent from one town to the next.

Shooting at Lexington and Concord. The first British troops reached Lexington, five miles short of Concord, at dawn. There they found some seventy minutemen drawn up in lines on the vil-

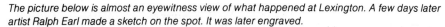

The picture below is almost an eyewitness view of what happened at Lexington. A few days later artist Ralph Earl made a sketch on the spot. It was later engraved.

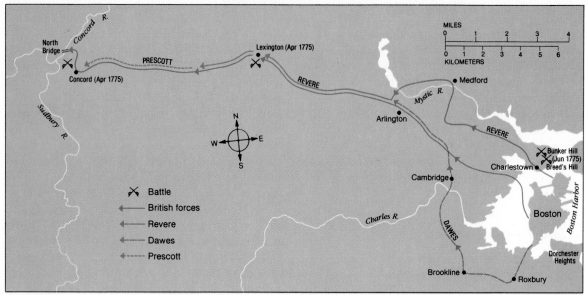

Map Skills   *The first battles of the Revolutionary War were fought near Boston. How far was the British march to Lexington? Who rode through the town of Brookline? Medford?*

lage green. The commanding British officer ordered them to disperse. The Americans began to do so but without laying down their arms. Someone fired—no one knows who—and the redcoats sent a volley of shots into the dispersing militia. Eight were killed.

The British troops then pressed on to Concord, which they reached at about half-past ten in the morning. They drove off a small group of minutemen and searched for the store of arms. All that remained were a few gun carriages, digging tools, and some flour. After burning the flour, the British lined up for the return march to Boston. They were tired, and they knew they had another twenty-one miles to go with their heavy packs and muskets. But they did not know that they were about to be involved in a kind of battle the likes of which they had never experienced.

The British Retreat.   The entire march was a disaster. The road to Boston seemed lined with minutemen who fired from behind trees and stone walls. Some 3000 to 4000 New England militia had assembled in about twelve hours. Redcoats fell by the dozen. Only the arrival of reinforcements from Boston saved them from complete dis-

aster. As it was, they suffered three times as many casualties as the country farmers whom they had held in contempt.

Bloodied, exhausted, humiliated, and bewildered, the redcoats found themselves back in Boston that night. Probably they were too tired to notice that the surrounding hills were dotted with campfires over which salt pork and johnnycake were cooking. The campfires belonged to English colonists who had somehow become their enemies.

Section 4 Review

COMPREHENSION   Developing Vocabulary

1. Explain these terms: Committees of Correspondence, minutemen, Boston Tea Party, Suffolk Resolves, Galloway Plan.

COMPREHENSION   Mastering Facts

1. Why did Lord North push the Tea Act through Parliament?
2. What colony were the Intolerable Acts designed to punish?
3. What was the purpose of the First Continental Congress?

CHAPTER 6 Review

Chapter Summary

New financial problems in England brought stricter regulations and more taxes after the colonial wars. In response to the Stamp Act, colonists began to protest their unfair treatment at the hands of Parliament and King George III. The Stamp Act Congress (1765) represented the colonists' first attempt at an organized, united action. The Townshend Acts and the arrival of additional British troops increased tension in the colonies; then the Boston "Massacre" (1770) and the Boston Tea Party (1773) moved both sides closer to the breaking point. In 1774 the first Continental Congress met. Within a year, fighting between British and Americans erupted at Lexington and Concord.

Questions for Critical Thinking

COMPREHENSION   Summarizing Main Ideas

1. Tell what effect the Treaty of Paris had on (a) Florida; (b) Canada; (c) the land drained by the Mississippi river system.
2. List three factors that led to Pontiac's uprising. Do you think the British could have done anything to prevent fighting from breaking out? Explain your answer.
3. List the economic differences that existed between Great Britain and the colonies. List the political differences.
4. What were the major provisions of the Quebec Act? Why did the British government pass it? Why were the American colonists opposed to it? Do you think the colonists were justified in their opposition? Why or why not?
5. What was the British view of the Empire? What was the colonists' view?

COMPREHENSION   Interpreting Events

1. Evaluate the Proclamation of 1763 in terms of (a) its objectives; (b) its results. Do you think the British government was wise to issue the proclamation? Why or why not?
2. Why did Grenville order the stationing of 10,000 British troops in the American colonies? How did the colonists react?
3. What political means did the colonists use to show their opposition to the Stamp Act? What economic means did the colonists use? Which proved to be more effective?
4. Explain how each of the following helped lead up to the American Revolution: (a) the publication of *Letters from a Farmer*; (b) the arrival of British soldiers in Boston; (c) the organization of Committees of Correspondence; (d) the passage of the Intolerable Acts.
5. Do you think the American Revolution might have been avoided if Lord North had not retained the tax on tea? Explain your reasoning.

APPLICATION   Using Skills To Understand Time

An important element in studying and understanding history is a sense of time. Suppose that you had entered elementary school at the end of the French and Indian Wars and were promoted one grade each year. In what grade would you have been when each of the following events took place?

1. The Ottawa chief Pontiac leads his warriors in an attack against Fort Detroit.
2. Patrick Henry urges the House of Burgesses to pass seven resolutions stating that only Virginians can tax Virginians.
3. A British bullet kills Crispus Attucks.
4. Colonials dump 15,000 pounds of tea into the waters of Boston harbor.
5. American minutemen fire at British troops on the road from Concord to Boston.

EVALUATION   Comparing Past to Present

1. What effect did the media have on the events preceding the outbreak of the American Revolution? How does this compare with their effects on the most recent presidential election?
2. Is the principle of "no taxation without representation" followed in the United States today? Explain.
3. How did Lord North attempt to help the British East India Company? How does the government help large corporations today?

Taxes

"In this world," wrote Benjamin Franklin, "nothing is certain but death and taxes." If you have a job, you probably know what Franklin meant. When you get your paycheck, some of your earnings have already been deducted for taxes. One figure lists the amount of income tax withheld; a second figure shows the deduction made for Social Security taxes. In some cases, another amount may be taken out for city or state taxes. After all taxes have been subtracted, the remainder—your take-home pay—is usually much less than your total earnings.

Public debate over taxes is part of our nation's English heritage. Throughout the 1600s, England's Parliament struggled with the king over control of the public purse strings. In this struggle, during the time after the Glorious Revolution in 1688, Parliament finally won the power to tax. After this event, the Crown could no longer take a person's property without consent. According to John Locke, when Parliament won the authority to tax, it also established a basic right of free people everywhere.

Battling for Power. During the 1700s the thirteen colonial legislatures were also trying to assert control over taxation. Colonists had always been concerned with the question of who had the authority to levy taxes. In Virginia the House of Burgesses claimed the power to tax for itself alone; one of its earliest laws prohibited the royal governor from imposing taxes without the representatives' consent. The same spirit pervaded the other colonies. Partly because of English neglect, colonial assemblies asserted the right to levy their own taxes rather than having Parliament do so.

These centers of power—one in England and one in America—functioned relatively well until the French and Indian War. Then, after 1763, changes in British tax policies helped bring about the American Revolution. Faced with huge war debts and the high cost of protecting their newly acquired territory, Parliament tried taxing the colonies. After 1763 many colonists felt that Parliament was taking away powers that belonged to colonial legislatures by tradition and right.

Thus, the Revolutionary War was not fought over paying taxes. Instead, the Revolution concerned the debate over the authority to impose taxes. In failing to understand the colonial opposition to taxes, the British Parliament did not appreciate the colonial struggle for responsible independence.

Protests Are Nothing New. Since Revolutionary times, tax protests have continued to characterize our nation. In 1846, for example, noted author Henry David Thoreau spent a night in jail because he failed to pay his taxes. Thoreau objected to paying the taxes because he opposed the way tax dollars were spent. He objected to the nation's war against Mexico and the practice of slavery. If the United States were to win the war, slavery would be extended into the Southwest. Paying taxes to support those activities violated Thoreau's conscience. He chose to go to jail rather than go against his personal principles.

Thoreau's protest struck at the heart of the relationship between government and the individual. Collecting taxes is a basic right of the legislature. Tax money enables a government to operate. Without tax payments, a government cannot carry out its programs. Paying taxes is a citizen's responsibility to a government dedicated to promoting the general welfare. On the other hand, refusing to pay taxes calls into question the very authority of those who govern.

Levying an Income Tax. Although local taxes have existed since colonial times, the federal tax on personal income began only in the early 1900s. An earlier income tax levied during the Civil War was challenged in the courts. The

Supreme Court finally upheld the constitutionality of the Civil War measure in the case *Springer* v. *United States* (1881), though the personal income tax by then had been dropped.

In 1893 severe circumstances. in the form of a depression once again strained the federal treasury. To remedy this money shortage, Congress passed the Wilson-Gorman Act in 1894. It levied a 2 percent tax on all kinds of income—rents, interest, dividends, salaries, and profits. Soon a case challenging the constitutionality of this federal income tax reached the Supreme Court.

This time, in the case *Pollack* v. *The Farmers' Loan and Trust Company* (1895), the Court decided that sections of the law dealing with an income tax were unconstitutional. The Court denied Congress the right to levy personal income taxes. Not until 1913 did ratification of the Sixteenth Amendment (see page 190) finally enlarge Congress's power to tax. That year the first modern federal income tax began. It is still in effect, though it has changed a great deal over the years.

Future Trends. Americans today pay much more in taxes than their ancestors ever would have imagined—or allowed. Anyone who has paid any type of taxes during the past several decades has felt the sharp increases. In 1902, for example, the revenues for all federal, state, and

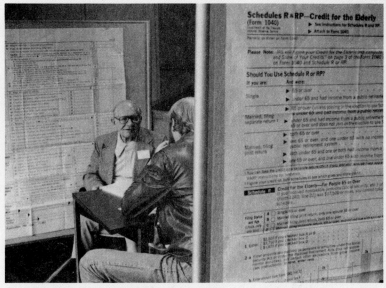

A senior citizen listens to advice concerning payment of his income tax.

local taxes collected in the United States totaled about $1.4 billion—representing an average tax payment that year of $17.34 per person. For 1980, all tax revenues in the nation totaled about $574.2 billion—an average payment of $2,535.24 per person. Despite some scattered tax decreases during the 1980s, the overall trend points to increased taxation of property, income, and consumer goods.

Today, the debate over taxes is no longer one of right, but of responsibility. Many people are concerned with the effects of high taxes on the nation's economic health. One of the country's most pressing concerns is a growing debt that has already surpassed $1 trillion. For a nation accustomed to abundance, the notion of living within limits—specifically within the

limits of tax revenues—has been difficult to accept.

Understanding Government

1. What basic conflict over taxes existed between the colonists and the British Parliament? What objections did Thoreau have to paying his taxes?

2. What issues regarding taxation concern many people today? What is being done to remedy these problems?

3. How do the concerns people today have about taxes differ from the concerns of colonists? How are they similar?

4. Which taxes may increase or decrease during your lifetime? How might different groups of people react to these changes? Why?

CHAPTER 7

War for Independence

1775–1783

Linking Past to Present

The American Revolution was one of the major events in the history of the modern world. It was the first major rebellion by overseas European emigrants against their parent country. It set on example that was widely followed, especially in France and in Latin America. The American Revolution was the first in modern times to be based on ideas about equal rights for all. American revolutionaries claimed that their principles applied to people everywhere, not just to themselves. They saw themselves as leaders in a universal struggle for liberty and hoped that people in other countries would follow their lead.

Looking back years afterwards, John Adams asked, "What do we mean by the Revolution? The War? That was no part of the Revolution. It was only an effect and consequence of it. The Revolution was in the minds of the people, and this was effected, from 1760 to 1775, in the course of fifteen years before a drop of blood was drawn at Lexington."

It is possible that John Adams was right: that the "real" Revolution took place in the hearts and minds of men and women.

1 OVERCOMING THE LAST DOUBTS

VOCABULARY   *Olive Branch Petition*   *Common Sense*

The Second Continental Congress assembled in Philadelphia as scheduled in May 1775. Among the delegates were three men who were later to have distinguished careers in the service of their country. George Washington of Virginia was already well-known as a military leader from the days of the French and Indian War. Benjamin Franklin, who had fled London to escape arrest, was someone every delegate wanted to meet. John Adams, a lawyer and author from Massachusetts, impressed many with his patriotic vigor and sound reasoning. Somewhat later, the delegates were joined by a young, red-headed lawyer from Virginia, Thomas Jefferson, who was also known as an able writer on colonial rights.

Military Maneuvering

It was clear from the beginning that the Continental Congress would support Massachusetts. Yet there was no formal creation of an American army. The Congress simply declared that the farmers and shopkeepers besieging Boston were the "Army of the United Colonies." John Adams urged that Washington be named commander in chief; and the latter accepted the post on June 16. He did not know that he was just about to miss the bloodiest battle of the entire war.

The "Bunker Hill Victory." Cooped up in Boston, General Gage had received reinforcements from England. His new "top brass" included three generals: Sir John "Gentleman Johnny" Burgoyne, Sir Henry Clinton, and Sir William Howe. They decided to dislodge the colonial militia from the hills around Boston. Learning of the British plan through spies in the city, the colonials beat their opponents to the punch. They dug themselves in on Breed's Hill on the Charlestown peninsula north of the city. (Refer to the map on page 124.)

On the morning of June 17, some 2200 redcoats crossed the Charles River and assembled in their customary broad lines at the bottom of the hill. They shouldered their heavy packs and began marching up the slope. They stopped only to fire volleys, which fell harmlessly on Americans grouped at the top behind mounds of earth and logs. The American militiamen held their fire until the last moment. When they did fire, the exposed rows of advancing redcoats went down one after the other. The survivors, including the walking wounded, retreated to the bottom of the hill. There they regrouped. A second and a third assault produced similar murderous results. A fourth assault finally succeeded when the Americans ran low on musket balls and powder. They fell back at bayonet point from the hill and then from the entire peninsula. The battle has gone down in history as the Battle of Bunker Hill, although it was actually fought on Breed's Hill. But the two hills are very close, and the first newspaper accounts made the mistake.

The Americans lost the battle with some 400 casualties. The British won the battle but sustained more than 1000 casualties. As General Clinton wrote, it was "a dear bought victory, another such would have ruined us." And as General Gage wrote in a private letter, "The trials we have had

At Bunker Hill the British showed a habit that lasted throughout the war. They massed together, were visible for miles, and failed to take advantage of ground cover.

show that the rebels are not the despicable rabble too many supposed them to be."

The British Retreat. Some nine months after the Battle of Breed's Hill, the siege of Boston finally came to an end. The Americans, led by a former bookseller named Henry Knox, brought fifty-nine cannon from Fort Ticonderoga, New York, to Boston. The men loaded the heavy guns on wooden sledges pulled by teams of oxen, and then trudged for 300 miles over snow-covered mountains to their destination. On the night of March 4–5, 1776, the Americans set the guns in place on Dorchester Heights, just south of Boston, where they commanded the city and much of the harbor. On March 17 General Howe and his troops evacuated Boston and sailed for Nova Scotia.

American arms also proved successful elsewhere during that first year of fighting. A British fleet was chased from the harbor of Charleston, South Carolina, on June 28, 1776. There, patriots and black slaves had built a fort out of soft palm logs which absorbed the cannonballs from the British ships. In Virginia the royal governor, the Earl of Dunmore, took refuge on a British warship anchored off the harbor of Norfolk. On November 5, 1775, he issued a statement freeing all slaves and in-

dentured servants if they would join the British in suppressing the rebellion. Several hundred men answered the call, but there was no general slave uprising. On December 9 the Virginia militia defeated Dunmore's troops. In revenge the British fleet bombarded Norfolk on January 1, 1776, and reduced the town's wooden houses to ashes.

The Americans Retreat. At the same time the Second Continental Congress appointed Washington commander in chief, it authorized Benedict Arnold to lead some 1100 Americans through Maine into Canada. The goal was to prevent the British from isolating New England by moving redcoats south through the Hudson River valley. Arnold led his men on a grueling march of 350 miles through untracked wilderness. Half the troops succumbed to the bitter cold and lack of food.

After six weeks, the Americans reached Quebec and laid seige to the city. Despite their lack of artillery, they remained there throughout the winter. But with the spring thaw came fresh British troops, and the Americans abandoned their hopes for a victory on the northern front. Four years later, Benedict Arnold turned traitor to the American cause. His plot to surrender West Point to the

British was discovered when a British secret agent, Major John André, was caught. Arnold escaped to the British forces, but Major André was hanged.

Political Maneuvering

In the meantime, the Second Continental Congress was acting more and more like an independent government. It issued paper money to pay the army and named a committee for dealing with foreign powers. It established a postal department with Benjamin Franklin as postmaster general. It organized three Indian commissions to make alliances with the frontier tribes or at least to persuade them not to side with the British. In the fall of 1775 it authorized the creation of a navy.

The Olive Branch Petition. All these actions were undertaken while the Congress was still expressing its loyalty to the king. Most Americans felt such loyalty deeply. They did not blame the war on King George. They blamed it on his ministers and referred to British forces as the "ministerial army" rather than the "king's troops." The idea of independence was so frightening that one of the delegates to the Congress said he felt "like a child being thrust violently out of his father's house." On July 8, 1775, the Congress even sent England the so-called Olive Branch Petition, urging a return to "the former harmony" that had existed between England and the colonies.

The Petition Is Rejected. King George's response to the colonial plea for peace was clear and to the point. He refused to read it. Then he issued a proclamation that a general rebellion existed throughout all of North America, not just Massachusetts. "Utmost endeavors," the king said, were needed to "suppress such rebellion, and to bring the traitors to justice." After two months of debate, Parliament adopted a resolution to that effect by a vote of two to one. Parliament then ordered the royal navy to blockade the American coastline.

Paine's *Common Sense*

Even before news of these events reached the colonies, public opinion about the king and independence had begun to change. One of the sparkplugs of the change was a poor London writer who had arrived in America two years earlier.

In an anonymous forty-seven page pamphlet entitled *Common Sense* (January 1776), Thomas Paine attacked King George in particular and monarchy in general. Responsibility for British tyranny, Paine argued, lay with "the royal brute of Britain." One honest man, in Paine's opinion, was worth "all the crowned ruffians that ever lived."

It was time, Paine declared, for Americans to proclaim an independent republic and have nothing further to do with hereditary kings. Independence was the "destiny" of Americans. And there were practical advantages as well. For example, an independent America could trade freely with other nations, thus obtaining money for guns and ammunition. If American soldiers were captured by the British, independence meant they would be treated as prisoners of war instead of rebels. They would be imprisoned instead of being shot.

Also, it would be easier for an independent America to obtain foreign aid. Spain and France, both monarchies, might not help rebels against a king. But they were almost certain to help an independent country at war with their common enemy, England. Without foreign aid, it was doubtful that the colonies could win.

There was yet another argument for independence, according to Paine. That was the chance to create a better society. Paine foresaw a nation where everyone would be free from tyranny, and where there would be equal social and economic opportunity for all.

Common Sense was widely read (some 500,000 copies were eventually sold) and widely applauded. It was, in fact, one of the most influential political pamphlets ever written. Within six months, the Second Continental Congress—encouraged by public opinion—did just what Paine suggested.

Section 1 Review

COMPREHENSION Developing Vocabulary

1. Explain these terms: Olive Branch Petition, *Common Sense*.

COMPREHENSION Mastering Facts

1. Why did the British suffer so many casualties at the so-called Battle of Bunker Hill?
2. What did Henry Knox do to help lift the siege of Boston?
3. Who led American troops into Canada to besiege Quebec?
4. What did George III do when he received the Olive Branch Petition?

VOCABULARY   *Loyalists*

In May 1776 the Second Continental Congress advised all the colonies to form new state governments if they had not already done so. On June 7, Virginia delegate Richard Henry Lee made a motion that "these United Colonies are, and of a right ought to be, free and independent States."

While debate on the motion went on, the Continental Congress appointed a committee of five men to prepare a formal declaration to explain to the world the reason for the colonies' actions. The five men were John Adams (Massachusetts), Benjamin Franklin (Pennsylvania), Thomas Jefferson (Virginia), Robert Livingston (New York), and Roger Sherman (Connecticut). They agreed on the main points to be covered and then chose Jefferson to give the declaration a "proper dress," or, in effect, to express the points suitably in writing.

In his first draft, or version, Jefferson included an eloquent attack on the cruelty and injustice of the slave trade. The two colonies most heavily dependent on the slave trade, South Carolina and Georgia, objected. In order to gain the votes of those two states for the Declaration, the offending passage was dropped.

Abigail Adams, the wife of Massachusetts delegate John Adams, wanted something about the status of women written into law. She wrote her husband:

66 Remember the ladies and be more generous to them than your ancestors. Do not put unlimited power in the hands of husbands. Remember all men would be tyrants if they could. If particular care and attention is not paid to the ladies, we are determined to foment rebellion, and will not be bound by any laws in which we have no voice or representation. 99

Nevertheless, the Declaration of Independence states that only "all men are created equal."

The Declaration of Independence

The Declaration was a masterpiece of political writing. The famous words of the preamble remain far better known than the long list of accusations aimed at King George. For people at the time, however, that list summarized the events of the preceding dozen years. The accusations were not entirely fair. The king did not bear personal, sole responsibility for many of the actions the Declaration condemned. But Americans were finally breaking their one remaining tie with Britain. That tie was the king, so Jefferson aimed his propaganda at that final link.

Many years later, John Adams belittled Jefferson's achievement in the preamble by claiming that it merely repeated what everyone had been saying all along. Jefferson replied that this was exactly what he had intended to do. The Declaration, he said, was "to be an expression of the American mind." He had simply expressed commonplace ideas about natural rights and the right of the people to rebel against tyranny.

Life, Liberty, Happiness. In fact, these ideas about natural rights, which were first stated by John Locke, had become basic beliefs in the American mind. They were the way most Americans automatically thought about government. It was "self-evident" that the powers of government came from the people. The people could take the pow-

This British engraving illustrates how the Declaration of Independence was read in each colony.

ers back if a government abused its powers and could set up a government that would not abuse natural rights. And what were these natural rights? They were life, liberty, and property.

When Jefferson came to list those rights, he made an interesting change in one of the three. Instead of "life, liberty, and property," he substituted "life, liberty, and the pursuit of happiness." This wording has prompted some people to jest that the Declaration gives everyone the right to pursue happiness but not the right to catch up with it. But Jefferson did not use the word "pursuit" to mean "chase." He used it in the older meaning of the word, which was "to cultivate or improve by attention and care."

All Men Are Created Equal.
The Declaration of Independence states flatly that "all men are created equal." At the time, it merely expressed the common assumption that free citizens were politically equal. Each had one vote of equal weight. It was not intended to mean that all men had the same ability or ought to be of equal wealth. It obviously did not apply to women, who could not vote, nor to blacks who were slaves.

Yet the Declaration's principle of equality later took on a life of its own. The phrase "all men" could very easily be regarded as meaning all human beings, not just the white men of America in 1776. Why shouldn't blacks and women be included? In later years, many people began to ponder this question.

On July 4, 1776, the Declaration was adopted by the Second Continental Congress, although the last signature did not go on until November. On July 8, 1776, the Declaration of Independence was read for the first time to a crowd in front of the red brick Pennsylvania State House, now Independence Hall. Everyone knew that if any of the delegates fell into British hands, they would be hanged as traitors. A thrill of pride and anxiety ran through the crowd when they heard the delegates' vow that ends the Declaration: "We mutually pledge to each other our Lives and Fortunes and our Sacred Honor."

The Loyalist Opposition

Many Americans opposed independence and the war that was being waged for it. These Loyalists varied in number from place to place and also from time to time. The best modern estimates suggest that they constituted about one-fifth of the white population.

Reasons for Loyalty.
But numbers do not explain why some people chose to remain loyal to the British crown. For many the decision was an agonizing crisis of conscience. For others it was a matter of self-interest. Those who had held posts as royal officials, for example, found it easy to retain their old loyalty. Some Loyalists were people of wealth who did not like popular rule or "mob rule" as they called it. Others were staunch believers in law and order. Certain ethnic groups in certain places tended to become Loyalists because other ethnic groups in the same area were becoming patriots. Quakers and German pacifists could not become active patriots because their beliefs did not allow them to support any war.

Probably the most important factor in pushing Americans toward one side or the other was the presence of British troops in the immediate neighborhood. This could make Loyalists out of wavering individuals who wished to pick the winning side. Or it could make patriots out of outraged farmers who watched helplessly as redcoats made off with their corn and livestock. As the major fighting moved from one part of the country to another, more and more Americans had to make a choice. Neutrality became difficult when there was fighting in one's own backyard. This pattern placed the Loyalists at a tremendous disadvantage. British troops came and went, but their American opponents remained.

Committees of patriots, backed with bayonets, drove many Loyalists from their homes and communities. The new state governments set up legal machinery for the confiscation of Loyalist property. There were brutalities on both sides, but few Loyalists lost their lives except in open battle against patriot forces. Throughout the war, the British constantly overestimated the number of Loyalists. At the same time, they failed to take full advantage of Loyalist support. Professional British army officers often treated the Loyalists with the same contempt they had for all colonial amateur fighters.

Peaceful Departure.
One basic fact about the opposition to the American Revolution has often been overlooked by historians. Many of the Loyalists could simply leave without fully going into ex-

Tension between Americans. The Loyalist (left) confronts the Patriot (with the Liberty Tree) in this French engraving.

British crown. Few exiled refugees from a major revolution have had the same opportunity. Many Loyalists even received money from the British government for their losses during the war.

The departure of so many Loyalists had an important effect on the future of the newly independent country. It meant that the people most vehemently against the Revolution were gone when victory and independence were finally won. Americans did not have to try or execute people who had opposed the war. There were no old scores to settle. There were no palaces to be invaded or hated symbols of the past government to be destroyed. The patriots were able to start immediately on the problems of building a nation.

Section 2 Review

COMPREHENSION   Developing Vocabulary

1.   Explain these terms: Loyalists, pursuit.

COMPREHENSION   Mastering Facts

1.   Why was the reference to the slave trade dropped from the Declaration of Independence?
2.   What two groups were not originally covered by the phrase "all men are created equal"?
3.   What were the natural rights listed in the Declaration of Independence?
4.   What was the most important factor in pushing Americans toward one side or the other in the Revolutionary War?

ile. Opponents of the French Revolution, which broke out in 1789, had to flee to foreign countries. But American Loyalists could return "home" to England (if they had enough money for the trip) or move to another part of the British Empire, especially to Canada. Many did so. When General Gage evacuated Boston, some 1000 Loyalists left with him for Nova Scotia. The same pattern was repeated whenever the British evacuated an American port. For many Loyalists, such journeys were heart-wrenching departures. Nevertheless, they were moving to lands where people had the same language and laws and held similar loyalties to the

3   THE STRUGGLE FOR INDEPENDENCE BEGINS

VOCABULARY   *mercenaries   Hessians   privateers   Continentals*

Few people thought the rebellion would last very long. A divided colonial population of about 2.5 million people, nearly one-fifth of whom were slaves, faced a nation of 10 million backed up by a worldwide empire.

The British Position

Loyalist warnings that Britain possessed enormous military advantages were well-founded. The British navy was easily the largest in the world, even though many of its ships were in poor repair. British factories were equipped to turn out large quantities of cannon, muskets, and other weapons. The British army had trained engineers

who knew how to build fortifications and besiege cities. Its non-commissioned officers, especially its sergeants, were experienced professionals.

On the other hand, the British army was short of manpower. Although the British Empire was worldwide, its army consisted of fewer than 35,000 men, of whom 7500 were busy occupying Ireland. Army pay was so low and living conditions were so bad that few Englishmen joined up voluntarily. Most were "pressed" into service. Press gangs went around kidnapping able-bodied men. Sometimes the press gangs beat the men or got them drunk. When the men woke up, they found they were in the armed forces. Desertions were common.

Accordingly, England was forced to hire *merce-*

134

naries (people who fight for money) from other nations. After being turned down by Empress Catherine the Great of Russia, England succeeded in obtaining some 30,000 soldiers from six small German states. Since half came from the state of Hesse-Cassel, the Americans called all the mercenaries "Hessians." As it turned out, almost 5000 Hessians deserted to try their luck in the New World.

The British faced other important disadvantages. Chief among them was 3000 miles of the Atlantic Ocean. In addition, they had to fight on unfamiliar, badly mapped stretches of territory. Also, the British were used to the better roads and more open countryside of the Old World.

On a one-to-one basis, British troops were sometimes outgunned. Most of them carried smoothbore muskets, which were less accurate than the "Pennsylvania" or "Kentucky" rifles many Americans carried. The rifles' bores were grooved, which made them more accurate. On the other hand, rifles were slow to reload and could not be equipped with bayonets.

The American Position

The Americans were fighting on their own ground. But they too faced serious difficulties despite having this advantage.

Military Handicaps. A major handicap was the lack of a sizable navy. Congress could afford to pay for only a few vessels. The British navy controlled the sea lanes and the American coastline (except at one brief and crucial moment). Hundreds of Americans known as *privateers* were given the right by the Continental Congress to prey on British merchant ships, and some enriched themselves considerably. But privateers had little effect on the course of the war.

The Americans also had great difficulty in keeping an army together. In any given place, Americans would turn out in large numbers to fight. But staying in the army and marching off through other states did not appeal to them. It meant low pay, rigid discipline, cold, hunger, and disease. There were no pensions for soldiers disabled by wounds, no insurance payments for their widows if they died. As a result, many American farmers continued the tradition of enlisting either for a single campaign or for three months. Then they went back to their farms.

Washington's Achievement. George Washington's great achievement was the fact that he managed to keep something of an army together for eight years. His command always consisted of two kinds of soldiers: militia from the individual states, and the men of the Continental Army. It was called the Continental Army because the men were paid directly by the Continental Congress rather than by the states from which they came.

The Continental soldiers, also called *Continentals,* served longer periods of enlistment and were therefore better trained and more reliable in battle than the militia. The Continentals began to take pride in themselves both as professional soldiers and as the truest of patriots. For the most part they were intensely loyal to their tall, somewhat aloof but always devoted commander. It was the kind of loyalty possible only in a small army where the men were actually able to see the commander-in-chief. (It was partly for this reason that many officers rode on horseback.) For his part, Washington was a firm yet fair administrator of military discipline, who spent much of his time pleading with the Continental Congress for supplies for his men.

The Role of Women. Many American women took their husbands' places on farms and at various trades when the men went off to fight. Women helped to make munitions and supplied soldiers

Molly Pitcher, the heroine of the Battle of Monmouth. This intensely patriotic picture is from a lithograph done by Currier & Ives.

with food and clothing. Other women followed their husbands. As one historian noted, they

66 cooked for the troops and nursed the wounded and sick. They mended and sewed and laundered. On the marches they carried their share of supplies and ammunition on their backs. . . . Women who could write performed clerical and copying tasks. . . . At night they crept over the battlefield. . . stripping (the dead bodies) of their clothes to help keep the ragged Revolutionary soldiers warm. 99

On occasion, women took part in the actual fighting. Two who did so were Margaret Corbin and Mary Ludwig Hays. In a battle at Fort Washington, New York (1776), Corbin replaced a gunner who had been shot and was herself wounded. Congress gave her a pension and a complete set of clothes every year for life. Mary Ludwig Hays is called "Molly Pitcher" by many historians because she carried pitchers of water to wash out the barrels of cannon before they were reloaded. When her husband was wounded at the Battle of Monmouth, she took his place on the battlefield. For her heroism, Washington made her a sergeant.

Financing the War Effort. A major problem that confronted Washington throughout the war was how to obtain supplies. With a British coastal blockade and almost no local munitions factories, arms and ammunition had to be smuggled from Europe. Most American families—except the very rich—made their own clothing at home. So it was difficult, if not impossible, for them to increase their output to equip soldiers. As Washington once wrote, "There are now in this Army . . . 4000 men wanting blankets, near 2000 of which have never had one, altho' some of them have been 12 months in service." There was also the problem of how to pay the troops.

The Continental Congress borrowed money by selling bonds to foreign governments, especially France, and also to domestic investors. It printed paper money, called continentals. But the value of this currency dropped so much that people used the phrase "Not worth a continental" to refer to anything that was worthless.

Finally, in 1781 the Congress appointed a rich Philadelphia merchant named Robert Morris as superintendent of finance. Morris was assisted by Haym Salomon, a Jewish political refugee from Poland who had been a Son of Liberty and had escaped from a British prison on the eve of being hanged as an American spy.

Morris and Salomon begged and borrowed on their personal credit. They obtained funds from Philadelphia's Quakers and Jews. They straightened out the government's finances enough to set up an adequate supply system for the American army. On September 8, 1781, a Continental major wrote in his diary, "This day will be famous in the Annals of History for being the first on which the Troops of the United States received one Month's Pay in Specie (coin)."

Section 3 Review

COMPREHENSION   Developing Vocabulary

1. Explain these terms: Mercenaries, privateers, Continentals, Hessians, press gang.

COMPREHENSION   Mastering Facts

1. Where did most of the mercenaries in the British army come from?
2. What were the disadvantages of an American rifle as compared to a British musket?
3. What was the biggest problem that confronted George Washington during the war?
4. What roles did American women play in the Revolution?

4 FARMERS AND SHOPKEEPERS DEFEAT AN EMPIRE
VOCABULARY   *amnesty*

After the British pulled out of Boston in March 1776, the theater of war shifted to the middle states. For fifteen months, American forces suffered one defeat after another. They lost control of their two largest cities, New York and Philadelphia. Then the British, having won all these victories, proceeded to lose an entire army. That loss was the turning point of the war.

Fighting in the Middle States

After pulling out of Boston, the British decided to take New York. Believing that only New England was rebelling, they figured that by taking New York they could isolate New England from the other "loyal colonies." Two brothers, General William Howe and Admiral Richard Howe, ar-

The War in the Middle States   1776–1778

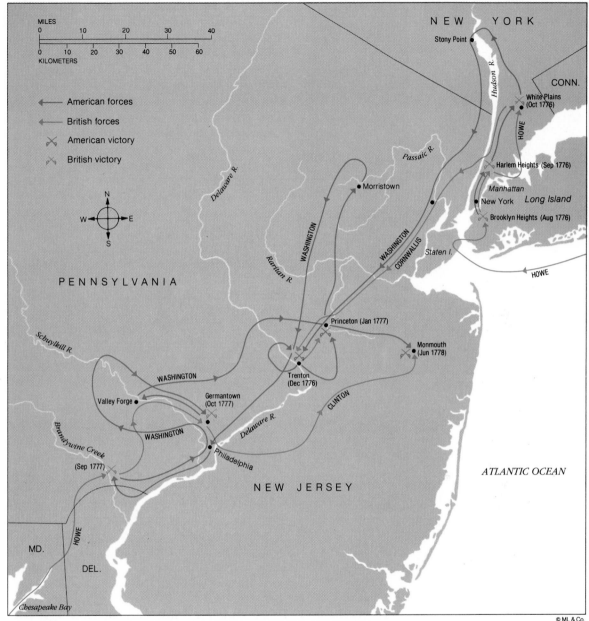

Map Skills   *Many early battles were fought around New York and Philadelphia. Who led the British forces at Brooklyn Heights? When and where was Washington's first victory?*

rived in New York harbor in the summer of 1776. The Howes carried instructions to discuss peace terms plus an offer of amnesty, or pardon, to all rebels who would lay down their arms and take an oath of allegiance to the king. But they also had 32,000 soldiers and 10,000 seamen to back their words.

Washington, forseeing the British plans, rallied some 23,000 men for New York's defense. Not only was he outnumbered, but most of his troops were inexperienced farmers who lacked equipment. The Americans retreated with heavy losses, first from the Brooklyn end of Long Island, then from Manhattan northward to White Plains, and from there across the Hudson River into New Jersey.

By the late fall of 1776, Washington's army had been pushed across New Jersey into Pennsylvania.

137

Two midwinter victories cheered the Americans: the Battles of Trenton and (above) Princeton.

Only some 8000 men remained under his command. The rest had gone back to their farms or had been killed or captured. Most Americans seemed to be in a state of apathy, waiting to see what would happen. As Paine wrote in his new pamphlet *The Crisis,* "These are the times that try men's souls. The summer soldier and the sunshine patriot will, in this crisis, shrink from the service of their country, but he that stands it now deserves the love and thanks of man and woman."

Washington was desperate for some sort of victory to revive the morale of his troops and to prove that the American cause was alive. He resolved to risk everything on one bold stroke.

On the freezing Christmas night of 1776, Washington led 2400 men in boats back across the ice-choked Delaware River into New Jersey. By eight o'clock the next morning, the men had marched the nine miles to Trenton. There they surprised a group of Hessians, most of whom were sleeping off the effects of a large quantity of rum they had drunk the night before. The Americans killed 46 of the enemy and took some 900 captives at the cost of only 5 casualties.

The victory was so stunning that many of the Americans promptly reenlisted. They were further cheered by another smashing victory at Princeton on January 5, 1777. Washington then marched his little army into winter camp near Morristown in northern New Jersey.

When spring came, General Howe decided to take another major American city. His troops left New York by sea, sailed up the Delaware River, and landed near Philadelphia. Washington's troops tried to block their way at Brandywine Creek. But the Americans lost the pitched battle. The British occupied Philadelphia in September, and the pleasure-loving General Howe settled back to enjoy the hospitality of the city's grateful Loyalists. A week later, Washington attempted an attack on the major British encampment outside the city at Germantown. At first, things went well for the Americans. But patches of dense fog created so much confusion that at one point they were firing on each other. Once again Howe won.

Victory at Saratoga

In the meantime, one of Howe's fellow British generals was marching straight into the jaws of disaster. General "Gentleman Johnny" Burgoyne had persuaded the high command in London to let him lead a major army down the route of lakes from Canada to Albany. There he intended to link up with Howe's troops, coming north from New York City. But when Burgoyne set out, he did not know that Howe had gone to Philadelphia.

Burgoyne also did not know how to lead an expedition through a forested wilderness. He had 4000 redcoats, 3000 Hessians, and 1000 Mohawk Indians. But he also had 138 pieces of artillery, a plentiful supply of wine and fine clothes, and his large four-poster bed. The farther south of Lake Champlain he went, the more resistance he met. Felled trees and thick underbrush slowed his progress. Food supplies ran low. Militiamen and Continentals were gathering from all over New York and New England. Every time the two sides clashed— as at Bennington, Vermont—Burgoyne lost several hundred men.

Meanwhile a British force under General Barry St. Leger was marching from Lake Ontario. But it was turned back at Oriskany and Fort Stanwix by the American Generals Nicholas Herkimer and Benedict Arnold. (The latter did not turn traitor until 1780.)

Finally halted at Saratoga by the massed Americans, Burgoyne surrendered his battered army on October 17, 1777, to General Horatio Gates. From that time on, the British dared not send troops into the countryside. They kept them along the coast, no more than 50 miles away from the big guns and supply bases of the British fleet.

Saratoga was important psychologically as well as militarily. Americans now had proof that they could defeat British regulars. Yet American forces were still outnumbered overall. The real impact of Saratoga came in Paris and London.

The French Alliance

France's desire to humiliate Great Britain was greater than its fear of encouraging revolution. Early in 1776, the Continental Congress had sent Silas Deane as its agent to seek assistance in Paris. Soon, the Americans were secretly getting about 80 percent of their gunpowder from the French. After the victory at Saratoga, the French were willing to support the Americans openly.

A formal treaty of alliance between the French and the Americans was concluded in February 1778. They agreed not to make peace with England unless American independence was recognized. The Americans would keep all territory conquered from the British. If war came between France and England, neither ally was to make peace without the consent of the other.

The American War of Independence was now transformed into still another full-scale European conflict. In 1779 Spain joined the war as France's ally. The Spanish port of New Orleans thus became available for the Americans to use as a base for the war at sea. Spain later reoccupied Florida. The Netherlands declared war on England in 1780.

Stalemate

In the long run, French seapower proved decisive. Yet the French alliance was followed by three years of discouragement for the Americans.

While American negotiators were at work in Paris, Washington's Continentals were in winter camp at Valley Forge, Pennsylvania. Of the 10,000 men living on snowy ground in makeshift wood-and-clay shelters, poorly fed and in rags, almost 2500 died. As seventeen-year-old Joseph Martin later wrote, "I endured hardships sufficient to kill a dozen horses." Yet the time was not spent in idleness. The men were engaged in learning the Baron von Steuben's new Prussian military drill. Friedrich von Steuben had joined the Americans at Valley Forge in February 1778, where he went to work "to make regular soldiers out of country bumpkins." He taught the Americans how to use the bayonet and how to load their cannon properly.

There were some other foreign officers who helped the Americans. Thaddeus Kosciuszko (kosh-*choosh*-ko), an artillery officer, came from Poland, as did Count Casimir Pulaski. Kosciuszko helped build the fortifications at West Point. Pulaski was asked by Congress to organize a U.S. Cavalry Corps. Pulaski died of wounds in the battle of Savannah. There are about 15 towns and counties in the United States named in honor of these two Poles.

Surrender at Saratoga 1777

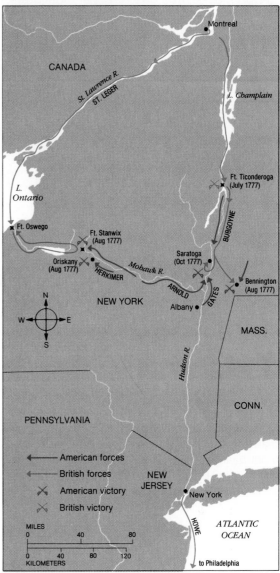

Map Skills *How different might the situation have been at Saratoga if Howe had marched north?*

139

While General Howe and his men relaxed in Philadelphia, Washington and his men camped out at Valley Forge. There they endured cold and hunger while being drilled by Von Steuben.

That spring, General Howe was replaced by Sir Henry Clinton. Hearing rumors about a French assault on New York City, Clinton set out from Philadelphia across New Jersey. Washington's forces pursued him but were unable to prevent his reaching New York. The Americans then camped outside the British-occupied city. There the two armies remained, facing each other, for three long years.

The War in the South

That same summer of 1778, the British decided to shift their main operations to the southern states. A British expedition took Savannah at the end of that year. By the spring of 1779, a royal governor was once more in charge of Georgia. Hopeful that the South might turn out to be the long-sought Loyalist stronghold, Clinton, assisted by General Charles Lord Cornwallis, embarked from New York with 8500 men and fourteen battleships. The fleet sailed to Charleston, where the British won their greatest victory of the war. They captured not only the city but the entire force of American defenders, some 5500 men. Thoroughly satisfied, Clinton retired to New York leaving Cornwallis in charge of mopping up the Carolinas.

At first Cornwallis was successful. At Camden,

South Carolina, he smashed the American forces. Within three months, South Carolina, like Georgia, was for all practical purposes again part of the British Empire. When Cornwallis advanced into North Carolina, however, he was hit by a series of reverses. Guerrilla bands—led by such men as Francis Marion, called the "Swamp Fox," Andrew Pickens, and Thomas Sumter—constantly harassed him. In October 1780, farmers and trappers came across a Loyalist force of 1400 men who were dug in atop a wooded ridge called Kings Mountain. It was, as one historian declared, "Bunker Hill in reverse." The frontier militia charged up the hill twice but were driven back. Finally, on the third charge, the guerrillas captured the position and the battle was won. Cornwallis retreated to South Carolina.

In the meantime, Washington sent 1000 Continentals commanded by his ablest general, Nathanael Greene, into the Carolinas. After a loss at Cowpens and a bloody victory at Guilford Court House in which he lost more than 30 percent of his troops, Cornwallis concluded that he might do better in Virginia. Greene did not pursue him but went to mop up the remaining British units farther south.

Cornwallis then made the fateful mistake of taking his army out onto the peninsula between

The War in the South   1778–1781

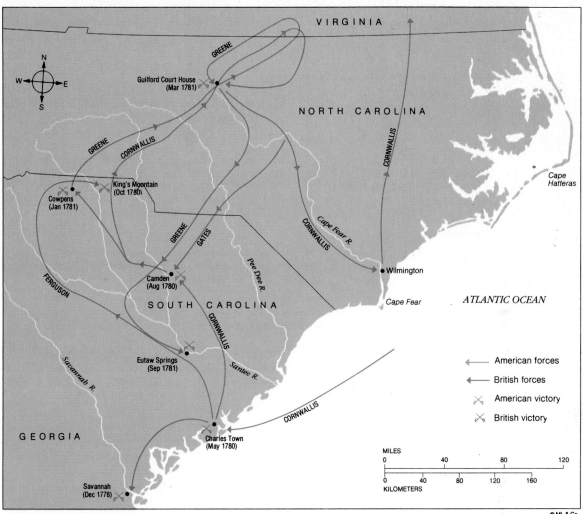

Map Skills   *Who were the British and American commanders at Camden? When was the battle of King's Mountain? To what city did the British go after the battle of Guilford Court House?*

the James and the York rivers. There his 8000 troops set up camp at Yorktown, just a few miles northeast of the original English settlement of Jamestown. It was Cornwallis's plan to fortify Yorktown, take Virginia, and then move north to join up with Clinton's forces which would move south from New York.

The End Comes at Yorktown

A combination of good luck and well-timed decisions now favored the American cause.

A French army of 6000 men had taken Newport, Rhode Island, in 1780. In addition to a fleet there, another French fleet was operating in the West Indies, attacking British ships wherever they were to be found. And Washington's army was still encamped at White Plains, besieging the British in New York City. The idea of first combining the two armies and the two fleets and then attacking Cornwallis in Virginia was the brainstorm of Marie Joseph Paul, the Marquis de Lafayette. Lafayette had joined the American cause even before the French alliance. Now he convinced Washington to try his plan.

Accordingly, the French troops left Newport and joined the Americans at White Plains. A German officer attached to the French troops described the American soldiers in the following words.

141

❝It was really painful to see these brave men almost naked, with only some trousers and little linen jackets; most of them without stockings, but, believe it or not, very cheerful and healthy in appearance. A quarter of them were Negroes, merry, confident, and sturdy.❞

From White Plains, the combined armies began the long march south to Yorktown.

In the meantime, a French naval force suddenly appeared within sight of the Yorktown peninsula. Clinton desperately sent a fleet of warships south from New York. But the French blocked the entrance to Chesapeake Bay. After two hours of flaming combat, the British fleet was forced to turn back. Now the jaws of the trap closed on Cornwallis. British soldiers could not escape by sea as they had from Boston more than six years before. On land they faced 8000 French troops and 9000 Americans. The siege of Yorktown lasted about a month. Finally on October 18, 1781, outnumbered more than two to one and cut off from reinforcements, Cornwallis agreed to have his men lay down their arms. He insisted, however, that they do so in front of the French troops rather than before the despised colonials. The next day, as the redcoats walked forward to stack their arms in a field, the British army band played a popular marching song, "The World Turned Upside Down." It went like this:

❝If ponies rode men and if grass ate the cows,
And cats should be chased into holes by the mouse...
If summer were spring and the other way round,
Then all the world would be upside down.❞

Indeed the world *was* turned upside down. The Americans had defeated the mighty British Empire. When Lord North heard the news of the surrender he cried out, "Oh God! It is all over." Then he resigned.

The world was amazed at what the Americans had done. One of the Hessian mercenaries serving with the British forces was filled with admiration when he saw some of the victorious colonials lined up for inspection.

❝The men looked haggard and pallid (pale) and were poorly dressed. Indeed, very many stood quite proudly under arms without shoes and stockings. What army could be maintained in this manner? None, certainly, for the whole army would gradually run away. This, too, is a part of that "Liberty and Independence" for which these poor fellows had to have their arms and legs smashed. But to what cannot enthusiasm lead a people!❞

Section 4 Review

COMPREHENSION Developing Vocabulary
1. Explain these terms: amnesty, pallid.

COMPREHENSION Mastering Facts
1. Why did Washington risk his troops at the Battle of Trenton?
2. How did France react to the Battle of Saratoga?
3. What battle was described as being the Battle of Bunker Hill in reverse?
4. What was Lafayette's plan for ending the war?

The French print below shows Yorktown. The British soldiers marched out and stacked their arms between the American army (left) and French army (right). The French Navy is in Chesapeake Bay.

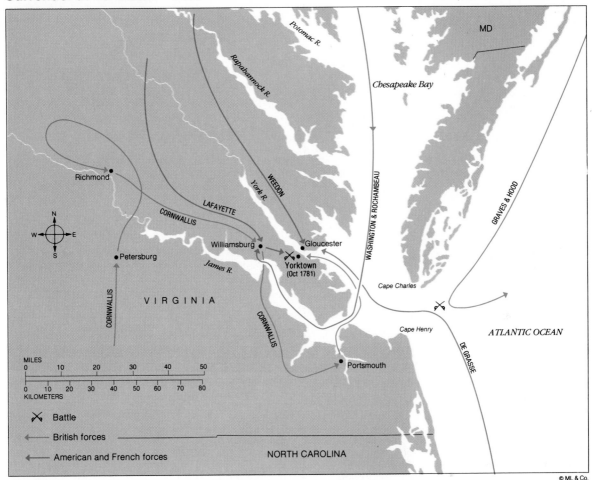

© ML & Co.

Map Skills   *Who were the commanders of the American and French forces that converged on Yorktown? How might the war have been affected if British Rear Admiral Thomas Graves had defeated French Admiral Francois de Grasse?*

5   THE AMERICAN REVOLUTION CHANGES THE WORLD

VOCABULARY   *emancipation*

Negotiating a peace treaty was a delicate and difficult business. In effect, four nations were involved—the United States, Great Britain, France, and Spain—each of which had different interests.

Spain had no formal ties with the United States. Indeed, Spain was hostile to the new nation's hopes both for independence and for a western boundary on the Mississippi River. One of the American negotiators, John Jay of New York, described France's position very accurately: "We can depend upon the French only to see that we are separated from England, but it is not in their interest that we should become a great and formidable (powerful) people, and therefore they will not help

us to become so." Jay was quite correct. About this time, French Minister of Foreign Affairs Charles Vergennes wrote to a friend, "We ask independence only for the thirteen states of America. . . . We do not desire that a new republic shall arise which shall become the exclusive mistress of this immense continent."

The Treaty of Paris

Fortunately for the United States, the Continental Congress sent an extremely able team of negotiators to Paris: John Adams, Benjamin Franklin, and John Jay. The negotiators soon got wind

143

North America After the Treaty of Paris 1783

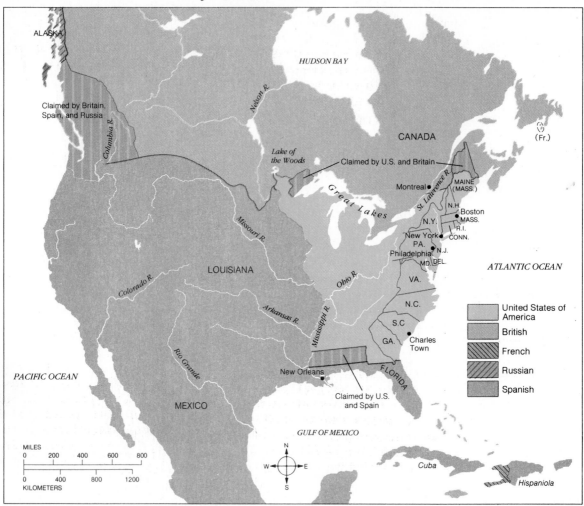

Map Skills *The new United States of America stretched from the Atlantic to the Mississippi. About how far was that? Who controlled Canada? Florida? Alaska? Louisiana?*

of the fact that the French were secretly encouraging the English to insist on a boundary well to the east of the Mississippi River. They decided to ignore the French for the moment and to deal directly with the British delegation. The British and the Americans worked out a tentative agreement that included a western boundary at the Mississippi. By agreeing to this, the British hoped to drive a wedge between the Americans and the French. The Americans in turn laid this agreement before the French as an accomplished fact. Franklin used all his charm to soothe the French.

The treaty was signed in September.1783, eight years after the war began. Britain formally acknowledged American independence. The boundaries of the new nation were set at Florida in the south, the Mississippi in the west, and a border with Canada much like the present one. The British recognized American fishing rights off Newfoundland. The Americans agreed that private British creditors could collect any debts owed them by citizens of the United States. Finally, the Continental Congress was to "earnestly recommend" to the various states that they return property seized from Loyalists. By separate treaty the British gave Florida back to Spain.

George Washington went to Harlem, which was then on the outskirts of New York City, and watched for three days as the last British troops boarded their transports in New York harbor.

Meanwhile, five miles away at the lower end of Manhattan, Loyalists were busily selling off their property and goods. Finally, the nearly 30,000 soldiers and Loyalists sailed away, and Washington entered the cheering city. He then bade farewell to his assembled officers and rode off to present his resignation as commander-in-chief to the Continental Congress. He told it that he was leaving "all the employments of public life." He had no idea that his country would call on him again.

How Revolutionary Was the Revolution?

Historians have often asked an obvious question about the American Revolution. How much change did it produce in American society? We usually think of revolutions as being periods of great and rapid change. Certainly the French Revolution of 1789 and the more recent Russian and Chinese revolutions produced profound changes in those societies. Was the American Revolution, in this sense, really revolutionary?

Economic Life Relatively Unchanged. The American Revolution produced fewer economic changes than almost any other major modern revolution. The principal reason is that a great deal of change had already taken place during the century *before* the Revolution. The great majority of white men already owned some property and had good hopes of getting more by their own labors. So during the Revolution, there were few demands for taking property from the wealthy. There were no calls for changing the economic system in basic ways because it was working well. By and large, Americans were well off. Prosperous people do not like to rock the foundations of their prosperity.

Slaves Freed When Convenient. One group of Americans had no share in this prosperity—the slaves. Slavery was the conspicuous exception to the principles of the Revolution.

The war itself considerably changed the lives of some slaves. Several thousand served in the armed forces of both sides. Usually they gained their freedom by doing so. Thousands of other slaves were taken by the British when they left Georgia and South Carolina. Some went to freedom in Nova Scotia; others, to continued slavery in the West Indies. For the great majority of blacks, however, the war meant only continued toil in the fields.

The ideas of the Revolution threw the entire institution of slavery into question. The net result was that a number of states took steps toward abolishing it.

From Pennsylvania northward, slaves were few; so it was relatively easy to bring slavery to a gradual end. In Massachusetts, court decisions found that slavery violated the state constitution's assertion that "all men are born free and equal." Elsewhere in the North, states passed gradual emancipation laws. Although these laws did not abolish slavery outright, they provided that slaves born from then on would become free at age twenty-one or twenty-eight. In many cases, the laws named July 4 as the date when they would go into effect. That date itself pointed to the force of revolutionary principles.

In the southern states, the principles were the same, but the number of slaves was much greater. In Virginia and Maryland, where slavery was less profitable than farther south, there was considerable discussion about abolishing it. The difficulty was that most whites did not want free blacks around. If slavery were abolished, where would the blacks go? However, a number of slaveowners went ahead on their own and privately emancipated some, or all, of their slaves.

Farther south, in the Carolinas and Georgia, there was little discussion and no action. There, slavery was highly profitable, and slaves were far more numerous in proportion to the white population.

Thus, white Americans lived up to their revolutionary principles where it was easy to do so but failed where it was difficult. The author of the Declaration of Independence continued to own slaves for his entire life. Eventually, Americans would have to pay a terrible price for slavery.

The Revolution had one other important impact on the pattern of American slavery. The outbreak of war stopped the importation of slaves from Africa, while the Continental Congress prohibited the importation of new slaves from the West Indies and elsewhere. When the war was over, many people wanted to keep the ban on the slave trade.

The Churches Lose Power. The Revolution led to certain changes in the relationship between church and state. In New York and the southern states, the established Anglican church lost its privileged position. People were no longer required to pay taxes to support it. Yet most states continued to tax their citizens for the support of the churches. But it wasn't for a particular church. The taxpayers could name the church to which the tax money would go.

Only Virginia provided for the complete separation of church and state, an arrangement that today prevails throughout the United States. Virginia's advanced position on this matter was largely due to the influence of Thomas Jefferson and his friend James Madison.

A Political Example to the World. The ideas of the American Revolution have echoed around the world for 200 years. As one of George III's descendants, Queen Elizabeth II of England, said when she visited Independence Hall in 1976, "We learned a great lesson." As a result, few colonies of the British Empire had to fight a revolutionary war for their freedom. Countries such as Canada, Australia, and New Zealand were given their independence gradually.

For generations, any people seeking freedom from oppression have looked with admiration and longing toward the United States. It was in the realm of government that the American Revolution was truly revolutionary. A nation was born whose government and social development became the wonder of the world.

Section 5 Review

COMPREHENSION   Developing Vocabulary

1. Explain these terms: emancipation, formidable, Treaty of Paris.

COMPREHENSION   Mastering Facts

1. How did the French government feel about an independent United States?
2. Where did the Treaty of Paris set the boundaries of the United States?
3. How did the American Revolution affect slavery?
4. How did the American Revolution affect the relations between church and state?

CHAPTER 7   Review

Chapter Summary

The Second Continental Congress met in Philadelphia in May of 1775. The delegates continued to seek political solutions to their problems, but public opinion changed rapidly. In July, 1776, the colonists issued a Declaration of Independence. Meanwhile, as the fighting continued, each side had certain advantages and disadvantages. Only George Washington's leadership saved the Continental Army on several occasions. Then the Americans won an important victory at Saratoga in 1777. Four years later, the Revolution ended when British forces finally surrendered at Yorktown.

Questions for Critical Thinking

COMPREHENSION   Summarizing Main Ideas

1. What were the arguments in favor of the colonists' break with Great Britain in 1776? What were the arguments against the break?
2. What advantages did Great Britain have over the Americans at the start of the Revolutionary War? What advantages did the colonists have over Great Britain?
3. List four groups of Americans who tended to become Loyalists.
4. Describe the political results of each of the following battles: (a) Breed's Hill; (b) Trenton; (c) Saratoga; (d) Yorktown.
5. Show how each of the following helped to bring about the American victory: (a) the military leadership of George Washington; (b) the geographic extent of the fighting; (c) the financial expertise of Robert Morris and Haym Salomon; (d) the exercises of Baron Friedrich von Steuben; (e) the French fleet.

COMPREHENSION   Interpreting Events

1. Why did the Second Continental Congress still feel loyal to King George III? Why did public opinion about the king begin to change?
2. If Thomas Paine had not written *Common Sense* and *The Crisis*, do you think the course of American history would have been different? Give reasons for your opinion.

3. Why did the British at first direct their main operations to the middle states? Why did they shift to the southern states in 1778?
4. Why did France join the American struggle against Great Britain? Why did Spain join the war as France's ally?
5. Did the American Revolution achieve the goals its supporters wanted? Explain.

APPLICATION   Using Skills To Evaluate Sources

In evaluating the significance of historical data, it is important to examine events from several different points of view. Explain how each of the following events might have been described by the individuals listed below each event.

1. The writing of the Declaration of Independence
   a. A Loyalist
   b. A black slave
   c. A member of Parliament
   d. Samuel Adams
2. Cornwallis's surrender at Yorktown
   a. General Benedict Arnold
   b. General Nathanael Greene
   c. The Marquis de Lafayette
   d. Baron von Steuben
3. The signing of the Treaty of Paris
   a. A Hessian mercenary
   b. A colonial soldier
   c. The French Minister of Foreign Affairs
   d. The head of the Iroquois Confederacy

EVALUATION   Forming Generalizations

1. Would you say that the United States has achieved the ideal of "equality" stated in the Declaration of Independence? Explain.
2. What nations have become independent within the last twenty-five years? How does the way in which they achieved independence compare with the way the United States achieved independence?
3. If you live in a community that is connected in some way with the Revolutionary War, prepare a report describing the relationship. Are any schools, streets, or other public places in your community named after Revolutionary War heroes or heroines?

Declaration of Independence

In Congress, July 4, 1776

The Unanimous Declaration of the Thirteen United States of America.

When, in the course of human events, it becomes necessary for one people to dissolve the political bands which have connected them with another, and to assume, among the powers of the earth, the separate and equal station to which the laws of nature and of nature's God entitle them, a decent respect to the opinions of mankind requires that they should declare the causes which impel them to the separation.

We hold these truths to be self-evident:—That all men are created equal; that they are endowed by their Creator with certain unalienable rights; that among these are life, liberty, and the pursuit of happiness. That, to secure these rights, governments are instituted among men, deriving their just powers from the consent of the governed; that, whenever any form of government becomes destructive of these ends, it is the right of the people to alter or to abolish it, and to institute new government, laying its foundation on such principles, and organizing its powers in such form, as to them shall seem most likely to effect their safety and happiness. Prudence, indeed, will dictate that governments long established should not be changed for light and transient causes; and, accordingly, all experience hath shown that mankind are more disposed to suffer, while evils are sufferable, than to right themselves by abolishing the forms to which they are accustomed. But, when a long train of abuses and usurpations, pursuing invariably the same object, evinces a design to reduce them under absolute despotism, it is their right, it is their duty, to throw off such government, and to provide new guards for their future security. Such has been the patient sufferance of these colonies; and such is now the necessity which constrains them to alter their former systems of government. The history of the present King of Great Britain is a history of repeated injuries and usurpations, all having in direct object the establishment of an absolute tyranny over these States. To prove this, let facts be submitted to a candid world.

He has refused his assent to laws the most wholesome and necessary for the public good.

He has forbidden his governors to pass laws of immediate and pressing importance, unless suspended in their operation till his assent should be obtained; and when so suspended, he has utterly neglected to attend to them.

He has refused to pass other laws for the accommodation of large districts of people, unless those people would relinquish the right of representation in the legislature—a right inestimable to them, and formidable to tyrants only.

He has called together legislative bodies at places unusual, uncomfortable, and distant from the depository of their public records, for the sole purpose of fatiguing them into compliance with his measures.

He has dissolved representative houses repeatedly, for opposing, with manly firmness, his invasions on the rights of the people.

He has refused for a long time, after such dissolutions, to cause others to be elected; whereby the legislative powers, incapable of annihilation, have returned to the people at large for their exercise; the State remaining, in the mean time, exposed to all the dangers of invasion from without, and convulsions within.

He has endeavored to prevent the population of these States; for that purpose obstructing the laws for naturalization of foreigners; refusing to pass others to encourage their migrations hither, and raising the conditions of new appropriations of lands.

He has obstructed the administration of justice, by refusing his assent to laws for establishing judiciary powers.

He has made judges dependent on his will alone, for the tenure of their offices, and the amount and payment of their salaries.

He has erected a multitude of new offices, and sent hither swarms of officers to harass our people, and eat out their substance.

He has kept among us, in times of peace, standing armies, without the consent of our legislatures.

He has affected to render the military independent of and superior to the civil power.

He has combined with others to subject us to a jurisdiction foreign to our constitution, and unacknowledged by our laws; giving his assent to their acts of pretended legislation:

For quartering large bodies of armed troops among us;

For protecting them, by a mock trial, from punishment for any murders which they should commit on the inhabitants of these States;

For cutting off our trade with all parts of the world;

For imposing taxes on us without our consent;

For depriving us, in many cases, of the benefits of trial by jury;

For transporting us beyond seas to be tried for pretended offences;

For abolishing the free system of English laws in a neighboring province, establishing therein an arbitrary government, and enlarging its boundaries, so as to render it at once an example and fit instrument for introducing the same absolute rule into these colonies;

For taking away our charters, abolishing our most valuable laws, and altering fundamentally the forms of our governments;

For suspending our own legislatures, and declaring themselves invested with power to legislate for us in all cases whatsoever.

He has abdicated government here, by declaring us out of his protection, and waging war against us.

He has plundered our seas, ravaged our coasts, burnt our towns, and destroyed the lives of our people.

He is at this time transporting large armies of foreign mercenaries to complete the works of death, desolation, and tyranny, already begun with circumstances of cruelty and perfidy scarcely paralleled in the most barbarous ages, and totally unworthy the head of a civilized nation.

He has constrained our fellow citizens, taken captive on the high seas, to bear arms against their country, to become the executioners of their friends and brethren, or to fall themselves by their hands.

He has excited domestic insurrections amongst us, and has endeavored to bring on the inhabitants of our frontiers, the merciless Indian savages, whose known rule of warfare is an undistinguished destruction of all ages, sexes, and conditions.

In every stage of these oppressions, we have petitioned for redress, in the most humble terms: our repeated petitions have been answered only by repeated injury. A prince, whose character is thus marked by every act which may define a tyrant, is unfit to be the ruler of a free people.

Nor have we been wanting in attentions to our British brethren. We have warned them, from time to time, of attempts by their legislature to extend an unwarrantable jurisdiction over us. We have reminded them of the circumstances of our emigration and settlement here. We have appealed to their native justice and magnanimity; and we have conjured them, by the ties of our common kindred, to disavow these usurpations, which would inevitably interrupt our connections and correspondence. They, too, have been deaf to the voice of justice and of consanguinity. We must, therefore, acquiesce in the necessity, which denounces our separation, and hold them, as we hold the rest of mankind, enemies in war, in peace friends.

WE, THEREFORE, the REPRESENTATIVES of the UNITED STATES OF AMERICA, in General Congress assembled, appealing to the Supreme Judge of the world for the rectitude of our intentions, do, in the name and by the authority of the good people of these colonies, solemnly publish and declare, That these United Colonies are, and of right ought to be, FREE AND INDEPENDENT STATES; that they are absolved from all allegiance to the British crown, and that all political connection between them and the state of

Great Britain, is and ought to be totally dissolved; and that, as free and independent states, they have full power to levy war, conclude peace, contract alliances, establish commerce, and to do all other acts and things which independent states may of right do. And, for the support of this declaration, with a firm reliance on the protection of Divine Providence, we mutually pledge to each other our lives, our fortunes, and our sacred honor.

John Hancock

The foregoing Declaration was, by order of Congress, engrossed and signed by the following members:—

NEW HAMPSHIRE.
Josiah Bartlett,
William Whipple,
Matthew Thornton.

MASSACHUSETTS BAY.
Samuel Adams,
John Adams,
Robert Treat Paine,
Elbridge Gerry.

RHODE ISLAND.
Stephen Hopkins,
William Ellery.

CONNECTICUT.
Roger Sherman,
Samuel Huntington,
William Williams,
Oliver Wolcott.

NEW YORK.
William Floyd,
Philip Livingston,
Francis Lewis,
Lewis Morris.

NEW JERSEY.
Richard Stockton,
John Witherspoon,
Francis Hopkinson,
John Hart,
Abraham Clark.

PENNSYLVANIA.
Robert Morris,
Benjamin Rush,
Benjamin Franklin,
John Morton,
George Clymer,
James Smith,

George Taylor,
James Wilson,
George Ross.

DELAWARE.
Caesar Rodney,
George Read,
Thomas M'Kean.

MARYLAND.
Samuel Chase,
William Paca,
Thomas Stone,
Charles Carroll
 of Carrollton.

VIRGINIA.
George Wythe,
Richard Henry Lee,
Thomas Jefferson,

Benjamin Harrison,
Thomas Nelson, Jr.,
Francis Lightfoot Lee,
Carter Braxton.

NORTH CAROLINA.
William Hooper,
Joseph Hewes,
John Penn.

SOUTH CAROLINA.
Edward Rutledge,
Thomas Heyward, Jr.,
Thomas Lynch, Jr.,
Arthur Middleton.

GEORGIA.
Button Gwinnett,
Lyman Hall,
George Walton.

Resolved, That copies of the Declaration be sent to the several assemblies, conventions, and committees, or councils of safety, and to the several commanding officers of the continental troops; that it be proclaimed in each of the United States, at the head of the army.

Understanding Government

1. Describe how the Declaration is organized.
2. Which of the complaints listed by Jefferson in the Declaration against King George III seem to you to be the most serious? Why?
3. What basic rights does the Declaration of Independence claim for all people?
4. Study the names of the people who signed the Declaration. Which do you recognize? Why?

UNIT 2   Review

Understanding Social Studies Concepts

History

1. Which early American best exemplified the ideas of the Englightenment? What scientific contributions did he make?
2. How did the libel case against John Peter Zenger set the basis for American freedom of the press?
3. How did George Grenville justify keeping ten thousand British troops in the colonies after the French and Indian War? How did the colonists react to the troops? How did this contribute to the growing tension between England and the colonies?
4. Who spoke for the colonial cause in Parliament? What arguments did he offer for improving British-colonial relations?
5. What were Committees of Correspondence? Why were they organized?
6. How did the American Revolution become an example for the world?

Geography

1. How did geography affect British military strategy during the Revolutionary War? Name several instances in which the Americans used geography to their advantage during battles.
2. Why was the Proclamation line of 1763 placed where it was? What geographical obstacles faced settlers moving westward? How did they overcome these obstacles?

Economics

1. What economic conditions caused Grenville to encourage passage of the Sugar Act?
2. How did the Townshend Acts contribute to Britain's growing economic problems?
3. Give an example of how Britain tried to follow mercantilist principles regarding its American colonies. Then give an example of how Britain went against mercantilist principles.

Government

1. The Albany Plan of Union was an early try at a united colonial government. Describe the plan. Who formed it? Why did it fail?
2. After the Declaration of Independence, what group exercised the power of government in the colonies? What specific government functions did it assume?

Extending Map, Chart, Picture Skills

1. Study the picture on page 142. What worthwhile information can be learned from it concerning the Battle of Yorktown? In what ways is the picture probably exaggerated? How does personal bias affect an artist as well as a writer?
2. Study the map on page 144. After the Treaty of Paris, what territory was claimed by the United States? Great Britain? France? Which territory was claimed by more than one nation?

Understanding Current Events

1. In what ways does Canada today reflect both a strong French and British heritage? Why?
2. Newspapers were an important source of public information during colonial times. Are newspapers still important for that reason today? What other means of communication are used now that colonists did not have?

Developing Effective Citizenship

1. Imagine that you are a colonist living in 1775. Which side would you have supported, Patriots or Loyalists? Why? Could it have depended on your occupation or where you lived? Why was the choice difficult for many colonists?
2. In what ways did women and blacks contribute to the Revolutionary War effort? Use specific examples in your answer.

THE UNITED STATES

THE WORLD

1781 Articles of Confederation adopted.

1788 Ratification of the Constitution.

1789–1800 Federalist Era.

1800 Thomas Jefferson elected president.

1780

1790

1800

1790s European nations begin to abolish slave trade.

1789 French Revolution begins.

1784 China begins trading with the United States.

1801 Ireland joins Great Britain.

UNIT 3

U.S.A., a New Nation

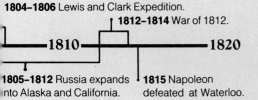

3 Louisiana Purchase.

1804–1806 Lewis and Clark Expedition.

                  1812–1814 War of 1812.

1810————————————**1820**

1805–1812 Russia expands   **1815** Napoleon
nto Alaska and California.   defeated at Waterloo.

Starting a New Nation

1781–1788

Linking Past to Present

In 1776 Americans did not know they were going to be a united country. They simply agreed that certain rights and principles were worth fighting for. And they knew the way a government ought to work. But after they gained their independence it took them twelve years to work out a suitable government. The first government established by the new country was unable to govern. It had to be scrapped and a new one devised. The main problem was that in order to function effectively, a central government had to have some powers which the colonies, now states, were reluctant to give up. This struggle between a national outlook and a local outlook caused difficulties and bad feelings.

The world watched skeptically to see what would happen. Few gave the Americans long to enjoy their new independence. The odds were against them. Some peoples before and many since have broken away from a larger political unit to form a new nation. But they have usually ended up either weak and confused, or under the heel of a dictator. The American colonies, thanks to their history and to some of the wisest leaders the world has ever known, escaped both fates. And the government they finally created has been hailed as "the most wonderful work ever struck off at a given time by the brain and purpose of man."

Let's see how they did it.

1 CREATING THE FIRST NATIONAL GOVERNMENT

VOCABULARY   *sovereign   confederation   Northwest Ordinance*

When the Revolutionary War broke out, the old colonial assemblies simply transformed themselves into the governing bodies of the newly independent states. But everyone realized that new constitutions were needed. So despite wartime difficulties, each state adopted one.

All the states, except Pennsylvania, set up a legislature with two houses. The upper house grew out of the old governor's council. Since Pennsylvania had not had a governor's council, it set up a unicameral, or one-house, legislature. All the states made an important change in the way the upper house was chosen. No longer were members appointed by the governor. They were elected either by the people or by the lower house.

The new state constitutions lowered property requirements for suffrage. Yet they did not abandon the old idea that a man ought to own some property in order to vote. And they continued the requirement that those seeking public office should have higher than usual educational and property qualifications. In contrast to Europe, however, so many persons were able to vote that it seemed the people really ruled themselves.

Drafting the Articles of Confederation

While the states worked on their individual constitutions, the Continental Congress tried to draft one for the states as a whole. That was much more difficult to do. There was considerable disagreement over what the role of the Congress should be. In fact, so great were the problems that it took two and a half years of work before the delegates could agree on a draft. There were some basic questions that had to be answered.

Representation: By Population or by State? The states had come together as independent political units. As such, they were equal to one another. But they were clearly unequal in land size, wealth, and population. This posed a dilemma. Should delegates to a national congress represent people or states? Should each state elect the same number of representatives regardless of its population? Or should states with large populations have more representatives than states with small populations? For example, if Georgia with 25,000 people could elect the same number of representatives as Massachusetts with 270,000 people, then a person in Georgia would have much more political power than a person in Massachusetts. But if delegates were elected on the basis of one delegate for every 4000 people, then large states like Virginia would have much more power in Congress than states with smaller populations like New Jersey.

For the time being, the members of Congress looked on themselves as representing independent states. Therefore, the decision was that each state would have one vote regardless of population. A state could send as many representatives as it wished, but it would still have only one vote.

Supreme Power: Can It Be Divided? Until this time, most people assumed that sovereign, or supreme, power could not be shared. That is, either a government had supreme power or it did not. If it did not, it could not function. There could not be two supreme governments.

Yet that is exactly what the Articles of Confederation proposed. They proposed a new kind of government where fundamental powers were shared between two levels of government. State

Western Land Claims by the States 1783

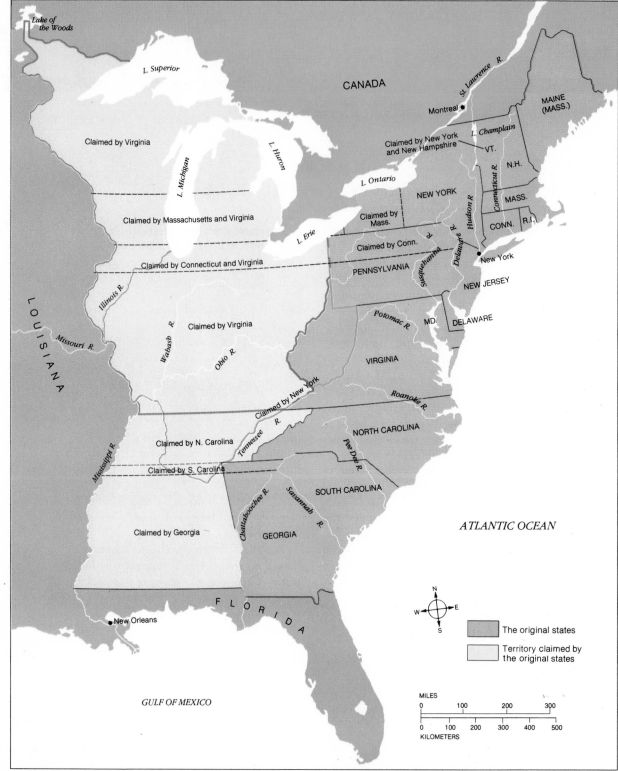

Map Skills *Claims to the Western lands overlapped. What states claimed the present states of Michigan? Tennessee? Mississippi? Vermont? What state claimed the largest area?*

© ML & Co.

governments were supreme in some matters, while the federal, or national, government was supreme in other matters. The delegates used an unusual word for this unusual form of government. They called it a *confederation*, or alliance.

The Articles of Confederation gave the new federal government power to declare war, make peace, and sign treaties. It could borrow money, set standards for coins and for weights and measures, establish a postal service, and deal with the Indians.

Western Lands: Who Gets Them? The framers of the Articles of Confederation expected the states to approve them quickly. But problems concerning western lands created almost a three-year delay.

In their original charters, seven states had claims to territory extending to the Mississippi River and even to the Pacific Ocean. The claims of these "landed" states often overlapped. The "landless states" had western boundaries that were fixed within a few hundred miles of the Atlantic. These states refused to confederate unless the landed states turned over their western claims to the United States. They argued that the landed states would be able to pay off their war debts by selling western lands while the landless states would be forced to tax their people. The landless states also feared the growth in wealth and power of the other states. They also made a less selfish argument. The war for independence, they said, was a common effort. Therefore the whole of the western territory should be used to support it.

The deadlock was broken by patriotic sentiment and by a group of Virginians led by Thomas Jefferson. Jefferson argued that all of the West should eventually be carved up into new states. These would be admitted into the confederation on an equal footing with the original states. It was a bold and novel idea at the time. Yet in later years it seemed natural and inevitable. Virginia and New York gave up their western claims to the national government. Other landed states followed suit, and the Articles of Confederation went into effect in 1781.

Weaknesses of the Articles

Adopting the Articles of Confederation was one thing. Maintaining an effective national government was another.

Short of food and pay, soldiers revolt against their brigade leader (later General) Anthony Wayne.

Most of the powers given to the Confederation Congress required the cooperation of the states. And the states feared a strong national government. As a result, although the central government could settle disputes between states, the states did not have to agree. The federal government could determine how many troops the states should furnish to the nation's army, but the states did not have to send the number of troops asked for.

In addition, the national government lacked many powers. It had no control over trade between the states. Nor did it have any control over foreign trade. Worst of all, the national government had no power to collect taxes. It had to ask the states for money with which to operate. And the states never gave the Congress anything like the amount of money it needed to function. Finally, all the states had to agree before any changes could be made in the Articles of Confederation.

As the Revolutionary War drew to a close, the feelings of unity among the states diminished. They no longer sent able delegates to Philadelphia, and sometimes they sent none at all. Ratification of the Treaty of Paris was delayed for months because there were not enough members to vote on it. In 1783 some Pennsylvania regiments mutinied and came to Philadelphia demanding their pay. The congressmen hastily left town.

The Confederation Congress met in a number of towns. No one seemed anxious to have it in any one place, and no capital had been chosen. The turnover in membership of the Confederation Congress was high because in many ways being a member was a thankless job.

The Old Northwest Territories

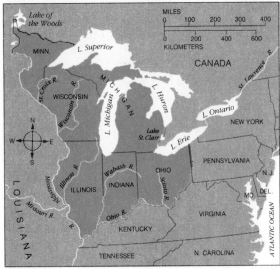

Map Skills *What present states make up the Old Northwest? Which ones touch the Ohio River? the Great Lakes?*

The Northwest Ordinance: Guide to the Future

In one field of administration, the government was extremely successful. In 1787 the Confederation Congress passed a law for the government of part of the western lands. The law was based in large measure on a plan suggested by Jefferson. It is called the Northwest Ordinance because it covered "the old northwest," the land north of the Ohio River and east of the Mississippi River. (The land south of the Ohio and east of the Mississippi is known as "the old southwest" and was covered by different legislation.)

The Northwest Ordinance of 1787 provided for the establishment of not less than three nor more than five territories. As soon as a territory had 5000 voting residents, it could elect its own government.

When the total population reached 60,000, the territory could write a constitution and become a state equal in all respects to other states.

The Ordinance also declared: "Religion, morality and knowledge being necessary to good government and the happiness of mankind, schools and the means of education shall be forever encouraged." A law passed in 1785 had provided the means for this. It reserved one lot in every township for the maintenance of public schools.

The Northwest Ordinance also touched on the question of slavery. It said, "There shall be neither slavery nor involuntary servitude in the said territory otherwise than in the punishment of crimes." Indian rights were likewise mentioned. "The utmost good faith shall always be observed toward the Indians; their lands and property shall never be taken away from them without their consent." However, the prohibition of slavery did not extend into the area south of the Ohio River, and the statement about Indian rights was simply ignored.

Although the Northwest Ordinance did not apply to all the western lands, it did establish an orderly procedure for creating new states. The nation followed this procedure for more than a century as it expanded to the Pacific.

Section 1 Review

COMPREHENSION   Developing Vocabulary
1. Explain these terms: confederation, sovereign, Northwest Ordinance.

COMPREHENSION   Mastering Facts
1. How many votes in Congress did each state have under the Articles of Confederation?
2. How was sovereign power divided under the Articles of Confederation?
3. What economic powers did the government lack under the Articles of Confederation?
4. What did the Northwest Ordinance say about education?

2   SURVIVING A CRITICAL PERIOD

VOCABULARY   *creditors   debtors*

Despite its limitations, the Confederation Congress tried its best to handle the problems that confronted the new nation. In some respects it succeeded, but in others it ran into a number of roadblocks. This was probably inevitable. The nation was new. Some of its leaders were in-

experienced. World opinion was that the country would not last long.

Foreign Problems

The most immediate problems facing the United States had to do with foreign relations.

The nations involved were Great Britain and Spain, and they caused the new government a great deal of embarrassment.

Britain Refuses To Leave.

According to the Treaty of Paris, the British were supposed to leave their military and fur-trading posts in the west "with convenient speed." But in the Great Lakes region, the British did not budge.

What the British really wanted was to dominate the valuable fur trade. But they said they were remaining in their forts because the United States was violating two clauses of the peace treaty. And they were quite right. The states refused to pay debts owed to British merchants. And they refused to return property taken from the Loyalists.

Great Britain also closed ports in both Canada and the British West Indies to American ships. The first ambassador to Great Britain, John Adams, tried in vain to get this policy changed. But Britain saw no reason to encourage the growth of a competitive merchant marine. Especially since there seemed to be nothing the United States could do about it. The Confederation Congress had no power to control foreign trade, and the states acted independently of one another. If New York boycotted Canadian goods, for example, Massachusetts was only too happy to import them.

Fort Niagara was one of those forts the British refused to vacate after the war.

Spain Closes the Mississippi.

Dealing with Spain was as frustrating as dealing with England. Spain refused to recognize the claims of the United States to the territory west of the Appalachians and south of the Ohio River. It established forts throughout the region and made alliances with the Indians there. Further, Spain refused to allow the states to use the port of New Orleans at the mouth of the Mississippi River. This effectively prevented Americans in the West from trading with the rest of the world. It was much too expensive to cart agricultural products over the Appalachian Mountains to ports on the Atlantic.

In 1785 Congress asked John Jay to try to persuade Spain to let Americans send goods down the Mississippi. But Jay was more interested in getting Spain to open up ports in the Spanish West Indies to New England shipping. Although the negotiations eventually fell through, westerners were outraged. They saw the negotiations as evidence that the new nation cared nothing about their interests. Many westerners began talking about setting up a separate republic west of the Appalachians. A few even held secret talks with Spain about such a possibility.

Domestic Problems

While coping with foreign problems, the Confederation Congress found itself confronted with problems at home. One of the most troublesome was the struggle between *creditors* (lenders of money) and *debtors* (borrowers of money).

Borrowers Versus Lenders.

During the Revolutionary War, the states had piled up huge debts. Wealthy people who had lent money to the states favored high taxes so that the states would be able to pay them back. But high taxes meant that many farmers had to go into debt. And since most creditors refused to accept repayment in farm produce, they often found themselves suing farmers in court. If a creditor won a case, the farmer's land and animals were seized and sold at auction. Even if the creditor lost, the farmer still had to pay a lawyer, which put the farmer further in debt.

Debtors and creditors argued about the usefulness of paper money. Almost everyone agreed it was essential. Debtors, however, wanted lots of money printed. This would lessen its value and enable them to pay off their debts in cheap currency. Creditors, on the other hand, wanted to keep the supply of money small so that its value would not decrease. Both groups had much to lose.

Shays's Rebellion.   The conflict between debtors and creditors reached the breaking point in Massachusetts in 1786. People in the coastal towns, where merchants had sold goods to farmers on credit, pushed through a state law taxing landowners. The burden fell most heavily on poor farmers in the western part of the state. The farmers petitioned the assembly for relief. But the western part of Massachusetts had only a few representatives in the legislature because its inhabitants were too poor to be eligible to vote. Their pleas fell on deaf ears.

All through the summer and fall, farmers kept demanding that courts be closed so they would not lose their farms to creditors. That winter, their discontent boiled over into mob action. Some 2000 farmers closed the courts and marched through the snow toward the arsenal at Springfield. They were led by Daniel Shays. A veteran of Bunker Hill and Saratoga, Shays was also an angry farmer who was about to be put in debtors' prison.

Shays's Rebellion, as the farmers' protest movement came to be called, was put down at the cost of three rebels shot by the state militia. The remaining rebels, including Shays, were pardoned. Although most people in Massachusetts did not approve of the farmers' actions, they agreed that the farmers had genuine grievances.

Shays's Rebellion caused dismay and panic throughout the nation. There were debt-ridden farmers in every state. Would rebellion spread from Massachusetts elsewhere? Not only was private property in danger but so was the new nation's reputation. As George Washington himself exclaimed, "What a triumph for our enemies. . .to find we are incapable of governing ourselves!"

A Local Versus National Outlook

Ever since the Treaty of Paris, there had been a division among American political leaders. Some took a local view, while others took a nationalist view.

Those with a local view were interested primarily in their own state and in local affairs. They felt that liberties are best defended by keeping sovereign power closely leashed to the state capital. They distrusted giving much power to a national government. Some of the people who thought this way did so partly because of their personal background. Men like Samuel Adams of Massachusetts and Patrick Henry of Virginia were highly successful politicians in their own states. But they lacked experience at the national level, in the Congress, in the Continental army, and in diplomatic posts abroad.

The nationalists were mostly individuals with considerable experience at the national level. George Washington was obviously such a man. So

Shays's Rebellion caused great embarrassment in the new nation. The engraving below shows Shays's men preparing to attack the courthouse in Springfield, Massachusetts.

were John Adams, Benjamin Franklin, Thomas Jefferson, and James Madison. Another nationally minded man was young Alexander Hamilton of New York, who had served throughout much of the war as an aide to General Washington.

These men, and many others, were greatly concerned about the weaknesses of the Confederation Congress. How could a government function when it was unable either to levy taxes or to enforce its decisions? As Washington wrote to a friend,

66 The consequences of . . . [an] inefficient government are too obvious to be dwelt upon. Thirteen sovereignties pulling against each other, and all tugging at the federal head, will soon bring ruin upon the whole . . . .Let us have [government] by which our lives, liberty, and property will be secured, or let us know the worst at once. 99

James Madison had Virginia call on all the states to send delegates to a general meeting at Annapolis, Maryland, in September 1786. The purpose of the meeting was to discuss problems of interstate trade. New York, for example, taxed goods coming from New Jersey. Maryland and Virginia were quarreling bitterly over which state had the right to use the Potomac River for navigation.

Only five states, however, responded to Madison's call. So at the suggestion of Hamilton, the Annapolis delegates called for another general meeting to be held in Philadelphia in May 1787. The new call arrived along with the news of Shays's Rebellion. This time, every state except Rhode Island responded favorably. They sent their best political leaders to Philadelphia. State squabbles were forgotten in the greater concern over how to strengthen the central government. But Patrick Henry refused to go because he did not want Virginia to give up any of its sovereign power.

The Constitutional Convention

As is true of most such political meetings, the fifty-five delegates were wealthier and better educated than the people they represented. Most were lawyers, merchants, or planters. In a day when very few people went to college, a majority were college graduates. And they were remarkably young for such a gathering. Their average age was forty-two. The most active member of the convention, James Madison, had just passed his thirty-sixth birthday.

All the delegates were convinced that this meet-

James Madison was an active member of the Continental Congress who later became the fourth president of the United States.

ing would be the final chance to put the national government on a firmer footing. They knew they had to succeed in giving the Confederation more powers. Otherwise it would break up into smaller and weaker regional alliances.

On shipboard, horseback, and at overnight stops at roadside taverns, they consulted with themselves and with chance companions. As they straggled into Philadelphia in the latter part of May, each of them found that his fellow delegates had been thinking along the same lines.

In Philadelphia many of them stayed in the same inns and boarding houses and so were able to meet often in small groups and talk things over. Their official meetings were held in a large room on the second floor of the Pennsylvania State House. The delegates decided to keep the proceedings secret. They were afraid that public discussion would interfere with debate. But they deliberately announced the fact that George

Washington—the most respected man in America—would chair the meetings. They knew this would inspire public confidence.

The delegates worked all through the long hot summer of 1787. They were physically uncomfortable, especially because the windows were usually kept closed to prevent outsiders from hearing the discussions. And the arguments that raged were hotter than the weather. Yet within seventeen weeks, they succeeded in what they called their "grand experiment." They created a new form of government for the United States.

Section 2 Review

COMPREHENSION **Developing Vocabulary**
1. Explain these terms: creditors, debtors, Shays's Rebellion, Annapolis Convention.

COMPREHENSION **Mastering Facts**
1. Why did the British refuse to leave their forts in the Great Lakes region?
2. What did Spain and the United States argue about?
3. Why did debtors want lots of money printed?
4. What did Shay's Rebellion have to do with the meeting in Philadelphia?

3 DRAFTING THE CONSTITUTION

VOCABULARY *bicameral delegated powers reserved powers impeach bills of credit Anti-Federalists Federalist*

The delegates were in general agreement about government, liberty, and the way human beings behaved. This agreement was the cement that prevented the convention from coming apart.

Philosophical Principles

In general, the delegates believed that humans are motivated primarily by self-interest and that society consists of many interest groups. The most important of these groups, however, were the economic groups. Some groups were landowners, slaveowners (who usually owned land as well),

William Paterson, author of the New Jersey Plan, is shown in this etching by artist Max Rosenthal.

bankers, merchants, small farmers, and business employees. The delegates believed that each group would favor itself at the expense of the rest of society. But they saw a way to prevent any group from becoming dominant. This was, as far as possible, to balance the interest of each group against those of the other groups.

The delegates wanted to strengthen the national government. At the same time, they feared giving too much power to any government. The delegates believed that "power belongs originally to the people." The liberties of the people would be in danger if government were too independent.

At the same time, the delegates believed that the people's power should not go unchecked. A majority could tyrannize a minority. The poor, for example, outnumbered the wealthy. But the rights of the minority had to be protected.

The delegates differed in just how much they trusted popular rule. At one extreme lay Alexander Hamilton, who at one point declared, "The people, sir, are a great beast." On the other hand, a number of delegates were less fearful about the mass of the people than they were about the grasping power of the few. As one Massachusetts man put it, "These lawyers and men of learning and moneyed men . . . expect to . . . get all the power into their own hands . . . and then they will swallow up all us little folks . . . just as the whale swallowed Jonah."

These philosophical differences came out clearly during the debates. But the delegates kept their eyes on the more practical matter of how the new government would work. The delegates were acutely aware that they were not writing an ideal instrument of government. They also knew that any document they drafted would have to be approved by the voters in the states.

On this latter matter, the delegates quickly took a revolutionary step. The convention had been called for the purpose of revising the Articles of Confederation. But the delegates soon decided that the Articles were hopeless for governing a nation. So they abolished them and started from scratch to invent a new form of government.

Conflict and Compromise

It took the convention only five days to elect a presiding officer, decide on secrecy, and scrap the Articles of Confederation. Then they began to consider what kind of government they wanted.

The Virginia Plan. On May 30, 1787, Virginia's Edmund Randolph proposed a plan of government. Although known as the Virginia or Randolph Plan, it had actually been drafted by James Madison.

The plan provided for a *bicameral*, or two-house, legislature. Instead of the previous unworkable one-state, one-vote arrangement, membership in both houses would be allotted among the states according to their free population. Members of the lower house would be elected by the voters. The lower house in turn would elect members of the upper house. Both houses would then vote for a national executive and a national judiciary. Each of the three branches of government would have specific powers to check and balance the other two.

This system of checks and balances already existed in many states, and Madison believed it ought to exist at the national level as well. The idea quieted the fears of many delegates and made them more willing to give the proposed national government more power. But as debate on the Virginia Plan went on, delegates from the small states grew anxious. They began to realize that the small states were being asked to give up their sovereignty to the larger ones. The states with the largest populations would have the most delegates and the greatest influence in Congress.

The New Jersey Plan. Accordingly, William Paterson introduced the New Jersey Plan. It proposed to keep Congress as a single house. That house would appoint an executive branch of several men and would also appoint a high court. Voting in the legislature would be, as it had been, by states; that is each state would have one vote. The New Jersey Plan also gave two new powers to the proposed legislature—the power to tax and to regulate commerce. The Confederation Congress had neither.

The New Jersey Plan was intended to be a counterproposal to the Virginia Plan. It also contained a provision, the importance of which was not realized at the time. It declared that the decisions of the national government would be "the supreme law of the land." This phrase later proved to be a key one, for it meant that national law should override state law if the two conflicted.

The Great Compromise. The conflict over representation was finally settled by compromise. The convention agreed on a two-house legislature. Representation in the House of Representatives would be according to population, with one representative for every 40,000 people in a state. In the upper house, the Senate, representation would be by states. Each state would have two senators regardless of its population. Members of the House of Representatives would be elected by all the voters who were eligible to vote in elections for their own state's lower house. As Madison pointed out, this would give the people a large voice in the government and make them more loyal to it. The Senate, however, would be elected by the state legislatures. The delegates expected the Senate to be friendlier to the interests of property owners than the popularly elected House of Representatives.

The Three-Fifths Compromise. This first compromise immediately raised an issue that divided southern from northern delegates. If representation in the House of Representatives was apportioned according to population, would slaves be counted as people? Northern delegates argued that slaves were property and therefore could not be represented. "Why should blacks . . . be in the rule of representation more than the cattle and horses of the north?" Southerners argued that "the labor of a slave in South Carolina was as productive and valuable as that of a freeman in Massachusetts . . . and that consequently an equal representation ought to be allowed for them."

Once again the convention compromised. Three-fifths of a slave would be counted for purposes of representation. None of the delegates were completely comfortable with this fraction. Yet there was logic to it. Slaves were in fact treated partly as people and partly as property. Like horses, they could be bought and sold. But unlike horses, they could be tried and punished for murder. The more the delegates discussed slavery, the more uneasy they became. Almost all of them were embarrassed by its existence among a supposedly free people. They were so anxious to avoid the subject that they managed to write the Constitution without actually using the word "slaves." They referred instead to "all other persons" or to "such persons as any of the states now existing shall think proper to admit."

The Slave Trade Compromise. At this point, economic interests came into play. The southern economy was based on the export of staple crops produced by slave labor. But the slave trade had stopped when the Revolutionary War broke out. Since then, only Georgia had resumed importing slaves. Now South Carolina also wanted to resume importation. However, if Congress were given the power to regulate foreign commerce, it might decide to do away with the slave trade. South Carolina and Georgia would never agree to that.

Once again the issue was resolved by compromise. Congress was given the power to regulate foreign commerce. But it could not do anything about the slave trade until 1808. In the meantime, importers would pay a duty of up to ten dollars for each slave brought into the country.

Division of Powers

There were several other areas in which the Philadelphia delegates divided the powers of government between the states and the national government. For example, under the Articles, the states had had the right to keep a standing army and to wage war. Now only the federal government had this right.

The powers which the national government received are called *delegated powers.* Those that were kept by the states are known as *reserved powers.* Thus, states control education, marriage and divorce, and their own highways and other means of transportation.

The delegates adopted this division of powers in order to maintain a balance. On the one hand, they did not want the states to have too much power as compared to the national government. That had been the situation under the Articles, and it had not worked. On the other hand, they did not want the national government to have too much power, for that would mean tyranny. The important thing was that both levels of government should protect the rights of the people.

At the same time, the delegates made it clear that the new government was to be truly national, with the central government supreme over the states. As Gouverneur Morris of New York said, "We had better take a supreme government now, than a despot twenty years hence—for come he must" unless the weaknesses of the Articles were corrected. Morris did not like it that people spoke of themselves only as Georgians or Pennsylvanians, and that they knew and cared almost nothing about people from other states. Yet he was hopeful. "This generation will die away and give place to a race of Americans."

Separation of Powers and Other Matters

In line with their belief in balancing one interest against another, the Philadelphia delegates separated the national government's power into three parts. The Constitution defines the powers of each branch of government.

The Executive. The delegates had briefly toyed with the idea of a monarchy, for some of them believed it had good points as well as bad. However, they soon agreed that popular hatred of King George made a monarchy impossible. Besides, how could the people really control a king?

Then the question arose whether to have a single executive or several of them. The head of a government ought to be vigorous, quick-acting, and responsible. Surely it was easier to find such qualities in three separate individuals rather than in one. In addition, each of the three executives could be "drawn from different portions of the country," thus providing each section with representation. The counter-argument was that each of the thirteen states had a single executive. Having three presidents would lead to conflict and chaos. So the delegates agreed that the executive branch would be headed by one person.

The president was given considerable power. He was to be commander-in-chief of the armed forces. He could make extensive appointments to federal offices, although Senate approval was required for the highest ones. And he could veto acts of Congress.

The Legislature.

Yet the convention was careful to place certain checks on presidential powers. Congress, the legislative branch (consisting of the House of Representatives and the Senate), could override the president's veto by a two-thirds vote. The House of Representatives could *impeach* (bring to trial) the president for "treason, bribery, or other high crimes and misdemeanors." If that happened, the president could be convicted by a two-thirds vote of the Senate. The chief check on executive actions was the fact that the president was an elected rather than appointed official.

As a result of the economic weakness of the Confederation government, the Philadelphia delegates gave Congress considerable financial powers. It received the power to regulate commerce among the states, with foreign powers, and with Indian nations. The clause permitting Congress to pay the debts of the existing United States passed unanimously. No one opposed giving the new Congress power to coin money and set its value, and to borrow on the credit of the new government.

At the same time, the delegates restricted the powers of the states in financial matters. They prohibited states from issuing *bills of credit* (paper money) and provided that no state could violate "the obligations of contracts." States were also banned from taxing commerce with other states.

The Judiciary.

The Articles of Confederation had made no provision for a national system of courts. The new Constitution provided for a Supreme Court to be appointed by the president with the advice and consent of the Senate. It also gave Congress the power to establish lower courts. Federal judges were to hold their offices "during good behavior."

The Supreme Court was given final jurisdiction over cases involving the Constitution, the laws of the United States, and treaties with other countries. The convention failed to make specific provision for judicial review; that is, the Supreme Court was not explicitly given the power to strike down state or federal laws if they violated the Constitution. But Article VI, Section 2, contained the key phrase from the New Jersey Plan—that the Constitution was to be "the supreme law of the land." It was not long before the Supreme Court successfully used this phrase to give itself the power to declare laws unconstitutional.

The Electoral College.

The president and vice-president were not to be chosen directly by the voters. Article 2, Section 1, of the Constitution states that they are to be elected by electors appointed by the states. Each state has as many electors as it has senators and representatives in Congress. But by the middle 1800s the electors were chosen directly by the voters. The person who received the largest number of electoral votes became president. The person receiving the next largest became vice-president.

Rules for Changing the Constitution.

The convention had the foresight to provide for a way to change the Constitution. Amendments could be made through two steps:

1.) approval either by a two-thirds vote of Congress or by a new Constitutional Convention
2.) ratification either by the legislatures of, or conventions in, three-quarters of the states.

The opening passage of the Federalist Papers. *This first in a series of essays appeared in 1788.*

THE

FEDERALIST:

ADDRESSED TO THE

PEOPLE OF THE STATE OF NEW-YORK.

NUMBER I.

Introduction.

AFTER an unequivocal experience of the inefficacy of the subsisting federal government, you are called upon to deliberate on a new constitution for the United States of America. The subject speaks its own importance; comprehending in its consequences, nothing less than the existence of the UNION, the safety and welfare of the parts of which it is composed, the fate of an empire, in many respects, the most interesting in the world. It has been frequently remarked, that it seems to have been reserved to the people of this country, by their conduct and example, to decide the important question, whether societies of men are really capable or not, of establishing good government from reflection and choice, or whether they are forever destined to depend, for their political constitutions, on accident and force. If there be any truth in the remark, the crisis, at which we are arrived, may with propriety be regarded as the æra in which

A   that

Ratification Squeaks Through

On September 17, 1787, the new Constitution was signed by all but three of the delegates present. The convention then sent it to Congress, which forwarded it to the states. This was an "end run" around the state legislatures. Many of those bodies were dominated by people with a personal stake in maintaining the powers of the states. Instead, the Constitution was to be ratified or rejected by special state conventions called solely for that purpose. Nine of the thirteen states had to approve the Constitution for it to go into effect.

The debate over adoption raged for eight months. New Englanders argued in their town meetings. Supporters and opponents alike wrote numerous articles in the press. The most widely circulated of these articles appeared in the *New York Journal* over the signature of Publius. Publius was occasionally James Madison and occasionally John Jay. Most of the time, however, he was Alexander Hamilton. This may seem surprising because Hamilton disapproved of many of the Constitution's provisions. Yet he felt strongly that the government it set up was far better than the "anarchy and convulsion" that had existed under the Articles of Confederation. The Publius articles are now known as *The Federalist Papers*.

Opponents of the Constitution offered numerous arguments that showed their fears of strong, centralized governmental power. Called *Antifederalists* by the *Federalist* friends of the Constitution, the opposition smelled tyranny in nearly every clause. There was no bill of rights. State sovereignty would be destroyed. The president might become king. The territory to be set aside for the national capital would become the nesting ground for an uncontrollable standing army. Tax collectors would swarm about the countryside. Commercial treaties would sell out the South and the West. Debtors would be at the mercy of grasping, monied aristocrats. Besides which, it was not possible for a single government to manage so large a country.

Despite these and other arguments, by July 1788, eleven states had ratified the document. Both North Carolina and Rhode Island rejected the Constitution. Since the new government was now in operation, however, they were left with the choice of ratifying or "going it alone." Both states held new conventions and reversed their earlier decisions.

Historians know something, although not a great deal, about who favored the Constitution and why. Many men seemed to think that the new, stronger government would be favorable to commerce. In general, cities and towns and the regions of the country most touched by commercial activity tended to vote Federalist and for the Constitution. Wealthy men were also inclined to vote for adoption.

In some instances, the opinion about ratification was set by local leaders. Individual local leaders like Patrick Henry and John Hancock were Antifederalist and they carried a great deal of influence. Small farmers in the West and the more rural areas tended also to be Antifederalist.

Finally, if George Washington had not favored the Constitution, it might have been doomed. It was almost universally assumed that the general who had led American troops to victory would be the nation's first president. No one else inspired so much trust.

Benjamin Franklin voiced the optimistic view. At the end of the Constitutional Convention, he pointed to the chair where Washington had sat as presiding officer. On the back of the chair was the painting of a sun. Franklin said, "I have often and often in the course of the session . . . looked at that behind the President without being able to tell whether it was rising or setting; but now at length I have the happiness to know that it is a rising and not a setting sun."

Section 3 Review

COMPREHENSION   Developing Vocabulary

1. Explain these terms: bicameral, delegated powers, reserved powers, impeach, bills of credit, Anti-Federalists, Federalist, New Jersey Plan.

COMPREHENSION   Mastering Facts

1. Why did the Philadelphia delegates decide to scrap the Articles of Confederation?
2. Under the "Great Compromise" how many representatives would each state have in the House of Representatives?
3. What was the three-fifths compromise?
4. How can the Constitution of the United States be changed?

CHAPTER 8 Review

Chapter Summary

The most important task for the new nation was to create a national government. Delegates to the Continental Congress responded by forming the Articles of Confederation; however, they proved to be too weak to deal with many important problems. Finally, at the Constitutional Convention in 1787, a distinguished group of delegates—through a series of compromises—shaped a new federal system of government. By 1788 the states had ratified the new Constitution.

Questions for Critical Thinking

COMPREHENSION Summarizing Main Ideas

1. What were the main accomplishments of the Confederation Congress? What were the main weaknesses of the Articles of Confederation?
2. What were the causes of Shays's Rebellion? What was its outcome?
3. What are the main differences between a federal union and a confederation?
4. How does the Constitution provide for the election of the president and vice-president?
5. How can Congress check the power of the president? How can the president check the power of Congress?
6. How can the federal judiciary check Congress and the president? How can Congress and the president check the federal judiciary?
7. Why is the Constitution regarded as "the supreme law of the land"?

COMPREHENSION Interpreting Events

1. How many states sent delegates to the Annapolis Convention? How many sent delegates to the Philadelphia Convention? How do you account for the difference in the response?
2. Why did the delegates to the Philadelphia Convention decide to keep the proceedings secret? Do you agree with their decision? Why or why not? How do historians know what happened at the convention?
3. Tell whether you would have favored or opposed ratification of the Constitution—and give reasons for your decision—if you had been (a) a Pennsylvania farmer who owed a large sum of money; (b) a free black; (c) a New York banker; (d) a Georgia plantation owner; (e) a government official in Maryland with no experience at the national level; (f) a woman living on a farm along the Virginia frontier; (g) a Boston shipbuilder.

APPLICATION Using Skills To Understand Time

Another factor in developing a sense of time is the ability to arrange facts in chronological order. For each of the following groups, indicate which event came first.

1. Virginia gives up its claim to western lands to the national government; Spain closes the port of New Orleans to American trade.
2. The Constitution is ratified; the Northwest Ordinance is adopted.
3. Benjamin Franklin spends a hot summer in Philadelphia; Daniel Shays leads a march on the arsenal at Springfield, Massachusetts.
4. Alexander Hamilton writes a series of articles for the *New York Journal;* James Madison convinces Virginia to call a general meeting of the states at Annapolis.

EVALUATION Comparing Past to Present

1. Which of the suffrage requirements that were included in the first state constitutions are still in effect today?
2. What arguments against a strong national government were presented in 1787? Do these arguments apply today? Why or why not?
3. In order to see how the Bill of Rights works in everyday life, class members should develop a bulletin board display on civil rights issues. Newspaper and magazine clippings, cartoons, and photographs should be brought in periodically and arranged under such headings as "Freedom of Speech," "Freedom of Religion," "Freedom of the Press," and the like. An explanation of the constitutional significance of each item should be included.

The Constitution

CONTENTS OF THE CONSTITUTION

"In framing a system which we wish to last for ages, we should not lose sight of the changes which ages will produce," said James Madison in 1787. Since then the *Constitution of the United States*, the document which established our system of government, has withstood the test of time. The fifty-five delegates who shaped the Constitution lived in a mostly rural America. For the most part they were planters, merchants, small farmers, and self-educated citizens. Two hundred years later, most Americans live in urban areas and are educated in public schools. They are pilots, computer operators, and factory workers. Still, the Constitution has managed to fulfill Madison's hope.

The Constitution, a remarkable document, has grown and changed with the times. But even as it has changed, the Constitution has maintained its original purpose: to protect the rights and diverse interests of Americans. Where does this protection come from? First, it comes from the idea that the government's power is specifically delegated by its people. Second, protection comes from the system of *federalism* that divides power between states and the national government. A third source of protection is the division of the federal government into three branches—legislative, executive, and judicial. This provides a system of checks and balances. Finally, a method of making changes exists through amendment and court interpretations.

In these pages you will learn: (1) what the Constitution means; (2) how the government is organized; (3) why the Constitution is a living document; and (4) why the Constitution is a source of pride.

The Constitution is printed on color panels. Following each panel is an explanation of that part. Each **Article,** or major part, is made up of **Sections.** Each paragraph within a section is called a **Clause.** Headings have been added, and the spelling and punctuation modernized for easier reading. Portions of the Constitution no longer in use have been crossed out. The final section explains how court cases have added to application of the Constitution.

Original Articles of the Constitution

THE PREAMBLE.
The Purpose of the Constitution

We, the people of the United States, in order to form a more perfect Union, establish justice, insure domestic tranquillity, provide for the common defense, promote the general welfare, and secure the blessings of liberty to ourselves and our posterity, do ordain and establish this Constitution for the United States of America.

Creating a new government is a momentous undertaking. The framers wanted to make their reasoning clear to other Americans and the rest of the world. The framers wanted the people to understand that their new government rested on great principles. These included freedom, equality, justice, and safety. The *Preamble*, or introduction, states the basic purposes of the government of the United States.

When the framers of the Constitution drafted it, they stated the source of their authority to do so. They said their authority came from the people. Basic to our form of government is the idea that the people have the right and the power to determine how they should be governed. The Constitution outlines the structure of the government of the United States. The Preamble challenges every generation to reestablish the principles of the Constitution.

ARTICLE 1. The Legislature

The First Article of the Constitution describes what the *legislative* branch is and what it can and cannot do. With the Second and Third Articles, this part of the Constitution assures the *separation of powers* of the central government into three components: the legislative, executive, and judicial branches.

SECTION 1. Congress

All legislative powers herein granted shall be vested in a Congress of the United States, which shall consist of a Senate and House of Representatives.

VOCABULARY FOR ARTICLES

Constitution of the United States, document that has been the basis of the government of the United States since 1788, when it replaced the Articles of Confederation. See pages 169–194.

Elastic Clause, clause 18 of the 8th section of Article 1 of the Constitution. This clause allows Congress to do what is "necessary and proper" to carry out its functions. Congress has used the vague wording of the elastic clause to allow it to adjust to changing conditions. See page 175.

Electoral College, group of individuals who actually elect the President; members are chosen by state elections. See page 177.

Executive, part of government that enforces laws and carries out policies. The President is head of the executive branch. See page 177.

Federalism, principle that divides governmental power between national, state, and local governments that are each directly responsible to the people who elected them. See page 168.

Felony, serious crime punishable by at least a year in prison. See page 183.

Judicial, part of government that has the responsibility to interpret the law. The judicial branch of our government is headed by the Supreme Court. See page 181.

Jury, body of citizens that judges an individual suspected of committing a crime. See page 182.

Legislative, part of government that makes laws and policies. See page 169.

Misdemeanor, minor crime usually punishable by a fine or a short prison sentence. See page 181.

Override, vote by Congress to pass a law despite a veto by the President; an override requires a two-thirds majority vote in each house of Congress. See page 174.

Preamble, introductory statement indicating the purpose of a document. The Preamble to the Constitution of the United States lists six purposes of that document. See page 169.

Republic, form of government where citizens elect representatives to serve in government. Republics are based on the belief that all power is ultimately held by the people. See page 183.

Separation of Powers, principle that divides powers of government among different branches of government. Each branch has specific powers. See page 169, also chart on page 177.

Only Congress has the power to make laws. Making laws is what is meant by legislative powers. Congress is made up of two houses—the Senate and House of Representatives. This **bicameral,** or two-house, legislature is the result of a "great compromise" agreed upon during the Constitutional Convention (see page 163).

SECTION 2. The House of Representatives

1. Elections. *The House of Representatives shall be composed of members chosen every second year by the people of the several states, and the electors in each state shall have the qualifications requisite for electors of the most numerous branch of the state legislature.*
2. Qualifications. *No person shall be a Representative who shall not have attained to the age of twenty-five years, and been seven years a citizen of the United States, and who shall not, when elected, be an inhabitant of that state in which he shall be chosen.*

The second paragraph of this section specifies the constitutional requirements for Representatives: age, citizenship, and state residence. In addition, the first paragraph, or clause, indicates that states must hold elections for their Representatives every two years. Such frequent elections, the framers of the Constitution thought, would keep Representatives responsive to the people. Voter qualifications are determined by the states. Some states used this power to limit voting to white males. Amendments 15, 19, 24, and 26 have extended voting rights to people who previously had not been allowed to vote because of state laws.

There are 435 Representatives, a number fixed by Congress in 1912. Over the years, however, each state's allotment of Representatives has varied. The number of Representatives for each state is based on that state's population.

3. Number of Representatives.
Representatives ~~and direct taxes~~ shall be apportioned among the several states which may be included within this Union according to their respective numbers, ~~which shall be determined by adding to the whole number of free persons, including those bound to service for a term of years, and excluding Indians not taxed, three fifths of all other persons~~.

The actual enumeration shall be made within three years after the first meeting of the Congress of the United States, and within every subsequent term of ten years, in such a manner as they shall by law direct. The number of Representatives shall not exceed one for every thirty thousand, but each state shall have at least one Representative; ~~and until such enumeration shall be made, the state of New Hampshire shall be entitled to choose 3, Massachusetts, 8, Rhode Island and Providence Plantations, 1, Connecticut, 5, New York, 6, New Jersey, 4, Pennsylvania, 8, Delaware, 1, Maryland, 6, Virginia, 10, North Carolina, 5, South Carolina, 5, and Georgia, 3~~.
4. Vacancies. *When vacancies happen in the representation from any state, the executive authority thereof shall issue writs of election to fill such vacancies.*
5. Officers and Impeachment. *The House of Representatives shall choose their Speaker and other officers; and shall have the sole power of impeachment.*

The portions of this section no longer in use were part of the "Three-fifths Compromise," which

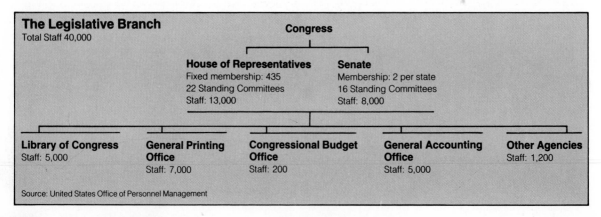

The Legislative Branch
Total Staff 40,000

Congress

House of Representatives
Fixed membership: 435
22 Standing Committees
Staff: 13,000

Senate
Membership: 2 per state
16 Standing Committees
Staff: 8,000

Library of Congress
Staff: 5,000

General Printing Office
Staff: 7,000

Congressional Budget Office
Staff: 200

General Accounting Office
Staff: 5,000

Other Agencies
Staff: 1,200

Source: United States Office of Personnel Management

counted three-fifths of the slave population in each state for purposes of representation and direct taxes. Here, the term direct taxes means poll and property taxes. The Thirteenth Amendment abolished slavery; the Sixteenth Amendment changed the direct taxes provision; and the Twenty-Fourth Amendment abolished poll taxes and other taxes that had been requirements for voting.

To determine the number of Representatives each state has, Congress counts Americans every ten years (five years beginning in 1985). Each member of the House now represents about 500,000 persons. When a Representative dies in office or leaves office before his or her term is over, the state governor is to call an election to fill the vacancy.

The final clause gives the House of Representatives the power to organize members into committees and the power to impeach. **Impeachment** is the process of accusing a public official of a crime or serious misbehavior. One President, Andrew Johnson, was impeached by the House, but the Senate found him not guilty of the charges made against him. Other federal officials have been impeached, tried in the Senate, and removed from office.

SECTION 3.   The Senate

1. Numbers. *The Senate of the United States shall be composed of two Senators from each state, chosen by the legislature thereof for six years; and each Senator shall have one vote.*

2. Classifying Terms. *Immediately after they shall be assembled in consequence of the first election, they shall be divided as equally as may be into three classes. The seats of the Senator of the first class shall be vacated at the expiration of the second year, of the second class at the expiration of the fourth year, and of the third class at the expiration of the sixth year, so that one third may be chosen every second year, and if vacancies happen by resignation or otherwise during the recess of the legislature of any state, the executive thereof may make temporary appointments until the next meeting of the legislature, which shall then fill such vacancies.*

3. Qualifications. *No person shall be a Senator who shall not have attained to the age of thirty years and been nine years a citizen of the United States, and who shall not when elected be an inhabitant of that state for which he shall be chosen.*

The Senate has two Senators from each state. Until 1913, Senators were elected by the state legislatures. The Seventeenth Amendment changed that rule by allowing the voters to choose their Senators directly. Each Senator is elected for a six-year term.

The third clause specifies the constitutional requirements for Senators. A Senator must be at least thirty, a citizen of the United States for nine years, and a resident of the state in which he is elected.

4. Role of Vice-President. *The Vice-President of the United States shall be President of the Senate, but shall have no vote unless they be equally divided.*

5. Officers. *The Senate shall choose their officers, and also a President pro tempore, in the absence of the Vice-President, or when he shall exercise the office of the President of the United States.*

6. Impeachment Trials. *The Senate shall have the sole power to try all impeachments. When sitting for that purpose, they shall be on oath or affirmation. When the President of the United States is tried, the Chief Justice shall preside; and no person shall be convicted without the concurrence of two-thirds of the members present.*

7. Punishment for Impeachment. *Judgment in cases of impeachment shall not extend further than to removal from office and disqualification to hold and enjoy any office of honor, trust, or profit under the United States; but the party convicted shall nevertheless be liable and subject to indictment, trial, judgment, and punishment, according to law.*

The Vice-President presides at Senate meetings but votes only when there is a tie.

The Senate also organizes into committees and chooses its other officers, including the **president pro tempore,** who presides over the Senate in the absence of the Vice-President. The Twenty-Fifth Amendment now provides for filling the vacant office of the Vice-President.

The last two clauses give the Senate the power to act as a court at impeachment trials. The Senate's power to punish a convicted official is limited, however. The Senate can remove the official from office and bar him or her from holding another United States government office. The convicted person can then be tried in the regular courts for the crime(s) that caused the loss of office and punished if found guilty.

How a Bill Becomes a Law

1
Bill Is Introduced.

A bill can be introduced in either the House or the Senate, where it is then assigned to a committee for study.

2
Approved by Committee.

Committee makes recommendation that the bill be placed on calendar.

3
Vote of House Members.

Either house reads, debates, and votes on bill. If approved by majority, bill is passed and referred to the other house.

4
Passed by Other House.

Committee reviews bill. Bill read, debated, and voted on by all members. Majority vote passes it.

SECTION 4. Congressional Elections

1. Regulations. *The times, places, and manner of holding elections for Senators and Representatives shall be prescribed in each state by the legislature thereof; but the Congress may at any time by law make or alter such regulations except as to the places of choosing Senators.*

2. Sessions. *The Congress shall assemble at least once in every year, and such meeting shall be on the first Monday in December, unless they shall by law appoint a different day.*

Federal law now requires all states to hold elections for Congress on the first Tuesday after the first Monday in November in even-numbered years. The Seventeenth Amendment provides for Senators to be elected at the same voting places as other officials.

The English kings had often kept Parliament from meeting simply by not calling it together. This is the reason for the provision that Congress must meet once a year.

The Twentieth Amendment changed Congress's meeting time to January 3, unless Congress itself rules otherwise.

SECTION 5. Rules and Procedures

1. Quorum. *Each house shall be the judge of the elections, returns, and qualifications of its own members, and a majority of each shall constitute a quorum to do business; but a smaller number may adjourn from day to day and may be authorized to compel the attendance of absent members in such manner and under such penalties as each house may provide.*

2. Rules and Conduct. *Each house may determine the rules of its proceedings, punish its*
members for disorderly behavior, and, with the concurrence of two-thirds, expel a member.

3. Congressional Records. *Each house shall keep a journal of its proceedings, and from time to time publish the same, excepting such parts as may in their judgment require secrecy; and the yeas and nays of the members of either house on any question shall, at the desire of one-fifth of those present, be entered on the journal.*

4. Adjournment. *Neither house, during the session of Congress, shall without the consent of the other adjourn, for more than three days, nor to any other place than that in which the two houses shall be sitting.*

Both the House and the Senate decide whether their members are legally qualified and have been fairly elected. On the basis of this section, members of Congress refused to seat members from the former Confederate states in the election following the Civil War (see page 360).

Each house disciplines its own members when the activities of those members are judged to be improper. Under this clause, Senator Joseph R. McCarthy was condemned in 1954 for his improper search for Communists. Representative Adam Clayton Powell was denied his seat in 1967 on the charge that he had misused government funds. Senator Herman Talmadge was "denounced" in 1979 for financial irregularities. Representative Charles Diggs was also censured in 1979 for financial misconduct. More recently, members of Congress have been disciplined for their roles in the Abscam investigations, and for improper moral behavior.

The proceedings of both the Senate and the House of Representatives have been published together in the *Congressional Record* since 1873. The *Record* comes out daily while Congress is in session. It will omit certain matters if Congress decides that they are

5
Differences Worked Out.

Joint Conference Committee works out differences in bill. Revised bill passes both houses.

6
Enrolled and Signed.

Bill is printed and verified. Vice-President signs bill and sends it to President.

7
Made a Law.

President signs bill—or holds it ten days without signing it—and it becomes a law.

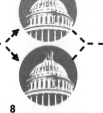

8
Passed over Veto.

If President vetoes bill, two-thirds vote of both houses makes it a law.

secret. It must show, however, how each member voted if one-fifth of the members present agree.

The last clause provides Congress with the power to decide when and where it should meet. Both houses must agree to any recess that extends beyond three days, and both must meet in the same city.

SECTION 6. Payment and Privileges

1. Salary. *The Senators and Representatives shall receive a compensation for their services, to be ascertained by law, and paid out of the Treasury of the United States. They shall in all cases, except treason, felony, and breach of the peace, be privileged from arrest during their attendance at the session of their respective houses, and in going to and returning from the same; and for any speech or debate in either house they shall not be questioned in any other place.*

2. Restrictions. *No Senator or Representative shall, during the time for which he was elected, be appointed to any civil office under the authority of the United States which shall have been created or the emoluments whereof shall have been increased during such time; and no person holding any office under the United States shall be a member of either house during his continuance in office.*

Senators and Representatives receive a salary of $60,662.50 a year, plus office space and allowances for office costs, staff salaries, travel, and similar expenses. Congressional **immunity,** freedom from arrest, protects members while going to and from congressional work. Like all Americans, both Senators and Representatives may be arrested for breaking the law. A member of Congress also has immunity

from prosecution for libel or slander during congressional debates or in official reports.

The second clause was included so that no member of Congress would be able to profit personally from laws that he or she helped make. This keeps Senators and Representatives from creating jobs to which they might later be appointed or from raising the salaries of jobs they someday hope to hold.

SECTION 7. How a Bill Becomes a Law

1. Tax Bills. *All bills for raising revenue shall originate in the House of Representatives; but the Senate may propose or concur with amendments as on other bills.*

The tradition of the tax bill originating in the lower house of the legislature is a part of our legacy from England, where tax measures start in the House of Commons. However, the Senate can amend the tax bill to the extent that it rewrites the whole measure.

2. Law-Making Process. *Every bill which shall have passed the House of Representatives and the Senate shall before it becomes a law be presented to the President of the United States. If he approves, he shall sign it; but if not, he shall return it with his objections to that house in which it shall have originated, who shall enter the objections at large on their journal and proceed to reconsider it. If after such reconsideration two-thirds of that house shall agree to pass the bill, it shall be sent, together with the objections, to the other house, by which it shall likewise be reconsidered; and if approved by two-thirds of that house, it shall become a law. But in all such cases the votes of both houses shall be determined by yeas and nays, and*

173

the names of the persons voting for and against the bill shall be entered on the journal of each house respectively.

If any bill shall not be returned by the President within ten days (Sundays excepted) after it shall have been presented to him, the same shall be a law in like manner as if he had signed it, unless the Congress by their adjournment prevent its return, in which case it shall not be a law.

3. Role of President. *Every order, resolution, or vote to which the concurrence of the Senate and House of Representatives may be necessary (except on a question of adjournment) shall be presented to the President of the United States; and before the same shall take effect, shall be approved by him, or being disapproved by him, shall be repassed by two-thirds of the Senate and House of Representatives, according to the rules and limitations prescribed in the case of a bill.*

A bill that gains a majority vote in both the House and the Senate must be sent to the President. The President can: (1) sign it and make it a law; (2) hold it for ten days without signing it, after which time it still becomes a law; or (3) veto, or refuse to sign it, and return it to Congress with his reasons for doing so. These clauses keep Congress from making laws without the agreement of the President. They are a strong check because only 5 percent of the bills have passed over presidential vetoes.

A bill can still become a law if each house *overrides* the President's veto and passes the bill by a two-thirds majority. When a bill is sent to the President near the end of a congressional session, the President can hold it. If Congress adjourns within ten days, it does not become law if the President does not sign it. This is called a **pocket veto.** Franklin Roosevelt used 263 such vetoes. The chart on pages 172-173 shows the process by which a bill becomes a law.

SECTION 8. Powers Granted to Congress

1. Taxation. *The Congress shall have power to lay and collect taxes, duties, imposts, and excises, to pay the debts and provide for the common defense and general welfare of the United States; but all duties, imposts, and excises shall be uniform throughout the United States.*

2. Credit. *To borrow money on the credit of the United States.*

3. Commerce. *To regulate commerce with foreign nations, and among the several states, and with the Indian tribes.*

This section lists the powers granted to Congress. Clause 1 grants Congress the power to establish uniform taxes. **Duties** are taxes on goods coming into the United States. **Excises** are taxes on the manufacture, sale, or use of goods made within the country. Imposts are other taxes on imported goods.

Clause 2 is the basis for national banks and the Federal Reserve System. There is no limit on the amount of money the government can borrow.

Clause 3 was intended to remedy a weakness of the Articles of Confederation. Over the years, the Supreme Court has interpreted this clause so that Congress can regulate many forms of interstate commerce. As a result, Congress is concerned not only about commercial activity that crosses state boundaries but also about activity that affects commerce in more than one state. For instance, Congress can pass laws and provide funds to improve waterways, to enforce air safety measures, and to forbid interstate shipment of certain goods.

Congress can also regulate the movement of people, of stocks and bonds, and of television signals. It is a federal crime for people to flee across state lines from state or local police. This clause sees that interstate travelers receive fair treatment regardless of race or nationality.

4. Naturalization, Bankruptcy. *To establish a uniform rule of naturalization, and uniform laws on the subject of bankruptcies throughout the United States.*

5. Money. *To coin money, regulate the value thereof and foreign coin, and fix the standard of weights and measures.*

6. Counterfeiting. *To provide for the punishment of counterfeiting the securities and current coin of the United States.*

Clause 4 insures uniform rules for **naturalization,** the process of becoming a citizen, and rules for people who owe debts they cannot pay.

Clause 5 gives Congress the right to make currency and to regulate its value.

Clause 6 allows Congress to decide punishment for people who make imitation government bonds, stamps, or money.

7. Post Office. *To establish post offices and post roads.*

8. Patents, Copyrights. *To promote the progress of science and useful arts, by securing for limited times to authors and investors the exclusive right to their respective writings and discoveries.*

9. Federal Court. *To constitute tribunals inferior to the Supreme Court.*

10. International Law. *To define and punish piracies and felonies committed on the high seas, and offenses against the law of nations.*

Congress has attempted to reform the Post Office Department, making it an independent agency. Postal workers now have the right to organize and to bargain collectively. (See chart on page 179.)

Clause 8 gives Congress the responsibility to promote science, industry, and the arts by making laws under which inventors, writers, and artists receive patents and copyrights to protect their own works. A **patent** is an official document that gives an inventor the exclusive right to make, use, or sell the invention for a specified number of years. A **copyright** is the exclusive right to publish or perform literary, artistic, or musical works for a certain number of years (usually twenty-eight).

Clause 9 allows Congress to set up the federal district courts, the United States Courts of Appeals, and other special courts.

Through Clause 10, Congress has the power to make laws regarding crimes committed on the seas or oceans. It also has power to make laws to punish persons who break international laws.

11. War. *To declare war, ~~grant letters of marque and reprisal~~, and make rules concerning captures on land and water.*

12. Armed Forces. *To raise and support armies, but no appropriation of money to that use shall be for a longer term than two years.*

13. Navy. *To provide and maintain a navy.*

14. Regulation for Armed Forces. *To make rules for the government and regulation of the land and naval forces.*

15. Militia. *To provide for calling forth the militia to execute the laws of the Union, suppress insurrections, and repel invasions.*

16. Regulations for Militia. *To provide for organizing, arming, and disciplining the mili-*

tia, and for governing such part of them as may be employed in the service of the United States, reserving to the states, respectively, the appointment of the officers and the authority of training the militia according to the discipline prescribed by Congress.

According to Clause 11, only Congress can declare war. However, the President has taken military action without the consent of Congress in the case of the Korean War (1950–1953) and the Vietnam War (1957–1975). **Letters of marque** or **reprisal** are documents that authorize vessels to attack enemy ships. They are outlawed by international law today and reference to them is deleted in the clause.

The next clauses, including the two-year limit for appropriations, were intended to keep the army under the control of civilians. The navy, which was young and small, was not placed under that limitation. An air force was not even imagined then.

Clause 16 provides for a National Militia, popularly called the National Guard. Congress has given the President power to decide when a state of emergency exists. Then, the President, as its Commander in Chief, can call out the National Guard.

17. District of Columbia. *To exercise exclusive legislation in all cases whatsoever over such district (not exceeding ten miles square) as may, by cession of particular states and the acceptance of Congress, become the seat of government of the United States; and to exercise like authority over all places purchased by the consent of the legislature of the state in which the same shall be, for the erection of forts, magazines, arsenals, dockyards, and other needful buildings.*

18. Elastic Clause. *And to make all laws which shall be necessary and proper for carrying into execution the foregoing powers and all other powers vested by this Constitution in the government of the United States, or in any department or office thereof.*

Congress is the legislative body for the District of Columbia and for all federal property on which forts, naval bases, arsenals, and other federal works or buildings are located.

This final clause of Section 8 is called the "necessary and proper" clause, or sometimes the *elastic clause*. It allows Congress to deal with many matters not specifically mentioned in the Constitution.

SECTION 9. Powers Denied Congress

~~1. Slave Trade. *The migration or importation of such persons as any of the states now existing shall think proper to admit shall not be prohibited by the Congress prior to the year one thousand eight hundred and eight, but a tax or duty may be imposed on such importation, not exceeding ten dollars for each person.*~~

2. Habeas Corpus. *The privilege of the writ of habeas corpus shall not be suspended, unless when in cases of rebellion or invasion the public safety may require it.*

3. Illegal Punishment. *No bill of attainder or ex post facto law shall be passed.*

4. Direct Taxes. *No capitation or other direct tax shall be laid, unless in proportion to the census or enumeration herein before directed to be taken.*

5. Export Taxes. *No tax or duty shall be laid on articles exported from any state.*

The first clause, now obsolete, refers to foreign slave trade. Congress passed a law in 1808 stopping the importation of slaves.

A **writ of habeas corpus** is a legal order that protects people from being held in jail on weak evidence or none at all. During the Civil War Abraham Lincoln suspended the writ of habeas corpus in certain areas. Chief Justice Taney ruled in the *Merryman* case (1861) that only Congress had the right to suspend the writ of habeas corpus. Lincoln disagreed and continued to follow his own interpretation. Several other Presidents have, too.

A **bill of attainder** is an act passed by a legislature to punish a person without a trial. An **ex post facto law** is one that provides punishment for an act that was legal when the act was committed. This clause indicates that punishment for disregarding a law is the responsibility of the courts, not Congress.

A **capitation** is a head tax; the word comes from the Latin designation for "head." Congress cannot levy head taxes, or poll taxes, unless all persons (men, women, and children) in the United States are taxed the same. Other direct taxes must also be based on population. The Sixteenth Amendment made it legal to have an income tax.

Clause 5 refers to **export taxes,** taxes on goods sent to other states or to foreign countries. Congress can regulate or prohibit shipment of certain items, but it cannot tax goods for being sent out of any state.

6. No Favorites. *No preference shall be given by any regulation of commerce or revenue to the ports of one state over those of another; nor shall vessels bound to or from one state be obliged to enter, clear, or pay duties to another.*

7. Public Money. *No money shall be drawn from the Treasury but in consequence of appropriations made by law; and a regular statement and account of the receipts and expenditures of all public money shall be published from time to time.*

8. Titles of Nobility. *No title of nobility shall be granted by the United States; and no person holding any office of profit or trust under them shall without the consent of the Congress accept of any present, emolument, office, or title of any kind whatever from any king, prince, or foreign state.*

Clause 6 says that Congress cannot make any laws that favor one state more than another in matters of trade and commerce. Interstate commerce was strengthened by the provision that ships from one state may enter the ports of any other state without paying charges.

Clause 7 requires that government money be spent only after Congress passes a law for that purpose. A statement of federal income and spending must be published.

According to Clause 8, a United States official cannot have titles of nobility. A federal officer may not accept a title, position, or gift from a foreign government without the consent of Congress.

SECTION 10. Powers Denied the States

1. Restrictions. *No state shall enter into any treaty, alliance, or confederation; grant letters of marque and reprisal; coin money; emit bills of credit; make anything but gold and silver coin a tender in payment of debts; pass any bill of attainder, ex post facto law, or law impairing the obligation of contracts, or grant any title of nobility.*

Clause 1 presents certain activities that State governments cannot do. States cannot: (1) make treaties; (2) permit private citizens to make war on other nations; (3) issue money; (4) disregard federal laws dealing with money; (5) pass the kinds of laws forbidden by

Federalism

Powers of the Federal Government	Powers Shared by State and Federal Governments	Powers of State Governments
declare war sign treaties regulate interstate commerce coin money	levy taxes build roads finance schools	issue marriage licenses pass state laws regulate intrastate commerce

Section 9, Clause 3; (6) pass laws excusing people from carrying out lawful agreements; or (7) issue titles of nobility.

> **2. Import and Export Taxes.** *No state shall, without the consent of the Congress, lay any imposts or duties on imports or exports, except what may be absolutely necessary for executing its inspection laws; and the net produce of all duties and imposts, laid by any state on imports or exports, shall be for the use of the Treasury of the United States; and all such laws shall be subject to the revision and control of the Congress.*
>
> **3. Peacetime and War Restraints.** *No state shall, without the consent of Congress, lay any duty of tonnage, keep troops or ships of war in time of peace, enter into any agreement or compact with another state, or with a foreign power, or engage in war, unless actually invaded, or in such imminent danger as will not admit of delay.*

Clauses 2 and 3 specify the following things that states may do only with the consent or approval of Congress: (1) tax goods entering or leaving a state beyond what is needed to cover costs of inspection; (2) tax ships; (3) keep state troops or warships in time of peace; (4) make separate alliances with other states or foreign countries; and (5) go to war.

ARTICLE 2. The Executive Department

The President is given a number of powers in the Constitution, but the Constitution is vague about how the President is to use these powers. The primary responsibility of the President is to **execute,** or carry out, the laws of the United States. The President's strength lies in his or her interpretation of the Constitution and how the powers are used.

The powers of the President have grown since the writing of the Constitution. Strong Presidents have expanded the powers of the chief executive and the *executive* department. Although the specified powers of the President have not changed, presidential customs have.

SECTION 1. The Presidency

> **1. Term of Office.** *The executive power shall be vested in a President of the United States of America. He shall hold his office during the term of four years and, together with the Vice-President, chosen for the same term, be elected as follows.*
>
> **2. Electoral College.** *Each state shall appoint, in such manner as the legislature thereof may direct, a number of electors, equal to the whole number of Senators and Representatives to which the state may be entitled in the Congress; but no Senator or Representative, or person holding an office of trust or profit under the United States, shall be appointed an elector.*
>
> ~~**3. Former Method of Electing President.** *The electors shall meet in their respective states and vote by ballot for two persons, of whom one at least shall not be an inhabitant of the same state with themselves. And they shall make a list of all the persons voted for, and of the number of votes for each, which list they shall sign and certify and transmit, sealed, to the seat of the*~~

Powers and Levels of Government

Powers	Federal	State	Local	
			City	School
Legislative	Congress	State Legislature	City Council	School Board
Executive	President	Governor	Mayor or City Manager	Superintendent
Judicial	Federal District Court	State Court	Traffic Court	School Board

government of the United States, directed to the president of the Senate. The president of the Senate shall, in the presence of the Senate and the House of Representatives, open all the certificates, and the votes shall then be counted. The person having the greatest number of votes shall be the President, if such number be a majority of the whole number of electors appointed, and if there be more than one who have such majority, and have an equal number of votes, then the House of Representatives shall immediately choose by ballot one of them for President, and if no person have a majority, then from the five highest on the list the said House shall in like manner choose the President. But in choosing the President, the vote shall be taken by states, the representation from each state having one vote. A quorum for this purpose shall consist of a member or members from two-thirds of the states, and a majority of all the states shall be necessary to a choice. In every case, after the choice of President, the person having the greatest number of votes of the electors shall be the Vice-President. But if there should remain two or more who have equal votes, the Senate shall choose from them by ballot the Vice-President.

4. Election Day. *The Congress may determine the time of choosing the electors and the day on which they shall give their votes, which day shall be the same throughout the United States.*

Requirements for Holding Federal Office

Position	Minimum Age	Residency	Citizenship
House of Representatives	25	state in which elected	7 years
Senate	30	state in which elected	9 years
President	35	14 years in the United States	natural-born
Supreme Court	none	none	none

Full executive power of the United States is vested in the President, who holds office for a four-year term. The people of the United States do not vote directly for the President. Each state chooses electors who in turn make up the *electoral college*. Each state has as many electors as it has members of Congress.

Clause 3 describes the original method for electing the President and Vice-President. This procedure was changed by the Twelfth Amendment after the election of 1796 resulted in a President and Vice-President of different political parties being elected (see page 214).

Clause 4 provides that the day when electors vote must be the same throughout the United States. When citizens go to the polls on the first Tuesday after the first Monday in November to vote for the

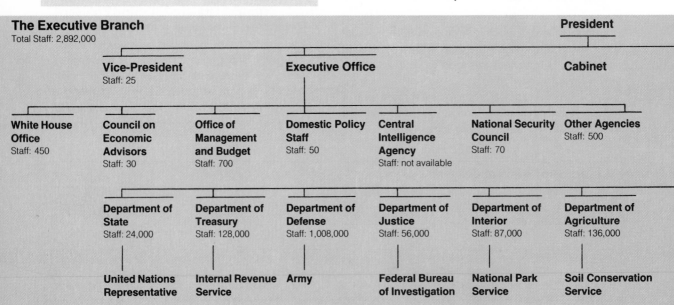

The Executive Branch
Total Staff: 2,892,000

President

Vice-President
Staff: 25

Executive Office

Cabinet

White House Office
Staff: 450

Council on Economic Advisors
Staff: 30

Office of Management and Budget
Staff: 700

Domestic Policy Staff
Staff: 50

Central Intelligence Agency
Staff: not available

National Security Council
Staff: 70

Other Agencies
Staff: 500

Department of State
Staff: 24,000

Department of Treasury
Staff: 128,000

Department of Defense
Staff: 1,008,000

Department of Justice
Staff: 56,000

Department of Interior
Staff: 87,000

Department of Agriculture
Staff: 136,000

United Nations Representative

Internal Revenue Service

Army

Federal Bureau of Investigation

National Park Service

Soil Conservation Service

President and Vice-President, they vote for the electors. The electors cast their votes on the first Monday after the second Wednesday in December. Only Congress has the power to set or change these days regarding electors.

> **5. Qualifications.** *No person except a natural-born citizen ~~or citizen of the United States at the time of the adoption of this Constitution~~ shall be eligible to the office of President; neither shall any person be eligible to that office who shall not have attained the age of thirty-five years and been fourteen years a resident within the United States.*
>
> **6. Succession.** *In case of the removal of the President from office, or of his death, resignation, or inability to discharge the powers and duties of the said office, the same shall devolve on the Vice-President, and the Congress may by law provide for the case of removal, death, resignation, or inability, both of the President and Vice-President, declaring what officer shall then act as President, and such officer shall act accordingly until the disability be removed or a President shall be elected.*

Clause 5 states that the President of the United States must be at least thirty-five years of age, a native citizen, and must have lived in the United States at least fourteen years.

Clause 6 has been changed by the Twenty-Fifth Amendment. This amendment clarifies the pro-

cedure for dealing with vacancies in the offices of President and Vice-President.

> **7. Salary.** *The President shall at stated times receive for his services a compensation, which shall neither be increased nor diminished during the period for which he shall have been elected, and he shall not receive within that period any other emolument from the United States, or any of them.*

The President's salary is $200,000 a year, with a $50,000 annual allowance for expenses and additional allowances for travel, staff support, and maintenance of the White House. After leaving office, the President is eligible for a pension of $69,630 per year, clerical assistants, office space, and free mailing privileges. Widowed wives of former Presidents get a pension of $20,000 per year. The President may not receive any other pay from the federal government or from the states.

> **8. Oath of Office.** *Before he enter on the execution of his office, he shall take the following oath or affirmation: "I do solemnly swear (or affirm) that I will faithfully execute the office of President of the United States, and will to the best of my ability preserve, protect, and defend the Constitution of the United States."*

The Constitution does not say who shall give the oath to the newly-elected President. Presidents have

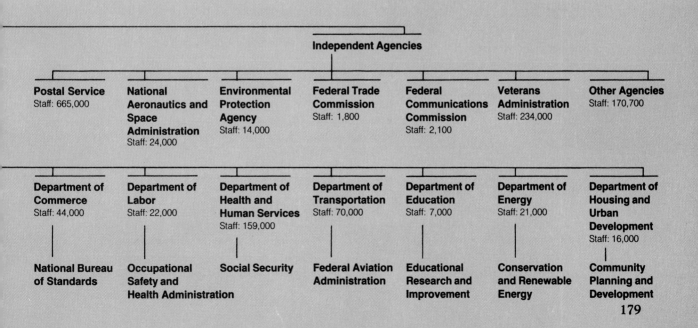

Independent Agencies

| Postal Service Staff: 665,000 | National Aeronautics and Space Administration Staff: 24,000 | Environmental Protection Agency Staff: 14,000 | Federal Trade Commission Staff: 1,800 | Federal Communications Commission Staff: 2,100 | Veterans Administration Staff: 234,000 | Other Agencies Staff: 170,700 |

| Department of Commerce Staff: 44,000 | Department of Labor Staff: 22,000 | Department of Health and Human Services Staff: 159,000 | Department of Transportation Staff: 70,000 | Department of Education Staff: 7,000 | Department of Energy Staff: 21,000 | Department of Housing and Urban Development Staff: 16,000 |

| National Bureau of Standards | Occupational Safety and Health Administration | Social Security | Federal Aviation Administration | Educational Research and Improvement | Conservation and Renewable Energy | Community Planning and Development |

179

The System of Checks and Balances

Branch		Powers	Checks
Executive (President)		**President** enforces laws; appoints officers; makes treaties; appoints Supreme Court judges; serves as commander in chief of the United States Army and Navy and of the state militia.	**Congress** shelves bills proposed by President; overrides vetoes; refuses to confirm appointments and to ratify treaties; impeaches the President. **Supreme Court** declares laws or executive acts unconstitutional.
Legislative (Congress)		**Congress** passes laws; approves treaties and appointments; provides for and maintains the navy and for calling of the militia; collects taxes; pays debts; borrows and coins money; regulates trade.	**President** vetoes laws; calls special sessions of Congress. **Supreme Court** interprets laws and treaties; reviews constitutionality of laws.
Judicial (Courts)		**Supreme Court** interprets laws and treaties; judges appointed for life; Chief Justice presides at impeachment of President.	**President** appoints judges but cannot remove them; grants pardons. **Congress** decides jurisdiction of federal courts; sets up lower courts; approves appointments of judges; impeaches judges; tries impeachments.

been sworn in by Supreme Court justices, by judges, and by ministers. Today, however, the Chief Justice usually administers the oath of office.

SECTION 2. Powers of the President

1. Military Powers. *The President shall be commander in chief of the Army and Navy of the United States, and of the militias of the several states when called into the actual service of the United States; he may require the opinion, in writing, of the principal officer in each of the executive departments, upon any subject relating to the duties of their respective offices, and he shall have power to grant reprieves and pardons for offenses against the United States except in cases of impeachment.*

2. Treaties, Appointments. *He shall have power, by and with the advice and consent of the Senate, to make treaties, provided two-thirds of the Senators present concur; and he shall nominate and, by and with the advice and consent of the Senate, shall appoint ambassadors, other public ministers and consuls, judges of the Supreme Court, and all other officers of the United States whose appointments are not herein provided for and which shall be established by law; but the Congress may by law vest the appointment of such inferior officers as they think proper in the President alone, in the courts of law, or in the heads of departments.*

3. Vacancies. *The President shall have power to fill up all vacancies that may happen during the recess of the Senate by granting commissions which shall expire at the end of their next session.*

Clause 1 ensures that the military is clearly under civilian control. The executive departments mentioned have grown in number and size over the years. This clause prompted President Washington to start a **cabinet,** or group of advisers.

Clause 2 is the basis of an important check on the powers of the President—the President's need for the "advice and consent" of the Senate. The President can make treaties and appoint officials only with a two-thirds approval from the Senate. Sometimes the President enters into an **executive agreement** with a foreign country. This has the force of a treaty and does not require Senate approval.

Clause 3 indicates that when the Senate is not in session, the President can make temporary appointments requiring no Senate confirmation.

SECTION 3. Presidential Duties

He shall from time to time give to the Congress information of the state of the Union, and recommend to their consideration such measures as he shall judge necessary and expedient; he may, on extraordinary occasions, convene both houses, or either of them, and in case of disagreement between them, with respect to the time of adjournment, he may adjourn them to such time as he shall think proper; he shall receive ambassadors and other public ministers; he shall take care that the laws be faithfully executed, and shall commission all the officers of the United States.

This section identifies four major responsibilities of the President: (1) legislative—the President must give a State of the Union message to Congress each year; (2) diplomatic—the President must receive the representatives of foreign countries; (3) executive—the President must faithfully carry out the laws of the land; (4) military—the President, as the nation's commander in chief, grants every military officer his or her **commission,** or rank and authority.

SECTION 4. Impeachment

The President, Vice-President, and all civil officers of the United States shall be removed from office on impeachment for, and conviction of, treason, bribery, or other high crimes and misdemeanors.

President Andrew Johnson was impeached by the House and tried by the Senate. The necessary two-thirds majority of Senators did not vote him guilty, so he remained President. President Richard Nixon resigned in 1974 before he could be impeached.

ARTICLE 3. The Judicial Department

The Constitution devotes fewer words to the *judicial* branch than the other two branches. Yet this branch is as powerful as the others.

SECTION 1. Federal Courts and Judges

The judicial power of the United States shall be vested in one Supreme Court, and in such inferior courts as the Congress may from time to time ordain and establish. The judges, both of the Supreme and inferior courts, shall hold their offices during good behavior, and shall at stated times receive for their services a compensation, which shall not be diminished during their continuance in office.

The Constitution keeps the courts independent from both the President and Congress. Unless judges are impeached and convicted, they can hold their jobs for life. This protects the judge from being dismissed by the President.

Only two Presidents have tried to change the membership of the Supreme Court. Jefferson did so by the attempted impeachment of Samuel Chase in 1805. Years later, Franklin D. Roosevelt attempted to place additional members on the bench. Neither President was successful.

1. General Authority. *The judicial power shall extend to all cases in law and equity arising under this Constitution, the laws of the United States, and treaties made or which shall be made under their authority; to all cases affecting ambassadors, other public ministers, and consuls; to all cases of admiralty and maritime jurisdiction; to controversies to which the United States shall be a party; to controversies between two or more states; between a state and citizens of another state; between citizens of different states; between citizens of the same state claiming lands under grants of different states, and between a state, or the citizens thereof, and foreign states, citizens or subjects.*

2. Supreme Court. *In all cases affecting ambassadors, other public ministers and consuls, and those in which a state shall be party, the Supreme Court shall have original jurisdiction. In all the other cases before mentioned, the Supreme Court shall have appellate jurisdiction, both as to law and fact, with such exceptions and under such regulations as the Congress shall make.*

3. Trial by Jury. *The trial of all crimes except in cases of impeachment shall be by jury; and such trial shall be held in the state where the said crimes shall have been committed; but when not committed within any state, the trial shall be at such place or places as the Congress may by law have directed.*

The first clause establishes the Supreme Court's right to declare laws of Congress unconstitutional. This right was established by Chief Justice Marshall's decision in *Marbury* v. *Madison* (see page 195). **Judicial review** is the power to review a law and decide whether it violates the Constitution.

According to the second clause, the Supreme Court has **original jurisdiction,** primary responsibility, in cases affecting representatives of foreign countries and in cases in which a state is one of the parties. These go directly to the Supreme Court.

The Supreme Court has **appellate jurisdiction,** the right to review appeals, in other kinds of cases. These cases are tried first in a lower court and then may come up to the Supreme Court for review if Congress authorizes an appeal. Congress can take away the right to appeal to the Supreme Court or fix the procedures to present an appeal.

Clause 3 guarantees trial by *jury* to anyone accused of a crime against the federal government, except an impeached official. The trial is held in the state where the crime was committed. If the crime occurred in a place other than a state, Congress can determine the trial site.

SECTION 3.   Treason

> **1. Definition.** *Treason against the United States shall consist only in levying war against them, or in adhering to their enemies, giving them aid and comfort. No person shall be convicted of treason unless on the testimony of two witnesses to the same overt act, or on confession in open court.*
>
> **2. Punishment.** *The Congress shall have power to declare the punishment of treason, but no attainder of treason shall work corruption of blood or forfeiture except during the life of the person attainted.*

The constitutional definition of treason is limited to starting war against the United States or joining or giving aid to its enemies. Because of the strict definition, Aaron Burr was found not guilty when he was charged with treason after the killing of Alexander Hamilton during a duel. Treason is the only crime defined in the Constitution. The phrase *no attainder*

of treason shall work corruption of blood means that the family of a convicted traitor does not share the guilt of the traitor. Formerly, a traitor's family could also be punished.

ARTICLE 4.   Relations Among States

Much of this article is based on the Articles of Confederation. States must honor one another's laws, records, and court rulings. Congress has the power to make laws forcing the states to respect each other's laws, records, and decisions.

SECTION 1.   State Acts and Records

> *Full faith and credit shall be given in each state to the public acts, records, and judicial proceedings of every other state. And the Congress may by general laws prescribe the manner in which such acts, records, and proceedings shall be proved, and the effect thereof.*

Section 1 demands that states respect each other's laws regarding public information about births, deaths, wills, and marriages.

SECTION 2.   Rights of Citizens

> **1. Citizenship.** *The citizens of each state shall be entitled to all privileges and immunities of citizens in the several states.*
>
> **2. Extradition.** *A person charged in any state with treason, felony, or other crime, who shall flee from justice, and be found in another state, shall, on demand of the executive authority of the state from which he fled, be delivered*

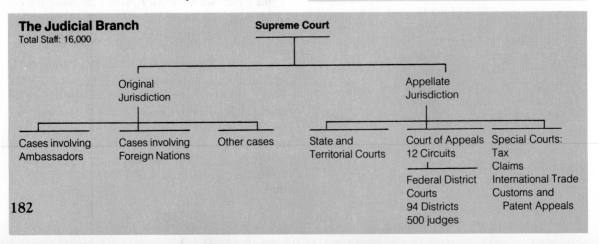

The Judicial Branch
Total Staff: 16,000

Supreme Court

Original Jurisdiction

Appellate Jurisdiction

Cases involving Ambassadors

Cases involving Foreign Nations

Other cases

State and Territorial Courts

Court of Appeals 12 Circuits

Federal District Courts 94 Districts 500 judges

Special Courts: Tax Claims International Trade Customs and Patent Appeals *up, to be removed to the state having jurisdiction of the crime.*

3. Fugitive Slaves. *No person held to service or labor in one state, under the laws thereof, escaping into another, shall, in consequence of any law or regulation therein, be discharged from such service or labor, but shall be delivered up on claim of the party to whom such service or labor may be due.*

Citizens traveling from state to state enjoy all the rights and privileges of the citizens of those states.

If a person is charged with a *felony* or other serious crime in one state and flees to another state, that person must be returned to the first state upon that governor's request. This is called **extradition.** Sometimes extradition of a person is refused.

The Thirteenth Amendment renders the third clause obsolete.

SECTION 3.   New States

1.   Admission. *New states may be admitted by Congress into this Union; but no new state shall be formed or erected within the jurisdiction of any other state; nor any state be formed by the junction of two or more states, or parts of states, without the consent of the legislatures of the states concerned as well as of the Congress.*
2.   Congressional Authority. *The Congress shall have power to dispose of and make all needful rules and regulations respecting the territory or other property belonging to the United States; and nothing in this Constitution shall be so construed as to prejudice any claims of the United States, or of any particular state.*

Congress can admit new states into the Union and control all federal property. This section also allows Congress to establish governments for land under United States guardianship, like Puerto Rico. Clause 2 also allows Congress to establish national parks.

This section once permitted Congress to deal with the question of slavery in the territories.

SECTION 4.   Guarantees to the States

The United States shall guarantee to every state in this Union a republican form of government, and shall protect each of them against invasion; and, on application of the

legislature, or of the executive (when the legislature cannot be convened), against domestic violence.

This section insures that each state is a republic. A *republic* is a form of government in which the people elect officials to represent them.

This section also guarantees each state federal protection against invasion and domestic violence. President Eisenhower used this power in 1957 when he ordered the Arkansas National Guard into federal service at Central High School in Little Rock.

ARTICLE 5.   Amending the Constitution

The Fifth Article explains the process of **amending,** or changing, the Constitution. This article gives the Constitution its flexibility, one of its strongest features. Custom has provided that all amendments (the Twenty-First Amendment being the only exception to the custom) be proposed by two-thirds vote in Congress and ratified by state legislatures.

The Congress, whenever two-thirds of both houses shall deem it necessary, shall propose amendments to this Constitution, or on the application of the legislatures of two-thirds of the several states, shall call a convention for proposing amendments, which, in either case, shall be valid to all intents and purposes, as part of this Constitution, when ratified by the legislatures of three-fourths of the several states, or by conventions in three-fourths thereof, as the one or the other mode of ratification may be proposed by the Congress, provided that no amendment which may be made prior to the year one thousand eight hundred and eight shall in any manner affect the first and fourth clauses in the Ninth Section of the First Article; and that no state, without its consent, shall be deprived of its equal suffrage in the Senate.

Over the years, seven thousand amendments have been proposed in Congress, but only thirty-three have been passed and submitted to the states. To date, twenty-six have been ratified, and at least one is still being considered by the states. Since the early 1900s, most of the proposed amendments have included a clause that ratification had to be obtained within seven years.

Amending the Constitution	
Proposing Amendments	**Ratifying Amendments**
1. 2/3 of each house of Congress	1. 3/4 of the state legislatures
2. convention called by 2/3 of the state legislatures	2. 3/4 of special conventions held in each state

Through the years, the Constitution has been changed by the interpretation of the Supreme Court as well as by amendment. In fact, the Court has been labeled "a continuing constitutional convention" because of its changing attitudes and opinions.

ARTICLE 6.
Supremacy of the National Government

1. Valid Debts. *All debts contracted and engagements entered into before the adoption of this Constitution shall be as valid against the United States under this Constitution as under the Confederation.*

2. Supreme Law. *This Constitution and the laws of the United States which shall be made in pursuance thereof, and all treaties made or which shall be made under the authority of the United States, shall be the supreme law of the land, and the judges in every state shall be bound thereby, anything in the constitution or laws of any state to the contrary notwithstanding.*

3. Loyalty to Constitution. *The Senators and Representatives before mentioned, and the members of the several state legislatures, and all executive and judicial officers, both of the United States and of the several states, shall be bound by oath or affirmation to support this Constitution; but no religious test shall ever be required as a qualification to any office or public trust under the United States.*

This article asserts that all debts under the Articles of Confederation will be honored. Clause 2 establishes that the supreme law of the land is based on: (1) the Constitution; (2) federal laws; and (3) all treaties. According to Clause 3, all government officials must promise to support the Constitution. The third clause also forbids religious qualifications as a condition for holding a government job.

ARTICLE 7. Ratification

The framers set up an orderly procedure for the Constitution to be approved by the states. The Constitution did not require unanimous support to become effective.

The ratifiction of the conventions of nine states shall be sufficient for the establishment of this Constitution between the states so ratifying the same.

Done in convention by the unanimous consent of the states present the seventeenth day of September, in the year of our Lord one thousand seven hundred and eighty-seven and of the independence of the United States of America the twelfth. In witness whereof, we have hereunto subscribed our names.

George Washington—*President and deputy from Virginia*

DELAWARE
George Read
Gunning Bedford, Junior
John Dickinson
Richard Bassett
Jacob Broom

MARYLAND
James McHenry
Dan of St. Thomas Jenifer
Daniel Carroll

VIRGINIA
John Blair
James Madison, Junior

NORTH CAROLINA
William Blount
Richard Dobbs Spaight
Hugh Williamson

NEW HAMPSHIRE
John Langdon
Nicholas Gilman

MASSACHUSETTS
Nathaniel Gorham
Rufus King

CONNECTICUT
William Samuel Johnson
Roger Sherman

NEW YORK
Alexander Hamilton

NEW JERSEY
William Livingston
David Brearley
William Paterson
Jonathan Dayton

SOUTH CAROLINA
John Rutledge
Charles Cotesworth Pinckney
Charles Pinckney
Pierce Butler

GEORGIA
William Few
Abraham Baldwin

PENNSYLVANIA
Benjamin Franklin
Thomas Mifflin
Robert Morris
George Clymer
Thomas FitzSimons
Jared Ingersoll
James Wilson
Gouverneur Morris

Section Review

COMPREHENSION Developing Vocabulary

Match each term with the correct definition:

1. writ of habeas corpus
2. elastic clause
3. patent
4. judicial review
5. impeachment
6. cabinet
7. republic

a. accusing a public official of a crime or misbehavior
b. legal order protecting people from being held in jail on little evidence
c. President's advisers
d. power to examine a law and see if it violates the Constitution
e. form of government in which people elect officials to represent them
f. official document that protects an invention
g. part of Constitution allowing Congress to deal with issues not specifically mentioned

COMPREHENSION Mastering Facts

Identify the article of the Constitution from which each excerpt has been taken:

1. _____ "The Congress shall have power to lay and collect taxes. . . ."
2. _____ "The judicial power of the United States shall be vested in one Supreme Court, and in such inferior courts as Congress may . . . establish."
3. _____ "This Constitution . . . shall be the supreme law of the land. . . ."
4. _____ "The citizens of each state shall be entitled to all privileges . . . of citizens in the several states. . . ."
5. _____ "The President shall be commander in chief of the Army and Navy. . . ."
6. _____ "We, the people of the United States . . . do ordain and establish this Constitution for the United States of America."
7. _____ "Amendments . . . shall be valid . . . when ratified by the legislatures of three-fourths of the several states. . . ."
8. What powers does the Senate have that the House does not have? What powers does the House have that the Senate does not have?
9. Indicate which branch of government has each of the following powers: (a) declare war; (b) collect taxes; (c) make treaties; (d) appoint ambassadors; (e) regulate trade with foreign nations; (f) coin money; (g) grant pardons.

APPLICATION Interpreting Charts

1. Refer to the chart on page 177. How is a state government organized like the federal government? How is it different?
2. This chart shows the organization of our government. Identify the missing parts:

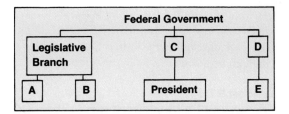

EVALUATION Relating Past to Present

1. Explain how Congress has the authority to regulate nuclear wastes, radio stations, and other issues that were unknown to the writers of the Constitution.
2. Which two powers of Congress listed in Article 1, Section 8, affect you directly? Explain.

CONCEPTS Understanding Government

1. Federalism: Write a paragraph explaining the concept of federalism.
2. Separation of Powers: Explain how this idea is used in the Constitution.
3. Checks and Balances: Name one "check" that each branch has over the other branches. How does this system create "balance"?

CONCEPTS Developing Effective Citizenship

1. Are amendments to the Constitution ever voted on directly by citizens? What role do individual citizens have in proposing and ratifying amendments?
2. Without using outside references, name as many of the following as you can: President; Vice-President; the two Senators from your state; your Representative; Chief Justice of the Supreme Court; members of the cabinet. Where could you find the names of the people currently holding these posts? Why is it important to know who these people are and how they vote on important issues?

Amendments to the Constitution

Bill of Rights

The first ten *amendments* to the Constitution are known as the *Bill of Rights*. These amendments were added to the Constitution on December 15, 1791—one year after the last state ratified the Constitution. James Madison drafted the Bill of Rights (see page 201). He had not forgotten that five states had approved the Constitution only after stressing the need for such an addition.

AMENDMENT 1.
Religious and Political Freedoms (1791)

Congress shall make no law respecting an establishment of religion, or prohibiting the free exercise thereof; or abridging the freedom of speech, or of the press; or the right of the people peaceably to assemble, and to petition the government for a redress of grievances.

The First Amendment protects the cornerstones of *civil rights:* (1) freedom of religious worship; (2) freedom of speech; (3) freedom of the press; (4) freedom to assemble; and (5) the right to voice complaints to the government. The Supreme Court has applied this amendment to a variety of situations.

AMENDMENT 2.   Right to Bear Arms (1791)

A well-regulated militia being necessary to the security of a free state, the right of the people to keep and bear arms shall not be infringed.

The First Amendment allowed Lemuel Haynes to become the first black minister of a Congregational Church.

A citizen's right to bear arms is related to the maintenance of a *militia.* Various restrictions have been placed on this right, including the requirement of gun licenses and the restricted right to carry concealed weapons.

AMENDMENT 3.   Quartering Troops (1791)

No soldier shall in time of peace be quartered in any house without the consent of the owner; nor in time of war but in a manner to be prescribed by law.

VOCABULARY FOR AMENDMENTS

Amendment, change in the provisions of the Constitution. Though interpretations of the Constitution change constantly, only twenty-six amendments have been ratified. See pages 186–194.

Bill of Rights, first ten amendments to the Constitution. They protect the basic civil liberties of citizens. The first three protect general rights. Amendments four through eight protect rights of people suspected of committing crimes. The last two protect rights not specifically mentioned in the Constitution. See pages 186–188.

Citizenship, condition in which a person gives allegiance to a government and has the civil rights granted by that government. See page 189.

Civil Rights, rights protected by a constitution or government. See page 186.

Due Process, proper and orderly working of the legal system. The Fifth and the Fourteenth Amendments protect individuals from loss of property or freedom without due process of law. See page 187.

Grand Jury, group of between twelve and twenty-four citizens who determine whether there is enough evidence to indict, or accuse, a person of a crime. If a person is indicted by a grand jury, a trial is held to determine whether the person is guilty or innocent. See page 187.

Militia, military force made up of civilians called upon during special emergencies. Today the National Guard serves as the militia in each state. See page 186.

Suffrage, right to vote. Since 1788, suffrage has been extended to blacks (1870), women (1920), and all citizens over the age of eighteen (1971). See page 191.

Soldiers cannot be stationed in a private home during peacetime without the owner's consent. Soldiers can be stationed in homes during wartime only if Congress passes such a law.

AMENDMENT 4.   Search and Seizure (1791)

The right of the people to be secure in their persons, houses, papers, and effects, against unreasonable searches and seizures, shall not be violated; and no warrants shall issue, but upon probable cause, supported by oath or affirmation, and particularly describing the place to be searched and the persons or things to be seized.

This amendment requires authorities to obtain a specific search or arrest warrant from a judge before searches or seizure of property can take place. If evidence is obtained illegally, it is not allowed in court. Recently, this amendment has been applied to evidence secured through wiretapping. This guarantees an individual's right to privacy. A person requesting a warrant has to furnish very specific information to legal authorities.

AMENDMENT 5.
Rights of Accused Persons (1791)

No person shall be held to answer for a capital or otherwise infamous crime unless on a presentment or indictment of a grand jury, except in cases arising in the land or naval forces, or in the militia, when in actual service in time of war or public danger; nor shall any person be subject for the same offense to be twice put in jeopardy of life or limb, nor shall be compelled in any criminal case to be a witness against himself, nor be deprived of life, liberty, or property without due process of law; nor shall private property be taken for public use without just compensation.

This amendment protects the rights of those who have been accused of some crime. A **capital crime** is one punishable by death. An **infamous crime** is punishable by death or imprisonment. A *grand jury* is a special group of people selected to decide whether there is enough evidence against a person to hold a trial. A person cannot be tried for the same offense by the same government twice. A person cannot be forced to say anything in a federal court that will incriminate him or her.

The federal government cannot take a person's life, freedom, or property except by *due process* of the law. The Fourteenth Amendment applies this law to the states, too.

The government cannot take private property for public use without fair payment. The government's right to take property for public use is called **eminent domain.** This land is usually used for public facilities such as parks, playgrounds, schools, highways, or government buildings.

AMENDMENT 6.
Right to a Speedy, Public Trial (1791)

In all criminal prosecutions, the accused shall enjoy the right to a speedy and public trial, by an impartial jury of the state and district wherein the crime shall have been committed, which district shall have been previously ascertained by law, and to be informed of the nature and cause of the accusation; to be confronted with the witness against him; to have compulsory process for obtaining witnesses in his favor, and to have the assistance of counsel for his defense.

A person accused of a crime is entitled to a prompt public trial before an unbiased jury chosen from the district where the crime was committed. The accused must be told what he or she is accused of and must be present when witnesses testify against him or her. The accused has the right to have the court call witnesses in his or her favor and to have an attorney. If the accused cannot afford a lawyer, one will be appointed at government expense. (See *Miranda* case on pages 198–199.)

AMENDMENT 7.
Trial by Jury in Civil Cases (1791)

In suits at common law where the value in controversy shall exceed twenty dollars, the right of trial by jury shall be preserved, and no fact tried by a jury shall be otherwise reexamined in any court of the United States than according to the rules of the common law.

Common law is unwritten law based on custom and use. **Statute law** is written law. Although trial by jury is guaranteed in cases involving more than twenty dollars, more is usually at stake before a case is heard in federal court.

AMENDMENT 8.
Limits of Fines and Punishments (1791)

> *Excessive bail shall not be required, nor excessive fines imposed, nor cruel and unusual punishment inflicted.*

An accused person cannot be required to pay an unnecessarily large bail. **Bail** is the security given by the accused to guarantee his or her appearance for trial. What constitutes "cruel and unusual punishment" is still debated. In 1972, for example, the Supreme Court ruled in *Furman* v. *Georgia* that in some cases the death penalty violated the Eighth Amendment. But in 1976 the Court said that capital punishment was "not unconstitutionally severe."

AMENDMENT 9.   Rights of People (1791)

> *The enumeration in the Constitution of certain rights shall not be construed to deny or disparage others retained by the people.*

The people have many rights. Some are listed in the Constitution; others are not. This amendment reaffirms that the people remain the source of power.

AMENDMENT 10.
Powers of the States and People (1791)

> *The powers not delegated to the United States by the Constitution, nor prohibited by it to the states, are reserved to the states respectively, or to the people.*

The United States has only the specific powers given to it by the Constitution. All other powers, unless they are specifically denied to the states, belong to the states or to the people. The source of power of the federal government rests on what the states and people give to it.

Additional Amendments

AMENDMENT 11.
Lawsuits Against States (1798)

> *The judicial power of the United States shall not be construed to extend to any suit in law or equity commenced or prosecuted against one of the United States by citizens of another state, or by citizens or subjects of any foreign state.*

Citizens of one state cannot sue another state in the federal courts. An individual, however, can sue state authorities in federal court for taking away his constitutional rights. This amendment changes part of Article III, Section 2, Clause 1.

AMENDMENT 12.
Election of Executives (1804)

> *The electors shall meet in their respective states, and vote by ballot for President and Vice-President, one of whom, at least, shall not be an inhabitant of the same state with themselves; they shall name in their ballots the person voted for as President, and in distinct ballots the person voted for as Vice-President, and they shall make distinct lists of all persons voted for as President and of all persons voted for as Vice-President, and of the number of votes for each, which lists they shall sign and certify, and transmit, sealed, to the seat of the government of the United States, directed to the president of the Senate; the president of the Senate shall, in the presence of the Senate and House of Representatives, open all the certificates, and the votes shall then be counted. The person having the greatest number of votes for President shall be the President, if such number be a majority of the whole number of electors appointed; and if no person have such majority, then from the persons having the highest numbers, not exceeding three, on the list of those voted for as President, the House of Representatives shall choose immediately, by ballot, the President. But in choosing the President, the votes shall be taken by the states, the representation from each state having one vote; a quorum for this purpose shall consist of a member or members from two-thirds of the states, and a majority of all the states shall be necessary to a choice. And if the House of Representatives shall not choose a President, whenever the right of choice shall devolve upon them, before the fourth day of March next following, then the Vice-President shall act as President, as in case of the death or other constitutional disability of the President. The person having the greatest number of votes as Vice-President shall be the Vice-President, if such number be a majority of the whole number of electors appointed, and if no person have a majority, then, from the two highest numbers on*

the list, the Senate shall choose the Vice-President; a quorum for the purpose shall consist of two-thirds of the whole number of Senators, and a majority of the whole number shall be necessary to a choice. But no person constitutionally ineligible to the office of President shall be eligible to that of Vice-President of the United States.

The Twelfth Amendment is designed to avoid the problems experienced in the election of 1800 (see page 214). It provides that members of the Electoral College (Electors) vote for one person as President and another as Vice-President.

In the event no presidential candidate receives a majority of votes, the House of Representatives is required to choose the President from the top three candidates. Each state has a single vote. In the event no vice-presidential candidate receives a majority of votes, the Senate must elect one from the top two candidates. The House has chosen two Presidents, Thomas Jefferson (1800) and John Q. Adams (1824).

The part crossed out was changed by Amendment 20 in 1933.

AMENDMENT 13.   Slavery Abolished (1865)

Section 1. *Neither slavery nor involuntary servitude, except as a punishment for crime whereof the party shall have been duly convicted, shall exist within the United States or any place subject to their jurisdiction.*
Section 2. *Congress shall have power to enforce this article by appropriate legislation.*

Since all slaves were not free at the end of the Civil War, this amendment was necessary to abolish slavery in the United States. This Amendment also guarantees that no one can be forced to work against his or her will except as punishment for a crime.

Congress can pass whatever laws are necessary to enforce this amendment.

AMENDMENT 14.   Civil Rights (1868)

Section 1. *All persons born or naturalized in the United States, and subject to the jurisdiction thereof, are citizens of the United States and of the state wherein they reside. No state shall make or enforce any law which shall abridge the privileges or immunities of citizens of the*

United States, nor shall any state deprive any person of life, liberty, or property without due process of law, nor deny to any person within its jurisdiction the equal protection of the laws.

The first section defined *citizenship*, applied the definition to the former slaves, and prohibited states from limiting the immunity and rights of citizens as stated in the Constitution. Many Supreme Court rulings on civil rights have resulted from the statement that a state cannot deny anyone "equal protection of the laws." The Supreme Court outlawed segregation in public schools on the basis of this statement, saying everyone, regardless of race, must have an equal opportunity for education.

Section 2. *Representatives shall be apportioned among the several states according to their respective numbers, counting the whole number of persons in each state, excluding Indians not taxed. But when the right to vote at any election for the choice of electors for President and Vice-President of the United States, Representatives in Congress, the executive and judicial officers of a state, or the members of the legislature thereof, is denied to any of the male inhabitants of such state, being twenty-one years of age, and citizens of the United States, or in any way abridged, except for participation in rebellion, or other crime, the basis of representation therein shall be reduced in the proportion which the number of such male citizens shall bear to the whole number of male citizens twenty-one years of age in such state.*

The second section specifies how Representatives shall be distributed among the states. It cancelled the Three-Fifths Compromise of Article 1, Section 2. It was supposed to extend the right to vote to all twenty-one-year-old males, including the former slaves. The penalty for a state's refusing to comply with this section was to be reduction of that state's representation in Congress. This provision was never enforced.

Section 3. *No person shall be a Senator or Representative in Congress, or elector of President and Vice-President, or hold any office, civil or military, under the United States or under any state, who, having previously taken an oath as a member of Congress, or as an officer of the United States, or as a member of any state legislature, or as an executive or judicial officer*

189

of any state, to support the Constitution of the United States, shall have engaged in insurrection or rebellion against the same or given aid or comfort to the enemies thereof. But Congress may by a vote of two-thirds of each house remove such disability.

Section 4. *The validity of the public debt of the United States, authorized by law, including debts incurred for payment of pensions and bounties for services in suppressing insurrection and rebellion, shall not be questioned. But neither the United States nor any state shall assume or pay any debt or obligation incurred in aid of insurrection or rebellion against the United States, or any claim for the loss or emancipation of any slave; but all such debts, obligations, and claims shall be held illegal and void.*

Section 5. *The Congress shall have power to enforce by appropriate legislation the provisions of this article.*

These sections were intended to punish Confederate leaders during the post-Civil War period. By 1898 all had been pardoned and had returned to political life.

The Union debt for the Civil War was paid, while the Confederate debt was declared void. No one was paid for loss of slaves.

AMENDMENT 15. Right to Vote (1870)

Section 1. *The right of the citizens of the United States to vote shall not be denied or abridged by the United States or by any state on account of race, color, or previous condition of servitude.*

Section 2. *The Congress shall have power to enforce this article by appropriate legislation.*

This amendment attempted to insure black males the right to vote. But blacks were often kept from the polls, and further federal action was needed.

AMENDMENT 16. Income Tax (1913)

The Congress shall have power to lay and collect taxes on incomes, from whatever source derived, without apportionment among the several states, and without regard to any census or enumeration.

Congress can pass and collect income taxes. These taxes do not have to be divided among the states according to the population. Today, income taxes are the federal government's greatest source of revenue. This amendment changes Article 1, Section 9, Clause 4 of the Constitution.

AMENDMENT 17.
Direct Election of Senators (1913)

Clause 1. *The Senate of the United States shall be composed of two Senators from each state, elected by the people thereof, for six years; and each Senator shall have one vote. The electors in each state shall have the qualifications requisite for electors of the most numerous branch of the state legislatures.*

Clause 2. *When vacancies happen in the representation of any state in the Senate, the executive authority of such state shall issue writs of election to fill such vacancies: Provided that the legislature of any state may empower the executive thereof to make temporary appointments until the people fill the vacancies by election as the legislature may direct.*

Clause 3. *This amendment shall not be so construed as to affect the election or term of any Senator chosen before it becomes valid as part of the Constitution.*

The Seventeenth Amendment changed Article 1, Section 3, Clause 1. By providing for their direct election, this amendment persuaded Senators to become more responsible to the voters of their state.

AMENDMENT 18. Prohibition (1919)

Section 1. *After one year from the ratification of this article the manufacture, sale, or transportation of intoxicating liquors within, the importation thereof into, or the exportation thereof from the United States and all territory subject to the jurisdiction thereof for beverage purposes is hereby prohibited.*

Section 2. *The Congress and the several states shall have concurrent power to enforce this article by appropriate legislation.*

Section 3. *This article shall be inoperative unless it shall have been ratified as an amendment to the Constitution by the legislatures of the several states, as provided in the Constitution, within seven years from the date of the submission hereof to the states by the Congress.*

This amendment which banned people from making, selling, or transporting liquor was later repealed by the Twenty-First Amendment.

AMENDMENT 19. Women's Suffrage (1920)

Clause 1. *The right of citizens of the United States to vote shall not be denied or abridged by the United States or by any state on account of sex.*

Clause 2. *Congress shall have power to enforce this article by appropriate legislation.*

For more than forty years, amendment after amendment regarding women's right to vote had been introduced in Congress. *Suffrage* was finally extended to women in 1920.

AMENDMENT 20. "Lame Duck" Sessions (1933)

Section 1. *The terms of the President and Vice-President shall end at noon on the twentieth day of January, and the terms of Senators and Representatives at noon on the third day of January, of the years in which such terms would have ended if this article had not been ratified; and the terms of their successors shall then begin.*

This amendment provides for the efficient transfer of power among elected officials. Originally, a defeated official would continue in office for several months before the replacement was installed. This situation was compared to that of a "lame duck" whose wings were clipped. Usually very little was accomplished during these months.

The terms of President and Vice-President end on January 20 instead of March 4, and the terms of the Senators and Representatives end on January 3 of the same year they ended prior to this amendment. All successors begin their jobs at that time.

Section 2. *The Congress shall assemble at least once in every year, and such meeting shall begin at noon on the third day of January unless they shall by law appoint a different day.*

Congress must meet once every year beginning on January 3 at noon unless another date is established by law. This amendment changes Article 1, Section 4, Clause 2.

Forty years after the first introduction of a bill in Congress, women secured voting rights. Susan B. Anthony was arrested for voting in 1872.

Section 3. *If, at the time fixed for the beginning of the term of the President, the President-elect shall have died, the Vice-President-elect shall become President. If a President shall not have been chosen before the time fixed for the beginning of his term, or if the President-elect shall have failed to qualify, then the Vice-President-elect shall act as President until a President shall have qualified; and the Congress may by law provide for the case wherein neither a President-elect nor a Vice-President-elect shall have qualified, declaring who shall then act as President, or the manner in which one who is to act shall be selected, and such person shall act accordingly until a President or Vice-President shall have qualified.*

This section describes the succession to the presidency if the President-elect should die before taking office on January 20. If the Vice-President-elect is unavailable, Congress must temporarily fill the office of President.

191

Section 4. *The Congress may by law provide for the case of the death of any of the persons from whom the House of Representatives may choose a President whenever the right of choice shall have devolved upon them, and for the case of the death of any of the persons from whom the Senate may choose a Vice-President whenever the right of choice shall have devolved upon them.*

Section 5. *Sections 1 and 2 shall take effect on the fifteenth day of October following the ratification of this article.*

Section 6. *This article shall be inoperative unless it shall have been ratified as an amendment to the Constitution by the legislatures of three-fourths of the several states within seven years from the date of its submission.*

If a candidate dies while his or her name is on a list from which the House of Representatives or Senate must choose a President or Vice-President, Congress then decides the proper procedure for the House and Senate to follow.

Sections 1 and 2 of this amendment became law on October 15 after three-fourths of the states ratified this amendment.

AMENDMENT 21.
Repeal of Prohibition (1933)

Section 1. *The eighteenth article of amendment to the Constitution of the United States is hereby repealed.*

Section 2. *The transportation or importation into any state, territory, or possession of the United States for delivery or use therein of intoxicating liquors, in violation of the laws thereof, is hereby prohibited.*

Section 3. *This article shall be inoperative unless it shall have been ratified as an amendment to the Constitution by convention in the several states, as provided in the Constitution, within seven years from the date of the submission hereof to the states by the Congress.*

In view of widespread violations of prohibition, there was a growing fear that disrespect for this one law would breed disrespect for all laws. This amendment repealed the Eighteenth Amendment. This is the only amendment that has ever been ratified through special state conventions.

AMENDMENT 22.
Limit on Presidential Terms (1951)

Section 1. *No person shall be elected to the office of the President more than twice, and no person who has held the office of President, or acted as President, for more than two years of a term to which some other person was elected President shall be elected to the office of President more than once. But this Article shall not apply to any person holding the office of President when this Article was proposed by the Congress, and shall not prevent any person who may be holding the office of President, or acting as President, during the term within which this Article becomes operative from holding the office of President, or acting as President during the remainder of such terms.*

Ever since George Washington served as President of the United States for two terms, a tradition limiting a President to two terms was established. The elections of Franklin Roosevelt in 1940 and 1944 broke the two-term tradition. This amendment gives that tradition the force of law. The obsolete portions were written so as not to apply to President Truman, who was in office at the time of ratification.

AMENDMENT 23.
Voting in District of Columbia (1961)

Section 1. *The District constituting the seat of Government of the United States shall appoint in such manner as the Congress may direct:*

A number of electors of President and Vice-President equal to the whole number of Senators and Representatives in Congress to which the District would be entitled if it were a state, but in no event more than the least populous state; they shall be in addition to those appointed by the states, but they shall be considered, for the purposes of the election of President and Vice-President, to be electors appointed by a state; and they shall meet in the District and perform such duties as provided by the twelfth article of amendment.

Section 2. *The Congress shall have the power to enforce this article by appropriate legislation.*

The District of Columbia has the right to participate in the election of the President and Vice-President of the United States. It has three electoral votes—the same number of votes as the state with the smallest population.

This amendment did not provide representation in Congress or a system of home rule municipal government for the district.

AMENDMENT 24.
Abolition of Poll Taxes (1964)

Section 1. *The right of citizens of the United States to vote in any primary or other election for President or Vice-President, for electors for President or Vice-President, or for Senator or Representative in Congress, shall not be denied or abridged by the United States or any state by reason of failure to pay any poll or other tax.*

Section 2. *The Congress shall have power to enforce this article by appropriate legislation.*

Poll taxes in federal elections are prohibited. Previously, some southern states had used a poll tax as a way to prevent blacks from voting.

AMENDMENT 25.
Presidential Disability, Succession (1967)

Section 1. *In case of the removal of the President from office or his death or resignation, the Vice-President shall become President.*

This amendment resulted from President Dwight Eisenhower's serious illnesses while in office. It clarifies Article 2, Section 1, Clause 6 regarding a President's disability. Its purpose was to avoid: (1) a lapse in the functioning of the presidency if the elected President was not able to perform the job; and (2) a situation in which the President's personal advisers might take over without legal authority.

In 1973, when Vice-President Spiro Agnew resigned, President Richard Nixon nominated Republican Representative Gerald R. Ford to take his place. Upon Nixon's resignation, Ford became President. President Ford then appointed Nelson Rockefeller as Vice-President. Mr. Rockefeller's appointment was confirmed by a vote of Congress.

Section 2. *Whenever there is a vacancy in the office of the Vice-President, the President shall nominate a Vice-President who shall take the office upon confirmation by a majority vote of both houses of Congress.*

Section 3. *Whenever the President transmits to the president pro tempore of the Senate and the speaker of the House of Representatives his written declaration that he is unable to discharge the powers and duties of his office, and until he transmits to them a written declaration to the contrary, such powers and duties shall be discharged by the Vice-President as Acting President.*

Section 4. *Whenever the Vice-President and a majority of either the principal officers of the executive departments, or of such other body as Congress may by law provide, transmit to the president pro tempore of the Senate and the speaker of the House of Representatives their written declaration that the President is unable to discharge the powers and duties of his office, the Vice-President shall immediately assume the powers and duties of the office as Acting President.*

Thereafter, when the President transmits to the president pro tempore of the Senate and the speaker of the House of Representatives his written declaration that no inability exists, he shall resume the powers and duties of his office unless the Vice-President and a majority of either the principal officers of the executive department, or of such other body as Congress may by law provide, transmit within four days to the president pro tempore of the Senate and the speaker of the House of Representatives their written declaration that the president is unable to discharge the powers and duties of his office. Thereupon Congress shall decide the issue, assembling within 48 hours for that purpose if not in session. If the Congress, within 21 days after receipt of the latter written declaration, or if Congress is not in session, within 21 days after Congress is required to assemble, determines by two-thirds vote of both houses that the President is unable to discharge the powers and duties of his office, the Vice-President shall continue to discharge the same as Acting President; otherwise, the President shall resume the powers and duties of his office.

The Vice-President becomes Acting President whenever the President makes a written declaration to the heads of Congress that he is unable to carry out his duties. The Vice-President also becomes the Acting President when the Vice-President and a majority of the cabinet make a written declaration to the president pro tempore of the Senate and to the speaker of the House of Representatives that the President is unable to perform his duties.

If the President later notifies the president pro tempore of the Senate and the speaker of the House of Representatives that he can resume his duties, he then does so. If a controversy occurs about the President's ability to perform his duties, Congress decides the question. If two-thirds of both the Senate and the House of Representatives decide that the President is unable to perform his duties, then the Vice-President continues as Acting President.

AMENDMENT 26.
Eighteen-year-old Vote (1971)

Section 1. *The right of citizens of the United States, who are eighteen years of age or older, to vote, shall not be denied or abridged by the United States or any state on account of age.*
Section 2. *The Congress shall have the power to enforce this article by appropriate legislation.*

This amendment gives eighteen-year-olds the right to vote.

Section Review

COMPREHENSION Developing Vocabulary

1. Explain each of the following terms: amendment, Bill of Rights, grand jury, eminent domain, suffrage, civil rights, citizenship, due process.
2. What is the difference between common law and statute law?
3. Explain why the Twentieth Amendment is called the "lame duck" amendment.

COMPREHENSION Mastering Facts

1. Use a short phrase to identify the content of each of the amendments in the Bill of Rights.
2. What "five freedoms" are guaranteed to Americans by the First Amendment?
3. According to the Fourth Amendment, under what conditions can a search warrant be issued? What must be described in the warrant?
4. What phrase in the Fifth Amendment protects individuals from being tried more than once for the same offense?

5. List the rights that are protected by the Sixth Amendment.
6. What is the purpose of the Ninth Amendment to the Constitution?
7. If no presidential candidate receives a majority of electoral votes, how is the President chosen? When has this occurred?
8. Which amendment outlawed slavery? Which amendment set up dual citizenship in both a state and the United States?
9. In what year did women obtain suffrage?
10. Which President began the tradition of not serving more than two terms? Which President broke the tradition? What is the maximum number of years one individual can serve as President?
11. Poll taxes were finally abolished in 1964. How had they once been used to get around provisions of the Fifteenth Amendment?
12. List the circumstances under which a Vice-President may become an Acting President.

EVALUATION Relating Past to Present

1. Which amendment allows the government to levy an income tax? How important is the income tax to the government today?
2. If the President died today, who would fill that office? What is the line of succession for the office of President?
3. In what cases does an individual have a right to a jury trial? How has the significance of these requirements changed over the years?

CONCEPTS Understanding Government

1. According to the Fourteenth Amendment, what is your status as a citizen?
2. List the states you can sue in federal court, according to the Eleventh Amendment.
3. Will you be eligible to vote in the next presidential election? How will the Twenty-sixth Amendment affect when you can vote?

CONCEPTS Developing Effective Citizenship

1. Which five amendments expand suffrage?
2. The Fourth Amendment protects innocent people from police searches. Does it also protect criminals? Explain your reasoning.
3. Explain how each clause of the First Amendment promotes effective citizenship.
4. The Fifth and Seventh Amendments, besides protecting certain rights, imply a duty on the part of citizens. Explain what that duty is, and why performing it is important.

Interpreting the Constitution

The Constitution is not just a piece of parchment for visitors to Washington to admire as a relic of a bygone age. It is very much alive, and it affects us on a day-to-day basis.

For instance, when you apply for a job, in many cases your minimum pay is determined by Congress and the courts. Congress has passed legislation establishing a minimum wage. That minimum wage applies, however, only to jobs with companies that are involved in interstate commerce (see Article 1, Section 8). If your job is with a company that operates only locally, then state laws govern it.

As times change, so do the needs of the people. One of the Constitution's outstanding qualities is its flexibility. Conflicts continue to arise as citizens, states, and the federal government deal with new problems. Some of these conflicts are ultimately decided by the Supreme Court. The Supreme Court has the final opportunity to preserve the balance of power between the three branches of government.

In our early days, the judicial branch was the weakest of the three departments. Several important Supreme Court decisions increased the power of the Court. During the Reconstruction era, Court decisions preserved the power of the states in order to maintain the Union. Recent decisions have enlarged the rights of individuals against expanding state and federal legislation. Let us examine several of these key Supreme Court decisions.

Marbury v. Madison (1803)

President John Adams was bitter. He had just lost the election to Thomas Jefferson. On his last night in office, Adams appinted some of his Federalist supporters to be judges. The Judicial Act of 1789 gave him power to do this. The commissions, including one for William Marbury, were put on the Secretary of State's desk to be sealed and then delivered the next day. The Secretary of State, John Marshall, neglected to have them delivered.

When Jefferson took office, his new Secretary of State, James Madison, refused to deliver the commissions. William Marbury asked the Supreme Court to issue an order requiring Madison to hand over the commissions. John Marshall, who had become Chief Justice, wrote the decision in 1803.

Chief Justice Marshall was indeed justified in ordering Madison to deliver the commission to Marbury. Suppose, though, that Madison ignored the order with Jefferson's approval? The Supreme Court would be seriously weakened. Future Presidents might also ignore its decisions.

Marshall looked to the Constitution for guidance. According to Article 3, the Supreme Court had original jurisdiction only in "all cases affecting ambassadors, other public ministers and consuls, and those in which a state shall be a party." In all other cases, the Court had only appellate jurisdiction.

VOCABULARY FOR COURT CASES

Abridge, to shorten a written document or a policy by cutting out words or by limiting its meaning. Colonists rebelled against the British because they felt the British were abridging their rights. See page 197.

Charter, legal document from a government that grants an individual or group specific privileges, often including permission to begin an enterprise. See page 196.

Commerce, any form of trade or business between people, groups, or nations. See page 196.

Contract, legal and binding agreement between individuals or companies stating what each will do for the other. The Constitution prohibits states, but not the federal government, from interfering with legal contracts. See page 196.

Emancipation, a freeing from restraint; often used when referring to the legal action of ending slavery. See page 196.

Judicial Review, power to examine a law and decide whether it is constitutional. See page 196.

Monopoly, sole control of a market, or any situation in which actual competition does not exist. See page 196.

Segregation, separation according to a certain trait, usually by race. Though racial segregation is no longer legal, it is still a serious problem today. See page 197.

Self-Incrimination, making statements indicating that one is guilty of a crime. Historically, force has often been used in order to get suspected criminals to make self-incriminating statements. See page 198.

Justice Marshall concluded that the section of the Judiciary Act of 1789 which gave Marbury the right to demand the delivery of his commission was unconstitutional. The Judiciary Act was adding to the original jurisdiction of the Court by giving it permission to issue orders.

Justice Marshall's decision cleverly avoided making a ruling the Court could not enforce. The real issue was not whether Marbury got his job as justice of the peace, but whether the Supreme Court had the power to declare a law unconstitutional. With this decision, the Supreme Court established itself as a check on the legislative and executive departments. The Court would strike down any law which contradicted the Constitution.

William Marbury never got his commission. His loss was the country's gain—the new concept of *judicial review*.

Dartmouth College Case (1819)

Eleazar Wheelock founded Dartmouth College under a *charter* from King George III. The charter permitted him to name his ne'er-do-well son, John Wheelock, to succeed him. Opposition developed between John and the college's governing board of trustees. Finally they removed him as president. John was rich, influential, and furious. He persuaded the state legislature to pass a law changing the Dartmouth charter.

The trustees of the original college brought an action to get back the college records and seal. The trustees lost their case in the state court. Daniel Webster, a Dartmouth alumnus, handled the appeal to the Supreme Court. Webster argued:

❝ This sir, is my case . . . it is the case of every college in our land. . . . It is more. It is, in some sense, the case of every man who has property of which he may be stripped, for the question is simply this: Shall our state legislature be allowed to take that which is not their own, to turn it from its original use, and apply it to such ends or purposes as they, in their discretion, shall see fit? ❞

The Supreme Court decided that a charter, like a *contract*, could not be changed by the state legislature. Under Article 1, Section 10, Clause 1 of the Constitution, states are forbidden to pass any law changing contract obligations. The *Dartmouth College* case extended national power at the expense of state power. It also encouraged businesses to grow without fearing state interference.

Individuals, corporations, and every private college in America can thank John Wheelock. By losing the presidency of Dartmouth, he preserved contract rights from state interference.

Gibbons v. Ogden (1824)

Thomas Gibbons and Aaron Ogden were partners in operating a steamboat between New Jersey and New York. The partnership broke up when Ogden accused Gibbons of cheating on business agreements. Each then began operating his own steamboat line. Ogden had a charter from the state of New York that gave him exclusive rights to the route. Gibbons had a charter from the federal government. Ogden took Gibbons to court for violating his exclusive charter.

The case worked its way through the court system. The Supreme Court finally ruled on it, with Chief Justice John Marshall writing the landmark decision. Settling the issue required Marshall to analyze the proper role of the federal government in regulating commerce. In a conflict between the federal government and a state, "the law of the state must yield," he said. Marshall gave a broad definition to the clause of the Constitution that says "Congress shall have power . . . to regulate *commerce* . . . among several states." Consequently, the charter Gibbons received from the federal government was legal, and Ogden's "exclusive" right was not. Because of Marshall's ruling, the federal government can regulate everything that crosses state boundaries, from air travel to radio signals.

In addition, by striking down Ogden's state-granted *monopoly*, Marshall paved the way for competition between companies. The authority of state governments to give exclusive charters to business firms was drastically limited. For this reason, the case is sometimes called "The Emancipation Proclamation of American Commerce."

Dred Scott Case (1857)

Dred Scott was born a slave, but he did not die a slave. Dred Scott, like William Marbury and John Wheelock, was an ordinary person who, by a series of ordinary events, changed the history of the entire nation. Dred Scott's failure to win his freedom became one of the issues leading to the Civil War and finally to the *emancipation* of all slaves.

In 1834 Dred Scott was the property of an army

surgeon living in the slave state of Missouri. The surgeon was transferred to the free state of Illinois, and later to the Wisconsin Territory, before returning to Missouri. Dred Scott accompanied the surgeon on all these moves.

After the surgeon died, Scott went to court to secure his freedom. Some abolitionists wanted to determine if a slave was freed when taken into free territory. Dred Scott became the test case. The case went through two Missouri courts. By this time the surgeon's widow had sold Scott to John Sanford.

A federal case has to involve citizens from different states (see Article 3, Section 2). Sanford was from New York. Scott had to prove he was a citizen of Missouri. The lower court ruled that Scott was a slave, and therefore not a citizen. Scott's lawyers appealed to the Supreme Court.

After much debate, the Supreme Court issued its fateful decision—that Dred Scott was a slave, not a citizen, and that slaves were property and did not even have the right to bring a suit. Congress could not interfere with property rights; therefore, Congress had no power to prohibit slavery in the territories—lands which were the common property of all the states. Although slavery was the issue in this case, the court declared that no black, free or slave, could claim United States citizenship. The Constitution was made by and for white people only.

Two judges disagreed with the majority opinion. They each wrote separate statements. In fact, none of the judges could agree on the exact reason for the decision. So, each judge wrote his own opinion.

Among lawyers there is a saying, "Hard cases make bad law." *Dred Scott* was the hardest of cases. It involved moral and political issues as well as legal questions. The consequences of the case were far-reaching. The Court suffered and the nation suffered. Perhaps the only one who did not suffer was Dred Scott; his owner freed him just weeks after the Court's decision. It took the passage of the Fourteenth Amendment to extend citizenship to blacks, thus reversing the *Dred Scott* decision.

Schenck v. United States (1919)

The First Amendment states clearly and simply, "Congress shall make no law . . . *abridging* the freedom of speech. . . ." That phrase, though, has been the subject of numerous difficult court cases. Can a person say anything at any time? If not, what restrictions are constitutional?

During every war in the history of the United States, civil rights have been challenged in the name of national unity. One task of the courts is to restrain the fears that develop during wars so that liberty is not destroyed. During World War 1, one act passed out of fear of subversion was the Espionage Act. The act made it illegal to disrupt recruitment efforts by the military. Richard Schenck was arrested for violating this act. He had distributed circulars to men urging them to resist the draft. His defense was that he was protected by the First Amendment.

In the case, the debate focused not on Schenck's action, but on the Espionage Act. Did it, as Schenck argued, violate the First Amendment? In the unanimous Supreme Court ruling, Justice Oliver Wendell Holmes explained what the First Amendment protected and what it did not. He wrote:

" We admit that in many places and in ordinary times the defendants [Schenck and others] in saying all that was said in the circular would have been within their constitutional rights. But the character of every act depends upon the circumstances in which it is done. The most stringent [strongest] protection of free speech would not protect a man in falsely shouting fire in a theater and causing a panic. The question in every case is whether the words used are used in such circumstances and are of such a nature as to create a clear and present danger that they will bring about the substantive [serious] evils that Congress has a right to prevent. It is a question of proximity and degree. When a nation is at war, many things that might be said in time of peace are such a hindrance to its effort that their utterance will not be endured so long as men fight and that no court could regard them as protected by any constitutional right. "

The Court ruled against Schenck. What the First Amendment protected depended on the conditions in society. This interpretation became known as the "clear and present danger doctrine."

Brown v. Board of Education (1954, 1955)

Racial discrimination continued to plague the United States long after slavery was abolished. The United States was, in many ways, two societies, one black and one white. In 1896 the Supreme Court ruled in *Plessy* v. *Ferguson* that *segregation* was legal as long as each race was provided equal facilities. "Separate but equal" became the law of the land. In practice, facilities such as schools were usually separate but unequal. White schools generally continued to have more money, better buildings, and higher paid teachers.

In 1951 the Topeka, Kansas, school system, like systems in half the nation's states, prohibited black and white children from going to school together. Oliver Brown, a black railroad worker, protested on behalf of his daughter, Linda. There was a school near their home, but she was not allowed to attend it because it was a white school. The case worked its way to the Supreme Court, which ruled on it in 1954.

The Court's ruling in the *Brown* case said that segregation in schools was unconstitutional. The reasoning the court used was unusual. They spent little time arguing complex interpretations of the law. Rather, they focused simply on how the law made people feel. According to Chief Justice Earl Warren, segregated schools led to a "feeling of inferiority" in black children. Such a feeling could put them at a permanent disadvantage as they grew up. Consequently, segregated schools violated the equal protection clause of the Fourteenth Amendment.

Members of the Court realized the implications of their decision. Segregation was deeply ingrained in the culture of the United States. The law could be changed overnight, but the minds of people could not. So, the Court followed up its unusual reasoning with an unusual implementation. Rather than order

schools desegregated at once, the Court requested that the lawyers for each side reargue the issue of how to enforce the decision. In effect, the Court ruled that school segregation was wrong, but it did not have to stop at once. People would have to wait to get their constitutional rights. A year later, the Court issued another ruling. This stated that schools were to be desegregated "with all deliberate speed." Based on the *Brown* decision, segregation in other public facilities was soon challenged and outlawed. Three decades after the *Brown* ruling, though, controversies over school integration continue.

Miranda Case (1966)

In the twentieth century the Supreme Court has championed the rights of the individual against both state and national governments. The Fifth Amendment protects an individual from *self-incrimination*. The Sixth Amendment states than an accused is entitled to have **counsel,** a lawyer, for his defense.

What is self-incrimination? A confession is incriminating. Can a confession be used against the accused? If the accused is entitled to a lawyer but cannot afford one, must the court provide one? In a series of cases before the Supreme Court, the rights of the accused were steadily expanded, culminating in the *Miranda* case.

Major Court Decisions Since 1960

Date	Case	Topic	Decision
1961	*Mapp v. Ohio*	Rights of the Accused	Illegally obtained evidence cannot be used in a trial.
1962	*Engel v. Vitale*	School Prayer	Students in public school cannot be required to recite prayers.
1963	*Gideon v. Wainwright*	Rights of the Accused	Persons accused of crime must be given free legal counsel if they cannot afford a lawyer.
1964	*Reynolds v. Sims*	Voting	State and local election districts must be roughly equal in population.
1971	*New York Times Co. v. United States*	Freedom of the Press	Government censorship of the Pentagon papers, a series of reports on Vietnam, was not justifiable.
1972	*Furman v. Georgia*	Death Penalty	The death penalty is unconstitutional unless applied in a fair and consistent manner.
1973	*Roe v. Wade*	Individual Rights	States have limited authority to prohibit abortions.
1974	*United States v. Nixon*	Separation of Powers	The President must submit to requests for evidence in a criminal trial.
1979	*United Steelworkers of America v. Weber*	Individual Rights	Women and minorities can be given preference in hiring and in promotions in "traditionally segregated job categories."
1983	*Immigration and Naturalization Service v. Jogdish Rai Chadha*	Separation of Powers	Congress cannot veto actions taken by agencies of the executive branch.

Ernesto Miranda was arrested on charges of kidnapping and rape. He was not told of his right to have a lawyer present during questioning. Nor was he told of his right to remain silent. He was questioned for two hours, after which be broke down and confessed to the crimes. Miranda was convicted of the crimes on the basis of his confession.

The Supreme Court had to decide whether Miranda's constitutional rights had been violated. Miranda did not know that he had a right to remain silent. When the police questioned him, he confessed, thus becoming a witness against himself. Nor did Miranda know that he had a right to have a lawyer to advise him during the questioning. Did the failure to advise Miranda of his rights mean that he had been "deprived of liberty without due process"?

The Court held that it did, and that Miranda's confession could not be used as evidence. The proper way to question a suspect was explained:

" Prior to any questioning, the person must be warned that he has a right to remain silent, that any statement he does make may be used as evidence against him, and that he has a right to the presence of an attorney, either retained or appointed. The defendant may waive . . . these rights, provided the waiver is made voluntarily, knowingly and intelligently. If, however, he indicates in any manner and at any stage of the process that he wishes to consult with an attorney before speaking, there can be no questioning. Likewise, if the individual is alone and indicates in any manner that he does not wish to be interrogated, the police may not question him. The mere fact that he may have answered some questions or volunteered some statements on his own does not deprive him of the right to refrain from answering any further inquiries until he has consulted with an attorney and thereafter consents to be questioned.**"**

These warnings outlined by the Court have come to be known as reading the suspect the "Miranda rights." There is an ironic twist to the Miranda case. In January, 1976, Ernesto Miranda was killed in a fight. He was carrying a pile of "Miranda cards" that informed suspects of their rights. One of these cards was carefully read to the suspect arrested for Miranda's murder at the scene.

The framers of the Constitution created a framework for government that has functioned well for two hundred years. Its flexibility has permitted it to adjust to change. For all its adjusting, the Constitution has retained its essential shape and balance of power. But there is always the danger that one branch of govern-

ment will become too powerful and the other branches too weak. It is every citizen's duty to prevent this. Like a delicate ecology system, the checks and balances must be maintained. Otherwise, America will lose the blessings of liberty which the Constitution has established.

Section Review

COMPREHENSION   Developing Vocabulary

1. Explain each of the following terms: judicial review, self-incrimination, commerce, separate but equal.
2. What is meant by "free speech"? What are some of the limits on free speech?

COMPREHENSION   Mastering Facts

1. What act of Congress was ruled unconstitutional in the case of *Marbury* v. *Madison?*
2. In the *Dartmouth College* case, what did the Supreme Court rule about the power of a state legislature over charters?
3. What was the Supreme Court ruling in the *Plessy* v. *Ferguson* decision?
4. What was unusual about the *Brown* decision?

EVALUATION   Relating Past to Present

1. How does the *Marbury* case make the Supreme Court the final authority on the Constitution? Does this make the judicial branch more powerful than the other branches? Explain.
2. Are monopolies legal today? How has the *Gibbons* v. *Ogden* case affected the status of monopolies?

CONCEPTS
Understanding Our Nation's Heritage

1. How are your rights protected by the decision in the *Miranda* case?
2. Do you attend an integrated school? Has your school district been affected by the *Brown* decision? How could you find out more about the impact of the *Brown* decision in your school district?

CONCEPTS   Developing Effective Citizenship

1. What did the Dred Scott decision say about citizenship? How did it make violent resistance to slavery more likely?
2. According to the *Schenck* case, how do conditions influence what is good citizenship?

199

CHAPTER 9

The Federalist Era

1789–1800

People in the Chapter

George Washington—*first president of the United States, whose aim is to keep the presidential office above political disputes.*

Alexander Hamilton—*the first secretary of the treasury, whose economic policies guide the new nation.*

Thomas Jefferson—*Washington's secretary of state and a political foe of Hamilton.*

John Jay—*diplomat who concludes a very unpopular treaty with Britain, and becomes the first Chief Justice of the United States.*

John Adams—*the second president of the United States, who puts national interest above his party in avoiding war with France.*

Linking Past to Present

When George Washington became the first president of the United States, he led a nation that seemed united in heart and mind. But soon he discovered that such was not the case. Washington hoped for unity in the national government. He did not like factions or political parties because he considered them enemies of the republic. But by the time he left office in 1797, two political parties had come into existence. They took the names of Federalist and Republican. Although the name was the same, this Republican party was completely different from the modern one.

One of the reasons for the development of parties was the public reaction to a series of economic proposals by Alexander Hamilton, Washington's secretary of the treasury. Hamilton's policies created such a disagreement in the House of Representatives that members split into two parties. The Federalists favored Hamilton's policies while the Republicans, led by James Madison and then by Thomas Jefferson, opposed them.

Few people expected this division and no one welcomed it. Each party looked on the other as a troublemaking faction made up of the enemies of good government. Changes of government in European monarchies were usually accompanied by great disorder if not bloodshed. That is why Americans at first had such a distrust, even fear, of political parties.

1 PRESIDENT WASHINGTON TAKES CHARGE

VOCABULARY   *Bill of Rights   cabinet   funding   bank notes   elastic clause   excise*

It was shortly after noon on April 30, 1789. George Washington, dressed in a plain brown suit but wearing a sword, stood on the porch of the Federal Hall on Wall Street in New York and said, "I do solemnly swear that I will faithfully execute the office of President of the United States and will, to the best of my ability, preserve, protect, and defend the Constitution of the United States. So help me God."

Cheers rose from the crowd as Washington repeated the words that made him the first president of the new nation. The cheers grew louder and bells rang as he kissed the red leather-bound Bible on which he had sworn his oath of office. Then he turned and entered the hall to talk to Congress about the "ocean of difficulties" that lay ahead.

The president and the first Congress had much work to do. They had to create a bureaucracy to help the president carry out laws. They had to provide for a judicial system. And they had to raise money for operating expenses and for paying off the debts of the United States. American leaders realized they were treading on fresh ground. "We are in a wilderness," James Madison wrote, "without a single footstep to guide us."

The Bill of Rights

Everyone agreed that the new government's first order of business should be the adoption of a bill of rights. These amendments to the Constitution would list the freedoms that the new federal government could not take away from the people.

The question of a bill of rights had come up several times during the Constitutional Convention, but the delegates had voted it down. Why? Apparently because they did not think it was necessary. To them, the Constitution as a whole was a bill of rights. It listed what the new government could do. It did not take away any of the rights for which Americans had fought the Revolutionary War. The delegates assumed that the people retained their rights. As one of them later wrote, "It never occurred to us that personal liberty could ever be endangered in this country."

Others, however, felt differently about the matter. Thomas Jefferson had been in Paris while the convention was going on. He wrote to Madison that "a bill of rights is what the people are entitled to against every government on earth . . . and what no just government should refuse." Patrick Henry felt it was foolish to take a chance that the rulers of the new nation would turn out to be good men. To him, the only way to guarantee liberty was through a system of law. In addition, some states had ratified the Constitution with the definite understanding that it would quickly be amended to include a bill of rights.

Accordingly, in September 1789, Congress approved twelve amendments to the Constitution and submitted them to the states. Two of them—dealing with congressmen's salaries and congressional reapportionment—were defeated. The remaining ten were ratified and became part of the Constitution in 1791. These first ten amendments are known as the Bill of Rights.

As you can see from reading the Bill of Rights on page 186, it protects people from government interference in certain areas. The Bill of Rights

Washington's Inaugural. It took him one week to go from Mount Vernon to New York. He had to stop along the way for speeches, fireworks, and hastily constructed triumphal arches.

protects freedom of religion, freedom of speech, freedom of the press, the right to assemble peacefully with other persons, and the right to petition the federal government to correct wrongs. It requires that authorities obtain a warrant from a judge before searching or seizing any property. The Bill of Rights also provides for trial by jury in criminal cases, and prohibits excessive bail and "cruel and unusual punishments." It gives individuals the right not to testify against themselves in court. The Ninth and Tenth Amendments restrict the powers of the federal government to those named in the Constitution. All other powers are reserved "to the States respectively, or the people."

The Judicial and Executive Branches

After approving the constitutional amendments, Congress turned its attention to the organization of the other two branches of the federal government.

Organizing the Judiciary. The Constitution had left the details of the federal court system up to Congress. Members of the first Congress faced many questions concerning the courts. How many judges should there be? How many courts? Who would prosecute the government's cases? How would court orders be enforced? Suppose federal court decisions conflicted with state laws?

The Judiciary Act of 1789 established a Supreme Court with a chief justice and five associate justices (a number since changed several times by Congress). In addition, the act established sixteen lower federal courts throughout the country (this number has likewise been changed).

The act also provided for prosecuting attorneys and for marshals who would enforce the decisions of the federal courts. These marshals were given the job of taking the first national census of 1790. This census was required by the Constitution mostly because no one knew exactly how many representatives each state should send to Congress. Finally, the Judiciary Act created the office of attorney general as the nation's chief law enforcement officer.

Organizing Departments and the Cabinet. In 1789 the executive branch of the federal government consisted of two men, the president and the vice-president. Obviously, they needed help in governing. Three executive departments were created to deal with the three most pressing problem areas: the Department of State to deal with foreign affairs, the Department of War to handle military matters, and the Department of the Treasury to handle financial problems.

Washington was careful in the secretaries he appointed to head each department. He chose able men whom he knew and trusted personally. He also chose them from various parts of the country.

He knew there were jealousies between different sections. Each section would be more interested in supporting the new government if one of its own leaders was appointed to a high executive office. Washington's most important appointments were Thomas Jefferson as secretary of state, Alexander Hamilton as secretary of the treasury, Henry Knox as secretary of war, and Edmund Randolph as attorney general.

Originally, the president had no intention that the three secretaries and the attorney general would form a cabinet. No such group is mentioned in the Constitution. Within a few years, however, the secretaries began meeting together to advise the president, and the cabinet became a lasting part of the executive branch.

Hamilton's Economic Policies

As secretary of the treasury, Hamilton felt he had a mission: to introduce "order into our finances" and to put the new nation on a firm economic footing. He turned his attention first to the public debt, that is, the money owed by the national and state governments.

Paying Off Foreign Debts. The public debt in 1790 came to about $80 million, a huge amount for those days. About two-thirds was owed by the United States; about one-third by various state governments.

The federal government owed money both at home and abroad. Most of the debt had been incurred during the Revolution. Patriots had lent the Continental Congress funds with which to carry on the struggle against Great Britain. Soldiers had received government bonds instead of hard cash as payment for their military service. In addition, both the Continental Congress and the Confederation Congress had borrowed money from such nations as France, the Netherlands, and Spain. In contrast, states owed money only to private citizens.

There was no argument about paying off the foreign debt at face value in order to establish the new government's credit with other nations. As Hamilton said, "The debt of the United States . . . was the price of liberty." There was, however, a tremendous amount of controversy about the domestic debt. Some people objected to the method of payment that Hamilton suggested. Others opposed Hamilton's idea that the federal government should simply assume, or take over, the debts of the states.

Funding Domestic Debts. Hamilton's suggested method of payment is known as *funding*, or paying off one debt by creating another. Hamilton proposed that the federal government issue new bonds in exchange for the old ones that had been issued by the Continental Congress and the Confederation Congress. The new bonds would have the same value as the old ones, plus any unpaid interest.

On the surface, this seemed like a fair exchange. But many people—including James Madison, who rapidly became the leader of the House of Representatives—strongly opposed Hamilton's plan. They felt that Hamilton was not being fair. The average person had bought the bonds to help support the government. But during the hard times following the Revolutionary War, many people had sold their bonds in order to make ends meet. Not only that. Since bond prices had fallen after the war, many people had sold their bonds for as little as 25 percent of the original value. And who had purchased the bonds? Wealthy speculators, most of them merchants in northern commercial cities. Madison and others resented the fact that these speculators would receive $100 from the government for a bond that had cost them only $25, especially since the money to buy the bonds would come from taxes. Why should speculators gain at the expense of ordinary, patriotic soldiers and citizens?

Far from being horrified by the situation, Hamilton had planned it. In his view, the best way to make the new federal government succeed was to get powerful, wealthy people behind it. This could be accomplished by making their interest the government's interest. People would support a government that allowed them to make money.

Assuming State Debts. Hamilton's suggestion that the federal government assume debts owed by the states also made many people furious, especially in the South. The southern states had already paid off most of their debts. They resented government debt assumption because it meant they would be taxed to help pay the debts of northern states.

Despite the opposition, Congress approved both funding and debt assumption. The congressmen felt that they had to establish a good credit reputation for the new government, and this meant paying all public debts. Also, Hamilton had made a suggestion that was particularly attractive to southerners. Rather than locate the capital in New York or Philadelphia, he said, why not build a new city on the banks of the Potomac? So Congress passed both parts of the Hamiltonian program as well as a bill establishing a new "federal city" on land donated by Maryland. The federal government was moved to Washington, D.C., in 1800.

Establishing a National Bank.
After Congress accepted his proposals for managing the public debt, Hamilton moved on to the second part of his economic program. He urged the establishment of a bank of the United States, with the power to issue *bank notes,* or paper money, and with branches in various cities.

Hamilton argued that such a national banking system had many economic advantages. It would handle tax receipts and all other government money. Since its notes would have the same value all over the nation, citizens of different states would find it easier to do business with one another. People would have more confidence in paper money that said "Bank of the United States" than in paper money printed by small local or state banks.

Alexander Hamilton. The young man from the West Indies believed that the government should depend on the support of the rich.

Hamilton also believed that there were political advantages in a national banking system. The government would own only 20 percent of the shares of stock in the bank. The remaining 80 percent would be owned by private investors. Naturally, these private investors would be "the rich and well-born" people whose allegiance to the federal government Hamilton wanted to encourage. In Hamilton's view, the bank would help cement the national Union.

Hamilton got his national bank, but only after arousing further suspicion and hostility to his entire financial program. Southerners argued, quite correctly, that the bank would make northern merchants richer but would offer few benefits to farmers. At the same time, in the House, Madison raised a new issue. The Constitution, he said, did not give the federal government specific authority to establish a bank. Thus, in Madison's opinion, establishing a national bank was unconstitutional.

When the bill chartering the Bank for twenty years reached Washington's desk, the president was very doubtful about signing it. He asked Jefferson and Hamilton for their opinions.

Jefferson agreed with Madison's "strict interpretation" of the Constitution. Yes, there was a so-called elastic clause, which said that Congress could make all laws "necessary and proper" for carrying out its powers. But such laws, in Jefferson's opinion, had to be really necessary, not just convenient. If Congress could carry out its powers *without* setting up a bank, for example, then it did not have the right to set up a bank.

Hamilton, on the other hand, favored a "loose interpretation" of the Constitution. Congress had the right "to lay and collect taxes" and "to borrow money." The national bank would help with both tasks. Since the Constitution did not specifically prohibit such a bank, Congress had the right to set one up. Washington took Hamilton's advice, and the first National Bank was established.

Levying Taxes.
"All taxes are odious (hateful)," said Congressman John Laurance of New York. "It is also true some are more odious than others." And indeed, the tax proposed by Hamilton as the third part of his economic program was so odious that it caused a tax revolt known as the Whiskey Rebellion.

One of the first acts of the new Congress had been the passage of an import tax on goods manufactured in Europe. By the time Hamilton took of-

The First Bank of the United States on Third Street in Philadelphia is shown here in a 1799 engraving.

distilled the corn into whiskey, which could be sent easily to market on the backs of mules.

Since whiskey was the main source of cash for these frontier farmers, Hamilton knew that the excise tax would make them furious. And so it did. Farmers in western Pennsylvania refused to pay. They beat up federal marshals in Pittsburgh and even threatened to secede from the Union.

Hamilton, however, was not upset. He looked upon the Whiskey Rebellion as an opportunity for the federal government to show that it could enforce the law without help from the states, even along the western frontier. Accordingly, some 15,000 militia were called up. Accompanied by Hamilton himself in uniform, the federal troops hiked over the Alleghenies and scattered the rebels without the loss of a single life.

fice as secretary of the treasury, this tax was bringing in a lot of revenue. But more money was needed to pay off the public debt and to run the national government. So Hamilton suggested that an *excise* (sales tax) be levied on every gallon of whiskey that was made and sold.

Why on whiskey? The reason was political. Most whiskey producers were small frontier farmers. Their major crop was corn. But corn was too bulky to carry across the Appalachians and sell in the settled areas along the Atlantic. So the farmers

Section 1 Review

COMPREHENSION   Developing Vocabulary

1.   Explain these terms: funding, bank notes, excise, elastic clause, Bill of Rights, cabinet.

COMPREHENSION   Mastering Facts

1.   What was the first order of business for the new Congress?

2.   Why did the Constitution require a census?

3.   Where did Hamilton suggest that the new national capital be established?

4.   Why did Hamilton favor a sales tax on whiskey?

2   THE FIRST POLITICAL PARTIES DEVELOP

VOCABULARY   *Federalists   Republicans*

Hamilton's view of the new nation's proper future was different from that held by Jefferson and Madison. As time went on, this difference resulted in the formation of two distinct political groups, or parties. People whose opinions were closest to those of Hamilton called themselves Federalists. Those whose views were closer to those of Jefferson and Madison became known as Republicans.

Hamilton's View

Hamilton wanted a powerful nation resting on a balanced economy of agriculture, trade, finance, and manufacturing. Agriculture, he thought, did not need any special encouragement since most people were farmers. Other, less developed parts of the economy, however, *did* need government help. Hamilton thought that the major weakness of the Confederation had been its inability to raise money. Therefore, he wanted to gain the support of financial leaders for the new government.

Hamilton believed that people in the mass were not to be trusted. He thought they often acted foolishly and needed a strong government to tell them what to do. The rich, the educated, and the well-born were the only people who counted, Hamilton believed. Only they could be depended on to govern wisely, because they had the most to lose from a weak or unstable government. Hamilton feared that if common people got too much

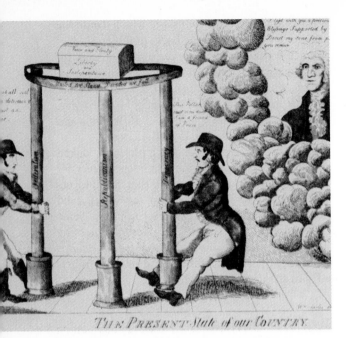

In the cartoon above the spirit of party threatens to destroy the nation. Washington urges restraint.

Washington's Role

As hostility rose between Hamilton and Jefferson, Washington tried evenhandedly to soothe things between them. He respected both men's abilities and hoped they could work together. But Washington was deeply convinced that as head of the nation he should remain above the quarrels over details of public policy.

Washington's idea of the presidency was to keep it formal. He held regular morning receptions as well as formal evening dances and dinners. Uniformed servants in powdered wigs stood at the doors. Some critics thought these occasions made the president seem too distant and cold. But Washington thought it was necessary for the dignity of the highest office in the new country.

Others thought all the social events were just dull. It is only necessary, one wrote, "to be clean shaved, shirted, and powdered, go make your bows with grace, and to be master of small chat on the weather . . . or newspaper anecdote of the day."

power, they might endanger private property. In other words, the have-nots might take it away from the haves.

Jefferson's View

Jefferson had a deep faith in the common people, especially the American farmer. "Those who labor in the earth," he once wrote, "are the chosen people of God." He distrusted special privilege. He also disliked the world of cities, commerce, and finance. Although he later modified his views somewhat, in general he felt that city life corrupted people through ignorance and poverty. "The mobs of great cities add just so much to the support of pure government as sores do to the strength of the human body."

Unlike Hamilton, Jefferson favored a weak central government and strong state governments. He believed that the liberties of individuals had to be protected against all governments, which is why he fought so strongly for the Bill of Rights. Again unlike Hamilton, he did not favor government help to manufacturing, trade, or finance. "For the general operation of manufacture, let our workshops remain in Europe." Jefferson's view of the American nation was a land of small independent farmers and educated leaders working together in perfect harmony.

The Parties Organize

Before 1791 the *Gazette of the United States* was the only newspaper that specialized in national politics. Its editor, John Frenno, was a Hamiltonian, and his paper reflected Hamilton's views.

To offset this publication, Madison and Jefferson set out to gain popular support for their position. They toured New England and New York to explain their views to political leaders there. In New York they won over Governor George Clinton, who had long been a rival of Hamilton's wealthy father-in-law and who controlled the upstate vote. They also gained the support of Aaron Burr, who had many followers in New York City. Then in October 1791, Madison and Jefferson established the *National Gazette*, edited by the poet Philip Freneau. The *National Gazette* was to criticize Hamilton's policies. Madison wrote several articles for this newspaper, referring to people who backed his views as "the Republican party." Many readers responded to this call for support. They began forming Republican clubs.

Hamilton was not a man to sit idle while his opponents organized. Like the Republicans, the Federalists began setting up local clubs of supporters. In this new kind of contest, the Federalists had several advantages. They had a well-thought-out, positive program. The great majority of newspaper editors and clergymen supported their ideas, as did most wealthy men. In addition, Federalists in the federal government were able to reward their party's workers with jobs.

At the time of the 1792 national election, the Republicans were not well enough organized to run a candidate for president. Besides, Washington had reluctantly agreed to serve again, and it would have been futile for the Republicans to oppose the great national hero. Washington was elected for a second term with John Adams again as vice-president.

Section 2 Review

COMPREHENSION   Developing Vocabulary

1. Explain these terms: Federalists, Republicans, balanced economy.

COMPREHENSION   Mastering Facts

1. According to Hamilton, which parts of the economy needed help from the federal government?
2. Which political party consisted of people who shared Jefferson's views?
3. Which groups of people did Jefferson consider most important? Which groups did Hamilton consider most important?

3   FOREIGN AFFAIRS BECOME TROUBLESOME

VOCABULARY   *neutrality   privateers*

The new government faced old problems with the British and the Indians in the Northwest Territory. Spain still claimed the land west of the Appalachians and south of the Ohio. But the greatest difficulties arose as a result of the French Revolution, which broke out only a few weeks after Washington took office in the spring of 1789.

The French Revolution

At first most Americans welcomed the French Revolution. They felt that their own principles of liberty were spreading to the Old World. Several cities showed their feelings against monarchy by changing street names. New York's Queen Street, for example, was renamed Pearl Street, while Crown Street turned into Liberty Street.

As the French Revolution grew bloodier, however, American public opinion began to shift. Hamilton and other Federalists expressed their fear that the Revolution's leaders were determined to destroy all authority and stability. President Washington tended to agree with Hamilton, and other Americans began to wonder if perhaps Hamilton was right when he said that the public was "a great beast."

Divided Opinions.   In 1793, after the beheading of Louis XVI, France declared war on Great Britain. When the news reached America, it immediately deepened the division between the two emerging political parties. The Republicans cheered for the cause of republicanism and against the British monarchy. Both sides traded insults. Cries of "British bootlickers" were met with such phrases as "lying dogs," and "frog-eating, man-eating, blood-drinking cannibals."

The insults masked a basic political question, namely: Should the United States enter the war? Republicans argued that France had helped the United States gain its independence. We were therefore obligated to help France, especially because we had signed a treaty of alliance in 1778. Federalists felt the United States had no choice but to support Britain, the former parent country.

Washington did not favor fighting for Great Britain. On the other hand, since France had started the war, he did not feel that the United States was bound by the treaty. So he issued a declaration of neutrality, saying that the United States would support neither side in the conflict.

Genet's Mission.   In the meantime, a minister from the new French republic had arrived in the United States to persuade the Americans to join the war against England. Edmond Genet (juh-*nay*) was an energetic, enthusiastic young man with a wooden leg and absolutely no common sense. He did not bother to present himself formally to the United States government, as required by the rules of international diplomacy. Instead, he organized military expeditions against the Spanish in Florida and New Orleans, and outfitted *privateers* (people with privately owned ships) to prey on British shipping. In short, he went about undermining United States neutrality.

When Genet finally got around to visiting the president, Washington treated him with a chilling coldness. That would have brought most men to their senses. But Genet continued to act in a way that no independent nation could tolerate from a foreign minister. Even Jefferson, who had been enthusiastic about Genet's arrival, was put off by the latter's lack of respect for the United States. The entire cabinet backed the president's formal request for Genet's recall. By then Genet's political backers had fallen from power in Paris. Fearing for his life, the young envoy remained in America, married Governor Clinton's daughter, and retired to a country estate on the Hudson River. Alexander Hamilton called him a "burned-out comet."

The effects of Genet's activities on the American government were less romantic. Jefferson's apparent sympathy with Genet's early activities and his continued approval of the French Revolution aroused Washington's suspicions. The president also disapproved of the grass-roots Republican clubs Jefferson was sponsoring. Washington did not like political factions. At the end of 1793 the president accepted Jefferson's resignation as secretary of state. Hamilton remained Washington's intimate advisor, his words no longer challenged by his rival.

Undeclared War with Britain

It proved easier to proclaim neutrality in the European contest than to maintain it. As neutrals, Americans claimed the right to carry non-military goods to the ports of any warring nation. In 1793 the French lifted their traditional mercantilist restrictions on trade with their West Indian islands. Soon the Caribbean was filled with the sails of American trading vessels. But the British took a different view of neutral rights. They claimed that no trade closed in peacetime could be opened in time of war. Without warning, they began seizing American vessels in large numbers and taking over both crew and cargoes.

Republicans called for stronger measures against the British. War hysteria swept the country as Americans railed against George III, that "prince of land and sea-robbers." Hamilton watched U.S. neutrality go down the drain. Although Hamilton favored Britain, he thought the young country should stay out of war. He urged Washington to send a special envoy to London to negotiate the various points of issue between the

two countries. Washington decided to send John Jay, the experienced diplomat whom he had earlier appointed as the first chief justice of the Supreme Court.

Jay's Treaty. Jay was in a strong negotiating position. The British did not want to again fight both France and the United States. Jay's secret instructions were to try to gain concessions from the British on neutral shipping. If he could not, then he was to get an agreement with other neutral powers in Europe about protecting their rights as neutrals. While Jay was crossing the Atlantic, Washington received just such an offer from two neutrals, Sweden and Denmark. But Hamilton persuaded him not to accept it. He argued that such an alliance of neutrals would anger the British and make Jay's task more difficult. Then Hamilton privately told his friend, the British ambassador, about Washington's decision. The ambassador, in turn, sent this news to the British negotiators in London. Jay remained unaware that Hamilton had undercut his position. No matter how much he threatened that the United States would join with other neutrals to protect neutral rights, the English knew that Washington would not allow such an action.

The result was that Jay could only make a treaty highly favorable to the British. They agreed, again, to evacuate their posts in the Northwest Territory, and they soon did so. But Jay had to give up a great deal in return. The British won the right to continue the fur trade with Indians on the American side of the Canadian–United States border. This concession angered westerners who had been suspicious of Jay ever since his unsuccessful talks with Spain in 1785. On the rights of neutral ships, the British refused to budge an inch. They would still seize neutral ships in certain waters. Both parties agreed that each should have the right of free navigation of the Mississippi River through Spanish territory.

The Country Objects. Jay's Treaty was so unsatisfactory that the public outcry was even greater than Washington and Hamilton feared. Nevertheless, the Senate ratified the treaty by an exact two-thirds majority. The Republican press echoed with outraged criticisms of Jay, of the Senate, and even of the president himself. The hostile mood of the country was demonstrated by someone who chalked in large letters on a Boston fence: "DAMN

JOHN JAY! DAMN EVERY ONE THAT WON'T DAMN JOHN JAY! DAMN EVERY ONE THAT WON'T SIT UP ALL NIGHT DAMNING JOHN JAY!!!"

The Western Frontier

Having made one of the most unpopular treaties ever ratified by the United States Senate, the Washington administration was fortunate to achieve two popular victories in the West.

Pinckney's Treaty. The first victory was a diplomatic one at the expense of Spain. Jay's apparently minor success concerning British and American rights on the Mississippi River frightened the Spanish. The Madrid government grew worried about possible joint British-American action against the Louisiana Territory. The American ambassador in Madrid, Thomas Pinckney, successfully played on these fears.

Pinckney's Treaty of 1795 won virtually every point with Spain that the Americans had been aiming for since the Revolution. Spain gave up its claims to all land east of the Mississippi and north of Florida, and also agreed to open the Mississippi River to American traffic. For three years American traders would be permitted to land goods at New Orleans for reloading onto ocean-going vessels. At the end of that time, the arrangement could be renewed.

Defeating the Indians. When the Revolutionary War broke out, the Indian tribes of the Iroquois League were not involved at first. As the Oneidas put it, "We are unwilling to join on either side of such a contest, for we love you both—old England and new." By 1776, however, the League was no longer neutral. And it was now the League of Six Nations, rather than Five Nations, since the Tuscaroras had joined the League in 1712. Four of the six nations—the Cayugas, Mohawks, Onondagas, and Senecas—joined forces with the British. The two remaining tribes—the Oneidas and Tuscaroras—threw their support to the Americans.

The Indian war in the northern states was bloody and destructive. During 1778 and 1779, combined British and Indian troops led a series of raids on American frontier settlements. They would strike unexpectedly out of the forest, burn houses and scalp victims, and then melt away into the wilderness. In response, General John Sullivan

This cartoon from a wood engraving shows Jefferson's followers burning John Jay in effigy because of the latter's unpopular treaty of 1794.

led an American army into Seneca territory from the west. The Senecas withdrew, and the Americans burned the Indians' villages and cornfields.

A similar pattern was followed in the southern states by the descendants of the Adapters you read about in chapter 1. The Cherokees, Chocktaws, and Creeks supported the British because American settlers had pushed into Indian lands in spite of agreements to the contrary. As in the North, the Indians raided white settlements along the frontier, and in return, American troops laid waste the Indian homelands.

209

Under the terms of the Treaty of Paris, the United States received title to the land between the Appalachians and the Mississippi River. However, as the Spanish negotiator pointed out, that land belonged to "free and independent nations of Indians." And these Indian nations were not represented in Paris. Furthermore, they would not admit their defeat. They wanted the Americans to negotiate with them directly.

The Americans refused. Instead, they sent a series of armies into Indian country to force the tribes to submit. The first army was led by General Josiah Harmar. In 1790 Harmar's troops were ambushed and defeated by a group of northern tribes under the command of a Miami warrior named Little Turtle. In 1791 the Miami Confederacy inflicted an even worse defeat on an army led by General Arthur St. Clair.

Finally, in 1793, Washington appointed General "Mad Anthony" Wayne. Wayne spent an entire year drilling his troops. Greatly impressed, Little Turtle told his allies, "We have beaten the enemy twice under different commanders. . . . The Americans are now led by a chief who never sleeps. . . . We have never been able to surprise him. . . . It would be prudent to listen to his offers of peace." The other Indian chiefs did not agree with Little Turtle's advice and replaced him with a far less able commander. In 1794 the Indians were decisively defeated at the Battle of Fallen Timbers, near what is now Toledo, Ohio.

The next year, United States authorities negotiated the Treaty of Greenville. In exchange for an annual payment of $10,000, the Miami Confederacy gave up most of the land that eventually became Ohio. The Indians also gave up the land on which Chicago now stands.

Section 3 Review

COMPREHENSION   Developing Vocabulary

1. Explain these terms: privateers, neutrality, League of Six Nations.

COMPREHENSION   Mastering Facts

1. Why did Washington issue a declaration of neutrality?
2. How did Genet antagonize the United States?
3. What did the United States obtain from Spain in Pinckney's Treaty of 1795?
4. What happened at the Battle of Fallen Timbers?

4   PRESIDENT ADAMS FACES POLITICAL STRIFE

VOCABULARY   *sectionalism*   *XYZ Affair*   *nullification*

In 1796, at the close of his second four-year term, Washington made it clear that he would not serve as president again. In his Farewell Address, he urged the United States to "steer clear of permanent alliances" with other nations. "Temporary alliances" were acceptable in "extraordinary emergencies," he said. But Americans should remember that nations never give one another real favors but are concerned only with their own interests. Washington then retired to his home at Mount Vernon, where he watched unhappily the developing political parties.

The First Partisan Election: 1796

To most Federalists, it seemed logical that the vice-president should succeed the retiring hero. John Adams was known as a friend of strong government and an enemy of the radical experiments that were taking place in France. Whom to nominate for vice-president, however, was a ticklish matter. Hamilton seemed the obvious choice. But Adams had always been suspicious of Hamilton, whom he considered sly and ambitious. Hamilton, for his part, knew Adams was a man he could not control. Hamilton also recognized that he himself did not have much popular following. So the Federalists selected Charles Cotesworth Pinckney as their vice-presidential candidate.

The Republicans saw the election as their first opportunity to gain control over national policy. They chose Jefferson as their candidate because he had wider popular appeal than Madison. They named Burr as their candidate for vice-president.

As things turned out, Adams received seventy-one electoral votes and Jefferson, sixty-eight. But the Constitution provided that the runner-up for president should become vice-president. Thus a Republican was elected vice-president to serve under a Federalist president! What had seemed sensible when the Constitution was written seemed almost unworkable with the unexpected rise of two political parties.

Washington got no reassurance from the election. What he feared most—sectionalism—was apparent. Almost all the electors from southern states voted for Jefferson, while all the electors from northern states voted for Adams.

Friction with France

No American politician had written more about human nature than John Adams. But in practice he was, as Jefferson observed, "a bad calculator" of people's motives. Benjamin Franklin had once written that Adams "is always an honest man, often a wise one, but sometimes, and in some things, absolutely out of his senses." He was also vain, stuffy, short, and overweight, which led to the unflattering nickname of "His Rotundity." And his administration began with a crisis with France.

The XYZ Affair. The French had been outraged by Jay's Treaty, which they regarded as a betrayal of the 1778 French-American alliance. Even before Adams took office in March 1797, French naval vessels had begun seizing American merchantmen bound for England. The French government refused to receive a new American ambassador. When news of this insult arrived in Philadelphia, Adams was faced with demands for war by members of his own political party.

Rather than agree, Adams chose to send a three-man team to Paris to negotiate about ship seizures. The French foreign minister, Talleyrand, appointed three low-level officials to meet with the Americans. The three Frenchmen explained that there could be no negotiations unless Talleyrand's palm was greased with a bribe of $240,000. Bribes were fairly common in diplomacy in those days. But the amount the French wanted was outrageously high.

In their indignant reports home, the American

This rare print (1799) shows a Federalist bias. The five-headed French government demands money from the Americans. Behind the French rob each other and chop off heads.

211

envoys referred to the three Frenchmen simply as "X, Y, and Z." When the reports became public, an uproar broke out over the so-called XYZ Affair. "Millions for defense but not one cent for tribute." Congress promptly created a navy department and authorized American ships to seize French vessels. For the next two years, an undeclared naval war raged in the Atlantic and in the Caribbean Sea.

Adams the Peacemaker. Extreme Federalists—or High Federalists, as they were called—continued to demand that the president ask Congress for a declaration of war. But Adams acted boldly and independently. In doing so, he split his party and ruined his own political future.

Adams had received word that a new French government would now welcome an American envoy without bribe money in his pocket. So in 1799 he sent another three-man team to Paris. The two sides agreed to abandon the 1778 treaty and to work out their differences peacefully. Republicans were delighted. High Federalists were furious. But Adams had won the point about freedom of the seas without getting into a needless war. He rightly remained proud of having placed the nation's interests ahead of his party's and his own. As he later wrote, "I desire no other inscription over my gravestone than: 'Here lies John Adams, who took upon himself the responsibility of peace with France in the year 1800.'"

This portrait of President John Adams captures some of his high-minded and independent character.

Dissent at Home

John Adams was not a man to take criticism lightly. Like Washington—and other presidents since—he thought he should rise above political parties. And again like Washington, he never fully realized that his own opinions were highly political. He thought of them as being simply patriotic. As a confirmed Federalist, he regarded the Republican opposition as something close to a criminal conspiracy against the welfare of the nation. He publicly denounced "those lovers of themselves who withdraw their confidence from their own . . . Government, and place it on a foreign nation, or Domestic Faction."

The Alien Acts. In fact, Adams was heavily and unfairly criticized in the Republican press. To many Federalists, this criticism seemed un-American. Some of the most vocal critics were foreign-born. They included French and English radicals as well as recent Irish immigrants who lashed out at anyone even faintly pro-British. (Britain had occupied Ireland for centuries, using force and bloodshed against its inhabitants.) In addition, the Republican party had chosen a "foreigner" as its leader in the House of Representatives. Albert Gallatin, an able Swiss immigrant, had taken over when Madison retired from Congress in 1798.

So the High Federalists decided to crush this criticism. At the height of war preparations in the early summer of 1798, they pushed four measures through Congress.

The first measure raised the residence requirement for American citizenship from five to fourteen years. The second, the Alien Act, gave the president the power in peacetime to order any alien out of the country. The third, the Alien Enemies Act, permitted the president in wartime to jail aliens at his pleasure. No arrests were made under either the Alien Act or the Alien Enemies Act. But the laws frightened some French refugees into leaving the country.

The Sedition Act. The fourth measure, the Sedition Act, was the one most dangerous to liberty. Its key clause provided fines and jail penalties for anyone speaking or writing "with intent to defame . . . or bring into contempt or disrepute" the president or other members of the government. Since the act was to remain in effect only until the next presidential inauguration, it was clear that it was directly aimed at silencing Republican opposition to Adams's administration.

A number of Republican editors, printers, and politicians were fined and jailed under the Sedition Act. With few exceptions, the judges in these cases were Federalist party members. The trials were often unfair. Many of the juries were handpicked by court marshals who were devoted Federalists.

Republicans were alarmed, and with good reason. They had looked to the courts for protection against tyrannous acts by the other two branches of government. Now it was clear that no branch of government was free from the spirit of political persecution. Both Jefferson and Madison recognized the Alien and Sedition Acts for what they were—violations of the First Amendment, and an excellent campaign issue for the election of 1800.

The Virginia and Kentucky Resolutions. The two Republican leaders decided to organize opposition to these acts by appealing to the states. Madison drew up a set of resolutions which his friends ushered through the Virginia state legislature. Jefferson wrote some similar resolutions that were adopted by Kentucky.

The Virginia and Kentucky Resolutions denounced the offending acts as unconstitutional. Both argued that the states were the original parties to the agreement known as the Constitution. Both resolutions claimed that the states had the power to say when that agreement had been violated. Jefferson argued that each of the states had the power of *nullification*. To nullify something means to declare it illegal and void. Jefferson's theory was that each state had the right to "nullify" any federal act within its borders if it thought the act unconstitutional.

Here was a direct challenge to the supremacy of the federal government. Both resolutions asked other state legislatures to adopt a similar position. None did so. In fact, Federalists in several northern states denounced Virginia and Kentucky for totally misinterpreting the nature of the Constitution. They argued that the Constitution was much more than an agreement among independent states. The Constitution, they said, was an agreement among all the *people* of the nation. They also argued that only the federal courts could decide whether actions of the other two branches violated the Constitution.

So the Virginia and Kentucky Resolutions had little effect at the time. But they reminded Americans that the relationship of the states to the national government was not a settled one. And in fact, the question would soon arise again.

A Transfer of Power: 1800

By 1798 everyone knew that the next presidential election would be a contest between the president and the vice-president. Both sides believed the future of the country was at stake.

Republicans accused Adams of being the tool of the wealthy. After all, one of the Federalist mottoes was: "Those who own the country ought to govern it." Adams, they said, wanted to destroy his enemies with measures like the Alien and Sedition Acts. He was said to be intent on turning the executive branch into a monarchy on the British model. And they urged a vote "For Jefferson and liberty."

Federalists accused Jefferson of being the friend of France and revolutionary disorder. He was described as a wild-eyed opponent of all property except slaves, and an atheist (one who doesn't believe in God). If Jefferson were elected, warned the president of Yale College, "the Bible would be cast into a bonfire."

None of these charges against either man was accurate. Yet neither side hesitated to question the other's patriotism.

The national mood was probably inevitable. The government was new. Americans were not accustomed to the peaceful transfer of power from one political group to another. Each party regarded the other much as Protestants and Catholics had in earlier times—as totally in error and dangerously threatening to all that was good and true. Nevertheless, both sides proved willing to fight with votes, not guns.

The electoral ballots were counted on a cold and snowy day in Washington. Adams received sixty-five votes while Jefferson received seventy-three votes. This constituted a victory for Jefferson. But there was a problem. Burr, who was running as the Republican vice-president, also received seventy-three votes. He realized that if he could get a majority of votes, he could become not vice-president but president! This meant that the House of Representatives, which was dominated by Federalists, would have to break the tie between the two Republicans.

For six feverish days the House took one ballot after another. Finally, Hamilton intervened. Although he opposed Jefferson's policies, he feared Burr even more. He persuaded enough Federalists to cast blank ballots to give Jefferson a majority of two votes. Burr became vice-president.

Most politicians now recognized the need to change the system of voting in the electoral college. The next Congress drafted the Twelfth Amendment, which was ratified in 1804. It provided that electors cast separate ballots for president and for vice-president. This system is still in effect today.

During the few weeks remaining before Jefferson's inauguration, the outgoing Congress passed a new judiciary act. Adams named strong Federalists as judges. Among them was John Marshall, whom Adams named chief justice of the Supreme Court. It turned out to be an act of lasting importance. Although the Republican party ruled for more than thirty years, Marshall kept handing down Federalist interpretations of the supreme law of the land.

Section 4 Review

COMPREHENSION Developing Vocabulary

1. Explain these terms: nullification, sectionalism, XYZ Affair, High Federalists, Sedition Act.

COMPREHENSION Mastering Facts

1. What act provided fines and imprisonment for anyone who criticized members of the government?
2. What was the major campaign issue of the 1800 presidential election?
3. What event led to the adoption of the Twelfth Amendment?
4. What important judicial appointment did Adams make in the final days of his administration?

CHAPTER 9 Review

Chapter Summary

The United States experienced much political change and development during the Federalist Era. George Washington feared the formation of political parties. However, from the debates over different interpretations of the Constitution and different economic and foreign policies, political parties developed anyway. The outbreak of the French Revolution and an undeclared war with Britain created serious problems in foreign affairs. In 1800 the United States experienced its first real transfer of power when Thomas Jefferson, a Republican, succeeded John Adams, a Federalist, as president.

Questions for Critical Thinking

COMPREHENSION Summarizing Main Ideas

1. Give two reasons why the Republicans did not run a presidential candidate in 1792.
2. What foreign policy did Washington urge in his Farewell Address? What reasons did he give? Do you agree or disagree with his point of view? Explain.
3. What intepretation of the Constitution was advanced by the Kentucky and Virginia Resolutions? Why were the resolutions not adopted by other state governments?

COMPREHENSION Interpreting Events

1. Why do you think George Washington was chosen the first president of the Untied States?
2. Why was the Bill of Rights not part of the original Constitution? Why was it added?
3. Which groups of people were in favor of funding the federal government's domestic debt? Which groups of people were against doing so?
4. What constitutional argument did Madison raise against the establishment of a national bank? How did Hamilton respond?
5. To what extent were the first political parties formed on the basis of geography? on the basis of economic interest?
6. If John Peter Zenger had been tried under the Sedition Act of 1798, what would the verdict in his trial probably have been?

7. Why was the presidential election of 1800 significant from the viewpoint of transfer of power?

APPLICATION Using Skills To Evaluate Sources

In using a reference book one must know how to look up information in the Index. For each item below, tell which of the two index entries would be more likely to yield the necessary material.

1. The duties of the attorney general
   a. Federal government
   b. Judiciary
2. Free navigation for Americans on the Mississippi River
   a. Pinckney's Treaty
   b. Mississippi River
3. The actions of the Iroquois League during the Revolutionary War
   a. Iroquois League
   b. Revolutionary War

EVALUATION Comparing Past to Present

1. What constitutional amendment did your state legislature consider most recently? Do you agree or disagree with the final vote? Why?
2. How many cabinet members are there today? Which have been added since Washington's presidency? What do you think accounts for the additions?
3. How many political parties ran candidates in the most recent presidential election? Did any of these parties exist in 1800?
4. What kinds of taxes brought in the most revenue during the nation's first two administrations? What kinds of taxes bring in the most revenue to the federal government today?
5. What criticisms have been raised against the electoral college in recent years? Do you agree or disagree with them?
6. Do you think Hamilton or Jefferson would be more pleased by the government and economy of the United States today? Give reasons for your answer.

Creating a National Capital

When John and Abigail Adams moved into the White House in 1800, the plaster was still damp and many of the rooms were cold and drafty. Quarters were so cramped that Abigail had to hang the family's laundry in the unfinished audience room, now known as the East Room. Outside, the White House itself occupied the middle of a muddy field. There were no fences around the building, so people and stray animals wandered on the lawn. Indeed, during its early days the White House hardly seemed to resemble a presidential residence.

From the start, politicians moving to Washington, D.C., had similar feelings about the new capital city. Living there around 1800 required an ability to put up with the inconveniences of temporary quarters. Many grumbled that the city would never be completed.

The Location. Like Philadelphia and Williamsburg, Washington, D.C., was a planned project. Because of political considerations, however, building the capital city proved extremely difficult. The question of location, for example, was the subject of extended debate. A dozen cities, including Kingston, New Jersey, and Wilmington, Delaware, made offers. But to avoid favoritism toward any established city,

Congress decided not to choose any of them as the capital.

To symbolize the new beginning of the American people, Congress determined to choose an entirely new site. That did not settle the issue, though, as Southerners favored a location along the Potomac River while Northerners opposed placing the capital in slave-holding territory. Thomas Jefferson and Alexander Hamilton finally broke the deadlock through a compromise that resulted in the Residency Bill of 1790.

The bill authorized the president to choose a site "not exceeding 10 miles square" in the Potomac region between Maryland and Virginia. The territory would serve as the permanent location of the American federal government. Since the capital was a federal one, it would not be located in any state. The area would be known as the District of Columbia.

President Washington appointed a surveyor, Andrew Ellicott, to map out the boundaries of the new federal district. As his first assistant in the surveying project, Ellicott selected Benjamin Banneker, a self-taught free black who distinguished himself in mathematics and would soon become famous as a compiler of almanacs.

The Design. To design and oversee the planning of the city,

Washington chose Major Pierre Charles L'Enfant, a French engineer who had served in the American Revolution. The design which L'Enfant produced was splendid, with malls, wide avenues, parks, and squares. He placed important public buildings like the Capitol on high ground. This highlighted structures and also created broad and impressive views of the city.

One unique feature of American city planning was emphasized in the L'Enfant plan: the square block. To early Americans, the geometric regularity of the block symbolized the taming of a hostile environment. L'Enfant used the block pattern, but he also cut some of them with broad diagonal streets that formed public squares—much like those in Europe—at strategic points.

The Problems. Like any urban proposal, L'Enfant's plan created controversy between the aesthetic-minded and the more practical. The plan was so grand that it disturbed many of the landowners in the federal district. L'Enfant's streets were to be 100 to 110 feet wide. Avenues were 160 feet wide, and one grand boulevard was 400 feet wide and a mile long! Business leaders and property owners protested this seeming waste of valuable real estate.

Hostilities between L'Enfant and the business community came to a head when he ordered the biggest landowner in the federal district to demolish his home to make way for an avenue. Such actions could not be tolerated, so Washington had to dismiss the designer.

After L'Enfant's dismissal, work continued haltingly on the city. By 1800 enough of the "President's Palace" and other buildings had been completed to be habitable. So, President John Adams ordered that the functions of the federal government should be transferred from Philadelphia to the "City of Washington . . . by the 15th of June." The man after whom the city had been named died just six months before it officially became the nation's capital.

The Result. From the beginning, Washington, D.C., was a city of contrasts. Despite magnificent governmental structures, the surrounding poverty was immediately visible. This condition persisted into the mid-1800s. One reason for this as well as the city's slow growth was that the nation had limited financial resources. In addition, there was considerable damage caused by the British attack during the War of 1812. A long depression, which began in 1837, also hampered progress.

Washington, D.C., assumed the look of a great capital in the late nineteenth century, when electricity and other inventions

The Capitol building under construction in the new city of Washington in 1800.

made urban improvements possible. After the Civil War, the water supply was improved, sewers were built, streets paved, and sidewalks laid. Spacious parks graced the city, and street lights glittered in the night. By the 1880s, Washington was a fitting capital for a dynamic, expanding nation.

The Present. The passage of nearly two centuries has brought continued additions to and modifications of L'Enfant's original design. Still, the spaciousness of his first plan remains, together with the block pattern of streets cut by diagonals.

Today, Washington, D.C., stands as a model of planned development. Its example has extended far beyond this nation. The United States was the first modern nation to plan a city exclusively as a seat of government. Since then, the planned capitals of Canada, Australia, Pakistan, and Brazil stand as testimonies to the originality and power of an American idea.

Understanding Geography

1. In what ways did political considerations influence the location and construction of America's new capital?

2. What was the main complaint against L'Enfant's design? Do most people still have the same complaint today? Explain.

3. If you were to visit Washington today, what sites would you choose to see?

4. In what ways did Washington, D.C., serve as an example for other nations?

CHAPTER 10

The Jeffersonians

1800–1815

People in the Chapter

John Marshall—*the chief justice of the Supreme Court whose opinions strengthen national power.*

Meriwether Lewis and William Clark—*the explorers who lead the first U.S. expedition across the continent to the Pacific Ocean.*

Aaron Burr—*the former vice-president under Jefferson who kills Alexander Hamilton in a duel.*

James Madison—*the fourth president of the United States. He and his cabinet must flee the capital when the British burn it during the War of 1812.*

Henry Clay—*a leading War Hawk who urges war against Britain and helps negotiate the Treaty of Ghent in 1815.*

Andrew Jackson—*the defender and hero of the Battle of New Orleans in 1815.*

Linking Past to Present

Thomas Jefferson called the Republican victory that placed him in office "the revolution of 1800." His election was indeed followed by change. Never again would Federalists control the presidency. However, they continued to control the courts through the judges appointed during the Washington and Adams administrations.

Jefferson and his hand-picked successors, James Madison and James Monroe, wanted to avoid further entanglement in European conflicts. Jefferson's eyes were on what he called America's "continental destiny." He looked forward to the day when much of North America would be an American "empire for liberty." He used that phrase unblushingly, despite the fact that the rest of the continent was claimed by European powers and occupied by Indians, while one-fifth of his own countrymen were slaves. As things turned out, Jefferson more than doubled the size of the United States. But then Madison allowed the country to become involved in a European war. Only after the war ended was the United States free to concentrate on its internal expansion.

1 PRESIDENT JEFFERSON LEADS THE NATION

VOCABULARY   *midnight judges*   *judicial review*

The new president's eloquent Inaugural Address extended the hand of peace to his opponents. "Every difference of opinion is not a difference of principle. . . . We are all Republicans, we are all Federalists." At the time the statement was more hopeful than accurate. But as Jefferson's administration proceeded, certain Federalist ideas did in fact become part of the nation's government. In a parting shot at Adams, Jefferson also announced his faith that enemies of the Republic should be left undisturbed as a sign that in the United States "error of opinion" may be tolerated. Bitter over his defeat, the former president did not attend Jefferson's inauguration. When Jefferson spoke, Adams was already in a coach rattling back to Massachusetts.

A Fresh Start Is Made

"Long Tom" Jefferson had triumphed in a strongly partisan election. And the new administration did seem quite different from the previous Federalist ones.

A New Capital and a New Style.   Jefferson's inauguration was the first to take place in the new federal city of Washington on the Potomac. The new president was sworn in by Chief Justice John Marshall.

The inauguration symbolized Jefferson's feeling that a simple government was the one best suited to a republic. Washington and Adams had favored a grand, almost royal, style. Washington had

The famous painting of Thomas Jefferson by Caleb Boyle. In the background is a natural bridge which can still be seen in Virginia.

219

Two important members of Jefferson's cabinet. General Henry Dearborn, *Secretary of War (left)* and Albert Gallatin, *Secretary of the Treasury (right).*

driven around in a coach with six horses, just like King George III. Martha Washington had been addressed as "Lady Washington." Instead of shaking hands, John Adams used to bow stiffly at his receptions. Jefferson, in contrast, actually walked from his boardinghouse to his inauguration.

Jefferson continued this informality while in office. There were few servants with powdered wigs. The president often opened the White House's front door to visiting diplomats. He met senators while wearing old clothes and carpet slippers "with his toes out." The British ambassador was so shocked at such behavior that he refused to attend Jefferson's dinners. But the "levelers" who had voted Republican were delighted.

Also in keeping with the more "common touch" he thought suitable for a republic, Jefferson did not deliver his first annual State of the Union address in person, as Washington and Adams had done. Instead, he sent it to Congress in writing.

Cutting Costs and Simplifying Finances. Jefferson's first appointments to his cabinet followed Washington's precedent. He appointed men who agreed with him, but he kept an eye on geographical balance. His most influential appointees were James Madison, who was named secretary of state, and Albert Gallatin, who became secretary of the treasury.

Since Jefferson believed in a weak national government, he cut costs wherever possible. He reduced the size of the army, halted the scheduled expansion of the navy, and lowered expenses for government social functions. Such reductions were easier then than they would be today. The federal bureaucracy was tiny. For example, when Jefferson took office, the State Department had eight employees. Now it has over 11,000.

Jefferson wanted to make the government's financial affairs so simple "that every member of Congress and every man of any mind in the Union should be able to comprehend them." He also wanted to tear down Hamilton's financial program. So all internal taxes were eliminated, and all tax collectors and inspectors were fired. Gallatin persuaded the president not to abolish the Bank of the United States, but its influence was nevertheless greatly reduced anyway.

Judicial Changes. Jefferson had been a strong opponent of the Alien and Sedition Acts. So he asked Congress to change the period of naturalization back from fourteen to five years. He also pardoned the men who had been convicted under the Sedition Act and ordered their fines returned with interest.

Jefferson also began what many called a "war" against the judiciary. During the four months between Jefferson's election in 1800 and his inauguration on March 4, 1801, the Federalists tried to increase their hold on the judiciary. They passed the new Judiciary Act of 1801 which increased the number of federal judges, and Adams promptly filled sixty-seven of the positions with members of his party. These judges were called "midnight judges," because, so the story went, Adams had signed the appointments up to midnight on the last day of his administration.

The election of 1800 had given the Republicans majorities in the House and Senate, but they still feared that the Federalist judges might threaten their legislation. There was reason for fear. The judges were appointed for life and were beyond the control of the voters. Because many of the judges were political friends of Hamilton and Adams, federal courts were likely to strengthen federal power and weaken state power in their decisions. Some of the judges were openly critical of Republican policies and denounced them to juries.

Jefferson could not dismiss the judges, but he did get the House of Representatives to impeach Supreme Court Justice Samuel Chase, who had insulted Republicans and denounced them as traitors. The Senate, however, refused to convict him. Although his words and behavior had been shameful, he was not actually guilty of "high crimes and misdemeanors."

Marbury v. *Madison.* A more significant incident in Jefferson's war on the judiciary was the case of *Marbury* v. *Madison* (1803). It arose out of one of Adams's last-minute appointments— William Marbury as a justice of the peace in the District of Columbia. Marbury's commission of office was signed so late that he did not receive it before Jefferson was inaugurated. The new secretary of state, James Madison, refused to deliver it. Marbury thereupon asked the Supreme Court to order delivery of the commission. The Judiciary Act of 1789 gave the Supreme Court the power to do so.

The Court concluded, in a decision written by Chief Justice Marshall, that Marbury had no case. Marshall argued that the 1789 Judiciary Act itself was unconstitutional. The Constitution, he said, stated what sort of cases the Supreme Court might deal with, and Marbury's complaint was not among them. According to Marshall, an act of Congress could not give the Court powers not named in the Constitution. Only a constitutional amendment could do that.

The Constitution, Marshall said, was the "supreme law of the land." It was up to the courts, and no one else, "to say what the law is." Neither the federal executive, nor Congress, nor the states had this power.

The *Marbury v. Madison* case was the first time that the Supreme Court declared an act of Congress unconstitutional. It established the principle of *judicial review*, that is, the power of the Supreme Court to decide whether an act of Congress is or is not constitutional. Marshall expanded this principle in later decisions which held that the Supreme Court could also declare acts passed by state legislatures unconstitutional. As a result of Marshall's opinions, judicial review—though not directly provided for by the Constitution—is part of the American system of government.

The West Is Opened

Jefferson was angry at the decisions of the Marshall Court. He feared that the federal judiciary was gaining great power at the expense of state governments. Yet it was Jefferson himself who was responsible for a tremendous expansion of federal territory and power.

Beyond the Appalachians. For centuries the valleys of the Ohio, Cumberland, and Tennessee rivers had been the hunting grounds of the Shawnee and the Iroquois. By 1800, however, some 250,000 white settlers had cleared homesteads in the area, and Kentucky and Tennessee had followed Vermont in becoming part of the United States.

The main gateway to the West in those years was through the Cumberland Gap in the Appalachian Mountains. The gap is located where Kentucky, Tennessee, and Virginia come together. This natural break in the Appalachians had been discovered in 1750. In 1775, under the leadership of woodsman Daniel Boone, a group of thirty men cleared a continuous road through the gap from eastern Tennessee to what is now Louisville, Kentucky. The men "picked up woodland paths, joined trails beaten down by wandering bison . . . rolled away rocks, and hacked down forest and brush." When it was finished, the Wilderness Road was almost 300 miles long. At first, people journeyed over it on foot or horseback. But by 1790 the Wilderness Road had been graded so that it was fit for wagons.

West of Louisville, people usually went by water. If you were traveling light, you paddled a birchbark canoe. Families generally used a Kentucky ark, a roofed barge large enough to carry household goods, grain, hay, and livestock. Groups of several families floated downstream on flatboats that ranged from twenty to one hundred feet in length and twelve to twenty feet in width. The flatboats were equipped with poles and oars for use in shallow water. Since they only had to last for a single voyage, arks and flatboats alike were built as simply and cheaply as possible. When they reached their destination, they were broken up and sold for lumber.

Although water travel was faster and easier than land travel, it had its dangers. One traveller wrote:

"River pirates sometimes seized loaded rafts and flatboats and threw the owners and passengers overboard. Hostile Indians were also a threat, for their arrows and gunfire from the wooded banks along narrow reaches of the rivers could be disastrous. The weather could be tricky, and sudden squalls could upset a boat or drive it onto a sandbar. The streams were filled with fallen trees and snags which had to be avoided. In short, navigating any craft on the great rivers required both courage and skill."

Pioneer Life. The lives of the pioneers who crossed the Appalachians were anything but easy. They consisted mainly of hard work and bouts of illness. First, settlers had to get to the new land.

Many traveled on foot, carrying their possessions in a wheelbarrow or pushcart, or strapped to the backs of a few scrawny cows. The lucky ones rode rafts piled with all their worldly goods as far as the rivers would take them. Then they had to walk. When they reached their destination, they had to clear the land and build shelters.

Illness came often but there were few doctors. Many suffered from the "ague," a fever we now know as malaria. The settlers learned to use many home remedies from the Indians. Even today there are still about sixty Indian remedies that are official drugs.

Every family had a book full of cures for various ailments. Exchanging remedies with neighbors was as common as exchanging recipes for pies or jam. Indians in the South used blue iris for liver trouble. The Cherokees used the hydrangea for stones in the bladder. Thyme was used for whooping cough, and trillium, called "birthroot" by the Indians, was given to a mother during childbirth. Calomel and bleeding were used for almost any ailment. And the few doctors in the backwoods of America relied heavily on patent medicines bought from peddlers. Some of these tonics were Dover's Powder, Dragon's Blood (twenty-five cents a dose), and Peruvian Bark (one dollar a dose). But the pioneers were a hardy lot and many survived despite, not because of, the medicines.

A steel engraving of American families going west along the Ohio River. This was the great waterway to the interior of the continent.

The life of Thomas Lincoln was typical of a pioneer who moved west. Born in the late 1700s in western Virginia, he grew up in Kentucky. There he did some carpentry and also worked as a hired hand on farms. He never went to school, and he married Nancy Hanks, who could neither read nor write. In 1809 she gave birth to their son, Abraham. The Lincoln and Hanks families rarely stayed long in one spot. By 1816 they had reached southern Indiana, where they settled as squatters on land they did not own. "We lived the same as the Indians," one of the Hankses said later, "exceptin' we took an interest in politics and religion."

Within a year of moving to Indiana, they built a typical log cabin with a dirt floor, no windows, and a mere opening for a door. They stuffed the cracks in the roof with mud and grass to keep out the rain. They lived in this home for ten years before moving on to Illinois.

A Remarkable Process. The process of westward expansion was a remarkable event in the history of a people. And it astonished everyone who saw any part of it. The last French governor of Louisiana watched thousands of Americans as they poured into the new land. He was moved by admiration and perhaps a little envy. This is how he described the event to a friend:

"They set up their huts, cut and burn the timber, kill the savages or are killed by them, and disappear from the country either by dying or ceding to some steadfast cultivator the land they have already begun to clear. When a score of new colonists are thus gathered in a certain spot, they are followed by two printers, one a federalist and the other an antifederalist, then by doctors, lawyers and adventurers; they propose toasts and nominate a speaker; they erect a city; they begat children without end; they vainly advertise vast territories for sale; they attract and deceive as many buyers as possible; they increase the figures of the population till they reach a total of 60,000 souls, at which they are able to form an independent state and send a representative to Congress . . . and there is one more star in the United States flag."

The Louisiana Purchase

As vast as the western territories were, Jefferson dreamed of an even larger America. Soon there was an opportunity to make the dream a reality.

Napoleon Wants Louisiana. In 1800 Napoleon Bonaparte of France persuaded Spain to return the Louisiana Territory it had taken in 1762.

The French dictator intended to use the territory as a breadbasket for the French West Indies. When news of the secret transfer leaked out in 1802, Americans reacted with alarm. Spain was weak but Napoleon's France was not. Jefferson feared that a strong French presence in the midcontinent would force the United States into an alliance with Britain. "The day that France takes New Orleans . . . we must marry ourselves to the British fleet and nation."

Then the Spanish, anticipating the transfer of Louisiana, closed New Orleans to American goods. American westerners immediately called for a war to reopen the lifeline of their trade. Jefferson decided to see whether he could resolve the problem by buying New Orleans and West Florida from the French. He sent James Monroe to join Robert Livingston, the American ambassador in Paris.

Napoleon Changes His Mind. Before Monroe arrived, however, Napoleon had abandoned his vision of a New World empire. Rather, his vision had been changed for him.

France's most important island colony was Santo Domingo. In 1791, under the leadership of Toussaint L'Ouverture (*too*-saint loo-ver-*tew*-er), the black slaves in Haiti, on the western half of the island, revolted and won their independence. When Napoleon tried to reconquer Haiti in 1801, he lost more than 30,000 men to guerrilla attacks and yellow fever. Without Santo Domingo, Napoleon saw no reason to keep Louisiana. Furthermore, he was expecting renewed war against Great Britain. So he offered to sell the entire Louisiana Territory to the United States.

With no time to consult their government, the surprised but jubilant Monroe and Livingston went ahead and closed the deal for $15 million in gold. French foreign minister Talleyrand told them, "You have made a noble bargain for yourselves, and I suppose you will make the most of it."

The Constitutional Question. The Constitution did not give the federal government the power to purchase territory. As a strict interpreter of the Constitution, Jefferson was deeply worried on this point. He admitted privately that the purchase was "an act beyond the Constitution." He toyed briefly with the idea of getting a constitutional amendment, but he was afraid that Napoleon might change his mind. So Jefferson swallowed his doubts and pressed the treaty of

The Louisiana Purchase 1803

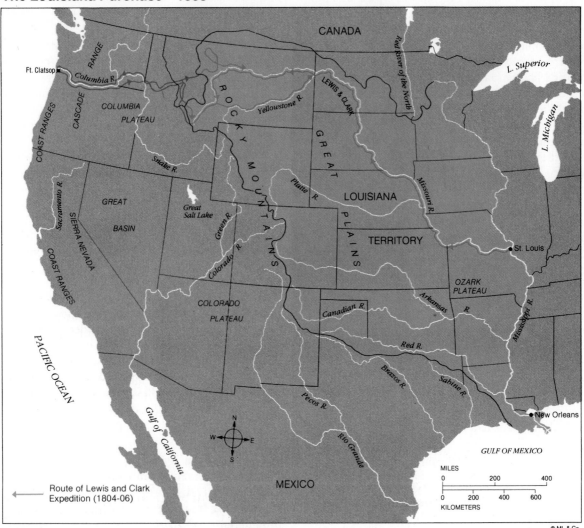

Map Skills   *Lewis and Clark left from what city? What river did they go up? What river did they follow to the Pacific? Why is the Louisiana Territory shown extending into Canada?*

purchase through the Senate. The United States had more than doubled in size.

Westerners were delighted by this enormous addition to United States territory. But no one knew exactly what the borders of Louisiana were. When the Americans in Paris asked Talleyrand, he avoided a direct answer, saying: "You must take it as we received it." This, the Americans assumed, meant they should claim as much territory as they dared at the expense of Spain and Britain.

The Lewis and Clark Expedition. Jefferson looked forward to the day when the American "empire for liberty" would extend clear across the

continent and perhaps beyond. Americans, he said, would eventually "cover the whole northern, if not the southern, continent with a people speaking the same language" and "governed . . . by similar laws." Even before the Louisiana Purchase, Jefferson had asked for—and Congress had granted—money to finance an expedition to explore beyond the Mississippi. Now that the Louisiana Purchase gave much of that land to the United States, Jefferson was even more eager to send out an expedition.

In general, the Louisiana Purchase covered the land drained by the western tributaries of the Mississippi. Its exact boundaries were not settled for decades. But within three years of the purchase, men crossed it from east to west for the first time. In 1803 Jefferson appointed Meriwether Lewis and William Clark to lead an overland party from the French settlement of St. Louis all the way to the Pacific coast if possible. The expedition consisted of some fifty young soldiers and woodsmen, organized as an army unit. Privates received five dollars a month pay, while sergeants received eight dollars.

Jefferson's scientific interests were evident in his instructions to the two leaders. Their first duty was to find, if possible "water communication" across this continent. But they were also to keep careful journals about the soil, climate, vegetation, and minerals. They were to record information about their meetings with Indian tribes, opportunities for fur trading, and possible routes for overland migration. They were even told to take along the recently developed smallpox vaccine and show the Indians how to use it.

A Shoshone Indian woman, Sacajawea (sak-ah-jah-*wee*-ah), served as their interpreter and guide. She helped them establish friendly relations with the Shoshone, who furnished horses for the expedition. The horses helped the expedition to get through the Rocky Mountain passes and finally to the Pacific Ocean.

The Lewis and Clark expedition took two years and four months. It was a great success for the United States, adding tremendously to American knowledge of the West. It showed that overland travel in that enormous region was possible. It opened the path for people who "would come for furs, then for gold, and then for the land itself." And it strengthened American claims to the vaguely defined Oregon country on the northwest coast.

Burr: Tragedy and Treason

In 1800, as you recall, Aaron Burr lost the presidency by two votes. He was disliked by those Republicans who had favored Jefferson, and was equally unpopular with the Federalists, particularly Hamilton. Aware that he had little future in either group nationally, Burr looked around for another outlet for his energy and ambition.

In 1804 Burr ran for governor of New York State. He accepted the aid of some Federalists who, angry at the thought of national Republican rule, wanted to establish an independent northern confederacy consisting of New York and New Jersey. Hamilton found out about the scheme and exposed it. He is supposed to have said that Burr was a "dangerous man and ought not to be trusted with the reins of government." Once again Burr lost a major election. Furious, he challenged Hamilton to a "gentlemen's duel" with pistols. On July 11, 1804, in Weehawken, New Jersey, Burr fatally wounded Hamilton, who had previously resolved to withhold his fire.

Burr fled with a charge of murder on his head and found refuge in Georgia where dueling was both common and acceptable. Since the murder charge only applied in New York and New Jersey, Burr returned to Washington after several months. For obvious reasons he was dropped as a vice-presidential candidate for reelection in 1804, and was forced to watch bitterly as Jefferson and the Republicans swept to a landslide victory.

Burr then set off to the west and became involved in an enterprise for establishing a settlement in Louisiana near the border of Spanish Texas. He won the support of an old army buddy, General James Wilkinson, governor of the Louisiana Territory. He also obtained financial backing from Harmon Blennerhassett, a wealthy Irishman who lived on an island in the Ohio River.

In this old print Hamilton fires, but not at Burr. The latter fatally wounds Hamilton in the stomach.

In the summer of 1806, Burr and about sixty men sailed down the Ohio. Wilkinson, however, was an informer on the Spanish payroll. He told Jefferson of Burr's intentions, accusing him of planning to seize New Orleans and set up an independent nation in Louisiana. Wilkinson also accused Burr of planning to launch an attack against Spanish possessions. Jefferson ordered Burr arrested and brought to trial for treason.

Since Blennerhassett's Island was part of Virginia, the trial was held in the Federal Circuit Court at Richmond. At this time Supreme Court justices had to sit in on circuit court cases. So the presiding judge at Burr's trial was Chief Justice Marshall. As one historian wrote,

❝Richmond promptly became the most crowded community in the country. Nothing to compare with this trial had ever occurred—a former vice-president facing death on the gallows for high treason. Spectators slept three and four to a bed in the town's inns and boarding-houses, camped beside their wagons in vacant lots, and argued deep into the night in taverns.❞

As the trial began, Burr's attorneys asked Marshall to define treason. Marshall argued for a very narrow definition. He pointed out that the Constitution had been written by men who had themselves been considered traitors by England. In drafting the Constitution, they were less afraid of treason than they were of giving the federal government the power to persecute citizens for their political opinions. Accordingly, Marshall gave the following instructions to the jury. To be found guilty, Burr had to be convicted of a war-like *act*, not just a conspiracy. Also, there had to be two witnesses to the specific act. The trial failed to produce such witnesses, and Burr was acquitted.

Section 1 Review

COMPREHENSION   Developing Vocabulary
1. Explain these terms: judicial review, midnight judges, Cumberland Gap.

COMPREHENSION   Mastering Facts
1. Why did Jefferson sometimes wear old clothes when meeting senators in the White House?
2. Why did Jefferson wage a "war" against federal judges?
3. What was the significance of Justice Marshall's decision in the *Marbury* v. *Madison* case?
4. How did Jefferson's instructions to Lewis and Clark reflect his scientific interests?

2   THE ROAD TO THE WAR OF 1812

VOCABULARY   *impressment   coercion*

In 1803 the expected war between France and Great Britain broke out and continued for a dozen years. Before it was over, the United States was drawn into the conflict.

American Ships and Men Are Seized

The basic problem was one that had existed for more than a century. The American economy was based on exporting agricultural products and importing manufactured goods from Europe. Any interference with American shipping caused economic troubles at home. And now that the colonies were an independent nation, such interference was a threat to national honor as well.

In 1806 Napoleon decided to exclude British goods from his "fortress Europe." In turn, Great Britain decided that the best way of attacking the fortress was to blockade it. Neutral American ships were caught in the middle. By 1807, Britain had seized more than 1000 American ships and confiscated their cargoes, while France had seized about half that number.

The Evils of Impressment. There was one thing, however, that made Great Britain seem more offensive than France—its policy of *impressment.* For centuries, the British had manned their fleet by impressing men into service. This meant kidnapping sailors off a British fishing vessel or using a press gang. Press gangs would often sweep the taverns of a British port for men to add to the crew. The British took the position that any man born in England was properly subject to the press.

Inevitably, this led to conflict over American seamen who had been born in England but had become naturalized citizens of the United States. The conflict was made worse by many incidents in which a longboat from a British man-of-war boarded an American merchantman and impressed likely-looking sailors without paying any attention to their actual citizenship. As one British captain arrogantly declared, "It is my duty to keep my ship manned, and I will do so wherever I find men that speak the same language with me." All told, British press gangs claimed about 10,000 American citizens.

The Chesapeake *Incident.* In June 1807 the newly launched frigate U.S.S. *Chesapeake* was cruising in international waters just outside the three-mile limit off Norfolk, Virginia. The British warship *Leopard* approached and ordered the *Chesapeake* to heave to in order to permit a search for British deserters. When the *Chesapeake's* captain refused, the *Leopard* opened fire. The *Chesapeake's* guns were not fully mounted, and its decks were cluttered by gear that had not been sorted and stowed away. Three Americans were killed and eighteen were wounded. The *Chesapeake's* captain then permitted a British search party on board. Four alleged deserters from the British navy—two black and two white—were rowed to the *Leopard* while the American frigate limped back to Norfolk.

An Embargo Boomerangs

To many Americans this humiliating attack meant war. "Never since the battle of Lexington," Jefferson wrote, "have I seen this country in such a state." But the president was determined to try what he called "peaceful coercion." He decided to keep American ships and foodstuffs off the high

The cartoon below shows how an attempt to smuggle tobacco is stopped by the Ograbme snapping turtle.

seas. He thought this would force European powers to respect neutral American rights. The Embargo Act sailed through Congress in December 1807.

As it turned out, the embargo hurt the United States much more than Britain or France. Despite shipping losses, American foreign commerce had doubled between 1803 and 1807. Now it came to a standstill. Shipping centers, particularly those in New England, closed down. Merchants, sailmakers, seamen, shipbuilders, stevedores, and so on—all reacted with outrage to Jefferson's "dambargo." A New Hampshire man put his anger into rhyme:

❝ Our ships all in motion once whitened the ocean,
They sailed and returned with a cargo;
Now doomed to decay, they are fallen a prey
To Jefferson—worms—and Embargo. ❞

Many people considered Jefferson's policy weak-kneed and unworthy of the Republic. Others turned the word embargo around and called it "O-grab-me," because it pinched their pocketbooks.

Not surprisingly, the Federalists made gains at the polls in 1808. They recaptured control of most New England state legislatures and doubled their numbers in Congress. But James Madison, the Republican candidate, easily won the presidency. Shortly before he took office, the Embargo Act was repealed. In its place Congress passed the Non-Intercourse Act, which allowed Americans to trade with all nations except England and France. But this did not improve the economy enough. Finally, in 1810, Congress allowed the new act to expire. American ships were again free to sail the Atlantic and to take their chances with seizure.

War Hawks Want War with Indians and Britain

In 1810, some bright new men in their early thirties were elected to Congress. They came mostly from the western states, where all white male citizens could vote regardless of how much property they owned. One historian has described them as "tough, outspoken, resentful of the Indians, fervently nationalistic, and eager to extend the U.S. boundaries northward into Canada." Known as the War Hawks, they felt that impressment was a major issue, not because they had maritime interests, but because it was an insult to the

227

The painting above is thought to be of Chief Tecumseh. It belonged to the family of William Clark, who explored the Louisiana Territory.

policy of absorbing Indians into the white man's culture by transforming them from hunters into farmers. But he had also told Harrison that any tribe "foolhardy enough to take up the hatchet" should be driven across the Mississippi.

Tecumseh Forms a Confederacy. The Indians did in fact take up the hatchet. And eventually they *were* driven across the Mississippi. But only after several years of fierce fighting and thousands of casualties on both sides.

The Indian leader in the struggle was a Shawnee chief named Tecumseh. Around 1805 he began to assert that no tribe could sell land to the whites unless all the tribes east of the Mississippi gave their consent. His dream was to combine the eastern tribes into a gigantic confederacy to fight for their common homeland.

    "The only way to check and stop this evil (white settlement), is for all the red men to unite in claiming a common and equal right in the land . . . for it never was divided, but belongs to all for the use of each. . . . The Great Spirit gave this great land to his red children. He placed the whites on the other side of the big water. They were not contented with their own, but came to take ours from us. They have driven us from the sea to the lakes. We can go no further."

Tecumseh was joined in his campaign by his brother Tenskwatawa, known to whites as "the Prophet." A powerful preacher, Tenskwatawa mounted a campaign for spiritual and moral revival among the Shawnee and various neighboring tribes. He preached a straightforward message: the Indians should "shun the white man's liquor, abandon his ways, [and] return to the old customs."

The Battle of Tippecanoe. In 1811 Tecumseh went on a six-month journey to gain support from the Creeks and other tribes in the South. While he was gone, Tenskwatawa, disregarding Tecumseh's instructions, mounted a premature attack on a force of 1000 men assembled by Governor Harrison. A full-scale battle took place near the mouth of the Tippecanoe River. The Indians fought bravely. For a long time no one could tell who was winning because both sides suffered high casualties. Eventually, the Indians withdrew. The battle made Harrison a popular hero. Almost thirty years later, it supplied him with a campaign slogan that helped him become president.

American flag. Unlike the older generation of Republican and Federalist leaders, the War Hawks had been born under that flag. These violently patriotic men included John C. Calhoun of South Carolina, Felix Grundy of Tennessee, and especially Henry Clay of Kentucky, who was elected speaker of the House of Representatives.

Indian Territory Is Invaded. Next to impressment, what bothered the War Hawks most was the "Indian problem" in the Indiana Territory. (Ohio had become a state in 1803.) The attitude of most white settlers in the area is shown in a statement made by General William Henry Harrison, the territorial governor. "Is one of the fairest portions of the globe to remain in a state of nature, the haunt of a few wretched savages, when it seems destined, by the Creator, to give support to a large population, and to be the seat of civilization, of science, and of true religion?"

In 1809 Harrison invited some elderly Indian chiefs to Fort Wayne. After getting them drunk, he persuaded them to sign away 3 million acres of tribal land. Jefferson had told Harrison about his

On to Canada! The War Hawks in Congress seized upon the Battle of Tippecanoe as another reason to attack Britain. Some of the firearms the Indians abandoned at Tippecanoe came from Canada. Here was another example, the War Hawks cried, of Britain insulting America.

New Englanders were generally opposed to the War Hawk position, partly because they had closer cultural contacts with Britain than westerners did. Henry Clay felt, however, that their patriotism was dampened by a desire to make money. And in truth, New England merchants were not overly upset about British trade restrictions. Even if only one ship in three got through the blockade, it could still make a fortune for its owners. But westerners were spoiling for a fight. Since the quickest way to attack Britain was to head northward, the War Hawk rallying cry was "On to Canada!"

Section 2 Review

COMPREHENSION   Developing Vocabulary

1.   Explain these terms: impressment, peaceful coercion, War Hawks, embargo.

COMPREHENSION   Mastering Facts

1.   What effect did interference with American shipping have on the nation's economy?
2.   Why were Americans angrier at Britain than at France?
3.   What were the results of the Battle of Tippecanoe?
4.   Why wasn't New England enthusiastic about war?

3   THE WAR OF 1812 BRINGS MIXED RESULTS

VOCABULARY   *Hartford Convention   Virginia dynasty*

By the middle of 1812, President Madison felt he had to give in to the war fever. So although the nation was unprepared and all the Federalists in the House of Representatives voted "No," war was declared.

At the time, the war was referred to by its opponents as "Mr. Madison's War." It might as well have been called the "War for Canada," or the "Indian War Beyond the Appalachians," or the "Second War for American Independence." Probably because the reasons for it were so mixed, the conflict has become known in American history only by a date—1812.

Successes and Defeats

Madison called for 50,000 volunteers for a year's service in the regular army. Five thousand signed up. The corps of top army officers consisted largely of tired old incompetents.

The Northern Front. Given this situation, it is not surprising that the first attempts to invade Canada were disastrous. Three separate armies tried different routes of attack. One proceeded to lose Detroit to a combined force of British soldiers plus Indian warriors led by Tecumseh. The remaining two American armies got nowhere when New York militiamen refused to cross the Canadian border.

The next year, things went better for the Americans. Determined to retake Detroit, they built a small squadron of ships on the shores of Lake Erie at Put-in-Bay. In September, under the command of Captain Oliver Hazard Perry, the American fleet defeated a British fleet. As Perry reported to Harrison, "We have met the enemy and they are ours—two ships, two brigs, one schooner, and one sloop."

The British abandoned Detroit, and Harrison pursued them into Canada. At the Thames River, he defeated a combined British-Indian force. Tecumseh was killed in that battle, and with his death his confederacy collapsed. To the east, on Lake Ontario, United States troops raided York (now Toronto) and burned the capital buildings. Then they turned south and took Fort George but lost to the British at Stoney Creek.

The War at Sea. At sea, American privateers captured nearly 1000 British merchantmen. But the superiority of the British fleet began to tell. By the end of 1813, most of the American navy and a good part of its merchant marine were bottled up in American ports.

The British Burn Washington. By 1814 British landing parties were burning towns all along the coast. That summer they sent a sizable force up Chesapeake Bay. The redcoats brushed aside some hastily assembled American troops and entered Washington on August 24. Madison and other federal officials had to flee from their own capital. In revenge for the American raid on York, the British burned the Capitol, the White House, and other public buildings. Although the burning of Washington had little military significance, it was a severe blow to national pride.

The Star-Spangled Banner. From Washington, the British mounted an attack on Baltimore. It was on that occasion that Francis Scott Key, a prisoner aboard a British warship, watched anxiously all night as British shells bombarded Fort McHenry at the entrance to the city's harbor. When morning came, he was thrilled to see that the American flag was still flying. On the back of an envelope he jotted down some verse which later became the words of the American national anthem.

War's End. After failing to capture Baltimore, the British high command planned a three-pronged attack. One was to smash across the border at Niagara into western New York. Another was to follow the same route of lakes that Burgoyne had taken thirty-five years before. And the third was to strike at New Orleans.

The British thrust at Niagara was stopped cold at Lundy's Lane, though neither side won a clear victory. The invasion down the lakes was halted by a stunning American naval victory at Plattsburg Bay on Lake Champlain.

Plattsburg Bay was the last battle before the war officially came to an end. A month earlier, British and American peace negotiators had met at the Belgian town of Ghent, and by Christmas Eve, 1814, they had reached an agreement. But two weeks later, well before the news from Ghent arrived in Washington, the Americans finally achieved their only really decisive land victory of the entire war.

Andrew Jackson: Hero of New Orleans. For more than a year, a vigorous man from Tennessee had been running a more or less independent campaign of his own in the "Old Southwest." At first it was aimed against hostile Indians, or at least against Indians he made hostile. Andrew Jackson was a born leader and a self-taught military genius. He led a band of Tennessee frontiersmen southward into the Mississippi Territory, fighting Indians wherever he could find them. At Horseshoe Bend in present-day Alabama, he routed a Creek army and virtually wiped out the Creek nation. He then forced the survivors to give up two-thirds of their land.

Never a man to pay much attention to legal niceties, Jackson next invaded Spanish territory in western Florida. He aimed at heading off any British attempt to take the port of Pensacola.

Jackson then turned westward to help defend New Orleans. There, on January 8, 1815, his collection of some 5400 frontiersmen, sailors, regular troops, and pirates took on 8000 invading redcoats. The Americans lay lodged behind walls of cotton

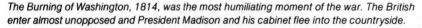

The Burning of Washington, 1814, was the most humiliating moment of the war. The British enter almost unopposed and President Madison and his cabinet flee into the countryside.

The War of 1812

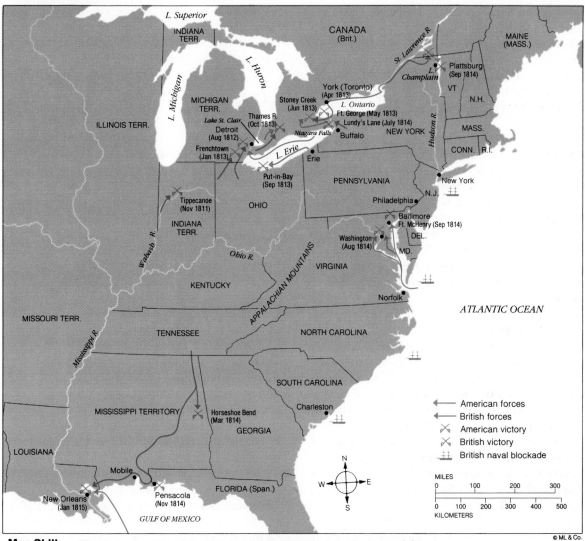

Map Skills *Was the battle of New Orleans before or after the attack on Washington? On what lake was the battle of Put-in-Bay? Who won it? What was the city of Toronto called in 1813?*

bales. The British commander ordered a frontal assault. Before he was killed, he watched his veteran soldiers go down in rows. British losses from the Battle of New Orleans stood at more than 2000. American casualties numbered seventy-nine. Jackson instantly became known as the Hero of New Orleans.

The Blacks' Contributions to the War. Black as well as white sailors were often impressed by the British. About one hundred blacks were part of Commander Perry's naval forces on Lake Erie.

When it became apparent that the British were going to attack New Orleans, General Jackson issued a "proclamation to the free colored inhabitants of Louisiana," who were almost as numerous as whites. "Through a mistaken policy," the proclamation said in part, "you have heretofore been deprived of a participation in the glorious struggle for national rights in which our country is engaged. This no longer shall exist." Jackson added that those who enrolled "will be paid the same bounty in money and lands now received by the white soldiers of the United States."

The black soldiers fought splendidly in the defense of New Orleans. When British General Sir

231

Edward Pakenham was killed, Jackson wrote to President Monroe, "I saw Pakenham reel and pitch out of his saddle. I have always believed he fell from the bullet of a free man of color who was a famous rifle shot and came from the Attakaps region of Louisiana."

New England's Discontent

From the beginning of the war, New Englanders had refused to support a conflict they thought would ruin their maritime interests. Furthermore, New Englanders saw their section as a shrinking corner of an expanding nation. Every time a new state entered the Union, the voting weight of New England lessened in Congress and in the electoral college.

New Englanders did everything they could to cripple the war effort. They boycotted federal bond sales. They refused to let their state militias serve beyond state borders. In Congress they successfully blocked a bill for a military draft. Congressman Daniel Webster of New Hampshire called it "unconstitutional and illegal" and warned that the people and the states would and should defy it. Some New Englanders traded with Canada and sold supplies to British ships. In fact, when the British occupied that part of Maine east of the Penobscot River, the people there took an oath of allegiance to their old sovereign, George III!

In 1814 the extension of the blockade to all New England, as well as British raids on coastal towns, brought a sense of crisis. The Massachusetts legislature called for a regional convention at Hartford, Connecticut. Some hotheads wanted to secede from the Union. But cooler minds prevailed, and the Hartford Convention contented itself with a report on coastal defense and some proposed constitutional amendments. These amendments showed a good deal about New England's grievances. One would have eliminated the three-fifths clause, thereby lessening the South's voting power in Congress. The South usually voted against New England's interests, and vice versa. Another amendment would have limited the presidency to one term and prohibited the election of successive presidents from the same state. This last proposal was aimed at the so-called "Virginia dynasty." Three of the first four presidents had been from Virginia.

The Hartford Convention ended by threatening to call a second convention if these demands were not met. Delegates packed off to Washington to present them. But, they found the capital wildly celebrating both a treaty of peace and Jackson's great victory at New Orleans. None of the New England proposals were adopted.

The Treaty of Ghent

Formal peace talks began at Ghent in August 1814. The British negotiating team had orders to give little and demand much, including pieces of territory along the United States–Canadian border. The five American negotiators were less bound by strict instructions. Yet their own quarreling almost broke up the talks. Henry Clay of Kentucky spoke for western interests. John Quincy Adams, the ex-president's son, had New England at heart. Each was suspicious that the other would sacrifice the interests of any section but his own. When Adams suggested that the British be allowed to navigate the Mississippi in exchange for fishing rights near Newfoundland, Clay exploded. "The navigation principle," he said, "is much too important to concede for the mere liberty of drying fish." Adams irritated his colleagues by his stiff manner. In turn, he found Clay and the others too fond of loose living. "They sit after dinner and drink bad wine and smoke cigars. Such behavior neither suits my habits nor my health, and absorbs time which I cannot spare." Fortunately, Albert Gallatin of Pennsylvania managed to keep a measure of peace in the delegation.

Britain's lack of success at Niagara and Plattsburg Bay forced the British negotiators to back off from their demands. They abandoned their idea of an Indian state north of the Ohio. Under the terms of the treaty, no territory changed hands. However, the issues of impressment and freedom of the seas were not mentioned. The treaty actually looked more like an armistice agreement than a peace treaty. Yet Americans welcomed it. They were eager for peace, and Jackson's victory tended to block all memories of earlier military humiliations. The United States had survived a major war. The result, as Gallatin put it, was that "The people . . . feel and act more as a nation."

The Aftermath of the War

Although the War of 1812 more or less ended in a stalemate, it was followed by a number of political and geographic changes.

United States Boundary Settlements 1818–1819

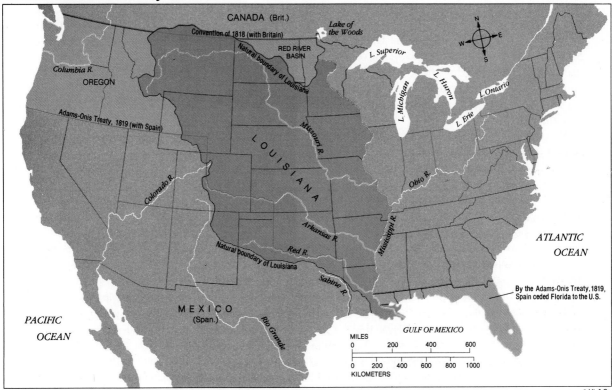

Map Skills   *The Adams-Onis treaty of 1819 set the boundary with what Spanish colony? The Convention of 1818 gave what river basin to the U.S.? When was Florida added to the U.S.?*

Anglo-American Accord. Within a few years, the United States and Great Britain were able to reach agreement on many of the issues left open at Ghent. In 1815 a commercial treaty reopened trade between the two countries. In 1817 the British minister in Washington, Charles Bagot, worked out a disarmament agreement for the Canadian border with Richard Rush, the acting secretary of state. The Rush-Bagot agreement restricted each side to four small warships on the Great Lakes. With certain technical changes, that agreement was still in force 150 years later.

In 1818, four separate British-American commissions reached agreements on fisheries and the Canadian–United States border. The coasts of Labrador and Newfoundland were reopened to American fishermen, while the northern boundary of the Louisiana Territory was set at the forty-ninth parallel as far west as the Rocky Mountains. Finally, the two nations agreed to a ten-year "joint occupation" of the Oregon Country.

No one knew it at the time, but these agree-

ments laid the groundwork for lasting peace between the two nations. The chief reason was that the overthrow of Napoleon brought an end to more than a century of conflict between Britain and France. The United States was thereby free to concentrate on its own internal development.

Florida at Last. There remained one outstanding piece of unfinished business. Most Americans assumed that Spanish Florida would eventually become part of the United States, and American settlers began to move in on their own. In 1817 there were outbreaks of violence between white settlers and Seminole Indians who were aided by fugitive slaves from Georgia. Andrew Jackson was given command of United States troops, and vague instructions to bring peace and order to the borderland region.

Jackson interpreted these instructions with great freedom. Many times he dealt with Indians simply by destroying their villages. He seemed to have little respect for international law. When the

233

Seminoles retreated into Florida, Jackson pursued them across the border and hunted them down in Spanish territory.

When he reached Pensacola he threw out the Spanish governor, set up his own garrisons, and claimed the territory for the United States. Not content with offending Spain, he hanged two British subjects whom he thought had sided with the Indians.

Secretary of State John Quincy Adams was left with the problem of picking up the diplomatic pieces. Though he did not approve of Jackson's behavior, he knew Jackson was popular with most Americans. He was already in the process of negotiating with the Spanish minister, Luis de Onis (o-*niece*), about the future of Florida. With one hand, Adams was able to quiet British protests about the two executions. With the other hand, he was able to persuade Onis that Spain would do well to give up Florida before impatient Americans simply seized it.

In the final Adams-Onis Treaty of 1819, Spain ceded Florida to the United States. In exchange, the United States government agreed to pay the $5 million that American merchants claimed they had lost to Spain during the Napoleonic wars.

Adams was not content to let matters rest there. An extraordinarily skillful negotiator, he persuaded Onis to include in the agreement a firm boundary between Spanish territory and the United States all the way from Louisiana to the Pacific coast. Adams held a vision of continental expansion which matched that of Thomas Jefferson. The taking of all North America by the United States, he wrote, is "as much a law of nature . . . as that the Mississippi should flow to the sea."

Section 3 Review

COMPREHENSION   Developing Vocabulary

1. Explain these terms: Virginia dynasty, Hartford Convention.

COMPREHENSION   Mastering Facts

1. What treaty officially ended the War of 1812?
2. What did the Rush-Bagot agreement settle?
3. What area did Britain and the United States agree to occupy "jointly" after the war?
4. What two territorial questions did the Adams-Onis Treaty of 1819 settle?

CHAPTER 10   Review

Chapter Summary

Jefferson was the first president to be inaugurated at the nation's new capital. Jefferson's appointment of John Marshall as Chief Justice permanently altered the role of the Supreme Court. Then the Louisiana Purchase in 1803 more than doubled the size of the nation. Meanwhile, settlements in the Ohio Valley created problems with Indians that were temporarily resolved at the Battle of Tippecanoe. However, unresolved problems with Britain led to the War of 1812. When the war ended in 1814, neither side had won. Still, the war encouraged American nationalism and set the stage for a period of internal growth and expansion.

Questions for Critical Thinking

COMPREHENSION   Summarizing Main Ideas

1. What use did Napoleon originally intend to make of the Louisiana Territory? Why did Jefferson agree to buy Louisiana although doing so was unconstitutional?

2. List three results of the Lewis and Clark expedition to the Louisiana Territory.

3. In the trial of Aaron Burr, how did Supreme Court Justice Marshall define treason? Why did he argue for a narrow rather than a broad definition of the term?

4. How did Tecumseh hope to prevent the continuing incursion of white settlers into the Indiana Territory? What approach did his brother Tenskwatawa favor? Was either approach successful? Were there other alternatives for the Indians? Explain.

5. Explain how each of the following helped bring about the War of 1812: (a) British impressment of American sailors; (b) American national pride; (c) Napoleon's economic struggle with Britain; (d) Battle of Tippecanoe.

6. What was the political reason why New England opposed the War of 1812? What was the economic reason?

COMPREHENSION   Interpreting Events

1. How did Jefferson's attitude toward the presidency differ from that of his predecessors?

Which attitude do you consider more appropriate? Give reasons for your opinion.

2. Did Jefferson "win" or "lose" his "war" against federal judges? Explain your answer.

3. If you had been a pioneer around 1800, would you have preferred moving westward by land or by water? Why?

4. Why did Andrew Jackson invade Florida? Do you think he was right to do so? Give reasons for your opinion. How did Secretary of State John Quincy Adams finally obtain the territory for the United States?

APPLICATION   Using Skills To Recognize Cause and Effect

Among the skills required for clear thinking is the ability to relate cause and effect. Below are five pairs of events. For each pair, tell whether the second event was caused by the first event or merely followed it in time.

1. The Federalists pass the Judiciary Act of 1801; Chief Justice John Marshall establishes the principle of judicial review.

2. Toussaint L'Ouverture leads a successful revolt for independence on Haiti; France offers to sell the Louisiana Territory to the United States.

3. Aaron Burr shoots Alexander Hamilton in a duel; Aaron Burr is tried for treason.

4. Jefferson persuades Congress to pass an Embargo Act; the War Hawks call for war against Great Britain.

5. The Americans and British sign a peace treaty at Ghent; Andrew Jackson successfully defends New Orleans against a British attack.

EVALUATION   Comparing Past to Present

1. What arguments did people raise against the draft during the War of 1812? What arguments do people raise against the draft today?

2. List the states that have been formed in whole or in part from land included in the Louisiana Purchase.

3. On a map of the United States, trace the route followed by the Lewis and Clark expedition. What large cities lie along the route today?

Individualism

*I celebrate myself, and sing
  myself,
And what I assume you shall
  assume,
For every atom belonging to me
  as good belongs to you.*

The poet Walt Whitman wrote these lines in "Song of Myself," which praised individualism. Whitman, like Ralph Waldo Emerson, Henry David Thoreau, and other mid-nineteenth century writers, believed in the uniqueness of each person. Moreover, they believed this recognition of the uniqueness of individuals was what contained the essence of America. Whether through heroic deeds or daily life, individualism stressed the importance of each person above the authority of groups and institutions.

Respect for the individual is linked to the origins of our nation. The relatively new idea that government exists to serve the individual is basic to our political system. Jefferson stated this belief in the Declaration of Independence when he asserted that all people had certain unalienable rights. The Bill of Rights expanded Jefferson's idea by specifically listing the rights which individual citizens enjoy under the Constitution.

Influence of the Frontier. As the nation grew, Americans continued to praise individualism.

This mural at the Harry S Truman Library in Independence, Missouri, illustrates the traditional American spirit of individualism.

The frontier, for example, attracted pioneers with the courage to face the wilderness. Pioneers needed bravery, self-reliance, and ingenuity to live on the edge of civilization.

Individualism also flourished during the early growth of capitalism. The Industrial Revolution required and demanded people who were willing to take risks. Nineteenth century Americans had great respect for the self-made barons of industry.

Individualism Today. More recently, the spirit of self-reliance, or individualism, has faced more and more restrictions. Yet individualism remains the spirit of America. The nation still contains thousands of individuals who succeed only through perseverance and self-reliance. The challenge for all Americans is to keep this spark of individualism alive—and to pass it on to the next generation.

Understanding Our Heritage

1. In what ways does the Constitution protect the concept of individualism?

2. What conditions in America encouraged individualism? How did individualism strengthen America?

3. Name some people you admire. Is individualism an important part of their personalities? Explain.

UNIT 3 Review

Understanding Social Studies Concepts

History

1. Arrange the following events in chronological order: (a) development of political parties; (b) election of George Washington; (c) Shays's Rebellion; (d) election of the first Republican president; (e) Constitutional Convention; (f) beginning of the French Revolution.

2. How long after the signing of the Declaration of Independence did it take Americans to establish a central government that functioned effectively? What dangers did the young nation face by operating during this critical period without a strong government?

3. How did most Americans react to the outbreak of the French Revolution? What dilemma did Washington face as a result of the revolution? What was his solution?

4. What political and geographical changes resulted from the War of 1812? What happened to British-American relations following the conclusion of the war?

Economics

1. Governments frequently make economic decisions for political reasons. Describe Hamilton's economic plan for the nation. What was the political goal of his economic plan?

2. What is an embargo? What were the economic results of the embargo of 1807?

Government

1. What is a federal system? What new concept of sovereignty did federalism establish?

2. After the Revolution, why was it easier to create new state governments than a new central government?

3. Define separation of powers. What was the purpose of separating the powers of the government? How did this separation of powers provide for built-in checks and balances?

4. Which branch of government deals with these problems: setting new taxes; appointing ambassadors; deciding constitutional issues; declaring war; settling disputes between states?

5. What were some of the major arguments against ratification of the Constitution?

6. Give examples of compromises on key issues that enabled the writers of the Constitution to reach a final agreement. What role does compromise play in our government today?

Sociology

1. Describe the attitude of most settlers toward Indians during and after the Revolution. Did this attitude encourage peace? Explain.

2. How did delegates to the Constitutional Convention deal with the issue of slavery? How might our history have been different if slavery had been abolished in the Constitution?

Extending Map, Chart, Picture Skills

1. Refer to the unit opening picture on pages 152–153. Which leaders can you identify?

2. In the cartoon on page 211, why is the French government depicted as a figure with five heads? Does the cartoon present a favorable opinion of the French Revolution? Explain.

3. Refer to the map on page 224. Which states were originally part of the Louisiana Purchase? What were the boundaries of the territory?

Understanding Current Events

1. What advice did Washington give to Americans regarding foreign affairs in his farewell address? Do you think that the nation has followed the path in foreign affairs that Washington envisioned? Explain.

2. How has the role of political parties changed since Washington's administration?

Developing Effective Citizenship

1. Summarize the activities of Daniel Shays in 1786. Do you think Shays chose the best course of action to register his protest concerning certain policies? Explain. What other actions could Shays have chosen?

2. Do you view yourself primarily as a citizen of your state or of the United States? Why? What separate responsibilities are associated with being a citizen of each?

GLOBAL TIME LINE
1815–1850

THE UNITED STATES

THE WORLD

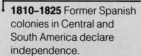

1817–1825 Era of Good Feelings.

1819 U.S. acquires Florida from Spain.

1823 Monroe Doctrine.

1828 Andrew Jackson elected president.

—1810— —1820— —1830—

1810–1825 Former Spanish colonies in Central and South America declare independence.

1829 Britain claims western part of Australia.

1832 Santa Anna elected president of Mexico.

The Nation Grows and Changes

1836 Texas declares independence.

1838 Cherokees endure "Trail of Tears."

1846–1848 Mexican-American War.

1848 First women's rights convention.

1840

1850

1842 Hong Kong becomes British colony.

1840 Act of Union unites Upper and Lower Canada.

CHAPTER 11

Nationalism and a New Economy

1815–1830

People in the Chapter

James Monroe—*fifth president of the United States and the last one from the old revolutionary generation.*

Eli Whitney—*inventor of the cotton gin and interchangeable parts.*

James Tallmadge—*sponsor of an amendment gradually banning slavery in Missouri.*

Samuel Slater—*English mechanic who establishes the first successful factory in America.*

Linking Past to Present

The years after the War of 1812 were like no others in the history of the United States. For the first time there was a long period of peace in Europe. The new country had no fear of being drawn into a war with England, France, or Spain. Now Americans could turn their attention to the development of their own country. There was a spirit of excitement and enthusiasm everywhere. For the first time there was a feeling of being united in a great national adventure.

New men took control of the government. They helped encourage and direct the nation's economic growth. The Supreme Court began handing down decisions that strengthened the power of the federal government. The unhappy political division between the two political parties almost disappeared as the Republicans began adopting measures that made them look very much like Federalists. Immigration increased and cities grew. Society began to change as a result of the Industrial Revolution. With industrialization came some hardships and injustices. But generally this was a time when Americans began energetically to develop and exploit the resources of the country.

1 ECONOMIC AND FEDERAL GROWTH

VOCABULARY   *Era of Good Feelings   commerce*

A sign of the new spirit that gripped the country came in 1817 when the new president, James Monroe, paid a visit to Boston and was warmly welcomed. The idea of a Republican president from Virginia being welcomed in the heart of Federalist-land astounded the nation. One Boston publication, the *Columbian Centinel*, which had been strongly against Monroe, declared that Americans were seeing an "Era of Good Feelings." Also, Monroe was admired because he was sixty-one years of age at his election and seemed likely to be one of the last living links with the old revolutionary generation. He was, for example, the last president to wear a powdered wig.

The American System

The postwar mood of the country showed itself in certain economic measures pushed through Congress by the Republicans. The measures were designed to encourage the growth of commerce and industry.

The theory behind the measures was called the American System. It was explained by former War Hawk Henry Clay in a famous speech delivered in 1824. Congressman Clay envisioned the United States as consisting of two sections—each one helping the other. An industrial North would turn out manufactured products. An agricultural section composed of the South and West would raise grain, meat, and cotton. Factory workers in the North would form a market for agricultural produce. Farmers in the South and West would buy manufactured goods. There were three kinds of measures that would help bring about the American System: they were tariffs, transportation, and the National Bank.

Protective Tariffs.   To help the North, the federal government would set up tariff barriers to protect industries from overseas competition. Immediately after the war, British merchants tried to flood the American market with iron, textiles, and other products at prices cheaper than the prices of those same goods produced in the United States. One member of Parliament explained the reason for this economic warfare. It was better, he said, to sell at a loss at first so as "to stifle in the cradle those rising manufacturers in the United States."

The National Road was part of the transportation system that helped to build the nation.

241

Major Roads in the United States in the Early 1800s

Map Skills   *Where did the National and Michigan roads cross? What road linked New York and Boston? Albany and Buffalo? Knoxville and Lynchburg?*

© ML & Co.

In 1816 Congress passed a mild protective tariff that helped America's infant industries. By the time Clay delivered his speech, however, manufacturers were calling for additional protection. Also, some of the states that had been formed from the old Northwest Territory—such as Indiana (1816) and Illinois (1818)—were hoping that they, too, could industrialize. So Congress raised rates in the tariff of 1824.

Transportation Improvements.   To help the West and South, the federal government would build roads and canals so goods could move to market. The government would get the money it

Some Principal Early Canals

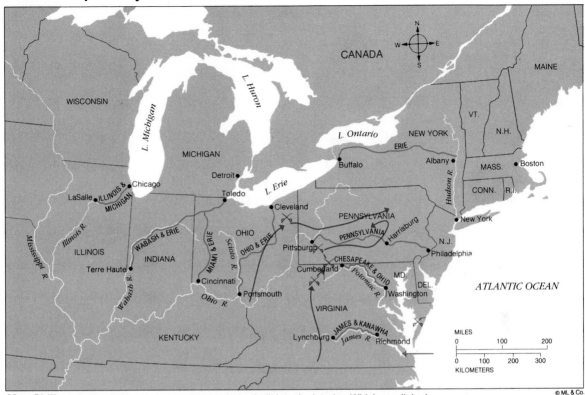

© ML & Co.

Map Skills *By the 1820s, many canals were being built into the interior. Which one linked the Hudson River and Lake Erie? How did the Illinois and Michigan Canal get its name?*

needed for these "internal improvements" from the protective tariff.

As early as 1806, Congress authorized a national road which ran from Baltimore to Wheeling in what is now West Virginia. By 1833 it extended to Columbus, Ohio, and eventually all the way to Vandalia, Illinois. As one historian described it, "Portions . . . were paved with flat stones and some not so flat, which caused complaints from travelers jolting over it in wheeled vehicles." Despite the discomfort, the National Road served as "the path of empire" for millions of Americans on their way west.

The Second Bank of the United States. To help the two sections of the country do business with each other, the federal government would set up a new national bank. The charter of Hamilton's first national bank had run out after twenty years. So starting in 1811, most of its business went to banks chartered by the states. The regulations for these state banks were lax and many of them, wanting to increase their lending business, issued a great deal more paper money. In fact, except for

banks in New England, they issued more paper money than they could back up with silver or gold. The money, therefore, quickly lost value. In addition, money issued in one state, or even one community, was often not accepted anywhere else. This made it difficult to conduct business.

In 1816 Congress chartered the Second Bank of the United States. The Bank set up twenty-five banks throughout the United States and proceeded to issue paper money in the form of national bank notes that could be used everywhere. Many local bankers did not take kindly to the new competitor because people preferred the national currency to what was issued by the state banks. In some states the local bankers got the legislature to tax the branches of the National Bank out of existence. Yet by increasing the money supply, the National Bank enabled many industries to expand.

Boom and Bust

The postwar economy went on a booming spree. Manufacturing flourished behind the protective wall of the tariff. British textile mills devoured as much cotton as American plantations could produce. Tobacco sold well on the peaceful European continent. Poor European harvests in 1816 and 1817 added to the demand for American grain and other farm products.

The boom in agriculture caused a boom in land speculation. People began pouring into the West. The new bank helped fuel this economic expansion by enlarging the money supply. Since both the Bank of the United States and the state banks wanted to lend as much as possible, they printed an oversupply of currency. At the height of the boom, in the summer of 1818, the Bank of the United States realized that it had issued too many banknotes. It also realized it had made loans without much security. So it ordered its branch banks to cut down on loans. It also asked the state banks to *redeem* their state money, that is, to pay the equivalent in gold and silver in exchange for their paper money. Thus began the economic crisis of 1819.

The state banks could not meet their debts, so they were forced to close their doors. People lost their savings and their property because they could not pay their debts. Now the National Bank was as unpopular with the public as it had always been with local financiers.

The Supreme Court and National Power

Supreme Court Justice John Marshall, like Monroe, represented a link with the revolutionary past. He had served as an army officer during that war. When appointed as chief justice in 1801, he was known as a skilled but undistinguished Virginia lawyer. Unlike so many Virginians, however, Marshall favored national over state power.

Marshall had a knack of cutting to the heart of a complex legal problem. He thought and wrote with force and clarity. He dominated the Supreme Court for thirty-four years, during which period he wrote nearly half its opinions and found himself in the minority only a few times.

Marshall's decisions not only enlarged the powers of the Supreme Court, as in *Marbury* v. *Madison*, they also affected the nation's economy. In general, they freed business enterprises from restriction by the states. Marshall realized that a new national economy was developing, and he tried to protect and encourage it through a loose interpretation of the Constitution. Four of his decisions dealt with the binding force of contracts, the authority of the federal government, and the meaning of the word "commerce."

Fletcher v. *Peck* (1810). In 1795 Georgia agreed to grant some land to a group of land speculators. After the next election, however, the new administration discovered that certain state officials involved in making the grant had been bribed. So the legislature passed a law saying the grant was illegal. The businessmen took the case to court.

Despite evidence that some of the men had indeed bribed state officials, Marshall ruled that the land grant had to stand. It was a contract between the state and the businessmen, and Georgia was bound by its own contract. The decision laid down the principle that once a contract is made, the motives that lead to it are no concern of the courts. But more important, this decision was also the first time that the Supreme Court declared a state law unconstitutional.

Dartmouth College v. *Woodward* (1819). New Hampshire had approved the old colonial charter of Dartmouth College, which had been granted under George III in 1769. But in 1816 the state legislature decided to change the old charter and turn Dartmouth from a private school into a

John Marshall (below) was the Supreme Court Justice whose decisions increased national over state power.

state college. The college took the case to the Supreme Court.

Marshall's decision was that a contract was binding. The state of New Hampshire had no power to alter a contract unless the other party agreed. The principle laid down in this decision was that the law of contracts applied to corporations as well as individuals. As more business corporations were established in the country, this ruling became very important.

McCulloch v. Maryland (1819). The State of Maryland passed a heavy tax on a branch of the Bank of the United States. Marshall ruled that such legislation violated the Constitution. "The power to tax involves the power to destroy," he said. If states were allowed to attack agencies of the federal government, it meant in effect that they were overturning a law passed by Congress. And the law establishing the National Bank was entirely constitutional.

Marshall declared that if the "end," or purpose, of a national law is "within the scope of the Constitution," then "all means . . . appropriate . . . to that end . . . which are not prohibited . . . are constitutional." Hamilton would have been delighted with this decision, for it upheld his own position against that of Jefferson.

Gibbons v. Ogden (1824). In this case Justice Marshall gave a very broad definition of what commerce was and ruled that the federal government,

not the states, had authority over interstate commerce. Aaron Ogden had a license from the state of New York giving him a monopoly to run a steam ferry between the states of New York and New Jersey. Thomas Gibbons also started running a ferry between the two states even though he did not have a state license. So Ogden sued him.

Justice Marshall declared that although a state could regulate commerce within its borders, only Congress had the power to regulate interstate commerce. Accordingly, he ruled against Ogden. The monopoly he had received from New York was unconstitutional. Marshall then went further to give a broad interpretation to the word "commerce." It included not only the exchange of goods between states but also within a state's borders under certain conditions. Federal regulation of radio, telegraph, telephone, and television, for example, is based on this decision.

Section 1 Review

COMPREHENSION   Developing Vocabulary

1. Explain these terms: Era of Good Feelings, commerce, redeem, American System, National Road.

COMPREHENSION   Mastering Facts

1. What kind of interpretation did Justice Marshall give to the Constitution, a loose interpretation or a strict one?
2. Why did the case of *Fletcher* v. *Peck* reassure businessmen?
3. How did the decision in the case of *Gibbons* v. *Ogden* support federal power?

2   THE MONROE YEARS BRING CHANGE

VOCABULARY   *Monroe Doctrine   Missouri Compromise*

On the political scene, Monroe's administration was noted for two significant developments. The first had to do with America's role in the Western Hemisphere. The second had to do with the admission of new states to the Union.

Foreign Affairs

In 1807 Napoleon invaded Portugal and Spain. Those two countries did not have the money or manpower to fight Napoleon and at the same time keep control of their overseas colonies. So beginning in 1810, Latin American patriots started revolutions for independence much as the United States had done. By 1822 Portugal had lost Brazil.

By 1825 all that remained of Spain's New World empire were Cuba and Puerto Rico.

Threats from Abroad. In 1815 Napoleon was defeated and sent into exile on the island of St. Helena. The kings of Russia, France, and Austria then formed the so-called Holy Alliance, aimed at restoring conditions to the way they were before the French Revolution. Groups agitating for political independence were to be stamped out. This alliance made Monroe nervous. Secretary of State Adams said, "I find him . . . alarmed, far beyond anything I could have conceived possible with the fear that the Holy Alliance are about to restore immediately all of South America to Spain."

The possibility of European aggression was not limited to South America. The Russians had been in Alaska since 1784. By 1812 they had established trading posts in what is now California. In 1821 the tsar of Russia claimed that Alaska's southern boundary was the 51st parallel, and he forbade all foreign vessels from using the coast.

This posed a threat to the flourishing American trade with China. For several decades, American traders had sailed from New England and New York around Cape Horn to the Pacific Northwest. There they would load the glossy skins of sea otters, which they obtained from the Indians, and sail to Canton, China. One to three years after leaving, they were back with tea, pepper, and silk, which fetched profits of as much as 800 percent.

The Monroe Doctrine. With Spain and Portugal trying to move back into their old colonial areas, and with Russia pushing in from the northwest, the United States felt it had to do something. Fortunately, it had an ally in Great Britain. Britain had developed profitable trading relations with many of the newly independent Latin Ameri-

can republics and did not want to see anything change that. So in 1823 British Foreign Secretary George Canning suggested to the United States that the two countries jointly declare their objection to having other European powers interfere in the affairs of the New World.

John Quincy Adams, however, argued against a joint declaration. He feared that Britain might use it to keep the United States from taking any more territory from Spain. And Adams had his eye on both Cuba and the northern portion of Mexico. He urged that the United States act alone on matters concerning the Western Hemisphere.

President Monroe agreed and, using some of the secretary's own words, set forth the American view in his 1823 message to Congress. He pictured the republican governments of the Western Hemisphere as different from, and more virtuous than, the corrupt monarchies of Europe. He warned all European powers not to interfere with affairs in the New World. They should not attempt to create new colonies or try to overthrow the newly independent republics. The United States would consider such action "dangerous to our peace and

The Monroe Doctrine is shown as strong and alive nearly 70 years after Monroe announced it. This 1896 cartoon shows Uncle Sam still warning the European powers to stay away.

The Missouri Compromise   1820

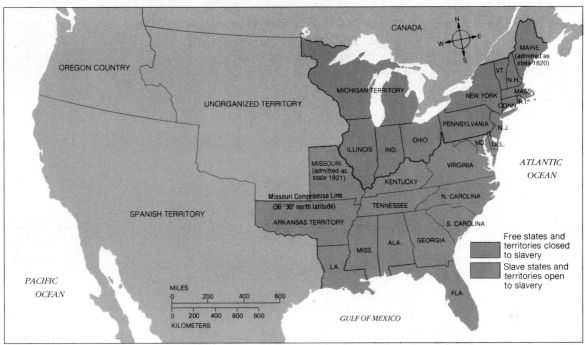

Map Skills   *Did the slave states include Delaware? Virginia? Missouri? Which free state extended farthest south? What present states lie along the Missouri Compromise Line?*

safety." At the same time, the United States would not involve itself in European affairs or interfere with existing colonies in the New World. These principles have since become known as the *Monroe Doctrine.*

At first, Monroe's words did not attract much attention in the United States. But in Europe there was anger and indignation. One French newspaper declared,

❝Mr. Monroe is the temporary President of a Republic situated on the east coast of North America. This republic is bounded on the south by the possessions of the King of Spain and on the north by those of the King of England. Its independence was only recognized forty years ago; by what right then would the two Americas today be under its immediate [influence] from Hudson's Bay to Cape Horn?❞

Other European government leaders were irritated at the upstart new republic lecturing them on how to behave in the New World. The British government was also furious that the United States had issued the declaration on its own. After all, it could not even enforce the Monroe Doctrine without the help of the British fleet which controlled the Atlantic.

Nevertheless, the Monroe Doctrine was important in the long run because Americans later adopted it as a major principle of foreign policy. And soon something happened that made the doctrine seem more important than it really was. In 1824 the Russian tsar decided to give up claims to the northwest coast of America south of the 54°40′ latitude. Actually, this decision had been made before the Monroe Doctrine was issued. Russia considered that Alaska was too far away to govern effectively or profitably. But to many Americans, the giving up of Alaskan territory seemed to be a result of their nationalist "lick all creation" spirit.

Domestic Affairs

On the home front, the new spirit of nationalism was challenged by an issue that had previously confronted the framers of the Constitution. That was the issue of slavery.

Debate over Spread of Slavery.   In 1787 slavery had been prohibited in the Northwest Territory. Then came the Louisiana Purchase of 1803. In 1818 the territory of Missouri, which was part of Louisiana, applied for admission to the Union. Its proposed state constitution recognized the right to

247

hold slaves. Immediately a dispute erupted. Would admitting Missouri with slavery set a precedent for the entire area included in the Louisiana Purchase?

Representative James Tallmadge, Jr., of New York proposed an amendment to the act admitting Missouri. The amendment barred the further introduction of slaves into Missouri, and also stated that children born of slaves in Missouri would become free when they reached the age of twenty-five.

There was an immediate uproar in Congress. For the first time, the merits of slavery were debated long and openly. A New Hampshire representative explained the importance of the issue. "An opportunity is now presented, if not to diminish, at least to prevent the growth of a sin which sits heavy on the soul of every one of us." Southerners took a different view. They defended the necessity of slavery and its extension westward. Many observers were alarmed by the bitterness of the controversy. This "momentous question," groaned the aging Thomas Jefferson, "like a fire-bell in the night, awakened and filled me with terror."

The Tallmadge Amendment narrowly passed the House, owing to the North's larger number of representatives. It failed in the Senate, however, despite the fact that free states outnumbered slave states eleven to ten. The reason was that several senators from northern states had been born and raised in the South and were sympathetic to it. The admission of Missouri was stalled.

Meanwhile, at the next session of Congress, Alabama, which was not part of the Louisiana Purchase, was admitted as a slave state. Now free states and slave states were balanced at eleven each. Then Congress received an application from the area now known as Maine. Here was a chance to break the deadlock over Missouri.

The Missouri Compromise. Under the leadership of Henry Clay, Congress passed a series of measures known as the Missouri Compromise. Maine was admitted as a free state and Missouri as a slave state, thus preserving the sectional balance in the Senate. The rest of Louisiana was split into two "spheres of interest, one . . . for the slaveholders and one for free settlers. The dividing line was set at 36°30' north latitude." South of the line, slavery was legal. North of the line—except for Missouri—slavery was banned.

President Monroe signed the Missouri Compromise in 1820, and the controversy came to an end. Many people were grateful that the issue had apparently been settled. Some, however, were jarred and frightened by the sectional anger that was revealed. They feared that the Missouri Compromise might not, in fact, last forever. Yet for a generation, the problem of slavery in federal territories remained where American politicians had carefully placed it—out of mind.

Section 2 Review

COMPREHENSION   Developing Vocabulary

1. Explain these terms: Monroe Doctrine, Missouri Compromise.

COMPREHENSION   Mastering Facts

1. How did Russia's attempt to move Alaska's boundary southward affect America's trade with China?
2. How did European nations react to the Monroe Doctrine?
3. What was the Tallmadge Amendment?
4. Who was the leader in getting the Missouri Compromise passed in Congress?

3 THE SOUTH BECOMES A COTTON KINGDOM

VOCABULARY   *King Cotton   cotton gin*

The Missouri Compromise was but one indication of the increasing importance of cotton in the national economy. Before the Revolution, tobacco, rice, and indigo were the important southern commercial crops. By the 1820s, however, "King Cotton" was the most important crop grown in the South. From fewer than 140,000 pounds in 1792, production soared to 35 million pounds by 1800.

Beginning in 1815, it doubled every ten years. By 1860 cotton was the nation's most valuable export.

Eli Whitney's Invention

Before 1793, southern slaveholders grew mostly long-staple cotton, also known as sea-island cotton.

The portrait of Eli Whitney was painted in 1822. At right is a patent model of his famous cotton gin. Whitney's first six gins which he took to Georgia were much larger.

(The word "staple" refers to the fibers within which cotton seeds grow.) Long-staple fibers were four to five inches long, and were easily twisted into thread. They also had a soft, silky texture. As a result, long-staple cotton commanded such a high price that it was profitable to have slaves spend hour upon hour removing the oily black seeds from the fibers by hand. In America, the soil and climate needed to grow this variety of cotton were found only in the semitropical coastal plains of South Carolina and Georgia, and on the sea islands off their coasts.

Another type of cotton, a coarser, short-staple variety sometimes called upland cotton, could be grown on the higher inland areas of the South. But it had a major drawback. Its green seeds were so tightly bound up in the fibers that a worker could clean only one pound a day.

In 1793 a talented young man from Massachusetts spent the winter as a guest on a Georgia plantation. Before graduating from Yale, Eli Whitney had set up a workshop on his father's farm where he built all sorts of tools. Now he turned his mechanical skills to the problem of inventing a cotton gin (gin is short for engine), a machine that would separate the seeds from the fibers. According to one historian,

"Legend has it that he was sitting on a farm fence brooding about the problem. As he sat there, a cat stole up to the fence and put a paw through it to clutch a chicken on the other side. The bird's body slammed against the fence, and it ran squawking away. But the cat came away with some feathers."

Whether or not the legend is true, Whitney applied the principle to a machine in which rollers were implanted with wire teeth. As a handle turned the rollers, they pulled the cotton seeds from the fibers. A worker using a gin could clean fifty pounds of short-staple cotton in one day. Later, other inventors found ways to operate gins by horsepower and steam engine, which increased production even more.

A Land Rush

An immediate result of the cotton gin's invention was a great land rush westward into the Old Southwest, the area between the Appalachians and the Mississippi south of the Ohio. The War of 1812 had effectively broken the power of the Adapter tribes in the area—the Creeks, Cherokees, Chickasaws, Chocktaws, and Seminoles—that you read about in chapter 1. And since short-staple cotton was now commercially profitable, tens of thousands of white settlers began moving in.

The first pioneers were mostly poor, non-slaveholding farmers. The soil on their farms had become worn-out and they were looking for new land to cultivate. They were soon followed, however, by wealthier, slaveholding planters who could afford to buy and work large areas of land. The poor farmers were forced to retreat to the hills of eastern Kentucky and Tennessee, western Georgia, and northern Alabama. The wealthy planters turned Louisiana, Mississippi, and Alabama into a booming frontier of cotton and slaves.

The Demand for Slave Labor Grows

The invention of the cotton gin and the resulting movement into the Old Southwest created an enormous demand for more slave labor. No slaves had been imported since the Revolution. But in 1803 South Carolina legalized importation, and for the next five years Africans flooded into Charleston in unprecedented numbers. In 1808 the twenty-year period of protection of the slave trade, which had been written into the Constitution, expired. Jefferson promptly signed a law banning the importation of slaves. But the law was not enforced very well, and slaves continued to be smuggled into the United States until 1859.

More important than the international slave trade, however, was the domestic slave trade. By 1820, as one historian put it, "slaves had become a valuable cash crop." Slaveowners in the eastern part of the South encouraged their slaves to breed as fast as possible, and then sold the blacks they could not use to planters farther west. The trade was handled by people called "soul-drivers." They would buy slaves from a plantation, trade them at auctions, and then send them in "lots" to their new destination. Some slaves were shipped by steamer on the Ohio and Mississippi rivers or along the Gulf coast. Others were driven overland. As with many human migrations, especially forced ones, families were often separated. Young blacks in particular were frequently sold away from their parents to unfamiliar surroundings in the land of cotton.

Life on a Cotton Plantation

The land of cotton it certainly was. As a British visitor to the Gulf port of Mobile, Alabama, wrote,

66 People live in cotton houses and ride in cotton carriages. They buy cotton, sell cotton, think cotton, eat cotton, drink cotton, and dream cotton. They marry cotton wives and unto them are born cotton children. 99

Cotton Planters. Some cotton planters lived a life of luxury and refinement. Their homes were white mansions with great columns supporting wide verandas. The gardens and grounds were carefully tended. Many of the furnishings came from Europe, and sons were often educated abroad. There was much social activity, with visits between families and huge parties. Even strangers were welcomed with gracious hospitality.

But such a life was in the minority. Most planters were tough, hardworking farmers whose living conditions were quite rough. A traveler who was charged one dollar for staying overnight at a plan-

A cotton plantation on the Mississippi river. Planters used Whitney's gin as well as slave labor, and then shipped the cotton by steamer to all parts of the world.

tation house described his visit. The house in which he stayed was indeed painted white, but there was a log cabin in the front yard that served as both a kitchen and a dining room. The planter and his wife slept in a bed in the parlor, while the traveler shared a straw mattress upstairs with one of the planter's sons. Everyone on this plantation walked barefoot in both summer and winter, and "nobody wore coats, except on holidays." Yet the planter was a rich man, having hundreds of acres of land, large herds of cattle and horses, and some thirty to forty slaves.

Actually, operating a cotton plantation required considerable effort. A planter who invested $200 in a slave had to make certain that the slave remained in good health. This was especially difficult since the hot, humid months of May through November usually brought malaria. Also, many blacks resisted slavery by performing their tasks as poorly as possible. So there was a constant struggle on the part of planters to keep their work force producing.

Cotton Slaves. Growing cotton was a year-round job for slaves. In January and February they would plow the fields with mule-drawn plows. In March and April they would seed the land. Within a few days, the plants would push their way above ground, signaling the start of hoeing time. The slaves would move in long lines across the fields, chopping weeds and grass away from the cotton. The weeds and grass would spring up

again, and the slaves would repeat the operation. Hoeing usually lasted until the middle of July.

By late August the cotton bolls had split open, and the fluffy white crop was ready to be harvested. Soloman Northrup, a free black who was kidnapped by a slave trader and sold in Louisiana, described its appearance this way: "There are few sights more pleasant to the eye, than a wide cotton field. . . . It presents an appearance of purity, like an immaculate (faultless) expanse of light, new-fallen snow."

Although the ripe cotton may have looked beautiful, picking it was a bone-weary job. The slaves would drag a coarse strong bag called a gunny sack behind them as they worked their way down the cotton rows picking the cotton out of the boll and dropping it into the sacks. Then they would empty the contents into a large basket. At day's end they would "tote," or carry, the basket to the gin-house for weighing.

Section 3 Review

COMPREHENSION   Developing Vocabulary
1. Explain these terms: King Cotton, staple, soul- drivers.

COMPREHENSION   Mastering Facts
1. What did a cotton gin do?
2. Why did the invention of the cotton gin cause a rush into the Old Southwest?
3. How did the invention of the cotton gin affect the demand for slave labor?

4   THE INDUSTRIAL REVOLUTION SPREADS TO AMERICA

VOCABULARY   *interchangeable parts   Waltham (Lowell) system*

At first, the cotton grown in the Cotton Kingdom went mostly to textile mills in Great Britain. But gradually a large textile industry developed in New England. In this, too, Eli Whitney played a major role.

The Use of Interchangeable Parts

After inventing the cotton gin, Whitney went north to obtain a patent from the federal government and also to open a factory to manufacture the new device. But his machine was easy to copy. So people simply adopted it and refused to pay a royalty. Whitney's enterprise failed.

Whitney's inventive mind then turned to an-

other mechanical problem: the fact that every gun was a unique unit, and if one part broke, the gun had to go back to its maker because only he could fix a part for that particular gun. Whitney looked at a gun, not as a unit, but as a combination of parts. He developed machines to produce these parts, each one exactly like all the others. A gun manufacturer no longer had to employ master mechanics but could use unskilled workers. The manufacturer could also turn out a great many guns in a short period of time.

Whitney's system of interchangeable parts was soon applied to dozens of other products, which moved from the hands of individual artisans to the noisy machinery of the factory. Soon cities and towns throughout the North, especially in New England, were turning out goods on a mass basis.

New England's Textile Industry

As was the case in England, America's industrialization started with textiles, specifically cotton goods. The textile industry soon became the largest in the nation.

The Growth of Mills. The American textile industry began in 1789, when a twenty-one-year-old Englishman named Samuel Slater stepped onto a New York dock. When he left England, he had declared himself to be a farmer. But he was actually a skilled mechanic. Because the British wanted to guard the secrets of their own industrial development, they banned the export of machine designs and even the emigration of mechanics. Slater, however, memorized the plans for a complete textile mill and then came to this country. With financial backing from Moses Brown, a wealthy Quaker merchant, he opened a cotton-spinning plant at Pawtucket, Rhode Island, in 1791. It was the first successful full-time factory in America and was soon widely imitated, although on a smaller scale.

In 1807 Jefferson's embargo caused many businessmen to turn from overseas trade to industry. The War of 1812 likewise encouraged Americans to produce their own cloth. In 1813 a group of wealthy Bostonians decided to band together as the Boston Associates and pool their capital resources. They established the world's first integrated cotton manufacturing plant. All operations, from the unbaling of the cotton to the dyeing of the finished cloth, were carried out under one roof.

During the 1820s and 1830s the Boston Associates expanded operations by establishing a series of plants, each of which specialized in a different textile product. They also founded insurance companies and banks in order to have a steady supply of capital. They set up real-estate firms to buy the best sites for their factories. And they organized water-power companies to develop the rivers whose falling waters powered their machines.

Working Conditions. Conditions in the New England textile mills were far from pleasant. The buildings, which fronted on a river, were six or seven stories high and looked very imposing. But

The print above was used to illustrate the 1840 English novel Michael Armstrong, the Factory Boy.

ceilings were low and ventilation, poor. Windows were kept closed even in summer in order to maintain the humidity that was supposed to prevent the cotton thread from breaking. Winter, with its short hours of daylight, was even worse. Then the smoky fumes from whale-oil lamps would mix with the thick cotton dust in the air, making it difficult to breathe.

Work began at five o'clock in the morning. At half-past seven there was a short pause for breakfast. Workers took half an hour for lunch at noon, and the day ended at half-past seven in the evening. The workweek was six days. On Sunday, workers were expected to attend church.

All the workers in Slater's first mill were children, and in 1832 it was reported that two out of five textile workers were between six and seventeen years of age. Some industrialists argued that small hands were best suited for the narrow slots of the textile machinery. More to the point, children could be paid lower wages than adults.

The balance of the textile work force consisted of young women from seventeen to twenty-four, who flocked to the mill towns from the worn-out farms of New England. Their workday was probably no longer than if they had stayed on the farm, and factory work was their only alternative to domestic service.

The Boardinghouses. Since these women workers did not come from the mill towns, and since many of them were young enough to require permission from their families in order to work, mill owners developed the so-called Waltham or Lowell system, named after two of the leading Massachusetts mill towns. Under this system, women textile workers lived in a boardinghouse. The company deducted room and board from their paychecks, and employed a housemother—usually a local widow—to cook meals, check up on church attendance, and in general provide an atmosphere of respectability.

Most boardinghouses were closely regulated. Boarders were expected to enter quietly, observe good manners at all times, and take turns making beds and sweeping out the bedrooms. Those who had worked in the mill the greatest length of time sat near the head of the dining room table; newer workers, at the foot. No lights were allowed in the bedrooms, and all doors were locked at ten o'clock. Workers who did not attend church were asked by the housemother "to keep within doors and improve their time in reading, writing, and in other valuable and harmless employment." The women were kept in line by the fact that they were paid only two or four times a year. If they did not obey the rules, they were fired without wages.

Industrialists thought the mills offered a beneficial education to women and children. After all, they were learning the value of labor, the worth of money, and the merits of strict moral behavior. Mill owners were also proud to point out, quite correctly, that working conditions in American factories were considerably better than those in England.

The First Factory Strike. Understandably, the women and children involved in these new conditions took a different view. For a time, they accepted the new industrial discipline, just as they had always accepted the authority of their fathers. By about 1830, however, there were signs of restlessness. The first recorded factory strike came in 1828. The mill owners in Paterson, New Jersey, tried to change the lunch hour from twelve to one o'clock. The children went out on strike, "for fear," said one observer, "if they assented to this, the next thing would be to deprive them of eating at all."

The First Unions

Until about 1830, most labor disputes involved skilled workers. Traditionally, such people started as apprentices and then moved up to become jour-

neymen. Some succeeded in reaching the top rank. They became master craftsmen, who themselves employed apprentices and journeymen. This pattern dominated such skilled trades as the carpenters, masons, stone-cutters, hatters, tailors, shoemakers, and sailmakers.

In the 1790s, journeymen in several northern cities began to join together in mutual-aid societies. They rightly sensed that their interests were no longer the same as those of their employers. The population had grown, and the market for goods was much larger. This permitted masters to accumulate capital and employ large numbers of journeymen. The fact that there were more journeymen tended to keep salaries low. If one journeyman refused to work for a low wage, another could soon be found who would. It was, therefore, getting more and more difficult for journeymen to become masters themselves.

The mutual-aid societies of journeymen were the nation's first labor unions. Their efforts to obtain higher wages and shorter hours, however, ran into a stone wall of tradition. The common law (which was tradition) held that it was illegal for workers to combine to withhold their labor. In other words, strikes were "criminal conspiracies." The courts convicted workers who went out on strike in an attempt to improve their working conditions.

New York Becomes Urban Leader

The development of industry also had an effect on the ranking of American cities. By 1810, the nation's largest city was no longer Boston or Philadelphia. It was New York, a situation that is still true today.

A New Sales Technique. One reason for New York's spectacular rise was the fact that its business people were more willing to try new techniques than were business people in other cities. For example, prior to 1817 imported goods were sold at auction. If the price offered was not high enough, traders would withdraw the goods from sale. This meant they had to pay storage charges, which were often quite high. It also meant their money was tied up in goods that were not being sold. In 1817 New York merchants agreed to sell imported goods no matter how low a price was offered. Sailing vessels immediately began unloading their cargoes at New York in preference to other ports, and

The Tontine Coffee House at Wall and Water streets in New York City was a center of social activity.

business boomed. Thereupon, merchants from other cities began to come to New York to trade, and business kept booming.

A *Regular Shipping Service*. The following year, 1818, New York merchants put another new business practice into operation. They started a regular shipping service between New York and Liverpool, England. Each month—"full or not full," as the advertisement put it—four ships sailed across the Atlantic carrying freight, passengers, money, and mail. Two went east and two went west. A black ball hanging from the foremast showed that the ships belonged to the Black Ball Line. Previously, ship captains had waited for full cargoes before setting sail. The new practice of regularly scheduled service was a tremendous aid to business. By 1828, New York's merchant fleet

was almost as large as those of Baltimore, Boston, and Philadelphia combined.

Financing the Cotton Kingdom. The flowing in of goods and business people meant that New York merchants had to have something staple to export. They found it in cotton. They would lend cotton planters money to buy land and slaves. They would also sell cotton planters hardware, foodstuffs, and luxury items that were not produced in the South. In exchange, they would send their ships to Charleston, Mobile, New Orleans, and other southern ports. They would load the ships with bales of cotton and bring them back to New York for shipment to New England and Europe.

By 1830 about forty cents of every dollar that southern planters received from the sale of cotton was going to New York. Its merchants earned a profit from interest on loans. They earned a profit on the markup of goods sold to the planters. And they earned a profit on the shipping and insurance commissions they charged. In short, the financial capital of the Cotton Kingdom was New York City.

Section 4 Review

COMPREHENSION   Developing Vocabulary

1. Explain these terms: interchangeable parts, Waltham or Lowell system, master craftsmen.

COMPREHENSION   Mastering Facts

1. What was the advantage of using interchangeable parts?
2. What did the first successful full-time factory in America make?
3. What caused the first recorded factory strike in America?
4. Why were strikes considered criminal conspiracies by the courts?

CHAPTER 11 Review

Chapter Summary

A period of nationalism brought new economic growth and increased federal power to the United States. Commerce and industry were encouraged by Henry Clay's American System; protective tariffs encouraged new manufacturing; road and canal building improved transportation; and the Second Bank of the United States increased the money supply. New threats from abroad prompted the United States to issue the Monroe Doctrine, which warned Europeans to stay out of the affairs of the Western Hemisphere. Meanwhile, with development of the cotton gin, cotton became the chief crop of the South—and this increased the demand for slave labor. As a thriving textile industry developed in New England, new factories led to the development of the first American labor unions.

Questions for Critical Thinking

COMPREHENSION   Summarizing Main Ideas

1. According to Henry Clay, what three kinds of measures were needed to help bring about the "American System"?
2. How did the National Road help northeastern manufacturers? How did it help westward-moving pioneers?
3. Explain how each of the following helped industry develop in the Northeast: (a) the establishment of protective tariffs; (b) the chartering of the Second Bank of the United States; (c) the immigration of Samuel Slater; (d) Eli Whitney's system of interchangeable parts; (e) Jefferson's embargo and the War of 1812.
4. What was Justice Marshall's attitude toward the new national economy?
5. What were the principles of the Monroe Doctrine? On what did enforcement of the Monroe Doctrine depend during the first half of the nineteenth century?
6. What effect did the debate over the admission of Missouri have on sectional feelings in the United States?
7. What factors led to the rise of New York as the nation's largest city and commercial center?

COMPREHENSION   Interpreting Events

1. Why was Monroe's administration known as the "Era of Good Feelings"?
2. If you had been a senator in 1820, how would you have voted on the question of admitting Missouri to the Union? Give reasons to support your position.
3. Why did most of the work force in the textile industry consist of women and children?

APPLICATION   Using Skills To Read Maps

When studying history, the ability to gain information from maps is an important skill. The relationship between history and geography can become more evident through the study of maps. Refer to the three maps in this chapter to answer the following questions.

1. Give several examples showing that the location of roads in the early 1800s was influenced by geographical features such as mountains and rivers.
2. In what ways did the Great Lakes affect where canals were built in the United States?
3. What natural boundaries were used to divide free and slave areas under terms of the Missouri Compromise?

EVALUATION   Forming Generalizations

1. Which of the principles put forth in the Monroe Doctrine are still followed by the United States today?
2. What problems did women textile workers of the 1830s face? What problems do women textile workers face today? How might you explain the similarities and differences?

The Industrial Revolution

The American Revolution was a dramatic event that captured the attention of the world. At the same time another revolution was going on, totally unplanned and unnoticed, which finally transformed the lives of Americans as much–some say more–than that of 1775–1783. This silent change was called the Industrial Revolution.

It began in England during the early 1700s and eventually spread to the rest of the world. As the Jeffersonian period ended, the Industrial Revolution (as you will read in the next chapter) had already begun to affect the new nation. If Americans had known what was going on in England at this time, they would have known their own future. The pattern of industrial growth and its accompanying social consequences would soon be repeated in the United States.

An early cotton factory with power looms. The hours in the factory were long, and machines noisy and dirty.

Basic Resources. Industrialization began in England because of certain geographic, social, and economic conditions. It was based on that country's ample supply of natural resources. Large coal and iron deposits were crucial for the construction of machinery and factories in all industries. The rapid currents of England's many rivers and streams provided the water power to keep machines running. England's coastline furnished numerous ports from which manufactured goods could be shipped to foreign buyers. In addition, English wool, as well as cotton from the colonies, helped spur the expanding British textile industry.

Great Britain could also draw upon a large labor force for its industrial needs. New advances in medicine and sanitation caused the population to double. Farms became overpopulated. With fewer jobs on the farm, men and women streamed into the factories in the cities, where there was hope of work.

Capital and Support. The Industrial Revolution was further advanced by the huge amounts of capital which British merchants and landowners had accumulated. These savings could now be invested with much profit in such expanding industries as mining, iron, and textiles.

Finally, the British government did its best to stimulate the growth of industry. Following the principles of laissez faire, it relaxed taxes and mercantilist regulations that hampered trade. In addition, the powerful British navy was sent out to defend English commercial interests around the world.

Flying Shuttle. Because of the increased demand for cloth both from new city dwellers and from expanding foreign markets, the search for new methods of production led to the mechanization of the textile industry. John Kay developed his "flying shuttle" in 1733, which cut weaving time in half. In 1769 Richard Arkwright's water-powered spinning machine made it possible to produce many strong threads at once. By 1785, Edmund Cartwright had invented the first successful power weaving loom.

To acquire these and other

inventions, business owners had to invest considerable amounts of money. To make a profit, they had to run the machines twenty-four hours a day and provide them with expert maintenance and repair. The new inventions also required a steady source of power, which at first had to come from swift streams. As a result, centralized factories rapidly dominated industrial production in England.

Steam Engines. The invention of a steam engine, however, was the greatest aid to factory building. Steam was a mobile source of power. Factories using steam engines could be built anywhere, not just along streams.

In 1698, Thomas Savery had built the first practical steam pump. Years later, John Watt and others had so perfected the engine that, by 1800, steam had replaced water as the chief source of power in British factories.

Industrial inventions were also appearing in other countries as well. In America, for example, Eli Whitney, best known for inventing the cotton gin, devised the first methods of using interchangeable parts in assembling muskets. This was the beginning of modern mass-production methods.

Changing Times. Overnight Great Britain had changed from an agricultural to an urban society, because factories and jobs were to be found in cities. The speed of the transfor-

mation is striking. At the beginning of the Industrial Revolution, England had only four cities with a population of over 50,000. By 1850, there were 31; and 50 percent of the English population lived in urban areas.

In many ways, the cities were not prepared to receive their new inhabitants. Crime and disease grew along with the population. Cities lacked sewers and paved streets. Workers' housing was dark, overcrowded, and poorly built. Their working conditions were no better. They worked 15 hours a day in the noise and dirt of the factory for a wage they could barely live on.

Women and children worked in the factories, as they would later in the United States. Many children rarely saw the sun, because they worked from five-thirty in the morning until eight at night. In addition, the work was dull and repetitive. Assembly-line workers could take little pride in their work because they contributed only a small part to the finished product. Even worse, the lack of safety devices on industrial machines resulted in frequent accidents, and a worker injured in the factory seldom received any compensation.

In its early stages, therefore, the Industrial Revolution seems actually to have lowered living standards for millions of working people.

Improvements. As the pace of technological change slowed and stabilized, however, conditions gradually improved. Beginning in the 1820s, a powerful

movement for workers' rights and for the reform of working conditions arose. By 1830, the wages of skilled laborers rose to a level where meat, a luxury in the 1700s, became a common item on the English table.

As the Industrial Revolution spread to Belgium, France, Germany, and the United States, the miseries bred by technological change were followed by efforts at reform. In England in 1842, a law was passed prohibiting the use of women, girls, and boys in underground mines. A bill passed in 1847 made the ten-hour day standard for British workers. In later years, workers managed gradually to improve their wages and working conditions. As a result, workers in industrialized countries now enjoy a standard of living and exercise a political influence unheard of in preindustrial times.

Pollution and stubborn pockets of poverty remain problems in developed countries. Nonetheless, in the long run, the Industrial Revolution resulted in longer lives and a better living standard for millions of people.

Understanding Free Enterprise

1. Why did the Industrial Revolution begin in England?

2. What were some unpleasant side effects of the Industrial Revolution?

3. Why is steam considered a "mobile source of power"?

4. Why did the growth of industry and cities occur at about the same time?

257

CHAPTER 12

The Age of Jackson

1824–1840

Linking Past to Present

The 1820s saw a change both in political types and the way politics were conducted. President James Monroe was the last president of the founding-father generation. His successor, John Quincy Adams, was, according to many historians, the last intellectual president until Woodrow Wilson in the twentieth century. Adams, however, was not popular with the public, which was ready for quite another type of man.

In 1828 the public elected Andrew Jackson, hero of New Orleans. He so dominated the political scene during the 1830s that this period is often called the Jacksonian Age. Jackson greatly enlarged the powers of the presidency. There also developed at this time certain political techniques, such as national conventions and campaign hoopla, which continue to this day. Also, for the first time the average person became more involved in politics. But at the same time, sectional interests began to strain the bonds among the states.

1 THE TWO-PARTY SYSTEM DEVELOPS

VOCABULARY   *two-party system   states' rights*

Everyone assumed that Monroe would not run for a third term largely because Washington had not done so. Monroe's heir-apparent was John Quincy Adams, for by this time it was traditional for the secretary of state to succeed to the presidency.

Adams's candidacy was challenged by three other rising politicians. Neither they nor Adams was associated with any political party. Everyone was assumed to be a Republican because the Federalist party had been dead during the "Era of Good Feelings." William Crawford of Georgia was a personally attractive man who claimed to be the true heir of Thomas Jefferson. Kentucky's Henry Clay had built a political power base as speaker of the House of Representatives. He also had a broad popular following because of his "American System," which you read about in chapter 11. Andrew Jackson of Tennessee had become an overnight hero at the Battle of New Orleans and had kept himself in the public eye by his exploits in Florida. Popularity and sectional interests rather than national issues dominated the campaign.

The Election of 1824 Enrages Jacksonians

The war hero won at the popular polls but lost the election. Jackson received the largest number of popular votes and the largest number in the electoral college. But since he did not have an electoral majority, the election went into the House of Representatives. Clay, with the least number of electoral votes, was thrown out of the running under the terms of the Twelfth Amendment. Crawford had suffered a stroke. So the contest came down to a struggle between Jackson's supporters and those representatives who favored Adams.

Clay, because of his power in the House, could swing the election either way. Jackson's supporters urged Clay to support their candidate because he had the largest popular vote. But Clay disliked Jackson personally and mistrusted his lack of political experience. "I cannot believe," Clay commented, "that killing 2500 Englishmen at New Orleans qualifies [him] for the various difficult and complicated duties of the [Presidency]." Adams, on the other hand, agreed with Clay's American System. The two men held a private talk, and Adams was elected president by a majority of the states represented in the House.

Everyone knew that Adams and Clay had consulted with each other, though no one knew (or knows today) what was said. Then, a few days later, Adams announced that he planned to appoint Clay as his secretary of state. Jackson's supporters were convinced a deal had been made to rob the general of his victory. "Unholy coalition!" "Bargain and corruption!" they shouted. Representative John Randolph of Virginia was so outraged that he denounced Clay as a man who "shines and stinks like rotten mackerel by moonlight." No sooner had Adams begun his term than the Jacksonians started campaigning to put their man in the White House at the next election.

Adams's Policies Are Not Popular

Adams's father was still alive in Quincy, Massachusetts, busily corresponding with Thomas Jefferson about statecraft, religion, and the nature of humankind. But while the younger Adams was president, a remarkable thing happened. Both his father and Jefferson died on the same day. And that day was July 4, 1826, the fiftieth anniversary

259

of the Declaration of Independence. Many people felt this was a sign that the hand of God was indeed guiding the American people.

Young Adams, however, was not the kind of man who attracted public sympathy. He was the last president to regard political parties with distaste. And because he was a proud, intensely patriotic, high-minded man, he never quite got over the fact that he was a minority president. With stubborn courage and conviction, he proceeded to propose a program that was political suicide. He tried to continue the strong national program the Republicans had taken over from the Federalists. But most voters now wanted less federal government and less influence by the East on national policy.

National Policy Defeated. In his first message, Adams reminded Congress that the Constitution gave it the power to provide for the common defense and general welfare. He then proceeded to stretch the concept of general welfare. The national government, Adams said, should establish a national university, finance scientific expeditions, reform the patent system, and promote literature and the arts. Above all, Congress should use income from the sale of public lands to finance national internal improvements. Adams's program got nowhere. He was ridiculed as an aristocrat. People said it was foolish to spend public money on such frivolous subjects as art and literature. And in any event, they were swinging away from the idea of a strong national government and toward the idea of states' rights.

Adams's program perhaps deserved more serious attention than it received. Much of it was eventually adopted years later. Adams was quite right when he claimed that "the spirit of improvement is abroad upon this earth." But many of his opponents thought he was stretching the Constitution too far. Many would also have opposed any proposals he offered no matter what their merits. Jackson's friends were determined that Adams's administration should look bad. More and more people began to believe the propaganda that Adams had "stolen" the election from Jackson.

Indian and Foreign Policies Defeated. Adams also irritated southern states when he tried to protect the rights of the Creeks. Georgia, under pressure from land speculators, began a survey of Creek territory in 1826 with the intention of selling land to white settlers. Adams threatened to send in federal troops to stop the survey and talked about the supremacy of the national government. The governor of Georgia defied him and talked about states' rights. Eventually the Creeks agreed to move west of the Mississippi. But Adams was humiliated.

Even in foreign affairs, Adams was far less successful than he had been as secretary of state. Political enemies in Congress blocked his attempt to send delegates to a convention of American republics in Panama.

The Democratic Party Is Born

The presidential campaign of 1828 marked a fundamental change in the national attitude toward political parties. Since 1800, people had gradually been moving away from Washington's view that parties were a danger to the republic. Instead, more and more people were coming to believe that a two-party system helped the nation. It enabled people of differing views to band together and express their beliefs. It provided a means by which citizens could challenge the way their government was functioning. And it enabled political power to pass from one group to another in a systematic manner without bloodshed.

Since the collapse of the Federalists in 1820, the only party in the United States had been the Republican party. But soon after the congressional elections of 1826, a new political party came into existence. Between 1826 and 1828, both Adams and Jackson called themselves Republicans. But while Adams called himself a National Republican, Jackson called himself a Democratic Republican. After Jackson's election in 1828, his party became known as the Democratic party.

The Democratic party was organized in large part by a short, charming, extremely discreet, and extremely ambitious politician named Martin Van Buren, also known as "the Little Magician." Van Buren started out by building a political machine in New York State. From there he decided to move onto the national scene. He believed that Jackson would make an excellent president. He also wanted to revive Jefferson's philosophy of government: namely, states' rights and as little federal spending as possible. Van Buren believed that the best way to achieve this was to unite "the planters of the South and the plain people of the North." And there was another advantage to such a move, Van Buren felt. It would reduce sectional feelings about slavery.

Martin Van Buren, shown here in the portrait by American artist G. P. A. Healy, was Jackson's secretary of state and later vice president. He served as president from 1837 to 1840.

Accordingly, Van Buren formed an alliance with several prominent political figures. Chief among them were John C. Calhoun of South Carolina and Thomas Hart Benton of Missouri. The three men proceeded to organize a national party from the bottom up.

A New Campaign Style Develops

Van Buren and his fellow politicians also developed a campaign style that is still popular today. As one historian described it:

❝They introduced songs and slogans into election campaigns. They inaugurated parades, barbecues, tree plantings, dinners, rallies. They provided buttons and clothes to designate one's party and

candidate; and through a chain of newspapers covering the nation they turned out a mountain of party propaganda, including cartoons, songs, and funny stories. . . . One of the more effective gimmicks invented by the Democrats was the use of the hickory as a symbol of their candidate and party. Jackson had been nicknamed "Old Hickory" during the War of 1812 by his soldiers because hickory was the toughest wood they knew. . . . Hickory sticks, hickory canes, hickory brooms shot up across the country, at crossroads, at steeples, on steamboats, in the hands of children—everywhere. Local Democratic clubs and military companies also organized ceremonies to plant hickory trees in their village and town squares as part of their campaign to heighten public interest in the election.❞

Jackson Wins the White House

Heighten interest it did. There was also the fact that western states had universal white male suffrage without property qualifications, which meant that many more individuals could vote. Also, Jackson was the first presidential candidate from west of the Appalachians and the first to come from a poor family. People felt that he was one of them, and they elected him. The turnout of voters in 1828 was three times what it had been in 1824. In 1824 only 27 percent of those who were eligible to vote actually did so. In 1828 the figure rose to 56 percent.

This portrait of Andrew Jackson reflects some of Jackson's strong character.

Jackson's inauguration was followed by a White House reception attended by many "common people."

the White House. As eyewitness Margaret Bayard Smith, wife of a Maryland senator, wrote, "Country men, farmers, gentlemen, mounted and dismounted, boys, women and children, black and white. Carriages, wagons, and carts all pursuing him to the President's house."

There they stood with their muddy boots on the satin-covered chairs, bawled out political slogans, tossed plates and glassware about, and got drunk. It was obvious to everyone that the American presidency now belonged to the masses. Others said, with mingled horror and disgust, that "King Mob" now ruled the nation.

Section 1 Review

COMPREHENSION   Developing Vocabulary

1. Explain these terms: two-party system, states' rights, National Republicans.

COMPREHENSION   Mastering Facts

1. Why did Jackson and his supporters feel so bitter about Adams's election as president?
2. Why was Adams's national policy not popular?
3. What were some of the new campaign techniques used in the 1828 election?
4. What was unusual about Jackson's inauguration?

The scene at Jackson's inauguration symbolized the new political spirit. An immense crowd gathered in Washington. Many had traveled hundreds of miles from the farms and backwoods of America to see their president. They surged through the city's unpaved streets and followed Old Hickory to

2   JACKSON SHOWS A NEW PRESIDENTIAL STYLE

VOCABULARY   *spoils system   caucus*

Jackson himself did nothing to discourage the popular mood. He thought of himself as a man of the common people. He had been born in poverty in the Carolina backcountry, the son of Scotch-Irish immigrants. He was the first president since Washington without a college education. He and his supporters made a great deal of these facts.

But at the time of his election at the age of sixty-one, Jackson was hardly one of the common people. He had built a highly successful career in Tennessee in law, politics, land speculation, cotton planting, and soldiering. His home, the Hermitage, was a mansion, not a log cabin. Anyone who owned more than a hundred slaves, as Jackson did, was a very wealthy man.

New Methods for New Leaders

Although he had been elected with the help of sectional interests, Jackson regarded himself as representing the nation as a whole. Because he

had a suspicious nature, he disliked special interest groups and men whose power came from privilege. Lurking beneath the surface of his iron will was a deep streak of anger. When crossed, he lashed back, whether it was at the British army, Indians, Spanish officials, or political opponents. He found it hard to forgive. He was the only president ever to have fought five duels and killed a man in one of them. His physical presence was more commanding than that of any public figure since George Washington. Yet while Washington had commanded widespread respect, Jackson commanded widespread popularity. He seemed to symbolize the virtues of the new America—a common man who climbed the ladder of success, ready to destroy aristocratic privileges wherever he found them.

The Kitchen Cabinet.   It was characteristic of Old Hickory that most of his cabinet appointments went to undistinguished men. The only exception was his secretary of state, Martin Van Buren. Jackson preferred to rely on the advice of personal intimates. Several western newspaper editors became the core of what soon became known as the "kitchen cabinet." This group of thirteen men supposedly slipped into the White House by the back door and then went through the kitchen on their way to see the president. Today they would be called White House advisors.

The Spoils System.

One of Jackson's first moves was equally characteristic of the man and his thinking. He fired nearly 10 percent of federal government employees, most of them holdovers from the Adams administration, and gave their jobs to loyal Jacksonians. Jackson restrained his political supporters who wanted even more heads to roll. The practice of making such replacements was not new, and later presidents followed it much more vigorously. Jackson called a "rotation in office, a leading principle in the republican creed." The president believed that common people should not only have the right to vote but the right to hold office as well. Why should government jobs be given only to those who were educated or wealthy? Besides, unless there was a regular turnover of personnel, Jackson declared, office holders would become inefficient and corrupt.

Jackson's action became known as the "spoils system," from an old saying that in war, "to the victor belong the spoils of the enemy." Actually, Jefferson had removed about the same percentage of office holders as Jackson. But by Jackson's time, the federal bureaucracy had grown, so the number of people who were fired was much larger. Ever since, Jackson's name has been associated with the system by which incoming political parties throw out old appointees and replace them with their own friends.

The spoils system did, in fact, make government officials more representative of the people as a whole. But it did not prevent corruption. In fact, one of Jackson's appointees turned out to be the first person to steal $1 million from the federal government. Samuel Swartwout received the post of collector of the Port of New York and was in charge of collecting tariffs on all imported goods that passed through the nation's busiest seaport. Eight years after being appointed, Swartwout fled to England with his loot.

A Political Alliance.

The 1820s and 1830s saw the arrival of large numbers of Catholic immigrants, especially from Ireland. The National Republicans disliked the new arrivals, but the Democrats welcomed them as friends and supporters at the polls in the Northeast's growing cities. Quite naturally, Irish immigrants supported those politicians who were the most friendly to them. This started an alliance between the Democratic party and the Irish in cities which exists to the present day.

Jacksonian Vetoes.

Jackson's belief that he was the voice of the people led him to veto more legislation than all previous presidents combined. One of his most famous vetoes concerned the proposed Maysville Road in Kentucky. As passed by Congress, the Maysville Bill required the federal government to purchase stock in a private road-building corporation. To Jackson, this smelled of privilege. Why should taxpayers help a private business? He justified his veto on the grounds that since the road was going to be built within the boundaries of a single state, the state—and not the federal government—should take the responsibility of paying for it.

Though internal improvements were very popular, Jackson had his eye on the politics of the situation. Kentucky was the home state of Henry Clay, so the veto was a blow at one of the president's arch enemies. Also, Pennsylvania and New York, which had supported Jackson's campaign, had spent a great deal of state money on their own internal improvements. They did not want the federal government to pay for such projects elsewhere.

Jackson's veto also pleased the South. Most of the money for the Maysville Road and similar projects would come from the protective tariff, and southerners were becoming increasingly unhappy about the tariff. While it helped northern manufacturers by keeping out cheaper foreign goods, it hurt the South. The southerners had to pay the high prices for northern goods when they could have gotten such products cheaper from Europe.

In the long run, continued vetoes of internal improvements would have thoroughly angered the West. But Jackson was easier on so-called pork-barrel legislation, that is, legislation that benefited his political friends. He signed a great many such bills to improve river traffic and harbor facilities in areas where Democrats were numerous. In return, he expected loyalty to the party and to himself.

Jackson "Removes" the Indians

Since the 1600s, the attitude of white settlers toward the Indians had fluctuated. Sometimes whites favored extermination. At other times they tried to convert the Indians to Christianity, turn them into farmers, and assimilate them into the white culture.

Both Washington and Jefferson had favored a policy of assimilation of the Indians. But by the time Jackson became president, most Americans agreed with Henry Clay that "it was impossible to civilize Indians . . . [because] they were essentially inferior to the Anglo-Saxon race." Or, to put it differently, the Indians stood in the way of a developing America. Many Americans definitely felt that the sooner they were eliminated, the better.

A New Policy. Jackson, despite his background as an Indian fighter, did not support extermination. Assimilation, he felt, could not work. A third possibility—allowing Indians to live in their own areas—would have required too many troops to enforce against white settlers who wanted Indian lands. The only solution was to move the Indians from their lands to areas farther west. "Say to the [Indians]," Jackson wrote,

❝ where they now are, they and my white children are too near to each other to live in harmony and peace. . . . Beyond the river Mississippi . . . their father has provided a country, large enough for them all, and he advises them to remove to it. There, their white brethren will not trouble them . . . and they can live upon it, they and all their children as long as grass grows or water runs in peace and plenty. **❞**

So Congress passed the Indian Removal Act in 1830 and followed it up with the Indian Intercourse Act of 1834. Under these laws, Indian lands in the existing twenty-four states were to be exchanged for lands in the Indian Territory, which later became the state of Oklahoma. About ninety removal treaties were signed by the federal government and various Indian tribes. For Jackson, the removal policy was "not only liberal, but generous," because it would enable the Indians to maintain their way of life.

Black Hawk and Osceola Resist. Some tribes, however, were unwilling to leave their ancestral lands. So removal was carried out with considerable brutality. The Creeks in Alabama, for example, were removed in chains. The Chocktaws were forced out of Mississippi in the dead of winter without proper clothing and provisions. In Illinois in 1832 some hungry Sac and Fox, led by Chief Black Hawk, tried to plant grain on their old farmland and were slaughtered by local militia. This became known as the Black Hawk War. The Seminole Indians in Florida, aided by some escaped black slaves, put up a fierce fight under the skillful and vigorous leadership of Chief Osceola. It took seven years before government troops finally wiped out the last pockets of resistance.

Robert Lindneaux's Trail of Tears *depicts some of the sufferings endured by the Cherokee during their forced thousand-mile march west from the Great Smoky Mountains in Tennessee.*

The Court Supports the Cherokees. One Indian tribe that tried to follow white ways fared no better. The Cherokees in Georgia had done what Jefferson had asked. They had turned from hunting to farming. They had established small manufacturing shops, built schools, and begun publishing a newspaper in their own language. In 1827 they decided to form a separate state with its own constitution. Georgia, however, refused to recognize the action of the Cherokees. Instead, it said that federal laws and treaties with the Indians interfered with Georgia's rights of government. Georgia then opened Cherokee land to white settlement.

The legality of the matter wound up before the Supreme Court. Marshall's decision in *Worcester v. Georgia* (1832) held that the Cherokees formed a nation with clearly defined boundaries within which "the laws of Georgia can have no force." Furthermore, citizens of Georgia could not enter Cherokee territory without Cherokee consent. In effect, Marshall claimed that the Cherokee nation existed because the federal government wanted it to exist. The state of Georgia had nothing to do with the matter.

Jackson Defies the Court. Jackson and Congress simply paid no attention to the Court's decision. No federal troops were sent to protect the Cherokees from the equally defiant state authorities. The land seizures continued until finally, in 1838, the Cherokees were forcibly evicted. Georgia militiamen rounded up some 17,000 Indians and packed them off to Oklahoma.

The 800-mile journey was made partly by steamboat and railroad and partly on foot. Along the way, government officials stole the Cherokees' money, while outlaws made off with their livestock. The Cherokees buried more than a quarter of their people along the "Trail of Tears." Some died from starvation; others were suffocated in the hot and overcrowded railroad cars. And as usual, when the Indians reached their final destination, they ended up on land far inferior to that which they had been forced to leave.

The National Convention System

In 1828 Jackson had been nominated in the traditional manner: that is, by a "caucus," or meeting, of the Democratic congressmen in Washington. Previous presidential and vice presidential candidates had likewise been nominated either by caucus or by state legislatures. The people were not consulted about which candidates they wanted.

But in 1831 a little party called the Anti-Masonic party appeared. Before it went into oblivion in 1832, it made a major contribution to the American political system. The Anti-Masons decided to hold a national convention to choose their candidates. The people would elect delegates to the convention and tell them whom to nominate. This was obviously such a more democratic method that it was immediately adopted by other parties. The system has been followed ever since.

Section 2 Review

COMPREHENSION   Developing Vocabulary

1. Explain these terms: spoils system, caucus, pork-barrel legislation, kitchen cabinet.

COMPREHENSION   Mastering Facts

1. What arguments did Jackson make in favor of the spoils system?
2. What was Jackson's solution to the "Indian problem"?
3. Who traveled the "Trail of Tears," and why?
4. What contribution to national politics did the short-lived Anti-Masonic party make?

3 DEBATING STATES' RIGHTS AND A NATIONAL BANK

VOCABULARY   *nullification   hard money*

The two most important problems Jackson had to struggle with during his presidency concerned states' rights and the Bank of the United States. Jackson did not try to avoid or postpone the difficult decisions that each demanded. He met the two issues straight on.

States' Rights Versus National Rights

The issue of how much power the federal government should have and how much power state governments should have is one that has confronted the United States since the Constitution was adopted. In the 1830s the issue grew so hot that it almost led to civil war. It began on the question of land, shifted to the question of tariffs, and ended up on the question of whether or not a state has the right to secede from the Union.

The issue arose in Congress over a proposal by Senator Thomas Hart Benton of Missouri. Benton wanted unsold federal lands to be reduced in price and finally to be given away if they remained unsold. Northerners saw this proposal as a scheme to draw off workers from the older sections of the country and thus increase the power of western states in Congress. Southern spokesmen, however, agreed to support Benton in hopes of winning western support for something the South wanted—a reduction in the 1828 tariff, which they felt not only discriminated against them but, some said, was unconstitutional.

Tariff of Abomination. As you recall, when the War of 1812 ended, British manufacturers wanted to destroy their U.S. competitors by flooding the U.S. market with cheap goods. For that reason, in 1816 Congress passed a tariff to protect the infant U.S. industries. The tariff was raised in 1824 and again in 1828.

Jackson's vice-president, John Calhoun of South Carolina, called it a "Yankee Tariff of Abomination." As an agricultural region dependent on a single crop, which was cotton, the South had to compete in an unprotected world market. Because of the high tariff on manufactured goods, England, for example, could not sell its goods in the United States. It had less money and therefore bought less cotton from the South. The South, on the other hand, could not buy the cheap manufactured goods it needed from England but had to buy the more expensive northern manufactured goods. The North was getting rich at the expense of the South. One observer remarked that when southerners "see the flourishing villages of New England they cry, 'We pay for all this.'"

Calhoun's Nullification Theory. John Calhoun was in a peculiar and dangerous position. He had long been known as a nationalist spokesman and had supported the protective tariff of 1816. He was on his way to a career as a national statesman and had served under both Adams and Jackson as vice-president. But the situation in his home state had made him change his views. South Carolina's economy failed to recover fully from the depression of 1819. Cotton prices remained low because planters and their slaves were moving to more fertile lands in Alabama and the lower Mississippi River valley. Some South Carolina politicians began to wonder if Calhoun really cared about the needs of his state. Calhoun soon showed them that he did.

Calhoun devised a theory of nullification much like that expressed in Jefferson's Kentucky Resolution against the Alien and Sedition Acts, which you read about in chapter 9. Nullification, you may recall, means to declare something not legal or not in force. Calhoun's argument was that the U.S. Constitution was based on a compact between the sovereign states. If the Constitution was established by thirteen sovereign states, he said, then they must still be sovereign, and each had the right to determine whether or not an act of Congress was constitutional. If it was not, then each state had the right to declare the offending law nullified within its borders. If the states did not have this right, Calhoun reasoned, a majority in the federal government might trample on the rights of a minority. Calhoun published his theory

The brilliant John C. Calhoun came to oppose Jackson over the doctrine of nullification.

in a pamphlet in 1826, but he did not sign his name to it. Nor did he come out and say what he privately felt: that if the federal government refused to permit a state to nullify a federal law, the state had the right to secede from the Union.

Robert Hayne Versus Daniel Webster.

The tariff question (and the underlying states' rights issue) was discussed in one of the great debates in American history. For more than a week in January 1830, visitors to the Senate listened to Senator Robert Y. Hayne of South Carolina debate Senator Daniel Webster of Massachusetts.

Hayne gave a lengthy condemnation of the tariff, listing southern grievances. He charged that southern planters were slaves of northern industrialists. Vice President Calhoun, who presided over the Senate's deliberations, listened with satisfaction as Hayne borrowed liberally from the pamphlet Calhoun had written. "The tariff is unconstitutional and must be repealed," Calhoun had written. "The rights of the South have been destroyed, and must be restored. . . . The Union is in danger and must be saved." Hayne also called for strict construction of the powers of the federal government. "The very life of our system is the independence of the States."

Hayne was answered by Senator Daniel Webster of Massachusetts. Webster was already the most famous orator of the age, at a time when people seemed to have an unlimited appetite for long and flowery speeches. In his reply to Hayne, Webster spoke for four hours without notes. His eloquent defense of the Union so impressed contemporaries that an entire generation of northern school children was set to memorizing passages from his speech.

The Union, Webster argued, was more than a mere compact among sovereign states. The national government was supreme in the powers given to it by the Constitution. Any disputes between the states and the federal government should be settled by the courts and the electoral process, not by the states refusing to obey the law. Webster made a direct attack on the theories of states' rights and nullification. "I go for the Constitution as it is, and for the Union, as it is. It is, Sir, the people's Constitution, the people's government, made for the people, made by the people, and answerable to the people." Webster concluded with the ringing phrase, "Liberty and Union, now and forever, one and inseparable!"

Jackson Versus Calhoun.

Once the Hayne-Webster debate was over, everyone looked to the president for a statement of his position. Jackson kept the public waiting for several months. Finally, at a public dinner in a Washington hotel, he confronted his vice-president, Calhoun. As was customary, the dinner included dozens of short speeches or toasts. After listening to a number of them about the right of the states to decide constitutional questions, the president rose and raised his glass. "Our Union: it must be preserved." Calhoun responded with a toast of his own: "The Union, next to our liberty, most dear." After the dinner the president changed his wording for the newspapers. So the public read that Jackson had said, "Our Federal Union: it must and shall be preserved." The president's attitude was now clear.

In the months following the famous dinner toasts in Washington, Jackson and Calhoun came to a complete break. The grounds for the split were personal as well as political. A social scandal involving the reputation of a cabinet member's wife found Jackson on one side of the controversy and Calhoun on the other. Then Calhoun's enemies let Jackson know that Calhoun had once denounced Jackson's military actions in Florida as being high-handed. The vice-president tried to explain his remark, but Jackson never forgave him. Finally, to top matters off, Calhoun cast the deciding vote in the Senate's rejection of Martin Van Buren as ambassador to Britain. Jackson promptly told Democratic party leaders to drop Calhoun from the 1832 national ticket and substitute Van Buren as Jackson's running mate.

South Carolina Threatens to Secede.

In 1832 Congress passed a new tariff law that actually lowered duties somewhat. But this did not satisfy most South Carolinians. Encouraged by Calhoun, states' rights supporters called a special state convention to nullify the hated act. It pronounced the tariffs of 1828 and 1832 "unauthorized by the Constitution" and, accordingly, "null, void, and no law."

The convention called for an end to customs collections and warned that if any federal forces were sent to collect the duties, South Carolina would immediately secede from the Union.

Jackson was furious. He took South Carolina's action as a challenge to him personally, as well as to the nation as a whole. He threatened to hang Calhoun and lead federal troops in the field if necessary. He did more than bluster, for he knew he had a strong hand to play. He had just been overwhelmingly reelected. No other southern state was willing to back nullification. So he issued a proclamation declaring that South Carolina's actions threatened "the existence of the Union" and violated "the letter of the Constitution." He warned that the laws of the United States required him to meet treason with force. "By the eternal," he said, he would "uphold the law even against the state of his birth."

Henry Clay's Compromise. In an atmosphere of mounting crisis, Congress passed the Force Bill in February 1833. Known in South Carolina as the "Bloody Bill," it authorized the use of the federal army and navy against South Carolina if state authorities resisted federal customs officials.

At this point Henry Clay, at Jackson's urging, once again stepped in as a compromiser. He introduced a new tariff bill that gradually lowered duties over a ten-year period. Thereupon, the South Carolina convention met once again and repealed its previous ordinance of nullification. To save face, however, the delegates passed another ordinance nullifying the Force Bill. But Jackson was wise enough to disregard this last defiant challenge.

Both sides claimed victory. Jackson boasted that, "I met nullification at its threshold." Cal-

This cartoon of the period has Jackson causing the downfall of the "party engine and corrupt monopoly."

houn, who was now a senator, asserted that the fight for states' rights had just begun. But most Americans were aware that the national government had successfully weathered a major crisis.

The "War" Against the "Monster Bank"

The second great crisis of Jackson's administration concerned the Bank of the United States. In this case, too, Jackson's actions strengthened the presidency and brought the nation safely through a difficult time.

Reasons for Opposition. In Jackson's eyes, the Bank symbolized eastern wealth and power. He regarded it as an agent of the aristocracy which cared nothing for the welfare of ordinary people. Because of its financial strength and influence on the economy, it was a threat to American democracy. It might bribe officials and even try to buy elections and control the government and change its character.

State banks hated the National Bank because it was a powerful competitor. Farmers hated the Bank because they distrusted paper money. The only real money, they said, was "hard money"– gold and silver. They also felt that they were the ones who created real wealth in the form of cotton, corn, tobacco, hogs, and other agricultural products. Bankers, in their opinion, did not create real wealth but made money by playing with pieces of paper called loans and mortgages—and often at the expense of people's happiness. For when loans were not paid, the Bank took away people's farms and homes. In addition, the National Bank had a monopoly on government business; the federal government turned all its funds over to the Bank for investment purposes. But the money these public funds earned did not go to the taxpayers. It went mostly to the wealthy stockholders of the Bank.

Adding to popular dislike of the Bank was its leader, Nicholas Biddle. A Philadelphia aristocrat, he was bright, articulate, and capable. He was also extremely arrogant and thought nothing of using Bank funds for loans to friendly congressmen at rates well below those the Bank usually charged.

In 1831 Senator Benton introduced a resolution against rechartering the Bank, even though recharter was not due for another five years. For several hours, Benton assailed the Bank for adding to the "inequality of fortunes." This privileged institution, Benton declared flatly, made "the rich richer and the poor poorer." No remark could have united so many Americans of the Jacksonian Age.

An Election Issue.

As the election of 1832 approached, Jackson's political opponents, Henry Clay and Daniel Webster, wanted to embarrass him. They badly underestimated public dislike of the Second Bank. So they urged Biddle to press for a recharter before the election. They knew that Jackson would be so furious he might veto the charter and thus make the Bank a major campaign issue. They gave Jackson the sort of election issue he wanted. He took it and used it vigorously.

First, Jackson denounced the pro-Bank people for their "grants of monopolies and special privileges." He described the Bank as a monster with horns, hooves, and tail that corrupted "our statesmen" and wanted "to destroy our republican institution." Then he vetoed the charter. As he told the man who would be his next vice-president, "The Bank, Mr. Van Buren, is trying to kill me, but *I will kill it.*"

The Bank became the principal issue of the 1832 election campaign. The National Republicans chose Clay as their candidate because he had a wider popular following than Webster. The National Bank contributed about $100,000 to Clay's campaign. There was little doubt about the final outcome. Jackson, with Van Buren as his running mate, won easily.

The long-range significance of the veto was the reason Jackson gave for his action. Previous presidents had vetoed bills only on the basis that they were unconstitutional. Jackson, however, vetoed the bill because he felt it was harmful to the nation. He asserted that it was both the right and the duty of a president to veto a bill "for any reason—political, social, economic, or constitutional" if, in his opinion, the bill damaged the welfare of the people. In effect, Jackson was telling Congress that before they passed a law, they should consider what the president thought of that law. Or, to put it another way—which is how men like Clay and Webster put it—Congress was no longer the most important of the three branches of government. The president was.

Jackson Beats the Bank.

The "Bank War" continued after the election, with results that were nearly disastrous to the American economy. Jackson was determined to weaken the Bank before its charter expired in 1836. He ordered the withdrawal of all government deposits from the Bank's branches and their placement in certain state institutions. His opponents immediately labeled them Jackson's "pet banks."

Biddle lashed back by calling in private loans. He also decided not to lend money for new business. He argued, quite reasonably, that such steps were necessary since the Bank was being forced to close. But his motives were thoroughly political. He hoped to generate public pressure to force Jackson to reverse his policy.

The financial community nearly panicked for a few months in the winter of 1833–1834. Bankruptcies became widespread as merchants and manufacturers found themselves without credit. Delegations of businessmen descended on Washington to appeal to the president. Jackson firmly told them they were talking to the wrong man. "Go," he said, "to Nicholas Biddle." Thus, Biddle's policy of shrinking credit was hurled back in his face.

Pressure from financial leaders finally forced Biddle into adopting a more generous loan policy. But the entire chain of events had by this time cost him much of his backing even with the eastern business community. In 1836 the Second Bank of the United States quietly expired.

Results of the Bank War

Jackson's war on the Bank was part of a fundamental hostility to special privilege which runs deep throughout U.S. history. It can be seen in Bacon's Rebellion, Shays's Rebellion, and the Boston Tea Party. It continues to the present day.

New York Becomes Financial Capital.

Biddle's bank became just one of many state institutions and finally went bankrupt in 1841. Other state banks and Jackson's pet banks—many of them in New York City—received the money that would have gone into the Bank of the United States. As one historian said:

❝ After the lapse of more than a century, it is clear that although democracy won the battle with the Bank, it lost the war. The bankers of New York City, almost splitting their sides laughing over the discomfiture of rivals . . . [in] Philadelphia, promptly picked up the pieces of the [Bank of the United States] and on Wall Street constructed a vastly bigger money power than anything ever dreamed of

269

by Mr. Biddle. Poor farmers, mechanics, and frontiersmen gained nothing by this bank war; the net result was to move the financial capital of the United States from Philadelphia to New York.**"**

There it has been ever since.

The Whig Party Is Formed. The Bank War, especially the panic of 1833–1834, resulted in the formation of a new political party. Its core consisted of Republicans. But they were joined by Democrats, mostly from the industrial North, who disapproved of Jackson's policy toward the Bank and who believed that his actions in general were those of a monarch rather than a president. "King Andrew the First," they called him. Also joining the new party were believers in states' rights.

In 1834 this new party was named the Whig party. The Whigs in Britain were a group that tried to limit royal power, and the term "Whig" is generally applied to a person who opposes a chief executive having too much political power.

Section 3 Review

COMPREHENSION Developing Vocabulary

1. Explain these terms: nullification, hard money, Whigs, pet banks.

COMPREHENSION Mastering Facts

1. What was Calhoun's theory of nullification?
2. Why was the South against the tariff of 1828?
3. Why did the general public oppose the Bank of the United States?
4. What were two results of the Bank War?

4 JACKSON'S SUCCESSORS FOLLOW HIS LEAD

VOCABULARY   *specie*

The sheer force of Andrew Jackson's personality has tended to make the presidents who followed him, such as Van Buren, Harrison, and Tyler, seem weak, shadowy figures. Yet each was associated with important developments in our nation's history and each followed policies of Old Hickory.

The Depression of 1837

Less than three months after Van Buren took office, the country was hit by a financial panic. Although "Martin Van Ruin" was blamed, a major cause lay in the previous administration.

You recall that after withdrawing federal funds from the National Bank, Jackson deposited them in various state pet banks. Many of these pet banks were located in western states. These banks began to print bank notes, which they lent to persons who wanted to buy federally owned land. As a result, the sale of public land boomed. But the state banks printed notes far in excess of the federal funds they had on deposit. This meant that the notes were not worth much. Thus, the federal government found that while it was selling millions of acres of land, it was receiving almost worthless currency in exchange.

Jackson decided to stop the land speculation. He issued an executive order stating that the Treasury would accept payment for land only in gold and silver, or in paper money that was backed by

gold and silver. This order is known as the Specie Circular, *specie* being another word for gold and silver. The state banks did not have enough specie to redeem the notes, so they closed their doors. This wiped out the savings of thousands of people. With fewer banks and less money available for loans, many businesses failed. Unemployment rose, and there were bread riots in New York City.

The Substitute for Banks. The new president spent much of his administration trying to deal with the vacuum left by the disappearance of the "monster" Bank. Van Buren, like Jackson, was convinced that banks in general were a threat to the livelihood of working people. He pressed continually for what he called an independent Treasury. The government would deposit its temporary surplus funds in vaults in various cities. They would not be tied in any way to state banks or a central federal financial institution. Whig leaders were not happy with the proposed system, but they lacked a better alternative. In 1840, in the darkest year of the depression, Congress finally went along with Van Buren's plan. It seemed to work no worse than the rest of the economy.

World Economic Forces. As the depression deepened, people looked for its cause. But there was no one cause, nor were all the causes to be found in local conditions. What few people real-

Elections and campaigns began to take on a carnival atmosphere in the big cities from early times, as this nineteenth century engraving shows. The scene is Philadelphia 1815.

ized was that the American economy had become intertwined with a world economy. What happened outside the country could affect the people throughout the United States. It was not understood that a drought in cotton-producing Egypt could cause the price of cotton in the United States to rise. The reverse could also occur.

A depression in one country could affect another. During the booming 1830s, for example, British investment in the United States rose from about $60 million to $175 million. British banks made huge loans to U.S. banks. But when hard times hit Britain, British banks asked for the loans to be paid. But the U.S. banks didn't have the money. They had lent it out to their customers who were, in turn, asked to repay their debts. This caused further economic hardship. Cotton planters, for example, had to sell slaves and cotton to repay their local bank. But since they were all trying to repay their debts, the market was flooded with cotton and slaves. Therefore, the price of both plunged.

The Election of 1840

In 1840 Van Buren still had enough clout in his own party to run again. But the Whigs smelled victory in the winds of economic disaster. They ran an old war hero from Ohio, ex-territorial Governor and ex-General William Henry Harrison. The Whig national convention rightly concluded that this pale imitation of Old Hickory would be liked by the voting public.

Campaign Hoopla. Whig politicians had learned from the Jacksonians and turned the campaign into a circus. But they outdid all efforts at transforming their candidate into a man of the common people. Van Buren never made a great deal of money, but the Whigs insisted that he lived a life of astonishing luxury while common folk starved. The president was described as spending his time sampling French cooking from golden plates while reclining on a cushioned sofa.

A tactless editor of a Democratic newspaper played into their hands. He declared that if Harrison were given an annual pension of $2000, the aging hero of Tippecanoe would be content to live in a log cabin with a barrel of hard cider as his sole companion. In fact, Harrison came from a wealthy family. He was college-educated and at the time lived in a sixteen-room mansion. But "log cabin and hard cider" became a campaign slogan. Torchlit parades rolled cider barrels through the streets to demonstrate Harrison's supposedly humble origins. Pictures of Harrison at a plow flooded the nation. Songbooks with such titles as *The Log Cabin Song Book* were published. As one historian put it, "Processions involved miles of marchers; [rallies] attracted acres of people."

A Voting Record. With all this hoopla, Harrison's portion of the popular vote was only 53 percent. But what was truly extraordinary was that 78 percent of those eligible turned out to vote. That figure is a record high in the history of American politics. The entire election, said one observer, was a "totally new phase in party politics."

President Tyler Enrages the Whigs

Clay, Webster, and other Whig politicians expected that they could easily control their successful candidate. But "Old Tippecanoe" Harrison died of pneumonia one month after his inauguration, and for the first time a vice-president succeeded to the presidency.

John Tyler was a strong-minded Virginia aristocrat who had broken with Jackson over nullification and the withdrawal of deposits from the National Bank. Whig leaders had chosen him in hopes of winning southern votes for their ticket. They soon wished they hadn't.

Clay thought the time had come for putting his American System into full effect. As a states' rights man, Tyler thought otherwise. He vetoed bills for internal improvements and reluctantly agreed to a somewhat higher tariff in 1842. He also agreed to repeal Van Buren's independent Treasury. But when the Whigs tried repeatedly to reestablish another national bank, Tyler vetoed one proposal after another. The federal government continued to use state banks. Gradual economic recovery made the issue of a national bank seem less important. As politicians turned to other matters in the 1840s, the banking issue disappeared as a major factor in American politics for more than twenty years.

Tyler's vetoes outraged Whig leaders, but they lacked enough votes in Congress to override them. National domestic legislation came almost to a standstill. Angry Whig congressmen issued a formal statement reading Tyler out of the party. His entire cabinet resigned except for Webster, who stayed on as secretary of state to complete certain diplomatic negotiations.

The victory of 1840 turned out to be a nearly fruitless one for the Whigs. Party leaders began arguing among themselves. They lost their majority in the House in the 1842 congressional elections. Clay resigned his Senate seat to try once again for the presidency.

The Jacksonian Legacy

Just as in the 1790s, when people divided politically between Jeffersonian Republicans and Hamiltonian Federalists, so did people in the 1830s divide into two distinct parties, each with a core of loyal followers. They identified themselves either as Jacksonian Democrats or Whigs. These parties occupied the political stage until the eve of the Civil War.

The style of politics, however, had drastically changed from the 1790s. Politicians appealed more to passions than to reason. They courted popularity in a way that John Quincy Adams and his predecessors never would have done. Political speeches became a form of mass entertainment. But in doing so, politicians involved far more Americans in the political process. The average citizen was more politically aware than ever before, and the average citizen had more political power than ever before. And that is what Andrew Jackson had wanted.

Section 4 Review

COMPREHENSION   Developing Vocabulary
1.   Explain these terms: specie, legacy.

COMPREHENSION   Mastering Facts
1.   What brought on the depression of 1837?
2.   What kind of propaganda did the Whigs put out about Van Buren during the election of 1840?
3.   Why were Whig leaders sorry they had chosen Tyler as Harrison's running mate?
4.   What two parties dominated politics in the United States during the 1830s?

CHAPTER 12 Review

Chapter Summary

The Republican party of Jefferson gradually became the Democratic party of Andrew Jackson. Jackson attributed his election in 1828 to the preferences of the "common people." "Old Hickory" firmly defended the Union while greatly expanding the influence of the federal government. Jackson tried to solve the issue of Indian lands by removing all Indians to lands west of the Mississippi River. Jackson also rejected the Second Bank of the United States. The nation became more democratic during the Age of Jackson.

Questions for Critical Thinking

COMPREHENSION   Summarizing Main Ideas

1. Describe Adams's concept of "general welfare." If you had been in Congress in 1825, would you have supported or opposed it? Give reasons for your position.
2. List three arguments in favor of a two-party political system.
3. In what ways did Jackson expand the power of the presidency? In what ways did he weaken the power of the judiciary?

COMPREHENSION   Interpreting Events

1. Why did the 1824 presidential election go into the House of Representatives?
2. Why did Henry Clay support John Quincy Adams rather than Andrew Jackson in 1824?
3. Which of Jackson's arguments in favor of the spoils system worked out in practice? Which argument did not?
4. How did Jackson's solution to the "Indian problem" differ from that of Washington and Jefferson? Which policy, if either, do you favor? Why?
5. Why did political parties adopt the method of holding a national convention to choose presidential and vice-presidential candidates?
6. How did Henry Clay's compromise tariff of 1833 satisfy northern industrialists? Southern planters? President Jackson?

7. Why did Jackson's opponents refer to him as "King Andrew the First"? Why did supporters call him "a man of the common people"?

APPLICATION   Using Skills To Recognize Similarities

When examining historical data, it is important to group similar items for purposes of analysis. For each group of items below, indicate the item that does not belong.

1. Principles of Jacksonian democracy
   a. A strong president
   b. The spoils system
   c. The right of a state to secede
   d. The abolition of the National Bank
2. The theory of nullification
   a. The U.S. Constitution is based on a compact between the sovereign states.
   b. The Supreme Court determines whether an act of Congress is constitutional.
   c. A state may refuse to obey a federal law within its borders
   d. A state has the right to secede from the Union.
3. Groups forming the basis for the Democratic party of the 1820s
   a. Southern cotton planters
   b. Irish immigrants
   c. Industrial workers
   d. Big businessmen

EVALUATION   Comparing Past to Present

1. In 1824 it was traditional for the secretary of state to succeed to the presidency. Is this true today? If not, what has been the governmental background of the last four presidents?
2. William Henry Harrison was the first president to die in office. Read the part of the Constitution that provides for the succession to the presidency. Read the Twenty-fifth Amendment. What happens if a president is unable to discharge the powers and duties of the office? What safeguards are there against a takeover of the presidency by a vice-president?

Business Cycles

Seasons of the year . . . stages of life . . . waves on the ocean. Almost everything has a pattern, a familiar rhythm. Historians identify patterns when they refer to certain periods such as the Atomic Age, the Federalist Era, or the Roaring Twenties. Labeling these historical periods gives a sense of order to history.

Boom and bust . . . inflation and depression . . . good times and hard times. These phrases describe patterns in business activity. The nation's economy constantly expands and contracts, alternating from periods of prosperity to economic slowdowns. Look at the graph on the opposite page. Over the years this expansion and contraction process seems like a roller coaster. Economists call these patterns in a free enterprise system *business cycles*.

Phases of Each Cycle. Four phases make up every business cycle. First there is a period of prosperity, a peak of productivity. In this phase, production, prices, and profits are high; unemployment is limited; and most people can buy the goods and services they need. The second phase is a period of decline. Here business activity slows down; fewer goods and services are produced; fewer people have jobs; and investment profits begin to go down. The third phase is the low period, also called the

trough. In this phase, everything is low: production, employment, income, and morale. The fourth phase is the upswing, or expansion, in which business gradually improves. This phase leads to a period of prosperity—and so the cycles continue.

Because of free enterprise, business activity always experiences the ups and downs of the economic roller coaster. Before the Industrial Revolution, these ups and downs depended on external forces like weather. Times were good when crops were plentiful, and times were hard when food was scarce. After the American Revolution ended the restraints of British trade policies, a free market economy based on the forces of supply and demand developed in the United States. More Americans began to produce goods for sale instead of for themselves, and to buy goods for their own use.

Encouraged by roads, canals and turnpikes, inventions, and western and foreign markets, the American economy gradually took on the features of capitalism. *Entrepreneurs*, individuals willing to take risks for the hope of profit, began to use their profits to invest in new and even larger enterprises.

All Kinds of Theories. What caused the recurrent cycles which characterized this new system? Some early observances

actually explained business cycles in terms of sunspots. However, even today economists do not agree on the causes of business cycles. Some hold to the theory that business cycles depend on psychology—people's moods of optimism or pessimism. They claim that if most people are optimistic about the future, business will be good; but if most people foresee doom and gloom, then business will be bad.

Another theory holds that business cycles are brought about by changes in the money supply. Economists who support this line of reasoning claim that if government and banks make money available through easy credit, business investments will go up, people will spend, and the economy will grow. If governments and banks tighten the money supply and reduce lending, business in general will tend to go down.

Still another theory deals with levels of saving and consumption. According to this explanation, saving and investing too much money creates more productive capacity than society needs. Then farmers and manufacturers cannot sell what they produce, goods pile up in warehouses, and people lose their jobs and businesses.

Probably no single factor explains business cycles. The Panic of 1837 (see page 270), for

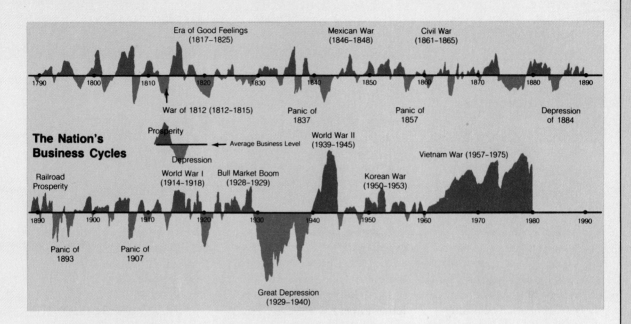

The Nation's Business Cycles

Era of Good Feelings (1817–1825)

Mexican War (1846–1848)

Civil War (1861–1865)

War of 1812 (1812–1815)

Panic of 1837

Panic of 1857

Depression of 1884

Prosperity

Average Business Level

Depression

World War II (1939–1945)

Vietnam War (1957–1975)

Railroad Prosperity

World War I (1914–1918)

Bull Market Boom (1928–1929)

Korean War (1950–1953)

Panic of 1893

Panic of 1907

Great Depression (1929–1940)

example, was brought about by easy credit and overspeculation in western lands, coupled with crop failures, a drop in cotton prices, and President Jackson's new specie requirements. On the other hand, the Panic of 1873 was caused by a shortage of gold, which in turn led to bank failures and slowdowns in railroad building, and gradually affected the entire economy.

The Great Depression.

Business cycles vary in length and intensity. Generally the four phases emerge about eight to ten years from peak to valley and back to peak. Usually the downward slumps (called recessions) bottom out without causing drastic hardships to large numbers of Americans. During the 1930s many Americans did suffer, however. Despite measures aimed at recovery, the Great Depression was long and severe. Unemployment stood at 25 percent. The nation's output of goods and services fell by one-half. Before it was over, 11,000 banks closed. Not until the boom of World War II did full production resume in the 1940s.

The Great Depression was so devastating that the federal government has tried to prevent another. Since World War II, the government has assumed responsibility for managing business cycles. It encourages the economy when business contracts and applies the brakes when business expands. Gradually, in trying to provide citizens with a more stable economic environment, the federal government during the past fifty years has assumed increasing control over production, jobs, and national wealth.

Most citizens now expect this control from their government. After all, roller coasters may be great fun at an amusement park, but most people do not want them in their economic life. They would much rather move along smoothly toward an ever higher standard of living.

Understanding Free Enterprise

1. Describe the four phases of a business cycle. Why do business cycles exist?

2. What reasons explained business downturns in 1837 and 1873?

3. How can government policies influence business cycles?

4. Give three examples that show how business cycles are related to important historical events.

CHAPTER 13

An Era of Reform

1830–1850

People in the Chapter

John Deere—*a blacksmith who invents the steel plow, making prairie plowing much easier.*

Cyrus McCormick—*invents a mowing and reaping machine, making it possible for farmers to do more work with less labor.*

William Lloyd Garrison—*outspoken abolitionist and editor of the* Liberator, *one of the first persons to declare publicly that blacks are also entitled to the rights set forth in the Declaration of Independence.*

Harriet Tubman—*an escaped slave who returns repeatedly to the South and eventually leads some 300 other slaves to freedom in the North.*

Dorothea Dix—*Maine-born reformer who agitates for the improvement of prisons and the establishment of separate hospitals for the mentally ill.*

Linking Past to Present

During the thiry years before the Civil War, American society changed more rapidly than ever before. In 1810 only one out of seven people lived west of the Appalachian Mountains. By 1840 one out of every three people lived there.

In 1810 farming was the chief occupation of Americans and the biggest source of national income. Then came a series of inventions that improved farm life and farm productivity. Other inventions improved manufacturing techniques and production.

Improvements in transportation and communication helped bring rural and city areas closer than they had ever been. By 1850 the value of American manufactured goods passed the value of all American agricultural production, including cotton.

At the same time, there was a rise in religious feeling and an urge to improve society. Many social injustices were attacked and some were eliminated. But two of the nation's gravest social ills—the status of slaves and women—remained uncured.

1 INVENTIONS IMPROVE AMERICAN LIFE

VOCABULARY   *installment plan   telegraph*

During the first half of the 1800s, the standard of living in the United States took a big jump. It had been fairly low during colonial years. But independence, followed by territorial expansion and the stimulus of the War of 1812, brought about changes and improvements for most white Americans. These were further reinforced by several significant inventions in agriculture, manufacturing, transportation, and communication.

New Plows and Harvesters

From the landing at Jamestown to the Revolutionary War, American farmers had continued to use traditional farming tools and methods. They turned the soil with wooden plows. They cut grain with a hand sickle. They threshed grain by having oxen or mules walk over a threshing floor trampling out the seeds.

In 1797 Charles Newbold patented a cast-iron plow. At first, farmers were reluctant to use it because they were afraid that iron "poisoned the land." But they soon found that they were able to turn many more acres of soil than before.

Then settlers moved into the area we now call the Middle West. There they ran into a problem. They no longer had to clear the land of trees before planting their crops. But the prairie soil, although very fertile, was hard-packed and difficult to plow.

A solution was found in 1837 when a blacksmith named John Deere invented the steel plow. It worked where the iron plow did not. Prairie soil does not contain stone and grit. So it sticks to iron—but not to steel. Also, Deere's plow cut fur-rows at an angle instead of straight up and down. Soil offers less resistance to a slanting blade than it does to a vertical blade. Still another advantage of the steel plow was its lightness. It could be drawn by horses rather than oxen, and horses cover much more ground than slow-moving oxen. In 1847 Deere established a factory at Moline, Illinois. By the late 1850s he was selling 13,000 of his plows each year.

Another invention enabled farmers to harvest more wheat than ever before. Cyrus McCormick patented a "mowing and reaping machine" in the early 1830s. The McCormick reaper became a tremendous success because it enabled farmers to do without large numbers of hired hands. The various parts of the reaper were packed and shipped

John Deere demonstrates to neighboring farmers how easily his steel plow cuts, lifts, and turns the soil.

277

In July 1831, a public exhibition is held to show how the McCormick Reaper harvests wheat rapidly and efficiently. The public was very impressed.

directly to the farmer, together with a handbook of directions for assembling and operating the machine.

These two inventions, along with others, raised wheat production in the United States so much that American farmers were soon exporting a surplus to Europe.

New Industrial Tools and Processes

Americans also invented a variety of non-agricultural tools and processes, all of which improved the quality of American life.

Some directly affected daily life. For example, there was a special bit for cutting chunks of ice large enough so they could be brought into cities without melting. Having ice for refrigeration meant that city dwellers, as well as farmers, could enjoy fresh food. There was the tin can, which made food preparation much simpler. There was vulcanized rubber, developed by Charles Goodyear in 1839. It not only protected boots and shoes from rain, snow, and mud but—unlike the previously used India rubber—did not become sticky or melt in hot weather.

In 1846 Elias Howe invented the sewing machine. In 1851, I. M. Singer improved it by invent-

ing the foot treadle. These two inventions made life for the homemaker much easier. She now had to spend daily only half an hour, instead of four hours, making and mending clothes. Even more important, clothing could now be mass-produced in factories. Prices tumbled by more than three-quarters, and even ordinary people could afford something that was "store-bought."

Singer also made two notable contributions to marketing. He came up with the ideas of advertising his sewing machine in newspapers and magazines, and of allowing customers to pay for it on the installment plan. His business boomed, and his ideas were soon adopted by other industires.

Among the new industries that developed during this period was the meat-packing industry. Many meat-packing plants used a kind of assembly-line method. The animal's carcass would slide down an inclined table. As it moved along, each worker would cut away a particular part.

New Forms of Transportation

The expansion of agriculture and industry created a demand for better transportation facilities. Farmers and manufacturers alike wanted faster, more direct ways of shipping their goods to market.

Boats Run by Steam. As early as 1804, Oliver Evans of Philadelphia had designed a high-pressure steam engine that was less bulky and more adaptable to various uses than earlier versions. Evans claimed that he could build a steam-driven wagon that would be able "to run on a level road against the swiftest horses." But he could not find any financial backing and so turned to other projects.

Robert Fulton of New York showed that the new engine could be made to propel a boat. In 1807 his *Clermont* made a 150-mile trip from New York City up the Hudson River to Albany in thirty-two hours. This successful demonstration marked the beginning of the steamboat era. The new method of transportation spread quickly to the Ohio and Mississippi rivers. Transportation on the Mississippi was particularly affected. Until this time, most travel on the river had been southward, with the current.

The steamboats were built of wood. They were propelled by either a stern wheel or side wheels, and were fueled by logs from woodpiles along the riverbanks. They were an exciting sight as they moved along, their three decks riding high above the water and their smokestacks giving off smoke and sparks. They were also dangerous; fires and boiler explosions were common.

By 1830 there were some 200 steamboats on the western rivers. Both freight rates and voyage time dropped dramatically. Steamboats were put to work on some eastern rivers as well. Above all, the steamboat cemented the economic life of the Northwest to the Southwest. New Orleans became one of the nation's major ports.

Canals Speed Up Transportation. Even on the best of roads, transporting bulky products, such as wheat, was slow. Since waterways were more efficient, Americans set about creating them where they did not exist naturally. However, canals cost far more to build than roads. Owing to the expense, most early canal projects were undertaken in the wealthier northern states. (Refer to the map of canals on page 243.)

In 1816 the country had one hundred miles of canals. Twenty-five years later it had more than 30,000. The granddaddy of these projects was the Erie Canal, which stretched a breathtaking 363 miles from Albany to Buffalo. It was the second-longest canal in the world (China's Grand Canal is longer). Building it involved much more than simply digging a big ditch. Towpaths for oxen, horses, and mules had to be laid out along the canal's banks. The banks themselves had to be shored up with cement in many places, to prevent the canal from becoming a muddy ditch. A system of locks was constructed that raised and lowered barges, since Lake Erie was slightly higher than the Hudson River at Albany.

The Erie Canal was an enormous success. Begun in 1816, it was completed in 1825. Within seven years, tolls paid off the cost of construction. And the cost of shipping goods through the canal was only one-tenth of what it was by road.

Dozens of other canal projects were less spectacularly successful, but many of them also paid off eventually. Now the Northwest was no longer tied by the strings of commerce only to New Orleans. Ohio farmers could ship grain by canal and river to New York City, which became the nation's major port. Thus the canals helped bind the two sections of the North together and, indeed, opened the heartland of America to the world markets.

In 1848 the Illinois and Michigan Canal linked Lake Michigan with the Mississippi River system. This canal started the rise of Chicago as a great port, years before that city became an important railroad center.

Railroads Shrink the Country. During the 1830s Americans began to experiment with the new steam engine set on rails. They liked its speed. By 1840 there was more than 3000 miles of railroad track in the United States, most of it in the Northeast. By 1850 there was almost 10,000 miles, and there was some track in almost every state east of the Mississippi. But because most of the lines did not join one another, there was no national network.

Nevertheless, travel by rail gradually began to replace travel by water. It was more expensive but it was much faster. Freight could be hauled at an average of eleven miles per hour. Passengers were whisked along at the astonishing speed of thirty miles per hour. European travelers objected to all the cigar smoke and the American habit of spitting tobacco juice on the floors of the railroad cars. But the speed was thrilling.

New Means of Communication

The expanding American economy called for better means of communication as well as transportation. The two major inventions in this field were the telegraph and the rotary-cylinder printing press.

The telegraph was invented by a New England painter named Samuel F. B. Morse. In 1844, with aid from the federal government, Morse set up a demonstration of his device. From Washington, he tapped out the words "What Hath God Wrought?" in code and sent them over an iron wire. Seconds later, the message was received in Baltimore and a reply was on its way.

Soon, business people everywhere were using the device to transmit orders and up-to-date information on prices and sales. Railroads used the telegraph to keep trains moving regularly and to warn engineers of safety hazards down the line. This is one reason why most telegraph poles were erected along the railroads' right of way, that is, the narrow strip of land on each side of the track which belongs to the railroad.

The telegraph also affected newspapers by creating a demand for daily publication of the latest news. In 1847 Richard M. Hoe met the demand

United States Railways in 1850

Map Skills *In what part of the United States was the only developed railway network in 1850? Could a rail trip have been made from Boston to Baltimore? to Buffalo? to Chicago?*

by inventing a printing press that could turn out 10,000 newspapers an hour.

Effects of Improvements

All these new developments contributed to each other. The growth of manufacturing stimulated agriculture because the industrial cities needed food. In return, American farmers stimulated industry. Farmers made fewer things of their own and, instead, bought more from the cities. Improved transportation and communication tied regions of the country more closely together.

Just as events overseas affected the American economy, so did events in one part of the nation affect the economy elsewhere. For example, a rise in the price of hogs in Mississippi could raise the price of shoes (made of pigskin) in Alabama, and the price of brushes (made of hog bristles) in Vermont.

Section 1 Review

COMPREHENSION   Developing Vocabulary

1. Explain these terms: installment plan, telegraph, McCormick reaper.

COMPREHENSION   Mastering Facts

1. How was John Deere's plow superior to those used previously?

2. What two new marketing techniques did I. M. Singer develop to sell his sewing machines?

3. What other seaport, besides New Orleans, did the new system of canals open up for farmers in the Northwest?

2   REFORMERS WORK FOR SOCIAL CHANGES

VOCABULARY   *anesthetics*

By 1830 several movements to reform society had sprung up in the United States. Individually or through organizations, thousands of Americans set out to fight a variety of social ills. Most of the reformers were middle-class northerners—farmers, housewives, business people, and educators and other professionals. Many of them became interested in reform for religious reasons. They saw social reform as a way of eliminating sin and creating a better, moral world.

Broadening Religious Horizons

In 1831 the Frenchman Alexis de Tocqueville, who was visiting America, noted that there was "no other country in the world where the Christian religion had a greater influence over the souls of men than in America."

The people of the United States had been deeply religious and mainly Protestant since the earliest settlements. There were hundreds of flourishing churches. In upstate New York, religious revivals were numerous. The fires of religious feeling burned so hot in the area that it became known as "the burned-over district." But in the late 1700s and early 1800s that religious feeling began to change, particularly in churches around Boston. There was a reaction against the emotional revivalism of preachers like George Whitefield and Jonathan Edwards. And there was a rejection of the stern Puritan and Calvinist view of the world. Humankind, many thought, was better than the Puritans believed. Increasingly, ministers told people that they could be saved if they only believed in God. One of the ways they could show this belief was by trying to reform society. Groups of people formed churches to serve God by showing concern for human welfare.

Channing and the Unitarians.   The stern Calvinist view of predestination had been questioned by many, but none objected more strongly to it than the *Unitarians*—a group of New England Congregationalists who eventually formed their own denomination. They also shocked other Christians by rejecting the Trinity and asserting that Jesus and God were two separate beings.

The principal spokesman of the Unitarians was William Ellery Channing. His pulpit eloquence and his published writings won prominent Bostonians to Unitarianism, and his interest in social reform and his opposition to slavery extended his influence far beyond Boston. His close friends and protegés included Horace Mann, Dorothea Dix, and Ralph Waldo Emerson.

William Ellery Channing (1780–1842) was born in Newport, R.I., but won fame as a preacher and reformer in Boston.

Expanding Education

President James Madison once stated: "A people who mean to be their own governors must arm themselves with the power which knowledge gives." Most Americans probably agreed with him. But the question of who should pay for educating the people was something else again.

The First Sixty Years. Before the 1850s, there was no uniform educational policy in the United States. Towns in New England maintained free public schools that were open to all, although families who could afford it were expected to pay tuition. Schools in the middle states, such as New York and Pennsylvania, were private. They were run by either church groups or independent citizens. In the South several planters would join together and hire a teacher for their children. In rural areas, parents "subscribed" to a school; that is, they all chipped in, put up a building, and paid a teacher. Part of the pay often included room and board at pupils' homes.

Education was not compulsory, and even those who managed to attend school rarely went beyond the fourth grade. The curriculum consisted of reading, writing, and arithmetic. Schools were not divided into grades. While the younger pupils recited their lessons, the older ones were supposed to study. To make sure they did, teachers had a supply of birch rods with which to thrash anyone who misbehaved.

The most popular textbooks were the *Blue Back Spellers*, written by Noah Webster, who also compiled the famous dictionary in 1828. Webster was a strong believer in "American education for Americans." He tried to get people to talk less like the British and more like people in his native state of Connecticut. As a result of his efforts, the spelling of many words was simplified—for example, "plow" instead of "plough" and "labor" instead of "labour."

Universal Free Education. Beginning in the 1830s, many Americans began to demand public, tax-supported schools for everyone. Pennsylvania led the way in 1834. Although the system was optional, there was a storm of opposition at first. It came mostly from well-to-do taxpayers who saw no reason to support schools which their children, who went to private schools, would not attend. Opposition also came from German immigrants who were afraid that their children would forget the German language and culture. Within three years, however, about 42 percent of children who were of elementary school age in Pennsylvania were attending a free school.

Massachusetts and other states soon followed Pennsylvania's example. By the 1850s every state had provided for a system of free elementary schools. In western and southern states, however, it took years before the schools were actually established. As a result, in 1860 only 15 percent of eligible children were attending school.

One of the leaders in the public school movement was Horace Mann of Massachusetts. In 1837 he became the first secretary of that state's Board of Education. Two years later he helped establish the first American college for training teachers.

Attacking Social Evils

Other areas, besides education, in which social reformers worked included the care of the mentally ill and of alcoholics.

Dorothea Dix and the Mentally Ill. The outstanding figure in the first area was Dorothea Dix, who grew up in Boston and taught for a while at a fashionable girls' school. She then became interested in the way insane people were treated. A quiet, gentle, but very determined person, she inspected the places where insane people were held. She found many of them in jails, where they were

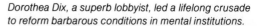

Dorothea Dix, a superb lobbyist, led a lifelong crusade to reform barbarous conditions in mental institutions.

mixed in with criminals. She found others hidden away in closets, attics, or cellars. Almost everywhere she found them "chained, naked, beaten with rods and lashed into obedience." In 1842 she sent a report of her findings to the Massachusetts legislature, which at first ignored her but later passed a law aimed at improving conditions.

Dix then visited other parts of the country. Between 1845 and 1852, she persuaded nine southern states to set up public hospitals for the insane. Also as a result of her lobbying, Congress established St. Elizabeth's Hospital in Washington.

Down with "Demon Rum."

During the colonial period, rum had been a major element in the triangular trade between West Africa, the West Indies, and New England. Other alcoholic drinks that were popular in the colonies included beer, wine, and cider. Americans found that drinking alcohol helped counterbalance the taste of the salted meat and fish that formed a common part of their diet. Until anesthetics (substances that reduce pain) were developed in 1842, doctors would dose patients with whiskey or brandy before operating. Politicians often distributed free drinks to voters before an election.

By the 1800s, however, many people had begun to realize that drunkenness was a serious problem. The American Temperance Society, which tried to restrict the amount of liquor a person consumed, was organized in 1826. Within a few years, there were about 1000 local temperance societies throughout the country. They held rallies and put out pamphlets. They organized children into clubs called "The Cold Water Armies." Lecturers went from town to town, describing the dreadful results of drunkenness through stories, such as the one about "a drunkard who fell into a pig sty. As the hogs grunted in alarm, he muttered, 'Hold your tongues; I'm as good as any of you.' "

The first state to prohibit the sale of liquor altogether was Maine. By 1857 twelve other states had done the same.

Utopian Communities.

A number of individuals decided that the evils of society were too great to be dealt with by piecemeal reforms. Small numbers of men and women established communities of their own where they could live in a utopian, or perfect, society. Sometimes all property was held in common. Sometimes children were raised in common. The two best-known communities were New Harmony, Indiana, and Brook Farm, near Boston. But although they aimed at perfection, most got into financial difficulties and collapsed after a few years of struggle.

Section 2 Review

COMPREHENSION   Developing Vocabulary

1. Explain these terms: anesthetics, lobbying, American Temperance Society.

COMPREHENSION   Mastering Facts

1. Who were the Unitarians, and what was their influence on American life?
2. What was Noah Webster trying to achieve with his *Blue Back Spellers*?
3. Why was there opposition in Pennsylvania to the idea of public tax-supported schools?
4. What were utopian communities?

3 AMERICANS SPEAK OUT ON SLAVERY

VOCABULARY   *underground railroad*

Until about 1830 many men and women, mostly in the North but some in the South, believed that slavery would eventually disappear. But as cotton became king and as the demand for slave labor increased, they grew uneasy. They began to call for an immediate end to slavery.

Early Antislavery Agitation

The first antislavery society in the United States was formed in Philadelphia in 1775. By the 1820s there were about 120 societies throughout the country. Their members were moderates. They favored gradual emancipation and payment to slaveholders for the loss of property. Most of them were also opposed to accepting free blacks as equals. They believed the solution lay in shipping all blacks back to Africa.

There were free blacks who also thought that their best hope was to go back to Africa. One such person was Paul Cuffe, a wealthy Massachusetts shipbuilder. He made a trip to Sierra Leone on Africa's west coast to investigate the possibilities of founding a black colony there. He was prevented

283

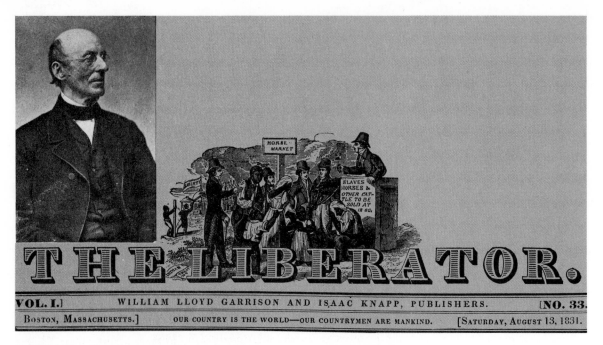

In 1831, William Lloyd Garrison published and edited The Liberator, a weekly newspaper dedicated to the principles of abolishing slavery and raising the status of blacks in America.

from carrying out his plans because of the War of 1812. But in 1815 he chartered a ship at his own expense and carried thirty-eight blacks to Africa. He quickly discovered, however, that the expenses involved in founding a colony were more than one person could bear. But his efforts inspired others. Two years later, the American Colonization Society was organized. Among its supporters were such leading figures as Senators Henry Clay and Daniel Webster, Supreme Court Justice John Marshall, and President James Monroe. With help from the federal government, the society obtained some land in West Africa, which it named Liberia, meaning "place of freedom." Its capital was named Monrovia, after the president.

The American Colonization Society was popular and well financed. Nevertheless, by 1830, only about 200 slaves had been freed and sent to Liberia. Some 12,000 free blacks, however, did eventually settle in Liberia.

William Lloyd Garrison and The Liberator

On the Fourth of July, 1829, a young man with wire-rimmed glasses stepped up to the pulpit of the Park Street Church in Boston to deliver an address. His name was William Lloyd Garrison, and his message was both new and revolutionary.

Garrison asserted that blacks were not Africans but Americans, and that they were not subjects but citizens. "This is their country by birth, not by adoption." Accordingly, blacks were entitled to the same rights set forth in the Declaration of Independence as other Americans were, and until blacks obtained those rights, "the American Revolution was not yet over." Garrison did not advocate using force to get rid of slavery. He was, in fact, a pacifist. He believed the answer lay in constitutional changes brought about by public opinion. Since the population of the free states was nearly double that of the slave states, it remained only to convince northerners that slavery was a sin and must be removed at once.

So Garrison set about to change public opinion. On New Year's Day, 1831, the first issue of his weekly newspaper, The Liberator, appeared in Boston. Garrison was both publisher and editor. Of its first 2300 subscribers, some 1725 were free blacks. Blacks were also Garrison's main financial backers and salespeople.

In the first issue of The Liberator, Garrison called for the immediate and unconditional abolition of slavery.

“I am aware, that many object to the severity of my language; but is there not cause for severity? . . . On this subject, I do not wish to think or speak or write, with moderation. No! No! Tell a man whose house is on fire, to give a moderate alarm . . . tell the mother to gradually extricate [remove] her babe from the fire into which it has fallen—but urge me not to use moderation in a cause like the present. I am in earnest. . . . I will not retreat a single inch—AND I WILL BE HEARD.”

And heard he was, for thirty-five years, until the last slave was free.

Nat Turner's Revolt

The same year *The Liberator* began publication, the bloodiest slave rebellion in American history broke out in Virginia's Southampton County. Southerners promptly blamed it on Garrison's writings, and a price was put on his head.

Actually, Nat Turner's revolt was born in the mind of a black slave. Nat Turner was taught to read and write by his parents. When he was about twenty-five years old, he fled from his master's plantation after a severe flogging and spent a month in the Virginia woods. However, instead of following his father's example and fleeing north, he decided to return to slavery. Apparently, while in the woods, he experienced a vision in which God told him that his task on earth was to "lead and organize his fellow slaves in a struggle for freedom."

For six years Nat Turner preached to the slaves with whom he worked in the fields. Then, on February 12, 1831, there was a partial eclipse of the sun. Turner took this as a sign that the time was ripe. Six months later, he led some fifty or sixty slaves against a number of plantation houses. The first four attacks resulted in the death of fifty-five whites. By the time the fifth house was attacked, however, the alarm had been given. The whites were armed and ready, and the members of Turner's band were either captured or killed.

Turner himself hid out for several weeks. But he was finally taken, tried, and hanged. Southern states then forbade the circulation of antislavery printed material within their borders.

Frederick Douglass

In 1833 Garrison helped found the American Antislavery Society. By 1840 the organization boasted some 600 local groups and 200,000 members. Among its most effective lecturers were former slaves who had escaped to freedom. Probably the most outstanding of these was Frederick Douglass.

Douglass was born a slave in 1817. He was taught to read and write by the wife of one of his owners. Later he continued to study on his own, buying books with the money he earned when not working for his owners. In 1838, while employed in a Baltimore shipyard, he decided to make a break for freedom. He borrowed the identity of a friend, a free black merchant seaman. Dressed as a sailor and carrying an official "protection" paper indicating that he was not a slave, Douglass took a train to Philadelphia and stepped out a free man. As he later wrote in his autobiography, "A new world had opened upon me. . . . I lived more in one day than in a year of my slave life."

In 1841 Garrison invited Douglass to become a lecturer for the Antislavery Society. Douglass was a superb speaker who thrilled his audiences with the power of his words. But he hoped that abolition would come about without violence. In fact, he believed that abolition was the only way to *prevent* violence. "Let us not forget that justice to the Negro is safety to the nation." Douglass also started a newspaper called *The North Star*. It was named after the steady star that runaway slaves kept before them so they would not lose direction as they fled northward to freedom.

Harriet Tubman and the Underground Railroad

Another ex-slave helped her people in a different way. Harriet Tubman had also escaped from slavery in Maryland. But time and time again, she returned to that state to assist some 300 other slaves in their flight to freedom.

Tubman thus became a leading "conductor" on the so-called "underground railroad." This was a network of persons—men and women, white and black—who helped fugitive slaves on their way north. They provided such things as hiding places, food, dry clothing, money, and guides. Although they risked being fined and imprisoned for breaking the law, they felt that their obligation to "the law of God" was more important.

Historians do not know for certain how many "running abolitionists" escaped from slavery before the Civil War. Thousands did, but not enough to undermine the institution of slavery.

Abolitionist Harriet Tubman is pictured (far left) with some of the slaves she helped to free. Sometimes called "the Moses of her people," she returned to the South many times to lead her people to freedom.

Opposition to Abolition

There was fierce opposition to abolitionists in the South. The abolitionists were attacking the South's most important social and economic institution. But there was also strong resistance to abolitionists in the North.

Prejudice Against Blacks. Many northerners called abolitionists fanatics who were out to wreck the Union. During the 1830s, mobs attacked abolitionist meetings. They burned Pennsylvania Hall in Philadelphia just prior to an abolitionist meeting there. A mob of citizens in Boston threatened Garrison's life. Elijah P. Lovejoy, an abolitionist editor in Alton, Illinois, was murdered by a mob when they attacked his printing press and threw it into the Mississippi River.

Why was there such hostility in the North? Apart from the sincere belief that abolitionists were wrecking the Union, there was a more common feeling: prejudice against blacks. Free blacks in the North were subject to all kinds of discrimination. In many states they could not vote or go to school with whites. Many blacks could get only the lowest-paying jobs. Many white northerners simply had no interest in a movement to give rights to black slaves. Even some of the abolitionists did not think that blacks could ever be the social and political equals of white people.

Slavery Is Declared a "Positive Good." Before 1830 many white people in the South thought of slavery as a "necessary evil." They would have liked to do away with it, but they could not do so. Slaves, they argued, were property, and men should not have their property taken away without their consent. Also they feared that freed slaves would become wandering bandits who would endanger the lives of all white people.

But after about 1830, white southerners' views on slavery changed rapidly. This was partly in response to the increased abolitionist agitation, which infuriated southerners. But a more important reason was that after 1830 the South became increasingly dependent on cotton for its economic prosperity. Cotton production required slaves to cultivate it.

The South now could not abolish slavery without suffering what it considered an unbearable economic loss. About this time southerners began declaring that slavery, far from being a "necessary evil," was in fact a "positive good."

Blacks in the South were much better off, said the defenders of slavery, than they were in the North. Virginia's George Fitzhugh wrote several books which claimed that northerners practiced "wage slavery" which was far worse than anything that existed in the South. Northern wage earners, Fitzhugh said, were totally at the mercy of their employers. When sick or old, they were simply thrown out of work. Fitzhugh argued that southern slaves were much better off since their owners took care of them in sickness and in old age.

It was not long thereafter that southerners began to describe their slaves as happy and contented. Indeed, they described the slaves as loving people who were devoted to their masters. So in the face of a great deal of evidence to the contrary, white southerners firmly decided that blacks were happy in their bondage. They thereby created a myth which did not begin to break down until many years later.

Section 3 Review

COMPREHENSION   Developing Vocabulary

1. Explain these terms: underground railroad, Liberia, extricate.

COMPREHENSION   Mastering Facts

1. What was the purpose of the American Colonization Society?

2. What was the effect of Nat Turner's rebellion in the South?

3. How did Frederick Douglass help the cause of abolition?

4. Why did southerners say that northern "wage slaves" were worse off than southern slaves?

4   WOMEN STRUGGLE FOR EQUALITY

To many people, one of the most disturbing things about the abolition movement was the active involvement of women. Female speakers sat on the same platforms with men. Some, like Lucretia Mott and the sisters Sarah and Angelina Grimké of South Carolina, became famous as eloquent spokeswomen for antislavery. Hundreds and then thousands of women began attending abolition meetings. They raised money, distributed literature, and collected signatures on petitions to Congress.

These women met a great deal of opposition. Southern spokesmen denounced the sexually mixed meetings. Many men in the North also thought that women were getting out of hand. A group of New England clergymen announced that when a woman "assumes the place and tone of a man as a public reformer . . . her character becomes unnatural." But that did not stop the women. Many saw the abolitionist cause as one that would help them as well. As Abby Kelley Foster said, "We have good cause to be grateful to the slave. . . . In striving to strike his irons off, we found most surely, that we were manacled [chained] ourselves."

Limitations on Women

Foster was right. Many laws limited the rights of women. They could not vote or sit on juries. When a woman married, her property became her husband's. Any money she earned, she had to turn over to her husband. She was not even entitled to protection against physical abuse. A husband had the legal right to beat his wife with "a reasonable instrument," which a Massachusetts judge defined as a "stick no thicker than my thumb."

Custom as well as law limited women's rights. Probably most Americans regarded women as weak and intellectually inferior to men. At the same time, they believed that women were morally superior to men. Accordingly, a woman's proper place was in the home where she could guard the family's morals and give religious training to the children. Since these beliefs about women were firmly held, it was especially shocking to hear a woman challenge them. Sarah Grimké, for one, did so as early as 1838. Speaking about women, she declared that man "has done all he could to . . . enslave her mind" and now he calls her "his inferior." She continued, "All I ask of our brethren is that

Mary Lyon founded Mount Holyoke Female Seminary, the first institution of higher learning for women in the U.S.

they will take their feet from off our necks and permit us to stand upright."

Early Attempts at Change

Women's first attempts to improve their status were directed to certain areas of immediate concern. These included education, health, and working conditions in the industrial marketplace.

In Education. Until the 1820s, women who wanted a high school education were more or less out of luck. As Sarah Grimké observed, a woman was considered sufficiently "learned" if she knew "chemistry enough to keep the pot boiling, and ge-

ography enough to know the location of the different rooms in her house." But in 1821 Emma Willard opened the nation's first high school for girls in Troy, New York. The curriculum included mathematics, history, geography, languages, art and music, and English writing and literature, as well as "domestic sciences." Despite tremendous ridicule—"They will be educating the cows next," people said mockingly—Willard's school prospered.

In 1837 it became possible for women in the United States to attend college. The first women's college, Mount Holyoke Female Seminary, was founded in South Hadley, Massachusetts, by Mary Lyon. That same year, Oberlin College in Ohio admitted four women, thus becoming the nation's first coeducational college.

The education of black women was even more limited than that of white women. In 1831 Prudence Crandall, a white Quaker, opened a school for girls in Canterbury, Connecticut. One of her pupils, Sarah Harris, was black. The townspeople protested so vigorously against this mixing of the races that in 1833 Crandall decided to have black pupils only. This aroused even more opposition. The following year Crandall was forced to close her school and moved away. In 1851 a white woman named Myrtilla Miner started a school in Washington, D.C., to train black women as teachers. But in general, education for black women had to wait until after the Civil War.

In Health. The state of women's health was as poor as the state of their education. Bathing was uncommon, outdoor exercise rare, and as for clothing! "Fashionable ladies wore tightly laced corsets lined with whalebone stays which tended to force the lungs up into the chest cavity, making breathing difficult and fainting common. They also wore several petticoats and long skirts that dragged on the floor or street."

Elizabeth Smith Miller, who liked to garden, tried to reform women's clothing with a "short dress." This was a dress or skirt that came about four inches below the knee and was worn over loose-fitting pants tied at the ankles. Amelia Bloomer, publisher of a women's rights paper called *The Lily,* wrote an article describing the costume and was promptly swamped with requests for sewing patterns. Gradually the costume became known as "bloomers." But few women had the courage to wear it outside the home.

Elizabeth Blackwell took a different approach to women's health. In 1849 she became the first woman to receive a degree in medicine in the United States. Unable to get practical experience here, she went to Paris. When she returned, she was still not accepted. So she and her sister Emily Blackwell opened their own medical clinic, the New York Infirmary for Women and Children.

In the Marketplace. The 1830s and 1840s also saw increasing numbers of women moving into the industrial labor force. By 1850 about one-fourth of the nation's manufacturing workers were women. Most were employed in textile mills. Others sewed, made straw hats, bound shoes, or worked as compositors in printing shops. In most instances, they received between one-fourth and one-half the wages men did for the same kind of work. Their hours, however, were equally long: usually fourteen hours a day, six days a week.

Some women tried to organize to improve their working conditions. In Philadelphia, for example, women workers from different industries formed a city-wide organization in 1835. The Female Im-provement Society for the City and County of Philadelphia succeeded in gaining some wage increases but then went out of existence. In Massachusetts, women textile workers organized the Lowell Female Labor Reform Association in 1844. Its main goal was a ten-hour day, which it failed to achieve. It did, however, set up sick funds for its members, organize a library, hold classes, and publish a newspaper called *Voice of Industry*.

The Women's Rights Convention

In 1840 a single incident sparked the beginnings of a formal movement for women's rights. Lucretia Mott and Elizabeth Cady Stanton traveled with other abolitionists to the World's Antislavery Convention in London. Once there, the two women were refused proper seating because of their sex, despite the protests of Garrison and some other American men.

Mott and Stanton began thinking about organizing a convention back in the United States, a convention that would be devoted solely to women's rights. Since neither wanted to abandon

At the first women's rights convention in Seneca Falls, New York, a woman calls for the assembly to resolve that women have rights and privileges that belong to them as citizens.

the cause of the slave, however, it took them several years to accomplish their aim. But in 1848 the women's rights convention was held at Seneca Falls, New York. Two hundred sixty women and forty men gathered there and elected Frederick Douglass to chair the meeting.

The convention boldly issued a Declaration of Sentiments, which was carefully modeled on the Declaration of Independence. It began: "We hold these truths to be self-evident: that all men and women are created equal." Then the group passed a series of resolutions that denounced the many unfair legal restrictions on women. All but one passed unanimously. The exception was the resolution demanding that women be given the right to vote.

Why was there opposition? Some people at the convention, even though a minority, were afraid that such a demand would create too much anger and ridicule on the part of the American people.

In any event, the convention marked the start of a national campaign for women's equality. The campaign still continues.

Section 4 Review

COMPREHENSION   Developing Vocabulary

1. Explain these terms: bloomers, manacled.

COMPREHENSION   Mastering Facts

1. What were some limitations on women's legal position?
2. What was the nation's first coeducational college?
3. How did clothing styles of the period affect women's health?
4. What was the one resolution that did not receive unanimous approval at the Seneca Falls Convention in 1848?

CHAPTER 13 Review

Chapter Summary

During the 1830s and 1840s, new inventions improved agriculture and business. The steel plow permitted cultivation of Midwest prairies. The steam engine revolutionized water transportation. Then railroads quickly became the largest industry in the nation. While all this was taking place, reformers tried to improve social conditions. Public education expanded, care for the mentally ill improved, and temperance societies began to appear. Slavery was attacked by a growing abolitionist movement, and the American Antislavery Society was founded by William Lloyd Garrison. The movement was greatly aided by ex-slaves such as Frederick Douglass and Harriet Tubman.

Questions for Critical Thinking

COMPREHENSION   Summarizing Main Ideas

1. List four inventions that helped improve daily life in the United States during the first half of the 1800s.
2. What were the advantages of rail over water transportation? What were the disadvantages?
3. Describe the contributions made to American education by (a) Noah Webster; (b) Horace Mann.
4. What effect did each of these have on the abolition movement? (a) *The Liberator*; (b) Nat Turner's revolt; (c) the speeches of Frederick Douglass; (d) the undergound railroad.
5. In what three areas did women first attempt to improve their status? In which area were they most successful? least successful?
6. Describe the relationship between the abolition movement and the movement for women's rights.

COMPREHENSION   Interpreting Events

1. Why were more canals built in northern rather than southern states?
2. If you had been a state legislator in 1850, would you have voted to prohibit the sale of liquor? Why or why not?

3. How did the early antislavery societies propose to eliminate slavery? What did they think the freed slaves should do?
4. Why did William Lloyd Garrison assert that "the American Revolution was not yet over"?

APPLICATION   Using Skills To Evaluate Sources

In analyzing historical data, it is important to arrange them in their order of significance. For each group of data below, indicate which is the most important and which is the least important.

1. By the 1850s, American farmers were able to expand their exportation of wheat because
   a. the soil in the Middle West was extremely fertile.
   b. the invention of the steel plow enabled them to cultivate prairie soil.
   c. new means of transportation enabled them to send wheat to distant markets.
2. The invention of the steamboat was significant because it
   a. made river travel exciting.
   b. lowered freight rates and travel times dramatically.
   c. cemented the economic life of the Northwest to the Southwest.
3. The idea of universal free education spread slowly because
   a. people could not agree on who should pay for it.
   b. there was no uniform policy throughout the nation.
   c. many immigrants were opposed to it.

EVALUATION   Comparing Past to Present

1. Which of the reform movements discussed in this chapter are still going on?
2. In the 1830s most goods were shipped by water. In the 1850s more and more goods were being shipped by rail. How are most goods shipped today?
3. Many Americans favor a voucher system for education. This means people would pay for vouchers, instead of paying taxes to local school boards, and then use the vouchers as tuition to the school of their choice. How might such a system affect public education?

The Mighty Mississippi

During the age of Jackson there was a renewed surge of settlers moving westward across Illinois and into the growing towns on the shores of the great river that Indian tribes called the "Mitchi-sipi," the "Missi-sippi," or the "Misipi." It was called the Mississippi by French explorers—Louis Joliet and Father Jacques Marquette among others—who came from the Great Lakes overland and worked their way downstream to where the river empties into the Gulf of Mexico.

The Mississippi is one of the most important geographic features of the United States. Not only has it been a highway of communication and commerce in the development of the nation's economy, it has also inspired much of America's folk music and literature. Songs like "Old Man River" and books such as *Tom Sawyer* and *Huckleberry Finn* all describe the influence of the river on the lives of people who live near it.

Geography of the River.
The Mississippi flows out of Lake Itasca in Minnesota. At its source it is small enough to jump across. But at Cairo, Illinois, the river has become nearly a mile wide. Finally it empties into the Gulf of Mexico south of New Orleans. At this point it carries with it the water drained from nearly one and a half million square miles of America—most of the land between the Rocky Mountains and the Appalachians. That is one of the reasons Indians called the Mississippi the "Father of Waters."

Between Minneapolis, Minnesota, and St. Louis, the river flows smooth and clear between rocky bluffs. It is joined at intervals by tributaries. Just above St. Louis it is joined by the Missouri River, which carries so much mud from the Great Plains that it turns the Mississippi's water a chocolate brown. Some two hundred miles downstream near Cairo, Illinois, the Mississippi is joined by another major tributary, the Ohio River. The Ohio's water is blue-green, and for miles below the junction, the Mississippi is a two-toned river: blue-green on the east and brown on the west.

The mouth of the Ohio is usually considered the dividing place between the upper and the lower Mississippi. Now the river, instead of flowing between rocky bluffs, is banked only by low stretches of land that become increasingly swampy as the river flows south. At three spots on the east bank, however, there are bluffs high enough not to be reached by floods. On these bluffs stand the cities of Memphis, in Tennessee, and Vicksburg and Natchez, both in Mississippi. There are also two west-bank bluffs, occupied by New Madrid, Missouri, and Helena, Arkansas.

The lower Mississippi is a meandering river. It is, as one observer said, "always changing, gnawing away one bank, building another, building itself islands and bars, or taking them away." In the past the river always flooded in the spring, often with severe loss of property and lives. Today, however, the danger of floods is lessened by an elaborate system of artificial levees, dams, and spillways.

Although New Orleans is considered the gateway to the Mississippi, the river actually flows an additional 107 miles before reaching the Gulf of Mexico. Much of the land below New Orleans consists of mud that the river has brought down and dumped there. This land is called the river delta because its triangular shape resembles the Greek letter delta. The Mississippi delta covers about 13,000 square miles and grows at a rate of about one mile every sixteen years. As the Mississippi enters the delta it breaks up into several channels, which reach the Gulf at places like South Pass, North Pass, and Main Pass.

Running a Steamboat.
The first steamboat appeared on the Mississippi in 1811. Within a few years—largely as a result of

the efforts of Captain Henry M. Shreve (after whom Shreveport, Louisiana is named)—tonnage on the Mississippi was larger than that on the Great Lakes and the Atlantic Coast combined. The average steamboat lasted about five years. It usually perished because its boilers exploded, or it caught fire, or it was ripped by snags, or it collided with another boat.

In addition to the captain, the most important person on board was the pilot. Actually, there were at least two pilots, one for the day watch, the other for the night watch. A pilot had to be extremely skillful and knowledgeable. As one pilot said, he had to memorize "every snag, bar, rock, caving bank, and bend, and to know what happened to the channel when the river rose five feet or when it dropped ten." He had to memorize it both ways, upstream and downstream. And he had to relearn it over and over, because the river changed so much between trips. Needless to say, pilots were well paid. A typical wage in 1857 was $500 a month, compared to a factory worker's yearly wage of less than $100. Mark Twain's *Life on the Mississippi* is this nation's classic account of piloting on the Great River.

Not all the boats that moved up and down the river carried people, goods, and mail. Some provided services. For example, a boat might contain a tinsmith's shop and float from one river town to another selling

A riverboat churns down the Mississippi River near La Crosse, Wisconsin.

pots and pans. A second boat might be fitted out as a dry goods store. A third might be equipped with a forge for the shoeing of horses and the production of such iron tools as axes and scythes. A boat might carry a barber or a cobbler or—in the case of a showboat—actors, singers, acrobats, and other performers.

River Traffic.   New Orleans today is our nation's second busiest port, exceeded only by New York. That has been the case since 1840, when the "queen of the river towns" saw almost 1000 steamboats and 2700 flatboats unload 3 million passengers and tons of freight from all parts of the Mississippi valley. The items that passed through the port reflected the nation's economy. The main product was cotton. Sugar and slaves were likewise important. Then there was produce: pork, flour, Indian corn, pumpkins, apples, potatoes, dried fruits, and several kinds of liquor. Industrial goods included salt, barrel staves, planks, hemp, rope, and

lead. And of course there were furs.

Today the Mississippi carries 40 percent of the freight transported on all the nation's inland waterways. Most freight on the river is now loaded on large barges and pushed by tugboats. This is one of the cheapest forms of transport.

The southbound traffic contains products such as corn, soybeans, and wheat plus coal and steel products which come down the Ohio River. At Baton Rouge, Louisiana, the Mississippi is deep enough for ocean-going vessels. From here the products of America's heartland are carried to all the world.

Understanding Geography

1. What are the two main tributaries of the Mississippi River?

2. How are deltas formed?

3. Why did steamboat pilots have to "relearn" the river?

4. Name several ways in which the Mississippi River has affected the economic growth of the United States.

CHAPTER 14

Expansion and Conflict

1830–1850

People in the Chapter

Samuel (Sam) Houston—*the leader of the Texas forces that defeat General Santa Anna. He serves twice as president of the independent Republic of Texas.*

James Polk—*the eleventh president. Known as "The Purposeful," he annexes Oregon, New Mexico, and California. Then, having fulfilled his ambitions, he declines to run for a second term.*

Henry Clay—*senator who desperately wants to be president but achieves fame as the "Great Pacificator." Balancing the interests of North and South, he proposes the Compromise of 1850, which averts civil war for a time.*

Linking Past to Present

On January 3, 1846, Congressman Robert C. Winthrop of Massachusetts stood up to make a speech. He was the great-great-grandson of John Winthrop, the leader of the original Massachusetts colony. John Winthrop had migrated 3000 miles across the ocean in 1630. Now, 216 years later, Robert Winthrop spoke in favor of people migrating 3000 miles farther westward to the Oregon Country.

Seven months later a congressman from Pennsylvania rose to offer an amendment to a bill. David Wilmot's amendment, later called the Wilmot Proviso, concerned the war which had broken out between the United States and Mexico. Wilmot's amendment stated that "neither slavery nor involuntary servitude shall ever exist in any part" of the land taken from Mexico.

Winthrop's speech and the Wilmot Proviso reflected the two most important political developments of the period: westward expansion and slavery. The latter divided the country so badly that the nation nearly came apart. But in 1850 a major compromise was worked out which people hoped would settle the issue once and for all.

1 THE SPIRIT OF EXPANSION SWEEPS INTO TEXAS

VOCABULARY *manifest destiny*

For some twenty-five years after the War of 1812, Americans did not seem much interested in adding to their already vast territory. They were busy exploring, settling, and developing what they had. In the 1840s, however, a feverish interest in expansion swept the country. As one person said, expansion was a way of "extending the area of freedom." The expansion fever was fed from time to time by the phrase *manifest destiny*.

Manifest Destiny

The word "destiny" implied that further expansion of the United States was inevitable. Nothing could stop it. The word "manifest" meant that this destiny was obvious. It was clearly inevitable that the United States would expand to the Pacific Ocean and into part or all of Mexico. And this expansion was not only inevitable, it was right and proper.

The origin of the term "manifest destiny" was not widely known at the time. It has been attributed to John L. O'Sullivan, a New York magazine editor, but the phrase was probably first used in Congress by Robert C. Winthrop in the speech you have just read about. The term rapidly became so common that most Americans knew instantly what it meant. It meant, according to one editor, to spread over "and to possess the whole of the continent" which God "has given us for the development of the great experiment of liberty and . . . self-government." Another editor assumed that this development would be an Anglo-Saxon triumph. The term "Anglo-Saxon" refers to people of English descent. The name comes from the Angles and the Saxons, two peoples from northern Germany and Denmark who invaded and settled in England 1500 years ago. The term has become part of a much more recent one, *WASP*—an abbreviation for white Anglo-Saxon Protestant.

The above editor wrote specifically about California, which was then part of Mexico:

66 The Anglo-Saxon foot is already on its borders. Already the advance guard of the irresistible army of Anglo-Saxon immigration has begun to pour down upon it, armed with the plough and the rifle, and marking its trail with schools and colleges, courts and representative halls, mills and meeting houses. . . . All this [is] in the natural flow of events. 99

Emanuel Leutze's painting Westward the Course of Empire Takes Its Way *idealized American expansion.*

Reasons for the New Mood

Why did so many Americans begin talking this way? Many historians think the following reasons were involved.

1. Since Jamestown, Americans had always hungered for land. Some wanted their own farms. Others were interested in land speculation. And still others, especially from New England and the eastern cotton states, sought new and fertile soil because the older lands had been worn out.

2. Merchants and manufacturers believed that expansion would create new markets for their goods and services.

3. Millions of immigrants—especially from Ireland, which had been severely hurt by potato rot—flooded into the United States. Population grew so rapidly, from 7 million in 1810 to 28 million in 1850, that more living space was needed.

4. Americans wanted to expand trade with China. Taking over Oregon, which was also claimed by England, would give the United States several excellent harbors that could also serve as naval stations for a Pacific fleet.

5. The panic of 1837 led many unemployed persons to decide that it would be easier to cope with hard times "anyplace but here." Moving west enabled them to escape their creditors and to make a fresh start.

6. Americans wanted to spread what they considered were the virtues of their system of government.

Mexico Invites Settlers

The first area to be touched by expansionist fever was Texas, which was then the northernmost province of the Mexican state of Coahuila (ko-ah-wee-lah). In 1821, when Mexico gained its independence from Spain, Texas was only sparsely settled. Three small towns—Goliad, Nacogdoches, and San Antonio—were inhabited by about 4000 Mexicans engaged in cattle ranching. And there were perhaps 8000 Apache Indians who often raided the towns for sheep, cattle, and horses.

The Mexican government wanted to develop Texas. So in 1821 and again in 1823, it offered land grants to people who would bring in settlers. The only conditions attached to the grants were that the settlers would obey Mexican laws and follow the official religion of Roman Catholicism.

In 1821 an American cotton planter named Moses Austin obtained a land grant and made plans to establish a colony of settlers from the United States. After his death, his son Stephen took over and in 1823 led 300 families to a fertile area along the Brazos River. Each family received 177 acres of farmland plus 13,000 acres of pasture at a very low price. They also received a six-year exemption from paying taxes. The colony prospered, and soon thousands of other Americans, most of them southerners, were streaming across the border.

Mexican-American Difficulties

By 1830 the population of Texas included about 20,000 Anglos, or English-speaking whites, and from 1000 to 1500 slaves who worked in the cotton and sugar cane fields. The presence of slaves was now a problem, for in 1829 Mexico had abolished slavery. Since then the Mexican government had made several attempts to enforce the law. It wanted the Texans to free their slaves.

The Mexican government was also becoming fearful of the continuing influx of people who spoke a different language—English—and who practiced a different religion—Protestantism. In addition, more and more Americans were talking about extending the boundaries of the United States to the Rio Grande (known in Mexico as the Rio Bravo). In fact, President John Quincy Adams had previously offered to buy Texas for $1 million, while President Jackson had upped the price to $5 million.

So in 1830 the Mexican government closed the border to immigration from the United States and slapped a heavy tax on the importation of American goods. It also sent Mexican troops north to Texas to see to it that the laws were obeyed. However, there were not enough troops to patrol the border, so Americans kept coming in.

In 1833 Stephen Austin went to the national capital of Mexico City with a petition that Texas be allowed to form a separate state within the Mexican union. His petition was rejected, and on his way home he was arrested for treason and imprisoned for eighteen months. Protest meetings erupted throughout Texas. But the response of the Mexican government was only to send in more troops.

By this time, too, a new kind of settler was coming into Texas. They were ambitious men with forceful personalities. They included people such

Texan War for Independence 1835–1836

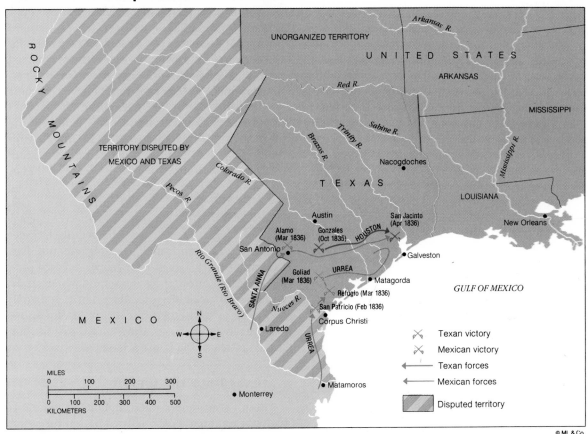

Map Skills *What river did Texas claim as its boundary with Mexico? Who was the Mexican commander at the Alamo? When was the battle of San Jacinto? Who was the American commander?*

as Sam Houston, former congressman from Tennessee and soldier of fortune who had been adopted into the Cherokee tribe when he was fourteen. There were also the Bowie brothers, James and Rezin, who invented the fifteen-inch single-edge knife that bore their name. Also, there was a pioneer named Davy Crockett, who had also served in Congress. These men and others like them saw no reason to live under Mexican law. And in truth, it was difficult to respect a government in Mexico City that kept changing all the time as general succeeded general as head of the country.

Battle of the Alamo

In 1835 President Antonio López de Santa Anna abolished all state governments in Mexico. He then marched north at the head of 6000 troops and besieged a group of Texans who were holed up

Among Americans killed at the Alamo was folk hero Davy Crockett, shown here with rifle upraised.

297

in the Alamo, a chapel-fort in San Antonio. The siege lasted from February 23 until March 6, 1836, and ended only after Mexican troops finally succeeded in scaling the Alamo's walls. All 187 defenders were killed, at a cost of some 1600 Mexican dead. Santa Anna then ordered his men to pour oil on the bodies of the defenders and burn them. The only Americans who survived were Susana Dickinson, wife of one of the defenders, and her infant child, and two black slaves.

Many Texans saw a clear similarity between the oppression suffered by the colonists under Britain during the time of George III and their situation under Santa Anna. They felt their fundamental rights were being threatened.

Texas Declares Independence

On March 2, 1836, the Texans declared their independence. Then they drew up a constitution based on that of the United States.

Even as the Alamo battle raged, the Republic of Texas set up a temporary government. The president was David G. Burnet, and the vice-president was Lorenzo de Zavala, a Mexican-American and foe of Santa Anna. These men guided the republic

Sam Houston, champion of Texan independence, also defended the cause of American Indians.

298

during the chaotic first months until the Mexican forces were driven out and a regular election could be held.

The Alamo victory proved to be a costly one for Santa Anna, for it aroused fighting fury among Texans. Six weeks later, an army led by Sam Houston met the Mexicans in a grove of live oaks by the San Jacinto River. Shouting "Remember the Alamo!" the Texans soundly defeated the Mexican forces and captured Santa Anna. After the battle of San Jacinto, when he signed a treaty pledging to recognize the independence of Texas, he was allowed to go free. But, understandably, the Mexican government refused to recognize the legality of a treaty Santa Anna was forced to sign.

Nevertheless, Texas had declared itself independent, and France and England recognized it. In September 1836 Sam Houston was elected president of the Lone Star Republic, and Mirabeau B. Lamar was named vice-president. The new nation had a flag with a "lone star" on it. It also had a small navy and a larger army, and a constitution based on that of the United States.

Texas Joins the Union

Most Texans hoped their republic would eventually be annexed by the United States, but opinion was divided in the states. Many people, especially in the South and West, wanted to take over this republic which had been won by Americans. Southerners also wanted to extend slavery, and it was already established in Texas. But northerners were opposed to taking over more slave territory. Still others feared that annexation would cause a war with Mexico. For a while, the situation drifted along, during which time the population of Texas increased to 142,000. President Van Buren opposed annexation. President John Tyler, who was a southerner, favored it but was unable to get the necessary two-thirds of the Senate to agree to a treaty.

Meanwhile, Great Britain began to take an interest in Texas. The British opposed slavery, but they welcomed the idea of an independent Texas. They thought it would be a counterweight to U.S. power. They also wanted to buy its cotton and to sell manufactured goods to Texas without paying a U.S. tariff. England even went so far as to get Mexico finally to recognize the independence of Texas.

But by now many Americans were alarmed. Just before he left office, President Tyler succeeded in

Trails to the West in the 1850s

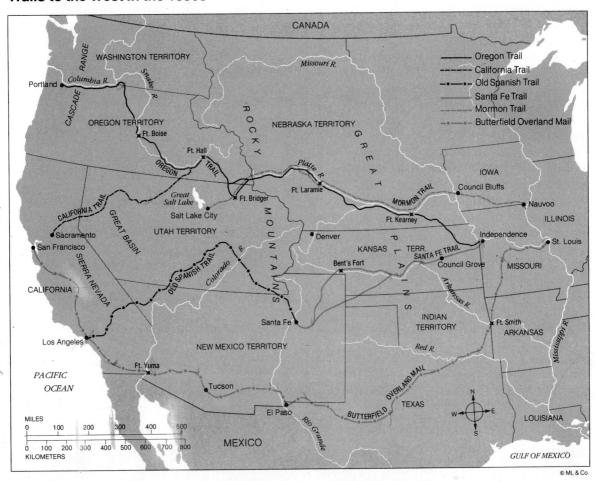

Map Skills *What two trails began at Independence? How long was the trail from Council Bluffs to Sacramento? At a wagon train speed of 15 miles a day, how long would that trip take?*

gaining congressional approval of annexation. On December 29, 1845, Texas became the twenty-eighth state. The Mexican government was furious and immediately recalled its ambassador from Washington.

The Santa Fe Trail

During the noisy dispute over Texas, a quiet but important trade continued between Americans and Mexicans. The trade route was called the Santa Fe Trail, and it led some 800 miles from Independence, Missouri, to Santa Fe, New Mexico. Each spring, between 1821 and 1843, American traders loaded their covered wagons with textiles, cutlery, and firearms, and then set off.

The first leg of the journey, about 150 miles to

Council Grove, was covered by each trader individually. But beyond Council Grove, there existed serious danger of attack from Kiowa, Comanche, and other Indian tribes. So at Council Grove, the traders would organize a caravan of up to a hundred wagons. First they elected a captain, who in turn selected four lieutenants. Each lieutenant was put in charge of twenty-five wagons. The wagons moved across the plains in four parallel columns. A few scouts on horseback rode ahead and to the rear to keep an eye out for Indians.

At night the caravan would draw up in a hollow square, twenty-five wagons to a side. By interlocking their wheels, the wagons formed a corral within which the horses, mules, and oxen slept. This prevented the possibility of a night stampede and also provided a defense against Indian attack.

299

The traders followed this system until Santa Fe came into view. Then it was every man for himself. The traders would whip their teams as they raced toward the town, each trying to be the first to pass through Mexican customs. After several days of selling and relaxation, the wagons would regroup into a caravan and head back to Independence with silver, furs, horses, and mules.

The results of the trade were not only economic. They also added to American expansionist fever. People learned about the Spanish Southwest and the vast stretches of land that seemed to be there for the taking. They learned that Mexican control over the area was weak. And they learned the techniques of covering hundreds of dusty miles in safety. More and more pioneers began to copy the technique as they headed west to Oregon, California, and Utah.

Section 1 Review

COMPREHENSION   Developing Vocabulary

1. Explain these terms: manifest destiny, WASP, Battle of San Jacinto.

COMPREHENSION   Mastering Facts

1. Why did Texans want to separate from Mexico?
2. What happened at the Alamo?
3. Why did the United States hesitate for so long before annexing Texas?
4. What made the United States finally agree to annex Texas?

2   THE NATION EXPANDS WESTWARD TO THE PACIFIC

VOCABULARY   *Conestoga wagons   dark horse candidate   Mormons*

During the 1840s the boundaries of the United States expanded to include even more than Texas. North, west, and south, the nation continued to spread across the continent.

The Webster-Ashburton Treaty

The War of 1812 had not fully resolved differences between the United States and Great Brit-

The grandeur of the American West is captured in The Oregon Trail *by landscape artist Albert Bierstadt, who traveled there himself and made sketches of the country and people.*

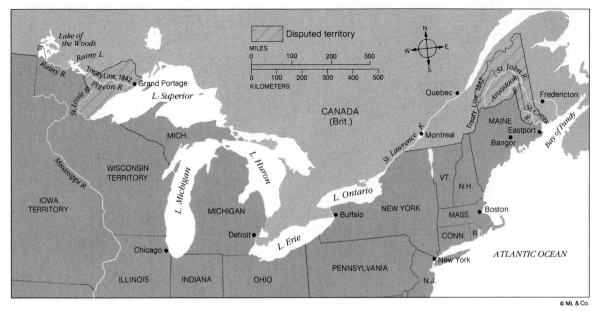

Map Skills   *What two rivers formed the U.S.-Canada border west of Lake Superior? About how close to the St. Lawrence River was the U.S. claim in Maine?*

ain. The biggest difficulty was the American-Canadian boundary.

Part of the land disputed by the two nations was a forested area that included the Aroostook River, now part of Maine. In 1839 Canadian lumberjacks began logging operations there but were soon chased out by Maine militiamen. Although no one was killed, the fight was known locally as the Aroostook War. Other areas where the boundary line was in dispute included the northern part of what is now Minnesota.

Fortunately, neither Great Britain nor the United States wanted to go to war over the matter. So in 1842 two skilled negotiators—Daniel Webster for the Americans and Lord Ashburton for the British—worked out a treaty that split the disputed territories roughly in half.

The treaty, however, did not settle the dispute over the boundary line in the Far West. It simply continued the "joint occupation" of the Oregon Territory that had first been agreed upon in the Treaty of Ghent, ending the War of 1812.

Oregon Fever

Originally, five nations—Britain, France, Russia, Spain, and the United States—had shown an interest in Oregon. In the early 1800s, France and Spain had given up their claims, while Russia had

fixed the southern border of Alaska at 54°40′. That left Britain and the United States to resolve their claims.

Both nations were represented mostly by fur traders who sold guns, tools, and liquor to the Nez Percé, Walla Walla, Yakima, and other Indian tribes in the area. In the 1830s some Methodist ministers made their way there and set up a number of mission schools. Their letters east spoke glowingly of the fertile soil and abundant rainfall, and soon hundreds of Americans were off on the Oregon Trail. The route led from Independence, Missouri, to Portland, Oregon, and was similar to the one followed by Lewis and Clark.

Some of the Oregon pioneers bought wagons, usually the famous Conestoga wagons that were covered with sailcloth and pulled by oxen. More of them walked, pushing handcarts loaded with a few precious possessions. They packed food to last the journey, such as dried pork, beans, and corn. They packed one or two iron pots for cooking. And they took leather bags for water to keep themselves and their animals going over the dry stretches between rivers.

The trip between Independence and Portland now takes three days of superhighway driving. In the 1840s it took several months—if all went well. Sickness was a common problem. Babies threw up

301

The Oregon Settlement 1846

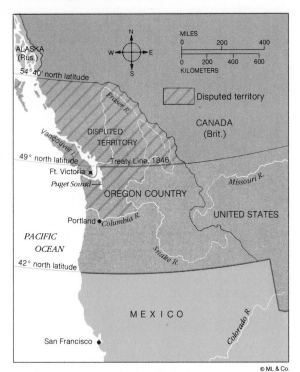

Map Skills *What river was the southern limit of the disputed area? At what latitude was the border set?*

from the heat or the altitude. Wagon axles broke, and coyotes howled at night. And of course there was always the danger of Indian attack. The caravans provided protection and also companionship. They helped combat the loneliness of traveling mile after mile without seeming to get anywhere.

What lay at the far end of the 2000-mile journey? The situation can be summarized by two entries in the diary of James Nesmith:

66 Friday, October 27—Arrived at Oregon City at the falls of the Willamette [River].
Saturday, October 28—Went to work. 99

By 1844 about 5000 Americans were farming in the green and fertile Willamette River valley. And demands for "the reoccupation of Oregon" became a major issue in the presidential campaign.

The Unusual Election of 1844

The election of 1844 was unusual in several ways. The Democrats nominated the first "dark horse" candidate, that is, a candidate who is not well known but receives unexpected support. The campaign revolved around a single issue: westward expansion. Finally, the results of the election were changed by the existence of a tiny third political party.

Who Is James K. Polk? The Whig party convention easily nominated their most popular man, "Glorious" Henry Clay of Kentucky. It looked as if the Democrats would nominate ex-President Van Buren. But Van Buren had opposed the annexation of Texas. Finally, after many ballots, the Democratic convention named James K. Polk of Tennessee. In turn, the Whigs adopted a campaign slogan asking, "Who is James K. Polk?"

How Much Do We Want? Polk deliberately made annexation of Texas an issue. He was for it, make no mistake about that. Clay, on the other hand, couldn't seem to make up his mind—at least in public. He announced that he was against it; that he was for it; and that maybe, possibly, and probably he was for it. By the time of the election, no one knew exactly where he stood. Polk went further. He wanted not only Texas. He declared that the United States should take the entire Oregon country. Uncle Sam (the United States) should tell John Bull (Great Britain) to get out and stay out. "The only way to treat John Bull," Polk told one congressman, "is to look him straight in the eye."

What Is the Liberty Party? Although the main issue was territorial expansion, the election was actually decided by a completely different matter. Polk won in the electoral college, 170 to Clay's 105. But the popular vote was extremely close. Clay lost because he failed to carry New York State by about 500 votes out of 500,000 cast. And he failed because a tiny abolitionist group called the Liberty party polled nearly 16,000 votes, most of which would otherwise have gone to Clay.

Settling the Oregon Border

As you know, just before Polk took office, outgoing President Tyler signed the resolution admitting Texas to the Union. But Polk was determined not to be outdone as far as enlarging the territory of the United States was concerned. In his Inaugural Address, he stated: "Our title to the whole of the Territory of Oregon is clear and unquestionable, and already are our people preparing to perfect that title by occupying it with their wives and children." His words were strongly approved by most Americans. Newspapers everywhere came forth with such war-like slogans as "All or None, Now or Never" and "Fifty-four Forty or Fight." You remember that 54°40′ was the northern limit of the Oregon Territory.

Nevertheless, the issue was settled peacefully. Since men had stopped wearing beaver hats, British fur traders were no longer particularly interested in territory along the Columbia River. Polk was advised that the land north of the 49th parallel was really not well suited to agriculture. So in 1846 the two nations agreed to extend the boundary along that parallel westward from the Rocky Mountains to Puget Sound. The only exception was the southern tip of Vancouver Island, which was ceded to Britain. The boundary Polk agreed to remains today.

Moving in on California

When the Spaniards first arrived in California, it was inhabited by some 200,000 Indians. They were hunters and food gatherers who lived in small communities of 100 to 500 persons. Each community was self-sufficient, and there was little trade or travel between them. In all, there were 135 different tribes, almost all of whom spoke a different language.

In 1765 British and Russian fur traders began casting their eyes on California. To counteract them, the Spaniards sent in soldiers and missionaries from central Mexico. They established a series of twenty-one missions along the coast from San Diego to San Francisco. These consisted of a central church, outlying buildings, and a fort. The missionaries converted the Indians to the Catholic faith. They also taught the Indians how to farm; how to herd horses and cattle; and how to perform such skills as blacksmithing, shoemaking, and pottery-making. Unfortunately, many of the Indians died of diseases that the newcomers brought in.

In 1834 the missions were taken over by the Mexican government. Within a few years, about 7000 Mexican settlers had moved into the area. They set up cattle ranches and used the Indians as workers. The ranches produced hides and tallow, which the Mexicans sold to American trading vessels to be taken to Boston and other eastern manufacturing cities of the United States.

Life in California was delightful, at least for the Mexicans. The weather was warm and sunny. There was plenty of beef, beans, and tortillas to eat. People learned to ride at the age of four, and women as well as men wore brightly colored jackets and silver spurs on their boots. Dancing was a passion. Weddings and parties often lasted for three days and, as an American visitor put it, "a Californian would have paused in a dance for an earthquake, and would be pretty sure to renew it, even before the vibrations had ceased."

By the mid-1840s there were also about 700 Americans in California. Most were sailors who had deserted from whaling vessels. The rest were merchants and traders who did business in such towns as Los Angeles, Monterey, and Santa Barbara.

Annexing California was not an issue in the 1844 presidential campaign. Nevertheless, some Americans began to think about its future possibilities, especially because it had two of the best harbors on the Pacific coast: San Diego and San Francisco. To Americans, California looked empty. It also seemed to be badly governed. The Mexican government did not think so, and in any event did not think it was any business of the United States. When President Polk offered to buy California, the Mexican government indignantly refused. Would Polk sell one of the United States, they wondered? Meanwhile, some settlers were moving into an area that no one else seemed interested in.

The Mormons Settle Utah

Most Americans in the Far West hoped that their new settlements would come under the American flag. This was true in Texas, in the Oregon country, and in California. Yet one migration to the Far West was undertaken by Americans who hoped to get away from the United States. These people were members of a religious group called the Church of Jesus Christ of Latter-day Saints. They are commonly known as Mormons.

Joseph Smith Founds a New Church. Mormon history dates back to 1823 in upstate New York, where eighteen-year-old Joseph Smith announced that he had received a special message from God. He said he had found a book "written upon golden plates" buried in a hillside. This Book of Mormon was written in an ancient language, Smith claimed, but he could translate what it said. His words attracted many followers. They

On inhospitable land the Mormons constructed a city (Salt Lake City) and a tabernacle (above).

So the Mormons began to walk north to Nebraska, across the Rockies to Wyoming, and then south. In 1847 they found themselves in a lonely land.

They were in a desert by a salt lake in the northern part of Mexico. The enormous lake lay like a giant drop of water at the bottom of a teacup. It was ringed by high mountains. The salty lake was useless for plants or animals. Dry and dusty winds swirled down the sides of the mountains and scorched the Mormons. Young realized they might be safe there. Who else would want such an unpleasant land? "This is the place," he said. And there the Mormons began to build Salt Lake City.

The Mormons dug irrigation ditches from streams in the mountains. They decided to give land to each settler according to his particular skill. Water and timberland were to be held by the people in common, not by individuals. After much hardship, the Mormons made the desert fruitful. They prospered in a land they called Deseret.

The Mormons developed settlements and farms out of land that seemed extremely unpromising. Despite all their troubles, they eventually gained the admiration of most Americans by their hard work, their steady faith, and the good character of their lives. The area they settled eventually became the state of Utah. But this was long after the fate of the Far West had been decided.

came to think of themselves as an entirely separate and different people. Smith and his associates formed the Mormon church in 1830. Then they established their church headquarters in Kirtland, Ohio.

However, some Mormon views and beliefs alarmed and angered many other Americans. Insults and violence followed. Smith and his growing band of believers decided to move west, eventually stopping at Nauvoo, Illinois, in 1839. There they stayed for five years and grew to some 15,000.

Serious conflict developed when Smith proclaimed that male members of the church could have more than one wife. This idea of *polygamy* shocked most Americans, especially Smith's neighbors in Nauvoo. Those who differed with Smith began publishing their disagreements. Smith was charged with destroying their printing press and for this he was jailed. An anti-Mormon mob then broke into the jail, hauled him out, and murdered him.

Brigham Young Founds Salt Lake City. Such a disaster would have crushed many religious movements. But the Mormons quickly rallied behind a remarkable new leader, Brigham Young. He urged them to band together to again move west.

Section 2 Review

COMPREHENSION   Developing Vocabulary

1. Explain these terms: dark horse candidate, Mormons, Conestoga wagons, Deseret, polygamy.

COMPREHENSION   Mastering Facts

1. Where did the Oregon Trail begin, and in what town did it end?
2. What effect did the Liberty party have on the 1844 election?
3. How did Mexico react to Polk's offer to buy California?
4. Who led the Mormons beyond the Mississippi, and what city did they build?

3   WAR WITH MEXICO RESULTS IN NEW TERRITORY

VOCABULARY   *Bear Flag Republic   Gadsden Purchase   Free-soil party*

Polk had been eager to compromise with Britain on Oregon because the United States was already at war with Mexico. That war came about for several reasons. Mexican patriots were still angry over the American annexation of Texas. Texas insisted that its southern border was the Rio Grande, while Mexico held that it was the Nueces River. Control of the Mexican government changed hands quite often, and these changes interfered with negotiations between the two countries.

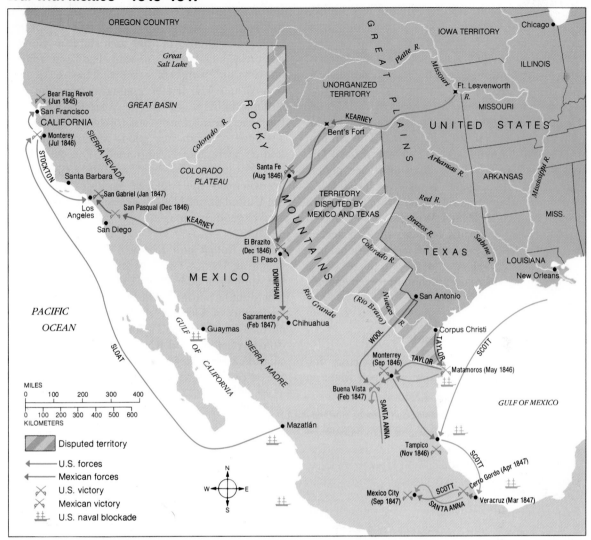

© ML & Co.

Map Skills   *What U.S. general marched to Mexico City? Who commanded Mexican forces at Buena Vista? Where and when was the only Mexican victory? How far north did Mexico extend?*

Polk Urges War

The most important reason for the war, however, was the attitude of "Polk the Purposeful," who was determined to take New Mexico and California. He was willing to buy these huge territories and offered $30 million for them. He was prepared to go up to $40 million. But when the Mexican government flatly refused even to consider the offer, Polk decided to use force.

Polk ordered General Zachary Taylor to move from the Nueces to the Rio Grande and build a fort to blockade the river. To Mexico, this was an invasion of its territory. So Mexican troops crossed the Rio Grande and in a small skirmish killed and

wounded sixteen American soldiers. Polk sat down at once to write a war message to Congress. In it he declared: "Mexico has passed the boundary of the United States, has invaded our territory and shed American blood upon the American soil. . . . War exists, and notwithstanding all our efforts to avoid it, exists by act of Mexico herself." After only two hours of debate, Congress overwhelmingly voted for war.

Thoreau and Webster Oppose War

The Mexican people were more united about the war than Americans were. Mexicans felt that they were defending their territory against invaders. In the United States, the war was popular in the South and West, where expansionist sentiment was especially strong. In the Northeast, however, it was not popular at all. Religious groups, such as the Unitarians and the Congregationalists, felt it was immoral to support a struggle that would extend slavery to new territory. Henry David Thoreau protested by refusing to pay his poll tax and was jailed for his action. This led him to write his famous essay, "The Duty of Civil Disobedience," in which he discussed what people should do when moral law conflicts with civil law.

Additional opposition came from Whigs in Congress, such as Daniel Webster, who believed that Polk had usurped Congress's right to declare war. "What is the value of this Constitutional provision," asked Webster, "if the President of his own authority may make such military movements as must bring on war?"

Some Victorious Leaders

For the Americans, one military victory followed another. Why? Because although Mexican troops gallantly defended their own soil, American soldiers were fired up by dreams of expansion. Most were volunteers from such states as Illinois, Kentucky, and Tennessee. Many had been frontier hunters and were crack shots. They were well trained and well led by graduates from the new national military academy of West Point. In contrast, the Mexican army was top-heavy with generals—none of them very good—while the ordinary soldiers were mostly ill-trained. The Americans were equipped with light, mobile artillery that overwhelmed the Mexican cavalry. In addition, the United States Navy was far superior, and it was used to good advantage.

"Old Rough and Ready." The American invasion of Mexico lasted about a year, starting in the summer of 1846. The Americans advanced on four different fronts. The first thrust, under the leadership of General Zachary Taylor, was into northeastern Mexico. Taylor, whom his men affectionately called "Old Rough and Ready," became a national hero after his victory over Santa Anna at the battle of Buena Vista.

In September 1847, General Winfield Scott's troops stormed the fortress of Chapultepec, which guarded the entrance to Mexico City. Scott then captured Mexico City itself.

Growth of the United States 1783–1853

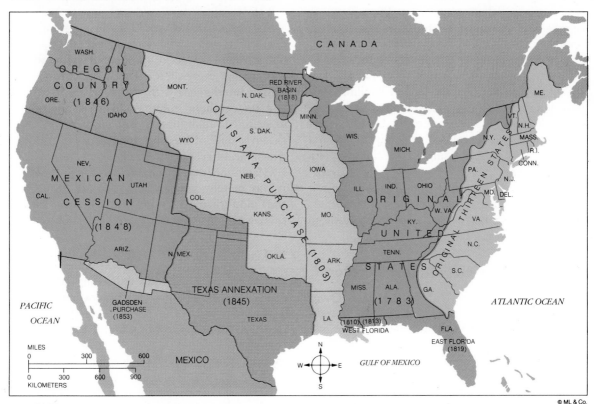

Map Skills *What territory was added to the United States in 1803? in 1853? In what years was Wyoming added? Which two states are not shown? How far is it from Maine to California?*

"Old Fuss and Feathers." An even more able general commanded the American thrust toward Mexico City itself. General Winfield Scott, at six feet four and one-quarter inches, looked the way a general should—especially when wearing his full-dress blue uniform with a yellow sash around his waist. His vanity and attention to discipline won him the nickname "Old Fuss and Feathers." He carefully supervised an amphibious landing at Vera Cruz. An army of 14,000 men disembarked from 200 ships within twenty-four hours. It was an extraordinary feat.

After capturing Vera Cruz, the army began a difficult march along the twisting route that took them thousands of feet upward from the coast to the great central plateau of Mexico. On September 14, 1847, Scott's troops finally forced their way into the Mexican capital.

"Long Marcher." In the meantime, a small group of Americans led by General Stephen Kearny (the "Long Marcher") went from Fort Leavenworth to Santa Fe. They captured the old trading town without firing a shot, probably because the Mexican governor there had been bribed to disappear. Kearny then led his troops off on another long march, this time to southern California.

The Bear Flag Republic. On the fourth front, in California, the situation was complicated by the fact that American settlers there had already proclaimed the area an independent republic called the Bear Flag Republic. (The grizzly bear remains on the California flag to this day, even though there are no longer any grizzlies in the state.) The American settlers and Kearny's men eventually joined forces with an American naval expedition. Mexican forces—few and scattered—were soon overcome, and California fell to the United States almost as easily as a ripe apple falls from a tree.

The Treaty of Guadalupe Hidalgo

Mexico had lost its northern territories, its capital city, and thousands of young men. Santa Anna stepped down as leader, and a new Mexican gov-

307

ernment agreed to make peace. The terms of the treaty of Guadalupe Hidalgo (1848) were fairly simple. Mexico recognized the Rio Grande as its boundary with Texas. The United States received a huge chunk of land, including New Mexico and California. In all, Mexico lost about one-third of its territory. In return, it received $15 million. Five years later, in 1853, the United States purchased a small piece of territory south of the Gila River for $10 million. This Gadsden Purchase included land which seemed especially suitable for the path of a transcontinental railroad.

The United States had won an aggressive war and an enormous amount of new territory. As things turned out, however, it had also uncaged the lions of sectional conflict.

Does Slavery Go with the Territory?

You may remember that Congressman David Wilmot raised the question of slavery in the territories almost as soon as the war began. If he had not offered his famous proviso, someone else would have; for the issue of slavery was on everyone's mind.

Slavery did not exist in Oregon or in any of the territories taken from Mexico. Why, then, did Americans feel so strongly about the possibility that it might spread to these areas, especially because the climate and soil were unsuited to plantation crops? The reason was that two questions were haunting people's minds:

1. Could slaves be used in other occupations? Many people argued that slavery had not reached its natural limits. By this, they meant that even if large plantations did not develop in the West, slaves could still be used on ranches, small farms, and in mining and lumbering. To prove their point, they correctly noted that some slaves already worked at such activities in the South.

2. Could slavery exist in any American territory? Many people wanted the United States to expand even farther. One possibility was Cuba, where plantation slavery already existed. With this in mind, both sides wanted to know whether slavery could or could not exist in any territory the United States might buy or occupy in the future.

Southerners felt strongly about the extension of slavery, even if it did not seem a practical possibility. Southerners saw themselves on the defensive. As a representative from Virginia put it, banning slavery in the territories was a "direct attack on the institutions" of the southern people, an "insult and injury, outrage and wrong, on them."

As you already know, an increasing number of northerners were beginning to see slavery as a moral issue. If in fact it *was* a moral wrong, then it was wrong everywhere. The Constitution prevented interference with slavery where it existed, and the southern states would never approve an amendment abolishing it. But northerners argued that it should at least be stopped from spreading, which meant keeping it out of the territories.

Many northerners opposed slavery not because it was morally wrong. They opposed it because they didn't like blacks and if slavery were banned there would be fewer blacks in the territories.

The Election of 1848

The entire subject was still being debated in Congress and the country at large when the time arrived for the 1848 presidential election. Would the United States split along party lines concerning the issue? Would the Democrats become a southern party and the Whigs a northern one?

As things turned out, the answers were "No." Many men voted for local reasons, or they voted for one party or the other because their fathers had. The great majority of Americans did not want slavery to become a political football kicked back and forth between the two political parties. And neither party could decide on an exciting candidate.

What happened was this: Polk refused to run again. He had said all along that he would serve only one term, and he had accomplished everything he had set out to do. The Democrats nominated colorless Lewis Cass and said nothing about slavery extension. A small group of antislavery Democrats were so disgusted that they nominated Van Buren to lead a new party, the Free-Soil party. The party stood for the abolition of slavery in the territories and supported federal internal improvements. It also wanted the government to give free land to settlers. The Whigs nominated General Zachary Taylor. Old Rough and Ready did not have many firm political beliefs, but he was ready to run.

The election of 1848 showed several things. It proved that a presidential election could be dull and boring. It showed that the two national political parties could avoid the issue of slavery. It demonstrated that an antislavery party could gain ten percent of the popular vote. And it showed that Taylor could beat Cass by a narrow margin.

Section 3 Review

COMPREHENSION   Developing Vocabulary

1. Explain these terms: Bear Flag Republic, Gadsden Purchase, Free-Soil party.

COMPREHENSION   Mastering Facts

1. How did Thoreau show his opposition to the Mexican-American War?
2. What advantages did American troops have in the war?
3. What did Mexico lose by the Treaty of Guadalupe Hidalgo?
4. Why did Polk not wish to run again in 1848?

4   THE COMPROMISE OF 1850 POSTPONES A CRISIS

VOCABULARY   *secession   omnibus bill*

Zachary Taylor was a good general but not a very good president. He had plenty of common sense but no experience with national politics. Soon after he took office, the sectional crisis reached the boiling point.

When Polk left the White House in March 1849, the signs of crisis were already apparent. The New Mexico and California territories still had no civilian government. Abolitionists were demanding an end to the slave trade in the District of Colum-bia. Proslavery people in the South were demanding that fugitive slaves be returned from the North.

Gold, Gold, Gold

Then something happened that riveted attention on California. In January 1848 a man named James Marshall discovered gold at the bottom of the American River. The few specks of shiny metal

The bustle and toil characteristic of the rush for mineral wealth in the new territory are reflected in this early photograph. California entered the Union in September 1850.

set off a frantic wave of gold fever throughout the nation and indeed throughout the world.

In California itself, some men abandoned their ranches and others abandoned their businesses, but all headed for the diggings. So many sailors jumped ship that San Francisco Bay looked like a forest of masts. Everyone expected to strike it rich and a few did. But most of the money ended up in the pockets of men and women who set up stores to sell food and mining supplies.

The result of the '49 gold rush was that California's population grew enormously almost overnight. Clearly, it was ready for statehood. In 1849 a constitutional convention met at Monterey and drew up a constitution outlawing slavery. But when California's application for statehood arrived in Congress, the storm broke.

Three Old Men and the Union

Southerners were furious. If California were admitted as a free state, to be followed by New Mexico, what then? The Union could fall into the grasp of men who were hostile to the special interests of the South.

Many people in the North became equally angry. Slavery, they said, must never find a footing in California or any other territory obtained from Mexico. A few wanted to go further. They called for the abolition of slavery in the District of Columbia. Such a step would be constitutional, as Congress had complete control over the federal district. Thousands of petitions poured in from the North in support of these positions.

Secession in the Air. The word *secession* was whispered or shouted in the halls of Congress, in dining rooms of Washington hotels, in the press, and in the nation at large.

At this point, Henry Clay moved to save the Union. It was his finest hour. Old and sick, he was still swallowing his disappointment at not winning the White House. But his vision of the nation's future had always been a broad one. Now he worked night and day to shape a compromise which both North and South could accept. He took the unusual step of consulting with Daniel Webster, his old Whig rival. Webster offered his support.

On January 29, 1850, Clay rose unsteadily from his seat in the Senate to offer his plan of compromise. Several days later he rose again to defend it. He spoke for two days. It was the last important speech of his life.

Henry Clay's Compromise. Clay proposed a series of seven resolutions which carefully balanced the interests of the North and the South. They were:

1. California should be admitted immediately as a free state;

2. Utah should be separated from New Mexico, and the two territories should be allowed to decide for themselves whether to have slavery or not;

3. The land disputed between Texas and New Mexico should be assigned to New Mexico;

4. In return, the United States should pay the debts which Texas had contracted before annexation;

5. Slavery should not be abolished in the District of Columbia without the consent of its residents and the surrounding state of Maryland, and then only if the owners were paid for their slaves;

6. Slave-trading (but not slavery) should be banned in the District of Columbia; and

7. A stricter fugitive slave law should be adopted.

Clay's resolutions were followed by one of the most magnificent debates in American history. The Senate galleries were crowded with senators' wives and important government officials. Eloquent speeches went on for hours and even days. They were widely reported in the press, where they were eagerly followed by the nation's citizens.

John Calhoun's Reply. John Calhoun led the attack on Clay's proposals. He was too old and weak to read his own speech. He sat in his Senate chair with a warm cloak around him as he listened to his words being read by another southern senator. He looked like an aging eagle, his fierce eyes peering over his nose and the deep lines of his face. He still wanted to preserve the Union, but he was willing to tear it apart if necessary to protect the interests of the South. "If you," he said to the senators from the North, "cannot agree to settle [these issues] on the broad principle of justice and duty, say so." If that was the case, then "let the States we both represent agree to separate . . . in peace. If you are unwilling [that] we should part in peace, tell us so." In that case, Calhoun warned, "we shall know what to do."

George P. A. Healy's dramatic painting shows Daniel Webster replying to Senator Robert Hayne of South Carolina on sectionalism. Calhoun is in the shadows on the left.

Daniel Webster's Speech. Three days after Calhoun delivered his grim warning, Daniel Webster raised his bulky body to deliver the last great oration of his life. In the flickering gas lights of the Senate chamber, his deep-set eyes still glowed. Sometimes he paused at strange moments, as his mind groped for the words he had memorized. Yet the old powerful logic and sentiment were still there. He would speak, he said, "not as a Massachusetts man, nor as a northern man, but as an American. I speak for the preservation of the Union. Hear me for my cause."

Webster denounced Calhoun's warnings about secession. But Webster also called upon the North to make concessions, especially in support of a new, strict fugitive slave law. He had private doubts about such a law, but he saw that the South must be given something in return for a free California. His support of the new fugitive slave law helped secure the compromise, but it brought down a flood of criticism from the North. Webster was widely denounced as a traitor to the cause of free men.

An Uneasy Agreement

The debate went on for months after Webster sat down. Almost every senator had his say. Some of them remained bitter enemies of the compromise right up to the end. Senator William H. Seward of New York raised a great many eyebrows when he claimed that there was "a higher law than the Constitution." The law of God, Seward claimed, prohibited slavery from all the territories. If this was the case, many of his listeners thought, what good was the Constitution at all? Southerners denounced Seward's claim as "fanaticism."

Early in July, President Taylor suddenly developed an inflamed stomach and died. He was succeeded by Vice President Millard Fillmore, who quickly indicated that he was willing to go along with the compromise. Members of Congress began to see light at the end of the tunnel. Henry Clay had become too feeble to continue the fight. So in the final few months, Illinois Senator Stephen A. Douglas took charge of the behind-the-scenes efforts to gain votes. Short and somewhat stout, the young senator from Illinois was a skillful political operator.

Clay had presented his compromise as an *omnibus bill*. The term *omnibus* means "covering everything." In other words, Clay had presented his resolutions as a package, to be considered on an all-or-nothing basis. Douglas realized that the compromise would fail if it was offered this way because every congressman hated at least one provision. So Douglas separated the contents of the Omnibus Bill into a series of bills to be voted on individually. Thus any individual congressman could vote for the provisions he liked and could vote against, or abstain from voting on, the provisions he disliked.

Douglas had found the key for passing the entire compromise. Things turned out as he hoped because so many opponents abstained.

By September 1850, the Great Compromise had been adopted, much in the form originally proposed by Clay. Calhoun had died during the crisis. Within two years, Clay and Webster were both dead, too.

The country seemed to sigh with relief. Newspapers everywhere hailed the settlement. Peace and harmony reigned in Washington. When Congress met at the end of that year, the sectional conflict over slavery seemed to be over. Stephen Douglas announced in the Senate, "I have determined never to make another speech on the slavery question." He urged his fellow senators to "drop the subject." If they did so, he predicted, the Compromise of 1850 would stand as a "final settlement." Most of the country agreed.

Section 4 Review

COMPREHENSION   Developing Vocabulary

1. Explain these terms: secession, omnibus bill.

COMPREHENSION   Mastering Facts

1. Why did California's application for statehood create a political storm?
2. What did Daniel Webster propose that made many people in the North angry?
3. What was the subject that Stephen Douglas urged his fellow senators to "drop"?
4. How did Henry Clay save the Union in 1850?

CHAPTER 14 Review

Chapter Summary

The phrase manifest destiny *that characterized the nation in the 1840s described the prevalent spirit of expansion. Seeking more territory, Americans went to war with Mexico. When the Mexican government closed the borders of Texas to further immigration, Texans revolted. Texas remained an independent republic until it entered the Union in 1845. Then President James K. Polk tried to purchase New Mexico and California from Mexico. When his offer was refused, he resorted to force. When fighting began, Americans in California revolted; eventually they, too, joined the Union. The treaty ending the Mexican-American War in 1848 added huge new sections to the southwestern area of the United States. As the war ended, the discovery of gold in California reopened arguments about slavery. However, sectional disagreements lessened when Congress passed the Compromise of 1850.*

Questions for Critical Thinking

COMPREHENSION   Summarizing Main Ideas

1. What effect did each of the following have on America's westward expansion? (a) land hunger; (b) trade with China; (c) rivalry with Great Britain; (d) slavery; (e) the gold rush; (f) religious prejudice against the Mormons.
2. What were three reasons for the outbreak of the Mexican-American War?
3. Give two reasons why many Americans opposed war with Mexico.
4. What concessions did the South make in the Compromise of 1850? What concessions did the North make?

COMPREHENSION   Interpreting Events

1. If you had been a U.S. senator in 1845, would you have voted in favor of admitting Texas? Give reasons for your position.
2. Why did wagon trains crossing the Great Plains form a hollow square at night?
3. Why did the United States and Great Britain agree to settle the Oregon border dispute peacefully? On what basis did they draw the boundary line?

4. Do you approve or disapprove of the way in which Henry David Thoreau expressed his opposition to the war? Explain your opinion.
5. Do you agree or disagree with Seward's claim that there is a higher law than the Constitution? Justify your position.
6. If you had been a senator in 1850, would you have voted in favor of the Compromise? Why or why not?

APPLICATION   Using Skills To Evaluate Sources

Historians must provide evidence to support their conclusions. For each of the following group of statements, indicate which statement would be the most difficult to prove.

Group 1
  a. Many Americans in the 1840s and 1850s believed that the United States should expand to the Pacific Ocean.
  b. It was inevitable that the United States should expand to the Pacific Ocean.
  c. Land hunger was an important factor in manifest destiny.
  d. Many Americans believed manifest destiny was desirable because it would expand freedom.

Group 2
  a. The Mexican-American War was partly the result of a clash between two different cultures.
  b. Most Mexicans felt the war was caused by the American invasion of their territory.
  c. The Mexican-American War could have been avoided if Henry Clay had defeated James Polk in the 1844 election.
  d. The Mexican-American War was fought on four separate fronts.

EVALUATION   Forming Generalizations

1. Describe the influence of Spanish culture in California today.
2. List the states that have been formed in whole or in part from land included in the Oregon country.
3. From which nation—France, Great Britain, Mexico, or Spain—did the United States obtain the most territory between 1783 and 1853?

Political Leadership

In a poll taken during the early 1980s, the *Chicago Tribune* asked historians to rate the nation's presidents. As in surveys taken in 1948 and 1962, Abraham Lincoln, George Washington, and Franklin Roosevelt were again ranked as the best Presidents, in that order. The top ten also included Thomas Jefferson and Andrew Jackson.

Most historians use five basic guidelines in judging previous presidents: (1) Were established goals achieved? (2) Were responses to crises effective? (3) Was a high level of integrity displayed? (4) Were all citizens treated fairly? (5) Were wise advisers chosen? These guidelines encourage a fair evaluation based on the same standards.

Though conclusions differ, all evaluators use the perspective of time. As time passes, leadership evaluation becomes somewhat less difficult. Events and decisions can be viewed more objectively after decades and centuries have passed.

Common Characteristics.

A look at past elections reveals only a few clear preferences expressed in voting behavior. For example, no women or blacks have been elected president. In all levels of government, minorities have generally been underrepresented.

Americans have also repeatedly voted for heroes. Military

Effective communication is necessary between a president and Congress. The president addresses Congress and the American public regularly.

leaders like Washington, Jackson, Harrison, Grant, and Eisenhower won elections by tapping public recognition, confidence, and admiration. Many successful candidates without military experience have projected images of courage or strength in other fields.

Some of the most admired politicians have been able to communicate effectively. William Jennings Bryan and John F. Kennedy, for example, were known for their stirring words. Though not forceful speakers, Jefferson and Lincoln wrote some of the most eloquent prose in the English language.

Concern Over Quality.

The democratic process does not always produce capable leaders, however. Many people are concerned about the quality of political leaders in the United States today. They argue that the high level of leadership established during the nation's early administrations has not been matched in recent years. Some blame the influence of the mass media. Candidates, they say, are now elected on the basis of image, not substance.

"The best presidents have been strong political leaders with a vision . . . of where they think the country should go," one historian has said. How to attract into politics people with vision, ability, and integrity is an immediate and important challenge for all democratic societies.

Understanding Government

1. What characteristics have winning politicians in the United States usually had?
2. How can the nation attract better leaders in the future?
3. Rate the nation's first sixteen presidents using the guidelines on this page.

UNIT 4 Review

Understanding Social Studies Concepts

History

1. Explain why Monroe's term as president is often described as an "Era of Good Feelings."
2. Name two major developments in transportation and communication that came about in the early 1800s. How did each of these affect life in the United States?
3. Describe the changing attitude of settlers toward the Indians between 1600 and 1830. How did Andrew Jackson finally solve the Indian "problem"? Did the Supreme Court agree with his methods? Explain.
4. Explain the phrase *manifest destiny*. Describe the sequence of events that led Americans to fulfill their manifest destiny.
5. What growing problem was not solved by Clay's Compromise of 1850?

Geography

1. Describe how the Mississippi River has contributed to the historical and cultural development of the United States.
2. Describe the different geographical areas and obstacles pioneers had to contend with as they traveled along the Oregon Trail.

Economics

1. How did Henry Clay's American System contribute to the economic development of the United States?
2. Describe the contributions of women to the American economy between 1820 and 1850.
3. What economic divisions between North and South were caused by the growth of cotton? Would these same divisions probably have developed if the South had had its own textile industries? Explain.

Government

1. In what ways did the United States become a more democratic nation during the Age of Jackson? What effect did Jackson have on the office of the presidency?

2. Explain the meaning of *states' rights*. Which state took the lead in promoting this philosophy? How did President Jackson react?

Sociology

1. List three areas of life that social reformers attempted to change during the mid-1800s.
2. Why were many of the nation's early social reformers women?
3. When did it first become possible for women to attend college in America? What general advancements in education were made during the mid-1800s?

Extending Map, Chart, Picture Skills

1. In the cartoon on page 246, who is Uncle Sam protecting? From whom is he protecting them?
2. Compare the maps on pages 242, 243, and 280. What generalizations can you make regarding transportation facilities in the United States during the early and mid-1800s?
3. Refer to the map on page 307. Which states were either completely or partially formed from the Texas Annexation? Oregon Country? Mexican Cession?

Understanding Current Events

1. The Democratic party developed a new style of campaigning in the 1820s. Who was chiefly responsible for this change? Compare campaign techniques then to those of the present.
2. Which reform movements that started during the early 1800s are still part of American life today? Which new movements now exist?

Developing Effective Citizenship

1. Who wrote the "Duty of Civil Disobedience"? According to the author, when was civil disobedience justified? Are his ideas still accepted today? Explain.
2. In what ways was Frederick Douglass an effective citizen? Explain.

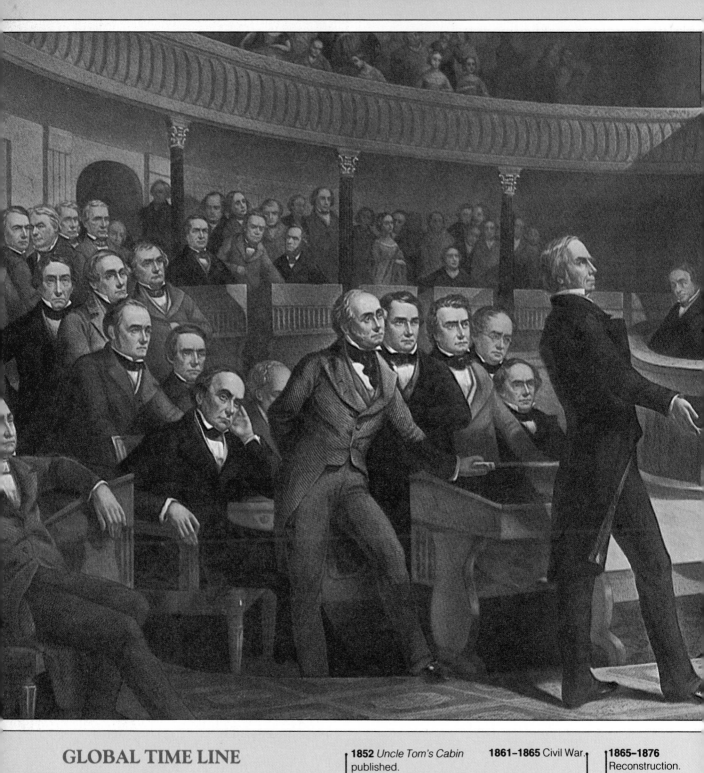

GLOBAL TIME LINE
1850–1876

THE UNITED STATES

THE WORLD

1852 *Uncle Tom's Cabin* published.

1854 Republican party formed.

1857 Dred Scott decision.

1861–1865 Civil War.

1865–1876 Reconstruction.

1865 Abraham Lincoln assassinated.

1850

1860

1858 British take over rule of India.

1853–1854 Perry opens two Japanese ports to U.S. trade.

1863 French troops occupy Mexico City.

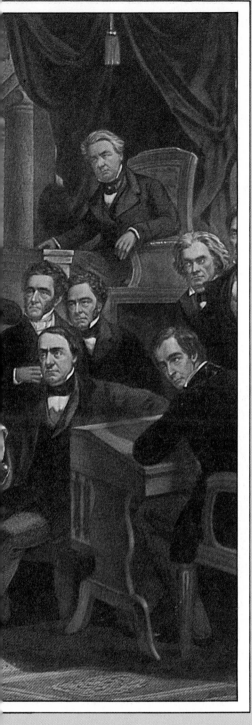

1869 Transcontinental railroad completed.

1873 Economic depression begins.

1877 Rutherford B. Hayes becomes president.

1870 ——————— 1880

1870–1871 Franco-Prussian War.

1869 Suez Canal opens.

1867 British grant dominion status to Canada.

CHAPTER 15

A Decade of Crisis

1850–1861

Linking Past to Present

From 1850 to 1860 most people in the United States were angry and resentful toward the national government. No matter that popular leaders had decided to drop the issue of slavery from their debates. It would not stay dead. Again and again during this period, events took place which threw the issue into the faces of citizens and congressmen alike. Positions gradually hardened into firm lines, separating Northern interests from Southern interests. As Lincoln was to state, the nation had become "a house divided against itself."

As the United States appeared to be drawn inevitably toward the abyss, the presidents during the decade—Fillmore, Pierce, and Buchanan—seemed helpless. Friends became enemies, old parties collapsed, and new ones were formed.

The Compromise of 1850 had broken down. It had been carefully and patriotically patched together. But as one crisis after another battered it, the compromise gradually fell apart like a sandcastle on a stormy beach.

1 THE SUBJECT OF SLAVERY REFUSES TO DIE

VOCABULARY *Fugitive Slave Law* *propaganda*

The decade of the 1850s began quietly enough. When people went to vote in November 1852, they had a very dull choice. In the South the majority voted for the Democratic candidate, Franklin Pierce of New Hampshire. He had been nominated as another dark horse. No one outside his native state knew much about him or what he stood for. Still, he was elected over the aging General Winfield Scott, whose strong antiforeign feelings antagonized a large number of German and Irish voters in Northern cities.

The Whig party more or less came apart. Both its old leaders, Clay and Webster, died during the campaign. Northern Whigs who did not like Scott refused to vote, or split their votes between Whig and Free-Soil candidates, or switched to the Democratic party.

At first, Americans hoped the new president would be able to keep the nation on an even keel. But soon President Pierce was seen to be as colorless as Fillmore had been and even less able to control the events that swirled around him.

The Fugitive Slave Law

The Fugitive Slave Law of 1850, part of the Compromise of that year, provided for the recovery of slaves who ran away to free states. Slaveholders, or their hired agents, could seize their runaway slaves in any Northern state. They could demand assistance from federal marshals. A slaveholder could then go before a federal judge to make a legal claim. If the judge decided in the slaveholder's favor, the slave could be taken south.

Unjust Practices. Abolitionists charged that the law made it easy to kidnap free blacks. The judges received $10 if they ruled that a black was a slave but only $5 if they ruled that he or she was legally free. In addition, a black accused of being a runaway was not entitled to a trial by jury and was not even allowed to testify in his or her own behalf. The law also provided for a fine of $1000 and six months in jail for anyone convicted of helping a fugitive slave.

The Fugitive Slave Law spread fear among blacks in the North, whether they were escaped slaves or legally free. Kidnapping of free blacks could and did happen. Some blacks became so alarmed that they migrated to Canada, where the law could not reach them. Black leaders, such as Frederick Douglass, called on the black community to resist the law with force.

Personal Liberty Laws. Many Northern states passed personal liberty laws in an attempt to get around the new federal statute. Those laws forbade state officials from cooperating with federal officials who were returning fugitive slaves to the South. As a result, state and federal officials often found themselves in conflict with one another. In Ohio, for example, a crowd of men from Oberlin College rescued a fugitive from a slave catcher. Members of the crowd were convicted by a federal jury. But then a state court ordered the arrest of the slave catcher and all federal officials who had cooperated with him. In this case a compromise was worked out, but it was clear that the Fugitive Slave Law would be difficult to enforce.

319

Author Harriet Beecher Stowe is seated beside her father, Lyman Beecher, and brother, Henry Ward Beecher, who is on the right.

Horrifying Cases. A number of dramatic incidents greatly inflamed Northern opinion about slavery and the South. Early in 1851, for example, a black man named Frederick Wilkins was working quietly as a waiter in a Boston coffeehouse. Suddenly, he was seized by a Virginia slave catcher—who knew him as Shadrach, a runaway slave. While Wilkins was being held for return to Virginia, a crowd of blacks burst into the courthouse and led him away to safety.

In New York City, James Hamlet, another escaped slave, was seized and packed off to Maryland so fast that he was not even allowed to say goodbye to his wife and children. In the end Hamlet was lucky, for his black friends and a few sympathetic whites managed to raise $800 and purchase his freedom.

Several years later the streets of Boston were lined with federal troops as Anthony Burns, a fugitive slave, was marched from the courthouse to a ship waiting to carry him back to slavery in Virginia. A gigantic crowd of 50,000 people hissed and shouted in protest. It cost the federal government $100,000 to return Burns to slavery.

About 300 blacks were returned to slavery under the terms of the Fugitive Slave Act. For every slave returned, however, thousands of Northerners became abolitionists. Previously, slavery had seemed distant and remote. Now it seemed much closer to home. A mere glimpse of Anthony Burns in chains was far more vivid than the most awful tales in abolitionist literature.

Uncle Tom's Cabin

In 1852 a woman wrote a book that brought slavery into the living rooms of a great many American homes. Her story had more impact than any single piece of writing since Thomas Paine's *Common Sense*. It reached more people and changed more minds than any TV series has done in modern times.

The Author. Harriet Beecher Stowe was the daughter of a Calvinist minister and the wife of another. One of her older brothers, the minister Henry Ward Beecher, had been a supporter of abolitionist Elijah Lovejoy. When the latter was murdered by proslavers, Harriet Stowe decided to make the cause of slavery her own. Her feelings were reinforced when her eighteen-month-old son died in a cholera epidemic. She saw the epidemic as a modern version of the Biblical plagues which struck Egyptians because their pharaoh refused to let Jewish slaves go free. She then sat down and wrote *Uncle Tom's Cabin, or Life Among the Lowly*.

At first the novel was published in a series of magazine articles. Then in the spring of 1852, the publisher brought out her story in book form. He printed only 5000 copies because he thought it would not sell well. It sold out in two days! Within another week 10,000 copies were swept up from the shelves of bookstores all over the North. Within a year the publisher had sold 300,000 copies. No other book except the Bible had sold so many copies. People everywhere talked about it. In the North it was hailed; in the South it was damned.

The Story. How could one book create such a fuss? Clearly, Harriet Stowe used her story to tell many Northerners what they wanted to hear about slavery and what many Southerners did not want to hear at all.

The story deals mostly with Uncle Tom, a loyal

and deeply Christian slave who grows to manhood in Kentucky. Tom's kindly master is forced to sell him because of financial difficulties. Thus, Tom is forced to leave his wife and his "old Kentucky home" for the long trip "down the river" to New Orleans.

While he is carried off by a vicious slave trader, Tom's daughter and her husband flee to Ohio. Tom spends some time with a kindly family in New Orleans but is later sold to a cruel slavemaster in Arkansas named Simon Legree. In the end, Tom is lashed to death at Legree's orders. As he dies, Tom forgives the two black overseers who have beaten him to death.

The Propaganda. Stowe's story was excellent propaganda. It exaggerated everything. It was as sentimental as a soap opera, and the characters and situations were often totally unbelievable. Ever since its publication, many people have said that *Uncle Tom's Cabin* did not deserve to be rated as a great novel.

Even so, the book deeply touched millions of Americans. It did so primarily for three reasons. It told a simple story. It showed that slavery was evil, even when good people were involved, because it was contrary to both Christian ethics and the Declaration of Independence. And it showed that slavery damaged families, white as well as black.

The Reaction. Reaction to the book in the North was extremely favorable. It increased agitation to abolish the Fugitive Slave Law. Southerners hated it, even if they couldn't put it down. Southerners viewed it as an attack, not just against slavery but against the South as a whole. Southerners felt that they did not treat their slaves any worse than factory owners in the North treated their workers. At least a dozen Southern writers wrote novels which attempted to show that *Uncle Tom's Cabin* was a pack of lies. The most successful, *Aunt Eva's Cabin*, had illustrations showing lace curtains in the windows of Aunt Eva's cabin. Northerners were reminded that Aunt Eva was happy. But they could not forget that she was a slave.

Section 1 Review

COMPREHENSION   Developing Vocabulary

1. Explain these terms: propaganda, Fugitive Slave Law.

COMPREHENSION   Mastering Facts

1. Why did many abolitionists believe that judges might not be fair in enforcing the Fugitive Slave Law?
2. What were personal liberty laws?
3. Who wrote *Uncle Tom's Cabin*, and why?
4. What made *Uncle Tom's Cabin* a best-seller?

2   A NEW PROPOSAL OPENS OLD WOUNDS

VOCABULARY   *popular sovereignty*

When Franklin Pierce took office at the age of forty-eight, he was the youngest man to become president up to that time. People liked him, for he was friendly and sociable. He named a strong cabinet, which included both Northerners and Southerners. But he could not control them or members of Congress. He tried to please extremists on both sides of the sectional controversy. The nation needed a steady hand to guide the ship of state. Pierce's hand was as weak as his smile was friendly, and he soon lost all control over political events.

The dynamic young senator from Illinois stepped into the political vacuum. Without meaning to, Stephen Douglas, the top Democratic party leader now that Calhoun was dead, wrecked the Compromise of 1850.

The Kansas-Nebraska Act

In 1854 Douglas introduced a bill to organize the vast Nebraska Country, which lay completely north of 36°30'. The bill divided the country, setting off the southern portion as the territory of Kansas and the northern portion as the territory of Nebraska. It also specifically repealed the Missouri Compromise, that there would be no slavery in the Louisiana Purchase north of 36°30'. Instead, both territories would have *popular sovereignty*—that is, settlers themselves would decide whether or not they wanted slavery in their territory.

There was an immediate howl of protest in the North. Douglas had seriously underestimated Northern hostility toward slavery in the territories.

At his home base in Chicago, Douglas was hooted off the platform by members of his own Democratic party.

Why did Douglas take this fateful step? Historians are still not certain. But they do know that Douglas wanted a transcontinental railroad. "No man can keep up with the spirit of this age who travels on anything slower than the locomotive. . . . We must therefore have Rail Roads . . . from the Atlantic to the Pacific." He wanted it to start at Chicago, where he owned considerable real estate, and to run west through the Nebraska country. Southerners, however, wanted the railroad to begin at New Orleans or Memphis and follow a southern route through El Paso to San Diego. Douglas did not favor slavery in Kansas and Nebraska. He believed it could not exist on the open prairies since none of the crops requiring slave labor could be grown there. But in order to win Southern support for his railroad route and for his own presidential hopes, he agreed to support repeal of the Missouri Compromise. He thought this would have no practical effect on the territories themselves. He proved to be dead wrong.

"Bleeding Kansas"

The Kansas-Nebraska Act inflamed opinions in both the North and the South. Although popular sovereignty seemed a logical way of deciding the fundamental issue of slavery in the territories, events showed that it did not work. There was a crucial question: *When* should settlers decide about slavery? Before the territory has an official government? After? Or when the territory becomes a state? The question was never really settled. Instead, a minor war broke out in Kansas.

Government Against Government. Proslavery settlers began moving into Kansas from Missouri. The first territorial election took place in March 1855. Although only 1400 residents were eligible to vote, some 6000 votes were cast. Most of the voters were from Missouri. They crossed the border just long enough to mark their ballots and then returned home. The new territorial legislature promptly passed laws in support of slavery, including one that required the death penalty for aiding a fugitive slave.

Antislavery residents of Kansas refused to recognize this new government and instead organized one of their own. Kansas now had two governments, one based on fraud and the other without any legal basis.

Settler Against Settler. In those days, Kansas was very much a frontier society. Violence and lawlessness were common. Also, most of the settlers were young, single men. The absence of women and families made them quick to draw their knives and pistols.

Soon, major incidents of violence broke out. A large group of tough proslavery men rode into Lawrence, Kansas, in search of several leading

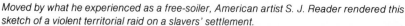
Moved by what he experienced as a free-soiler, American artist S. J. Reader rendered this sketch of a violent territorial raid on a slavers' settlement.

Free-Soilers. The proslavery legislature had indicted those Free-Soilers for treason, so the raiders of Lawrence felt they had legal backing. They burned the only hotel in the tiny town, destroyed several homes, and smashed the presses of a new Free-Soil newspaper. When Northern newspapers learned about the raid, they called it the "Sack of Lawrence" and exaggerated every detail.

In Kansas a single-minded abolitionist decided on revenge. John Brown gathered four of his sons and two other followers. In May 1856 they rode into the small proslavery settlement at Pottawatomie Creek, dragged five men out of their homes, and killed them. Brown claimed that he had God's support for this murderous action.

Soon all of Kansas was an armed camp. More settlers moved in from Missouri and other slave states. In the North, abolitionists organized the New England Emigrant Aid Company to assist Free-Soilers who would migrate to Kansas. One of Harriet Beecher Stowe's brothers, Henry Ward Beecher, was a popular preacher with strong antislavery views. He said that guns would be more useful against slavery than Bibles. Crates of "Beecher's Bibles" began arriving in free-soil Kansas settlements—crates packed with rifles and ammunition. Kansas turned into a battleground on which more than two hundred people eventually died in a miniature civil war.

Congressman Against Congressman. The spirit of violence spread to the heart of the nation. Late one day in 1856, Senator Charles Sumner of Massachusetts was writing at his desk on the Senate floor. He hated slavery and used vulgar language to defend his high principles. He had just finished a speech about "the crime against Kansas." He had demanded the immediate admission of Kansas as a free state. He lashed into Douglas and Senator Butler of South Carolina, using language sometimes heard in the streets but not on the floor of the Senate. Many people were deeply

shocked. Sumner went on with a cruel remark about Butler's speech difficulties, which had been caused by a heart condition. While he was speaking, someone overheard Douglas grumble, "That damn fool will get himself killed by some other damn fool."

As Sumner sat writing, a young cousin of Butler approached him. Preston S. Brooks was a representative from South Carolina and he had been driven to fury by Sumner's remarks. He held in his hand a heavy cane with a gold head. Sumner did not even notice the approaching man. Brooks waited for a minute while a woman left the back of the hall. Then he rushed forward and began pounding Sumner over the head. Sumner struggled to rise, but his knees were caught under his desk. Soon he was on the floor with blood pouring from his head.

In the South, Brooks was cheered for having supported the honor of his family and the honor of the South. In the North, Brooks was denounced as a bully. His action was described as typical of a violent slaveholding society. The entire incident confirmed each section's suspicions about the other. Sumner lived although it took him three years to recover from his injuries. In the meantime, his empty desk stood like a silent accusation.

Section 2 Review

COMPREHENSION   Developing Vocabulary

1. Explain these terms: popular sovereignty, Beecher's Bibles.

COMPREHENSION   Mastering Facts

1. What effect did the Kansas-Nebraska Act have on the Missouri Compromise?
2. What happened as a result of the first territorial election in Kansas?
3. What did John Brown do at Pottawatomie?
4. Why did Representative Brooks attack Senator Sumner?

3   NEW ARRIVALS LEAD TO NEW POLITICAL PARTIES

VOCABULARY   *nativism   Know-Nothings*

During this violent and dramatic time, other events, equally significant but less startling, were taking place. From 1845 to 1853 a great flood of immigrants came to the United States from Europe. Many were from Scandinavia and Germany, but the majority came from Ireland. New York City was the great immigrant port but Boston, Philadelphia, Baltimore, and New Orleans also received large numbers.

Most of these immigrants settled in the free

states. More jobs were available there in factories and construction work, and they would not have to compete with slave labor. Most of the Germans and Scandinavians bought farms and settled in the Midwest. The Irish were usually too poor to buy even cheap farmland, so many of them remained in eastern cities. Soon, however, many Irish followed the railroad and canal lines that were spreading through the North.

Immigrants Face Opposition

In the long run, the immigrants prospered. The nation's economy was vigorous and expanding very rapidly. In 1850 the United States had only one-tenth the number of people it has today. There seemed to be room for everyone who wanted to come. But these new immigrants faced opposition.

Nativism. The policy of favoring native-born people over immigrants is called *nativism*. Nativist sentiment grew rapidly in the 1840s and 1850s. In the cities the main reason was fear of job competition. Immigrants had to have work and they were desperate. They would work for much less than the native Americans who were, at the same time, trying to get higher wages. But there were other causes of hostility.

Anti-Catholicism. Nativists objected to so many immigrants being Roman Catholics. They resented the increasing numbers of priests and nuns, parochial schools, and Catholic colleges. At that time many Americans had grown up in an anti-Catholic tradition as old as the Reformation in England. They believed the pope headed an organization that wanted to wipe out Protestantism and take over the world. They were convinced that Catholics could not understand democracy because they were used to following orders from the pope.

As a result, anti-Catholic books and magazines circulated widely. Shops and factories carried "NINA" signs—"No Irish Need Apply." On some occasions, mobs turned to violence against Catholics. In Massachusetts one mob burned a convent to the ground. They would never have believed that the United States would one day have a Catholic president (John F. Kennedy)—or that in 1979 Pope John Paul II would make a tour of the United States and be warmly welcomed by millions of American Protestants as well as Catholics.

German immigrants encountered much less hostility at least on religious grounds—but they were often referred to as "damned Dutchmen." Nativists made fun of their strange-sounding language and their habit of group singing in social halls. Nativists were also suspicious of what they regarded as German clannishness or unwillingness to Americanize. They resented Germans forming their own clubs, organizing German-language schools and churches, and publishing German-language newspapers.

New Parties Develop

During the 1840s nativist Americans organized a number of secret societies with such names as the Sons of America and the Sons of '76. They aimed at "protecting" Americans from the threat of Catholic immigration. In the early 1850s many of these societies united as a single national organization, the Supreme Order of the Star-Spangled Banner. Its members were pledged to secrecy about the organization's structure and leaders. If asked, a member was supposed to say, "I know nothing." Soon, members of the organization were being called Know-Nothings.

The Know-Nothings. The Know-Nothings decided they could best achieve their aims by entering politics. They wanted to restrict the flow of immigration. They called for changes in the naturalization laws which would require aliens to wait twenty-one years before they could apply for citizenship. And they pledged to support only white, native-born Protestants for public office.

The Know-Nothings were extremely successful at the polls. In 1854 they obtained 25 percent of the vote in New York State and 40 percent of the vote in Pennsylvania. They elected numerous state legislators and governors and at least seventy-five members of Congress. In 1856 they became the American party and nominated ex-President Millard Fillmore for president on the slogan "Americans Must Rule America."

Why were the Know-Nothings such a success? Two reasons seem especially important. First, nativist sentiment was strong and widespread. Second, the American party was stepping into the political vacuum caused by the collapse of the Whigs. It remained to be seen whether the American party would replace the Whigs as one of the national political parties.

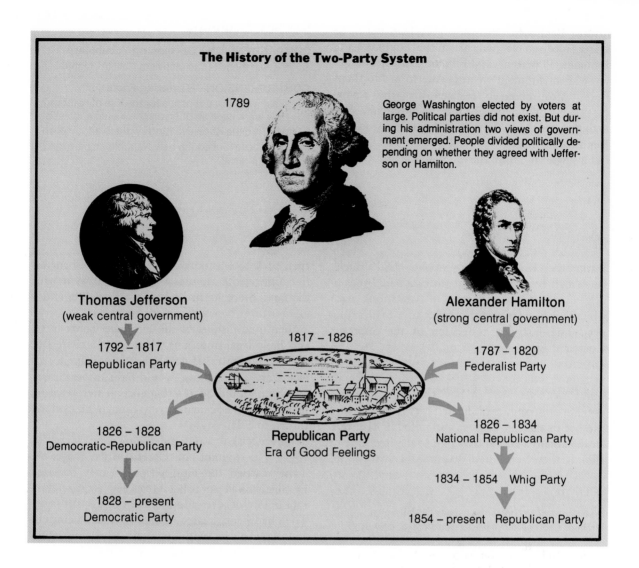

The History of the Two-Party System

1789

George Washington elected by voters at large. Political parties did not exist. But during his administration two views of government emerged. People divided politically depending on whether they agreed with Jefferson or Hamilton.

Thomas Jefferson
(weak central government)

1792 – 1817
Republican Party

1817 – 1826
Republican Party
Era of Good Feelings

1826 – 1828
Democratic-Republican Party

1828 – present
Democratic Party

Alexander Hamilton
(strong central government)

1787 – 1820
Federalist Party

1826 – 1834
National Republican Party

1834 – 1854   Whig Party

1854 – present   Republican Party

A New Republican Party. While the American party was gaining ground, another new party was doing the same. But unlike the Know-Nothings, this party was based entirely in the North.

In the summer of 1854 a group of people representing Whigs, Free-Soilers, and antislavery Democrats met at Jackson, Michigan, and formed the present-day Republican party. (It had no connection with the old Republican party of Jefferson and Madison.) Unlike the American party, it was not organized around a single issue. It favored certain economic policies, such as higher wages for labor and construction of a transcontinental railroad. It supported a high protective tariff on the basis that if business flourished, so would the worker. Nonetheless, what united the party and made it grow was the belief that slavery must be barred from all territories.

The 1856 Election

In 1856 the Democrats nominated James Buchanan of Pennsylvania for president. Although the Democratic platform advocated popular sovereignty in all the territories, Buchanan himself was "Kansasless." He had been out of the country during the Kansas-Nebraska uproar and so had not offended anyone on the subject. The Republicans turned to a hero from the Mexican War, Colonel John C. Frémont. Millard Fillmore headed the American ticket.

The Democrats won the three-way race, but the Republicans showed they were the party of the

325

future. Buchanan, the only president never to marry, received 45 percent of the popular vote; Frémont, 33 percent; and Fillmore, 22 percent. Almost all of Frémont's votes came from Northern states. Most observers realized that the Know-Nothings would never capture the presidency. But if they voted Republican in the next election, the Republicans might win—and quite possibly without a single vote from the less populous South.

Section 3 Review

COMPREHENSION   Developing Vocabulary

1. Explain these terms: nativism, "NINA" signs.

COMPREHENSION   Mastering Facts

1. What were three reasons for the rise of nativism?
2. How were the Irish often discriminated against?
3. What did the Know-Nothings want to accomplish?
4. What belief united the new Republican party and made it grow?

4 CRISES LEAD TO A SHOWDOWN

From the time sixty-six-year-old "Old Buck" Buchanan became president with John C. Breckinridge as vice-president, a series of events took place which led like a train of powder to a final explosion. The first was a decision of the Supreme Court.

The Dred Scott Decision

The case concerned Dred Scott, a black who was born a slave in Virginia and raised in Missouri. In 1834 Scott's master took him to the free state of Illinois, then to the free Wisconsin Territory, and

Dred Scott lost his fight for freedom in 1857, when the Supreme Court ruled that blacks were not U.S. citizens.

then back to Missouri. In 1843 Scott sued for his freedom on the grounds that freedom went with the land. Since he had lived in a free state and a free territory, he was therefore a free man.

The nine justices of the Supreme Court faced two basic legal questions. Was Scott a citizen of the United States? If not, he could not sue in federal court, and the case would have to be thrown out. Second, did Scott's residence in free territory make him a free man, even though he had returned to a slave state?

The decision was handed down on March 6, 1857. The opinion of Chief Justice Roger B. Taney carried the most weight. Taney declared that blacks had never been regarded as citizens, either before or after adoption of the Constitution. They had been treated, Taney said, as "beings of an inferior order," with "no rights which any white man was bound to respect." National citizenship was for whites only. Two justices disagreed strongly, pointing out that several colonies and states had allowed blacks to vote. But a majority of the Court agreed that Scott had no standing to sue in federal court.

The Court also ruled that being on free territory did not make a slave free. For territories to exclude slavery, Taney said, would be to take away an owner's property "without due process of law." This was a violation of the Fifth Amendment. In effect, the Supreme Court declared the Missouri Compromise unconstitutional. This was the first time since *Marbury* v. *Madison* (1803) that the Court struck down an act of Congress.

The decision in *Scott* v. *Sandford* was one of the most important the Court has ever made. *All* blacks were declared non-citizens of the United States. And slavery could exist in any territory of

326

the United States. The decision wiped out the main plank of the new Republican party. It undercut the idea of popular sovereignty. And, of course, it infuriated the North and delighted the South. What particularly irritated Northerners was the realization that the majority of Supreme Court justices were Southerners. Chief Justice Taney came from a Maryland slaveholding family, although he had freed his own slaves long before. In short, many people believed that the Court had not made an impartial or fair judgment.

Chaos in Kansas

While people were still arguing about the Dred Scott case, events in Kansas again shocked the public. The situation there was becoming less violent but more confused. More settlers had come in from free states than from slave states. Each group tried to set up a legal territorial government. Then each government applied for admission as a state. Men on both sides stuffed the ballot boxes with illegal votes.

President Buchanan sent out several territorial governors to see if they could find a compromise. Because they were unable to do so, Kansas was not admitted to the Union. Northerners thought the South was still trying to grab the territory. Southerners thought Northerners were trying to do the same.

Economic Differences

In 1857 the national economy suffered a depression. Banks and businesses folded, and tens of thousands of people were thrown out of work. The effects of the depression were greater in the North than in the South, because the Southern economy depended on agriculture rather than business and finance. Southern writers and politicians were quick to point this out. They said that the cynical and greedy attitude of Northern merchants and manufacturers was largely responsible for the depression. Northerners snapped back that the only reason the Southern economy was more stable was because it rested on the unspeakable evil of slavery.

The dispute illustrated the enormous economic differences between the North and the South. The latter may have believed its way of life was superior, but at the same time it feared it was being overwhelmed by Northern economic power. Hin-

ton Rowan Helper, a Southerner, wrote a book about the matter called *The Impending Crisis of the South: How to Meet It.* Helper claimed that slavery was actually holding back the economic development of the South. Other Southerners were outraged, but they agreed that Helper did present some facts of Southern life:

       In one way or another we are slaves to the North. As babies, we are wrapped in Northern muslin. In childhood, we have toys made in the North. In maturity we serve as a market for all sorts of Northern industries. In old age, we wear glasses made in the North. When we die, our bodies are draped in Northern sheets. We are taken to the grave in a Northern carriage, buried with a Northern spade. Over us rests a Northern gravestone.

In other words, Helper felt that the South should abandon slavery and become industrialized.

The Lincoln-Douglas Debates

In 1858 Stephen A. Douglas ran for reelection to the United States Senate. Everyone thought that if elected, he would run for president in 1860. But the Republican party hoped it could stop him now. So Republicans in Illinois chose Abraham Lincoln to challenge Douglas. And Lincoln did challenge him to a series of seven open-air debates to be held in various parts of the state. These debates drew wide attention. They concerned the most important issue of the day—slavery's expansion in the territories. The speakers were stimulating because of the dramatic contrast in their words and manner. Also, the speeches were taken down in shorthand by newspaper correspondents who accompanied the candidates. Thus, people everywhere were kept abreast of what the two men said.

How They Looked. Although short and stocky, Douglas was called "the Little Giant" by his admirers. He dressed in the latest fashion, including a colorful vest. He traveled from place to place with a large group of followers in a private railroad car. When he arrived for a debate, he rode at the head of a large parade, complete with blaring band. When he spoke he was all energy and self-confidence. He paced back and forth and used his hands to pound home his points. If one wanted a man who seemed to know everybody and everything, one would choose "the Little Giant."

By contrast, Abraham Lincoln was extremely

Denouncing the extension of slavery, Lincoln attracts widespread attention as Douglas, with hand on hip, waits to defend the idea of popular sovereignty.

tall and thin. He seemed even taller because of his stove-pipe hat, in which he kept his notes and other odd pieces of paper. He appeared plain and even awkward as he stood solemnly addressing crowds. His clothes were far from fashionable and were usually rumpled. He often slept in them because he traveled in a regular railway car. When speaking, Lincoln talked in direct and plain language.

Lincoln was born in Kentucky but moved first to Indiana and then later to Illinois. By age twenty he had reached his full height of six feet four inches. He enjoyed wrestling and other feats of strength. But he also showed qualities that were not common to most frontier youths. Despite little formal education, he was very well read. All his life, his language reflected the Bible and Shakespeare. He was a great storyteller. Most of his stories were frontier tales and jokes which probably would not seem funny today. But at the time they appealed to people in frontier Illinois.

Lincoln had a successful career as a lawyer and state politician. He took all kinds of cases, including arguing both for and against the return of fugitive slaves. He did legal work for a large railroad corporation. As a state legislator and a one-term congressman, he voted, like other Whigs, in favor of internal improvements. As a young and middle-aged man, Lincoln went through long periods of depression. He was, in the term of the day, a "melancholy" man. But there was something attractive about him. He always spoke straight out, without beating around the bush. He was clearly a man one could trust. It was no accident that he earned the nickname "Honest Abe."

What They Said. In their speeches, Lincoln and Douglas kept their arguments consistent. Douglas believed deeply in popular sovereignty. Lincoln believed just as strongly that Congress could and should keep slavery out of the territories. This was the main issue. Neither man wanted slavery in the territories. But they disagreed as to how to keep it out.

In the course of the debates, each candidate tried to distort the views of the other. Lincoln tried to make Douglas look like a defender of slavery and of the Dred Scott decision. Neither charge was true. In turn, Douglas tried to show that Lincoln was an abolitionist. And that charge was not true. Lincoln said, "I am not, nor ever have been, in favor of bringing about in any way the social and political equality of the white and black races." But he insisted that slavery was a moral, social, and political wrong, and hoped it would eventually disappear where it existed in the South. He confessed he had no idea how or when it would happen. But he stressed again and again that the moral wrong of slavery should not be allowed to spread.

Douglas had a difficult time defending popular sovereignty. At first he thought the concept would prove popular in Illinois and throughout the nation. After all, he was saying, "Let the people decide." What position could be more acceptable to American voters?

But Lincoln discovered a major weakness in Douglas's argument. At Freeport, Lincoln asked his opponent a crucial question: Could the settlers of a territory vote to exclude slavery before the territory became a state? Everyone knew the Dred Scott decision said no.

Douglas's Freeport Doctrine. Douglas immediately retorted with an answer that became known as the Freeport Doctrine. Slavery could not exist without laws to support it—laws dealing with runaways, the sale of slaves, and the like. If the people of a territory refused to pass such laws, Douglas said, slavery could not exist in practice, no matter what the Supreme Court said about the theory of the matter.

Douglas convinced many Illinois voters who simply wanted to keep slavery out of the territories. He won the senatorial election. But his Freeport Doctrine cost him most of his support in the South. Many Southerners had considered the Dred Scott decision a major victory. Now they heard Douglas saying that settlers could easily get around it.

Although Lincoln lost the election, he was now more than just another ambitious state politician. Suddenly, many Republicans saw him as a possible candidate for the presidency. Lincoln knew this and was not displeased.

John Brown Strikes Again

John Brown disappeared for several years after his murders at Pottawatomie Creek in Kansas. When he surfaced again in 1859, his name became a household word overnight.

Brown had studied the slave uprisings in ancient Rome and on the French island of Haiti. He decided the time had come for something similar in the United States. He obtained secret financial backing from several prominent Boston abolitionists. On October 16, 1859, with only seventeen free blacks and white men, Brown attacked the federal arsenal at Harpers Ferry on the Virginia side of the Potomac River. He and his followers hoped that such an act would encourage the blacks of Virginia to revolt. Brown captured some arms and took several slaveholders hostage, together with several slaves. Then he and his men dug in and waited for news of a general slave rebellion.

But no revolt took place. Instead, Virginia militiamen and federal troops from Washington, under the command of Colonel Robert E. Lee, raced to Harpers Ferry and surrounded the arsenal. The raiders found themselves pinned down by rifle fire. Dangerfield Newby, a free black man, was the first to die. His widow and children were still slaves in Virginia. Brown held out for two days but then, with more than half his men dead, he surrendered.

Horace Pippin, a black American artist, painted this scene of John Brown on his way to be hanged.

The episode shocked the nation. What followed did nothing to heal the new sectional wound. Brown was placed on trial for his life and was found guilty. Throughout the trial he insisted calmly that his cause had been just. Some men began to call him a martyr for the sacred cause of freedom. On December 2, 1859, Brown was hanged in the presence of federal troops and a crowd of curious observers. As he walked straight and proud to the gallows, Brown predicted, "The crimes of this guilty land will never be purged away; but with Blood."

The entire episode aroused fierce emotions in both sections of the country. For months, little incidents continued to inflame both sides. In the South, outraged mobs assaulted whites who were suspected of being antislavery. The wife of the governor of Massachusetts wrote to the wife of Virginia's governor asking if she could come south and nurse Brown's wounds while he was in jail. She got back a stinging letter of refusal. A North Carolina man, who said he was a long-time supporter of the Union, wrote angrily, "I am willing to take the chances of . . . disunion, sooner than submit any longer to Northern insolence and Northern outrage."

Lincoln Elected President

The presidential election of 1860 was a four-way race. The parties, their platforms, and their candidates were as follows:

1. Southern Democrats took the position set forth in the Dred Scott decision; namely, that the federal government was obligated to protect slavery in the territories. They nominated Vice President Breckinridge of Kentucky.

2. Northern Democrats lined up behind Stephen A. Douglas, declaring that the best way to decide the slavery question in the territories was by popular sovereignty.

3. The remnants of the Whig and American parties formed the Constitutional Union party,

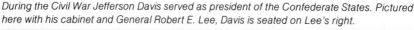
During the Civil War Jefferson Davis served as president of the Confederate States. Pictured here with his cabinet and General Robert E. Lee, Davis is seated on Lee's right.

Presidential Election of 1860

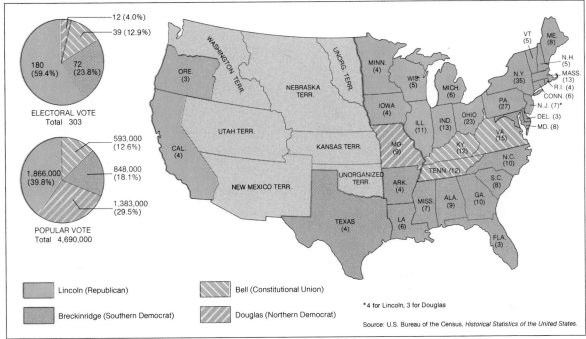

ELECTORAL VOTE
Total 303

180 (59.4%)
72 (23.8%)
39 (12.9%)
12 (4.0%)

POPULAR VOTE
Total 4,690,000

1,866,000 (39.8%)
848,000 (18.1%)
1,383,000 (29.5%)
593,000 (12.6%)

Lincoln (Republican)
Breckinridge (Southern Democrat)
Bell (Constitutional Union)
Douglas (Northern Democrat)

* 4 for Lincoln, 3 for Douglas

Source: U.S. Bureau of the Census, *Historical Statistics of the United States.*

© ML & Co.

Map Skills   *The electoral votes were split by four candidates. How many did Lincoln get? Was that a majority? Which state did Douglas win? Who won the states of the Deep South?*

which did not say much except that it supported "the Constitution, the Union, and the laws." Its candidate was John Bell of Tennessee.

4. The Republican party ran Abraham Lincoln on a platform opposing the extension of slavery into the territories.

Lincoln won with only 40 percent of the popular vote but 59 percent of the electoral vote, all from the Northern states. Lincoln's election was a clear signal to the South that their way of life was in grave danger.

Six weeks later, South Carolina seceded from the Union. It was soon followed by six other states in the Lower South: Alabama, Florida, Georgia, Louisiana, Mississippi, and Texas. These were the states where slavery was well established and very profitable. White people in the Lower South knew that slavery was essential to their way of life. They were ready to leave the Union in order to defend it.

Forming the Confederacy.   In February 1861 representatives of the secessionist states met in Montgomery, Alabama. There they formed a new confederation of states, the Confederate States of America. The new government's constitution re-

sembled that of the United States except for two clauses. Each state in the Confederacy was to be "sovereign and independent." And people were guaranteed the right to own slaves. Ex-Senator Jefferson Davis of Mississippi was chosen president of the Confederacy. Shortly after, Confederate soldiers began occupying federal post offices, courthouses, customshouses, arsenals, and forts throughout the Lower South.

What Happens Now?   During the early months of 1861, the weather was milder than usual in much of the nation. But a dark thundercloud hung over the American people and their elected officials. Seven slave states had seceded and formed a new nation. Eight slave states remained within the Union. Would they secede also? What was to be done?

People were more confused than angry. In the White House, President Buchanan tried his best to keep the Union together. When one of his cabinet ministers resigned to return to Georgia, the president replaced him with a supporter of the Union. But Buchanan's lack of firmness was obvious. He announced that secession was illegal but

331

that it would also be illegal for him to do anything about it. In effect, he tied his own hands. But even if he hadn't been so timid, there was not much he could do.

Washington was really a Southern city. There were secessionists in Congress, and in all the departments of the federal government, as well as in the president's cabinet. There were mass resignations. To some people, it seemed as if the federal government were melting away.

There was no great ground swell of opinion to give an indication of what the public thought. The North had heard threats of secession so often that when it finally happened, the news was received calmly. Horace Greeley may have expressed the feelings of many people when he wrote to the Southern states: "Wayward sisters, depart in peace."

The president-elect sat quietly in Springfield, Illinois. He could do nothing until he was inaugurated in March. He said little publicly. But he wrote privately that he would not agree to any "compromise in regard to the extension of slavery."

As he watched and waited in Illinois, Lincoln took time to answer a letter from an eleven-year-old girl in upstate New York. She had written him before the election, asking why he didn't let his whiskers grow. "All the ladies like whiskers and they would tease their husbands to vote for you and then you would be President. My father is going to vote for you and if I were a man I would vote for you, too." Lincoln replied that people would think him "silly . . . if I were to begin it now."

And then he grew a beard.

Section 4 Review

COMPREHENSION Developing Vocabulary

1. Explain these terms: Freeport Doctrine, impartial, Confederacy.

COMPREHENSION Mastering Facts

1. What did the Dred Scott decision say?
2. How did people throughout the country learn about the Lincoln-Douglas debates?
3. What did John Brown hope to achieve by attacking the arsenal at Harpers Ferry?
4. What was the immediate cause of secession?

CHAPTER 15 Review

Chapter Summary

The issue of slavery refused to die. After the Kansas-Nebraska Act (1854) permitted popular sovereignty concerning slavery in the territories, Kansas became a battleground. Tensions also increased as migration patterns gave rise to strong nativist sentiment, and new political parties developed. During the 1850s, growing economic and political differences between the North and South set the stage for the final break. The split became a reality in late 1860 when Southern states began to secede after the election of President Abraham Lincoln.

Questions for Critical Thinking

COMPREHENSION   Summarizing Main Ideas

1. How did each of the following events increase hostility between the South and the North? (a) the Fugitive Slave Law of 1850; (b) *Uncle Tom's Cabin*; (c) the Kansas-Nebraska Act; (d) the attack by Congressman Preston S. Brooks against Senator Charles Sumner; (e) the Dred Scott decision; (f) the depression of 1857; (g) John Brown's raid at Harpers Ferry.
2. What effect did competition for jobs have on the rise of the Know-Nothing movement?
3. What was the main difference between Stephen Douglas and Abraham Lincoln regarding the issue of slavery?

COMPREHENSION   Interpreting Events

1. Why did popular sovereignty fail to decide the issue of slavery in the territories?
2. Why was Kansas known during the 1850s as "bleeding Kansas"?
3. How did the election of 1856 indicate that the Republicans were the party of the future?
4. Why did Hinton Rowan Helper believe Southerners were slaves to the North? What did he want the South to do? Do you agree or disagree with his recommendations? Give reasons for your opinion.

5. Why did the Republican party in Illinois run Abraham Lincoln for senator in 1858?
6. Why did Lincoln's election in 1860 lead to the secession of seven states?
7. How did the constitution of the Confederacy differ from that of the United States?

APPLICATION   Using Skills To Recognize Similarities

1. Are there any groups in the United States today that favor restricting immigration? If so, what arguments do they use?
2. Which of the parties that ran candidates in the 1860 election still exist today?

EVALUATION   Forming Generalizations

Write a generalization for each of the following groups of statements.

Group 1
   a. The Fugitive Slave Law of 1850 permitted slave owners to recover their slaves who had run away to free states.
   b. A federal jury convicted a group of men in Ohio for rescuing a slave from a slave catcher.
   c. Many Northern states passed laws forbidding state officials to cooperate with federal officials who were returning fugitive slaves to the South.

Group 2
   a. Proslavery settlers began moving into Kansas from Missouri.
   b. The New England Emigrant Aid Company was organized to help Free-Soilers migrate to Kansas.
   c. More settlers from free states than from slave states moved into Kansas.

Group 3
   a. Southern Democrats believed the federal government was obligated to protect slavery in the territories.
   b. Northern Democrats believed popular sovereignty was the best way to decide the issue of slavery in the territories.
   c. Republicans opposed the extension of slavery into the territories.

Public Opinion

Everyone has opinions. They are judgments people make about individuals and events around them. Opinions are based on certain beliefs that each person has acquired about the world. Often these beliefs are not consistent with facts, but they are still thought of as facts.

Our view of the world is learned gradually from birth. Families shape our earliest attitudes and beliefs. Then, as we acquire more knowledge about the world—from books, teachers, friends, television, and so on—experience modifies our attitudes and beliefs. Since each person has unique experiences, each person's view of the world is likewise unique. That is why ten witnesses to the same event will each describe it in a different way.

Forming Opinions. How accurate is anyone's view of the world? Actually, what people believe to be true may not correspond to reality at all. Ponce de León went searching for the fountain of youth because he believed the tales he heard. Convinced he had reached the Far East, Columbus never considered that he had bumped into a new continent.

The perspective of time enables people to see when others in the past have acted with false notions of reality. However,

many people today also think and act without the benefit of correct information. In a democracy, factual knowledge and an informed public are crucial. *Public opinion* involves the process of open or public debate over important issues.

People often form opinions based on what they read, see, or hear. "All I know is what I read in the papers," humorist Will Rogers once joked. Indeed, newspapers, magazines, television, and radio provide vital sources of information that influence the formation of public opinion. Even two hundred years ago, publications such as *The Federalist Papers* and Thomas Paine's *Common Sense* did much then to shape public opinion. The right of free expression plays a key role in permitting the public to receive ideas and form opinions about various issues.

Emotion and Propaganda. Unfortunately, the right of free expression sometimes becomes confused with extreme propaganda efforts or emotional agitation. When facts and critical thinking skills are ignored, a responsible debate over issues does not take place. Some critics believe that this was the case during the 1850s. They argue that extremists such as Charles Sumner and Preston Brooks (see

page 323) created a climate in which compromise was impossible. In the end, public opinion concerning the Union and slavery became bitterly divided between North and South.

Special interest groups also play a role in shaping public opinion. Public opinion lobbying, as it is called today, seeks to convince the majority of voters of the merit of a particular view. In the mid-1800s, the abolitionists were an example of a group which attempted to shape people's ideas—in this case, to change their view of slavery. A century later, during the 1950s and 1960s, civil rights organizations such as the NAACP and the Urban League joined forces to end segregation. They used massive demonstrations, sit-ins, and peace marches to mobilize a sympathetic public and win its support of equal rights.

Influence of Government. The government itself has an influence on public opinion, for the most important opinion-shaper in our nation is the president. The president is the nation's leading spokesperson. As the representative of all the people, the chief executive is in a unique position to influence, persuade, and lead the public.

Although the opportunity to lead is unparalleled, however, not every president has a clear sense of direction on every issue. After reading public opinion polls during 1941, President Franklin D. Roosevelt wavered between detachment and involvement for the United States in World War II. "The president," concluded one of his advisers, "would rather follow public opinion than lead it."

Still, virtually all politicians do pay attention to public opinion. In order to create majorities and stay in office, elected officials must know what voters think. Of course, the most important public opinion poll of all is an election.

Surveying Public Opinion. Since the 1930s, public opinion polling has also become a popular method for finding out how citizens feel about social issues. The news media regularly conduct polls on a wide variety of social, economic, and political issues. Reporting the public pulse has become an accepted practice, and many pollsters have become quite successful at measuring public opinion. By interviewing people who have just voted, for example, pollsters are often able to accurately project the winner of an election long before the voting itself has ended.

Many of the most popular politicians, however, are not those who measure public opinion. Instead, they are able to accurately sense what is impor-

Pollsters measure public opinion on a wide variety of important issues.

tant to their constituents. Other politicians capitalize on changes in public opinion before the changes are well-defined. For instance, in 1980 President Reagan took advantage of a conservative shift in the mood of the nation—a shift that was not evident until just before the election itself.

Forming educated opinions is important for citizens in a democracy, but it is not easy— even though Americans today have much better access to information than ever before. Prejudices and stereotypes often get in the way of reason. Other opinions sometimes scream loudly for attention, and conflicting claims can cloud or confuse understanding. Our opinions will have greater validity if we learn to distinguish truth from fiction, reason logically, and reflect critically on our own unique experiences.

Understanding Government

1. What is public opinion? Why is it important in a democracy?

2. Why is the president able to have such a strong influence on public opinion?

3. Do you believe that legislators should vote on issues according to public opinion or according to their own beliefs? Explain.

4. What sources do you use to gain information about local, national, and world events? Which sources do you trust the most? the least? Do you believe that you are strongly influenced by public opinion polls and surveys? Explain.

CHAPTER 16

The Civil War

1861–1865

People in the Chapter

Ulysses Simpson Grant—*the veteran commander of the Union armies who finally succeeds in defeating the Confederacy.*

Robert Edward Lee—*the commander in chief of the Confederate armies whose military genius prolongs the war but cannot avoid the final surrender at Appomattox.*

William Tecumseh Sherman—*the Northern general who proves his remark "war is hell" by marching his forces through Georgia to the sea, burning and wrecking everything in his path.*

Dorothea Dix—*former teacher at a girls' school in Massachusetts who serves through the Civil War as the superintendent of women nurses.*

Linking Past to Present

The Civil War was a gigantic struggle which lasted for four years. It was also the first modern war. For the first time, machine guns, railway guns, and electrically exploding torpedoes were used. The first recorded sinking of a ship by a submarine took place in the Civil War. Many of the inventions of modern science—such as ironclad ships—were used as weapons of destruction. It was also a total war—that is, the battlefields were often in the towns, the cities, and the farms of the South. Everyone was involved. As one historian noted, it seemed that after every battle, frantic parents rushed around the battlefields in horse and carriage looking for lost children. When families fled in confusion before the oncoming troops, children were often left because one family member thought another was taking care of the baby. The fighting killed more people than any other war in the world between 1815 and 1914 except for one war in China. One white person died for every six slaves who became free.

The results of the Civil War were unexpected. The South was wrecked and impoverished. The Union was "saved" but the relationship between the federal government and the states was greatly changed. Slavery came to an end but the freed slaves were not, as you will read, truly free. Finally, despite slaughter and destruction, the United States came out of this great war a more powerful nation than ever before.

1 BLOODSHED

VOCABULARY *Copperheads* *border states*

When Lincoln took his oath of office on March 4, 1861, seven states of the Lower South had seceded. Within a few months, four more left the Union. Another four looked as if they might secede, too. Still, many Americans thought there would be a way to avoid actual war. Indeed, probably a majority of Americans opposed the idea of war. Yet within six weeks, fighting broke out between the North and the South.

Fort Sumter Leads to War

As you know, soon after the Confederacy was formed, it began taking over federal offices and forts. By the time Lincoln was inaugurated, only four forts remained in Union hands. The most important of these stood at the mouth of the harbor of Charleston, South Carolina. Fort Sumter was built of heavy brick, but it was in easy range of cannons on the nearby shore. The Confederates wanted to take that fort because it was a symbol of Federal power. Over it flew the Stars and Stripes rather than the Confederate flag, the Stars and Bars. Lincoln was equally determined to keep the fort. But he did not want to shed first blood.

Major Robert Anderson, who commanded the fort, sent Lincoln word that he could not hold it for more than six weeks unless he received reinforcements and supplies. Lincoln announced that he would send no fresh troops to Fort Sumter since that would look like an attack on the Confederacy. But he did order supplies sent to the troops already there.

Now the burden lay with the Confederates. If the fort remained in Federal hands, their new government would appear weak. But if they attacked peaceful ships carrying food and medical supplies, they would be guilty of firing the first shot.

In the early morning dark of April 12, 1861, cannons began firing. The Union supply fleet stood off at a distance, helpless against the shore-based cannons. The walls of the fort began to crumble. After 34 hours, Major Anderson surrendered. He and his men were allowed to sail back north on one of the supply ships. The Stars and Bars flew over Fort Sumter. Miraculously, no one was killed in the heavy shelling.

This print by Currier and Ives dramatizes the firing on Fort Sumter, opening salvo of the Civil War.

The Union Splits 1861

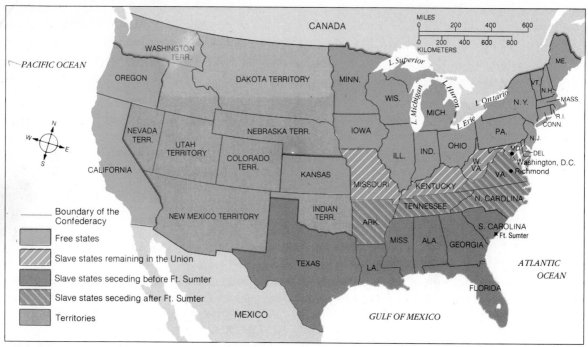

Map Skills *Which were the free states? Which states seceded from the Union? Which slave states did not? Where in the Confederacy were the states that seceded after Ft. Sumter?*

The incident electrified the North. Until then, there had been a considerable difference of opinion as to whether or not the Federal government should oppose secession. Many Northerners felt that the Southern states had entered the Union peacefully and therefore had the right to withdraw peacefully. Abolitionists such as Garrison were actually pleased by secession. They did not want slave states in the Union, and they figured that in a South cut off from the industrial North, slavery would wither away. So-called "Copperheads," or Northern Democrats, asked "Why fight?" To them, a war was a needless sacrifice. Northerners should concentrate instead on turning the United States into a world-wide industrial power.

But the news from Fort Sumter united most Northerners. As Senator Douglas himself said, "Every man must be for the United States or against it. There can be no neutrals in this war—only patriots and traitors."

Other Southern States Secede. On April 15, President Lincoln issued a proclamation calling for volunteers to fight in the Union army. Two days later, Virginia seceded on the ground that the call for volunteers was an act of war. Virginia was followed by Arkansas, North Carolina, and Tennessee. The western part of Virginia had few slaves and little sympathy with the Confederacy. With some military help from the Federal government, the area seceded from Virginia and applied for admission to the Union. West Virginia became a separate state, the thirty-fifth, on June 20, 1863.

The Border States. The big question at this time was: what would the border states do? They were Maryland, Missouri, Kentucky, and Delaware. And they were all slave states.

Delaware had few slaves and remained loyal to the Union. Maryland had many more. In fact, on the way to his inauguration in Washington, Lincoln had to go through Baltimore in disguise because he thought he might be killed by Southern sympathizers. During this time a Massachusetts regiment on its way to the capital was mobbed in Baltimore. Troops and civilians were killed. Yet despite all this pro-Southern opinion, Maryland remained within the Union. The state of Kentucky was also divided. Kentuckians fought on both sides during the Civil War but the state government remained under the control of Unionists.

In the fourth border state, Missouri, fighting between the Confederate and Union forces went on for nearly two years. But in the end, Missouri remained within the Union too.

The North Against the South

Now that war had broken out, what advantages and disadvantages did each side have?

The Northern Position. The Union had a great advantage in terms of sheer numbers. Its overall population was 22 million, compared to the South's 9 million. More important, the North had almost three times as many men of fighting age, about 4 million to 1.5 million. The Confederacy could have had more, but it refused to arm any of its 3 million blacks, although they were used to build fortifications. In a short war, this advantage did not mean a great deal, since it is not possible to organize and arm millions of men overnight. But in a long war, the Northern armies could afford to suffer huge numbers of casualties. The Confederate armies could not.

The North had an even greater advantage in manufacturing and food production. The free states produced four-fifths of the nation's industrial goods. They also produced two-thirds of the nation's food. The North produced far more grain than the South. Indeed, after a while, the plantations and farms of the South were forced to switch from cotton to food just in order to feed the people of the Confederacy. In addition, the North contained two-thirds of the country's railroad mileage. It could transport men and supplies much faster and in greater numbers than the South.

Civilian leadership in the North proved to be very effective. Lincoln himself was a patient, yet decisive administrator. He appointed the most capable Republicans he could find to his cabinet. Among others, he made Salmon Chase his secretary of the treasury and William H. Seward his secretary of state. A little later he appointed, as secretary of war, Edwin M. Stanton. Lincoln also removed known secessionists from the bureaucracy and replaced them with individuals who favored the Union.

The Southern Position. The South also had certain advantages, especially in the early years of the struggle. In order to exist as a new nation, the Confederacy had merely to defend its own soil. In contrast, Northern armies had to attack, capture, and occupy territory far from their home bases. On the whole, Confederate troops had better leadership in the field than Northern troops did. And Southerners were more accustomed than Northerners to handling guns and horses.

The South also had "King Cotton," on which the English textile industry relied. Southern leaders were convinced that England would be forced to recognize and assist the new Confederate nation. At the very least, the South could make up for its lack of industry by selling cotton abroad and using the money to buy guns and other needed manufactured goods. As you will see, however, Southern hopes about the power of cotton came to nothing. But at the outset, Southern leaders were convinced that cotton would prove a powerful weapon against the North.

One of the South's weaknesses was its civilian leadership. Jefferson Davis was president of the Confederacy throughout the war. Davis looked and acted like a Southern aristocrat. He had gone to West Point and served in the Mexican War, but most historians consider him a poor military strategist.

Even a man of far greater skills, however, would have had difficulties. Perhaps the worst problem was that the Southern states had seceded in the name of states' rights. Davis's associates never let him forget that fact. They claimed that he was taking too much power for the central Confederate government. His vice-president, Alexander H. Stephens, spent most of the war at home in Georgia, criticizing the president for becoming a dictator. The governors of North Carolina and Georgia refused cooperation while they talked about the sovereign rights of individual states. In addition, Judah P. Benjamin, whom many historians considered the ablest member of Davis's cabinet, was repeatedly attacked in the Confederate press as "the hated Jew" whenever he pointed out the Confederacy's economic and political problems.

Surprise at Bull Run

When Virginia seceded, the capital of the Confederacy was transferred from Montgomery to Richmond, Virginia. Thus the capitals of the two

Peninsula Campaign 1861-1862

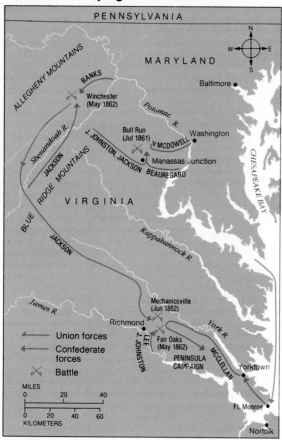

Map Skills *Were the battles shown fought on Union or Confederate Land? When was the battle of Bull Run?*

those terms were nearly up. The newspapers and politicians of Washington were calling "On to Richmond." So Lincoln sent some 30,000 inexperienced young soldiers on the road south toward the Confederate capital.

At the little creek of Bull Run, the Northern soldiers confronted an equally inexperienced Confederate army. The civilian population was equally unacquainted with the realities of war. In Washington, ladies and gentlemen put on their best clothes and mounted their carriages and horses. With picnic baskets and iced champagne they rode out to observe the battle!

At first the Federal forces had the upper hand. But in the middle of the day more Virginia troops arrived under the command of Thomas J. Jackson. Their strong stand turned the tide and gave Jackson a permanent nickname, "Stonewall."

As often happens with untrained and inexperienced soldiers, the Northern army's retreat became a rout. The men streamed back to Washington, jamming the roads along with the carriages of the civilian "observers." For days the city of Washington expected invasion. But the Southern troops were also disorganized and exhausted, and they failed to seize this opportunity·

Section 1 Review

COMPREHENSION   Developing Vocabulary

1.   Explain these terms: Copperheads, border states.

COMPREHENSION   Mastering Facts

1.   What event united most Northerners in the war against the South?
2.   What advantages did the North have?
3.   What advantages did the South have?
4.   What city became the symbol of the Confederacy?

nations were only one hundred miles apart. Richmond became the symbol of the Southern rebellion. If Richmond fell, the Confederacy would fail.

Like most people, Lincoln expected a short war. His first call for volunteers had provided for only three-month terms of enlistment. By July 1861,

2   THE REAL WAR BEGINS

VOCABULARY   *ironclads   blockade-running*

The Battle of Bull Run shocked people on both sides of the Potomac. For the first time they began to realize what was happening. They were at war in earnest. This was not a skirmish, and it was not going to be over by Christmas. Time was needed for training and equipping real armies. The victory at Bull Run gave the people of the Confederacy a great boost in morale. But Northerners grew grim and determined.

Machinery of Modern War

At first both sides in the great conflict relied on volunteers for their armies. When the two governments first called for volunteers, more men signed up than could be used effectively. Each of the states raised its own regiments. At first the various regiments did not wear the same colors. It was only in the later years of the war that Confederate soldiers wore grey and the Federal forces blue.

New Guns. At first troops on both sides were armed with old-fashioned muskets. These were not much more efficient than the ones used in the American Revolution. They had smooth bores, or interior cylinders, and hardly reached more than 100 yards. This meant that until troops came within a hundred yards of the enemy, nothing much happened. Once they were within range, however, victory usually depended on numbers, especially if the attackers used fixed bayonets.

Within a year, however, soldiers on both sides were using breech-loading rifles. "Breechloaded" meant that the powder and ball went into the gun at the near end of the barrel, not the muzzle at the far end. And the guns no longer had smooth bores but rifled ones. This means the guns had spiral grooves which made the bullet turn round on itself. In the same way that a "spiral" football pass is more accurate than a wobbly one, a rifled or spiralled bullet was much more accurate and went farther than a non–rifled one from the older muskets.

Using the new type of gun had several results. First, it made fighting much more impersonal. In the past, soldiers saw their opponents as recognizable human beings. Now, as historian Bruce Catton put it, the enemy "was simply a line of snake-tail fence or a grove of trees or a raw length of heaped-up earth, from which came clouds of powder smoke and a storm of bullets."

Second, cavalry lost its importance. It could no longer be used successfully to attack infantry or artillery. Instead, it was used mostly for scouting and to screen an army's movements.

Third, frontal infantry charges were no longer effective. They only resulted in extremely heavy casualties. This made tactics more important than ever before.

Better Warships. Other technological changes took place on naval vessels. Now most warships were driven by steam rather than sail. The newer steamboats had screw propellers rather than paddle wheels, and they were much faster. And in the early years of the war, both sides began to build "ironclads," wooden ships with ironplate armor.

One such ironclad was the Federal ship *Monitor*. This ship was the first to have a revolving gun turret. The South had previously captured another Federal ironclad called the *Merrimac*, but had changed its name to the *Virginia*. The two ships engaged in battle in 1862 off the coast of Virginia.

A detail of H. O. Tanner's painting recreates the historic naval engagement between the Monitor *and the* Merrimac *(renamed the* Virginia *by the Confederacy). Both were ironclad ships.*

It was the first naval battle in history between ironclads. The result was a draw but the *Virginia* had to withdraw to Norfolk for repairs.

Neither ship won a decisive victory. Still, the new ironclads made it clear that the days of all-wood naval ships were over.

Early Battles

After Bull Run, Lincoln decided that he needed a new commander for the Army of the Potomac. He chose thirty-five-year-old George McClellan, who, like most generals on both sides, was a veteran of the Mexican War. But McClellan refused to move until he had organized his army and drilled his troops for months on end.

As the fall of 1861 turned into the winter of 1862, Northerners grew increasingly impatient with "Tardy George" McClellan. Finally, even Lincoln remarked that he would "borrow McClellan's army if the general himself was not going to use it."

The Battle of Shiloh. The eastern campaign to take Richmond was only one part of a three-pronged Union strategy. The second part was a western campaign to drive Confederate troops from the Mississippi River valley and split the Confederacy in two. So, while McClellan polished and repolished his army, the western front was where full-scale fighting began.

In February 1862, a Union army invaded western Tennessee. It was led by a veteran U.S. Army officer named Ulysses Simpson Grant. Grant usu-

ally ended up wearing a wrinkled uniform; generally his appearance did not create a strong impression. Despite these characteristics, while McClellan sat, Grant moved. With the help of gunboats, he captured two major Confederate forts, Fort Henry on the Tennessee River and Fort Donelson on the Cumberland River. The latter exploit gained him a nickname. When the Confederate commander asked for surrender terms, Grant replied, "No terms except unconditional and immediate surrender can be accepted." From then on, Grant was known as "Unconditional Surrender" Grant.

As Grant's army drove south toward Mississippi, it paused for the night near a crossroads called Shiloh. Early the next morning the Union troops were surprised by an all-out Confederate assault. Many of the Federals were shot while making coffee; some died while they were still lying in their blankets. The charges and countercharges went on all day. Woods and meadows became filled with corpses and the bodies of thousands of wounded men. By nightfall, Union forces were on the edge of disaster. Then more Federal troops arrived. Grant reorganized his men and artillery, and the next day he drove the Confederates from the field.

The Battle of Shiloh taught both sides several lessons. First, generals began thinking more about sending out scouts, communicating with divisional commanders, digging trenches, and building fortifications. In short, they began to think more defensively. Second, people gave up any hope of an easy victory. More than 13,000 Union soldiers were dead or wounded, while the Confederates suffered more than 10,000 casualties. The appalling slaugh-

The McCormick Harvesting Machine Company of Chicago commissioned this painting of the Battle of Shiloh. The Union army paid a heavy price in casualties for its victory.

ter made people realize that war was not all bravery and glory. It could kill men in numbers that no one had imagined.

Although the Battle of Shiloh seemed to be a draw, it was actually decisive. The Confederates needed to win in order to maintain their Ohio-Kentucky frontier. Their failure to win meant that they would not be able to hold the Mississippi valley and that one part of the three-way Union strategy would succeed.

A Naval Blockade. Along with an eastern campaign and a western campaign, Union strategy called for a blockade of the Confederate coast in order to cut its commercial lifeline with Europe. Union ships took up positions outside each major Southern seaport. They succeeded in keeping regular ocean-going vessels from entering or leaving the harbors. But they were unable to prevent blockade-running. Small, low boats would dash in under cover of darkness with a cargo of weapons or luxury goods, and dash out again with a load of cotton. However, as the war progressed, fewer and fewer blockade-runners were able to get through. And in any event, they could not carry enough cargo to make up for the regular trade which the blockade had cut off.

The Federal government combined the blockade with direct attacks on Southern ports. The most significant took place in the spring of 1862. A Union naval force, commanded by David Farragut, steamed forty miles up the Mississippi from the Gulf of Mexico and captured New Orleans. By May it had advanced upriver and taken Baton Rouge. With Grant moving south, the Confederate States were now dangerously close to being split in two. Southern forces controlled only one section of the Mississippi, between Vicksburg in the north and Port Hudson near Baton Rouge in the south. If Union troops and sailors could close that gap, they would cut off Texas, Louisiana, and Arkansas from the rest of the Confederacy. But it took them another year to do it.

The Peninsula Campaign. McClellan's army finally got under way a few days before Shiloh. After successfully occupying Yorktown, it advanced at a snail's pace up the peninsula between the York and James rivers toward Richmond. McClellan was terribly cautious and kept asking for reinforcements. Lincoln, however, refused to send them because of a brilliant maneuver by General

War in the West   1862–1863

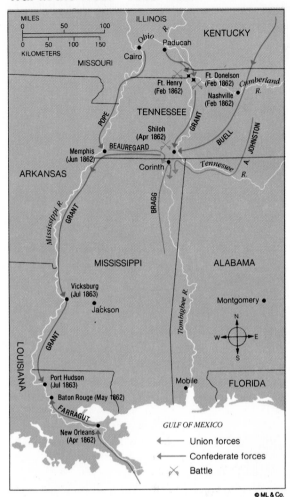

Map Skills   *What three states came together near the battle of Shiloh? When did Grant capture Port Hudson?*

Stonewall Jackson. The Confederates swept through the Shenandoah valley and threatened an attack directly on Washington. But then Jackson's troops pulled away to help defend Richmond against McClellan's slow-moving army.

During the month of June 1862, one battle followed another outside of Richmond. The two armies were fairly evenly matched in numbers. But McClellan was clearly out-generaled by a new Confederate commander named Robert E. Lee.

In many ways Lee was the opposite of McClellan. He was bold and imaginative, and he directed many of the most brilliant military movements of the war. A quiet, modest, but forceful man, Lee won more respect from Northerners than any other Confederate leader. He was also greatly

343

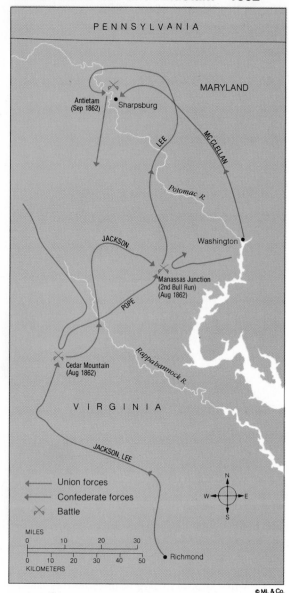

Map Skills *Who led the Union and Confederate forces at Antietam? Near what river was the battle?*

won a clear victory at Manassas Junction, also called the second battle of Bull Run. (For some reason Northerners usually identified battles by rivers and streams; Southerners named them after nearby towns.) Union forces were now no nearer Richmond than they had been at the beginning of the war. A desperate President called on McClellan to head the Army of the Potomac once again.

Antietam. Following this victory, the South shifted from a defensive strategy to an offensive one. Lee boldly decided to push his forces into enemy territory. McClellan at first pursued him northwest of Washington with his usual caution. Then he had a stroke of luck. Some Union soldiers found a copy of Lee's secret army orders being used as a wrapping for a bunch of cigars. Months earlier Lincoln had complained that McClellan had "the slows." But now McClellan grew bolder because he knew something of Lee's plans. He caught up with Lee just north of the Maryland border.

A major and crucial battle took place near the village of Sharpsburg on Antietam creek. Federal forces outnumbered Lee's army, 70,000 to 40,000. When night fell on September 17, more than 22,000 men lay dead or wounded on that bloody ground. The casualties were about even on both sides, but McClellan had far more fresh troops at his command. A bolder general would have ordered an all-out attack at dawn. Instead, McClellan did nothing. Lee's troops watched and waited for the entire day. That evening the battered army began limping back toward Virginia. Many dead and wounded had to be left behind. McClellan had "won" the Battle of Antietam, but he had let a really decisive victory slip through his fingers. This time, Lincoln fired him permanently.

Section 2 Review

COMPREHENSION Developing Vocabulary

1. Explain these terms: ironclads, blockade-running, breechloaded.

COMPREHENSION Mastering Facts

1. What changes in warfare resulted from the use of guns with rifled bores?
2. What was the significance of the battle between the *Monitor* and the *Virginia*?
3. What were the three parts of the Northern military strategy?
4. Why was the Battle of Shiloh decisive?

loved by his fellow officers and soldiers. Lee had freed his slaves some years earlier, and had been informally offered command of the Union armies by Lincoln. But he had decided to go with Virginia.

At the beginning of July, after a series of defeats and one draw, Lincoln pulled the Army of the Potomac out of the peninsula and back to Washington. While he did not officially remove McClellan, he gave effective command of the army to General John Pope. Lee, however, went on the attack. On the last two days of August, Lee's troops

THE GOALS OF WAR CHANGE

VOCABULARY   *Radicals*   *conscription*

Although Antietam's military effect was limited, its political effect was tremendous. After Antietam, England and France decided to postpone recognizing the Confederacy. Also, Antietam persuaded Lincoln to issue his Emancipation Proclamation. He told his cabinet that he had made a promise to God. If the rebels were driven out of Maryland, he would free the slaves. Antietam had cleared the rebels from Maryland.

England Remains Neutral

In the fall of 1861, England had almost slipped into war against the North. The captain of a United States warship had stopped a British merchantman, the *Trent*, on its way home from Havana, and had seized two Confederate diplomats, James M. Mason and John Slidell, who were traveling to Europe. This was a clear violation of neutral rights. The British cabinet drafted an angry protest and sent 8000 troops to Canada. The United States, not wanting to fight against two foes at the same time, finally released the diplomats. It also sent England a note congratulating it on accepting the principle of freedom of the seas over which the War of 1812 had been fought.

Another grave problem arose between the United States and Britain over Confederate warships built in Britain. The *Alabama*, the *Florida* and the *Shenandoah* were three such ships. They left Britain in 1862 and began destroying Union merchant ships. The *Alabama* alone sank more than sixty before it was itself sunk in 1864 by the U.S.S. *Kearsage*. The United States warned Britain that such construction was an act of war. Britain thereupon ceased building ships for the South.

After the war the United States presented a bill, called the *Alabama* claims, to Britain for $419 million. This was to pay for the damage done to the Union cause during the Civil War by the *Alabama* and similar ships. Britain and the United States agreed to submit the bill to arbitration. (In 1871 both sides presented their case to an international jury in Geneva, Switzerland. The tribunal declared in 1872 that an award of $15 million should be made by Britain to the United States. This was the first time that such a tricky matter of national honor was settled by the majority vote of an international jury.)

Although Britain ceased building warships for the South during the Civil War, its neutrality was still in doubt. Public opinion in England was divided on the question of whether or not to recognize the Confederate States. Many leading Englishmen were pleased that their former colonies had been unable to maintain their unity. On the other hand, most English people disliked slavery.

In addition, cotton did not turn out to be nearly as important as the South had hoped. The cotton crop of 1860 was enormous. Since English merchants knew a crisis was coming, they bought it up. So when the war began, British mills had a good supply on hand. They also found alternate sources of cotton in Egypt and India.

Furthermore, an industrialized England depended heavily on imports of grain to feed its workers. And much of this grain came from Northern farms. To Britain, the fear of losing its breadbasket was stronger than the fear of losing one of its sources of cotton. As one Northern magazine put it, "Old King Cotton's dead and buried; brave young Corn is King." There was, therefore, no economic reason to aid the Confederacy. But soon an event occurred that insured British neutrality.

Slavery Becomes the Main Issue

At the beginning of the Civil War, neither side declared slavery to be the central issue. It was, but neither side was willing to admit it. Lincoln and most Republicans insisted that the Federal government had no power over slavery in the states where it already existed. Southerners agreed.

As the war dragged on into its second year, however, this opinion began to change, especially in the North. Some Republicans became known as *Radicals*. Radical means one who favors great or extreme changes. Radicals believed that abolition was in fact the main reason for the war. These Radicals insisted that Lincoln should free the slaves and they passed several laws in Congress to this effect. But Lincoln did not think the laws were constitutional. So he did not enforce them. He believed that the purpose of the war was to save the Union—and nothing else. He doubted that most Northerners would fight for the freedom of blacks.

Three developments caused Lincoln to change

his mind. First, the bloody fighting made many Northerners want to hurt the South as much as possible. Abolishing slavery would help do that. Second, slavery helped the Southern war effort. Slaves helped to build military fortifications and they produced food. Third, slavery was a crucial issue on the Union's diplomatic front with England. Britain's leaders would not support a war to keep the United States together. But English public opinion would back a war against slavery.

Lincoln realized that he could use emancipation as a weapon of war. He could also satisfy his own personal hope that everyone everywhere would eventually be free.

The Emancipation Proclamation

In June 1862, Congress passed a law prohibiting slavery in the territories. On January 1, 1863, Lincoln issued the final form of his Emancipation Proclamation. No slaves became free immediately because it applied only to areas behind Confederate military lines. It did not apply to the slave states that had remained loyal to the Union, nor did it apply to Confederate territories already occupied by Union forces. Critics commented that it applied only in areas where Lincoln did not have the power to enforce it.

Yet the Proclamation had a powerful symbolic effect. It broadened the base of the war and turned it into a fight for freedom as well as union.

It gave the Northern cause the weight of a moral crusade.

White Southerners were of course deeply angered. They realized that if they lost the war they would lose their entire way of life. In England, the Emancipation Proclamation had just the effect that Lincoln hoped for. Now that the Union was clearly fighting against slavery, British public opinion supported the Union's cause.

The Emancipation Proclamation also encouraged the recruitment of black soldiers in the Union Army. Two of the first and most famous units were the Fifty-fourth and Fifty-fifth Regiments of Massachusetts Volunteers. All told, nearly 300,000 blacks served in the Union army. They were not always well treated, and until 1864 were paid only half as much as white soldiers. But they proved their bravery and skill in numerous battles.

Drafting Begins

At first both sides relied on volunteers for their armies. But by 1863 both the North and the South were forced to pass *conscription*, or draft, acts. Although individual states had used the draft in the past, this was the first time it was applied by a central government.

The Confederacy led off in 1862 with a law calling up all able-bodied white men between eighteen and thirty-five (later extended to seventeen

These soldiers of the Fifty-fourth Massachusetts Regiment fought bravely but served without pay for a year to protest the fact that they were not paid as much as white Northern soldiers.

and fifty.) Few Southerners were actually drafted, however. They considered it shameful, and preferred to volunteer instead.

However, several provisions of the draft created considerable resentment. Men in certain industries were exempt, and many persons could not see why teachers and mailmen did not have to serve. A man could hire a substitute to go in his place, and the price rose to $10,000 in Confederate money, which most Southern whites could not afford. Still another provision aroused even more bad feeling. It said that for every twenty slaves on a plantation, one white man—the planter, his sons, or his overseer—would be exempt from the draft. The provision was included because of fears of slave uprisings. But it led to widespread grumbling about "a rich man's war and a poor man's fight."

The Union adopted the draft in 1863, calling up men between twenty and forty-five. Here, too, draftees were allowed to hire substitutes to go in their place. In addition, many Northern states offered bounties, or cash payments, to volunteers. The practice led to considerable abuse, for a man could enlist, take his bounty, desert his regiment, and do the same thing all over again. Patriotic Northerners resented this "bounty jumping."

Feelings in the North against the draft led to several riots, especially in New York City. The city was filled with working poor, who could not afford to pay the going rate of $300 to a draft substitute.

In addition, many of them—especially the newly arrived Irish, who made up one-third of the city's voters—were competing with free blacks for jobs. In 1863 blacks were used to break up a dockworkers' strike for higher wages and better working conditions. That did it for the Irish workers. It wasn't bad enough, they complained, that the blacks were the cause of the war. Now they were taking bread out of their children's mouths! The resulting riot lasted for four days. The houses of antislavery leaders were attacked. Shops and taverns were looted. A black orphan asylum was burned, and blacks of draft age were tortured and lynched. In all, more than 100 persons were killed and hundreds were injured. Priests and the police (also mainly Irish) did their best. But it was not until troops were poured into the city that order was restored.

Section 3 Review

COMPREHENSION   Developing Vocabulary

1. Explain these terms: Radicals, conscription, bounty jumping.

COMPREHENSION   Mastering Facts

1. What was the *Trent* Affair?
2. To whom did the Emancipation Proclamation apply?
3. How did some Southerners escape the draft? How did some Northerners escape it?
4. Why did Irish workers in New York City riot in 1863?

4 LIFE GOES ON BEHIND THE LINES

VOCABULARY   *greenbacks   Homestead Act*

The Civil War changed the lives of Americans, both in the South and in the North. On both sides, the war brought grief to hundreds of thousands of families. Grief could arrive in many ways. It came with news that sons and fathers were dead, either on the field of battle or from disease in camp. It came with a man limping up the steps on crutches, with one leg of his trousers empty. It came with no news at all. Sometimes the soldier just did not come back—ever.

Life in the South

The Confederate government seemed more harmful than helpful. Early on, it passed a tax on farm products. Then it began to print paper

money to finance the war. It printed so many Confederate dollars that they began to fall in value.

Even with high prices, many goods were impossible to get. There were no linens, shoes, or clothing. People wrote letters on the back of wallpaper because there was no stationery. Meat was served once a week at the most. In 1863 the food shortage in Richmond became so severe that a huge mob of men and women staged a bread riot in front of the government buildings. The mob broke up only when President Davis climbed up on an overturned wagon and promised the rioters that he would distribute food from government warehouses to those in need.

At the same time, a small group of people, mostly blockade-runners, gunmakers, and contractors who provided food and supplies to the army, grew rich. As one historian described them, they "dined on caviar, lobsters, oysters, roast beef, sugar ham, roast fowl, and thick steaks, while the children of soldiers went to bed whimpering with hunger."

For blacks in the South, the first few years of the war made little difference in their lives. The only significant change was that many of the men were pulled out of the cotton fields and put to work building fortifications and repairing roads. But as Union troops conquered more and more Southern territory, thousands of blacks ran away from their masters and joined the Yankees. Since there was no official policy about escaped slaves, each military commander did what he thought best. A few returned the runaways. But most protected them, and the blacks reciprocated by working for Union forces as teamsters, cooks, laundresses, and guides.

Life in the North

In the North there was a wartime boom. Immigration increased, because wartime industries created a large demand for workers. Agriculture flourished. The government was buying all kinds of equipment for the armed forces. Some businessmen profited so much that they laid the groundwork for famous millionaire fortunes. You will read more about such men later on.

To help pay for the war, Congress passed the first income tax in United States history. It levied a 5 percent tax on incomes between $600 and $5000 and a 10 percent tax on incomes above $5000. The Federal government also issued some $450 million worth of "greenbacks" or paper money. However, the government refused to redeem the greenbacks with gold, so the value of the currency went up and down depending on the latest news from the warfront.

Congress also passed several important laws to aid both business and agriculture. Before the war, Southern representatives had opposed a high tariff. Now Congress passed the Morrill Act of 1861 which raised the average import duty on manufactured goods to 25 percent. By 1864 the rates reached an all-time high of 47 percent. This protected American manufacturers from European competition. Next, Congress voted to build a transcontinental railroad over a north-central route, and supported the proposal with vast grants

of public lands and large government loans. Third, in 1863 and 1864, Congress adopted a new banking system. It did away with state banks and set up a system of national banks. This gave the United States a new currency, the national banknote, which was uniform throughout the country. Fourth, Congress passed the Homestead Act in 1862. It gave 160 acres of public land free to any citizen or intending citizen (which, until the Fourteenth Amendment was passed in 1868, excluded blacks). All a citizen had to do was occupy and cultivate the land and pay registration fees ranging from $26 to $34. Fifth, the Morrill Land Grant Act of 1862 gave land to states and territories for the support of colleges that would teach agricultural and mechanical skills.

Taken together, these laws showed an important new trend. Now it was clear that the national government could and would give aid to agriculture and business. These acts also showed that the government was becoming much more actively involved in the nation's economy than ever before.

Women and the War Effort

The Civil War brought great changes in the lives of millions of American women. On both sides, they were left to run plantations and farms on their own. And some American women were doing completely new jobs, ones they had never dealt with before.

Factory and Office Work. Women found work in wartime factories, especially in the North. Since sewing was a traditional task for women at home, many women took sewing jobs in factories making uniforms for the army. They were paid very low wages—from seventeen to twenty-four cents for a fifteen hour day—and they were always supervised by men. The long hours and low pay were so clearly unfair that some women organized to protest them. Their organizations had little success, but they won a good deal of sympathy. In New York, middle-class women organized a Protective Union to provide women workers with free legal services for settling grievances, and also to serve as an employment agency.

For the first time women found jobs working for the government. Both the Union and the Confederate governments grew during the war. Most of the "government girls" worked as clerks and copyists. (In those days, all letters and documents

Sarah Edmonds, a Union spy, disguised herself as a man and fought in the Battle of Bull Run.

had to be copied by hand, for there were no typewriters or copying machines.) Indeed, the Civil War was the first time that large numbers of women did office work of any kind.

Dorothea Dix and Nursing. The Civil War opened one other major area of work for women. Fighting on the battlefields resulted in a great need for nurses to care for the wounded. Many women on both sides volunteered their services. The Union government appointed Dorothea Dix as superintendent of nurses. Dix was well aware of the doubts that many Americans had about women in army hospitals. Would they "distract" the men? Did a proper woman belong in a tentful of men, even if many of them were groaning and screaming? And could women themselves stand the awful smells of sweat, blood, and gangrene? Dix met some of these doubts by requiring that government nurses be over age thirty and "plain in appearance." In fact, the women fulfilled their duties with great skill and efficiency.

The Prison Camps

The large numbers of men involved in the Civil War had an unexpected result other than high casualty figures. That was the large numbers of prisoners that were taken by both sides and the miserable conditions under which they were kept.

Probably the worst prisoner-of-war camp was the Confederate Military Prison near Andersonville, Georgia. One historian described it as "a pesthole of a place, a ghastly, stinking sore which blighted the ground on which it stood. . . . Union prisoners were . . . reduced to living like animals. They ate scraps of food, wore rags, and were surrounded by filth, vermin, disease and death." More than 12,000 of them died. Part of the problem was the fact that the South was short of food and so was unable to feed its captives much. Part of the problem was the brutality of Captain Henry Wirz, the camp commander. After Andersonville was captured by Union forces in 1864, the Yankees hanged him as a war criminal.

Northern prisoner-of-war camps—such as those at Elmira, New York, and Camp Douglas, Illinois—were not much better. There was more food but little or no heat. Unused to cold winters, hundreds of Confederate soldiers contracted pneumonia and failed to recover. Other hundreds died from dysentery and malnutrition.

Section 4 Review

COMPREHENSION   Developing Vocabulary

1. Explain these terms: greenbacks, Homestead Act, Morrill Land Grant Act.

COMPREHENSION   Mastering Facts

1. How did the war affect blacks in the South?
2. How did Congress help pay for the war?
3. Who were "government girls" and what did they do?
4. What were conditions like in prisoner-of-war camps?

5   THE ROUGH ROAD TO PEACE

The year 1863 saw the tide turn toward a clear-cut Union victory. The superior power of the North gradually wore the South down. But the cost in human life was terrible. Northern newspapers began calling the Union's most successful general, "Grant, the butcher."

The Tide Turns at Gettysburg

In the first battles after Antietam, Confederate forces came off very well. Lincoln, still searching for a general who would bring him victories, chose Ambrose E. Burnside to command the Army of

349

The Road to Gettysburg   1862–1863

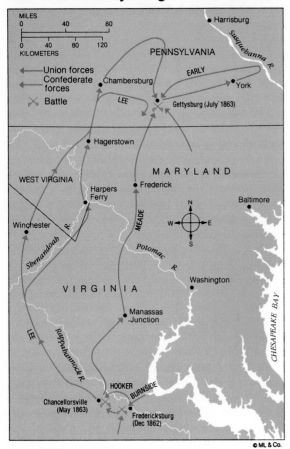

Map Skills   *How might the war have been affected if Union forces had lost the battle of Gettysburg?*

the Potomac. Burnside had a good military record. He also had bushy sidewhiskers which were called "Burnsides" and have since become known as "sideburns." But he had doubts about his own abilities and accepted command reluctantly. Unfortunately his doubts were justified. On December 13, 1862, at Fredericksburg, Virginia, he ordered an all-out attack on Confederate troops who were well dug in on several hills. The result was a bloody defeat for the Union forces, some 13,000 casualties to the Confederacy's 5300. Lincoln replaced Burnside with General Joseph "Fighting Joe" Hooker.

Victory at Chancellorsville. Hooker almost lost the Army of the Potomac. At Chancellorsville, Lee pulled a daring maneuver. He split his army and sent Stonewall Jackson with 30,000 men to attack Hooker from the side. Hooker was totally surprised. The battle began at six o'clock in the evening. If it had started earlier in the day, Lee might

have captured the entire Union army. As it was, the next dawn found the Union forces better organized. Since they outnumbered the Confederates two to one, they were able to avoid complete defeat and to withdraw northwards.

The Confederate victory at Chancellorsville was a costly one. Lee lost 12,000 troops. And Stonewall Jackson was hit by a bullet from one of his own men when he returned from patrol in the darkness. A surgeon amputated his left arm in an effort to save his life, and Lee sent him a message: "You have lost only your left arm while I have lost my right." Eight days later, Jackson was dead.

A saddened Lee decided to press his advantage. If he could invade the free states, perhaps the Union would come to terms. Also, he had another reason for wanting to invade the North. In the West, Grant's army was threatening to take Vicksburg and finally cut the Confederacy in two. Perhaps invading the North would cause Grant to pull back.

On June 15, 1863, Lee's army marched off, and a larger force of Union troops moved directly north so as to keep themselves between Lee and the city of Washington. A discouraged President Lincoln replaced Hooker with General George Meade. But it soon became clear that Lee was not aiming at the capital. His army crossed Maryland into southern Pennsylvania.

The two armies met each other more or less by accident. Near the village of Gettysburg some Confederate soldiers, many of whom were barefoot, were out searching for shoes and boots. They stumbled onto a Union patrol and the minor shooting attracted more troops from both sides. Meade drew up his army just south of the village. Each end of the Union line was anchored on a hilltop. The center ran along a ridge since named Cemetery Ridge. Lee's infantry and artillery occupied Seminary Ridge, about a mile to the west. In between the armies lay an open field. The stage was set for a fight to the finish.

Slaughter at Gettysburg. The two armies battled each other for two days. On the second day the morning air thundered with the heaviest artillery fire of the entire war. Wave after wave of Confederate soldiers bravely charged across the field and up the slope of Cemetery Ridge. On July 3 General George Pickett led a massive charge at the center of the Union lines. For a moment, Confederate troops broke through. But by this time they had lost so many men that they could not hold the ridge. Pickett's charge had failed. For the first time, Lee had clearly been defeated.

Lincoln telegraphed Meade, "Call no council of war. . . . Do not let the enemy escape." But Meade hesitated. He called his officers together, and the guns were silent throughout the Fourth of July. The next day, Lee's battered army moved southward in the pouring rain. No Federal troops followed them. The Union had won, but as Lincoln said later, "Our army held the war in the hollow of its hand and would not close it."

That same Fourth of July, Grant's army finally captured Vicksburg. Port Hudson fell to Union forces shortly afterwards. The strategy of cutting the Confederacy in two had finally worked.

The field at Gettysburg remained carpeted with bodies. Even veterans of other battles were shocked by the slaughter. One experienced Union officer described those awful days:

" We see the poor fellows hobbling back from the crest, or unable to do so, pale and weak, lying on the ground with the mangled stump of an arm or leg, dripping their life-blood away; or with a cheek torn open, or a shoulder mashed. And many, alas! hear not the roar as they stretch upon the ground with upturned faces and open eyes. "

For some a trip to the field hospital proved to be fatal. Soldiers in the camps sickened and died simply because the camps of large numbers of men spread disease very fast. Many died from simple wounds, such as a musketball in the elbow. Surgeons knew nothing of germs. So they did not sterilize their knives and saws but simply cleaned them. In the Civil War more men died from wounds and sickness than on the battlefield.

The Gettysburg Address

There were so many bodies at Gettysburg that they remained unburied for months. Buzzards circled overhead and then dropped down to feed. The smell was so overpowering that no one wanted to go near the place. Northern newspapers raised a cry about this scandal, and the Union government decided to erect a national cemetery on the scene. At the dedication ceremonies in autumn, Edward Everett of Massachusetts gave the major speech. He was famous as a public speaker, nearly as eloquent as Daniel Webster had been. Everett spoke for two hours. The President spoke also—for about two minutes. Today no one remembers what Everett said. But many people are familiar with Lincoln's eloquent words.

" Four score and seven years ago our fathers brought forth on this continent a new nation, conceived in liberty, and dedicated to the proposition that all men are created equal.

Now we are engaged in a great civil war, testing whether that nation, or any nation so conceived and so dedicated, can long endure. We are met on a great battlefield of that war. We have come to dedicate a portion of that field as a final resting place for those who here gave their lives that that nation might live. It is altogether fitting and proper that we should do this.

But, in a larger sense, we cannot dedicate—we cannot consecrate—we cannot hallow—this ground. The brave men, living and dead, who struggled here, have consecrated it far above our poor power to add or detract. The world will little note nor long remember what we say here, but it can never forget what they did here. It is for us, the living, rather, to be dedicated here to the unfinished work which they who fought here have thus far so nobly advanced. It is rather for us to be here dedicated to the great task remaining before us—that from these honored dead we take increased devotion to that cause for which they gave the last full measure of devotion; that we here highly resolve that these dead shall not have died in vain; that this nation, under God, shall have a new birth of freedom; and that government of the people, by the people, for the people, shall not perish from the earth. "

Grant Heads the Armies

Lincoln finally found a general who would fight. In March 1864 he named Ulysses S. Grant, the hero of Vicksburg, as general in chief of all the Union armies. Grant adopted a simple yet costly strategy. He appointed William Tecumseh Sherman to command the Union army in Tennessee. Sherman's army was to fight its way from Tennessee through Georgia to the Atlantic coast and then move north through the Carolinas. In the meantime, Grant's Army of the Potomac would keep Lee's forces pinned down in Virginia.

Wearing Them Down. Grant believed in pushing ahead at all costs. "When in doubt, fight." His main purpose was not necessarily to take Richmond but rather to grind up Lee's forces. The North's manpower pool was several times the size of the South's. Grant figured that even if his casualties were twice as large as Lee's, the Union side would still come out ahead.

So Grant ordered his men into one battle after

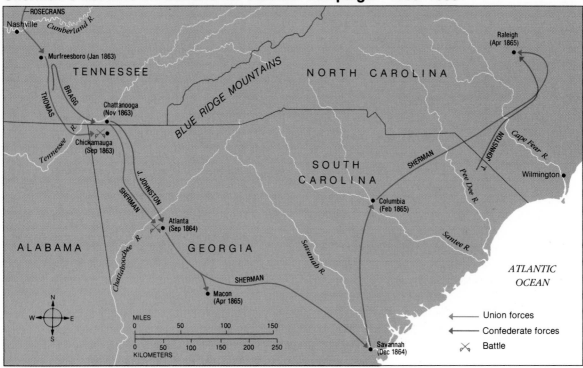

Sherman's March to the Sea and the Carolina Campaign   1863–1865

Map Skills *Who led the Union forces marching from Nashville to Murfreesboro? How far was Sherman's march from Chattanooga to Savannah? When did Sherman take Raleigh?*

another in central Virginia—the Wilderness, Spotsylvania, Cold Harbor, Yellow Tavern, and Petersburg. In one month, his army suffered 60,000 casualties, and Lee's army half that number. But the Federals were able to replace their losses, while the Confederates were not. Grant was slowly but steadily wearing Lee down, not by superior tactics or better fighting, but by sheer brute strength. The Union armies drove south through Tennessee toward Georgia. In January 1863 Murfreesboro fell and, despite a Southern victory at Chickamauga in September, Chattanooga was in Union hands by the end of the year.

Sherman's March to the Sea. Sherman had lived in the South for several years, and when war broke out, the Confederacy offered him a high military post. Just the opposite of Lee, Sherman decided to support the Union. He believed the best way to end the horrors of war was to defeat the other side as quickly as possible.

In September his troops captured Atlanta. They then set off on a famous "march to the sea," which he reached at Savannah. Sherman was not a cruel man, but he wanted to crush Confederate

morale. Announcing that "war is hell," he deliberately led his troops on a path of destruction. He aimed to destroy the countryside and strike at the civilian population. His troops burned houses and barns. They destroyed food and killed livestock. They terrorized the people, even though there was not much actual killing of civilians. "To realize what war is," Sherman said, "one should follow in our tracks."

Sherman's invasion of the Lower South marked a turning point in the history of modern warfare. This was because Sherman's march illustrated a shift in the belief that only military targets should be destroyed. Now civilian centers of population were fair game also.

Lincoln Reelected

The mounting death toll deepened Lincoln's natural sadness. He had not been back to Springfield since becoming president. Even then, in 1861, he had wondered whether he would ever see home again. The tragedies of the war had deeply lined his face. He began to dream about his own death.

352

The fall of 1864 brought an election campaign. Lincoln faced a great deal of opposition. Many Northerners were unhappy with the way the war was going, and especially with the high casualty figures. So the Democrats, who had made gains in the congressional elections of 1862, nominated George McClellan on a platform of a negotiated peace. On the other side, Radical Republicans opposed Lincoln's renomination because of his plans for handling the rebel states when they were finally defeated. Lincoln favored readmitting them into the Union as soon as 10 percent of the voters in each state took an oath of loyalty to the United States. Radical Republicans wanted a majority of the voters in each state to take the oath. The Radical Republicans also wanted the Southern states to free their slaves before being readmitted.

Lincoln's backers decided to drop the name Republican in order to win some Democratic votes. They called themselves the National Union party in order to emphasize their major purpose of saving the Union. And they chose a Unionist Democrat from Tennessee as Lincoln's running mate. His name was Andrew Johnson.

Lincoln was reelected because of Union victories. First, Admiral Farragut captured Mobile, Alabama. Then General Sherman telegraphed "Atlanta is ours." Finally, General Philip Sheridan swept the Confederates out of the Shenandoah valley. Public opinion in the North shifted in Lincoln's favor and he won the election with 55 percent of the popular vote.

Lee Surrenders

On April 2, 1865, as the Virginia countryside burst into bloom, the smoking city of Richmond finally fell to Union troops. The badly outnumbered Confederate army retreated west. On April 7, Lee sent a message to Grant. Two days later, the generals met at a farmhouse near Appomattox Court House. Lee was dressed in his best uniform, with a silk sash tied around his waist, and wearing a sword. Grant, whose baggage had been lost, wore his usual rumpled and mud-spattered uniform. He had no sword. Soldiers of both armies stood close by. They were so tired that they stood in uneven lines. Grant was not a man of words. He had orders from the president. "Let them have their horses to plow with, and, if you like, their guns to shoot crows with. I want no one punished." Lee himself hinted that the horses would be welcome. He was too proud to ask directly. The two generals looked each other in the eye and shook hands. For those two men, the great war ended in mutual respect.

Lincoln Assassinated

Five days later, Abraham Lincoln did something unusual. He went to the theater to see a play, *Our American Cousin*. He had not relaxed for a long time. He sat with Mrs. Lincoln in a special box which nearly hung over the stage. No one saw the man creep up behind him. When the pis-

Artist H. G. Ferris suffused his painting of Lee's surrender to Grant with humanity and gentleness.

A tragic moment in American history is captured: Abraham Lincoln is assassinated at Ford's Theater.

The Road to Appomattox   1864–1865

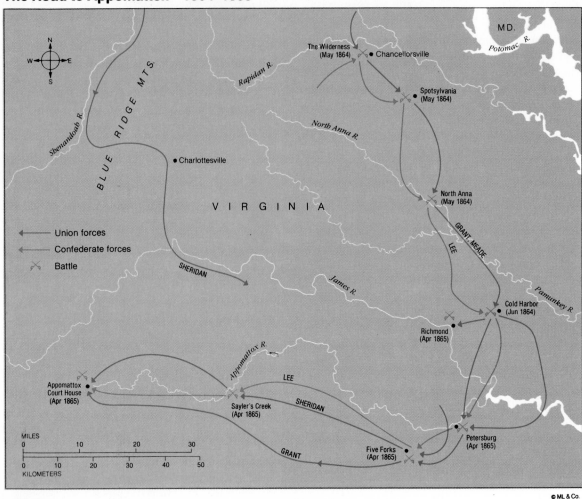

Map Skills   *Grant pursued Lee from the battle of the Wilderness to the surrender at Appomattox. How many months did it take? How far was Appomattox from Richmond? In what direction?*

tol shot rang out, Lincoln fell forward with a bullet in his head. But he was not dead. The man jumped down onto the stage, breaking his leg, but then managed to escape. John Wilkes Booth was an actor, a Southern sympathizer, and perhaps slightly mad. He was later caught and shot. Several others were convicted of a conspiracy to assassinate the President and were hanged.

There was difficulty in moving the tall, unconscious president to a hotel room across the street. Finally he lay stretched out on the hotel bed, surrounded by a dozen worried people. The sun rose over the Potomac and the capital city. He still breathed a little. The sun turned from red to yellow. He still breathed. And then he stopped.

Section 5 Review

COMPREHENSION   Developing Vocabulary

1. Explain these terms: National Union Party, Pickett's charge.

COMPREHENSION   Mastering Facts

1. In what battle were Lee's forces decisively defeated?
2. Why did so many men die even though their wounds were not fatal?
3. What were the two parts of Grant's battle philosophy?
4. What helped Lincoln win reelection?

CHAPTER 16   Review

Chapter Summary

The Civil War began when Confederate guns fired on Fort Sumter in April, 1861. Four border slave states decided to remain in the Union. Northern advantages included more industry, railroads, soldiers, and military supplies. Still, the Confederacy was defending its own territory, and it had superior military leadership. During the early years of the war, Southern forces won a number of victories. Then in 1863 Abraham Lincoln issued the Emancipation Proclamation. That same year the Battle of Gettysburg proved to be a turning point. The costly war ended when Lee surrendered to Grant on April 9, 1865. The nation suffered another tragedy five days later, however, when President Lincoln was assassinated.

Questions for Critical Thinking

COMPREHENSION   Summarizing Main Ideas

1. Give three reasons why England decided to remain neutral in the Civil War.
2. What changes did the Civil War bring about in the roles of women?
3. In the Gettysburg Address, what did Lincoln say the Civil War was testing? To what task did he call the American people? What democratic ideals were expressed in the speech?

COMPREHENSION   Interpreting Events

1. Before the firing on Fort Sumter, why did many Northerners believe the national government should not oppose secession?
2. Why was Lincoln against emancipating the slaves at the start of the Civil War? What caused him to change his mind?
3. Why did many Southerners oppose the draft? Why did many Northerners oppose it?
4. Why did the Confederacy print large quantities of paper money? What was the result?
5. Why did agriculture and industry in the North boom during the war? Why didn't the same thing happen in the South?

6. Do you agree or disagree with General William Sherman's concept of total war? Give reasons for your opinion.
7. What do you consider to be the most important result of the Civil War? Justify your opinion.

APPLICATION   Using Skills To Infer Information

Drawing inferences from data is another important skill in critical thinking. Reread the first paragraph under "A Naval Blockade." Then indicate whether you can infer that the statements below are true or false, or whether the paragraph does not contain sufficient information for you to infer anything.

1. There were three parts to the Union's military strategy.
2. The South's navy was weak.
3. The Union navy was stronger than that of the South.
4. The Southern economy depended heavily on foreign trade.
5. The South did not produce all the industrial goods it needed.
6. Southern naval commanders were skillful sailors.
7. The coast of the South contains many small natural harbors.
8. Southerners were willing to pay more for luxury goods than for necessities.
9. Many blockade-runners became rich.
10. The Union blockade was a success.

EVALUATION   Comparing Past to Present

1. Are there any reminders of the Civil War in your community (statues, street names, forts, and the like)? If so, make a list of them and the reasons why you think they are in your community.
2. Were any of your ancestors involved in the Civil War either as soldiers or civilians? If so, find out what you can about them and prepare a report on what you have heard of their experiences.

Geography and Civil War Strategy

Even today—despite the development of devastating modern weapons—geography plays an important role in military strategy. In the past, geography was even more important to such strategy. Consider the influence of geography on both sides during the Civil War. Since virtually all Civil War battles were fought on Southern land, the geography of the South was crucial to military planning for both Union and Confederate forces.

From the beginning of the Civil War, the two sides operated with different goals. To restore the Union, the North had to invade and defeat the South. The South, on the other hand, did not seek Northern territory. Its goal was to defend itself until the North was tired of fighting and chose to withdraw. Thus, it was evident from the start that Southern geography would greatly influence the outcome of the war.

Divide and Conquer. Several geographical features influenced Northern strategy. The Ap-palachian Mountains, for example, divided the South. This meant that the North would have to fight a war on two fronts, one in the west and one in the east. So, this natural mountain division helped determine Union strategy.

Southern rivers also played a key role in Northern strategy. Rivers formed an excellent transportation system in the South, particularly the Mississippi, Tennessee, and Cumberland Rivers. Therefore, controlling these rivers became an important Union goal. When General Grant captured Vicksburg, the divide and conquer strategy began to succeed.

Blockading the Coastline. Likewise, another geographical feature—the enormous length of the South's coastline—meant that the Civil War would also be a naval conflict. Because the Southern states had so many Atlantic ports, they could easily import war supplies. Therefore, the Union navy blockaded the entire Southern coastline.

The maps on these two pages present views of three different geographic regions of the South during the Civil War. Study each one, and then answer the following questions concerning geography and military strategy.

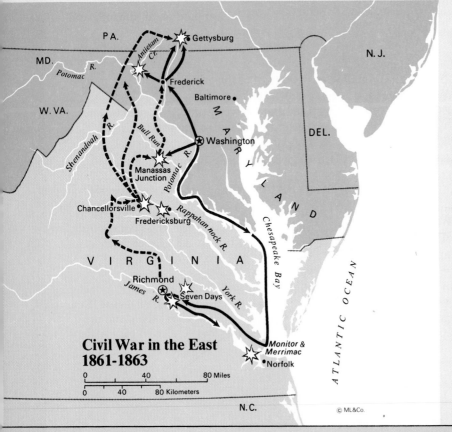

Civil War in the East 1861–1863

0   40   80 Miles

0   40   80 Kilometers

Understanding Geography

1. Why was the South's geography more important to military strategy than the North's geography?

2. In which state did the most fighting take place?

3. What major southern ports did the Union attempt to seal off with a blockade?

4. Use the key of the map on page 356 to estimate how far it is from Washington, D.C., to Richmond. Which rivers separated the two capitals? Which battles took place near the capitals?

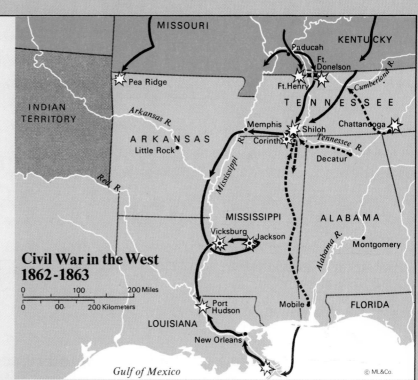

Civil War in the West 1862-1863

0 ____ 100 ____ 200 Miles
0 ____ 00. ____ 200 Kilometers

© ML&Co.

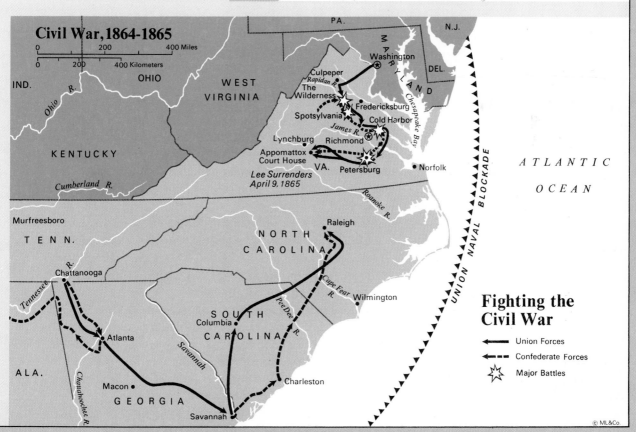

Civil War, 1864-1865

0 ____ 200 ____ 400 Miles
0 ____ 200 ____ 400 Kilometers

Lee Surrenders April 9, 1865

UNION NAVAL BLOCKADE

Fighting the Civil War

⟵ Union Forces
⟵⟵ Confederate Forces
✶ Major Battles

© ML&Co.

Reconstruction and Its Effects

1865–1876

People in the Chapter

Andrew Johnson—*becomes president at Lincoln's death and fights to preserve the power of the president from Radicals, whose attacks on him include impeachment.*

Thaddeus Stevens—*one of the Radical Reconstructionists who hates slavery and wants to punish all who had tolerated it.*

Senator Hiram Revels—*black Union army chaplain who is elected to the Senate seat that once belonged to Jefferson Davis when he was senator.*

Samuel J. Tilden—*the Democratic candidate who loses the disputed presidential election of 1876 to Republican candidate Rutherford B. Hayes. Tilden won more popular votes and, many historians believe, he won more electoral votes as well.*

Linking Past to Present

Wars often create as many problems as they solve. The Civil War was no exception. To be sure, it put an end to the system of slavery, and it settled the question of whether or not a state could withdraw from the Union. On the other hand, it severely damaged one part of the nation and left a legacy of hatred and racial injustice that has not disappeared. The war lived on in stories handed down from generation to generation. In fact, a former slave was still alive in 1979. Charlie Smith, when he died at the age of 130, was the oldest known person in the United States, and he remembered being sold in New Orleans when he was a child.

The nation's wounds took so long to heal because of what happened during the twelve years after Lincoln's death. This period is called Reconstruction, a time during which the country's leaders were struggling to reconstruct, or rebuild, the nation.

In this effort, the American people entered another tragic period. The South was occupied by Union armies again. Graft and corruption became a way of life in both North and South, and for the first time in history, a United States president was put on trial for "high crimes and misdemeanors." A presidential election was decided by a political deal. Later a pattern of racial segregation was established in the South.

1 THE PRESIDENT VERSUS CONGRESS

VOCABULARY   *amnesty   pocket veto   manifesto   Freedmen's Bureau   black codes*

At war's end there were three main problems. The first was a human one. What were the 4 million newly freed blacks in the South to do? They had no land, no jobs, and few skills outside of farming. How would they feed and clothe themselves? How would they live?

The second problem was political. What was to happen with the Southern states? Were they to be received back into the Union as Lincoln wished, "with malice toward none"? Or were they to be treated as conquered territories that would be occupied and punished, as some Northerners wished?

The third problem was a constitutional one. Who had the right to determine how the Confederate states would be readmitted to the Union?

Was it the president, as head of the executive branch of government, or Congress, the legislative branch?

Lincoln's Proclamation of Amnesty and Reconstruction

Even in the midst of war, Lincoln had wondered how to treat the Confederate states. In general he believed they had never legally seceded. In fact, an important purpose of the war was to prove that secession was not constitutionally possible. Lincoln felt that it was individuals who had rebelled and that the president had the power to pardon individuals.

Mathew Brady, the famous Civil War photographer, recorded this scene of devastation. Much of Richmond, Virginia, was destroyed during the Confederate evacuation of the city.

Lincoln was eager to restore the Union as quickly as possible. So he wanted a reconstruction which would be mild and forgiving. He wanted the South's return to be as easy and painless as possible. In December 1863 he announced his Proclamation of Amnesty and Reconstruction. *Amnesty* means a pardon for crimes against the government. Pardons were granted to all Confederates who would swear allegiance to the Union and promise to obey its law. This did not include high officials of the Confederacy and those accused of crimes against prisoners of war.

A Confederate state could form a state government as soon as 10 percent of those in the 1860 voting lists took an oath to uphold the U.S. Constitution. That state could then send its representatives and senators to Congress.

Lincoln's Reconstruction plan by no means satisfied Congress. Many Northerners, particularly the Radicals, wanted the political power of the slave-owning class destroyed and the Southern blacks given full citizenship. By that, Radicals meant all civil rights, including the right to vote. This does not seem radical or extreme now, but it did at that time.

The Radicals' Plan for Reconstruction

In July 1864 the Radicals in Congress adopted their own blueprint for Reconstruction—the Wade-Davis Bill. It proposed that Congress, not the president, be responsible for Reconstruction. The bill declared that for a state government to be acceptable, a majority—not 10 percent—of those eligible to vote in 1860 would have to take an "ironclad" oath to support the Constitution. In addition they would have to swear that they had never supported the Confederacy in any way. Clearly, if more than half a state's voters had been loyal to the Union, the state would not have seceded in the first place.

Lincoln did not condemn the Radical plan outright. He waited until Congress adjourned, and then he killed the bill with a pocket veto. According to the Constitution, the president may, within ten days of the end of a congressional sitting, use a pocket veto. He simply ignores a bill (puts it in his pocket), and it automatically fails to become law.

The Radical Republicans responded by issuing a manifesto, or proclamation, in which they called Lincoln's pocket veto a "stupid outrage" and declared the authority of Congress supreme. They warned Lincoln to confine himself to his executive duties and to leave Reconstruction up to Congress. The Radicals took the position that the Confederate states actually had seceded. Now they were territories seeking admission to the Union. And it was Congress, not the president, that controlled territorial matters. A serious quarrel was shaping up.

After the fall elections of 1864, Arkansas and Louisiana, acting under Lincoln's plan, sent representatives to Washington. The Radicals barred them from taking their seats. That was early in March 1865. Within a month, the war was over and Abraham Lincoln was dead.

Many historians believe that had Lincoln lived, he might have been able to deal with this difficult situation. But his successor, Vice President Andrew Johnson, a man with many good qualities, lacked the quiet dignity and diplomatic skill of Lincoln.

Johnson Continues Lincoln's Policy

Andrew Johnson was always aware that he had not been elected but had become president by accident. This bothered him a bit at first but not for long. What he could not forget was that he had been a poor boy who had to work his way to the top. He scorned people who had had an easier time. He was a man of strong conviction and great energy. His political ideas were a mixture of Jefferson's and those of an earlier Tennesseean, Andrew Jackson. Like them, he disliked cities and manufacturing, distrusted banks and bondholders, and feared wealth that was not based on land.

White Southerners did not know what to make of this man. They considered him a traitor to his region. The Radicals thought he was one of them. Both were wrong.

Almost at once, Johnson surprised everybody by announcing that he would continue Lincoln's plan of Reconstruction. He declared that any state could be readmitted if it would declare its secession illegal, swear allegiance to the Union, promise not to pay any Confederate debts, and ratify the Thirteenth Amendment, which abolished slavery.

The Southern states quickly took advantage of these easy terms. Within a few months, these states—except for Texas—held constitutional conventions, set up state governments, and elected

The Freedman's Union Industrial School in Richmond (above) was one of many such schools set up in the Reconstruction period to help train former slaves for their new life of freedom.

representatives to Congress. In December 1865, the newly elected Southerners arrived in Washington to take their seats. Fifty-eight of them had previously sat in the Congress of the Confederacy, six had served in its cabinet, and four had fought against the United States as rebel generals. Johnson gave them all pardons, a gesture that shook the Radicals deeply.

Johnson's Vetoes Enrage Republicans

In the last month of the war, President Lincoln established a special bureau to assist former slaves and poor whites in the South. He took this step at the urging of Josephine Griffin, a prominent abolitionist.

The Freedmen's Bureau gave food and clothing to former slaves and needy whites. In all, it set up over forty hospitals, 4000 primary schools, sixty-one industrial institutes, and seventy-four teacher-training establishments. The backbone of the bureau's schools was its women teachers, both black and white. They came from all over the country and worked almost around the clock to meet the former slaves' demand for schooling.

Charlotte Forten, a black teacher from Philadelphia, was one of seventy Northern teachers who went to Georgia to teach. She wrote: "I never before saw children so eager to learn. . . .The older ones, during the summer, work in the fields from early morning until eleven or twelve o'clock and then come to school, after their hard toil in the hot sun, as bright and as anxious to learn as ever." Former slave and educator Booker T. Washington recalled those times: "It was a whole race trying to go to school. Few were too young and none were too old." By 1869 about 600,000 blacks of all ages were in elementary schools.

Life was not always pleasant for the students or the teachers. Sometimes the teachers could not find rooms to rent. Other times they could not get credit at local stores. Whites threw stones at the students as they went to and from school. But neither teachers nor students would give up.

In February 1866, Congress voted to continue and enlarge the Freedmen's Bureau by backing it with more money. One month later, Congress passed the Civil Rights Bill of 1866. This act gave blacks citizenship and forbade states from passing discriminatory laws.

President Johnson stunned everyone when he vetoed both measures. It was the opening gun in his battle with Congress over Reconstruction of the South. Johnson said Congress went far beyond "anything contemplated by the authors of the

Constitution." The Radicals believed Johnson was protecting Southerners who had no intention of giving blacks their full rights. Indeed, there was good reason to think so, because the Southern states had passed some repressive laws.

The Black Codes

Black codes were laws aimed at regulating the economic and social lives of freed slaves. Immediately after the war many blacks, delighted to be free, nevertheless did not know what to do. There were no jobs; the old plantation life was gone. Many of them drifted from place to place around the South seeking work. Others traveled about in the hope of finding relatives from whom they had been separated during slavery days. Seeing this great mass of free black men and women wandering around infuriated Southern whites. So they passed black codes, which put blacks in an inferior position. As one historian said, they were in a "kind of twilight zone between slavery and freedom."

The black codes varied. Generally they all stated that blacks could legally marry, own property, sue in court, and go to school. Thus the codes recognized that blacks had certain rights they did not have before. But at the same time, blacks could not serve on juries, carry weapons, testify against whites, or marry whites. Blacks had to obey a curfew. They needed permits in order to travel. They were not allowed to start their own businesses. In some states, blacks could not rent or lease farm land. In South Carolina, blacks needed special licenses to work other than as servants or farm laborers.

The codes confirmed the Radicals' darkest suspicions about the South. Northern voters now began asking themselves if they had won the war after all.

Section 1 Review

COMPREHENSION   Developing Vocabulary

1. Explain these terms: amnesty, pocket veto, manifesto.

COMPREHENSION   Mastering Facts

1. What was the main constitutional problem that arose at the beginning of the Reconstruction period?
2. Why did Northern Radicals oppose Lincoln's Reconstruction policies?
3. How did the Freedmen's Bureau help educate Southern blacks?
4. What did the black codes attempt to do?

2   THE RADICALS GAIN CONTROL

VOCABULARY   *impeachment*

Andrew Johnson had not been president a year when his "easy" Reconstruction program reached a dead end. Congress refused to recognize the state governments he had encouraged to be set up. Control of events, therefore, passed from the executive branch to Congress. That meant the power passed into the hands of the Radical Republicans and their leader, Thaddeus Stevens.

The Battle Gets Hotter

Stevens had piercing eyes and a thin-lipped mouth in a tall, thin body. In spite of a crippled foot, he was a famous horseman and swimmer. Before being elected to Congress, he had practiced law in Pennsylvania. There he had used his considerable talents to defend runaway slaves. Stevens hated slavery, and in time he came to hate white Southerners as well. He was determined to teach them a hard lesson they would never forget. As he

Thaddeus Stevens of Pennsylvania was the leader of the Republicans in the House and a foe of Johnson's.

said, "I look upon every man who would permit slavery . . . as a traitor to liberty and disloyal to God." When he died, he asked to be buried in a cemetery for black people. He said that he wanted to show in death "the principles which I advocated throughout a long life: equality of man before his Creator."

Fourteenth Amendment Is Adopted. In mid-1866 the moderate Republicans, who felt that Johnson was stepping on Congress's toes, joined with the Radicals to override the president's veto of the bill extending the Freedmen's Bureau. Then the leaders in Congress finished drafting the Fourteenth Amendment. It was to take the place of the Civil Rights Act that Johnson had vetoed.

The first clause of the Fourteenth Amendment made "all persons born or naturalized in the United States" citizens of the country. All were entitled to equal treatment before the law, and no state could deprive any person of life, liberty, or property without due process of law. The amendment did not grant black citizens the right to vote because that was still viewed as a matter to be decided by the states. But if a state barred blacks from taking part in elections, that state would lose some of its seats in Congress.

Another provision of the Fourteenth Amendment barred most Southern leaders from holding federal or state offices. The ban could be lifted only by a two-thirds majority of Congress.

The South Rejects the Amendment. Congress adopted the Fourteenth Amendment and sent it to the states for their approval. If the Southern states had ratified it, most Northerners would have been satisfied. But Johnson believed that it was too harsh, that the Southern states should be guided gently back to partnership in the Union. More important, he believed Congress did not have the constitutional power to treat states in this fashion. So he advised the states to reject the amendment, and all of them except Tennessee did. The amendment was not ratified. Congress was now convinced that stronger measures were called for.

Putting More Pressure on the South

In 1866, congressional elections focused partly on the question of who should control Reconstruction: the president, or the Radicals. Johnson went on a long speaking tour, urging voters to elect to Congress those men who agreed with his policy of an easy Reconstruction. His trip was a disaster because he was his own worst enemy. He had a hot temper, and he embarrassed many people with his rough language and undignified behavior.

In addition, vicious race riots erupted in the South, particularly in Memphis and New Orleans. This strengthened the belief of many people that the federal government had to take action to protect freed slaves against their former masters.

The voters gave the Radicals a two-thirds majority in Congress, which meant that Radicals could now override presidential vetoes. Now they felt strong enough to move, and in the spring of 1867 they began putting their policy into effect.

The First Reconstruction Act. This act, which was followed by two others, divided the seceded states—except Tennessee—into five military districts. The civilian courts in these districts were replaced by military tribunals. Each district was placed under a major general who was to oversee the drawing up of new constitutions in the states under his control. The constitutions were required to give black males the right to vote. In addition, before states could be readmitted to the Union, their legislatures had to ratify the Fourteenth Amendment.

Johnson vetoed the First Reconstruction Act, saying that it was "without precedent and without authority, in clear conflict with the plainest provisions of the Constitution." Congress promptly overrode the veto.

The Reconstruction Act stunned Southern whites. Had they not surrendered their armies? Had they not admitted that secession was impossible? Hadn't they freed their slaves? What more could be expected of them? The fact was, of course, that white Southerners could not bring themselves to regard blacks as equals. They did not want to give blacks more civil rights than were absolutely necessary. And they had passed harsh, unjust laws against their ex-slaves. So the First Reconstruction Act was the price they had to pay. Some 20,000 federal troops were sent to the South during the spring and summer of 1867 to keep law and order.

Tenure of Office Act. Now Radical leaders then turned their energies to getting rid of the hated President Johnson. The Radicals felt that

Johnson was not carrying out his Constitutional obligation to enforce the First Reconstruction Act. He removed military officers who were helping blacks. Also, members of his cabinet ignored the test-oath law and appointed many Confederates to positions in their department.

Accordingly, the Radicals decided to lay the groundwork for *impeachment*, that is, to charge a public official with misconduct in office. In fact, they made a bold attempt to seize control of the presidency by passing the Tenure of Office Act. That law stated that presidents could not remove cabinet officers they had themselves appointed without first obtaining a two-thirds vote of the Senate. So that no one would doubt the real purpose of the act, one clause flatly stated that breaking the act would be a "high misdemeanor." The words "high crimes and misdemeanors" are used in the Constitution (Article 2, Section 4) to define an impeachable offense.

Johnson, as well as many others, was sure that Congress had overreached itself, that the act was unconstitutional. But it had to be tested in court. So Johnson fired Secretary of War Edwin M. Stanton, a Radical sympathizer.

Johnson Impeached

On February 24, 1868, the House voted to impeach the president. His trial before the Senate lasted from mid-March to May 26, 1868.

There were two questions to be decided at Johnson's trial. One was a narrow constitutional case. That was easily knocked down by the president's lawyers. The Tenure of Office Act, they

pointed out, did not even apply to Stanton. He had been appointed by Lincoln, not Johnson. So there was no criminal act as defined by the Constitution.

The second question had to do with Johnson's conduct in office. He was accused of "intemperate language" and of having brought "disgrace, ridicule, contempt, and reproach" on Congress. To press criminal charges against a man because Congress did not like the way he talked or behaved seemed ridiculous to those not caught up in the passion of the moment. But there was an underlying issue. Senator Charles Sumner of Massachusetts stated that Johnson personally stood for the "tyrannical slave power." Keeping him in the presidency, Sumner went on, would mean leaving loyal Unionists of the South, both black and white, at the mercy of their enemies. The question was political, not legal. Impeachment, said Sumner, is "as broad as the Constitution itself." It applied, he said, to "any act of evil example or influence."

The Massachusetts senator had raised a serious issue. There is no doubt that the Radicals were trying to change the way the Constitution worked. They were trying to destroy the system of checks and balances, and to make the executive answerable to the legislature (as it is in the British system).

On the day when the final vote at the trial was to be taken, the streets leading to the Senate were packed with people. The atmosphere was tense in the crowded Senate galleries. Would the Radicals get the two-thirds vote needed for conviction? Finally the moment came. People in the Senate chamber leaned forward and held their breath as

Crowds rushed to the visitors' galleries on the first day of Andrew Johnson's impeachment in the Senate (February 25, 1868) to hear Thaddeus Stevens deliver the impeachment message.

Presidential Election of 1868

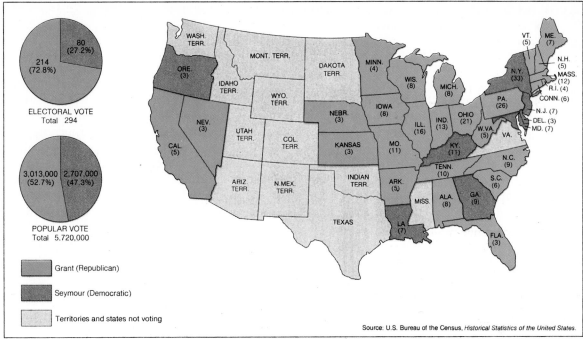

ELECTORAL VOTE
Total 294

POPULAR VOTE
Total 5,720,000

Grant (Republican)

Seymour (Democratic)

Territories and states not voting

Source: U.S. Bureau of the Census, *Historical Statistics of the United States.*

© ML & Co.

Map Skills *Which candidate and party won the election? What was his electoral vote? his percentage of the popular vote? Which state gave the most electoral votes to the loser?*

the senators were asked one by one to give their verdict. As each one said "Guilty," or "Not guilty," they heaved a great sigh: some of hope, others of despair.

When the last senator was asked his verdict and declared "Not guilty," the vote was thirty-five to nineteen, one vote less than the two-thirds needed to convict the president. Johnson was saved by one vote. Roars, shouts, and jeers rang down from the gallery. Some people were delighted, others were furious. Thaddeus Stevens was seen leaving the chamber, his face red with rage. Waving his arms, he cried, "The country is going to the devil."

The 1868 Election and the Fifteenth Amendment

The Democrats knew they could not win the 1868 election with Johnson. Instead they nominated the wartime governor of New York, Horatio Seymour. The Republicans put up Ulysses S. Grant, the hero of the Civil War. In November he was elected president with an impressive majority of 214 to 80 in the electoral college. But the popular vote was something else. With almost 6 million ballots cast, Grant led by only 310,000. About 500,000 Southern blacks had voted (only 1 percent

of the nation's black population lived in the North at that time), most of them for Grant. The importance of the black vote to the Republican party was obvious.

The Radicals feared that Southern whites might try to limit black suffrage in the future. So the Radicals introduced the Fifteenth Amendment. It stated that no one could be kept from voting because of race or color or for having once been a slave. Most Northern states at this time barred blacks from voting, so these states also were affected by the Fifteenth Amendment. It was ratified in 1870.

Section 2 Review

COMPREHENSION   Developing Vocabulary

1. Explain these terms: impeachment, misdemeanor.

COMPREHENSION   Mastering Facts

1. What were the main provisions of the Fourteenth Amendment?
2. Give two reasons why Radicals obtained a two-thirds majority in Congress in 1866.
3. What did the First Reconstruction Act provide?
4. Why did Johnson want to test the Tenure of Office Act in court?

365

3 RADICAL RECONSTRUCTION

VOCABULARY   *sharecropping   tenant farming   scalawags   carpetbaggers*

The period of Radical Reconstruction lasted from 1867, when the First Reconstruction Act was passed, to 1877, when the last federal troops were withdrawn from the South. However, Reconstruction was not uniform. For example, in only three states—Florida, Louisiana, and South Carolina—did it last the full ten years. In the other ex-Confederate states, reconstruction governments were soon replaced—sometimes within one year—by governments that represented traditional white rule.

New Farm Practices

Thaddeus Stevens and other Radicals had promised every freedman "forty acres and a mule." They intended to take the plantations belonging to the 70,000 or so "chief rebels," as Stevens called them, and redistribute the land. But they never did. The reason was that moderate Republicans considered private property a basic American right. It could not be taken away from its owners without due process of law. Congress therefore made no land provisions for the freed people.

The land arrangements that developed in the South were *sharecropping* and *tenant farming*. Plantation owners had land but no workers and no cash to hire them. Blacks, and poor whites, were able to work but had no land, no tools, and sometimes no place to live. Here were grounds for an economic bargain. Landowners divided their land and gave each worker a few acres, seed, tools, and food to live on. When the crops were harvested, the grower gave a share—usually two-thirds—to the landowner. This paid the owner back, and the arrangement was over until the next year.

As sharecroppers, ex-slaves had some independence. At least they could now keep part of what they produced. Also, there was flexibility in the system. In theory, "croppers" who saved a little and bought their own tools could drive a better bargain with landowners. Those who got their own horses or mules might even become tenants, renting the land for cash. Eventually they might move up the economic ladder to become outright owners of their farms.

But it seldom worked that way. By the time sharecroppers had shared their crops and paid their debts, they rarely had any money left. Also, most sharecroppers grew only cash crops such as cotton or tobacco. This put them at the mercy of the market. Sometimes the demand was high and the prices were good; sometimes they were not. But because the croppers' plots of land were small, they did not have enough space to increase the crop yield when prices were high. And the production, year after year, eventually exhausted the soil.

The war had devastated Southern agriculture. Sharecropping and tenant farming were means of coping with the situation. They may not have been the most desirable means, but they worked. The problem was that they kept Southern farmers dependent on one or two crops. The farmers would have been better off either growing food for themselves or diversifying into such commercial crops as fruits, vegetables, and livestock.

Blacks in Government

One legend of Reconstruction is that it was a time of black rule in the South, when whites were not permitted to use the ballot. The fact is that under Radical Reconstruction, some 704,000 blacks and 660,000 whites were registered to vote. In 1860, the last year before the Civil War, 721,000 voters had been registered—all white. In other words, there was a drop of at most 10 percent in the registration of white voters. Most of these included in this 10 percent figure were not allowed to register because they were former Confederate leaders. Some could have registered if they had wanted to; they refused in order to show their opposition to black suffrage.

Although there were more black than white voters in the South, out of 125 Southerners elected to Congress during Reconstruction, only 16 were black. South Carolina was the only state where blacks were even a majority in the state legislature. No state elected a black governor.

Many of the blacks elected to office were ministers or teachers who had gone to school in the North. Some had educated themselves. One had learned to read by watching through the window of a white schoolroom that stood across an alley from the shop where he worked.

The sixteen blacks elected to Congress during Reconstruction, two senators and fourteen representatives, were at least as well prepared as the whites with whom they sat. For instance, Senator Hiram Revels of Mississippi had graduated from Knox College in Illinois and had become a minister. During the war he served as a chaplain with the Union army. In the Senate he held the seat that had once belonged to Jefferson Davis, president of the Confederacy. Senator Blanche K. Bruce, also from Mississippi, had been a slave in Virginia but had escaped to freedom before the war. Bruce attended Oberlin College in Ohio before settling in Mississippi, where he became a planter and entered politics.

Another charge made against the Radicals is that they gave the vote to large numbers of blacks who could neither read nor write. This is true. But the drive to extend voting rights to all adult males had gone on since before Andrew Jackson's time. And nowhere had the ability to read and write been made a voting requirement.

In eastern cities at the time of Reconstruction and after, even citizenship was not always necessary in order to vote. Immigrants fresh off the boat, who could neither speak English nor write in any language, were regularly lined up at the polls. There, a party worker, almost always a Democrat, told them how they should mark their ballots. Whatever its effects at the time, this policy came

to be regarded as useful. It gave the immigrant a crude but helpful introduction to politics. The same reasoning could be applied to black citizens as well.

Scalawags and Carpetbaggers

In addition to blacks, the Radical Reconstruction governments in Southern states were supported by people known as "scalawags" and "carpetbaggers."

Scalawags were white Southerners who joined the Republican party. Some had been Whigs before the Civil War. They wanted the South to industrialize as quickly as possible, and believed this could best be done under the Republicans. Other scalawags had opposed slavery and secession, and they did not want the former planter aristocracy to return to power. And some scalawags were selfish individuals who hoped to get themselves into office with the help of black voters and then steal as much as they could. These scalawags would parade blacks to the polls, pad voting lists, and stuff ballot boxes. Whatever their motives, scalawags were considered traitors by most white Southerners. (The word "scalawag" means "scoundrel.")

Carpetbaggers were Northerners who moved

This Currier and Ives print shows the first black senator and representatives to serve in Congress. Senator Hiram R. Revels of Mississippi is seated at the far left.

This illustration was typical of many that reflected the southern bias against those northerners who went south after the Civil War to make money, often by exploiting poor whites and blacks.

south after the war. (The nickname came from the belief that they carried all their belongings in a bag made of carpeting material.) Like the scalawags, carpetbaggers had mixed motives for supporting Radical Reconstruction. Some were teachers and members of the clergy who felt a moral duty to help former slaves. Some were Union soldiers who preferred to live in the warm climate of the South. Some were business people who hoped to start new industries. The iron works at Birmingham, Alabama, and Chattanooga, Tennessee, for example, were founded by Ohioans John T. Wilder and Willard Ware. And some carpetbaggers were dishonest, irresponsible adventurers. Horace Greeley, editor of the *New York Tribune*, described them as having "both arms around the Negroes, and their hands in their rear pockets, seeing if they can't pick a . . . dollar out of them."

The Reconstruction Governments

The results of Reconstruction were as mixed as the motives of the people who supported it. On the one hand, many political and social conditions were improved. On the other hand, there was widespread corruption.

The new constitutions drafted by the Southern states under Reconstruction not only set up black suffrage. They eliminated property qualifications for voting and holding office. This gave poor whites their first chance to take part in politics. The new constitutions also abolished imprisonment for debt. Reconstruction governments wrote the region's first laws establishing a system of public schools. Except in New Orleans, though, it was a segregated system, with separate schools for whites and blacks.

The reconstruction governments faced the immense problem of rebuilding a land that had been devastated by war. Roads, bridges, railroads, and factories had to be repaired or replaced. This cost money. So did the public schools, as well as the orphanages, hospitals, and other social welfare institutions that were now open to blacks as well as to whites. Since there was little capital available in the South, state governments borrowed funds by selling bonds in the North. But Southern credit was so poor that for every $100 bond sold, the re-

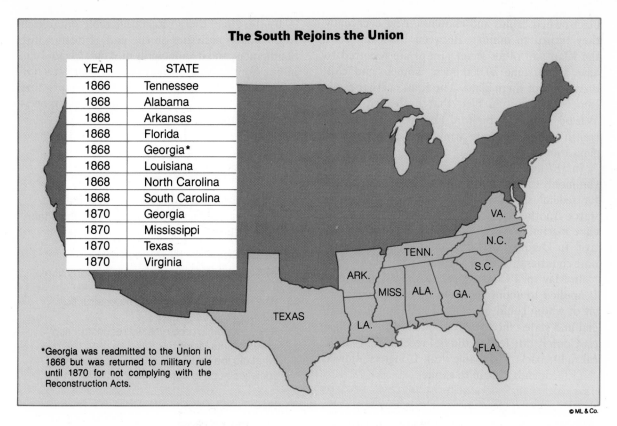

The South Rejoins the Union

YEAR	STATE
1866	Tennessee
1868	Alabama
1868	Arkansas
1868	Florida
1868	Georgia*
1868	Louisiana
1868	North Carolina
1868	South Carolina
1870	Georgia
1870	Mississippi
1870	Texas
1870	Virginia

*Georgia was readmitted to the Union in 1868 but was returned to military rule until 1870 for not complying with the Reconstruction Acts.

© ML & Co.

construction government often received only $25 while the Northern investor received $75! Taxes on real estate kept going higher and higher, which made it harder than ever for planters to get out of debt. The situation became even worse after the 1873 depression, which led to a sharp drop in prices for the South's agricultural products.

Another factor that pushed government costs up was graft. Some officials took bribes from companies in return for construction and printing contracts. Some officials spent public funds for carriages, liquor, furniture, and other personal items. One carpetbagger governor managed to earn $100,000 during his first year in office although his official salary was only $8000.

Secret Societies

Most white Southerners had been taught from infancy that blacks were inferior. They found it very difficult to accept the idea of blacks voting and taking part in government. They blamed blacks for the high taxes. In addition, they resented the presence of federal troops in the South, although there were never more than 20,000, and they were usually confined to army camps.

Most white Southerners swallowed their resentment. Some expressed their feeling by refusing to register to vote. A few white Southerners, however, turned to terrorism and violence. They did so through secret societies, of which the most notorious was the Ku Klux Klan.

The Ku Klux Klan began in Tennessee in 1866, even before Radical Reconstruction. A group of Confederate veterans, supposedly as a joke, covered themselves and their horses with bedsheets and hid their faces behind white masks. Costumed in this way, they rode to a nearby meeting of freedmen, pretending to be the ghosts of Confederate soldiers killed in battle. The meeting broke up at once.

Soon, such costumes were no longer a joking matter. They were taken over by whites who were determined to bring down reconstruction governments and drive blacks from the polling booths back to the fields "where they belonged." At first the Ku Klux Klan, as well as other secret groups, such as the Knights of the White Camelia, simply warned blacks not to vote. They also tried to persuade white workers for the Freedmen's Bureau to quit their jobs.

After a while, the secret societies began burning

369

black-owned cabins and churches. And eventually they turned to murder. Between 1868 and 1871 the Klan and other secret groups are reported to have killed some 20,000 men, women, and children, most of them black. The Klan's activities became so violent, in fact, that its leader, Grand Wizard Nathaniel Bedford Forrest, a former general in the Confederate army, tried to get the organization to disband.

In 1870 and 1871 Congress passed several acts commonly called the Force Acts. One act provided for federal supervision of elections in Southern states. Another act gave the president power to declare martial law in areas where the Klan was active. In October 1871 President Grant did so in nine counties in South Carolina.

In May 1872 Congress passed the Amnesty Act. It applied to about 160,000 former Confederates, all of whom could once again vote and hold federal and state offices. Only about 500 of the highest Confederate leaders did not receive their political rights back. That same year, Congress allowed the Freedmen's Bureau to expire.

By this time, there was considerable opposition to the Klan's activities on the part of many white Southerners, and it temporarily died out. Meanwhile, in one Southern state after another, reconstruction governments were replaced by governments that represented traditional white rule. This process was called "redemption."

Section 3 Review

COMPREHENSION   Developing Vocabulary

1. Explain these terms: sharecropping, tenant farming, scalawags, carpetbaggers, redemption.

COMPREHENSION   Mastering Facts

1. Why didn't blacks get the promised "forty acres and a mule"?
2. What educational reform did reconstruction governments carry out?
3. What economic problems did reconstruction governments face?
4. What did the Ku Klux Klan and other secret societies hope to accomplish?

4 RECONSTRUCTION EFFORTS COME TO AN END

VOCABULARY   *literacy test   poll tax   grandfather clause   Jim Crow laws*

The Radical plan of Reconstruction for the South ended in 1877. It ended partly because giving blacks voting rights was not combined with giving them help in achieving economic independence. It ended partly because of white resistance, violent and otherwise. And there were other reasons too. One was growing Northern indifference. Another was the fact that the Republican party was torn by scandal and corruption.

Apathy in the North

Outside the South, the idea grew that, having achieved freedom, blacks should now take care of themselves. Northerners were weary of the seemingly endless trouble in the South. Both Thaddeus Stevens and Charles Sumner were dead, and the Radicals were losing their influence within the Republican party. Pressing for full civil rights in the South would have raised embarrassing questions about segregation in the North. In addition, Northern business interests wanted stability in the South. That usually meant having traditional white leadership in control. In addition the dominant Republican party no longer needed the black vote and perhaps they didn't even need the South.

Grant's Corrupt Administration

As you have learned, there was considerable graft in the reconstruction governments of the South. But it was more than matched by the corruption that existed at the national level.

President Grant, who was elected for a second term in 1872, was an honest man. But he had had no political experience before being elected to the presidency, and he apparently found it hard to believe that his friends might use him for their own advantage. As some historians explained it, the main trouble with Grant was that he could not tell the difference between an honest person and a crook. And in fact, he surrounded himself with crooked individuals.

Beginning in 1873, a series of long-simmering scandals erupted. First came the Treasury Department scandal involving kickbacks on a tax-

Presidential Election of 1876

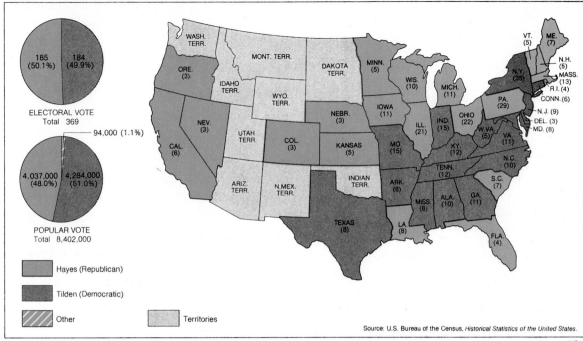

ELECTORAL VOTE
Total 369

185 (50.1%) 184 (49.9%)

94,000 (1.1%)

POPULAR VOTE
Total 8,402,000

4,037,000 (48.0%) 4,284,000 (51.0%)

Hayes (Republican)

Tilden (Democratic)

Other

Territories

Source: U.S. Bureau of the Census, *Historical Statistics of the United States.*

© ML & Co.

Map Skills *Which candidate won the popular vote? the electoral vote? Who was elected? How does the map reveal which three southern states had the disputed election returns?*

collection contract. It led to the resignation of the secretary of the treasury.

Then came the so-called "Whiskey Ring," in which it turned out that internal revenue collectors had helped defraud the federal government of millions of dollars of revenue taxes on whiskey. The scandal reached up to Grant's private secretary, General Orville E. Babcock, who was one of 238 persons indicted.

Then it turned out that Secretary of War William W. Belknap had accepted bribes from merchants in Indian Territory who wanted to keep their profitable trading concessions. The House of Representatives impeached Belknap, who promptly resigned. The secretary of the navy had taken bribes from shipbuilders. The secretary of the interior had had dealings with land speculators. And so it went, with the bribe money being used both for personal enrichment and to build up the Republican political machine.

An Economic Depression

As if political scandals were not enough, in 1873 the nation was hit by a depression. The economy had been expanding since the end of the Civil War. People in railroads and manufacturing thought business would always be good and profits would always go up. So they borrowed enormous amounts of money and built new facilities as quickly as possible. Unfortunately, many bankers and businessmen got overextended—that is, they assumed more debts than they could pay. In September 1873 Jay Cooke and Company, a major banking firm, went bankrupt, setting off a series of financial failures. Within a year, eighty-nine railroads went broke. Hundreds of companies folded. In the four-year depression that followed, 3 million workers lost their jobs. Dislike of the Grant administration grew, and white interest in black welfare declined.

The Disputed 1876 Election

In 1876 the Republicans decided, understandably, not to run Grant for a third term. Instead they chose the stodgy governor of Ohio, Rutherford B. Hayes. Scenting victory, the Democrats put up one of their ablest leaders, Governor Samuel J. Tilden of New York. Tilden had helped clean up the graft that had flourished in New York City under the Tweed Ring. (You will read about the Tweed Ring in chapter 20.)

As most people expected, Tilden carried the

371

Samuel J. Tilden, the Democratic reformist governor of New York, won a larger number of popular and electoral votes than Hayes, but lost the election.

Rutherford B. Hayes became the nineteenth president in 1877. He ended the Reconstruction era that year by withdrawing federal troops from the South.

popular vote—by a margin of 250,000. He also received 184 electoral votes to 165 for Hayes. But Tilden needed 185 electoral votes to win—and there were twenty electoral votes in dispute. One was from Oregon. The rest were from Florida, Louisiana, and South Carolina. In those three Southern states, Radical Republicans were still in control. Local Democrats, however, had frightened away enough blacks and Radical voters to win. Each state's Radical leaders had then thrown out a quantity of Democratic ballots and made up returns to show that Republicans had carried the state. Since no one knew which set of returns was the accurate one, Florida, Louisiana, and South Carolina sent both sets to Washington.

Historians are now quite sure that the Democrats would have carried Florida even if the election had been run honestly. In other words, Tilden deserved that state's four electoral votes—and the presidency. But he did not get them.

To deal with the problem, an electoral commission was appointed, made up of eight Republicans and seven Democrats. The commission voted along straight party lines. All the disputed votes were given to Hayes, who thus became president with a minority of the popular vote.

Why did the nation stand for this bold-faced robbery? The answer is that, in the oldest tradition of politics, a largely secret deal was made. Southern Democrats were willing to accept Hayes if they could get something in return. The price they demanded was, first of all, assurance that federal troops would be withdrawn from Florida, Louisiana, and South Carolina. That would enable local Democrats to overthrow the last Radical regimes. Second, they wanted federal money for a railroad from Texas to the West Coast, and for improving their rivers, harbors, and bridges. Their third demand was for a conservative Southerner in the cabinet. The Republican leaders agreed to these demands, and Hayes was peacefully inaugurated.

White Supremacy and Jim Crow

For at least ten years or so after the end of Radical Reconstruction, blacks in the South continued to vote and were occasionally elected to office. The last Southern black elected to Congress served until 1900. There were black policemen in some Southern cities, too. But beginning in 1890, Southern states adopted various techniques to keep blacks away from the polling booths. Beginning in 1881, they also adopted a policy of rigid legal separation of whites and blacks.

Emergence of Poor Whites. Because of the long history of slavery, many whites—especially poor ones—found it hard to form new attitudes about blacks. Middle class whites did not have to compete with blacks for jobs. Poor whites did. In the 1880s and 1890s agricultural conditions were so bad that many poor farmers were forced to leave their farms. They came to Southern cities to work in coal mines, in the growing iron and steel foundries, and in the cotton mills. Their pay varied from 40 cents to 50 cents a day, which meant that women and children had to work also if the family were to survive. These people did not want competition from free blacks. And because their economic position was so low, the only thing that gave them a sense of pride was the feeling that they were whites and that the white race was superior.

The poor white farmers who did not leave their farms also had problems. They needed back-country roads so they could bring their crops to market. They needed credit facilities so they could borrow money to carry them over until harvest time. They also needed schools and hospitals.

As you will read in chapter 23, these farmers became active in the Populist movement. In many cases, they courted the black vote. Then, under the leadership of Governor "Pitchfork Ben" Tillman of South Carolina, the elected representative of the poor whites made a deal with the Democratic party. If the Democrats would work to improve the economic condition of poor whites, the Populists would join the Democratic party and help end black participation in politics. This is precisely what happened.

Political Restrictions. By the end of the century, new voting regulations had been adopted in all Southern states. These were carefully drawn to stay within the bounds of the Fourteenth and Fifteenth Amendments, but they were subtly discriminating. For example, a requirement for voting might be the ability to "read and understand" the law. Tests of understanding were administered orally. Blacks and others who might vote Republi-

can were given hard questions and were told they had failed. Democratic party members would receive easy questions.

In addition to literacy tests, there were laws calling for the payment of poll taxes. An individual had to pay a poll tax before being allowed to vote. The tax was small, usually a few dollars, but it had to be paid long before election day. Blacks might not get reminders of the due date, but whites would. Those blacks who remembered on their own were often unable to find an official to accept their money.

The literacy test and the poll tax kept many poor whites as well as blacks away from the polls. So beginning in 1898, several Southern states added a "grandfather clause" to their constitutions. The clause stated that even if a man failed the literacy test or could not afford the poll tax, he was still entitled to vote provided that he had been eligible to do so on January 1, 1867—before Radical Reconstruction—or provided that his father or grandfather had been eligible to do so. The "grandfather clause" enabled many poor whites to vote. But it did not apply to blacks, because blacks did not have suffrage before Radical Reconstruction. (The "grandfather clause" was declared unconstitutional in 1915.)

As a result of these tactics, most Southern blacks stopped voting. In Louisiana, for example, 130,334 blacks voted in 1896. Eight years later, only 1342 cast ballots.

"Separate but Equal." At the same time that blacks were losing their voting rights in state after state, a pattern of segregation in all public facilities was being put into effect. The laws establishing this pattern were called "Jim Crow" laws. The term comes from the name of a character in a minstrel show who sang a song that ended with the words "Jump, Jim Crow." How the name became attached to the laws enforcing segregation is uncertain.

Prior to Jim Crow, there was a period of fifteen or twenty years during which black and white Southerners mingled to some degree. At least in cities, railroad lunch counters, ice cream parlors, and theaters were often unsegregated.

The first Jim Crow law was passed in 1881 in Tennessee. It provided that whites and blacks ride in separate railway cars. Other states adopted similar laws. By the 1890s, Jim Crow was being applied to schools, hospitals, restaurants, railroad stations, parks, playgrounds, water fountains—every imaginable place where whites and blacks might come together. There were Jim Crow entrances to factories and theaters. Black taxicab drivers were not even allowed to pick up white fares.

Then in 1896, in the case of *Plessy* v. *Ferguson*, the Supreme Court ruled that such separation of the races was legal. Plessy, a black man living in Louisiana, had sued because he was denied a seat in a railroad car reserved for white passengers. The railroad replied that the separate facilities for black people were just as good as the ones for whites. The Supreme Court sided with the railroad. Facilities might be separate, the Court said, as long as they were equal. (The only dissent came from Justice John Marshall Harlan, a Southerner. Harlan argued that "Our Constitution is color-blind, and neither knows nor tolerates classes among citizens. In respect of civil rights, all citizens are equal before the law.")

What happened after *Plessy* v. *Ferguson* was that public facilities in the South were separate but far from equal. As one historian said, what blacks got was "the old battered schools and beat-up railroad cars, the rundown tenements and the muddy parks." Jim Crow continued as the legal way of life in the South for another fifty-eight years, until the Supreme Court case of *Brown* v. *Board of Education* (1954). You will read about this case in chapter 36.

Summing Up Radical Reconstruction

The purpose of Radical Reconstruction was to give black Americans equality. That goal was not achieved in the years after the Civil War. Radical Republicans sincerely wanted to help the former slaves, but they made two serious mistakes. They assumed that giving southern blacks the vote would enable them to protect themselves politically. Second, Radical Republicans, although willing to give millions of acres of land to railroad companies, were unwilling to give land to the freed slaves so that they could become economically independent. Black abolitionist Frederick Douglass summed up this last failure when he said, "You gave us no acres. You turned us loose to the sky, to the storm, to the whirlwind, and worst of all, you turned us loose to the wrath of our infuriated masters."

But Radical Reconstruction should not be written off as a failure. Historian Kenneth Stampp says that the Fourteenth and Fifteenth Amendments were the greatest achievements of Reconstruction and could have been passed only at that time. And the amendments had to be passed because they were the springboards from which blacks, after a very long struggle, could at last achieve full political and civil rights.

Section 4 Review

COMPREHENSION Developing Vocabulary

1. Explain these terms: literacy test, poll tax, grandfather clause, Jim Crow laws.

COMPREHENSION Mastering Facts

1. What was the price Southerners asked for accepting Hayes in the disputed election of 1876?
2. Why were poor whites more likely to be antiblack than middle-class whites were?
3. What was the Supreme Court ruling in *Plessy* v. *Ferguson*?
4. What were two reasons why Radical Reconstruction did not give blacks equality?

CHAPTER 17 Review

Chapter Summary

President Andrew Johnson and the Radical Republicans in Congress became embroiled in a struggle to control Reconstruction policies. Johnson's vetoes of Radical legislation enraged those who wanted to punish the South. When Southern states began to pass black codes, the Radicals gained enough power to assume control of Reconstruction efforts. The House voted to impeach Johnson, but the Senate failed by one vote to convict him. Meanwhile, under Radical Reconstruction blacks were able to participate in many Southern governments. Reconstruction continued during the corrupt Grant administration. It ended in 1877 when Hayes became president following a disputed election.

Questions for Critical Thinking

COMPREHENSION   Summarizing Main Ideas

1. Compare the views of Lincoln and the Radical Republicans with regard to the following: (a) who had seceded, states or individuals; (b) who had the right to control the admission of Confederate states to the Union; (c) the conditions under which Confederate states could form governments.

2. What two major political changes were brought about by Reconstruction constitutions? Did these changes make state governments more or less democratic? Explain.

3. What effect did Reconstruction have on the education of blacks? of poor whites?

4. Give four reasons why Radical Reconstruction ended by 1877.

COMPREHENSION   Interpreting Events

1. How did the condition of blacks under the black codes differ from their condition as slaves?

2. If you had been a member of the House of Representatives in 1868, would you have voted to impeach President Andrew Johnson? Give reasons for your position.

3. Why was the Fourteenth Amendment adopted? Why was the Fifteenth Amendment adopted?

4. Why were tenant farming and sharecropping widespread in the South after the Civil War? What were the advantages and disadvantages of these systems of working the land?

5. For what reasons did the Southern states adopt Jim Crow legislation?

APPLICATION   Using Skills To Recognize Similarities

1. Compare the attitude and policies of the federal government toward blacks during Radical Reconstruction with its attitude and policies today.

2. What institutions in the United States are still racially segregated?

3. One criticism of Radical Reconstruction is that it gave blacks the vote without a period of education. What requirements for suffrage does the federal government have today? What requirements does your state government have? What standards, if any, do you think should be required of voters in a democracy? Justify your answer.

EVALUATION   Forming Generalizations

Which of the statements below support the generalization that "The readmission of the Confederate states to the Union raised certain constitutional questions"?

1. The main purpose of the Civil War was to prove that secession was impossible.

2. Radical Republicans wanted blacks to have the right to vote.

3. The president has the power to pardon individuals.

4. Congress has the power to determine on what basis states may enter the Union.

5. Andrew Johnson came from the Southern state of Tennessee.

6. People who take up arms against their government are rebels and traitors.

Alaska

When it comes to buying large chunks of real estate, the United States has proven that it knows how to recognize a bargain. In 1803 the Louisiana Purchase cost only pennies per acre; then in 1867 Secretary of State William H. Seward engineered the purchase of Alaska from Russia for $7.2 million.

Seward's action was not popular at first. Newspapers then referred to Alaska as the "national icebox." Some called the new territory "Seward's folly." But Seward recognized the immense value of the 600,000 square-mile peninsula.

Russian Alaska. Under Russian control, Alaska did not become a thriving colony. Furs attracted hunters and trappers, but other resources went undeveloped. Then in 1863, Poland revolted against the Russian government. Fearing that their biggest rival, Great Britain, might attempt a takeover of Alaska during this unsettled period, Russian leaders decided to sell it. They hoped the United States would be interested. Some Americans—including Seward—quickly saw a chance for the nation to expand its power.

Incredible Riches. Gold was discovered in Alaska around the turn of the century. With further exploration, Alaska yielded valuable deposits of coal, iron ore, chromite, silver, and tin. Today

Alaska

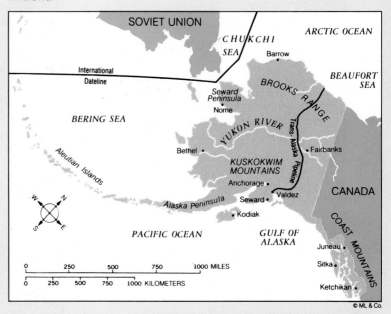

Alaska also produces many forest products, and its coastal waters are rich in salmon, halibut, king crab, herring, trout, and other fish. Over the years, Alaska has paid for itself many times over.

Today, Alaska's biggest contribution to the American economy is oil. In 1968 the largest known oil pool in North America was discovered on Alaska's North Slope. This discovery led to the construction in 1974–1977 of the 789-mile Alaska Pipeline.

Alaska, which became America's forty-ninth state in 1959, is still one of the nation's last frontiers. Its harsh climate, rugged landscape, and isolated location make living there a challenge. The construction in recent years

of new roads, airports, and the pipeline have helped integrate the state more closely into the American economy. Still, those who choose to live in Alaska interact with their environment in ways that most urban Americans never experience.

Understanding Geography

1. Compare the sizes of Alaska and the Louisiana Territory (see page 224). Which was larger? What resources were contained in each?

2. Name several of Alaska's largest cities. Why are they located along the coast?

3. Why is Alaska often called America's "last frontier"?

UNIT 5 Review

Understanding Social Studies Concepts

History

1. Arrange the following events in chronological order: (a) Kansas-Nebraska Act; (b) Dred Scott decision; (c) Bleeding Kansas; (d) Lincoln-Douglas debates; (e) John Brown's raid; (f) secession of South Carolina.

2. What new political parties emerged during the two decades prior to the Civil War? Which was the most successful? the least successful?

3. How did the Lincoln-Douglas debates contribute to Lincoln's election as president?

4. How did Northerners react to the Battle of Bull Run? How did Southerners react?

5. Explain the political significance of the Battle of Antietam.

6. When did the North add abolition of slavery to its war aims?

7. What years comprised the period known as Reconstruction? What positive results were accomplished during this time? In what ways did reconstruction efforts fail?

Economics

1. How did newly arriving immigrants contribute to the economy of the United States? What economic problems did they face? Where did most new immigrants settle? Why?

2. Compare wartime economic conditions in the North with those in the South. What were the similarities? differences?

3. Describe the Southern economy after the Civil War. What skills did former slaves need to acquire to participate in a growing economy?

Government

1. Which constitutional amendments were direct results of the Civil War?

2. What two legal questions were involved in the impeachment trial of Andrew Johnson?

3. Who were the Radical Republicans? How did they influence the nation's government during the late 1860s?

4. Why was Lincoln worried about his chances for reelection in 1864? What did he do to improve his chances? How did results on the battlefield help him?

Sociology

1. Describe the methods used by the Ku Klux Klan to intimidate blacks and other minorities. Why did the influence of the Ku Klux Klan finally weaken?

2. What roles did women perform for both sides during the Civil War? What happened to ex-slaves during and after the war?

Extending Map, Chart, Picture Skills

1. Refer to the map on page 331. Which candidate received the largest number of popular votes? Was that a majority of all votes cast? For which candidate was the popular and electoral vote percentage nearly the same?

2. Refer to the maps of Civil War battles in Chapter 16. In which states did the most fighting take place? Which major battle was fought in a Northern state? What role did the Mississippi River play in the formation of the North's overall military strategy?

3. Estimate the distance traveled by Sherman's army on its march from Chattanooga to Raleigh (see map on page 352).

4. Use the chart on page 325 to write a paragraph outlining the history of either the present Republican or Democratic party.

Understanding Current Events

1. Give examples of sectionalism that are still evident in the nation. What can sectionalism accomplish today? Explain.

2. Why is the Civil War called the first modern war? What weapons and techniques used then are still used today?

Developing Effective Citizenship

1. Several amendments—especially the Fifteenth—deal with the right to vote. Why is voting such an important right in a democracy?

2. How did the Freedmen's Bureau aid ex-slaves in becoming more effective citizens?

GLOBAL TIME LINE
1876–1915

THE UNITED STATES

THE WORLD

1871 Great Chicago Fire.

1876 Sioux Indians defeat Custer's troops.

1882 Chinese Exclusion Act passed.

1886 Haymarket Riot in Chicago.

1892 Homestead strike.

1896 *Plessy* v. *Ferguson* decision.

1870 — 1880 — 1890 — 1900 —

1879 Britain defeats Zulu kingdom in Africa.

1871 Rome becomes capital of Italy.

1889 Brazil becomes an independent republic.

1897 Britain's Queen Victoria celebrates 60th year of her reign.

The Industrial Revolution Creates the Modern Age

1907–1908 Japan limits emigration
to U.S. under terms of
Gentlemen's Agreement.

1910 ———————————— 1920

1911 Roald Amundsen of Norway
is first to reach South Pole.

1910 Union of South
Africa formed.

The Passing of the Old Frontier

1876–1900

People in the Chapter

George Custer—*U.S. military commander who is killed with all his men at the Battle of Little Big Horn in 1876.*

Tashunka Witko—*brilliant Indian commander known as Crazy Horse, who defeats Custer in the last and greatest Indian victory.*

Martha Jane Canary—*known as Calamity Jane, this mule-skinner and scout for Custer's forces is a great friend of famous western outlaws.*

Joseph G. McCoy—*the first cattle dealer to ship cattle from Abilene, Kansas, by rail to the packing plants of Chicago, thereby creating a great new industry.*

Linking Past to Present

In 1865 about half the national territory of the United States, that part west of the Mississippi River, was considered a wilderness. It had an average of fewer than two people per square mile. Most of those were Indians. Twenty-five years later, in 1890, the director of the United States Census announced that so many people had gone west that the frontier hardly existed anymore.

As irresistible as an incoming tide, people poured across the Mississippi River and spread all over the West. There were explorers, prospectors, cattlemen, and, finally, farmers. In the process, the first inhabitants of the land were simply overwhelmed. Most Indians were pushed from their lands by trickery or force. Many were killed. All were forced to change their way of life.

For a while, life on the old frontier was dominated by cattlemen and the cowboys who helped in organizing the cattle industry. Later, farmers came to take advantage of the cheap land. Finally, even the frontier life of the farmer disappeared and with new inventions and new technology the West became firmly tied to the growing industrial society of the United States.

Chapter Outline

1 INVADING THE INDIANS' HOMELAND

VOCABULARY   *reservations   Chivington massacre*

At the time of the Civil War, the Great Plains grew mostly short grass, with only an occasional clump of trees along the banks of a river. The animal life included several hundred million jack rabbits and prairie dogs that furnished food for the wolves and coyotes. It also included some 15 million buffalo that provided almost everything the Plains Indians needed. As one observer noted:

"With the buffalo skins they make their houses; with the skins they clothe and shoe themselves; of the skins they make thread with which they sew their clothes and also their tents. From the bones they shape awls; the dung serves them for firewood, because there is no other fuel in that country. The stomachs serve them for pitchers, vessels from which they drink. They live on the flesh; they sometimes eat it roasted and warmed over the dung, at other times raw."

Indian Cultural Changes

Before the arrival of the Spaniards, there were only a few thousand Indians on the Great Plains. The Indians were primarily farmers who grew maize, beans, and squash. By the Civil War, the Indian population of the region had climbed to about 225,000. The reason for the population explosion was the introduction of the horse.

Horses had been brought to the New World as early as 1598 by the Spanish but up until about the 1700s, Plains Indians still hunted buffalo on foot. Since it was difficult to creep close enough to shoot without scaring the herd, the Indians had to make do with young or weak animals that fell behind the main body.

The use of the horse enabled the Indians to become more efficient hunters, which meant that the region could support more people. By the 1700s, the Great Plains were filled with some thirty different tribes which had moved there from all directions. At the same time, the horse extended an individual tribe's hunting range—and sometimes brought it into conflict with another tribe. After the early 1700s, almost all the Indian tribes on the Great Plains gave up farming. They became nomadic warriors, used to fighting and resentful of anyone who interfered with the buffalo hunt.

On the other hand, the warfare the Plains Indians practiced—although frequent—was not particularly bloody. The main object was to either steal horses or avenge a defeat. Casualties were few. A warrior who "counted coup"—that is, touched a live enemy with his hand and got away unharmed—received much more honor and praise than did a warrior who killed an enemy. Skill and individual courage were considered more important than force.

The Reservations Policy Begins

Until the middle of the 1800s, there was little conflict between Americans and Plains Indians. This was primarily because Americans tried to avoid the region as much as possible. Early explorers, who came from wooded areas with abundant rainfall, considered it unsuitable for farming. It was shown on maps as the Great American Desert. Even most of the Forty-niners preferred to reach California by sailing clipper ships around dan-

Charles Russell's painting The Buffalo Hunt *vividly portrays the action of the hunt, which underlay the economy of the Plains Indians. Great skill was required to shoot from a speeding horse.*

gerous Cape Horn at the southern tip of South America or by portaging through the jungle at the Isthmus of Panama.

Indians Are Restricted. Gradually, however, reports began coming eastward that many parts of the Great Plains were very good for farming. Railroad companies began sending out survey parties to determine the best place to lay transcontinental tracks. The United States Army, responding to appeals from settlers on their way to Oregon, built a series of forts on the plains. And in 1858 the discovery of gold in Colorado drew 100,000 miners into the region.

The United States government had first planned to keep the entire Great Plains as "one big reservation" for the Indians. But as pressure from traders, travelers, and miners built up, the government changed its mind. It began signing treaties with Indian tribes. Under the treaties, the Indians were to remain within certain boundaries. The remainder of the land was to be opened to white settlement. Also, the federal government was allowed to build roads and railroads across Indian territory. In exchange for limiting themselves to reservations, the Indians were to be helped to become farmers. The federal government promised to give them supplies, including food, blankets, and seed corn.

Indians Are Cheated. The policy did not work. It was the same old story of trickery and greed. The treaties were usually made not with real tribal leaders, but with Indians who for one reason or another opposed their chiefs. So most Indians never agreed to the treaties. Also, many of the government officials in charge of supplying the reservations were crooks. The agents for the Indian Bureau looked upon their government jobs as a chance to make money. For example, the annual salary of an Indian Bureau agent was $1500. Yet many agents racked up as much as $15,000 a year by such methods as mixing flour with sawdust, or stealing goods and selling them instead of distributing them to the Indians.

A third reason the reservations policy did not work is that the Indians did not want to give up their culture. As Chief Gall of the Sioux said,

❝[We] have been taught to hunt and live on the game. You tell us that we must learn to farm, live in one house, and take on your ways. Suppose the people living beyond the great sea should come and tell you that you must stop farming and kill your cattle, and take your houses and lands, what would you do? Would you not fight them? **"**

Indians Fight Back

The Indians fought on and off from 1862 to 1890. Leaders in the struggle against the encroaching Americans were the Sioux and the Cheyenne.

The struggle was touched off in 1862 when a small band of young Sioux, while searching for food, killed five whites near a reservation in Minnesota. The white farmers in the area promptly fled for their lives. Equally frightened, the Sioux split into two groups. One also fled the vicinity, but the other, afraid of retaliation, decided to attack first. Hundreds of settlers were killed and their farmhouses burned before the state militia succeeded in defeating the Sioux. Most of the Indians who were taken prisoner were later pardoned by President Lincoln, but thirty-eight were hanged "at a great hanging-bee" the day after Christmas, 1862. The following year, the remaining Sioux in Minnesota were defeated and forced to leave the state after yielding their land to the Americans.

The Sioux were more successful in Montana and Wyoming. There they were able to prevent the construction of a wagon road along the Bozeman Trail that would have cut through their best hunting grounds. In fact, under the terms of the peace treaty signed in 1868, the United States government abandoned several forts it had built on Indian land. This was one of the few Indian-American peace treaties in which the Americans retreated.

The Chivington Massacre

Farther south, however, in the Colorado Territory, the situation was quite different. There, miners had forced the Cheyenne into a barren area known as the Sand Creek Reserve. Short of food, bands of Indians began raiding nearby trails and settlements. Colorado Governor John Evans immediately called out the militia. But he also urged those Indians who did not want to fight to report to Fort Lyon where they would be safe from harm.

In the fall of 1864, some 500 Cheyenne were encamped on Sand Creek. Two flags fluttered above the camp: the Stars and Stripes, and a white flag—both symbols of the Indians' desire for peace. In the meantime, General S. R. Curtis, United States army commander in the West, had sent a telegram to the head of the Colorado militia, Colonel J. M. Chivington: "I want no peace till the Indians suffer more." So at daybreak of November 29, Chivington and his troops fell upon the sleeping Indians and killed about 450 of them.

The Chivington massacre led to four more years of savage fighting between the United States and

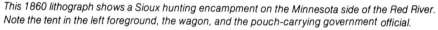

This 1860 lithograph shows a Sioux hunting encampment on the Minnesota side of the Red River. Note the tent in the left foreground, the wagon, and the pouch-carrying government official.

various Indian tribes. Finally, in 1868, most of the Plains Indians agreed to withdraw to two reservations, one in the Black Hills of the Dakota territory, the other in what is now Oklahoma.

Destruction of the Buffalo

One reason American troops were victorious was that they had the Winchester repeating rifle. The new weapon enabled the Americans to fire bullets faster than the Indians could shoot arrows. Another reason was the construction of a railroad network across the Great Plains. The railroad lines split up the buffalo herds, thus making it harder for Indians to hunt. They also brought in millions of settlers.

But the main reason for the American victory was simply the slaughter of the buffalo. Out of 15 million animals in 1865, only 600 remained in 1886. Some were killed by hunters hired by the railroads, who did not want to risk having a stampeding herd overturn their trains. Some were killed by rich European visitors enjoying a new form of recreation.

In 1871 a Pennsylvania tannery discovered that buffalo hides could be tanned into leather for harnesses, furniture, floor covering, and other products. With railroad lines available to take the hides to market, as many as 3 million buffalo were killed each year for the next three years. One man said, "I saw buffaloes lying dead on the prairie so thick that one could hardly see the ground. A man could have walked for twenty miles upon their carcasses."

And, of course, with the disappearance of the buffalo went the economic basis for the Plains Indians' way of life. As the herds dwindled, so did the Indians' ability to maintain their independence and resist the invaders. They were forced to find another way to live or to depend on the doubtful kindness of the settlers.

United States Army leaders encouraged the killing of buffalo as part of their military tactics. Buffalo hunters, said General Philip Sheridan, "have done more in the last two years, and will do more in the next year, to settle the vexed Indian question, than the entire regular army has done in the last thirty years. . . . For the sake of peace let them kill, skin, and sell until the buffalo are destroyed."

Section 1 Review

COMPREHENSION   **Developing Vocabulary**

1. Explain these terms: reservations, Chivington massacre, Bozeman Trail.

COMPREHENSION   **Mastering Facts**

1. Why did the government change its policy of keeping the Great Plains as one large Indian reservation?
2. Give three reasons why the reservations policy did not work.
3. What was the result of the Chivington massacre?
4. How did the slaughter of the buffalo affect the Plains Indians?

2   BROKEN TREATIES

The treaty of 1868 had promised the Sioux that they could live forever in *Paha Sapa*, the Black Hills area of what is now South Dakota and Wyoming. To the Sioux the area was sacred. It was the center of their land, the place where warriors went to await visions from their guardian spirits. It was also the only good hunting ground they had left.

Unfortunately for the Sioux, the Black Hills contained large deposits of gold. And as soon as Americans learned that gold had been discovered, they poured into the Indians' territory and began staking claims.

Leaders in the Indian Wars

The Indians appealed to Washington to enforce the treaty terms and remove the miners. The government responded by sending out a commission to either lease mineral rights or buy *Paha Sapa* outright. The Indians refused the commission's offer. Whereupon the government sent in the Seventh Cavalry to remove, not the miners, but the Indians.

The Seventh Cavalry was under the command of a tall, handsome man with blue eyes and long, curly blond hair. He was Lieutenant-Colonel

This painting is said to be the most accurate representation of the aftermath of the tragedy at Little Big Horn. The artist, J. K. Ralston, based his work on 39 authenticated incidents.

George Armstrong Custer. He had gained an enviable military reputation during the Civil War. In fact, he became a general when he was only twenty-three. When the war ended, his regiment was transferred to the frontier and he resumed his prewar rank. A Democrat who opposed Radical Reconstruction, Custer was rumored to have presidential ambitions.

Tatanka Yotanka ("Sitting Bull") was a medicine man whose visions often showed him what actions to take. He was also a remarkable politician. Plains Indians usually took orders only from the leader of their clan. When different clans or different tribes held joint conferences, every chief was considered equal to every other chief. But Tatanka Yotanka was acknowledged as being "above all the others." And in 1876 he succeeded in forming an alliance between the Arapaho, the Cheyenne, and the Sioux.

Tashunka Witko ("Crazy Horse") was the Indians' field commander. He was always coming up with new ways of moving his troops around and attacking the enemy where they least expected it. He was especially skilled at making charges and fake retreats that would draw off part of the opposing forces.

Custer's Last Stand

The battle known as Custer's Last Stand took place on June 25, 1876, along the banks of the Little Big Horn River in Montana. When it was over, Custer and all 215 of the officers and men with him were dead. It was the greatest victory the Plains Indians scored against United States forces. It was also the last.

The death of Custer and his men shook the United States. Buildings in major cities were draped in black cloth. Newspapers wrote editorials about the disgrace of a group of "savages" humiliating a nation of 50 million. Calls for vengeance were common. And Congress promptly voted money to enlarge the army and to send thousands of additional troops to the frontier.

In 1877 Crazy Horse chose to surrender. He was murdered at Fort Robinson, Nebraska, later that year. Sitting Bull escaped across the border into Canada, where he and other Indian refugees succeeded in holding out for four years. Finally, in 1881, Sitting Bull also surrendered. For the next nine years, he spent part of his time on a reservation and part touring with Buffalo Bill's Wild West Show. Ironically, Buffalo Bill—whose real

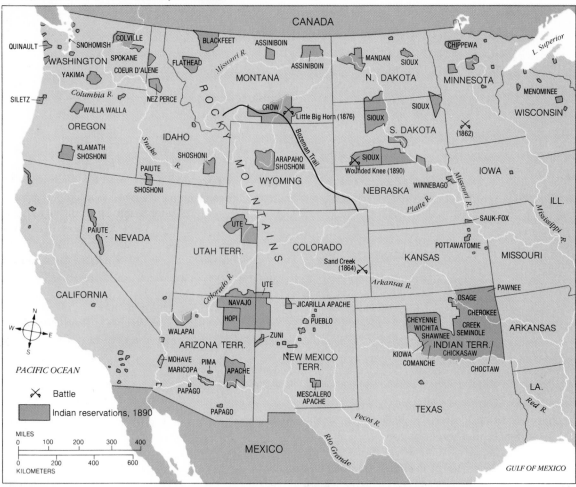

Map Skills *Which modern state was mostly Indian territory in 1890? In which state were the Mandan? the Navajo? the Crow? In what state was the battle at Wounded Knee? Sand Creek?*

name was William F. Cody—had earned his nickname by killing more than 4000 buffalo for the Kansas Pacific Railroad.

"Bury My Heart at Wounded Knee"

In 1889 the Sioux made one more attempt to keep their way of life. A Paiute (pie-*yute*) Indian named Wovoka presented himself as the Messiah. He said:

❝In the beginning, God made the earth, and then sent the Christ to earth to teach the people, but white men had treated him badly, leaving scars on his body, and so he had gone back to heaven. Now he had returned to earth as an Indian, and he was to renew everything as it used to be and make it better.❞

Then as one historian wrote:

❝In the next springtime, when the grass was knee high, the earth would be covered with new soil which would bury all the white men, and the new land would be covered with sweet grass and running water and trees. Great herds of buffalo and wild horses would come back. The Indians who danced the Ghost Dance would be taken up in the air and suspended there while a wave of new earth was passing, and then they would be set down among the ghosts of their ancestors on the new earth, where only Indians would live.❞

And so the Sioux began to dance. They danced on all the reservations. They danced instead of farming or trading or going to school. And the reservation agents, terrified that the dancing would lead to an armed uprising, sent for the Seventh Cavalry.

On December 29, 1890, the cavalry rounded up a group of about 350 Sioux—mostly old men, women, and children—and searched them for weapons. Two rifles were found. There was a scuffle, and a shot rang out. At once, soldiers on a nearby hill opened up with Hotchkiss machine guns. When the smoke cleared from the so-called Battle of Wounded Knee, about 200 Indians and 35 whites lay dead. Most of the whites had been killed by bullets from their own side.

Years later, Hehaka Sapa ("Black Elk") of the Sioux, who had been thirteen years old at the time of the "battle," spoke these words:

> " When I look back now from this high hill of my old age, I can still see the butchered women and children lying heaped and scattered all along the crooked gulch as plain as when I saw them with eyes still young. And I can see that something else died there in the bloody mud, and was buried in the blizzard. A people's dream died there. It was a beautiful dream. "

"Americanizing" the Indians

Though some military officials wanted to eliminate all Indians, many Americans had different opinions. Anthropologist Lewis Morgan, for example, argued that the Indians were only acting in self-defense. Helen Hunt Jackson, a well-known writer, published two books—*A Century of Dishonor* and the novel *Ramona*—in which she called people's attention to the government's broken promises to the Indians. Even President Grant, in his farewell speech in 1876, acknowledged that white miners should not have been allowed to enter the Black Hills.

Gradually, the mood in Congress shifted. Realizing that the Indians had been treated shamefully, congressmen now asked, "Why not 'Americanize' them?" The idea was to make them give up the tribal system and become individual farmers. As you know, this was what Thomas Jefferson hoped would eventually happen.

The Dawes Act. In 1887 Congress passed the Dawes Act. Under the act, Indian tribes were officially abolished. Each male head of an Indian family could claim 160 acres of reservation land as a farm. Bachelors and women could claim a smaller acreage. The federal government would hold the land in trust for twenty-five years while the Indians supposedly learned how to handle their own affairs. Then the Indians would receive legal title to the land. In the meantime, however, they would become American citizens. In 1906 the Burke Act postponed citizenship until the twenty-five-year period was over.

Failure of Dawes Act. The Americanization policy was a dismal failure. The Indians were not given any farm equipment, or even taught how to farm. Speculators managed to buy up more than two-thirds of the reservation land through loopholes in the law. The Office of Indian Affairs did not provide the Indians with proper health services. Disease and malnutrition were common on the reservations, and the death rate was high.

In addition, although the government set up schools for Indian children, most of the teachers were poorly trained. Worse still, they taught the children that Indians were "skulking savages" and that the Indian way of life consisted of "idleness, superstition, and barbarism." When the children left the schools, they found themselves between two cultures. They felt uncomfortable on the reservations. But if they left the reservations to work in the cities, they were discriminated against by the whites.

Section 2 Review

COMPREHENSION   Developing Vocabulary
1. Explain these terms: anthropologist, Paiute, Wounded Knee.

COMPREHENSION   Mastering Facts
1. What caused settlers to invade the Sioux reservation of *Paha Sapa*?
2. What did Wovoka teach?
3. How did the government hope to "Americanize" the Indians?
4. Why did the Dawes Act fail?

3 EXPLORING THE COWBOY IMAGE

VOCABULARY   *Longhorns   vaqueros   ranchero   drought*

Probably the greatest American folk hero is the cowboy. Young, slim, and wearing jeans and a ten-gallon hat, he slouches in his saddle, his eyes gazing into the distance. Then off he gallops after the herd of cattle he is driving north to market.

The Mexican Background

The American cattle industry that thrived on the Great Plains from 1866 to about 1890 was born in Mexico. This includes the cattle that were driven along the trails, the horses that cowboys rode, and the cowboys' clothes, equipment, and techniques.

The cattle were a sturdy breed called Texas Longhorns, a cross of Spanish and British stock. They had long legs and needle-pointed horns that measured five to six feet across. They stood heat well, could travel many miles without water, and were able to forage for food on their own. Their only drawback was nervousness. Any sudden noise or movement was liable to panic them and start them running in all directions.

The Spaniards brought cattle and horses with them to the New World. By the mid-1600s, there was a flourishing cattle industry in Mexico centered in the province of Texas. In 1821, as you know, Stephen F. Austin led a group of people from the United States into Mexico where they settled in the valley of the Brazos River. The climate was mild, and there was plenty of water, grass, and shade trees—perfect cattle country. The Anglos proceeded to learn about ranching from the Mexican *vaqueros* (vah-*care*-ohz), or "people who work with cows." They learned what kind of clothing and equipment they should have. They learned how to break in horses, how to rope cattle with a lasso, and how to use a branding iron.

The Anglo-Americans also adopted many Mexican words. *Corral, bronco, loco, and sombrero* were taken straight from Spanish. Other Spanish words became corrupted because of the English-speaking immigrants' inability to pronounce them clearly. Examples are ranch from the Spanish *ranchero*; rodeo from *rodear*, and stampede from *stampida*.

Organizing a Cattle Industry

Following their war for independence in 1836, the Texans expanded the ranching industry. They sent Longhorns to New Orleans by steamboat, and drove them overland to Sedalia, Missouri. In the 1850s a cattle disease called "Texas fever" broke out in Missouri and eastern Kansas. It was caused by ticks that the Longhorns carried but to which they themselves were immune. Missouri and Kansas farmers, however, were furious that their cattle were affected. They seized their shotguns and pitchforks, and forced the Texas herds to turn back at the state borders. In addition, both states passed quarantine laws against Longhorns.

When the Civil War broke out, Texas men

joined the Confederate army and left their cattle to fend for themselves. The animals managed so well that by 1865 they had increased from several hundred thousand head to at least 3.5 million.

Texans returning from the war thus found themselves with a prime asset. But they also faced a problem. How could they get all that beef to the industrial workers and European immigrants who were flooding northern cities? Quarantine laws blocked them to the north. There were no railroads into the Texas cattle country. And Mississippi River steamboats could carry only a few animals at a time.

The person who solved the problem was an Illinois cattle dealer named Joseph G. McCoy. In 1867 he built a shipping yard at Abilene, Kansas. The village was situated on the Kansas Pacific Railroad. Not only that, it lay 150 miles west of Sedalia, in central Kansas. And that part of Kansas contained only a few farmers. So despite the state's quarantine law against Longhorns, McCoy figured that no one around Abilene would try to stop cattle coming up from Texas.

McCoy's gamble paid off. That first season, some 35,000 Longhorns moved along the Chisholm Trail. From Abilene, 1000 cattle cars shipped the animals to packing plants in Chicago. The next year, 75,000 Longhorns plodded northward. And by 1871, more than 600,000 head of cattle were making the long drive.

The Long Drive

The typical herd on the long drive consisted of 1000 to 3000 cattle. The trail crew consisted of eight to eighteen cowboys, depending on the size of the herd. There was a trail boss, who was in command of the drive. And there was also a horse wrangler, who was in charge of the extra horses. Each cowboy used five or six horses in the course of a drive. Finally, there was a cook, usually Mexican, who drove the mule-drawn chuckwagon carrying food, bedding, and other camp equipment.

Life on the Drive. The cowboys worked from sunrise to sunset, with an additional two hours of night duty. Their morning alarm clock was the cook's call for breakfast, "Wake up Jacob, day's a-breakin', beans in the pan and sourdough's a-bakin'." Or, if the cook was not poetic, a simple "Grab a plate and growl." The cowboys would put on their trousers, boots, and hats; roll up their bedding and place it in the chuckwagon; gulp down their food; and saddle and mount their horses.

The cowboys kept the herd moving until about an hour before noon. Then they would camp for several hours. The cattle would be watered and allowed to graze. The men would take turns eating lunch. In late afternoon, the herd would be started up again and kept on the move until sundown, when the animals would sink to their knees and bed down for sleep. A herd could cover ten to twenty miles a day. So a long drive lasted about three to four months.

Dangers of the Drive. There were four things cowboys dreaded on the long drives: stampedes, thunder and lightning, rivers, and drought. Stampedes were probably the worst. It took hours to round up the scattered animals, and many were so badly injured they had to be shot. The cowboys were sometimes hurt, too. They might be thrown from their horses over a bluff or crushed to death by the cattle in their headlong flight. Stampedes are one reason there are so many cowboy songs. Cowboys used to sing lullabies to calm the cattle as they rode around the herd at night.

Although thunder and lightning were the most common cause of a stampede, lightning was equally dangerous to the cowboys. They took their chances while riding. In camp, however, they would always remove their six-shooters, spurs, belt buckles, and other metal objects, and pile them on the ground away from the campfire.

Rivers were a problem because they were difficult to cross. If something frightened the herd, the lead animals would try to turn back. The result was that the herd would mill around in the water, unable to either advance or retreat. After a time, the animals would become so tired that they would lose their footing and be swept downstream.

In order to save the animals, the cowboys rode their swimming horses into the tangle of horns and kicking hooves. They hit at the steers, shouting and trying to make them head for the bank. Many a man was swept off by the current and his body never found.

The rivers caused other problems—mostly in spring, when snow melting in the Rocky Mountains caused them to rise in their banks. In summer the problem was just the opposite: no rain, in a land without trees. Then the animals' tongues

A rare early photograph of cowboys rounding up cattle, preparing to continue a drive across the barren plains.

389

would swell up and turn black. The cowboys' lips would crack in the heat. And an alkali dust would settle on men and cattle alike.

Ending the Drive. As you may imagine, by the time the herd reached a cow town and the Longhorns were sold, the cowboys were raring to go. With their pay in their pockets, they would head first for the barbershop and the dry goods store. Next came a restaurant where they would order such delicacies as eggs, ice cream, and oysters. Then they would drop in on a saloon, a gambling parlor, or a dance hall. After several days of blowing off steam, they would head back home to Texas. They would spend winter on the ranch, telling yarns about their experiences up north. And in the spring they would start all over again.

The Myth About Cowboys

Your parents and grandparents would probably not recognize the cowboy's life you just read. What they learned was very different. Their cowboys were always having knock-down, drag-out fistfights in saloons. Their villains wore black hats and scowled. Their heroes were six feet tall, wore white hats, and held shootouts with the villains on dust-covered streets at high noon. Billy the Kid and Wild Bill Hickok were handsome and dashing, while Calamity Jane was a petite, spunky blonde. And, of course, there was not a black face among them.

The images portrayed in old westerns began in the late 1800s with dime novels. Buffalo Bill's Wild West Show and Owen Wister's best-seller *The Virginian* helped spread the myth throughout the United States. Then came the movies.

The first big cowboy film was *The Great Train Robbery*, made in 1907. Although a silent movie with subtitles, it was full of excitement. A gang of desperadoes tie up a telegrapher, stop a train carrying a shipment of gold, kill a man, and ride off with their loot. A group of cowboys chase the desperadoes and succeed in catching them and bringing them to justice. The high point of the film—apart from the chase—was the scene in which a cowboy fired his six-shooter directly at the audience! *The Great Train Robbery* earned so much money that other filmmakers began turning out westerns by the dozen. About one out of every four films made in Hollywood has been a western. Later, radio and television carried on the legends.

The Truth About Cowboys

What was the truth? Well, for one thing, a cowboy didn't like to fight with his fists. He needed strong, healthy hands in his work and could not afford to take the chance of injuring them in a fight. The typical cowboy was only five and a half feet tall. Shootings were rare. One out of every seven cowboys was black. One of the best-known black cowboys was Nat Love; his nickname was "Deadwood Dick."

What was Billy the Kid really like? His real name was Henry McCarty, and he was said to have been born in New York City. A cattle thief, he committed his first murder at age thirteen and boasted of twenty others. He was killed by a sheriff when he was twenty-two.

Wild Bill Hickok was a drifter, unable to hold down a job for more than a few months. He was a crack shot, though, and served as a U.S. marshal in Abilene during the summer of 1871. But the town trustees failed to renew his contract. In 1876 Hickok was shot in the back of the head while playing poker in a Deadwood, South Dakota, saloon. Since then, poker players refer to the cards he held as the "Dead Man's Hand"—the ace of spades, the ace of clubs, the eight of spades, the eight of clubs, and the queen of diamonds.

Nat Love (above) claimed to have won the title of "Deadwood Dick" in a roping contest, in Deadwood, S.D.

Calamity Jane poses beside the grave of a "pistol-shot" comrade—one of Custer's men.

Calamity Jane, born Martha Jane Canary, was "rough and burly" and passed as a man for most of her life. Two of her jobs were that of a mule-skinner and a scout in Custer's command. Luckily for her, she was hospitalized during June 1876. Otherwise, she might have been killed at the Battle of the Little Bighorn. Instead, she lived until 1903 and was buried beside Wild Bill Hickok in Mt. Moriah Cemetery in Deadwood.

Disappearance of the Cowboys' Frontier

By 1872, the prairie around Abilene had filled up with farmers. They did not like Longhorns trampling their crops. So the cattle trails shifted to western Kansas, ending up at such cow towns as Dodge City, Ellsworth, and Wichita.

In the meantime, the buffalo herds were killed off, and the Plains Indians were pushed onto reservations. This left millions of square miles of publicly owned grasslands that were unfenced and unused. Cattle could be fed on this pasturage free of charge. So northern cattlemen stopped bringing grown steers to market from Texas. Instead, they took to buying young animals and then fattening them for two or three years on the open range of Colorado, Montana, Wyoming, and the Dakotas. Since the pasturage was free, they stood to make a great deal of money.

The early 1880s were a boom period for the cattle industry. Demand was high, as Americans shifted from eating mostly pork to eating mostly beef. The invention of refrigerator cars and canning machinery helped get western beef to all parts of the United States and even to Europe. Prices kept rising. And hundreds of investors, many of them British, flocked to the region to make their fortunes.

Then came disaster. From December 31, 1885, through January 2, 1886, the worst blizzard in the history of the West hit the Great Plains. More than 300 persons, mostly cowboys attempting to bring cattle to safety, froze to death. Many ranchers lost up to three-fourths of their stock, and hundreds of cattlemen were ruined.

That summer there was a drought. Streams and rivers dried up, while temperatures of 120 degrees in the shade were common. Prairie fires raged continuously, filling the air with ash and smoke. With little grass left, tens of thousands of cattle starved to death.

The final blow came that winter. Once again, blizzards hit the Great Plains. When the spring thaw finally came, it revealed the frozen carcasses of 1.5 million animals!

The blizzards and drought resulted in wholesale bankruptcy and a basic change in the cattle industry. If the cattle were to survive, it was obvious that they could no longer be left to fend for themselves. They had to be protected. Instead of using public lands for grazing, cattlemen would have to buy their own grazing land and fence it in. They would also have to raise hay for winter feed.

Soon the cattle industry changed even more. Ranchers began to limit themselves to breeding and raising cattle. Then they would ship the animals by rail to farmers farther east who would fatten them for market. By 1890 the open range was fenced in, the cattle industry was a part of the meat-packing industry, and the cowboys' frontier had disappeared.

Section 3 Review

COMPREHENSION   Developing Vocabulary

1. Explain these terms: vaqueros, ranchero, drought, chuckwagon.

COMPREHENSION   Mastering Facts

1. Why were Texas Longhorns so well suited to the Southwest?
2. What was the long drive?
3. What did cowboys fear most on the drive?
4. What made cattlemen change their practice of letting their animals graze on the open range?

4 FARMERS TAME THE FRONTIER

VOCABULARY *exodusters soddy*

It took Americans 263 years—from the first settlement at Jamestown until 1870—to turn 400 million acres of forests and prairies into flourishing farms. Changing the second 400 million acres took only thirty years, from 1870 to 1900. This rapid settlement of the West was due to federal land policy and the transcontinental railroads.

Settling the Land

In 1862 Congress passed the Homestead Act giving 160 acres to anyone who would live on it for five years. About 400,000 families took advantage of the government's offer. Some were from the South. Some were New Englanders anxious to exchange their worn-out fields for more fertile land farther west. Some were German and Scandinavian farmers unable to earn a living in their native lands. About 6000 were *exodusters*—blacks who moved from the post-Reconstruction South to Kansas in a great exodus.

Free land, however, was not enough to lure farmers onto the Great Plains. What was needed was good transportation, both to bring people in and to take crops out. During the 1870s and 1880s, four transcontinental railroads were built. As the tracks moved westward toward the Rocky Mountains, they were followed by streams of settlers.

To encourage construction, the federal government had given the railroads huge tracts of land. In fact, the railroads were given about twice as much land as had been set aside under the Homestead Act. Both the Union Pacific and the Central Pacific, for example, received ten square miles of public land for every mile of track laid in a state, and twenty square miles of public land for every mile laid in a territory. Because of its location along the railroad tracks, such land was very desirable to farmers. So they bought it from the railroads for two to ten dollars an acre.

To further encourage land sales, the railroads took to advertising up and down the frontier, calling their lands "better than a homestead." Some railroads opened offices in London and sent agents all over Europe urging people to come to the Great Plains. They were very successful in their

Once the Oklahoma border was opened in the last government distribution of homesteads, a wild rush for the free land was on. A fast horse was an advantage in reaching one's preferred claim.

THE RUN FOR HOMES IN OKLAHOMA.

Cattle Trails and Early Transcontinental Railroads

Map Skills *In what part of Texas did the cattle trails begin? Which one went to Cheyenne? to Kansas City? About how long was the Sedalia Trail? To what railroad did it go?*

campaign. The 1880 census showed that the percentage of foreign-born settlers in the West ranged from 44 percent in Nebraska to more than 70 percent in Minnesota and Wisconsin.

The Great Land Giveaway

Although most Plains farmers bought their land, either from the government or from railroads, there *was* one final distribution of free homesteads. It took place in 1889 in what is now Oklahoma. The American writer Edna Ferber described what happened in her novel *Cimarron*.

"Folks, there's never been anything like it since Creation. . . . Thousands and thousands of people from all over this vast commonwealth of ours . . . traveled hundreds of miles to get a bare piece of land for nothing. . . . They came from Texas, and Arkansas and Colorado and Missouri. They came on foot, by God, all the way from Iowa and Nebraska! They came in buggies and wagons and on horseback and muleback. In prairie schooners and ox carts and carriages. . . .

Well, the Border at last. . . . No one was allowed to set foot on the new land until noon next day. . . .

There we stood, by the thousands, all night. Morning, and we began to line up at the Border, as near as they'd let us go. Militia all along to keep us back. They had burned the prairie ahead for

393

miles. . . . so as to keep the grass down and make the way clearer. To smoke out the Sooners, too, who had sneaked in and were hiding in the scrub oaks, in the draws, wherever they could. Most of the killing was due to them. They had crawled in and staked the land and stood ready to shoot those of us who came in, fair and square, in the Run. . . .

Ten o'clock, and the crowd was nervous and restless. . . . Well, eleven o'clock, and they were crowding and cursing and fighting for places near the Line. They shouted and sang and yelled and argued, and the sound they made wasn't human at all, but like thousands of wild animals penned up. The sun blazed down. It was cruel. The dust hung over everything in a thick cloud, blinding you and choking you. . . .

Eleven forty-five. Along the Border were the soldiers, their guns in one hand, their watches in the other. Those last five minutes seemed years long; and funny, they'd quieted till there wasn't a sound. Listening. The last minute was an eternity. Twelve o'clock. There went up a roar that drowned the crack of the soldiers' musketry as they fired in the air, . . . You could see the puffs of smoke from their guns, but you couldn't hear a sound. The thousands surged over the Line. It was like water going over a broken dam. **"**

In less than twenty-four hours, the land-hungry settlers had claimed two million acres. Ironically, Oklahoma is known as the Sooner State after those settlers who jumped the gun.

Everyday Life on the Prairie

"The hinges are of leather and the windows have no glass,
While the roof, it lets the howling blizzard in,
And I hear the hungry coyote, as he sneaks up through the grass,
'Round my little old sod shanty on the claim. **"**

The sod shanty of this song was the typical prairie house of the period. Why sod? Because trees were scarce on the Plains, and there was neither stone nor clay for bricks.

Life in Sod Houses. In making a "soddy," farmers would plow a strip of turf about a foot wide and five inches thick. Then they would chop the strip into blocks and place the blocks on the ground, grass side down, to start the wall of the house. The typical wall was thirty inches thick. After leveling the first layer of sod, farmers would put on the second layer, mismatching the two layers so as not to leave any cracks for mice and snakes. Window and door frames were made out of pack-ing boxes; the door, of planks nailed together; and the windows, of heavy oiled paper.

The biggest problem was the roof. Usually it consisted of thin wooden planking nailed to rafters and topped with a layer of sod, grass side up. Such roofs were very pretty in the springtime, when wildflowers bloomed on them. Unfortunately, if there was a heavy rain, they also leaked like a sieve. However, the sod did provide insulation against the winter cold.

Dug-out Homes. After the Civil War, the governor of Kansas, John P. St. John, invited as many black people as could come to settle in Kansas. Many joined with the exodusters. Nearly 20,000 blacks settled there in one year. By 1881, they had built ten settlements. One of the settlements was in the Solomon River valley of western Kansas. The town was named Nicodemus in honor of a former slave. Because of the lack of wood, this settlement began as a collection of dug-outs. They were even more primitive than sod houses. At least most sod houses were on the surface of the ground. But for these Kansas dwellings, settlers dug out a space on a bank or into a hill. Then they covered the opening with a roof of sod. People were living under the ground but it was a protection against snow and rain. One of the early settlers was Mrs. William Hickman, who arrived in Kansas on a cold and wet March evening. Years later she recalled that night.

"The men shouted, "There is Nicodemus." . . . I said, "Where is Nicodemus? I don't see anything."

My husband pointed out some smoke coming out of the ground in several places. . . .

Then I could see that people really were living in dugouts really in holes in the ground. **"**

What Mrs. Hickman had seen was her first prairie home. Later they were improved and became somewhat more comfortable.

Physical Strain. Rain and cold were not the only natural hazards that homesteaders faced on the Plains. Dry summers often brought raging prairie fires in their wake. Hailstorms pounded people and animals with stones the size of marbles. In the early 1870s, the region suffered a series of grasshopper plagues in which hundreds of millions of insects destroyed all the wheat and corn. They lay from four to six inches deep on the ground and even prevented the Union Pacific trains from moving along the tracks.

A Nebraska farmer and his family pose for their picture in front of their house. It is part cave, part sod blocks piled in horizontal layers. The treeless plains supplied no lumber.

Emotional Strain. Another problem that Plains farmers faced was not physical but emotional. It was loneliness. The land stretched for miles on end without even a tree to break its flat monotony. There was no place to go for recreation, no neighbors to drop by in the morning for coffee and conversation. Winter snows kept homesteaders indoors for weeks and sometimes months at a time—and without a telephone, radio, or television! People became cranky and restless. They would strike out, verbally or physically, at other members of the family. And once in a while, they would break under the strain and go insane.

About four out of five families that tried homesteading on the Plains between 1865 and 1890 never made it. After a while, they moved back east to easier surroundings. The ones who lasted had to be tough.

Technological Changes

Fortunately for Plains farmers, the technological boom that took place in the United States before and after the Civil War included agriculture. Thanks to four major inventions—barbed wire, the steel windmill, the steel plow, and the reaper—the Plains in the 1880s became America's breadbasket.

Historians usually credit the invention of barbed wire to Joseph F. Glidden, who received his patent in 1874. Farmers needed barbed wire for two reasons: to prevent their own cattle from wandering off, and to keep stray animals from trampling their crops. Longhorns could walk through a fence of ordinary wire without much trouble. But barbed wire was an effective barrier even to a stampeding herd.

Cattlemen hated barbed wire when it was first introduced. As one of them said, he wished that the "man who invented barbed wire had it all around him in a ball and the ball rolled into hell." But as the open range gave way to ranches, cattlemen, like farmers, found barbed wire of great value.

The steel windmill enabled Plains farmers to cope with the water shortage. Since rainfall was inadequate, subsurface water was the only alternative. However, farmers had to sink wells as much as 200 or 300 feet under the ground in order to tap a water supply. Hand-operated pumps and old oaken buckets obviously could not do the job of bringing the water to the surface.

The steel windmill was developed in the 1860s. The huge fan on top was powered by the constant prairie wind. And the windmill powered machinery that pumped water up to the surface. Factories in Illinois and Wisconsin began manufacturing windmills near the end of the decade, and by the 1870s they were a fairly common sight.

You will recall that the steel plow had been invented in 1837 by John Deere. This enabled the Plains farmers to grow large quantities of wheat. But because of hailstorms and sudden frosts, farmers also needed a faster means of harvesting their crops. The answer was Whitely's reaper, an improvement on the McCormick reaper. Whitely's reaper not only cut the wheat but threshed it as well. Before the Civil War, the average Plains farmer had sowed about eight acres for each worker on the farm. By 1890, the figure was 135 acres per worker.

Changing Farm Life

In these ways, improved technology helped Plains farmers increase their productivity. But it also made them increasingly vulnerable to forces over which they had little control. All that labor-saving machinery was expensive, which meant that most farmers could only buy it on credit. So long as wheat prices were high, farmers had no trouble paying their debts. But when wheat prices fell, the only way out, other than bankruptcy, was to grow more wheat. This in turn meant farmers had to mortgage the land they already owned in order to buy more land.

In addition to being dependent on banks, Plains farmers were dependent on the railroads. Without railroads, they could not get their crops to eastern and overseas markets. The railroads naturally charged whatever the traffic would bear. Farmers resented being gouged. Railroad officials looked at it this way: "What would it cost for a man to carry a ton of wheat one mile? What would it cost for a horse to do the same? The railroad does it at a cost of less than a cent."

By the 1890s, the farmers' frontier had disappeared from the Great Plains. There was no more free land available. Farms were large and required investments of tens of thousands of dollars. And farmers were as concerned about railroad rates and the cost of credit as they were about the weather or the opposition of Indians and cattlemen.

Section 4 Review

COMPREHENSION Developing Vocabulary

1. Explain these terms: exodusters, soddy, Sooners.

COMPREHENSION Mastering Facts

1. What was needed, in addition to free land, to lure farmers onto the Great Plains?
2. What physical problems did Plains farmers face?
3. What percentage of people who tried homesteading on the Great Plains did not succeed?
4. How did the invention of barbed wire and the steel plow help the prairie settler?

CHAPTER 18   Review

Chapter Summary

Following the Civil War, the old frontier began to disappear. Indians were forced onto reservations, and farmers began to cultivate the Great Plains. Completion of the transcontinental railroad in 1869 heightened the conflict between Indians and settlers. The growth of railroads attracted ranchers with their cattle drives and farmers with their crops. When farmers began to fence in the open range, the cowboys' frontier began to disappear. The last free distribution of land under the Homestead Act (1862) took place in 1889. Meanwhile, though the frontier disappeared, life was still extremely difficult for those who lived on the prairies and Great Plains. Only gradually did technology improve conditions and increase farmers' productivity.

Questions for Critical Thinking

COMPREHENSION   Summarizing Main Ideas

1. What effect did the introduction of the horse have on the Indian population of the Great Plains? on inter-tribal relations?
2. How did each of the following contribute to the eventual defeat of the Plains Indians? (a) the slaughter of the buffalo; (b) the invention of the Winchester repeating rifle; (c) the building of transcontinental railroads; (d) the discovery of gold in the Black Hills; (e) anti-Indian prejudice.
3. What did Mexico contribute to the American cattle industry?
4. What effect did the railroads have on the long drive?
5. What effect did each of the following have on the settlement of the Great Plains? (a) the Homestead Act of 1862; (b) the railroads; (c) barbed wire; (d) grasshopper plagues; (e) loneliness.

COMPREHENSION   Interpreting Events

1. Why did Congress pass the Dawes Act? How did it change the policy of the federal government toward Indians? What were its results?
2. Why did most Americans have a mistaken idea of what the cowboy's life was like? What was the truth?
3. Why did the cowboys' frontier disappear?
4. Why did the farmers' frontier disappear?

APPLICATION   Using Skills To Read Maps

Data can be obtained from maps as well as from text. Look at the map on page 393 and answer the following questions.

1. What was the approximate size of the area that made up the original range of the Texas Longhorns?
2. Which cattle trail led from South Texas to Ogallala?
3. To what towns did the Chisholm Trail go?
4. Through what states did the Goodnight-Loving Trail go?
5. What was the approximate distance between Abilene and Chicago?
6. Name two railroads that took cattle to market.
7. In general, the cattle trails ran in what direction?

EVALUATION   Comparing Past to Present

1. Americans are still moving West in large numbers. Compare the reasons for today's migration with the reasons for the migration after the Civil War.
2. Is an adequate water supply a problem in the West today? Give evidence to support your answer.
3. Do you think the space frontier will have as much influence on Americans of the future as the western frontier had on Americans after the Civil War? What makes you think so?

The Great Plains

Before the Civil War, most Americans thought of the territory west of the Missouri River as a vast, uninhabitable wilderness. In 1820, Major Stephen Long had led an army expedition through what is now Nebraska, eastern Colorado, northern Texas, and Oklahoma. He labeled the treeless, short-grass plain east of the Rocky Mountains the "Great American Desert." Because of the scarcity of wood and water, a member of the expedition described the region as "almost wholly unfit for cultivation."

This perception of the region—now known as the Great Plains—stuck for many years. As a result, most of the tens of thousands of pioneers winding their way up the Platte and Arkansas River valleys along the Oregon and Santa Fe trails did not stop.

The Land. The Great Plains covers a large area of the United States—more than 600,000 square miles. It lies between the Rocky Mountains and the Central Lowland, extending some 1600 miles from Canada to Mexico and averaging about 400 miles wide. The Great Plains crosses ten states, including the western parts of North Dakota, South Dakota, Nebraska, Kansas, Oklahoma, and Texas, and the eastern parts of Montana, Wyoming, Colorado, and New Mexico. The total population of the Great Plains in 1980 was about 7 million.

In the east at about 98 degrees west longitude, where the Great Plains merges with the Central Lowland, the land is about 2000 feet above sea level. The land gradually slopes upward at about ten feet per mile toward the west, where at between 5000 and 6000 feet above sea level the Great Plains reaches the Rocky Mountains. Occasionally there is some dramatic relief from the otherwise flat appearance of the western plains. In southwestern South Dakota, for example, are the Badlands, an area of rainbow-colored, sharp-angled hills and buttes. In western South Dakota are the Black Hills, whose wooded slopes rise above the plains to more than 7000 feet above sea level.

Except for the reservoirs formed behind dams in modern times, there are no lakes on the Great Plains. The rivers generally flow to the east, most of them eventually reaching the Mississippi. The rivers are fewer and shallower than back east. Many, like the Platte, are braided streams, dividing into crisscrossing channels threaded with sandbars. Only on the eastern margins of the Great Plains are there many trees, and then usually along the well-watered

In the eastern half of North Dakota is found some of the nation's most fertile soil. Treeless and without rocks, the flat land of this part of the Great Plains was transformed in the 1880s into rich wheat country.

bottomlands of the rivers. In the west there are almost no trees.

In the east, precipitation, both rain and snow together, averages 25 inches or more per year; in the west it is as little as ten inches.

The Climate. The climate of the Great Plains is marked by wide contrasts of weather and seasons. Winters are very cold in the far north, with average daily low temperatures close to 0 degrees F in January. Winters are much milder in the south. Except for northern Montana and North Dakota, summers are warm throughout the Great Plains, with average daily high temperatures in the upper 80s or the 90s in July.

With few hills or forests to block them, winds sweep freely over the northern Great Plains in winter. Blizzards can pile up huge snowdrifts across roads and along fences. On the other hand, hot, drying winds in summer often wither the growing crops and may blow away loose, plowed topsoil.

The Changes. The Great Plains, populated mainly by nomadic Indians, lay almost empty of farmers well into the nineteenth century. Occasional army posts were established to protect the pioneers from the Indians. There also were stagecoach stations, which provided fresh horses for travelers making the rough overland journey to the West Coast.

In 1862, the U.S. Congress passed a law that would radi-

The Great Plains

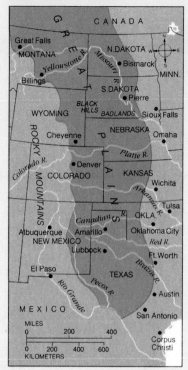

cally alter the character of the Great Plains. The Homestead Act brought in many thousands of settlers, with the promise of 160 free acres of land to any head of a family over 21 years of age who was willing to live on the land and farm it. A popular song of the day hailed this generous law with the lyric: "Uncle Sam is rich enough to give us all a farm!"

The completion of the transcontinental railroad in 1869 not only enabled travelers to journey from New York all the way to California, but it boosted trade and settlement on the Great Plains.

The discovery of gold in the Black Hills lured thousands more to South Dakota in the

1870s. A few years later, cheap land sold by the railroads brought farm families to North Dakota, where they soon began planting large expanses of wheat. Today wheat is the main crop on the Great Plains.

The Dust Bowl. In the 1930s, prolonged drought, along with the strong winds characteristic of the Great Plains, turned large parts of it into a giant "dust bowl." Tens of thousands of destitute farmers fled. Since then, however, agriculture in the region has more than recovered from that natural disaster, with increased reliance on well irrigation and dry farming methods.

Today. In recent years the Great Plains, while still largely rural, has become increasingly industrialized and urban. Of the nation's largest cities, only Denver is actually on the Great Plains. But several, such as Wichita, Oklahoma City, Fort Worth, and San Antonio, are near its edge. With an economy based solidly on agriculture and expanding industry, the future prosperity of the Great Plains seems assured.

Understanding Geography

1. What happened to the Great Plains in the 1930s?

2. What is the main crop today on the Great Plains?

3. What kind of climate does the Great Plains have?

4. How did the Homestead Act change the Great Plains?

CHAPTER 19

A New Industrial Age

1876–1900

People in the Chapter

Thomas Alva Edison—*the genius whose applications of electricity in a series of inventions help industrialize the nation and the world.*

Professor C. F. Dowd—*the man who suggests the idea of time zones and names those which cover most of the United States.*

Andrew Carnegie—*a Scottish-born telegraph messenger who revolutionizes the steel industry and becomes a millionaire and a great philanthropist.*

John D. Rockefeller—*a financial wizard who builds up a monopoly in the oil refining and marketing industries.*

Linking Past to Present

Between the end of the Civil War and the turn of the century, the United States underwent striking changes. One was the passing of the old frontier. Another was the development of an industrial society. By 1894 the United States had surpassed Great Britain, where the Industrial Revolution had begun, to become the mightiest industrial power on earth.

The growth of industry was based on a series of inventions which were used by men of vision and determination to create the great industries of oil, steel, and railroads. The leaders of industry were, by and large, men of poor background who had risen by their own efforts to become rich and famous. Their careers seemed to prove what people had said for years: America was the land of golden opportunity. But to be successful in the highly competitive world of business, one had to be shrewd and even ruthless. The assumption was that success belonged to the best. In time, however, some people began questioning whether whatever was best for business was always best for the rest of society.

1 INDUSTRIES EXPAND

VOCABULARY   *technology   incandescent light   Bessemer process*

Like the Industrial Revolution itself, the new industrial age grew out of new *technology*—that is, the application of scientific discoveries to industry. But the basic power source was different. The Industrial Revolution had been sparked by the steam engine. The new industrial age was based on electricity.

Electricity: The Silent Servant

The great advantage of electric power was the fact that it was portable. Thus you no longer had to build a factory near a waterfall. Instead, you could build it near your raw materials, or market, or labor supply, or in an area of cheap land or low taxes. The use of electric power helped spread factories to all parts of our nation.

In addition, electric motors were much more flexible than steam engines. Steam engines had to be large, because they used large quantities of fuel and water. But you could make an electric motor in whatever size was best suited for your needs. In a factory, for example, you could have several different-size motors, each adapted to a different task and each operating on its own.

Electric motors became important in transportation as well as manufacturing. Many cities followed the example of Richmond, Virginia, and installed public trolley systems to replace horse-drawn cars. Some added electric snowplows, electric mail cars, and electric taxis. As trolley-car lines spread outward from the center of town, so did new construction. Cities grew larger, and their population became more dispersed.

People also applied electric power to communication. The American version of the electric telegraph had been developed in the 1830s and 1840s by Samuel F. B. Morse. During the Civil War, President Lincoln received campaign news via telegraph directly from the field; he sent instructions to his generals the same way. The South did not have this direct communication. Thus the North was able to respond to changing battle conditions much more rapidly than the South.

Gradually, too, newspaper columns headed "by telegraph from . . ." became common. People grew accustomed to learning about events within twenty-four hours after they happened. Newspaper sales increased, and so did the influence of the press. Papers began carrying detailed national as well as local news. Americans began to get more of a sense of what they were like as a nation.

When the Civil War ended, the United States had about 76,000 miles of telegraph lines. This included a transcontinental line from New York to San Francisco. By 1900, the telegraph network was about a million miles long, and Americans were sending some 63 million business and personal messages a year.

The Wizard of Menlo Park

Another area to which people applied electric power was illumination. Here the great name is Thomas Alva Edison. He is often called "the Wizard of Menlo Park" because in later life he worked in his own laboratory at Menlo Park, New Jersey. Actually, it was more of an invention factory than a laboratory, for Edison knew little about basic science. He was essentially a "tinkerer," that is, someone who tries to solve specific problems and who likes to experiment.

Edison was born in 1847. He started school at the age of seven but quit after only three months

Thomas Edison's invention of the incandescent lamp had far-reaching effects in transforming the appearance of American towns and cities and changing home and business life.

when the headmaster called him "addled" (confused). Instead, he took to reading and exploring the world around him. He was immensely curious. He built a fire in his father's barn just to see what would happen. What happened was that he got a spanking. To find out why a goose squatted on eggs, he would get as close as he could to the nest and watch for hours. He also experimented with chemicals and built his own telegraph set. Later, he worked as a telegraph operator, choosing the night shift so that he could spend his days reading. The most important book he read was *Experimental Researches in Electricity*, by British scientist Michael Faraday, inventor of the dynamo.

Edison soon began turning out inventions of his own. They included the phonograph, the motion picture camera, and the microphone. All told, he took out more than 1000 patents with the United States Patent Office. But perhaps the most revolutionary of his inventions was the incandescent light bulb.

Electric arc lamps were already being made during the 1870s. They were called arc lamps because an arc of light was created by jumping an electric current between two sticks of carbon. In 1878 merchant John Wanamaker of Philadelphia got ahead of his competitors by putting arc lights in his department store and doing business at night. By 1880 several cities had installed arc lights on their major streets.

Arc lights, however, were not an efficient way to use electricity. They made a noise. One had to keep adjusting the distance between the carbon sticks to make the light steady. And the light was really too strong for private homes. The problem was twofold: 1. how to replace the carbon sticks with a filament that would glow for a long time without melting or exploding; and 2. how to take only a small amount of current off a main line so that turning a few lights on or off would not affect the entire system.

Edison solved both problems. He tried thousands of possible filaments, including hairs from his assistants' beards. Fortunately for the assistants, the best substance turned out to be carbonized bamboo from Japan. Later, the bamboo was replaced by tungsten. Edison also invented a system for stepping down electric current.

But Edison did not stop there. He realized that people could not really use light bulbs unless there was a central source of supply. After all, it was impossible for every household to have its own dynamo chugging in the backyard! So Edison worked out the details for a complete light-and-power system. And in 1882, just two years after patenting the light bulb, he opened the first central power station on Pearl Street in New York. At first he supplied current to downtown stores; later, to individual customers. By 1900, 25 million light bulbs were burning in the United States.

New Forms of Communication

Two other inventions that helped change American life between 1865 and 1900 were the telephone and the typewriter.

The Telephone. The telephone first appeared in public at the 1876 Philadelphia Centennial Exposition, a year after it had been invented by Alexander Graham Bell. The machine did not make much of an impression at first. Then Dom Pedro II, the visiting emperor of Brazil, walked by. He had met Bell during an earlier visit to Boston and had liked the way Bell was teaching deaf-mutes how to speak. When Dom Pedro saw Bell sitting with his machine, he insisted on being shown how it worked. "My God, it talks!" he exclaimed. The emperor's excited shouts immediately drew a large crowd. More important, the exposition's judges, who had passed by the exhibit just a few minutes before, turned back to see what the fuss was about.

The telephone soon became extremely popular. The first switchboard in New Haven, Connecticut, began operating in 1878, with twenty-one subscribers. Two years later, there were 54,000 telephones in service in the United States. By 1900, there were 1.5 million. Forests of telephone poles sprouted in all major cities and then began to move cross-country. By 1887, New Yorkers were talking long-distance to Philadelphia. The New York–Chicago line went into operation in 1892. And the first transcontinental line was in service in 1915.

Bell's invention not only speeded up communication and helped tie the different parts of our nation together. It also had a profound effect on the role of women in the economy.

The first telephone switchboard operators were men. Then employers discovered that women

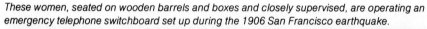

These women, seated on wooden barrels and boxes and closely supervised, are operating an emergency telephone switchboard set up during the 1906 San Francisco earthquake.

could do the work just as well for less pay. By 1888, women were handling most daytime exchanges. They moved onto the night shift around 1900. Soon there were some 77,000 female telephone operators, or about 96 percent of the total.

The Typewriter. Even more significant in its consequences for women workers was the typewriter, which was invented by Christopher Latham Sholes in 1867. Sholes, who had worked as an editor and a postmaster, looked on his invention as an amusing toy. The Remington Arms Company, however, took a different view. In 1874 the firm bought Sholes's patent rights to the machine and proceeded to revolutionize offices throughout the nation.

In 1870 women made up less than 5 percent of office workers. By 1900, they made up more than 75 percent, or about 500,000. Most of them were between fifteen and twenty-four years old, single, and living at home. Most of them were also white and native-born. If a woman were black, Jewish, an immigrant, or even the daughter of an immigrant, she was out of luck. White-collar work was reserved for "real Americans." It was cleaner and easier than factory or domestic work. One was paid by the week rather than by the hour. And the work was usually steady, so one was less likely to be laid off. With such an economic base, women began to press more strongly for voting rights.

Sholes received only $12,000 from the Remington Arms Company (later Remington Rand) for his revolutionary invention. His financial backer, who took royalties from Remington rather than cash, ended up with $1.5 million. But Sholes was a philosophical person. "All my life I have been trying to escape being a millionaire," he said, "and now I think I have succeeded."

Muscles of Steel

The new industrial age would not have been possible without steel. Both wood and cast iron, which people used in earlier machines, are brittle and wear out easily. Also, it is difficult to make them to exact specifications. Steel, on the other hand, is strong, long-lasting, and easily shaped.

Bessemer Process. Before the Civil War, only a few thousand tons of steel were produced in the United States. Consequently, it was very expensive and was used only for such special items as swords and high-grade tools. Then two men, an American named William Kelly and an Englishman named Henry Bessemer, came up almost at the same time with a new manufacturing technique. Eventually known as the Bessemer process, it made steel production more efficient and much less expensive. Some years later another technique, known as the open-hearth process, was introduced. It cost more than the Bessemer process, but it made it possible to control the steel's quality. By the 1890s, most of the millions of tons of steel produced in our nation were made on the open hearth.

And what a spectacular process it was! The ovens were huge. The heat was intense. Showers of sparks rose to the sky as air blasts hit the molten iron. And the liquid steel poured down like a river of fire.

Joe Magarac. Most of the nation's steel mills were concentrated in Pennsylvania, and most of the steelworkers were Slavs. They created a new folk hero named Joe Magarac. Arriving one Sun-

Author Mark Twain (below) submitted his manuscript for Tom Sawyer *(1876) in typewritten form to the printer—the first American writer to do so.*

Mining and Industry in the United States 1850–1900

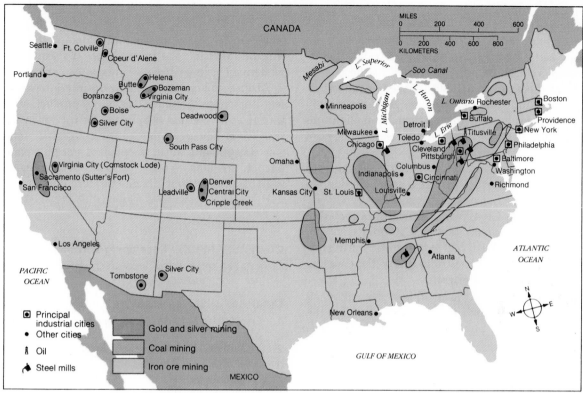

Map Skills *What principal industrial cities are shown? In what part of the U.S. were they? Around what city were several steel mills? What was mined in the Butte-Helena area?*

© ML & Co.

day at a local contest of strength, so the legend goes, this seven-foot giant "with a back as broad as a door, easily lifted in one hand an 800-pound bar. . . . All he needed was five good meals a day. His home was the mill where he worked night and day, feeding the open-hearth furnace, stirring the molten steel with his fingers and shaping rails with his bare hands."

Tin Cans and Barbed Wire. The rails Joe Magarac reputedly shaped with his hands were but one of dozens of steel products that poured from American factories. Among the most significant were barbed wire and tin-plated cans. Barbed wire, as you know, changed both the cattle industry and farming on the Great Plains.

The first tin can was introduced into the United States in 1818 by an Englishman named Peter Durand. The following year Ezra Daggett and Thomas Kensett started one of the first canning businesses in America when they began canning fish. But now the cans could be produced in greater quantities and at cheaper prices. More

people could benefit from this new way of preserving food. Marketing became easier, and meals became more varied.

Riches from the Earth

Making steel requires iron and coal. Fortunately for the United States, it has ample supplies of both.

Iron Ore Discovered. Iron ore came mostly from eastern deposits. Around the middle of the century, prospectors discovered new ore fields in the Lake Superior region. In 1855 the Soo Canal was built between Lake Superior and Lake Huron. This enabled iron ore to be shipped by water to the Pennsylvania steel mills. In 1887 the iron-ore deposits in the Mesabi Range of Minnesota were found. The Mesabi fields have yielded more iron ore than any other deposit in the world. In addition, Mesabi ore lies near the surface, so expensive underground mining is not necessary.

Coal. Most U.S. coal comes from an area that lies along the Allegheny Mountains from Pennsylvania to Alabama. People had used coal since colonial times for domestic heating and cooking. In the early 1800s, locomotives and other steam-driven vehicles used coal as a fuel. As the United States became more industrialized, demand increased. And so did production, jumping from 33 million tons in 1870 to more than 250 million tons in 1900.

Oil. Besides iron ore and coal, oil was needed in the new industrial age. Here again, the United States seemed to have ample resources.

Before the Civil War, Americans did not drill for oil. They simply skimmed it from creeks or other places where it had seeped to the earth's surface. They used it mostly to grease their wagons and as a rub for rheumatism.

For generations, whale oil had been used all over the world for lighting lamps. But by the 1850s, the whale population was beginning to decline. Whale oil was becoming scarce, and the price was going up. Kerosene seemed a possible substitute. So in 1857, a lawyer named George H. Bissell sent a railroad conductor named E. L. Drake to Titusville, Pennsylvania. Drake, imitating the production technique of the salt industry started drilling the nation's first commercial oil well. In 1859, after going down almost seventy feet, "Drake's folly" finally gushed in, and the petroleum industry was on its way. (By contrast, modern oil wells go down as much as two miles.)

At first, the oil was refined primarily into kerosene for lamps. Gasoline, an oil by-product, was thrown away because people had no use for it. In the 1890s, however, the internal-combustion engine was put into a car. It operated not on steam but on gasoline. Today, gasoline is the most valuable product that oil refineries turn out.

Section 1 Review

COMPREHENSION Developing Vocabulary

1. Explain these terms: technology, Bessemer process, incandescent light.

COMPREHENSION Mastering Facts

1. On what kind of power was the new industrial age based?
2. How did the typewriter revolutionize office work?
3. What advantages does steel have over wood and cast iron?
4. What three minerals were needed for the new industrial age?

2 RAILROADS CONNECT THE NATION

VOCABULARY   *National Grange   public utility*

Of all the industries that developed during the period between 1865 and 1900, perhaps the one that most affected people's lives was the railroad.

The Influence of the Iron Horse

Statistics bear out the immense importance of railroads in the new industrial age. In 1870 the railroads employed 163,000 persons. In 1900 they employed more than a million. In fact, by 1880 they were the largest industry in the nation, and the value of their stocks and bonds was more than the national debt.

Cultural Effects. People hung pictures of famous trains on the walls of their living rooms and dens. They used railroad phrases in their conversation. As one historian said:

"They got sidetracked or came uncoupled; or, if things were going better, they got up a full head of steam, highballed it, and warned their neighbors to clear the track. Expressing disapproval of almost anything, we exclaim even today, "That's a heck of a way to run a railroad!" . . . Nor was it long before the railroad achieved a special place in literature, song, and folklore. . . . From early tributes to those who built the roads, like John Henry and the singer of "I Been Working on the Railroad," to . . . pop tunes like "Chattanooga Choo Choo" and "The Atchison, Topeka, and the Santa Fe," the railroad has forever occupied our song."

Standard Time. Railroads influenced time. Originally, each railroad followed its own time. Thus, if there were five different railroad lines using the same station, there would be five different clocks on the wall, no two of them alike. In addition, there were different times within a state.

Illinois, for example, had twenty-seven, while Wisconsin had thirty-eight. If you were traveling from coast to coast, you had to change your watch at least twenty times along the way if you wanted to keep up with local time. The confusion was tremendous.

In 1870 Professor C. F. Dowd started a campaign for uniform time. He suggested that the earth's surface be divided into twenty-four time belts, or zones, beginning at Greenwich, England (which is at 0 degrees longitude). Each zone would represent one hour. The continental United States would have four such zones, which Dowd named Eastern, Central, Mountain, and Pacific. Thus, when it was noon in New York City, it would be eleven o'clock in Chicago, ten in Denver, and nine in San Francisco.

In 1872 the railroads decided to adopt Dowd's suggestion. But it took until 1883 before the plan went into effect. However, no sooner did the railroads adopt standard time zones, then the rest of the nation did the same. As one newspaper declared, "The sun is no longer boss of the job. People, 55 million of them, must eat, sleep and work, as well as travel, by railroad time." In 1918 Congress passed an act making the time zones official. In 1966 Congress passed another act that set up eight time zones, thus including Alaska, Hawaii, and all U.S. possessions. Later, Congress also adopted daylight saving time in summer as a fuel-saving measure. The only holdouts are Arizona, Hawaii, Puerto Rico, and part of Indiana.

From Sea to Shining Sea

The first railroad locomotive arrived in the United States from England in 1829. Twenty-five years later, the railroad reached the Mississippi River at Rock Island, Illinois. A few years later work began on the first transcontinental railroad in America.

Choosing a Route. The idea of a railroad that would run from the Atlantic to the Pacific was first raised in 1832. No one gave the idea much attention, however, until gold was discovered in California. Then people became very interested indeed, and several possible routes were discussed in Congress. There was a southern route by way of El Paso and San Diego; a central route from St. Louis through Colorado; and a northern route from Chicago toward the Columbia River between the present states of Washington and Oregon. As it turned out, none of the three was chosen. The outbreak of the Civil War removed the southern route as a possibility. And President Lincoln even-

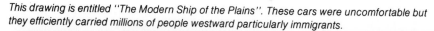

This drawing is entitled "The Modern Ship of the Plains". These cars were uncomfortable but they efficiently carried millions of people westward particularly immigrants.

Railroad Land Grants and Time Zones   1850–1900

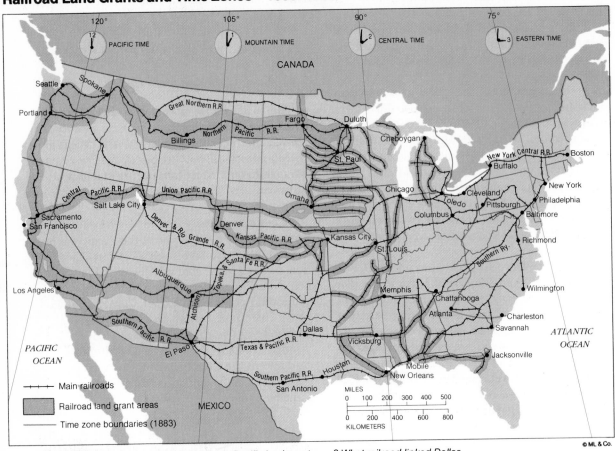

Map Skills   *How wide was the Northern Pacific land grant area? What railroad linked Dallas and El Paso? Kansas City and Denver? In what time zone was Cleveland in 1883?*

tually decided that the first line should run from Omaha, Nebraska, to Sacramento, California.

In 1862 Lincoln signed the Pacific Railroad Act. A second Railroad Act was passed in 1864. Under these acts, the Union Pacific and Central Pacific Railroad companies received about 20 million acres of land, as well as federal loans in the amount of $60 million. Additional money was invested by individuals hoping to make a profit, and by towns that wanted to make certain that the railroad would not pass them by.

The Two Tracks Begin.   Construction of the two lines moved slowly at first, for the nation's attention was focused on the Civil War. In 1865, however, thousands of young veterans found themselves at loose ends. They were strong, used to danger, and trained to do what they were told. They were as eager to work as the railroad was eager to

hire them. The majority of those who laid tracks for the Union Pacific were Irish immigrants. But there were native-born Americans as well, both white and black.

The Union Pacific work gangs were headed by a former Union general, Jack S. Casement, and his brother Dan. Jack Casement stood only five feet four inches; his brother was "five feet nothing." They were said to resemble a pair of bearded midgets. But as they organized men and equipment and moved out across hundreds of miles of almost uninhabited land, it soon became obvious that they were "the biggest little men you ever saw."

And indeed, the difficulties were tremendous. Lines had to be surveyed despite the danger of attacks by the Sioux and Cheyenne. Materials—iron rails, hardware, timber for ties and trestles—had to be transported from 500 to 1500 miles. So did food and water for the workers. In addition, accidents were common, many men were killed in drunken brawls, and pneumonia and other diseases took a heavy toll.

The Chinese Workers. The Central Pacific had its problems, too. The main difficulty was a shortage of labor, for there were few Civil War veterans in California. Then Charlie Crocker, the railroad's general superintendent, decided to hire some Chinese. About 25,000 had come from Canton in 1850 to take part in the gold rush.

Crocker's decision was greeted with skepticism. How could men who only weighed 110 pounds move earth and stone? "Did they not build the Chinese Wall," Crocker exclaimed, "the biggest piece of masonry in the world?" And he went ahead with his plan.

The Chinese, soon known as "Crocker's pets," turned out to be excellent workers—steady, patient, and brave. Some of the tasks they performed were astounding. In 1866, for example, it was necessary to drive a tunnel through a mountain. The tunnel was only a quarter of a mile long. But the granite of the mountain was so hard that it took twelve hours to chip away eight inches. (Dynamite had just been invented but was not in general use.) The entire tunnel took a full year to dig. And for five months of the year, the work was done with work camps buried under forty feet of snow. Chimneys and air shafts had to be dug to the surface. Lanterns burned twenty-four hours a day. The Chinese lived and worked "like moles, in dim passages far below the earth's surface." Avalanches made life even more difficult. Hundreds of Chinese were swept away by snowslides and their bodies not recovered until the spring thaw. Some were found "with shovels or picks still clutched in their frozen hands."

And what did the Chinese receive for their efforts? Less than white workers. The Chinese worked from sunrise to sunset; white workers, eight hours a day. The Chinese earned thirty-five dollars a month; white workers, from forty to sixty dollars. The Chinese had to buy their own dried fish, rice, and tea; white workers were fed by the railroad free of charge.

A Workers' Duel. The last few months of construction were sparked by a duel between the workers of the Union Pacific and those of the Central Pacific to see which group could lay the most

track in a single day. Both sides kept increasing production until finally Casement's men laid 7.5 miles of track in twelve hours. Crocker thereupon promised that *his* men would lay ten miles in one day. When Thomas C. Durant, vice president of the Union Pacific, heard about the promise, he bet Crocker $10,000 that it couldn't be done. To everyone's amazement, it was. And that record has never been broken.

Finally, on May 10, 1869, the greatest engineering and construction effort undertaken since the arrival of the first Europeans on the American continent was over. The two rail lines were joined at Promontory Point, Utah, and the United States was joined from coast to coast with rails of steel.

Traveling on the Transcontinental

The greatest adventure Americans could experience during the 1870s and 1880s was to travel across the continent by rail. Just think of all the wonderful things you could see on the eight- to ten-day trip! The Missouri River bridge, which

Rail travel—at least for more affluent Americans—was quite luxurious, as this train interior shows.

framed the seemingly endless prairies beyond; the snow-topped ranges of the Rockies; the strange shapes and colors of canyon rocks; Salt Lake City, an oasis of flowers, trees, and stream-lined streets; the 105-mile long stretch down a 7000-foot-drop from the top of the Sierra Nevada Mountains to Sacramento, half of which was made with the brakes on; prairie-dog villages and antelope that raced the train (the antelope usually won); and, especially, herds of buffalo and "real wild Indians." The vast size and variety of the West created a feeling of awe among travelers, as well as an intense sense of patriotism.

Until the late 1880s, when regular food service on trains was introduced, travelers ate their meals at dining stations along the road. These stations were not run by the railroads but were contracted to private individuals, and the food and service ranged from "wretched to middling-fair." Breakfast, lunch, and dinner were usually the same. They consisted primarily of beefsteak, fried eggs, and fried potatoes. Meal prices averaged a dollar, and passengers were allowed from twenty to thirty minutes per meal.

Sleeping accommodations depended on whether you rode a Pullman car, a day coach, or a Zulu car. A Pullman car, first introduced in 1859 by George M. Pullman, was the best. For one hundred dollars, plus four dollars a day, travelers could ride from Omaha to Sacramento on a comfortable sofa that converted into a bed with warm blankets and a certain amount of privacy. For day-coach passengers, who paid seventy-five dollars, the seat back was lowered at night and the footrest extended. Zulu cars cost forty dollars to ride and were used mostly by European immigrants to whom the railroads had sold land. Some Zulu cars contained rows of backless benches; passengers took turns sleeping under the benches or in the aisles. Other Zulu cars contained wooden cubicles in which people could either sit or stretch out, depending on the number of passengers.

And then there were the private cars of wealthy businessmen and politicians. They contained such items as "marble baths, plate-glass mirrors, wood-burning fireplaces, a pipe organ, masterpieces of art, and solid-gold light fixtures." They cost as much as $50,000 to build.

A grand ceremony marked the joining of the Union Pacific and Central Pacific railroads, when a golden spike was driven to celebrate the country's first coast-to-coast rail link (1869).

Crédit Mobilier and Other Scandals

One reason many businessmen and politicians were able to afford private railroad cars was the Crédit Mobilier. This was the construction company that built the Union Pacific Railroad, and it operated in the following way. Crédit Mobilier and Union Pacific were both run by the same individuals. These men realized that it was not the owners or operators who made the most money out of railroad building. It was the construction contractors. So, in their capacity as officials of Union Pacific, these men formed a construction company called the Crédit Mobilier. Then, in their capacity as officials of the Union Pacific, they gave their own construction company a contract to lay track at two to three times the actual cost! Then they divided the excess profits among themselves. These profits were later estimated as ranging from $33 million to $50 million. Similar tactics were followed by the Central Pacific Railroad, which was paid $120 million to build a line that actually cost about $58 million.

Nor was this all. The railroad officials wanted to be sure that Congress would continue giving the railroads land grants and construction subsidies. They also wanted to prevent a congressional investigation of their financial dealings. So they gave shares of stock in Crédit Mobilier to such political figures as Schuyler Colfax, vice-president during Grant's first term, and about twenty or so congressmen, including James Garfield of Ohio, who later became president of the United States. The stock paid dividends of several hundred percent.

In 1872 a crusading newspaper, the *New York Sun*, exposed the bribery. The following year a congressional committee investigated the matter. Two congressmen were censured, but otherwise the result was a complete whitewash. As one congressman said when asked what his constituents would think about his having accepted stock in Crédit Mobilier, "They would ask why I didn't take more!"

The Crédit Mobilier was only another example of the graft and corruption among President Grant's cabinet and friends that you read about in chapter 17. There was corruption at lower levels of government, too. For example, railroads commonly gave state officials passes entitling them and their families to travel by rail at any time, anywhere, free of charge. In fact, rail passes were one of the main reasons many people ran for state office. Collis Huntington of the Central Pacific openly helped California legislators with "pleasant social gifts." Naturally, such officials were reluctant to tax railroads, or to pass safety laws or other legislation that would increase the railroads' costs.

The Grangers and Interstate Commerce

In 1867 a farmer named Oliver Hudson Kelley organized the Patrons of Husbandry, popularly known as the National Grange. Its original purpose was to provide a way for isolated farm families to get together socially and also learn more about scientific methods of farming. By the 1870s, however, farmers in the Grange lodges were spending most of their time and energy fighting the railroads. And since there were more than 20,000 lodges with a membership of more than 1.5 million—women as well as men—they put up an extremely effective fight.

Restrictive Railroad Policies. What angered the Grangers were the rate policies the railroads followed. Since most communities were served by only one line, there was no price competition. Furthermore, there were no alternative means of transportation. If farmers wanted to send their crops to market, they had to pay whatever shipping rate the railroad set. And all too often, the railroad charged all that the traffic would bear.

In addition, the railroad usually owned the grain elevators in which the farmers stored their wheat and corn before it was shipped out. Here again, the farmers had no choice but to pay whatever price was demanded.

The Fight Against Railroads. The Granger idea was that railroads were a public utility, that is, they were public in nature even though they were privately owned and managed. Since they were public utilities, the public had the right to regulate them through their government.

Accordingly, the Grangers, by voting as a bloc, elected enough state legislators to get so-called Granger legislation passed in fourteen states, including the breadbasket states of Illinois, Iowa, Minnesota, and Wisconsin. In general, these laws established state railroad commissions with the power to set freight rates according to distance—lower for a short haul, higher for a long haul. The commissions were also supposed to regulate the storing and shipping of grain.

411

The railroads fought back in every way they could. They spent huge sums of money to defeat state legislators who had voted in favor of the Granger laws. They refused to let trains stop in towns that had Granger lodges and they kept filing suits against the Grangers.

Railroad attorneys argued that Granger legislation took away private property without due process of law. In 1877, however, in the case of *Munn v. Illinois*, the Supreme Court ruled that state Granger laws *were* constitutional. Owners of property "in which the public has an interest . . . must submit to be controlled by the public for the common good."

In 1886 the Supreme Court took most of the teeth out of *Munn v. Illinois* by a new ruling. In the *Wabash* case, the Court held that even within its own borders, a state could not set rates on railroad traffic that either came from another state or was headed for another state. Only the federal government, the Court said, had the power to regulate interstate commerce.

The Interstate Commerce Act. So in 1887, responding to public pressure, Congress passed the Interstate Commerce Act. The act required railroad rates to be "reasonable and just," and established a five-member Interstate Commerce Commission. But all the ICC could do was prohibit railroads from charging more for short hauls than for long hauls. It had no power to set maximum rates. Also, the only way it could enforce a decision was by suing the railroad, and cases dragged on for years. The ICC did not really become effective until after Theodore Roosevelt became president in 1901 (see chapter 26). As for the Granger movement, it lost its drive and again became a social and educational organization.

Nevertheless, the Granger movement marked a turning point in American history. It helped establish the principle that the federal government has the right to regulate private business under certain conditions: 1. if it is in the public interest; and 2. if the states are not able to do so.

Section 2 Review

COMPREHENSION   Developing Vocabulary

1. Explain these terms: National Grange, public utility.

COMPREHENSION   Mastering Facts

1. Why were the Casement brothers called "the biggest little men you ever saw"?
2. Why did many towns buy railroad stock?
3. How did the officials of the Union Pacific benefit from the Crédit Mobilier?
4. Why did the Grangers fight the railroads?

3 BUSINESSES BECOME MORE COMPLEX

VOCABULARY   *subsidiaries   holding company   pool   trust   interlocking directorate   rebates*

Industrial development requires more than energy, technology, and resources. It also requires individuals who can organize business. And during the period between 1865 and 1900, hundreds of such individuals helped change both the shape and size of American industry.

Carnegie: Captain of Industry

Andrew Carnegie got his first job in 1848, when he was thirteen years old. He worked as a bobbin boy, changing spools of thread in a cotton mill twelve hours a day, six days a week. His wages were $1.20 per week, plus another 80 cents for firing the furnace. Fifty-three years later, he sold his own steel company for almost $500 million. More than half that sum went to his associates. But the balance, invested, gave Carnegie a monthly income of more than $1 million. And in those days there was no income tax!

Preparing. Carnegie started his climb from rags to riches by leaving the cotton mill and becoming a telegraph messenger. He immediately began enlarging the possibilities of his new job. He learned the faces and names of Pittsburgh's leading businessmen and was able to deliver telegrams to them in a club or office without delay. While waiting to be sent out on deliveries, he studied Morse code so that he could become a telegraph operator instead of just a messenger. He also utilized his free time, spending it reading literature, histories, and science books to make up for his limited formal education.

Andrew Carnegie was one of the great tycoons of industry. He was also an avid reader, and gave many millions to build libraries throughout America.

Seizing Opportunities. At seventeen, Carnegie became a telegraph operator with the Pennsylvania Railroad and proceeded to learn all he could about the railroad business. One day, there was an accident on the line. The division superintendent, Thomas A. Scott, was not available. So Carnegie took it on himself to send several telegrams signed with Scott's name, giving orders to untangle the traffic snarl and get the trains moving again. When Scott learned about Carnegie's actions, he made Carnegie his private secretary. Seven years later, Carnegie had Scott's job.

Finally, in 1865, Carnegie left the Pennsylvania Railroad and devoted himself full-time to looking after his investments. After a while, he decided to concentrate on the steel industry, and in 1873 he launched what later became the Carnegie Steel Corporation.

Making It Better Cheaper. Carnegie stressed certain business practices that are now widespread. For example, he was always trying to turn out a better product at a lower cost. He spent large sums of money to install new technology in his steel plants. He hired chemists and metallurgists to improve the steel's quality. He installed detailed accounting systems so that he knew precisely what each process cost. He hired top-notch assistants, offered them stock in the firm, and then set them competing against one another to increase production and to cut costs.

Carnegie was also interested in controlling as much of the steel industry as possible. He bought out rival plants whenever he had the chance. He lowered his prices—which he could afford to do—and undersold his competitors, many of whom went out of business. He developed an operation that included not only steel plants but also coal and iron mines, ore freighters, and railroad lines, as well as the steel plants. This is called an "integrated" operation. That is, it controls every step in the manufacturing process, from mining the raw materials to delivering the finished product to the consumer. In 1901, when Carnegie sold his property, he was producing 25 percent of the nation's steel.

Corporate Combinations

The United States Steel Corporation, which was formed in 1901 by combining Carnegie Steel with eleven other steel firms plus 170 *subsidiaries* (companies totally owned by another), was the largest business organization in the world. It was a prime example of how companies combine to form bigger and stronger businesses. But there were several other kinds of combinations.

The Holding Company. A holding company, like U.S. Steel, did not actually produce goods or services. It sold stock in itself and then used the money to buy control of companies that *were* producing goods and services. Thus, U.S. Steel did not make steel; it owned the companies that did.

The Merger. The easiest way of forming a larger business unit was the merger. In a merger, two or more corporations combined to form a single corporation. Usually, one corporation would buy the stock of the others.

The Pool. Another way of forming a larger business unit was the pool. Under a pooling agreement, several companies agreed to function as if they were a single organization. For example, a group of steel mills might agree to divide the market into areas, with each mill selling only within a particular area. Or, the steel mills might decide to charge a uniform price for their products so that no single mill could undersell its competitors. Unlike mergers, however, pooling agreements had no legal standing. If one of the steel mills in a pool violated the agreement, the other mills could not sue to enforce it. The Interstate Commerce Act of 1887 declared pools illegal in interstate commerce, after which most of them disappeared.

The Trust. Under a trust agreement, the stockholders of several competing companies would turn their stock over to a group of trustees. In return, the stockholders received trust certificates that entitled them to receive dividends from the trust's profits. In the meantime, the trustees ran the various companies in the trust as if they were one.

The Interlocking Directorate. A fifth way of combining companies was the interlocking directorate. This existed whenever directors of one firm also served as directors of another firm. The two firms might have completely separate ownership, yet because they had the same directors their operating policies and practices were the same.

The Growth of Trusts. Although there were different ways in which large business units were formed, all were popularly known as trusts. And by 1900, trusts dominated about four-fifths of the industries in the United States. In addition to steel and oil refining, there were trusts in sugar refining, whiskey distilling, meat packing, and tobacco processing, as well as the production of wire and nails, bicycles, agricultural machinery, salt, matches, crackers, lead, copper, electrical supplies, and many other items.

What made trusts so popular? In many instances, large-scale businesses are more efficient than small businesses. They can reduce waste by getting rid of duplication. They can afford to install new and more productive equipment. Since they buy supplies in large quantities, they pay lower prices and can therefore sell their products for less. And they can afford to introduce new products and wait several years for the products to return a profit.

Corporate Excesses

Why, then, did antitrust feelings develop in the United States during the 1880s and 1890s? Primarily because some trusts behaved in a destructive way. Instead of lowering prices, they raised prices. Since they dominated an industry, there was nothing that other companies or customers could do.

John D. Rockefeller. John D. Rockefeller, who founded the Standard Oil Trust in 1882, carried this further. He would sell products below cost until he had driven all his competitors out of business. Then he would jack up his prices to several times their previous level. He also forced railroads to give him *rebates*, or refunds, of part of his payments for shipping his products. This was against the law. But the railroads felt they had no choice, because they could not operate if they lost Standard's business. After all, the trust controlled at least 90 percent of the nation's oil refining and marketing.

Sherman Antitrust Act. Gradually, many people came to feel that an economic giant like Standard had too much power—especially in a de-

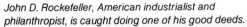

John D. Rockefeller, American industrialist and philanthropist, is caught doing one of his good deeds.

mocracy. So in 1890, Congress passed the Sherman Antitrust Act. The act stated that "Every contract, combination in the form of trust or otherwise, or conspiracy, in restraint of trade . . . is hereby declared to be illegal."

Enforcing the act, however, proved almost impossible. It was vaguely worded and did not define such terms as "trust" and "conspiracy." Many trusts simply reorganized as holding companies or single corporations, thus avoiding prosecution. In addition, seven of the first eight cases the federal government brought against trusts were thrown out.

The American Sugar Case. Finally, in 1895 came the so-called *Sugar* case. The American Sugar Refining Company controlled about 95 percent of the nation's sugar-refining business. Nevertheless, the Supreme Court held that the company was not violating the Sherman Act. Monopoly in itself is not illegal, said the Court. It is illegal only if it restrains interstate commerce. The Court indicated that manufacturing and trade were not the same.

As a result of this decision, the federal government stopped trying to break up trusts, and business consolidations continued to increase. By 1900, about 2 percent of the firms in the United States were making 50 percent of the products.

The Philosophy of Getting Ahead

One philosophy that helps explain why Carnegie, Rockefeller, and other industrialists acted the way they did is called *Social Darwinism.* Charles Darwin was an English biologist who developed a theory of biological evolution. He observed that no two creatures are exactly the same, and that children are not exactly the same as their parents. Also, in any generation, some survive while others do not. Darwin concluded that some individuals in a species are better able to adapt to their environment than others. To put it another way, Darwin said, there is a process of *natural selection* at work. Those individuals who are best fitted to survive, do. The weaker individuals drop by the wayside.

Herbert Spencer's First Principles. Darwin's ideas were transferred from biology to business by the English philosopher Herbert Spencer. In his book *First Principles,* published in 1862, he argued that free competition was a natural law and that it

was dangerous to interfere with it. If the government would just leave business and businessmen alone, the fittest would naturally survive. The more productive the business, the larger it would grow. The more competent the individual, the richer he would become. Whatever survived must be good, and the more effectively it survived, the better it was. Is it any wonder that Social Darwinism appealed to people like Carnegie and Rockefeller?

Horatio Alger and Success. Social Darwinism did not appeal just to the 4000 millionaires who had made their money in business since the Civil War. It had mass appeal as well. Again, it was the written word that spread the message. The writer was Horatio Alger, Jr. The word was a series of more than a hundred books that sold between 125 million and 250 million copies. (Spencer's *First Principles* sold about 300,000 copies.) Some of the titles were: *Bound to Rise, Luck and Pluck, Making His Way, Struggling Upward, Helping Himself, Frank and Fearless, In Search of Treasure, Strive and Succeed, Brave and Bold, Do and Dare, Risen from the Ranks,* and *The Young Adventurer.* Each book had a similar plot. One historian described it as about

> 66 the rise to riches of a street urchin. . . . Alger heroes . . . demonstrated beyond any doubt that the poor boy who worked hard and cheerfully, who was kind, decent, took baths, was respectful to his betters and elders, and was always more or less honest in his dealings, why, this boy was sure to become rich and honored. 99

Not only that—he was practically certain to marry the boss's daughter.

Many a young American must have had satisfying dreams when reading such scenes as this from *Herbert Carter's Legacy:*

> 66 "Is that the latest style?" inquired James Leech, with a sneer, pointing to a patch on Herbert Carter's pants.
> Herbert's face flushed. He was not ashamed of the patch, for he knew that his mother's poverty made it a necessity. But he felt it was mean and dishonorable in James Leech, whose father was one of the rich men of Wrayburn, to taunt him with what he could not help. Some boys might have slunk away abashed, but Herbert had pluck and stood his ground.
> "It is my style," he answered firmly, looking James boldly in the face. 99

For some millionaires, their first job was selling newspapers. These paper carriers in New York City look like a collection of Horatio Alger's typical heroes.

Horatio Alger's books inspired thousands of Americans to take advantage of the opportunities that opened up during the new industrial age. The books had a political effect as well. Although there was widespread poverty in the United States during this period, as will be seen later on, the majority of Americans tended to lay the blame entirely on individuals. There was nothing wrong with the economic system. The old Puritan idea of the value and meaning of work surfaces from time to time throughout our history. It did so now. Thrift, hard work, and honesty would lead to material success. Riches were a sign of God's favor. If people were poor, said these nineteenth-century businessmen, they must be either lazy or inferior. There was really no need to pass social legislation or to change the way businesses and other institutions operated. As a consequence, movements for economic reform had a difficult time.

Section 3 Review

COMPREHENSION Developing Vocabulary

1. Explain these terms: holding company, trust, pool, interlocking directorate, subsidiaries, rebates, merger, Social Darwinism, natural selection.

COMPREHENSION Mastering Facts

1. What are the advantages of large-scale businesses?
2. What was the purpose of the Sherman Antitrust Law?
3. How did Herbert Spencer apply Darwin's ideas to businesses?
4. How did the books of Horatio Alger influence young people?

CHAPTER 19   Review

Chapter Summary

New technology led to a new industrial age. As electrical power was harnessed, cities were lighted and new forms of urban transportation appeared. The invention of the telephone totally revolutionized communications. Plentiful supplies of coal and iron ore, along with the new Bessemer process for making steel, fueled spectacular growth in that industry. But the emergence of powerful businesses caused responses from other groups in the nation. Suffering from unfair railroad freight rates, farmers organized the Grange movement. As the federal government became more involved in the nation's economy, the Interstate Commerce Act was passed. Then Congress also approved the Sherman Antitrust Act. Meanwhile, both government and business had to contend with widespread corruption.

Questions for Critical Thinking

COMPREHENSION   Summarizing Main Ideas

1. How did each of these affect industrial growth in the United States? (a) use of electric power; (b) the telephone; (c) the typewriter; (d) the open-hearth process; (e) "Drake's folly."
2. How were blacks, Jews, and immigrants discriminated against in office employment? How were the Chinese discriminated against while working on the transcontinental railroad?
3. List five areas other than transportation in which the railroads affected American life.
4. What was the original purpose of the Grange? Why did it change its aims? What effect did it have on the role the federal government played in the economy?
5. How did the Supreme Court help big business during the new industrial age?

COMPREHENSION   Interpreting Events

1. Why did the federal government encourage the building of railroads? What methods did it use?

2. Why were many state legislators reluctant to pass safety laws or other legislation that would increase the railroads' costs?
3. What new forms of business organization developed between 1865 and 1901? How effective were they? Why did many people oppose them? Was the opposition successful? Explain your answer.
4. Why were people such as Carnegie and Rockefeller called "captains of industry"? Why were they also called "robber barons"?
5. Why did movements for reform of the economic system have a difficult time?

APPLICATION   Using Skills To Understand Time

In addition to arranging events in chronological order, it is important to appreciate the relative length of time during which events occur. For each set of events below, tell which covered the longer time span.

1. The telegraph is invented and becomes a major means of communication; the incandescent light bulb is invented and becomes common in American homes.
2. The telephone is invented and people can talk long distance from coast to coast; the first telephone switchboard is installed and women take over operation of telephone exchanges.
3. Women enter office work and make up more than 75 percent of office employees; the nation's first commercial oil well is drilled and gasoline becomes the most valuable product that oil refineries turn out.

EVALUATION   Forming Generalizations

1. Compare the boundaries of the time zones that existed in the United States before 1883 with the time zones that exist today. Why do you think the boundaries have changed?.
2. What industries or business corporations does the federal government subsidize today? Do you approve or disapprove of such subsidies? Give reasons for your opinion.

Government Regulations

A political cartoon poking fun at government "red tape" shows a business executive filling out forms in a plush office. The desk is swamped with mounds of paper, and the job looks impossible to complete. A secretary, arriving to lend the boss a hand, comments: "This all started with the New Deal."

The secretary's comment echoes a belief held by many concerning our federal bureaucracy and government regulations in general. Governments have always issued *regulations*, which are rules or laws that govern certain actions. Government *bureaucracy*—the administration of government through various departments and subdivisions, each headed by an official who must follow certain guidelines—is relatively new, however. Only as empires and populations grew did large bureaucratic governments become widespread.

In our complex, modern society, most people have come to accept the need for bureaucratic organization in governments and businesses. It is the increasing amount of regulations and bureaucratic paperwork that bother most Americans.

During a typical year, Americans now spend an estimated 1.2 billion hours filling out six thousand different kinds of federal forms. But contrary to popular belief, these government regulations did not first appear during the New Deal. Instead, their origins can be traced at least back to the growth of monopoly capitalism following the Civil War.

A New Economic Order. Government involvement in the nation's economic and social workings grew out of the excessive power accumulated by America's big business empire. In the decades after Appomattox, the opportunities for success afforded by mass production, new inventions, and a national market encouraged fierce competition among companies. Powerful business leaders attempted to restrain competition by consolidating industries into large-scale operations. They used pools, trusts, and holding companies (see pages 413–414) to accomplish their goals. As a result, vast concentrations—in oil, iron and steel, lead, meatpacking, coal, tobacco, sugar— dominated the new economic order.

Government Steps In. The failure of states to regulate big business finally led public opinion to demand federal intervention. A century ago there were hardly any rules for the game of capitalism except one: survival. In that sense, the Interstate Commerce Act of 1887 can be seen as the first government attempt to establish order and fairness in what seemed to be uncivilized economic behavior.

That act also established the Interstate Commerce Commission (ICC), the nation's first regulatory agency. Three years later Congress went even further and passed the Sherman Antitrust Act, which on paper made monopolies illegal. Though neither of these laws proved effective at the time, both established the principle of federal supervision of business activity. They sent a clear signal that there were certain economic practices the American public would not tolerate.

Federal Involvement Grows. Principle was put into action during the twentieth century. Beginning around 1900, Congress and the executive branch began to see themselves as a countervailing power to big business. This meant a drastic change in the role of government. Instead of doing as little as possible, government began to get involved in a variety of public welfare issues.

Before World War I, federal legislation enacted by reformers expanded government authority over such areas as health, child labor, banking, conservation, and the income tax. These reformers, who called themselves Progressives, did not want to eliminate capitalism; instead, they only wanted to establish rules for fair play—with the government acting as a referee.

Believing that the problems of an industrial society would never be entirely solved, the Progressives created regulatory agencies as permanent fixtures of government to manage and control these problems. The Federal Reserve Board, the National Conservation Commission, the Department of Commerce and Labor, the Federal Trade Commission, and the Federal Board for Vocational Education were but a few set up during this period. Progressive reformers hoped that government agencies and regulations would serve as watchdogs over corporations.

Administrations ever since then have been building on the foundations established by the Progressives. Subsequent governments have extended this practice of managing the economy and modifying free market practices. The 1984 breakup of the nation's largest monopoly, American Telephone and Telegraph, is one recent example.

The Situation Today.

Federal regulations now abound in areas which would have been unimagined several decades ago. To build a bridge which uses federal funds, a locality must obey civil rights laws; satisfy environmental protection requirements; insure access for the handicapped; and include the public in policy decisions. Guidelines for the school milk program, clean air and water

Many government regulations have appeared only recently. However, the practice of federal involvement in the nation's economy began a century ago.

standards, rules for auto seat belts, speed limits on interstate highways, and warnings on cigarette packages affect virtually every American citizen.

Do federal regulations strangle free enterprise? Do too many rules stifle risk-taking and discourage investment? Many people think so. One of the themes which helped Ronald Reagan become president concerned "getting the government off peoples' backs." He proposed *deregulation* in certain areas to ease some of the many restrictions on businesses.

Still, few people believe that the federal government will be able to eliminate many regulations. Some people believe that even more regulations are needed to insure greater honesty and fairness. Striking the best

possible balance between government regulation and government noninterference is still a challenge that faces our free enterprise system.

Understanding Government

1. When did federal government regulation actually begin? Why did people begin to demand it?

2. How responsible are today's industries to the public? Do you believe that businesses would behave differently without regulation? Why?

3. How did Progressives affect the growth of government regulation?

4. Name several ways in which the federal government affects your daily life.

Mushrooming Cities

1876–1900

People in the Chapter

George Washington Plunkitt—a precinct captain in the New York City Democratic machine who is very successful in winning political support in exchange for favors.

Marshall Field—the Chicago merchant who pioneers in department store operation.

Frank W. Woolworth—establishes the five-and-ten-cent store, the earliest chain store.

Jane Addams—one of the founders of Hull House, a settlement house designed to improve the life of Chicago slum dwellers.

Frederick Law Olmsted—a pioneer in municipal planning, who directs the development of city parks, including Central Park in New York City.

Linking Past to Present

When the Civil War broke out, the United States was largely rural. Only one out of five Americans lived in a city. The cities themselves were small. Only sixteen had a population of more than 50,000.

By 1900 the nation's urban population had doubled. Now there were seventy-six cities with more than 50,000 inhabitants. The older large cities—New York, Boston, Philadelphia, Baltimore, Washington, Pittsburgh, Cincinnati, Louisville, St. Louis, Chicago, New Orleans, and San Francisco—had become even larger. With so many people crowded together, there were physical and social situations never before faced by Americans.

There was the simple problem of where all the people would stay. How would they get from place to place in a large and crowded city? In addition to problems of housing and transportation, there were the problems of lighting and sanitation. There also had to be an efficient system for keeping law and order.

These problems generally had to be solved by politicians. With all those voters so conveniently massed in one location, it was inevitable that politicians in large cities would not only help but influence the voters and, in some cases, take advantage of them.

Despite crowding and political corruption, city life had many enriching qualities. Indeed, a growing number of Americans had decided that they could live happily nowhere else.

1 PROBLEMS ARISE AS CITIES GROW

VOCABULARY   *row house   tenements   dumbbell tenement   de facto segregation*

Urbanization was concentrated in the northeastern part of the United States. That was natural because the Northeast was the region where most of the nation's industrial development was taking place.

The cities grew because the factories, mines, mills, and transportation systems needed millions of workers to turn out the goods that were making the nation rich. Additional millions were needed in trade and service occupations—to sell goods, to clean houses, and to work in laundries, restaurants, real estate offices, and banks.

People flocked to the cities for the same reason they had flocked to the western frontier—seeking opportunity. The majority of newcomers came from American farms. The rest came from overseas, mostly Europe. But like their American counterparts, most of them left a rural environment to enter an urban one.

As a result of their tremendous growth, American cities in the new industrial age faced a variety of problems. The most fundamental was housing.

Finding a Roof Overhead

For rich urban dwellers, housing was no problem. They lived in large private homes, with a staff of servants to take care of the cooking, cleaning, and children, and with a flock of horse-drawn carriages to take them wherever they wanted to go. The only inconvenience was the absence of zoning laws. Consequently, an elegant mansion might be

Crowded city scenes like this Labor Day celebration in Buffalo, New York, became more and more a part of American life as the nation's urban population doubled between 1860 and 1900.

situated near a slaughterhouse or a gasworks. Wealth was no protection against polluted city air.

Middle-Class Options.

The situation for middle-class families was different. When the new industrial age began, they had a simple choice. They could buy a house on the outskirts of town, where land was cheap, and commute into the central business district when necessary. Or, they could live in a centrally located boardinghouse where they shared the kitchen and the dining room with several other families.

As the industrial age developed, builders began to offer two additional possibilities: the apartment house and the row house. The first apartment house was built in 1870 on East 18th Street in New York City. Each apartment contained six rooms and a bath. Rent ranged from $1000 to $1500 a year. The idea caught on quickly. By the 1880s there were numerous six- and eight-story apartment buildings throughout the city. They had such modern conveniences as elevator service, a built-in kitchen range, and a hot-water heater.

It was the *row house*, however, that really captured the fancy of middle-class urban dwellers. With row housing, each family could own a home. At the same time, construction costs were low because a row house shared its side walls with its neighbors and took up comparatively little land. By the 1880s, New York contained hundreds of "brownstone blocks," whose row houses, looking very much alike, were built of reddish-brown sandstone with a cast-iron fence in the front. Baltimore's red-brick houses, one just like another, were distinguished by shining white steps that led up to the front door and were faithfully scrubbed each morning.

Row-House Living.

Living in a row house was comfortable. Each room had a brass fixture for gas jets or electric bulbs. The furnace fire glowed all night, so you did not wake up shivering with cold. A gas flame heated the water in the water tank and fueled the stove. And every house had a bathroom with "tiled walls, an indoor water closet, running water and porcelain or enameled fixtures." In larger families, however, people continued to wash out of pitcher and bowl.

Middle-class housewives particularly enjoyed row-house living. The houses were usually some distance from the husband's work place. So husbands no longer came home for lunch. Women no longer had to spend the morning cooking. They could serve themselves and the children with leftovers from the previous night's meal, or with a cold luncheon of sandwiches and fruit. This plus the invention of the refrigerator meant you only had to shop for food twice a week. And if you owned a telephone, you did not even have to make a trip to the store because grocery stores delivered to homes. In addition, you no longer had to bake your own bread but could have it delivered fresh to the house each morning. You could also buy milk and vegetables in season from the wagons of the milkman and the grocer.

Cleaning was likewise easier. The newly invented carpet sweeper was much more efficient than the broom. There was an abundance of hot water for doing dishes. Commercial laundries took care of most of the family wash. And the development of new soaps, oils, and waxes which could be used on a regular basis meant that you no longer had to go through the ordeal of a thorough spring cleaning.

The Development of Tenements.

Poor people made up at least half a city's population. In the case of a factory town with a single major industrial enterprise, they made up almost the entire population. In either case, the poor lived in multifamily dwellings called *tenements*. They were concentrated in neighborhoods that often bore such names as Bone Alley, Hell's Kitchen, and Poverty Gap.

Tenements usually developed as industrial areas expanded. When this happened, middle-class families moved away from the factories to more desirable areas. After they left, their residences were converted into housing for several families rather than one. Because each family was on a different level, some had no water or plumbing. After a while, rooms as well as floors were divided, so most tenants found themselves without windows. Outhouses and stables were likewise converted into dwellings. Thousands of people even lived in cellars. Rents were high. And because building codes—if they existed—were not enforced, landlords seldom if ever maintained their property, although their profits ranged from 30 to 100 percent a year.

The first tenement designed expressly for working-class families was built in New York. As the new industrial age developed, other cities followed suit. Unfortunately, with rising land costs on the one hand and with a need to provide cheap housing on the other, these tenements soon became as overcrowded, airless, filthy, and disease-ridden as converted housing.

Jacob Riis, a Danish-born newspaper reporter, described the relationship between tenements and disease in his book *How the Other Half Lives.*

" Suppose we look into one? . . . Be a little careful, please! The hall is dark and you might stumble over the children pitching pennies back there. . . . Close? Yes! What would you have? All the fresh air that ever enters these stairs comes from the hall-door that is forever slamming. . . .

   Here is a door. Listen! That short hacking cough, that tiny helpless wail—what do they mean? . . . Oh! a sadly familiar story. . . . The child is dying with measles. With half a chance it might have lived; but it had none. That dark bedroom killed it. "

And, in fact, the infant and child mortality rates in such buildings were three to four times higher than the average mortality rates.

Attempts at Reform. New York, as the largest city in the nation, had the largest slum areas with the worst tenements. It also had the first laws designed to improve slum conditions. They were passed in 1867.

In 1879 a major attempt at slum reform resulted in the construction of the "dumbbell tenement." The floor plan called for a long, narrow building (five- or six-stories high) that covered the entire lot of twenty-five feet by one hundred feet except for a tiny yard at one end. However, the central part was indented on either side to allow for an air shaft, and thus an outside window for each room. In addition, the law called for fireproof stairways and a toilet for every two families.

But soon these "old law" tenements likewise became overcrowded, with up to 400 persons per building. Also, people dumped their waste into the air shafts. And since there was no way to clean the bottom of the shafts, they quickly became breeding places for rats and vermin. The stench was so bad that people had to nail the air-shaft windows shut. As a result, the air shafts created drafts; and the drafts made the fires which often broke out even more fearsome and destructive than they otherwise would have been.

By 1900, about 1.7 million New Yorkers were living in some 40,000 dumbbell tenements, most of which were without bathtubs, toilets, or running water. The New York housing commission, which met that same year, concluded that the situ-

Many of the urban poor lived packed together in tenements similar to these in New York City.

ation in the slums was worse than it had been thirty-three years earlier when the first tenement reform law had been passed.

Beginning of Black Ghettos. When the Civil War ended, most of the nation's black population was rural. Fewer than 5 percent lived in cities. By 1890 the proportion had increased to 12 percent and by 1910 it had reached 25 percent. About three out of four urban blacks lived in Washington and in such southern cities as Atlanta, Baltimore, Memphis, New Orleans, Savannah, and Shreveport. The rest were concentrated in such northern communities as Chicago, New York, Philadelphia, and St. Louis.

Until about 1890, urban blacks and whites often shared the same neighborhood. After 1890, Jim Crow legislation brought about strict racial segregation of housing in the South. The North and the West did not adopt Jim Crow laws. But increasing racial prejudice, spurred by competition for industrial jobs, brought about *de facto* segregation, that is, a pattern of segregation supported by custom rather than law.

And what were the results of de facto segrega-

423

The back porches of tenements were places for meetings and exchange of gossip, particularly on wash days. These tenements are on Roosevelt Street in New York City's lower east side.

tion? As the New York *Freeman*, a black newspaper, said in 1885: "[Blacks] are not only forced to colonize in the worst sections of the city, and into the very worst tenements, but they are charged fabulous prices for the luxury of having a place to sleep and eat." It was estimated that urban blacks had to pay between one-third and one-half of their earnings for rent.

At the same time, however, the concentration of blacks in a particular area encouraged them to set up their own commercial institutions. Some were in businesses that provided personal services to blacks, such as hairdressing and undertaking. Others entered areas of finance that whites considered too risky—such as insuring blacks' lives and property or arranging credit for them. Thousands of such enterprises were established in New York's Harlem and other black ghettos. Most were small, and many failed. Nevertheless, a black middle class gradually developed in the nation's cities.

Getting from Place to Place

Housing was not the only problem confronting American cities. Traffic was another.

Before the new industrial age, people moved around town on foot or by horsecar. But horsecars were small and only went six miles an hour. New means of transportation were needed to move large numbers of workers to and from their jobs.

In 1867 New York became the first city to build an "el," or elevated railway that ran on a track above the street. It was driven by a coal-burning steam locomotive. The "el" could carry hundreds of passengers at a time. But it had several disadvantages. The track structure cut off light and air from buildings along the way. Trains dropped soot and hot ashes on pedestrians below. And the structure was very expensive to build.

In 1873 San Francisco, a city of steep hills, installed a cable car driven by a moving underground chain. It was a great success, and similar lines were soon opened in such cities as Denver, Los Angeles, Omaha, and Seattle. Even more successful was the electric trolley car, or street car, which was first introduced in Richmond in 1888. Since the trolley carried its own motor and ran on the ground, it was both flexible and cheap. By 1890 it had been adopted by some 200 cities. In 1897 another mass-transit innovation, the electric subway, was introduced in Boston. New York built its first subway in 1904.

Providing Water and Sanitation

At the start of the new industrial age, urban Americans bought their drinking water in bottles that were sold from horse-drawn carts. By the turn of the century, most cities had installed water mains and were piping water directly to houses.

Sanitation was more difficult to handle. True, scavenger pigs no longer roamed about, and some cities employed workers to sweep the streets and dampen down the dust. But the following account of Baltimore by writer H. L. Mencken describes the typical situation.

❝ All the sewers of Baltimore, whether private or public, emptied into the Back Basin in those days, just as all those of Manhattan empty into the North and East rivers. . . . But I should add that there is a difference, for the North and East rivers have swift tidal currents, whereas the Back Basin . . . had only the most lethargic. As a result it began to acquire a powerful aroma every Spring, and by August smelled like a billion polecats. ❞

Establishing Law and Order

Another problem that confronted American cities was how to maintain law and order. Full-time, salaried police forces with special uniforms were first established as late as the 1850s—and then only in such large cities as Boston, New York, and Philadelphia. These forces were usually small. Certainly they were too small to handle the increased crime that went along with the increased population of the cities. Pickpockets and shoplifters flourished in urban crowds, while confidence men found it easy to sell counterfeit money to country folk and non-English-speaking immigrants.

Violent crimes were likewise commonplace. Tourists in 1876, for example, were warned to "Reach the city in the daytime," and "Take the car or stage which passes nearest your stopping place." Areas of certain cities were known as Robbers' Roost and Murderers' Alley. Gangs of young toughs controlled such areas and it was dangerous for police to enter them.

Yet another difficulty was corruption on the part of the police themselves. The worst police scandal was uncovered in New York in 1892 by Dr. Charles H. Parkhurst, a Presbyterian minister. Dressed as a tramp and accompanied by a similarly disguised private detective, Parkhurst spent four nights visiting saloons, gambling parlors, and policy shops. Everywhere he went, he found evidence of payoffs to police for protection. He found so much evidence, in fact, that a state legislative committee investigated the matter. The result was the forced resignation of all top police officials in the city.

Fighting Fires

On October 8, 1871, a wagon driver named Daniel "Peg Leg" Sullivan was drinking whiskey in his neighbor's barn as he often did. The reason he drank there and not at home was that his mother disapproved of the habit. As things turned out, she was right to do so. That night, so the story goes, Sullivan took one drink too many and dropped a kerosene lamp into a hay pile. Mrs. Catherine O'Leary's barn caught fire, and "the most destructive accidental blaze in history" swept through Chicago. When it was over, about 500 persons were dead; 18,000 buildings, destroyed; and more than 100,000 persons—almost one-third of the city's population—left homeless.

Almost every American city suffered a major fire during the 1870s and 1880s. Part of the reason was that most houses were still built of wood. Another reason was the existence of volunteer rather than salaried fire departments. Although volunteers were skilled fire fighters, they were also very competitive. Instead of cooperating to put out a blaze, they would fight over which company's hose would get attached to the fire hydrant.

Gradually, however, the situation improved. The city of Cleveland had set an example by establishing the nation's first salaried fire department in 1853. By 1900, the only volunteer fire departments left were in suburbs or small towns. Another aid to fighting fires was the automatic fire sprinkler, which was invented in 1877. Most important, however, was the fact that wooden buildings were replaced by those made of brick, stone, and concrete.

Section 1 Review

COMPREHENSION Developing Vocabulary

1. Explain these terms: row house, tenements, de facto segregation, dumbbell tenement, el.

COMPREHENSION Mastering Facts

1. What were the advantages of row-house living?
2. In what two ways did tenements develop?
3. What new means of urban transportation came into use in the new industrial age?
4. Why was fire such a problem in American cities during the 1870s and 1880s?

VOCABULARY   *political machine*   *Tammany Hall*   *philanthropy*

Many of the problems you have just read about are now handled by local government. In the new industrial age, local government was itself a problem. As scholar James Bryce wrote in 1888: "There is no denying that the government of cities is the one conspicuous failure of the United States." Two years later, another scholar called American cities "the worst [governed] in Christiandom—the most expensive, the most inefficient, and the most corrupt."

The Rise of the Political Machine

Perhaps local government was so inept because cities mushroomed almost overnight. Their governments did not have a chance to learn how to handle a few problems gradually. Instead, they found themselves facing a tremendous number of problems within a short period of time.

Consider New York, for example. It doubled five times in less than a generation. Its population was swamped by immigrants: white southerners seeking to rebuild their prewar fortunes; southern blacks seeking a more favorable atmosphere; and Europeans from the farms and rural villages of Italy, Poland, and Russia. Millions of new people, speaking a variety of languages, entering a new type of environment and all eager to get ahead.

And what did they find in the way of local government? An old-line leadership that generally looked down on the newcomers. And a structure in which no one had clear responsibility for anything. The powers of government were divided among a mayor, a city council, various judges, and independent boards. In addition, the state legislature—which chartered cities—had the right to interfere in municipal affairs.

The absence of responsible government, combined with the sheer size of urban problems, opened the way for a new power structure. This was the political machine, dominated by a political boss.

Machine Politics

The typical party machine worked on two levels. It provided services to the general population in exchange for their votes. And it provided opportunities to businesses in exchange for money.

Working a District.   George Washington Plunkitt, a precinct captain for Tammany Hall—the Democratic political machine in New York City—explained why the people in his district voted the way he wanted.

> If there's a fire in Ninth, Tenth, or Eleventh Avenue, for example, any hour of the day or night, I'm usually there . . . as soon as the fire engines. If a family is burned out I don't ask them whether they are Republicans or Democrats, and I don't refer them to the Charity Organization Society, which would investigate their case in a month or two and decide they were worthy of help about the time they are dead from starvation. I just get quarters for them, buy clothes for them if their clothes were burned up, and fix them up till they get things runnin' again. It's philanthropy, (charity) but it's politics, too, mighty good politics. . . . The poor are the most grateful people in the world, and, let me tell you, they have more friends in their neighborhoods than the rich have in theirs. . . .
>
> Another thing, I can always get a job for a deservin' man. I make it a point to keep on the track of jobs, and it seldom happens that I don't have a few up my sleeve ready for use.

Nor did Plunkitt stop with helping people who were hit by fire or unemployment. He helped immigrants with their naturalization proceedings. He put in a good word for youngsters who got into trouble with the police. He paid court fines for constituents who were picked up for being drunk. And he paid attention to people's needs for social outlets.

> I hear of a young feller that's proud of his voice. . . . I ask him to come around . . . and join our Glee Club. He comes and sings, and he's a follower of Plunkitt for life. Another young feller gains a reputation as a base-ball player in a vacant lot. I bring him into our base-ball club. That fixes him. You'll find him workin' for my ticket at the polls next election day. . . . I rope them all in by givin' them opportunities to show themselves off. I don't trouble them with political arguments.

Stealing Votes.   Sometimes, however, even the loyalty of the poor was not enough to carry an election. Under those circumstances, political machines turned to fraud. The voting list has the names of all people who are eligible to vote in a certain district or division. Lincoln Steffens, a reporter, once described how the Republican machine in Philadelphia operated.

> " The assessor's list is the voting list, and the assessor is the machine's man. . . . The assessor pads the list with the names of dead dogs, children, and non-existent persons. . . .
>
> Rudolph Blankenburg, a persistent fighter for the right and the use of the right to vote . . . sent out just before one election a registered letter to each voter on the rolls of a certain selected division. Sixty-three percent were returned marked "not at," "removed," "deceased," etc. . . . "

Municipal Graft. Once a political machine got its candidates into office, there were numerous opportunities for making money. The basic technique was the same one that businessmen involved in the Crédit Mobilier scandal had used; namely, padding bills. If you worked for the city, you simply turned in a bill that was a fixed percentage higher than the actual cost of the materials or service. Then you paid the difference to the machine.

The most extravagant example of graft was probably the New York County Courthouse, which was built while Tammany Hall was under the control of William Marcy "Boss" Tweed. The building cost about $11 million, or 1.5 times as much as it cost to buy Alaska. Expenditures included such items as $179,729.60 for three tables and forty chairs, and $41,190.95 for brooms. Although the entire building was made of marble and iron, the plastering bill came to $2,870,464.06. And $1,294,684.13 of this amount was for repair work before the building was even finished! There were checks endorsed to such names as Phillip F. Dummey and T. C. Cash. All in all, it was a grand boondoggle for everyone involved. The only people who suffered were the taxpayers.

Boss Tweed Takes a Tumble

The wholesale graft practiced in Tammany Hall under Tweed's leadership gradually aroused public anger. *The New York Times* printed one scathing editorial after another. Thomas Nast's cartoons in the *Times* and in *Harper's Weekly* were even more devastating. As Tweed himself said, "I don't care what people write, for my people can't read. But they have eyes and they can see as well as other folk."

The Tweed ring was finally broken in 1871

Thomas Nast used satirical cartoons like this to expose New York City's corrupt political machine led by ''Boss'' Tweed. Nast's work was effective in publicizing the machine's deeds.

WHO STOLE THE PEOPLE'S MONEY ? " — DO TELL . N.Y.TIMES.   'TWAS HIM.

when a disgruntled member of the machine provided the *New York Times* with direct proof of corruption. That year, reformers were elected to every municipal office in New York. Tweed himself was indicted on 120 counts charging him with—among other things—"felony, forgery, grand larceny, false pretenses, and conspiracy to defraud." His first trial ended without a verdict; his second, with a twelve-year sentence. He escaped from jail but was recaptured in Spain. Spanish officials recognized him from a drawing by Nast. In 1878 Tweed died in prison.

Similar situations existed in other cities. Why did voters tolerate this? Because, as *The Nation* pointed out in its farewell to Tweed,

66 Let us remember that he fell without loss of reputation among the bulk of his supporters. The bulk of the poorer voters of this city today revere his memory, and look on him as the victim of rich men's malice; as, in short, a friend of the needy who applied the public funds to the purposes to which they ought to be applied—and that is to the making of work for the working man. 99

So long as municipal governments did not address themselves to certain social needs, the majority of voters supported the machines that gave at least some help to the poor.

Section 2 Review

COMPREHENSION   Developing Vocabulary

1. Explain these terms: political machine, Tammany Hall, philanthropy.

COMPREHENSION   Mastering Facts

1. Why were American cities so badly governed early in the industrial age?
2. Why would immigrants vote for machine candidates?
3. What were some opportunities for graft in machine politics?

3 AMERICANS IMPROVE CITIES AND SERVICES

VOCABULARY   *skyscrapers settlement houses*

The American city of the new industrial age was unquestionably filled with problems. But it was also filled with wonders. There were skyscrapers that soared twenty stories high; electric lights that turned the streets from night into day; trolleys that moved at the "incredible speed" of twenty miles an hour; and giant bridges, like the Brooklyn Bridge, which leaped across rivers almost one-third of a mile wide.

Coupled with these wonders were attempts to make the city more livable. Some of these attempts had to do with the physical environment. Others had to do with the mind and the spirit.

Creating Parks

As cities grew larger and more crowded, open space for recreation became increasingly important. The movement for planned urban parks began with Frederick Law Olmsted. In the 1850s he designed Manhattan's Central Park with a zoological garden, boating and tennis facilities, and bicycle paths in a natural setting. In the 1870s he planned the landscaping for Washington, D.C. Olmsted was also responsible for the initial design of the Fenway, the park system in Boston.

Another well-known urban planner was Daniel H. Burnham. He helped design the general plan for the Columbian Exposition, a world's fair that was held in Chicago in 1893 and drew more than 27 million visitors. Burnham also developed an overall park plan for the city. As a result, most of Chicago's lakefront is a curving bank of green instead of a mass of piers and warehouses.

Although only a few other cities set up extensive park systems, most did manage to scatter small playgrounds and playing fields here and there for their residents' use. Many cities also boasted amusement parks on their outskirts. These were usually built by trolley-car companies that wanted more people to use their lines. These parks contained picnic grounds, bathing beaches, and a variety of rides. The first roller coaster began operating at Coney Island in 1884; the first Ferris wheel turned in Chicago in 1893. Some amusement parks offered outdoor spectaculars. Twenty thousand people would jam the amphitheater at Brooklyn's Manhattan Beach to watch a re-creation of the London Fire complete with rockets.

"Give the Lady What She Wants"

With concentrated urban markets on the one hand and vast quantities of reasonably priced manufactured goods on the other, it was inevitable that city merchants would change their sales methods. Among the major retailing innovations of the new industrial age were: 1. the department store, 2. the chain store, and 3. the shopping center.

The Department Store.
Marshall Field of Chicago led the way in department-store operations. He began his career as a sales clerk in a dry goods store. He soon discovered that by paying close attention to each woman customer, he increased sales considerably. So in 1865 he decided to open his own store and practice the motto "Give the lady what she wants." Fields allowed women to take merchandise home on approval and return it if they were not satisfied, regardless of the reason. Field's store aimed its advertising directly at women in such specialized publications as the *Chicago Magazine of Fashion*. In 1885 Field's pioneered the bargain basement, which carried goods that were "less expensive but reliable." And in 1890 Field's opened a restaurant where women shoppers might lunch at their leisure.

Other department stores, such as Wanamaker's in Philadelphia and Lord & Taylor in New York, followed suit.

The Chain Store.
In 1879 a clerk in Lancaster, Pennsylvania, named Frank W. Woolworth found himself with a group of miscellaneous items. On an impulse, he placed them on a tray and priced them at five or ten cents apiece. By the end of the day, the tray was almost empty. Woolworth was soon in business for himself. Within six years, he had a chain of twenty-five stores. By 1911, there were more than 1000 F. W. Woolworths throughout the United States.

The five-and-ten-cent store chain was followed by the establishment of chain grocery stores and chain drug stores. They did not carry what shoppers today would consider a large number of items. Yet they had such modern characteristics as brand-names, standard packages, high volume, and low-cost sales.

The Shopping Center.
The nation's first shopping center opened in Cleveland in 1890. A glass-topped arcade contained four levels of jewelry, leather goods, and stationery shops. In all, there were 112 shops. The arcade also provided band music on Sundays, and it was a popular pastime for Cleveland residents to spend Sunday afternoons strolling through the arcade and looking at the window displays.

Dining Away from Home

City dwellers changed their eating habits as well as their shopping methods. Having meals away from home, especially at noontime, became common.

Business executives impressed potential customers at such elegant and expensive restaurants as Delmonico's, located on Fifth Avenue at Fourteenth Street in New York. White-gloved waiters, imported wines, flowers, and music provided the proper background for the sumptuous meals.

Lower on the scale were short-order houses. These were designed to serve as many people as possible in the shortest period of time. An English visitor in 1876 estimated that the average urban American needed only six minutes and forty-five seconds to bolt down a full meal of pudding, pastry, vegetables, and meat. And the noise! "There was as much din in the order of dishes and the clash of plates and knives and forks, as if a brass band had been in full blast." The meal was a financial bargain, though—only ten cents.

If all you could afford was five cents, you went to a saloon and bought a nickel beer. Then you walked over to the buffet counter and helped yourself to cold meats, hard-boiled eggs, sausages, and pickles.

This was F. W. Woolworth's first store. His "chain store" concept began a new trend in retailing.

The work of Jane Addams (right) became a model for those seeking to improve slum dwellers' lives.

The Settlement House Movement

Along with places in which to play, shop, and eat, a few American cities provided places where people could obtain help and friendship, but without requiring votes in exchange. These places were known as *settlement houses*, and they were set up by private reformers in slum neighborhoods.

Settlement houses provided classes in such subjects as English, health, crafts, drama, music, and painting. There were college extension classes "for ambitious young people," and reading circles in which books were read aloud to illiterates. Settlement houses also emphasized social services. They tried to get "support for deserted women, insurance for bewildered widows, damages for injured operators, furniture from the clutches of the installment store." And they sent visiting nurses into the homes of the sick.

The leading settlement houses in the United States were Hull House, founded in Chicago in 1889 by Jane Addams and Ellen Gates Starr, and the Henry Street Settlement House, established in New York in 1893 by Lillian D. Wald. Janie Porter Barrett founded the first settlement house for blacks—the Locust Street Social Settlement in Hampton, Virginia—in 1890.

Soon there were some fifty such centers operating in the United States. This was because an increasing number of groups and individuals realized that as more and more of American life centered in and around cities, it was vital that urban surroundings be improved, particularly for the poor. That was the beginning of a program that continues to this day.

Section 3 Review

COMPREHENSION   Developing Vocabulary

1. Explain these terms: skyscrapers, chain store, short-order houses.

COMPREHENSION   Mastering Facts

1. What did Burnham's plan provide for Chicago's lakefront?
2. How did Marshall Field attract women customers to his store?
3. How did city dwellers change their eating habits?
4. What kind of services did settlement houses provide?

CHAPTER 20   Review

Chapter Summary

The expansion of business and industry stimulated the development of new cities and brought rapid growth to the older ones. During the late 1800s, the United States faced serious urban problems. Half of the urban population was poor, and many lived in rundown tenements. Urban blacks faced increased racial prejudice and segregation. City government tended to be inept and frequently dominated by newly developing political organizations called machines. Machine activity—exemplified by the Tweed Ring in New York City—came to be virtually synonymous with graft and corruption. However, during this time there were efforts to improve cities and services. People like Jane Addams and Jacob Riis took the lead in promoting social welfare and reform.

Questions for Critical Thinking

COMPREHENSION   Summarizing Main Ideas

1. Give three reasons why living in tenements could lead to bad health.
2. Give two reasons for the de facto segregation of blacks in northern and western cities.
3. What effect did urban political machines have on each of the following? (a) unemployment; (b) enabling some business people to become rich; (c) meeting people's needs for social outlets; (d) the level of taxes; (e) public morality.
4. What were the major retailing innovations of the new industrial age? Why did each one turn out to be a success?

COMPREHENSION   Interpreting Events

1. Why did urbanization increase in the United States after the Civil War?
2. Why was polluted air a problem for rich city dwellers as well as poor ones?
3. Why were slum reform laws in New York City ineffective? Can you think of any legislation that might have improved slum conditions? Explain your answer.

4. Why was it difficult to maintain law and order in most American cities during the new industrial age?
5. Why were parks increasingly important in the nation's cities?

APPLICATION   Using Skills To Evaluate Sources

For each of the following, tell whether it is a primary or a secondary source.

1. Jacob Riis's *How the Other Half Lives*
2. The text of the New York slum reform law of 1879
3. Edna Ferber's novel *Saratoga Trunk*
4. A cartoon by Thomas Nast
5. An advertisement in the *Chicago Magazine of Fashion*
6. A menu from Delmonico's dated 1876
7. Jane Addams's *Twenty Years at Hull House*
8. A photograph of a San Francisco cable car
9. The 1877 patent on an automatic fire sprinkler
10. *The Urbanization of America, 1816–1915*, by Blake McKelvey.

EVALUATION   Comparing Past to Present

1. Describe a problem that your local community faces and tell what is being done about it. Are efforts for improvement being made by public officials or by private reformers? What role, if any, is being played by your local newspaper or other mass media?
2. Is there a political machine in your local community? If there is, compare the services it provides with those provided by Tammany Hall. Which of these services are also provided by other institutions? Explain your answer.
3. Compare the first shopping center in Cleveland with a shopping center near your home. What are the differences? What are the similarities?

Democracy

At the dedication of the national cemetery at Gettysburg in 1863, President Lincoln renewed a pledge that "government of the people, by the people, for the people, shall not perish from the earth." His remark has often been used as a definition of democracy: government of, by, and for the people.

Lincoln did not say "all" the people, however. Only gradually have increased numbers of people participated in government as various laws extended *suffrage*—the right to vote—to more individuals. In that way Americans have proven democracy to be a process that constantly changes while adapting to new ideas and conditions.

Limited Colonial Views.
Most colonial leaders did not think much of democracy. The idea that all community members could participate intelligently in the decision-making process of government seemed unrealistic. Those early colonial leaders were accustomed to the unquestioned exercise of authority. "I do not conceive that ever God did ordain [democracy] as a fit government either for church or commonwealth," said Puritan minister John Cotton. He asked, "If the people be governors, who shall be governed?"

So, in colonial times the people enjoyed only partial self-government. Voting was basically limited to men who met certain property or religious requirements; qualifications for holding office were equally restrictive. Throughout the colonies, women, slaves, Indians, and poor people were never able to participate in the political process.

Democracy Expands.
After the Revolution, the founding fathers feared mob rule and used indirect methods of election and other means to insulate the government from popular control. However, they did continue the practice of the direct election of representatives to Congress. In addition, they encouraged conditions which strengthened other democratic practices. The Bill of Rights, for example, guaranteed citizens the right to speak freely, criticize leadership, publish without censorship, and assemble freely.

Over the years, improvements in our nation's political process made it more democratic. The emergence of a two-party system encouraged an open contest between political opponents. Gradually, new state constitutions took the lead in extending voting rights to more people. Eventually the electorate included all white males without regard to property or religious restrictions. Then ex-slaves and other black males were guaranteed the right to vote through adoption of the Fifteenth Amendment in 1870.

Democracy in the United States has continued to expand during the twentieth century, too. For example, five constitutional amendments ratified since 1900 have made our nation's election process more open: the Seventeenth (direct election of senators, 1913); the Nineteenth (women's suffrage, 1920); the Twenty-third (voting in the District of Columbia, 1961); the Twenty-fourth (abolition of poll taxes, 1964); and the Twenty-sixth (eighteen-year-old vote, 1971). Still other reforms, such as the direct primary to nominate party candidates and the referendum to submit issues to the people for approval, have been enacted in most states. These, too, have expanded citizen participation in the democratic process.

Ingredients for Democracy.
Why did democracy thrive from the beginning in America but not in many other parts of the world? One reason centered on the land itself. A nation abundant in resources, especially land, helped democracy prosper. In order to function, democracy requires a reasonable level of economic well-being for its citizens. In America the availability of cheap or even free land allowed many people to own property and therefore have a

strong interest in the well-being of society.

Prosperity from the widespread use and distribution of resources contributed to the growth of a substantial middle class. This middle class consisted of people who could afford to be public-spirited citizens. In addition, public education became available to all Americans. As a result, citizens were informed about the processes and issues of government.

On the other hand, democracy did not flourish in cities where the poor and newly arriving immigrants jammed together in tenements. In New York City and other cities, many newcomers cared more about day-to-day survival than they did about exercising their right to vote in a responsible manner. Political machines took full advantage of this situation. Even Tammany Hall's Boss Tweed boasted that he was not worried about newspaper attempts to expose his corruption since his constituents could not read. Though living in a democracy, many urban immigrants remained far removed from the democratic process. This situation changed only gradually with the impact of political reforms.

American Democracy Today.
How well is democracy working today? Some critics argue that democracy is outmoded. They doubt the ability of most citizens to understand the complexity of

A first-time voter learns how to use a voting machine. The right of suffrage is one cornerstone of our nation's democracy.

military issues, nuclear energy debates, and economic problems. Others cite the Vietnam War and Watergate as the worst examples of the abuses of power. In addition, mass media advertising campaigns often suggest that politics now consists of manipulating large numbers of people. Even during the elections themselves, only a small percentage of eligible voters often end up going to the polls.

Yet despite these criticisms, democracy in America has worked amazingly well thus far. But to improve and expand their democracy, Americans must insure that education continues to receive a high priority. Only well-informed, responsible citizens can make the important decisions needed to protect our

unique system of government. To survive, democracy requires constant care and attention.

Understanding Government

1. How did Lincoln define democracy? What can you add to this definition?

2. Why did democracy thrive in early America but not in many other areas of the world? How has our democracy expanded during the past two centuries?

3. Why is education important to democracy?

4. How do you participate in our nation's democratic process? What responsibilities do citizens have who live in a democracy?

CHAPTER 21

Workers and Unions

1876–1915

People in the Chapter

George M. Pullman—*owner of the Pullman Car Company who requires his workers to live in a company town.*

Isaac Myers—*ship-caulker who heads the first black national labor union.*

Samuel Gompers—*founder of the American Federation of Labor (a union for skilled workers) and long-time president of the union.*

Eugene V. Debs—*labor leader who helps organize the American Railway Union, the first national industrial union.*

Mary Harris Jones—*labor organizer known as "Mother Jones," who mobilizes mine workers and their wives and leads a children's march to New York to demonstrate for child labor laws.*

Pauline Feldman—*the first woman organizer for the International Ladies Garment Workers Union.*

Linking Past to Present

During their first hundred years, Americans on the whole were an optimistic people. In part this was a result of the open frontier. If things got too difficult in one place, there was always the possibility of pulling up stakes and moving somewhere else. But by 1890 the land frontier had closed. And the new urban-industrial frontier presented different kinds of challenges. It also created among many workers strong feelings of dissatisfaction and even despair.

A new situation had developed in America. Industrialization reduced the importance of the traditional skilled workers. Mass production needed no artisans; it needed people to tend the machines and service assembly lines. This required no special talent or education. As a result, workers felt a loss of pride in their work and in themselves.

At the same time they knew they could easily be replaced by employers who had become increasingly indifferent and remote. In those days it seemed sensible, and even right, to employers that their primary function was not looking after the welfare of workers but producing the most at the least amount of cost and bother. It was perhaps inevitable, therefore, that hostility should erupt occasionally between factory owners and labor. As owners sought support from government, labor sought strength by forming unions.

1 WORKERS HAVE CAUSE FOR COMPLAINTS

VOCABULARY *breaker boys sweatshop system*

When the Civil War broke out, there were about 1.3 million factory workers in the United States. By 1900, the figure had risen to 5.3 million, with an additional 4 million persons employed in construction and transportation.

But a growing work force was not the only effect of industrialization. More important were changes in the conditions of labor and the development of a new spirit on the part of many workers. These were basic changes in American life.

The Changing Status of Work

Perhaps the biggest change for workers in the new industrial age was the fact that they were no longer artisans. For example, a shoemaker no longer made an entire shoe, but only a small part of a shoe, such as the sole. And he or she made it over and over again, hundreds and often thousands of times a day. In a sense, the worker became almost an extension of the machine. Since no par-

The rise of industrialism meant that more Americans became factory workers, whose living standards continued to decline. In the early 1900s pickets became a familiar sight in this country.

435

ticular ability was needed to run the machine, there was little or no satisfaction in doing the job. And since anyone could do the job, the worker had no security. She or he could easily be replaced.

Loss of Freedom. In addition to losing skills, workers lost a sense of comradeship and personal freedom. A cigarmaker described conditions in earlier times this way.

66 The craftsmanship of the cigar maker was shown in his ability to utilize wrappers to the best advantage, to shave off the unusable to a hairbreadth, to roll so as to cover holes in the leaf and to use both hands so as to make a perfectly shaped and rolled product. These things a good cigar maker learned to do more or less mechanically, which left us free to think, talk, listen, or sing. . . . Often we chose someone to read to us who was a particularly good reader, and in payment the rest of us gave him sufficient of our cigars so he was not the loser. 99

But with the introduction of machines, there was no longer any talking or singing or listening. The machines made too much noise. And besides, the emphasis was on continually increasing production. Most factories prohibited workers from speaking at all during working hours. If they did, they were fired at once.

Loss of Identity. Still another result of industrialization was a growing gap between workers and employers. In the past, a boss knew all those who worked in the shop, saw them as distinct human beings, and often took a personal interest in their welfare. But to Andrew Carnegie, for example, the thousands of workers in his steel mills could only be abstract numbers. Not much attention was paid to the conditions under which they worked.

Wages Too Low. In 1864 *The Printer*, a New York newspaper, published the following information on the weekly cost of living for a family of six—including father, mother, and four children.

66 1 bag of flour 1.80
small measure of potatoes at 17 cents per day for 7 days 1.19
1/4 pound of tea .38
1 pound coffee (mixed or adulterated, can't afford better) .35
3 1/2 pounds sugar 1.05
milk .56
meats for the week (being on 1/2 ration supply) 3.50
2 bushels of coal 1.36

4 pounds of butter 1.60
2 pounds of lard .38
kerosene .30
soap, starch, pepper, salt, vinegar 1.00
vegetables .50
dried apples (to promote health of children) .25
sundries .28
rent 4.00
Total $18.50 99

That same year, the average wage for printers was $16 a week. This meant that even without spending any money for clothing or entertainment, the family's weekly expenses were higher than its income. And printers were skilled and comparatively well paid! Workers in other trades averaged between $3 and $12 a week!

Hours Too Long. If wages were low, working hours were long. As late as 1919, a steel mill's shift was twelve hours. Textile mills averaged twelve to fourteen hours a day. The usual workweek was six days, but the seven-day week was the rule in oil refineries, paper mills, steel mills, restaurants, laundries, and most stores. A poster read: "If you don't come in on Sunday, you needn't come in on Monday." There were no vacations or days off for sickness. Nor was there any unemployment compensation or payment for injuries on the job.

Work Too Dangerous. The lack of workers' compensation was especially significant because working conditions in many industries were extremely hazardous. Take the railroads, for example. Between 1890 and 1917, some 72,000 employees were killed, and almost 2 million were injured on the trains and tracks. An additional 158,000 were killed and 237,000 were injured in the repair shops and roundhouses. These figures are several times higher than the casualties, on both sides, of all the Indian wars put together.

Or take the coal mines. A reporter describing conditions in 1906 wrote,

66 Crouched over the chutes, the boys sit hour after hour picking out the pieces of slate and other refuse from the coal as it rushes past to the washers. . . . The coal is hard, and accidents to the hands, such as cut, broken or crushed fingers, are common. . . . Sometimes there is a worse accident: a terrified shriek is heard, and a boy is mangled and torn in the machinery, or disappears in the chutes to be picked out later smothered and dead. Clouds of dust fill the breakers and are inhaled by the boys, laying the 99 foundations for asthma and miners' consumption.

These "breaker boys" in a coal mine were some of the many children employed at an early age. By 1914 most states prohibited child labor under a specified age, usually 14.

Child Labor

"The most beautiful sight that we see is the child at labor." The statement was made by one company president, but it was typical of what many Americans in the new industrial age believed: namely, that idleness for children was bad, and that factories were a godsend that would keep children from wasting their lives. A second argument in favor of child labor was economic necessity. Because wage rates were so low, the only way many families could survive was to have everybody work.

As a result, by 1910 one out of every five children under the age of fifteen was earning wages. Many child workers were as young as five. They did all kinds of work. They made artificial flowers. They tended rows of machines in huge factories. But mostly they worked in textile mills and coal mines.

Employers were anxious to use child labor because they could pay children lower wages than they paid adults. The children, however, suffered a great deal from the long hours and dangerous working conditions that existed. For example, in 1903, reporter Maria Van Vorst wrote about textile workers in South Carolina. She described how the children would come home at eight o'clock in the evening or even later if the mill was working overtime. "They are usually beyond speech. They fall asleep at the table, on the stairs; they are carried to bed and there laid down as they are, unwashed, undressed; and the . . . bundles of rags so lie until the mill summons them with its . . . cry before sunrise . . ."

There was another way child workers suffered as well. Going to work meant giving up school—and thus giving up the possibility of a better life as adults.

The Sweatshop System

Despite the tremendous growth in the number of factories, certain products—especially clothing—were actually manufactured in people's homes. The system worked this way.

A wholesale clothing manufacturer would parcel work out to a group of contractors. Each contractor in turn would sublet the work to a group of "sweaters." The sweater's shop was usually one of the two larger rooms of a tenement flat. It held anywhere from six to twenty "sweating" employees who would eat at their work and sleep on the goods. The sweater himself would live, sleep, and cook in the other large room of the flat. In addition, the sweater would sometimes subcontract work to other tenement dwellers—families with several children and one or more lodgers. These "homeworkers" would work in their own rooms.

The contractor provided the supplies, but the workers were required to furnish the tools, such as sewing machines, needles, scissors, and the like. Payment was on a piecework basis. The more goods the worker turned out, the more money the worker received. In 1910 average weekly earnings were $5 for about one hundred hours.

Mr. Pullman's Town

"We are born in a Pullman house, fed from the Pullman shop, taught in the Pullman school, catechized in the Pullman church, and when we die we shall be buried in the Pullman cemetery and go to the Pullman hell." So said one of the 5000 workers at the Pullman Palace Car Company, which manufactured dining, sleeping, and club cars for three-fourths of the nation's railroad trackage. The worker was referring to the town of Pullman, which George M. Pullman had built on the outskirts of Chicago in 1880.

Like hundreds of other communities—especially Pennsylvania's coal and steel towns and the mill villages built around southern textile mills—Pullman was a company town. Every resident either worked for the company or belonged to a family whose head worked for the company. The company owned everything in the town. This included not just the land and the houses, but also the stores, bank, school, library, churches, and water and gas systems. George M. Pullman determined the wages his workers received. He also fixed the rents they paid for their housing and the prices they paid for their food and clothing.

Pullman also controlled the town's government. The company appointed all town officials, including policemen, firemen, and school teachers. Spies reported anyone who criticized the company. Non-residents who disagreed with company policy were not allowed to use public facilities to express their opinions. As the New York *Sun* stated in 1885, "The people of Pullman are not happy. . . . They want to run the municipal government themselves, according to the ordinary American fashion. They secretly rebel because the Pullman Company continues its watch and authority over them after working hours."

Section 1 Review

COMPREHENSION   Developing Vocabulary
1. Explain these terms: sweatshop system, breaker boys, company town.

COMPREHENSION   Mastering Facts
1. How did industrialization affect workers' skills?
2. How long was the usual workweek in the 1870s?
3. What were some of the dangers that railroad workers and coal miners faced?
4. Why did some people believe that factory labor was good for children?

2   THE LABOR MOVEMENT TAKES SHAPE

VOCABULARY   *yellow-dog contract   arbitration   craft unions   industrial unionism*

As the new industrial age developed, many workers began to feel that they had to do something to improve their lot. An individual worker could not stand up to an employer. But a group of workers would have power to bargain on more equal terms.

Labor organizations were not new in the United States. Workers had begun to organize as far back as the 1790s. During the first half of the 1800s, many local unions of skilled workers such as mechanics, carpenters, and seamstresses, were formed. But it was only in 1866 that the first *national* labor federation came into being. Why then? Because business was becoming national, with manufacturers selling goods throughout the country. If businessmen were operating nationally, it seemed reasonable for workers to do the same.

The National Labor Union

The new organization was called the National Labor Union (NLU). It consisted of about 300 local unions from thirteen states, led by an iron molder named William H. Sylvis. Its main demand was for an eight-hour day. And how would labor get the eight-hour day? Sylvis's answer was political action. He urged labor to organize its own national party, the way workers in Europe were doing.

Sylvis also argued in favor of including women and blacks in the NLU. Accordingly, the 1868 Congress of the NLU had four women delegates. Kate Mullaney, head of the Laundry Workers Union in Troy, New York, became assistant secretary of the national federation. Black delegates were seated at the 1869 convention, and carpenters and joiners agreed to open their locals to black members. Other unions, however, refused to follow suit. So black workers formed their own national union, the National Colored Labor Union (NCLU), under the leadership of ship-caulker Isaac Myers of Baltimore. But workers were soon outnumbered in the NCLU by middle-class ministers and government clerks. Frederick Douglass replaced Isaac Myers, and the NCLU, after becoming almost an affiliate of the Republican party, simply disappeared.

The NLU grew to 650,000 members. In 1868 it persuaded Congress to pass an eight-hour law for government workers. In 1872 it ran a candidate for president on the Labor Reform party ticket.

Then came the depression of 1873. The National Labor Union did not survive.

The Great Strike

Early in 1877 the New York *Commercial and Financial Chronicle* told its readers: "Labor is under control for the first time since the war." A few months later, newspapers throughout the country were carrying such headlines as CITY IN POSSESSION OF COMMUNISTS. What had happened? The first nation-wide strike in U.S. history had broken out.

The Cause. The strike was begun by workers for the Baltimore and Ohio Railroad in West Virginia. Ever since the depression of 1873, the railroad industry had been in trouble. Many lines had gone bankrupt. In an effort to lower costs and still maintain annual dividends of 8 to 10 percent, which stockholders expected, railroad management had cut wage rates 35 percent in three years. In addition, the railroads had lengthened the working day to fifteen to eighteen hours. Also, trains were double-headed, which meant that a crew had to handle twice as many cars as before.

Then on July 11, the Baltimore and Ohio Railroad announced yet another pay cut. It would bring a fireman's wages, for example, down to $6 for a four-day week. On July 16, when the new scale went into effect, forty firemen and brakemen quit their jobs in protest. They were replaced at once, and the freight trains started down the line. But when they reached Martinsburg, West Virginia, sympathetic trainmen surrounded the railroad depot. No trains would leave, they said, until wages were restored to their original level. The wives and mothers of the trainmen, who joined the demonstration, agreed. "Better to starve outright," said one of them, "than to die by slow starvation."

The Reaction. The Baltimore and Ohio immediately asked the governor to request federal troops. In the meantime, county militia were sent to Pittsburgh, where a sympathy strike had broken out. But instead of dispersing the strikers, the militia went over to their side. Only when federal troops arrived was the demonstration broken up, at a cost of twenty-six strikers killed and hundreds wounded. Enraged by this bloodshed, some 20,000 persons, including thousands of workers from Pittsburgh's steel mills and coal mines, attacked the federal troops and drove them out of the city. Then they began to destroy railroad property.

Similar strikes flared up all along the nation's railroad lines. Everywhere, federal troops were used against peaceful strikers and rioters alike. Sometimes state militia supported the strikers. At other times, the state militia fought alongside the federal forces.

The Results. By August 2, order had been restored and trains began running again. Most workers who had gone out on strike lost their jobs. However, the workers had made their point. Most railroads decided either to restore wage cuts, or at least not to lower wages any further.

At the same time, railroads and many other corporations began to organize against unions. They hired private detectives known as Pinkertons, named after Allan Pinkerton, the Scottish-born founder of a leading detective agency. It was the job of the Pinkertons to find out which workers were union members. Such workers were promptly fired. Pinkertons also hired out as strikebreakers. In addition, corporations required new employees to sign a *yellow-dog contract*, that is, a pledge not to join a union.

Nevertheless, the American union movement continued to develop. And a new national organization rose to prominence.

The Knights of Labor

The Noble Order of the Knights of Labor was organized in 1869 by Uriah Stephens, a garment cutter from Philadelphia. It started out as a secret society, with a password and a distinctive hand grip that members used when greeting one another. Its motto was, "An injury to one is the concern of all."

Unlike the NLU, the Knights of Labor was an organization of individuals rather than unions. Membership was open to all workers, regardless of race, sex, or degree of skill. The only occupations that were excluded were lawyers, bankers, professional gamblers, and liquor dealers.

Like the NLU, the Knights supported the eight-hour day. They were also opposed to child labor and convict labor, and were in favor of health and safety laws. They advocated "equal pay for equal work" for men and women. In later years, they came out in favor of government ownership of railroads, telephones, and telegraphs.

The Knights did not favor the use of strikes except as a last resort. They preferred *arbitration*, that is, the settlement of disagreements between employers and workers by an impartial third party.

These women attend an 1886 convention of the Knights of Labor, an organization that welcomed all workers.

A Successful Leader. At first the Knights grew slowly. Skilled trade unions did not like the idea of one big union, and the Catholic church was opposed to secret societies such as the Knights. Then in 1879, a mechanic named Terence V. Powderly of Scranton, Pennsylvania, became the order's Grand Master Workman. Under his leadership, the Knights began a headlong growth from 28,000 members in 1880 to about 700,000 in 1886.

Part of the reason for the Knights' success was the fact that Powderly was an excellent leader. Although short and mild-mannered, he was an energetic organizer and a superb orator. He electrified people wherever he spoke. Also, Powderly dropped the Knights' veil of secrecy and made the organization public.

A Series of Strikes. A second reason for the Knights' success was, ironically, a series of successful strikes. The most important were those against Jay Gould's railroads. The first strike broke out spontaneously in 1884. As a result of the strike, the Union Pacific canceled a 10 percent wage cut. In 1885, workers on three more of Gould's lines struck for the same reason and won again. Later that year, Gould's Wabash line fired several hundred men for being union members. The Knights at first tried to arbitrate the dispute. When this did not work, the Knights ordered all members who worked on any of Gould's railroads "to refuse to repair or handle the rolling stock of his Wabash line." Gould had boasted, "I can hire one half the working class to kill the other half." But he could not afford to have all work stop on 20,000 miles of railroad track. He rehired the fired workers.

As a result, membership in the Knights grew by leaps and bounds. Many states, except in the South, passed laws prohibiting the sale of goods made by convict labor. Congress set up a Federal Bureau of Labor, and by 1900 there were similar agencies in thirty states.

But the Knights' days of glory were numbered. By the mid-1890s, the organization was practically extinct. Its downfall can be laid to two main factors: the Haymarket affair, and the rise of the American Federation of Labor.

The Haymarket Affair

The evening of May 4, 1886, was windy and chilly, with a hint of rain in the air. Haymarket Square, in Chicago, was filled with some 1200

Samuel Gompers favored organizing workers by crafts and helped found the American Federation of Labor.

bomb. However, the police arrested Parsons, Spies, and Fielden. They also arrested five other radicals who in the past had advocated violence. Although only three of the accused men were actually in Haymarket Square, and although there was no proof that any of them had either planted or thrown a bomb, all eight men were convicted. Four of them, including Parsons and Spies, were hanged. One committed suicide. Governor John P. Altgeld pardoned the remaining three by 1893. After studying the record, Altgeld concluded that the defendants had not received a fair trial. The presiding judge was biased; much of the evidence was false; and the jury had been especially selected by a bailiff who said, "Those fellows are going to be hanged as certain as death."

Altgeld paid for the pardon with his political career. But even before the pardon was granted, the Knights of Labor paid for Haymarket. Although they condemned the incident, they were pictured in the press as a gang of radicals with bombs in their pockets. Public opinion swung sharply against them.

The American Federation of Labor

The Knights of Labor were concerned mostly with what historians call "uplift unionism." Powderly dreamed of a classless society, and believed that the road to labor's success lay in political activity and in educating the public. The Knights were organized on the basis that all workers had the same interests. Therefore, there was no need for specialized unions.

But a different kind of unionism was developing in the United States. It was known as "bread-and-butter unionism." Its interest was less in political reform and more in shorter hours, higher wages, and better working conditions for skilled, specialized workers. The ideas came mainly from a man named Samuel Gompers.

A Strong Leader. Gompers was born in London of Dutch Jewish parents. His father, a cigarmaker, was active in the British cigarmakers' union. Young Gompers absorbed both his father's skill and his views on unions. At the age of thirteen, he came to the United States and went to work in a cigar-making shop. Later he became secretary and then president of the cigarmakers' union in New York.

In 1881 Gompers helped found the Federation

people. They were listening to three men—Albert Parsons, August Spies, and Samuel Fielden—who were arguing in favor of the eight-hour day and were condemning a police action that had taken place on May 3. There had been a fight between pickets and strikebreakers at the McCormick Harvester plant. In attempting to restore order, the police had killed four workers and wounded several others.

Shortly after ten o'clock, rain began to fall. As the crowd broke up, about 180 policemen appeared in the square. Their commanding officer declared: "In the name of the people of the State of Illinois, I command this meeting immediately and peaceably to disperse!" "But, captain, we *are* peaceable," came the reply.

Suddenly, there was a terrific explosion. Someone had thrown a dynamite bomb! It hit the ground near the police column, killing seven officers and wounding sixty-seven others. The police immediately opened fire and then charged on horseback. When the shooting and clubbing were over, ten workers lay dead and another fifty, wounded.

No one knows, even today, who threw the

of Organized Trade and Labor Unions of the United States of America and Canada. The name was shortened in 1886 to the American Federation of Labor (AFL). Gompers was elected president in 1885 and, except for one year, continued to lead the organization until his death in 1924.

The AFL Program.

Like the NLU, the AFL was a federation of unions. But the unions were national rather than local. And they included skilled workers only; unskilled workers were not permitted to join. Women and blacks, except in the United Mine Workers, were also excluded. Unions that include only skilled workers in a particular craft are known as *craft unions.*

The AFL was, in Gompers's words, "the business organization of the workers." It avoided third-party political activity. Instead, it supported whichever candidate or party agreed with its demands. It did not oppose capitalism. It used peaceful bargaining whenever possible, and strikes whenever necessary. And it succeeded in its basic goals. Between 1890 and 1915, average weekly wages in unionized industries rose from $17.57 to $23.98, while the average workweek fell from 54.4 to 48.9 hours. (For unorganized workers, weekly earnings rose from $8.82 to $11.52, while the workweek dropped from 62.2 to 55.6 hours.)

The Limitation of Craft Unionism.

The problem was that artisans made up less than 30 percent of the labor force. The great majority of workers were unskilled or semiskilled. And their numbers kept growing as big business broke production down into increasingly simpler tasks.

Some labor leaders began to feel that craft unionism, no matter how effective, was not the answer. In their opinion, the future of labor lay in *industrial unionism,* that is, in organizing workers—whether skilled or unskilled—who worked in the same industry. Two groups tried to do this: the American Railway Union, and a more radical group called the Industrial Workers of the World.

The American Railway Union

The man who made the first major attempt at industrial unionism was Eugene V. Debs. He was born in 1855 in Terre Haute, Indiana, and went to work in the railroad yards when he was fourteen years old. Later he became an officer of the Brotherhood of Locomotive Firemen and Enginemen,

to which only skilled workers belonged.

In 1893 another railroad union, the Switchmen's Union, went on strike. But the four railroad brotherhoods—Locomotive Engineers, Railway Conductors, Firemen and Enginemen, and Trainmen—refused to support the strike. Disgusted, Debs resigned his union position and organized the American Railway Union to include all railroad workers. Most of its members were unskilled and semiskilled workers who were not eligible for the brotherhoods. But many skilled engineers and firemen joined, too. The only workers not admitted were blacks. Debs led a strong fight against this discrimination but was defeated at the organizing convention.

The next year, the American Railway Union won a strike for higher wages against the Great Northern Railroad. Within two months, its membership climbed to 150,000 compared with 90,000 in the four brotherhoods. Debs's idea that workers had to "march together, vote together, and fight together" seemed to be on its way. But as you will read later in this chapter, the attempt failed.

The Industrial Workers of the World

In 1905 a group of radical unionists and socialists made a second attempt at industrial unionism. The new organization was called the Industrial Workers of the World (IWW), and its members became known as Wobblies.

The head of the IWW was William "Big Bill" Haywood, a former hard-rock miner. Haywood used to explain the difference between craft unionism and industrial unionism in the following way:

66 "The A. F. of L. organizes like this!" [he would say], separating his fingers, as far apart as they would go, and naming them—weavers, loom-fixers, dyers, spinners. Then he would say, "The I.W.W. organizes like this!"—tightly clenching his big fist, shaking it at the bosses. 99

Most of the IWW's organizing took place in the West, and most of its members were miners, lumbermen, and cannery and dock workers. Unlike the AFL, the IWW included both women and blacks. But the IWW never attracted more than 150,000 workers at its peak. Its only major strike victory took place in the textile town of Lawrence, Massachusetts, in 1912. Then during World War I, IWW membership dwindled. Yet the IWW influenced the American labor movement. It proved that unskilled workers *could* be organized. It gave unskilled workers a sense of dignity and self-worth.

Section 2 Review

COMPREHENSION   Developing Vocabulary

1. Explain these terms: yellow-dog contract, arbitration, craft unions, industrial unionism.

COMPREHENSION   Mastering Facts

1. Why did the Knights of Labor gain so many members between 1880 and 1886?
2. How did the Haymarket affair affect the Knights of Labor?
3. What were the main goals of the AFL?
4. How did the IWW influence the American labor movement?

3   LABOR EXPERIENCES SETBACKS AND VICTORIES

VOCABULARY   *lockout   scabs   blacklist   injunction*

As things turned out, industrial unionism did not become widespread in the United States until the 1930s. Even craft unionism found it difficult to make much progress. Why? Primarily because government used its powers to support management against labor.

The Government Supports Carnegie Steel

One example occurred in 1892 at Homestead, Pennsylvania. The Carnegie Steel Company had a contract with the Amalgamated Association of Iron and Steel Workers, an affiliate of the AFL. The union asked for a wage raise in the new contract. Instead of bargaining, Carnegie's lieutenant, Henry Clay Frick, announced a wage cut. The workers refused to accept this. Frick then instituted a "lockout"; that is, he closed down the plant. The workers responded by forming a picket line around the plant to prevent *scabs* from coming in. Scabs are people who go to work despite a strike by their co-workers. Frick in turn hired 300 Pinkertons and tried to smuggle them in on barges. Thereupon some 10,000 men, women, and children lined the banks of the Monongahela River. When the barges carrying the Pinkertons tried to land, fighting between the two groups broke out.

The workers won the first battle. But a few days later, the governor sent 8000 National Guardsmen to Homestead. The militia remained in town for more than three months, while the company brought in 2000 scabs to operate the steel mill. At last the workers gave in and voted to return to work. Most of them, however, never got their old jobs back. That was not all. Wages were cut even more than originally proposed. And the Amalgamated Association of Iron and Steel Workers was put on an industry-wide blacklist. This meant that no steel company would hire any worker who belonged to the union.

It was the governor's duty to maintain law and order. Also, most people felt that the union had no right to prevent strikebreakers from entering the plant. On the other hand, the Carnegie Steel Company had refused to live up to its contract and bargain with the union. By sending in troops, the state government made it impossible for the union to use its major weapon, the strike.

The Government Supports Pullman

Another example of government support of industry took place in 1894. When the 1893 depression hit, the Pullman Company cut wages by 24 to 40 percent. Rents and prices in the town of Pullman, however, remained the same. As a result, many workers found themselves deep in debt. So they sent a committee to the company management asking that the wage cuts be restored. The company replied by firing the committee members. The workers struck and asked the American Railway Union for help.

Debs tried several times to arbitrate the dispute, but the Pullman Company refused to negotiate. So the American Railway Union declared a boycott of Pullman cars. ARU members cut the cars out from trains and put them on sidetracks. When these men were fired, other members of the ARU quit in protest. Within four days, 125,000 railroad workers were out on strike, and traffic between Chicago and the West Coast was practically at a standstill.

At this point, the General Managers Association, an organization of twenty-four of the nation's biggest railroads, decided to step in.

First, the managers brought in strikebreakers. Then they asked U.S. Attorney General Richard Olney, who had been a railroad lawyer for many years, for help. Olney convinced President Cleveland to send in federal troops on the grounds of guaranteeing the delivery of mail. (As a matter of fact, the ARU had not interfered with mail trains at all, and mail was being delivered without interruption.)

Olney also appointed Edwin Walker, another railroad lawyer, as special federal attorney in Chicago. Walker promptly issued an *injunction*, that is, a court order prohibiting all strike activity against the railroads. The argument was that railroads were not a private business but "a public highway." If workers quit as a group, they were interfering with interstate commerce. Walker also swore in almost 3600 special deputies, which brought the total of armed troops in Chicago to 14,000.

The combination of federal troops and the injunction was too much for the union. The boycott collapsed, while Debs was sentenced to six months in jail for trying to keep the strike going in spite of the court order. Soon after, the strike ended and the American Railway Union fell apart.

Court Decisions Support Business

The Pullman strike was the first time that employers were able to use an injunction to break up a strike. This gave business a strong edge over unions. It was no longer necessary for a company to hire Pinkertons, for example, or even to call in federal troops. All the company had to do was say that a strike, a picket line, or a boycott would hurt its sales. A federal or state court would then issue an injunction on the gounds that such activity by a union was "a conspiracy in restraint of trade" and violated the Sherman Antitrust Act of 1890.

Some judges went even further. They prohibited unions from promoting or endorsing strikes "in any manner by letters, printed or other circulars, telegrams or telephones, word of mouth, oral persuasion, or suggestion, or through interviews to be published in newspapers." One court in Boston ruled that unions could not pay strike benefits to any of their members who walked off a job.

Congress did not outlaw injunctions against strikers until 1932. In the meantime, unions found it difficult to organize workers. In 1910 only 8.3 percent of the industrial workers were in unions.

Women in the Labor Movement

There had always been women who worked for wages in the United States. As the new industrial age developed, their numbers increased until, by 1910, they made up about 21 percent of the labor force. Most were concentrated in certain industries, such as the garment trade, textiles, tobacco, and retail sales, as well as nursing and teaching. In general, they held so-called "women's jobs." These trades were usually unskilled and offered very little opportunity for moving up the job or pay ladder. Wages, in fact, were a far cry from "equal pay for equal work." Women earned about one-half as much money as non-union men and about one-third as much as union men, even for the same kind of work.

As the union movement developed in the United States, several women organizers became prominent. Among them were Mary Harris Jones and Pauline Feldman.

Mother Jones of the Mines and Mills. During the 1880s and 1890s, almost every mining town had a "mother." Her job was to mobilize the miners' wives when their husbands went out on strike. The women would bang on tin pans to frighten the mine mules and would throw garbage on the scabs whom the mining companies hired. If they were imprisoned for disturbing the peace, they would take their babies to jail with them. The more their babies cried at night, the less time the women usually had to spend behind bars.

The most famous mine town "mother" was Mother Jones. Born in Ireland about 1830, she emigrated when she was seven years old. She taught school and later ran a dressmaking shop that burned down in the Chicago fire of 1871. In 1877, after her husband and four children died, she took part in the great railroad strike. From then on, she devoted her life to the labor movement.

Mother Jones did not limit her organizing activities to mining towns. In the spring of 1903, she was in Kensington, Pennsylvania, where some 75,000 textile workers were on strike. About 10,000 were children, and Mother Jones was horrified by how many were stooped and old at the age of ten, or were missing fingers and even hands that had been cut off by mill machinery. What could she do to arouse public opinion against child labor?

The idea that Mother Jones came up with was a children's march to see President Theodore Roose-

Mary Harris ("Mother") Jones became active in the labor movement in the great railroad strike of 1877, in her late forties. She became most strongly identified with the mine labor movement, but she helped organize strikes and demonstrations in several industries. She died in 1930.

velt at his home in Oyster Bay, Long Island. She received permission from Kensington mothers to take about eighty children on a week's march. Each child packed a little knapsack. Accompanied by a few men to help them, Mother Jones and the children marched away. The signs they carried read, "We want more schools and less hospitals"; "We want time to play"; "Prosperity is here. Where is ours?"

In New York, Mother Jones addressed a crowd of some 20,000 sympathetic people. "Fifty years ago," she said, "there was a cry against slavery and men gave up their lives to stop the selling of black children on the block. Today the white child is sold for two dollars a week to the manufacturers. Fifty years ago the black babies were sold C.O.D. Today the white baby is sold on the installment plan."

Despite the large audience, in the short run the children's march was a failure. President Roosevelt refused to see them and did not answer Mother Jones's letters. The Kensington textile workers lost their strike for shorter hours and higher wages, and the children had to return to the mills. In the long run, however, the march was a success. It drew a tremendous amount of publicity. And a year later, Pennsylvania passed a law prohibiting child labor under the age of fourteen.

Pauline Feldman of the Garment Trade. Pauline Feldman went to work for the Triangle Shirtwaist Company in 1901 when she was eight years old. In 1909, at the age of sixteen, she became the first woman organizer for the International Ladies Garment Workers Union. Her first task was raising money to support the "Uprising of the 20,000." This was a general strike that broke out in New York City's garment industry. About three-fourths of the strikers were young women between the ages of sixteen and twenty-five, and almost all were either Jewish or Italian.

The strike lasted thirteen weeks and achieved many of its goals, including a fifty-two-hour, instead of a fifty-nine-hour, workweek. The Triangle

Union Membership in Selected Industries

	Auto Workers	AFL	AFL-CIO	Airline Pilots	Garment Workers	Horseshoers	Teamsters
1897		264,800			4,000	2,000	
1904		1,676,200			45,700	4,200	84,000
1912		1,770,100			46,400	5,200	41,500
1920		4,078,700			45,900	5,400	110,800
1924		2,865,800			47,500	2,000	75,000
1930		2,961,100			47,200	700	98,800
1935		3,218,400		700	37,100	100	161,900
1939	165,300	3,878,000		1,000	40,000	200	441,600
1945	891,800	6,890,400		6,000	40,000	200	644,500
1955	1,260,000		12,622,000	9,000	40,000	200	1,291,100
1965	1,150,000		12,919,000	18,000	35,000	200	1,506,700
1975	1,400,000		14,066,000	46,000	32,000	200	1,973,200

Shirtwaist Company, however, refused to settle with the union. Eventually, its 500 employees returned to work under the same bad working conditions as before the strike. Two of these conditions were: 1. Factory doors opened inward rather than outward, and, with one exception, were kept locked all day; and 2. There was no sprinkler system and only one fire escape, which went down only to the second floor.

On March 25, 1911, fire broke out on the seventh, eighth, and ninth floors of the Asch Building, where the Triangle Shirtwaist Company was housed. It spread swiftly through the oil-soaked machines and the piles of cloth and cuttings. The workers tried desperately to escape the searing heat. Some jumped from the windows, only to crash through the fire department's safety nets to the street below. (The department's fire ladders extended only to the sixth floor.) Some jumped into one of the two elevator shafts, putting the elevator out of commission. In all, 146 workers died from burns, suffocation, or leaps from the windows.

On April 5, about 120,000 men, women, and children marched in silence in the pouring rain to honor the Triangle dead. The two owners of the Triangle Shirtwaist Company were tried on manslaughter charges but were acquitted. The jurors felt that no one person was responsible. They regarded the accident as an act of God. One of the jurors said, "I think the girls who worked there were not as intelligent as those in other walks of life and were therefore the more susceptible to panic."

The public in general, however, took a different view. The New York Factory Investigating Commission, popularly called the Triangle Commission, was set up to look into working conditions throughout the state. Its members included two Tammany leaders, Alfred E. Smith (the 1928 Democratic candidate for president), and Robert F. Wagner, Sr. A third member was Frances Perkins, who later became the nation's first woman cabinet member as secretary of labor.

After four years of investigation, Smith and Wagner convinced the New York legislature to pass laws improving working conditions. The new legislation provided for, among other things, strict fire safety codes in factories; a fifty-four-hour workweek for women and minors; the prohibition of Sunday work; and the abolition of child labor under fourteen years of age. In the meantime, the ILGWU established itself as one of the nation's strongest unions. Pauline Feldman was its director of education as late as 1976, when she was in her mid-eighties.

Section 3 Review

COMPREHENSION   Developing Vocabulary

1. Explain these terms: scabs, injunction, lockout, blacklist.

COMPREHENSION   Mastering Facts

1. What caused the Pullman strike to collapse?
2. How did judges apply the Sherman Antitrust Act to unions?
3. What was the job of a mining town "mother"?
4. What were the results of the Triangle Commission investigation?

CHAPTER 21 Review

Chapter Summary

Industrialization and mass production methods created dissatisfaction among many workers. Factory conditions were poor; children were often employed in factories, mines, and sweatshops. To combat these conditions, workers began to organize labor unions. Strikes, often accompanied by violence, brought some gains. However, many government and court decisions tended to support the wealthy owners. Women played an important role during the early days of the labor movement. But by the turn of the century, American workers still faced an uphill battle.

Questions for Critical Thinking

COMPREHENSION Summarizing Main Ideas

1. Compare labor-management relations in small, privately owned shops with those in large, corporation-owned factories.

2. What brought about the first nationwide strike in U.S. history? How did the federal government respond? What were the economic results of the strike? How did many corporations respond to the strike?

3. What special problems did women workers face in the new industrial age?

COMPREHENSION Interpreting Events

1. Why were people who lived in such company towns as Pullman, Illinois, unhappy? Do you think they were justified in their feelings? Give reasons for your opinion.

2. Why were many employers anxious to use child labor? In what ways did child workers suffer? Do you believe that child labor under the age of fourteen should be prohibited? Why?

3. Why did national labor organizations first develop after the Civil War?

4. Which type of unionism—craft unionism or industrial unionism—do you favor? Give reasons for your opinion.

5. How did corporations use each of the following against workers? (a) Pinkertons; (b) the yellow-dog contract; (c) the lockout; (d) the blacklist; (e) injunctions.

6. Why did the federal government and state governments in the 1880s and 1890s usually support management against labor?

7. If you had been a member of the jury at the trial of the owners of the Triangle Shirtwaist Company, which verdict would you have supported? Give reasons for your answer.

APPLICATION Using Skills To Distinguish Fact from Opinion

For each of the statements below, indicate whether it is a fact or an opinion.

1. Workers were worse off in the new industrial age than they had been before the Civil War.

2. Industrialization led to a large increase in the work force.

3. Most workers in the new industrial age were unskilled.

4. The sweatshop system was common in the clothing industry.

5. George M. Pullman liked to control his employees' lives.

6. The first labor organizations in the United States developed in the 1790s.

7. The first local unions consisted of skilled workers.

8. It is easier to organize skilled rather than unskilled workers.

9. The first nation-wide strike in the United States was led by communists.

10. The Haymarket trial was a miscarriage of justice.

EVALUATION Comparing Past to Present

1. Both companies and unions have come up with ideas for coping with the repetitiveness of the assembly line. Report on one such idea.

2. Interview a local labor leader regarding the major concerns and goals of his or her union. How do these compare with the concerns and goals of the Knights of Labor? the A.F.L. in 1900? the I.W.W.?

3. Interview a local business executive regarding the major concerns and goals of his or her company. How do they differ from the concerns and goals of business people in the 1870–1915 period?

Alternatives to Capitalism:
Socialism and Communism

As Americans, we have come to understand and appreciate the workings of our economic system called capitalism. Basically, capitalism is a system of free enterprise—that is, private individuals seeking a profit on their investments which include the means of production (machines, factories, land, and so on). Over the years the United States has become the world's leading capitalist society.

However, there are other ways to organize an economy. Two other systems, *socialism* and *communism*, operate in large areas of the world today. Both are fundamentally different from capitalism.

Socialism. Socialism is an economic system in which the government owns the means of production. Decisions concerning how much to produce, what prices to charge, what wages to pay, and so on, are made by government officials.

Like capitalism, the principles of socialism originated in Europe. Because early socialists believed people could be persuaded to work without a profit, they were considered idealistic. Some were called "utopians"—believers in a perfect world. Utopians thought it was possible to reform the economic system to distribute wealth more fairly. In the United States, experi-

ments in socialism—such as the community in New Harmony, Indiana—ended in failure.

Marx's Philosophy. Karl Marx (1818–1883), the most influential socialist thinker of the nineteenth century, eventually went beyond socialism. With Friedrich Engels, Marx wrote a pamphlet in 1848 entitled the *Communist Manifesto*. The word communism comes from the Latin word *communis*, meaning "belonging to all in common." Marx used this word in his title because he believed that the world's goods should belong to everyone in common, not to private individuals. But at that time communism was just another name for socialism.

Marx's pamphlet presented its readers with an economic interpretation of history. In it, Marx argued that the group controlling economic power also has political and social power. He believed that history was a conflict between opposing economic forces—a class struggle. These classes, the "haves and have-nots," have struggled for control throughout history. With the coming of the Industrial Revolution, many saw the class struggle developing between the *bourgeoisie* and the *proletariat*—that is, between the owners of the means of production and the laborers in factories and mines

who owned nothing but their ability to work.

In Marx's view, workers did not receive the entire value of their labor. Instead, the capitalist system deprived workers of most of the value of their labor. Capitalists took most labor value as profit and, as a result, the bourgeoisie got richer and richer while the proletariat became poorer and poorer.

But Marx was encouraged by the lessons he saw in history. He believed class struggle was a law of society that would continue to operate whenever economic inequality existed. Eventually, Marx predicted, economic conditions would become so bad that the proletariat would rise up and seize power from their capitalist oppressors.

Communism. Although the ideas of Marx have had worldwide influence, their greatest impact occurred in Russia. There, radical socialists favored quick, drastic action to achieve their goals. Headed by V. I. Lenin, these revolutionaries called themselves Communists and declared that socialism was only a temporary stage through which a nation passed on the way to a truly Communist state. After the start of the Russian Revolution in 1917, the Soviet Communists broke completely with other socialist groups.

Eventually, the Communists under Lenin's direction won a bloody civil war and then established a Communist government called the Union of Soviet Socialist Republics (USSR). In setting up their economic system, Communist leaders also set up a political system that left no room for individual rights or personal freedom.

The Communist leaders demanded complete ownership of factories, machines, land, and other basic means of production. Private enterprise was outlawed. They held that the government should be run by the Communist party, which would plan all of the nation's economic activity. The Soviets encouraged other Communists around the world to unite in overthrowing capitalism—if necessary, by using force and violence.

U.S. Rejects Other Systems.

Though the Communist takeover in Russia caused concern in the United States, the economic ideas included in that system did not have a strong impact on the nation. Socialists never received more than a small percentage of votes in any American presidential election.

Why did socialism fail to attract a significant following in the United States? One important reason lies in the adaptability of capitalism. Over the years, Americans and their elected representatives have successfully modified the less desirable features of capitalism.

V. I. Lenin, portrayed here rousing Russian workers to action with Stalin and Trotsky in the background, gave Marxists a revolutionary political program.

Without regulations, capitalism can lead to unfair monopolies that restrict competition. When that happens, workers can be excluded from receiving just wages for their labor.

Responding to the problems involved in the growth of capitalism, the federal government became involved in the regulation of business in the United States during the late 1800s. To balance the growth of capitalism, the government eventually encouraged the growth of labor unions. Thus, our current economic system is actually a modified capitalist system. But the additional rules and regulations have created more overall equity and justice. They have also made systems such as socialism and communism unattractive to most Americans.

The goals of many socialists have changed over the years, and today socialist democracies are common in European nations. Communism, however, continues to have a strong appeal in poorer, more undeveloped nations. It is that struggle between capitalism and communism—two basically different economic and political systems—that continues today.

Understanding Free Enterprise

1. How does capitalism differ from communism?

2. Explain Marx's view of history. Have his predictions proven to be correct?

3. Why did socialism and communism fail to thrive in the United States?

4. Why does communism appeal to many people living in poorer, more underdeveloped nations? What can the United States do to counteract this appeal?

CHAPTER 22

The New Immigrants

1880-1915

Linking Past to Present

For nearly two hundred years, the English colonies and then the United States had been a place of welcome for all sorts of people. But when immigrants came to these shores, it was expected that they would, in time, take on the habits and customs of the majority. These included the English language, the Protestant religion, and a whole set of Anglo-Saxon attitudes. These expectations were to be achieved by what many considered America to be—a "melting pot." According to the melting pot theory, differences of nationality were to be melted away, leaving a generally homogenized population.

This appeared to have worked pretty well until many new immigrants began to arrive who could not, or would not, melt into the social soup. Moreover, their language, looks, and customs were often strikingly different from those of the American majority. Many such immigrants declared that they did not think of America as a melting pot but as a "mixed salad," in which each immigrant group contributed to the whole but still kept its individual flavor. Others regarded new immigrant groups as additions to the great mosaic of American society.

But most people at this time were made uneasy by these views. In addition, there were economic differences which caused problems. The new immigrants were willing to work for lower wages. As a result, there was a movement to close the "golden door" against most new immigrants.

1 EASTERN EUROPEANS ARRIVE IN AMERICA

As you know from chapters 1 and 2, the migration of peoples to what is now the continental United States occurred in several massive waves. The first was that of people from Asia, who crossed over to Alaska thousands of years ago and gradually made their way south. The second wave arrived during the 1600s. It consisted mostly of English and Spanish peoples, with a sprinkling of other nationalities such as the Dutch, the French, and the Swedes. The third great influx took place during the 1700s. It included primarily Scotch-Irish, Germans, and black Africans.

The forty years before the Civil War saw the next great wave of immigrants. They were mostly Irish, Germans, and English who went to the East Coast, and Chinese who went to the West Coast. The fifth wave, from 1860 to 1880, likewise featured immigrants from Britain, Germany, and Scandinavia.

But the sixth wave, between 1880 and 1915, had a different source. Instead of coming mostly from northern Europe, it was drawn mainly from southern and eastern Europe, especially Austria-Hungary, Italy, and Russia. There were also newcomers from the Balkans, Turkey, French-speaking Canada, and Japan.

It was not the number of immigrants during this last period that caused controversy. True, the absolute number of foreign-born people in the United States rose from 4 million in 1860 to 13 million in 1910. But the overall population increased as well. Thus, the proportion of immigrants to native-born Americans remained about the same: 12 percent.

What caused controversy were two conditions. First, there were considerable cultural differences between the so-called "new immigrants" and those who preceded them. Second, most of the new immigrants were concentrated in certain areas, which made for economic friction.

Cultural Differences

Many people today disagree with the idea that a nation's citizens must resemble one another. Most Americans of the new industrial age, however, felt very threatened by immigrants of different cultures. How was it possible for such strange people to become Americans?

This photograph from 1902, by William H. Raw, shows immigrants huddled on a ship approaching Ellis Island.

451

Language. One major cultural difference was language. Until the 1880s, most immigrants—except for Germans and blacks—spoke English. But the majority of new immigrants spoke a variety of languages.

Furthermore, they tended to retain their language in the United States. They used it in daily conversation. They shopped only at stores that carried signs in their native tongue. And they read newspapers in their native language rather than English. In 1920, for example, the foreign language press in the United States included 276 German papers, 118 in Spanish and Portuguese, 76 in Polish, 51 in Czech, 46 in French, 42 in Slovenian, and 39 in Yiddish.

Religion. Another cultural difference was religion. A majority of the new immigrants were Roman Catholic. Catholics had been coming to the United States since the 1500s. But many of the newcomers, especially those from Italy and what is now Poland, did not care for the predominantly Irish clergy they found in the United States. They preferred national parishes in which priests of their own nationality conducted services. German and Scandinavian Lutherans likewise preferred services in their native languages rather than in English.

Then there were the Orthodox Catholics from eastern Europe and the Balkans. Their bearded clergy and their church buildings with onion-shaped roofs were very different from anything previously seen in the United States.

Also very different were the Jews. Earlier Jewish immigrants had come mostly from Portugal and Germany. The great majority of Jews who arrived after 1880 came from Russia and what is now Poland, where they had been forced to live in areas apart from the rest of the population. They spoke and read Yiddish, observed religious dietary laws (which included the prohibition of pork and shellfish), and sent their children to Hebrew school after public school was over for the day. Most of the men did not shave, while most of the women either wore wigs or covered their hair with kerchiefs.

Race. The third difference was race. The great majority of Americans were white. To many of them, Chinese and Japanese immigrants did not look like "real Americans."

Melting Pot Theory

In 1782 Jean de Crèvecoeur (krev-*kur*), a French writer living in New York, asked the question,

“ What then is the American, this new man? He is . . . a strange mixture of blood, which you will find in no other country. I could point out to you a family whose grandfather was an Englishman, whose wife was Dutch, whose son married a French woman, and whose present four sons have now four wives of different nations. . . . Here individuals of all nations are melted into a new race . . . whose labors and posterity will one day cause great changes in the world. ”

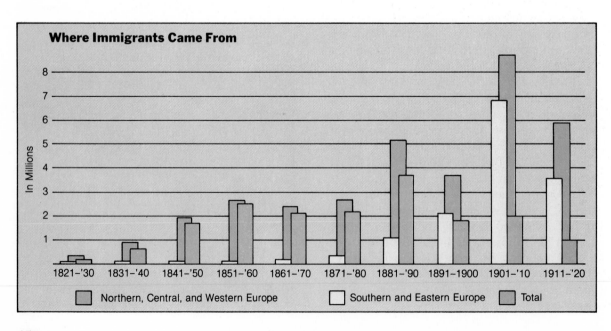

Where Immigrants Came From

In Millions

1821–'30 1831–'40 1841–'50 1851–'60 1861–'70 1871–'80 1881–'90 1891–1900 1901–'10 1911–'20

☐ Northern, Central, and Western Europe   ☐ Southern and Eastern Europe   ☐ Total

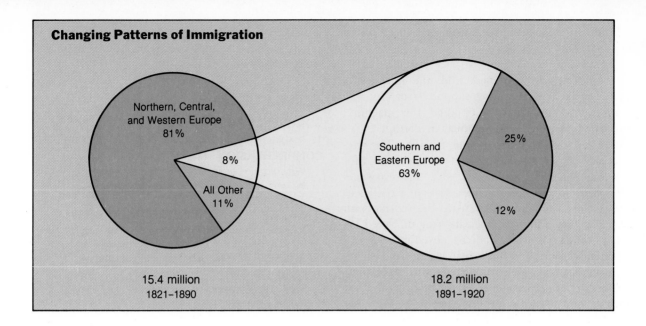

Changing Patterns of Immigration

Northern, Central, and Western Europe 81%

8%

All Other 11%

Southern and Eastern Europe 63%

25%

12%

15.4 million
1821–1890

18.2 million
1891–1920

In other words, Americans were becoming a new people, blended from many nations.

In 1909 British playwright Israel Zangwill wrote a play called *The Melting Pot*, which glorified this concept. At the end of the play, Vera and David are looking at New York City.

> **David:** . . . There she lies, the great Melting Pot—listen! Can't you hear the roaring and the bubbling? (He points east.)—the harbor where a thousand mammoth feeders come from the ends of the world to pour in their human freight. Ah, what a stirring and a seething! Celt and Latin, Slav and Teuton, Greek and Syrian—black and yellow—
> **Vera:** Jew and Gentile—
> **David:** Yes, East and West, and North and South, the palm and the pine, the pole and the equator, the crescent and the cross—how the great Alchemist melts and fuses them with his purging flame! Here shall they all unite to build the Republic of Man and the Kingdom of God. Ah, Vera, what is the glory of Rome and Jerusalem . . . compared with the glory of America, where all races and nations come to labor and look forward! . . .
> (An instant's solemn pause. The sunset is swiftly fading. . . . Far back, like a lonely guiding star, twinkles over the darkening water the torch of the Statue of Liberty. From below comes up the softened sound of voices and instruments joining in "My Country 'tis of thee." The curtain falls slowly.)

The concept of the melting pot was a very idealistic one. But it had a price. It called for immigrants to throw away their past, to give up their entire history and culture in order to become Americans.

Immigrants and the Cities

Another reason the new immigrants created controversy was the fact that they settled mostly in the area north of the Mason-Dixon line and east of the Mississippi River. Half of them were concentrated in just four states: Illinois, Massachusetts, New York, and Pennsylvania. And all of them were concentrated in cities where they were highly visible. In Boston and Cincinnati, for example, more than 60 percent of the population in 1880 either were born abroad or had parents who were foreign-born. In Chicago and New York, the figure stood at 90 percent. By 1890 there were twice as many Irish in New York as in Dublin, while the largest Polish city in the world was not Warsaw but Chicago.

Concentration. Why did the new immigrants settle where they did? Because that was where they could earn a living. By the time they reached the United States, the land frontier was closed. There was no more free or cheap land available. The language barrier made working as farm laborers almost impossible.

The cities, on the other hand, were teeming with mills and factories looking for workers. Not only that, as industrialization increased, many new machines and processes were put into use. This lessened the demand for skilled labor while increasing the demand for unskilled labor. Thus, even with a language barrier, inexperienced immigrants could find jobs.

Friction. As you have read, the immigrants tended to become strong supporters of city machines. So people who opposed the machines began to regard the newcomers as corrupt.

There was also economic friction. The tremendous supply of immigrant labor meant that for a long time, employers were able to keep wages down. If workers struck for a raise in pay, it was easy for an employer to replace the strikers with immigrants. This was especially true in New England, where French Canadians moved into the textile industry, and in California, where Chinese immigrants were widely employed. Also, since most immigrants did not read or speak English, they could not understand the arguments of the labor unions. As a result, many native-born workers began to resent the newcomers, regarding them as cheap scabs who took their jobs.

Section 1 Review

COMPREHENSION   Developing Vocabulary

1.   Explain these terms: new immigrants, melting pot.

COMPREHENSION   Mastering Facts

1.   Why did the immigrants who came to America between 1880 and 1915 cause so much controversy?

2.   What were the main cultural differences between the "new immigrants" and those who preceded them?

3.   Why did new immigrants settle mostly in the cities?

4.   How did native-born factory workers feel about the immigrants?

2 DIFFICULTIES CONFRONT THE NEW IMMIGRANTS

VOCABULARY   *steerage   culture shock*

While many native-born Americans looked on the new immigrants mainly as a threat and source of problems, the immigrants naturally saw things from a very different point of view.

The Journey

Before the Civil War, immigrants came to the United States mostly by sailing ship. By the 1870s, almost all immigrants were arriving by steamship. This cut the Atlantic crossing from about two months to a mere ten days. The Pacific crossing fell from three months to about twenty days. Yet despite the shorter time, crossing the ocean was uncomfortable and scary.

Physical and Psychological Difficulties. Most immigrants traveled in *steerage,* that is, in the cargo holds below the ship's waterline. There were no portholes, so the only ventilation came from open doors, while the only light came from a few scattered lanterns. There were perhaps six toilets for every hundred passengers. Although food was adequate, passengers were seldom allowed on deck. They spent most of the time crowded together in the gloom, unable to stretch their legs or to catch a breath of fresh air.

Coupled with physical discomforts were psychological ones. Unlike the early colonists, who came mostly in organized groups, the new immigrants came mostly as individuals. How do you think you would feel if you had to leave your parents and the home where you grew up, and journey thousands of miles by yourself to a strange land? As a Japanese woman immigrant wrote in later years:

❝ In spite of aging,
Still the homesick child in me
Who sailed so far out
From Yokahama harbor . . .
I still long for my hometown. ❞

Passing Through Ellis Island. In addition to loneliness and homesickness, the new immigrants faced the anxiety of not knowing whether they would be admitted to the United States when they arrived. First they had to pass inspection. If they had tuberculosis, or trachoma (an eye disease), or head lice, back they went. If they were fifteen years and eight months old instead of sixteen years old, and were not accompanied by a parent, back they went. If they were ex-convicts, or believed in the forcible overthrow of government, back they went. And if they did not have $25 with them, that too was grounds for return. Sometimes a family would be split apart, with one member accepted and another rejected. In a few instances, it took as long as eleven years before a family was reunited.

Another hazard of inspection involved a change of name. Immigration inspectors often could not pronounce or spell the new immigrants' names. So they simply wrote down an Anglicized version. Jievute became Eva, Czernovitsky turned into Charnow, and Iorizzo ended up as Rice.

From 1892 to 1924, the chief immigration station of the United States was Ellis Island, in New York Bay. Historians estimate that more than 16 million people passed through its facilities. During the peak immigration years, from 1905 to 1907, 10,000 immigrants a day, smelling of Ellis Island disinfectant, would walk down the long staircase to take the ferryboat to Manhattan. If you visit the main building today, you can still see the "kissing balcony" in the great hall, from which friends and relatives used to search for newcomers in the crowds below.

Images of a New World. Once the new immigrant stepped on shore, there was an immediate culture shock, an awareness of new things. Edward Corsi, who arrived in the United States from Italy in 1907, observed that

“ I was first struck by the fact that American men did not wear beards. In contrast to my own fellow countrymen, I thought they looked almost like women. Also on this boat (the ferry that ran from Ellis Island to Manhattan) I saw my first Negro. But these wonders melted into insignificance when we arrived at the Battery (a park at the southern tip of Manhattan) and our first elevated trains appeared on the scene. There could be nothing in America superior to these! ”

Abraham Cahan, a Jewish immigrant who escaped from Russia in 1882, was impressed by other sights.

“ When I found myself on the street and my eye fell on an old rickety building, I expressed a feeling akin to surprise. I could only conceive of America as a brand-new country, and everything in it, everything made by man, at least, was to be spick-and-span, while here was an old house, weatherbeaten and somewhat misshapen with age. How did it get time to get old? ”

Becoming Assimilated

Many of the problems confronting the new immigrants were the same problems that confronted all Americans: finding a place to live, earning a liv-

This early photograph of immigrant children being lined up in almost military formation is called Drilling the Gang on Mulberry Street *in New York. Gangs were formed for protection.*

455

ing, establishing a family. But there were special difficulties as well.

Language Barriers. The major difficulty was language. Carl Christian Jensen, a Dane who arrived in 1906, described the situation this way.

❝ I was a man and stronger than most men. Yet my second childhood began the day I entered my new country. . . . I had to learn life over in a brand-new world. And I could not talk. My first desire was for chocolate drops, and I pointed my finger at them. My second was for fishing tackle, and I pointed my finger at a wrapping cord and heaved up an imaginary fish. I used baby talk. "Price?" I asked. . . . Saleswomen answered with motherly grimaces. ❞

Adult immigrants who wanted to learn English attended night classes in the public schools and the libraries of the cities. Settlement houses offered daytime and evening instruction. And youngsters who did not have to work full-time attended public school during the day.

Ethnic Islands. A second difficulty was of special concern to youngsters. As the new immigrants crowded into the ever-growing cities of the industrial Northeast and Middle West, they formed national districts, with each language group living in its own section of town. People from one section were not welcome in another. The late comedian Harpo Marx described his experiences in New York in the early 1900s.

❝ The upper East Side was subdivided into Jewish blocks (the smallest area), Irish blocks, and German blocks, with a couple of independent Italian states thrown in for good measure. That is, the cross streets were subdivided. The north-and-south Avenues—First, Second, Third and Lexington—belonged more to the city than the neighborhood. They were neutral zones. But there was open season on strangers in the cross streets.

If you were caught trying to sneak through a foreign block, the first thing the Irishers or Germans would ask was, "Hey, kid! What Streeter?" I learned it saved time and trouble to tell the truth. I was a 93rd Streeter, I would confess.

"Yeah? What block 93rd Streeter?"

"Ninety-third between Third and Lex." That pinned me down. I was a Jew.

The worst thing you could do was run from other Streeters. But if you didn't have anything to fork over for ransom you were just as dead. I learned never to leave my block without some kind of boodle in my pocket—a dead tennis ball, an empty thread spool, a penny, anything. It didn't cost much

to buy your freedom; the gesture was the important thing.

It was all part of the endless fight for recognition of foreigners in the process of becoming Americans. Every Irish kid who made a Jewish kid knuckle under was made to say "Uncle" by an Italian, who got his lumps from a German kid, who got his insides kicked out by his old man for street fighting and then went out and beat up an Irish kid to heal his wounds. "I'll teach *you!*" was the threat they passed along, Irisher to Jew to Italian to German. Everyone was trying to teach everybody else, all down the line. ❞

Generation Gap. Even when the new immigrants had learned English and no longer fought with one another, there often remained a cultural gap between generations.

On one hand were the immigrants themselves. They seldom sounded like the teachers in school or looked like the people whose pictures appeared in the newspapers. As author Mario Puzo wrote: "They wore lumpy work clothes and handlebar mustaches . . . and they were so short that their high-school children towered over them. They spoke a laughable broken English and the furthest limit to their horizon was their daily bread." The immigrants' children, eager to move into the mainstream of American life, were sometimes embarrassed by their parents.

On the other hand were the immigrants' children. They no longer recited the traditional prayers. They no longer spoke their parents' native tongue or knew anything about their parents' native land. "Why did we come to America," many immigrants wondered, "if our own children are strangers in our house?"

And if immigrants were anxious to adopt American standards as quickly as possible, that too created difficulties. Why? Because in most instances, parents could only learn about American ways from their children. Instead of parents teaching children, the situation was reversed. The effect was often to disrupt the traditional structure of family life.

After a time, the generations grew to understand one another better. The first generation born in America began to respect their parents' courage in immigrating, while the next generation began to take greater pride in its cultural heritage. In turn, the immigrants came to realize that new ways were not necessarily evil. Spending money for pleasure, for example—which European peasants did not do because they had no extra money—did

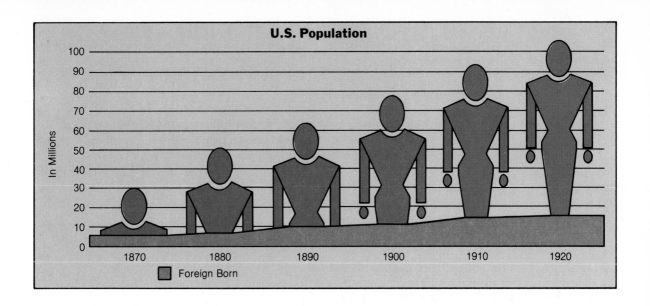

U.S. Population

In Millions

100 90 80 70 60 50 40 30 20 10 0

1870 · 1880 · 1890 · 1900 · 1910 · 1920

☐ Foreign Born

not mean their children lacked character. It only meant that their circumstances and values were different.

Helping Each Other

The new immigrants tried in many ways to ease the difficulties of adjusting to a new life. For example, people from the same village in Italy or Poland or Russia would pool their money to build their own church or synagogue. They formed social clubs where people could meet to talk and read letters from home. The clubs also provided facilities where their sons and daughters could meet young people of similar background. They set up mutual benefit societies that furnished medical treatment and helped with medical costs. They

founded orphanages and old people's homes. And they established cemeteries so that they would not have to be buried among strangers.

Section 2 Review

COMPREHENSION   Developing Vocabulary

1. Explain these terms: steerage, culture shock.

COMPREHENSION   Mastering Facts

1. What problems confronted immigrants on their way to the United States?
2. What special problems did new immigrants face in the United States?
3. Why did children in immigrant families often teach the parents?
4. How did new immigrants help each other to adjust to a new life?

3   DEMANDS GROW FOR IMMIGRATION RESTRICTIONS

Beginning in the late 1870s, demands for restricting immigration to the United States grew increasingly strong. There were several reasons for this development.

The Rebirth of Nativism

As you have read, the Know-Nothing movement was undercut by the issue of slavery in the election of 1856. During the Civil War and Reconstruction, there were few signs of nativism. Then

the old frontiers disappeared, to be replaced by an increasingly urban and industrial society that presented all sorts of new challenges. Just as sectionalism in the 1850s led to feelings of "us against them" on the part of both North and South, so too did conditions in the 1880s lead to similar feelings about immigrants.

Anti-radicalism. The Haymarket affair of 1886 convinced many Americans that the government was being undermined by wild-eyed foreign

457

radicals. Within a month after Haymarket, the American party was organized in California. Its program called for restricting immigration and prohibiting aliens from owning real estate. But the party failed to expand nationally and soon disappeared.

More permanent were various veteran and fraternal organizations such as the Order of United American Mechanics. Their members were mostly professionals, white-collar workers, small merchants, and skilled mechanics. They were proud of their standing in the new industrial society and were very concerned about maintaining it. As a result, they were extremely suspicious of immigrants who supposedly believed in revolution and who, at the very least, would unionize, go out on strike, and generally threaten the status quo.

Anti-Catholicism. Along with fears of foreign radicals, there developed a fear of growing Catholic political influence. This was partly due to the prominence of Irish politicians in the governments of such cities as Boston, Chicago, New York, and San Francisco.

Another cause of anti-Catholicism was the appointment of Cardinal Satolli in 1893 as the first Apostolic Delegate. Such a delegate is a political representative of the pope to the United States. Many Americans regarded that appointment as violating the principle of separation of church and state.

And then there was the demand of Catholic parochial schools for a share of public school funds. Catholics argued that they were paying twice for education, once by being taxed for public schools and again by paying tuition for parochial schools. Many Protestants regarded the Catholic position as a foreign attack on the traditional classroom.

As a result, a number of secret anti-Catholic societies sprang up pledged to defend the public school system and to oppose Catholic influence in politics. The largest was the American Protective Association, which was organized at Clinton, Iowa, in 1887. By 1894 the APA had 500,000 members. It broke up soon after, however, as a third element in nativism became more important.

Anglo-Saxonism. The third element was race prejudice. As sociologist Robert Hunter wrote in 1904: "The direct descendants of the people who fought for and founded the Republic, and who gave us a rich heritage of democratic institutions,

This 1893 cartoon makes fun of those immigrants who, once they were established in the United States, tried to keep other immigrants from following their example.

LOOKING BACKWARD.
THEY WOULD CLOSE TO THE NEW-COMER THE BRIDGE THAT CARRIED THEM AND THEIR FATHERS OVER.

are being displaced by the Slavic, Balkan, and Mediterranean peoples. . . . This is . . . race-suicide." Or, as Prescott F. Hall explained it, the question was whether Americans wanted their nation "to be peopled by British, German, and Scandinavian stock, historically free, energetic, progressive, or by Slav, Latin, and Asiatic races, historically down-trodden . . . and stagnant."

This emphasis on the importance of heredity over environment was especially strong in New England. There the traditional Yankee leadership was being successfully challenged by the Irish. That was bad enough, many Yankees felt. But when they began to consider the increasing number of new immigrants, they became afraid that American civilization would not be able to assimilate the newcomers and would fall apart. So in 1894, a group of race-conscious "Boston blue-bloods" set up the Immigration Restriction League. The organization began a campaign to keep out the "undesirable classes" from southern and eastern Europe.

The Literacy Test

The Immigration Restriction League was reluctant to exclude immigrants for the stated reason of "race." So they came up with the idea of a literacy test. Only immigrants who could read and write forty words, either in their own language or in some other language, would be admitted. In 1896 Senator Henry Cabot Lodge of Massachusetts introduced a bill to this effect. As he stated quite openly, the test would "bear most heavily upon the Italians, Russians, Poles, Hungarians, Greeks, and Asiatics, and very lightly, or not at all, upon English-speaking immigrants or Germans, Scandinavians, and French."

The bill passed both houses of Congress but was vetoed by President Cleveland just two days before he left office. In his veto message, Cleveland argued that the literacy test measured opportunity, not ability. Just because people had never had a chance to learn how to read and write did not mean that they were incapable of learning. Besides, Cleveland pointed out, some of the nation's "best citizens" had been illiterate when they arrived.

It took twenty-one years before the literacy test became law. Opposition to the measure came from several sources. The National Association of Manufacturers did not want to restrict the supply of labor. Immigrant groups—led by Russian Jews, the German-American Alliance, and the Ancient Order of Hibernians—wanted others to have the same opportunity they had had for a better life in America. Also, the gradual movement of Italian, Slavic, and Jewish voters from the Democratic party into the Republican party made anti-restriction a bipartisan matter. Republican President Howard Taft vetoed a literacy test in 1913. Democratic President Woodrow Wilson vetoed a similar bill in 1915. It was only in 1917, after the United States entered World War I, that Congress overrode a second veto by Wilson and enacted the literacy test. You will read more about the reasons for this in chapter 27.

Anti-Asian Legislation

The one area in which nativists triumphed was that of Asian exclusion. Between 1882 and 1913, Chinese immigrants and then Japanese immigrants were subjected to restrictive legislation.

Keeping Out the Chinese. As you know, Chinese people first came to California during gold-rush days. Later they helped build the nation's first transcontinental railroad, as well as other western roads. When the railroads were completed, the Chinese turned to jobs in farming, mining, and domestic service. Nevertheless, they labored under a cloud. They were not allowed to vote and they could not testify in court.

Most Chinese immigrants were men. They did not bring their wives with them because they expected to go back to China someday. Not having a family in the United States, they lived in bachelor quarters, several men to a room, in certain areas where most Chinese lived. These areas of shops, temples, restaurants, and homes were called Chinatowns.

Not only did Chinese immigrants live differently from most Americans, they looked different. And it was not just a matter of skin color. At that time, a Chinese man wore his hair in a "queue," or long braid, down his back. Men also wore quilted cotton jackets, cotton pants, and conical hats. Their dress and hairstyles looked odd to most Americans.

Then came the depression of 1873. As economic conditions worsened, anti-Chinese feeling in California grew more intense. The Chinese were disliked because they would work for less than white men. Dennis Kearney, himself a recently naturalized immigrant from Ireland, spearheaded the anti-Chinese movement. He founded the Workingmen's party and made hundreds of speeches throughout the state, each speech ending with the words: "The Chinese must go!"

Anti-Chinese feelings increased. The Chinese were often subject to physical attacks. And since they were not allowed to testify in court against white people, they had no legal way of defending themselves.

Finally, in 1882, Congress passed the Chinese Exclusion Act. This prohibited Chinese workers from entering the United States during the next ten years. In 1892 the law was extended for another ten years. And in 1902 all Chinese immigration was indefinitely suspended. In addition, Chinese already living in the United States were prohibited from sending for their wives.

Resisting the "Yellow Peril." In 1886 Japan allowed its people to emigrate for the first time in almost 300 years. Several hundred Japanese men, women, and children began arriving in the United States each year. After the turn of the century, the number rose to several thousand a year. By 1910 there were about 130,000 Japanese, mostly men, in the country.

At first, the Japanese settlers were welcomed. As a California newspaper commented:

66 These groups of Japanese are of the better class, talk English, and are very anxious to find a permanent home in this state. . . . There is probably much knowledge in the possession of these Asiatics that we could profit from. . . . They will at all events teach us how to produce teas and silk, some useful lessons in frugality, industry, and possibly politeness. 99

Gradually, however, the same fears about economic competition that had led to anti-Chinese agitation also resulted in anti-Japanese agitation. Newspapers began carrying articles with such headlines as these: JAPANESE INVASION THE PROBLEM OF THE HOUR: MORE THAN 100,000 OF THE LITTLE BROWN MEN ARE NOW IN THE UNITED STATES; and CRIME AND POVERTY GO HAND IN HAND WITH ASIATIC LABOR; and JAPANESE SWEATSHOPS ARE A BLOT ON THE CITY. In addition, Japan's victory in the 1904

war with China and again in the Russo-Japanese War of 1905 frightened many Californians. Suppose Japan were to wage war against the United States? Why, the whole country might be inundated with the "Yellow Peril"!

The issue came to a head in 1906. A scandal about municipal graft in San Francisco was about to explode. In an attempt to distract the people's attention, the city's political leaders apparently decided to exploit the racial issue. The local board of education ordered all Chinese, Japanese, and Korean children removed from neighborhood schools and segregated in special Oriental schools.

Anti-American demonstrations broke out immediately in Japan. Alarmed, President Theodore Roosevelt persuaded the San Francisco authorities to withdraw the segregation order. In exchange, he urged the Japanese government to limit emigration on its own. Under the Gentlemen's Agreement of 1907–1908, Japan agreed not to issue passports to workers unless they had already been in America or had relatives in this country. Some 30,000 Japanese had come in 1907; by 1909 the figure had dropped to 3000.

In addition, in 1913 the California state legislature passed an Alien Land Law. Since the Japanese and other Asians were "aliens ineligible for citizenship," they were prohibited from owning agricultural land. Not only had the golden door slammed shut; even those who had successfully gotten through found stiff discrimination against them.

Section 3 Review

COMPREHENSION   Developing Vocabulary

1. Explain these terms: prejudice, queue, American party, Workingmen's party.

COMPREHENSION   Mastering Facts

1. Give three reasons for resentment against Catholic immigrants.

2. Which immigrant groups did the Immigration Restriction League want to keep out?

3. What reasons did President Cleveland give for vetoing the literacy test bill?

4. What restrictions were placed on Chinese and Japanese immigration?

CHAPTER 22 · Review

Chapter Summary

As American industries grew, new immigrants filled many of the new jobs. The new immigrants tended to cluster in the larger cities. To many Americans, the cultural, language, and religious characteristics of the new immigrants seemed strange. New arrivals from eastern and southern Europe, and also from Asia, soon found themselves in conflict with other Americans. Also, some people feared foreign radicalism and the growing political influence of Catholics. In response to the new immigrants, a rebirth of nativism developed in the United States. The depression of 1873 helped increase anti-Chinese feelings, and the Chinese were excluded from further immigration in 1882. Later, the number of Japanese immigrants was also limited.

Questions for Critical Thinking

COMPREHENSION   Summarizing Main Ideas

1. How might immigrants benefit from the concept of the melting pot? What was the price immigrants had to pay for these benefits?
2. What effect did the new immigrants have on each of the following: (a) public schools; (b) city political machines; (c) labor unions?
3. List four things about which immigration inspectors at Ellis Island used to carefully check new arrivals.
4. What were the three main reasons why demands for restricting immigration grew stronger after 1880?
5. What civil rights were Chinese immigrants deprived of? Why did the Workingmen's party want to prevent further Chinese immigration? Was the party successful in its efforts? Explain.

COMPREHENSION   Interpreting Events

1. Did cities help or hinder the Americanization of immigrants? Explain your answer.
2. Why was the journey to the New World more difficult in some ways for the new immigrants than it had been for earlier immigrants?

3. Why were the children of immigrants often ashamed of their parents? In what way was the attitude of the next generation often different from that of the first generation born in America?
4. If you had been a U.S. senator in 1896, would you have voted in favor of Senator Lodge's bill for a literacy test for immigrants? Why?
5. Why were Japanese immigrants welcomed to the United States at first? Why did opposition to them develop during the 1890s and 1900s? What effect do you think California's Alien Land Law had on relations between the United States and Japan?

APPLICATION   Using Skills To Interpret Charts and Graphs

Data can be obtained from charts and graphs as well as from text and maps. Look at the charts and graphs on pages 452, 453, and 457, and answer the following questions.

1. Which source of immigration rose less from 1821 to 1920?
2. In what year did the number of immigrants from southern and eastern Europe first exceed the number from northern, central, and western Europe?
3. Was the percentage of foreign-born people in the United States larger or smaller in 1870 than in 1880? By what year did the percentage of foreign-born people rise above 10 percent?

EVALUATION   Comparing Past to Present

1. Interview someone in your local community who is an immigrant to the United States. Compare that person's experiences in this country with the experiences of the new immigrants of the late 1800s and early 1900s.
2. Find out how many foreign-language newspapers are published in the United States today and in what languages they appear. How do the number and the languages compare with those in 1920? Were any of today's newspapers being published in 1920?

Ethnic Diversity

The United States is a nation of immigrants. Even the very first Americans, now called Indians, once came here from an "old country." Can you name the nationalities that are part of your background? Many Americans take great pride in discovering their ethnic heritage.

Over the years more than one hundred ethnic groups have been represented in the United States; *ethnic groups* refer to groups of people who share a certain language, religion, history, and some physical characteristics. But even though the nation has been settled by people from around the world, most Americans can trace their individual origins to Europe. At the beginning of colonization, the English dominated migration to the New World. Then they were joined by Scotch-Irish, Germans, French Huguenots, and black Africans.

Because of ethnic diversity, the United States is really a nation of many nations.

New Immigration Patterns. Around the time of the Civil War, millions of newcomers again swelled the population. Northern Europeans dominated this wave of immigration as Irish, Germans, Swedes, Danes, and Norwegians came by the thousands. Later, in the years around the turn of the century and before World War I, the origins of newcomers expanded to include people from southern and eastern Europe—Poland, Russia, Italy, Greece, Yugoslavia, and Romania.

Since World War II, immigrants have often been refugees. Since the mid-1970s, immigrants from Spanish-speaking nations—Cuba, Haiti, El Salvador, and Mexico—as well as Asians from Korea, Cambodia, Vietnam, and Thailand have filled the roster of new arrivals.

A Nation of Diversity. Over the years tens of millions of people have reached American shores and begun new lives. As they held onto what they could of the past, America became a nation of many nations.

Immigrants were altered by their new surroundings, but they shaped their new environment as well. And, because immigra-tion continues to keep the nation in a constant state of renewal, America's family tree of future generations will continue to branch out in many directions.

Understanding Our Heritage

1. Where did most immigrants to America come from during the early years of colonization? during the years before World War I?

2. Why have recent years often been described as the age of the refugee?

3. What national groups comprise your background? What aspects of your ethnic heritage are a part of our national heritage?

UNIT 6   Review

Understanding Social Studies Concepts

History

1. How did the Bessemer process affect the development of the steel industry?
2. How did post-Civil War technology contribute to settlement of the Great Plains?
3. What was the purpose of the Interstate Commerce Commission? Was it effective in accomplishing its purpose? Explain.
4. List several benefits and several problems that increased industrialization brought to American society.
5. What was meant by the phrase "new immigrants"? What reactions did many Americans have to the arrival of these people?

Geography

1. How did Western geography complicate the building of a transcontinental railroad?
2. What geographical features made the Great Plains a good location for development of the cattle industry? What events in the mid-1880s led to basic changes in this industry?

Economics

1. What was the Crédit Mobilier? Who owned it? How were excess profits assured? What scandals were connected with the Crédit Mobilier?
2. How did the growth of industrialization lead to the development of labor unions? Which side did the government seem to support at first, business owners or unions?
3. What was a company town? Who controlled the economy of a company town?

Government

1. What is a political machine? What finally caused the downfall of the Tweed Ring in New York City?
2. Name the men who served as president during the time span of this unit. Then rate them according to the guidelines found on page 314.

Sociology

1. Explain *Social Darwinism*. How did it apply to the American work environment?

2. List several reasons why the policy regarding Indian reservations did not work. Also explain how destruction of the buffalo affected the lives of Indians living on the Plains.
3. How did Jacob Riis and Jane Addams improve social conditions in urban areas?

Extending Map, Chart, Picture Skills

1. Compare the maps on pages 405 and 408. Which major rail centers were also located near important mining areas?
2. Explain the cartoon on page 427. Which character is Boss Tweed? How can you tell?
3. Examine the picture on page 435. What were some of the demands of the picketers?
4. Refer to the graph on page 452. In which decade did southern and eastern European immigration first surpass that from northern, central, and western Europe? Write a paragraph that describes the general pattern of immigration to the United States during the years shown on the graph.

Understanding Current Events

1. Do you think that the Horatio Alger "rags to riches" success story is still possible to achieve during the 1980s? Why?
2. During the late 1800s, the city became a "New Frontier" for many Americans. What new frontiers do many people point to today?
3. How has the role of women changed in the world of work? Use examples in your answer.

Developing Effective Citizenship

1. Over the years the United States did not live up to the commitments of many treaties made with various groups of Indians. Do people today have an obligation to try to correct the mistakes made by government leaders long ago? Explain.
2. Find examples in a newspaper showing that corruption in government is still a problem today. What can individual citizens do about such corruption?

GLOBAL TIME LINE
1876–1920

THE UNITED STATES

THE WORLD

1881 President Garfield assassinated.

1883 Brooklyn Bridge completed.

1891 Populist party formed.

1901 President McKinley assassinated.

1898 Spanish-American War.

— 1870 — 1880 — 1890 — 1900 —

1885 Canadian Pacific Railway spans Canada.

1900 Boxer Rebellion in China.

1882 British troops occupy Egypt.

1894 France, Russia sign military alliance.

UNIT 7

Dawn of a New Century

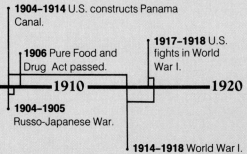

1904–1914 U.S. constructs Panama Canal.

1906 Pure Food and Drug Act passed.

1917–1918 U.S. fights in World War I.

1910 ——— 1920

1904–1905 Russo-Japanese War.

1914–1918 World War I.

Populism

1876–1910

Linking Past to Present

Beginning about 1875 the United States entered onto the world stage. For the first time the rest of the world—particularly Europe—became fully aware of the vast resources and power of the United States. Visitors to this country were amazed at the energy of the people and the seemingly unlimited possibilities of making money.

In 1865 a millionaire was a rarity in the United States but by 1890 there were 4047 of them. Making money was the American dream, and politicians were as eager to do so as business people. In fact, the level of corruption that existed in national politics from 1870 to 1896 led writer Mark Twain to name the period the "Gilded Age." (To gild means to cover something with gold or silver.) In a novel called The Gilded Age (written in collaboration with Charles Dudley Warner), Twain had a U.S. senator declare, "I think I can say, and say with pride, that we have some legislatures that bring higher prices than any in the world."

At the same time, the Gilded Age saw the beginning of several movements to bring about political reforms. Some had lasting effects, others had none at all. But they represented a growing belief that as society changed, government should change as well.

1 DEMANDS FOR REFORMS GROW

VOCABULARY   *patronage   merit system   tariffs*

From James K. Polk on, every president complained about the amount of time he spent on problems of *patronage*. Patronage is the practice of paying off people who vote for a certain candidate or party or those who in any way may help that candidate or party get elected. If the candidate wins, to him or her belong the spoils—hence, the phrase "spoils system." As you may remember, the phrase was used during Jackson's Administration.

Not only cabinet members were involved in patronage. Even people who mopped floors and scrubbed steps in federal buildings got their jobs only through the approval of a political boss. Of course, many federal officials remained in office despite changes in the presidency. But there were always thousands of positions to fill. And it was up to the president to make the final decision.

Gradually, many people began to press for a federal merit system to replace the spoils system. Under the merit system, jobs would go to the most qualified persons, no matter what political views they held or who recommended them.

Hayes and Executive Action

About one month after being declared winner of the 1876 election, Republican President Rutherford B. Hayes wrote in his diary, "Now for Civil Service Reform." Unfortunately for his goals, Hayes, although honest and conscientious, lacked both personality and political power. Unable to get legislative support for his ideas, even from members of his own party, he did what he could through executive orders and appointments.

Hayes began by naming able independents to his cabinet. A leading appointee was Carl Schurz, a German immigrant and a well-known newspaper editor, who became secretary of the interior. Schurz promptly set up a merit system in his department. Another cabinet appointee was John Sherman as secretary of the treasury. Sherman took a step that was almost unheard of for a government bureaucrat. He fired from his department all clerks who did not have enough work to do.

Hayes's next act was to appoint a commission to investigate the nation's customshouses. These customshouses were a source of great corruption. The New York Customs House, for example, had more than 1000 employees, all of whom spent most of their time working for the Republican party. The city's collector of customs, who received half of all the fines that were levied on importers, took in more than $40,000 a year.

When the commission turned in its report, Hayes fired the two top officials at the New York Customs House. Senator Roscoe Conkling, the Republican boss of New York State who had sponsored the fired officials, promptly declared political war on the president. At the Republican state convention, Conkling's supporters, who were known as Stalwarts, booed and insulted Hayes at the top of their lungs. When Hayes submitted the names of two honest men to replace the fired officials, Conkling persuaded the Senate to vote them down.

Hayes, however, would not give up. When the new Congress met in the fall, he again submitted the names of two honest replacements for the fired officials. This time, a combination of reform Republicans and Democrats voted to confirm the president's men.

467

The hopeful applicants in this etching await interviews with President Hayes in his office. Hayes opposed Senator Roscoe Conkling on the issue of a merit system of federal hiring.

Garfield and Arthur Continue Reform

Hayes decided not to run for reelection in 1880. So there was a free-for-all at the Republican convention. Conkling's Stalwarts supported former President Ulysses S. Grant for a third term. The reform Republicans rallied behind Senator James G. Blaine of Maine. Since neither side could obtain a majority, the convention finally settled on an independent candidate, Congressman James A. Garfield of Ohio. However, Garfield was a close personal friend of Blaine. So the Republicans decided to balance the ticket by nominating a friend of Conkling for vice-president. He was Chester A. Arthur, one of the two officials of the New York Customs House whom Hayes had fired.

The Democrats also nominated a compromise candidate, General Winfield Hancock. The election campaign dealt mostly in personalities, since neither party spoke clearly on issues. After weeks of heavily financed electioneering, Garfield squeaked into office by 9500 votes.

Garfield appointed Blaine as secretary of state and gave anti-Conkling Republicans most of the patronage positions at his disposal. He even appointed one as head of the New York Customs House. The Stalwarts were furious, and Conkling went so far as to resign from the Senate in protest.

Garfield Assassinated   On July 2, 1881, the president went to the Washington railroad station to travel to his twenty-fifth college reunion. As he and Blaine strolled arm in arm through the station, two shots rang out. They were fired by a mentally unbalanced lawyer named Charles Guiteau, who had previously applied for a government job and had been turned down by Garfield. As police officials seized the assassin, he shouted, "I did it and will go to jail for it. I am a Stalwart and Arthur will be president."

Chester Arthur did not become president until seventy-nine days later when Garfield finally succumbed to a massive blood clot. But as Garfield lay on his deathbed, public indignation against Conkling and the Stalwarts was rising. Many people felt they were to blame for Guiteau's attack. Hadn't they laughed at what they called "snivel service reform"? MURDERED BY THE SPOILS SYSTEM screamed a headline in the *New York Tribune*. And membership in the Civil Service Reform League jumped by leaps and bounds.

Arthur Urges Reform.   Nevertheless, when Arthur moved into the White House, no one knew what to expect. After all, he was one of Conkling's most trusted lieutenants. But high office apparently brought out the new president's best qualities. As the nation's highest leader, he turned reformer. He kept Garfield's appointee as head of the New York Customs House. He ordered the attorney general to prosecute post office employees who were accused of theft. And in his first message to Congress, he urged the legislators to pass civil service legislation.

The Pendleton Act. In 1883 Democrats and Republicans joined in support of the Pendleton Act. Under the act, the president was authorized to appoint a three-member, bi-partisan civil service commission. The commission was to give "open competitive examinations" to all applicants for "classified" jobs. These constituted about 10 percent of all federal jobs and included almost all the Customs House workers and about half the postal workers.

The act also gave the president the power to add to the "classified list." Every president after Arthur did so. By 1900 the merit system covered about 40 percent of federal jobs. It now covers about 85 percent.

In addition, the Pendleton Act said that federal employees could no longer be forced to kick back part of their salaries to a political party. Nor could they be fired if they refused to make such payments.

The Pendleton Act had mixed consequences. On the one hand, an ever-growing proportion of federal jobs came to be held by people with qualifications other than just political ones. Public administration became more honest and more efficient.

On the other hand, as politicians lost patronage, they had to find other sources of campaign funds. The most obvious source was wealthy business people. So the alliance between the federal government and big business became stronger than ever. As editor William Allen White wrote, "A United States senator . . . represented something more than a state. . . . He represented . . . powers in business. One senator, for instance, represented the New York Central, still another the insurance interests. . . . Cotton had half a dozen senators. And so it went."

Efforts To Regulate Tariffs

Most Americans agreed that tariffs were necessary to protect domestic industries from foreign competition. Without tariffs, the reasoning went,

American firms could be forced out of business and American workers would lose their jobs. The chief questions were: Which industries should be protected? How high should the tariff be?

During the Civil War, tariffs were very high. When the war ended, a general tariff reduction seemed reasonable. But every suggestion for lowering the duty on a particular item—shoes, for example—was opposed by those members of Congress who came from districts where many voters were shoe-makers. Economists might argue that high tariffs raised domestic prices and encouraged monopolies to develop. But members of Congress were more concerned with getting reelected.

A Democratic President. In 1884, the Democratic party captured the presidency for the first time in twenty-eight years. Their successful candidate was Grover Cleveland, a former mayor of Buffalo and governor of New York. He won over the Republican candidate, Senator James G. Blaine.

The campaign, like that of 1880, was one of personalities rather than issues. For example, one of Blaine's supporters, a Presbyterian clergyman named Dr. Samuel D. Burchard, referred to the Democratic party as the party of "rum, Romanism, and rebellion." Although Blaine later disclaimed the remark, the damage was done. Tens of thousands of Irish Catholics voted for Cleveland.

Tariffs had not been an issue in the 1884 campaign, but Cleveland felt that high tariffs were "a burden upon those with moderate means and the poor."

Cleveland Versus Harrison over Tariffs. In 1887 President Grover Cleveland asked Congress to lower tariff rates. His suggestion was supported by the Democratic majority in the House of Representatives but rejected by the Republican majority in the Senate. Since neither house would change its mind, tariff rates remained unchanged.

Cleveland was renominated in 1888 on a party platform of lower tariffs. The Republicans nominated Benjamin Harrison, the grandson of President William Henry Harrison. Supported by large contributions from companies that wanted even higher tariff protection, the Republicans ran the most expensive election campaign in U.S. history up to that time. The price of a vote rose from the usual $2 to $15 in gold or $20 in paper money. Some manufacturers printed warnings on the pay envelopes of their employees that their factories would close if Cleveland were reelected. Although Cleveland polled about 100,000 more popular votes than Harrison, it was Harrison who received a majority of the electoral votes.

The McKinley Tariff Act of 1890.   The new Congress accordingly set to work on a high protective tariff bill. The McKinley Tariff Act of 1890 raised duties on manufactured goods to the highest level ever. Those on some products were so high that similar foreign products were kept out of the United States entirely. The act also placed sugar on the free list. This meant that manufacturers of refined sugar, which was protected, could buy raw sugar from abroad at low prices. Since this hurt the raw sugar producers of Louisiana, the act gave them a bounty of two cents for every pound of sugar they grew.

Tariff Reform Ends in Failure.   In 1892 Cleveland was returned to the White House for a second term, thus becoming the only president to serve two terms that were not consecutive. The Wilson-Gorman Tariff Act of 1894 ended the bounty on domestic raw sugar and restored the duties on raw sugar from abroad. The 1896 election, however, was won by the Republicans. And in 1897 the Dingley Tariff Act raised duties once again. Thus, the attempt at tariff reform ended in failure. The special interests of industry and agriculture were too strong.

Section 1 Review

COMPREHENSION   Developing Vocabulary
1. Explain these terms: tariffs, merit system, Gilded Age, Stalwarts.

COMPREHENSION   Mastering Facts
1. What is meant by patronage in politics?
2. What effect did the Pendleton Act have on federal employees?
3. What group replaced government employees as a source of campaign funds?
4. Why did efforts to reduce tariffs end in failure?

2   ANGRY FARMERS BEGIN THE POPULIST MOVEMENT

VOCABULARY   *Populism   initiative   recall   referendum*

Reforming public administration was not the only political issue that aroused America in the Gilded Age. The last decade of the 1890s saw tremendous unrest among the nation's farmers and, as a result, the rise of a movement that threatened to realign the Democratic and Republican parties. This movement, begun by farmers, is called *Populism*. It comes from the Latin word "populus" meaning "the people." The widening gap between the farmer and other economic interests can be felt in this song of the time:

66 When the banker says he's broke
And the merchant's up in smoke,
They forget that it's the farmer feeds them all.
It would put them to the test
If the farmer took a rest;
Then they'd know that it's the farmer feeds them all. 99

Demands for Cheaper Money

The period after the Civil War was one of deflation. In other words, the purchasing power of the dollar rose. That was good news for consumers. But it was bad news for farmers. Why? Because the dollars with which they had to repay their loans were worth more than the dollars they had borrowed. At the same time, deflation meant that farmers received lower prices for their cattle, wheat, and cotton.

Under these circumstances, American farmers refused to understand that such factors as overproduction or competition from wheat and cotton growers overseas helped to lower prices. They were interested only in cheaper money. How could they get it?

More Greenbacks.   The farmers' first attempt had to do with greenbacks, the paper currency issued by the federal government during the Civil War. When the war ended, the farmers wanted the government to print more greenbacks, thereby making them cheaper. But the government began retiring the number of greenbacks in circulation, which made them more expensive. This was the opposite of what the debtor farmers wanted. So they organized the Greenback party in 1874 and called on the federal government to reverse its position and print more paper money.

But the government refused. Instead, in 1875 Congress passed the Resumption Act. This act ordered the treasury to redeem greenbacks in gold as of January 1, 1879. That is, everyone who turned in paper money was to receive the equivalent in gold. As the resumption date approached, the value of greenbacks kept rising. By two weeks before the date, greenbacks were on a par with gold; that is, they were worth their face value in gold. Or, as one banker put it, they were "as good as gold." As a result, most people did not bother to turn their greenbacks in to the treasury.

Congress finally decided to allow the remaining 346 million bills to stay in circulation. The Greenback party, which had combined with certain labor groups in 1877, declined.

Unlimited Silver Coinage. Since the idea of printing more greenbacks had been rejected, debtor farmers began to consider another technique to help pay off their debts. This was the unlimited coinage of silver.

In order to understand this issue, it is important to remember that over a period of years, the supply of silver and gold increased tremendously because new mines were being opened. But the discoveries of gold and silver took place at different times. If lots of silver was suddenly found, the value of silver dropped in comparison to the value of gold. If silver became scarce in comparison to gold—as it did when a gold discovery was made—then the value of silver went up and the value of gold went down.

The relative value of these two precious metals affected the supply of money in the country. Why? Because most people regarded paper money as worthless if it could not be turned in for silver or gold. They thought that only those two metals were real money. If paper money was not backed by gold, or silver, or both, people felt that it was not worth anything.

Years before, in 1834, the federal government had said it would mint both gold and silver dollars at a ratio of 16 to 1. That is, the government

This cartoon from 1891 pokes fun at the Grange's demands to increase the money supply. Many farmers' organizations sought cheaper money to offset the disastrous deflation after the Civil War.

471

would pay the same price for 16 ounces of silver as it paid for 1 ounce of gold. To put it another way, 16 ounces of silver were worth as much as 1 ounce of gold.

This 16 to 1 ratio worked well for a time because the amount of gold and silver in circulation was fairly steady. Then came the gold rush of 1849. So much gold poured into the market that silver prices went up and gold prices went down. Instead of selling silver to the government for coinage, silver producers found they could make more profit by selling it to private buyers.

Then came the western silver strikes of the 1870s. The situation was reversed. So much silver poured into the market that gold prices went up and the price of silver went down. Well, thought silver producers, we will go back to selling silver to the government at the old 16 to 1 ratio. But when they approached the Treasury Department, they discovered that Congress had passed a law in 1873 ending the minting of silver dollars. And there was more: silver dollars were no longer legal tender; that is, they were no longer accepted as money.

The uproar against the so-called "Crime of '73" was tremendous. Silver people from the Far West joined debtor farmers from the South and the Middle West in insisting that Congress do some-

thing. In 1877 Representative Richard "Silver Dick" Bland of Missouri introduced a bill calling for the unlimited coinage of silver at a ratio of 16 ounces of silver to 1 ounce of gold.

Banking interests, however, argued that it would not be possible to sell government bonds for gold in the future if silver again became legal tender. So when the Bland Bill reached the Senate, it was amended by Senator William Allison of Iowa. The Bland-Allison Act of 1878 provided for limited rather than unlimited coinage of silver, namely, between $2 million and $4 million a month. This helped silver producers. But gold dollars remained in circulation, and money still did not become any cheaper.

The People's Party

When the Granger movement died out as a political force for farmers, its role was taken over by three groups known as alliances. One was the National Farmers' Alliance of the Northwest, commonly called the Northern Alliance. Its main strength lay in the wheat-growing states of Kansas, Nebraska, Minnesota, and the Dakotas. The Southern Alliance was the largest of the three groups, with an estimated membership of more than a million white farmers throughout the southern states. Black farmers in the South belonged to a separate group, the Colored Farmers' Alliance.

The alliances started out by supporting state laws to limit the foreclosing of mortgages and to restrict unfair railroad practices. Gradually, however, farmers in the western states began to feel that the only way to get results was to organize a third party.

In May 1891 the Northern Alliance, along with some of the Southern Alliance and other reformers, held a convention in Cincinnati. They founded the National People's party. In June 1892 the party's first national nominating convention met in Omaha. General James B. Weaver, who had fought on the Union side in the Civil War, was nominated for president. Former Confederate General James G. Field of Virginia was named as Weaver's running mate.

Populist Leaders. Although most Populists were farmers, the Populist party's leaders were mainly lawyers and other professionals. On the whole, they were poor politicians; some can only

The diverse membership and radical views of the Populists inspired this 1891 cartoon by Bernard Gillam.

A PARTY OF PATCHES.
Grand Balloon Ascension—Cincinnati, May 20th, 1891

be described as crackpots. But they were remarkably talented orators who roused listeners wherever they spoke.

One Populist member of Congress from Minnesota, Ignatius Donnelly, had fought hard for a national bureau of education and for reforesting public lands. He was also the author of several books in which he tried to prove that Shakespeare's plays had really been written by Francis Bacon, and that the mythical island of Atlantis had actually once existed somewhere in the mid-Atlantic.

Another Populist member of Congress was "Sockless" Jerry Simpson of Kansas. He got his nickname because he was supposedly "too much a man of the people to wear socks."

From the South came Thomas E. Watson of Georgia. Watson was a strong advocate of rural free delivery of mail. He was also the first Populist leader to favor cooperation between southern white and black farmers. In later years, however, Watson changed his views. He wrote violent books against blacks, and against Jews and Catholics as well.

Women in the Party. Women were also represented among the Populist leadership. Sarah Emery of Michigan wrote a popular pamphlet called "Seven Financial Conspiracies." The conspiracy to keep women down was one of them.

Annie L. Diggs and Eva McDonald-Valesh traveled from town to town preaching the cause. They often had to sleep on open ground or in barns. Men, and even some women, treated them badly. They were viewed as trying to bring down the traditional social order.

Mary Elizabeth Lease of Kansas was a woman with a grand style and resonant speaking voice. She could practically hypnotize her audiences as she declared, "What you farmers need to do is to raise less corn and more *Hell!* We want the accursed foreclosure system wiped out. . . . We will stand by our homes and stay by our firesides by force if necessary, and we will not pay our debts to the loan-shark companies until the Government pays its debts to us."

The Populist Platform

The main demands of the Populists fell into three categories. These had to do with money, transportation, and government.

Mary Elizabeth Lease was a leàder in the Populist party. Her style and oratory attracted many.

The proposed financial reforms were as follows:

1. Currency inflation (making money cheap), to be accomplished by either printing paper money or coining silver.

2. A graduated federal income tax that would take a higher proportion of large incomes than of small incomes.

3. The establishment of postal savings banks.

4. The establishment of a sub-treasury system. Under the system, farmers could store non-perishable products in government warehouses and then borrow up to 80 percent of the value of those products from the United States Treasury.

In the field of transportation, the Populists called for government ownership and operation of the railroads. They also wanted the government to take over the telegraph and telephone systems.

Among the governmental reforms the Populists proposed were the following:

1. The election of United States senators by direct popular vote instead of by state legislatures.

2. A single term for the president and the vice-president.

3. The secret Australian ballot, so as to end vote frauds.

4. The *initiative*, which would enable the people to introduce bills in Congress and in state legislatures by petition.

5. The *recall*, which would enable voters to remove officials from elected positions before their terms were completed.

6. The *referendum*, which would allow the people to vote on bills after they had been passed by a legislature.

The Populists hoped to become a party of labor, as well as of farming, interests. Accordingly, they called for the eight-hour workday in factories and for restrictions on immigration. They also opposed any subsidies to private corporations. They did, however, come out in favor of liberal pensions for ex-Union soldiers and sailors.

Conservative Objections

Conservative response to the Populists was strongly negative. Conservatives were often self-made men—men who had become successful on their own. They did not think people should be given help to get what they, the conservatives, had worked so hard to attain.

William Allen White wrote scornfully of the Populist movement.

" That's the stuff! Give the prosperous man the dickens! Legislate the thriftless man into ease. Whack the stuffing out of the creditors and tell the debtors who borrowed the money five years ago . . . that the contraction of currency gives him a right to repudiate. . . . Whoop it up for the ragged trousers. . . . What we need is not the respect of our fellow men, but the chance to get something for nothing. "

Nevertheless, in the 1892 presidential election, the Populists polled more than a million votes against a combined 11 million votes for the Democratic and Republican parties. They also elected 5 senators, 10 representatives, 3 governors, and some 1500 state legislators. It was the best first-year showing of any third party.

Section 2 Review

COMPREHENSION   Developing Vocabulary

1. Explain these terms: Populism, initiative, recall, referendum.

COMPREHENSION   Mastering Facts

1. Who started the Populist movement, and why?
2. What happened to the price of silver as a result of the 1849 gold rush?
3. What was the "Crime of '73," and who suffered most from it?
4. Why did many conservatives disapprove of the Populist movement?

3   THE INFLUENCE OF POPULISM ENDURES

VOCABULARY   *Bimetallism   gold standard*

The Populists did even better in the 1894 campaign because of widespread unemployment and farm foreclosures caused by the panic of 1893. It was the worst depression the United States had suffered up to that time. Some 500 banks and 15,000 businesses failed. Some 3 million people lost their jobs. It seemed that, as one Populist said, the nation would be "brought to the verge of ruin." Farmers and cheap-money advocates were more frightened and angry than ever. Then came the election of 1896.

Battle To Control the Economy

The central issue of the 1896 campaign was the question: What would be the basis of the nation's monetary system?

On one side were the "free silverites," who favored *bimetallism*. Bimetallism means two metals. Bimetallists wanted the dollar to be defined as equal to both one ounce of gold and sixteen ounces of silver. Under bimetallism, the government would give people either gold or silver in exchange for other forms of money, such as paper currency and checks.

On the other side were the "goldbugs," who favored the gold standard. That is, they wanted the dollar to be defined only in terms of gold. The government would exchange gold for other forms of currency.

You recall that the Bland-Allison Act of 1878 had provided for limited coinage of silver. In 1890 the Sherman Silver Purchase Act went a step further. It required the government to buy an amount of silver almost equal to all the silver

Presidential Election of 1896

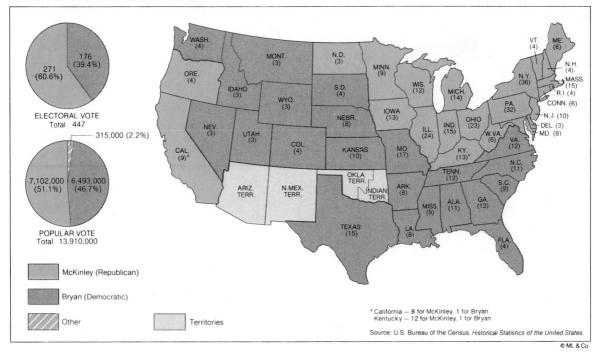

Map Skills *Which candidate won the northeastern states? Was he elected President? What was his percentage of the popular vote? What state gave the most electoral votes to the loser?*

mined in the United States. But so much silver was being produced that the value of the silver in a dollar fell to 49 cents. So everyone hurried to turn in their silver coins for gold ones.

Gold flowed out of the treasury. So much gold flowed out, in fact, that it looked as if the federal government might not be able to back up its currency with gold. It would have to use silver instead. And that would lead to runaway inflation because the value of money would be cut in half.

In 1893 the Sherman Silver Purchase was repealed. But that did not stop the outflow of gold. Although the government no longer had to buy silver, it still had to give people gold in exchange for other forms of money. By January 1895 the nation's gold reserves were down to $41 million and shrinking fast. If withdrawals continued at the same rate, the treasury would run out of gold in eleven days.

At this point, President Cleveland worked out an arrangement with a group of bankers headed by J. Pierpont Morgan, the nation's leading financier. The bankers agreed to supply the federal government with 3.5 million ounces of gold, half of it from Europe, in exchange for government bonds.

They also agreed to do everything they could to prevent gold from leaving the country for money markets overseas. Thus, the nation's government was rescued by a group of private financiers.

The arrangement was a success. The run on gold stopped and the business climate improved. Silverites, however, were convinced Cleveland had sold out to Wall Street. Mary Elizabeth Lease declared that the government "is no longer a government of the people, by the people, for the people, but a government of Wall Street, by Wall Street, and for Wall Street."

Agriculture Versus Industry

The 1896 campaign was basically a struggle between different regions and different economic interests. In the Republican camp were the financial and business interests of the nation. Their strength lay in the industrialized Northeast. In the Democratic camp were the farmers and laborers of the United States. They were based in the agrarian South and West.

Although some Republicans walked out of the national convention in protest, the Republican

475

party came out firmly in favor of the gold standard. They nominated Governor William McKinley of Ohio.

The Democratic party, after a bitter struggle, came down on the side of currency inflation. "We demand the free and unlimited coinage of both silver and gold at the present legal ratio of sixteen to one." They nominated William Jennings Bryan, a former member of Congress from Nebraska and the editor of the *Omaha World-Herald.* The Populists also nominated Bryan but, unable to accept his running mate—a wealthy shipbuilder and banker from Maine—put up their own Thomas E. Watson instead.

Bryan: "Boy Orator of the Platte." The thirty-six-year-old Bryan had not been the immediate choice of the Democratic convention. In fact, the front runner for the nomination had been Representative Bland. But Bryan was famed as a speaker and had been called the "boy orator of the Platte," the Platte being the river that runs through Nebraska. At the convention Bryan had gotten up to speak on a motion and had delivered what historians refer to as the "Cross of Gold" speech.

" You come to us and tell us that the great cities are in favor of the gold standard; we reply that the great cities rest upon our broad and fertile prairies. Burn down your cities and leave our farms, and your cities will spring up again as if by magic; but destroy our farms and the grass will grow in the streets of every city in the country. . . .

Having behind us the producing masses of this nation and the world, supported by the commercial interests, the laboring interests, and the toilers everywhere, we will answer their demand for a gold standard by saying to them: You shall not press down upon the brow of labor this crown of thorns, you shall not crucify mankind upon a cross of gold.**"**

For a moment, the thousands of delegates stood silent. Then bedlam broke loose, like "a great sea thundering against the dikes." For a full hour, according to an observer, the delegates were "shouting, weeping, rejoicing. They lifted this orator upon their shoulders and carried him as if he had been a god. At last a man!"

Populist William Jennings Bryan addresses a Madison, Indiana, crowd in 1901. Note the variety of people present. The map on page 475 shows clearly the sectional appeal of Bryan and his platform. Nominated for president in 1896, 1900, and 1908, Bryan lost each time.

Bryan's campaign broke new grounds. For the first time, a presidential candidate stumped the country. Traveling some 18,000 miles by train, Bryan visited 27 states and delivered approximately 600 speeches to audiences totaling 5 million people.

McKinley: "The Front Porch Campaigner." McKinley received his party's nomination for two main reasons. First, his appearance was solid, stable, and reassuring. Second, he was backed by Marcus Alonzo Hanna—an extremely successful businessman, the Republican boss of Cleveland, and one of the best political organizers the United States has ever known.

Hanna realized that McKinley was a poor orator but an impressive-looking individual. So he arranged for McKinley to conduct a front porch campaign. McKinley stayed in his hometown of Canton, where he received delegation after delegation of supporters brought there "with the help of free tickets and cheap excursion rates." Dressed in a frock coat, he would come out on the porch, deliver a set speech, and shake several thousand hands. In all, some 750,000 people from 30 states came to see the Republican candidate.

Hanna did not stop there. He raised some $3.5 million in campaign contributions from oil companies, meat-packing firms, railroads, and other big businesses. (Bryan, in comparison, was able to raise only one-tenth that amount.) Then he organized a "campaign of education" to persuade city workers that "any threat to the gold standard was a threat to their jobs." He sent thousands of speakers—from Civil War generals to Terence V. Powderly, former grandmaster of the Knights of Labor—to all parts of the country. He had 200 million pieces of literature, an average of fourteen per voter, printed in twelve languages besides English—Danish, Dutch, French, German, modern Greek, Hebrew, Hungarian, Italian, Norwegian, Polish, Spanish, and Swedish. It was the nation's first modern political advertising campaign.

Almost every newspaper in the United States came out in support of McKinley. Preachers thundered that cheap money was the same as stealing. And employers had their shop supervisors lecture workers on the best way to cast their ballots. As one Democratic senator said, "Boys, I'm afraid it beats us. If I were a working man and had nothing but my job, I am afraid when I came to vote I would think of Molly and the babies."

Aftermath

That is precisely what city workers did. When the returns were in, McKinley had approximately 7 million votes; Bryan, about 6.5 million. As expected, McKinley carried the East while Bryan swept the South. The West split; higher prices for agricultural products had lessened farmer discontent. But it was the voters of the industrial Middle West—Ohio, Illinois, Wisconsin, and Michigan—who brought McKinley into office. It was also the rising middle class, who were afraid that inflation would lower the value of their savings accounts, insurance, and stocks. "God's in his Heaven, all's right with the world!" Hanna telegraphed happily to his victorious candidate.

Bryan ran against McKinley again in 1900 and was again defeated. That same year, the Gold Standard Act made gold the legal basis for United States currency. Soon after, the Populists faded away.

Populist Reforms Adopted

Yet many Populist reforms were eventually adopted: some during the Progressive movement of the early 1900s, others during the New Deal of the 1930s. The graduated income tax, postal savings banks, government loans to farmers, the direct popular election of United States senators, the secret ballot, the recall, the initiative, the referendum, and a shorter workday—all became the law of the land. Though the Populist party was short-lived, it nevertheless profoundly influenced American political life. Third parties seldom get their candidates elected, but they often present new ideas that the major parties later adopt.

Section 3 Review

COMPREHENSION **Developing Vocabulary**

1. Explain these terms: bimetallism, gold standard, front porch campaign.

COMPREHENSION **Mastering Facts**

1. What two factors led to a run on gold?
2. What group of people did Bryan criticize in his "Cross of Gold" speech?
3. What new techniques did Marcus Alonzo Hanna use in the 1896 campaign?
4. Name three proposals of the Populist party that were later adopted.

Another area in which reformers attempted to bring about political change was women's rights, specifically the right to vote. The struggle had gotten off to a rocky start.

Woman Suffrage Delayed

Ironically, the enfranchisement of black men proved a major setback to woman suffrage. The Fourteenth Amendment (1868) had added the word "male" to the United States Constitution for the first time. The amendment said that any state denying *male* citizens the right to vote could lose some of its representation in Congress. This seemed to imply that women were not citizens. The Fifteenth Amendment (1870) declared that the right to vote could not be denied because of race or color. But discrimination on the basis of sex was not mentioned.

The women objected bitterly. But even their former co-workers in the abolitionist cause, such as Wendell Phillips, William Lloyd Garrison, and Frederick Douglass, felt that women should remain silent for the time being. As one of them said, "This is the Negro's hour. . . . Do not embarrass the Republican Party with any new issue. . . . The Negro once safe, the woman comes next."

The Fourteenth and Fifteenth Amendments split the women's movement, with some supporting the amendments and others opposing them. But by 1890, most suffragists were united in the National American Woman Suffrage Association. Among its leaders were Susan B. Anthony, Elizabeth Cady Stanton, Lucy Stone, and Julia Ward Haine.

The women used three main approaches in their campaign. They tried to convince state legislatures to change voting laws. They tried to test the Fourteenth Amendment in the courts. And they pushed for a national constitutional amendment.

Efforts in the States

In 1869 the territory of Wyoming gave women the right to vote. In 1889 the territory applied for statehood. However, because its constitution contained a woman suffrage provision, there was considerable resistance in Congress.

The Wyoming delegate wired home for instructions. The Wyoming legislature promptly wired back: "We will remain out of the Union a hundred years rather than come in without the women." Wyoming was admitted as a state the following year.

The territory of Utah gave women the right to vote in 1870. Congress took away the vote of Utah women in 1887 when it outlawed polygamy. But they regained the vote when the territory was admitted to statehood.

The legislatures of Colorado and Idaho also passed woman suffrage bills in the 1890s. Efforts in fourteen other states, however, ended in defeat for the suffrage cause.

Efforts in the Courts

In 1871 and 1872 there were some 150 attempts by women to vote in ten states and the District of Columbia. The most famous court case arising from these attempts was that of Susan B. Anthony in Rochester, New York.

Anthony felt that women were entitled to vote under the first article of the Fourteenth Amendment. The article stated that "All persons born or naturalized in the United States . . . are citizens . . . [and] no State shall make or enforce any law which shall abridge the privileges . . . of citizens." In other words, since the article did not forbid women to vote, they were entitled to do so if they were born or naturalized in this country.

Accordingly, on November 1, 1872, Anthony and fifteen "sturdy, determined, and respectable housewives" appeared at the registration desk in Rochester's Eighth Ward and asked to be listed as voters. The inspectors agreed. On November 5, the sixteen women went to the polls and voted. That night, Anthony wrote to Stanton, "Well, I have been and gone and done it! Positively voted the Republican ticket, straight, this A.M. at 7 o'clock."

Nothing happened for more than three weeks. Then, on November 28, Thanksgiving Day, Anthony and her followers were arrested for voting illegally. Her case was tried in June 1873 before Justice J. Ward Hunt, a political hack who did not even poll the jury for its verdict. Justice Hunt hostilely pronounced Anthony guilty and imposed a $100 fine, which she angrily refused to pay. She

Susan B. Anthony (standing) and Elizabeth Cady Stanton took part in women's long struggle for the vote.

hoped the judge would imprison her so that the case would go to the Supreme Court. But this did not happen.

The following year, however, the Supreme Court *did* rule on the relationship between the Fourteenth Amendment and woman suffrage. In the case of *Minor* v. *Happensatt*, the Court agreed unanimously that women were citizens. But citizenship, the justices said, did not automatically include the right to vote. If the states could withhold suffrage from certain men—such as criminals, the mentally unfit, and those under twenty-one—then the states could withhold it from all women.

Efforts in Congress

In 1878 Senator A. A. Sargent of California introduced an amendment to the United States Constitution. Known as the Anthony amendment, it read: "The right of citizens of the United States to vote shall not be denied or abridged by the United States or by any state on account of sex."

The measure was sent to the Senate Committee on Privileges and Elections. The committee held hearings at which representatives of the women's organizations testified. Elizabeth Cady Stanton described her experience:

"I have never felt more exasperated than on this occasion, standing before a committee of men many years my junior, all comfortably seated in armchairs. . . . The peculiar aggravating feature of the present occasion was the studied inattention and contempt of the chairman, Senator Wadleigh of New Hampshire. . . . He alternately looked over some manuscripts and newspapers before him, and jumped up to open or close a door or a window. He stretched, yawned, gazed at the ceiling, cut his nails, sharpened his pencil, changing his occupation and position every two minutes. . . . It was with difficulty that I restrained the impulse more than once to hurl my manuscript at his head."

Senator Wadleigh's committee did not recommend passage of the bill. Even so, supporters of woman suffrage reintroduced it every year for the next eight years. In 1886 the bill was finally called up for debate, but it was voted down in January 1887. It was reintroduced again for the next nine years without success.

Anti-Suffrage Opinions

The opposition to woman suffrage came from both men and women. The reasons given for opposing woman suffrage included the following:

1. The "woman's place" argument. For generations this idea had been firmly fixed in most people's minds. As a woman antisuffragist declared,

"Scripture [indicates] a different, and for us, a higher sphere apart from public life. . . . That we find a full measure of cares, duties, responsibilities devolving upon us, and are therefore unwilling to bear other and heavier burdens and those unsuited to our physical organization."

2. The argument that voting increases divorce. Many people felt that if women voted, it would only "increase the already alarming prevalence of divorce throughout the land." The New York *Tribune*, less kindly but more directly, snapped that all the suffragists needed was a "cradle and a dimple-cheeked baby."

3. The factory owners' argument. Many factory owners could not, of course, argue that woman's place was only in the home because much of their labor force consisted of women. Their argument against woman suffrage was the fear that women

voters would support legislation for shorter work hours and safer working conditions. Such legislation would cost employers money.

4. The suffrage-temperance link. Members of the liquor industry were nervous about suffragists. They saw that many of those women fighting for the right to vote were also active in the temperance movement. So distillers spent hundreds of thousands of dollars opposing woman's suffrage.

5. White southerners' fears. In the South, one state after another passed Jim Crow laws, which deprived black males of their right to vote. White southern politicians were afraid that the issue of woman suffrage would reopen the entire black suffrage question and would lead to "another period of reconstruction horrors, which will introduce a set of female carpetbaggers as bad as their male prototypes (original examples) of the sixties."

As a result of all these arguments, the campaign for woman suffrage made little headway during the Gilded Age. Between 1896 and 1910, it almost disappeared from public view. The leaders of women's organizations either retired or died, and new leaders did not appear right away. Nevertheless, in 1910 the movement began again, as you will see, and finally achieved success.

Section 4 Review

COMPREHENSION   Developing Vocabulary

1. Explain these terms: Anthony amendment, prototypes.

COMPREHENSION   Mastering Facts

1. What effect did the enfranchisement of black men have on the cause of woman suffrage?

2. What three approaches did women use in their suffrage campaign?

3. Why did many factory owners oppose woman suffrage?

4. What was the suffrage-temperance link?

CHAPTER 23 Review

Chapter Summary

The assassination of President Garfield prompted calls for reform in the nation's civil service system. The result was passage of the Pendleton Act in 1883. Meanwhile, during the late 1800s the nation's farmers experienced increasing difficulties. When the Grange Movement died out, farmers helped organize the National People's party. This Populist movement called for economic and political reforms. Populists championed the free coinage of silver and paper currency. The Populist movement died out by the late 1890s, but many of its suggested reforms were eventually adopted. Though women had played important roles for the Populists, they still failed to win widespread suffrage during this period. However, some western states did allow women to vote.

Questions for Critical Thinking

COMPREHENSION   Summarizing Main Ideas

1. Which groups benefit from high tariffs? Which groups suffer from high tariffs?

2. What were the original goals of the farmers' alliances? What change occurred in 1892?

3. Which groups were mainly responsible for Bryan's defeat in 1896? Why did these groups vote the way they did?

4. What was the main effect of the Populist party on the United States? Would you say that the party was a success or a failure? Give reasons for your opinion.

COMPREHENSION   Interpreting Events

1. If you had been a member of Congress in 1883, would you have voted in favor of the Pendleton Act? Why or why not?

2. Why was there tremendous unrest among the nation's farmers during the 1890s?

3. Which groups benefit from deflation? Which groups suffer from deflation?

4. Why did people want paper currency to be backed by gold or silver or both?

5. Why do you think the Populists in 1892 made the best first-year showing of any third party in United States history? Why did they do even better in 1894?

6. Why did the campaign for woman suffrage make little headway during the Gilded Age?

APPLICATION   Using Skills To Evaluate Sources

Here is a list of reference works.
   a. *Historical Statistics of the United States*
   b. *The New Columbia Encyclopedia*
   c. *Dictionary of American Biography*
   d. *Webster's Seventh New Collegiate Dictionary*
   e. Morris and Woodress, ed., *Voices from America's Past*
   f. Glad, *McKinley, Bryan, and the People*
Which of the above would you use to locate information about each of the following?

1. The number of votes cast in each state for the different candidates in 1896

2. A brief history of Populism

3. The life of Tom Watson

4. The fight for woman suffrage during the Gilded Age

EVALUATION   Forming Generalizations

1. Research the provisions of the 1978 Civil Service Reform Act. What problems does this act attempt to solve? Has it been successful? Explain your answer.

2. Where do political parties today obtain campaign funds for state and local elections? How are national election campaigns funded? How much did the last presidential election campaign cost? Can third parties obtain funds for a national campaign on the same basis as the Democratic and Republican parties? What restrictions, if any, do you think should be placed on campaign contributions? Give reasons for your opinion.

3. Compare the role of the media in presidential campaigns today with their role in 1896.

4. What is the backing behind U.S. paper currency today?

Justice

Clarence Darrow, a famous trial lawyer during the early 1900s, is reported to have made this comment about justice: "There is no such thing as justice—in or out of court." Yet the Preamble to the Constitution lists the establishment of justice as one of its main goals; "liberty and justice for all," claims the pledge of allegiance; "Equal Justice Under Law," says a message engraved in marble on the Supreme Court building. Exactly what is justice? Is justice possible to achieve in a complex society?

Justice implies fairness, an equality of opportunity, an assurance that actions will not inflict injury on others. Justice requires difficult decisions when the law must be applied to real situations in which rights are in conflict. Sometimes, however, the choice is not clear-cut. For this reason, Americans have responded by trying hard to eliminate gray areas of confusion regarding the law.

"There Oughta Be a Law."
Since its very beginning, the United States has tried to be a "nation of laws, not people"— that is, not of people's ideas of what the law ought to be at a given time. So, justice is often defined by what is lawful. "Scarcely any question arises in the United States that is not resolved, sooner or later, into a judicial question," observed the

French social commentrator Alexis de Tocqueville in 1834. "There oughta be a law" was the name of a comic strip which poked fun at an American tendency to pass too many laws.

What does it mean to be a "nation of laws"? In practice, it means that no one, including the president, stands above the law. That is the principle on which the Judiciary Committee recommended the impeachment of Richard Nixon in 1974.

Changing Views of Justice.
A nation's ideas about justice continue to change. What is thought to be just during one decade can turn out to be reversed years later. That was the case in 1896 when the Supreme Court upheld segregation in the case Plessy v. Ferguson. Not until 1954, after attitudes had changed, did the Court reverse itself by ruling that "separate but equal" facilities were unequal.

Nor have civil rights issues characterized the only aboutface in the nation's conscience. The prohibition against alcohol, amended into the Constitution in 1919, was removed by another amendment just fourteen years later. Likewise, women were denied the right to vote for well over a century—until another amendment officially changed that policy in 1920. As times changed, so did people's ideas of justice.

Legal issues are decided in courts of law—however, resolution of conflict in the courts is no guarantee of justice. For example, five of the eight men tried and convicted for the Haymarket bombing in Chicago in 1886 were not even present the night of the incident. Those men were victims of individual motives and prejudices. Despite tragic occurrences like that, our judicial system still requires that guilt be proved beyond a shadow of a doubt before a verdict is announced. It has been said that one hundred guilty people going free would be preferable to misjudging one innocent person.

The idea of change sometimes seems to conflict with the very nature of justice, at least to some people. Thus, the concept of justice becomes caught in a difficult position: on one hand, many people believe that justice, in order to be completely fair, must rest on certain firm, unyielding principles. On the other hand, most people also believe that justice should be flexible enough to fit each individual set of circumstances. Can laws be interpreted to accomplish both purposes?

Role of the Supreme Court.
In the United States, the Supreme Court has the final authority for deciding the constitutionality of a law. Some people question this process of

judicial review. Critics charge that the Supreme Court itself too often becomes an instrument for social change rather than remaining totally objective and simply administering justice. They point to recent decisions concerning criminals, school prayer, abortion, and busing as examples of the judiciary making law instead of applying it.

Controversy, however, has been a tradition in America's judicial history. "John Marshall has made his decision; now let him enforce it," was President Andrew Jackson's reaction to the outcome of one case involving Cherokee Indian rights.

Building a More Just Society. In addition to the courts, Americans have pursued many other avenues to achieve justice. The United States has a long tradition of dissent, protest, and reform. Countless people working outside the judicial system have dedicated their lives to making our nation more just. Some of the people have included abolitionists, civil service reformers, teachers, populists, suffragists, union organizers, news editors, and other champions of human rights. For example, during the same period that suffragists were working for the right to vote, members of the Women's Christian Temperance Union were involved in establishing kindergartens, improving prison conditions, and supporting the eight-hour work day.

One important element of justice in our society is the Sixth Amendment, which guarantees to all Americans "the right to a speedy and public trial."

The overall result of these efforts was that our nation became a more just society.

It is probably safe to say that perfect justice will never be achieved anywhere on earth as long as humans are involved in the decisions. This is probably what Clarence Darrow was actually saying in the opening paragraph. Still, that fact does not keep Americans from continually trying to establish a more just society. During its two-hundred-year history, the United States has moved in that direction, though advances have not always been steady. Continued progress is the goal for present and future generations.

Understanding Our Heritage

1. What progress toward a more just society has the nation made during the past century? Give examples.

2. How do laws change attitudes? behavior? What are some ways of promoting justice besides passing a law?

3. What role do courts play in our nation's judicial system? What does it mean to say that ours is a "nation of laws, not people?"

4. Name some situations in society that seem to you to be unfair. What can you do about them?

Americans in the Gilded Age

1876–1910

People in the Chapter

William McGuffey—*author of the most popular school book ever written.*

Booker T. Washington—*founds Tuskegee Institute in Alabama, the first teacher training school for blacks in the South.*

Joseph Pulitzer and William Randolph Hearst—*owners of newspapers whose scandalous and often fictional stories give news reporting a bad reputation that lasts for many years.*

Sarah Bernhardt—*famous French actress who makes several coast-to-coast tours of the United States and is one of the first European artists to discover that Americans will pay high prices and travel far to attend cultural events.*

Linking Past to Present

During the last quarter of the nineteenth century, there was a great urge among Americans to improve themselves not only financially but also culturally. This usually meant becoming familiar with the arts and with what were called the more refined pleasures of the mind. It also meant a very serious interest in education.

This was a time when the great American fortunes were made. The Vanderbilts, Astors, Goulds, Morgans, and Singers not only made millions, they spent them. And they spent them in a showy fashion. They were willing at times to flaunt their wealth before others. They went to Europe and bought paintings, furnishings, and jewels. Some of the wealthy returned home and erected huge palaces to rival those they had seen in Europe.

Millions of other Americans of more modest means were as busily engaged in the pursuit of self-improvement. At no time in our history was there more interest in education and culture.

1 MORE PEOPLE RECEIVE AN EDUCATION

VOCABULARY   *eclectic   vocational education   normal school*

In 1894 a Russian Jewish girl named Mary Antin, age thirteen, arrived in Boston with her mother, brother, and two sisters. Her father had emigrated several years earlier and then sent for his family when he had earned enough money for their passage. In her book *The Promised Land*, Antin wrote about one of the wonders she found in an American city.

"Education was free. That subject my father had written about repeatedly, as comprising his chief hope for us children, the essence of American opportunity, the treasure that no thief could touch, not even misfortune or poverty. It was the only thing that he was able to promise us when he sent for us; surer, safer than bread or shelter. . . . No application made; no questions asked; no examination, rulings, exclusions . . . no fees. The doors stood open for every one of us."

In Russia at that time, Jewish girls received no formal education at all, while only one Jewish boy out of ten was allowed by the government to enter high school.

Compulsory Elementary Education

Between 1865 and 1895, thirty-one states passed laws making it compulsory for children between the ages of eight and fourteen to attend elementary school twelve to sixteen weeks a year. By 1900 about 72 percent of all school-age children were in school, most of them in the cities. The curriculum was straightforward: the three Rs, physical education, domestic science (cooking and sewing), and manual training (woodworking). And just

The rich learned too. They lavishly copied the style and architecture of Europe. This summer home of the Vanderbilt family at Newport, Rhode Island, resembled an Italian palace.

485

about every pupil used the same basic text: one of the six *Eclectic Readers* put together by William H. McGuffey. ("Eclectic" means choosing whatever is best from various sources.)

Like the works of Horatio Alger, the McGuffey *Readers* sold about 125 million copies. They not only helped students to read better, but also stressed moral behavior and the importance of work. Here is an example from one *Reader*.

" 1. Henry Bond was about ten years old when his father died. His mother found it difficult to provide for the support of a large family. . . . By good management, however, she contrived to do so, and also to send Henry, the oldest, to school . . .

2. At one time, however, Henry wanted a grammar, in order to join a class in that study, and his mother could not furnish him with the money to buy it. He was very much troubled about it, and went to bed with a heavy heart, thinking what could be done.

3. On waking in the morning, he found that a deep snow had fallen, and the cold wind was blowing furiously. "Ah," said he, "it is an ill wind that blows nobody good."

4. He rose, ran to the house of a neighbor, and offered his services to clear a path around his premises. . . . Having completed this work and received his pay, he went to another place for the same purpose, and then to another, until he had earned enough to buy a grammar.

5. When school commenced, Henry was in his seat, the happiest boy there, ready to begin the lesson in his new book.

6. From that time, Henry was always the first in all his classes. He knew no such word as fail, but always succeeded in all he attempted. Having the will, he always found the way. "

The Growth of High Schools

High school attendance, unlike that of elementary school, was not compulsory. However, as the new industrial age developed, it became clear that the economy needed certain technical and managerial skills. Also, as Andrew Carnegie (and other business leaders) pointed out, one way to keep workers loyal to capitalism was to "provide ladders upon which the aspiring can rise."

The number of "ladders," or public high schools, jumped from 100 before the Civil War to 6000 in 1900. The curriculum expanded to include history, literature, and vocational courses designed to help graduates find jobs. By 1910 the majority of urban white teenagers, especially boys, took going to high school for granted.

Higher Education

Going to college was another matter. Although the number of colleges doubled from 500 at the time of the Civil War to 1000 in 1900, only a small percentage of the population were college graduates. Nevertheless, here too the new industrial age brought about changes in both curriculum and admission policies.

Before the Civil War, colleges emphasized theology, mathematics, and the classics. After the war, the curriculum became more practical. Courses in agriculture, engineering, economics, foreign languages, and the physical sciences became more important.

At the same time, colleges opened their doors wider. State universities in the Midwest and California admitted high school graduates without a test and charged only token tuition. More important was the admission of women. By 1900 about four out of five colleges were coeducational. The proportion of co-eds, however, averaged less than ten percent of the student body.

Education of Blacks

In the fall of 1872, a sixteen-year-old former slave, wearing the only suit he owned, began a 500-mile journey, most of it on foot, from West Virginia to Hampton, Virginia. His name was Booker Taliaferro Washington, and he had left his job as a coal miner to seek an education at the all-black Hampton Normal and Agricultural Institute. (A normal school taught students to be teachers.) Hampton emphasized vocational education: mostly farming and handicrafts, plus some geography, history, grammar, and science.

In 1881 Washington opened his own normal school in the little Alabama town of Tuskegee. It was called the Tuskegee Normal and Industrial Institute. Like Hampton, Tuskegee stressed courses that would enable its graduates to teach and to do agricultural, domestic, or mechanical work. Other areas were ignored. Washington felt that the best way blacks could advance was first to convince southern whites that the education of blacks was also in the interests of the South. He did not want blacks to compete economically with whites. Nor did he believe they should seek social equality at that time. As one historian explained:

" He never tired of urging blacks to develop habits and skills that would win places for them in their

George Washington Carver maintained this laboratory at Booker T. Washington's Tuskegee Institute.

would not disturb southern society. In fact, it seemed to many that Washington's ideas would keep blacks in a position of permanent inferiority.

As the years passed, many blacks began to disagree with Washington's philosophy about black education and the place of blacks in American life. They wanted a more energetic push toward equal rights, as you will read in chapter 28.

Nevertheless, Washington's ideas were generally accepted by whites and blacks until the early 1900s. Tuskegee graduates, especially botanist George Washington Carver, spread a knowledge of scientific farming throughout the South. Carver, in fact, revolutionized southern agriculture by developing hundreds of new uses for the sweet potato and the peanut. He helped end the dependence of southern farmers on cotton.

Southern communities. Intelligent management of farms, ownership of land, habits of thrift, patience, and perseverance and the cultivation of high morals and good manners were encouraged. . . . He was greatly distressed by the mass movement of blacks from the country to the city, and did what he could to persuade them to return. **"**

Most white people in both the North and the South accepted Washington's ideas with interest and some relief. Northerners were tired of racial and regional conflicts. They thought that Washington pointed a way for whites and blacks to live productively and peacefully side by side. Southerners were relieved because Washington did not seem to be pushing for political and civil rights for blacks. His idea of a good education for blacks

Section 1 Review

COMPREHENSION   Developing Vocabulary

1.   Explain these terms: normal school, vocational education, eclectic.

COMPREHENSION   Mastering Facts

1.   What was the great free cultural benefit in America?
2.   What did the McGuffey *Readers* teach?
3.   Why did Booker T. Washington not want blacks to move from the country to the city?
4.   How did George Washington Carver help the economy of the South?

2   SOURCES OF INFORMATION MULTIPLY

VOCABULARY   *lyceum   photojournalism   yellow journalism*

Many U.S. millionaires did more than just install art treasures in their palatial homes. They established large and beautiful art galleries throughout the country. Experts say that in 1870 there was scarcely one good art gallery in the United States, but by 1900 there was at least one in every large city. Efforts were also made to provide public information facilities.

The Growth of Libraries and Lyceums

Education in the city did not stop with public schools and colleges. Beginning in 1881, Andrew Carnegie donated about $45 million to build some

2800 public libraries. The cities in which the libraries were built provided the land and levied taxes to buy books and pay librarians.

The *lyceum* movement was also a popular form of adult education. Lyceums were organizations that provided public information and entertainment. They arranged for people to travel about giving lectures, extension courses, and concerts. Audiences got all sorts of information from the people the lyceums sent out. Here is a sample of some lecturers, their subjects, and their fees. Note the sometimes peculiar words and spelling.

" **Ames, Mrs. Nellie**
   Subject—"Working Women of New York."
   Mrs. Ames is the author of the serial, "Up

People flocked to Chautauqua, N.Y., where they heard lectures on culture and self-improvement.

magazines poured in ever-increasing numbers from new types of presses. Advertising began to play a crucial role in the media. Information and entertainment were transmitted everywhere, helping to tie the nation together.

The technology that changed printing in this period covered four main areas: paper, presses, typesetting, and photography.

Paper. Prior to the Civil War, paper was made mostly from wastepaper and rags. In the 1860s, several German chemists discovered that you could make paper from wood pulp. By the 1880s, American paper mills were turning out huge quantities of paper that was strong enough to be used in high-speed presses and, at the same time, cheap enough so that newspapers could be sold for a penny a copy. This put newspapers within the economic reach of many more Americans than before. Magazines likewise dropped in price, from the typical twenty-five cents to a nickel.

Presses. Printing was speeded up tremendously by William Bullock's invention of the web-perfecting press. Instead of printing on paper sheets, Bullock's press, which was electrically powered, printed on both sides of a continuous paper roll. It also cut the roll into pages, folded the pages, and counted the papers as they came down the line.

Typesetting. With strong, cheap paper and fast presses, the next problem was how to set type more quickly. Ottmar Mergenthaler invented a Linotype machine that was first used by a newspaper in 1886. The operator used a typewriter-like keyboard to cast an entire line of metal type at one time instead of going through the old laborious process of hand-assembling separate bits of metal, one for each letter.

Photography. At about the same time, there occurred changes in photography. Before, photography had been a profession rather than a hobby. Equipment and materials were so heavy that it was almost impossible to get a shot of a moving object. In the 1870s, however, new techniques eliminated the need for photographers to develop pictures right away. Instead, they could send the film to the factory for processing.

Then, in 1888, came the major change. George Eastman invented the Kodak camera. It was light

Broadway.". . . Recommended by a distinguished N.Y. author as "a lady of great talent, a fine speaker, and has the magnetism necessary to enchain an audience."

Terms—$100.

Billings, Josh

Subjects—"Milk," "A Plaintive Discourse on Natural Hist'ry."

Terms—Outside of New England, Mr. Billings' average terms are $90.40, "with privilege of throwing off the $90 if I was a mind to, but never to discount the 40 cents." In New England, his terms range from $75.40 to $100.40.

Time—All December. Lyceums who desire to secure him should apply soon. . . .

Gunning, W. D.

Subjects—Eight lectures on Geology, to be delivered either as a course, or separately. A syllabus of these lectures will be sent on application.

Terms—$50 and expenses, and upwards, for one lecture, or $250 for the course—one lecture weekly, for eight successive weeks—with modifications.

Mr. Gunning is recommended by Profs. Agassiz, Wood, Harley and others. **"**

The Spread of Information

As cities grew and the literacy rate rose from 70 percent to almost 90 percent, the United States became a reading nation. Newspapers, books, and enough to be easily held in the hand and it was simple to operate. It turned millions of Americans into amateur photographers. The Kodak camera also created photojournalism, for now reporters could photograph events as they occurred. In addition, the halftone process of chemical engraving, invented in 1880, made it possible to reproduce photographs and paintings accurately. Soon, illustrations became common in newspapers, magazines, and books.

The Growth of Advertising

Improvements in printing pictures reinforced the rapid growth of newspaper and magazine advertising. Expenditures for advertising rose from $20 million in 1870 to more than $70 million in 1890 and kept climbing.

Patent medicines received the largest number of advertising lines. Next came soaps, followed by baking powders. Royal Baking Powder, in fact, had the largest advertising budget of any product in the world: $600,000 a year. Next in order were cereals such as Cream of Wheat and Quaker Oats, the Eastman Kodak Company, and manufacturers of shoes, trousers, shirts, collars, and undergarments.

Pulitzer, Hearst, and the Yellow Press

JERKED TO JESUS and THE VALLEY OF DEATH are two of the typical headlines that newspapers of the new industrial age splashed in thick black type across their front pages. The first, from the *Chicago Tribune*, had to do with the 1875 hanging of four murderers who repented on the gallows. The second, from the *New York World* of June 3, 1889, referred to the horrors of a flood in Johnstown, Pennsylvania. In it at least 6000 persons were drowned, burned, or crushed to death. This was quite a change from such previous staid headlines as POLITICS IN ALBANY and CHARMING DOG SHOW. But then, newspapers were no longer written primarily for the upper class. They were designed to attract the urban masses.

The use of huge, black, screaming headlines was only one of the techniques that newspapers followed in their drive for higher circulations. Equally popular were promotional stunts and crusades. For example, in 1871 the *New York Herald* sent reporter Henry M. Stanley to Africa to look for explorer Dr. David Livingstone, who had not been heard of for several years. In 1881 the *New York Tribune* started a fresh-air fund to send children from the slums to the countryside for a week in summer. In 1890, the *New York World* sent reporter Nellie Bly (whose real name was Elizabeth Cochrane) around the world in imitation of a fictional character in Jules Verne's novel *Around the World in Eighty Days*. Bly, who traveled by "ship, sampan, jinriksha, burro, and train," made it in a little more than seventy-two days. Her reports, filed from places with exotic names, kept the *World's* readers in a constant tizzy wondering what would happen next.

In 1894 that same paper printed a full page of comic strips in color. Several years later, H. C. Fisher's "Mutt and Jeff" became the first comic strip to appear every day. Other innovations included a large Sunday edition, a daily sports section, and a daily women's section.

The individuals most responsible for these changes were Joseph Pulitzer and William Randolph Hearst. Pulitzer, a Hungarian immigrant, began his career as a reporter on a German-language newspaper in St. Louis. He then bought two bankrupt local papers and combined them into the *St. Louis Post-Dispatch*. It soon became a flourishing enterprise. From there Pulitzer moved to New York, where he bought the *World* in 1883. With a circulation of 15,000 and an annual loss of $40,000, the *World* did not seem much of a bargain. But by 1889 its circulation had jumped to 300,000, and Pulitzer was earning a million dollars a year.

How did Pulitzer do it? He hired talented writers and editors, and set them competing against one another. He tried to arouse his readers to the evils of slum life and the need for tax and election reforms. And he emphasized "sin, sex, and sensation." Since the *World* used yellow ink in its cartoons, the latter tactics became known as "yellow journalism." Papers that used such tactics were referred to as the "yellow press."

In 1895 Pulitzer's newspaper leadership in New York was challenged by Hearst, whose father had made a fortune in mining. Hearst already owned the *San Francisco Examiner*. His next step in building a mass chain of papers was to buy the *New York Morning Journal*. Hearst decided that the only way to compete against Pulitzer was by outdoing him in yellow journalism. So he proceeded to fill the *Journal* with exaggerated stories about personal scandals, animal cruelty, hypnotism, the imaginary conquest of Mars, and the like.

As the circulation war escalated, both papers became more and more sensational. The climax came in 1898, when, as you will read in chapter 25, the *Journal* and the *World* actually helped to prod the United States into a shooting war with Spain. By that time, each was selling 1.5 million copies a day.

When the Spanish-American War was over, Pulitzer apologized for the role the *World* had played. "The great mistakes which have been made . . . have been caused by an excess of zeal. Be just as clever as you can. Be more energetic and enterprising than any other man if you can, but above all, be right." Since then, yellow journalism has more or less faded from the scene.

Literature

The outstanding literary figure of the Gilded Age was the person who gave the period its name: Mark Twain. He was born Samuel Langhorne Clemens and grew up in little Hannibal, Missouri, on the Mississippi River. He worked as a printer, a newspaperman, and a gold miner before becoming a humorous lecturer. His pseudonym comes from his experience as a steamboat pilot on the Mississippi. "Mark Twain" is the river call for a water depth of two fathoms or twelve feet.

Twain's most famous books deal with his boyhood in Hannibal. *The Adventures of Tom Sawyer* contains one of the great scenes in American literature, the one in which Tom gets his chums to pay him for the privilege of whitewashing Aunt Polly's fence. *The Adventures of Huckleberry Finn*

describes how Tom helps the runaway slave Jim escape from his pursuers.

Twain's work combines humor with social criticism. His main target was people's hypocrisy. From a literary viewpoint, his books are significant because they broke the near monopoly of eastern writers. His books are also significant because they described life in such areas of the country as the Middle West and the Far West.

Other writers of the period also wrote about characters from various walks of life. They used vivid language and occasionally introduced violence into their plots. William Dean Howells, for example, dealt with the triumphs and tragedies of a self-made man in his book *The Rise of Silas Lapham*. Stephen Crane in *The Red Badge of Courage* portrayed the feelings of a young soldier in battle for the first time. Jack London "drew a host of characters from the waterfront bum to the working stiff of the western wheat fields." Theodore Dreiser in his book *Sister Carrie* told about a girl from the slums who ends up with a career.

Section 2 Review

COMPREHENSION   Developing Vocabulary

1. Explain these terms: linotype machine, photojournalism, yellow journalism.

COMPREHENSION   Mastering Facts

1. How did lyceums contribute to adult education?
2. What were two results of the invention of the Kodak camera?
3. How did the "yellow press" attract readers?
4. How did Mark Twain get his pseudonym?

3 AMERICANS ENJOY LEISURE

VOCABULARY   *melodrama   revues*

The cities of the new industrial age provided the setting for changes in the way Americans spent their leisure time.

Baseball

❝ Oh, somewhere in this favored land the sun is
    shining bright,
The band is playing somewhere, and somewhere
    hearts are light,
And somewhere men are laughing, and
    somewhere children shout,
But there is no joy in Mudville—mighty Casey
    has struck out. ❞

Legend has it that the game of baseball was invented at Cooperstown, New York, by Abner Doubleday in 1839. It seems more likely, however, that baseball began as a children's game in the late 1700s and gradually evolved into its present form.

At any rate, the first professional baseball team, the Cincinnati Red Stockings, took to the field in 1869. In 1876 the first professional league was organized. The National League included teams from Boston, Chicago, Cincinnati, Hartford, Louisville, New York, Philadelphia, and St. Louis. In 1887 the New Yorks, later known as the Giants,

The 1887 home schedule of the New Yorks (later the Giants) sported this romantic lithograph of the Polo Grounds. Baseball established itself as the national pastime during the Gilded Age.

drew so many people to the Polo Grounds that the overflow had to stand in the outfield. In 1899 the Western League was formed; it was renamed the American League in 1901. Players earned about $1400 a year, and intercity rivalry was fierce. Even fiercer was the "world championship" competition between the champions of the two leagues.

Other Sports

Another spectator sport that flourished in the cities was boxing. By the 1800s, it had become sufficiently respectable that women could attend.

The first great heavyweight boxer was the "Boston Strong Boy," John L. Sullivan, who won his title in Mississippi City in 1882. "The Great John L." fought most of his bouts with bare knuckles. He was a flamboyant personality and extremely popular with the crowds. People were shocked when he was knocked out in the twenty-first round by James J. "Gentleman Jim" Corbett at a fight held in New Orleans in 1892.

What defeated Sullivan was the fact that boxing was becoming more scientific because of the adoption of the Marquess of Queensbury rules. Corbett had practiced using the new five-ounce gloves. He also took full advantage of several new punches, as well as feints and quick footwork that confused his opponent.

Corbett was defeated in turn by Robert L. Fitzsimmons at Carson City, Nevada, in 1897. Fitzsimmons held the heavyweight crown for two years before losing it to James J. Jeffries at Coney Island in Brooklyn. Jeffries retired undefeated in 1905.

A third great urban sport of the period was cycling. In 1876 Colonel Albert A. Pope began to mass-produce bicycles. By 1890 indoor ovals in Chicago, New York, and Philadelphia were drawing even more spectators than the local major league baseball clubs. In 1893 the first cycling championship race was held at Springfield, Massachusetts. And in 1898 Charles Murphy gained the nickname of "Mile-a-Minute Murphy" by cycling one mile in less than sixty seconds.

Drama and Spectacle

One day in 1880, the great French actress Sarah Bernhardt and her troupe, who were touring the United States, settled in at the Palmer House in Chicago. One of the young actresses, Marie Colombier, wrote to a friend that Chicago "is a city of iron with locomotives smoking in the streets . . . telegraph wires so numerous they hide the sky, banks the size of the Louvre (a great museum in Paris), insurance houses like the Palace of Versailles. All this, swarming with 600,000 inhabitants who come and go, frantically running after the almighty dollar."

And Madame Bernhardt was one of the fastest runners. She and all the great artists of Europe soon discovered that America was a gold mine for performers. People would come from hundreds of miles and pay high prices to see a play. Madame Bernhardt spoke hardly a word of English and all her plays were in French. Nevertheless, people thronged to see her as she made several coast-to-coast tours of the country. And people came to see other actresses, such as Lily Langtry of England, as well as singers such as Jenny Lind, the "Swedish Nightingale."

Like sports, the theater of the Gilded Age became highly organized. For example, Bostonians B. F. Keith and E. F. Albee controlled a chain of more than 400 theaters throughout the country into which they booked talent.

Star Attractions. Other managers specialized in productions with a particular star. Producer Charles Frohman, for example, created the first "matinee idol" in 1892 when he starred John Drew in *The Masked Ball*. Audiences, mainly women, came to afternoon performances and watched the handsome Drew with worshipful attention. Frohman was also responsible for the stage success of Maude Adams, with whom Drew frequently co-starred. Miss Adams was famous for her role as Peter Pan.

Sports figures also appeared in the theater. John L. Sullivan played Simon Legree in *Uncle Tom's Cabin*. He also toured in a play especially written for him called *Honest Hearts and Willing Hands*. The big scene showed Sullivan working at a real forge with sparks flying all over the stage. Jim Corbett likewise had a play especially written for him, *Gentleman Jack*, which featured a boxing scene. Not to be outdone, Bob Fitzsimmons toured with

Americans of the Gilded Age had an insatiable hunger for celebrities. The fact that the performances of the gifted actress Sarah Bernhardt were in French did not daunt her audiences.

his special play, *The Honest Blacksmith.* Fitzsimmons had been a real blacksmith before becoming a boxer, and he sometimes made extra horseshoes on stage and gave them to people in the audience as souvenirs.

There were three main kinds of theatrical entertainment at this time: serious drama, melodrama, and the revue.

Serious Drama. To most Americans this "meant intrigue, discovery, swordplay, gasping death, and exalted language." In other words, Shakespeare's tragedies, preferably starring Edwin Booth. Booth had temporarily retired from the stage after his brother assassinated President Lincoln. But the public welcomed him on his return, apparently feeling that family tragedy had increased his already great talent. Tickets for his production of *Romeo and Juliet,* for example, were sold for $125 apiece. In Kansas City, the opera house in which Booth performed had not yet been roofed over. The audience shivered but did not leave. In New York, his *Hamlet* set a record by playing for one hundred consecutive performances.

One of the great Shakespearean actors of the time was the American Ira Aldridge. This black artist took Europe by storm and received both public and critical success as he performed in most European capitals.

Melodrama. This had two forms. The most popular were the so-called "Tom Shows," or dramatizations of *Uncle Tom's Cabin.* They emphasized complicated staging. People sat at the edge of their seats as real bloodhounds chased Eliza on ice floes that moved on a rotary belt. And when Tom died, angels opened a series of silver and gold gates to show him entering heaven. In 1890 there were almost 500 "Tom Shows" on the road.

The second form of melodrama was symbolized by such plays as *Under the Gaslight.* In it the heroine was tied to the railroad tracks and rescued by the hero just as the mail express came pounding down the line. Another melodrama featured the hero tied to a sawmill log, with the chain saw coming ever closer. Sometimes the roles were reversed, with the hero being rescued by the heroine.

Revues. The most popular form of theater was the revue. It included songs, dances, comedy skits, and such specialty acts as magicians and ventriloquists. Sometimes there was a chorus line of

Edwin Booth as Hamlet drew audiences by the thousands from 1883 to 1893.

scantily clad females. Minstrel shows were performed in blackface, although one minstrel show, Primrose & West, had forty white and thirty black performers on stage together, with equal billing.

Architecture

Perhaps one of the most striking and permanent cultural influences of the Gilded Age was in architecture. The boundless optimism, enthusiasm, and energy of a rich society was caught in the soaring steel, iron, and concrete skyscrapers.

Up until the Civil War, most public and office buildings in the United States were three or four stories tall, constructed along classic Greek lines. But in the 1880s, with the invention of the elevator and the growing cost of land in the cities, the skyscraper building became popular. One of the

Louis Sullivan's Wainwright Building in St. Louis was one of the first to use a structural-steel framework.

first was the Monadnock Building in Chicago. But to support its sixteen floors, it was necessary for the stone walls at the base to be about fifteen feet thick. In 1890 the great architectural pioneer Louis Sullivan designed the Wainwright Building in St. Louis. This was one of the first buildings to have a framework of structural steel on which hung thin sheathings for the building's sides.

Many experts believe that the skyscraper is the greatest American contribution to world architecture. It solved the practical problem of how to make the best use of limited and expensive real estate. The skyscraper was also the proud symbol of a rich and optimistic society.

Section 3 Review

COMPREHENSION   Developing Vocabulary

1.   Explain these terms: melodrama, revues.

COMPREHENSION   Mastering Facts

1.   What were the three main urban spectator sports of the Gilded Age?
2.   Who was America's first matinee idol?
3.   What were Tom Shows?
4.   What inventions made the skyscraper possible?

CHAPTER 24 Review

Chapter Summary

During the Gilded Age, some Americans made huge fortunes and developed a new interest in all things cultural. Great strides were made in education, too, as compulsory education laws were passed in thirty-one states. By 1900, four out of five colleges were co-educational. Hampton and Tuskegee Institutes increased educational opportunities for blacks. The number of public libraries increased, and the lyceum movement became an important source of adult education. The growing numbers of educated Americans aided the growth of newspapers and magazines. Similar growth occurred in the arts, and spectator sports became more popular than ever before. A new style of "yellow journalism" stressed sensationalism in an attempt to increase newspaper circulations.

Questions for Critical Thinking

COMPREHENSION   Summarizing Main Ideas

1. Give two reasons why many business leaders supported the idea that young people should have a high school education.

2. What effect did the new industrial age have on college admission policies? What effect did it have on the courses offered in colleges? Do you approve of these changes? Why or why not?

3. What did Andrew Carnegie contribute to the public library system of the United States? What did local communities provide?

4. How did each of the following affect newspapers? (a) the discovery that one could make paper from wood pulp; (b) the invention of the web-perfecting press; (c) Ottmar Mergenthaler; (d) George Eastman; (e) the circulation war between Pulitzer and Hearst.

5. Where were the three main kinds of theatrical entertainment during the Gilded Age?

COMPREHENSION   Interpreting Events

1. Why did immigrants consider free education one of the wonders of American life?

2. If you were an elementary school teacher, would you recommend using the McGuffey *Readers*? Why or why not?

3. Do you agree or disagree with Booker T. Washington's ideas about the kind of education most desirable for blacks? Give reasons for your opinion.

4. How did the literature of the Gilded Age reflect a democratic attitude?

5. How did the skyscraper reflect the economic conditions of the new industrial age? How did it reflect the spirit of American society?

APPLICATION   Using Skills To Recognize Cause and Effect

Below are four pairs of events. For each pair, tell whether the second event was caused by the first or merely followed it in time.

1. Elementary school pupils use the McGuffey *Readers*; the literacy rate rises to almost 90 percent

2. George Eastman invents the Kodak camera; expenditures for newspaper and magazine advertising increase

3. Pulitzer and Hearst compete for readers; yellow journalism becomes popular

4. The first professional baseball league is organized; spectator sports flourish in the cities

EVALUATION   Comparing Past to Present

1. Compare the elementary school curriculum in your local community with the typical elementary school curriculum at the turn of the century. How might you explain the changes in content that have occurred?

2. What changes in curriculum, if any, do you think should be made in high schools today? Give reasons for your opinion.

3. Which of the spectator sports that developed during the Gilded Age are still popular today?

4. Have any sports figures of the past ten years also appeared in the theater or in films?

Public Education

If you were to evaluate your education, what grade would you give it? In 1983, America's educational system received a report card—and the marks were not good. A National Commission on Excellence in Education found startling evidence of much mediocrity.

According to the commission report, curriculums were overloaded with "soft" courses, and student enrollment had declined in English, math, and other basic subjects. As a result, Scholastic Aptitude Test (SAT) scores had dropped significantly, and in competition with twenty-one other nations, American students came in last on seven of the achievement tests. Perhaps worst of all, the commission's findings revealed that about 13 percent of the country's seventeen-year-olds could not read.

Colonial Education.
Three hundred years ago, education in the United States was neither free nor public. In those years children began work early in life, and many never learned to read or write. Going to school was reserved for the wealthy few. The rest learned at home, under the direction of parents who used the *Bible*, the *Bay Psalm Book*, and church sermons as textbooks. Education beyond these basics was the exception.

Arrangements for formal education varied from colony to colony. Instruction might be available in church schools or from private tutors hired by wealthy merchants and planters. Massachusetts stood alone in establishing a colonywide system of education. By a law of 1647, each town of fifty households was required to hire a schoolmaster to teach reading and writing. At that time, Massachusetts already had the first institution of higher education in the colonies: Harvard College, founded in 1636. Most colonies, however, did not establish school systems.

Public Support Expands.
Slowly, as Americans placed increased emphasis on child development, they accepted the idea of a state-supported public school system that was financed by citizen taxpayers.

By the 1830s, many parents saw schools as an avenue of success; they expected education to enable their children to get ahead. As free public education became more widespread, immigrants—and especially their children—took advantage of that tremendous opportunity to become educated Americans.

Through the efforts of such educational reformers as Horace Mann, legislators implemented plans for state-wide school systems. As early as 1785, the Land Ordinance required that one section of each township in the Northwest Territory be kept for support of the public schools. By the 1850s, all the states had made a start toward establishing public elementary schools.

Progress in the 1800s.
Attempts to provide equal access to education for all continued throughout the nineteenth century. After the Civil War, many black children and adults attended school for the first time. Land grant colleges opened the doors of higher education to students of modest means who wanted to study subjects such as agriculture or mechanics.

However, breaking down barriers of prejudice took time. It was widely believed, for example, that a woman's mind was inferior to a man's. Only the most determined women received a college education, and fewer still could train for careers in law, medicine, or engineering.

Because it was viewed as an extension of woman's mothering role, teaching was one of the first professions open to women. Emma Willard and Catherine Beecher, who saw the growing need for trained teachers, pioneered in founding schools of education for that purpose.

Recent Advancements.
Three important themes have characterized education during the twentieth century. One has been continuing research into

how children learn; another has been continuing improvements in the way instructors teach. These trends go back to the years before World War I, when John Dewey's ideas about how learning occurred challenged traditional teaching methods. He recommended replacing memorization of facts with "learning by doing," so that knowledge would have practical meaning. More recently, the introduction into classrooms of television and computers represents another revolution in teaching and learning.

The third important trend in education has been toward specialization. This development is the natural outcome of a society strongly dependent on science and technology. In some fields, specialization has often meant years of additional training beyond college. Thomas Jefferson, for example, read widely in many areas and studied Greek, Latin, moral philosophy, history, rhetoric, grammar, and other subjects in the humanities. Today's students are more likely to take courses with direct applications in special areas such as hotel management or computer science.

Federal Involvement Grows.
Besides changes in instructional methods, during recent decades there has been another development: the federal government has assumed a much greater role in the education process. First, federal child labor laws have

Americans have traditionally emphasized the importance of education.

strengthened compulsory school attendance by preventing young children from entering the labor market. During World War I, Congress subsidized vocational courses in secondary schools. Since then, federal aid to education has continued and expanded in many ways.

The judicial branch has also had an important hand in public education. In 1954 the Supreme Court ruled that segregated schools were inherently unequal. Later rulings expanded on this decision and touched on issues such as busing.

Like virtually all areas of society, education has been—and will continue to be—a changing field. How will your children be educated? At home? At school? By their own efforts? By television? Will increased emphasis be placed on creative thinking? Or will students only learn pre-

cisely what they need to perform a specific job? Whether public education the way we know it endures or not, education itself will most likely retain a high importance. After all, education is a cornerstone of democracy.

Understanding Our Heritage

1. List several examples that show education has had a high priority in the United States since colonial days.

2. What three trends in education became evident during the twentieth century?

3. What role has the Supreme Court played in American education?

4. Why is education called a cornerstone of democracy? In your opinion, what improvements need to be made in the public education system as a whole?

497

The Nation Claims an Empire

1880–1914

People in the Chapter

Dr. Carlos Finlay—*Cuban doctor who correctly theorizes that yellow fever is carried by mosquitoes.*

Dr. Walter Reed—*leader of a medical team that rids Cuba of yellow fever.*

Theodore Roosevelt—*leader of the Rough Riders. He later becomes president and is a vigorous supporter of expanding American interests abroad.*

Queen Liliuokalani—*ruler of the Hawaiian Islands who is deposed by a group of American businessmen. Her kingdom becomes the Republic of Hawaii and, later, a United States territory.*

Linking Past to Present

During the 1840s, the cry of "Manifest Destiny" helped justify the expansion of the United States to the shores of the Pacific Ocean. In the 1890s, the nation's spirit was similar. But this time the spread of American political and economic control moved overseas rather than overland. The United States changed from a continental to a world power.

The change took place with great fanfare. As one military officer declared: "Whether they will or no, Americans must now begin to look outward." Americans needed no encouragement. Republicans, Democrats, and Populists all joined in the cry for, as one historian noted, "more land, more trade, and more power."

This was understandable because a race for national prestige was going on all over the world. European nations were carving up Africa and were also seeking empires in Asia.

There were some, however, in the United States who were made uneasy by the idea of owning overseas land. They felt that a republic should not have "subject" peoples. But their doubts were drowned in the patriotic pride of Americans who liked the idea of possessions that stretched across the world from the Caribbean to the Philippine Islands.

1 AMERICA READY TO EXPAND

In the years immediately following the Civil War, the American people focused their attention on domestic matters. Even the purchase of Alaska from Russia in 1867 was of little interest. If Secretary of State Seward wanted to waste $7 million on a frozen wasteland, well, that was "Seward's folly." Reconstructing the South, conquering the West, and developing industry were far more important.

Reasons for Imperialism

As the 1880s progressed, however, Americans began to give more attention to the idea that the United States should obtain colonies overseas. There were several reasons for this.

The Need for Markets and Materials.

American farmers and workers, backed by machines, were extremely productive. As Senator Albert J. Beveridge of Indiana argued, "Today we are raising more than we can consume. Today we are making more than we can use. . . . Therefore we must find new markets for our produce, new occupation for our capital, new work for our labor." Also, American factories needed certain raw materials, such as rubber and tin, that could only be obtained abroad. Imperialism seemed to offer a solution to both these problems.

Anglo-Saxon "Superiority."

Economic factors, however, were not the only reasons for the change in public opinion. Equally significant was the concept that combined Darwin's ideas about the "survival of the fittest" with a belief in the racial superiority of Anglo-Saxons.

As Josiah Strong, a Congregational minister and writer, put it in 1885:

"It seems to me that God, with infinite wisdom and skill, is training the Anglo-Saxon race for an hour sure to come in the world's future. . . . The . . . lands of the earth are limited, and will soon be taken. . . . Then will the world enter upon a new stage of its history—the final competition of races. . . . Then this [Anglo-Saxon] race of unequaled energy, with all the majesty of numbers and the might of wealth behind it—the representative . . . of the largest liberty, the purest Christianity, the highest civilization . . . will spread itself over the earth."

Already the nations of Europe were dividing Africa into colonies and seemed ready to do the same with China. Surely the United States could not afford to fall behind.

Admiral Mahan Calls for Sea Power.

Among the leading exponents of American expansion overseas was Captain, later Admiral, Alfred Thayer Mahan. In 1886 he became president of the newly established Naval War College at Newport, Virginia. There he gave a series of lectures, which were later published under the title *The Influence of Sea Power upon History 1660–1783.*

Mahan argued that sea power was essential if a nation wanted to be rich in peacetime and unbeatable in wartime. A nation needed a navy to defend its shipping lanes. And it needed strategically located bases where its fleets could coal and repair. Specifically, according to Mahan, the United States should acquire four things: a modern fleet; naval bases in the Caribbean; a canal across the Isthmus of Panama; and Hawaii and other islands in the Pacific.

Mahan's book had a tremendous influence. And gradually the United States acquired all the things Mahan said it needed.

First came a modern fleet. Prodded by Secretary

of State James Blaine, one of Mahan's staunchest supporters, Congress set about building up the American navy. Between 1883 and 1890, nine steel cruisers were completed, and construction was started on the nation's first modern battleship, the U.S.S. *Maine*. By 1898 the United States was the third-largest naval power in the world. Only Great Britain and France ranked higher.

After the modern fleet came naval bases in the Caribbean. The United States obtained these, as well as a number of Pacific islands, as a result of the Spanish-American War. That war was fought in 1898. It was a brief conflict, lasting only three months and twenty-two days. It was almost bloodless. Out of 200,000 American troops, fewer than 400 were killed in battle, while about 4000 died from yellow fever and dysentery. The war was also, in the opinion of many historians, unnecessary and unjustified. It all began over Cuba.

Crisis over Cuba

American interest in Cuba dated back to the early 1800s. President Thomas Jefferson had considered the possibility of annexing the island. President James Polk had tried to buy it from Spain. The Democratic party's national platform prior to the Civil War contained a plank calling for Cuba's admission as a slave state.

First War of Independence. In 1868 the First War for Independence broke out in Cuba. It lasted for ten years and resulted in some 250,000 casualties. Although the rebels lost, Spain agreed to abolish slavery and to allow a certain amount of self-government. The latter promise, however, was not kept.

After emancipation, American capitalists began investing tens of millions of dollars in Cuba. In particular, they bought large tracts of land and set up sugar-cane plantations. Sugar was the basis of the Cuban economy, and now the United States became the island's main market. In 1884 the United States abolished its tariff on Cuban sugar. This sent sugar production skyrocketing even higher than before. Ten years later, however, the Wilson-Gorman Tariff restored a 40 percent duty—and the Cuban economy was ruined.

Second War of Independence. The Second War for Independence broke out in 1895. It was led by José Martí (hoe-*zay* mar-*tee*), a poet and

journalist who had spent much of his life in exile in New York City. There he organized Cuban resistance against Spain. Unable to defeat Spanish troops in battle, the rebels took to the hills and began an active guerrilla campaign. This included destroying property, especially American-owned sugar mills and plantations. The rebels did this deliberately, for they hoped the United States would intervene. Apparently they were willing to have their rebellion put down if, in exchange, Cuba would become free from Spain.

Public opinion in the United States was split. Many business people wanted the government to support Spain in order to protect their investments. Other Americans, however, were enthusiastic about the rebel cause. Wasn't the cry of "Cuba Libre!—A Free Cuba!" a bit like Patrick Henry's cry of "Give me liberty or give me death"?

The Road to War

In 1896 the Spanish government sent to Cuba a new general, Valeriano Weyler y Nicolau (vah-lay-ree-*yah*-no *way*-ler e knee-ko-*lah*-oo), with orders to put down the revolt. Weyler decided that regular military methods would not work against the rebels' guerrilla tactics. The rebels would sneak into the villages at night where they got food and some recruits. So Weyler began a policy of *reconcentration*. The rebels were particularly active in areas of central and western Cuba. Weyler moved the entire rural population of these areas into reconcentration camps, which were surrounded by barbed wire. Weyler figured this would cut off the rebels' source of food and recruits.

Unfortunately for the people in the camps, sanitation facilities were miserable and food was in short supply. Disease and famine took a high toll. Of the 1.6 million people whom Weyler reconcentrated, about 200,000 died within two years.

The Yellow Press

While Weyler was attempting to put down the Cuban revolt, supporters of the rebel cause were active in the United States. Large quantities of money and arms were collected and then smuggled into the island.

More important, newspaper tycoons William Randolph Hearst and Joseph Pulitzer were carrying on a circulation war. Each was determined that his paper would outsell the other. So both began

Spanish General Valeriano Weyler's harsh action against Cuban rebels was attacked by the U.S. press.

to play up Spanish "atrocities." General Weyler was nicknamed "the Butcher." Legitimate accounts of suffering in the reconcentration camps were mixed with fake stories of wells being poisoned and little children being thrown to the sharks. American correspondents, who were not allowed to enter areas where fighting was going on, would sit around the bars in Havana and make up reports about battles that never took place. Once, artist Frederic Remington, who had been illustrating reporters' dispatches, cabled Hearst saying that a war between the United States and Spain seemed very unlikely. Back came Hearst's reply, "You furnish the pictures and I'll furnish the war."

Section 1 Review

COMPREHENSION   Developing Vocabulary

1. Explain these terms: circulation war, atrocities.

COMPREHENSION   Mastering Facts

1. What were the four things that Admiral Mahan said were necessary for the U.S. to have if it wished to be a strong and wealthy nation?
2. Who was the leader of Cuba's Second War of Independence?
3. What was the purpose of Weyler's reconcentration policy?
4. What kind of press coverage did Cuba get from U.S. newspapers?

2   THE UNITED STATES GOES TO WAR WITH SPAIN

VOCABULARY   *rations   Rough Riders*

Both the Democratic and Republican platforms of 1896 had proclaimed sympathy for the Cuban rebels. President McKinley, however, did not want the United States to fight against Spain. He had been through the Civil War and, as he told a friend, "I have seen the dead piled up, and I do not want to see another [war]." With regard to Weyler's actions, McKinley observed that "there were some outrages on both sides if the truth were known."

Toward the end of 1897, it seemed as if McKinley's hope might turn into reality. A new government took power in Madrid. It recalled Weyler, closed down the reconcentration camps, and offered Cuba self-government in all matters except defense, foreign relations, and the court system. The rebels, however, rejected the offer. They would settle only for complete independence.

Nevertheless, in his first annual message to Congress, McKinley urged American firebrands to give Spain "a reasonable chance to realize . . . the new order of things." But two incidents changed that.

The De Lôme Scandal

The first had to do with a private letter written by Enrique Dupuy de Lôme (in-*re*-kay duh-poo*wee* duh *lowm*), the Spanish minister to the United States. A Cuban rebel stole the letter from a Havana post office and leaked it to Hearst's *Journal*. In the letter, de Lôme called McKinley a weak president and a common politician, who took both sides of an issue and always tried "for the admiration of the crowd."

This was much milder than some of Theodore Roosevelt's comments. Roosevelt considered

501

McKinley "a white-livered cur" with "no more backbone than a chocolate eclair!" But foreign ministers are supposed to be discreet and not put critical statements down on paper. Before an indignant State Department could demand his recall, de Lôme resigned. Six days later came the second incident.

The U.S.S. *Maine* Explodes

Early in 1898 McKinley had ordered the U.S.S. *Maine* to Havana harbor. Officially it was a courtesy call. Actually, the battleship had responded to a telegram from the American consul general in Havana. He was afraid that American citizens there might be in danger from local rioters.

When the *Maine* arrived in the city's harbor, all seemed calm. The ship's officers went sightseeing ashore and even took in a bullfight. The evening of February 15, Captain Charles D. Sigsbee was sitting in his cabin writing a letter to his wife. Suddenly there was a terrible explosion, and the ship's ammunition went up in flames. Some 260 of the 350 officers and men on board lost their lives.

Even today no one really knows what caused the *Maine* to explode. A naval court of inquiry decided that the ship had hit a submarine mine. Other investigators believe there was an internal explosion in the coal bunkers. But Hearst had no doubts about the matter at all. His *Journal's* headline read: THE WARSHIP MAINE WAS SPLIT IN TWO BY AN ENEMY'S SECRET INFERNAL MACHINE. The paper offered a reward of $50,000 for the capture of the evil Spaniards who had committed the outrage.

Now there was no holding back the forces that wanted war. Everyone seemed to be crying, "Remember the *Maine*!" As the *New York Times* put it, "It would have been as easy to end the war of the Revolution at Bunker Hill or the Civil War at Bull Run as to turn back now." It made no difference that the Spanish government agreed on April 9 to almost everything the United States demanded, including a six-month cease-fire.

On April 11 McKinley sent a message to Congress asking for the right "to use the military and naval forces of the United States" to bring peace to Cuba. On April 19 Congress agreed. And on April 20 the United States went to war with Spain. It was the first conflict with a foreign power since the Mexican War of 1846.

"Remember the Maine" became the rallying cry of those favoring war with Spain after the American battleship mysteriously exploded in Havana harbor, killing some 260 Americans.

Dewey Takes Manila

The Spanish-American War was fought on both sides of the globe. Engagements included sea and land forces alike. Some of them inspired songs:

> "O Dewey was the morning
> Upon the first of May,
> And Dewey was the Admiral
> Down in Manila Bay;
> And Dewey were the Regent's eyes,
> Them orbs of royal blue!
> And Dewey feel discouraged?
> I Dew not think we Dew. "

On February 25 John Long, secretary of the navy, left his office for some badly needed rest. No sooner was he gone than the assistant secretary, Theodore Roosevelt, sent a cable to Commodore (later Admiral) George Dewey, head of the Pacific fleet, telling him to sail for the Philippine Islands in case war with Spain broke out.

On May 1, Dewey steamed into the harbor of Manila, capital of the Spanish-owned Philippine Islands. Thanks to Secretary of State Blaine's preparedness campaign, the squadron included four heavily armed cruisers. The Spanish fleet, although larger, carried only a few obsolete guns. Even the Spanish land batteries were old-fashioned and slow-firing.

The Spanish-American War in the Philippines

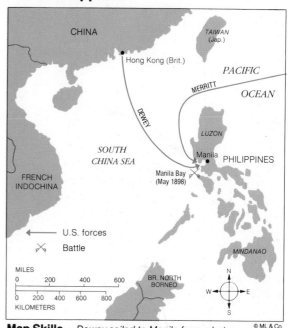

Map Skills *Dewey sailed to Manila from what British colony? When was the battle of Manila Bay?*

As one historian wrote, it "was more a practice shoot than a battle." Dewey brought his ships within three miles of the Spanish fleet and then re-

The guns of the American fleet under George Dewey overwhelmed the ill-equipped Spanish forces as the U.S. Navy gained an easy victory at Manila Bay in the Philippine Islands.

The Spanish-American War in the Caribbean

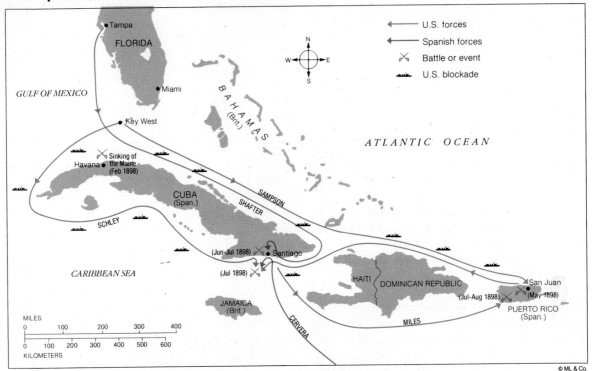

Map Skills *Shafter sailed from what U.S. city? Who sailed to Puerto Rico? When was the naval battle off Cuba? Who commanded the Spanish forces? How far is Havana from Key West?*

marked to an officer, "You may fire when ready, Gridley." And back and forth went the American squadron, spitting black powder for several hours, until the entire enemy fleet was destroyed. Spanish casualties numbered 381. American casualties numbered one: an overweight engineer who died of heat prostration.

Over the next two months, some 11,000 American troops landed in the Philippines. There they joined forces with Filipino rebels led by General Emilio Aguinaldo (ah-ghee-*nal*-do). The rebels had been fighting for freedom since 1896. In August the Spanish troops in Manila surrendered. But they surrendered only to the Americans. Aguinaldo's troops were not allowed into the city.

U.S. Troops Invade Cuba

Back in the New World, hostilities began with a naval blockade. After searching for the main Spanish fleet for almost a week, Rear Admiral William T. Sampson located it in the harbor of Santiago, Cuba. He immediately bottled it up.

In the meantime, American troops organized to invade the island. Unfortunately, unlike the navy, the army was ill-prepared. About 125,000 Americans had volunteered to fight, including a large number of blacks who hoped the war would help achieve "justice at home as well as abroad." But there were not enough up-to-date guns to go around. Nor was there any khaki cloth for lightweight uniforms. This meant the soldiers had to wear heavy blue wool in a tropical climate. There were not enough boots. Rations consisted of cans containing uneatable and sometimes rotten meat, popularly known as "embalmed beef." And most of the officers were Civil War veterans, who spent a great deal of time reminiscing about old battles and almost no time training the volunteers.

Nevertheless, in mid-June about 17,000 men managed to sail from Tampa, Florida, and land in Cuba. They included all four black regiments of the regular army, as well as the First Volunteer Cavalry Regiment. The latter had been organized by Theodore Roosevelt, who had resigned as assistant secretary of the navy in order to fight. Roose-

504

velt's "Rough Riders" were an unusual mixture. There were cowboys, Indians, and former sheriffs from the western territories of Arizona, New Mexico, and Oklahoma. There were also "polo players and gentlemen riders from New York's Harvard, Yale, and Princeton clubs."

Rough Riders Take Santiago

The most famous land battle in Cuba was the Battle of San Juan Hill, which occurred on the outskirts of Santiago on July 1. The first part, which took place on nearby Kettle Hill, featured a gallant uphill charge by the Rough Riders and two black regiments, the Ninth and Tenth Cavalry. The second part consisted of an infantry attack on San Juan Hill proper.

Two days later, on July 3, the Spanish fleet, under Admiral Pascual Cervera (pahs-*kwahl* sair-*vair*-ah), made a dash for freedom. The Spanish ships succeeded in slipping out of Santiago harbor. But they were quickly overtaken by the American ships, and were either sunk or forced to shore. The next day, Admiral Sampson cabled Washington,

"The fleet under my command offers the nation as a Fourth of July present the whole of Cervera's fleet."

On July 17 Santiago surrendered. On July 26 American troops invaded Puerto Rico. An armistice was declared on August 12. And on December 10 the United States and Spain signed the Treaty of Paris.

An Imperial Peace

The American and Spanish commissioners in Paris agreed on most issues. Cuba was to become independent. The United States would take over Puerto Rico and the Spanish-owned island of Guam in the Pacific. The sticking point was what to do with the Philippines.

When the war broke out, the idea of annexing a group of islands 6000 miles west of California was probably the last thing in most Americans' minds. McKinley admitted that he didn't even know where they were. Mahan, Roosevelt, and their followers, however, believed the islands had strategic and commercial importance.

The "Rough Riders," a motley group of volunteers that included western frontiersmen and eastern gentlemen, pose with their leader Theodore Roosevelt (center) at the top of San Juan Hill.

As the war progressed, more and more Americans began to feel that annexation was a good idea after all. McKinley waffled at first. Then, in late October, he came to a decision. Here is how he explained it to a group of Methodist ministers.

" I walked the floor of the White House night after night until midnight; and I am not ashamed to tell you, gentlemen, that I went down on my knees and prayed Almighty God for light and guidance more than one night. And one night late it came to me this way—I don't know how it was, but it came: (1) That we could not give them back to Spain—that would be cowardly and dishonorable; (2) that we could not turn them over to France or Germany—our commercial rivals in the Orient—that would be bad business and discreditable; (3) that we could not leave them to themselves—they were unfit for self-government . . . ; and (4) that there was nothing left for us to do but to take them all, and to educate the Filipinos, and uplift and Christianize them, and by God's grace do the very best we could by them, as our fellow-men for whom Christ also died. "

McKinley apparently did not remember that most Filipinos had been Christians for several hundred years. In any event, under the Treaty of Paris the United States took over Spain's role as ruler of the Philippines. In exchange, the United States promised to pay Spain $20 million.

The struggle for ratification was touch-and-go.

Although a majority of Americans favored ratification, many vocal people opposed it. These included former Presidents Benjamin Harrison and Grover Cleveland, as well as Jane Addams, Andrew Carnegie, and Mark Twain. They believed that colonial expansion went against American tradition. One said, "A republic can have no subjects." Speaker of the House Thomas B. Reed felt so strongly about the matter that he later resigned his congressional seat in protest. In addition, labor leaders such as Samuel Gompers were afraid that Filipino workers would compete against Americans for jobs, while racists like "Pitchfork" Ben Tillman did not want any more dark-skinned Americans. Still, the treaty passed the Senate with one vote to spare—and the United States had an empire.

Section 2 Review

COMPREHENSION   Developing Vocabulary

1. Explain these terms: rations, Rough Riders.

COMPREHENSION   Mastering Facts

1. What event started the Spanish-American War?
2. Who ordered Admiral Dewey to sail to Manila?
3. What reasons did McKinley give for deciding to annex the Philippines?
4. What objections did some Americans raise to our country's colonial expansion?

3 NEW LANDS COME UNDER THE AMERICAN FLAG

VOCABULARY   *protectorate   commonwealth*

As of 1898 the United States found itself for the first time with possessions overseas: Puerto Rico and the Philippines. It also had military control over Cuba. Also in that year the United States acquired Hawaii, as you will soon read. How did the people fare under American rule?

Cuba Becomes a Protectorate

A *protectorate* is a country whose affairs are controlled by a stronger power. A few months before he died fighting in Cuba, José Martí warned his compatriots against depending too much on the United States. What worried Martí was the fear that the United States would try to take Spain's place in controlling the island.

For the first three years of Cuban independence, it seemed as if Martí had been right. The United States set up a military government, first

under John R. Brooke, then under Dr. Leonard Wood. American occupation forces appointed the same local officials who had served the Spaniards. Cubans who protested such actions were either put in prison or exiled.

At the same time, the American military government did its best to improve the people's well-being. It gave food and clothing to thousands of families. It built roads, railroads, and dock facilities. It helped farmers put land back into cultivation. It reopened the University of Havana and organized a large number of elementary schools.

Conquering Yellow Fever. Perhaps the most spectacular accomplishment of the military government was the almost complete elimination of yellow fever. Each year, about 800 persons had died from the disease in Havana alone. In 1900 an epidemic swept the island. Wood appointed a team of four army surgeons under Dr. Walter Reed to try to find out what caused the disease.

The team decided to work on a theory that had been proposed by a Cuban, Dr. Carlos Finlay. Dr. Finlay believed that yellow fever is carried from person to person by a species of mosquito. Within a year the theory was proven correct. The doctors identified the guilty species of mosquito and cleared out its breeding places. By 1901 Havana was free of yellow fever.

The U.S. Writes a Constitution. That same year, Cuba adopted a constitution. Many of its provisions, however, were not written by the Cuban constitutional assembly. They were drafted in Washington and were simply presented to the assembly for its approval. Collectively they are known as the Platt Amendment, because they took the form of an amendment to a military appropriations bill.

The Platt Amendment provided the following: (1) Cuba was not to make any treaties that might limit its independence; (2) Cuba was not to permit any foreign power to control any part of its territory; (3) the United States was to have the right to intervene in Cuba's internal affairs "for the protection of life, property, and individual liberty"; (4) Cuba was not to go into debt; and (5) the United States could buy or lease land on the island for coaling or naval stations.

The result of the Platt Amendment was to make Cuba a protectorate of the United States. As the stronger of the two nations, the United States protected weaker Cuba by partially controlling its affairs. A major American naval base was set up at Guantánamo Bay. Although American troops were removed from the island in 1902, they were sent back three times between 1906 and 1920 to support a particular political group. In addition, it was common practice for the American ambassador in Havana to present his government's views to the Cuban president about the policies that he was following.

U.S. Economic Domination. There was economic influence on Cuba as well. The United States made large loans to the Cuban government. American corporations invested heavily in the island's sugar plantations and refineries; its public utilities, especially telephone and electricity; and its railroads. The bulk of Cuba's foreign trade was with the United States, which bought about 90 percent of the island's sugar.

The United States was concerned about conditions in Cuba because of the island's location. Only ninety-two miles off the coast of Florida, Cuba offers a good base for any nation that wants to threaten the United States. From the Cuban viewpoint, however, it seemed as if the United States was treating it like a child. Also, American businesses in Cuba paid low wages and low taxes while the high profits they earned went back to the United States.

The Platt Amendment was finally *abrogated*, or abolished, in 1934. American economic influence in the island, however, continued until the early 1960s, as you will read in chapter 37.

Puerto Rico Becomes a Commonwealth

The changeover from military to civilian rule was far smoother in Puerto Rico than in Cuba. The Foraker Act of 1900 provided for a governor to be appointed by the president of the United States. The president also received the power to appoint members of the legislature's upper house. Members of the lower house were popularly elected.

In 1917 Puerto Ricans were given the right to elect members of both legislative houses. They also became citizens of the United States. In 1950 Puerto Ricans drafted their own constitution. Two years later the island became a commonwealth. That means Puerto Rico makes its own laws and handles its own finances while the United States takes care of defense and tariffs. Residents of Puerto Rico may move freely between the island and the United States.

Several elections have taken place in Puerto Rico on the issue of whether to remain a commonwealth, become a state of the Union, or become an independent nation. Thus far, the Puerto Ricans have voted to continue their commonwealth status.

Hawaii Is Deeply and Permanently Changed

United States interest in Hawaii had been of long standing. No sooner was the Revolutionary War over than American merchants set out in their tall sailing ships to obtain a share of the lucra-

Queen Liliuokalani was the last monarch to rule Hawaii before the United States annexed it in 1898.

tive China and East India trade. On their way across the Pacific, they would stop at the Hawaiian Islands for fresh supplies of fruits and vegetables. The merchants were followed in the 1820s by Yankee missionaries, who transformed the Hawaiian capital of Honolulu into "a pleasant replica of a New England town." After 1840 Hawaii became the center of the Pacific whaling industry.

In the 1850s the islands' economy changed. Sugar-growing replaced whaling as the main industry. Almost all the sugar plantations were owned by white planters from the United States. This change had several significant consequences.

Hawaiians Lose Control.

First, it led to the importing of contract laborers. As one historian explained, Hawaiians "could see no sense in working hard all day in the hot sun in the cane fields to earn money, when the sea was full of fish, and a man could eat well off his own small taro (edible roots) patch." Wages for American workers were too high for plantation owners to make a profit. So young male Chinese, then Portuguese, and finally Japanese were brought into Hawaii by the tens of thousands to work in the cane fields. By 1872 the Hawaiians were a minority in their own nation. They were outnumbered almost two to one by foreigners and immigrant laborers.

A second result of the economic change was a desire on the part of plantation owners for closer ties with the United States. In 1875 a treaty between the two nations removed American tariffs on Hawaiian sugar, as well as Hawaiian tariffs on American goods. The treaty was renewed in 1887, at which time the United States acquired Pearl Harbor as a coaling station for its Pacific fleet.

That same year, Hawaiian-born white businessmen forced King Kalakaua to change the constitution. Under the change, only men who owned land or had a certain income were allowed to vote. Since most Hawaiians either were poor or did not own land, and since immigrant laborers were not citizens, the result was that control of the government passed into the hands of businessmen of American descent.

Queen Liliuokalani Deposed.

The Hawaiians grew more and more resentful. In 1891 King Kalakaua died and his sister Liliuokalani became queen. She did not like white rule. So she announced her intention of issuing a new constitution that would remove property qualifications from the right to vote. She wanted "Hawaii for the Hawaiians."

The result was a revolution, organized by white business groups with the help of John L. Stevens, the United States minister to Hawaii. On the night of January 16, 1893, the U.S.S. *Boston* appeared without warning in Honolulu Harbor. Following Stevens's orders, American marines moved ashore to "protect American lives and property in case of riot." As they marched through the streets, volunteer troops organized by the white business groups took over the government building. The Hawaiian flag was pulled down, and the Stars and Stripes raised in its stead. The queen was imprisoned in her palace.

Stevens immediately recognized the provisional government, which sent a commission to Washington asking that the islands be annexed. Queen "Lil" also sent a representative, asking for justice.

Kingdom to Republic to State.

President Cleveland in turn ordered a special investigator to Hawaii to learn what was going on. The investigator reported that, "in his judgment, Minister Stevens had been responsible for the revolution." Cleveland then demanded that the provisional government restore Queen "Lil" to the throne. Instead, the provisional government formed the Republic of Hawaii, wrote a constitution, and elected pineapple grower Sanford B. Dole as president.

By this time, it was clear to the United States that only force could put the queen back on her throne, and Congress did not want to use force. So in 1894 it adopted a resolution saying that the United States should not interfere further in Hawaii.

Then came the Spanish-American War. Public opinion in the United States changed. When the Republic of Hawaii again petitioned for annexation, Congress agreed. On August 12, 1898, the Hawaiian Islands became a territory of the United States. In 1959 Hawaii became the fiftieth state in the Union.

War with the Philippine Islands

The Filipino rebels led by Emilio Aguinaldo had proclaimed their independence from Spain in June 1898. Two months later, as you know, the Spanish troops in Manila made a deal to surrender only to the Americans. Then in December the Treaty of Paris gave the United States ownership of the Philippine Islands. In the meantime, a Filipino constitutional assembly had drafted a document similar to the Constitution of the United States. In January 1899 the first Philippine Republic was inaugurated. General Aguinaldo was sworn in as its first president. But he was president not of an independent country but of a country that was about to become a U.S. possession. The Filipinos were furious over what they considered betrayal on the part of the United States.

Conflict Erupts. Throughout the month of January, tension between American and Filipino soldiers kept rising. The Americans were demoralized by the heat, the humidity, the torrential rains, and the lack of anything to do.

On the night of February 4, as the annexation debate in the United States Senate was nearing a climax, a Filipino soldier began to walk across a bridge on the outskirts of Manila. An American enlisted man, seeing the shadowy figure in the dark, fired—and the Philippine-American War was on.

The conflict lasted for three years. At first the United States was confident that it would be over in a few weeks. But as Filipino resistance continued, more and more American troops were sent in. Unable to defeat them in regular battle, Aguinaldo turned to guerrilla tactics.

Gradually, the fighting became bloodier and more brutal on both sides. Wounded soldiers were killed instead of becoming prisoners. Villages were burnt to the ground in an attempt to flush out guerrillas. Even torture was sometimes used.

Some Blacks Condemn the War. Complicating matters was the fact that many of the 70,000 American troops were black. Once an area was conquered, ties of friendship soon developed between the Filipinos and the blacks. White Americans, on the other hand, tended to look down on the Filipinos because of their skin color.

A number of black newspapers in the United States wondered why black soldiers were "fighting to curse the country (the Philippines) with colorphobia, jimcrow cars, disfranchisement, lynchers, and everything that prejudice can do to blight the manhood of the darker races." Many blacks deserted to the Filipino side.

Commonwealth to Independence. The war began to wind down in 1901 when Aguinaldo was captured. Sporadic fighting continued for another year. But except for an outbreak on the island of Mindanao, where a treaty with some Muslim tribes broke down, peace was more or less in effect by mid-1902.

On July 4, 1901, William Howard Taft became civilian governor of the Philippines. Legislative

Among the American troops fighting rebels in the Philippine Islands were a large number of blacks.

functions were in the hands of an appointed commission and an elected assembly. In 1916 the Jones Act replaced the appointed commission with an elected senate. In 1934 the Tydings-McDuffie Act offered the Philippines complete independence after a ten-year trial period as a commonwealth. The Filipinos accepted the offer in 1936. Ten years later, on July 4, 1946, the islands became an independent republic.

U.S. Youth Lend a Hand. During the years between annexation and independence, Americans brought about several changes. Perhaps the most significant was in public education. Within six weeks after Taft's administration began, the U.S.S. *Thomas* docked in Manila Harbor. Aboard were 540 young American college graduates who soon became known as the "Thomasites." Settling in various communities throughout the islands, they taught day and evening classes for children and adults, and trained Filipino teachers. During the first year and a half, twenty-seven of them died from cholera or bandits. But the work continued.

It continued so well that the literacy rate more

than doubled between 1902 and 1935. In 1898 only 5000 Filipino students were attending elementary school. By 1920 there were over a million and by 1946, over two million. As Filipino diplomat Carlos Romulo said, "Public education transformed a nation ready to be transformed. . . . The American schoolteachers joined with us in creating the literacy, the knowledge, the self-confidence, and devotion to democracy on which it was possible to establish our Republic."

Section 3 Review

COMPREHENSION   Developing Vocabulary

1. Explain these terms: protectorate, abrogated, Thomasites.

COMPREHENSION   Mastering Facts

1. How did the Platt Amendment affect Cuba?
2. As a commonwealth, how is Puerto Rico governed?
3. How did Hawaiians lose control of their government?
4. Why did the United States go to war with the Philippines?

4   THE UNITED STATES BECOMES A WORLD POWER

VOCABULARY   *spheres of influence   extraterritoriality   Open Door policy   Dollar Diplomacy*

An overseas empire meant that the United States had to develop policies for defending its possessions and also for dealing with other imperialist nations. The two areas of greatest concern were the Far East and Latin America.

The Open Door Policy in China

When the United States "arrived" in the Far East as ruler of the Philippines, it found that the vast but weak nation of China was in danger of being carved up by France, Germany, Great Britain, Japan, and Russia. Each nation had its *spheres of influence*, areas where it had special trading privileges and where numbers of its merchants, missionaries, and other nationals lived. In these areas the people who might be charged with breaking Chinese laws were tried according to their own laws and by their own courts, not by Chinese laws and courts. This right of *extraterritoriality* had been forced on China by the stronger powers. These nations were anxious for even more Chinese territory.

The United States was not interested in acquiring colonies on the Asian mainland. Nor did it want to risk a war. On the other hand, it *did* want a larger share of the rich China market.

A solution to the difficulty was proposed by Secretary of State John Hay. He sent notes with the same message to Britain, Germany, and Russia and later to France, Italy, and Japan. Hay asked the powers to promise two things with regard to their spheres of influence:

1. They would not prevent other nations from doing business there.

2. They would not charge other nations higher railroad, harbor, and tariff rates than they charged their own merchants.

In other words, there would really be no advantage in having a sphere of influence because every other nation would be allowed to compete there on equal terms.

The nations involved more or less said "No" to Hay's note. Nevertheless, on March 20, 1900, Hay announced that the Open Door policy had been accepted and was in effect.

The United States and Its Possessions   1917

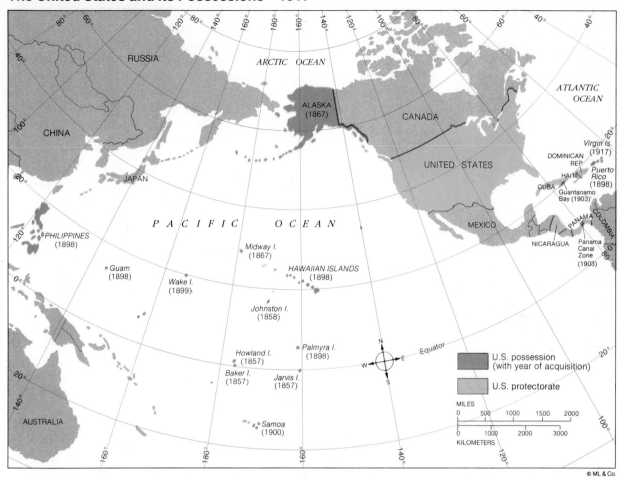

Map Skills   *When did the United States acquire Puerto Rico? Alaska? Guam? Where is Guantanamo Bay? How far are the Philippine Islands from the United States?*

The Boxer Rebellion.   At this point, a Chinese secret society, known to Westerners as the Boxers, began an armed movement to, as they said, "expel the barbarians." The Boxers objected to what they saw as a foreign takeover of their country.

The Boxers began by burning foreign missions, schools, and houses, and by killing several thousand Chinese Christians in northern China. Then they laid siege to the foreign legations in Peking and the foreign settlement in Tientsin. In turn, an international military force, including Americans, British, Japanese, and Russians, relieved Tientsin within a month and Peking within two months.

The colonial powers now had an excellent excuse to take over more territory from China. But Hay moved to prevent this from happening. Even before the siege at Peking was lifted, he announced that it was United States policy to "preserve the Chinese territorial and administrative entity" and to "safeguard for the world the principle of equal and impartial trade with all parts of the Chinese Empire."

Results of the Rebellion.   As a result of Hay's statement, the colonial powers agreed not to occupy additional parts of China after all. Instead, they accepted $333 million as payment for property damage and loss of life. The American share of this indemnity was almost $25 million. Only half of this, however, was actually needed to compensate American citizens. So the United States returned the balance to China, which in turn used the money to educate a number of Chinese students in America.

511

Foreign Spheres of Influence in China 1900

Map Skills *Which foreign enclaves in China were German? British? Russian? French? Portuguese? American?*

Preventing the further division of China was not the only result of Hay's Open Door policy. Even more important, the policy paved the way for greater American influence in Asia. Within a few years, that influence showed itself in the settlement of the Russo-Japanese War of 1904–1905.

Relations with Russia and Japan

Japan and Russia came to blows over Korea. Japan had received Korea from China in 1895 and had set it up as a partly independent state within the Japanese sphere of influence. After the Boxer Rebellion, the Russians set up Manchuria within *their* sphere of influence and began to cast their eyes at Korea. Japan suggested that the two imperialist nations agree to give each other a free hand within their respective spheres but to stay off the other nation's turf. Russia refused. Japan thereupon gave Russia "a last and earnest warning" and in February 1904 launched a surprise attack.

Japan the Victor. To everyone's amazement, Japan not only destroyed the Russian Pacific fleet. It also destroyed Russia's European fleet, which was ordered to the Far East after the Pacific fleet was defeated. And through a series of land battles in China, Japan obtained firm control over not only Korea but much of Manchuria as well.

Japan's victories, however, cost it a great deal of money. So the Japanese asked the United States to mediate the conflict. President Theodore Roosevelt agreed. In the summer of 1905 he invited Russia and Japan to send delegates to a conference at Portsmouth, New Hampshire.

Roosevelt the Peacemaker. The first meeting took place at lunch on the presidential yacht *Mayflower*. It was prickly at first. But Roosevelt had a way of grasping a person's hand and saying in his special way, "*Dee*-light-ed." His smile was so broad and so genuine that few people were not charmed by him. The Russians and the Japanese began to enjoy themselves. After an excellent lunch, they shook hands cordially with one another.

Japan wanted Sakhalin Island and a large sum of money from Russia. Russia refused. Finally, Roosevelt persuaded Japan to accept half of Sakhalin and to forget about the cash indemnity. In exchange, Russia agreed to let Japan take over its interests in Manchuria and Korea.

In 1906 Roosevelt was awarded the Nobel Peace Prize.

On the yacht Mayflower *President Theodore Roosevelt greets diplomats from Russia and Japan. He successfully mediated a conflict between the two nations.*

512

Locating the Panama Canal　1903

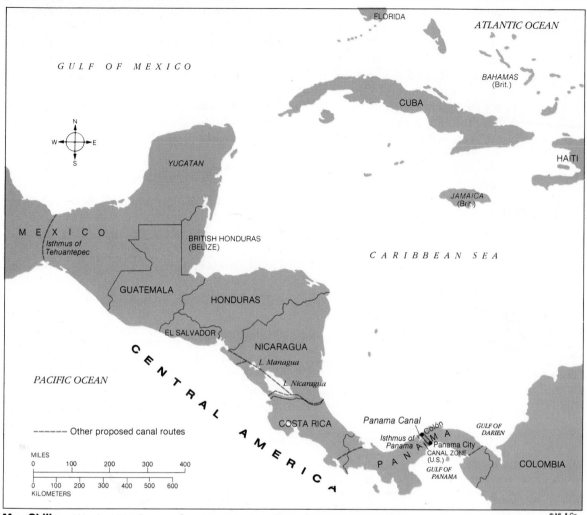

Map Skills　*How far is the Panama Canal from the tip of Florida? In what country is the Isthmus of Tehuantepec? Through what two lakes did the canal route through Nicaragua go?*

© ML & Co.

"The Path Between the Seas"

By 1900 the United States had acquired three of the four things Mahan said it needed to become a world power. It had a modern fleet, naval bases in the Caribbean, and Hawaii. What it did *not* have was a canal across the Isthmus of Panama.

Preparing the Way. Interest in a water passage between the Atlantic and the Pacific dated back to Spanish times. A relative of Cortes had hoped to "open the land of Castilla del Oro . . . from sea to sea." In 1552, a priest named Francisco Lopez de Gomara wrote about isthmian geography. "There are mountains," he acknowledged,

"but there are also hands, and for a king of [Spain], few things are impossible." However, not until the mid-1800s did the steam engine and improvements in hydraulic engineering actually make a canal possible.

In 1850 the United States and Great Britain agreed that they would have equal rights in any canal that might be built between the Atlantic and Pacific oceans. In 1901 the two nations made a new agreement. Under the Hay-Pauncefote Treaty, the United States received exclusive rights to build, control, and presumably fortify a canal across the narrow part of Central America. In return, the United States promised that all nations would be allowed to send their commercial and fighting ships through such a canal without discrimination.

Choosing a Route.

Now the question arose of where to build the canal. The two possibilities were Nicaragua and the province of Panama in Colombia. Nicaragua was several hundred miles closer to the United States. It contained lakes and rivers which could form part of the route and thus reduce construction costs. And the government of Nicaragua was cooperative. Nevertheless, the final decision was in favor of the Panama route.

The man largely responsible for this choice was Philippe Bunau-Varilla (fee-*leep* boo-*no*-vah-ree-*yah*). Born in France, he graduated from college with a degree in engineering. In 1878 a French company headed by Ferdinand de Lesseps, who had directed the construction of the Suez Canal, began digging in Panama. Bunau-Varilla joined the company in 1884 and soon became its chief engineer.

The French Project Fails.

But the French project was doomed to failure. The excavating machinery was not equal to the task. And the environment was appalling.

66 The men worked in constant fear of poisonous snakes (coral, bushmaster, fer-de-lance, all three among the world's most deadly reptiles) and of the big cats (puma and jaguar). Days and nights were made a living hell by *bichos*, the local designation for ticks, chiggers, spiders, ants, mosquitoes, flies, or any other crawling, buzzing, stinging form of insect life for which no one had a name.... The jungle ... was so "thickly matted that one could only see a few yards in any direction." 99

In addition, eight months of the year were the wet season, when it not only rained every day, it rained in torrents! Six inches in twenty-four hours or less was not uncommon. Topping it all off was the prevalence of malaria and yellow fever.

The United States Takes Over.

In 1889 the French abandoned the project and sold the concession and the rusted machinery to the New Panama Canal Company. This consisted of a group of speculators, one of whom was Bunau-Varilla. After negotiating first with Russia and then with Great Britain, the company approached the United States. Both President Roosevelt and Congress were receptive to the idea of America building the canal. But an investigating committee recommended Nicaragua, and the House of Representatives agreed.

At this point, Bunau-Varilla, who was acting as the company's agent in the United States, pulled a brilliant public relations coup. He sent each of the ninety-two senators in the United States Senate a Nicaraguan stamp with a picture of an erupting volcano. The Senate voted to build the canal in Panama.

Trouble with Colombia

In March 1903 the Senate ratified the Hay-Herrán Treaty between the United States and Colombia. The treaty stated that the United States would give Colombia $10 million, plus an annual rent of $250,000, for a six-mile-wide strip across the isthmus of Panama.

But a new government had just come to power in Colombia, and it resented the treaty for a number of reasons. First, the Senate was offering the New Panama Canal Company four times as much money, $40 million. Second, Colombia was afraid it might lose all sovereignty within the canal zone. Finally, Secretary Hay had responded to Colombian suggestions for changes in the treaty with harsh and insulting words. So in August the Colombian Senate turned the treaty down.

On October 10, 1903, Bunau-Varilla met with President Roosevelt at the White House. Bunau-Varilla predicted that there might soon be a revo-

This Nicaraguan stamp of an erupting volcano led Congress to choose Panama as the site for a canal.

lution in Panama. The canal would have meant an economic boom for the area, and the Panamanians were very disappointed.

Roosevelt did not say flat out that the United States would prevent the landing of Colombian troops on the isthmus. But, as he observed some time later, "He [Bunau-Varilla] is a very able fellow, and it was his business to find out what he thought our Government would do. I have no doubt that he was able to make a very accurate guess, and to advise his people accordingly. In fact, he would have been a very dull man had he been unable to make such a guess."

On October 30, 1903, the commander of the U.S.S. *Nashville* received instructions from Washington to head for the harbor of Colon in Panama. If a rebellion broke out there, he was to take over the Panama Railroad. He was also to "prevent the landing of any armed forces with hostile intent" within fifty miles of the city. The only way the Colombian government could send troops to Colon was by sea.

Panama Becomes Independent

The *Nashville* entered Colon harbor on November 2. The next day a rebellion against Colombia broke out. On November 4, ten American warships appeared in Panamanian waters, and Panama declared its independence. On November 6 the United States recognized the new republic. Bunau-Varilla became the first Panamanian minister to the United States. And on November 18 the Hay–Bunau-Varilla Treaty was signed. It gave the United States a ten-mile-wide canal zone "in perpetuity," or forever. It gave Panama $10 million plus $250,000 a year after nine years. The treaty also guaranteed Panama's independence but added that the principles of the Platt Amendment—including the right of American intervention—would apply.

In 1911, commenting on his actions, President Roosevelt said the following:

66 The Panama Canal I naturally take special interest in because I started it.

There are plenty of other things I started merely because the time had come that whoever was in power would have started them.

But the Panama Canal would not have been started if I had not taken hold of it, because if I had followed the traditional or conservative method I would have submitted an admirable state paper occupying a couple of hundred pages detailing all of the facts to Congress and asking Congress' consideration of it.

In that case there would have been a number of excellent speeches made on the subject in Congress; the debate would be proceeding at this moment with great spirit and the beginning of work on the canal would be fifty years in the future.

Fortunately the crisis came at a period when I could act unhampered. Accordingly I took the Isthmus, started the canal and then left Congress not to debate the canal, but to debate me. 99

The Panama Canal greatly strengthened the position of the United States as a world power. But it severely damaged relations with Latin America. As the American minister to Colombia explained in 1912:

66 By refusing to allow Colombia to uphold her sovereign rights over a territory where she had held dominion for eighty years, the friendship of nearly a century disappeared; the indignation of every Colombian, and millions of other Latin Americans, was aroused. . . . The confidence and trust in the justice and fairness of the United States, so long manifested, has completely vanished. 99

The Canal Is Completed

The canal was completed after ten years of monumental effort. Mud slides, rock slides, and premature dynamite explosions were only some of the engineering problems. The amount of earth that had to be removed was staggering: enough to fill a train of dirt cars four times around the equator. About 5600 workers, 4500 of whom were black, lost their lives from disease and accidents.

This illustration of the cutting of the Panama Canal gives an idea of the vastness of the project.

Costs ran higher than anything the United States government had built up to that time. In fact, building the Panama Canal cost more than five times as much as buying the Louisiana Territory, Florida, California, and Alaska put together.

On August 15, 1914, the waterway was finally opened for business. In 1921 Congress paid Colombia $25 million for its loss of Panama. An apology for Roosevelt's actions, however, was dropped from the treaty that authorized payment.

Expanding the Monroe Doctrine

Latin America was now the United States's major sphere of influence. And like all imperialist nations, the United States wanted to keep its sphere of influence as free as possible from foreign competition or control.

The main problem had to do with the financial condition of the smaller nations, especially those in the Caribbean. Most of them had borrowed heavily from European bankers to build railroads and other public works, and to develop their mines, farms, and industries. However, they were not always able to pay the interest on their loans. This made a very tempting situation for European

imperialist nations. If Haiti, for example, owed money to France but could not pay, why shouldn't France move into Haiti in order to protect the investments of its citizens? And once in, there was always the possibility of remaining.

France had actually done just that in Mexico in 1863. Napoleon III sent troops to Mexico which overthrew the government. He also set up Maximilian of Austria as his puppet Emperor of Mexico. The United States, at that time in the midst of a civil war, could do little but protest. However, after Appomattox, Secretary of State Seward warned Napoleon III to remove his troops. He did so, and the foolish but brave Maximilian died before a Mexican firing squad.

President Roosevelt was well aware of such dangers. So in 1904, in a message to Congress, he expressed what historians call the Roosevelt Corollary to the Monroe Doctrine. In sum, if any foreign nation was to interfere in the affairs of a Latin American country, it would be the United States that would do the interfering. "The adherence of the United States to the Monroe Doctrine may force the United States, however reluctantly . . . to the exercise of an international police power."

This 1904 cartoon of "Teddy" Roosevelt reflects the nationalistic spirit of the times. European and Latin American nations found this attitude highly distasteful.

Dollar Diplomacy

During the next decade or so, the United States did intervene in Latin America on several occasions. American bankers took over the foreign debt of the Dominican Republic in 1905. In 1911 there was a revolution in Nicaragua, and the nation was on the verge of bankruptcy. Roosevelt's successor, William Howard Taft, quickly arranged for U.S. bankers to loan Nicaragua enough money to pay its debts. In return the bankers were given the right to recover their money by collecting Nicaragua's customs duties. The U.S. bankers also received control of Nicaragua's state-owned railroad system and the nation's national bank.

When the Nicaraguan citizens heard about this deal, they revolted against President Adolfo Díaz. To prop up Díaz's government and to protect U.S. economic interests, some 2000 marines were sent to Nicaragua. The revolt was put down but some marine detachments remained in the country until 1933. This was to insure that U.S. business interests did not suffer.

This policy of using the U.S. government to guarantee loans made to foreign countries by U.S. businessmen was called "Dollar Diplomacy" by those who opposed it. But the policy was followed again in Haiti in 1916. It was justified as a method of keeping Europeans out of the Caribbean area.

The United States and Mexico

American intervention in Mexico was justified on different grounds. Shortly after taking office in 1913, President Woodrow Wilson announced what historians call a "missionary policy" toward Latin America. He wanted to insure that the nations in the Western Hemisphere established democratic governments.

The Mexican Revolution. In 1910 the Mexicans had revolted against Porfirio Díaz, who had ruled as a dictator since 1877. During Díaz's regime, the Mexican government had offered tax benefits and other privileges to foreign investors to develop the nation's mineral and industrial resources. One result was that by 1913, U.S. investments in Mexican oil wells, mines, ranches, and railroads stood at almost $1 billion.

In 1911 Francisco Madero was elected president. A well-meaning but politically timid person, Madero could not handle the conflicting demands of different Mexican groups. Poor peasants wanted land of their own to farm, while rich landowners did not want any limitations on the amount of land they owned. Many factory workers wanted the government to nationalize industries, including those owned by foreigners. But the urban middle class wanted continued foreign investment.

After two years the government was taken over by Victoriano Huerta (*where*-tah), a hard-drinking general who had Madero shot. The American ambassador, Henry Lane Wilson (no relation to the U.S. president), urged the United States to recognize Huerta at once.

A New Foreign Policy. Ever since the time of Jefferson, it had been the policy of the United States to recognize any government that controlled a nation. It did not matter how that government had come to power. Nor did it matter whether the government was democratic or dictatorial in nature. President Wilson, however, felt strongly that only a democratic government supported by the people deserved American recognition. So he changed United States policy. Instead of recognizing Huerta, he placed an arms embargo on Mexico and urged other nations to do likewise. Wilson hoped this would cause the Huerta government to collapse.

Wilson's policy did not work. Moreover, American business people with investments in Mexico grew increasingly unhappy over the possibility that their property would be either damaged or confiscated. Wilson then reversed himself and lifted the arms embargo. Soon bands of Mexicans led by Venustiano Carranza, Emiliano Zapata, and Francisco "Pancho" Villa (*vee*-yah) were waging guerrilla warfare against Huerta.

In April 1914 two incidents occurred. A group of American marines were arrested near Tampico for supposedly violating martial law. Although they were quickly released, Huerta refused to apologize. The refusal gave Wilson an excuse to order American ships to blockade the port of Veracruz, toward which a German ship carrying weapons for Huerta was heading. When the German government protested, Wilson ordered the marines to seize Veracruz in order to keep the munitions cargo from being unloaded.

For a few weeks, it seemed as if war might again break out between the United States and Mexico. The governments of Argentina, Brazil, and Chile suggested a conference to try to resolve matters,

The wily Mexican rebel Pancho Villa (front) managed to elude an American expedition sent to capture him.

and one was held at Niagara Falls, Canada. But Wilson stood firm. Under no circumstances would the United States recognize a government that had come to power as a result of force and violence. So in July 1914 Huerta resigned and went into exile in Spain.

After some maneuvering, Carranza assumed the presidency in August 1914 and soon after, American troops were withdrawn from Veracruz. In 1915 Carranza promised that his government would not confiscate foreign-owned property and would protect the lives of foreigners. Wilson thereupon recognized the Carranza regime as the official government of Mexico.

Pershing and Pancho Villa. In the meantime, both Villa and Zapata had revolted against Carranza, fearing that he would not reform the na-tion's land-owing system enough to help the great mass of peasants. Villa in particular was infuriated by Wilson's recognition of Carranza and made threats against the United States.

Then, in January 1916, about fifteen American mining engineers working in northern Mexico were taken off a train by Mexican bandits and shot. Two months later, some of Villa's guerrillas raided the border town of Columbus, New Mexico, and killed a number of Americans. Although there was no direct evidence that Villa had had a hand in either action, it was generally agreed that he was to blame.

Wilson immediately sent 5000 American troops under General John J. "Black Jack" Pershing across the border with orders to capture Villa "dead or alive." For eleven months, the Americans pursued the elusive guerrilla, but without success. In the meantime, the Mexicans got angrier and angrier over the American invasion of their territory. In June 1916 there was even an armed clash between the Americans and Carranza's army. Finally, in February 1917, Wilson withdrew Pershing's soldiers, and relations between the two nations became normal once again.

Section 4 Review

COMPREHENSION Developing Vocabulary

1. Explain these terms: spheres of influence, extraterritoriality, Dollar Diplomacy, indemnity.

COMPREHENSION Mastering Facts

1. How did Secretary of State Hay try to keep China from being carved up even more by the European powers?
2. What was the cause of the Boxer Rebellion?
3. How was the U.S. government persuaded to choose Panama, rather than Nicaragua, as the site of a canal?
4. Why did U.S. policy over Panama damage its relations with Latin America?
5. What new foreign policy did President Wilson try to establish?

CHAPTER 25   Review

Chapter Summary

America's search for empire was related to its need for new markets because of its increased productivity. Congress ordered the building of a modern navy, and by 1898 the United States had the third largest fleet in the world. Then a revolt in Cuba gave yellow journalists an opportunity to demand war with Spain. When the U.S.S. Maine *exploded in Havana Harbor, American troops were sent to Cuba and the United States fleet steamed to the Philippines. After the Spanish-American War, the United States had an empire that included Puerto Rico, Guam, and the Philippines. Soon Hawaii also became an American possession. As a world power, the nation then exerted its influence in the Far East and Central America, and began building the Panama Canal.*

Questions for Critical Thinking

COMPREHENSION   Summarizing Main Ideas

1. Give three reasons why more and more Americans supported colonial expansion during the late 1800s.
2. What effect did each of the following have on the outbreak of the Spanish-American War: (a) Mahan's book on seapower; (b) American business investments in Cuba; (c) the circulation war between Pulitzer and Hearst; (d) the Weyler reconcentration policy; (e) the de Lôme letter; (f) the destruction of the U.S.S. *Maine?*
3. What advantages and disadvantages did the United States have in the war with Spain?
4. What improvements did the United States bring about in Cuba? Why did many Cubans object to American influence on the island?

COMPREHENSION   Interpreting Events

1. How was American expansion during the 1890s different from that which occurred in the 1840s and 1850s?
2. If you had been a U.S. Senator in 1898, would you have voted to annex the Philippines? Why or why not?

3. Why did a revolution break out in Hawaii in 1893? Why did President Cleveland refuse to recognize the government of the Republic of Hawaii? Why did Congress agree to annex Hawaii in 1898?
4. Why did President Theodore Roosevelt receive the Nobel Peace Prize in 1906?
5. How would you justify Roosevelt's actions regarding the Panama Canal? What criticisms would you make?
6. Would you have supported the sending of the Pershing expedition into Mexico in 1916? Why or why not? Can you think of any other way in which President Woodrow Wilson might have handled the situation? Explain your answer.

APPLICATION   Using Skills To Evaluate Sources

For each of the following events, explain the point of view of the individuals listed below each event.

1. U.S. annexation of the Philippines
   a. Admiral Alfred Thayer Mahan
   b. The governor of a southern state
   c. Emilio Aguinaldo
   d. A black newspaper editor
   e. An American factory worker
2. The Boxer Rebellion
   a. Secretary of State John Hay
   b. The prime minister of Great Britain
   c. A Chinese nationalist
   d. A Japanese businessman
   e. A Christian missionary in China

EVALUATION   Forming Generalizations

1. Report on the arguments presented by Puerto Ricans who favor the island's (a) remaining a commonwealth, (b) becoming a state, and (c) becoming an independent nation. Which status do you support?
2. Compare the relations between the United States and China today with those existing in the early 1900s.
3. What is the current status of the Panama Canal Zone?

Foreign Policy

After suffering a paralyzing stroke, President Woodrow Wilson was visited at the White House by Senator Albert Fall of New Mexico. The Republican Senator had ardently opposed Wilson's proposal that the United States join the League of Nations. Standing over the President's bed, Fall told the Chief Executive: "Well, Mr. President, we have all been praying for you." The ailing Wilson had not lost his sense of humor. "Which way, Senator, which way?" he replied.

Though Wilson was able to make light of it, he had touched a sensitive nerve with respect to American foreign policy. Specifically, his joke referred to the bitter opposition of the Senate to the Treaty of Versailles, which required United States membership in the League of Nations. But his comment had a wider application that went beyond this particular issue to encompass the whole problem of decision-making in foreign affairs. From the start of our nation, the struggle between Congress and the chief executive over foreign policy has been a continuing theme. These two branches of government have traditionally competed for control of foreign policy.

A Case of Shared Powers.
The Constitution has provided for shared responsibilities in the realm of foreign affairs. No one questions that the president, with the assistance of State Department officials and other advisers, has the right to conduct foreign policy. That tradition was established by our first president. At the same time, Congress has the power to appropriate funds for foreign aid, to regulate commerce with foreign nations, to raise and support the armed forces, and, in the case of the Senate, to ratify or reject treaties made by the president. In addition, only Congress can declare war.

Such a division of powers is bound to make for conflicts. In 1846, for example, many Whigs opposed "Mr. Polk's War" with Mexico. Likewise, during President Reagan's tenure in office, prominent members of Congress not only questioned his policies toward the nations of Central America, but also refused to give him all the funds for the military support he wanted to send there. Thus, Wilson's difficulty was but one instance in an ongoing congressional-executive struggle that still continues.

Cooperation Among Allies.
Foreign policy matters have also been a matter of contention between the United States and its allies. The problem was first illustrated in 1900 when Secretary of State John Hay tried to get other nations to practice an Open Door Policy in China. Most nations said "No" to Hay's proposal. Similarly, President Reagan met opposition when he tried to persuade allies to adopt a get-tough policy with the Soviet Union during the early 1980s. Most European allies refused to impose the economic sanctions against the Soviet Union that Reagan wanted.

Diplomacy: Secret or Open?
In addition to conflicts over the nature and direction of foreign policy, the problem of secrecy in diplomatic negotiations remains a subject for debate. To what extent must the conduct of foreign policy be kept secret from the public? President Wilson thought that diplomacy should be conducted in the open. Many experts, however, consider this idea to be unrealistic.

Former Secretary of State Henry Kissinger argued that open diplomacy hindered progress in achieving the compromises necessary for nations to reach agreement. While he was secretary of state, many of the negotiations to end our participation in the Vietnam War were held in secret.

A related consideration concerns the role of the public and the press in influencing foreign policy. American public opinion has played an important role in many foreign policy decisions. For example, public opinion did much to cause the Spanish-American War, and to end the Vietnam War. Just how much should the public participate in foreign policy decisions? When is national security more important than the public's right to know certain information?

Foreign Policy Goals.

Finally, there remains the problem of properly defining the goals of American foreign policy. Although the general purpose of American foreign policy is the advancement of United States interests, it is not always clear exactly what those interests are. Do they include the expansion of national territory? the protection of American businesses abroad? an increase in military might? What role should our nation's traditional ideals play in the conduct of foreign relations?

Perhaps the greatest difficulty of all comes in the need to reconcile conflicts between competing American interests. Our relations with Central American nations offer a good example of that difficulty. Under President William Howard Taft, for instance, United States Marines were sent to Nicaragua in 1911. At first these troops bolstered a pro-American government in order to protect the investments of American financiers. In 1912, however, the president sent more marines, this time to crush an uprising against the unpopular puppet government. So anti-American did the people of

Leaders of the executive and legislative branches discuss our foreign policy for the Caribbean island of Grenada in October, 1983.

Nicaragua become that some United States forces remained in that nation until 1933. Was stability in the Caribbean really at stake—or did the pursuit of "Dollar Diplomacy" override simple American notions of respect and fair play?

Because of the very nature of our democratic system, American foreign policy sometimes appears hesitant and undecided. Disagreements over foreign policy led to the formation of the first political parties, and foreign policy decisions remain extremely political today. Public opinion does count—especially when Americans elect a new leader every four years. Thus, every four years our foreign policy takes a new direction.

One important future goal could be the formation of a broad foreign policy (agreed upon by Democrats and Republicans) that clearly outlines America's worldwide goals. This could provide much needed stability and direction for both the nation and the world.

Understanding Government

1. Which branches of government are responsible for conducting our nation's foreign policy? Why does conflict often occur?

2. In your opinion, should the public play a major role in foreign policy decisions? Explain.

3. What qualities should a good diplomat possess?

4. Which do you think are the most important foreign policy issues facing the United States right now? Be specific with your answer.

CHAPTER 26

The Progressive Era

1900–1916

Linking Past to Present

The first two decades of the 1900s resembled the Jacksonian Era in many ways. A concern for the average citizen was in the air. People became interested in the reform of government and society. Although they did not form a single group, they are generally known as Progressives, and the period is commonly called the Progressive Era.

Progressives realized that large corporations were necessary and in many cases desirable. They had, after all, helped create the material wealth that made America the wonder of the world. The problem lay in how to encourage the development of business and the creation of wealth and, at the same time, protect society from the excesses that characterized some large corporations.

Three successive presidents—Theodore Roosevelt, William Howard Taft, and Woodrow Wilson—were leaders in this Progressive movement. Roosevelt called his politics the "Square Deal." Wilson called his the "New Freedom." But all three men were determined to use the power of government to curb what they considered the excesses of big business.

1 THE PROGRESSIVE MOVEMENT BEGINS

VOCABULARY   *social gospel   muckrakers   direct primary*

The immediate stimulus to the Progressive movement came from three main sources: religion, the press, and a number of radical political groups.

Social Christianity

A basic strand in the reform movement was religion. Baptist minister Walter Rauschenbusch was an early exponent of what was called the "social gospel." He put it this way: "It is true that any regeneration (reform) of society can come only through the act of God and the presence of Christ, but God is now acting, and Christ is now here." In other words, if the church were to save souls, it should "save society first."

After the Civil War, several religious associations had been transplanted to the United States from Great Britain. They included the Young Men's Christian Association (YMCA), the Young Women's Christian Association (YWCA), and the

Meetings like this one of a Granger group in Illinois reflected the growing public interest in political action and social reform that was to culminate in the Progressive movement.

This engraving shows health officials in New York City chasing dealers in illegal meat. Abuses in the meat industry were among the targets of muckraking journalists.

Salvation Army. All three concentrated their efforts on helping newcomers adjust to life in the big cities. They encouraged the establishment of settlement houses, investigated slum conditions, and provided food and clothing to people in need.

Gradually, many religious leaders and organizations began to shift their efforts from private charity to public reform. In 1908, twenty-seven Protestant churches formed the Federal Council of the Churches of Christ in America. The council called for legislation on several issues, including the abolition of child labor and the sweating system, one day of rest in seven, a living wage in every industry, and safety rules in factories and shops.

The Muckrakers

A second strand in the reform movement came from a group of journalists known as *muckrakers*. They were given the name by Theodore Roosevelt. He compared them to a character in John Bunyan's novel *Pilgrim's Progress* who is so busy raking the muck or dirt on the floor that he does not see the good things that are above his head. Roosevelt felt the muckrakers were making people discontented by pointing out what was wrong with

society. The muckrakers felt that unless people got angry about social wrongs, they would not fight for change.

Actually, journalists had been writing muckraking articles for years. What made the difference in the early 1900s was the rise of mass-circulation magazines. These appealed to a nationwide audience through their romantic fiction, their advertisements for new consumer products, and their low price of ten cents. Chief among them was *McClure's*, founded by Irish immigrant Samuel Sidney McClure. *McClure's* and other magazines, such as *Hampton's*, *Cosmopolitan*, the *American*, *The Ladies' Home Journal*, and *Everybody's*, not only published muckraking articles. They also paid the journalists while they did their research, and reinforced the articles with vivid illustrations. Readers reveled in one sensational disclosure after another.

The exposés covered many topics. Lincoln Steffens wrote about the links between big business and crooked politicians in "The Shame of the Cities." Ida M. Tarbell, in her "History of the Standard Oil Company," described that firm's cutthroat methods of eliminating competition. Ray Stannard Baker raked over the railroads and their stock swindles. Edward Bok went after the manufacturers of patent medicines. William Hard explained the relationship between "Making Steel and Killing Men." Edwin Markham attacked child labor in southern cotton mills. Thomas W. Lawson revealed in "Frenzied Finance" how financial speculators deceived the public. Burton J. Hendrick told how "The Gould Fortune" was really made.

And then there was Upton Sinclair. In 1906 his novel *The Jungle* appeared. It described in graphic detail the lives of stockyard workers and the operations of the meat-packing industry. Here is Sinclair's account of how the packers handled meat.

66 There would be meat that had tumbled out on the floor, in the dirt and sawdust, where the workers had trampled and spit uncounted billions of consumption (tuberculosis) germs. There would be meat stored in great piles in rooms; and the water from leaky roofs would drip over it, and thousands of rats would race about on it. . . . These rats were nuisances, and the packers would put poisoned bread out for them, they would die, and then rats, 99 bread, and meat would go into the hoppers together.

Socialist Critics

In addition to being a muckraker, Sinclair was an on-and-off member of the Socialist party. The party had been organized in 1901 by, among others, labor leader Eugene V. Debs. Debs had become a socialist while sitting in jail after the Pullman strike. Later, he was the Socialist party's presidential candidate in several elections, receiving almost a million votes in 1912 and again in 1920. Commenting on the relationship between big business, government, and the people, Debs said:

66 As long as a relatively few men own the railroads, the telegraph, the telephone, own the oilfields and the gasfields and the steel mills and the sugar refineries and the leather tanneries—own, in short, the sources and means of life—they will corrupt our politics, they will enslave the working class, they will impoverish and debase society, they will do all things that are needful to perpetuate their power as the economic masters and the political rulers of the people.

Competition was natural enough at one time, but do you think you are competing today? Many of you think you are competing. Against whom? Against Rockefeller? About as I would if I had a wheelbarrow and competed with the Santa Fe (railroad) from here to Kansas City. 99

The Progressives did not agree with Debs's proposed solution of socialism. They wanted to keep the capitalist system. But there was no denying that many of Debs's criticisms were true. Big business *was* ruthless. It *did* enjoy special privileges from government. Women and children *did* have difficulty protecting themselves in the urban industrial marketplace. Wages and working conditions in most mines, shops, and factories *were* shocking.

So the Progressives tried to steal socialism's thunder without adopting socialism. They concentrated on improving capitalism by making government more responsive to social problems.

Progressivism at the Local Level

The nation's large cities contained the most obvious problems of the new industrial age. Accordingly, the Progressives began by trying to improve municipal government. This took two forms: 1. "throwing the rascals out," and 2. making institutional changes.

Reform Mayors. The best examples of reform city mayors were Hazen Pingree of Detroit, Thomas L. Johnson of Cleveland, and Samuel M. "Golden Rule" Jones of Toledo.

Pingree, who served from 1889 to 1896, concentrated on economic issues. He built schools, parks, and a municipal lighting plant. He lowered streetcar and gas rates. And he set up a system of work relief for unemployed persons.

Johnson governed from 1901 to 1909. He appointed competent, honest men to city jobs. He reassessed property values for tax purposes, which had not been done for more than thirty years. He believed people should take an active part in government. So he held meetings in a large circus tent and invited citizens to ask officials any questions they wished about the way the city was being run. Johnson did so well in office that Cleveland gained the reputation of being the best-governed city in the United States. Even muckraker Lincoln Steffens was impressed.

Jones, who held office from 1899 to 1904, believed in applying the teachings of Christ to government. The story is told that one evening a tramp came up to him and asked for the price of a night's lodging. Not having any coins, Jones gave the tramp a five-dollar bill and asked him to bring back the change. When the tramp returned, Jones put the money in his pocket without counting it.

"Ain't you goin' to count it?" asked the tramp. "Did you count it?" asked Jones. Yes he had, and it was all there. "Well, then, there's no need for me to count it, is there?" And Jones gave the tramp a half-dollar.

In addition, there were eighteen Socialist mayors, including Emil Seidel and Daniel W. Hoan of Milwaukee. In general, they practiced "gas and water socialism." That is, they threw out the crooked private owners of gasworks, waterworks, and transit lines, substituting municipal ownership of utilities.

New Forms of Government. In 1900 a hurricane and tidal wave swept out of the Gulf of Mexico and almost demolished Galveston, Texas. The job of relief and rebuilding was a huge one, and the politicians on the city council botched it. They were so incompetent, in fact, that the Texas legislature appointed a five-member commission of experts to take over. Each expert was put in charge of a different city department. The commission soon got Galveston back on its feet, and the city decided to adopt the commission form of government. By 1914 some 400 cities had followed Galveston's example.

In 1913 another natural disaster—this time a flood in Dayton, Ohio—led to the widespread adoption of the city-manager form of government. This system was already being used in Staunton, Virginia. People elected a nonpartisan board of commissioners to make laws. In turn, the board appointed a manager, usually someone with training and experience in public administration, to run the city's departments. By 1923 about 300 cities were being governed by managers.

In both instances, the Progressives were transferring sound management principles from business to public life. If specialists improved business, they believed, specialists would improve government as well.

Progressivism at the State Level

From reforms at the local level, the Progressives moved on to reforms at the state level. In a way, they had to. Cities are created by state legislatures. So municipal reforms could only be maintained if state governments were also reformed.

Reform Governors. The outstanding reform governor of the period was Robert M. "Fighting Bob" La Follette of Wisconsin. First elected in

1900, he served three terms before entering the United States Senate in 1906. He remained in the Senate until his death in 1925.

La Follette's goal, as he explained it, "was not to *smash* corporations, but to drive them out of politics, and then to treat them exactly the same as other people are treated." A major target was the railroad industry. He taxed railroad property at the same rate as other business property. He set up a railroad commission to regulate rates, and he forbade railroads from issuing free passes to state officials, as they had been doing. Some of his reforms, interestingly enough, helped the industry as well as the public. Lower rates, for example, created enough new traffic to increase the railroads' income.

Other governors who attacked "the interests" included Charles B. Aycock of North Carolina, Albert B. Cummins of Iowa, John A. Johnson of Minnesota, and Joseph W. Folk of Missouri. "Holy Hiram" Johnson of California smashed the control of the Southern Pacific Railroad over the

The dynamic leader of the Progressive movement, Robert M. La Follette, campaigns in Wisconsin, where he achieved many reforms as governor.

state legislature. Charles Evans Hughes became governor of New York after exposing corrupt practices in the insurance business.

"The Oregon System" and Other Reforms.

In some cases, state reforms came about through the efforts of ordinary citizens rather than governors. The most effective such individual was probably William S. U'Ren (you *wren*) of Oregon. As a result of his leadership, Oregon adopted the secret ballot, the initiative, the referendum, and the recall. By 1920 another twenty states had adopted at least one of these techniques.

Even more significant was the adoption of the *direct primary*. Instead of being chosen by political machines, candidates for public office were chosen through a special popular election. The direct primary was first adopted by Wisconsin in 1903. By 1916 every state except three had done the same.

Adopting the direct primary led to the Seventeenth Amendment to the Constitution. Before 1913 United States senators were chosen by state legislatures. As a result, most senators were either party bosses or directors of their state's leading corporations. Progressives agreed that the level of intelligence in the Senate was high. But they believed that it represented special business interests rather than the public.

The Senate at first refused to go along with the idea of popular election. Gradually, however, more and more states began choosing senators by means of the direct primary. They would vote on candidates and then expect the state legislature to select the primary winner as senator. So in 1912 the Senate approved the Seventeenth Amendment. It became a part of the Constitution in 1913.

Social Legislation.

The Progressives pushed for social reforms as well as political ones. In this activity the leaders were mostly women. Some were members of the National Child Labor Committee; others belonged to the National Consumers' League. Most of them agreed that a woman's place was in the home but that her interests should also include public affairs. Women's groups did research on social problems and hired lobbyists to present their views in state capitals. They succeeded in bringing about a number of changes.

By 1914 almost every state had passed a law either prohibiting the employment of children under fourteen or requiring them to attend school until age fourteen. Some states also prohibited minors from working at night or in certain dangerous occupations. Unfortunately, most of these laws did not cover farmwork or domestic service. Also, the opposition of southern textile mill owners kept them from being enforced in some areas.

In 1908 the Supreme Court, in the case of *Muller* v. *Oregon,* reversed itself on the issue of whether or not a state could limit the working hours of women. In the past, the Court had held that such limits interfered with freedom of contract. But this time, lawyer Louis D. Brandeis, assisted by Josephine Goldmark and Florence Kelley, submitted a 112-page brief. Instead of limiting himself to legal arguments, Brandeis (who later became the first Jewish justice on the Supreme Court) presented statistics on disease and other sociological data to prove that long hours were harmful to women's health. He also argued that freedom of contract was unrealistic. In theory, freedom of contract meant that women were as free as corporations to sign or not to sign a contract. But in reality, Brandeis argued, a woman was much more economically insecure than a giant corporation. The "Brandeis Brief" convinced the Court, which said that Oregon's law limiting women to a ten-hour day was constitutional. In 1917 a similar brief in *Bunting* v. *Oregon* persuaded the Court to uphold a ten-hour law for men. As a result of these two decisions, many states passed laws limiting working hours.

A third area in which Progressive reforms succeeded was workers' compensation. Every year about 35,000 workers were killed on the job and another 700,000 injured. Beginning with Maryland in 1902, one state after another passed legislation requiring employers in dangerous occupations to pay benefits to injured employees.

Section 1 Review

COMPREHENSION   Developing Vocabulary

1. Explain these terms: direct primary, social gospel, regeneration.

COMPREHENSION   Mastering Facts

1. Why were certain writers called "muckrakers"?
2. How did the Progressives differ from the Socialists?
3. What two new forms of city government were adopted during the Progressive period?
4. What social reforms did Progressives push for?

2 ROOSEVELT BECOMES A PROGRESSIVE LEADER

VOCABULARY *square deal   closed shop*

It was at the national level that the Progressive movement really made its mark. And if you were to ask which president personified Progressivism, most historians would answer: Theodore Roosevelt.

A Rough Rider in the White House

Theodore Roosevelt was born in 1858 into an old Dutch merchant and banking family in New York State. Asthmatic and near-sighted as a child, he overcame his physical weaknesses by hard exercises and sheer force of will. After graduating from Harvard, he became a cattle rancher in the Dakotas. He fell in love with the out-of-doors and developed a deep and lifelong interest in the conservation of natural resources. He wrote two historical works: one on the War of 1812, the other on the winning of the West. He entered politics and moved from assemblyman and police commissioner in New York City to civil service commissioner and assistant secretary of the navy in Washington, D.C.

Roosevelt's spectacular charge up Kettle Hill during the Spanish-American War brought him to the attention of Senator Thomas C. Platt, the Republican boss of New York State. Platt needed a Republican governor, to help him in his business

Theodore Roosevelt, here on safari, pursued politics and leisure activities with the same enthusiasm.

affairs. He had misgivings about Roosevelt's interest in Progressive legislation, but he decided to run the former Rough Rider for office anyway.

No sooner was Roosevelt elected, however, than he began attacking the ties between business and government. He refused to appoint Platt's choice for state insurance commissioner. He also forced through a law requiring streetcar companies to pay taxes on the value of their franchises. Platt was furious. If such actions continued, New York's Republican machine would lose its financial support from big business. It was unthinkable to renominate Roosevelt for the governorship. The only solution was to nominate him for vice-president on the national ticket headed by William McKinley. The vice-presidency was considered a political graveyard.

Mark Hanna objected. Didn't Platt realize that "that damned cowboy" would be only one heartbeat away from the White House? But Platt's scheme worked, and "Mack and Teddy" were swept into office in 1900. Then, in September 1901, Hanna's worst fears came true. McKinley was shot by an assassin and Theodore Roosevelt became president of the United States.

Achievements of the Square Deal

The new president represented a great change from his predecessor. For one thing, he simply crackled with energy. While in the White House, he boxed with professionals, one of whom blinded him in the left eye. He played strenuous tennis. He galloped a hundred miles on horseback in one day (using several horses) to prove that it could be done. And he energetically shot bears while on what he called a "restful" vacation. His red-blooded advice to boys was, "Don't flinch, don't foul, and hit the line hard."

In politics, as in sports, Roosevelt believed in action. The federal government was responsible for the national welfare. He believed it should step in whenever the states proved incapable of handling problems. The president represented all the people and thus should play a major role in shaping legislative policy. If big business was squeezing farmers, workers, and small business people, then he, Roosevelt, would see to it that they received a "square deal." "I believe in a strong executive," he said, and proceeded to put his beliefs into practice.

Increasing Federal Power.

There was another aspect to Roosevelt's political behavior. It was based on a knowledge of American history and a vision of national unity. Americans had filled out a continent and built an industrial empire. But they had not, in Roosevelt's opinion, developed the political tools for managing what they had created. "A simple and poor society can exist as a democracy on the basis of sheer individualism. But a rich and complex society cannot so exist." In other words, in the 1900s, according to Roosevelt, it was necessary for the federal government to manage certain areas of society so the nation could develop in an orderly manner.

Mediating a Coal Strike.

One example of Roosevelt's approach was his handling of a coal strike in 1902. Coal miners in Pennsylvania struck for higher wages, an eight-hour day, and the right to organize a union. The mine operators refused to bargain. They even refused to meet with the labor leaders at the White House. George Baer, a mine owner and president of the Reading Railroad, said it was his "religious duty" to defeat the strikers. "The rights and interests of the laboring men will be protected and cared for—not by labor agitators, but by Christian men to whom God in his infinite wisdom had given control of the property interests of the country."

Roosevelt threatened to seize the mines and have the army run them. Finally, he decided to appoint a commission to make recommendations for settling the strike.

The mine operators finally agreed to arbitration. The settlement was a compromise. The workers received a 10 percent pay hike and a nine-hour day. But they did not obtain a *closed shop*, that is, an agreement under which operators will not hire anyone who does not belong to the union. In addition, the workers agreed not to strike again for three years.

More important than the actual settlement, however, was the establishment of a new principle. In the past, presidents had sent in federal troops only to protect private property or to keep such services as the United States mail going. Now, Roosevelt was saying that the federal government could intervene in a strike if the public welfare was involved. And since much of the nation used Pennsylvania coal for heating, there was no question but that the welfare of the public was involved. In some northern cities, riots even broke out as people found themselves facing winter with empty coal bins. In addition, Roosevelt was emphasizing the Progressive belief that disputes should be settled in an orderly way with the help of experts.

Regulating Trusts.

In the public mind, trusts were bad and should be smashed. Roosevelt, however, believed that how a trust acted was more significant than how big it was. He wanted to curb trusts if their actions become oppressive to the public, but he did not want to destroy large corporations.

At first, Roosevelt tried to persuade Congress to pass a law defining "good" and "bad" business practices. Congress, however, refused. So the president concentrated his efforts on filing suits under the Sherman Antitrust Act of 1890. He attacked the Northern Securities Company, which had established a monopoly over western railroads. He sued the beef trust, the oil trust, the steel trust, the sugar trust, and the tobacco trust. All in all, his administration filed forty-four antitrust suits. But although the government won a number of cases and broke up a number of trusts, it did not stop the merger movement in business.

Regulating Transportation.

Roosevelt was more successful in railroad regulation. Under his urging, Congress put some teeth in the Interstate Commerce Act of 1887.

The Elkins Act of 1903 made it illegal for railroad officials and shippers to either give or receive rebates. It also said that once a railroad had set rates, it could not change them without notifying the public.

The Hepburn Act of 1906 went several steps further. It gave the Interstate Commerce Commission power to set maximum railroad rates, subject to court approval, whenever shippers complained. Within two years, the commission received more than 9000 complaints and lowered a great many rates. The Hepburn Act also gave the ICC power to regulate express companies, sleeping-car companies, oil pipelines, railroad terminals, interstate ferries, and bridges. In addition, the railroads were told to use uniform methods of accounting and to stop giving out free passes.

Chemist Harvey W. Wiley (at table) worked to secure a law regulating the use of preservatives in food.

Protecting Health. President Roosevelt—like millions of Americans who stopped eating canned meat—was horrified when he read *The Jungle.* He promptly appointed a commission to investigate Upton Sinclair's charges. The commission reported that the charges were true. So in 1906 Congress passed the first federal Meat Inspection Act.

That same year, Congress passed a Pure Food and Drugs Act. Credit for this legislation belonged mostly to Dr. Harvey Washington Wiley, chief chemist in the U.S. Department of Agriculture. For years, Wiley had lectured around the country criticizing the harmful preservatives that were added to food. There was coal-tar dye and borax in sausage, formaldehyde in canned pork and beans, and so on. Wiley wanted such information printed on the labels of cans and other food packages. The 1906 act placed some restrictions on the manufacturers of prepared foods and patent medicines. And an amendment in 1911 prohibited the use of misleading labels. As one historian commented, "American stomachs and insides generally have been better than they would have been had Wiley not lived and labored."

Conserving Natural Resources. Before the Square Deal, the federal government had paid almost no attention to the nation's natural resources. The Forest Bureau had been established in 1887. Presidents Harrison, Cleveland, and McKinley had withdrawn several million acres of timberlands from public sale and put them into a national forest reserve. But other than this, nothing had been done.

This was not surprising. From the time the first Europeans landed in the New World, the resources of the continent seemed limitless. Forests stretched as far as the eye could see. Clear rivers tumbled down to the sea. No matter how far west people moved, there was always more land beyond the horizon.

In fact, Americans regarded the environment as something to be exploited rather than conserved. Pioneer farmers leveled forests by cutting and burning. They plowed up the prairies. Cattle raisers overgrazed the Great Plains. Coal companies mined only ore that was easily reached. Lumber companies ignored the effect of their logging operations on flood control and did not bother replanting what they cut down. Cities dumped untreated sewage and industrial wastes into rivers, creating health hazards and destroying fish.

By the end of the 1800s, however, people began to realize that the nation's natural resources were not limitless after all. Millions of acres of farmland were either unusable or required large amounts of fertilizer to be productive. Most of the nation's forests had disappeared. There were tens of thousands of abandoned mines.

When Roosevelt became president, he called the forest and water problems "perhaps the most vital internal problems of the United States." And he proceeded to attack them with his usual gusto. He withdrew about 150 million acres of forestland from public sale. (This was an area larger than Germany.) He withdrew 1.5 million acres of land containing some 2500 water-power sites. And he withdrew another 85 million acres of land, which he asked the United States Geological Survey to explore for mineral and water resources.

Roosevelt established fifty-three wildlife sanctuaries and sixteen national parks and monuments where people might enjoy the wonders of nature. He put Gifford Pinchot, a professional conservationist, in charge of supervising national forests. He also pushed for passage of the Newlands Reclamation Act. Under it, money from the sale of public lands in the West was set aside to build irrigation projects which would enable farmers to cultivate the desert. Both the Roosevelt Dam in Arizona and the Shoshone Dam in Wyoming were built under this act.

In 1908 Roosevelt called a White House conservation conference. As a result, forty-one states set up conservation agencies. A national commission began a study to find out what the nation's resources were. Perhaps most important, people began to realize how important conservation was.

Section 2 Review

COMPREHENSION   Developing Vocabulary

1. Explain these terms: closed shop, square deal.

COMPREHENSION   Mastering Facts

1. How did Governor Roosevelt of New York anger that state's Republican machine?
2. What was Roosevelt's view on the role of the federal government?
3. How did Roosevelt differ from his predecessors in using federal troops in case of strikes?

3   PROGRESSIVISM CONTINUES UNDER TAFT AND WILSON

VOCABULARY   *seniority   Grand Old Party   Bull Moose party*

In 1904 Theodore Roosevelt ran for president in his own right. He swamped his Democratic opponent, a conservative judge named Alton B. Parker. Delighted with his victory, Roosevelt impulsively promised not to "be a candidate for or accept another nomination." He would be serving almost eight years. And even though he was eligible to run for another term, he did not think he should.

So in 1908 Roosevelt looked around for a man who would carry out "my policies." His choice was William Howard "Smiling Bill" Taft. The Democrats nominated William Jennings Bryan for the third time. Instead of "free silver," Bryan campaigned on the slogan of "Let the people rule." He called for a federal income tax, a lower tariff, and new antitrust laws. But he polled even fewer votes than he had in 1896. As the Republicans said, "Vote for Taft This Time—You Can Vote for Bryan Any Time." And the voters did exactly that.

Taft in the White House

Taft's background and personality were excellent for a Supreme Court justice, which he later became. But they were not really suited for a president, especially a president following such a hard act as Roosevelt's. Taft was cautious and legalistic, a "horse-drawn carriage" in comparison with Roosevelt's "automobile." He believed in compromise rather than leadership. He hesitated to bring problems to public attention or to organize opinion around an issue. He did not even know how to handle members of his own party. As one congressman remarked, Taft was "a well-meaning man who was born with two left feet."

Stumbling over a Tariff.   Taft soon found himself in hot water on a number of issues. The first was the tariff. Taft had run on a platform of lowering tariffs. And the House did in fact pass the Payne Bill, which lowered rates on many manufactured goods. But when the bill reached the Senate, conservative Republicans, led by Senator Nelson

President William Howard Taft, shown here with his family, was not so strong a leader as Roosevelt. He lost the support of many in his own party.

W. Aldrich of Rhode Island, restored most of the cuts. Under pressure from big business, they boosted other rates as well. Taft signed the Payne-Aldrich Tariff Act amid cries that he had betrayed the Progressive movement.

Taft then went out on the stump to defend the new tariff. In Winona, Minnesota, before a hostile audience of grain growers, he asserted that the new law was "the best [tariff] bill the Republican party ever passed." Farmers everywhere groaned because the tariff would make the manufactured articles they needed more expensive. Later, Taft made matters even worse by saying that he had dictated the speech hurriedly between two railroad stations and had not bothered to reread it for meaning.

Carelessness over Resources. The next area in which Taft ran into difficulty was conservation. He removed Roosevelt's secretary of the interior and appointed his own man, Richard A. Ballinger. Ballinger returned to public sale many water-power sites plus extensive coal and timber lands that Roosevelt had previously withdrawn. When Pinchot, Roosevelt's appointee as head of the forestry service, protested, Taft restored some of the lands to the forest reserve. But he fired Pinchot.

Supporting Unpopular Officials. Still another of Taft's mistakes was his support of Joseph "Uncle Joe" Cannon, speaker of the House of Representatives. Cannon was a heavy-swearing, cigar-chomping man who referred to himself as a "hard-boiled hayseed." At that time, the speaker had the power to choose the members of all House committees. Cannon, who hated "this babble for reform," appointed only conservatives. He ignored congressmen whose *seniority,* or length of service, entitled them to committee posts. In addition, Cannon appointed himself head of the Committee on Rules, which decided what bills Congress would or would not consider. He rarely decided on progressive bills. He was a virtual dictator of the House.

Blocked in their efforts to pass Progressive legislation, a group of reform-minded Republicans decided that the only thing to do was to strip Cannon of his power. In March 1910, with the help of the Democrats, they succeeded. One of them, Representative George W. Norris of Nebraska, introduced a resolution calling for the entire House to elect the Committee on Rules. Furthermore, the speaker was not even to be *on* the Rules Committee. Cannon fought desperately. But after

thirty-six hours of violent debate, the new rules were adopted. As *The Wall Street Journal* observed, "The clock has struck for Uncle Joe. He has stood between the people and too many things that they wanted and ought to have." The next Congress changed the rules even further, to have the House elect *all* committees, not just the Rules Committee.

Taft did not like Cannon, but he felt he should support the speaker against the reformist Republicans. As a result, people condemned Taft for Cannon's policies. When Cannon lost his power, Taft lost his prestige.

Losing Power. By 1910 the *Grand Old Party,* as the Republican party was known, was splitting at the seams, with the Progressives on one side and the "old guard" on the other. People were unhappy about the rising cost of living, which they blamed on the Payne-Aldrich Tariff. They were upset with Taft's stand on conservation. Even the fact that Taft extended civil service, established an eight-hour day for government employees, and filed ninety anti-trust suits (more than twice the number Roosevelt had) did not soften Progressive criticism. As a result, the Republicans lost the 1910 election. For the first time in sixteen years, Democrats controlled the House of Representatives.

The Bull Moose Party

Following Taft's election, Roosevelt had gone to Africa to shoot lions and other big game. In 1910 he came home to a hero's welcome. People sang such songs as "When Rough and Ready Teddy Dashes Home," "Ho, Ho! For Teddy!" and "Mr. Roosevelt Our Country Calls for You." Roosevelt responded by delivering a speech at Osawatomie, Kansas (where John Brown had spoken out against slavery). "Property shall be the servant and not the master." And he went on to say that the country needed a "new nationalism" under which the federal government would use its power for "the welfare of the people."

Roosevelt—Again! Taft felt that Roosevelt was attacking him unfairly. Roosevelt felt that Taft had fallen down on the job. "Taft means well; but he means well feebly." By 1911 Roosevelt was regretting his pledge of no third term. And in February 1912 he decided after all to throw his hat into the presidential ring. As he explained, just because a man says he does not want a third

Presidential Election of 1912

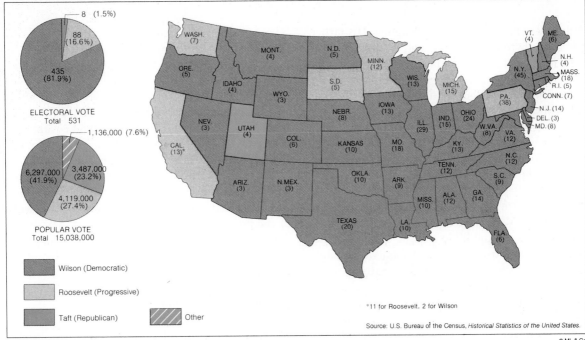

ELECTORAL VOTE
Total 531

8 (1.5%)
88 (16.6%)
435 (81.9%)

POPULAR VOTE
Total 15,038,000

1,136,000 (7.6%)
3,487,000 (23.2%)
6,297,000 (41.9%)
4,119,000 (27.4%)

WASH. (7)
ORE. (5)
MONT. (4)
IDAHO (4)
WYO. (3)
N.D. (5)
MINN. (12)
S.D. (5)
WIS. (13)
MICH. (15)
NEV. (3)
UTAH (4)
COL. (6)
NEBR. (8)
IOWA (13)
ILL. (29)
IND. (15)
OHIO (24)
CAL. (13)*
ARIZ. (3)
N.MEX. (3)
KANSAS (10)
OKLA. (10)
MO. (18)
ARK. (9)
KY. (13)
TENN. (12)
W.VA. (8)
VA. (12)
N.C. (12)
MISS. (10)
ALA. (12)
GA. (14)
S.C. (9)
TEXAS (20)
LA. (10)
FLA. (6)
VT. (4)
ME. (6)
N.H. (4)
MASS. (18)
R.I. (5)
N.Y. (45)
CONN. (7)
PA. (38)
N.J. (14)
DEL. (3)
MD. (8)

Wilson (Democratic)
Roosevelt (Progressive)
Taft (Republican)
Other

*11 for Roosevelt, 2 for Wilson

Source: U.S. Bureau of the Census, *Historical Statistics of the United States*.

© ML & Co.

Map Skills *Who got a majority of the electoral vote? the popular vote? Which states did Taft win? What was Taft's and Roosevelt's combined percentage of the popular vote?*

cup of coffee at breakfast does not mean he is never going to take another cup of coffee.

The Republican Party Splits. An incumbent president, however, has certain advantages. In Chicago in June 1912, Taft's supporters seized control of the Republican convention. They refused to seat delegates who were backing Roosevelt. Then they renominated Taft on the first ballot. Roosevelt's supporters—screaming "Fraud!"—stormed out and held their own convention in Chicago in August. They formed a new third party, the Progressive party. It was commonly called the Bull Moose party after a statement Roosevelt made to Mark Hanna in 1900: "I am as strong as a bull moose and you can use me to the limit." Then, in an atmosphere of near-hysteria, they nominated Roosevelt as their candidate for president. After hearing Roosevelt, William A. White wrote later, "Roosevelt bit me and I went mad."

The Bull Moose platform called for various Progressive reforms, including the direct election of senators and the adoption in all states of the initiative, referendum, and recall. It also advocated woman suffrage, national workers' compensation, an eight-hour day, minimum wages for women, a federal law against child labor, and a federal trade commission to regulate business.

The split in Republican ranks had two main results. In the long run, it changed the nature of the Republican party. Since the Civil War, the GOP had been "the party of new ideas and positive leadership." Now, liberal and Progressive elements had shifted to the Bull Moose party. Few of them ever returned. In the short run, the Republican split provided the Democrats with their first real chance at the presidency since Grover Cleveland. In the 1912 presidential election, they put forward as their candidate a reform governor of New Jersey named Woodrow Wilson.

Section 3 Review

COMPREHENSION Developing Vocabulary

1. Explain these terms: seniority, Grand Old Party, Bull Moose party.

COMPREHENSION Mastering Facts

1. Why did Progressives want to get rid of "Uncle Joe" Cannon?
2. Why did some people believe that Taft had betrayed the Progressive movement?
3. Where did Roosevelt go after Taft's election, and why?
4. Why did the Republican party split?

533

Wilson was born in Staunton, Virginia. His father was a Presbyterian minister, and his mother was the daughter of a Presbyterian minister. Wilson received a strict moral upbringing. After graduation, he became a lawyer but soon shifted into teaching political science at the college level. In 1902 he became president of Princeton University. In 1910, like Roosevelt, he was picked by the state's political boss to run for governor. And again like Roosevelt, once he was elected he declared his independence of the party machine and proceeded to reform the state government.

A critic of Wilson once wrote that he was "born halfway between the Bible and the dictionary and never got away from either." Wilson was a calm, cool, highly logical thinker. He had a strong sense of justice and a conviction that he knew what was right and what was wrong. He was a humanitarian who cared deeply about people as a whole. But he found it difficult to relate to individuals. So he often seemed cold-blooded and an intellectual snob. He believed that social problems could and should

be solved. But he failed to realize that people are often moved by emotion rather than reason.

Wilson, again like Roosevelt, believed in a strong executive. But he favored a different role for the federal government than Roosevelt did. Wilson did not think that trusts should be regulated. He thought they should be broken up. He did not think government should get bigger; he thought business should be made smaller.

When the votes were counted, Wilson was the winner, and the Democrats controlled the House and the Senate. Wilson received only 42 percent of the popular vote, the lowest figure of any president since Abraham Lincoln. However, the combined vote for Wilson, Roosevelt, and Debs, all of whom supported Progressive ideas, came to 75 percent. The nation was obviously in favor of more political and social reforms.

Wilson's campaign theme had been "The New Freedom," and it involved an attack on the "triple wall of privilege": the tariff, high finance, and the trusts.

President Woodrow Wilson delivers his Inaugural Address. In his "New Freedom" program, Wilson pledged to attack privileged groups and to restore opportunity for the individual.

Income Tax Replaces High Tariff

Wilson began by reviving an old tradition. In 1801 Thomas Jefferson had sent his message to Congress to be read by a clerk. Since then, no president had appeared on Capitol Hill. But when the new Congress met in 1913. Wilson, an excellent public speaker, strode onto the rostrum and delivered a stirring appeal for tariff reform. He also appealed to the people through the press. He asked them for help against the "Third House of Congress." This, he said, included the lobbyists who tried to get tariffs for certain industries raised. Wilson's appeal to public opinion was a technique that he had used as governor, and one he was to use many times as president.

The Underwood-Simmons Tariff Act of 1913 marked the first real lowering of the tariff since the Civil War. Overall, tariff rates were reduced from about 41 percent to about 29 percent.

The new tariff changed the entire revenue basis of the federal government. Before 1913, almost all federal income came from tariffs. The lower rates of the Underwood-Simmons Tariff obviously meant a loss of revenue. But the Sixteenth Amendment, which provided for a federal income tax, had just been ratified. Congress added a section to the tariff act levying a 1 percent tax on incomes over $3000 for single persons and $4000 for married couples. A graduated tax ranging from 2 to 6 percent was imposed on incomes over $20,000. At the time, few congressmen realized the possibilities of the income tax. Today, it is the federal government's main source of revenue.

Improving the Banking System

After tackling tariff reform, Wilson turned his attention to financial reform. Both liberals and conservatives agreed that the nation needed some way to move credit out of such financial centers as New York and Boston and make it easily available everywhere. The nation also needed an elastic currency. That is, the amount of money in circulation should change depending on the needs of the economy.

The Federal Reserve System. Wilson's solution was a decentralized private banking system under federal control. Under the Federal Reserve Act of 1913, the nation was divided into twelve regions, or districts. Each district had a Federal Reserve bank, to which all the national banks within the district belonged. State banks within the district could join if they wanted to. Member banks had to subscribe 6 percent of their capital to the Federal Reserve bank in their district. In return, the Federal Reserve bank had the power to issue a new currency, Federal Reserve notes. The member banks could then use the new currency to make loans to their customers. The Federal Reserve System could regulate the amount of notes it issued by raising or lowering the interest it charged to member banks. If it raised the interest—which is known as the rediscount rate—it reduced the amount of money in circulation. If it lowered the rediscount rate, then there was more money available for loans. In addition, Federal Reserve banks could transfer funds to member banks that ran into trouble, thus keeping them from closing.

The Federal Reserve Board. The Federal Reserve System was put under a Federal Reserve Board. This consisted of the secretary of the treasury plus seven other persons appointed by the president. By 1923 about 70 percent of the nation's banking resources belonged to member banks of the Federal Reserve System.

Farm Loan Banks. In 1916 a similar system was set up especially for farmers. Under the Federal Farm Loan Act, twelve regional Farm Loan banks were authorized to lend money to cooperative farm-loan associations. Interest was limited to 6 percent, and profits were distributed to association members.

Bringing Trusts in Line

Two main antitrust measures were passed during Wilson's administration. One was the Federal Trade Commission Act of 1914. The other was the Clayton Act of 1914.

The Federal Trade Act. This act set up a five-member Federal Trade Commission. The commission had power to investigate unfair business practices, such as inaccurate labeling, false patent claims, and the adulteration of products. If the commission found that a corporation was doing something it should not be doing, the commission could tell the corporation to "cease and desist," or stop such practices. Both the commission and the corporation could then turn to the courts. There the commission might have its ruling enforced or the charge against the corporation might be struck down.

The Clayton Act. This legislation was designed to strengthen the Sherman Antitrust Act. It declared certain business practices illegal. For example, a corporation could not acquire the stock of another corporation if that would create a monopoly. A company could not make a purchaser sign a "tying contract," that prevented the purchaser from doing business with a competitor. Interlocking directorates in companies worth more than $1 million were prohibited. If a company violated the law, company officers could be prosecuted.

In addition, the Clayton Act said that labor unions and farm organizations were not subject to antitrust laws. In other words, they had a legal right to exist. Also declared legal were strikes, peaceful picketing, boycotts, and the collection of strike benefits. Injunctions in labor disputes were prohibited unless there was "irreparable (unable to be remedied) injury to property."

The FTC handed down almost 400 cease-and-desist orders during Wilson's administration. Samuel Gompers called the Clayton Act labor's "Magna Carta." But the outbreak of war slowed down the Progressive movement and—as you will read later on—the effect of both acts gradually lessened.

Section 4 Review

COMPREHENSION   Developing Vocabulary
1. Explain these terms: rediscount rate, cease-and-desist order, Federal Reserve System, irreparable, humanitarian, elastic currency, New Freedom.

COMPREHENSION   Mastering Facts
1. What was Woodrow Wilson's background before he became governor of New Jersey?
2. What was Wilson's view on the role of the federal government?
3. Where did the federal government get most of its income after 1913?
4. What were the powers of the Federal Trade Commission?

CHAPTER 26   Review

Chapter Summary

The turn of the century brought the rise of the Progressive Movement. Progressive Americans pressed for social and political reforms, first at the local level and then in state and national government. At the national level, Theodore Roosevelt became the leader of the Progressives. His administration increased federal power, regulated trusts, protected public health, and preserved the nation's natural resources. Progressivism continued during the presidencies of Taft and Wilson. Under Wilson's "New Freedom" administration, the income tax replaced the high tariff, and the Federal Reserve System was created.

Questions for Critical Thinking

COMPREHENSION   Summarizing Main Ideas

1. Which groups were the main supporters of the Progressive movement? Why did each group take the position it did?
2. What contributions did women make to the Progressive movement?
3. Describe three issues over which Taft ran into difficulty. In what other ways might he have handled each issue? Explain.
4. What were the two main reasons for the establishment of the Federal Reserve System?
5. Compare Roosevelt's view on the role of the federal government with Wilson's view. Which view do you favor? Give reasons for your opinion.

COMPREHENSION   Interpreting Events

1. Why did Theodore Roosevelt disapprove of muckrakers? How did muckrakers justify their actions? With whom do you agree? List five abuses that muckrakers uncovered.
2. Why did the Progressives begin by trying to improve municipal government? Why did they move from reforms at the local level to reforms at the state level?
3. Before the Square Deal, why did most Americans regard the environment as something to be exploited rather than conserved? What made people change their attitude?
4. If you had been a voter in 1912, which presidential candidate would you have supported? Give reasons for your choice.
5. Why did Samuel Gompers call the Clayton Act labor's "Magna Carta"?

APPLICATION   Using Skills To Infer Information

For each of the following references in the first section of this chapter, indicate the paragraph's main theme.

1. Paragraph 1 under "New Forms of Government"
   a. Galveston was the first city to adopt the commission form of government.
   b. Galveston's city council was incompetent.
   c. A natural disaster resulted in Galveston changing its form of government.
2. Paragraph 4 under " 'The Oregon System' and Other Reforms"
   a. Senators did not like the idea of being elected by state voters rather than state legislatures.
   b. The direct primary helped change the way in which U.S. senators are chosen.
   c. The Seventeenth Amendment was adopted in 1913.

EVALUATION   Comparing Past to Present

1. Which of the evils that the Progressive movement attacked still exist? What, if anything, are people doing about them?
2. What conservation problems exist in the United States today? What is the attitude of the federal government toward these problems? What, if anything, is your local community doing about the conservation of natural resources? What, if anything, is your state doing? Judging from your answers to these questions, would you say that people are more interested or less interested in conservation today than they were in Roosevelt's day? How might you explain this?

Free Elections

In many nations of the world there are no free elections. In some, dictators seize power and rule for as long as they desire. In others, elections do take place—but with only one candidate listed for each office, the elections can hardly be called free and open.

American citizens are fortunate to participate in the most open election process in the world. "Ballots, not bullets" decide elections in the United States—meaning that there are no armed guards stationed by polling places waiting to make certain that the "right" outcome is achieved. Our free election process is a legacy deeply cherished by Americans.

Sometimes elections in the United States, however, still include irregularities that point to dishonesty. In an era of modern computerized voting procedures, corruption can and does exist. Voting lists can be altered, and eligibility requirements can be skirted. In an extremely close election, such dishonest occurrences can make a difference. Still, the majority of elections in the United States are honestly and openly run.

Colonial Elections. During the colonial period, irregularities of any kind almost never occurred. In eighteenth-century Virginia, for example, the highly public method of conducting elections discouraged fraud. On election day, eligible voters assembled at the county courthouse, often traveling long distances to participate. Inside, behind a long table, sat the sheriff, local justices, the candidates, and several recording clerks with poll sheets.

The sheriff opened the election. One by one the voters presented themselves to the table of officials. As each voter stepped forward, his name was called out and the sheriff asked how he would vote. Orally, without a ballot, the voter then announced his choice, and the appropriate clerk entered his name on the poll sheet. Often, the candidate for whom he had voted stood up, bowed, and publicly expressed thanks.

Of course, this method of voting did not completely prevent fraud, and sometimes a committee in the House of Burgesses had to investigate an election dispute. In addition, the pressure to vote the same way as one's friends, relatives, or other acquaintances would have been great during an oral election. Nonetheless, this voting procedure encouraged honesty.

Changing the Process. Although some colonial voting procedures survived, after the Revolution elections slowly became more like those we are familiar with today. For example, more liberal suffrage requirements enlarged the electorate considerably over the years. The evolution of a two-party system aroused interest in politics, and the percentage of people voting increased. In the election of 1840, for instance, 78 percent of white adult males went to the polls.

The election process, however, still had weaknesses. After the Civil War, mass numbers of people concentrated in cities meant greater opportunity for fraud or coercion. Urban immigrants who could barely read became easy targets for machine politicians who were eager to exchange favors for votes.

Not long after the Civil War, most Southern states began using poll taxes and other gimmicks to disenfranchise blacks. Likewise, a certain amount of intimidation remained since oral voting was not widely replaced by the secret ballot until the Progressive period.

Progressivism and Reform. The Progressives made significant gains in opening up the election process and making it more responsive to citizens' wishes. With Oregon taking the lead, other states adopted election reforms. Some allowed for initiative and referendum, the processes whereby citizens could introduce new legislation or ratify bills passed by legislative bodies. Another reform provided for the recall of officials, that is, their removal from office if enough citizens decided that they were not performing their duties in a responsible manner.

During the Progressive period, most states also adopted the direct primary. This allowed voters to choose which candidates would run for office. The effect of this and other changes made the election process more democratic than ever before.

Elections Today. Today our national election process is still not perfect. Some people continue to question the fact that the president is still chosen indirectly, by electors. Under this system, the Hayes-Tilden election of 1876 became tangled in disputed electoral results. Finally, politicians decided the outcome in committee. Under the electoral college system, it is still possible for a presidential candidate to win a majority of votes and lose the election.

More people have criticized the campaign process that precedes elections. Candidates often begin running for office years before election day. The amount of money spent running for office has also skyrocketed. In the 1982 election, for example, a record $300 million was spent on congressional campaigns. The need to raise such large sums of money to conduct a

As this workers' poster by artist Ben Shahn indicates, one of the most important rights of all Americans is the right to vote in free and open elections. The poster title is from a speech by Franklin D. Roosevelt.

campaign can make a candidate vulnerable to influential lobbyists and political action groups.

Despite these faults, the American election process has withstood the test of time. Other nations watch with wonder as elected officials in the United States enter and leave office peacefully without resorting to force or violence. Still, there are dangers that threaten this free process—and one of the greatest threats comes from within. In the presidential election of 1980, only 53.95 percent of eligible voters cast their ballots. This was the lowest turnout in thirty-two years.

If our free election process is to survive, it must remain healthy—and if it is to remain healthy, more Americans must participate. How to open the

election process to greater participation remains a challenge for Americans.

Understanding Government

1. How have elections changed since colonial times? How have these changes affected the democratic process?

2. What reforms would improve political elections today? How can these reforms be enacted?

3. Why is voter apathy dangerous for our free election process? How can this trend be reversed?

4. Do you plan to register and vote when you become eighteen? What steps should you take to become an informed voter?

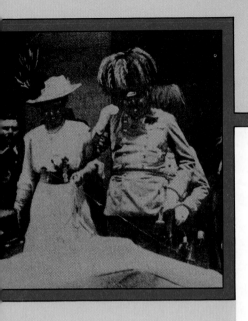

The First World War

1914–1920

People in the Chapter

Woodrow Wilson—*idealistic president who originates the League of Nations but fails to persuade Americans that the United States should join it.*

Senator Henry Cabot Lodge—*isolationist and bitter foe of Wilson. He fights desperately and successfully to keep the United States from joining the League of Nations.*

Kaiser Wilhelm II—*emperor of Germany who, after his nation's defeat in World War I, abdicates and flees to exile in the Netherlands.*

General John J. Pershing—*commander of American land forces in Europe.*

Linking Past to Present

On June 28, 1914, two pistol shots rang out in Sarajevo, a town in the Austro-Hungarian Empire. They struck and killed the Archduke Franz Ferdinand and the Archduchess Sophie. Ferdinand was the heir to the throne of the Austro-Hungarian Empire. The double assassination set off the bloodiest war in history up to that time.

World War I lasted four years, involved thirty nations and six continents, and resulted in the death of some 13 million soldiers and another 13 million civilians. In addition, 20 million more were wounded and additional millions were made refugees. The war also rearranged the map of Europe. Three ancient monarchies collapsed: the Austro-Hungarian, the German, and the Russian. From their ruins new nations as well as new kinds of governments were formed.

Life was completely changed not only in Europe but in the United States, which finally was drawn into the war. After the war, the American people were determined to oppose any further involvement in European affairs. Many Americans became suspicious of "foreigners" and even "foreign ideas."

1 THE UNITED STATES TRIES TO REMAIN NEUTRAL

VOCABULARY   *contraband   unterseeboot   munitions*

The United States did not enter World War I until three years after hostilities began. And until almost the last minute, there was considerable doubt as to whether or not we would take part. Woodrow Wilson even won a second term in 1916 on the slogan "He Kept Us Out of War." What, then, made the United States change its mind?

Sympathy for the Allies

Most Americans in 1914 saw no reason for being drawn into a struggle 3000 miles away. No American lives or property were threatened. Whether or not the Allies, which were France, Great Britain, and Russia, beat the Central Powers of Germany, Austria-Hungary, and Turkey did not seem a matter of direct national concern.

This does not mean that individual Americans were indifferent to who would win the war. Quite the contrary.

Overall, there was a general feeling of sympathy for Great Britain and France. Many Americans felt close to England as a consequence of sharing a common ancestry, language, and literature, as well as similar democratic institutions and legal systems. Ties with France, although much weaker, went back to 1778 when France had helped the thirteen colonies in their fight for independence. As a New York editor put it: "Forget us, God, if we forget the sacred sword of Lafayette."

But millions of naturalized citizens favored the nation from which they had emigrated to the United States. For example, many Germans sympathized with Germany. Many Americans of Irish descent remembered the centuries of British oppression in Ireland. They saw the war as a chance for Ireland to gain its independence.

In addition, there were certain Americans who believed the war was evil. Pacifists such as William Jennings Bryan argued that it was the obligation of the United States, "the greatest of the Christian nations," to set an example of peace for the world. Socialists such as Eugene V. Debs criticized the war as an imperialist struggle between German and English businessmen. Since both groups wanted to control raw materials and markets in China, Africa, and the Middle East, it was "a plague on both your houses."

The majority of Americans, however, undoubtedly favored victory for the Allies rather than the Central Powers. But they did not feel strongly enough to want to help the Allies. As President Wilson said, "Our whole duty for the present, at any rate, is summed up in the motto 'America First: Let us think of America before we think of Europe.' "

The Invasion of Belgium

The first shift in American public opinion began with the German invasion of Belgium. Belgium was a neutral nation, but it was the gateway to France. And since Germany was fighting on two fronts, Russia on the east and France on the west, German war lords decided to follow a plan that had been drawn up in 1905 by Count Alfred von Schlieffen (von *shlee*-fan), chief of the German General Staff. The Schlieffen Plan called for a holding action against Russia, which was always slow to mobilize. This was to be combined with a quick drive in strength through the Belgian lowlands to Paris. Then after France had fallen, the two German armies would unite to defeat the tsar.

So the Germans invaded neutral Belgium. The

541

Europe During World War I 1914–1918

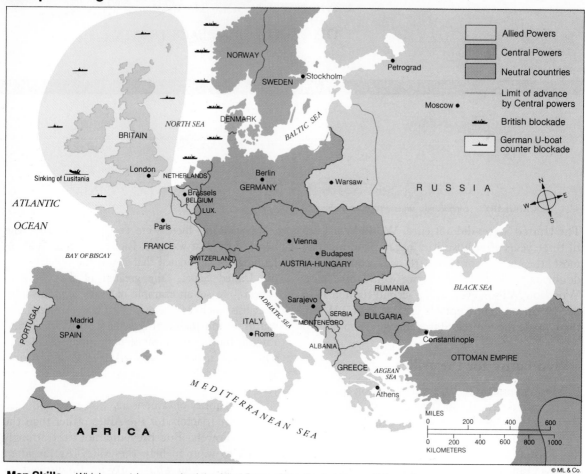

Map Skills *Which countries comprised the Allied Powers? the Central Powers? Around what country was the German naval blockade? Off what country was the* Lusitania *sunk?*

accounts sent back by American correspondents presented a frightening image of a military juggernaut on the move. Here is Richard Harding Davis's account of the German army's entry into Brussels:

❝ At the sight of the first few regiments of the enemy we were thrilled. After, for three hours, they had passed in one unbroken steel-gray column, we were bored. But when hour after hour passed and there was no halt, no breathing time, no open spaces in the ranks, the thing became uncanny, unhuman. You returned to watch it, fascinated. It held the mystery and menace of fog rolling toward you across the sea.

For seven hours the army passed. . . . Like a river of steel it flowed, gray and ghostlike. Then, as dusk came and as thousands of horses' hoofs and thousands of iron boots continued to tramp forward, they struck tiny sparks from the stones, but the horses and the men who beat out the sparks were invisible. ❞

German troops invade neutral Belgium. They are shown moving through the city of Antwerp.

542

> **❝** At midnight, packwagons and siege-guns were still passing. At 7 this morning I was awakened by the tramp of men. . . . For twenty-six hours the gray army has rumbled by with the mystery of fog and the pertinacity of a steamroller. **❞**

German soldiers inspired fear and so did the terrible new weapons they used. One such was called Big Bertha—for Bertha Krupp, the wife of Gustav Krupp, the Krupp munitions king. This cannon hurled an 1800-pound shell a distance of nine miles. Another terrifying weapon was the zeppelin, a gas-filled airship which enabled Germans to drop bombs behind the battle line. And there were tubes that spewed poison gas rather than bullets.

Equally frightening were the tactics Germans employed after they had conquered an area. For example, they leveled the entire town of Louvain because a Belgian sniper killed a German soldier. They charged hundreds of civilians, including women and children, with armed resistance and shot them without trial. They executed priests on the charge (often false) that they were organizing civilian resistance. They destroyed cathedrals, libraries, and even hospitals. Some "atrocity" stories, such as the cutting off of children's hands, later proved to be false. But so many proved to be true that within a month after the war broke out, one magazine was referring to Germany as "the bully of Europe." Newspapers warned Americans about the menace of the "Hun," comparing the Germans with *Hunni,* a brutal people who invaded Europe from the East around A.D. 400.

Struggle at Sea

In the fourth century B.C., the struggle between the ancient Greeks and the Persian Empire was described as a conflict between a whale and an elephant. The greatest sea power of the time, Greece, confronted the mightiest land power. Now, in 1914, a similar situation existed. Great Britain controlled the sea lanes of the world. Germany was the strongest force on the European continent.

Britain Blockades Germany. Fighting on land soon reached a stalemate, with neither side able to conquer the other. So Great Britain began to make more use of its naval strength. It set up a blockade along the German coast to prevent *contraband,* that is, smuggled goods (usually weapons), from getting through. The British, however, enlarged the definition of contraband to include such items

This sketch of The Prisoners and the Wounded, *reflects the grueling existence of men on the battlefields of World War I.*

as cotton and foodstuffs. The British also extended the blockade to neutral ports in the Netherlands, Denmark, Norway, and Sweden. The British mined the entire North Sea. And instead of searching neutral merchant ships at sea, which was the customary practice, they insisted that neutral vessels go to British ports for examination.

All of these actions were contrary to the international law of freedom of the seas. Many Americans reacted as angrily as their ancestors had in 1812. President Wilson protested sharply, calling the blockade "ineffective, illegal, and indefensible." But feelings against Great Britain did not last long because the Germans began using submarine warfare.

Germany Unleashes the U-Boats. By 1915 the British blockade had almost eliminated the flow of military supplies to Germany from neutral nations. So Kaiser Wilhelm II, the German ruler, announced a counter-blockade by U-boat (from *unterseeboot,* the German word for submarine). All cargoes moving toward Britain, food as well as *munitions* (weapons and ammunition), would be considered contraband, he said. Any ship found in the waters around Britain would be sunk. And he added that it would not always be possible to warn crews and passengers. Since U-boats had no room to take aboard people from a ship before sinking it, the kaiser's declaration meant that many more neutral lives would be lost.

543

Unleashing the U-boats turned out to be a colossal blunder on Germany's part. For one thing, Britain declared a counter-blockade of its own that led to the starvation of the German people. The importation of foodstuffs fell off, as did the importations of chemical fertilizers. Germany had to use its available nitrates for the production of munitions. It could not produce fertilizer. Without fertilizers, German soil became less productive. This increased Germany's need to import food.

The Germans began rationing food in 1915. But by 1917 famine invaded Germany. It is estimated that 750,000 Germans starved to death as a result of the British "hunger blockade." This is one hundred times the number of persons who lost their lives from submarine warfare.

But the British blockade worked slowly, and its effect was not visible except inside Germany. U-boat attacks, on the other hand, were spectacular events. News services flashed accounts of sinking ships and drowning persons around the world within a matter of minutes. And gradually, neutrals who had been angry at Britain because of damage to their property became outraged with Germany because of the loss of life.

The Lusitania Is Sunk.   On March 28, 1915, a U-boat sank the British steamer *Falaba* with the loss of one American life. On April 28 the American steamer *Cushing* was attacked by a German seaplane, but without any fatalities. On May 1 a U-boat torpedoed the American tanker *Gulflight*; two Americans drowned, and one died of heart failure.

Then, on May 7, a German submarine sank the British liner *Lusitania* off the southern coast of Ireland. Of the 1198 persons who lost their lives, 128 were Americans. The Germans defended their action on the grounds that the liner was carrying arms and possibly heavy explosives. Most Americans, however, agreed with the New York minister who said,

66This sinking . . . is not war; it is murder! . . . This is organized murder and no language is too strong for it. . . . If I see a ruffian in the street beating a boy I may want to be neutral. I may say I know neither ruffian nor boy. But God help me, I am less than a man if I don't thrust in my hand. It is too much to ask me to keep out. So it is getting to be too much to ask America to keep out when Americans are drowned as part of a European war.99

The *Sussex* Pledge

The United States protested sharply against the sinking of the *Lusitania*. Two months later, a U-boat sank another British liner, the *Arabic*. Al-

Torpedoed by a German submarine, the British liner Lusitania sinks. Among the victims were 128 Americans. Such German attacks on unarmed vessels outraged American public opinion.

Presidential Election of 1916

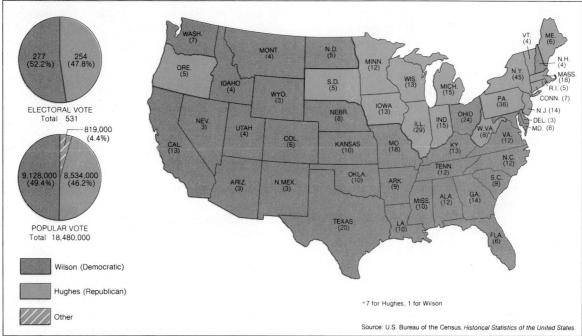

ELECTORAL VOTE
Total 531

277 (52.2%)   254 (47.8%)

POPULAR VOTE
Total 18,480,000

819,000 (4.4%)

9,128,000 (49.4%)   8,534,000 (46.2%)

Wilson (Democratic)

Hughes (Republican)

Other

*7 for Hughes, 1 for Wilson

Source: U.S. Bureau of the Census, *Historical Statistics of the United States.*

© ML & Co.

Map Skills *Who was the Republican candidate? the Democratic candidate? Who won the election? What was his percentage of the popular vote? Which state had the most electoral votes?*

though only two Americans were drowned, anti-German sentiment in the United States was so intense that Germany agreed not to sink any more liners without warning "provided that the liners do not try to escape or offer resistance."

In March 1916 Germany broke its promise and torpedoed an unarmed French passenger steamer, the *Sussex*. The *Sussex* did not sink. But about eighty passengers, including Americans, were killed or injured. Once again the United States warned that it would break off diplomatic relations unless Germany changed its tactics. Germany agreed, in the so-called "*Sussex* pledge." But there was a string attached. If the United States could not persuade Britain to lift the "hunger blockade," Germany said, it would consider itself free to renew unrestricted submarine warfare.

The 1916 Campaign

Although many Americans now believed that war was inevitable, President Wilson made several attempts to mediate the conflict. He sent his personal advisor, Colonel Edward M. House, to Europe. But House's peace missions came to nothing. So Wilson decided to take Theodore Roosevelt's advice and push for a program of preparedness.

This involved increasing the size of the regular army, establishing officers' training camps, and expanding the navy. The Council of National Defense was created to make plans for mobilizing national resources in the event of war. And the United States Shipping Board was set up to build and buy merchant ships.

But people had not yet succumbed to war fever, as a popular song of the time illustrates:

❝ I didn't raise my boy to be a soldier,
I brought him up to be my pride and joy.
Who dares to place a musket on his shoulder,
To shoot some other mother's darling boy?
Let nations arbitrate their future troubles,
It's time to lay the sword and gun away,
There'd be no war today,
If mothers all would say,
"I didn't raise my boy to be a soldier." ❞

In November came the presidential election. The Democrats renominated Wilson. The Progressives renominated Theodore Roosevelt. But Roosevelt realized that the only way to defeat Wilson, whom he despised as "that damned Presbyterian hypocrite" and "pacifist professor," was for the Progressives to rejoin the GOP. So he declined the nomination and threw his support to the Republican candidate, Supreme Court Justice Charles Evans Hughes.

545

The election revolved around two issues: peace and progressivism. Wilson appealed to voters with differing views about the war. He campaigned on the slogan "He Kept Us Out of War." At the same time, he pointed to the preparedness campaign and to the *Sussex* pledge as evidence of his concern about America's honor. In domestic matters, Wilson won the support of labor by pushing the Adamson Eight-Hour Law through Congress in time to avert a nationwide strike by the railroad brotherhoods.

Hughes likewise appealed to voters with differing views about the war. On the one hand, he pledged to uphold America's right to freedom of the seas. On the other hand, he tried to keep German-Americans in their traditional Republican ranks by promising not to be too severe on Germany. However, Hughes's vague speeches and lack of forcefulness led many to call him "Charles Evasive Hughes." And Roosevelt antagonized thousands of potential Hughes supporters by comparing Wilson to Pontius Pilate, "with apologies to the latter."

The results of the election were uncertain. First Wilson moved ahead, then Hughes moved ahead. By evening it was clear that Hughes had won the industrial Northeast and most of the Middle West. The next morning, even Democratic newspapers were conceding the election and displaying pictures of "The Republican President-Elect" on their front pages. But later that day the returns from California came in and by 3800 votes out of a million, they gave Wilson the necessary margin for victory in the electoral college. Wilson also won a majority of the popular vote.

Last Efforts Fail

Following the election, Wilson made yet another attempt to end the war. He sent both sides a note, asking them to indicate the terms on which they would be willing to stop fighting. Unfortunately, Germany had put out a peace feeler a few days before. The Allies felt that the timing of Wilson's note meant that he was supporting the Central Powers. So they rejected Wilson's offer.

On January 22, 1917, Wilson appealed to world public opinion through a speech before the Senate. He called for "a peace without victory . . . a peace among equals" in which neither side would impose harsh terms on the other. Instead, all nations would join in a League for Peace. The league would work as a group to extend democracy, maintain freedom of the seas, and reduce armaments.

Nine days later came the German response. German leaders felt they had a good chance to knock out Britain by resuming unrestricted submarine warfare. So on January 31, the kaiser announced that all ships in the waters around Britain, France, and Italy would be sunk on sight.

Wilson was stunned. In view of his earlier statements, the German action meant that the United States would have to go to war. But the president held back, saying that he would wait for "actual overt acts" before breaking diplomatic relations.

The Zimmermann Telegram. The overt acts came. First was the "Zimmermann telegram," sent by the German foreign secretary to the German ambassador in Mexico. The telegram suggested an alliance between Mexico and Germany, and promised that if war with the United States broke out, Germany would support Mexico in recovering "the lost territory in Texas, New Mexico, and Arizona." Next came the sinking of four unarmed American merchant ships with a loss of thirty-six lives.

Final Straws. In March of 1917, the tsarist regime in Russia was overthrown and replaced by a constitutional, democratic government. Now one could say that this made the war against Germany and Austria-Hungary a war of democracies against brutal monarchies.

Also, American trade with the Allies had risen from $825 million in 1914 to $3.2 billion in 1916. American bankers had also lent the Allies about $2 billion. Business leaders did not press for war. But America's economic ties with the Allies were stronger than their economic ties with the Central Powers.

Section 1 Review

COMPREHENSION   Developing Vocabulary

1. Explain these terms: contraband, unterseeboot, munitions, Big Bertha, Hunni.

COMPREHENSION   Mastering Facts

1. Who were the Allies and who were the Central Powers?
2. Why was the U-boat campaign considered a German blunder?
3. What was the *Sussex* pledge?
4. What was the message of the Zimmermann telegram?

THE NATION GOES TO WAR

VOCABULARY   *croix de guerre*   *victory gardens*   *convoy system*   *Lafayette Escadrille*

A light drizzle fell on Washington on April 2, 1917 as senators, representatives, ambassadors, members of the Supreme Court, and other guests crowded into the Capitol building to hear President Wilson deliver his "War Message."

Wilson began by stating: "Property can be paid for; the lives of peaceful and innocent people cannot be." German submarine warfare was "nothing less than war against the government and people of the United States." Therefore, he said, the United States had no choice but to enter the war that had been thrust upon it.

Then Wilson moved on to speak of larger goals. "We are glad . . . to fight thus for the ultimate peace of the world and for the liberation of its peoples, the German peoples included; for the rights of nations great and small and the privilege of men everywhere to choose their way of life. . . . The world must be made safe for democracy. . . . We have no selfish ends to serve. We desire no conquest, no dominion. We seek no indemnities."

The president closed by saying: "It is a fearful thing to lead this great peaceful people into war. . . . But the right is more precious than peace, and we shall fight for the things which we have always carried nearest our hearts."

The Senate declared war on April 4. The House of Representatives declared war on April 6.

America's entry into World War I assured the Allies' final victory in 1918. Without our troops, ships, food, and military supplies, the war could have gone the other way and the whole history of the world since 1918 would have been very different indeed!

Mobilizing the Military

❝ They marched me twenty miles a day to fit me for the war.
I didn't mind the first nineteen but the last one made me sore. ❞

The first task that confronted the United States was that of raising an army. When war was declared, only about 200,000 men were in service. Few officers had any combat experience or any training in the new methods of trench warfare. Almost all the army's weapons were out-of-date, while the air force consisted of fifty-five rickety planes and 130 pilots.

Posters like this, seeking public support for the war effort, were a familiar sight during World War I.

The lack of manpower was soon solved by a draft. Almost 10 million men registered for the draft on June 5, 1917 and, unlike the Civil War experience, not a single riot took place. Two additional registrations were held in 1918, raising the total number of men to 24 million. About 4.2 million were inducted into service. Of this number, about 2 million reached Europe before the armistice was signed. Three-fourths of these saw actual combat. The ages of the inductees ranged from eighteen to forty-five. However, since married men and those with dependents were generally excused, the overseas army consisted mostly of young men. Training lasted for nine months: "six months on this side, two months in Europe before going to the front, and a final month on the battle line in a quiet sector." Then the men were moved to wherever fighting was hottest.

The proportion of black Americans in service was double their proportion in the general population. As in earlier wars, black soldiers were segregated in separate units. They had separate living quarters and separate recreational facilities. Although most officers were white, the United States

Army for the first time trained some black officers and placed them in command of black troops. Most black troops were assigned to noncombat duties, but not all. The all-black 369th Infantry Regiment saw more continuous duty on the front lines than any other American regiment. Two soldiers of the 369th, Henry Johnson and Needham Roberts, were among the first Americans to receive the French military honor, the croix de guerre.

Mobilizing the Economy

The second task facing the United States was to transport millions of soldiers overseas and equip and feed not only our own troops but those of our allies as well. It was an immense task, and it was ultimately accomplished by increasing the powers of the federal government.

Industry. Congress gave President Wilson the power to fix prices. He could also regulate, and even nationalize, certain war-related industries.

The main regulatory body was the War Industries Board. It was established in 1917 and was reorganized in 1918 under the leadership of Bernard M. "Barney" Baruch. The board did a great deal to improve production by encouraging the use of mass production techniques. The board also did psychological testing to help a person find the right job. Civilians were urged to use substitutes for products containing steel or tin. Price controls, however, were applied only at the wholesale level. As a result, retail prices soared. Corporate profits soared as well, especially in such industries as chemicals, copper, lumber, meat-packing, oil, and steel.

Other federal agencies included the Railway Administration, which operated the nation's railroads as a single system, and the Fuel Administration, which regulated supplies of coal and oil. In addition, many people adopted "gasless Sundays" and "lightless nights" to help conserve fuel. The Emergency Fleet Corporation built some 10 million tons of shipping. However, most of the ships were finished too late to be of much use. The majority of American troops moved across the Atlantic either in British vessels or German ships that had been taken over in American ports when war was declared.

Labor. Wages in certain industries, especially the metal trades, shipbuilding, and meat packing,

rose during the war years by as much as 20 percent. White-collar workers, on the other hand, lost about 35 percent of their purchasing power because of inflation. As a result, union membership increased 70 percent and there was a wave of strikes in 1917 protesting the high cost of living.

In 1918 President Wilson established the National War Labor Board to deal with disputes between management and labor. In general, labor agreed not to strike in exchange for the right to organize and bargain collectively, and to keep the eight-hour day wherever it already existed. Workers who were reluctant to go along with board decisions were warned that they would lose their exemption from the draft. "Work or fight," they were told.

The wartime need for labor brought over a million more women into the work force. As one writer observed: "Suddenly a male-dominated America was confronted with the spectacle of women auto mechanics, telegraph messengers, elevator operators, and streetcar conductors—and that was not all. They toiled on factory assembly lines, carried ice, plowed fields, and became traffic cops. Women invaded even the sanctuary of the armed forces, about 11,000 female yeomen enlisting in the Navy as clerks and stenographers." However, although President Wilson called for equal pay for equal work, women in war work received less than men. And almost all of them were fired when the war ended.

Food. Yet another task that confronted the United States was that of producing and conserving food. As one joke went:

> ❝ My Tuesdays are meatless,
> My Wednesdays are wheatless,
> I'm getting more eatless each day. ❞

The person in charge of the Food Administration was Herbert Hoover. A former mining engineer, he had successfully headed the Commission for Relief in Belgium.

Hoover relied heavily on voluntary cooperation. His entire staff, except for clerks, consisted of volunteers. Instead of rationing food, he organized a tremendous publicity campaign that called on people to follow the "gospel of the clean plate." Since Europeans were accustomed to eating wheat, Americans were urged to eat corn so they could send their wheat abroad. Homeowners planted "victory gardens" in their yards. School children joined the United States School Garden Army and spent their after-school hours raising vegetables in public parks.

Hoover also set a high government price on wheat and other staples. Farmers responded by putting an additional 40 million acres of land into production. In the process, they increased their income by almost 30 percent. Also in 1918, as a food control measure, the Food Administration forbade the manufacture of intoxicating liquors from grain.

Paying for the War

The war cost the United States about $33 billion in direct expenses. About one-third of this amount was raised through taxes, the rest through public borrowing.

As Treasury Secretary William G. McAdoo explained, "We capitalized the profound impulse called patriotism." Government bonds were sold to the people. No one received a commission or made a profit on bond sales. Instead, tens of thousands of volunteers, sparked by such movie stars as Douglas Fairbanks and Mary Pickford, spoke at rallies in factories, schools, and street corners. Newspapers and billboards carried advertisements for the bonds free of charge. There were four-minute sales talks between theater acts. War-bond pa-

The all-black 369th Infantry Regiment returns home after having fought extensively "over there."

rades were held in the center of almost every town. All told, four great "Liberty Loan" drives and one "Victory Loan" drive were held. And on the average, every adult American lent the government $400.

The Great Witch Hunt

Early in 1917, President Wilson said, "Once lead this people into war, and they'll forget there was ever such a thing as tolerance." The president's prediction turned out to be correct. As soon as war was declared, conformity became the order of the day. Civil liberties were attacked both unofficially and officially.

Super-Americanism. The main target of the drive for conformity were so-called "hyphenated Americans," that is, Americans who had emigrated from other nations, especially those from Germany and Austria-Hungary. The most bitter attacks were directed against the 2 million Americans who had been born in Germany. But other foreign-born persons and native-born Americans of German descent suffered as well.

Many Americans unfortunate enough to have German-sounding names were fired from their jobs. The music of Mozart and Beethoven was not played. Books by German authors were removed from libraries.

Finally, in a burst of anti-German fervor, Americans changed the name of German measles to "liberty measles." Hamburger became "liberty steak" and sauerkraut was renamed "liberty cabbage." Dachshunds became "liberty pups."

The Espionage and Sedition Acts. In June 1917 Congress passed the Espionage Act, and in May 1918 it passed the Sedition Act. Under these laws a person could be fined up to $10,000 and/or sentenced to twenty years in jail for interfering with the draft, obstructing the sale of government bonds, or saying anything disloyal or profane or abusive about the government or the war effort.

Like the Alien and Sedition Acts of 1798, these laws clearly violated the spirit of the First Amendment. Their passage led to some 6000 arrests and 1500 convictions. A man named Walter Mathey was imprisoned for attending an antiwar meeting and contributing twenty-five cents. The Reverend Clarence Waldron received fifteen years in the penitentiary for telling a Bible class that "a Christian can take no part in the war." Farmer John White was sentenced to twenty-one months in jail for complaining about conditions in the army.

Socialists and labor leaders were major targets of the Espionage and Sedition Acts. Eugene V. Debs was sentenced to ten years in prison because he opposed the war. (He was pardoned by President Warren G. Harding after serving three years.) Anarchist "Red Emma" Goldman received a two-year sentence and a $10,000 fine for organizing the "No Conscription League." (When she came out of jail, she was deported to Russia.) "Big Bill" Haywood and other leaders of the Industrial Workers of the World were accused of sabotaging the war effort because they urged workers to strike for better conditions and higher pay. Haywood received thirty years; most of the other Wobblies received five to ten. The IWW finally faded away.

Other results of the law included the loss of mailing privileges for newspapers and magazines that opposed the war or even criticized the British Empire. Victor Berger, a Socialist congressman from Wisconsin, was denied his seat in the House of Representatives because of his antiwar views.

Over There

American military might first showed itself at sea. Rear Admiral William S. Sims persuaded the British that the best way to defeat the U-boats was the convoy system. It had been the practice for merchant ships to cross the Atlantic either singly or in small groups. While this lessened the chance of being spotted by a submarine, it also made defense difficult. Sims suggested instead that merchant vessels travel in a large group with a guard of circling destroyers and cruisers. The British agreed, and by midsummer of 1917 shipping losses had been cut in half. Eventually the United States put a hundred submarine chasers and 500 airplanes into the anti-U-boat campaign.

In Europe. American land forces were under the command of General John J. "Black Jack" Pershing. At first they were used mostly as replacements for European casualties. By April 1918, however, Pershing had convinced the Allies that the Americans should fight as a separate army, albeit under the overall direction of French Marshal Ferdinand Foch, commander of all Allied armies in Europe. American troops played a major role in throwing back German attacks at Chateau-Thierry, Belleau Wood, and Reims, near Paris. They mounted offensives against the Germans at St. Mihiel and in the Meuse-Argonne area. All told, the United States lost 48,000 men in battle, with an additional 56,000 dying of disease.

Also active on the western front were American fighter pilots. Even before the United States entered the war, Americans had flown in a special

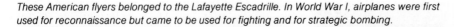

These American flyers belonged to the Lafayette Escadrille. In World War I, airplanes were first used for reconnaissance but came to be used for fighting and for strategic bombing.

The Western Front in World War I

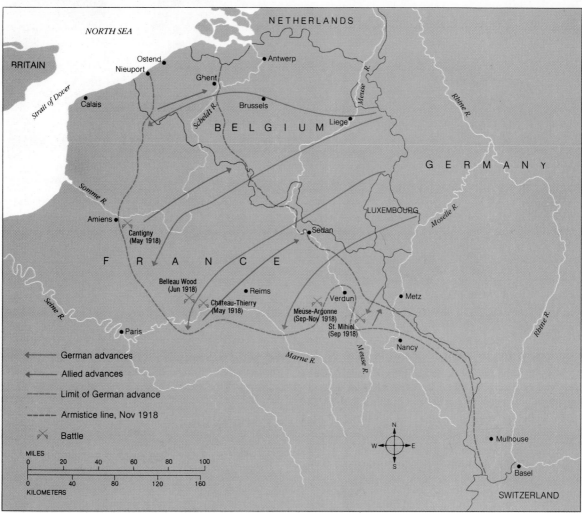

Map Skills *How close did German forces get to Paris? Near what river was the battle of Chateau-Thierry? Through what nation does the Rhine River flow? the Seine River?*

unit of the French Flying Corps called the Lafayette Escadrille. After the United States entered the war, the Lafayette Escadrille was disbanded, and its pilots joined one of the American units.

In Russia. In November 1917 the democratic government, which had been formed after the overthrow of the tsar, was itself replaced by a Communist government. The new government wanted to consolidate its power rather than continue the war. So, the new government signed a peace treaty with Germany on March 3, 1918.

The American and Allied leaders were shocked.

They feared that many of the munitions and foodstuffs in Russia might fall into German hands. While the Allies had no love for the new Communist government, they still did not want Russia's northern ports to be occupied by Germany. The United States, therefore, joined with thirteen other Allied nations in sending troops to Russia.

In September some 5000 infantrymen from the Middle West found themselves camping in the frozen forests of Arctic Russia near Murmansk. A joint U.S. and Japanese force also landed in Vladivostok some 5000 miles to the east in Siberia.

By the time the U.S. forces arrived in Russia,

551

Many women served overseas in World War I. Others, such as these women shown here, took training courses in civilian defense. They were called Home Guards.

law and order had completely broken down. Anti-Communist troops formed into what were called White Armies. This was to distinguish them from the Red Armies—so called because of the color of the new government's flag. Gradually the Allied soldiers began fighting with the White armies against the Reds.

American troops withdrew from Russia in 1920. The last Allied forces (the Japanese) left in 1922. The Soviet government never forgot this invasion, however.

The End. By September 1918 the superior power of the Allies was evident. On November 3 a mutiny broke out at the German naval base of Kiel. On November 9 Kaiser Wilhelm abdicated his throne and took refuge in the Netherlands. Two days later Germany signed an armistice with the Allies. Peace treaties were later signed in

France at the Palace of Versailles, once the home of Louis XVI who had done so much to help the American colonies gain independence.

Section 2 Review

COMPREHENSION   Developing Vocabulary

1. Explain these terms: convoy system, croix de guerre, victory gardens, Lafayette Escadrille.

COMPREHENSION   Mastering Facts

1. What was the first task confronting the United States after it entered the war?
2. How did the War Industries Board aid the war effort?
3. How did the United States finance the war?
4. What role did American troops play on the western front? What role did American fighter pilots play?

3   THE FIGHT FOR A PEACE TREATY

VOCABULARY   *covenants   self-determination   mandates   isolationists*

When the United States entered World War I, it was almost like embarking on a crusade. What could be more idealistic than ending war forever and making the world safe for democracy? Yet after the war, the Senate twice rejected the Ver-

sailles Treaty, refused to join the League of Nations, and, in the words of one historian, "broke the heart of the world." Let's see how it happened.

When the Communists seized power in Russia in 1917, they immediately urged an end to the war on terms of no takeover of territory and no indemnities. When the Allies did not respond, the Communists signed a separate peace treaty with Germany. They also threatened to publish the secret treaties which the Allies had drawn up at the start of the war. These treaties spelled out the territorial gains the Allies wanted in the event of victory.

Wilson's Fourteen Points

President Wilson, however, wanted nothing to do with those secret treaties. He had a different idea of what the ground rules for peace should be. So on January 18, 1918, he went before Congress and delivered his famous Fourteen Points speech.

The fourteen points were divided into three groups.

First were five points designed to remove what Wilson believed were the causes of war.

1. Open *covenants* (agreements) openly arrived at, that is, open diplomacy and no secret treaties.

2. Freedom of the seas.

3. The removal of tariffs and other economic barriers between nations.

4. Arms reduction "to the lowest point consistent with domestic safety."

5. Colonial policies that would take into account the interests of the colonial people as well as the interests of the imperialist powers.

Next were eight points dealing with boundary changes. These were based on the principle of "self-determination along historically established lines of nationality." In other words, national groups were to decide for themselves what nation they wanted to be part of. Specifically, Wilson called for the following:

6. The creation of an independent Poland.

7. German evacuation of Russian territory.

8. German evacuation of Belgium.

9. German evacuation of French territory, including the return of Alsace-Lorraine, a part of France that Germany had seized in 1870.

10. German evacuation of Rumania, Serbia, and Montenegro.

11. A readjustment of Italy's frontiers.

12. The establishment of new nations in the non-Turkish part of the Ottoman Empire.

13. The establishment of new nations in the Austro-Hungarian Empire (these later included Austria, Hungary, Czechoslovakia, and Yugoslavia).

The Fourteenth Point called for the formation of a League of Nations to keep world peace. The members of the league would be bound to protect any nation that was attacked by another.

Wilson at Versailles

President Wilson himself headed the United States delegation to the Versailles Peace Conference. Accompanying him were personal aide Colonel House, Secretary of State Robert Lansing, General Tasker H. Bliss, and diplomat Henry White. Only one of the four, White, was a Republican, although the 1918 congressional campaign had given the GOP a majority in both houses. None was a senator, although the Senate would have to ratify the peace treaty. Wilson's failure to include a senator was due to his bitter political feud with Senator Henry Cabot Lodge, who later became chairman of the Senate Foreign Relations Committee.

Before going to Versailles, Wilson visited England and Italy. Everywhere he went, people welcomed him. Italians displayed his picture in their windows and cheering crowds waited hours for him to pass. Parisians strewed the road with flowers. Representatives of one minority group after another—Armenians, Jews, Ukrainians, and Poles—approached him with appeals for help in setting themselves up as independent nations.

Once the peace conference began, however, Wilson's idealism ran into practical politics. Premier Georges Clemenceau (klem-on-so) of France had lived through two invasions of his country by Germany, and he was determined to prevent this from happening again. British Prime Minister David Lloyd George had just won reelection on the basis of "Make Germany Pay." Prime Minister Vittorio Orlando of Italy wanted Austrian territory.

The peace conference did not include either the defeated Central Powers or the smaller Allied nations. Instead, the "Big Four"—Wilson, Clemenceau, Lloyd George, and Orlando—worked out the treaty's details among themselves. In general, Wilson gave in on some of his Fourteen Points in return for European support for the League of Nations.

The Treaty of Versailles was signed on June 28, 1919. As you see by the map on page 555, nine new nations emerged as a result, and the boundaries of other nations were shifted. Some areas were carved out of Turkish territory and given to France and England as *mandates*. A mandate was to be administered by the victorious Allied country until the area was ready for self-rule and then independence. Such mandates included Iraq, Syria, Lebanon, and Palestine (now Israel and Jordan). Former German colonies in Africa and the Pacific region were likewise turned over to one or another of the Allied nations as mandates. Germany's armed forces were drastically reduced. Germany was also required to acknowledge sole responsibility for World War I and pay war damages in the amount of $32 billion. It was also forced to return the province of Alsace-Lorraine which it had taken from France in the war of 1870.

The Senate and the Treaty

When Wilson returned to the United States to get Senate approval for the peace treaty, he found several groups in opposition to it. Some, like Herbert Hoover, believed that the peace terms were too harsh. It did not seem possible for Germany, which had lost much of its coal resources as well as its colonies, to pay reparations, and failure to do so could only lead to trouble.

Others objected to the treaty because they doubted that national boundaries could be drawn to satisfy every group's demand for self-determination. For example, before the war Poles under German rule did not have self-determination. But now, there were Germans in Poland who would not have self-determination. Still others felt that the war-guilt clause was not justified, that Germany alone had not started the war. Italian-Americans were unhappy that Italy did not receive all the Austrian territory with a majority of Italian inhabitants. Irish-Americans were bitter because Wilson had not secured the independence of Ireland from Britain.

Isolationist Fears.   The main opposition, however, came from the "isolationists," those people who believed that America should isolate itself

Woodrow Wilson meets with Allied leaders at the Paris Peace Conference in 1919. Wilson's idea of "peace without victory" clashed with the harsher demands of the other Allied nations.

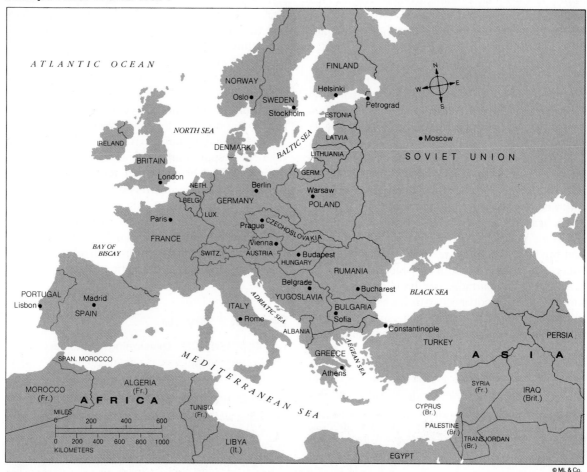

© ML. & Co.

Map Skills *Compare this map with the one on page 542. What new country lies between Germany and the Soviet Union? between Berlin and Vienna? on the Adriatic Sea? north of Petrograd?*

from the problems of Europe. They objected to the League of Nations. The covenant (or agreement) providing for the league's establishment formed the first section of the Versailles treaty. Wilson had put the covenant in because if the treaty was ratified by the Senate, the league would be ratified automatically. To Wilson, the league was the "only hope of mankind," and it could not be voted on separately from the treaty.

Nevertheless, the league was opposed by a powerful group of isolationist senators, such as William Borah, Hiram Johnson, and Henry Cabot Lodge, chairman of the Senate Foreign Relations Committee. They were convinced that the league represented a betrayal of America's traditional foreign policy of staying clear of European problems

as long as possible. Even though the league could not make its members go to the aid of any country attacked, the isolationists were still suspicious.

They pointed out that the covenant (1) did not recognize the Monroe Doctrine; (2) did not acknowledge that member nations had authority over their own internal affairs; (3) did not indicate that a member nation had the right to withdraw from the league if it wished; and (4) did not recognize that Congress had to approve any action the United States might take in the league.

If Wilson had been either more tactful or more willing to accept a compromise on the league, it is possible that the Senate might have approved both the treaty and the League of Nations. But Wilson was exhausted from his efforts at Versailles. His manner, to some, changed. He seemed to become cold, aloof, and even dictatorial. Things had to go exactly as he wished or they would not go at all.

Last Ditch Fight. Realizing the Senate might not approve of the league, Wilson decided to go directly to the people. Despite warnings from friends and doctors that his health was very fragile, he set out in September 1919 on an 8000-mile tour. He made thirty-five speeches in twenty-two days, explaining the need for the United States to join the league. But Senators Borah and Johnson followed in his footsteps, speaking in the same towns against the league. The effort was finally too much for Wilson. He fell ill in Pueblo, Colorado, and was rushed back to the White House. On October 2 he suffered a stroke (a blood clot in the brain) and lay partially paralyzed for over two months. He did not meet with his cabinet for six months. His health was broken, and it became more difficult for him to consider any compromise on his league.

The treaty came up for a vote in the Senate in November 1919. Senator Lodge introduced a number of amendments, called reservations, to the treaty. Wilson appealed from his sick bed to "all true friends of the treaty" to defeat the Lodge reservations. The Senate did so by a majority vote. But when the Senate voted on the treaty itself, Wilson's supporters could not obtain the necessary two-thirds.

Failure. The treaty came up again in March 1920, but again Wilson urged Democrats to reject it if the Lodge reservations were included. Wilson was willing to scrap the treaty entirely if the league provisions were not as he wanted. Democratic Senator Henry Ashurst explained the outcome: "As a friend of the President, as one who has loyally followed him, I solemnly declared to him this morning, 'If you want to kill your own child because the Senate straightens out its crooked limbs, you must take the responsibility and accept the verdict of history.'" The Senate again rejected the Lodge reservations, but again failed to muster enough votes to ratify the treaty.

The United States finally signed a separate peace treaty with Germany in 1921. But it never joined the League of Nations. Instead, the nation turned its attention to domestic issues.

Section 3 Review

COMPREHENSION   Developing Vocabulary
1. Explain these terms: covenants, mandates, isolationists, self-determination.

COMPREHENSION   Mastering Facts
1. What was Wilson's policy of self-determination?
2. List four objections to the Treaty of Versailles.
3. Why did the isolationists object to the League of Nations?
4. What was the outcome of the Senate fight over the treaty?

CHAPTER 27   Review

Chapter Summary

When war erupted in Europe in 1914, the United States tried to remain neutral. However, the sympathies of many Americans were with the Allies. As German submarines took more American lives, the nation edged closer to active participation. Woodrow Wilson was reelected by reminding Americans that he "kept us out of war." By 1917, however, Germany's unlimited submarine warfare forced Wilson to issue his war message. American troops were sent to Europe under the command of General Pershing, and the United States made the difference in the Allies' victory. At Versailles, Wilson presented fourteen points for peace that included formation of a League of Nations. The Senate, however, rejected both the treaty and the League.

Questions for Critical Thinking

COMPREHENSION   Summarizing Main Ideas

1. Give two reasons why many Americans were sympathetic toward Great Britain and France. Give two reasons why many Americans favored the Central Powers. What two groups favored neither side?

2. Tell what effect each of the following had on American public opinion: (a) the German invasion of Belgium; (b) the British blockade; (c) the sinking of the *Lusitania*; (d) expanded trade with the Allies.

3. According to Wilson, what was the purpose of World War I? Compare his attitude with that of Great Britain, France, and Italy.

4. What effect did the war have on the powers of the federal government? On the role of women in the labor force?

5. List six examples of super-Americanism during the war. Do you approve or disapprove of such actions? Why?

6. Explain how each of the first five points in Wilson's Fourteen Points might prevent a war.

COMPREHENSION   Interpreting Events

1. If you had been the president of Mexico in 1917, how would you have reacted to the Zimmermann telegram? Why?

2. Why did Wilson ask for a declaration of war only a few months after being reelected on the slogan "He Kept Us Out of War"?

3. Do you think the federal government should have the right to limit free speech during wartime? Give reasons for your opinion.

4. If you had been a U.S. senator in 1919, would you have voted in favor of the Lodge reservations to the Treaty of Versailles? Would you have voted in favor of the treaty? Why?

APPLICATION   Using Skills To Read Maps

Look at the maps on pages 542 and 555 and answer the following questions.

1. Name the nine new nations that emerged as a result of the Treaty of Versailles.

2. How did Germany's borders shift as a result of the treaty?

3. What happened to Serbia as a result of the treaty?

4. What territories did Russia lose during World War I?

5. What was the Polish Corridor?

EVALUATION   Forming Generalizations

1. Do you think a highly industrialized nation that carries on a great deal of international trade can follow a policy of isolation? Give reasons for your opinion. What might such a nation do if it wanted to encourage isolationism?

2. Does a world war seem more likely or less likely today than it was in the early 1900s? What makes you think so?

3. What is the present status of each of the nine new nations that emerged as a result of the Treaty of Versailles?

4. What is the present status of the areas that became mandates under the treaty?

European Geography

Central and Eastern Europe 1919

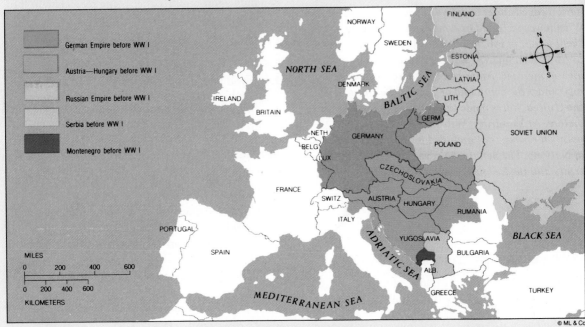

German Empire before WW I

Austria—Hungary before WW I

Russian Empire before WW I

Serbia before WW I

Montenegro before WW I

© ML & Co.

No treaty negotiations either before or since have attempted such an ambitious geographic rearrangement of a continent. When leaders of the Big Four (the United States, Great Britain, France, and Italy) gathered at Versailles in 1919, they set out to rearrange the boundaries of Europe as if the entire region were a giant puzzle.

Eventually, the final rearrangement reflected everyone's motives. The map shows that Germany was hemmed in on the east and south by the creation of buffer nations such as Poland and Czechoslovakia. These nations were created not only to isolate, surround, and punish Germany, but also to reflect the national majority of peoples living within these territories.

A second major change involved the reorganization of territory which had once been part of the Austro-Hungarian Empire; this led directly to the formation of Yugoslavia. As a result of the Treaty of Versailles, peoples who were once minorities within former nations became majorities in new nations.

"There never was a good war or a bad peace," said the wily diplomat, Ben Franklin. In the case of the Treaty of Versailles, however, many historians would disagree. Looking back through the perspective of time, it now appears that this geographic rearrangement of Europe actually sowed the seeds of future conflict. Resentments and fears later drew nations into World War II.

Understanding Geography

1. What were some of the goals that leaders of the Big Four had for attempting to reorganize Europe?

2. Which new nations were created after World War I? Which exist today?

3. Study the map of Europe following World War I. Which boundaries could have been better drawn so as to avoid future conflict?

UNIT 7   Review

Understanding Social Studies Concepts

History

1. What conditions in the United States prompted the rise of the Populist movement? What were some of the similarities that existed between Populism and Progressivism?
2. Explain the Roosevelt Corollary to the Monroe Doctrine. How did it change United States foreign policy?
3. Why were Americans eager to act against Spain in 1898 but reluctant to move against Germany in 1914?
4. What effect did American forces have on the outcome of World War I?
5. Explain why the period of the late 1800s is often referred to as the "Gilded Age." Who coined the phrase?

Geography

1. Why were the French unable to complete the Panama Canal? What problems did the United States face in building the canal? Why is the canal still important and useful today?
2. What geographical barriers helped isolate and protect United States territory during World War I? Are these barriers as important as they once were? Explain.

Economics

1. What is the purpose of tariffs? Which groups generally like to see them raised? lowered?
2. Why did farmers favor the unlimited coinage of silver during the late 1800s? How was this interest transformed into political action?
3. What economic interests in the United States were in favor of the nation gaining an overseas empire? Why? Explain the meaning of the phrase "Dollar Diplomacy."

Government

1. Though the Populist and Progressive parties both disappeared from the American scene, which of their suggested reforms eventually became part of our system?
2. What were the main objections of various Senators to the peace treaty ending World War I? What role did isolationists play in the defeat of the treaty? What might President Wilson have done differently to help get the treaty approved by the Senate?

Extending Map, Chart, Picture Skills

1. Use information from the map on page 511 to make a chart about United States overseas possessions. List the names of the possessions; when they were acquired; and their approximate distances from the United States.
2. What is your interpretation of the cartoon on page 516? Identify as many people and objects in the cartoon as you can.
3. Refer to the population chart of the United States on page 840. What was the increase in the nation's population during the time span of this unit (1876–1920)?

Understanding Current Events

1. In 1883 the Pendleton Act created the Civil Service Commission. Has civil service eliminated the patronage system? Explain.
2. Explain the connection between increased leisure time and the popularity of spectator sports. Does that connection exist today as it did around the turn of the century? Explain.
3. Through research, determine whether new national parks and wildlife areas have continued to be set aside during recent years. Do you believe that more such areas are needed? Explain.

Developing Effective Citizenship

1. Who were the muckrakers? Were they effective citizens? Explain.
2. How have direct primary elections increased the role of citizens in government? Does your state have a presidential primary during election years? What percentage of voters participated in the last presidential primary?

GLOBAL TIME LINE
1920–1940

THE UNITED STATES

THE WORLD

1920 Nineteenth Amendment grants woman suffrage.

1925 Scopes Trial.

1927 Lindbergh completes first solo flight across Atlantic.

1929 Great Depression begins.

1932 Franklin D. Roosevelt elected President.

1920

1930

1922 Union of Soviet Socialist Republics (USSR) established.

Late 1920s European colonial rule becomes firmly established in Africa.

1920 Gandhi becomes leader of National Congress in India.

1933 Hitler becomes dictator of Germany.

1931 Japanese invade Manchuria.

UNIT 8

Between World Wars

1933–1938 New Deal aids economic recovery.

1935 Congress passes Social Security Act.

1940 FDR elected to third term as president.

——1940——

1936–1939 Spanish Civil War.

The 1920s Bring Social Change

1920–1929

People in the Chapter

William Edward Burghardt Du Bois—*author, teacher, and a founder of the National Association for the Advancement of Colored People. His position concerning black demands for equal rights is more militant than that of Booker T. Washington.*

Alice Paul and Lucy Burns—*founders of the Women's Party who use picketing and other measures, considered radical at the time, to obtain woman suffrage.*

George Herman Ruth—*this great baseball star, called "the Babe" by adoring crowds, hits sixty home runs, then a record, for the New York Yankees in 1927.*

Sinclair Lewis—*American novelist and playwright from Sauk Centre, Minnesota, whose work criticizes much of American life. He is the first American to win a Nobel Prize for literature (1930).*

Linking Past to Present

The 1920s were a time of great social change. World War I had exposed many Americans to new ideas and new ways of living. The United States had become an urban nation, with more than half its population living in cities. After years of struggle, women won the right to vote. Blacks began moving from southern farms to northern cities. These factors, and others, affected the way people thought and behaved.

The popular music of the decade gave the period a name: the Jazz Age. Jazz is highly syncopated, or off a regular beat, and is often improvised by the musicians. Jazz was the decade's musical example of revolt against tradition. Other examples included new ideas about education and new styles of dress, appearance, and personal habits. The new lifestyles shocked more traditional Americans.

The decade also saw a great burst of literary and artistic creativity. From Harlem to Paris, American writers, musicians, and painters turned out works that often criticized the nation's pursuit of money making and what they saw as the narrowness of rural life.

1 MANNERS AND MORALS CHANGE

VOCABULARY   *Prohibition   speakeasies   bootleggers*

The 1920 census was the first to show that a majority of the United States population was urban. A little more than half of the nation's 106 million people now lived in cities and towns. Ten years later the population had increased by 17 million, with an increase of 15 million in urban areas.

America: Two Ways of Life

Living in cities, especially for people who moved there from rural areas, often meant a change in behavior. Standards of conduct were more relaxed in the city. City dwellers tended to be more tolerant of such activities as drinking and gambling. Social relations between men and women were less carefully regulated. Many small-town people were shocked by this. They felt that city life must inevitably lead to moral decay. City dwellers, on the other hand, felt that behavior was a matter of personal choice rather than public decision.

At the same time, life in urban communities was unquestionably lively and stimulating. There were many things to see—museums, art exhibits, plays, athletic events, trade expositions, and the like. New ideas in science were examined and often accepted. People tended to be judged on their accomplishments rather than on their social background. As a result, the city held great appeal for thousands of young men and women who had fought in Europe. That experience had broadened their horizons, and as a popular song of the time wondered, "How ya gonna keep 'em down on the farm, after they've seen Paree?"

Evolution: Court Cases

The most vigorous clash between modern and more traditional Americans took place over religious matters. An example was the so-called Monkey Trial held in Dayton, Tennessee, in 1925. John T. Scopes, in teaching his high school biology class, used a textbook outlining Darwin's theory of evolution. This theory was accepted by the majority of scientists. Many fundamentalists, however, were shocked by the idea that humans had evolved over millions of years from lower life forms. They

Clarence Darrow (in suspenders) and William Jennings Bryan championed opposite sides at the Scopes trial.

563

The "still" above was used to make illegal liquor which was then put in jars. Federal agents like these made many arrests but nothing could stop bootlegging.

pointed to the Bible's clear statement that the universe and humanity had been created in six days. To deny that, fundamentalists said, was to deny the Scriptures and to blaspheme against God. They did not want the theory of evolution taught to their children.

Earlier in March 1925 Tennessee passed a law that forbade the teaching of evolution. Scopes went on trial for violating the state law in July. The American Civil Liberties Union (ACLU) engaged Clarence Darrow, the most famous trial lawyer of the day, for the defense. William Jennings Bryan, three-time Democratic candidate for president, appeared as a special prosecutor. There was no question of guilt or innocence; Scopes was open about his action. The trial was supposed to hinge on a teacher's freedom to teach. Actually it became a battle of wits between Darrow—who did not believe in organized religion—and Bryan—a fundamentalist Christian—over the meaning of the Scriptures.

Reporters and photographers from big-city dailies, who had come to make fun of rural values, gave the trial a circus air. The jury found Scopes guilty and he was fined, but the Tennessee Supreme Court set the verdict aside on a technicality. After that, other states held back from passing laws against teaching evolution, but Tennessee's act stayed on the books until 1967—and even then the dispute was not over.

In 1981 fundamentalists in California filed a lawsuit contending that the state schools were presenting evolution as a fact. This, they claimed, violated the religious rights of children who believed in the biblical version of creation. The judge ruled against the fundamentalists but reminded the schools of the state's position that evolution was only a theory, not a scientific fact.

Prohibition: A "Noble Experiment"

Some of the abuse heaped on traditionalist America in the 1920s resulted directly from its greatest victory. On January 16, 1920, the Eighteenth Amendment—prohibiting the manufacture, sale, or transportation of alcoholic beverages—went into effect. Progressive reformers saw in the liquor trade a prime source of corruption. They felt that drunkenness led to crime, child abuse, accidents on the job, and similar problems. They had pushed the measure, but it took the church-affiliated Anti-Saloon League and the Women's Christian Temperance Union—which regarded drinking as a sin—to put the amendment across. As with woman suffrage, large areas of the country had adopted Prohibition by state law even before the constitutional amendment was ratified.

Use of Alcohol Declines.   The persistent myth that drinking increased under Prohibition is not true. Among workers, women, and children, drunkenness and alcoholism declined significantly in spite of "speakeasies" (places where liquor was illegally sold) operating almost openly in working-class neighborhoods. But for some people, liquor's illegality added to its attractiveness, and such persons may have increased their alcoholic consumption. At least in sophisticated circles, serving illegal liquor was a sign of being modern. Many films, plays, and novels helped reinforce that attitude.

Bootlegging Flourishes.   Providers of illegal drink were known as bootleggers. They smuggled beer and whiskey in from Canada or stole it from government warehouses. Often they mixed the liquor with other substances including embalming fluid. Like large-scale gambling, bootlegging was controlled by hoodlums, such as Al Capone. And again like large-scale gambling, bootlegging could exist only by bribes paid to police and judges. As a result, many people grew skeptical about the honesty of public officials, and disrespect for the law increased.

Prohibition Repealed.   Before the 1920s were far advanced, many Americans decided that Prohibition's social benefits were not worth the costs. Organized crime had increased to a fantastic extent, and taxes to pay for enforcement had gone up. In addition, many Americans felt that Prohibition invaded their individual rights. Why should society control how they behaved in private? Yet the supporters of Prohibition—especially religious fundamentalists and rural dwellers—would not yield. Alfred E. Smith's open opposition counted heavily against him in two national elections. Other politicians, such as Robert La Follette, Herbert Hoover, and Franklin D. Roosevelt, skirted the issue. Hoover, for example, called Prohibition "a noble experiment," that is, something that may or may not work. Nevertheless, the Eighteenth Amendment was finally repealed by the Twenty-first Amendment, which was ratified in 1933.

Section 1 Review

COMPREHENSION   Developing Vocabulary
1.   Explain these terms: bootleggers, speakeasies.

COMPREHENSION   Mastering Facts
1.   By what year did the United States become an urban nation?
2.   Why were many people offended by Darwin's theory?
3.   What did the Eighteenth Amendment provide?
4.   Give three reasons for the passage of the Twenty-first Amendment.

2   WOMEN ENJOY NEW CAREERS AND LIFESTYLES

VOCABULARY   *suffrage   flappers*

After a long and difficult struggle, women began the decade with a new freedom: the right to vote.

During World War I, women served their country in almost every possible capacity. They took jobs in steel foundries, chemical plants, and munitions factories. Many went overseas as nurses in the newly created U.S. Army Corps of Nurses. Their experiences away from homes and traditional women's work gave them a strong moral argument for the right to vote. As the war progressed, an increasing number of men joined women in seeing the absurdity of fighting for freedom in Europe but denying full freedom to women at home.

Although women were urged not to disrupt the war effort and to put aside their struggle for the vote until later, some women refused to be put off. They had been told to wait after the Civil War and were reluctant to do so again. In 1914 Alice Paul and Lucy Burns formed the Women's party and began a campaign of parades and picketing, patterned after the English suffrage movement, to draw attention to the issue. Beginning on January

The 1920s saw many social changes, and one of the first and most important was the 19th Amendment.

In 1923 Carrie Chapman Catt, president of the National American Woman Suffrage Association, described the effort it had taken to secure adoption of the Anthony amendment:

❝ To get the word "male" in effect out of the Constitution cost the women of the country fifty-two years of pauseless campaign. . . . During that time they were forced to conduct fifty-six campaigns of referenda to male voters; 480 campaigns to get legislatures to submit suffrage amendments to voters; 47 campaigns to get State constitutional conventions to write woman suffrage into state constitutions; 277 campaigns to get State party conventions to include woman suffrage planks; 30 campaigns to get presidential party conventions to adopt woman suffrage planks in party platforms; and 19 campaigns with 19 successive Congresses. ❞

New Look

For some people, concern over the changing status of women did not center on participation in politics. Instead, it centered on such matters as wearing short skirts, cutting hair, painting faces, and smoking and drinking in public. Many women and men were deeply shocked by such behavior. They believed it was a symptom of moral decay. Others, in contrast, regarded it as a symbol of freedom and progress.

After 1910, women's skirts rose above their traditional street length. That length had been diffi-

10, 1917, they took a stand outside the White House, and for almost a year—in sunshine, rain, sleet, and snow—they carried purple, white, and gold banners urging passage of the Anthony amendment. President Wilson invited them into the White House for hot coffee but otherwise did nothing to help. The women were subjected to jeers and even physical abuse by onlookers. Finally, they were carried off to jail as public nuisances. When they went on a hunger strike to protest their treatment, they were force-fed.

New Political Status

But the tactics of the women and the shameful way they were treated forced Congress to deal with the issue. On January 9, 1918, President Wilson declared himself in favor of woman suffrage, and on January 10 the Anthony amendment passed the House with the bare two-thirds majority. The crowd in the gallery clapped and shouted approval. Women broke into the hymn "Praise God from Whom All Blessings Flow." Still, it took another year and a half, as well as the election of a new Congress, to get the amendment through the Senate. Finally, on August 26, 1920, the last of the necessary thirty-seven states ratified the Nineteenth Amendment and it became law.

Amelia Earhart was a hero of aviation in the 1920s. She disappeared on a flight over the Pacific in 1937.

Magazines of the time often portrayed the new freedom of women. A "flapper" does the Charleston while (on the right) the "new" woman takes charge of a situation.

cult to walk in and had collected street dirt as well. Since fashion is changeable, people predicted skirts would soon go down again. But wartime shortages of fabric and more active occupations kept them nine inches above the ground. Then in the twenties they climbed even higher, finally reaching just above the knee. It was a style of women's dress not seen in the Western world in over 2000 years. During the twenties, too, the whalebone-reinforced corset, which constricted the waist and sometimes damaged the body's internal organs, was thrown into the trashcan, along with layers of petticoats.

During these years women's hairstyles were next to undergo drastic changes. The short haircut that swept the nation in the 1920s was called a "bob," or a "boyish bob" if very short. As were the new clothing styles, it was sensible, healthy, and neat—and the subject of loud public outcry.

New Interests

Young women who adopted all or most of the new styles were called flappers. But the truly "emancipated" or "new" women of the twenties were something more. They had received upbringings and educations similar to those of men. Progressive Era reforms had sharpened their interests in social, economic, and political problems. Victorious in the suffrage struggle, they had gained self-assurance and were able to deal with men on equal terms.

One of the most active and controversial women of the period was Margaret Sanger. As an obstetrical nurse in some of the worst slums of New York City, she saw firsthand the burden placed on poor women who had many children in rapid succession. That led her to open the nation's first birth-control clinic in 1916. She was arrested and imprisoned eight times for violating the Comstock Law, which prohibited the distribution of birth-control information. But the courts of New York State eventually recognized the right of women to obtain such information. The subject of birth control continues to be an extremely controversial subject.

New Goals

In addition to voting, some women attempted to enter politics. However, the highest elective offices were still closed to them. There were two women governors, Nellie Ross of Wyoming and Miriam "Ma" Ferguson of Texas, but they had been chosen as successors to their husbands. In 1916 Jeannette Rankin of Montana was elected to the House of Representatives on her own, but her opposition to America's role in World War I brought defeat in 1918. Most women in Congress got there the same way as the two governors: "widow's succession." In fact, not until 1978 was a woman elected to the Senate in her own right. She was Nancy Landon Kassebaum of Kansas.

Other political goals of women during the decade ended in disappointment. Florence Kelley led the movement for a constitutional amendment barring child labor but it was never ratified. An equal rights amendment fared worse; it could not even win the approval of Congress. For most of the public, both measures had become associated with radicalism—a fatal drawback in the 1920s.

New Jobs and Low Pay

Between 1910 and 1930, the proportion of women in the labor force remained at about 20 percent. But there was a notable change in the kinds of work some women did. The number of female cooks, dressmakers, household servants, and farmhands dropped. The number of women doctors, bankers, lawyers, police and probation officers, social workers, and hairdressers rose.

Nevertheless, most women remained in the lowest-paying occupations. And in any occupation, women were often preferred only because they would work for lower wages than men. As veteran suffragist Anna Howard Shaw explained: "You younger women have a harder task than ours. You will want equality in business, and it will be even harder to get than the vote." As the nation entered the mid-1980s, equal pay for equal work still had not been achieved in many instances.

New Roles

For all the changes in status during the twenties, it was still generally accepted—even by most women—that "woman's place is in the home." Men should earn more than women, it was thought, because usually they supported wives and children. Women workers generally were single. In some states, teachers who married lost their jobs.

In this light, the subject matter of Dorothy Canfield Fisher's 1924 novel *The Homemaker* is all the more remarkable. Fisher's heroine goes to work after her husband's business fails. She is highly successful and finds in her career a satisfaction she never got from raising children. At the same time, her husband is happy rearing the children, a task for which he is clearly better suited than working in business. Not for another fifty years were many Americans willing to consider such a possibility.

Section 2 Review

COMPREHENSION   Developing Vocabulary

1. Explain these terms: flappers, suffrage.

COMPREHENSION   Mastering Facts

1. Why were members of the Woman's party put in jail?
2. How many years did it take for women to win the right to vote?
3. Why did women's clothing styles change in the 1920s?
4. What did Nellie Ross and Miriam "Ma" Ferguson have in common?

3   A BLACK RENAISSANCE EMERGES

VOCABULARY   *Niagara Movement   filibuster   Harlem Renaissance*

Until about 1900 most blacks in the United States generally accepted Booker T. Washington's advice which you read about in chapter 24. He advised blacks to learn vocational skills, live a quiet life (preferably in the country), and avoid strife and competition with whites. Gradually, however, many blacks grew dissatisfied with a life that seemed to promise little future for them economically or intellectually. Consequently, several new movements arose in the black community.

The Great Migration

Beginning in 1910 the black population of the United States became more urban than the white population. It also began to shift from the South to the North.

In 1914 Henry Ford opened his assembly line to black workers. The outbreak of World War I and the drop in European immigration increased job opportunities in steel mills, munitions plants, and stockyards. In addition, many southern cotton fields were ruined by the boll weevil, an insect that had come to the United States from Mexico.

Floods and drought added to the economic difficulties of black sharecroppers and field hands.

So southern blacks boarded railroad trains and headed for "the top of the world." Between 1910 and 1920 about 1 million migrated to such northern cities as Chicago, New York, and Philadelphia. Another 800,000 migrated during the 1920s. This movement is known as the Great Migration.

Black migrants faced considerable prejudice in their new surroundings. Part of the prejudice was economic. Blacks not only competed with unskilled whites for jobs but also were used as strikebreakers in many northern industries. Part of the prejudice was racial.

Sometimes the prejudice took violent form. The worst race riot in United States history occurred in 1919 in Chicago. Before it ended, some 10,000 persons were involved; 38 were killed (23 blacks and 15 whites), 520 were injured (342 blacks and 178 whites), and 1000 were left homeless. The riot was sparked on July 27 when a seventeen-year-old black youth swimming in Lake Michigan swam from the water off the so-called "black beach" to the "white beach." There, white bathers threw

W. E. B. Du Bois, a founder of the NAACP, thought that Booker T. Washington's goals were too limited.

rocks at him until he drowned. Blacks who were bathing in the area attacked whites in retaliation and within a few hours mobs were fighting throughout the city. State troops finally restored order after three days.

"We Return Fighting"

Events such as these increased the appeal of more militant black leaders. One was the Massachusetts-born writer and teacher William Edward Burghardt Du Bois. The holder of three academic degrees, he was a professor of history and economics at the University of Atlanta from 1897 to 1919. In 1905 he helped found the Niagara Movement, the "first organized attempt to protest the shameful treatment [blacks] had suffered since the end of Reconstruction." In 1909 he helped found the National Association for the Advancement of Colored People (NAACP) and in 1910 he became a director of that association, a position he held for twenty-four years. He was also editor of its official magazine, *The Crisis*.

Du Bois disagreed with Booker T. Washington regarding goals and tactics. He accused Washington of educating blacks only to be farmers and artisans. Du Bois wanted blacks to strive toward higher education and the industrial mainstream of America. He also was more militant than Washington. In the May 1919 issue of *The Crisis*, he spoke for many returning black soldiers when he wrote: "We *return*. We *return from fighting*. We *return fighting*. Make way for Democracy! We saved it in France—and by the Great Jehovah we will save it in the U.S.A., or know the reason why!"

"Black is Beautiful"

Another important figure was Marcus Garvey, who began the Universal Negro Improvement Association in his native Jamaica in 1914. Two years later, he moved the UNIA to New York City and by the mid-1920s, he had enrolled more than 500,000 blacks in its ranks.

Garvey's organization was based on two ideas. First, blacks should go back to their African homeland and build a country of their own. This was an idea as old as Paul Cuffe's effort in Sierra Leone in 1815 and the founding of Liberia (chapter 13). Garvey wanted blacks to found "a free, redeemed and mighty nation. Let Africa be a bright star among the constellation of nations." The second idea was the slogan: "black is beautiful." Blacks should not envy or imitate whites or seek integration. "You are better than white people," Garvey told his followers. And he reminded them of their African heritage and urged them to be proud of it.

To finance his colonization scheme, Garvey collected money from his followers and started a successful newspaper, *The Negro World*. But his plan for a steamship company, the Black Star Line, failed and led to his being sent to prison for mail fraud. Upon release, he was deported to England.

Many blacks, especially from the working class, were swept along by Garvey's oratory and developed a strong pride in being black. But his scheme for resettlement in Africa held no appeal. Blacks were, after all, Americans and had been for generations. Instead of trying to redeem Africa, they felt they should redeem their own country by fighting for equal rights.

Legislative and Legal Battles

The NAACP attempted to do just that, mostly through court cases and legislation. In 1919 its president, poet and lawyer James Weldon Johnson, managed to have an antilynching law introduced in Congress. (Between 1889 and 1919, 3224 black men and women had been shot, burned, or hanged without trial. Between 1919 and 1927, another 400 blacks were lynched, 10 while wearing their World War I uniforms.) The bill passed the House but was filibustered to death in the Senate. A *filibuster* means holding the floor by talking at length, sometimes for days, in an attempt to postpone or avoid a vote being taken on a subject. However, the NAACP kept up its campaign, and the number of lynchings gradually diminished. The last lynching of a black was reported in 1960.

The NAACP had little success in its legal battle to do away with white primaries. In most parts of the South, there was virtually no Republican party after Reconstruction. November elections, therefore, were no more than empty formalities. The real decisions were made in Democratic primary elections. And because primaries were open only to party members, it was easy to keep blacks from voting since only whites could join the Democratic party. Court victories to bar this practice were obtained in 1927, 1932, 1944, and 1953. But they proved hollow. Each time, state officials were able to get around the ruling and find another way to keep black voters from the polls. Not until the 1960s, in an entirely different national climate, was the practice finally put to rest.

The Harlem Renaissance

Living conditions in the black ghettos of northern cities were appalling. Like European immigrants before them, blacks moved into run-down buildings in slum neighborhoods, where they paid high rents for cramped and unsanitary quarters. They were likely to be victimized by landlords and criminal elements, and their children often died of diseases which, in other circumstances, were preventable.

Nevertheless, the move north, especially to New York City's Harlem, released a great burst of creative energy. Harlem was the center of the nation's black intellectual and cultural life, and out of it flooded achievements in literature, music, drama, dance, and painting. These achievements are known collectively as the Harlem Renaissance, though some of the best work was done elsewhere.

Writers. The most lasting contribution of the Harlem Renaissance may have been in poetry. James Weldon Johnson was already well established in 1920, but Claude McKay, Langston Hughes, and Countee Cullen made their reputations during the decade. Here is part of Cullen's poem "Saturday's Child."

" Some are teethed on a silver spoon,
With the stars strung for a rattle;
I cut my teeth as the black raccoon—
For implements of battle. . . .
Some are swaddled in silk and down,
And heralded by a star;
They swathed my limbs in a sackcloth gown
On a night that was black as tar. . . .
For I was born on Saturday—
"Bad time for planting a seed,"
Was all my father had to say,
And, "One mouth more to feed." "

Actors and Musicians. It was in the performing arts that blacks gained their widest audiences. Tenor Roland Hayes won renown as a concert singer, as did Paul Robeson, the son of a runaway slave. Robeson, after making a brilliant record as a student and athlete at Rutgers, went on to Columbia University Law School. His magnificent bass voice and commanding presence brought him early fame as an actor. He was the original

Josephine Baker, who reached the peak of her fame in Europe, made France her permanent home.

Emperor Jones in Eugene O'Neill's play of the same name, and his performance in Shakespeare's *Othello* in London and New York made stage history. But the slights and indignities he experienced turned him away from America. He spent most of his later years in England and the Soviet Union.

Jazz is generally considered America's outstanding musical achievement. It originated in the latter part of the nineteenth century and was based mostly on black work songs and spirituals, or deeply emotional religious songs. In 1915 New Orleans, or Dixieland, jazz found its way to Chicago. There, King Oliver and a small group, including trumpeter Louis Armstrong, played what was probably the first jazz heard north of the Mason-Dixon line. The music quickly spread from Chicago to Kansas City, Los Angeles, and New York. Black composers and performers such as W. C. Handy, Cab Calloway, Eubie Blake, Ethel Waters, and Bessie Smith helped plant it in American culture.

Many black musical artists achieved great fame in Europe. Perhaps the most popular was Josephine Baker, who lived and worked in Paris. She was a star dancer and singer for forty years. After World War II the French government awarded her the Legion of Honor for her devotion to her adopted land.

Section 3 Review

COMPREHENSION   Developing Vocabulary

1. Explain these terms: filibuster, Niagara Movement, Harlem Renaissance, NAACP.

COMPREHENSION   Mastering Facts

1. What were the causes of the Great Migration?
2. How did W. E. B. Du Bois's hopes for the future of black people differ from those of Booker T. Washington?
3. What did Marcus Garvey want black people to do, and why did many blacks object?
4. What techniques did the NAACP use in trying to achieve its goals?

4   HEROES AND ISSUES OF THE TWENTIES

VOCABULARY   *tabloids   materialism*

Recreation, education, and communication were other areas in which changes took place during the twenties.

Going to the Movies

The first motion pictures were one-reel, 10-minute sequences consisting mostly of vaudeville skits or faked newsreels. In 1903 *The Great Train Robbery* introduced both westerns and a plot to the silver screen. By 1914, films consisted of two-hour features with such stars as Mary Pickford, Lillian and Dorothy Gish, Fatty Arbuckle, Charlie Chaplin, John Barrymore, William S. Hart, Harold Lloyd, and Douglas Fairbanks. There were also serials, such as *The Perils of Pauline*, starring Pearl White. As Pauline Marvin, a headstrong heiress seeking adventure, she fought off Indians, fell off cliffs, disappeared through trap doors in haunted houses, and was tied to a railroad track in front of an oncoming train. But to the relief of her enraptured audience, she was always saved in the nick of time by her courageous boyfriend.

Probably the most significant motion picture of the decade was D. W. Griffith's *Birth of a Nation*, which opened in 1915. Three hours long, it told the story of the Civil War and Reconstruction from the viewpoint of the Confederacy. Audiences thrilled to its blockbuster scenes with hundreds of extras. In the North, they also rioted in protest against scenes that favorably showed the Ku Klux Klan and the lynching of blacks.

By 1925, making and exhibiting films had grown to be the nation's fourth-largest industry, and more than 20,500 movie houses were operating throughout the United States. The smallest community had at least one cranking away for seven or eight hours a day and showing six pictures a week in three "double bills" (two movies for the price of one). Larger communities had one or more first-run houses downtown, where new films played before being shown in neighborhood theaters. The downtown "palaces" featured a "mighty Wurlitzer" organ or even a small symphony orchestra to accompany the films. Neighborhood theaters made do with tinny pianos.

Hollywood, a small town near Los Angeles, became the film capital of the country and, later, of the world. There, director D. W. Griffith introduced the close-up and the moving camera. In

Hollywood, actor Charlie Chaplin invented his world-famous character of the Little Tramp, a funny-looking little man, pretentious and impish, but warmhearted under it all. There, in 1927, the first major film with sound was produced. It was *The Jazz Singer*, starring Al Jolson, and it marked the start of a new age in motion pictures.

Challenges to Education

American education was also a growth industry during the twenties. Its chief area of expansion was in the high school. Until that time, the eighth grade had been the end of formal education for most children. High school—even though it was free—meant financial sacrifice, because most children were counted on to work and to provide a share of the family income until they married and established families of their own.

Increasing Enrollment. In 1914 only half a million Americans were in high school preparing for college or for better jobs in industry. By 1926 the number had jumped to 4 million. Yet this eightfold increase still accounted for only half the population of high school age. The remarkable increase was due to prosperous times and to higher educational standards for jobs in mass-production industries. If one wanted a good job, one needed a high school education.

Increasing Taxes. The greater numbers of high school students meant a steep increase in taxes for taxpayers. School costs doubled from 1913 to 1920, and they doubled again by 1926. The first jump was a result of inflation, but it was a staggering sum nevertheless. In fact, the total cost of American education in the mid-1920s—2.7 billion dollars a year—was half the amount spent on education by all other countries combined!

The modern high school appeared during this time. Before, high school was designed primarily for those going on to college. Now it had courses for the entire community. Larger student bodies meant wider offerings of courses, including vocational training, shop work, and home economics.

Educating Immigrants. A special challenge schools faced in the 1920s was educating children of immigrants. Although schools had been doing that for over fifty years, the period just before World War I saw the largest immigration in the

Cecil B. DeMille's Cleopatra (1934) is an example of the "epic" film that developed during the 1920s.

nation's history—close to a million newcomers a year. Unlike the earlier English and Irish immigrants, many of them did not speak the language of the country. By the 1920s their children were filling city classrooms. It is a measure of the schools' accomplishment and the students' determination that a higher proportion of such children learned to read and write than did the children of native-born whites.

Expanded News Coverage

One result of increased education was a higher readership of newspapers and magazines. During the war, interest in the news had risen. To meet the demand, *Time*, the first weekly newsmagazine, appeared in 1923 and soon became extremely popular. Newspapers also expanded their coverage, and some brought out huge, magazine-type Sunday supplements. Others bought or opened radio stations. Most of the money for this expansion came not only from higher circulation, for city papers cost only two cents on weekdays and ten on Sunday. The growth was paid primarily out of the great increases in advertising revenues, of which newspapers got a large portion. Never before had Americans been able to get so much news from so many places.

To catch an even wider readership, *tabloids* were introduced. These were half the regular page size and made liberal use of pictures. They were something like the sensationalist yellow press of the late-nineteenth century. They specialized in news of murders, kidnappings, and activities of gangsters and show people. Pictures were large, and often violent, and bold headlines screamed the news. The *Daily News* and the *Daily Mirror*, both in New York, were the most widely imitated.

Ballyhoo. Largely because of tabloids, the twenties produced its version of what is now called "media hype." That is, insignificant events were blown way out of proportion to their real importance. In those days it was called "ballyhoo," but the result was the same.

Lindbergh, the Hero. Even when the ballyhoo specialists had a genuine hero, they misrepresented him. On May 20–21, 1927, Charles A. Lindbergh flew alone, non-stop, from New York to Paris. It was a startling thirty-one-hour feat, and the papers played it up to the hilt. But they did it in such terms as "Lucky Lindy" and "the Flying Fool." Lindbergh was no fool, and luck had nothing to do with his achievement. He succeeded by working out every possible detail of his flight in advance. But the press had to present him in the most startling way possible.

Ruth, the "Babe." Interest in what has been called "children's games played by grown men for money," that is, professional athletics, reached a new peak in the twenties. Each sport had a single figure of legendary accomplishment.

In baseball the figure was George Herman Ruth, commonly known as Babe Ruth. He was a hard-drinking, salty-talking character whom the fans took to their hearts as they would a good-natured, unruly younger brother. Ruth's record of sixty home runs hit in one season—for the New York Yankees in 1927—has been surpassed. But many claim that only a longer playing season and a livelier ball made it possible. In any event, Ruth led the Yankees to seven world-series pennants between 1921 and 1932. Yankee Stadium, which opened in 1923, was known as "the house that Ruth built." Ruth was noted for paying visits to youngsters in hospitals, and shortly before his death in 1948, he set up a foundation to help underprivileged children.

Grange, the "Galloping Ghost." College football had its hero in Harold Edward "Red" Grange, otherwise known as the "Galloping Ghost" for his feats at the University of Illinois. Why a college

sport caught the attention of so many people who never finished high school is hard to determine—perhaps because in those years its dominance passed from eastern Ivy League schools to the huge midwestern universities. Loyal citizens of Michigan or Ohio could pile into new stadiums seating 70,000 or 80,000 people on Saturday afternoons and scream themselves hoarse for "their" team. The "Fighting Irish" of Notre Dame appealed to Americans of Irish descent. This was despite the school's legendary coach having the Norwegian name of Knute Rockne, as well as many of its players being sons of Slavic coal miners from Pennsylvania.

Dempsey, the "Manassa Mauler." Heavyweight boxing was particularly open to ballyhoo treatment. It was easy to work up popular frenzy over the periodic world-championship bouts. Here, a "million-dollar gate," (in paid admissions) was the goal. One of the most popular figures was Jack Dempsey of Manassa, Colorado. Thousands watched the career of this champion fighter. In 1927, when ex-champion Dempsey met Gene Tunney for their second bout, the promoters raked in $2,650,000.

Other Sports Idols. Men's tennis had its hero in "Big Bill" Tilden, and the women's game was dominated by Helen Wills. Their games and lives were followed by millions of people through radio, the press, and newsreels. Atlanta's Bobby Jones was the only golfer in history to make a "grand slam" by winning all British and American open and amateur matches in a single year (1930), after which he retired. Even racing had its wonder horse, Man-of-War, whose descendants are still prized animals.

The Yiddish Theater

The theater also bloomed during the 1920s, especially the Yiddish theater in New York City. Many of the developments that took place on the Yiddish stage showed up a few years later in the English-speaking theater on Broadway.

One such development was the theater-party benefit. Most Russian Jewish immigrants were organized into lodges that not only provided health insurance and burial benefits but also sponsored theater outings. For $300 a lodge could, and did, buy out the house.

Sinclair Lewis (left), Ernest Hemingway (center), and F. Scott Fitzgerald spoke for the social discontent of their generation.

The Yiddish theater also pioneered in the psychological approach to acting. The first theater was located near the Lower East Side of New York—within walking distance of the main Jewish immigrant neighborhood. Later, plays were produced on Broadway. Yiddish theater continued the traditions of the Gilded Age—broad melodramas, comedies, and Shakespeare. Later it performed works by Henrik Ibsen, Maxim Gorky, and others.

The outstanding actor of the Yiddish theater was Jacob P. Adler. When he died in 1926, most New York stores closed for the funeral, while church bells rang all afternoon.

Speaking for the Twenties

A common theme of most novels of the period was opposition to *materialism*. Materialism is usually defined as the single-minded pursuit of money and possessions. Most writers were against the modern business culture. F. Scott Fitzgerald, fresh from Princeton and the army and as handsome as a film star, published *This Side of Paradise* in 1920. He won instant acclaim as the spokesman for the twenties generation. In this novel and others, he described the confusion and tragedy caused by a frantic search for material success.

Sinclair Lewis (*Babbitt, Main Street*) was the most violent critic of materialism and of the hypocrisy and narrowness of American small-town life. He also attacked American medicine (*Arrowsmith*) and religion (*Elmer Gantry*). His novels were too savage to be very effective, but he never-

theless won the Nobel Prize for literature in 1930.

Ernest Hemingway, in *The Sun Also Rises* and *A Farewell to Arms*, expressed disgust with prewar codes of behavior and the glorification of war. He also developed a clear, straightforward prose that set a new, tough, "hard-boiled" literary style.

Poet T. S. Eliot's *The Waste Land* was perhaps the most agonizing view of the dehumanizing effects of the machine age. It is considered by some critics to be the great poem of the twentieth century.

Many American writers and artists felt stifled in what they called the "vulgar, money-grubbing" society of the 1920s. They fled to Europe where they felt they could live a richer cultural and intellectual life. From there they watched with dismayed fascination the fast-paced business life of the United States, which you will read about in the next chapter.

Section 4 Review

COMPREHENSION   Developing Vocabulary

1. Explain these terms: tabloids, materialism, ballyhoo, double bills.

COMPREHENSION   Mastering Facts

1. How did *The Jazz Singer* change motion pictures?
2. How did high schools change in the 1920s?
3. What were the most popular professional sports of the twenties?
4. What attitude did many American writers of the twenties have toward the society of their day?

CHAPTER 28　Review

Chapter Summary

Social change characterized the 1920s. For the first time, a majority of Americans lived in cities, and their modern values differed from those found in rural areas. Those values clashed in the Scopes Trial. Prohibition became national policy with the Eighteenth Amendment, but it created widespread illegal activities. Meanwhile, women finally gained the right to vote. Although there was little overall improvement in urban areas, New York's Harlem area gave birth to a Renaissance of black culture. All Americans enjoyed new forms of literature, music, and popular entertainment during the 1920s, and only a few criticized the materialism of the age.

Questions for Critical Thinking

COMPREHENSION　Summarizing Main Ideas

1. What were the attractions of urban life in the 1920s? What criticisms did many rural people make about life in the big city?

2. Compare the arguments in favor of the anti-evolution law passed in Tennessee with the arguments raised by the Puritans when they expelled Anne Hutchinson and other dissenters from Massachusetts.

3. List five results of Prohibition. Which do you consider desirable? Which do you consider undesirable? Give reasons for your opinion.

4. How did women change each of the following during the 1920s? (a) political status; (b) social roles; (c) appearance; (d) jobs.

5. What two factors contributed to the race riots of 1919?

6. What forms of recreation became popular in the 1920s? Which of them do you enjoy today?

COMPREHENSION　Interpreting Events

1. Why did Progressive reformers favor Prohibition? Why did church-affiliated groups favor it?

2. If you had been a black in the 1920s, would you have supported Marcus Garvey's back-to-Africa movement? Why or why not?

3. Explain the meaning of Countee Cullen's poem "Saturday's Child." Where does the title come from? Why do you think Cullen chose it?

4. What objections did many writers of the twenties raise against American society? Do you think they were justified in their opinion? Why or why not?

APPLICATION　Using Skills To Evaluate Sources

For each item below, tell which of the two index entries would be more likely to yield the necessary information.

1. The decision in the Monkey Trial
   a. John T. Scopes
   b. Evolution

2. Women in politics
   a. Politics
   b. The Anthony amendment

3. Dixieland jazz
   a. Dixieland
   b. Jazz

EVALUATION　Forming Generalizations

1. What groups currently oppose the teaching of evolution in schools? What states, if any, have laws either prohibiting or limiting such teaching? Do you agree or disagree with this type of legislation? Why?

2. Why was Prohibition difficult to enforce?

Freedom of the Press

To Americans, freedom of the press sometimes means the freedom to be controversial. It is true that newspapers, magazines, television, and radio—the media—provide much information and entertainment. However, it is controversy and difference of opinion that really command public attention. Americans are indeed fortunate to live under a political system that not only allows but encourages controversy.

A Free Press Does Its Job.
Without the freedom to provide people with news and information, our democratic system could not function. The media strengthen our republican institutions by keeping the public informed, exposing official mistakes, and helping the citizenry make educated decisions. For example, during Richard Nixon's administration, reporters at the *Washington Post* spearheaded an investigation into the Watergate break-in. This was the greatest example ever of investigative reporting. It led to the resignation of an American president.

Likewise, televised coverage of the Vietnam conflict was instrumental in bringing the war directly into people's living rooms and ultimately causing many to oppose American participation in the war.

As our society becomes in-creasingly complex, the media seem to gain greater and greater influence. Newspapers and television networks exercise tremendous power over readers and viewers by either reporting or not reporting certain items—or by reporting them from a positive or negative viewpoint. That is why the media have a strong responsibility to be fair and accurate in their coverage of the news. Sometimes the media have erred in their judgment, such as during the "yellow journalism" days that helped push the nation into the Spanish-American War. Overall, however, the media have generally accepted the challenge to exercise responsibility.

Before the Bill of Rights.
How did freedom of the press find its way into the Bill of Rights? Until ratification of the First Amendment in 1791, freedom of the press was not a widely accepted right. Before publishing almanacs or newspapers, for instance, colonial printers needed a license; this amounted to censorship before publication. As a matter of course, legislatures and colonial councils punished publishers for seditious libel—statements critical of or encouraging resistance to the government.

Even after the acquittal in 1735 of John Peter Zenger (see page 100), freedom to criticize the government did not become an accepted right. During the Revolution, Loyalist editors were sometimes tarred and feathered for publishing anti-patriot sentiments. Indeed, colonial legislatures construed freedom of the press so narrowly that one historian has called it a "legacy of suppression."

The First Amendment to the Constitution departed from this restrictive heritage. Quite simply, the Amendment prohibited Congress from making any law abridging freedom of the press. This was a bold statement for 1791, but at that time its meaning was still somewhat unclear. Were there really to be no limits on freedom of the press? In other words, could anyone print absolutely anything?

War and a Free Press.
Over the years, Congress and the courts have decided that there are indeed some limits to freedom of the press. They have agreed that the right depends on time and circumstances. During World War I, for example, the Supreme Court ruled that Congress could indeed suppress written material that posed a "clear and present danger" to the nation's survival during war. Thus, the nation's free press was not completely free.

But even though wartime has historically tested individual rights, it does not necessarily follow that those rights have always been limited. In contrast to World War I, the press enjoyed remarkable freedom during the Civil War.

Despite a few temporary suspensions of newspaper publications by military officers, the government made almost no effort to control the news. Reporters during the Civil War had wide latitude in covering events and expressing editorial opinions. In fact, so much valuable military data appeared in northern newspapers that it was General Lee's practice to read them for information.

The Debate Goes On.

Though the First Amendment has been a fundamental principle of our democratic system for two centuries, the debate goes on concerning freedom of the press. In 1983, for example, newspapers and major networks protested strongly when the government would not allow reporters to accompany American troops when they landed on Grenada. The government said that it would provide films of the military operation. The media responded with accusations of censorship; they reminded the government that reporters had provided full coverage of much larger battles in Vietnam, the Middle East, and Europe.

Discussions of freedom of the press are not limited to military cases. One of the most difficult situations the Supreme Court has had to deal with concerns

The First Amendment guarantees the right of newspaper, magazine, television, and radio reporters to interview public officials.

pornography and obscenity in magazines, movies, and television. Does the First Amendment permit—and even protect—the right of people to print or distribute obscene materials? Where do the rights of other individuals fit into all of this—the rights of those who want to be protected from such materials? So far the Court has tried to let local communities formulate their own definitions of what is and is not obscene.

While newspapers and magazines are an important part of our heritage, the day approaches when they may be replaced by home electronic information centers. But whatever their form, the media will still play an important role in the future of our nation. A free press is yet another cornerstone of American

democracy. After all, Thomas Jefferson once said that if he had to choose, he would prefer having newspapers without government to having government without newspapers.

Understanding Our Heritage

1. Do the press and government often find themselves in conflict? Explain your answer using examples from the past and present.

2. How will technology help or hinder the free press in maintaining republican institutions? What problems might arise from reporting news by computer?

3. What limits are there on freedom of the press? Are these limits necessary? Explain your reasoning.

CHAPTER 29

Politics and a Thin Prosperity

1920–1929

Linking Past to Present

The Republican administrations of the 1920s, those of Harding, Coolidge, and Hoover, made a sharp break with the policies of the three preceding presidents—Theodore Roosevelt, Taft, and Wilson. It was as if the nation had become weary of the struggles for social reform of the Progressive Era and of the sacrifices of World War I.

Making money again became for many people an exciting adventure. The federal government encouraged business and industry to grow and prosper without paying much attention to how it was done. The government imposed few restrictions on business leaders. The close connections between business and government led to the same sort of corruption and scandals that had marked the Gilded Age.

Business boomed and people began to think prosperity might go on forever. But in 1929 the stock market crashed, and the United States fell into the deepest depression of its history.

1 A TROUBLED POSTWAR WORLD

VOCABULARY   *Comintern*   *anarchists*

The police of Boston were angry. They had not had a raise since the beginning of World War I and by now, 1919, the cost of living had doubled. So they sent a group of representatives to the police commissioner to ask for what they considered a living wage. The commissioner promptly fired everyone in the group, and the remaining police responded by going out on strike. In the absence of police protection, some looting took place in downtown Boston. A number of windows were smashed, and people openly rolled dice on Boston Common. After an appeal from the mayor, Governor Calvin Coolidge called out the National Guard. Peace was restored, and the police called off the strike.

The police commissioner, however, refused to allow the men to return to their jobs. Instead, he hired a new police force which, ironically, received everything the strikers had asked for. Months later, when Coolidge received an appeal on behalf of the fired men from AFL President Samuel Gompers, he replied, "There is no right to strike against the public safety by anyone, anywhere, anytime." His statement made headlines throughout the country, and he was praised for saving Boston, if not the nation, from anarchy.

The Red Scare

If the public seemed to be over-reacting to events in Boston, there were reasons for such behavior. What frightened many Americans was the threat of communism.

In 1919 there were Communist attempts to overthrow the governments of Germany and Hungary. Also in March of 1919, The Third Communist International—consisting mostly of delegates from the Russian Communist party—convened in Moscow for the stated purpose of encouraging worldwide revolutions. The Communist International, called the *Comintern*, for short, advocated the overthrow of the capitalist system, and the abolition of free enterprise and private property.

Many radicals in the United States were Communists but many more were not. The public, however, found it difficult to distinguish between the two. Many Americans feared that radical support of unions was, really, an attack on the free enterprise system. Their fears were fed by the numerous strikes of 1919.

During World War I strikes were few because nothing was allowed to interfere with the war effort. But 1919 saw more than 3000 strikes with some 4 million workers walking off the job at one time or another. Wages had not kept up with prices but employers did not want to raise them. Nor did they want their employees to join unions. Some employees, either out of sincere belief, or because they saw a way to keep wages down, tried to show that union members were trying to start a revolution. Newspaper headlines screamed: CRIMES AGAINST SOCIETY, CONSPIRACIES AGAINST THE GOVERNMENT and PLOTS TO ESTABLISH COMMUNISM.

In April 1919 some bombs began turning up in the U.S. mails. They were hidden in packages addressed to various government and business leaders. During the next week, random explosions and outbreaks of violence in a number of cities caused

579

Soldiers of the Massachusetts National Guard break-up a demonstration of Boston policemen (in street clothes) in 1919. Many people thought public servants should not strike.

something like panic to grip the nation. On May 1, or May Day, the international worker's holiday, the violence was intense. That was followed throughout the summer by heavy labor unrest. And in the fall, two major strikes closed down the nation's coal mines and steel mills.

That same fall, agents of U.S. Attorney General A. Mitchell Palmer raided the offices of *anarchists* (who oppose all forms of government) as well as Socialist and Communist organizations. Most Americans were unaware that the three were different kinds of radical movements and that not all believed in violent revolution. It scarcely mattered. Most of their members were recent immigrants or people with foreign-sounding names, and that was enough to prove that they were un-American and undesirable.

In his earnestness, Palmer ran roughshod over people's civil rights. The "Palmer raids" were often conducted without search warrants. People were kept locked up for long periods without being allowed to see a lawyer. Many were arrested not because of their actions or affiliations but because they were friends of persons Palmer considered suspicious. Many of those arrested were not American citizens, and in December 1919, 249 of these aliens were put on board the ship *Buford* and deported.

During the next month, an additional 3000 persons were arrested. They were rumored to be armed to the teeth. But government agents found no explosives and only three pistols, so most of those arrested were released.

Palmer was a great hero for a time. But he kept predicting riots that never came. Finally, he said there would be serious trouble on May Day, 1920. After a calm May 1, people began to lose interest in him and his anti-Red crusade.

The Klan Again

Meanwhile, another movement, the Ku Klux Klan, was growing swiftly. The Klan of Reconstruction days had more or less died out in the 1870s. Revived in 1915, it reached a peak membership of 4.5 million "white male persons, native-born Gentile citizens" in 1924. The old practices of wearing hoods and burning crosses were still used, but the KKK widened its interests and its appeal. As well as keeping blacks "in their place," it sought to drive Catholics, Jews, and other "foreigners" from the land. It opposed union organizers and helped enforce Prohibition.

Klan members, as Grand Wizard Hiram Evans explained, were "plain people . . . the everyday, not highly cultured, not overly intellectualized, but entirely unspoiled and not de-Americanized, average citizen of the old stock." In other words, they were people who felt very threatened by the changes taking place in American society. They resented the small advances made by blacks during the war. They felt that their moral values were being attacked by urban intellectuals. They feared job competition from immigrants. They were convinced that foreigners were going to overthrow the American way of life.

Klan members expressed some of their frustrations in racial violence. They expressed some by trying to influence national and state politics. But Klan leaders in Indiana, the only state to fall under its control, committed such outrages that the law finally moved against them. After a while, most of the Klan's members drifted away.

Steel Mills: A Twenty-Four-Hour Workday

Public opinion had been outraged by the Boston police strike. It was equally opposed to the steel strike that began in September 1919.

Most steel workers put in seven, twelve-hour days every week in hot and noisy foundries. Since steel furnaces must operate around the clock, there were two shifts. Once every two weeks, a steel worker "swung" from the day shift to the night shift. This "swing shift" meant he had to work an incredible twenty-four hours! And that was at labor as hard, uncomfortable, and dangerous as any in American industry.

The steel industry was not unionized, although more than twenty unions belonging to the American Federation of Labor wanted to represent various occupations in the mills. This unwieldly group formed an organizing committee under William Z. Foster, but its efforts were badly coordinated. The AFL unions were jealous of one another, and Foster offended and frightened many with his radicalism. He later joined the Communist party and was its presidential candidate in 1924, 1928, and 1932.

The steel strike was broken in January 1920, after eighteen workers had been killed by a combination of U.S. Steel security police, state militia, and federal troops. At first people in general were relieved that another threat by "un-American elements" had been turned back. Then, in 1923, a Protestant interfaith committee published a report on working conditions in the mills. The report shocked the public, and the steel companies agreed to establish an eight-hour day. But steel workers remained unorganized.

John L. Lewis and the Coal Miners

Unionism was more successful in America's coalfields. In 1919 the United Mine Workers, organized since 1890, got a new president. He was a burly young man equally ready to throw an insult or a punch at anyone who got in his way. His family came from Wales, and they had been mining coal, and organizing miners, for generations.

John Llewellyn Lewis called his union's members out on November 1, 1919. On November 9 Attorney General Palmer got a court order sending the miners back to work. Lewis declared the strike over. "We cannot fight the government," he said with uncharacteristic meekness. But he quietly gave the word for the strike to continue.

The mines stayed closed for another month. Finally, President Wilson promised to have an arbitrator decide the issues between the miners and the mine owners. In due course the miners received a 27 percent wage increase, and John L. Lewis became a national figure. He fought often and hard, and with great success, to get better wages and working conditions for the miners. As a result, he was one of the most admired and hated men of the time.

The Sacco-Vanzetti Trial

Other figures in the 1920s were even more controversial than Lewis. Two of them, Italian immigrants Nicola Sacco and Bartolomeo Vanzetti, described themselves as "a good shoemaker and a poor fish peddler." They were also anarchists who had evaded the draft during World War I.

On May 5, 1920, they were arrested for a payroll robbery in South Braintree, Massachusetts, in which the paymaster and his guard were shot and killed. Although anarchists sometimes committed such crimes to get money for their cause, the evidence against Sacco and Vanzetti was circumstantial. Nevertheless, they were found guilty and sentenced to death. The state supreme court refused to grant a new trial, and Governor Alvan T. Fuller refused to pardon them or to change the sentence. But he postponed execution while a committee of three distinguished citizens exam-

The trial and execution of Bartolomeo Vanzetti (left) and Nicola Sacco drew worldwide furor.

At the time, many believed that America's reputation for justice had been tarnished forever. Looking back, it seems that public feeling against anarchists was so strong that the men would have been found guilty—even if they were not.

In 1961 new ballistics tests showed that the pistol found on Sacco had in fact been used to murder the guard, although there was no proof that Sacco had been the one to pull the trigger. However, many authorities now believe that Sacco was probably guilty but Vanzetti was probably innocent.

Section 1 Review

COMPREHENSION   Developing Vocabulary

1. Explain these terms: anarchists, Comintern, swing shift, May Day.

COMPREHENSION   Mastering Facts

1. Why did Ku Klux Klan membership increase during the 1920s?
2. What caused people to finally lose interest in Palmer and his anti-Red crusade?
3. What changes did John L. Lewis bring about in the nation's coal mines?
4. Why were there protests against the Sacco-Vanzetti trial?

ined the case. The committee strongly criticized the behavior of the judge, who had not remained impartial during the proceedings. But the committee upheld the conviction. In spite of protests and demonstrations in the United States, Europe, and Latin America, Sacco and Vanzetti were electrocuted on August 23, 1927.

2 A RETURN TO NORMALCY AND ISOLATION

VOCABULARY   *capital ship   reparations*

Sometimes when a political party has been out of office for a time and sees a chance for victory, it searches for its best possible candidate. The Republicans in 1920 did not do so. They nominated Senator Warren G. Harding, whom the *New York Times* called "a respectable Ohio politician of the second class." Some people believed that the *Times* had been too generous; they felt that Harding was not a respectable politician. However, he was handsome, good-natured, and, as one of his followers said, he "looked like a President ought to look." Governor Coolidge of Massachusetts, the hero of the Boston police strike, was nominated as his vice-president.

In November 1920, Harding and Coolidge swamped Democratic candidates James M. Cox and Franklin D. Roosevelt by 16 million votes to 9 million. The electoral count was even more of a landslide: 404 to 127.

Harding's Policy and Cabinet

The new president favored a two-part policy. On the domestic front, it involved a "return to normalcy." By this, Harding apparently meant the simpler days before the Progressive Era. He was opposed to the federal government's taking a role in business affairs, and he disapproved of most social reforms. On the foreign front, Harding disagreed with Wilson's ideas about the League of Nations. "We seek no part in directing the destinies of the Old World."

Harding made some excellent cabinet appointments. Charles Evans Hughes, secretary of state, was an able and dedicated public servant who went on to be chief justice of the United States. Herbert Hoover, secretary of commerce, was a popular figure because of his masterly handling of food supplies and refugee problems during the war. Andrew Mellon, Pittsburgh banker and financier, served twelve years as a cabinet member and was considered by many the greatest secretary of the treasury since Alexander Hamilton. Henry C. Wallace, secretary of agriculture, was a pioneer in advanced farming methods.

Unhappily, the cabinet also included the so-called "Ohio gang," the president's poker-playing cronies from back home. There was Attorney General Harry M. Daugherty, a lobbyist for tobacco and meat-packing companies who had been the first to push Harding for the presidency. And there was Interior Secretary Albert B. Fall, a close friend of various oil executives, about whose behavior you will read more.

The International Washington Conference

During the presidential campaign, the Republicans had talked of having some form of international cooperation as a substitute for the League of Nations. In August 1921 Harding invited all important nations except Russia to a conference in Washington to discuss naval armaments and the Far East.

Naval Force Reductions. When representatives of the nations gathered in Washington that November, they were expecting a routine speech

President Harding (left) and his cabinet whose members, with some exceptions, were weak and corrupt.

of welcome from Secretary of State Hughes. Instead, they were startled to hear a series of concrete proposals about arms control.

First, Hughes suggested a ten-year "naval holiday" during which time the nations would not build any warships. In addition, he suggested that the five major powers—the United States, Great Britain, Japan, France, and Italy—adjust the size of their fleets. The United States, Hughes said, would scrap 845,000 tons of *capital ship*, that is, battleships and cruisers. Britain would do the same with 583,000 tons and Japan with 480,000 tons. That would leave the United States and Britain with 500,000 tons of capital ships each and the Japanese with 300,000 tons—a ratio of 5:5:3. France and Italy were to restrict themselves to 175,000 tons each.

In the end the conference agreed to accept this proposal. The agreement was called the Five-Power Treaty.

Preserving Peace in the Far East. The Washington Conference also attempted to keep things calm in the Far East. The United States, Britain, Japan, and France signed the Four-Power Treaty to respect one another's interests in the Pacific area. The same nations joined with China, Italy, Belgium, the Netherlands, and Portugal to sign the Nine-Power Treaty. They promised to uphold the Open Door Policy and to keep China from being carved up further.

The Five-Power Treaty probably headed off a costly arms race. The other agreements may also have eased tensions between the United States and the rising power of Japan. In all, the conference was an admirable first step to world peace. But a second step was never taken. Efforts to limit the number of submarines and other small vessels met with no success, nor did efforts to reduce land armaments.

War Debts and Reparations

Behind the international glow of the Washington Conference, the Harding administration was actually turning its face away from Europe. The United States was trying to defuse trouble spots in the Far East and to cut down on the cost of armaments. But it was not retreating from its stand on war debts.

Through American bankers, Allied nations had borrowed over $10 billion to finance their war ef-

Presidential Election of 1920

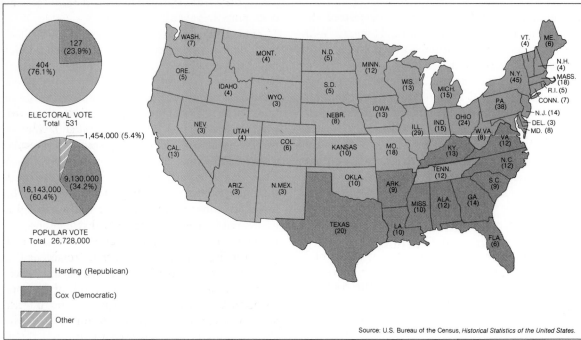

ELECTORAL VOTE
Total 531

404 (76.1%)
127 (23.9%)

POPULAR VOTE
Total 26,728,000

1,454,000 (5.4%)
16,143,000 (60.4%)
9,130,000 (34.2%)

Harding (Republican)

Cox (Democratic)

Other

Source: U.S. Bureau of the Census, *Historical Statistics of the United States.*

© ML & Co.

Map Skills *Who won almost all of the Southern states? Who won the election? What was his electoral vote? What was his percentage of the popular vote? What was his party?*

fort. When the fighting ended, Britain and France expected that some part of that would be written off as a contribution to the common struggle. Not at all. The American government insisted on payment in full. But the bankrupt Allies could raise the money in only two ways. One was through *reparations,* (payments for war damages) which Germany had promised to give the Allies. The other was by exporting more goods to the United States.

Higher Tariffs. U.S. policy in the 1920s was firmly against either solution. From the first moment of peace, America had urged Britain and France not to press their demands on Germany. Then, in 1922, the United States raised its tax on imported goods to the highest level to date. The Fordney-McCumber Tariff Act openly aimed at keeping foreign goods out of American markets. And it did. European exports to the United States fell from $5 billion in 1920 to $2.5 billion in 1922. Since England and France could not sell their products in the States, they were even less able to pay their debts.

The Dawes Plan. A series of international conferences tried to cope with the tangle of wartime debts and reparations. American banker Charles

G. Dawes and Owen D. Young of General Electric were responsible for the system that emerged. Between 1923 and 1930 American investors loaned about $2.5 billion to the German government and to German corporations. During the same years, Germany paid $2 billion in reparations to Britain and France, who in turn paid $2.6 billion on their war debts to the United States.

While this was going on, the United States still officially held that there was no connection between German reparations and Allied war debts. American business sense at the time was outraged that Britain and France would not pay their debts unless they could get the money from Germany. But the war had exhausted and bankrupted the two Allied nations, who had borne much of the war burden. America's unwillingness to lower or cancel their debts led to great bitterness between them and the United States.

Limited Immigration

Another sign of isolationism that appeared after World War I had to do with immigration. As you know, nativist sentiment had been growing ever since the 1880s, when "new immigrants" from southern and eastern Europe began coming to the

584

United States in large numbers. Nativist feelings were strengthened by the fact that many of the people involved in post-war labor disputes were immigrant anarchists and socialists. In addition, there was less demand for unskilled labor after the war. The railroads had been built, and basic industries such as coal mining, steel, and textiles were well developed.

In 1921 the immigration rate, a modest 110,000 in 1919, shot up to 805,000, and Congress decided that the time had come to limit immigration from Europe. (Immigration from China had already been suspended in 1902.) Congress pushed through a series of measures ending with the National Origins Act of 1924. Under this act, the United States established a quota system based on national origins.

Each European nation was given a quota of 2 percent of the number of its nationals who were living in the United States in 1890. This discriminated against people from eastern and southern Europe who did not start coming in large numbers until after 1890.

The base year was shifted to 1920 under the National Origins Act of 1929, but this change was offset by reducing to 150,000 the total number of persons to be admitted in any one year. As a result, some national quotas were pitifully small. In 1963, for example, the one for Greece was 1/337th of the number who applied for permission to enter the United States.

In addition, only applicants who might one day be naturalized were allowed to come in. That was an insult to Japan, whose Gentlemen's Agreement with Theodore Roosevelt had been faithfully kept. By ignoring that agreement, the United States wiped out much of the good will that had resulted from the Four-Power Treaty.

The "national origins" system was not applied to immigrants from the Western Hemisphere. During the 1920s, about a million Canadians, many of them Catholics, and at least 500,000 Mexicans crossed the nation's borders.

Teapot Dome and Other Scandals

Before the Harding administration was well into its third year, it began to come apart. And for the same reason as Grant's had nearly fifty years before: graft among the president's friends.

In spring 1923 Jesse Smith, an assistant to Attorney General Daugherty, was exposed as a "bag-man." A bagman carries a bribe from the person giving it to the person getting it. The money is often carried in a black bag, hence the name. Banished from Washington, Smith committed suicide in May. Shortly thereafter, Charles Cramer, principal legal advisor of the Veterans Bureau, took his life for similar reasons.

Next, it turned out that Charles R. Forbes, the head of the Veterans Bureau, had swindled the country of at least $250 million through kickbacks from contractors building veterans' hospitals. Forbes was sentenced to prison in 1925 for fraud and bribery. Colonel Thomas W. Miller, head of the Office of Alien Property, was also convicted for fraud. In exchange for bribes, he had taken valuable German chemical patents that the government had seized during the war and sold them to American firms for far less than their worth.

The most spectacular wrongdoing, however, concerned naval oil reserves. As a result of the conservation movement of the Progressive Era, oil-rich public lands at Teapot Dome, Wyoming, and Elk Hill, California, had been set aside for use by the U.S. Navy. Secretary of the Interior Fall managed to get the reserves transferred from the navy to the Interior Department. He then secretly leased the land to two private oil companies. Soon after, Fall,

A cartoon of the time indicating the connection between corrupt practices and the White House.

585

who had been having financial troubles, became the owner of $325,000 in bonds and cash, as well as a large herd of cattle.

By the summer of 1923, Harding realized what had been going on. He knew that a day of reckoning was coming. A hurt and confused man, he declared, "I have no trouble with my enemies. . . . But my damned friends . . . they're the ones that keep me walking the floor nights!" At that point he left on a goodwill trip to Alaska. Everyone noticed how tired and distracted he was. Returning from San Francisco, he suffered a severe heart attack. On August 2, 1923, Warren G. Harding died.

The American people sincerely mourned their good-natured president. Few of them realized the extent to which his friends had betrayed him and the country.

Section 2 Review

COMPREHENSION   Developing Vocabulary

1. Explain these terms: reparations, capital ships.

COMPREHENSION   Mastering Facts

1. Why was the Washington Conference of 1921 considered a step toward world peace?
2. How did the high tariff of 1922 make it harder for Great Britain and France to pay their war debts to the United States?
3. What kinds of restrictions were placed on immigration during the 1920s?
4. How did Secretary of the Interior Albert Fall become rich so quickly?
5. What specific political scandal of the 1920s is being referred to in the cartoon on page 585? How do you know?

3   COOLIDGE CONDUCTS THE NATION'S BUSINESS

VOCABULARY   *economic multiplier   assembly line   planned obsolescence*

The new president, Calvin Coolidge, was sworn into office by his father, a notary public, between two and three o'clock in the morning in the family farmhouse in Plymouth, Vermont. It was a moving scene—lighted by a kerosene lamp as the men stood over the family Bible. Americans who had grown up on the farm were deeply touched. And

An artist's reconstruction of that scene in early morning when Calvin Coolidge became president.

in the following months, as one scandal after another came out concerning Harding's administration, the new chief executive looked even more reassuring. He seemed, and was, a simple, honest man who obviously wouldn't steal a nickel.

Business leaders also liked Coolidge because he wanted to keep taxes down and profits up. "The business of America is business," he intoned. And, "The man who builds a factory, builds a temple." Such sentiments seemed to foretell a golden age for business.

To many people, the solemn Coolidge seemed to be an unusual president for the rapidly changing United States. Careful about what he said, he never said much. "I have never been hurt by what I haven't said." Many persons called him "Silent Cal." Still, America was ready to take it easy for a while and let the good times roll. As one campaign poster put it: "Keep Cool with Coolidge."

The 1924 Election

Coolidge easily won the Republican nomination in 1924. The Democrats, on the other hand, were divided. Their southern and rural members favored Prohibition, while their northern, big-city members wanted it repealed. Those same factions were at odds over the religion of one prominent contender for the nomination, Gover-

Presidential Election of 1924

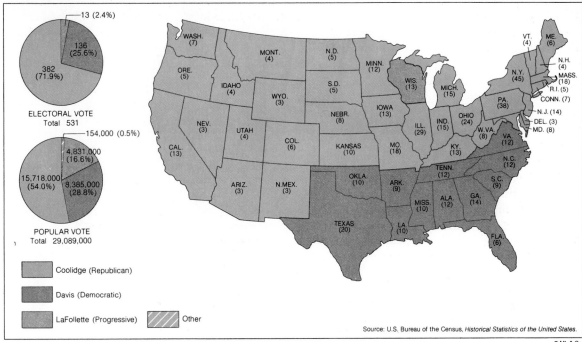

ELECTORAL VOTE
Total 531

13 (2.4%)
136 (25.6%)
382 (71.9%)

POPULAR VOTE
Total 29,089,000

154,000 (0.5%)
4,831,000 (16.6%)
15,718,000 (54.0%)
8,385,000 (28.8%)

Coolidge (Republican)

Davis (Democratic)

LaFollette (Progressive)   Other

Source: U.S. Bureau of the Census, *Historical Statistics of the United States.*

© ML & Co.

Map Skills   *Who won almost all of the Southern states? Who won the election? What was his electoral vote? his percentage of the popular vote? What state did La Follette win?*

nor Alfred E. Smith of New York, a Catholic. The Ku Klux Klan threw its considerable weight against Smith, and the Democratic Convention dragged on for an incredible 102 ballots.

The compromise candidate, wealthy corporation lawyer John W. Davis, had no chance against Coolidge. Even the presence on the ballot of Progressive candidate Robert La Follette of Wisconsin did not make a difference. Coolidge got almost 16 million of the 29 million votes cast.

Prosperous Times

Coolidge kept most of those in the Harding cabinet who had not been involved in its scandals. The kingpin of the group was Treasury Secretary Mellon, the only secretary of the treasury, as one wit later said, "under whom three presidents had served." Mellon was a multimillionaire, the head of the aluminum trust and the owner of several steel mills, oil companies, banks, and utilities. His policies were everything the business community wanted. He favored cutting the excess profits tax and reducing the public debt left over from the war, which meant keeping government spending

down. He also wanted to lower taxes on incomes over $66,000 a year while raising taxes for poorer citizens. "Let the rich keep their wealth," Mellon said. "They will invest it and so create jobs." He also favored raising postal rates.

The economy responded well to Mellon's policies. Business had never been so good. No less than 40 percent of the world's wealth belonged to Americans. The number of millionaires rose from 4500 in 1914 to 11,000 in 1926. Low interest rates, set by the Federal Reserve Board, made borrowing easy. Construction of industrial plants, homes, office buildings, and hotels boomed. The soaring 102-story Empire State Building in New York, the world's tallest building at that time, was the era's architectural triumph.

Technological developments added to the nation's well-being. Using an alternating electric current, it became possible to step up electric power by means of a transformer. Now electricity was no longer restricted to central cities but could be transmitted over great distances to outlying suburbs and even farms. Between 1913 and 1927, there was a 465 percent increase in the number of electrified households. Such labor-saving devices as

587

vacuum cleaners, washing machines, toasters, and electric irons, and stoves became widely used. By the end of the decade, household current made it possible for a radio to look like living room furniture rather than a piece of laboratory equipment.

Henry Ford and the Automobile Age

The chief engine of American prosperity in the 1920s was the automobile. Its demand for steel, rubber, glass, and textiles, not to mention petroleum, made it the great *economic multiplier*. That is, it caused all those other industries to prosper. And it remained the nation's major multiplier for half a century.

The person most responsible for putting the automobile on the road was Henry Ford. In 1908 he had developed his famous Model T. Americans told jokes about the homely "Tin Lizzie" everywhere. "Can I sell you a speedometer?" "I don't use one. When my Ford is running five miles an hour, the fender rattles; twelve miles an hour, my teeth rattle; and fifteen miles an hour the transmission drops out." But while Americans laughed at the Model T, they also loved it. It was actually a very efficient piece of machinery. It was also tough, easy to fix, and was priced under $300. By 1920, 15 million Model Ts had been sold.

The Assembly Line. By 1914 the Model T was being built on the nation's first true *assembly line*. Until then, the car's different parts were built in separate areas. Then they were brought to a specified place where one or two mechanics put them together. Ford soon found, however, that this method did not produce cars fast enough to keep up with demand. So he hired Walter Flanders, a student of Frederick Winslow Taylor. Taylor was an advocate of *scientific management*; that is, he believed you could increase efficiency by reorganizing and standardizing the way work was done.

Flanders put Taylor's theory of "line production" into effect. Instead of grouping all machines of one kind together, Flanders arranged them in sequence according to what was being done to the car. He also assigned the final assembly to a group of mechanics, each of whom handled only one part of the job. Soon, all the work was being broken up into increasingly smaller and simpler tasks.

Next, an electric conveyor belt was installed to carry the gradually assembled car from one worker

An unusual photo of Henry Ford (third from left) in 1895 when he was a $100-a-month engineer with the Edison Illuminating Company in Detroit.

to another. Production soared. Before, it had taken twelve hours and twenty-eight minutes to put a Model T together. In 1914, after the conveyor belt went into operation, it was taking only ninety-three minutes. The assembly-line technique has since been applied to most industries here and abroad.

The Five-Dollar Day. Ford also announced another idea in 1914. His company would pay workers five dollars for an eight-hour day which was more than twice the going rate. The idea, which actually came from Ford's associate James Couzens, was designed to counteract the high rate of labor turnover at the Ford plant. The plant employed 14,000 workers. But so many people left that it had to hire 53,000 workers every year to maintain that constant workforce.

Why were Ford workers quitting in such huge numbers? Mostly because of poor working conditions. Workers were treated as if they were parts of machines. They had to repeat the same motions for four hours at a time without a break, and the pace of work kept increasing as the conveyor belt was moved faster and faster. Also, although workers were crowded very close together, no personal contact or conversation between them was allowed.

Yet despite the poor working conditions, Ford's new wage rate stabilized employment at his plant. It also cost the company $12 million in 1914. But the company's profits that year rose from $25 million to $30 million. And in 1915 they doubled, from $30 million to $60 million.

What Ford showed was that profits can increase if production and sales increase. When that happens, even though individual wages go up, the labor cost per unit of production goes down. In 1913, the Ford plant produced 30,000 cars. In 1915, the figure stood at 300,000. So the company was making much more money per automobile. And since workers were earning more, they themselves were now able to afford a Model T.

Changing the Nation. / During the twenties the automobile helped change both the American landscape and American society. It stimulated construction of paved roads suitable for year-round driving in all weather. It changed architecture: houses were now built with a garage and a driveway. It created filling stations, repair shops, public garages, motels, and tourist camps. It enabled workers to live miles from their job/It led to urban sprawl—the spread of cities in all directions. It broke down the isolation of rural families and substituted "joy-riding" for sitting on the front porch. It spawned a variety of new industries and provided economic underpinning for such cities as Akron, Dearborn, Detroit, Flint, and Pontiac. It attracted people to such oil-producing states as California and Texas. And it became a symbol of the success of American free enterprise. In no other country did the people—even those with a good deal of money—move about so freely and in their own cars.

By the mid-1920s, the Model T began to lose ground. Essentially, it had not changed since 1908. And, as Ford said, you could have it any color "as long as it was black." However, General Motors' Chevrolet had appeared, costing little more than a fully equipped Ford sedan and providing much more comfort. To meet the challenge, Ford shut down his enormous operation for several months to retool. Then he unveiled his 1928 Model A, a well-designed four-cylinder automobile with a standard stick gearshift. A popular song of the day said that "Henry made a lady out of Lizzie." But the Model A never captured people's imaginations as had the Model T.

A Retailing Revolution

Ever since the Gilded Age, Americans had been familiar with the chain store. Frank W. Woolworth's "five and tens" had set the pattern of buying goods in large quantities, storing them in warehouses, and then selling them in several stores—all of which looked more or less alike and all of which carried the same merchandise. The technique eliminated wholesalers and middlemen. During the twenties the technique was adopted by A&P, United Drug, Thom McAnn, J. C. Penney, and United Cigar, among others.

At the same time, Sears, Roebuck and Company opened retail stores as its customers, mostly farmers, began throwing away their mail-order catalogs and driving to town in their Model Ts. Also, Clarence Saunders of Memphis, Tennessee, introduced his Piggly-Wiggly stores. Called "grocery-cafeterias," these self-service stores were forerunners of the modern supermarket.

In addition to these methods of distribution, industry came up with several solutions to the problem of finding consumers for the mountain of goods it turned out each year. One solution was easy credit, then called the installment plan, or "a dollar down and a dollar forever." It enabled people to buy goods without having to put up much money at the time of purchase. Banks provided the money at low interest rates. Other techniques for moving goods included annual model changes, such as in automobiles, as well as *planned obsolescence*, that is, a policy of making goods that last only a few months or years before they become obsolete and must be replaced.

Advertising: Creating Desire

Still another technique was advertising. In those days, business advertising was almost entirely in print. Of $1.5 billion spent in 1927 to sell various products, two-thirds went to newspapers and magazines. Another $300 million was spent on direct mail, and $200 million went to outdoor advertising, such as signs and billboards.

Advertising people no longer just sold space. They hired psychologists to study the best way of appealing to the buyer. What colors were best for what packages? What were the best words to use in an advertisement? These and similar questions aided the new field of motivational research, and no executive could fail to be impressed with the results. The slogan "Say It With Flowers" doubled the florist business between 1921 and 1924. "Reach for a Lucky Instead of a Sweet" turned weight-conscious Americans on to cigarettes and away from candy. And some variation of "Even Your Best Friend Won't Tell You" helped sell a great many deodorants, as well as cures for bad breath and athlete's foot.

There were gaps in the twenties' booming prosperity, and by decade's end they had begun to worry some careful observers. But while Calvin Coolidge occupied the White House, most Americans believed good times would last forever.

Section 3 Review

COMPREHENSION   Developing Vocabulary

1. Explain these terms: economic multiplier, planned obsolescence, scientific management.

COMPREHENSION   Mastering Facts

1. Why did Secretary of the Treasury Andrew Mellon want to cut taxes for the rich but not the poor?
2. How did the assembly line increase production?
3. How did the automobile change American life?
4. How does motivational research help to sell products?

4   SIGNS OF ECONOMIC TROUBLES

VOCABULARY   *farm bloc   floor price   margin*

Tremendous wealth was being created in the 1920s, but it was not evenly distributed. Certain industries were in deep trouble. Many corporations made fortunes, but did little for their workers. About half the population lived at or below the Labor Department's estimate of a decent living standard. As one song proclaimed: "The rich get richer and the poor get poorer." Yet no one seemed to question the economic ideas of Andrew Mellon.

Industries in Trouble

High on the list of industries not enjoying good times were those that had helped build the nation.

Railroads.   America's experience during World War I had shown that rails could be more efficiently run as a unified system. William G. McAdoo, who had administered the system during that time, proposed a five-year peacetime trial. Glenn E. Plumb, a lawyer for the railroad brotherhoods, drew up a detailed plan.

Continued government ownership of a basic industry, however, smacked of socialism. So the Plumb Plan got nowhere. Instead, Congress passed the Esch-Cummins Act of 1920, which placed rails under government control as to rates and service but left ownership in private hands. However, the railroads were never able to earn the modest 6 percent return on investment which the new act allowed. Part of the reason was that the government was unwilling to allow the railroads to abandon lines that were losing money. A more important reason was growing competition from trucks, buses, and private cars.

Textiles.   Even before World War I, the textile industry began shifting from New England to the South. It made economic sense to manufacture cotton cloth nearer the source of raw material. A stronger motive was the desire for cheap labor. There were many labor unions in northern mills but few in the South, and southern wage rates were considerably lower than northern ones.

There was no escape, though, from two other developments. One was foreign competition from Japan, India, China, and Latin America, all of whom produced cheap goods for the world textile market. The second development was the radical change in women's clothing, which eliminated yards of skirt and petticoat material and thus lowered the demand for cloth.

Coal Mining.   Another industry that felt an economic pinch was coal mining. It had expanded to meet wartime needs. But during the twenties, the increased demand vanished. In addition, oil, natural gas, and hydroelectric power became widely available. By the early 1930s they were filling more than half the energy needs that had once depended on coal. The price of soft coal fell to a point at which high-cost mines were forced to close. Since some of the high costs came from paying union wages, it was the non-union mines that remained open.

590

Agricultural Problems

Serious though they were, none of these problems threatened the nation's economic welfare as did the problems of agriculture.

Overproduction. During the war, farmers had expanded their operations. They had plowed up lands in the West which did not regularly get enough rainfall for planting. They had replaced scarce human labor with new kinds of farm machinery. And they had astonished the world with their productivity.

\At the same time, farmers had paid for expansion with borrowed money. Then, in 1920, mostly as a result of world competition, prices of such staple crops as wheat, corn, and cotton tumbled almost 50 percent. To make matters worse, overproduction was coupled with a drop in demand as clothing manufacturers turned from cotton to rayon fabrics and as families began eating less beef, pork, and flour and more fruits and vegetables./

Farmers tried to improve matters through further investments, such as electrifying their farms. But this only piled up more debts. By 1930 staple farmers owned three times as many tractors as in 1920—and also owed three times as much on mortgages as they did in 1912. Better seeds and fertilizers, and still more tractors, continued to expand American output. But there was no comparable rise in demand.

Price Supports. In 1921 a group of congressmen from the farm states became known as the "farm bloc." It included members of both political parties who aimed at improving the economic well-being of their constituents.

In 1924 Senator Charles L. McNary of Oregon and Representative Gilbert N. Haugen of Iowa introduced several pieces of legislation. The McNary-Haugen Bills proposed that the federal government buy surplus wheat, corn, cotton, and tobacco at a reasonable price. In that way the government would set a *floor price*, or minimum price, for each crop, as no farmer would be likely to sell it for less. The government could then unload the surplus abroad for whatever price it would bring. As the world price would be lower than the domestic price, the difference was to be made up by a special tax on all farm crops. The theory was that while farmers would lose something by paying the tax, on balance they would be better off.

The McNary-Haugen Bills were introduced repeatedly from 1924 to 1928. But when passed, they were vetoed by President Coolidge, who felt they were an unconstitutional use of federal power. And in any event, as he observed, "Farmers have never made money. I don't believe we can do much about it."

Uneven Distribution of Income

In 1929 a national study of family income showed that three-fifths of the nation's wealth was owned by 2 percent of its people. "The 27,500 wealthiest families in America had as much money as the 12 million poorest families." Miners and lumbermen, for example, earned $10 a week. Andrew Mellon paid an income tax of almost $2 million, while Henry Ford's income tax was $2.6 million.

This uneven distribution of income might not have been serious if the lowest-income families had been living at a decent level. But nearly half the nation's families earned less than $1500 a year, then considered the minimum amount for a decent life. Even families earning twice that sum could not afford most of the products that manufacturers were turning out in such numbers and at such speed. It is estimated that the average man or woman bought a new outfit of clothes only once a year. Scarcely half the homes in many cities had electric lights or furnace heat. Only one city home in ten had electric refrigeration.

The starkness of midwestern U.S. farm life is shown in this detail of Grant Wood's Dinner for Threshers. *Notice the use of the wood-burning stove.*

Low consumer demand was not the only consequence of the uneven distribution of income. Wealthy people can spend only so much, because they can eat just so much food, wear just so many clothes, and the like. So the wealthy people of America invested their surplus funds in the stock market. Less wealthy people did the same, hoping to get rich quickly. Some bought stocks on *margin;* that is, they paid only a percentage of the stock's cost and borrowed the rest from the stockbroker, intending to pay him back when they sold the stock at a higher price. The more speculators entered the stock market, the higher stock prices rose beyond the real value of businesses.

President Coolidge might say, as he did in a rare public utterance: "Everything is fundamentally sound." But in fact, some of the foundations on which prosperity rested were shaky indeed.

Section 4 Review

COMPREHENSION   Developing Vocabulary

1.   Explain these terms: farm bloc, floor price, margin.

COMPREHENSION   Mastering Facts

1.   How did women's fashions in the 1920s affect the textile industry?
2.   How did farmers' wartime expansion of productivity hurt them after the war was over?
3.   Why did President Coolidge veto the McNary-Haugen bills?
4.   What happened to stock prices when speculators entered the stock market?

5   A SLIPPING ECONOMY SIGNALS THE END OF AN ERA

VOCABULARY   *Roosevelt Corollary   Black Tuesday*

The decade's last political drama was the election of 1928, which pitted two remarkable men against each other. Personally they were as different as night and day. Herbert Hoover, secretary of commerce for eight years, was stiff, serious, and reserved, and had never run for office in his life. Alfred E. "Al" Smith was governor of New York, a witty, outgoing politician who could get along with anyone.

President Hoover in a rare and relaxed pose, fishing for trout in a California stream.

But in some ways the two presidential candidates were alike. Both had been born poor: Hoover on an Iowa farm, Smith in a slum of New York City known as the Lower East Side. Both had succeeded on their own with brains, and guts, and by hard work. Each was a superb administrator. Hoover had proved it by making a fortune in the mining engineering business before he was forty. He had also organized efforts to feed and house thousands of refugees during World War I. Smith had given New York the most efficient and up-to-date government of any state in the nation. Both had admired Woodrow Wilson. Both believed in American capitalism but knew it needed reform.

Another Republican Victory

Ordinarily, one would have expected the Republican candidate to be Coolidge. But in 1927 he announced, without warning or explanation, that he did not "choose to run." So party leaders turned to Hoover, "the Great Engineer," who was the favorite choice of forward-looking business leaders.

On the Democratic side, Smith could not again be denied a chance to run. Too many loyal party members had been angered when he lost to Davis in 1924. This time Smith got the nomination on the first ballot.

The weakened Ku Klux Klan roused itself to attack Smith once more because he was a Catholic.

Presidential Election of 1928

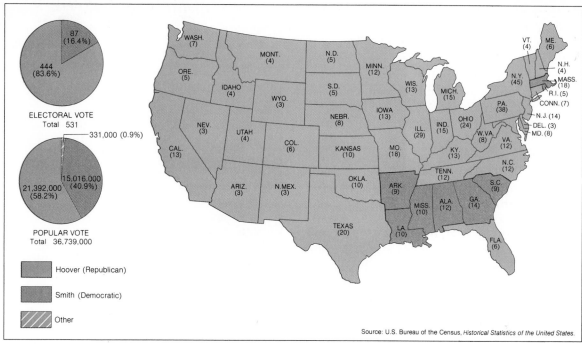

ELECTORAL VOTE
Total 531

87 (16.4%)
444 (83.6%)

POPULAR VOTE
Total 36,739,000

331,000 (0.9%)
15,016,000 (40.9%)
21,392,000 (58.2%)

Hoover (Republican)

Smith (Democratic)

Other

Source: U.S. Bureau of the Census, *Historical Statistics of the United States.*

© ML & Co.

Map Skills   *Compare this map with those on pages 584 and 587. Which states did the Democrats win in all three years—1920, 1924, and 1928? Who won the presidency in 1928?*

But Smith's call for repeal of Prohibition may have cost him as many votes as his religion. In addition, radio was widely used in the campaign. It carried Smith's rasping voice and exaggerated New York City accent straight to the people of rural America. It was a big-city accent they suspected and disliked.

More than anything else, though, Smith lost because the Republicans were in the majority and there was no reason to oust them. The Coolidge prosperity was at its peak. Smith's defeat by 21 million votes to 15 million was all the more stinging because "the solid South" broke ranks. Five southern states voted Republican for the first time since Reconstruction.

A Good Neighbor

One of Hoover's solid accomplishments was to continue improving relations with Latin America.

Coolidge had already made a start in that direction. Mexico's 1917 constitution had sharply curbed the activities of foreign oil companies. In 1927 the Mexican government further limited the rights of outsiders in Mexican oil fields. This action led hotheads to call for an invasion of Mexico. Instead, Coolidge appointed Dwight W. Morrow

as ambassador and told him to try conciliation. Within a year, economic restrictions on American oil companies were lifted.

Morrow's efforts began a policy of not overreacting to nationalist economic changes in Latin America. Hoover continued the policy and expanded it. Before assuming office, he made a good-will tour of eleven Latin American nations. In 1930 he repudiated the Roosevelt Corollary to the Monroe Doctrine, which had stated that the United States would act as a policeman in the Western Hemisphere. Hoover also denounced dollar diplomacy. He withdrew American marines from Nicaragua and started withdrawing those stationed in Haiti. He attempted to treat Latin American nations as equals. It was he who first used the term "good neighbor," though it is part of his political ill-luck that most people associate it with his arch-rival Franklin D. Roosevelt.

An Economic Downturn

Hoover's worst luck, though, was having the Great Depression begin during his first year in office. The myth about the depression being brought about by the stock market crash of October 1929 is as false as the belief that Prohibition caused people to drink. Actually, all through the year there were signs the boom was over. A number of the indicators which economists and business leaders carefully watch were pointing to a downturn.

Beginning in 1926 and continuing through 1929, housing starts and other construction were declining. Construction is an important multiplier industry. Not only does it use enormous resources but it stimulates other businesses. New construction means new furnishings, new equipment, and new appliances. Insurance and other services are called for. All this creates jobs. On the other hand, a decline in construction creates a downward spiral in other industries.

In 1929, too, business inventories were three times higher than the previous year. In other words, people were not buying. Orders were likely to be cut back until products had moved. And sure enough, freight shipments fell, indicating that orders were shrinking. Industrial production and wholesale prices soon followed.

The Stock Market Crash

Given these signs, shrewd stock market speculators began to unload their holdings and take their profits. Bernard Baruch, the wartime production head, was one who did so. Joseph P. Kennedy, father of future President John F. Kennedy, was another. But thousands of little, and not so little, investors went on buying, so prices continued to rise. The days of reckoning came in the fall.

After Labor Day the market did not bounce up as had been expected. Instead, it faltered. On October 21 it took a big drop. On October 24 there was a wave of selling orders as people who had bought on margin were forced to sell in order to cover their loans. Almost 13 million shares changed hands. But several banks and insurance companies bought stocks in order to stabilize prices.

Then, on October 29—"Black Tuesday"—the bottom fell out. People and corporations alike frantically tried to sell their stocks before prices went lower still. The number of shares dumped that day was a record 16 million. And additional millions of shares could not even find buyers. The panic continued for two more weeks. By mid-November, as one historian described it, "$30 billion had blown away—the same amount of money America had spent on World War I."

Hundreds of worried stock holders gather at the Stock Exchange after the news of the market collapse.

A depression had begun, but no one realized it until the stock market crashed. Economist John Kenneth Galbraith summed up conditions just before the crash in a single sentence. "The end had arrived," he wrote, "but it was not yet in sight."

Section 5 Review

COMPREHENSION   Developing Vocabulary

1. Explain these terms: Black Tuesday, Roosevelt Corollary.

COMPREHENSION   Mastering Facts

1. Give four reasons for Hoover's victory over Smith in 1928.
2. What was Hoover's "good neighbor" policy?
3. How did changes in the construction industry between 1926 and 1929 indicate that the boom was over?
4. What did Galbraith mean when he wrote that "The end had arrived but it was not yet in sight"?

CHAPTER 29 Review

Chapter Summary

After World War I, the world—and nation—remained troubled. World finances were shaky, but a Washington naval conference helped create some stability. The Communist Revolution in Russia produced the first "Red" scare in the United States. The Ku Klux Klan movement increased prejudices, and labor unrest also occurred—though this time labor unions finally made some gains. Meanwhile, the administration of Warren G. Harding was rocked by scandals at the cabinet level. During the 1920s the nation's economy boomed, but wealth was unevenly distributed. An economic downturn began as early as 1926, and the stock market finally crashed in 1929. The Great Depression had begun.

Questions for Critical Thinking

COMPREHENSION Summarizing Main Ideas

1. Give four reasons for the Red Scare of 1919. Do you think any of the reasons were valid? Explain your answer.

2. What techniques did Henry Ford use to increase production of the Model T?

3. What changes in retailing took place during the 1920s?

4. Explain why each of the following were in economic trouble during the 1920s: (a) railroads; (b) textiles; (c) coal mining; (d) agriculture.

COMPREHENSION Interpreting Events

1. Do you agree or disagree with Governor Coolidge's statement concerning the right of police to strike? Explain your opinion.

2. What effect did the war have on the rise of the Ku Klux Klan? What influence did the Klan have on the Democratic national convention of 1924?

3. How did labor unions improve their position during the 1920s? What setbacks did the labor movement receive during that period?

4. If you had been a U.S. senator in the 1920s, would you have voted in favor of higher tariffs? In favor of reducing naval armaments? Why?

5. How did business conditions contribute to the election of Republican presidents in 1924 and 1928?

6. Do you think anything could have been done to prevent the Great Depression? Explain.

APPLICATION Using Skills To Read Maps

Look at the maps on pages 584, 587, and 593 and answer the following questions.

1. For which political party did your state cast its electoral votes in each of these three elections? Was your state on the winning side?

2. What state or states supported the candidacy of Robert La Follette in 1924?

3. Was the South solidly Democratic in each election?

4. Which political party did the more industrialized part of the nation support?

EVALUATION Comparing Past to Present

1. Do you think a Red Scare could occur at the present time? What makes you think so?

2. What is the present status of the Ku Klux Klan?

3. Compare advertising in the 1920s with advertising today in terms of: (a) the amount of money spent to sell various products, (b) the media used. What changes have taken place during the past sixty years?

4. What percentage of the population today lives at or below a decent living standard? How does this compare with the situation during the 1920s?

5. Compare the distribution of family income in 1929 with its distribution today.

The Stock Market

In 1929 John J. Raskob, financial wizard for DuPont and General Motors, offered some investment advice for Americans. If one purchased $15 worth of stock every month, Raskob counseled, then one would accumulate an $80,000 investment at the end of twenty years. With dividends yielding $400 per month, a careful saver could then retire. "I am firm in my belief that anyone not only can be rich, but ought to be rich," said Raskob.

Owning stock is a tradition older than the nation itself. The English relied on the corporate form of ownership to finance colonization of the New World. Instead of using the Crown's money to underwrite the costs of settlement, entrepreneurs raised money by selling shares in a joint-stock company. This method was the one used in 1606 by merchants who formed the Virginia Company of London. The formation of this corporation spread the risk of loss among many rather than just a few investors. Likewise, investors would share in the profits (if any) of the venture.

Birth of the Stock Exchange. The birthday of the stock market is usually given as May 17, 1792. On that day, twenty-four stock dealers met under a buttonwood tree in New York City and set up a formal arrangement for doing business. They agreed to meet several mornings a week, to trade with each other rather than with other dealers, and to charge customers a uniform commission rate.

Since then the Wall Street area of New York has remained the nation's financial capital. The New York Stock Exchange has grown to its present average daily trading volume of some 40,000,000 shares. As many as 100,000,000 shares have changed hands in a single day.

Two Dark Days. Americans buy stock for a variety of reasons, but the basic goal is to earn a reasonable profit. However, the stock market also attracts a number of speculators—people who are willing to take large risks in order to earn high profits. Overspeculation has caused at least two dark days in the history of the stock market. One came in 1869, when Jay Gould and Jim Fisk tried to buy up all the gold, hold it, wait for prices to go sky-high, and then sell at an enormous profit. The scheme, however, depended on the government withholding its normal supply of gold to the market.

At first the plan seemed to work, but when the price of gold soared on "Black Friday," panic swept through the stock exchange. When President Grant finally realized what was going on, he ordered the Treasury to

This is the New York Stock Exchange, where people have earned and lost millions of dollars.

release the gold, whereupon the scheme collapsed. However, dozens of businesses and individuals were ruined.

The 1869 stock market fiasco illustrated the hazards of a completely unregulated economy. Unfortunately, nothing was done to reform trading practices at that time.

Then came the stock market's darkest day of all—October 29, 1929 ("Black Tuesday"), when the bottom fell out of the market. Critics began to point out that the government had done nothing to regulate the market or stop speculation during the boom times of the 1920s. As a result, Congress took action in a variety of ways during the 1930s to reform the system.

Regulating the Market.

Since the New Deal era, the federal government has served as a watchdog over the activities of the stock market. The government now tries to prevent fraudulent and unfair practices in the sale and listing of stocks. For example, new stocks must be registered before they can be sold. The registration statement must provide complete and honest information about a stock's true value.

When someone buys a stock on *margin*, it means that only a percentage of the total price must be paid at the time of purchase. The rest is owed. If the price goes up, people make a profit. But if the price goes down, people lose because they must still pay the cost of the stock when they bought it. Usually a buyer has to put up 50 percent of the purchase price. During the 1920s, however, many investors bought stock with only 10 percent down, a practice that added greatly to speculation fever and led to the stock market "crash" of 1929.

These and other requirements are administered by the Securities and Exchange Commission (SEC), set up in 1934. The SEC has five members, who are appointed by the president for five-year terms.

A Key Part of Our System.

Why is the stock market the object of so much interest? Economists follow the market's activities because it provides important clues to the nation's overall economic status. Even though ups and downs are common to the market, it has always been a sensitive indicator of the nation's economic health.

The stock market is an appropriate symbol of the American free enterprise system. All the actions that comprise our system—taking risks, making investments, earning profits, settling for losses, buying, selling, speculating, and many others—can be observed as they occur every business day on the trading floor of the New York Stock Exchange. Owning stock is one way that people show faith in the nation and in the future.

New York Stock Exchange Prices

Tuesday, May 26, 1981

Stock	Div.	PE	Sales in 100s	High	Low	Close	Net Cha.
			– A – A –				
AAR	.44	7	4	10⅜	10⅜	10⅜	...
ACF	2.76	11	43	48⅛	47¾	48	+ ½
AMF	1.24	13	72	26¼	25⅞	26	– ¼
APL		...	14	6⅜	6¼	6¼	...
ARA	1.94	6	x24	32½	32½	32½	– ⅛
ASA	5.00a	...	226	51⅝	50¼	50⅞	–1
ATO	.60	5	x52	16⅞	16½	16¾	+ ¼
AVX	.32	22	36	32	31¾	32	+ ⅛
			– B – B –				
Bache	.60a	9	2	31⅜	31⅜	31⅜	...
Bairnco		...	35	13⅝	13½	13⅝	...
BkrIntl	.60	16	227	42⅛	42	42	...
Baldor	.28	15	21	22⅞	22⅝	22⅝	...
BaldwU	1.60	8	x32	45	44⅝	45	+ ⅜
BallCp	1.60	7	x22	29¼	29¼	29¼	+ ¼
BallyMf	.10	12	336	28⅛	27⅞	27⅞	...
BallGE	2.56	6	17	22⅝	22½	22⅝	+ ¼

Part of an alphabetical listing of stocks that appears daily in U.S. papers. The last columns on the right represent the high, low, and closing stock prices for that day plus the net changes in prices.

Understanding Free Enterprise

1. What is the purpose of the New York Stock Exchange? Why was the SEC created?

2. How were the 1869 stock market panic and the 1929 crash alike? different?

3. Imagine that you have $1,000 to invest in a corporation listed on the New York Stock Exchange. In which one would you invest? Why? Check that corporation's listing on the Stock Exchange; keep track of the stock for a month. Make a graph showing the change in value from day to day.

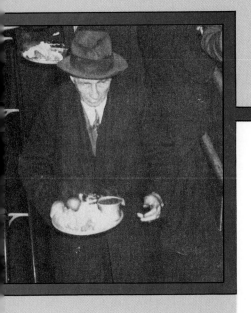

CHAPTER 30

The Great Depression

1929–1933

People in the Chapter

Franklin Delano Roosevelt—*the president who is ready to try anything reasonable to fight the depression.*

Eleanor Roosevelt—*a shy person who, as President Roosevelt's wife, becomes one of the most politically active women of her day as well as a champion of social causes all over the world.*

Frances Perkins—*secretary of labor under Roosevelt and the first woman member of a presidential cabinet.*

William Waters—*the leader of the Bonus Army, a group of World War I veterans who march on Washington demanding the immediate payment of bonuses which the government had promised would be paid them in 1945.*

Linking Past to Present

As the boom of the twenties collapsed, the period between World War I and World War II moved into its second phase: the Great Depression. In the White House a tired, harassed President Hoover did all he could to restore prosperity but nothing worked. The values on which business had been based—those of almost unhampered capitalism—came into question. There was little real evidence that people were turning either to socialism or to a right-wing dictatorship. Yet some feared they might if the depression went on much longer. At that time democracy was in great danger throughout the world. Sinclair Lewis's novel It Can't Happen Here portrayed the rise of an American Hitler. Despite the title, the point was that it could happen here, just as it had in Italy, Germany, and a half dozen other European countries. When great masses of people are hungry, anything can happen.

Continued bad times also convinced old Progressives and a number of young intellectuals that the economic system must better serve the needs of the people. Some of them gathered around the governor of New York, a man with his eyes firmly fixed on the White House: Franklin Delano Roosevelt.

1 THE NATION'S ECONOMY CRASHES

VOCABULARY   *national income*

At first people found it hard to believe that economic disaster had struck the country. On October 25, for example, President Hoover told Americans that "Business is on a sound and prosperous basis." Several days later Henry Ford declared that "Things are better today than they were yesterday." The following month Hoover again reassured the people. "Any lack of confidence in the economic future . . . is foolish."

Yet despite the comforting words, the most severe depression in American history was well on its way. What had brought it about?

Causes of the Depression

Historians and economists believe the Great Depression was the result of several factors rather than one. Although there is considerable disagreement, they usually include the following.

Uneven Distribution of Income. As discussed in chapter 29, about half the nation's families lived at or below a minimum level. They could not afford to buy most goods. Profits from production generally went to stockholders and business owners, or were put back into increased production. If, instead, businesses had paid workers higher wages, they would have been able to sell more goods. Similarly, if farmers could have received higher prices for their crops, they too would have been able to buy what factories were turning out.

Another way of putting the matter is that there was a lack of balance between production and consumption. American industry was extremely productive, as were American farms. But many American consumers lacked purchasing power. And little, if anything, was done during the twenties to increase it.

Easy Credit. Individuals had piled up huge debts during the twenties. People bought goods on the installment plan, and then were unable to buy more goods, or even to keep up payments on those they had already purchased. Others borrowed money to speculate on the stock market.

Federal banks were forbidden to lend money for stock market speculation. But private banks could—and did. Then, when the stock market turned down and people could not repay their loans, many banks were forced to close their doors. Sometimes there was a chain reaction of bank failures. One bank would call in its loans from other banks which, in turn, would press a third set of banks. People had their lifetime savings swept away in a single day.

Unbalanced Foreign Trade. All through the twenties the United States followed a high-tariff policy designed to keep out foreign products so that Americans would buy American-made goods. In 1930 the United States passed the Hawley-Smoot Tariff, the highest protective tariff in U.S. history. But it was, one can see now, a mistake. Nations unable to sell their goods in the American market were also unable to buy American products. In addition, some nations took the high-tariff policy as a declaration of economic warfare and retaliated by cutting back their purchases of American goods. United States exports kept dropping.

The problem was complicated by the after-effects of World War I. Not only had vast amounts of property in Europe been destroyed, but European nations were faced with heavy debts. This made them reduce their purchases of American goods even more.

Mechanization. During the postwar boom, new plants had been built, many with the latest technological improvements. But while the plants turned out increasing quantities of goods, they employed fewer workers as the new machines required fewer people to operate them. But machines do not buy goods. Fewer workers meant less money paid out in wages, which in turn meant less money to buy the goods rolling off the assembly lines.

The Human Results

Between 1929 and 1932, economic conditions grew steadily worse. The *national income,* or total payments to producers of the nation's goods and services, fell almost in half from $81 billion to $41 billion. During that same three-year span, 85,000 businesses shut their doors. About 400,000 farms

Soup kitchens provided free food for the unemployed. Note that most men still wore coats and ties.

were lost through foreclosure and bankruptcy sales. Some 6,000 banks, or one-fourth of the country's total number, failed, wiping out 9 million savings accounts. Each week, an additional 100,000 workers lost their jobs until 16 million persons, or about one-third of the labor force, found themselves unemployed.

Hunger and Suffering. In human terms, all this spelled hunger and suffering. There was no federal system of government relief, no public welfare, no social security. Facilities for the poor in most states and cities were swamped within a few months. Although every other industrialized country in the world had some form of unemployment insurance, the United States, except for the state of Wisconsin, had none.

Desperate poverty led to scenes never witnessed in the nation before or since. It became common to see men, women, and children digging through piles of rotting garbage for food. More than a million men, and some women, became hoboes. They stole rides on freight trains and rode back and forth across the country looking for work, any kind of work. Thousands were reduced to panhandling, or begging.

For people who had believed in the American dream that hard work would bring rewards, the mental suffering caused by the depression was as bad as the physical. As one social commentator observed: "Men who have been sturdy and self-respecting workers can take unemployment without flinching for a few weeks, a few months, even if they have to see their families suffer: but it is different after a year . . . two years . . . three years." It is hardly surprising that admissions to state hospitals for the insane tripled. The suicide rate climbed as the depression worsened.

The Position of Women. During the depression's first months, female workers generally did better than males, possibly because they worked for less. But as the depression wore on, unemployed women often had a harder time finding jobs than men, particularly if they were no longer young. Although government surveys showed that 13 percent of working women were the sole supporter of two or more persons, it was assumed that men needed work more than women did.

Some people even believed that the depression would end as soon as all married women left the job market and were replaced by men. In 1931 this belief led three-fourths of the nation's cities to bar married women from teaching jobs. If single female teachers got married, they were fired. The practice continued into the 1940s.

One reason it was assumed that women had it easier than men was that few women were seen begging or standing in breadlines. But as one social worker pointed out, women were reluctant to do so because their shame was too great. As a matter of fact, many were starving to death in cold garrets and rooming houses.

The Position of Children.

The weight of the depression fell on children as well as adults. At one New York City health center, for example, cases of malnutrition rose from 18 percent in 1928 to 60 percent in 1931. State after state reported big drops in milk consumption. Child welfare was one of the first services to go when cities and states cut budgets. A school principal in Chicago testified that he told his teachers, "Whenever you have a discipline case, ask this question first, 'What has he had for breakfast?' Which usually brings out the fact that he has had nothing at all."

Many children were not even in school. Instead they were forced to look for work and many found it in sweatshops. By 1933 some 2,600 schools across the nation had shut their doors for lack of funds. Other schools were open perhaps sixty days during the year.

The Plight of Farmers.

Farmers had been in trouble all during the twenties as the demand for staple crops declined. Then, in 1930, they were struck by a terrible drought. From Virginia westward to Arkansas, ponds, streams, and wells dried up. Even the mighty Mississippi sank to the lowest level ever recorded.

Foreclosures and bankruptcy sales increased, and many farm owners were forced to become tenants. But landlords were often in almost as bad shape as their tenants. They owed for supplies. They owed the mortgage company. And they owed the tax collector.

By 1932 the situation in farm states had grown so desperate that farmers began destroying their crops. What was the point in spending $30 to fatten a hog for market when the selling price was only $21? Much better to slit its throat. Apples spoiled in the orchards and cotton rotted in the fields because low prices did not cover the cost of harvesting.

Some farmers tried to solve their problems by force. When a farm was put on the auction block, neighbors of the farmer whose land was up for sale would keep potential buyers away. They would puncture the tires of their automobiles and cut telephone lines to prevent anyone from calling the sheriff. Then they would stand quietly but grimly around the auctioneer until he sold the land back to its original owner for next to nothing.

One Family's Story.

Some families managed to keep fairly cheerful despite the hard times. One woman remembers how the depression affected her family in Cleveland.

"I remember all of a sudden we had to move. My father lost his job and we moved into a double-garage. The landlord didn't charge us rent for seven years. It was awfully cold when you opened those garage doors. We would sleep with rugs and blankets over the top of us and we would dress under the sheets.

In the morning we'd get out and get some snow and put it on the stove and melt it and wash around our faces. Never the neck or anything. Put on our two pairs of socks on each hand and two pairs of socks on our feet, and long underwear and lace it up with Goodwill shoes. Off we'd walk, three, four miles to school.

My father owned three or four houses. His father left them to him. But he lost these one by one. One family couldn't pay the rent. But they owned a bakery and for awhile they paid him half in money, half in cookies. We lived on crumbled cookies and those little bread things. So my father was pretty sharp in a way. He always had something for us to eat. We lived about three months on candy cods, they're little chocolate squares. We had these melted in milk. And he had a part-time job in a Chinese restaurant. We lived on those fried noodles for weeks. I can't stand them today.

My mother used to bake bread, put it under a blanket to raise. Oh, that was tasty. I have never tasted such good bread since."

The Bonus Army.

On July 28, 1932, American soldiers, wearing gas masks, holding fixed bayonets, and backed by cavalry and tanks, marched from Washington, D.C., to Anacostia Flats, an open field at the outskirts of the capital. The troops were led by Army Chief of Staff Douglas MacArthur and his aide, Major Dwight D. Eisenhower. Firing tear gas canisters and wielding their bayonets and cavalry sabers, the soldiers soon cleared out those camping on the Flats and set fire to their shacks. In the course of the operation, more than 1000 persons were gassed, including an eleven-month-old baby who died and an eight-year-old boy who was partially blinded.

It was a sad end for a group of World War I veterans who called themselves the Bonus Expeditionary Force. The name was a reminder that fifteen years earlier, they had served in the American Expeditionary Force that sailed to France. In 1924 Congress had voted veterans a cash bonus, to be paid in 1945. In 1931 veterans were allowed to borrow money against the bonus. The bonus was to make up for the wages the men had missed by serving in the army at only thirty dollars a month while others back home worked at high-paying wartime jobs. The next year, in desperate financial straits, the veterans asked for full payment of what was due, an average of $500 to each man. Representative Wright Patman introduced such a bill.

Led by William Waters, an unemployed cannery worker, the first Bonus Marchers left Oregon and started across the country to lobby for passage of the Patman Bill. Others followed. By June,

about 17,000 veterans, some with wives and children, had arrived in the nation's capital and were camped on Anacostia Flats. On June 17 the Senate voted down the Patman Bill. The government then offered the veterans money for transportation home. The money was to be deducted from their bonuses when paid. Most of the veterans agreed to leave. But about 2000, without jobs and without homes, remained and were driven away on July 28.

Section 1 Review

COMPREHENSION   Developing Vocabulary

1.   Explain these terms: national income, Bonus Army.

COMPREHENSION   Mastering Facts

1.   How did easy credit help cause the depression?
2.   What effect did the Hawley-Smoot Tariff have on the depression?
3.   Why did many cities refuse to employ married women as teachers?
4.   What did the Patman Bill provide for?

2 HOOVER'S POLICIES HAVE LITTLE EFFECT

VOCABULARY   *humanitarian   Hoovervilles   moratorium   Brain Trust   bank holidays*

Treasury Secretary Mellon favored a hands-off policy on the part of the federal government in dealing with the depression. He believed depressions were a normal part of the business cycle. Business bankruptcies and human suffering were a way for the economy to correct the lack of balance between production and consumption. In his opinion, the federal government should stand back and let the capitalist system recover on its own.

President Hoover believed the twentieth-century industrial economy was too complicated for Mellon's do-nothing policies. By taking an active role in bolstering business, Hoover went far beyond what any previous president had done during a depression.

Hoover's Attempts at Solutions

First, Hoover set about trying to restore confidence. He convinced business leaders not to cut payrolls and labor leaders not to ask for higher wages or shorter hours. Then he put through a tax cut and had the Federal Reserve Board make it easier to borrow money. He set aside almost $800 million for public works so people would have

jobs. Among the projects begun under this program was Boulder Dam (now known as Hoover Dam) on the Colorado River. Hoover asked farmers to limit their production voluntarily so that prices would not fall further. And he persuaded Congress to set up the Federal Farm Marketing Board to help farmers market their crops.

Conditions, however, failed to improve. So Hoover recommended some additional measures. The most important was the establishment of the Reconstruction Finance Corporation to make loans to banks, railroads, and other industries so they could get back on their feet. Another new agency was the Home Loan Bank Board, which was designed to prevent foreclosures on homes and farms.

In the meantime, other things in the president's program got bogged down in politics. As a result of the 1930 election, the Republicans had lost control of the House, while their majority in the Senate had been reduced to one vote. By 1932 relations between the president and Congress were cool. Congressmen believed that Hoover's programs were too little and too late. For instance, the RFC had made loans of almost $2 billion.

Congress wanted to spend $40 billion over the next five years to end the depression.

Hoover dismissed Congress's spending plans as trying to "squander our way to prosperity." He also accused the legislators of dragging their feet on his program. He said, probably correctly, that Democrats hoped the depression would continue until the presidential election. People would then blame Hoover and vote Democratic.

Hoover's View of Society

Of course Hoover was not responsible for the depression. But his actions puzzled and angered many people. Hoover was a great *humanitarian*, one who wanted to help others. In one of his first speeches after becoming president, he said:

❝Our first objective must be to provide security from poverty and want. We want security in living for every home. We want to see a nation built of home owners and farm owners. We want to see their savings protected. We want to see them in steady jobs. We want to see more and more of them insured against death and accident, unemployment and old age. We want them all secure.❞

Hoover, however, believed that individuals and local government agencies were the ones to care for children and the sick, old, and disabled. The federal government should direct and guide relief measures, Hoover felt, but *not* through a vast federal bureaucracy. His reasons were philosophical.

❝You cannot extend the mastery of government over the daily working life of the people without, at the same time, making it the master of the people's souls and thought.❞

Hoover also feared that direct federal handouts weakened people's self-respect. In short, he thought the depression could best be cured by individual initiative and private charity. Hoover lent money to the states for relief. He also lent millions to corporations to help them resume production and employ workers. But he refused to permit federal payments to the poor and hungry.

The unemployed and homeless were not comforted by Hoover's philosophy. Nor did they understand why money was going to support failing corporations while people starved. The Democratic National Committee hired a public relations expert to further damage the president's image. Hoover's name was linked to the depression's worst features. The collection of shacks, filled with homeless men and women, that grew up outside many cities were called "Hoovervilles." Old newspapers worn under clothing for greater warmth were called "Hoover blankets." Empty pockets turned inside out were "Hoover flags." It was a cruel comment on a great humanitarian.

Hoover's Lack of Adaptability

President Hoover was often called "the Great Engineer," because he had indeed been a very good one before entering government. Engineers are known for the efficient and precise way they deal with blueprints and figures. But politicians deal with people, so they should be flexible and adaptable. Hoover lacked those political qualities. For example, instead of simply denouncing Congress's $40 billion spending plans, he might have said what was good about the program and then challenged Congress to act.

Another example of Hoover's unbending quality occurred in the summer of 1932 during the bonus march. The veterans had repeatedly invited the president to address them. A number of people urged Hoover to do it. "Explain why the country can't meet their demands, but give them something to hope for. Remind them that you're their commander-in-chief, speak to them from the heart." Hoover refused. James Watson of Indiana, Republican leader of the Senate, advised the president to invite Bonus Army leader Waters and a few others to the White House for dinner, talk to them frankly, and ask them to leave peacefully. There would be no need to use troops. Instead, Hoover wanted the marchers rounded up and fingerprinted.

Hoover also showed his unbending quality in certain of his dealings with other countries. By 1931 Europe was feeling the effects of the depression. American investors withdrew their money, and the United States government stopped all loans. In May, Austria's largest bank collapsed, and financial panic swept central Europe. A month later, Hoover proposed a *moratorium*, or postponement of payments, on Allied war debts and German reparations. But before anyone could agree, Britain and other European countries went off the gold standard. That is, their paper money could no longer be exchanged for gold. This made it drop in value, which meant that Europeans would be buying American goods and repaying American loans in cheap currency.

Hoover was furious at the abandonment of the gold standard. His administration was committed to paper money backed by gold. The president was further upset when the former Allies agreed to reduce Germany's war reparations by 90 percent. All Hoover wanted was a postponement. Although his own secretary of state, Henry L. Stimson, had been trying for over a year to persuade him that cancelling war debts would aid world recovery, Hoover insisted the obligations be paid.

The 1932 Campaign

By mid-1932 the situation was grim indeed. One historian described it this way.

"Travelers crossing America that summer saw a land of harsh contrasts. Surplus food was being spilled into the ocean or piled high in grain elevators while men were breaking store windows to steal a loaf of bread. Shoe factories were shut down in New England while children stayed home from school because they had nothing to put on their feet. . . . Families went in ragged clothing while farmers could not market millions of bales of cotton. All this in the richest country on earth, with the fattest acres, the tallest buildings, the mightiest machinery, the biggest factories."

Something had to be done.

It was clear that the American people were unhappy with Hoover. However, he *had* tried to deal with the depression. And the Republicans knew that if they did not nominate him, they would be blaming him publicly for the nation's economic woes. So Hoover again became the Republican standard bearer, although many observers thought the party's convention in Chicago was about as joyful as a funeral.

A Dramatic Entrance. By contrast, Democrats came to Chicago a few weeks later certain of victory in November. A majority of delegates were pledged to Governor Franklin Delano Roosevelt of New York. But at that time the nomination required a two-thirds majority. Roosevelt's main opponents, former candidate Alfred E. Smith and Speaker of the House John Nance Garner of Texas, hoped for a deadlock and a compromise candidate. After three ballots, however, Garner, the favorite of southern and western delegates, threw his votes to Roosevelt and accepted the vice-presidential slot.

Roosevelt flew to Chicago for the acceptance speech. This tradition-breaking move added a

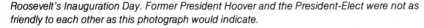

Roosevelt's Inauguration Day. Former President Hoover and the President-Elect were not as friendly to each other as this photograph would indicate.

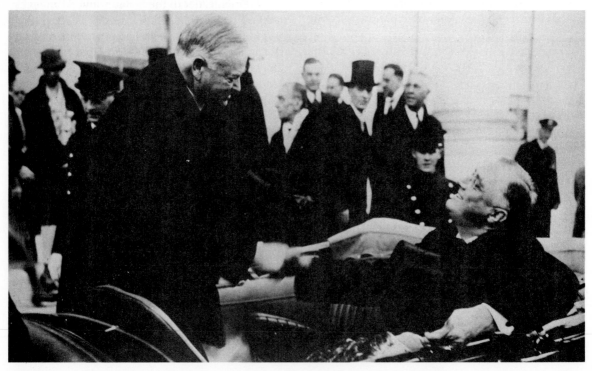

Presidential Election of 1932

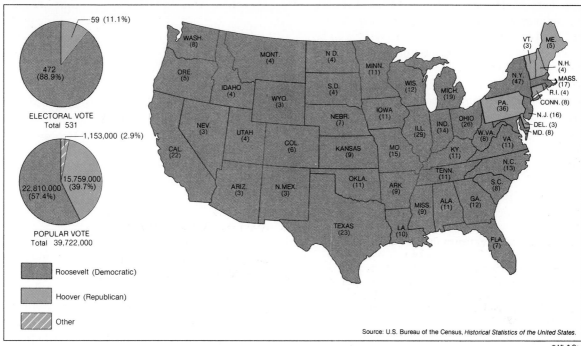

ELECTORAL VOTE
Total 531

59 (11.1%)
472 (88.9%)

POPULAR VOTE
Total 39,722,000

1,153,000 (2.9%)
15,759,000 (39.7%)
22,810,000 (57.4%)

Roosevelt (Democratic)

Hoover (Republican)

Other

Source: U.S. Bureau of the Census, *Historical Statistics of the United States.*

© ML & Co.

Map Skills   *Which party won the election? Who was its candidate? How many popular votes did he get? How many electoral votes? In what part of the country did Hoover win any states?*

touch of urgency and drama to the convention. Then, in a rousing speech, the candidate pledged "a new deal" for the American people. No one knew exactly what the New Deal program was. But it brought to mind the successful Square Deal of the candidate's favorite cousin, President Theodore Roosevelt.

The "Brain Trust."   It is possible that Roosevelt himself was not sure at the time about the details of the New Deal. Meanwhile, a group of his close advisors labored in Albany, outlining various economic and social programs. At the center of the group were three Columbia University professors: Adolf A. Berle, Jr., Raymond Moley, and Rexford Guy Tugwell. Newspapers were soon referring to them as the "Brain Trust." Their ideas formed a background for Roosevelt's campaign speeches. But the candidate was careful to avoid making definite promises. He did not want to say anything which might anger large groups of voters.

A Democratic Landslide.   Actually, neither party platform gave voters much guidance. The

most visible difference was over Prohibition. Democrats called for outright repeal, while Republicans favored "revision."

But if the campaign lacked a focus on issues, it clearly showed the deep contrast between the candidates. The tired, gloomy, worn-out president was no match for his handsome, optimistic challenger. Even the upward tilt of Roosevelt's head bespoke confidence—a quality the nation sorely needed in 1932.

In the November election Roosevelt's popular vote was 23 million to Hoover's 16 million. Democrats carried the South, the West, and all but six states in the Northeast. In the Senate they had nearly a two-thirds majority. And in the House they won 318 of the 435 seats. It was the greatest Democratic victory since the Civil War.

A Period of Waiting

If Americans were curious to know what sort of president they had elected and what he planned to do about the depression, they had a long wait. Still in effect was a four-month period between the November election and the March inauguration. (The Twentieth Amendment, which moved presidential inaugurations up to January, was not ratified until February 1933.)

The economy, however, did not wait. It steadily declined. More businesses went bankrupt, more people lost their jobs, more homes and farms were foreclosed, and the production of goods and services dropped farther than ever.

The banking situation was even worse. Thirty-eight states declared "bank holidays" to keep people from withdrawing their savings. By Inauguration Day, scarcely a bank was open.

Section 2 Review

COMPREHENSION   Developing Vocabulary

1. Explain these terms: moratorium, Hoovervilles, Brain Trust, bank holidays, humanitarian.

COMPREHENSION   Mastering Facts

1. Why did Hoover refuse to give federal aid directly to people?
2. What did Secretary of State Stimson want Hoover to do about European war debts, and why?
3. Why did the Republicans renominate Hoover for president?
4. Why did Roosevelt have to wait until March for his inauguration?

3 ROOSEVELT FACES A DIFFICULT CHALLENGE

VOCABULARY   *pragmatist   fireside chats*

Outgoing President Hoover blamed worsening conditions on people's fear of Roosevelt and what his administration might do. He called on the president-elect to continue the policies of the past four years. However, FDR, as the headline writers were beginning to call him, rejected Hoover's suggestions. He also refused, until he was president in his own right, to take part in international talks to stabilize the world's money supply.

A Reassuring Confidence

Saturday, March 4, 1933, dawned cold and raw across much of the nation. At noon millions of Americans gathered by their radios as Franklin Delano Roosevelt swore to uphold and defend the Constitution. Then the thirty-second president turned to the microphones and to the 100,000 persons gathered before the east front of the Capitol. His firm, clear voice rang out,

“This great nation will endure as it has endured, will revive and will prosper. . . . Let me assert my firm belief that the only thing we have to fear is fear itself—unreasoning, unjustified terror, which paralyzes needed efforts to convert retreat into advance.”

Roosevelt continued with reassurances. He would provide the action which the people wanted. He would call Congress into session and ask for executive power to wage war against poverty and pessimism. He wanted, he said, a power "as great as the power that would be given me if we were in fact invaded by a foreign foe."

Outgoing Secretary of State Stimson was "scared" by the president's words. One writer saw them as "grim," and others saw in them the threat of dictatorship. But comedian Will Rogers spoke for most frustrated Americans. "If he burned down the Capitol, we would cheer and say, 'Well, we at least got a fire started somehow.' "

A Determined President

Who was this man to whom Americans were entrusting their future? What did he stand for?

Franklin Roosevelt was born into a branch of the same well-to-do old New York family that had produced President Theodore Roosevelt. Though a loyal Democrat, young Franklin Roosevelt admired his famous cousin and followed in his footsteps by winning election to the New York State Senate, becoming assistant secretary of the navy (in the Wilson administration), and running for vice-president (with James M. Cox in 1920).

Overcoming a Physical Handicap.   The following year, 1921, Roosevelt was severely stricken with poliomyelitis, or polio, which left his legs almost totally paralyzed. Everyone thought his political career was finished. But calling on inner resources no one dreamed he had, he fought and worked to walk again. Month after month, he clamped heavy iron braces on his legs, pulled himself upright, more often than not crashed painfully to the floor, and began the entire process again. Through it all he was supported, literally and psy-

606

chologically, by his wife, Eleanor Roosevelt, and his aide Louis M. Howe.

By the time of the 1924 Democratic convention, Roosevelt was ready to appear in public without crutches. Wearing fifty-pound braces and supporting himself by holding the speaker's stand, he nominated Al Smith for president and took up public life once more. In 1928 he succeeded Smith as governor of New York and was reelected in 1930.

Political Beliefs.   Roosevelt, like Abraham Lincoln, was an extremely complex person. He had always liked people, and his physical problems, coming late in his forties, made him deeply compassionate toward others who suffered. He was interested in new ideas, but those around him were often confused as to what he was thinking. Sometimes his dislike of hurting people made it seem he was agreeing with them when in fact he was not.

Roosevelt was more interested in reforming capitalist institutions than in changing them. He believed in capitalism as he did in a strict moral code, and he was a sincerely religious man. Like many of his generation, Roosevelt was a product of the Pro-

gressive Era. He clung to its values. Philosophically he was a *pragmatist*, that is, one who believes that the value of an idea is whether or not it works. He was also creative and adventurous. He once said, "It is common sense to take a method and try it. If it fails, admit it frankly and try another. But above all, try something."

The Roosevelt Team

The New Deal attracted to Washington the brightest group of people since the Progressive Era. Dozens of young lawyers, economists, political scientists, and social workers flooded the nation's capital. Some became junior members of the Brain Trust, while others worked in the White House or the new federal agencies. Many went on to start Washington law firms or, in later administrations, to serve as cabinet officers or to sit on the Supreme Court.

Aides and Advisors.   One of the most influential of the new people was Harry Hopkins. A young social worker, he had supervised relief activities in New York State while Roosevelt was governor. Apart from his administrative ability, his main

The Brain Trust: The men who helped Roosevelt plan his New Deal program. Among the best-known were Professors Raymond Moley and Rex Tugwell (third and fourth from left)

contribution to the New Deal was his strong preference for work relief rather than money relief. Money helped people buy food, Hopkins acknowledged. But work not only enabled them to eat, it also gave them confidence and self-respect. Other non-official cabinet members included Thomas C. "Tommy the Cork" Corcoran, whose quick wit enlivened many a serious discussion, and Benjamin Cohen, who provided a scholarly base for much New Deal legislation.

A Bipartisan Cabinet.   Roosevelt's official cabinet represented a balance. It combined the statesman's realization that people in key positions should be able as well as loyal, and the politician's awareness that various interest groups should be satisfied. It included Republicans as well as Democrats.

As secretary of state, Roosevelt named Senator Cordell Hull, a courtly gentleman from Tennessee. Hull had no particular experience in foreign affairs, but he was highly regarded by his fellow legislators, with whom he had served for thirty years. He supported the South's traditional stand in favor of lower tariffs. William H. Woodin, FDR's first secretary of the treasury, was a conservative Republican businessman. He also played the guitar and composed songs. Because of poor health, however, Woodin remained in the cabinet for less than a year. He was succeeded by Henry Morgenthau, Jr.

James A. Farley, the skillful New York political leader who had managed FDR's campaign, became postmaster general. He was also put in charge of patronage. For attorney general, Roosevelt had wanted Senator Thomas J. Walsh of Montana, who had unearthed the Teapot Dome scandal. When Walsh died before the inauguration, Homer Cummings, former member of the Wilson administration, was appointed.

Reform members of the cabinet included Henry A. Wallace and Harold L. Ickes. Wallace's father had been secretary of agriculture in the Harding and Coolidge cabinets, and Roosevelt appointed the son to the same position. Ickes, a Chicago attorney and a strong conservationist, was put in charge of the Interior Department. He was described as "elderly, peppery, persnickety," and he soon became known as "the Old Curmudgeon" (an ill-tempered person).

In some ways, FDR's most interesting appointment was that of Frances Perkins as secretary of labor. The position had usually gone to a labor union official. "Madam Perkins," as she was called, had no such connection. But she was a nationally recognized expert on industrial safety. The first woman to sit in a president's cabinet, she was somewhat resented in the beginning. But her quiet manner and administrative ability soon won widespread respect.

An Energetic Wife.   A key member of Roosevelt's team had no official standing in the administration and drew no salary.

Eleanor Roosevelt was the niece of Theodore Roosevelt, who "gave her away" at her wedding. The bride should have been the center of attraction, but because President Theodore Roosevelt was there, she was hardly noticed. Being put in the background was the story of her young life. Her parents died while she was still a child, leaving her to be brought up by a bullying grandmother. Her childhood was bleak and friendless, and she grew into a tall, awkward girl. She had inherited a lot of her famous uncle's driving energy, most of which she devoted to social work.

Eleanor Roosevelt's work among the poor brought her into contact with her cousin Franklin. As their friendship turned to romance, his mother, Sara Delano Roosevelt, did her best to stop it. She then went on to bully her daughter-in-law, much as Eleanor's grandmother had. While raising five children in New York and Washington, Eleanor Roosevelt kept up her interest in helping the less fortunate. Her husband's illness was as much a turning point in her life as in his. Sara Roosevelt wanted her son to be a permanent invalid who would depend on her. Eleanor Roosevelt fought for his right to lead a useful life. Later, she represented him at public meetings and private conferences, and campaigned for him when he ran for governor. She handled these duties with considerable political skill.

Many of the things Eleanor Roosevelt did are now expected from the wives of political leaders. In the thirties they were not. After FDR became president, she traveled widely and reported back to him. The president often introduced an idea to his cabinet by beginning, "My missus says . . ." She took a particular interest in young people and often spoke to them about possibilities for the future. She also helped to make policy, especially in matters concerning women or blacks and other minorities. Rexford Tugwell said that no one could ever doubt her influence when they heard her say, as she looked the president firmly in the eye, "Franklin, I think you should . . ." or "Franklin, surely you will not . . . "

A Tough Banking Act

On Monday, March 6, two days after his inauguration, FDR ordered every bank in the nation closed. On March 9, Congress met in special session. It listened to the terms of Roosevelt's Emergency Banking Relief Bill and passed it in four hours. Before the day was over, the bill had been signed into law. It authorized the Treasury Department to inspect the country's banks. Those that were sound could reopen at once, those that needed help could receive loans, and the rest were to stay closed. About one out of ten banks fell into the last category. Although the measure was drastic, it ended the banking crisis. Now people would not have to wonder whether or not a bank was sound. If its doors were open, its deposits were safe. The federal government said so.

The Emergency Banking Relief Act also forbade the hoarding or exporting of gold. In effect, it took the United States off the gold standard. Conservatives were outraged. Radicals were likewise outraged, for they had wanted the federal government to nationalize the banking system. But FDR chose a middle road combining private ownership with government regulation. It was a road down which most Americans were likely to follow the president.

Straight Talk

Some of the renewed confidence in the banking system resulted from a radio talk Roosevelt delivered to the nation Sunday evening, March 12, the day before the first banks were to reopen. In his broadcast, he explained in clear, simple language how the banking system worked:

“When you deposit money in a bank, the bank does not put the money into a safe deposit vault. It invests your money in many different forms of credit: bonds, commercial paper (business loans),

"My fellow Americans." With these words Roosevelt began a series of "fireside chats" explaining domestic and international affairs to the American public.

mortgages, and many other kinds of loans. In other words, the bank puts your money to work to keep the wheels of industry and agriculture turning around. A comparatively small part of the money you put into the bank is kept in currency—an amount which in normal times is wholly sufficient to cover the cash needs of the ordinary citizen. In other words, the total amount of currency in the country is only a small fraction of the total deposits in all of the banks. "

Roosevelt then went on to explain that when too many people demanded their deposits in cash, banks would fail, not because they were weak, but because even the soundest banks could not meet such heavy demands.

FDR thanked the people for their patience during the crisis and praised their patriotism. Finally, he asked them as soon as their bank reopened to return any money or gold they might have drawn out. After assuring them it would be safe to do so, the president finished with these words:

" After all, there is an element in the readjustment of our financial system more important than currency, more important than gold, and that is the confidence of the people. Confidence and courage are the essentials of success in carrying out our plan. You people must have faith; you must not be stampeded by rumors or guesses. Let us unite in banishing fear. We have provided the machinery to restore our financial system; it is up to you to support and make it work.

It is your problem no less than mine. Together we cannot fail. "

This radio talk was the first of what came to be called fireside chats. They were the best means FDR discovered for explaining New Deal meas-ures to the voters. They were also the most creative use of radio by any political leader up to that time. Roosevelt never overlooked the fact that though his audience numbered millions, it was made up of individuals and families, each seated in a room. He spoke directly to them in friendly, intimate tones.

On this optimistic note, the Roosevelt administration got underway. Over the next few weeks, a billion dollars in gold and currency was dug up from backyards or removed from mattresses and deposited in banks. Listening to people talk, anyone might have thought the depression was already over. Even responsible leaders in the government expected a rapid end to the nation's economic ills. But the problems were too basic and too deep for quick, easy solutions. The depression had at last reached bottom, but the road to recovery was long and steep.

Section 3 Review

COMPREHENSION   Developing Vocabulary
1.   Explain these terms: pragmatist, fireside chats.

COMPREHENSION   Mastering Facts
1.   How did Roosevelt react to his polio attack?
2.   What factors did Roosevelt consider in choosing his cabinet?
3.   What role did Eleanor Roosevelt play in her husband's administration?
4.   Why did Roosevelt want all banks to close for four days?

CHAPTER 30   Review

Chapter Summary

The Great Depression had several causes, including uneven distribution of wealth; easy credit often used for stock market speculation; an unfavorable balance of foreign trade; and the need for fewer workers as industry mechanized. After 1929, unemployment rose rapidly, and hunger and suffering were widespread. President Hoover lacked the adaptability to deal with the situation, and he received most of the blame for the depression. In 1932, Franklin D. Roosevelt won the presidency by a landslide. He took action immediately by working for banking relief and restoring the confidence of Americans through fireside chats that promised a New Deal. Roosevelt assembled a talented group of advisers that also included his energetic wife, Eleanor.

Questions for Critical Thinking

COMPREHENSION   Summarizing Main Ideas

1. Explain how each of the following helped bring on the Great Depression: (a) the lack of consumer purchasing power; (b) the increased mechanization of factories.
2. What effect did the depression have on each of the following? (a) farm ownership; (b) savings accounts; (c) unemployed persons' self-respect; (d) the suicide rate; (e) women in the labor force; (f) public schools.
3. Compare Franklin D. Roosevelt's view of the role of the federal government with that of Theodore Roosevelt; of Herbert Hoover.
4. What was the purpose of FDR's fireside chats? Give two reasons why they were successful.

COMPREHENSION   Interpreting Events

1. Why did many farmers begin destroying their crops? In what other ways did they try to solve their problems? Were these methods successful? Explain.
2. Do you think the federal government was right to break up the Bonus Army by force? Why or why not? What else might the government have done?

3. How did Hoover attempt to solve the nation's economic problems? Why do you think his attempts did not succeed?
4. If you had been a delegate to the Republican national convention in 1932, would you have voted to renominate Hoover? Why or why not?
5. Why did FDR choose a bipartisan cabinet?
6. Why did conservatives object to the Emergency Banking Relief Act? Why did radicals object? What effect did the act have on the nation's banks?

APPLICATION   Using Skills To Evaluate Sources

Below are several topics. Under each is a list of three sources of information. For each topic, indicate which source is the most reliable, which is second best, and which is the least reliable.

1. People's experiences during the Great Depression
   a. *The Grapes of Wrath,* a novel about farmers in the 1930s
   b. Louis Adamic's description of how the depression affected Lawrence, Massachusetts
   c. Andrew Mellon's diary entries covering the 1930s
2. Hoover's philosophy of government
   a. Newspaper editorials from 1929 to 1932
   b. A history of the Hoover administration
   c. A collection of Hoover's speeches
3. The operation of the banking system
   a. FDR's first fireside chat
   b. An economics textbook
   c. The annual reports of the Federal Reserve Board

EVALUATION   Comparing Past to Present

1. How many women have sat in the president's cabinet since Frances Perkins?
2. What is the unemployment rate in the United States today? How does it compare with the highest unemployment rate during the Great Depression? Does any particular group of workers have a higher than average unemployment rate? How might you account for this?

Jobs and Productivity

In a famous 1930s movie entitled *Modern Times*, film star Charlie Chaplin works under the shadow of an enormous factory clock. As it ticks off the minutes, Chaplin and his co-workers stand along an assembly line doing the same task all day long. When the owner announces that he wants higher profits, he increases production by speeding up the assembly line belt. Always alert to ways of improving efficiency, the owner even considers purchasing a feeding machine so workers can eliminate time spent at lunch.

Out-of-work viewers during the Great Depression years loved the movie. They applauded wildly when Chaplin began to sabotage the system. In effect, movie-goers were cheering for the triumph of the common worker over unfair bosses.

Increasing Productivity.
Though the boss's actions in the movie may have been a little extreme, they do point to one important trend: since the very beginning of the Industrial Revolution, business owners and managers have searched for new ways to increase the productivity of workers. Productivity can be measured by dividing the quantity of goods or services by the time needed to make the products. Our standard of living has increased largely because of steadily improving productivity.

During the early years of the Industrial Revolution, new production methods required a number of basic changes in workers' thinking. Mass production techniques led to new attitudes toward work. In the past, farmers and artisans could work at their own pace until a task was completed. In factories, however, workers needed to keep pace with others and performed the same task day after day regardless of circumstances. Factory owners became more concerned about productivity than about the people who worked for them.

As the Industrial Revolution picked up steam, worker productivity also increased at a faster rate. Throughout the nineteenth century, statisticians at the Census Bureau recorded a transformation in American productivity. Machines, resources, and labor, along with efficient business management techniques, combined to accomplish astounding economic feats. In many industries, technical advances enabled production to increase ten or fifteen times over in just fifty years.

As a result, by 1890 the United States alone produced over one-third of the world's total annual supply of iron and steel. Production in other areas—oil, copper, lead, sugar, coal—followed similar patterns. In the sheer quantity and value of goods produced, the United States became the leading manufacturing nation in the entire world by the beginning of the present century.

Influence of "Taylorism."
The relationship between machines and human labor has led to many exhaustive studies regarding more efficient means of production. Always, the emphasis has been on more —more output in less time from fewer people and machines. For example, around the turn of the century an efficiency expert named Frederick Taylor developed the process of scientific management. Taylor found that workers could produce more if wasted efforts were eliminated. His theories of time and motion were called "Taylorism."

Taylor became famous by going into factories, conducting experiments, and recommending ways to increase productivity. In one such time and motion study, Taylor discovered that a worker shoveled more tonnage per day with a 21-pound shovel load than with an 18 or 24-pound load on his shovel. All these experiments had the same goal: to wring the maximum profit from the most effective organization of work patterns. Though this was exactly what Charlie Chaplin had ridiculed in his movie, the bottom line continued to revolve around numbers—those of time, amounts, and profits.

Productivity Today. We know that these same numbers are still important to businesses today, and new technology continues to increase worker productivity. However, efficiency experts now realize that even more is involved. People are not machines, and therefore other factors such as job satisfaction, working conditions, bonus incentives, and so on must be taken into account if the productivity of workers is to increase even further.

It has taken Americans some time to learn lessons that foreign competitors—notably the Japanese—have used for years in order to dramatically raise their production levels. After World War II, some rebuilding nations eventually surpassed the United States in worker productivity. During the early 1980s, Americans still trailed some of these nations in certain categories (see accompanying graphs).

Perhaps one of the most pressing needs right now concerns discovering ways to match available workers with skills that are in demand. It is puzzling to many people that, while unemployment remains relatively high, thousands of jobs remain unclaimed. The "Help Wanted" sections of most newspapers demonstrate that jobs are indeed available. The problem is that most of the jobs require technical skills of some kind while a

Worldwide Worker Productivity Index 1981 (1975 = 100)			
Chemicals, Energy, and Plastic Products		**Metal Products, Machinery, and Equipment**	
Belgium	129.2	Belgium	129.0
Canada	116.2	Canada	116.8
France	115.4	France	124.6
Germany	126.3	Germany	118.0
Italy	115.0	Italy	137.9
Japan	149.1	Japan	179.5
Netherlands	124.6	Netherlands	124.4
United Kingdom	116.3	United Kingdom	109.8
U.S.A.	123.7	U.S.A.	111.3

certain percentage of those unemployed are unskilled.

This gap between needed skills and available labor is likely to grow as more and more industries and businesses become computerized and mechanical. Some experts predict that the jobs many of today's high school students will one day have will be in fields that do not yet exist. Thus, the challenge remains to educate workers for the jobs of tomorrow, not yesterday. When that occurs, the American economy will become both more productive and more efficient.

Understanding Free Enterprise

1. How did machines eventually transform the nature of work? of people?

2. What factors contribute to high productivity by workers? What challenges face our economy in increasing productivity? in lowering unemployment?

3. The graphs on this page show a worker productivity index for 1981, with 1975 serving as the base year (1975 = worker productivity index of 100). In which category has United States worker productivity increased the most since 1975? Which nations continue to lead the United States in each category?

4. What career do you plan to pursue in the future? What changes might come to that field before you ever begin your work?

CHAPTER 31

The New Deal and Reform

1933–1940

People in the Chapter

Mary McLeod Bethune—*a member of Roosevelt's "Black Cabinet" and founder of Bethune-Cookman College.*

Amelia Earhart—*the first woman to fly the Atlantic Ocean (in 1928), who is on a round-the-world flight in 1937 when her plane disappears over the Pacific.*

Huey P. Long—*a governor of Louisiana and later senator who, through his powerful personal political machine, dominates Louisiana until his assassination in 1935.*

Harold Ickes—*Roosevelt's secretary of the interior who becomes head of the Public Works Administration. Under the direction of "Honest Harold," new jobs are created on some 34,000 public works projects.*

Linking Past to Present

During this period Franklin D. Roosevelt probably had more power than any other president except Lincoln during the Civil War. But Roosevelt's energy, personality, and confidence were a tonic to a frightened and confused people. At Roosevelt's urging, Congress set up so many government agencies that some of them were known simply by their initials. For example, AAA meant Agricultural Adjustment Administration and WPA meant Works Progress Administration. This alphabet soup of social relief helped get the nation back on its feet. But the measures were so unusual, so sweeping, and so different from the traditional view of sturdy American self-reliance that many people feared the worst. They believed, along with Herbert Hoover, that the federal government was becoming dangerously powerful. They also believed that the New Deal was eroding the moral character of Americans as fast as it was crushing their fundamental freedoms.

1 THE FIRST HUNDRED DAYS

VOCABULARY   *boondoggle*   *pump-priming*

In his Inaugural Address, President Roosevelt declared "Our greatest primary task is to put people to work. This is no unsolvable problem if we face it wisely and courageously."

Then he called Congress into a special session. It sat from March 9 to June 16, 1933, exactly one hundred days. In that brief time, it passed more significant legislation than Congress usually manages in two years. This haste was considered necessary because of the country's urgent problems.

Creating Jobs

The task was to increase consumers' purchasing power and also to restore prices to a level that allowed producers sufficient profit to make it worthwhile for them to produce goods. To increase purchasing power, people needed money—not through a handout, but through productive jobs.

The Civilian Conservation Corps.   In the first month of the new administration, a Civilian Conservation Corps (CCC) was established. Unemployed single males from seventeen to twenty-eight were put to work building roads, planting trees, and helping in soil erosion and flood control projects. The young men lived in camps run by army officers. The work was directed by experienced foresters and construction foremen. Members of the CCC got thirty dollars a month, twenty-two of which were sent to their dependent families. They also received free food and uniforms of forest green.

Many of the camps were located on the Great Plains. There, within a period of eight years, the men of the CCC planted more than 200 million trees. This tremendous reforestation program was aimed at preventing another dust bowl. You recall that much of the nation had been hit by a severe

A group of Civilian Conservation Corps (CCC) workers is shown here planting ponderosa pine on burned land near Sutter Creek, Montana. This kind of public works activity provided much-needed jobs as well as a healthy, active outdoor life.

drought in 1932. East of the Mississippi, the drought dried up streams and ponds. West of the Mississippi, it dried up crops and turned the land to dust. Beginning in fall 1933 and continuing through spring 1935, winds blew the dust eastward in a "black blizzard." As one historian described it:

" The skies were darkened. . . . The dry soil drifted like snow; automobiles had to use their headlights at noon; families stuffed door and window cracks to keep from being choked; livestock died of thirst; and the dust blew farther east and fell into the Atlantic Ocean. Millions of acres of farm land lost their topsoil and thousands of families fled their homes. Most of them headed for California, in battered trucks and limping passenger cars, with such furniture and other possessions as they could stuff inside or fasten to the sides and roof. Although they came from a dozen states, they were known mostly as "Okies" since Oklahoma was especially hard hit. "

The CCC lasted until 1941. By the time the program ended, almost 3 million young men had passed through the Three Cs.

Federal Emergency Relief. A second act, the Federal Emergency Relief Act, gave more general help to the unemployed. It provided $250 million in direct grants-in-aid to the states to be used to furnish food and clothing to the unemployed, the aged, and the ill. An additional $250 million was distributed on the basis of one federal dollar for every three state dollars. Harry Hopkins was placed in charge of the program.

This was not enough, however, so Hopkins set up the Civil Works Administration (CWA). Instead of channeling aid through the states, it gave it directly to people in need. Within two months, more than 4 million persons were working for the federal government at jobs that did not compete with existing jobs. The pay was minimal, and some of the jobs were so unnecessary that the word *boondoggle* came to describe them. Still, as a Michigan county administrator reported, men left her office "weeping for sheer happiness" at the idea of working again after years of being unemployed.

Raising Farmers' Incomes

The nation's farmers were caught between huge surpluses and low prices. Hoover had tried to persuade farmers to limit production, but the voluntary program had not worked. Now Roosevelt decided to follow the same approach, but with a twist. Instead of using words, the federal govern-

ment would pay farmers cash for reducing production. The money for the benefit payments would come from a tax on processors, that is, the people who mill flour, pack meat, manufacture cloth, and so on. By limiting production, farmers would also get more money for the crops and livestock they did produce.

The Agriculture Adjustment Act was launched in May. Under it, the federal government agreed to pay farmers a certain amount for every acre of land left unseeded. Some crops, however, were too far advanced for the acreage reduction to take effect. So the government paid cotton growers $200 million to plow under 10 million acres of their crop. It also paid hog farmers to slaughter 6 million swine.

These crop-control measures aroused a great deal of criticism. A few newspapers wrote sentimental articles about the "slaughter of baby pigs." A more serious objection came from people who were upset by the deliberate destruction of food at a time when many Americans were hungry. In addition, the tax on processors was passed along to consumers in the form of higher prices for food and clothing.

Still, the AAA program *did* succeed in its goals. Prices of farm commodities rose, and farmers received more income.

Developing Natural Resources: the TVA

Among the longest-lasting New Deal projects was the Tennessee Valley Authority (TVA). Ever since World War I Congress had been arguing about what to do with some hydroelectric plants the government had built at Muscle Shoals, Alabama, to produce nitrites for explosives. When the war ended, private utility companies wanted to buy or lease the plants. But a group of congressmen led by Senator George W. Norris of Nebraska insisted that the federal government should continue the Progressive policy of conserving and developing the country's natural resources.

In May 1933 the TVA was established. It was the first example of regional planning in the United States. The TVA takes in parts of seven states—Alabama, Georgia, Kentucky, Mississippi, North Carolina, Tennessee, and Virginia—all of which are drained by the Tennessee River and its tributaries. TVA policy is to develop all the region's natural resources at the same time. TVA dams help control floods and improve navigation. TVA hydroelectric plants produce electricity and agricultural fertilizers. The TVA has even helped local authorities control malaria and tuberculosis.

At first the TVA was strongly opposed by private utility companies in the region. Regulating industry was one thing, they said, but the federal government had no right to compete with private enterprise. The utilities also resented the fact that the low electricity rates the TVA charged customers served as a "yardstick" against which to measure the much higher rates that the private companies charged. In 1936, however, the Supreme Court ruled that the TVA's activities were legal.

Since 1933 the Tennessee River valley has been transformed. There are new factories and new jobs. Farms are more productive, farmhouses have been electrified, health and education have improved, and the region is filled with lakes for fishing, swimming, and boating. Today most people would agree that the TVA is one of the most successful accomplishments of the New Deal.

Regulating Finance

FDR's first act had been to declare a bank holiday, and the first law passed during the First Hundred Days was the Emergency Banking Relief Act. Congress permitted sound banks in the Federal Reserve System to reopen but under carefully controlled conditions. The hoarding of gold and its export were forbidden. This act, which gave the president broad powers over the financial affairs of banks, reassured many people's faith in the banking system. A series of other acts dealing with financial matters increased public confidence.

The Economy Act lowered the salaries of government workers and reduced payments to veterans. FDR hoped this act would appease people who were worried about excessive federal spending.

The Home Owners' Loan Act provided government loans to home owners who were facing foreclosure because they could not meet their mortgage payments. By 1936, when the act expired, it had saved the homes of almost a million families.

The Securities Act gave the Federal Trade Commission the power to supervise new securities. Now companies that wanted to sell stock had to give the public full information. The Glass-Steagall Banking Act set up the Federal Deposit Insurance Corporation to protect bank deposits up to $5000. (The current amount insured by FDIC is $100,000.) Depositors did not have to worry about losing their life savings if a bank failed.

Helping Industry: the NIRA

The National Industrial Recovery Act, called NIRA for short, was one of the most controversial agencies set up by the New Deal. At first, however, it was so popular with some people that a number of babies born at the time were named "Nira."

The act created the National Recovery Administration, or NRA. Beginning in June 1933 and continuing through May 1935, almost every store, factory, and office building in the United States displayed in its windows posters with an enormous Blue Eagle, under which were the words "We Do Our Part." The brainchild of General Hugh Johnson, the blue bird was a symbol of the NRA.

The administration was designed to limit production in industry so that prices would go up and producers would make a profit. There were two main parts to the act. They had to do with industry codes and public works projects.

By displaying the blue eagle companies showed that they abided by the new hour and wage labor codes.

Setting Up Fair Trade Codes. The NRA helped about 500 industries set up codes of "fair competition." Even such industries as shoulder pad manufacturers and the dog food industry took part. Each code fixed the prices to be charged for that industry's products. This was designed to end cutthroat competition in which goods were sold for less than it cost to make them. The workweek was limited to forty hours; minimum wages of thirty to forty cents an hour were established; and child labor was abolished. The right of workers to unionize was recognized, and a National Labor Board was set up to settle disputes.

Priming the Pump. The second part of the act set up the Public Works Administration (PWA). The PWA was to be a *pump-priming* operation. That is, the government would spend lots of money on creating jobs. It undertook projects that required lots of workers and materials. This would provide wages and would give workers greater buying power, thus stimulating the economy. The PWA was placed under "Honest Harold" Ickes,

who was also secretary of the interior. Ickes lived up to his nickname. He moved carefully to make sure that each public works project was worthwhile and a good buy for taxpayers. Eventually, more than $4 billion was spent on some 34,000 projects, including the Triborough Bridge in New York; the causeway connecting the Florida mainland and Key West; the port of Brownsville, Texas; hospitals with 120,000 beds; and fifty military airports and two aircraft carriers.

Section 1 Review

COMPREHENSION   Developing Vocabulary

1. Explain these terms: boondoggle, pump-priming, dust bowl.

COMPREHENSION   Mastering Facts

1. What were the two major accomplishments of the CCC?
2. How did the AAA raise farmers' incomes?
3. What benefits did the TVA bring to people in the Tennessee River valley?
4. What were NRA codes designed to do?

2 ROOSEVELT SEEKS TO REFORM THE SYSTEM

VOCABULARY   *Second New Deal   interest rates*

The relief and recovery activities of the First Hundred Days did not improve the nation's economy as much as had been hoped. In the area of unemployment, although 4 million persons were working for the federal government, there were still 10 million Americans without jobs. Purchasing power had risen somewhat, but not enough to lift prices a great deal. Industrial production had also increased somewhat, but business people lacked the confidence to invest their surplus funds.

The congressional elections of 1934 gave the Democrats even more of a landslide than they had received in 1932. In the House they had 318 members to the Republicans' 104. In the Senate the balance was 69 to 27.

In January 1935, President Roosevelt announced a somewhat different approach to the nation's problems. "When a man is getting over an illness, wisdom dictates not only cure of the symptoms but removal of their cause." He recommended that the federal government shift its emphasis from relief and recovery to reform. "I want to save our system, the capitalistic system." The

period of legislation that began in 1935 is usually called the Second New Deal.

Increasing Employment

The federal government reorganized its relief activities. People who were not employable because they were too old or too young or too ill were to be taken care of by the states. The CCC and the PWA were continued. All other work programs were put under the Works Progress Administration (WPA), headed by Harry Hopkins.

The WPA set out "to create as many jobs as fast as possible." It received a budget of $5 billion, the largest sum any nation had ever spent for public welfare at one time. Between 1935 and 1941, it employed more than 8 million persons. WPA workers, most of them unskilled, built 600 airports throughout the country. They built or repaired 651,000 miles of roads and streets. They put up 110,000 libraries, schools, and hospitals. Sewing groups, in which most women workers were employed, made 300 million garments for the needy.

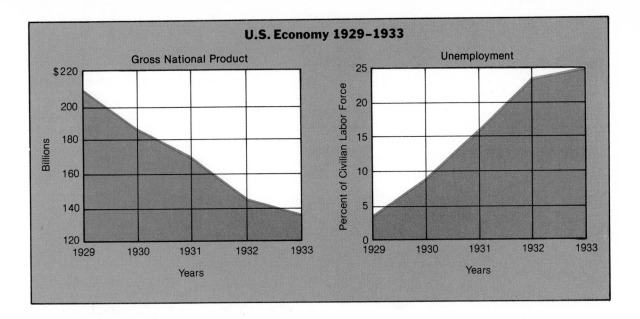

U.S. Economy 1929-1933

Gross National Product

Billions	
$220	
200	
180	
160	
140	
120	

Years: 1929 1930 1931 1932 1933

Unemployment

Percent of Civilian Labor Force

| 25 |
| 20 |
| 15 |
| 10 |
| 5 |
| 0 |

Years: 1929 1930 1931 1932 1933

The WPA also found work for unemployed writers, artists, musicians, and actors. Soon post offices and other public buildings were decorated with murals by such painters as Thomas Hart Benton. Newly formed symphony orchestras gave free public concerts and helped to make known the music of Aaron Copland, Virgil Thomson, and other American composers. People who had never seen a play were able to attend such productions as Clifford Odets's *Waiting for Lefty,* which dealt with a taxi drivers' strike, and *The Hot Mikado,* a black version of a Gilbert and Sullivan operetta.

The Construction of a Dam *by William Gropper commemorates the building of Boulder (Hoover) Dam.*

Authors who became well known later, such as Nelson Algren and Richard Wright, received training and help.

The WPA was efficiently and honestly run on the whole. However, it was criticized for encouraging people to vote Democratic in return for handouts. And some WPA officials *were* guilty of shady election practices. Also, many Americans did not believe the federal government should support cultural activities. They resented the fact that about 20 percent of WPA funds went into the arts instead of construction.

Establishing Social Security

In 1935 the United States followed the example of other industrial nations and established a system of social insurance. The centerpiece of the Social Security Act was a pension system for retired workers and their spouses. Also included were death benefits and support for surviving children up to the age of eighteen. None of these provisions were tied to need. Anyone, even a millionaire, could collect. The benefits were to come out of a payroll tax paid half by workers and half by employers. The Social Security Act also established a joint federal-state unemployment insurance system and provided for aid to crippled and blind persons, the needy elderly, neglected children, and others.

Not all groups of workers were covered. Farm workers and domestics, for example, were exempt.

In the long run, however, the Social Security Act has probably affected the lives of more people in the United States than any other legislation passed under the New Deal.

Reforming Business

Under the NIRA, the federal government had favored big business. Under the Second New Deal, more attention was given to small business.

Overseeing the Stock Market. The Securities and Exchange Commission (SEC), which had been established in 1934, was given the power to prevent people with inside information about companies from "rigging" the stock market, that is, making prices go up or down for their own profit regardless of the real value of the stock. Placed in charge of the new SEC was Joseph P. Kennedy. The business community at first objected to government interference in what had been a type of private club. However, when Richard Whitney, president of the New York Stock Exchange, was sent to prison, insiders saw the need for a change.

Reforming Utility Companies. In 1935 about 75 percent of electric light and power companies were controlled by a dozen holding companies. Now the purpose of holding companies is supposedly to provide economies in management. So the Public Utility Holding Company Act said that holding companies that failed to promote efficiency and savings over the next five years would be dissolved. Lobbyists for the holding companies immediately launched a million-dollar attack against the "death sentence" clause. They did not succeed, but enforcing the act proved difficult.

Taxing the Wealthy. The Revenue Act of 1935 was an attempt to break up large accumulations of wealth. It increased the rates of gift and estate taxes. It increased the tax rates for people with large incomes. And it provided for a graduated corporation income tax that favored small businesses over large ones. The act was described as "soaking the rich," although most rich people found many ways to avoid paying the highest rates. The act did, however, establish the idea that the well-to-do should carry a heavier tax burden than the poor.

Controlling Banks. The Banking Act of 1935 replaced the old Federal Reserve Board with a seven-member board of governors, to be appointed by the president for fourteen-year terms. The board was given the power to decide whether to raise or lower the nation's money supply by printing more or less paper money. It was also given the power to raise or lower *interest rates,* or the cost of borrowing money. As a result, economic decisions which until then had been made by private bankers were now made by public officials.

Section 2 Review

COMPREHENSION   Developing Vocabulary
1. Explain these terms: interest rates, Second New Deal.

COMPREHENSION   Mastering Facts
1. What was the outcome of the 1934 congressional elections?
2. What was the purpose of the Works Progress Administration?
3. What were two of the criticisms leveled at the WPA?
4. What act was described as "soaking the rich"?

3   THE NEW DEAL COMES UNDER ATTACK

VOCABULARY   *parity price   Townsend Plan*

As the New Deal struggled with the nation's economic problems, criticisms of its activities grew stronger and stronger. Some came from radicals on the left, who felt the New Deal was not doing enough to correct the evils of capitalism. Criticism also came from conservatives on the right, who felt that FDR was antibusiness and was leading the nation into socialism or even communism. Roosevelt's opponents complained to their congressmen. Some brought suit against the government.

In 1935 and 1936 the Supreme Court handed down decisions that eliminated certain New Deal agencies.

NIRA Declared Unconstitutional

The first decision came in the case of *Schechter Poultry Corporation* v. *United States,* otherwise known as the "sick chicken" case. It involved a Brooklyn poultry company that supposedly sold an unfit chicken to a butcher. The Court ruled that the National Industrial Recovery Act was unconstitutional for two reasons: (1) it gave legislative powers to the executive branch of government; and (2) some of the industry codes covered business that took place entirely within a state, whereas the federal government had power to regulate commerce only between states.

As a result of the Court's decision, the labor provisions of the NIRA likewise were no longer in effect. So Congress passed the National Labor Relations Act, more commonly known as the Wagner Act after its sponsor, Senator Robert F. Wagner of New York. The act reversed the attitude of the federal government toward collective bargaining. Instead of supporting employers, the federal government was now on the side of unions.

The Wagner Act said that employers had to bargain with their workers. It listed "unfair labor practices" that companies could not follow. Among these were threatening workers, firing union members, and interfering with union organizing efforts. The act also set up the National Labor Relations Board to hear testimony about unfair practices and to hold elections among workers to find out if they wished to be represented by a union.

To replace that part of the NIRA that dealt with wages and hours, Congress in 1938 passed the Fair Labor Standards Act. For the first time, there was a national minimum hourly rate for wages: twenty-five cents an hour at first, forty cents an hour in two years. There was also a national maximum work week: forty-four hours to begin with, forty hours in two years. Those under age sixteen were banned from factory work (age eighteen if the work was hazardous). Although industries not involved in interstate commerce were not covered, about 750,000 workers got raises when the law went through, and millions benefited from the shorter hours.

AAA Declared Unconstitutional

In 1936 the Supreme Court struck down the Agricultural Adjustment Act. It ruled that the processing tax out of which farmers were paid to restrict production was not a tax at all. It was a way of regulating agriculture—and that went beyond the proper powers of Congress.

Congress responded at first by passing a law based on conservation. It provided for government payments to farmers who planted crops and grasses that enriched the soil instead of commercial crops that took nutrients out of the soil. Then, in 1938, Congress passed a new Agricultural Adjustment Act, which the Supreme Court later declared constitutional.

The new act was based on the idea of an "ever-normal granary." It worked like this: If two-thirds of the farmers in a district agreed, each was given a certain quota of acres to plant in staple crops. If a farmer produced a surplus, it was not destroyed as it had been under the old act. But it could not be put on the market because that would cause prices to drop. So the AAA kept it in storage. Meanwhile, it lent the farmer money for living expenses.

Under the act, farmers were supposed to receive "a fair price" for their crops. What was considered a fair price? It was one that gave farmers the same purchasing power they had in the years between 1909 and 1914. That period was considered to be the last one during which farmers got a fair price for their goods. Another name for this fair price was *parity price*. (The word *parity* means equal to or equivalent). When prices reached parity, farmers sold their stored crops and repaid their loans to the government. If the market price remained below parity, farmers did not pay back the loans, and the government kept the crops in storage.

The Liberty League Charges

By the mid-1930s, the air was filled with charges that the New Deal was "endangering the Constitution" and slowly establishing a dictatorship. The charges were made by an organization called the Liberty League. Although it invited all classes of people to join, most of its members were rich industrialists, bankers, and corporation lawyers. Ironically, Alfred E. Smith, the 1928 Democratic presidential candidate, belonged but former President Hoover refused to join.

The kindest thing the Liberty League called FDR was a "traitor to his class," that is, to the well-born and the well-to-do. But the League was no real threat politically. As one observer said, its slogans had appeal only "to anyone with an income of a hundred thousand dollars a year."

Extremist Opposition

A more serious challenge to the New Deal came from those who said it was not doing enough for the country.

Upton Sinclair. A leading muckraker of the Progressive Era, Upton Sinclair helped bring about passage of the first Federal Meat Inspection Act with his novel *The Jungle*. In the 1930s he wrote a book called *I, Governor of California, and How I Ended Poverty*. This novel helped him win the Democratic nomination for governor of the state in 1934. In his campaign, Sinclair called for higher income and inheritance taxes, fifty-dollar-a-month pensions for the elderly, and consumer cooperatives. Sinclair lost. But the real significance of the election was the fact that the Republicans used a professional public relations firm for the first time. Since then, the practice has become common in political campaigns, especially those for the presidency of the United States.

Dr. Francis E. Townsend. When Sinclair lost his election bid, many of his followers turned to Dr. Francis E. Townsend. Townsend was a South Dakota physician who had become an assistant health officer in Long Beach, California. Many of the town's residents were retired farmers and business people, impoverished by the depression. Dr. Townsend devised a scheme that would pay everyone over sixty–five years of age $200 a month. The only requirement was that the entire amount be spent within 30 days. This was to keep money circulating which, in turn, would keep business healthy. The pensions were to be paid for by a 2 percent tax on business transactions. Economists pointed out that the "Townsend Plan" would give one-eleventh of the population about one-half the

New Deal Legislation

THE ACT OR AGENCY	THE PURPOSE
Farm Relief and Rural Development	
Agricultural Adjustment Administration AAA (1933)	To aid farmers and to regulate crop production.
The Tennessee Valley Authority TVA (1933)	To develop the resources of the Tennessee Valley.
Rural Electrification Administration REA (1935)	To provide cheap electricity for isolated rural areas.
Business Assistance and Reform	
Emergency Banking Relief Act EBRA (1933) ·	To regulate bank transactions in credit, currency, foreign exchange, gold, and silver.
Federal Deposit Insurance Corporation FDIC (1933)	To protect bank deposits up to $5,000. The amount now protected by the FDIC is $100,000.
National Recovery Administration NRA (1933)	To provide "codes" of fair competition and to give labor the right of collective bargaining.
Securities and Exchange Commission SEC (1934)	To supervise the stock exchanges and eliminate dishonest practices.
Public Utilities Holding Company Act (1935)	To eliminate holding companies of utilities that did not operate efficiently and economically.
Banking Act of 1935	To create a seven-member board of public officials to regulate the nation's money supply and the interest rates on loans.
Food, Drug and Cosmetic Act (1938)	To require manufacturers to list ingredients in food, drugs, and cosmetics.
Employment Projects	
Civilian Conservation Corps CCC (1933)	To provide jobs for young single males on conservation projects.
Federal Emergency Relief Act FERA (1933)	To help states provide jobs for the unemployed.
Civil Works Administration CWA (1933)	To provide work even if it means "making work" in federal jobs.
Public Works Administration PWA (1933)	To create jobs in public works which would increase worker buying power and stimulate the economy.
Works Progress Administration WPA (1935)	To create as many jobs as possible as quickly as possible, from jobs in the construction industry to jobs in symphony orchestras.
National Youth Administration NYA (1935)	To provide job training for unemployed youths and part-time jobs for students in need.
Housing and Social Security	
Home Owners Loan Corporation HOLC (1933)	To give loans at low interest to home owners who could not meet mortgage payments.
Federal Housing Administration FHA (1934)	To provide loans for the building and repair of houses.
Social Security Act (1935)	To provide a pension for retired workers and their spouses and to aid the handicapped.
United States Housing Authority USHA (1937)	To provide federal loans for a nation-wide home improvement program.
Labor Relations	
National Labor Relations Act (Wagner-Connery Act of 1935)	To define "unfair labor practices" and to establish a National Labor Relations Board to settle differences between employers and employees.
Fair Labor Standards Act (1938)	To set up a national minimum hourly wage, a maximum work week and to prohibit children under sixteen from working in factories.

national income. A bill to set up the plan was defeated in Congress. But Townsend's movement helped to push through the Social Security Act.

Father Coughlin.   A more startling voice than Townsend's was that of the Reverend Charles E. Coughlin, a Catholic priest in the Detroit suburb of Royal Oak. Even before the depression began, Father Coughlin was delivering Sunday afternoon sermons over a local radio station. As his audience grew, the talks moved from religious to social and political topics. Other stations picked up the broadcasts, and soon they were being carried nationwide. By 1934 some 10 million persons were listening to Father Coughlin each week and were sending him half a million dollars a year.

Father Coughlin had originally supported FDR, telling his listeners that it was "Roosevelt or ruin." But before long, he was attacking "international bankers" and calling for greater inflation than FDR was willing to risk. In late 1934 he formed the National Union for Social Justice, which came out for nationalizing banks, public utilities, and natural resources. As time went on, it became clear that Father Coughlin was strongly anti-Semitic. Eventually, his superiors in the Roman Catholic Church made him stop broadcasting.

Senator Huey P. Long.   The most able, and therefore the most dangerous, of the New Deal's extremist foes was Senator Huey P. Long of Louisiana. Starting as a dirt-poor salesman of patent medicines, Long studied law and was soon skillfully fighting cases against the oil and utility companies that controlled the state. He was an extremely effective speaker, although his loud clothes—orchid shirts, pink ties, and brown and white shoes—startled some people. His championship of the poor against corporate giants made him a hero to many people, and in 1928 he was elected governor. He gave the state badly needed schools, roads, bridges, and hospitals. He provided free textbooks for public school students and spent lavishly on the state university, providing it with the Sugar Bowl and "the best team that money could buy." In 1930 the people of Louisiana sent him to the U.S. Senate.

"The Kingfish," as Long was called, spent the next few years building a personal political machine in his home state and eyeing the presidency. In 1934 he introduced a nationwide social program called "Share Our Wealth." Its motto was "Every Man a King," and its key point was a $5000 guaranteed annual income for every family in the United States. The money for this was to be raised by taking over the wealth of the millionaires and by dividing up some of the nation's land and mineral treasures. According to "the Kingfish," every American family was entitled to own a house, an automobile, and a radio.

At the height of his popularity, Long was shot to death in the statehouse at Baton Rouge. The lone killer, whose family had quarreled with Long, was gunned down on the spot by the senator's bodyguards. Protestant minister Gerald L. K. Smith took over the "Share Our Wealth" program, but Long's family continued to dominate Louisiana politics.

Until his death, Long was Roosevelt's greatest political threat. Though unquestionably dictatorial, he was intelligent, colorful, and lively. He was also unique among southern politicians of his time and type—he appeared to be without racial prejudice. He said he wanted black people to share the wealth and be kings, too.

The Landslide of 1936

"America is in peril. We invite all Americans, [regardless] of party, to join us in defense of American institutions." So began the 1936 Republican platform. To lead their campaign, the Republicans nominated Alfred M. Landon, the able governor of Kansas, and Frank Knox, a Chicago newspaper publisher. During the campaign Landon was called a "Kansas Coolidge" because he had balanced his state's budget. Actually, both he and Knox were Progressives who had supported Theodore Roosevelt's Bull Moose campaign. Landon probably would have continued many New Deal programs.

Roosevelt and Garner were renominated by acclamation. In his acceptance speech, Roosevelt told his listeners that "To some generations much is given. Of other generations much is expected. This generation of Americans has a rendezvous with destiny." On that note, he kicked off a campaign directed against not his Republican opponent but the Liberty League. The strongest issue raised against Roosevelt was that 9 million people were still unemployed. He countered it by asking campaign crowds, "Are you better off than you were four years ago?" And the crowds roared back, "Yes."

Presidential Election of 1936

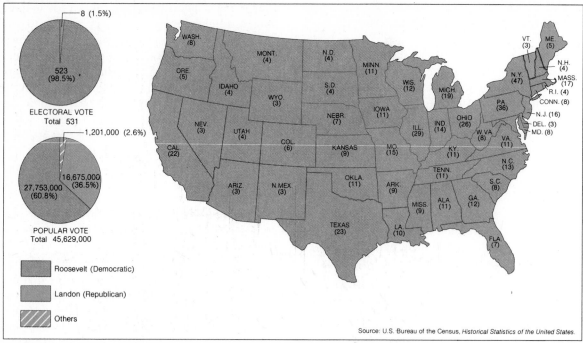

ELECTORAL VOTE
Total 531

8 (1.5%)
523 (98.5%)

POPULAR VOTE
Total 45,629,000

1,201,000 (2.6%)
16,675,000 (36.5%)
27,753,000 (60.8%)

Roosevelt (Democratic)

Landon (Republican)

Others

Source: U.S. Bureau of the Census, *Historical Statistics of the United States.*

© ML & Co.

Map Skills   *Roosevelt won the largest percentage of electoral votes in over 100 years. What was his percentage of the popular vote? Which states were won by the Republican candidate?*

On election day, FDR carried every state except Maine and Vermont. The popular vote was 27.7 million to 16.6 million, while the electoral vote was 523 to 8. The Democratic congressional majority stood at 330 to 90 in the House and 76 to 16 in the Senate. It was the biggest landslide victory since 1820, when James Monroe had swamped John Quincy Adams. It also represented the first time that most blacks voted Democratic rather than Republican. And it represented the first time that labor unions gave their united support to a single candidate, Roosevelt, instead of dividing their votes between the major parties.

Packing the Supreme Court

In his second Inaugural Address, Roosevelt spoke about the need for more reform. He pointed out that "one-third of a nation" was still "ill-housed, ill-clad, ill-nourished." And he promised to do something about it. But instead of proposing new economic legislation, Roosevelt asked Congress to reorganize the federal judiciary.

Roosevelt's message to Congress claimed that federal courts could not keep up with their case loads, that more judges were needed, and that part of the problem was that too many judges were "aged or infirm." He proposed that federal judges retire within six months after reaching the age of seventy. If they did not, then the president should have the power to appoint additional judges.

The measure was obviously aimed at the Supreme Court. Since six of its justices were seventy years or older, Roosevelt would be able to enlarge it to fifteen members. He had not yet had the opportunity to appoint a single Supreme Court justice. And he undoubtedly felt that the Court had been too conservative in knocking down the NIRA, the AAA, and other New Deal measures. What if it declared the Social Security Act and the National Labor Relations Act unconstitutional as well?

The president's bill set off a storm of protest in Congress and in the newspapers. Cries about "separation of powers" and "independence of the judiciary" were heard from all sides. People began calling the measure a "court-packing bill" that would fill the Supreme Court with judges who would agree with FDR's personal economic ideas. FDR replied that the "Nine Old Men" were already deciding cases on the basis of *their* personal economic ideas.

The bill Roosevelt wanted never got through Congress. But in the meantime, several changes took place. Two Supreme Court justices shifted their votes in favor of giving the federal government power to regulate the economy. In a series of 5–4 decisions, the Court declared both the Social Security Act and the National Labor Relations Act constitutional. Then one of the older, more conservative justices retired. That opened the way for the president to appoint New Dealer Hugo L. Black of Alabama.

In the end, Roosevelt got the kind of Supreme Court he wanted. He appointed seven justices in the next four years. But the attempt to pack the Court turned out to be a serious political mistake. It antagonized many congressmen and others who felt the president had been dictatorial. It also strengthened opposition to the New Deal. As a result, the 1938 congressional elections brought into office a number of conservative southern Demo-crats as well as many more Republicans. After the second Agricultural Adjustment Act and the Fair Labor Standards Act—both already described—no more major New Deal legislation was passed. By 1939 the New Deal, for all practical purposes, was over.

Section 3 Review

COMPREHENSION   Developing Vocabulary

1. Explain these terms: parity price, Townsend Plan, Liberty League.

COMPREHENSION   Mastering Facts

1. Why did the Supreme Court declare the NIRA unconstitutional?
2. How did the Wagner Act change the attitude of the federal government toward labor unions?
3. What was Senator Huey P. Long's program for ending poverty?
4. Why was Roosevelt unhappy with the Supreme Court?

4   THE NEW DEAL TRANSFORMS LIFESTYLES

VOCABULARY   *sit-down strike*

The 1930s saw a number of changes in the way Americans lived. Some were direct results of New Deal legislation. Others were brought on by the depression. Still others were outgrowths of developments in radio and film which had begun in earlier decades.

Labor Unions Grow

Until the 1930s, "organized labor" meant mostly the craft unions that made up the American Federation of Labor. However, a number of labor leaders considered the AFL's attitude old-fashioned. They wanted to organize industrial unions, particularly in such mass-production industries as automobiles, steel, textiles, and rubber.

After the Wagner Act was passed in 1935, John L. Lewis of the United Mine Workers Union, along with David Dubinsky of the International Ladies Garment Workers Union, Sidney Hillman of the Amalgamated Clothing Workers, Philip Murray, and Walter P. Reuther, among others, formed the Committee for Industrial Organization. The CIO began signing up unskilled and semiskilled workers as fast as it could, and within two years it had succeeded in gaining union recognition in the steel and auto industries. Among the techniques the CIO used was the *sit-down strike*. Instead of walking off their jobs, workers remained inside the plant, but did not work. This prevented the plant owners from carrying on production with strikebreakers.

The sit-down strike was declared unconstitutional in 1939. By that time the CIO was no longer part of the AFL. Its organizing success had caused jealousy among the older, more traditional unions. Also, John L. Lewis did not like AFL president William Green, claiming that he was only a figurehead and did not actively work for the union. Lewis also publicly traded punches with "Big Bill" Hutcheson, head of the carpenters' union. In 1937 the AFL kicked the CIO unions out. But they went ahead with their organizing drives and by 1938 claimed 4 million members. That same year the CIO changed its name (but not its initials) to the Congress of Industrial Organizations. The split in the labor movement lasted until the AFL and CIO combined in 1955.

The Sit Down Strike. Workers engage in a new kind of strike in Flint, Michigan in 1937. They relax in empty seats in an automobile factory. They are striking against General Motors.

More Attention Paid to Minorities

During the 1930s, the position of minorities in the United States improved somewhat.

Blacks. Black Americans benefited from New Deal relief measures. Officially, these were "color blind," that is, they applied equally to whites and blacks. The CCC and WPA gave help to blacks. There were a number of black administrators in New Deal agencies. For example, Secretary of the Interior Ickes, who had been president of the Chicago NAACP, hired William H. Hastie, later governor of the Virgin Islands and an appeals court judge. He also hired Robert C. Weaver, who went on to be the first secretary of housing and urban development. FDR often sought the opinion of highly placed government workers, who were sometimes referred to as the "Black Cabinet."

The new CIO unions included black members, something that most AFL unions had not done. The Supreme Court, too—in 1932 and 1934 cases—upheld the right of accused blacks to have competent legal advice and to be tried by juries that included blacks.

In those years Washington was still a Jim Crow town. President and Mrs. Roosevelt often trampled on the feelings of its white inhabitants by entertaining distinguished blacks at the White House. Eleanor Roosevelt's most spectacular step in recognizing black achievement involved the singer Marian Anderson. In 1939 the Daughters of the American Revolution refused Anderson the use of Constitution Hall in Philadelphia for a concert because of her color. Eleanor Roosevelt publicly resigned from the organization and arranged for the concert to be given at the Lincoln Memorial in Washington.

American Indians. The year 1924 had been a turning point for American Indians. They won full citizenship in acknowledgement of their services to the nation during World War I. In 1933 President Roosevelt appointed John Collier, a former officer of the American Indian Defense Organization, to be Commissioner of Indian Affairs. Collier made several suggestions that became part of the Howard-Wheeler Act, or Indian Reorganization Act, of 1934.

The act strengthened the claims of the Pueblo Indians to their ancient lands. It ended the allotment policy that had been established by the Dawes Act of 1887, under which parts of reservations were granted to individual Indians. And it tried to restore reservation land to tribal authority. In addition, Indians were now allowed to enter any business they wished and to sue and be sued in court. The act also provided more practical education for Indians, including farming, animal husbandry, soil conservation, and marketing.

Eleanor Roosevelt presents a medal of achievement to the famous contralto Marian Anderson.

Indians who wanted to return to traditional tribal life were pleased with the act. Those who had become more "Americanized" felt the act would make it harder for Indians to improve themselves economically.

Mexican-Americans. Like blacks and other minorities, Mexican-Americans suffered more from the depression than the general population. Since 1920 they had been moving in great numbers to Texas, California, and other parts of the Southwest, increasing the Hispanic population in the region. Mexican-Americans worked most often as farm laborers, an occupation less well protected by federal and state laws than other kinds of work. When the creation of the dust bowl sent thousands of ruined farmers to California, Mexican-Americans found it harder than ever to make a living. Competition among workers drove some farm wages as low as nine cents an hour. Efforts to unionize were often met with legal action and guns. The CCC and WPA were helpful to some Mexican-Americans, but migrant workers could not qualify if they had no permanent address.

Family Life

The typical or average middle-class family of 1936 was not on relief. The family consisted of two adults and their two children. The husband worked outside, and his wife kept house. The family lived in a six-room home or a four-room apartment. Their gross annual income was $1348. Fewer people were getting married. The rate fell from 10.14 marriages per 1000 people in 1929 to 7.8 per 1000 in 1932. The birthrate fell from 19 births per 1000 couples in 1929 to 16.5 per 1000 in 1933. Babies were expensive.

The main source of amusement was the radio. By 1931, 29 million families, or 85 percent of the population, owned radios. In the afternoon were serials portraying romantic adventure and small-town life, such as "The Romance of Helen Trent," "The Guiding Light," and "Ma Perkins." The main characters in these stories were female. Later in the afternoon, there were adventure stories for children, including "Little Orphan Annie," "The Green Hornet," and "The Lone Ranger."

The evening had excellent dramas and variety programs featuring such stars as Bob Hope, Orson Welles, Eddie Cantor, Jack Benny, and George Burns and Gracie Allen.

For outside entertainment the family usually went to a movie. Stars such as Greta Garbo, Joan Crawford, Marlene Dietrich, and Loretta Young played in dramas that reflected a life of sophistication and luxury. This was done deliberately, because people in pinched economic circumstances got vicarious, or second-hand, pleasure in watching the make-believe frolics on the silver screen.

Women in the News

In the 1930s women were the most popular movie stars. That was the reverse of the 1960s and early 1970s, when the most popular stars were men. In the thirties women were competing successfully with men in the literary field. Margaret Mitchell's *Gone with the Wind* sold over 12 million copies and won the Pulitzer Prize for literature in 1937. Other novelists were Pearl Buck and Edna Ferber. Famous short story writers were Dorothy Parker and Katherine Anne Porter. Dorothy Thompson was the most celebrated journalist for a time. Playwright Lillian Hellman wrote some of the most memorable plays to appear on Broadway, and she also wrote movies.

Male-dominated fields were also opening up for women. Amelia Earhart became the first female passenger on a transatlantic flight in 1928. In 1932 she flew alone across the Atlantic. In 1937, while attempting an around-the-world flight, she was lost in the Pacific. In the 1932 Olympics, Mildred "Babe" Didrikson won two gold medals and one silver medal in track and field events. In the field of anthropology, Ruth Benedict became internationally known for her work. Margaret Mead, a student of Benedict, won international acclaim with her first work, *Coming of Age in Samoa*. Maud Slye did cancer research at the Rockefeller Foundation, while Florence Sabin made valuable discoveries concerning blood and bone marrow. Ruth Bryan Owen, a former member of Congress, served as ambassador to Denmark. Mary McLeod Bethune, founder of Bethune-Cookman College in Florida, gave the Roosevelts advice on the needs and interests of black Americans. Margaret Bourke-White and Dorothea Lang made reputations in the new art form of photography.

Summing Up the New Deal

The New Deal was a daring experiment about which historians are still divided. On the one hand, it raised the incomes of farmers and workers, helped preserve natural resources, provided a cushion for the sick and the aged, enabled unions to organize, and added to the material wealth of the nation. It eliminated business excesses, guaranteed the safety of bank deposits, and reduced unemployment. On the other hand, it raised the national debt, doubled the federal bureaucracy, and failed to increase private business activity. Despite the CCC and the WPA, in 1940 there were still 7.5 million people without jobs. Economically, the New Deal was a mixed success. The real end of the Great Depression was brought about by World War II.

Politically, however, the New Deal is generally considered a rousing success. In the 1930s, many Americans believed that government participation in the economic life of a nation inevitably led to socialism, communism, or some form of dictatorship. They believed there was no middle ground between a more-or-less unregulated capitalism and a strictly regimented society. They saw, with fear and loathing, such regimented societies developing on the European continent and already established in the Soviet Union. But the New Deal showed it was possible to provide a certain amount of economic security without destroying fundamental political freedoms. By helping those who needed aid while at the same time turning back demands for more radical measures, the New Deal probably saved both democracy and the free enterprise system.

The New Deal also marked a shift in the relationship between the federal government and the American people. In the Progressive Era, the role of the federal government had been that of an economic regulator. As a result of the New Deal, the federal government began to play a more positive part in the economy. For better or worse, most Americans now believe that a government is responsible for the economic welfare of its people.

Section 4 Review

COMPREHENSION Developing Vocabulary
1. Explain these terms: sit-down strike, organized labor.

COMPREHENSION Mastering Facts
1. In what ways was the CIO different from the AFL?
2. Why was the sit-down strike an effective weapon of labor?
3. How and why did Eleanor Roosevelt show her displeasure with the Daughters of the American Revolution?
4. How did the Howard-Wheeler Act change government policy toward Indians?

CHAPTER 31   Review

Chapter Summary

During the first one hundred days of the Roosevelt administration, jobs were created for the unemployed and emergency relief was provided. Americans became familiar with an "alphabet soup" of new agencies: CCC, AAA, TVA, NRA, and many others. Then a second New Deal concentrated on reforming the system itself. Relief activities were improved, and the Social Security Act was passed. Roosevelt easily won reelection in 1936. Soon afterwards, however, the Supreme Court found some New Deal legislation unconstitutional. Still, the New Deal had a profound effect on the American system of government and on American life in general.

Questions for Critical Thinking

COMPREHENSION   Summarizing Main Ideas

1. What were the two main purposes of the legislation passed during the First Hundred Days? To what extent were these purposes achieved?

2. What was the main difference in approach between the First New Deal and the Second New Deal? Why did Roosevelt propose the change? Do you agree with him? Why or why not?

3. What were the arguments in favor of Roosevelt's court-packing proposal? What were the arguments against it?

4. What gains did the labor movement make under the New Deal?

5. What effect did the New Deal have on these? (a) the position of minorities; (b) the role of women; (c) the aged; (d) the stock market.

COMPREHENSION   Interpreting Events

1. How did the "black blizzard" affect farmers in the dust bowl? How did the farmers react?

2. Why was the TVA controversial? Why is it considered a major achievement of the New Deal? Do you agree with that evaluation?

3. Why did conservatives criticize the New Deal? Why did radicals on the left criticize it?

4. How did the balance of power between the legislative, executive, and judicial branches of government shift during the New Deal?

5. Do you think the federal government should be responsible for the economic welfare of the people? Give reasons for your opinion.

APPLICATION   Using Skills To Understand Time

For each of the following pairs of events, indicate which came first.

1. The Civilian Conservation Corps is established; Okies and other farmers migrate to California.

2. FDR attempts to pack the Supreme Court; FDR is reelected in the biggest landslide since 1820.

3. The NIRA is declared unconstitutional; Congress establishes a minimum wage.

4. The CIO is recognized in the steel and auto industries; the Wagner Act provides government backing for collective bargaining.

5. Eleanor Roosevelt resigns from the Daughters of the American Revolution; Margaret Mitchell wins the Pulitzer Prize for literature for her novel *Gone with the Wind*.

EVALUATION   Comparing Past to Present

1. Which of the alphabetic agencies set up under the New Deal exist today?

2. What is the minimum wage today? Why do some people believe it should be abolished?

3. How has the Social Security system changed since it was first established? What are some difficulties that confront the system today?

The Tennessee Valley Authority

Until fifty years ago, people living in "the Valley" came to accept annual floods as a way of life. Each year the Tennessee River and its tributaries would rise over their banks to destroy crops, cover towns, and sweep people and property before them. But since the Tennessee Valley Authority (TVA) was established, there has not been a major flood in the Valley.

In 1933 the federal government established the TVA. This corporation had the power to construct dams, generate and sell electric power, establish flood control, and "advance the economic and social well-being of the people" in the area.

The River's Course. "The Valley"—as it is called by the people who live there—is shown on this page. The river basin covers an area of about 40,000 square miles, approximately the same size as England, Scotland, and Wales put together. To the east are the Blue Ridge Mountains; the five major tributaries of the Tennessee rise there. Upstream from Chattanooga, the countryside is open and rolling. Downstream the landscape becomes more rugged, with many narrow valleys. Eventually the lower Tennessee flows into the Ohio River.

TVA Accomplishments. The TVA consists of nine major

The Tennessee Valley

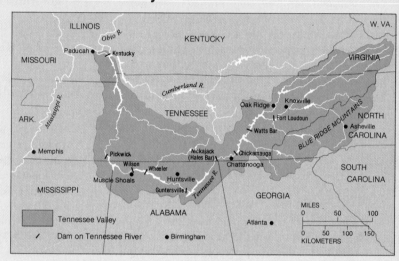

dams on the Tennessee River, plus eighteen smaller dams on the tributaries. There are also six small dams owned by the Aluminum Company of America.

The nine major dams have multipurpose uses. In addition to storing water, they have resulted in the creation of a 650-mile-long inland waterway. The lakes behind the major dams are connected by a system of locks. This means that boats and barges can travel through a nine-foot-deep navigable channel from the Ohio all the way to Knoxville. The Tennessee now carries millions of tons of products each year. Also, the major dams produce much electric power.

A few years after the TVA was established, millions of acres of land, once ruined by floods,

were returned to cultivation. Industry took advantage of the available water power, and tourists began to enjoy the artificial lakes and the river. Thus, the geography of the Tennessee River Valley has changed a great deal over the past fifty years—all because of a New Deal project called the TVA.

Understanding Geography

1. What conditions used to exist in the Tennessee Valley before the TVA?

2. Why is the TVA considered to be an important example of federal involvement in a free enterprise system?

3. How did the TVA change the geography of the area?

UNIT 8 Review

Understanding Social Studies Concepts

History

1. Most New Deal legislation was classified as either a relief or a reform measure. Place each of the following into one of those two categories: (a) Civilian Conservation Corps; (b) Civil Works Administration; (c) Works Progress Administration; (d) Security Exchange Commission; (e) Revenue Act of 1935. Which New Deal reforms still operate today?
2. What are reparations? How did they cause difficulties for many nations following World War I?
3. Write a paragraph summarizing the history of the Eighteenth Amendment (Prohibition). When was it passed? repealed? What positive and negative results did it produce?
4. What was the purpose of the Washington Conference? Did it accomplish its goal? Explain.

Economics

1. How did the advertising business contribute to the economic boom of the 1920s? What new techniques did advertisers use?
2. Why do Americans refer to the 1930s as the years of the "Great Depression"?
3. Which indicators had already begun pointing to a downturn in the nation's economy as early as 1926? Why is the beginning of the Great Depression usually considered to be on "Black Tuesday" in 1929? What conditions led up to this day?
4. Name several economic measures taken by the federal government during the 1930s that were aimed at preventing another Great Depression. Which are still important today?

Government

1. What was President Roosevelt's "courtpacking bill"? Why was it unpopular with many people?
2. Franklin D. Roosevelt has been described as a *pragmatist*. Define this word; then show how the philosophy of pragmatism was used by Roosevelt during the New Deal years.
3. Write several paragraphs summarizing both the positive contributions and the negative aspects of the New Deal.

Sociology

1. How did expansion of the American public school system during the early 1900s influence the growth of newspapers and magazines?
2. How did the coming of the automobile age change the lifestyles of many Americans?
3. In what ways did women express a new sense of freedom during the 1920s?

Extending Map, Chart, Picture Skills

1. Refer to charts on pages 619 and 841. About how many times greater was the Gross National Product in 1980 than in 1930?
2. Compare the presidential election maps on pages 605 and 624. Which states did Roosevelt win in 1936 that he did not win in 1932?

Understanding Current Events

1. Research some of the action taken recently by Congress concerning Social Security benefits for older Americans. What changes have been proposed? Why is the Social Security program becoming increasingly expensive?
2. Compare the program offerings of radio in the 1930s to those of television today. Is radio still an important source of information for Americans today? Explain.

Developing Effective Citizenship

1. Reread the quote by Carrie Chapman Catt on page 566. Does any single person or group deserve credit for passage of the Nineteenth Amendment? Explain.
2. What did President Roosevelt mean when he said in his first inaugural speech that "the only thing we have to fear is fear itself"? What was he calling on Americans to believe? How important is the quality of confidence to the well-being of a nation?
3. What role has the NAACP performed in the civil rights movement? Why can groups often have a greater effect on the legislative process than individuals?

GLOBAL TIME LINE
1933–1960

THE UNITED STATES

THE WORLD

1930

1940

1934 Nye Committee investigates war profits.

1940 Congress approves Lend-Lease Act.

1941 Japanese attack Pearl Harbor.

1945 FDR dies; Harry S. Truman becomes president.

1940 France surrenders to Germany.

1939–1945 World War II.

1937 Japan attacks China.

1946 United Nations General Assembly holds first meeting.

UNIT 9

War and World Leadership

1952 Dwight D. Eisenhower elected president.

1954 *Brown* v. *Board of Education* decision.

1959 Alaska, Hawaii become states.

1950 — 1960

1950–1953 Korean War.

1957 Soviet Union launches Sputnik I.

1957 North Vietnam begins attacks on South Vietnam.

1946–1949 Chinese Civil War.

The Road to War

1933–1940

Linking Past to Present

In 1933, the year that Franklin D. Roosevelt took office as president for the first time, another man in another country came to power and for partly the same reason: an economic depression. Germans, frightened and confused, turned to a man who seemed to have an answer or at least would do something to help. His name was Adolf Hitler.

Roosevelt's second Inaugural Address in 1937 made no mention of foreign affairs, yet he was deeply troubled by them. Japan had attacked China, and dictators were springing up in many European countries. For the next four years, Roosevelt was to spend more and more time on foreign affairs. He extended the Good Neighbor Policy with Latin America. He opened diplomatic relations with the Soviet Union and made preparations to grant independence to the Philippines.

Meanwhile, Italy was carving out an empire in Africa, Spain erupted into civil war, and Hitler began a series of European conquests. These horrifying years had begun with a promise by most nations that they would never again go to war.

1 STORM CLOUDS GATHER

VOCABULARY   *Fascism   Sturmabteilung   Schutzstaffel   sanctions   Rhineland*

On January 15, 1929, the United States Senate, by a vote of eighty-one to one, ratified the Kellogg-Briand Pact. Named after French Foreign Minister Aristide Briand and U.S. Secretary of State Frank B. Kellogg, the pact was eventually signed by sixty-four nations, or almost all the nations then in existence. They promised never to make war again and to settle future disputes by peaceful means. But the only way of enforcing the pact was through public opinion. There were no provisions in the treaty for the use of economic or military force against any nation that broke the agreement.

Some writers and historians believe that the Kellogg-Briand Pact is an example of what was wrong with American diplomacy during the thirties. One historian has characterized the pact as peace through incantation, that is, through the mumbling of magic words. It might have worked, he said, in a world that longed for peace. But it could not work in a world where three nations—Japan, Germany, and Italy—wanted war. As the depression deepened through the thirties, each of the three saw war as a solution to its problems.

Japan Attacks Manchuria

The island kingdom of Japan depended on world trade for the food and raw materials its 70 million people required. Even before the depression, its economic position had been shaky. Now, faced with the loss of overseas markets for its manufactured goods, the Japanese government became increasingly imperialistic. Military leaders, ignoring the objections of moderate officials, invaded the Chinese province of Manchuria in September 1931 and took over its rich coal and iron deposits.

When news of the Japanese attack reached Washington, Secretary of State Henry L. Stimson proposed an international boycott of Japanese goods. This would damage Japan's economy and presumably force it to withdraw from China. President Hoover, however, rejected Stimson's suggestion. He wanted only a statement of disapproval. So the United States declared, in the Stimson Doctrine, that it would not recognize any territorial gains made by force.

The Stimson Doctrine had no effect on Japan, which proceeded to conquer Manchuria and set up the *puppet state* of Manchukuo in 1932. (A puppet state is one that is independent in theory but whose officials and actions are actually controlled by another nation.) When the League of Nations criticized Japan for its actions, Japan simply quit the League. Then, in violation of the Five-Power Treaty that had been signed in Washington in 1922, it began to build up its navy.

Hitler Comes to Power

Meanwhile, Adolf Hitler was threatening the democratic government of Germany. The German economy had been shaky since the end of World War I. During the twenties, it had suffered a disastrous inflation. Also, it depended on heavy borrowing from U.S. banks and investors. When those sources of funds dried up in 1930 and 1931, business failures and unemployment spread throughout the country. None of the political parties was able to win a majority of votes. So the aged and ailing president, Paul von Hindenburg, called on the largest party to form a government. That was Hitler's National Socialist German Workers' party, commonly called the Nazi party. On January 30, 1933, the Nazis came into power.

635

The word "socialist" in the Nazi party's title is misleading. The Nazis were not socialists. They were fascists. *Fascism* is the belief that the state is more important than the people, and that a nation should have a strong centralized government headed by a dictator with absolute power. Individuals have no rights, and all opposition to the government is suppressed by force. Fascism was given its name by Benito Mussolini, who seized power in Italy in 1922. Hitler, however, added racism to Mussolini's fascist doctrine. In his book *Mein Kampf* (My Struggle), Hitler proclaimed his belief that Germans, especially those who were blond and blue-eyed, made up a "master race" that was destined to rule the world. Other "races," such as Jews, Slavs, and certain non-whites, were inferior "races" that contaminated society and were fit only to serve the Germans or to be exterminated.

The Nazi party, like Mussolini's Fascist party, was strongly anticommunist. As a result, it was supported by many conservative business leaders who gave it funds during the twenties when it was trying to come to power. The Nazi party was also intensely militaristic. War veterans made up much of its membership. Many belonged to one of Hitler's two private armies: the brown-shirted storm troopers (the *Sturmabteilung* or SA) and the black-shirted SS (*Schutzstaffel*, which means "protective group"). Their armbands showed the party symbol, a hooked black cross called the "swastika." During the ten years before Hitler took office and suspended the German constitution, they paraded about, shouted slogans, and beat up anyone who opposed them. Their particular targets were union leaders, Communists, and Jews. Hitler blamed the Jews, who made up less than one percent of the population, for Germany's defeat in World War I. It was a chief goal of the Nazis to undo the results of that war—the Treaty of Versailles—and to make Germany once more the dominant power in Europe. "One state! One people! One leader!" was their motto.

European Aggression Begins

For all his talk, Hitler at first moved cautiously on the international scene. In October 1933 he pulled Germany out of the League of Nations. Then he began a secret buildup of the nation's armed forces. But publicly, nothing else happened until 1936.

Mussolini Attacks Ethiopia. It was Mussolini who next threatened world stability. For years he had been boasting about his plans to turn the Mediterranean Sea into an Italian lake and to revive the glories of the ancient Roman Empire. In 1934 Italian and Ethiopian troops clashed along the border of Ethiopia and Italian Somaliland in Africa. That event was followed by a ten-month

The Nazis were experts at staging dramatic political demonstrations. Here Hitler and his officials salute the German Labor Corps. The soldiers bear shovels instead of guns.

drumfire of charges by Italy, manufactured "incidents," and propaganda. In the next few years the world was to see this scenario replayed often. It meant that a stronger country was getting ready to attack a weaker one. The Italian invasion began in October 1935. By May 1936 it was all over. In June, Ethiopia was annexed to Italy.

The League Does Not Act. Four days after the invasion began, the League of Nations branded Italy the aggressor and tried to apply *sanctions* (penalties), including an arms embargo as well as a boycott of Italian goods. But other nations would not agree to deny Mussolini oil for his highly mechanized army. Nor would Great Britain and France agree to keep Italian troops and munitions from passing through the Suez Canal. By this time it was clear that the League of Nations was more or less useless as a means of preventing war.

Aggression Condemned. Many groups and individuals bitterly protested Italy's actions. Black communities in the United States were particularly outraged by Italy's aggression. They responded by raising money and collecting medical supplies for the Ethiopians. Years later, Ethiopian Emperor Haile Selassie said, "We can never forget the help Ethiopia received from Negro Americans during the terrible crisis. . . . It moved me to know that Americans of African descent did not abandon their embattled brothers, but stood by us."

Blacks were also among the first Americans along with labor unions and the American Jewish community to denounce Hitler. As early as 1933 when Hitler came to power, educator and author Kelly Miller wrote an article called "Hitler—the German Ku Klux." In it he compared Hitler's persecution of the Jews to American Klan attacks on blacks. Another writer declared, "An individual who becomes a world menace on a doctrine of racial prejudice, bigotry, and oppression of minorities . . . is our concern."

Hitler Arms the Rhineland. Taking advantage of the international distraction over Ethiopia, Hitler made his first aggressive moves. In 1935 he announced that Germany would rearm despite the Versailles Treaty. In March 1936 he sent troops into the Rhineland, an area in western Germany that was supposed to remain free of soldiers and fortifications. Hitler's remilitarization of the Rhineland was a threat to France and Britain. If at

that time the two democracies had moved their own troops into the Rhineland, it is quite likely that Hitler would have backed down, for the German army was still weak. But the two democracies could not agree on joint action—so Hitler was not stopped.

The United States Offers Friendship

It is possible that President Roosevelt could have eased European tensions somewhat during this period by wiping out Allied war debts. But Congress would not have gone along with such action. Most Americans agreed with Calvin Coolidge. "They hired the money, didn't they?" that stern Yankee had said. However, the United States did take several important steps in the area of foreign affairs.

Recognizing the Soviet Union. Ever since the Russian Revolution of 1917, the United States had refused to recognize that country's government. This was partly because of opposition to communism, and partly because the Soviet government had taken over American property and refused to repay loans that the United States had made to the Russian monarchy. In November 1933, however, President Roosevelt agreed to exchange ambassadors with Moscow. The Soviet Union did not attempt to alter its often-stated policy of overthrowing the capitalist system of government wherever and whenever it could. Nor did the Russians pay the debt. Still, the fact that American diplomats could now be stationed in Moscow—where they could study Russians—was useful. It was useful to know more of what was going on inside the Soviet Union. Even more useful, the Soviet Union was now opened up as a possible market for American exports. It was also a possible counterweight to Japanese aggression in the Far East.

Reciprocal Trade Agreements. As you know, the Hawley-Smoot Tariff of 1930, which raised American tariffs to their highest point ever, had resulted in a sharp decline in American trade. So in 1934 Congress passed a Reciprocal Trade Agreement Act giving the president the power to make agreements with other countries to reduce tariffs by as much as 50 percent. Under the leadership of Secretary of State Hull, a strong supporter of low tariffs, the United States signed more than twenty agreements over the next five years. America's foreign trade increased, and other nations, especially in Latin America, became much friendlier toward the United States.

The Good Neighbor Policy. Roosevelt continued the Good Neighbor policy begun by Coolidge and Hoover. A Pan-American conference at Montevideo, Uruguay, in 1933 heard the U.S. representative promise to end all armed intervention in Latin American nations. The words were soon matched by action. In 1934 the United States signed a treaty with Cuba *abrogating*, or abolishing, the Platt Amendment but retaining the naval base at Guantánamo Bay. That same year, the last U.S. marines were withdrawn from Haiti, where they had been stationed since 1915. American fiscal control, however, was maintained until 1942.

Roosevelt then traveled 7000 miles to Buenos Aires, a long way for presidents to travel in those days, to attend the 1936 Inter-American Conference for Peace. There the president declared that he was a "traveling salesman for peace," and again stated the new U.S. policy of non-intervention in Latin American affairs.

Section 1 Review

COMPREHENSION   Developing Vocabulary

1. Explain these terms: Fascism, Sturmabteilung, Schutzstaffel, sanctions, Rhineland, puppet state, abrogating.

COMPREHENSION   Mastering Facts

1. What was one reason Italian and German business leaders supported Hitler and Mussolini?
2. What was Hitler's theory of the "master race"?
3. Why was Emperor Haile Selassie grateful to American blacks?
4. What advantages did the United States acquire by recognizing the Soviet Union?

2 AMERICA STRUGGLES TO REMAIN NEUTRAL

VOCABULARY   *collective security   quarantine   Anschluss   Sudetenland*

During the 1930s the Girl Scouts of America changed the color of their uniforms from khaki to green to make them appear less militaristic. The same antiwar spirit was behind other campaigns. One sought to end the sale of toy soldiers lest their owners develop a taste for battle. Another campaign tried to abolish Memorial Day on the ground that decorating soldiers' graves glorified past wars. Such campaigns reflected a widespread feeling in the United States that the country should isolate itself from the possibility of war.

The Nye Committee and Isolationism

Gerald P. Nye was a senator from North Dakota. Beginning in April 1934, he headed a committee to investigate the reasons for U.S. entry into World War I. Specifically, Nye's committee wanted to know what made Woodrow Wilson change from the candidate who "kept us out of war" in 1916 to the president who led us into war in 1917. The committee conducted hearings for three years and then published its findings.

The main point of the Nye committee's report was that certain American corporations, particularly those in munitions and banking, had made lots of money during World War I. There was also a suggestion, but without evidence to back it up, that some large corporations had urged Wilson to go to war so they could make a profit.

These findings were published as sensational exposés by newspapers and magazines. The public was horrified. The term "merchants of death" was applied to the corporations, and the number of isolationists in the nation skyrocketed.

The isolationists' belief was that the United States *could* remain at peace in a future war. All it had to do was avoid financial entanglements, keep its ships and its citizens at home, and refrain from exercising its neutral rights. Accordingly, Nye and other isolationists in Congress passed a series of neutrality acts designed to keep America out of the next world war.

The Neutrality Acts

The first Neutrality Act was passed in 1935 after the invasion of Ethiopia. According to the act, once the president declared that a state of war existed, it would be unlawful to ship or sell arms to those countries that were fighting. The president

As the threat of war increased in Europe, isolationist forces in the United States grew louder.
Members of the American Peace Mobilization (above) picket the White House.

could also warn American citizens traveling on ships of warring countries that they were doing so at their own risk. This was designed to prevent another *Lusitania* incident.

The second Neutrality Act was passed in February 1936. It expanded the terms of the first act to prohibit loans and credits, as well as arms, to warring nations.

The following month, an army revolt in Spain set off a civil war. Hitler and Mussolini made common cause with fascist-minded General Francisco Franco, who had attacked the Spanish republican government. Both dictators gave Franco all-out aid, including arms, planes, and "volunteers" from their own armed forces. It was an opportunity to try out their soldiers and weapons in a sort of dress rehearsal for bigger battles. The Soviet Union gave similar, but considerably less, assistance to the Loyalists, as the Spanish republican government forces were called. (This made the Loyalists look like communists, which most of them were not.) Also, about 3000 volunteers from the United States formed the Abraham Lincoln Brigade to fight against Franco. The civil war ended in March 1939 with the fall of Madrid to Franco. Another fascist state was established in Europe. In the meantime,

Italy and Germany had cemented their friendship with a formal alliance called the Rome-Berlin Axis.

When the Spanish Civil War broke out, Roosevelt asked Congress to apply the provisions of the neutrality acts to civil wars as well as international ones. This was done in January 1937. In May 1937, the third Neutrality Act was passed. It made the first and second acts permanent. It also made them more flexible. The president could now permit the sale of goods other than weapons on a "cash-and-carry" basis. They had to be paid for on delivery, and they had to be taken from a U.S. port by the buyer.

Challenging Isolationism

President Roosevelt was not an isolationist. He was aware of the dangers of fascism and Nazism, and he felt it was important to take a firm stand against them. At the same time, however, he did not want to be considered a warmonger.

Neutrality and the "China Incident."   In July 1937 Japanese militarists struck again in China. Chinese and Japanese troops had clashed at the

639

Marco Polo Bridge near Peking. Using the clash as an excuse, Japanese forces moved swiftly and were soon in control of most of China's seacoast.

Most Americans favored China rather than Japan. So Roosevelt did not invoke the Neutrality Act. His excuse was that Japan itself referred to the conflict as an "incident," not a war. Americans continued sending arms and other supplies to China. And American engineers helped the Chinese build the 700-mile-long Burma Road, a supply highway that led from the port of Rangoon in Burma across rough mountain country into China's interior.

The "Quarantine Speech." On October 5, 1937, Roosevelt delivered a speech in Chicago. The president expressed his fears about the international situation and the behavior of Germany, Italy, and Japan. What was needed, he said, was *collective security* on the part of the peace-loving nations of the world. They should behave the way a community behaves when faced by an epidemic. It "joins in a quarantine of the patients in order to protect the health of the community against the spread of the disease." In other words, instead of the United States isolating itself from the rest of the world, Roosevelt was suggesting that democratic nations get together and isolate the aggressor nations.

The president was deluged with mail. Some was favorable. But most of the letters accused him of trying to lead the country into war. Two months later, Americans got a real war scare.

The Panay *Incident.* On December 12, 1937, on the Yangtze River in China, a navy gunboat, the U.S.S. *Panay,* and three oil tankers it was escorting were attacked without warning by Japanese planes. Two servicemen were killed and several others wounded. The *Panay* had been clearly marked and had a legal right to be where it was. The attack obviously was no accident. But Japanese authorities apologized at once, offering to pay for damages and promising to punish those responsible. The United States accepted Japan's offer, and most Americans heaved a deep sigh of relief. A Gallup poll the next month showed that 70 percent of the public felt it would be better to pull out completely from China—withdrawing ships, marines, missionaries, and business people—rather than run the risk of getting into war. It was difficult to find any vital U.S. interest in China.

Hitler Annexes Austria

In Europe the smell of gunpowder grew stronger. For months the German propaganda machine had trumpeted the charge that Germans living in Austria were being treated as a despised minority. Hitler declared that Germany would have to do something to help them.

In February 1938, Austrian Chancellor Kurt von Schuschnigg was summoned to meet Hitler at the dictator's villa at Berchtesgaden, high in the Bavarian Alps. When Schuschnigg arrived, diplomatic niceties were thrown out the window. After being verbally abused by Hitler, Schuschnigg was told that unless Austria signed an agreement dismissing members of its present government and installing Austrian Nazis in their place, Germany would attack.

Schuschnigg was appalled. He protested that he had no power to sign such an agreement. He would have to refer it to his cabinet in Vienna. He was allowed to return to the Austrian capital, but immediately after, the German propaganda machine again began denouncing the "wrongs" suffered by Germans in Austria. The charges were false. But, as Hitler once remarked, no matter how big the lie, if it is repeated often enough, eventually people will believe it.

A month later Hitler declared that he had no choice but to help his "fellow Germans." On March 12, 1938, German forces marched into Austria without opposition and annexed it to Germany. By this *Anschluss* (union), one of Europe's oldest states vanished.

The shock of events in Europe was felt in the United States. That same spring the United States set about building a two-ocean navy. Until then, the country had concentrated its naval forces in the Pacific, believing that the Atlantic sea frontier was reasonably secure in British hands. Now Congress voted to spend a billion dollars over a ten-year period to expand the American fleet so it could protect both the Atlantic and Pacific coasts by itself.

Hitler Takes Czechoslovakia

Once Hitler had annexed Austria, he began threatening another neighbor. In the western part of Czechoslovakia, along its border with Germany, is a mountainous region called the Sudetenland. There, lived a large German minority. Hitler

Axis Conquests in Europe   1936–1939

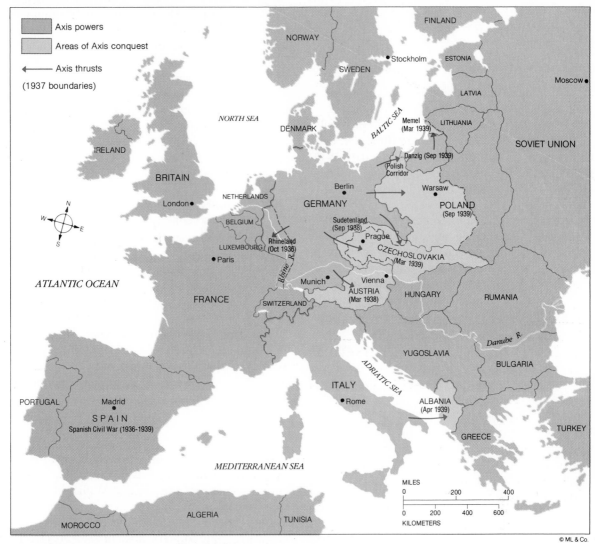

Map Skills   *Which countries were the Axis Powers? When did they conquer Albania? Czechoslovakia? Danzig? Western Poland? To what countries did the Rhineland and Sudetenland belong?*

charged that the Sudeten Germans were being persecuted by the Czechoslovakian government. By then, this was such a familiar story that everyone knew what it really meant. Hitler wanted to annex Czechoslovakia!

That spring and early summer saw a buildup of German military strength along the Czech border. Then, in late summer, Hitler summoned Czechoslovakia's aged president, Emil Hacha (ha-kuh), to Berlin. After the long train ride, the elderly man was not allowed to rest but was taken immediately before the German dictator. Hitler promptly went into his carefully calculated fit of rage. He

screamed that Hacha must submit to German military occupation of the Sudetenland, or else the entire country would face complete destruction. Hacha sat as if turned to stone as Hitler declared he must sign such an agreement immediately. Hitler warned that German troops were massed at the borders and bomber planes were already loaded and warming up their engines at airfields throughout Germany.

Hitler indicated a table where the papers and pens were lying. He left the room, and his aides practically thrust a pen into the old man's hand. The shock was too great and Hacha fainted. But

641

Hitler's doctor brought him around with an injection of vitamins. Hacha signed and returned home a broken-hearted man.

The Munich Pact

Both France and England had promised Czechoslovakia that they would protect it from a German takeover. Now British Prime Minister Neville Chamberlain asked for a meeting with Hitler. President Roosevelt sent messages to all the nations involved expressing his fear of war. Chamberlain flew to Berlin three times to talk with the German dictator.

Finally, at the end of September 1938, Hitler, Mussolini, Chamberlain, and the French premier, Edouard Daladier, met in Munich. Neither Czechoslovakia, which was the subject of discussion, nor the Soviet Union, which had a friendship treaty with Czechoslovakia, was included. At Munich, Hitler told the assembled diplomats that the Sudeten area would be his "last territorial demand." The English and French leaders feared war so much, and wanted to believe Hitler so desperately, that they agreed to let him have the Sudetenland. They did so simply because their hopes triumphed over their experience. They should have known what would happen. But they also believed that their people would not fight, as Chamberlain put it, "over a far-off country of which we know little." The Munich Pact was signed on September 30 and German troops immediately crossed the border into Czechoslovakia.

Section 2 Review

COMPREHENSION   Developing Vocabulary

1. Explain these terms: collective security, Anschluss, Sudetenland.

COMPREHENSION   Mastering Facts

1. How did isolationists believe the United States could keep out of a future war?
2. What did Roosevelt suggest in his "quarantine speech"?
3. What reason did Hitler give for attacking first Austria and then Czechoslovakia?
4. What did the Munich Pact provide?

3   THE CRISIS DEEPENS

VOCABULARY   *Aryans   Kristallnacht   non-aggression pact*

Chamberlain declared that the Munich Pact had brought about "peace in our time," and he was wildly cheered on his return to London. His rival in Parliament, who would also be his successor, was Winston Churchill. Churchill, and a small but growing part of the British people, took a different view. They felt that Britain and France had failed to act in the face of German aggression in Austria. Then, they had broken their promise to protect Czechoslovakia. As Churchill put it, "Britain and France had to choose between war and dishonor. They chose dishonor. They will have war."

Within six months of the Munich Pact, Hitler broke his promise not to seek additional territory. In March 1939, Germany took over the rest of Czechoslovakia. Not to be outdone, Mussolini invaded the tiny kingdom of Albania the following month and soon added it to the Italian Empire.

On-the-Scene Reports

One reason why people followed events in Europe with such horrified attention was the presence there of a group of extremely talented newspeople. Journalists such as Dorothy Thompson, Anne O'Hare McCormick, and William L. Shirer were tireless in covering the news for their papers and magazines. Also, for the first time, correspondents were able to make firsthand reports directly to people back home by radio. Americans were able to hear history unfold in their own living rooms. It was a stunning new experience in communication.

Both the Columbia Broadcasting System (CBS) and the National Broadcasting Corporation (NBC) signed up many correspondents. CBS employed as its European director a young man under thirty named Edward R. Murrow, who became one of the most famous broadcasters in history.

The Campaign Against Jews

One of the subjects which journalists covered was the plight of Germany's Jews. On coming to power in 1933, Hitler had announced a national economic boycott against them. They were forbidden to enter the medical or legal professions or to obtain business licenses. All Jewish teachers and other civil service employees were fired, as were Jews who worked in firms owned by non-Jews. It became increasingly difficult for German Jews to earn a living.

The Nuremberg Laws. Two years later, in 1935, the Nuremberg Laws took away the Jews' political rights. They lost their citizenship. They were expelled from German schools. They were denied medical care in German hospitals. They were not allowed to use the beaches. They were segregated on railroads and other means of transportation. They could not even have telephones in their homes. They could go shopping only during special hours. And they had to be off the streets after 8:00 P.M. To make identification easier, all Jews over the age of six were required to wear a Jewish star—black on a yellow background—over the left breast of their clothing.

The new laws also forbade "Aryans," by which Hitler meant non-Jews of "pure" German blood, from marrying Jews. Jews who left Germany were not allowed to take any of their property or money with them. To prevent the smuggling of valuables out of the country, later laws forced Jews to register everything they owned. This measure was applied to Austrian Jews after Germany and Austria were united in 1938.

Crystal Night. Worse was to come. On November 7, 1938, a seventeen-year-old Jewish refugee assassinated a German diplomat in Paris. Two nights later came *Kristallnacht*, the "night of broken glass." Throughout Germany, Nazi gangs entered and burned most of the nation's synagogues. They broke into Jewish homes and places of business, looted them, and beat up the occupants. Shattered glass littered the streets. Several hundred Jews committed suicide, more than 1000 were murdered, and 26,000 were thrown into concentration camps. In addition, a fine of one billion marks—about 20 percent of what they owned—was levied on the entire German Jewish community.

Plight of the Refugees. Many German Jews still loved their homeland and decided to remain in Germany, hoping that the Nazi storm would soon blow over. But others were extremely anxious to get out. They had begun to think about the unthinkable—that Hitler actually meant to get rid of the entire Jewish population one way or another.

The morning after Kristallnacht in Berlin. This is only one of thousands of Jewish businesses throughout Germany that were wrecked, looted and their owners beaten.

The League of Nations set up a High Commission for Refugees from Germany, but it had only limited success. England agreed to accept some 80,000 refugees. About 60,000 fled to the United States, and many more wanted to come. But the Roosevelt administration did little to help them. This was partly because the United States was suffering from widespread unemployment. It didn't want to take in additional people who might add to unemployment or take away jobs which Americans could have. Still, there were some 400,000 openings in the nation's immigration quotas that were available for people from countries under Hitler's rule—and the openings were not filled.

Illustrious Names. Many of those who succeeded in gaining entry were artists, scientists, and business people. In other words, they were the kind of newcomers who are more likely to create jobs than to take them away. The list—headed by mathematician Albert Einstein, conductor Arturo Toscanini, author Thomas Mann, physicist Enrico Fermi, and architect Walter Gropius—is impres-

World War II in Europe 1940

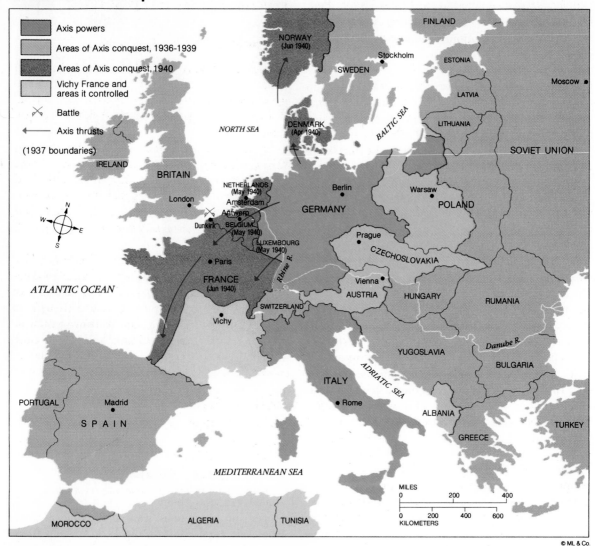

Map Skills *In what chronological order were the Netherlands, France, Denmark, and Czechoslovakia conquered? How far is Paris from Berlin? In what country was the battle of Dunkirk?*

sive. They and others who came here from Germany and Italy had much to do with America's leap to the forefront in science and the arts immediately after World War II. Many also went to Canada where they eventually rose to top positions in government and in private industry.

Russia and Germany Shock the World

Great Britain and France became increasingly nervous during the summer of 1939. Hitler was once again giving his usual signs of wanting more

territory. This time his target was the "Polish Corridor" and the free city of Danzig. The Versailles Treaty had given the Corridor to Poland so it would have an outlet to the Baltic Sea; Danzig was the seaport at the Corridor's end. The population of both was mostly German and, in addition, the Corridor separated East Prussia from the rest of Germany.

Accordingly, Hitler went into his usual routine. He declared that Germans in both places were being brutalized by unfeeling Poles and that he must rescue them. There were some who thought the Nazi leader was bluffing this time. After all, an invasion of Poland would bring Germany into contact with its avowed enemy, the Soviet Union, Poland's eastern neighbor. Furthermore, an attack on Poland would probably mean a two-front war for Germany: against the Soviet Union in the east and against France and Great Britain in the west. (Chamberlain had announced in March that Britain would help Poland if it were attacked.) Fighting on two fronts had helped bring about Germany's defeat in World War I. Surely, some people thought, Hitler would not be so stupid as to repeat *that* mistake!

In April, Russian dictator Joseph Stalin suggested to Britain that his nation and France follow the principle of collective security and back Britain's guarantee to Poland. Chamberlain turned down the idea. It would have given the Soviets the right to send their armies into Poland to fight the Germans—and the Poles refused to have Russian troops on their soil. Russians and Poles were enemies of long standing, and the eastern part of Poland had been Russian territory before World War I. Poland suspected—correctly, as it turned out—the Soviet Union wanted that territory back.

Stalin realized that Britain and France had no love for the Soviet Union. Nor was he sure how much help he would get from them in case Germany attacked his country. So he changed his policy. On August 23, 1939, he signed a non-aggression pact with Nazi Germany. The two nations agreed not to fight one another. They also signed a secret agreement in which Hitler promised that German troops would take only part of Poland and would let Soviet troops take over the eastern section. Stalin, many historians believe, was certain that Germany would attack the Soviet Union sooner or later, but the peace pact gave him more time to train and arm Russian forces.

Hitler had outwitted the democratic countries.

He had removed the threat of a two-front war. His way was now clear to attack Poland.

War Breaks Out in Europe

The next day, August 24, President Roosevelt asked Germany and Poland to settle their differences peacefully. Would they, he asked, accept the decision of an outside third party? Poland agreed. Hitler refused.

At dawn on September 1, Germany attacked Poland with planes, tanks, and ships, and almost two million troops. But this time Hitler misjudged the Western powers. There was a limit beyond which they could not be pushed. Britain and France declared war on Germany on September 3. World War II had begun.

That same evening, President Roosevelt discussed the war in a fireside chat. He said, "This nation will remain a neutral nation, but I cannot ask that every American remain neutral in thought as well. Even a neutral has a right to take account of the facts. Even a neutral cannot be asked to close his mind or his conscience." Roosevelt made no secret of his pro-British sympathies.

Section 3 Review

COMPREHENSION   Developing Vocabulary

1. Explain these terms: non-aggression pact, Kristallnacht, Aryans.

COMPREHENSION   Mastering Facts

1. How were Americans able to follow events in Europe so closely?
2. What actions did the Nazis take against German Jews?
3. How did many of the refugees from Nazi Germany turn out to be helpful to the United States?
4. What did Hitler gain from the non-aggression pact with the Soviet Union?

4 GERMANY UNVEILS A NEW KIND OF WARFARE

VOCABULARY   *blitzkrieg   panzer   genocide*

As soon as war broke out in Europe, the United States declared itself neutral. But three weeks later, President Roosevelt called Congress into special session and asked for passage of a fourth Neutrality Act. The act, approved in November, repealed the arms embargo. Great Britain, France, and their allies could now purchase American weapons and ammunition on a "cash-and-carry" basis. American ships were forbidden to enter the war zone. The United States and the Latin American countries agreed to establish a "safety belt" from 300 to 1000 miles around the coast of North and South America, and warned others not to engage in naval action in those waters.

New Horrors Are Unleashed

While the United States and other nations tried to protect themselves, the Germans proceeded to carry new military and political tactics into effect. Not since the Mongol invasions of the thirteenth and fourteenth centuries had there been such rapid conquests or such open contempt for human life and dignity.

Blitzkrieg. The German army raced through Poland. The world had never seen anything like it and learned a new word: *blitzkrieg,* or "lightning war." It began with dive-bomber attacks that destroyed Polish airfields and then smashed the large cities, disrupting communications and creating general confusion. The bombers were followed by mechanized *panzer* (armored) divisions that moved swiftly over roads which had been strafed, or machine-gunned, by lowflying planes to clear them of defense forces and refugees. Except for guerrillas, who fought in the forests to the end of the war, Polish resistance was over in less than a month. In the third week of the fighting, Stalin's armies attacked from the east. The Soviet Union got slightly more than half of Poland's territory, while Germany took almost two-thirds of its population.

Slave Labor. With the victory in Poland, the Nazis gave full play to their racist ideas. According to these fantasies, Slavic people such as the Poles were inferior to Nordic Germans. Hundreds of thousands of able-bodied Polish soldiers and civilians, regardless of education or past accomplishments, were shipped to Germany as slave labor for German factories and farms. Towns were emptied of their Polish inhabitants and refilled with German settlers. Poles were removed from the best farmlands to make way for German farmers.

The Nazis were also determined to wipe out Poland's culture. They burned Polish libraries. And they murdered or imprisoned a quarter of a million clergymen, intellectuals, and other leaders.

Genocide. Another horrifying word that became known to many people for the first time was *genocide,* the deliberate and systematic killing of a group of people. In 1939 the Nazis proceeded toward a "final solution of the Jewish question." The plan was to exterminate all the Jews of Europe, beginning with the 2 million in German-occupied Poland.

Special mobile killing units were assigned to round up Jewish men, women, and children; strip

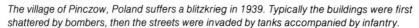

The village of Pinczow, Poland suffers a blitzkrieg in 1939. Typically the buildings were first shattered by bombers, then the streets were invaded by tanks accompanied by infantry.

them of their clothing; and then shoot them in cold blood. Other Jews were herded into special areas of Polish cities called ghettos. There they were left to starve or die of disease.

In time, these methods proved "inefficient." They did not kill fast enough. Late in 1941 the Germans set up six death camps in Poland: Auschwitz, Belzec, Chelmno, Maidenek, Sobibor, and Treblinka. Each camp contained several huge gas chambers in which as many as 6000 persons could be suffocated by cyanide gas each day. The corpses were then taken to a room where their gold dental fillings were removed and their hair was shaved off to be used for stuffing mattresses and pillows.

At first the bodies were buried in mass graves. But as one historian explained:

> " The decaying corpses left odors that spread for miles, and when the rate of killing increased, the space needed for graves was enormous. Worse, mass graves were evidence of mass killings. . . . [So the Germans] turned to burning the bodies in open pits. This proved to be the cheapest and most efficient method. "

All told, by the time World War II ended in 1945, about 6 million Jews, as well as several thousand gypsies, were slaughtered in these death camps. The enormity of the crime was unique in history.

The West Is Surprised

While Poland was being overrun by the Germans, what was happening on the western front? Nothing—for seven months! The French and the British sat in the Maginot Line, a system of fortifications along France's eastern border, and stared at the Germans, who sat in the Siegfried Line a few miles away and stared back. Soldiers ate, dozed, played cards, wrote letters home. There was no fighting. Planes flew over enemy territory but only to observe and drop leaflets. People called this period the "phony war." Later it became known as the "winter of illusion."

Illusion let the Allies believe they could win the war by blockading Germany and starving Hitler out. Beginning in April 1940, they learned otherwise. Early that month the German blitzkrieg struck without warning at the neutral nations of Denmark and Norway. Denmark was overrun in a few hours, but Norway resisted for several weeks. The Norwegians even managed to sink several German ships. By month's end, however, the king and his ministers had fled to Britain, where they joined the Poles as a government-in-exile.

The following month, the German blitzkrieg struck at the neutral nations of the Netherlands, Belgium, and Luxembourg. Before the end of May, all three had been overrun by Hitler's war machine.

The Fall of France. Hitler's strike into the Low Countries soon led to even greater disaster for the Allies. The Maginot Line did not extend as far as the English Channel but stopped at the French-Belgian border. The invading German armies simply swung around to the north of it. In four weeks they had pinned the British against the English Channel, cut the French army to pieces, and taken Paris. Hitler had accomplished in four weeks what the kaiser's armies had failed to do in four years. That was truly a blitzkrieg!

A third of a million British troops were miraculously rescued from the beaches of Dunkirk by a makeshift flotilla of tugboats, power launches, fishing craft, and private yachts which shuttled back and forth across the Channel for almost a week. It was a remarkable achievement, but heavy arms and equipment had to be left behind.

A few days later, Italy declared war on the side of Germany and invaded France from the south. On June 22, 1940, France surrendered—in the same railway coach in the forest of Compiègne where, twenty-two years earlier, Germany had signed the armistice that ended World War I. The Germans occupied the northern part of the country. A puppet government for France's southern region was set up at Vichy under aged Marshal Henri Philippe Pétain. In the meantime, yet another government-in-exile was organized in London. The Free French were headed by a very tall general who for years had been advocating the theory of mobile warfare, the kind of warfare that had just crushed his nation. His name was Charles de Gaulle.

Nazi occupation of Western Europe was not as savage as in the east. But hostages, including women and children, were shot in reprisal for sabotage and other guerrilla activity against the Germans. In time, the occupied countries had to pass laws against their Jewish citizens and round them up for shipment to the death camps. Others of their people were sent to work in war industries in Germany. Some of them were made to work as servants and others were picked as farm workers.

Events Leading to World War II in the Decade Before Pearl Harbor

THE DATE	THE EVENT
Sept. 1931	Japan occupies Manchuria starting an unofficial war with China that lasts—off and on—until 1945.
Jan. 1933	Adolph Hitler becomes Chancellor of Germany.
March 1934	Germany begins to rearm in violation of the Treaty of Versailles. The League of Nations condemns the action but does nothing more.
Oct. 1934	Italy begins invasion of Ethiopia. The League of Nations denounces Italy and imposes sanctions, but they are incomplete.
May 1935	Italy conquers Ethiopia. The League of Nations loses its prestige and effectiveness because it does nothing for Ethiopia even though that nation is a member of the League of Nations.
March 1936	Germany reoccupies the Rhineland in violation of international treaties.
July 1936	Civil War begins in Spain. Germany and Italy send troops and the Soviet Union sends war material and advisors to Spain.
Oct. 1936	Germany and Italy form the Berlin-Rome Axis and pledge friendship and mutual aid.
March 1938	Germany occupies Austria.
Sept. 1938	Hitler demands the annexation of the Sudetenland area of Czechoslovakia and is given a free hand by France and Britain at the Munich Conference.
March 1939	Hitler takes over all of Czechoslovakia.
April 1939	Italy invades Albania.
August 1939	Germany and the Soviet Union sign a non-aggression pact.
Sept. 1, 1939	Germany invades Poland.
Sept. 3, 1939	France and Britain declare war on Germany.
Nov. 30, 1939	Russia attacks Finland.
June 10, 1940	Italy declares war on Britain and France.
June 22, 1940	France surrenders and three-fifths of the country is occupied by Germany. Most of continental Europe is now under German control.
August 1940	Canada and the United States agree to set up a joint Board of Defense.
Sept. 1940	The United States begins a military draft.
March 1941	Lend Lease Act passes, whereby any country, whose defense the president deems necessary for the defense of the United States, may obtain arms and supplies from the United States by loan, lease or sale.
June 1941	Germany invades the Soviet Union.
June 7, 1941	U.S. forces land in Iceland, at the government's request, to help the British troops defend the island.
Dec. 7, 1941	Japan attacks Pearl Harbor and the Philippine Islands.
Dec. 8, 1941	The United States declares war on Japan.
Dec. 11, 1941	The United States declares war on Germany and Italy.

The Battle of Britain. After the fall of France, Nazi officials declared "We have just one more battle to win." Who could doubt that Hitler had a master plan prepared for the invasion of Britain? In fact, he had none. But he did have the illusion that Britain would recognize how hopeless its position was and ask for terms. He completely misjudged the British. Even before France's fall, Winston Churchill, who had replaced Chamberlain as prime minister, had told Parliament, "We shall defend our island, whatever the cost may be. We shall fight on the beaches, we shall fight on the landing-grounds, we shall fight in the fields and in the streets, we shall fight in the hills. We shall never surrender." So the Germans began assembling barges and landing craft along the French Channel coast. But first they had to establish air supremacy. They had to destroy the Royal Air Force (RAF).

The Battle of Britain was fought through the summer and autumn of 1940 to break the RAF. Hitler had 2600 bombers at his disposal. In a single day, August 15, he sent 1000 of them to range over Britain. Every night for two solid months, 200 bombers pounded London.

When the attacks concentrated on airfields and aircraft factories, they were a severe threat to the RAF. But when the Germans switched to cities

Presidential Election of 1940

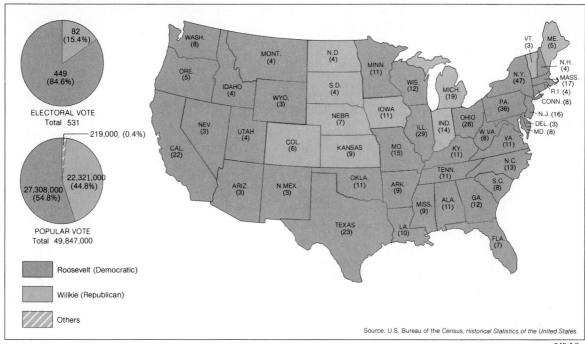

Map Skills *Compare this map with those on pages 605 and 624. Which states did the Democrats lose in all three elections? In what part of the country are they located?*

and land transportation, the RAF won a breather. Its resistance was deadly. Alerted by the new device of radar, which British scientists had perfected, British pilots soared aloft day after day, and sometimes night after night as well, to destroy the German planes. Eventually German losses became so great that Hitler decided to postpone his attempt to invade Britain. In fact, the idea was never considered again.

Terrible night raids against British cities continued through the winter of 1940–1941 in an effort to crack the people's morale. But that too failed. The lights of freedom had gone out on the European continent, but they continued to burn on the British Isles.

In the meantime, Japan joined in a three-power agreement with Germany and Italy. Each was to help the others against any future enemies. That made the Rome-Berlin-Tokyo Axis official.

The United States Prepares

In June 1940 Roosevelt responded to an appeal from Churchill. Using a 1917 law, he sent Britain 500,000 rifles, 80,000 machine guns, 900 field guns,

and 130 million rounds of ammunition to help replace what had been lost at Dunkirk. On September 3, Britain received fifty destroyers for use against German submarines in the North Atlantic. They were "four-stackers" from World War I but were still useful. In return, the United States obtained ninety-nine-year leases on eight naval and air bases in Newfoundland, Bermuda, the West Indies, and British Guiana (now Guyana).

A Bipartisan Cabinet. That same summer of 1940, FDR brought two distinguished Republicans into his cabinet. Henry L. Stimson, who had been Hoover's secretary of state, became secretary of war. Frank Knox, the 1936 Republican candidate for vice-president, was made secretary of the navy. Having two such able Republicans in key positions strengthened the administration for the coming struggle and broadened its popular base.

Selective Service. A further defense measure was the adoption of the nation's first peacetime draft. Under the Selective Training and Service Act, 16 million men between the ages of twenty-one and thirty-five were registered. Of this num-

649

Men got numbers when they registered at their local draft boards. Federal officials in Washington D.C. held a series of lotteries. Men whose numbers were drawn were drafted.

ber, 1 million were selected for training the first year, and 800,000 reserves were called up.

FDR Wins a Third Term

Meanwhile, in 1940, the nation was in the midst of a historic election campaign. If he won, Roosevelt would break a two-term tradition that went back to George Washington's time. The third term was a major issue in the campaign, but the war was not. The Republican candidate, a public-utilities executive named Wendell L. Willkie who had never before run for political office, supported FDR's program of aid to Britain.

Isolationists organized the America First Committee and urged the country to abandon Britain and concentrate on building its own strength. Some well-known Republicans were in the America First Committee, but the committee lost its bid to control the Republican convention. They could not make the war an election issue.

In the end, a majority of Americans decided in favor of Roosevelt. With so little difference in the views of the two candidates, it seemed safer not to change horses in mid-stream. FDR's 27 million votes were about 54 percent of the total; the electoral vote was 449 to 82. That was firm backing for the president's policy of giving Britain "all aid short of war."

Section 4 Review

COMPREHENSION   Developing Vocabulary
1. Explain these terms: blitzkrieg, panzer, genocide, strafed.

COMPREHENSION   Mastering Facts
1. How did the Nazis treat the Poles?
2. What was the "final solution" of the Jewish question?
3. Why did the Maginot Line fail to stop the Germans?
4. How did the election of 1940 shatter tradition?

CHAPTER 32　Review

Chapter Summary

While the world tried to cope with the depression, war clouds became more ominous. In 1931 Japan invaded Manchuria, withdrew from the League of Nations, and began to build up its navy. Hitler came to power in Germany in 1933, a year after Mussolini took over Italy. Both initiated dictatorships, and soon both began grabbing territory. While Americans tried to find ways to stay out of European conflicts, World War II began when Hitler's forces invaded Poland in 1939. Germany's shocking tactics included use of blitzkrieg against other armies and genocide against Jews. By 1940 only Britain held out against Hitler as the United States prepared for war.

Questions for Critical Thinking

COMPREHENSION　Summarizing Main Ideas

1. What were three basic principles of Nazism? Do you think such a philosophy could become popular in the United States? Give reasons for your opinion.
2. Give three reasons for the rise of fascism and Nazism in Europe during the 1930s.
3. Give three examples of how FDR practiced the Good Neighbor policy.
4. How did America's experiences in World War I affect its attitude toward such events as Italy's invasion of Ethiopia, Japan's attack on the U.S.S. *Panay*, and Germany's takeover of Czechoslovakia? What do you think the American government's reaction should have been?

COMPREHENSION　Interpreting Events

1. Why do you think that President Roosevelt wanted the neutrality acts to apply to civil as well as international wars?
2. If you had been Prime Minister Chamberlain, would you have signed the Munich Pact? Why or why not?
3. Do you think Stalin was justified in signing a non-aggression pact with Germany? Give reasons for your opinion.

4. What do you think the League of Nations might have done to prevent military aggressions in the thirties? What do you think the United States might have done?
5. Why did the United States gradually shift from a policy of isolationism to a policy that favored the Allies? What three actions did the U.S. take in 1940 to strengthen itself?
6. If you had been a voter in 1940, would you have voted to reelect FDR? Why or why not?

APPLICATION　Using Skills To Infer Information

For each group of items below, indicate the item that does not belong.

1. The Nuremberg Laws
   a. Jews lose their citizenship.
   b. Jews are expelled from schools.
   c. All Jewish property is confiscated.
   d. Jews are required to wear a Jewish star over the left breast of their clothing.
2. The first three neutrality acts
   a. The U.S. will not ship or sell arms to belligerent nations.
   b. The U.S. will not sell foodstuffs to belligerent nations.
   c. The U.S. will not lend money to belligerent nations.
   d. The U.S. will not protect American citizens traveling on ships of belligerent nations.

EVALUATION　Forming Generalizations

1. What do you think the United States learned from the events that led up to World War II? What effect, if any, do you think this has on American foreign policy today? Explain your answer.
2. From what countries are political refugees coming today? What, if anything, is being done to help them by the United States and by international organizations?
3. When was the Twenty-second Amendment ratified? What might have happened if it had been in effect in 1940? Do you approve of this amendment? Why or why not?

Multinational Corporations

By the end of the 1800s a new type of company was beginning to emerge. It was called a multi national corporation. By the end of the 1900s, economists predict that more than half of the world's business will be run by multinational corporations. As recently as 1970, these giant firms together sold more than was produced by any nation except the United States and the Soviet Union. In fact, there are several multinationals that are more productive all by themselves than most nations. If General Motors, for example, were a country, it would be the fourteenth richest in the world.

Economists usually define a multinational as a corporation that obtains its raw materials and capital, and produces and sells its goods and services, in at least two nations. Some economists say the corporation must operate in at least six nations; they also require that the company do at least $100 million worth of business a year. On that basis, there are about 200 American multinationals, 80 European multinationals, and 20 Japanese multinationals. Multinationals are also known as global corporations. Some of them are: Ford, Standard Oil of New Jersey, Royal Dutch Shell, and General Electric.

Beginnings. The first firms to become multinationals were

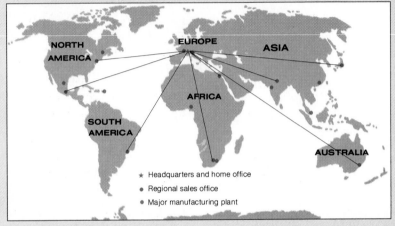

A Multinational Corporation

- ★ Headquarters and home office
- ● Regional sales office
- ● Major manufacturing plant

in mining and plantation agriculture. A company that mined for copper, drilled for oil, or raised tropical fruit obviously had to invest wherever it could find natural resources. Thus, the nineteenth century saw the rise of such multinationals as Anaconda Copper, British Petroleum, and United Fruit.

After World War I, many nations put up tariff barriers against the importation of manufactured products. But these barriers did not apply if the same products were made domestically by foreign-owned companies. As a result, many firms got around the tariff barriers by investing directly in other nations' businesses.

Growth. The Great Depression and World War II slowed the process down. It picked up after 1945 as American firms realized what a profitable market

there was in helping war-torn countries rebuild their economies. Another reason for direct overseas investment was the desire to produce cheaply abroad for sale at home. Wage rates in such places as Taiwan, Hong Kong, and Singapore were much lower than those in the United States. It cost less to send a product's components abroad for assembly and then reship it home than it did to manufacture the product in the United States. Most foreign subsidiaries of U.S. firms were in industries such as autos, cameras, chemicals, clothing, computers, electronics, and television sets—all of which grew rapidly during the 1950s and 1960s.

Adjustments. During the same period, however, feelings against multinationals were becoming stronger. This was especially true in areas that had formerly been European colonies. One result was that some nations expropriated, or took over, foreign-owned companies within their borders. Another result was that multinationals began working out more flexible arrangements. Instead of 100 percent ownership of foreign subsidiaries, they often agreed to an ownership ratio of less than 50 percent. In place of direct investment, they entered into management contracts under which they agreed to provide technology, managerial skills, and capital in exchange for a fee plus a share of the profits. As a consequence, multinational corporations have continued to grow in the 1970s and the early 1980s.

Benefits.   The impact of American business on Europe since World War II has been enormous. It has encouraged mass consumption of goods. It has increased the number of supermarkets and automobiles.

Less-developed countries—where many multinationals have established subsidiaries—also benefit. Multinationals bring in modern technology and modern methods of organizing business. They often increase local income in a dramatic way. For example, when an American engine manufacturer first opened a plant in India, it used three buses to pick up its workers. After a few years, the plant's biggest problem was the lack of parking space for the workers' bicycles and cars.

Drawbacks.   In the long run, global companies often raise living standards, but in the short run they often disrupt the way people live. One example is what happened in Mexico when Sears, Roebuck brought in mass merchandising. The stores offered a greater selection of goods than most Mexicans had ever seen. But they also did away with the social life of the old-fashioned local markets. Fewer social contacts meant a loss of neighborliness. Many Mexican housewives found themselves lonelier and more cut off from their friends.

Some multinational corporations may grow high-profit luxury crops for export. That is good business. They search the world for the best place to grow them. Often this may be in some of the poorer countries. They use land on which the people formerly grew their food. As a result, many less-developed countries produce luxury items (carnations, strawberries, asparagus, and the like) but also find it necessary to import basic foodstuffs.

These drawbacks may turn out to be relatively insignificant, however, when one looks at the best possible long-term benefit of multinational corporations. Many economists predict that multinationals will dominate world markets by the twenty-first century. Thus, the global economic interdependence among nations created by these giant corporations could serve as a key unifying force for the world. If

Largest United States Corporations

1909
1. United States Steel
2. Standard Oil Company of New Jersey
3. American Tobacco Company
4. International Mercantile Marine
5. Amalgamated Copper Company
6. International Harvester
7. Central Leather Company
8. The Pullman Company
9. Armour and Company
10. American Sugar Company

1980
1. Exxon Oil
2. Mobil Oil
3. General Motors Corporation
4. Texaco Oil
5. Standard Oil of California
6. Ford Motor Company
7. Gulf Oil
8. International Business Machines
9. Standard Oil of Indiana
10. General Electric

this happens, the world may edge a little closer toward peace and cooperation.

Understanding Free Enterprise

1. How do some economists define a multinational corporation?

2. In what ways do you think multinational corporations can be a help to societies? Give several reasons for your answer.

3. In what ways can multinational corporations disturb a society?

4. How have multinationals changed in the 1970s and early 1980s?

CHAPTER 33

The Second World War

1939–1945

Linking Past to Present

World War II began for the United States with a horrifying defeat at Pearl Harbor, Hawaii, at the hands of the Japanese. But the nation's geographic location and the sacrifices of the Allies gave it the time needed to build a mighty armed force and use it against the common enemy. Military engagements took place all over the world. The United States unleashed a new weapon of almost unimaginable power: the atomic bomb. At the same time, it took several steps toward building what it hoped would be a world of peace, liberty, and justice for all.

The United States emerged from World War II as the most powerful nation in history. But even as the guns of war cooled, the possibility of a future conflict with the Soviet Union began to loom.

1 THE UNITED STATES PREPARES FOR WAR

VOCABULARY   *lend-lease*

President Roosevelt's measures "short of war" were just barely short of it. In fact, one might say the United States was waging an undeclared war against the Axis during most of 1941. Earlier that year, American military leaders held secret talks with British officials in Washington and later with British and Dutch in Singapore. The conference laid plans for joint military operations after the United States entered the war.

Lend-Lease

As 1940 drew to a close, FDR gave a fireside chat to the American people. In it he declared his belief that the United States must become "the great arsenal of democracy." But by now Britain was almost bankrupt. Cash-and-carry was no longer of any use. So on January 6, 1941, in his first State of the Union Address after his unprecedented election to a third term, Roosevelt proposed a different means by which Britain could obtain military equipment and supplies. He called it *lend-lease;* in other words, the president would lend or lease arms and other goods to "any country whose defense was vital to the United States."

FDR compared lend-lease to letting a neighbor use a hose when his house was on fire to keep the blaze from spreading. Once the emergency was over, the hose might be returned, replaced, or paid for. Senator Robert A. Taft of Ohio, an isolationist, compared the process to lending someone chewing gum; he said you would not want it back. Nevertheless, Congress passed the measure in March by sizable majorities in both houses and appropriated $7 billion for it. In all, $50 billion was spent under the Lend-Lease Act.

Britain was not the only nation to benefit from lend-lease. On June 22, Hitler ignored his peace treaty with the Soviet Union and sent 3 million soldiers across the Russo-German border. At first people everywhere were convinced the Soviet Union would collapse within a month or two. But the Russians fought grimly in defense of their country. They adopted a "scorched earth" policy, destroying everything—even their first great hydroelectric project, the Dnieper dam—that could be of use to the advancing Germans. Some tied bombs to their belts and threw themselves at German tanks. Hitler's troops managed to reach the outskirts of Moscow and Leningrad. But then the terrible Russian winter set in, and the invading army came to a frozen halt. In November the Soviets got a billion dollars in lend-lease credits.

The Battle of the Atlantic

Keeping the supply lines from the New World open was vital to Britain (and, later, to the Soviet Union). Hitler was just as determined to close the lines, and he had the means to do it. Hundreds of submarines, traveling in groups of fifteen to twenty known as "wolf packs," and a few of Germany's new "pocket battleships," which were the size of cruisers but with the firepower of battleships, roved the Atlantic. During five weeks in April and May 1941, they sank 2.3 million tons of British shipping. This was more than three times the losses of the previous six months. And it was done despite the fact that American naval forces were "trailing" German U-boats and radioing their locations to the British.

German submarines paid no attention to the so-called safety zones off the coasts of North and South America. In May the *Robin Moor,* an American merchantman, was sunk off Brazil. In September the American destroyer *Greer* was attacked in the North Atlantic. FDR responded by ordering the navy to "shoot on sight" any Axis ships they might run into. In October the American destroyer *Kearney* was torpedoed off Iceland and eleven of its crew were killed. A few weeks later, in the same waters, the destroyer *Reuben James* was sunk with the loss of almost a hundred American lives. The United States began arming its merchant ships.

In the meantime, in August Congress agreed to continue the draft. The vote was very close, with only a one-vote margin in the House. The reluctance was partly due to the fact that men who had been drafted the previous October would now have their enlistment period extended for an additional eighteen months. There was fear of mass desertions, and the letters OHIO (standing for Over the Hill in October) began appearing on the walls of barracks. But no one actually tried to leave an army camp. Uncle Sam's draftees did not like the extension, but they accepted it.

The Atlantic Charter

The same month in which the draft was extended, Roosevelt and Churchill met secretly aboard a warship off the coast of Newfoundland. Churchill had come hoping for a military commitment from the United States, but had to settle for a general statement of war aims somewhat similar to Wilson's Fourteen Points. Called the Atlantic Charter, it contained the following principles: (1) no territorial expansion, (2) no territorial changes without the consent of the inhabitants, (3) self-determination for all people, (4) freer trade, (5) cooperation for the improvement of other nations, and (6) the disarming of all aggressors.

Churchill indicated that the principle of self-determination applied only with reservations to the British Empire. As he later said, "We mean to hold our own. I have not become the King's First Minister in order to preside over the liquidation of the British Empire." In any event, the Atlantic Charter was endorsed within a month by fifteen countries, including the Soviet Union. It later became the basis for the United Nations.

Japan Attacks Pearl Harbor

The German attack on the Soviet Union had effects half a world away. It encouraged Japan to

act. The most pressing need of the Japanese war machine was oil. The Dutch East Indies (now Indonesia) was the most convenient source, but to invade there would mean war with the United States and Britain. However, with Japan's old enemy, the Soviet Union, fighting for its life, the gamble looked more attractive.

Setting the Stage. In July 1941, Japan forced the French puppet government of Vichy to give it bases in southern Indochina (now Vietnam and Cambodia). FDR promptly froze all Japanese assets in the United States; that is, Japanese companies and individuals could no longer use any money or investments they had in this country. Japan immediately did the same with American assets in Japan and trade between the two nations came to a halt.

In October 1941 General Hideki Tojo, a strong militarist, became premier of Japan. A month later, Secretary of State Hull began a series of talks with the Japanese ambassador and a special envoy. The Japanese wanted the United States to unfreeze their assets, supply them with oil, and stop sending lend-lease aid to China. The United States, instead of yielding, demanded that Japan withdraw from China and Southeast Asia.

As it happens, that previous December the United States had broken Japan's secret diplomatic code. Hull knew that Japan was preparing a military attack. But he expected it to come either in the Malay Peninsula or in the Dutch East Indies. In the meantime, the United States was strengthening its defense of the Philippines. No one in Washington knew that on November 25 a force of six aircraft carriers, two battleships, two heavy cruisers, and eleven destroyers had sailed east from Japan's Kurile Islands. Aboard the carriers was a strike force of 423 planes. Their destination: the headquarters of the United States Pacific Fleet in Hawaii. The Japanese warlords had taken the gamble.

The Attack. At 7:55 on the sleepy Sunday morning of December 7, 1941, the Japanese bombing planes struck the naval base at Pearl Harbor. Of the eight United States battleships docked side-by-side, three were sunk, one was run aground, and another capsized. The remaining three were badly damaged. Eleven smaller ships were also sunk or disabled, some 170 planes were destroyed on the ground, and almost 2400 people, including

Disaster at Pearl Harbor. The USS Arizona *(right) sinks as Japanese bombs explode through its decks. Over 1100 men went down with the ship which today still remains their tomb.*

68 civilians, were killed. In a single hour on the day Roosevelt called "a date which will live in infamy," the United States Navy suffered more damage than it received during all of World War I. In carefully coordinated operations, Japan also struck at the Philippines, Guam, Midway, Hong Kong, and the Malay Peninsula.

Far away in Washington, it was 1:20 in the afternoon when the first bombs fell on Pearl Harbor. The Japanese envoys had been sent coded orders to give Secretary Hull their government's final rejection of American terms at precisely one o'clock Washington time. Due to a delay in the decoding, they reached Hull's office an hour late—just as he was getting the first incredible reports from Hawaii. For a few minutes, the courtly statesman lost his self-control. He dressed down the two diplomats in the colorful language of his native Tennessee hills.

The following day the United States declared war on Japan. Hitler, who had not been told about his ally's Pearl Harbor scheme, at first thought it

was a propaganda trick. But when the news was verified, he and Mussolini declared war on the United States.

The attack on Pearl Harbor was one of the most successful military actions in history. Even Hitler had never managed anything like it. With one swift blow the Japanese high command had apparently removed the only real obstacle to their country's domination over a third of the world's surface.

Section 1 Review

COMPREHENSION   Developing Vocabulary

1. Explain these terms: lend-lease, wolf packs, pocket battleships.

COMPREHENSION   Mastering Facts

1. What happened to the Russo-German peace treaty?
2. How did Hitler try to close the supply lines from the United States to Great Britain?
3. What were the terms of the Atlantic Charter?
4. What was the most pressing need of the Japanese war machine?

657

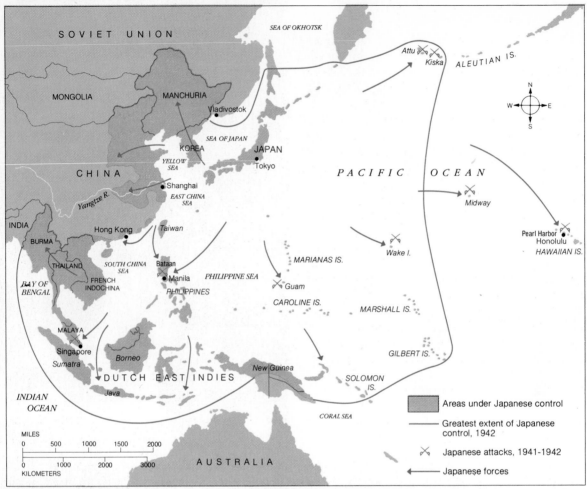

© ML & Co.

Map Skills *What islands in the Aleutians were occupied by the Japanese? What city was near the battle of Bataan? How far is Tokyo from Honolulu? from Singapore? from Vladivostok?*

2 THE NATION PERFORMS A PRODUCTION MIRACLE

VOCABULARY *Nisei*

The Japanese had counted on one thing when they attacked the United States. They believed the American people were "soft" and incapable of the discipline, courage, and hard work required for a long war. That was a serious mistake. By 1944 the United States industrial machine was grinding out as much war material as all the Axis countries combined. The figures are almost unimaginable: 86,000 tanks, nearly 300,000 planes, 2.5 million machine guns, and 64,000 landing craft for tanks and infantry. There were also 6500 naval ships, ranging from small minesweepers and destroyers— or "tin cans," as the sailors called them—all the

way to mighty aircraft carriers and battleships. There were also some 5400 cargo ships, most of them a type called Liberty Ships. Although slow-moving and squat in appearance, they could be turned out by shipyards in the then record time of 56 days.

Mobilizing for War

People are the chief ingredients of military and production machines. The selective service system provided 16.5 million of them to the armed forces. Eventually, all males from sixteen to sixty-five were registered, but early in the war the military stopped drafting men over thirty-eight.

Women in the Service. For the first time, women were permitted to volunteer for the armed forces, and about 216,000 of them enlisted. Most joined the Women's Army Corps (WACS), headed by Texas newspaper executive Oveta Culp Hobby. Others joined the navy, the Coast Guard, or the marines. Those in the navy and the Coast Guard were given names that translated, respectively, into WAVES and SPARS. The female component of the U.S. Marines was, simply, the Women's Reserve of the Marine Corps.

To become a WAC, a woman had to be between twenty and forty-nine years old, have no children under fourteen, and have completed at least two years of high school. WACS served in separate, non-combat units as accountants, bakers, bookkeepers, clerk-typists, drivers, and radio operators. Nurses in the Navy Nurse Corps received sea duty so they could train hospital corpsmen.

The Air Force (then part of the army) had a Women's Air Ferry Service (WAFS) that piloted planes across the Atlantic. The WAFS also flew planes that towed targets for antiaircraft and gunnery practice. But despite the hazards of their duty, WAFS were considered civilian government employees without military status or veterans' benefits.

Black Americans. About one million blacks entered the armed forces, and about half of them served overseas. Like women, blacks were segregated in the service, except at army officer-candidate schools and briefly, as an emergency measure, during the Battle of the Bulge (fought in Europe in December 1944–January 1945). The navy and the Coast Guard restricted them to non-combat service jobs, such as cooks, messengers, and mess-hall attendants, until almost the end of the war. Nevertheless, some black navy personnel won combat decorations. The Merchant Marine was more liberal: four of its ships' captains were black. One of the army's black units, the 761st Tank Battalion, saw 183 days of combat in Europe. The 332nd Fighter Group, commanded by Colonel Benjamin O. Davis, Jr., son of the army's first black general officer, flew escort sorties into central Europe with the Fifteenth Air Force.

Japanese-Americans. Yet another group of Americans who were segregated in the service were

These women undergo physical training loaded down with helmets, field packs, and water canteens.

Nisei, or Americans of Japanese descent. About 17,000 of them enlisted in the armed forces. Some served in the U.S. intelligence service. Others fought in Italy, France, and Germany. The 442nd Regiment, popularly known as the "Go for Broke" regiment, received more decorations than any other American combat unit.

Relocating the Japanese Americans

The performance of the Nisei was especially impressive considering how people of Japanese descent from California, Oregon, Washington, and Arizona were treated during the war. Some

112,000, two-thirds of them citizens, were rounded up by the army and the FBI on the grounds that they posed a threat to the nation's security. Forced to abandon their homes and property, they were shipped to ten hastily built internment camps. The camps were located in the desert regions of California, Arizona, and other western states, and in the swamplands of Arkansas. Except for the men who enlisted in the armed forces, most Japanese-Americans remained in the camps, surrounded by barbed wire and guarded by soldiers, until almost the end of the war.

In 1944 the Supreme Court upheld the relocation order in the case of *Korematsu* v. *United States*. Speaking for the majority, Justice Hugo Black argued that the government's action was caused by "military necessity." (Strangely enough, Japanese-Americans living in Hawaii, which contained many military installations, were left alone.) Speaking for the minority, Justice Frank Murphy said the relocation reminded him of the Nazi treatment of the Jews.

Historians today agree that the relocation order grew out of more than military necessity. The order also reflected anti-Japanese racism. Not a single Japanese-American was charged with committing a disloyal act, such as spying or sabotage, during the war. And no relocation orders were even considered against people of German or Italian descent. After the war, the federal government paid Japanese-Americans $35 million to compensate them for their lost property. The actual value of the property, however, has been put at $400 million.

Organizing Workers

The need for people in the armed forces and in war industries wiped out the depression's unemployment figure of 7 million. Not only that, the work force increased from 46.5 million to 53 million. In addition, by 1944 the average workweek was 45.2 hours. Since union representatives were able to maintain the standard forty-hour week with time-and-a-half for overtime, average weekly wages rose 70 percent during the war years. Union membership grew from 10.5 million in 1942 to almost 15 million in 1945.

Limiting Strikes. Immediately after Pearl Harbor, both the AFL and the CIO pledged not to strike while the war lasted. In return, the federal government set up the National War Labor Board to enforce settlements on wages, hours, and working conditions. To enforce the board's rulings, the government could seize a business and operate it.

In general, most unions kept their promise. Only one-ninth of 1 percent of working time was

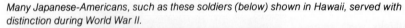

Many Japanese-Americans, such as these soldiers (below) shown in Hawaii, served with distinction during World War II.

lost during the war because of strikes. However, in 1943 the United Mine Workers went out on strike. Although wages had been frozen the previous year, the miners felt that rising prices and business profits justified a wage increase. FDR promptly seized the coal mines. Congress then passed the Smith-Connally Act over his veto. The act said that unions had to give thirty days' notice before striking; it also said that a strike in an industry being run by the government was a federal crime.

Utilizing Women in War Plants. About 2 million women joined or replaced men in the nation's war plants. In all, there were 4 to 5 million women workers by 1945. However, they were under two disadvantages: they received 60 percent less pay than men, and they had little job security. A wartime equal-pay-for-equal-work drive got nowhere. This was partly because of FDR's desire to hold down inflation and partly because the view was still widely held that married women should not work outside the home. Even those supporting families knew they would be laid off as soon as the war was over and servicemen returned to claim their old jobs.

Nevertheless, the efforts of women on the assembly line were widely recognized and applauded. One of the most popular songs of the time was "Rosie the Riveter."

Banning Discrimination. Other additions to the industrial work force included more than 1 million blacks, as well as Mexican-Americans and also American Indians who left their reservations to take part in the war effort. In June 1941 President Roosevelt issued an executive order barring racial discrimination in the hiring and firing of workers in plants that held government contracts. The order was to be enforced by a Fair Employment Practices Committee (FEPC). But the order was issued only after A. Philip Randolph, president of the Brotherhood of Sleeping Car Porters, threatened to arouse the nation's conscience and pressure the government by leading a march of 10,000 blacks on Washington, D.C.

Opening up industrial employment to blacks and other minorities had several effects. The movement of black families from the South into northern and western cities continued the change in the nation's racial map that had started during World War I. It also led to a series of lynchings and race

riots. The worst outbreak took place in Detroit in June 1943. Twenty-five blacks and nine whites were killed, and countless others were injured. Despite the violence, however, the economic standing of blacks improved considerably during the war.

Organizing Industry and Agriculture

Lend-lease and war production ended the depression in American industry. But despite America's great production achievements, there was much confusion, especially in the first years of the war. Some companies were wary of again being branded "merchants of death." Others feared that they would be caught after the war with more production capacity than they could use. As a result, about 85 percent of the new plants needed for war production were built by the federal government. The government then leased the plants for operation to private firms.

Allocating Materials. The government also set up a War Production Board (WPB). Its first chief was Donald M. Nelson, a former executive of Sears, Roebuck and Company. The WPB decided which firms would receive raw materials. It told certain companies to convert from peacetime to wartime production. It rationed gasoline in order to conserve oil and rubber. And it organized nation-wide drives to collect scrap iron, tin cans, and fats. To aid the WPB, the office of Economic Stabilization was formed and headed by James F. Byrnes.

Supervising Contracts. To supervise government buying, the Senate set up a committee headed by Senator Harry S Truman of Missouri. The committee uncovered a great deal of inefficiency and bungling on war contracts, but, although more than $300 billion were spent, there was very little wrongdoing. Senator Truman, as a result of his vigorous work, became a national figure.

Increasing Farm Production. Like manufacturers, American farmers outdid themselves in producing for the war. Although the work force declined, improved equipment and greater use of fertilizers, combined with good weather, resulted in a doubling of output per worker. Farm prices likewise doubled.

Curbing Inflation

Larger incomes plus fewer civilian goods meant higher prices. In order to prevent inflation from skyrocketing the way it had in World War I, Congress set up the Office of Price Administration (OPA).

The OPA. The OPA was given the power to fix rents and to set maximum prices on goods. It also had the power to set up a rationing system. People could buy meat, shoes, butter, sugar, coffee, and other items needed by the armed forces only if they had stamps from ration books. Some people cheated by shopping at "black markets," where they bought goods without stamps at prices above those set by the OPA. But overall, the combination of price controls and rationing kept inflation below 30 percent for the entire war period. This was about half the increase that had taken place in the First World War. It should be noted, however, that prices did not rise equally. Clothing, for example, went up forty percent, while food shot up fifty percent. Rents, on the other hand, were practically stable, increasing by only four percent.

Taxes. The government adopted several other techniques to curb inflation. It raised income tax rates and also extended the tax to millions of Americans who had never paid it before. In addition, in 1943 Congress passed a payroll deduction law. Since then, employers withhold income taxes from workers' paychecks each month and send the money in to the federal government.

Bonds. People were also encouraged, as in World War I, to buy government bonds. And they bought bonds to the tune of $100 billion. In all, they came out of the war with $129 billion in savings that they could not wait to spend on homes, cars, and other things they had gone without during sixteen years of depression and war.

Organizing Science

Science played a key role in the eventual defeat of the Axis.

Rocket Research. During the Battle of Britain, you recall, radar gave the Royal Air Force a great advantage in its fight with Hitler's bombers. The Allies also had antibiotics such as penicillin, as well as the powerful insecticide DDT. Allied armies in World War II were probably the first in history to be relatively free of body lice. Germany, on the other hand, had the first jet aircraft engines, while its rockets were superior to anything the Allies developed. When the war ended, some German scientists went to the Soviet Union to help in rocket research and the development of intercontinental missiles. Other German scientists went to the United States to do the same kind of work.

Splitting the Atom. But the greatest scientific achievement of the war resulted from the splitting of the atom, which Nazi scientists had accomplished in 1939. The energy thus released opened up the possibility of making an atomic bomb. Albert Einstein, a refugee from Hitler's Germany, wrote a letter to FDR warning him that such a bomb was possible and that the Germans might well develop it first. In 1941 Roosevelt set up the Office of Scientific Research and Development to organize a "crash program" to develop the atomic bomb as quickly as possible.

In 1942 a controlled nuclear reaction was achieved in a small laboratory under the concrete football stands at Stagg Field, at the University of Chicago. Colonel, later General, Leslie Groves of the Army Corps of Engineers was then given the task of producing the uranium-235 and plutonium-239 needed for an explosive device. Under the code name of Manhattan Project, two plants for this purpose were built at Oak Ridge, Tennessee

Dr. J. R. Oppenheimer (second from left), director of the Los Alamos Bomb Project, examines the effects of the first bomb blast on particles of sand.

where they could make use of the vast water and electric power resources of the TVA. A third plant was located at Hanford, Washington.

Creating the A-Bomb. At the same time, a group of American, British, and European-refugee scientists headed by Dr. J. Robert Oppenheimer put together the first atomic bomb at Los Alamos, New Mexico. At 5:30 on the morning of July 16, 1945, it was exploded in the desert near Alamagordo air base. There was a burst of blinding light (visible 180 miles away), a deep-growling blast, scalding wind, and then a gray mushroom cloud that rose slowly toward the sky. Words from the *Song of God*, a sacred Hindu text, came into Dr. Oppenheimer's mind as he watched. "I am become Death, the shatterer of worlds, waiting that hour that ripens to their doom." And in truth, the world has never been the same since.

Section 2 Review

COMPREHENSION   Developing Vocabulary

1. Explain these terms: Nisei, black markets, WACS, Liberty Ships.

COMPREHENSION   Mastering Facts

1. What happened to U.S. citizens of Japanese descent who lived on the West Coast?
2. What effect did the war have on unemployment?
3. How were prices held down during the war?
4. What was the greatest scientific achievement of World War II?

3 WAR RAGES ACROSS NORTH AFRICA AND EUROPE

VOCABULARY   *Afrika Korps   partisans   Operation Overlord*

The Allies and the Axis waged their struggle everywhere: on land, in the air, on the sea, and beneath the ocean. Although China and Russia ran their own operations, the United States and Great Britain worked closely together.

The Anglo-American Command

Decisions concerning the two English-speaking nations were made by their combined chiefs of staff, headquartered in Washington, after consultation with Roosevelt and Churchill.

These two men were unlike in many ways, but they came from a similar aristocratic tradition. They had the same kind of education and experience, and many of the same ideas about honor, discipline, and gentlemanly conduct. Churchill also had an American mother. As a result of all this, there was an easy friendship between the two leaders that added greatly to Anglo-American cooperation.

The Commanders. Both nations had strong military and civilian teams. In particular, there was General George Marshall, U.S. army chief of staff, a forceful yet sensitive man who thought nothing of working seventy hours a week. Marshall was regarded by subordinates and equals alike with the same mixture of respect and awe that George Washington had received.

General Dwight D. "Ike" Eisenhower, commander in the European theater of operations, had the military and political skills needed to run a two-nation command. Bright, energetic, and outgoing, he did all he could to encourage Anglo-American teamwork. He had pamphlets about English life and customs given out to American troops before they left the United States for Britain. He even sent an American officer home for cursing a British officer. "If you had called him a so-and-so, I wouldn't have minded," Ike told the American. "But you called him a British so-and-so."

The First Decisions. Far-reaching decisions were arrived at early in the war. The first was to give priority to defeating Hitler and to let the all-out effort against Japan wait. There were several reasons for this. One was the possibility that Germany might succeed in building an atomic bomb. Another was that Germany might be able to cut Britain off from America, something Japan would never be able to do.

The second major decision was—like that of Grant in the Civil War—to accept only the "unconditional surrender" of the enemy. Some historians, however, believe this second decision was a mistake. They feel it led Germany and Japan to fight longer and more desperately than they might otherwise have done.

The Atlantic Front

With destroyers escorting merchant ships across the North Atlantic, the waters off the east coast of the United States were left weakly defended. The Germans were quick to take advantage. By January 1942 submarine packs were striking from Newfoundland to New Orleans. In three months 200 ships were sunk; in the next two months, 182. Silhouetted against the bright glow of shore lights, merchant vessels and oil tankers made easy targets for enemy torpedoes.

By the end of the year, however, several tactics succeeded in lowering American losses. The tactics included tighter air and sea patrols (some making use of private boats) and a strict "brownout" of coastal cities that cut the use of electricity and thus reduced skyglow.

Meanwhile, the North Atlantic battle went on. The "polar bear route," from Iceland around the North Cape of Norway, above the Arctic Circle, to the Russian port of Murmansk, was the only route by which large amounts of American supplies could reach the Soviet Union. It was a dangerous route, for German planes and submarines based in Norway sank one merchant ship after another. Even seamen who were not blown up or drowned, suffered from exposure to Arctic weather. Yet the convoys kept sailing, bringing the Soviets badly needed supplies which they were soon using to good advantage.

The Russian Front

The initial German push into the Soviet Union had stalled in front of Leningrad and Moscow. With the coming of spring in 1942, Hitler decided to try a different tactic. His war machine was beginning to run low on oil and there were large oil fields in the Caucasus Mountains. In addition, Hitler wanted to cut the movement of military supplies along the Volga River to Moscow. So he decided to kill two birds with one stone. He flung his troops at the city of Stalingrad (now Volgograd) on the river's west bank.

For two months the Germans besieged the city, conquering it house by house and street by street. Then the Russians launched a counter-offensive, moving in one army from the north and another from the south. All through the bitter winter, the fighting went on. It was so cold—about 44 below zero—that tanks would not start, rifles misfired,

and food turned hard as stone. Finally, on the last day of January 1943, some 91,000 "dazed and frost-bitten [German] scarecrows hobbled into captivity." They were all that remained of the original force of 500,000.

Russian losses in the battle ran somewhere between 400,000 and 600,000. Yet despite the staggering death toll, Stalingrad was the turning point on the Eastern Front. From there, the Soviets began to move steadily west.

The Mediterranean Front

While the battle of Stalingrad was raging, Stalin kept urging the United States and Britain to open a "second front," an attack on Hitler's western frontier in Europe. The Americans were anxious to try it, but the British held back. Going in too soon, they said, would result in disaster. They wanted neither another Dunkirk nor a repetition of the trench warfare of World War I.

Invading North Africa. The compromise was Operation Torch, an invasion of French-held North Africa. On November 8, 1942, landings were made at Casablanca, Oran, and Algiers. The American and British forces then drove eastward toward the German base in Tunisia. The previous month, German General Erwin Rommel and his *Afrika Korps* had been defeated by British forces in Egypt at the battle of El Alamein. Now Rommel rushed back from Egypt to Tunisia and had the area well fortified by the time the Allied armies reached it in early 1943. After three months of sharp fighting, however, the remnants of the *Afrika Korps* surrendered. The triumphant Allied forces then crossed the narrow sea between Tunisia and Sicily, and secured that island in a month.

The Italian Campaign. The Allied forces were now ready to attack what Churchill called "the soft underbelly of the Axis"—Italy, Yugoslavia, and Eastern Europe. At that point, the king of Italy arrested Mussolini and prepared to surrender unconditionally.

Unfortunately, the Germans moved faster than the Allies. They took over Italy and dug themselves in. They even rescued Mussolini by dropping a hundred parachutists at his mountain prison and then flying him off to Munich. The Allied landings at Salerno in September 1943 and at "Bloody Anzio" the following January gave Ameri-

Axis Power at Its Peak in Europe in World War II

Map Skills *What did Ireland, Spain, Sweden, and Turkey have in common? Did the Axis Powers control Britain? France? the Soviet Union? How far is Berlin from London? from Moscow?*

© ML & Co.

can troops some of the hardest fighting they encountered in Europe. At Salerno, only the timely drop of two paratroop battalions saved them from being pushed back into the sea. In all, it took eighteen months of mud and mountain warfare before the Allies were able to drive the Germans from the Italian peninsula.

Mussolini ended up being captured on April 28, 1945, by Italian *partisans*. Partisans were members of the underground resistance movement that existed in the Nazi-held countries. They hid Allied fliers who were shot down, derailed trains, sabotaged factory machinery, smuggled Jews to neutral

countries, and did everything else they could to help defeat the Nazis. The Italian partisans shot Mussolini and then hung his body upside down in a Milan square.

The Invasion of "Fortress Europe"

As Anglo-American troops pushed north through Italy and the Russians pushed west into Poland, plans for invading Hitler's "Fortress Europe" moved ahead. But before the Allies could mount their cross-Channel invasion of France, they had to control the air. From October 1943

665

through May 1944, the Americans bombed by day, while the British bombed by night. By June 1944, the Allies had a thirty-to-one superiority over the German air force.

The Beaches of Normandy.

The invasion of France on D Day—June 6, 1944—carried the code name *Operation Overlord*. It was the largest amphibious, or combined land and sea, operation in history. In all, there were 176,000 troops involved, as well as 4000 landing craft, 600 warships, and 11,000 planes. It had taken two years of planning and work to set into motion.

German defenses were enormous. They included about 250,000 troops protected by every conceivable type of underwater mine, tank trap, and guns mounted in concrete forts. But by clever deception, the Allies kept the enemy off balance for twenty-four hours after the landing. They bombed an area east of the actual landing place so heavily that the Germans—certain it was the real invasion point—shifted men and equipment there. Even so, German fire at one of the five real landing beaches, Omaha Beach, was so withering that the invaders were almost wiped out. But all the beach-heads were held. And within a month, they had taken in a million troops, 567,000 tons of supplies, and 170,000 vehicles.

By September 1944 France, Belgium, Luxembourg, and part of the Netherlands had been liberated. British and American armies had fought their way through much of the Siegfried Line. There was talk that the war would be over by the end of the year. The good military news helped elect Roosevelt as president for the fourth time. His vice-president was Senator Truman.

Then a snag developed.

The Battle of the Bulge.

Three things upset the Allied timetable. First, the port of Antwerp held out longer than expected. As a result, American tanks under the command of General George Patton ran out of gas. Second, an airborne landing at Arnhem in the Netherlands fizzled badly. Third, when least expected, the enemy counterattacked.

War comes to a French village. This painting entitled Tank Breakthrough at St. Lo *shows American troops moving through a nightmarish landscape that is only too real.*

The Crushing of Nazi Germany   1944–1945

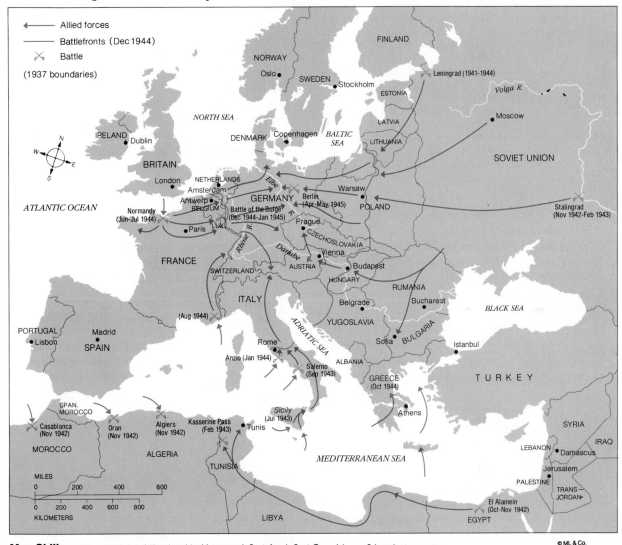

Map Skills   *When did the Allies land in Normandy? at Anzio? at Casablanca? In what country was the battle of the Bulge? Leningrad? El Alamein? How far is Berlin from Stalingrad?*

On December 16, under cover of fog, German troops hit an eighty-mile front along the Belgian border of the Ardennes Forest. The area was thinly defended by inexperienced American troops. Nevertheless, they put up a heroic defense of Bastogne, a key road center, holding out until Christmas. Then relief arrived. The weather cleared, American planes took to the air once more, and the German threat was over.

The idea for the attack had been Hitler's. After it failed, his forces were never able to make another, although there were continual sharp battles as the Germans retreated.

A Meeting at the Elbe.   At the end of March 1945, the western Allies crossed the Rhine River, the last major obstacle between them and the heart of Germany. In April, the Russians entered the outskirts of Berlin after having pushed the Germans back for more than a thousand miles. As one eyewitness remembered that time:

❝ Throughout those April days you could see a nation collapse. Tens of thousands of people fled westward toward the approaching American and allied troops. German soldiers, civilian men and women, and children—some in their mothers' arms—scurried along the ruined roads and across shell-pocked fields.

667

They were eager to reach the western armies because they did not wish to be captured by the Russians. Few troops are considerate to their enemies in the heat of battle. But the Russian troops, because of the great damage their country had suffered during the war, were considered more than ordinarily . . . brutal to those Germans who fell into their hands.

At the broad, swift-flowing Elbe River, the masses hardly halted. Across the water they came in boats and rafts. Some plunged into the river and swam. Others held onto whatever floating driftwood they could find. Many were carried away by the current.

Gratefully the survivors surrendered to American and British soldiers and disappeared behind their lines. **"**

On April 25, American and Russian infantrymen stood looking at each other from opposite banks of the broad Elbe River. Some Americans, against orders, rowed quietly across the river. Russians met them with hearty hugs and handclasps. For most, it was the first time they had seen a Russian or an American.

The End of Hitler. In his underground headquarters in Berlin, Hitler, his longtime friend Eva Braun whom he had recently married, and a few faithful followers waited for the end. Deep as they were, they could feel the shudder as bombs hit the ground above their heads. Hitler, determined to avoid capture by the Russians, decided to go out in flames like a warrior of old. On April 30 he shot himself, while his wife took poison. Then, following instructions, their bodies were taken up to the garden, doused with gasoline, and burned. Two days later, Berlin fell to the Soviets.

On May 7 Eisenhower accepted the unconditional surrender of Nazi Germany. The next day, V-E (Victory in Europe) Day marked the official end of one part of the war.

Section 3 Review

COMPREHENSION   Developing Vocabulary

1. Explain these terms: partisans, Afrika Korps, amphibious, polar bear route.

COMPREHENSION   Mastering Facts

1. What overall military strategy did Roosevelt and Churchill decide to follow?
2. What was the result of the Battle of Stalingrad?
3. What was Operation Overlord, and who commanded it?

4 JAPAN SURRENDERS UNCONDITIONALLY
VOCABULARY   *kamikaze*

Although Roosevelt and Churchill had agreed that victory over Germany came first, the Americans did not wait until V-E Day to move against Japan. On the contrary, as soon as possible, the United States began to wage an aggressive military campaign in the Pacific.

Early Japanese Victories

During the first five months after Pearl Harbor, the Japanese made tremendous advances in all directions. They overran Hong Kong, French Indochina (now Laos, Cambodia, and Vietnam), Malaya (including the naval base at Singapore), Burma, Thailand, and the Dutch East Indies, reaching as far south as New Guinea and the Solomon Islands. To the east, they captured Guam and Wake Island, as well as three islands in the Aleutian chain in Alaska.

In the Philippines, some 36,000 American and Filipino troops under General Douglas MacArthur succeeded in holding off a Japanese army of 200,000 for four months in the Bataan peninsula and then for another month on the fortress island of Corregidor, at the entrance to Manila Bay. When it became clear that the situation was hopeless, Marshall ordered MacArthur to escape to Australia. He did so, saying as he left, "I shall return."

As a result of Japan's conquests, the prestige of white people in Southeast Asia, which had been based on their hitherto unquestioned military power, was destroyed forever. Even after the Japanese were gone, people in the area were never again willing to live under white rule.

Stemming the Japanese Tide

By the spring of 1942 Japanese armies were at the gates of India, the Japanese fleet was menacing Australia, and even the Pacific coast of the United States was threatened. But in April the gloom lightened. Sixteen B-25 bombers, commanded by

The Crushing of Japan 1942–1945

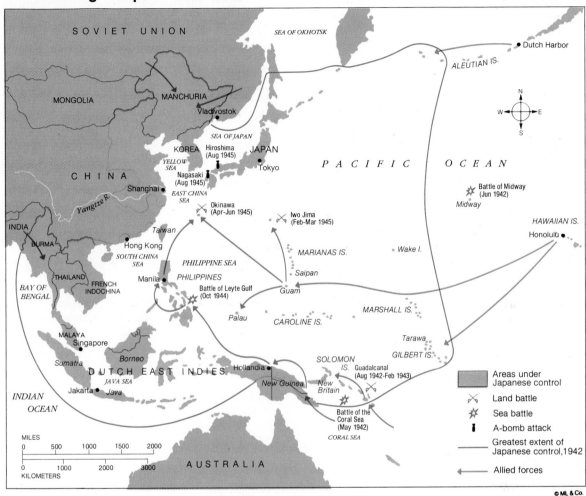

Map Skills *When was the battle of Midway? Guadalcanal? Iwo Jima? Which Japanese cities were hit by A-bombs? When? From what country did Allied forces go into Burma? Manchuria?*

Colonel James H. Doolittle, took off from the aircraft carrier U.S.S. *Hornet* and dropped a few bombs on Tokyo. The daring daylight raid had no strategic value, and all the planes went down in China, where the crews were forced to bail out. But the raid made the Japanese realize that their islands were vulnerable to bombs. It also made Americans feel a lot better.

Then, early in May, a combined American and Australian fleet intercepted a Japanese fleet in the Coral Sea. In the battle that followed, there was no ship-to-ship contact. All fighting was done by carrier-based planes. Although the Americans and Australians lost more ships than the enemy, they halted Japan's attempt to invade Australia.

The next month, the Japanese suffered an even worse defeat at the Battle of Midway. Four aircraft carriers, a cruiser, and several crowded troop ships were sunk and 253 planes were shot down. American losses totaled one carrier, one destroyer, and 150 planes. In this battle also, carrier aircraft rather than ships were the decisive element. The Japanese, who had been heading for Hawaii, turned back to their base. They no longer held unchallenged control over the Pacific.

"Leapfrogging" to Japan

The Pacific theater posed several serious problems for the United States and its allies. Japan was protected by some 3000 miles of water in which were literally hundreds of fortified islands. Even small coral atolls contained an air strip, guns, and determined Japanese. To storm every island would probably have taken a generation. Instead, MacArthur came up with a different tactic, which he called "leapfrogging." That is, the Americans would mount attacks only on selected islands. The Australians and New Zealanders would then bomb and mop up the Japanese garrisons that had been bypassed.

The Battle of Guadalcanal.
The American offensive began in August 1942. U.S. marines landed on Guadalcanal in the Solomon Islands, which form a thousand-mile-long barrier east of New Guinea and Australia. Two days after they had established a beachhead, Japanese cruisers sank almost all the American transport ships.

For the next six months, the marines, short of food and equipment, clung to the island's air strip while Japanese and American ships and planes fought one engagement after another. The tropical sun and rain created a steaming hell by day, while the strange bird and animal sounds made the jungle nights a time of uneasy rest. Finally, early in 1943, the Japanese withdrew from Guadalcanal, leaving the Americans with a valuable base from which to launch their offensive.

Return to the Philippines.
The American return to the Philippines was actually made from two directions. MacArthur's troops moved toward the islands from the south, while Admiral Chester W. Nimitz's forces moved toward the islands from the east. By February 1944 Japan's outer defenses had been cracked with the capture of the Solomon, Gilbert, and Marshall Islands. By June 1944 the Americans were attacking Japan's inner defenses in the Mariana Islands. The Japanese fought a tremendous naval engagement, the Battle of the Philippine Sea, in an effort to prevent the landings in the Marianas. But the battle dealt a crippling blow to Japan's carrier planes, 345 to a loss of only 17 for the Americans. It also placed Japan's home islands within reach of American land-based bombers for the first time.

In October MacArthur's and Nimitz's forces—consisting of 174,000 soldiers in 738 ships—converged on Leyte Island in the Philippines. MacArthur himself and a few officers, most of whom had fled the Philippines two years earlier, headed for land in a small barge. Fifty yards from shore, MacArthur stepped off into the knee-deep water and waded to the beach. "I have returned," he said into a microphone.

The Japanese threw their entire fleet into the

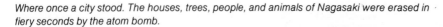

Where once a city stood. The houses, trees, people, and animals of Nagasaki were erased in fiery seconds by the atom bomb.

Battle of Leyte Gulf. Kamikaze suicide pilots crashed their bomb-laden planes into American ships, killing themselves and large numbers of the ship's crews. The word *kamikaze* means "divine wind," after a typhoon that in 1281 destroyed Kublai Khan's fleet when it attempted to invade Japan from China. But after three days of fighting, it was the Japanese fleet that was crushed. Three battleships, four aircraft carriers, thirteen cruisers, and almost 400 planes disappeared beneath the sea.

The Ultimate Weapon

After the capture of the Philippines, only two major battles remained. But they were among the worst of the war—Iwo Jima and Okinawa. Each island held out for many weeks in the spring of 1945. And each was so savagely defended, that it gave Americans a chilling foretaste of what the invasion of Japan's home islands would be like. Churchill thought the cost would be "a million American lives and half that number of British."

As matters turned out, no invasion of Japan was necessary. A few weeks after the capture of Okinawa, the first atom bomb was tested at Alamagordo. On July 26, 1945, a warning was sent to Japan that it faced "prompt and utter destruction" unless it surrendered. On August 6, a 9000-pound atomic bomb was put aboard a B-29 bomber called the *Enola Gay*, after the mother of pilot Colonel Paul W. Tibbets, Jr. At 9:15:30 A.M. the bomb was dropped on the city of Hiroshima, an important military center. It killed about 71,000 people, horribly injured another 68,000, and flattened four square miles of the city. Three days later a second atomic bomb hit Nagasaki, killing 36,000 persons, injuring 60,000, and leveling almost half the city. Together, though, the two atomic bombs took fewer lives than the regular air raids on Tokyo had done.

On August 14 Emperor Hirohito, despite opposition from some of his military leaders, made the decision to surrender unconditionally. Dozens of American and British ships sailed into Tokyo Bay. There, on September 2, 1945, the formal surrender was signed on the deck of the battleship U.S.S. *Missouri*. The greatest war in history was over.

Section 4 Review

COMPREHENSION   Developing Vocabulary
1. Explain these terms: kamikaze, leapfrogging.

COMPREHENSION   Mastering Facts
1. What were two effects of the Doolittle raid on Tokyo?
2. What naval battle destroyed Japan's supremacy in the Pacific?
3. What made an invasion of Japan's home islands unnecessary?
4. On what two cities were the first atomic bombs dropped?

5   THE ALLIES PLAN FOR THE POSTWAR WORLD

VOCABULARY   *Byelorussia   demokrashi*

The World War II Allies learned some lessons from 1919. One was to prepare for peace even as they were making war and not put off questions about the postwar world until the fighting ended.

The Wartime Conferences

Beginning with the August 1941 meeting in which Roosevelt and Churchill signed the Atlantic Charter, the United States took part in fifteen major international conferences. Most of them were between Roosevelt and Churchill; three included Soviet dictator Joseph Stalin; and one, establishing the United Nations, was attended by representatives of fifty nations.

Cairo. The early conferences between Roosevelt and Churchill dealt with military matters, such as the decision to invade North Africa and the setting of a target date for the Normandy invasion. Later conferences concerned political questions about the postwar world.

In November of 1943 FDR, Churchill, and Chiang Kai-shek of China met in Cairo, Egypt. They agreed on two issues: (1) Korea, then under Japanese domination, would become independent; and (2) Formosa (Taiwan) would be returned from Japan to China.

Teheran. In late November, Roosevelt and Churchill proceeded from Cairo to Teheran, Iran.

The Big Three at Yalta. Churchill, F.D.R., and Joseph Stalin. Roosevelt was ill and died two months later.

Yalta. In his next meeting with Stalin, at Yalta on the Black Sea, FDR may have had doubts. It was now February 1945, and the European war was drawing to a close. The Soviet armies were deep in Central Europe. Many doubted that these troops would draw back to the Soviet Union.

The Big Three reached some tentative decisions about what to do with Germany after the war. The three leaders also agreed that German and Japanese leaders would be tried as criminals for the atrocities they had committed. It was decided to set up the United Nations later in the year. Stalin, in exchange for Japan's Kuril and Sakhalin Islands, again promised to enter the war against Japan two or three months after Germany surrendered. (The atomic bomb had not yet been developed. The United States felt it would need Soviet help for the invasion of Japan.)

While these issues were fairly easily resolved, the question of Poland proved sticky. The Soviet Union supported a Communist regime for that nation. Great Britain and the United States favored the Polish government-in-exile that had been in London since 1939. From Stalin's point of view, the Soviet Union had to have friendly governments on its western borders. It had suffered 25,000,000 casualties during the war, as well as tremendous property damage. It had neither oceans nor mountains to protect it against invasion. Finally, Britain and the United States agreed to support the Polish Communist government provided that it was expanded to include a few representatives from the government-in-exile in London. Stalin then promised that, after the war, there would be "free and unfettered elections" in Poland and other Eastern European countries occupied by Soviet troops. But he never kept the promise.

There they promised Stalin that a second front would soon be opened. Stalin in turn promised to attack Japan after Germany was defeated.

The Teheran meeting was FDR's first encounter with Stalin. The American president had looked forward to it. He was sure he would be able to establish the same kind of relationship with the Soviet leader that he had with Churchill. Out of this he hoped would come a lasting postwar alliance. Roosevelt apparently regarded Stalin in the same way he regarded a tough Democratic political boss, that is, as someone whom he could handle by a combination of charm and political favors. FDR was wrong. Stalin had climbed to the top of a system quite different from that of the United States, one that involved murder, treachery, and the belief that the end justifies the means. It was a measure of Stalin's skill that Roosevelt came away from Teheran pleased. He assured Congress and the American people that future relations with the Soviet Union would be easy sailing.

San Francisco. In April 1945, representatives of fifty nations met at San Francisco to establish an international peace-keeping body. By now the Soviet Union was displaying considerable signs of suspiciousness and stubbornness. That country is made up of fifteen separate Soviet republics and the Soviet Union wanted to have all fifteen represented in the United Nations. The other countries refused. It would be much like having all the states of the United States represented. But there was a compromise. Two Soviet republics—the Ukraine and Byelorussia (White Russia)—as well as the Soviet Union as a whole were each given a seat.

Potsdam. The final wartime conference took place at Potsdam, Germany in July 1945. Although final decisions were reached about the postwar treatment of Germany, it seemed to many observers that the wartime alliance was definitely breaking up. Stalin made it clear that he had no intention of allowing free elections in Eastern Europe. Nor could the Big Three decide on Poland's western boundary. They did, however, decide to move 6.5 million Germans out of Czechoslovakia, Hungary, and Poland into Germany.

The United Nations

The charter establishing the United Nations was signed in June 1945. Like the League of Nations it had a large deliberative body and a smaller executive body. It provided for a General Assembly of all member nations. Real power, however, was placed in the hands of the Security Council. On this council, the United States, Britain, France, the Union of Soviet Socialist Republics, and China were to have permanent seats, with six other nations elected on a rotating basis. Voting in the Security Council would be by a majority, but the majority would have to include all five permanent members. Thus, each of the Big Five nations would have a veto power over any council action. The Economic and Social Council, the Trusteeship Council (for former colonies), The International Court of Justice, and the Secretariat for Administration completed the UN's main structure.

In 1919 and 1920, the United States Senate had spent eight months debating whether or not to join the League of Nations and had finally decided against doing so. In 1945 it took the Senate only six days to approve the country's membership in the United Nations. In fact, the United States was the first nation in the world to accept the UN charter. The organization began its work on a great wave of goodwill and optimism.

Dealing with the Enemy

As suggested at Yalta and confirmed at Potsdam, Germany was divided into four zones, or sections. The United States, Britain, France, and the Soviet Union were each to occupy and administer one zone. Germany's capital of Berlin, although within the Soviet Zone, was also divided into four separately administered sectors.

The Occupation of Japan. Japan was handled differently. Technically, there was an eleven-nation Far Eastern Commission, which met in Washington and made recommendations to a four-power Allied Council for Japan in Tokyo. This council in turn sent instructions to the Supreme Commander for the Allied Powers (SCAP). In practice, control lay in the hands of the Supreme Commander, General Douglas MacArthur.

The U.S. occupation of Japan lasted for six years. During that time, MacArthur brought in many aspects of *demokrashi.* They included freedom of the press, no secret police, woman suffrage, and recognition of labor's right to form unions. MacArthur also brought about extensive land reforms that freed farmers from paying rents to absentee landlords. He also helped break up the large business organizations that had previously controlled about 80 percent of Japan's economy. By retaining the emperor and working through officials of the former Japanese government, MacArthur was able to accomplish these and other changes with fewer than 40,000 troops.

The occupation ended with the signing of a peace treaty between the United Nations and Japan in September 1951. The Soviet Union, however, refused to sign because no restrictions were put on the Japanese economy.

The War Crimes Trials. During 1945 and 1946, Nazi leaders went on trial at Nuremberg, Germany, before an international tribunal representing 23 nations. Some 30 American judges took part in the proceedings. Supreme Court Justice Robert H. Jackson was a chief counsel for the prosecution. Defendants included industrialists and government officials as well as generals and admirals. The charges were: (1) waging aggressive war; and (2) violating generally accepted rules about how to treat prisoners of war and how to behave toward civilians in occupied territory. Twelve of the 22 defendants received death sentences, 7 received prison terms, and 3 were acquitted. Later, trials of lesser leaders were held. In all, about 500,000 Nazis were found guilty of war crimes.

Similar trials were held in Tokyo. Top officials were charged with war crimes and atrocities. Former Premier Hideki Tojo and six other Japanese leaders were executed, while about 4000 Japanese were convicted and received prison terms of varying length.

Some survivors of Buchenwald concentration camp. This famous photo was taken by Margaret Bourke-White.

A New President

Roosevelt did not live to see the final victory of the allies. He had returned from Yalta a dying man and troubled by what he saw as a growing coolness between the Soviet Union and its former allies. The wartime alliance was rapidly coming apart. On the morning of April 12, 1945, thirteen days before the date set for the UN organizing meeting, the president was posing for an artist who was painting his portrait. He sat in an armchair in the living room of the Little White House in Warm Springs, Georgia. Suddenly he put his hand to his forehead and said, "I have a terrific headache." Then he slumped over. He was put to bed and the doctors were called. He had suffered a stroke. Within hours he was dead.

He was mourned throughout the world. There were people in the armed services who could not remember a time when FDR had not been president. Harry Truman, uneasy and inexperienced, took over the reins of office.

Section 5 Review

COMPREHENSION   Developing Vocabulary

1. Explain these terms: Byelorussia, demokrashi, General Assembly, Security Council.

COMPREHENSION   Mastering Facts

1. How did Roosevelt misjudge Stalin?
2. How was Germany to be governed after the war?
3. What changes did MacArthur bring about in Japan?
4. What were the charges against the defendants in the Nuremberg war crimes trials?

CHAPTER 33 Review

Chapter Summary

As the United States officially continued a neutral policy, the nation provided much military equipment and many supplies for the Allies. Finally, when Japan attacked Pearl Harbor in 1941, the United States declared war on the Axis powers. Women and blacks greatly contributed to the American military buildup. Eventually, American involvement turned the tide in World War II. After the Normandy invasion in 1944, the Allies pushed the Germans back until they surrendered in 1945. When two atom bombs were dropped on Japan, that nation surrendered in 1945. The United States then tried to plan for a more peaceful postwar world.

Questions for Critical Thinking

COMPREHENSION Summarizing Main Ideas

1. Tell what role each of the following played in the war effort: (a) women; (b) labor unions; (c) farmers; (d) scientists.
2. Tell how the war affected each of these: (a) unemployment; (b) discrimination against black and other minority workers; (c) income taxes; (d) individual savings; (e) factory construction; (f) federal government power.
3. What personal qualities do you think members of the underground possessed?
4. What effect did Japan's conquests in Southeast Asia have on the prestige of whites in the area?
5. What were the differences between the war in Europe and Africa and the war in Asia? What were the similarities?

COMPREHENSION Interpreting Events

1. Why were many U.S. citizens of Japanese descent sent to relocation centers? Do you approve or disapprove of this action? Give reasons for your opinion.
2. How did the underground resistance movement help to defeat the Nazis?
3. Why did MacArthur come up with the tactic of "leapfrogging"?

4. If you had been president in 1945, would you have ordered the dropping of the atomic bomb on Japan? Give reasons for your answer. Can you think of any other way by which the power of the bomb might have been demonstrated?
5. Why do you think the Allies won World War II? What might your life be like today if we had lost?

APPLICATION Using Skills To Infer Information

For each of the following groups of statements, indicate which statement would be the most difficult to prove.

Group 1
1. Hitler's invasion of the Soviet Union was a major military blunder.
2. If Hitler had not invaded the Soviet Union, Nazi Germany would have won World War II.
3. Germany's invasion of the Soviet Union resulted in some 25,000,000 Russian casualties.
4. The Battle of Stalingrad was the most decisive battle between the Russians and the Germans.

Group 2
1. The U.S. inflation rate during World War II was about half that during World War I.
2. The federal government tried to combat inflation by price controls, rationing, and higher taxes.
3. Food prices rose more than rentals during World War II.
4. The OPA was one of the most desirable agencies established during the war.

EVALUATION Forming Generalizations

1. What is the present status of the French, British, and Dutch possessions in Southeast Asia that were conquered by Japan during World War II?
2. Which of the changes introduced by MacArthur during the American occupation of Japan are still in effect?

The Pacific Coast

At the end of World War II, millions of service veterans streamed back home, faced with the task of resuming their lives. For many this meant starting afresh, finding a new location that would provide wider employment opportunities and the hope of a richer, freer life.

Attractive Area. With its mild climate and attractive vistas of sea and mountains, California beckoned to millions across the nation. The state's booming industry and agriculture, spurred at first by the war effort, created large numbers of job openings. Before the war, in 1940, California's civilian labor force totaled 3,000,000. By 1950 the work force had soared to 4,640,000. The migration to California continued through the 1960s and 1970s, helped by the state's tolerance for innovation and eccentricity, which attracted many who felt discontented in more conservative parts of the country.

California's population rose from 6,900,000 in 1940, to 15,700,000 in 1960, to almost 23,700,000 in 1980. In the mid-1960s California passed New York to become the nation's most populous state. It also took the lead in personal income, consumer expenditures, and other indicators of economic growth.

Shaky Foundations. But was everything rosy in California? Not quite. Those moving there were at least faintly aware that life in California, as well as in Oregon and Washington, had some distinct dangers as well as advantages. The Pacific coast region was unique in the continental United States because of its frequent earthquakes and numerous volcanoes.

The memory of the devastating 1906 San Francisco earthquake had become a permanent part of American folklore. This hilly coastal city had already been shaken by damaging earthquakes in 1864, 1898, and 1900. But early in the morning of April 18, 1906, the rock masses along the nearby San Andreas fault heaved once again, dooming San Francisco as it then stood. (The fault is a long fracture in the earth's crust that stretches along the Pacific coast of California.)

When an accounting was finally made, it was discovered that four square miles with 28,000 buildings having a total value of $500,000,000 had been destroyed. Some 700 people were dead, and 250,000 were left homeless. The tragedy left a lasting mark on the look of the city as it was rebuilt. New buildings in San Francisco's business district were allowed to rise no more than 20 stories. The fear of skyscraper collapse in future quakes put a tight lid on the upward growth of the city.

An earthquake along the fault in 1933 wrecked Long Beach, California, leaving 117 dead and $1 billion in damage.

Volcanic Activity. Another example of the region's geological instability is its volcanic activity. The U.S. West Coast forms a segment of a "ring of fire"—a system of active volcanoes (60 percent of the world's total) that circles the Pacific Ocean basin from New Zealand to Japan, Alaska, California, and Chile. In recent times the West Coast's most troublesome "ring" volcanoes have been Lassen Peak, in northern California, which last erupted in 1917, and Mt. St. Helens, in the Cascade Range in southwest Washington. After intermittent eruptions between 1831 and 1857, Mt. St. Helens remained silent until May 18, 1980, when a violent eruption left 62 people dead or missing. Huge falls of volcanic ash and flooding of blocked streams did damage to the area's flourishing lumber industry estimated at more than $1 billion. The disastrous volcanic explosion had been preceded by months of tremors and warnings by earthquake experts.

Other peaks in the Cascades are also sleeping giants. Mt. Baker, in northwest Washington, began smoking in October 1975. The country around Mt. Hood, in northern Oregon, was shaken by several small quakes in 1980. Mt. Baker, Mt. Rainier, and Mt. Adams, in Washington, and Mt. Shasta, in California, have a potential for eruption, since they have been active in centuries past.

Plate Tectonics. Geologists, studying the instability of the Pacific basin, have only recently developed a theory to account for earthquakes and volcanic eruptions. The theory is called "plate tectonics." Tectonics is the branch of geology concerned with folding and cracking processes in the Earth's crust. The theory has been hailed as "the all-time breakthrough in geology."

According to plate tectonics, the Earth's crust (the thin surface layer of the Earth about 5 to 30 miles deep containing all the mountains, valleys, plains, and ocean basins) consists of giant interlocking parts known as "plates." The plates fit together like the pieces of a jigsaw puzzle. They float on a hot sea of molten material called the "asthenosphere" (as-*then*-oh-sphere). Below this molten sea is the Earth's mantle of hot rock 1800 miles deep. The mantle in turn is wrapped around the Earth's dense, metallic core, whose diameter is about 4000 miles.

Earthquakes occur most frequently at the boundaries, or faults, marking the meeting of

Tectonic Plates

two plates. As the plates move side by side in opposite directions—either vertically or horizontally as at the San Andreas fault—they sometimes hook together. The stress created between the two plates builds up, and when it becomes too great the plates snap violently apart. Energy is released in shock waves that cause the Earth's surface to tremble or "quake."

As can be seen from the map, three of the plates intersect along the West Coast of the United States, producing conditions for a geologic disturbance.

The motion of the Pacific plate against the North American plate has caused the most serious recent upheavals. Some geologists warn that increasing stresses in the region will produce another disastrous earthquake before the end of the century.

According to the theory of plate tectonics, the motion of surface plates also accounts for outbreaks of volcanic activity.

Calm Acceptance. Oddly enough, the potential for natural disaster has not inspired a hurried exodus from the West Coast. On the contrary, California and the Pacific Northwest continue to lure many thousands of migrants from other parts of the United States.

Even in San Francisco, a spurt of high-rise construction has been "Manhattanizing" the city. Ignoring the traditional 20-story limit on skyscrapers in the earthquake zones, one building is 52 stories tall. Another is 48 stories but has a pyramidal shape and was planned to provide stability in case of a quake.

Critics accuse West Coast residents of flirting with disaster. But others point to the vibrant business and cultural life as evidence of the optimism and courage of West Coast residents.

Understanding Geography

1. Why are there so many earthquakes and volcanoes on the Pacific coast?

2. What is the study of "plate tectonics"?

3. What is the asthenosphere?

677

An Uneasy Peace

1945–1950

People in the Chapter

Harry S Truman—*the president who has the task of succeeding FDR but surprises critics by guiding the nation firmly through the difficult postwar period.*

Jackie Robinson—*the player who first breaks the color line on a major league baseball team.*

General George Marshall—*the secretary of state whose Marshall Plan to aid war-torn Europe is called one of the most generous international acts ever made.*

Senator Joseph R. McCarthy—*a senator from Wisconsin who, preying on people's legitimate concerns about communism, creates a climate of hysteria and witch hunting never before seen in the United States.*

Linking Past to Present

Harry S Truman led the United States out of World War II and into the first years of peace. It was a difficult journey. Many things that Americans wanted in the early postwar years were impossible to achieve, or contradictory, or both. For example, people wanted the armed forces to be instantly demobilized but they did not want the nation to lose its military power. They wanted government to remove wartime economic restrictions but they did not want inflation. Finally, everyone wanted continued prosperity, yet many hoped to see labor stripped of its wartime gains.

In domestic affairs Truman announced his Fair Deal, which continued many of FDR's New Deal social programs. Truman also achieved great advances in civil rights legislation. But in foreign affairs the situation was less satisfactory.

The old wartime alliance of Britain, the United States and the Soviet Union began breaking up. Now that fascism and Nazism had been defeated in Europe, there was little to hold the Western democracies and the Soviet Union together. Theirs had only been a friendship of convenience. Now the two super powers, the Soviet Union and the United States, faced each other over the ruins of a divided Germany. The Soviet Union was determined to surround itself with Communist nations that it could control. The United States was determined to hinder the USSR's efforts to extend its influence beyond its borders.

1 A NEW LEADER FACES DOMESTIC PROBLEMS

VOCABULARY *demobilized   G.I. Bill of Rights*

Harry S Truman learned that he had become the thirty-third president of the United States from his predecessor's widow. When he asked Eleanor Roosevelt if there was anything he could do for her, she replied, "Is there anything *we* can do for *you?* You are the one in trouble now."

Truman's Background

And in fact, Truman was in many ways unprepared for the responsibilities of national and world leadership. For example, in the eighty-two days that FDR and Truman shared the highest offices in the land, they had been alone together only twice. Truman had not been briefed on military matters or on the continuing peace negotiations. He was completely unaware that the atomic bomb existed.

He was also very different personally from Roosevelt, which made it difficult for some people to accept him. He was neither tall nor handsome, and he spoke not with an upper-class accent cultivated at Harvard but with the twang of Missouri. Except for Cleveland, Truman was the only president since Lincoln who did not attend college. He had failed in business, a Kansas City men's clothing store. However, instead of declaring bankruptcy, he spent the next fifteen years paying off his debts. He was direct and down-to-earth and what many people would call "square." He also had self-confidence, combined with a sense of proportion and an awareness of the pitfalls of power. His mind was quick and his memory was good; he never had to be told the same thing twice. And he had the ability to make difficult decisions, such as whether or not to drop the atomic bomb, and to accept full responsibility for them. As the plaque on his White House desk read, "The Buck Stops Here."

Returning to Civilian Life

In the last months of 1945, most Americans seemed to have a single objective. It was to "bring the boys home"—to take apart, as quickly as possible, the military machine put together during the war.

The Point System. In order to choose who would be *demobilized* (released from service) first, a point system was established. It gave credit for time in the service, combat duty, decorations for bravery, and injuries caused by enemy action. There were also special provisions for fathers and for WACS whose husbands were being discharged. Those with the highest number of points came home first.

The new first family. President and Mrs. Truman and their daughter Margaret.

679

The pace of demobilization was breakneck. On one day, almost 32,000 soldiers clambered off transports in New York City. More than 125,000 veterans were flown across the Atlantic during one three-day period. In December 1945 over a million were released from the army, and half a million from the navy. When the army announced in January that there would be a slowdown in the rate of discharge, there were protest demonstrations by troops in Japan, the Philippines, and Germany.

By the summer of 1946 about 12 million servicemen and women had been released from the armed forces. The army was down to 1.5 million and the navy to 980,000. That was just enough to perform occupation duties and meet minimum security requirements.

Reorganizing the Military. The following year, Truman reorganized the military. The three services—army, navy, and air force—were combined into one under a secretary of defense. The National Security Council was established to coordinate the country's defense policies. Under the council was the Central Intelligence Agency (CIA), which was to gather intelligence abroad. Two years later, in 1949, the CIA received special powers so that it could operate with greater secrecy. Money can be spent in almost any way the CIA director wishes. No one—except the director and a few others—knows how big the agency's staff is.

The G.I. Bill. To express the nation's gratitude and to ease the return to civilian life for those whose schooling and careers had been interrupted, Congress in 1944 passed the Servicemen's Readjustment Act, commonly called the G.I. Bill of Rights. (The initials "G.I." stand for "government issue," and American soldiers had been known as G.I.s during the war.) Under the G.I. Bill, veterans attending college or technical school had their tuition paid and received a small monthly income as well. Between 1944 and 1956, more than 7.8 million veterans took advantage of these educational provisions. Many went to study the war they had just endured in hopes of preventing another.

The G.I. Bill also provided that the federal government would guarantee loans to veterans for buying homes and farms and for establishing businesses. Because the guarantee assured banks and other lenders that they would not lose their investments, billions of dollars in mortgage money were made available at low interest with small down payments. Home or farm ownership became possible for millions of young families that might otherwise never have been able to afford it. The G.I. Bill also provided for one year's unemployment payments and for treatment at veterans' hospitals.

Economic Ups and Downs

Most economists foresaw a postwar depression. After all, war industries would close down. What would companies do with their plants and equipment? Also, there were millions of veterans and war workers who would be seeking jobs. Where would they find them?

Financier Bernard Baruch, however, took a different view. In April 1945 he said, "No matter what is done or not done for five or seven years after the war ceases, there'll be more work in the U.S. than there will be minds or hands with which to do it."

Boom Times. Baruch was right. The economists who foresaw bad times failed to consider the backlog of consumer needs and wants. People had done without during the depression and the years of wartime shortages. Now, with more than $135 billion in savings from defense work, service pay, and war bond investments, they could and would pay for consumer goods.

Americans began buying. Automobiles and appliances were snapped up as fast as they appeared. Houses and apartment buildings could not be constructed fast enough. Spot shortages occurred in men's suits, beef, and nylon stockings.

The results of the shopping spree showed up quickly in employment and production, both of which rose. Unfortunately, prices rose as well. Wartime price controls ended June 30, 1946. In the next two weeks, prices soared 25 percent, or double the increase of the previous three years. They continued to rise for the next two years until the supply of goods caught up with the demand.

Labor Is Restless. At the same time prices were climbing, many workers found themselves earning less. Gone were the high-paying war jobs. Gone too was the weekly overtime. Workers began striking for higher wages in the automobile, electrical, lumber, oil, and textile industries.

Peace brought unexpected changes—in fashion. After World War I women's skirts got shorter. After World War II the "New Look" had them going lower.

By spring 1946, newspapers were sounding alarms about "labor's rebellion." In January there was a strike of 750,000 steelworkers that lasted eighty days. No sooner had they returned to their jobs than 400,000 soft coal miners left their pits on April 1. Eighteen days later, two railroad brotherhoods, the engineers and the trainmen, announced that *they* would go out on strike in thirty days.

Truman was generally a strong supporter of organized labor. But the walkout by the railroad unions threatened to stop all rail traffic throughout the nation. So on May 17, the president seized the railroads under his wartime powers. Two days later, he appeared before a special session of Congress and began to deliver a speech asking for authority to draft the striking workers into the army. Before he could finish the speech, the brotherhoods gave in.

A few days earlier, Truman also seized the coal mines. Federal authorities then worked out a contract, which the mine owners refused to accept. So the government continued to operate the mines.

In October, following unofficial word from John L. Lewis that the men should observe the policy of "No contract, no work," the miners struck against the government. The following month Lewis and the UMW were fined $3.5 million, the largest fine in labor history. Truman then announced that he would broadcast a direct appeal to the striking miners to save their country and return to work. Lewis ordered his men back to their mines.

The Taft-Hartley Act. The 4.6 million workers who went out on strike in 1946 set a record. There were strikes in the soft coal mines and on the railroads. The public became frightened. It felt that "labor tsars" like Lewis were abusing their power, and that the booming economy would be seriously hurt unless organized labor was curbed.

In the 1946 election the Republican party gained control of both the Senate and the House of Representatives for the first time since 1930. The Eightieth Congress then passed a new labor law, the Taft-Hartley Act, over Truman's veto. The law prohibited the closed shop, which requires that a person be a union member before being hired. It abolished the checkoff system by which employers collect union dues. Union officials had to take a loyalty oath, swearing they were not Communists. Union funds could not be used in political campaigns. (This provision was later declared unconstitutional.) And finally, if a strike threatened the nation's health or safety, the president could obtain an injunction delaying the strike for an eighty-day "cooling off" period.

Labor leaders were furious. They felt the loyalty oath was an insult, and they called the act a "slave-labor law." But most people apparently disagreed. Despite Taft-Hartley, though, union membership climbed from 14.6 million in 1945 to 17 million in 1952.

Other Economic Legislation. Earlier in the Truman administration, Congress passed two other important laws. One was the Employment Act of 1946. For the first time, the federal government committed itself to promoting "maximum employment, production, and purchasing power." Americans could now expect the government to act early and vigorously to counter a depression. The act also established the three-member Council of Economic Advisors. Its job is to analyze economic trends and recommend programs to the president.

The second law, also passed in 1946, created the five-member Atomic Energy Commission. The AEC was authorized to promote research into the peaceful uses of atomic energy and to develop facilities for producing it.

The act passed only after considerable controversy over who should control atomic energy, the military or civilians. Congress's final decision was for civilian control. The first head of the AEC was David E. Lilienthal, who had previously won approval as head of the TVA from 1941 to 1946.

Section 1 Review

COMPREHENSION   Developing Vocabulary

1. Explain these terms: demobilized, G. I., closed shop, point system.

COMPREHENSION   Mastering Facts

1. What was the purpose of the Central Intelligence Agency?
2. What benefits did G.I.s receive under the G.I. Bill?
3. What factors led to the postwar boom?
4. Why were there so many strikes after World War II?

2   TRUMAN INITIATES A PERIOD OF CHANGE

VOCABULARY   *Dixiecrats*

Truman's first three years in office were difficult. Inflation, labor strife, Soviet stubbornness in Europe—all were blamed on the man in the White House. The president's own party considered him a liability and wished it had someone else. But in 1948 it nominated him anyway, with Senator Alben W. Barkley of Kentucky for vice-president.

The Great Upset

Truman's difficulties, however, did not end with the nomination. He insisted on a strong civil-rights plank in the Democratic party platform. This caused southern delegates at the national

Another media mistake. A victorious Truman kids those who wrote him off as a loser.

convention, the so-called Dixiecrats, to withdraw. Instead, they formed the States' Rights Democratic party and ran their own candidate, Governor J. Strom Thurmond of South Carolina. At the other extreme, former Vice President Henry A. Wallace led supporters into a new Progressive party. Wallace disapproved of Truman's "get tough with Russia" policy, about which you will read later in this chapter.

The Republican candidate, Governor Thomas E. Dewey of New York, was an able administrator. All the opinion polls gave him a comfortable lead. And as election day approached, newspapers and magazine articles pointed to a Dewey victory.

But Republicans, pollsters, and writers alike overlooked one thing. That was Truman's fighting spirit. He had filled out Roosevelt's fourth term, and now he was determined to be elected on his own. He knew he could do it.

First, Truman called the Republican-dominated Congress back into session. He asked it to pass laws supporting planks in the Republican party platform such as an end to inflation, more housing, aid to education, a higher minimum wage, civil rights, and extended Social Security coverage. But Congress did not pass any of these requests.

Truman then took his campaign to the people. He traveled from one end of the country to the other in a railroad train, speaking from the rear platform. Day after day he spoke to crowds that numbered up to 250,000. The president denounced "the do-nothing, good-for-nothing Eightieth Congress." As he later commented, "I met the people face to face, and I convinced them, and they voted for me."

Presidential Election of 1948

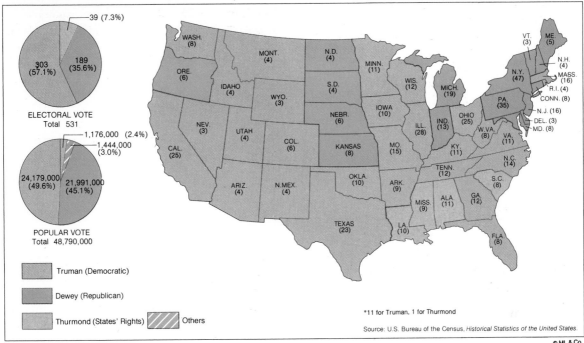

ELECTORAL VOTE
Total 531

303 (57.1%)
189 (35.6%)
39 (7.3%)

POPULAR VOTE
Total 48,790,000

24,179,000 (49.6%)
21,991,000 (45.1%)
1,176,000 (2.4%)
1,444,000 (3.0%)

Truman (Democratic)

Dewey (Republican)

Thurmond (States' Rights) / Others

*11 for Truman, 1 for Thurmond

Source: U.S. Bureau of the Census, *Historical Statistics of the United States.*

© ML & Co.

Map Skills *Which candidate won the election? What was his victory margin in the electoral vote? in the popular vote? In which part of the country were the states won by Thurmond?*

It was the greatest upset in the nation's political history. The morning after the election, the *Chicago Daily Tribune,* for example, was out on the streets with its early edition. The headline screamed: DEWEY DEFEATS TRUMAN. In actuality, the Democrats won by 24 million votes to 22 million for the Republicans. Wallace and Thurmond each got a million votes. In the electoral college Truman had 303 votes; Dewey, 189; and Thurmond, 39. The Democrats won without the Solid South, which they had carried since Reconstruction days. The Republicans even lost control of Congress.

Why, apart from Truman's "give 'em hell" campaign, did the Republicans lose? In part, it was the result of overconfidence. Dewey's belief in victory added a touch of arrogance to a manner which many felt was already cold and distant. His speeches were thin. He talked in generalities, as one historian described it, "for unity, cleanliness, better water, and faith." Truman dealt with what he felt were the specific economic and social issues that concerned the people. In addition, labor, despite its arguments with Truman, felt that Dewey would pay much less attention to its concerns.

And farmers, who often vote Republican when times are good, saw the bad crop figures for the 1948 growing season and went Democratic.

THE "FAIR DEAL"

Theodore Roosevelt had his Square Deal, and Franklin D. Roosevelt had his New Deal. Following his victory, Truman began pushing for what he called a "Fair Deal" for the American people. It was an extension of the New Deal—only stronger.

Truman proposed a steady income for farmers instead of price supports, and a nationwide system of compulsory health insurance. Southern and some northern Democrats combined with Republicans in Congress to defeat both measures. Truman's other proposals, however, did win congressional approval. They included: (1) an increase in the minimum wage from 40 to 75 cents an hour; (2) extension of Social Security coverage to almost 10 million more people; (3) more flood control and irrigation projects; and (4) financial help to cities for slum clearance and the construction of 810,000 housing units for low-income families.

683

Advances in Civil Rights

Someone asked J. Strom Thurmond why he had broken with the Democrats on civil rights. "After all," said the questioner, "FDR used to run on almost the same promises." "That's right," said Thurmond, "but Truman really means it." It was an exaggeration, but it showed Truman's determination to apply the Bill of Rights to everyone.

"To Secure These Rights." As early as 1945, Truman asked black leaders what they regarded as their top priorities. The first was a federal anti-lynching law that would make prosecution of lynching a federal rather than a state concern. Authorities in certain states sometimes "looked the other way" when mobs took violent action against blacks accused of serious crimes. The second priority was for abolition of the poll tax as a voting requirement. As explained in chapter 17, it was not the amount of the poll tax that concerned blacks, but the selective manner in which it was collected. The third priority was for a permanent Fair Employment Practice Commission to replace the wartime FEPC that was due to expire in 1946.

Congress did not pass any of these measures. So in 1946 Truman appointed a biracial Committee on Civil Rights to investigate the situation and report to the nation. Writing about it later, the president said:

❝ I took this action because of the repeated anti-minority incidents after the war in which homes were invaded, property was destroyed, and a number of innocent lives were taken. I wanted to get the facts behind these incidents of disregard for individual and group rights which were reported in the news with alarming regularity, and to see that the law was strengthened, if necessary, so as to offer adequate protection and fair treatment to all of our citizens. ❞

The report of the committee, which was issued in 1947, was called "To Secure These Rights." In addition to the antilynching, poll tax, and FEPC measures, it recommended that a permanent civil rights commission be established and that federal legislation be passed to eliminate discrimination in voting. In February 1948 Truman sent these recommendations to Congress, but they were not acted on. They were declared to be an interference with states' rights.

In July 1948, Truman issued an executive order calling for "equality of treatment and opportunity" for members of the armed forces "without re-

Jackie Robinson of the Dodgers. The famous player gets ready to hit the ball.

gard to race, color, religion, or national origin." The order was issued despite the opposition of almost every general and admiral. As matters turned out, the shift to full integration of the services went more smoothly than anyone had hoped. Truman also established the Fair Employment Board in the Civil Service Commission.

A Turning Point. Although Truman's civil rights program did not pass Congress, the year 1948 was in some ways a turning point in the struggle for racial equality. For one thing, blacks themselves became more active in the civil rights movement. Second, Truman showed that it was possible to take a strong civil rights stand, lose some southern support, and still get elected. Third, the federal government moved to assume an active role in race relations.

Jackie Robinson. One sign of change that should not be overlooked took place in major league baseball. The "color line" there was broken in 1947 when Jackie Robinson signed a contract to play for Branch Rickey's Brooklyn (later, Los Angeles) Dodgers. Until then, black baseball players, no matter how talented, were allowed to play only in all-black leagues. Rickey, however, believed the time had come for a change and, after much searching, chose Robinson to be the pioneer.

At first there was resistance to Robinson. Unhappy baseball fans shouted insults from the stands, and some threw bottles and other objects onto the playing field. Several of Robinson's teammates refused to eat or socialize with him. But his skill and personality soon impressed colleagues and public alike. In 1949 the spectacular Robinson was voted the most valuable player in the National League.

Other teams soon followed the example of the Dodgers and began signing black players. Robinson remained with the Dodgers for his entire career, until 1956. In 1962 he became the first black to be elected to the Baseball Hall of Fame.

Section 2 Review

COMPREHENSION   Developing Vocabulary

1.   Explain these terms: Dixiecrats, color line.

COMPREHENSION   Mastering Facts

1.   What two new parties were organized in 1948?
2.   What was the basis for Truman's campaign?
3.   What did Truman's Fair Deal provide?
4.   What were the three major recommendations of Truman's civil rights committee?

3   A FORMER ALLY BECOMES AN ENEMY

VOCABULARY   *Dardanelles   Truman Doctrine*

When Averell Harriman, United States ambassador to Moscow, learned of Roosevelt's death, he rushed home to warn the new president about Stalin. He feared that Truman might be taken in, as he thought FDR had been, by the wily Soviet leader. A few minutes of conversation with the new chief executive reassured Harriman. Truman, like the ambassador, considered Stalin a slippery character and believed the best way to handle the Soviet Union was to take a blunt, hard line.

The Soviet Union Dominates Eastern Europe

For the first time in history, the Soviet Union was now a power as far west as the Elbe River. And no one believed that Soviet troops would retreat back into the Soviet Union anytime soon.

The great wartime alliance of the United States, the Soviet Union, and Britain had been based on a common enemy—Adolf Hitler. Since Hitler no longer existed, what would be its new foundation? High hopes were held for the new international organization, the United Nations, but it was an untried group. And would the Soviets put their faith in a body in which they were outvoted by capitalist countries?

To the West, the USSR was a state dedicated to "world revolution" and to establishing a worldwide communist regime. But the Soviet Union in 1945 was so drained by its war effort, not to mention the years of Stalinist terror, that it had another, more pressing desire. It had to guard its own security. Without oceans or mountains to protect it from invasion and with vast open borderlands to their west, Russian leaders wanted none but friendly countries as neighbors. To the Soviets, that meant Communist countries whose governments they controlled.

The United States and Great Britain were insistent on free, open elections in Poland and other Eastern European nations. To the Soviets, this attitude was both puzzling and infuriating. "After all," the Russians seemed to be saying, "you have the whole Western Hemisphere. We are giving you a free hand in Italy and even with our old enemy Japan. Why do you begrudge us Eastern Europe?"

This deep disagreement surfaced again at a meeting of foreign ministers in London during September 1945. Despite the pleas of the British, Americans, and French, and despite the fact that the United States had the atomic bomb, the Soviet minister V. M. Molotov would not budge. He would not allow any kind of free elections in Eastern Europe. With the Red Army occupying the area, nothing could be done. The meeting ended in complete failure. A year later a Paris peace conference confirmed the West's helplessness. Settlements were made with Russia's neighbors on terms satisfactory to the Soviets.

In March of 1946 Winston Churchill, who was

no longer British prime minister, delivered a speech at Fulton, Missouri, that graphically described the situation in Europe. "A shadow has fallen," he said, "upon the scene so lately lighted by the Allied victory. . . . An iron curtain has descended across the Continent. Behind that line lie all the capitals of the ancient states of Central and Eastern Europe."

Early Squabbles

Differences between the United States and Great Britain on the one hand, and the Soviet Union on the other hand, showed themselves in several other ways during 1946.

No Atomic Inspection. The United States had taken the lead in establishing the Atomic Energy Commission in the United Nations. The American representative on the commission was Bernard Baruch. What came to be known as the Baruch Plan called for the setting up of the International Atomic Development Authority. The United States, Britain, and Canada would give this UN body their atomic weapons and their nuclear secrets. In return, all nations would permit UN inspection of their atomic facilities to insure that they were being used only for peaceful purposes and not to manufacture atomic bombs.

The Soviets found the inspection feature totally unacceptable. They made a proposal of their own that nations having weapons destroy them and promise never to make or use any others. However, there would be no inspection of any kind to see who might be cheating.

When the UN Security Council voted on the two proposals, the Baruch Plan was favored by all members except the Soviet Union and Poland. The Soviet vote meant it was vetoed.

Differences over Iran. Russian and Anglo-American troops had moved into Iran in 1941 to prevent Germany from capturing that nation's oil fields. At the Teheran conference in 1943, the three occupying powers agreed to withdraw these troops within six months after Germany's defeat.

In 1944 the Communist-dominated Tudeh party led a revolt in Iran's northernmost province, which adjoins the Soviet border. It succeeded in establishing two puppet states there. In 1946, when the Soviet Union did not withdraw its troops from the rest of the nation as it had promised, Iran protested to the UN. Truman then sent Stalin a stiff note asking him to live up to his agreement. A few months later, Stalin did so, but only after Iran promised to let the Soviet Union take part in developing Iran's oil fields. With help from the United States, the Iranian government then reestablished its control in the north. In 1947 it turned down the proposed Iranian-Soviet oil company.

Differences over Turkey. One of Russia's goals for several hundred years has been a seaport on the Mediterranean. Stalin asked for control of the Dardanelles, the Turkish straits that lead out from the Black Sea, after the war. The United States and Britain refused. But the Soviet Union kept pressuring Turkey for bases in the area. So in 1946 Truman sent a naval task force into the eastern Mediterranean.

The prospect of Soviet dominance in the Near East and the Mediterranean raised disturbing possibilities. If the USSR could bring Iran, Turkey, and Greece under its influence, much of the Muslim world would be threatened.

Truman was determined to stop Soviet influence in that area. As he wrote to his secretary of state in January of 1946, "Unless Russia is faced with an iron fist and strong language, another war is in the making. . . . I'm tired of babying the Soviets."

The Truman Doctrine

On February 4, 1947, Great Britain told the United States it could no longer afford to give economic help to Turkey. It also said it could no longer help the Greek monarchy, which was trying to put down a revolt by Communist-led guerrillas. As one historian said, "Rarely in history had there been so dramatic a moment when one nation turned over the responsibilities of empire to another."

The next month Truman went before Congress and asked for $400 million in economic and military aid for the two Eastern European nations. In his speech, the president said, "I believe that it must be the policy of the United States to support free peoples who are resisting attempted subjugation (conquest) by armed minorities or by outside pressures." This statement later became known as the Truman Doctrine.

The Truman Doctrine aroused considerable controversy. Some people felt it meant interfering in the internal affairs of other nations. Some people felt Truman should have tried to work through the U.N. Henry A. Wallace argued that "getting tough never brought anything real or lasting—whether from schoolyard bullies or world powers." He favored trying to improve American-Soviet relations. Political theorist Walter Lippmann believed the United States was trying to do too much. He was afraid America's power would be spread too thin if it tried to help free peoples everywhere. And some people were opposed to helping dictatorial governments even if they were against communism.

Congress, however, decided it was essential to keep Soviet influence from spreading in Europe. Aid for Turkey and Greece was approved. And between 1947 and 1950, about $660 million was sent. The Communist danger there was reduced.

The Marshall Plan

In the meantime, an even more dangerous situation had developed in Western Europe. The nations there were in economic chaos as a result of the war. Most of their factories had either been looted by the Germans or bombed to the ground by the Allies. And in any event, there were no raw materials or power. As a result, millions of Europeans could not find work, and many turned to black marketeering and theft in order to survive. Additional millions of people, who had either been uprooted by the Nazis or had fled before the advancing Russians, were living in refugee camps while European governments tried to figure out where they could go.

A Bitter Winter. On top of everything else, in January 1947 the continent was hit by the bitterest winter in several centuries. Temperatures remained below zero while snow piled up in record-breaking amounts. Crops were severely damaged, and a fuel shortage developed when all the rivers froze, cutting off water transportation. In England, things were so bad that electricity was limited to a few hours each morning, while food rations were lower than during the war. Former President Herbert Hoover, whom Truman sent to visit twenty-two countries and report on conditions, said that many people, especially children, were on the brink of starvation.

All this probably suited the Soviet Union just fine. Communists believe that when people become hungry enough, miserable enough, and angry enough, they will turn to communism. And indeed, the Communist party in many European nations was growing.

An Important Speech. In June 1947 General George Marshall, who was now secretary of state, delivered a historic speech at the Harvard College commencement exercises. He offered U.S. aid to all European nations that needed it, saying that this move was directed "not against any country or doctrine but against hunger, poverty, desperation, and chaos." However, the nations receiving aid had to agree to remove trade barriers and otherwise cooperate economically with one another.

Sixteen Western European nations applied for aid. The Soviet Union, which had been included in Marshall's offer, refused. Taking part would have meant revealing information about its economy to the West. Not only that, it would mean helping capitalist nations grow strong. Both ideas were completely unacceptable to the Soviets. So, the Soviet Union denounced the plan as an "imperialist plot" by the U.S. to dominate Europe.

The Policy of "X." The Soviets were even more annoyed by the appearance of an article in the influential magazine *Foreign Affairs.* It was signed "X," but everyone soon knew that the author was George F. Kennan, one of the State Department's experts on the Soviet Union.

Kennan called the policy of the USSR "a fluid stream which moves constantly, where it is permitted to move toward a given goal [namely, the establishment of communism everywhere in the world].... But if it finds ... barriers in its path it ... accommodates itself to them." The right answer to Soviet challenges, Kennan said, was "containment." By this he did not mean all-out war or a totally military response. Rather, he called for steady pressure to contain the Russians, to keep them from expanding their power. This would either cause the Soviet leaders to modify their goals, or would lead to such strains within the USSR and its satellites that communism would eventually weaken.

To the USSR, Kennan's words made the Marshall Plan look even more like a power grab for control of all Europe. The United States viewed Soviet rejection of the plan as a clear sign of hostility.

Jan Masaryk (left) in happier days with
Czechoslovakia's president Eduard Benes.

Results of the Plan. Congress debated the
Marshall Plan for several months. It was expensive,
about $12.5 billion, and there was opposition from
people who felt the United States could not afford
it. They thought of further aid to the Old World
as "Operation Rathole." Then in February 1948,
Soviet tanks rumbled into Czechoslovakia and
took over the country, which had a sizable Communist minority. The takeover was followed by a
purge in which many democrats disappeared or
died, including foreign minister Jan Masaryk, son
of the nation's founder, who reportedly fell to his
death from his office window. Congress promptly
approved the plan.

The Marshall Plan was a great success both politically and economically. Communism in Western Europe declined. Malnutrition declined,
people were warmly dressed in winter. The industrial life of Germany improved rapidly. By 1952
Western Europe was flourishing.

The Question of Germany

Another major issue between East and West
was the question of German reunification. The Soviet Union, whose land had been invaded and devastated by German armies twice in thirty years,
wanted Germany to remain weak and divided.
The United States, Great Britain, and France disagreed. They believed Europe would be more
stable if German industry were producing and if
the German people were not agitating all the time
for unity. In 1948 they met to discuss combining
the three western zones. The Russians reacted by
interfering with traffic between the western zones
and Berlin. They stopped trains and trucks with all
sorts of excuses, closed bridges for "repairs," and
generally made life difficult.

The Berlin Blockade. Then a currency dispute
arose. The Russians had been flooding West Berlin with paper money and causing a severe inflation. So the western authorities issued new
money. Thereupon the Russians, angry because
the West marks were worth more than the East
marks, cut off all surface traffic into the city.

West Berlin's 2.1 million inhabitants had food
for only thirty-six days and coal for forty-five.
American and British officials gambled on an airlift, using every transport and cargo plane their
two air forces could make available. For 327 days
planes took off and landed every few minutes
around the clock. In 277,000 flights they brought
in 2.5 million tons of supplies—everything from
food, fuel, and medicine to Christmas presents
that the planes' crew members bought with their
own money. By May 1949 the Russians realized
they were beaten and lifted the blockade.

The Division of Germany. That same month,
voters in the three western zones of Germany approved a constitution. By fall the Federal Republic of Germany, commonly called West Germany,
was established, with its capital in Bonn. The Soviet Union thereupon turned *its* zone into the
German Democratic Republic, commonly called
East Germany, with its capital in East Berlin.

NATO Is Formed

The Soviet advance into Czechoslovakia not
only led to American approval of the Marshall
Plan. It also led to the formation of a defensive
union called the North Atlantic Treaty Organization (NATO). Members at first included Belgium,
Canada, Denmark, France, Great Britain, Iceland,
Italy, Luxembourg, the Netherlands, Norway, Portugal, and the United States. In 1951 Greece and
Turkey joined, and in 1955 West Germany, which
had been allowed to rearm, was admitted, making
a total of fifteen. All the countries promised that
an attack on one would be regarded as an attack
on all. They also promised to resist such an attack
by armed force, if they thought it necessary.

When West Germany became a NATO member, the Soviet Union formed its own defensive
union. Called the Warsaw Pact, the organization
included that nation's Eastern European satel-

Europe After World War II

Map Skills *Which nations belong to NATO? to the Warsaw Pact? Compare this map with the one on page 555. What nation became divided into East and West?*

lites—Albania, Bulgaria, Czechoslovakia, East Germany, Hungary, Poland, and Rumania.

On September 23, 1949, Americans heard some startling and depressing news. "We have evidence," Truman said, "[that] an atomic explosion occurred in the USSR." The forties were ending and with them the security the United States had enjoyed, first from its ocean frontiers and then from its nuclear weapons. The shock drove some Americans into behavior they had not exhibited since the end of World War I.

Section 3 Review

COMPREHENSION **Developing Vocabulary**

1. Explain these terms: Dardanelles, containment, iron curtain, subjugation, NATO.

COMPREHENSION **Mastering Facts**

1. What kind of countries did the Soviet Union want as neighbors?
2. Why did the Soviet Union reject the Baruch Plan for controlling atomic energy?
3. What was the purpose of the Truman Doctrine?
4. What was the purpose of the Marshall Plan?

THE NATION SEEKS INTERNAL SECURITY

VOCABULARY   *perjury* *espionage*

Communism has never been popular in the United States. Its political and economic principles stand in sharp contrast to the beliefs of almost all Americans. During World War II, however, anticommunist feelings took a back seat to admiration for Russia's fight against Hitler. Then the war ended, and it again became clear that the two superpowers held very different views about what the world should be like. As the Soviet Union expanded into Eastern Europe, Americans became increasingly concerned about the possibility of Communist subversion within their own country.

Loyalty Checks

In September 1945, Igor Gouzenko, a Russian clerk at the Soviet embassy in Ottawa, Canada, *defected* (deserted) and sought political asylum. He brought with him a stack of documents that he turned over to the Canadian government. Investigation revealed that a few Canadian government workers had been giving secret information about the atomic bomb to the USSR.

By executive order President Truman set up the Loyalty Review Board to make sure no similar situation existed within the United States government. The Attorney General drew up a list of 90 or so "subversive" (treasonable) organizations, membership in which was grounds for suspicion. From 1947 to 1951, 3.2 million government employees were investigated. Of these, 212 were dismissed as security risks. Another 2900 resigned, some because they did not want to be investigated, others because they felt the investigation violated constitutional rights. Individuals being investigated were usually not allowed to see the evidence against them. Nor were they usually allowed to cross-examine or even know who had accused them of disloyalty.

Congress, however, felt Truman's action was not enough. In 1950 it passed the McCarran Internal Security Act. This measure made it unlawful to plan any action that might lead to the establishment of a totalitarian dictatorship in the United States. Communist and "Communist-front" organizations (organizations that were not Communist themselves but were either backed by Communist groups or had Communist officers) were required to register with the Attorney General. The act forbade the hiring of Communists in private employment related to national defense.

The act also sought to keep out of the United States anyone who had been a member of any Communist or Fascist organization. The last provision was seen to be hard on those who as children had belonged to some Communist or Fascist children's organization or who had been forced to join the Communist party to keep a job. A later amendment sought to correct this injustice.

President Truman saw far greater injustices in the McCarran Act and vetoed it saying, "In a free country, we punish men for crimes they commit, but never for the opinions they hold." Congress repassed the measure over Truman's veto.

Spy Cases

One reason for Congress's attitude can be found in several spy cases that were going on at the time.

The Alger Hiss Case. In 1948 Whittaker Chambers, an editor for Time, the weekly newsmagazine, told the Un-American Activities Committee of the House of Representatives (HUAC) that he had been a Communist during the 1930s. Furthermore, he said he had passed on secret documents to the Communist party. He then named as a fellow spy, Alger Hiss.

The accusation seemed absurd. Hiss had been among the bright young men who came to Washington to work for the New Deal. Hiss's denial of any previous contact with Chambers was immediate and public. It was easy to believe Hiss. He was neat, slim, well-dressed, and charming. Chambers was fat, his clothes were usually rumpled, and he often had a dogged and unpleasant manner. In addition, he had been expelled from Columbia University and had been a thief. Hiss remained in government, rising to ever higher positions until 1947. That year he resigned from the State Department to become president of the Carnegie Endowment for International Peace.

Most members of HUAC were willing to let the matter drop. Congressman Richard M. Nixon of California, however, insisted on pursuing the investigation. Chambers then produced *classified*, or

Whittaker Chambers (right) takes the stand before the House Un-American Activities Committee and accuses Alger Hiss (circle) of being a Communist in the 1930s.

secret, State Department documents which he had kept in a hollowed-out pumpkin in his garden. These were shown to have been copied in Hiss's handwriting and on his typewriter. Hiss was eventually convicted for *perjury* (lying) and sent to jail.

The case was a sensation and troubled people deeply. If Hiss was guilty, they thought, then anyone might be.

The Rosenberg Case. Julius and Ethel Rosenberg were minor activists in the Communist party in New York City. In 1950 they were arrested shortly after British physicist Klaus Fuchs admitted giving the Soviet Union information about America's atomic bomb. The information he gave probably enabled Russian scientists to develop their own atomic bomb eighteen months sooner than they would otherwise have done.

Evidence against the Rosenbergs came from Ethel Rosenberg's brother. He had been an army sergeant at Los Alamos and claimed to have passed atomic secrets through the Rosenbergs to the Soviets. The Rosenbergs were convicted of wartime *espionage* (spying). They died in the electric chair in 1953.

McCarthyism

The public figure who received the most personal publicity out of anticommunism in the late 1940s and early 1950s was Senator Joseph R. McCarthy of Wisconsin. He had been a small-town lawyer and judge until World War II, when he served as an intelligence officer with a marine air unit in the Pacific. After the war he entered politics, and on the strength of a war record (which he exaggerated) won the Republican senatorial nomination. Then he won the election.

In 1950, facing reelection, McCarthy looked about for an issue and hit on anticommunism. At various times he claimed to know the names of either 57 or 81 or 205 Communists in the State Department. A Senate committee that investigated his claims could not find any evidence to support them. McCarthy also charged that the Democratic party had been guilty of "twenty years of treason." During the period under Roosevelt and Truman, McCarthy said, American interests had been sacrificed to the interests of the Soviet Union. A Senate committee declared the charges "a fraud and a hoax."

691

Senator Joseph McCarthy makes one of his many
unfounded accusations about communists and traitors.

Only in the atmosphere of the Hiss and Rosenberg cases and the growing tension between the United States and the Soviet Union would most people have paid attention to McCarthy. As it was, he went about the country conducting hearings, badgering witnesses, and terrifying politicians. He made one reckless accusation after another, even questioning the loyalty of Secretary of Defense General George Marshall, who he said "would sell his grandmother for any advantage."

McCarthy's technique was never to explain a charge he made or offer evidence to support it. When he was questioned, he would respond by making another accusation. He thus gave the impression of being so overwhelmed by the monstrous conspiracy he had uncovered that he had no time to waste on petty details. However, he was always careful to do his name–calling only inside the Senate, where he had legal immunity. Thus he could not be sued for defamation of character and slander.

The Republicans hoped for a victory in the 1952 election and did nothing to stop McCarthy's attacks. But after General Dwight D. Eisenhower was elected, McCarthy turned on the new president and on other Republicans. Finally, in 1954 he cooperated in his own downfall by accusing the United States Army of "coddling" Communists and of mistreating an assistant of his who had been drafted. The result was a televised Senate investigation. Some 20 million persons watched in fascination for thirty-six days during the spring and summer of 1954 as McCarthy bullied witnesses, refused to reveal where he had obtained information, interrupted proceedings, and made one empty charge after another. He soon lost both supporters and power. The Senate condemned him for improper conduct that tended "to bring the Senate into disrepute." McCarthy died a broken man three years later.

In his memoirs, Eisenhower said that "McCarthyism took its toll on many individuals and on the nation. No one was safe from charges recklessly made from inside the walls of congressional immunity. . . . The cost was often tragic." And indeed it was, for thousands of people lost their jobs as a result of "guilt by association"—for knowing someone who had once attended a Communist meeting. However, McCarthyism did reflect the fears of many people about the growing menace of communism throughout the world.

Section 4 Review

COMPREHENSION   Developing Vocabulary

1. Explain these terms: perjury, espionage, defected, classified, subversive.

COMPREHENSION   Mastering Facts

1. What were the functions of the Loyalty Review Board?
2. Why did Truman veto the McCarran Internal Security Act?
3. How did Senator McCarthy play on the public's concern about communism?
4. What was the result of McCarthy's limiting his name-calling to the Senate Chamber?

CHAPTER 34 Review

Chapter Summary

Under the leadership of new President Harry Truman, the American military was demobilized and veterans were aided by the G.I. Bill. The economy boomed as peacetime production resumed. New demands by labor led to a series of strikes and government regulation of the labor movement. In 1948 Truman upset Republican Thomas Dewey, and Truman then initiated his Fair Deal program. In world affairs, a Cold War developed between the United States and the Soviet Union. The Soviet Union dominated eastern Europe; the United States countered with the Marshall Plan in an attempt to deal with the economic chaos of western Europe. The Soviets blockaded Berlin; the Allies formed NATO. Meanwhile, Soviet activities led to a new "Red Scare" in the United States.

Questions for Critical Thinking

COMPREHENSION   Summarizing Main Ideas

1. Give four reasons for Truman's victory in the 1948 election.
2. What advances in civil rights took place during Truman's administration? Which occurred as a result of legislation? of executive action by the president? of action by private individuals?
3. Explain how each of the following helped to contain communism in Europe: (a) Churchill's "Iron Curtain" speech; (b) economic aid for Greece and Turkey; (c) the Marshall Plan; (d) the Berlin airlift; (e) establishment of NATO.
4. What objection did Walter Lippmann raise against the Truman Doctrine? Do you agree or disagree with his argument? Why?
5. Compare the conditions that led to McCarthyism with the conditions that led to the Red Scare after World War I.

COMPREHENSION   Interpreting Events

1. Why did Congress pass the Taft-Hartley Law?
2. Why was the Soviet Union suspicious of the West? Why did it want Communist countries as neighbors? What attitude did the West take in this matter? Do you think there was any way in which this disagreement could have been resolved? Explain.
3. Why were people upset by the Alger Hiss case?
4. If you had been a member of Congress in 1950, would you have voted in favor of the McCarran Internal Security Act? Give reasons for your position.
5. Why did the Senate vote to condemn Joseph McCarthy in 1954?

APPLICATION   Using Skills To Interpret Charts

Look at the employment charts on pages 838–839 and answer the following questions.

1. What proportion of the labor force was unemployed before the United States entered World War II?
2. What happened to the number of unemployed during the 1940s? during the 1950s? during the 1960s?
3. Which decade saw the greatest improvement in employment?
4. By about what percentage did the labor force increase during the years from 1940 to 1980?
5. On the basis of this chart, would you say that the American economy has been successful in providing jobs for people? Explain your answer.

EVALUATION   Forming Generalizations

1. What is the present status of NATO?
2. What nations besides the United States and the Soviet Union possess the atomic bomb?
3. What checks on internal security does the federal government have today?

World Leadership

After World War II, the Middle East nation of Iran appealed to the United Nations for help in removing Soviet troops from its territory. UN protests, however, brought no results. What did work was a sharply-worded note from President Truman to Soviet Premier Joseph Stalin. Stalin withdrew Soviet forces several months later. With further help from the United States, the Iranian government then reestablished authority over northern areas which had fallen under Soviet control. Throughout this postwar period, Iran— like many nations—looked to the United States for both protection and leadership.

In 1945 the United States had emerged from World War II as clearly *the* most powerful—and therefore the leading—nation in the world. But times change, and now the United States shares its world leadership role with other nations. This altered position has affected our relations with many nations.

Nearly thirty-five years after World War II, for example, the Iranian attitude toward the United States had changed drastically. No longer did Iran look to the United States for advice or protection. Instead, Iran criticized the United States for interfering in its affairs. In 1979, when a mob of Iranian militants stormed the American embassy in Teheran and took over fifty

American hostages, the Iranian government encouraged the action. Iran enjoyed the chance to embarrass a powerful nation.

Leadership Based on Power.
Throughout history, leadership roles by nations have been based on military power. In earlier times, Rome, Spain, and Britain ruled vast empires and were world leaders through the strength of their armed forces. They were leaders because no one could counter their military power. The United States found itself in this position after World War II, but not for long. The Soviet Union soon achieved superpower status with its military and industrial advances, and Americans were forced to share the role of world leader.

Membership in the club of world leaders changes with time and circumstances. Though the United States successfully stood up to powerful nations such as Britain and France during its early years, the nation did not become a world leader until the late 1800s. At that time world leadership involved the acquisition of an overseas colonial empire. By the turn of the century, an American empire stretched from the Caribbean to the Pacific. This empire increased the economic and military influence of the United States around the world and made the nation a world leader.

World Leadership Roles.
One important question to be asked is this: How has the United States viewed its role as a world leader? In general, our leaders have envisioned the American leadership role in several ways.

In some cases the aggressive pursuit of American interests has led to direct intervention in the affairs of other nations. President Theodore Roosevelt encouraged a rebellion in what is now Panama in order to build a canal there. Likewise, President Kennedy agreed to train some Cuban refugees to invade Cuba in the hope of starting a rebellion against Fidel Castro.

The United States has also pursued another approach to world leadership. As a world leader, the United States has championed the rights of other democratic nations. During World War I, President Wilson wanted "to make the world safe for democracy." Likewise, President Franklin Roosevelt convinced Congress to make the United States the "arsenal of democracy" during World War II.

The Nation as a Rescuer.
Another view of the United States as a world leader places the nation in the role of being a rescuer. The practice of giving foreign aid is based on the belief that the nation has a responsibility to assist poor nations whose undeveloped economies make

communism attractive. The Marshall Plan assumed that economic aid would stop communism from gaining ground in postwar Europe.

The American view of the nation as a rescuer underwent fundamental changes after the Vietnam War. This was really the first time that the nation failed to achieve what it had set out to accomplish through military strength. The nation is still reevaluating its role as a world leader because of Vietnam.

Promoting Peace. In another approach to world leadership, the United States often acts as a peace promoter. In 1905, President Theodore Roosevelt personally mediated an end to the Russo-Japanese War, a feat which earned him the Nobel Peace Prize. In 1977, President Carter not only managed to get Israel and Egypt to the bargaining table, but also to sign a historic peace agreement.

None of these approaches have exclusively dominated the United States role as a world leader; nor have any of the roles proved wholly satisfactory. The policy of intervention, for example, led to a feeling of resentment by many Latin American nations. The role of rescuer saw the United States become bitterly divided over a war in Vietnam. The role of peacekeeper found United States troops being placed in a dangerous position in Lebanon in 1983–1984.

At the United Nations, the United States shares its leadership role with both larger and smaller nations.

World Leadership Today. Nevertheless, what choices does the United States have today? The nation cannot simply give up its role as a world leader—for if it did, the Soviet Union would probably emerge as the overwhelmingly dominant force in the world. As frustrating as the nation's position often becomes, it is a necessary one. To protect our own freedoms, the United States must remain a world power and a world leader.

World leadership status, however, does not carry the right to become a bully. Rather, restraint is required of powerful nations, and it must be recognized that there are limits even to the power of a world leader. Most importantly, the United States needs to exhibit its world

leadership abilities by exercising the power of its ideals: equality, justice, and freedom. After all, the best leaders are usually those who lead by example.

Understanding Our Heritage

1. In what ways does the United States have a legacy of world leadership? How did America become a world power?

2. What approaches often characterize American relations with other nations? Which do you prefer? Why?

3. Compare the position of the United States in the world today with its position after World War II. What changes have taken place?

695

CHAPTER 35

The Cold War Turns Hot

1950–1956

People in the Chapter

Chiang Kai-shek—*president of the Republic of China, whose conversion to Christianity, anti-Communist background, and struggle against the Japanese make him and his American-educated wife very popular in the United States. But his regime is riddled with corruption and inefficiency.*

Mao Tse-tung—*guerrilla leader who overthrows the Chiang government and establishes the Communist People's Republic of China.*

Syngman Rhee—*leader of the Republic of Korea, whose country is invaded by North Korea. This act begins the Korean War.*

General Douglas MacArthur—*American hero of World War II whose outspoken and critical views on the Truman war policy in Korea lead the president to fire him.*

Linking Past to Present

Five years after helping to defeat the Axis, the United States found itself fighting a limited war on the mainland of Asia. A limited war is one that is fought to achieve certain aims short of total victory. In Korea that aim was, as President Truman said, "to stop aggression and to prevent a big war." Specifically, it was to turn back the North Koreans who had invaded South Korea, but without having the war spread to China. Truman thought this goal could be achieved fairly quickly.

Fighting a limited war, however, was very different from the total effort that had gone into World War II. Many people found the change frustrating. The Korean War was one of the major reasons why Americans in 1952 voted out the Democratic party that had run their government for twenty years.

General Dwight D. Eisenhower, who became the nation's thirty-fourth president, had never held an elective office. Like most professional soldiers of his generation, he had avoided party politics. Nevertheless, as Supreme Commander of the Allied forces in Europe during World War II, then as the first commander of NATO troops, Eisenhower had shown great political and diplomatic skills. He used them during his two terms in office to give the American people a generally calm, moderate, and business-oriented administration.

1 WARS IN CHINA AND KOREA

VOCABULARY   *Long March*   *mediate*

No sooner had the United States adopted a policy of containing communism in Europe than trouble broke out in the Far East. Japan's surrender set the stage for the final showdown in China between the Nationalist forces of Chiang Kai-shek (jang ki-*sheck)*, and the Chinese Communists led by Mao Tse-tung (mow-zuh-doong).

The Communists Take Over China

In 1931, you recall, Japanese armies seized China's northeast province of Manchuria. The president of China was Chiang Kai-shek, who had been in office most of the time since 1928. (The first president of China, Dr. Sun Yat Sen, had died in 1925.) But Chiang did not act vigorously enough, some thought, against the Japanese. Apparently he first wanted to fight the Chinese Communists, who had been receiving aid from the Soviet Union. (Even in the 1920s he feared the growing power of the Communists. All the Russians were expelled from China but even so, Chinese Communists had continued to gain influence.) In 1934 Chiang attacked the Communists and forced them to begin their famous *Long March.* This march covered 6000 miles and took nearly a year to complete because they had to avoid Chiang's armies. The marchers took a long and complicated route through mountains and deserts finally arriving in the distant province of Shensi in northern China. Of the 100,000 people who began the march only a few thousand finished it. One who did was a former library worker named Mao Tse-tung. In 1921 he had helped found the Chinese Communist party and after this march he emerged as the leader of the party.

As the Japanese became more powerful in Manchuria, some members of the Chinese army became dissatisfied with Chiang's lack of aggression against the enemy. In 1936 Chiang was captured by some troops in the town of Sian. He was released only after he promised to unite with the Communists to fight the Japanese. It was an uneasy union.

In 1937 Japan launched a massive invasion of the rest of China. For the next nine years, the Chinese people resisted as best they could, with the Nationalists leading the struggle in the south and the Communists in the north.

Two Views of Chiang Kai-shek. For many Americans, Chiang Kai-shek was one of the most admired of world leaders. In 1938 he had moved his government 1400 miles inland in order to continue to fight against Japan. Millions of Chinese had· followed him westward, carrying factory equipment, school books, and household goods on their backs. Americans were impressed by the courage and determination the Chinese showed. Chiang's popularity was also increased by his conversion to Christianity and by the fact that his wife had been educated in the United States.

U.S. military and State Department officials who dealt with Chiang, however, held a different view. They found his government dictatorial, inefficient, and hopelessly corrupt. For example, of the $3.5 billion in aid that the United States sent the Nationalist regime, it is estimated that $750 million ended up in the pockets of Chiang's relatives and friends. Furthermore, the land policies the Chiang government followed were in sharp contrast to those practiced by the Communists. When the latter took over an area, they would redistribute the land and reduce rents. China's farmers found that very attractive.

Civil War.   During World War II, differences between the Nationalists and the Communists

President and Madame Chiang Kai-shek at the Presidential headquarters in Taipei, Taiwan.

ever, send $2 billion in military equipment and supplies to Chiang over the next two years.

A Communist Victory. Unfortunately for the Nationalists, their military leadership was poor. Nationalist troops outnumbered Communist troops three to one. But instead of attacking the center of Communist strength in northern China, Nationalist forces holed up in the cities. The Communists were thus able to cut Nationalist supply lines. Gradually, one isolated city after another surrendered to Mao's troops. The last Nationalist stronghold of Shanghai fell in May 1949. Chiang and what remained of his government and army fled to the island of Formosa (Taiwan).

The Search for a Scapegoat. The American public was astounded at the turn of events. They were also set back on their heels by the announcement that the Soviet Union had exploded its first atomic bomb. A debate on the nation's China policy promptly broke out.

In Congress a group of conservative Republicans and Democrats attacked the Truman administration for supplying only limited aid to Chiang. If containing communism was important in Europe, they asked, why wasn't it equally important in Asia? The State Department replied by stating that what had happened in China was a result of internal forces. The United States had tried to influence these forces, unfortunately without success. But trying to do more would only have meant a new war, which people were not in a mood for. However, the United States would continue to recognize the Nationalists as China's legal government and would oppose the admission of Red China to the United Nations.

Most Americans accepted the State Department's arguments, but some did not. They could not believe that Chiang himself and his regime were responsible for the Nationalist defeat. They were convinced that somehow the United States had "lost" China. Some were even prepared to believe that the American government was riddled with Communist agents. They spoke out bitterly on the matter.

were played down. As soon as Japanese soldiers left the mainland, however, civil war between the two groups broke out.

The United States tried to *mediate,* or act as peacemaker in, the dispute. In September 1945 U.S. ambassador Patrick J. Hurley held six weeks of meetings with Chiang and Mao, but to no avail. In 1946 President Truman sent special envoy General George Marshall over with a plan for setting up a coalition government that would include both sides. The plan failed.

In 1947 Truman sent yet another general, Albert C. Wedemeyer, to China on a fact-finding mission. Wedemeyer recommended that the United States continue helping the Nationalists. However, he felt the only way the Nationalists could win the civil war was if Chiang changed his economic policies and if the United States sent in several hundred thousand troops. Truman was unwilling to commit American soldiers. He did, how-

War Erupts in Korea

The peninsula of Korea, which means "Land of the Morning Calm," juts out from the mainland of Asia toward Japan. In 1910 Japan took over Korea

698

Communist Victory in China 1949

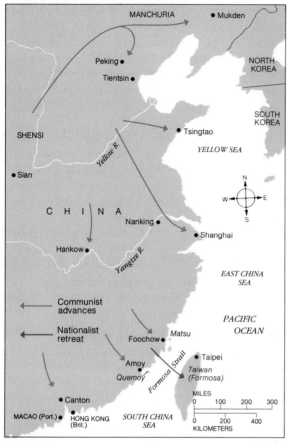

Map Skills *To what island did the Nationalists retreat? How far was it from the mainland of China?*

© ML & Co.

and ruled it until August 1945. As World War II ended, Japanese troops there surrendered to the Allies. Troops north of the 38th parallel surrendered to the Russians. Troops south of the parallel surrendered to the Americans.

The 38th parallel was not supposed to be a permanent boundary. But as was the case in Germany, two nations developed, one in each zone of occupation.

South Korea and Syngman Rhee. In 1947 the United States brought the question of a unified Korea before the UN. The next year UN elections in the American zone led to the establishment of the Republic of Korea, usually called South Korea. The government was headed by the elderly Syngman Rhee (sing-man rhee), who had spent many years, both in the United States and China, working for his country's independence. South Korea included Seoul, the country's traditional capital. South Korea also had two-thirds of the peninsula's people, and most of its farmland.

Rhee was eager to extend his control northward, but the United States would give his army only defensive weapons. In June 1949, at the suggestion of the UN General Assembly, the United States withdrew all its troops from South Korea except for 500 military advisors.

North Korea and Kim Il Sung. The Soviets, who had boycotted the UN elections, set up their own Democratic People's Republic of Korea, with a capital at Pyongyang. North Korea contained most of the mineral wealth of the peninsula and a good part of its industry. At its head was Kim Il Sung, who had been a guerrilla fighter against the Japanese since the 1930s. Kim's government, like that of Rhee, claimed the right to rule all of Korea. The Soviets withdrew their troops from North Korea in December 1948 after arming the North Koreans heavily.

A Fateful Speech. In January 1950, Secretary of State Dean Acheson addressed the National Press Club in Washington. He said that the United States had a military interest in the western part of the Pacific. American troops were stationed along a "defense perimeter" that ran from Alaska to Japan to the Ryukyus Islands (which include Okinawa) to the Philippines. If an attack were made anywhere east of the perimeter, he warned, the United States would fight. Formosa and Korea, which lay west of the perimeter, were not listed. Their defense, Acheson said, would have to depend on their own efforts and on the United Nations.

Acheson may only have been letting Chiang and Rhee know that the United States would not automatically jump to their aid if they attacked mainland China or North Korea. But without intending to, the secretary of state may have given the Communists a green light in Korea. In any event, at dawn on June 25, 1950, troops from North Korea crossed the 38th parallel and invaded South Korea.

The United Nations Takes a Stand

As soon as news of the invasion reached Washington, President Truman decided to resist. As he pointed out later,

"What the Communists, the North Koreans, were doing was nothing new. . . . Hitler and Mussolini and the Japanese were doing exactly the same thing in the 1930s. . . . Nobody had stood up to them. And that is what led to the Second World War. The strong got away [with] attacking the weak, and I wasn't going to let this attack on the Republic of Korea . . . go forward. Because if it wasn't stopped, it would lead to a third world war, and I wasn't going to let that happen. Not while I was President."

Accordingly, Truman ordered General MacArthur, who was in Japan, to air-drop food, weapons, and ammunition to the South Korean army. The president also sent the U.S. Seventh Fleet to Formosa Strait to make certain there would be no attack from the mainland against Formosa, or the other way around. Truman wanted to keep Red China out of the conflict. The next day, he ordered naval and air support for South Korea. When the announcement of his action was made, Congress stood up and cheered. The move was very popular. Only Republican Senator Robert A. Taft of Ohio (the son of President William Howard Taft) pointed out that the president, by acting on his own, had "usurped," or wrongfully seized, the power of Congress to declare war. Several days later, Truman ordered U.S. ground forces from Japan into South Korea.

In the meantime, the United Nations Security Council met on June 27 and adopted an American resolution calling on member nations to give all possible aid to the Republic of Korea. The next month the Security Council asked that all nations sending troops to Korea place them under MacArthur. The general thus became UN commander-in-chief for the so-called "police action." (In all, nineteen nations sent troops to resist North Korea's aggression; about four-fifths of the troops were Americans.)

It was possible for the UN to take such strong action because the Soviet Union was not there to use its veto. The Soviets were boycotting all UN meetings as a protest against the Security Council's refusal to seat Communist Chinese delegates.

Section 1 Review

COMPREHENSION   Developing Vocabulary
1. Explain these terms: mediate, Long March, limited war, police action.

COMPREHENSION   Mastering Facts
1. What were three reasons for the downfall of Chiang Kai-shek's Nationalist government?
2. How did the 38th parallel come to be the dividing line between North Korea and South Korea?
3. What was Truman's objective in Korea?
4. Why did the Soviet Union not veto the UN recommendation to send UN troops to Korea?

2 THE UNITED STATES FIGHTS A LIMITED WAR IN KOREA

VOCABULARY   *stalemate*

The first months of the Korean conflict were grave ones for the United States. With only a few under-manned and underequipped divisions available, MacArthur was barely able to slow down the enemy advance. North Korean armored units drove steadily southward, forcing South Korean and UN troops into an area around Pusan, in the southeastern part of the peninsula. There MacArthur and his men dug in, while tanks, heavy artillery, and especially fresh troops from the United States began to arrive. By mid-September, MacArthur was ready to launch a counter-attack.

South Korea Is Freed

Within two weeks, UN and South Korean forces had recaptured Seoul. This was accom-plished by a brilliant strategic maneuver—an am-phibious landing behind enemy lines at Inchon, on Korea's west coast. At the same time, other troops moved north from the Pusan area, thus creating a pincer movement that trapped the North Koreans. About half of them, almost 130,000, surrendered; the rest fled back across the 38th parallel.

On to North Korea. The sudden military triumph posed a serious political problem. MacArthur and his troops had achieved their objective, namely, clearing the invaders out of South Korea. What was to happen now? If UN forces crossed the 38th parallel, that would change the war from a defensive one to an offensive one. On the other hand, the Allies had agreed at Potsdam that Korea should be unified.

The War in Korea   1950–1953

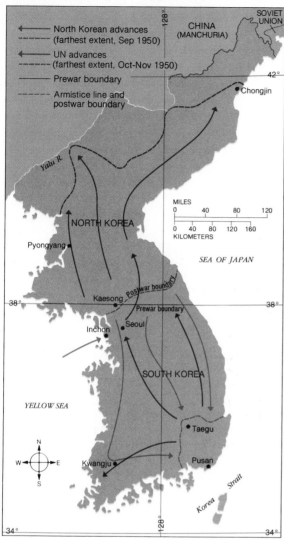

North Korean advances
(farthest extent, Sep 1950)

UN advances
(farthest extent, Oct-Nov 1950)

Prewar boundary

Armistice line and
postwar boundary

CHINA
(MANCHURIA)

SOVIET
UNION

Chongjin

NORTH KOREA

Pyongyang

MILES
0   40   80   120

0   40   80   120   160
KILOMETERS

SEA OF JAPAN

Kaesong

Prewar boundary

Postwar boundary

Inchon

Seoul

SOUTH KOREA

YELLOW SEA

Taegu

Kwangju

Pusan

Korea Strait

© ML & Co.

Map Skills   *Which cities in the South did not fall to the North Koreans? To what river did the UN advance?*

"Back . . . by Christmas."   On October 7 the UN General Assembly recommended that Mac-Arthur cross the 38th parallel and reunite Korea. However, days earlier, Communist China's foreign minister, Chou En-lai (joe on-lie), let it be known that his country would not stand idly by and see its North Korean ally destroyed. This warning was repeated again and again during the first weeks of October.

On October 14 President Truman flew halfway around the world to Wake Island. There he conferred with General MacArthur on the possibility of Chinese intervention. MacArthur told the president with complete assurance that this was not go-

ing to happen. The Chinese, he said, had only scattered forces along the Yalu River, the boundary between North Korea and Manchuria. With no air support, the Chinese would at best be able to move 60,000 troops across the border. "Mr. President, the war will be over by Thanksgiving and I'll have the American troops back in Tokyo by Christmas."

China Enters the War

The advance into North Korea went on, pressing ever closer to the borders of China. On October 20, Pyongyang fell. Then, on October 26, a Chinese Communist soldier was captured about ninety miles south of where he was supposed to be according to army intelligence. Four days later, sixteen more Chinese soldiers were caught. By the following week, eight Chinese divisions had been identified. Russian-made planes, also flown by Chinese, were engaging UN fighters in air combat.

The UN Retreats.   Then, on November 26, some 300,000 Chinese "volunteers" poured across the Yalu River into Korea. The UN forces had to retreat. It was done quickly and efficiently, but it was clearly a defeat. And it had to be carried out in the bitter cold of a North Asian winter.

By Christmas the UN had been driven seventy-five to one hundred miles below the 38th parallel.

General Douglas MacArthur and President Truman on Wake Island. They were not to be friendly for long.

701

Communist Party Chairman Mao Tse-tung attends a mass rally in Peking in the 1950s. This peasant and party organizer rose to become ruler of mainland China.

It had lost Seoul for the second time. More than 100,000 of its troops had to be evacuated from North Korea by British and American naval forces.

MacArthur now called for an extension of the war into China. He proposed a naval blockade of the China coast and the dropping of thirty to fifty atomic bombs on that nation's industrial and transportation centers. He also wanted the right to strike at Red air bases north of the Yalu River. For good measure, he asked for the use of Chiang Kai-shek's troops both in Korea and to invade southern China.

Truman rejected MacArthur's requests. The president did not want the United States involved in a massive land war in Asia. As General Omar N. Bradley, chairman of the Joint Chiefs of Staff, said, an all-out conflict with China would be "the wrong war, at the wrong place, at the wrong time, and with the wrong enemy." Furthermore, the Soviet Union had a mutual assistance pact with Red China. Attacking the latter would probably set off World War III.

Back to the Beginning. MacArthur predicted that if his requests were not granted, his army would be wiped out. But an able field commander, Matthew B. Ridgway, had been appointed head of the U.S. Eighth Army. With it as a spearhead, the UN forces began once more to advance. They were outnumbered, but by mid-March 1951 Ridgway had retaken Seoul and once more moved north of the 38th parallel. The situation was just what it had been before the fighting began.

General MacArthur Is Removed

MacArthur continued to urge a full-scale war against China as the best means of bringing a quick end to the Korean conflict. Every time he raised the subject, he was informed by the president or the Joint Chiefs of Staff that he was expected to fight only a limited war. Finding this intolerable, and certain that his views were correct, MacArthur tried to go over the president's head. He spoke and wrote privately to newspaper and magazine publishers and especially to leaders of the Republican party in Congress.

In March 1951 he sent a letter to Joseph Martin of Massachusetts, Republican leader in the House of Representatives. He stated his view that the place to crush world communism was Asia and closed his argument with the words, "There is no substitute for victory." When Martin released the general's letter to the press, Truman felt he no longer had a choice. On April 11, with the unanimous approval of the Joint Chiefs of Staff, he relieved MacArthur of his command. "I could do nothing else and still be President," Truman said.

The public outcry that followed the general's dismissal rocked the nation. He was given a hero's welcome to the United States, which he had not visited since before World War II. An address to Congress, which is an honor usually accorded only to heads of governments, capped MacArthur's triumph. He gave a highly emotional talk, ending with a reference to "old soldiers" who have served their country not dying but just fading away. A Gallup poll taken at the time showed that 69 percent of the American public thought the general was right, while only 29 percent agreed with the president. Apparently it was difficult for Americans to accept a military *stalemate*, or deadlock, no matter what the reasons.

Throughout the fuss, Truman kept in the background. He gave people full opportunity to express their gratitude to MacArthur for his leadership in World War II and for the way he had brought democracy to the people of Japan. Then it was the administration's turn. Before a congressional committee investigating MacArthur's dismissal, a parade of witnesses set forth the arguments for a limited war. The committee agreed with them. The public began to swing around to the view that Truman had properly defended his constitutional position as commander in chief. And MacArthur, while still admired for his fifty-two years of service to his country, soon "faded away" as a political figure.

A Limited Victory

As the Truman-MacArthur controversy died down, a suggestion for settling the Korean War was unexpectedly made by the Soviet Union. Negotiations for a cease-fire began in July 1951 and went on for months. By the following spring, agreement had been reached on two points: the location of the cease-fire line at the 38th parallel, and the establishment of a demilitarized zone between the opposing sides.

Another year of wrangling was taken up with the question of prisoners. Usually, when a war is over, prisoners are sent back to their homelands. But about 45,000 Chinese and North Koreans did not want to be sent home, and the United States felt they should not be forced to return. The North Koreans, who were furious at this damage to their prestige, insisted that the prisoners be handed over. At last a compromise was worked out. But before it could be put into effect, South Korean guards solved the problem by letting all the prisoners escape. After several more weeks of indignant speeches from both North and South Korea, an armistice was finally signed in July 1953.

It was a limited victory in a limited war. On one hand, the North Korean invaders had been pushed back, and communism had been contained without a major war or the use of atomic weapons. On the other hand, Korea had become two nations rather than one. And the cost had been high: about 2 million casualties, 80 percent of them Korean civilians. The figures for the United States were 33,000 dead, 103,000 wounded, and 410 missing. In addition, America's military expenditures had run over $15 billion, several billion more than the Marshall Plan.

This famous anti-administration cartoon by Leo Joseph Roche reflects the feeling of many Americans at that time.

A Republican Victory

In 1952 Republicans had no shortage of issues on which to challenge the Truman administration. There was the rise of communism in China and Eastern Europe, although its spread had been slowed or stopped by the Marshall Plan and the Korean War. There was the issue of Communists in government raised by Senator McCarthy. There was an issue called "the mess in Washington," by which people meant the growing power of the federal government and the examples of corruption that were coming to light. The war had set off another round of inflation, and Truman's failure to arbitrate a steel strike in 1952 had caused prices to rise even more. Above all, the negotiations for a Korean armistice had been dragging on for over a year. In addition, there was a general feeling that after twenty years of a Democratic presidency, it was time for a change.

Eisenhower Versus Stevenson. The Republicans were split over who their candidate should be. Conservatives preferred Senator Robert A. Taft, co-sponsor of the Taft-Hartley act. Moderates supported General Dwight D. Eisenhower. After a sharp battle over which of the two slates of delegates from Georgia, Louisiana, and Texas should be seated at the convention, the moderates won on the first ballot. But to please Taft's followers, they nominated Richard M. Nixon, now a senator, as Eisenhower's running mate.

A few weeks later, the Democrats chose Governor Adlai E. Stevenson of Illinois to be their standard bearer. Their candidate for vice-president was Senator John J. Sparkman of Alabama.

Stevenson's witty speeches delighted many of his supporters. But his remarks led other voters to distrust him. Along with the Puritan tradition of education, there has always been, historians say, a streak of anti-intellectualism in the United States—a belief that some highly educated individuals live in an ivory tower and don't know what the real world is like. It is said that they come up with schemes for spending money on people who don't deserve it, and that they think they are the only ones who know how to solve problems. Stevenson seemed to touch off this anti-intellectual streak. He and his followers were called "eggheads."

Eisenhower, on the other hand, looked and sounded like everyone's favorite uncle. He had a delightful grin and a genuinely warm personality. While Stevenson appealed to people's minds, Eisenhower appealed more to their emotions. As one historian put it, the general "might not always have had his facts quite right, but like his audiences, he knew something had gone wrong for America, and it had put his dander (temper) up."

TV and Nixon. For the first time in a presidential campaign, television played a major role. At one point it also added considerable excitement.

Eisenhower after the final speech in his 1952 campaign for president on the Republican ticket. To the cheering crowds, he gives his famous wave and flashes a sunny smile.

Presidential Election of 1952

ELECTORAL VOTE
Total 531

89 (16.8%)

442 (83.2%)

POPULAR VOTE
Total 61,542,000

291,000 (0.5%)

33,936,000 (55.1%)

27,315,000 (44.4%)

- Eisenhower (Republican)
- Stevenson (Democratic)
- Others

Source: U.S. Bureau of the Census, *Historical Statistics of the United States.*

© ML & Co.

Map Skills *Which candidate and party won the Presidency? What was his percentage of the popular vote? In what section of the country were his opponent's electoral votes?*

A newspaper article revealed that Nixon had benefited from a trust fund set up by California businessmen. The article was written as though the fund were secret, illegal, had been used to raise Nixon's living style, and was something totally new in American politics. It was none of these things. But it *was* a great embarrassment to a party running against corruption in government.

Nixon replied to the charges in a television address that made masterly use of the new medium. In it he showed that no one had received favors for contributing to the fund. The money had been used only for legitimate political expenses, such as travel, recordings of speeches, and Christmas cards to former campaign workers. Nixon's own resources were badly stretched by the demands of public life. He owed $10,000 on his California house (in which his parents were living) and $20,000 on his Washington house. His wife Pat did not wear a mink coat but, as he said, "a respectable Republican cloth coat."

Nixon finished with a reference to the family dog, a black-and-white cocker spaniel named Checkers. It was, he said, the only out-right gift he had ever accepted, and he would never give it up

because his two daughters loved it so. His performance was known thereafter as the "Checkers Speech." It saved Nixon's place on the Republican ticket once messages of support started pouring in.

"I Shall Go to Korea." The turning point in the hard-fought campaign occurred when Ike firmly grasped the number one issue: Korea. On October 24 the general promised that if elected he would go to Korea to see first-hand what could be done to bring the war to an end.

After that it was no contest. Eisenhower carried every state outside the South, and even there, in traditionally Democratic territory, he took Florida, Tennessee, and Virginia. His electoral total was 442 to Stevenson's 89; the popular vote was 33.9 million to 27.3 million. But Eisenhower's triumph was more of a personal than a party victory. The Republicans captured Congress by a majority of only one in the Senate and ten in the House of Representatives.

A New Voting Pattern. The 1952 election was a turning point. It ended twenty years of Democratic rule and restored the Republicans to na-

705

tional power. It also established a new voting pattern. The suburbs then springing up were filled with people from the central cities, most of whom had been loyal Democrats. In 1952 large numbers of them voted for Ike. One Republican newspaper implied that the fresh air must have cleared their heads. Actually, the change was part of a general breakdown in party loyalty. Two out of ten voters now considered themselves independents who would vote for the individual rather than the party. That trend continued, and at the beginning of the 1980s the proportion of independents had doubled and showed no signs of decreasing.

Section 2 Review

COMPREHENSION   Developing Vocabulary
1.   Explain these terms: stalemate, eggheads.

COMPREHENSION   Mastering Facts

1.   What happened when UN troops marched into North Korea?
2.   On what grounds did Truman fire MacArthur?
3.   What issue delayed the signing of a Korean armistice?
4.   What new voting pattern first appeared in the 1952 election?

3   EISENHOWER LEADS THE NATION

Americans who expected some spectacular development from Eisenhower's trip to Korea were disappointed. Ike was photographed eating army rations and talking to G.I.s, which raised morale. But the July 1953 armistice terms were the same as they had been under the Truman administration. In other matters of foreign policy, as you will learn in the next chapter, Eisenhower more or less followed in Truman's footsteps. On the domestic scene, however, there were a number of changes.

Eisenhower's Style

Eisenhower took a different view of the presidency than either FDR or Truman. He believed they had made the office too powerful, and he wanted to restore what he considered was a proper balance among the three branches of government. Also, he felt that as president, he should be above partisan politics and should try to resolve differences rather than suggest specific laws.

A Strong Cabinet.   In line with his view of the presidency, Eisenhower relied strongly on his cabinet. He believed department heads should develop their own policy to a great extent and should run their own show. Eisenhower also had great respect for business people. Accordingly, almost every member of his cabinet was a high-powered business executive or corporation lawyer. For example, the secretary of the treasury was George M. Humphrey, president of M.A. Hanna and Company (the firm organized by President McKinley's campaign manager, Mark Hanna). The post of de-

fense secretary went to Charles E. "Engine Charlie" Wilson, president of General Motors. Secretary of State John Foster Dulles was from a prominent law firm. Even Oveta Culp Hobby, whom Eisenhower appointed to head the newly created Department of Health, Education, and Welfare, had a business background. After heading the WACS in World War II, she had become co-publisher with her husband of the *Houston Post*.

As one magazine put it, Eisenhower's cabinet consisted of "eight millionaires and a plumber." The "plumber" was Labor Secretary Martin P. Durkin, who had been president of the Plumbers and Steamfitters Union. Both Durkin and his union had endorsed Democratic candidate Stevenson in the election. But by appointing a union official, Eisenhower acknowledged that many rank-and-file members of organized labor had voted for the Republican ticket.

The Presidential Office.   Just as significant as the makeup of the cabinet was Eisenhower's system of handling information and making decisions. It was organized along military lines. Everything went through a chain of command that was headed by a chief of staff. In this powerful post, Ike placed Sherman Adams, former governor of New Hampshire. Under Adams, new programs and routine decisions alike were thoroughly discussed and compromises were worked out before anything arrived on the president's desk. Except for Dulles, anyone who wanted to talk with Eisenhower had to approach the president through Adams. It was an orderly system.

Secretary of State John Foster Dulles at the United Nations. His stern manner disturbed many diplomats.

Eisenhower's "Dynamic Conservatism"

President Eisenhower's economic philosophy, which he called "dynamic conservatism," suited the temper of the times. It favored continuation of the chief New Deal programs, combined with an attempt to move the federal government out of some areas of operation.

A Middle-of-the-Road Policy. Congress extended Social Security to include farm workers, household servants, and employees of small businesses. In all, about 10.5 million people were added to the program. There was some additional money for public housing. The federal government continued to supervise labor-management relations. In 1959, the Labor-Management Reporting and Disclosures Act prohibited groups that were not directly involved in a strike from picketing. It also said that Communists and persons convicted of felonies could not run for union office or be employed by a union.

The Eisenhower administration tried to turn over the electric power operations of the TVA to private utilities but did not succeed. It did, however, abolish the government's monopoly of nu-

clear power. Under the Atomic Energy Act of 1954, private utilities can obtain a license from the Atomic Energy Commission to produce electricity by means of atomic energy.

Changing the Way We Live. In another area, however, the Eisenhower administration greatly expanded the economic role of the federal government. In fact, many people consider the Federal Interstate and Defense Highway Act the most far-reaching measure passed in the Eisenhower years. As implied by the word "defense" in the act's title, the 42,000-mile highway network would be an advantage in wartime. That justified the federal government's 90 percent contribution to construction costs. They were originally estimated at $40 billion; current estimates place the total cost at $90 billion.

The vast system of four- and six-lane roads was begun in the late 1950s. It soon changed patterns of work, residence, and travel for millions of Americans. The high-speed highways encouraged the movement of people and light industry away from central cities. They encouraged the development of thousands of suburban shopping centers. And they increased the dependence of Americans on the automobile.

The Continuing Farm Problem. In general, the mid-fifties were a time of booming business. The inflation rate remained below 2 percent, and most Americans enjoyed an ever-higher standard of living.

But while business and labor were pleased with the "Eisenhower prosperity," farmers were not so content. Between 1952 and 1956, farm income declined by about 25 percent, mostly as a result of higher production costs. At the same time, there was a pileup of farm surpluses in government warehouses. Secretary of Agriculture Ezra Taft Benson believed that the government price support program was encouraging farmers to produce more than the market could absorb. At his urging, Congress passed the Agricultural Act of 1954, which provided for a sliding scale of price supports. But the Benson program did not improve matters much. Farm income continued to decline, and surpluses continued to pile up.

In 1955 the Eisenhower administration tried a different approach. The federal government would pay farmers if they did *not* grow surplus crops. In addition, soil banks were established; that is, farm-

The Eisenhower appeal to many U.S. voters was enduring. He led his party to victory again in 1956.

ers were paid for the acres they did *not* plant. The land was in effect put away in a bank for some future time. These New Dealish measures helped somewhat but did not solve the farmers' basic problem.

A Divided Leadership

Despite his great popularity, Ike's political coattails were short; that is, he carried few Republicans into office with him. The small 1952 Republican majority in Congress was swept away in 1954 and was not regained. In 1956 Eisenhower won reelection by the greatest majority since FDR's triumph in 1936, but the Democratic majority in Congress increased. Ike's opponent again was Stevenson. The president's victory was a particularly personal triumph because of his age (he would be seventy at the end of his second term) and his health. His heart attack, suffered in 1955, and serious intestinal blockage in 1956 (with a mild stroke during his second term) helped bring about the passage in 1967 of the Twenty-fifth Amendment. This provides for temporary or permanent replacement of a president who is incapable of performing his duties.

Democratic control of Congress, however, did not change domestic policy much. The modest social programs that were passed in the 1950s were usually vetoed on the ground that they were too costly, or were an uncalled-for extension of federal power, or both. Back on Capitol Hill, Republicans could usually pick up enough votes from conservative Democrats to uphold the president's veto.

Section 3 Review

COMPREHENSION   Developing Vocabulary

1. Explain these terms: dynamic conservatism, political coattails, soil banks.

COMPREHENSION   Mastering Facts

1. What was the result of Eisenhower's trip to Korea?
2. What was Eisenhower's view of the presidency?
3. How did the Interstate and Defense Highway Act change the way Americans live?
4. What does the Twenty-fifth Amendment provide?

Chapter Summary

American attention focused on Asia when Communist forces drove the Nationalists from the mainland of China to the island of Formosa. Another shock came when the Soviet Union announced detonation of its first atomic bomb. When North Korea invaded South Korea in 1950, the United Nations voted to act. General MacArthur commanded UN forces. When the war expanded to the North, a struggle developed between MacArthur and Truman. It culminated in MacArthur's removal by the president. Eventually a limited victory was accepted and the independence of South Korea was assured. In 1952 Americans elected a war hero, Dwight D. Eisenhower, as president. His victory was the first by a Republican in twenty years.

Questions for Critical Thinking

COMPREHENSION Summarizing Main Ideas

1. What advantages did North Korea have in the Korean War? What advantages did South Korea have?

2. What were the arguments in favor of MacArthur and his troops crossing the 38th parallel into North Korea? What were the arguments against such action? 700

3. According to President Truman, did the United States succeed in achieving its objectives in the Korean War? Explain. 707

4. Give some reasons for Eisenhower's victory over Stevenson in 1952.

5. In what ways did Eisenhower continue the domestic reforms that had been started under the New Deal? In what ways did he move away from such reforms?

COMPREHENSION Interpreting Events

1. Why did many Americans admire Chiang Kai-shek? How did U.S. military and State Department officials view the Chinese leader? How do you explain the difference in perception?

2. How did the United States try to settle the conflict between the Nationalists and the Communists in China? What else, if anything, do you think this nation should have done? Give reasons for your opinion.

3. Why did many Americans look for someone to blame for the Nationalist defeat in China?

4. Do you agree or disagree with Senator Taft's statement that President Truman's actions in Korea had "usurped the power of Congress" to declare war? Defend your opinion.

5. If you had been President Truman, would you have fired MacArthur? Why or why not?

APPLICATION Using Skills To Understand Time

For each set of events below, tell which covered the longer time span.

1a. Japanese armies seize China's northeast province of Manchuria and Japanese troops pull out of China.

1b. Japanese troops pull out of China and the Communists take over control of the Chinese mainland.

2a. Japanese troops in Korea surrender and General MacArthur becomes UN commander in chief in Korea.

2b. North Korea invades South Korea and the Korean War ends.

3a. Negotiations for an armistice begin in Korea and the armistice agreement is signed.

3b. MacArthur becomes UN commander in chief in Korea and is relieved of his command.

EVALUATION Forming Generalizations

1. Do you think it is possible for one nation to determine the government of another nation? If so, under what circumstances? Do you think it is right for the United States to determine what kind of government other nations have? Give reasons for your opinion.

2. What is the present status of South Korea? of North Korea?

Guides to Economic Health

What do a baseball player and an economist have in common? One answer is that both rely on statistics to better understand and perform their jobs.

Statistics are numerical facts that have been carefully organized to present information about a certain subject. For example, baseball statistics could include the number of runs and hits made by each player during a game. Economic statistics could provide information about many topics, including the strengths and weaknesses of different parts of our nation's free enterprise system. Three important statistics that economists pay special attention to are the Gross National Product (GNP), the Consumer Price Index (CPI), and the unemployment rate.

Gross National Product.

The GNP is the market value of all the goods and services our economy produces in a year. It includes (1) the goods and services we buy as consumers; (2) what we spend for new housing; (3) everything that federal, state, and local governments buy; (4) what business and non-profit institutions invest in plant and equipment; (5) what business spends on inventories; (6) our net exports, or the differences between our exports and imports; and (7) profits earned overseas and invested there by U.S. companies.

GNP can be measured either in *current dollars* or in *constant dollars.* The term current dollars refers to what dollars can currently buy in the marketplace. GNP in current dollars is known as the *nominal GNP.* The term constant dollars refers to what dollars were worth in a base, or earlier, year. GNP in constant dollars is known as *real GNP* because it corrects or adjusts the dollar amount to take inflation into account. For example, in 1974 the nominal GNP rose 8.1 percent over the previous year. But the real GNP, based on constant dollars (what they were worth in 1973), dropped 1.4 percent. That was because the nation experienced a price rise of 9.5 percent between 1973 and 1974.

Economists use the GNP to determine whether the nation's economy is growing and if it is, how fast. This information helps business and government make plans for the future. Some people, however, feel the GNP is not as accurate as it should be. It does not include goods and services that have no market value. The work women have traditionally done, for example, managing households and children, has no monetary value and so is not included in the GNP.

The Consumer Price Index.

Economists define the Consumer Price Index as an average of prices for certain goods and services commonly bought by consumers. The prices are expressed in terms of their relationship to 100, the number given to the base year of 1967. In other words, a CPI of 200 means you have to pay twice as much today to buy the same things you bought in 1967.

There are about 400 items listed in the index of goods and services. They range from doctors' fees to bowling balls, including food, housing, transportation, clothing, and so on. These are the things most often bought by most people.

Changes in the nation's CPI probably upset more people than any other statistic. That is because so many things are tied to it. For example, many union contracts have cost-of-living clauses that provide for automatic wage increases to keep up with CPI increases. The benefits paid to people on social security and to retired government and military workers are keyed to the index. Food-stamp allotments go up when the index does. Such items as insurance coverage and child-support payments are often readjusted. It is estimated that a 1 percent rise in the CPI leads to a $2 billion rise in wages and benefits.

The Unemployment Rate.

The unemployment rate is another economic statistic that upsets many Americans—especially those who cannot find a job. Like the CPI, the unemploy-

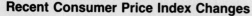

Recent Consumer Price Index Changes

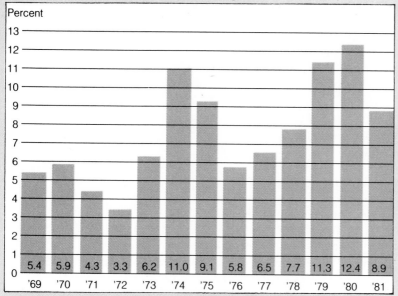

Percent												
5.4	5.9	4.3	3.3	6.2	11.0	9.1	5.8	6.5	7.7	11.3	12.4	8.9
'69	'70	'71	'72	'73	'74	'75	'76	'77	'78	'79	'80	'81

ment rate is linked to certain federal programs. For example, the Employment Act of 1946 (see chapter 34) committed the federal government to promoting "maximum employment." Economists nowadays define this as an unemployment rate of 5 percent.

Determining the unemployment rate is simple. You divide the total work force into the number of unemployed persons. The work force includes about 65 percent of Americans over sixteen years of age. Those not included are mostly retirees, full-time housewives, and students. The number of unemployed people is determined by a monthly sampling of 47,000 households across the country.

But the unemployment rate by itself does not tell the whole story. For one thing, unemploy-ment does not hit all groups the same way. Blacks in general have an unemployment rate double that of whites. Teenagers in general have an unemployment rate about four times as high as that of older people.

Second, the unemployment rate does not indicate how many unemployed people are "job losers." Some may have quit their last jobs. Some are new workers, having just graduated from high school or college. And some—usually women and teen-agers—are "reentering the work force." In general, about one-third to one-half of those who are unemployed have actually been fired.

Third, the unemployment role does not take into account those who are working only part-time or who have stopped looking for work.

In measuring unemployment hardship, economists usually look at how long people have been out of work. Anything over 26 weeks is considered long-term and much more serious than short-term unemployment.

These three measurements— the Gross National Product, the Consumer Price Index, and the unemployment rate—are important guides to the nation's economic health. The statistics they provide measure the current functioning of economic activity as well as help government agencies determine future economic policies. Hopefully, they also help build a healthier free enterprise system.

Understanding Free Enterprise

1. What is the difference between the nominal GNP and the real GNP?

2. Why are changes in the CPI likely to disturb consumers?

3. Why is the unemployment rate not an accurate picture of the unemployment situation?

4. The graph on this page shows the *percentage* of change in the Consumer Price Index since 1969. During the 1970s, in which year did the CPI increase the most? the least? By what percentage did the CPI rise in 1980? Through research, determine the percentage change in the CPI in the latest year available.

CHAPTER 36

Adjustments of the 1950s

1950–1960

People in the Chapter

William J. Levitt—*the Henry Ford of the housing industry whose real estate development on Long Island helps change the way Americans live.*

Rosa Parks—*the black woman who refuses to sit in the black section of a bus in Montgomery, Alabama. Her action triggers the black civil rights struggle of the 1950s.*

Martin Luther King, Jr.—*the young minister who leads the black boycott of Montgomery, Alabama's segregated bus system and urges his followers to resist peacefully, confronting physical force with a stronger "soul force."*

Ignacio Lopez—*founds the Unity League in California to encourage Mexican-Americans to vote.*

John Foster Dulles—*the tough-talking U.S. secretary of state who warns the Soviet Union that the United States will not hesitate to use nuclear arms against an aggressor.*

Linking Past to Present

Americans of the World War II generation are apt to look back on the 1950s as "the good old days." They see the decade as a time when the nation's place in the world was reasonably secure and when their personal goals were certain and their futures bright. Many Americans of the succeeding generation—who grew up during the 1950s—see it differently. They often claim that the period was too quiet and uninteresting.

The two generations arrive at their views from the same starting point. Each is comparing the decade with the violent and disorderly sixties and seventies. Yet despite the relative calm of the fifties, there were several indications of what lay ahead.

In foreign affairs there was a further chilling of relations between the United States and the Soviet Union. The interests of the two nations clashed in Europe, the Middle East, and Asia. On the domestic front, the Supreme Court in 1954 struck down the "separate but equal" doctrine that had existed since 1896 and opened the door for what many historians call the Second Reconstruction.

Also, the United States acquired two new states. In January 1959 Alaska became the forty-ninth state, and in August of the same year Hawaii was admitted as the fiftieth state.

1 NEW PATTERNS OF LIVING DEVELOP

During the 1950s a new trend developed. People began moving out of large cities into suburbs. Census figures for central cities went from 53.7 million in 1950 to 59.9 million in 1960, an increase of about 11 percent. But the figures for suburbs jumped almost 50 percent, from 40.0 million to 59.6 million. By the early 1960s every large city in the United States was surrounded by a heavily populated ring of smaller communities.

Suburban population also increased as a result of the movement of farmers. About 17 million left the land during the fifties. But most of them, instead of going to a large city, went either to a suburb or a small city.

The Growth of Suburbia

Fifteen years of depression and war had left the nation with a shortage of at least 5 million dwelling units. At first the construction industry was slow in meeting the demand. With the removal of wartime controls on prices and materials, builders concentrated on putting up factories rather than houses which were less profitable. Construction was further hampered by make-work rules that forbade the use of power tools and other labor-saving devices. Some ex-G.I.s made do with converted army barracks. About a million families doubled up. Then in 1949 William J. Levitt bought a 1500-acre potato field on Long Island, thirty miles east of New York City, and a new American lifestyle was inaugurated.

Levittown. Levitt was the Henry Ford of the housing industry. He pioneered the use of mass production in the building of private homes. He did it just as Ford had, by means of standardization. Ford used to say that people could buy a Model T in any color they wanted as long as it was black. Residents of Levittown could buy any kind of house they wanted as long as it was a four-room, one-story ranch house in the standard two-tone color scheme.

Levitt not only standardized the houses themselves. He also standardized the way they were built. First came the bulldozers to level the land. They were followed by street pavers, who laid down pavement. Next came electricians to install the light poles, and other men to put up the street signs. Once the streets were in, the lots were marked off.

Then it was time to put up the houses. As one historian described the process: "Convoys of trucks moved over the hardened pavements, tossing out prefabricated sidings at 8 A.M., toilets at 9:30, sinks and tubs at ten, sheetrock at 10:45, flooring at eleven." Within days, several hundred identical houses were ready for occupancy. (By 1951 Levittown contained 17,500 homes.)

It was a second Oklahoma Land Rush. Levitt did not advertise his houses. News spread by word of mouth. When his sales office opened on March 7, 1949, more than a thousand "Young Marrieds," some of whom had been waiting for four days, were already in line, ready to pay the standard price of $6990. With kitchen appliances, landscaping, and bank charges included, the whole package came to less than $10,000.

The package also included certain restrictions. For example, you were not allowed to put up a picket fence, and you were required to cut your lawn regularly. Laundry could dry on the line only on Monday, never on Sunday. Door signals had to be chimes; no buzzers or bell pulls were allowed. However, you *could* choose the particular chime you preferred.

Ten years after Levittown opened, its more rigid restrictions had been relaxed, and its geomet-

A second Levitt development in Pennsylvania. A popular song lamented the fact that people lived in "little boxes" that "all looked the same." But many people were happy to have homes they could afford.

rically planted trees had taken root. Patios, sun-decks, and dormers had added space and value to the basic ranch houses. By 1960 they were selling for two and three times their original cost, and the community had a varied and attractive look.

Suburban Sprawl. A year after Levitt had shown the way, housing starts rose to almost 2 million. They remained at about 1.5 million a year throughout the 1950s. The greatest part of this housing was in suburban developments. It had long been the American dream to own a single-family home with grass and some trees around it. The dream included a safe place for children to play, good schools, and friendly neighbors. Levitt and his imitators made it a reality for millions. Their customers did not seem to care that their daily commuting to the city took an hour or so each way, or that lawn care consumed much of their leisure time. The dream was worth it.

Dependence on the Auto. Suburban living made the automobile a necessity, not a luxury or a convenience. Public transportation was almost non-existent in rural areas plowed up by developers. Most suburbanites had to drive to work. In addition, schools, churches and synagogues, shopping centers, and doctors' and dentists' offices were seldom within walking distance. As a result, most suburban families owned two cars, one for the husband, another, usually a station wagon, for the wife to use while chauffeuring the children and doing errands.

Sales of new cars averaged about 6.7 million each year of the 1950s. The total number of private cars on the road went from 40 million in 1950 to 60 million in 1960. At the same time, public transportation dropped. There were 17.2 billion passenger trips in 1950 but only 9.4 billion ten years later.

A Trend Toward Conformity

Suburban life encouraged conformity. First of all, the houses were similar. Then, homeowners were all about the same age. There were no unmarried adults, and hardly any elderly or even middle-aged couples. Nearly all the males shared the same

714

background of wartime experiences and schooling under the G.I. bill. And because houses in any development cost about the same, homeowners had similar incomes. Some might be on their way up and a few on their way down but, for the time being, all were at nearly the same level.

Similar Lifestyles. People's lifestyles were about the same in housing developments. The emphasis was on friendliness and informality. People helped newcomers get settled and were generous with advice and the loan of tools. Children exchanged toys, clothing, and bikes. Carpooling children to school was common, as was the exchange of babysitting services. Buffet-style casserole dinners replaced sitdown dinners for entertaining, in part because the formal dining room no longer existed. It had given way to a combination living-dining room area that sometimes flowed into the kitchen as well. Men walked around in open-necked sport shirts on weekends, and women thought nothing of going to the grocery store with their hair in curlers. Almost everyone used first names, even youngsters talking to adults. But despite the casualness of manners and clothes, people were expected to "keep up" their property and take an active part in community affairs.

Probably no one in suburbia felt greater pressure to conform than children, who often outnumbered adults two to one. Childless couples were rare in the new developments, and by the middle fifties, families with four and five children were common. The PTA and Little League were among the most important community organizations. What with Scouts, music lessons, and religious classes—on top of regular school activities—children scarcely had an unorganized minute in their lives.

Education for Success. Both boys and girls were encouraged to be popular and well adjusted. If the boys could not "get along well" with their peers, how would they fit into a corporate organization when they grew up? And if the girls could not "get along well" with their peers, how would they be able to help their husbands advance in business or government?

Fitting into a corporate structure was particularly important by the fifties. One reason was that by 1956, the majority of workers were no longer blue-collar but white-collar. Instead of manufacturing goods, they produced services. And they produced services not for small firms but either for large corporations or for large government agencies—federal, state, and local.

As a result, the rising suburban middle class considered a good education an absolute necessity. Children were expected to outdo their parents in income and in social status. They could achieve that, it was believed, only if they were better educated than their parents. Although school budgets sometimes amounted to over half of the total expenditures in new communities, suburban parents seldom complained. What they wanted were programs that would raise school standards and enable their children to go to college.

Cloverleaf highways, like this one in a 1950 picture at Hackensack, N.J., were built to help reduce traffic jams. But before long, even these highways were crowded.

The Rise of Consumerism

Suburbanites also wanted, and were increasingly able to get, more consumer goods. Certainly one of the outstanding characteristics of the fifties was the high standard of living that most Americans enjoyed. Nearly 60 percent were now members of the middle class. The depression was only a bad memory. The country was producing half of the world's goods. And one new item after another was appearing in the marketplace. There were push-button phones and combination washer-dryers; cars with automatic transmissions; stereo FM sets and transistor radios and all sorts of things—even electric toothbrushes!

Most items were purchased on credit. Between 1952 and 1956 consumer debt rose from $27 billion to $43 billion. Instead of saving, Americans were spending, in full confidence that good times would continue indefinitely.

Section 1 Review

COMPREHENSION Developing Vocabulary

1. Explain these terms: conformity, white-collar workers, suburbia, standardization.

COMPREHENSION Mastering Facts

1. Who is considered the Henry Ford of the housing industry?
2. What effect did suburban living have on the use of the automobile?
3. What effect did suburban living have on people's clothes and manners?
4. What happened to the standard of living during the 1950s?

2 CHANGES COME TO THE WORLD OF ENTERTAINMENT

During the 1950s, old forms of entertainment changed and a new one arose. Beyond a doubt, television was *the* entertainment marvel of the postwar era. In 1950 there were not quite 4 million TV sets in use, and fewer than one household in ten had one. By 1960 there were 52 million sets in American homes—in almost nine out of ten households.

The average set was turned on six hours a day, seven days a week. One survey indicated that on the day of graduating from high school, the average American youngster would have spent 11,000 hours in the classroom and 15,000 hours in front of the television screen. Another survey pointed out that Americans spent more time watching the tube than they did earning a living.

The Triumph of the Little Screen

"A telegraph that could see" had been theoretically possible since the 1870s. A few experimental broadcasts were made in the 1920s, and very limited service began in 1939. Real expansion was touched off by the development of coaxial cable and microwave relays that could send television beams over the horizon. The first coast-to-coast television broadcast took place on September 4, 1951. It was President Truman's address at the Japanese Peace Treaty Conference in San Francisco, and was carried by 94 stations to 40 million viewers. As of 1952 the Federal Communications Commission (FCC) had issued licenses for 400 stations to operate on the twelve very-high-frequency (VHF) channels and 2000 stations on the seventy ultra-high-frequency (UHF) channels. About 12 percent of these stations presented educational and other non-commercial material.

Television Programming. Among the most popular programs of the decade were the *Toast of the Town* starring Ed Sullivan, which resembled the vaudeville shows of the Gilded Age; situation comedies such as *I Love Lucy* and *Adventures of Ozzie and Harriet*; game shows, of which *The $64,000 Question* and *What's My Line?* were typical; and newscasts by such reporters as Edward R. Murrow and the team of Chet Huntley and David Brinkley. Sports events filled many hours, and there were several dramatic presentations, including *Playhouse 90* and *Hallmark Hall of Fame*. Policemen were the heroes of such crime shows as *Dragnet*, while sheriffs played the starring roles in *Gunsmoke* and other westerns.

Occasionally a television-inspired fad came along. One in 1956 had millions of boys and girls between the ages of five and fifteen putting on coonskin caps in imitation of Davy Crockett of *Disneyland*. Other favorite children's shows of the time included *The Lone Ranger, Lassie, Hopalong Cassidy,* and *Howdy Doody.* Every once in a while there appeared a spec-

One of the first CBS television studios in Hollywood in 1952. TV opened up hundreds of new jobs. Sound and light experts were needed as well as cameramen, directors, and performing artists.

tacular—an extra-long, one-time only, carefully and expensively produced show.

Most programs were not produced by local stations but by one of three nationwide networks. The reason was economic. The larger an audience, the more money a TV station can charge to show an advertisement. Only a nationwide network could produce the kind of advertising revenue needed to fill all the hours of broadcast time. This had an effect on the type and quality of the programs. There were just so many writers, actors, actresses, musicians, and dancers. And shows had to be put together in a hurry. Minutes counted! As a result, much of the material tended to be commonplace or violent or both. The shows seemed thrown together. And they were! There was little emphasis on dialogue but considerable attention to slapstick, crashing cars, and murders. In 1954, in fact, more people were killed on television than in Korea. Controversial issues were more or less avoided so as not to offend advertisers or their potential customers. FCC Chairman Newton Minow gained considerable applause in the 1960s when he declared that television was "a vast wasteland."

Videotape Arrives. Meanwhile, TV's technical quality kept improving. An important engineering breakthrough of the late fifties was *videotape.* Live programs were visually bright and clear, but filmed programs lacked sharpness and definition. A videotaped performance, however, could not be distinguished from a live one. And the tape (like movie film) could be edited or redone to eliminate mistakes. As a result, by 1960, except for sports, news broadcasts, and a few other programs, live television was a thing of the past.

Radio and Motion Pictures Adjust

The media directly affected by the rise of television were radio and motion pictures. Radio was radically changed but not financially hurt. Expensive drama and variety shows disappeared. Instead, radio stations became local institutions, providing popular music, capsule news, and community services. The number of stations rose by 50 percent and advertising revenues went up 35 percent in ten years.

The change in the film industry was more drastic. The studio system of Hollywood was a highly industrialized operation that turned out 600 or more feature films a year. The films were distributed through 18,500 theaters which, in 1946, drew an incredible 90 million paid admissions per week. From the very beginning, TV cut into this rich market. People stayed home to watch the little screen. By 1950, 5000 theaters had turned into bowling alleys and supermarkets or simply stood dark, while the number of paid admissions had fallen by half.

As the decade progressed, business became even worse. Studios terminated the contracts of their stars and rented their facilities to independent producers or sold the land to real-estate developers for office buildings, apartment houses, and hotels. In 1960 only fourteen feature films were made by studios. The rest were turned out by independents or by filmmakers in Europe and elsewhere.

To compete with the little screen in the living room, movie makers concentrated on color and spectacle. Elaborate musical numbers, panoramic battle sequences, and numbing special effects were commonplace. Along with color and stereophonic sound, several widescreen techniques were used to make movies seem more realistic. There was even a brief revival of three-dimensional films for which the audience had to wear cardboard eyeglasses with polarized lenses. Nothing helped. By 1960 only 27 percent of the population over five years of age was going to the movies each week, down from 70 percent in 1946. And the bottom had not yet been reached.

One result was that motion pictures were no longer a national unifying force. Once, they had appealed to all ages and classes. Every war film made in the 1940s had representatives of at least four or five different ethnic groups as members of the army platoon or flying squadron that performed heroic deeds against the Axis. Now the motion picture market fragmented. Films were made to appeal to special markets such as young children, or teen-agers, or adults, or science fiction fans, or martial arts fans, or, as in the 1970s, blacks. Their subject matter and stars varied. So did the values they presented.

Elvis Presley, the most popular singer in the history of American rock music. For over twenty years, his movies, records, and public appearances captivated millions of teenagers.

A New Music

In popular music, the 1950s brought a change as radical as jazz had been more than a generation earlier. Jazz musicians had turned to progressive jazz; that is, they played a complex and sophisticated style that was best appreciated in concert or on records. It was no longer suitable for dancing.

In 1954 a black singing group called the Chords wrote a hit tune entitled "Sh–Boom." The next year performer Bill Haley and his band, the Comets, recorded "Rock Around the Clock." The music of both records combined country-western, black rhythm and blues, and black gospel singing.

Country-western is folk music that is usually played on guitars, fiddles, and harmonicas; its songs often deal with love, crime, and prison life. Rhythm-and-blues stresses saxophone solos. Gospel music evolved out of plantation work songs and Protestant church hymns.

The powerful beat, simple lyrics, and deafening volume of the new music appealed to young people. Disc jockey Alan Freed coined the term "rock and roll" to describe it. And in 1956 it became the ideal music of American teen-agers. Its star was a young country blues singer and former truck driver from Memphis named Elvis Presley. In short order, his long-playing records and such singles as "Heartbreak Hotel" and "Love Me Tender" were selling in the millions, while his vocal style and way of moving were widely imitated.

Section 2 Review

COMPREHENSION   Developing Vocabulary

1. Explain these terms: videotape, rock and roll, TV spectacular.

COMPREHENSION   Mastering Facts

1. Why were most television programs produced by nation-wide networks rather than local stations?
2. What are the advantages of a videotaped performance as compared with a live performance?
3. What effect did television have on radio?
4. What effect did television have on motion pictures?

3   MINORITIES MAKE SOME PROGRESS

VOCABULARY   *state interposition   termination policy*

The years after World War II saw considerable progress in the continuing struggle to end racial discrimination in the United States. Some of the progress resulted from court action, some from the political technique of civil disobedience.

Equal and Integrated Education

Beginning with the mid-1930s, the National Association for the Advancement of Colored People (NAACP) had concentrated its limited resources on winning equal educational opportunities for black Americans. By the mid-1950s the effort resulted in a precedent-shattering decision by the Supreme Court.

Early Cases.   The first significant challenge of the "separate but equal" doctrine established by *Plessy* v. *Ferguson* (1896) occurred in 1938. Lloyd Gaines, a black, wanted to study law at the University of Missouri. Since the state did not have a law school for blacks, it offered to pay Gaines's tuition at a Canadian school. Gaines sued. The Supreme Court held that since Gaines expected to practice law in Missouri, he was entitled to receive his legal training there. If Missouri did not have a black law school, then it would have to admit Gaines to the all-white state university.

Over the next fifteen years, the Supreme Court heard several similar cases. In each instance it held that unless facilities were in fact equal, blacks had to be admitted to all-white schools. A typical case was *Sweatt* v. *Painter* (1950). Texas had organized a separate law school for a single black applicant, Herman N. Sweatt. Sweatt refused to attend on the grounds that the school was inferior. The Court agreed and ordered him enrolled at the University of Texas Law School. In another decision handed down the same day, the Court ruled (in *McLaurin* v. *Oklahoma State Regents*) that a black student admitted to a state university could not be compelled to sit, study, or eat apart from other students.

The Brown Case.   All this was a rehearsal for the 1954 decision in the case of *Oliver Brown et al.* v. *Board of Education of Topeka, Kansas.* The case applied not to graduate schools but to the more sensitive area of elementary and secondary education.

Oliver Brown, a black resident of Topeka, brought legal action against the school board on behalf of his eight-year-old daughter Linda. She had been denied admission to the all-white elementary school a few blocks from her house. Instead, she had to cross a railroad yard and then take a bus for twenty-one blocks to an all-black school. The attorney for the NAACP, which represented Brown, was Thurgood Marshall (who later became the first black Supreme Court justice).

The case was not a simple one. Decades of law and custom, as well as the tradition of states' rights, stood on one side. On the other side was the argument that segregating students on the basis of race denied them the equal protection guaranteed by the Fourteenth Amendment. In this case, for the first time, the Supreme Court accepted psychological evidence. Leading psychologists submitted studies showing the effects of segregation on black children.

A Unanimous Decision. The Supreme Court handed down its decision on May 17, 1954. The opinion was delivered by Chief Justice Earl Warren. He was a recent appointee to the Court, having been active in California politics most of his life. He had served as state attorney-general and governor, and was the Republican candidate for vice-president in 1948.

The Court's opinion was unanimous. And it is worth noting that three of the justices—Hugo L. Black of Alabama, Tom C. Clark of Texas, and Stanley F. Reed of Kentucky—were southerners. As stated by Justice Warren, the Court held that

" To separate [black children] from others of similar age and qualifications solely because of their race generates a feeling of inferiority as to their status in the community that may affect their hearts and minds in a way never to be undone. . . . We conclude that in the field of public education the doctrine of 'separate but equal' has no place. Separate educational facilities are inherently unequal. **"**

In other words, public schools should be integrated.

Reaction to the Decision. The *Brown* case, which affected 12 million children, has been called the most important event in black history since the Emancipation Proclamation. Blacks throughout the nation greeted it with joy and hope.

White southerners were less happy. Public officials in the border states, however, announced they would go along with the decision. But in Virginia and the states of the Deep South, negative feelings were much stronger. The legal doctrine of state "interposition," another name for John C. Calhoun's nullification, was proposed by Senator Harry Byrd of Virginia. Other members of Congress brought forward a manifesto declaring the *Brown* decision an abuse of judicial power. In Mississippi, White Citizens Councils vowed "total resistance." The Ku Klux Klan rose again, and the sale of small arms increased. Virginia passed laws permitting state financing of private schools.

After the *Brown* decision the Supreme Court waited a year to give school authorities a chance to evaluate their situation. Then the Court ordered them to make a "prompt and reasonable start" toward carrying out the decision with "all deliberate speed." School districts in the border states and in large cities throughout the South began admitting a few blacks to all-white schools. But elsewhere there was no change. And in one instance, white resistance led to a major crisis.

Resisting School Integration. Governor Orval E. Faubus of Arkansas was seeking a third term. He faced several difficulties. The state had a two-term tradition, and the governor had offended various groups by raising taxes and allowing utilities and railroads to increase their rates. He needed a strong campaign issue.

The city of Little Rock had carefully worked out a plan for integrating its schools over a seven-year period. In the fall of 1957, the plan called for nine black students to be enrolled with 2000 white students in the city's Central High School. Suddenly, the night before classes were scheduled to begin, Governor Faubus called out the National Guard and stationed it around the school. The next day, soldiers with fixed bayonets turned the nine black youngsters away. Several days later, a federal court ordered the guardsmen removed. But when the black students again tried to go to class, a white mob created so much turmoil that they were forced to leave.

Faced with a virtual revolt, President Eisenhower did not hesitate. As he told the nation, "Mob rule cannot be allowed to override the decisions of our courts." He promptly ordered 1000 paratroopers of the 101st Airborne Division into Little Rock to uphold the law. This was the first

Members of the 101st Airborne Division stand guard outside Little Rock's Central High School. When classes began inside, black students were present for the first time in history.

time since Reconstruction that the power of the federal government was used to protect blacks in the South. For good measure, Eisenhower also federalized the Arkansas National Guard, thus taking it out of the governor's control.

The nine blacks were admitted to Central High School. Most of the federal troops were withdrawn in November, although a few remained until the end of the school year. In 1958 Governor Faubus, who had won his campaign for reelection, closed the school. After a legal battle it reopened in 1959 with only three black students enrolled.

Integrated Public Facilities

Even before Little Rock had shown that the struggle for school integration would be long and difficult, blacks in the South had begun using direct action rather than court cases to bring about change. The shift in tactics was triggered by a black woman in Montgomery, Alabama.

Rosa Parks. On December 1, 1955, seamstress Rosa Parks was returning home on a city bus. Tired after a long day's work, she sat down in the front section, which was reserved for whites. A white passenger entered, and the bus driver ordered her to give up her seat, as the law said she must. As Rosa Parks told it afterwards, "For a long time I had resented being treated a certain way because of my race. We had always been taught that America was the land of the free and the home of the brave and that we were all equals." So Rosa Parks said, "No." At the next bus stop she was arrested and later fined ten dollars.

Within forty-eight hours the black community of Montgomery had organized a one-day boycott of the city's bus line. It was a complete success, and it set black leaders thinking. There were 25,000 blacks in the city and they made up about 75 percent of the bus company's customers. Suppose they refused to ride the buses until certain conditions were met, such as allowing blacks to sit wherever they wanted to, hiring black drivers for buses in black areas, and instructing white bus drivers to be polite to black passengers. If the bus company lost three-fourths of its customers, surely it would eventually be forced to either agree to the conditions or go out of business.

Martin Luther King, Jr. At the head of the association formed to carry out the boycott was a twenty-six-year-old minister named Martin Luther King, Jr. Holder of a Ph.D. degree from Boston University, King preached a philosophy called "soul force." It was based on the teachings of several people: (1) Henry Thoreau, who believed individuals should refuse to obey unjust laws and had set an example by going to jail rather than pay taxes in support of slavery; (2) Mahatma Gandhi, who had helped his native country of India achieve its independence through non-violent resistance to the British; and (3) A. Philip Randolph, who had urged blacks to organize mass demonstrations.

King persuaded his fellow blacks to keep their protests entirely non-violent. "This is not a tension between the Negroes and whites," he told his followers. "This is only a conflict between justice and injustice. We are not just trying to improve Negro Montgomery. We are trying to improve the whole of Montgomery. If we are arrested every day; if we are exploited every day; if we are triumphed over every day; let nobody pull you so low as to hate them." King believed most whites were basically decent and, when faced by love, would not allow injustice and brutality to continue.

The struggle in Montgomery was not easy. Negotiations between black leaders and the bus company broke down early. The boycott continued for more than a year, as blacks walked, rode bicycles, or used a car pool that King organized. Some whites supported the boycott by giving blacks rides or paying taxi fares for their black cooks and handymen.

Then the Supreme Court handed down another ruling. Segregation in public transportation, as in public education, violated the Fourteenth Amendment and was unconstitutional. In December 1956, a little more than a year after Rosa Parks had refused to give up her seat, King boarded a Montgomery bus and sat down in the front. As he said later, "It was a great ride."

Hope for the Sixties

The Montgomery bus boycott was a bright spot in the civil rights movement. It had produced an organization, a leader, and a technique. Additional groups, mostly church centered, sprang up and were brought together by King in the Southern Christian Leadership Conference (SCLC). This organization was to play a major role during the 1960s.

Also significant for the future was the Civil Rights Act of 1957. It was the first such act since Reconstruction, and it was passed only after a legislative struggle that included a Senate debate lasting sixty-three days. The act set up a Civil Rights Commission and gave the Justice Department the power to file suits on behalf of black citizens who were being denied the right to vote. Black voter registration in the South was 1.2 million in 1956, but it was estimated that throughout the region, at least 5 million blacks were eligible to vote.

Mexican-Americans Gain Greater Recognition

Another minority that began to develop a stronger political awareness during the 1950s was the Mexican-Americans, or Chicanos.

Many Mexicans had become American citizens in the mid-1800s when the United States annexed the Southwest following the Mexican-American War. During and after World War I, large numbers of Mexicans crossed the border to work in the

After the Supreme Court decision, Rosa Parks returned to Montgomery, Ala., for an unsegregated ride.

Cesar Chavez (center), soon to become famous as an organizer and spokesman for Mexican-American farmworkers.

States. Most of them were either migrant farm laborers in the area's orchards, vegetable farms, and cotton fields or miners and railroad workers. Many came under a legal work contract. But many also crossed the Rio Grande without a passport. But regardless of how they came, Mexican-Americans played a major role in the economic growth of the Southwest.

During World War II, many Mexican-Americans served in the armed forces. When they returned to civilian life, they were determined to do something about the poor conditions under which most of them lived. Chicanos often suffered from discrimination in housing and wages. In addition, many were handicapped by the lack of job skills and the inability to speak English well. They wanted better opportunities to become educated and to earn a living.

Mexican-Americans were shocked into organized action by an insult to the family of Felix Longoria, a Mexican-American war hero killed in the Philippines. The only undertaker in his home town in Texas refused to let the Longoria family use his funeral home because they were Chicanos. The American G.I. Forum was organized to protest this and other injustices to Mexican-American veterans.

Soon after, Ignacio (eeg-*nah*-see-oh) Lopez founded the Unity League in California to register Mexican-American voters and to promote candidates who would represent them. The league also succeeded in having segregated classes for Chicano children outlawed in the state. Similar voter registration groups were formed under various names in Arizona and Texas.

American Indians Struggle To Survive

From the passage of the Dawes Act in 1887 until 1934, the policy of the federal government toward Indians was one of Americanization. This idea was as old as Jefferson's time. Indian tribes were officially abolished and in 1924 all Indians were made citizens of the United States.

That same year, the American Indian Defense Organization was formed. Under the leadership of such people as John Collier, Sr.—who later became head of the federal Bureau of Indian Affairs—the organization worked to change the government's policy.

Reorganizing Indian Affairs. In 1934 the Indian Reorganization Act took several significant steps away from assimilation. On the economic level, Indian lands would no longer be broken up into individual farms but would belong to a tribe as a whole. On the cultural level, the number of boarding schools for Indian children was cut back. Instead, children could attend day schools on the reservations and, in some cases, even have Indian teachers. On the political level, Indian tribes were given permission to elect a tribal council to govern their reservation. One result of the government's new policy was a rapid growth in the Indian population.

In 1943 the National Congress of American Indians was established. The organization eventually grew to include some 90 tribes containing two-thirds of the nation's Indians. The goals of the Congress were two-fold. First, it wanted Indians to have the same civil rights white Americans have.

Second, it wanted Indians on reservations to be allowed to retain their own customs and values, even if those were different from the customs and values of mainstream society. For example, Indians generally believe in cooperation rather than competition. No Indian language has a word for

723

Traditional life continues in many Indian settlements. The woman at the left is straining parts of a prickly pear cactus and will then boil them to make jam.

"time," and most Indians do not live by the clock the way most whites do.

During World War II, some 65,000 Indians left the reservations for military service and war work. As a result, they became very aware of anti-Indian discrimination. Then the war ended, and Indian family allotments and wages stopped. At the same time, the general prosperity meant there was greater pressure from non-Indians to get hold of tribal lands, primarily to explore them for mineral deposits.

The Termination Policy. In 1953 Congress again changed its Indian policy. The new approach was one of "termination." It was announced that the federal government would give up its responsibility for the Indian tribes as soon as possible. In other words, the reservation system would be discontinued and tribal land would be distributed among individual Indians. In the meantime, tribal leaders would no longer have authority over civil and criminal cases on the reservations. That authority was given to the states. In line with the termination policy, the Bureau of Indian Affairs began a relocation and job-training program to help Indians move to the city.

The termination policy was a failure. Although thousands of Indians left the reservations, they were often unable to find jobs in their new homes. Other Indians lost out when communally owned land was sold at too low a price. Federal medical and other assistance programs were abolished without anything to take their place. The number of Indians on state welfare rolls soared. Indians and whites alike protested vigorously and in 1963 the termination policy was abandoned.

Section 3 Review

COMPREHENSION   Developing Vocabulary
1. Explain these terms: state interposition, termination policy, soul force.

COMPREHENSION   Mastering Facts
1. What effect did *Brown* v. *Board of Education of Topeka* have on public schools?
2. Why did President Eisenhower send federal troops to Little Rock?
3. What were the results of the Montgomery bus boycott?
4. How did the federal government change its Indian policy in 1953?

VOCABULARY *Cold War* *massive retaliation* *Eisenhower Doctrine* *domino theory* *Sputnik I*

The 1950s ended on a note of doubt and uncertainty, much as they had begun. The Cold War between the United States and the Soviet Union, in which each side tested the other without actually engaging in direct conflict, heated up and then cooled down several times. A number of new concepts in foreign policy were enunciated. And Americans became increasingly involved in a conflict in Indochina which, in the next decade, was to develop into a major war.

In Europe

Following the death of Joseph Stalin in 1953, there was a slight thaw in U.S.-Soviet relations. The Soviets recognized the West German republic, and peace treaties were concluded with Austria and Japan. Attempts to control the nuclear arms race, however, were unsuccessful. In 1955 a summit conference at Geneva between American, British, French, and Russian heads of government broke down over an old issue: the fact that the Soviets refused to allow aerial inspection of their factories.

Dulles and Massive Retaliation. Although the Republican party had denounced Truman's policy of containing communism, Eisenhower continued it after he was elected president. The only real difference was a shift in the budget of the Defense Department.

In line with his belief in a strong cabinet, Eisenhower gave most of the responsibility for foreign affairs to his secretary of state, John Foster Dulles. Dulles was a staunch opponent of communism, but was a rather rigid individual who viewed compromise as immoral.

Dulles proposed a new policy he called *massive retaliation*. It said, in effect, that if the United States considered it necessary, it would not hesitate to use all of its force, including nuclear arms, against an aggressor nation. Application of the policy meant greater dependence on nuclear weapons and less on conventional ground forces. Accordingly, in the mid-1950s, the United States cut back on its army and navy but built up its air force and began stockpiling nuclear weapons.

Opponents of massive retaliation pointed out that the United States would no longer be able to wage wars for limited objectives, as in Korea. Ob-viously, they said, no nation would risk nuclear war unless its existence was at stake. And in fact, when the Soviet Union attacked Hungary in 1956, the United States did not take any military action.

The Soviets Invade Hungary. In October 1956 a revolt broke out in Hungary. Spearheaded by students and other young people, it called for an end to Soviet control of that nation's government. The new premier denounced the Warsaw Pact, and Soviet troops withdrew from Budapest. For a while it seemed as if the Hungarians had succeeded in freeing themselves.

But in November, Soviet forces returned and smashed the uprising with tanks and artillery. Joseph Cardinal Mindszenty (men-*sen*-tay) took shelter in the American embassy, where he remained for more than fifteen years. Thousands of other refugees fled the country, many of them eventually coming to the United States. Eisenhower sent Hungary $20 million for food and medicine. But his protests to the Soviet government on the invasion were rejected.

A U-2 Is Shot Down. Following the failure of the 1955 Summit Conference at Geneva, the CIA began making secret high-altitude flights over Soviet territory. The plane used for these missions, the U-2, was designed to fly higher than Russian fighter planes and beyond the reach of antiaircraft fire. As a U-2 passed over the USSR, its infrared cameras took detailed photographs of everything below.

On May 1, 1960 a U-2 flown by American pilot Francis Gary Powers was shot down by the Soviets. The United States issued a false story that one of its planes had disappeared while on a weather mission over Turkey and might have strayed over the Russian border. Soviet Premier Nikita Khrushchev (kroos-*choff*) then personally announced that the U-2 had been brought down 1300 miles inside the Soviet Union by a Russian rocket and that Powers had been captured "alive and kicking" and had confessed his activities.

It was a bad moment for the United States, especially since another summit conference on the arms race was to be held in Paris. But President Eisenhower regained credit for the nation by frankly owning up to the truth of the charge. In addition, the president took full personal responsibility for authorizing the flight. Such an admission was unprecedented for the head of a government. Although all nations use spies, they do not admit it publicly.

Khrushchev then insisted that the summit conference be postponed for six months and that the United States apologize for its past "aggressions" and punish the people responsible for them. Eisenhower, who had announced the suspension of further U-2 flights over Soviet territory, refused. The summit conference broke up.

Powers was tried for espionage and sentenced to ten years in a Soviet jail. After seventeen months, however, he was returned to the United States in exchange for a Soviet spy, Colonel Rudolf Abel, who had been convicted in an American court.

In the Middle East

The Cold War showed itself in the Middle East as well as in Europe. The first major event had to do with developments in Egypt.

The Suez Canal Crisis. In 1954 Great Britain agreed to withdraw its troops from the area of the Suez Canal, which was owned mostly by British and French stockholders. In 1955 Great Britain and the United States, anxious to keep Soviet influence out of Egypt, agreed to help finance construction of the Aswan Dam on the Nile River. But instead of signing the agreement, Gamal Abdel Nasser, head of the Egyptian government, delayed. Apparently he hoped to get better terms from the Soviet Union.

After seven months of waiting, the United States and Great Britain withdrew their offer in July 1956. Furious at what he considered an insult to his nation, Nasser seized the Suez Canal. In the future, he said, canal tolls would not go to the European stockholders. Instead, they would be used to help build the Aswan Dam.

Now it was the turn of the British and French to be furious, especially since two-thirds of the oil they needed for heat and industrial production came through the canal. In the meantime, the Egyptians had been making terrorist raids into Israel. Also, contrary to international law, Israeli ships had not been allowed by Egypt to use the canal. So in October 1956 Great Britain, France, and Israel joined forces against Egypt. British and French troops occupied the canal area, while Is-

raeli soldiers took over the Gaza Strip and the Sinai Peninsula. The Egyptians thereupon blocked all traffic through the canal by sinking some two dozen ships.

The attack on Egypt shocked Eisenhower, who felt there was no excuse for aggression, even by one's allies. The United States accordingly asked the United Nations to order a cease-fire in Egypt and the withdrawal of British, French, and Israeli troops. However, when the Soviet Union threatened to use missiles against England and France, the United States warned it would not tolerate such action.

Eventually matters simmered down. Britain and France withdrew their troops. So did Israel, after receiving a promise that its ships would be allowed to use the canal in the future. United Nations troops were sent into the area to help keep the peace. The UN also sent in a salvage operation to help clear the canal, and in April 1957 traffic again began moving along the waterway.

The Eisenhower Doctrine. As a result of its support for Egypt, the prestige of the Soviet Union in the Middle East was now high. To counterbalance this, and also as a reaction to events in Hungary, President Eisenhower issued a warning in January 1957. In it he said the United States would defend the Middle East against Soviet attack. This warning became known as the Eisenhower Doctrine.

In March Congress officially approved the doctrine. It gave the president authority to use American forces, at his discretion, against armed aggression in the Middle East from any nation "controlled by international communism." Accordingly, in 1957 Eisenhower sent the Sixth Fleet to the eastern Mediterranean, while in 1958 he dispatched 14,000 marines to Lebanon. In both cases, the president was countering moves by Soviet-supported Syria.

In Indochina

The Cold War was not limited to Europe and the Middle East. It showed up in Asia as well. There, however, the United States ran into a somewhat different problem: how to tell the difference between anticolonial nationalists and anticolonial communists. Both groups wanted to remove foreign control, a principle most Americans agreed with. But what sort of government was to

Indochina and Vietnam

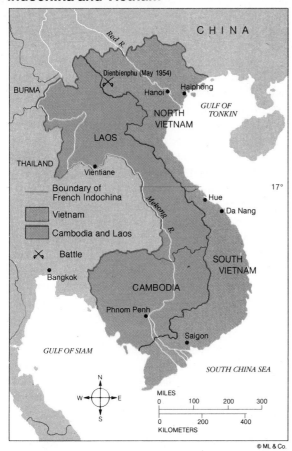

Map Skills *What countries were part of French Indochina? How long ago was the battle at Dien Bien Phu?*

replace the foreign power? And how was that government to be chosen?

The Japanese had occupied the French colony of Indochina (Laos, Cambodia, and Vietnam) during World War II. The United States had sent weapons and medical supplies to various nationalist groups in the area who were fighting the Japanese. One such group was the Viet Minh (*vee*-yet min) which was led by a Soviet-trained Communist named Ho Chi Minh (ho chee min).

In 1946 a war broke out between the Viet Minh and the French, who were trying to regain their colony after the defeat of Japan. In 1949 the French, in an agreement with non-Communist nationalists, recognized the State of Vietnam. Its head of state was Bao Dai (*bah*-oh dye), and the capital was Saigon. The following year Ho Chi Minh, apparently with help from Red China, mounted a major offensive against the French.

American Aid Begins. At first the United States remained neutral. But in 1950 President Truman decided to take action. He recognized Bao Dai's regime and sent it money, arms, and technicians. When Eisenhower was elected, he ordered the economic and military aid increased. He believed that if the Communists were to capture Indochina, all the remaining nations in Southeast Asia would come under Communist control one after another, the way a row of dominoes falls when the first domino is hit. This became known as the "domino theory." But even so, Eisenhower refused to send U.S. troops to Vietnam.

In 1954 the Viet Minh surrounded a large French army in the city of Dien Bien Phu (*dee*-yen *bee*-yen foo). The French begged the United States to send in troops but the appeal was turned down. Within a few weeks Dien Bien Phu fell, and it was clear that the French, like the Japanese, would have to clear out.

The Geneva Accords. In the meantime, an international peace conference to settle the Indochina question was held in Geneva. France and Great Britain represented one side, Red China and the Soviet Union the other side. Everyone agreed to a cease-fire. Then, as had been the case in Germany and Korea, Vietnam was divided, at the 17th parallel. The Democratic Republic of Vietnam, or North Vietnam, was headed by Ho Chi Minh. The State of Vietnam, or South Vietnam, was headed by Bao Dai. Elections to form a government for the entire country were to be held after two years. Laos and Cambodia received their independence.

A few months later, Bao Dai's government was overthrown by Ngo Dinh Diem (no din *zee*-em). Diem said he would not go along with the agreements made at Geneva because they had not been signed by the South Vietnamese government. And in 1956, the time set for the all-Vietnam election, he refused to take part. Anti-Diem forces, known as the Vietcong, thereupon began a guerrilla campaign in South Vietnam against the Diem government.

Some of the Vietcong were Communists receiving aid from Ho. Others were Buddhists who did not like Diem's favoritism toward Roman Catholics. There were also liberals who wanted a free press and trial by jury, neither of which Diem allowed. Finally, there were simply nationalists who wanted Vietnam to be united. But since it was clear that many of those opposed to Diem were Communists, Eisenhower sent more and more aid to Diem over the next four years.

Sputnik Starts the Space Race

The Cold War was not limited to geographic areas. It took place in scientific and scholastic areas, too.

The United States began the year 1957 confident that it was ahead of the Russians in military technology. It had guided missiles that could deliver nuclear warheads with great accuracy at dis-

The Soviet Union's scientific triumph is featured in Time *magazine. Premier Khrushchev beams at Sputnik I.*

tances of 1500 to 3000 miles. Then in August 1957, the Soviets announced they had developed a rocket capable of firing much greater distances, a true intercontinental ballistic missile (ICBM).

The real shock came on October 4, when the Russians proved their claim. On that day they used one of the rockets to push the first unmanned space satellite to a point above the friction of the earth's atmosphere. There the satellite, Sputnik I, traveled around the earth at a speed of 18,000 miles per hour, circling the globe every 96.2 minutes. Its weight of nearly 200 pounds indicated that 200,000 pounds of thrust had been used to lift it into orbit. That was more than enough force to deliver a nuclear warhead anywhere in the world.

The launching of Sputnik I had an enormous effect on Americans. It led to a space race that landed two American astronauts on the moon in 1969. It also led to several changes in education. The study of science, mathematics, and foreign languages was upgraded as federal programs were adopted to improve teaching in these disciplines. The National Science Foundation was expanded and charged with increasing the number and quality of scientists. Two results were greater attention to basic research and a new physics curriculum for schools.

Section 4 Review

COMPREHENSION   Developing Vocabulary
1. Explain these terms: massive retaliation, domino theory, Cold War, Eisenhower Doctrine, Sputnik I.

COMPREHENSION   Mastering Facts
1. How did the United States respond to the Soviet attack on Hungary?
2. What was the purpose of the U-2 flights?
3. What decisions about Vietnam were reached in Geneva in 1954?
4. What effect did the launching of Sputnik I have on American education?

CHAPTER 36   Review

Chapter Summary

New patterns of living developed in the 1950s. Americans moved to the suburbs, where conformity was encouraged. New methods of housing construction produced look-alike communities. Network television and the wide-screen motion picture became the focus of the entertainment world. The 1950s were a relatively quiet decade, but in 1954 a Supreme Court decision ended the "separate but equal" doctrine in public schools. Dr. Martin Luther King, Jr., led Americans to work for new civil rights reforms. In world affairs, the Soviets invaded Hungary, and Egypt took over the Suez Canal. The Eisenhower Doctrine committed the United States to defense of the Middle East. Then in 1957, the Soviet Union launched the Space Age when it orbited Sputnik I.

Questions for Critical Thinking

COMPREHENSION   Summarizing Main Ideas

1. What were the advantages of buying a house in Levittown? What were the disadvantages?
2. In what ways did the everyday lives of Americans change during the 1950s? Do you think the changes are permanent? Explain.
3. What reasons did the Supreme Court give for overturning the "separate but equal" doctrine?
4. How did each of the following contribute to the technique of non-violent protest? (a) Henry Thoreau; (b) Mahatma Gandhi; (c) Rosa Parks; (d) Martin Luther King, Jr.
5. Name three ways in which Mexicans came under the jurisdiction of the United States. How did they contribute to the economic growth of the Southwest?
6. What are the arguments in favor of massive retaliation? What are the arguments against it?

COMPREHENSION   Interpreting Events

1. Do you agree or disagree with the statement that television is " a vast wasteland"? Give reasons for your opinion.

2. Why did blacks shift from court cases to direct action to obtain civil rights?
3. Do you think the policy of termination is desirable? Why or why not? What were the results of the policy?

APPLICATION   Using Skills To Understand Time

1. A generation is usually considered to be a period of thirty years, the average difference in age between parents and their children. How many generations separate your lifetime from the 1950s? How many generations separate your lifetime from the Civil War era? from Revolutionary times?
2. Make a time line of your parents' lives. Include significant personal events as well as important world and national occurrences.

EVALUATION   Forming Generalizations

Write a generalization for each of the following groups of statements.

Group 1
  a. Most of the houses in a suburban development cost about the same.
  b. Most of the people who bought homes in suburban developments after World War II were young married couples.
  c. Most of the families who lived in suburban developments had several children.
  d. Most of the homes in suburban developments were bought with the help of the G. I. Bill.

Group 2
  a. Senator Harry Byrd of Virginia proposed the doctrine of state "interposition" with regard to the Supreme Court decision in *Brown* v. *Board of Education*.
  b. The Virginia state legislature passed laws permitting the use of state funds for private schools.
  c. Governor Orval E. Faubus of Arkansas stationed the National Guard around Central High School in Little Rock in order to keep out black students.

Yankee Ingenuity

Artist Norman Rockwell portrays the inventive spirit of Henry Ford.

"Yankee ingenuity" is a familiar phrase that refers to the American spirit of inventiveness. It means, quite simply, that no problem is too tough to solve. For example, when shocked Americans found themselves trailing in the space race in 1957, the nation set a goal to put a person on the moon before the end of the 1960s. In a classic example of the "can-do" spirit, the United States accomplished its awesome goal—with six months to spare. This same American determination has built transcontinental railroads, the Panama Canal, superhighways, and space shuttles.

Over the years, Americans have clearly been pioneers of applied science and technology. What conditions have fostered such inventiveness? From the beginning, America was an open society. Individuals were free to express curiosity, free to ask questions, free to experiment and explore. America was also a material society, with abundant resources readily at hand.

Originality Needed. As a new nation, the United States had distinctly new problems that required original solutions. In order to survive, Americans simply *had* to solve these problems. For that reason our history is filled with inventive geniuses who put "Yankee ingenuity" into practice.

What has the inventive spirit done for America? Most noticeably, it has provided a wealth of labor-saving devices that make our culture unique. There is some question, however, whether in controlling our environment we have invented machines that in turn master us. Have material inventions made us freer—or more dependent?

Many Challenges Remain. Whatever the consequences of our inventive spirit, one fact is certain: no one can turn back the clock or attempt to keep certain discoveries secret. Atomic power, for example, has the potential for many positive results, but it can also be incredibly destructive. Similar statements can be made regarding advances in genetics, chemicals, drugs, and other areas. Thus, although American ingenuity has brought unparalleled material well-being to ourselves and others, many serious problems still await inventive solutions.

Understanding Our Heritage

1. What evidence suggests that Yankee ingenuity is alive and well today?

2. What technological problems do you hope the American spirit of inventiveness will solve in your lifetime?

3. Has Yankee ingenuity been applied to social problems in the past? in the present? Give examples.

UNIT 9 Review

Understanding Social Studies Concepts

History

1. Arrange the following events in chronological order: (a) Munich Pact signed; (b) Mussolini invades Ethiopia; (c) Japan attacks Manchuria; (d) Germany invades Poland; (e) Germany occupies the Rhineland; (f) Nazi party comes to power in Germany.
2. After World War I, isolationism was popular in the United States. That was not the case after World War II. Why?
3. What was the Truman Doctrine? the Marshall Plan? NATO? How did each attempt to contain the growth of communism?
4. Though their attack on Pearl Harbor was an unquestioned military success, what did the Japanese underestimate about America?
5. Explain the meaning of the term *Cold War*.
6. What actions might the Allies have taken during the 1930s to prevent World War II?

Economics

1. In what ways did World War II represent a triumph of American economic power as well as military might?
2. Why did the United States experience a postwar economic boom rather than a depression in the late 1940s?
3. Why was President Eisenhower's economic philosophy called "dynamic conservatism"?
4. What important change in Americans' attitude toward personal savings took place during the decade of the 1950s?

Government

1. Describe the government action that led to the case of *Korematsu* v. *United States*. How do many historians today view the government isolation of Japanese Americans?
2. What strategy did Harry Truman use in 1948 to register the biggest political upset in the nation's history?
3. What effect did Senator McCarthy have on the government? on Americans in general?
4. Why was Dwight D. Eisenhower such a popular president?

Sociology

1. How did women contribute to the United States military effort in World War II? Did the changes in their status continue after the war?
2. What was the significance of the *Brown* v. *Board of Education* decision by the Supreme Court in 1954? What other gains did blacks and other minorities make during the 1950s?
3. What new patterns of living developed in the United States during the 1950s?

Extending Map, Chart, Picture Skills

1. Refer to the map on page 658. How does the information on the map demonstrate the American strategy of "leapfrogging" in the Pacific? Name specific islands in your answer.
2. Refer to the map on page 689. Along what borders did Winston Churchill say that an "iron curtain" had descended across Europe?
3. What is your interpretation of the cartoon on page 703? Why is "Public Opinion" providing the fuel for the flame?

Understanding Current Events

1. How old is the United Nations? In what ways has that organization changed since it was founded? Do you believe that the UN serves a worthwhile purpose? Explain.
2. What event marked the beginning of the Space Age? Over the years, what benefits have Americans received from the nation's commitment to explore space?

Developing Effective Citizenship

1. Why did virtually all unions agree not to strike during World War II? How did these and other patriotic actions aid the American war effort?
2. How did the G.I. Bill of Rights attempt to repay Americans who had fought for their country during World War II?
3. In what ways did Mexican-Americans, blacks, and other minorities assert more strongly their rights as Americans during the 1950s?

GLOBAL TIME LINE
since 1960

THE UNITED STATES

THE WORLD

1963 President Kennedy assassinated.

1965 American troops begin
fighting in South Vietnam.

1967 First black appointed
to Supreme Court.

1974 Richard Nixon resigns
as president.

1976 Americans
celebrate
bicentennial.

1960 — 1970

1967 First human
heart transplant.

1960 Thirteen nations form OPEC.

1975 South Vietnam
surrenders to
North Vietnam.

1971 Communist China
admitted to United Nations.

UNIT **10**

Continuity and Change

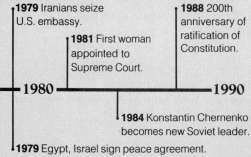

1979 Iranians seize U.S. embassy.

1981 First woman appointed to Supreme Court.

1988 200th anniversary of ratification of Constitution.

1980 ———————————— 1990

1984 Konstantin Chernenko becomes new Soviet leader.

1979 Egypt, Israel sign peace agreement.

CHAPTER 37

A Time of Progress and Peril

1960–1963

People in the Chapter

John Fitzgerald Kennedy—*the first Roman Catholic president whose youth, courage, and lifestyle delight the public but whose career is cut down by an assassin's bullet.*

Fidel Castro—*the young leader who overthrows the Cuban government and becomes the first Communist premier of Cuba.*

Nikita Khrushchev—*the premier of the Soviet Union whose actions disturb much of the Western world during the early 1960s.*

Ho Chi Minh—*the Communist-trained leader of North Vietnam who fights to bring South Vietnam under his control.*

Ngo Dinh Diem—*the leader of South Vietnam who, as corrupt as his government, loses the support of the Vietnamese and, eventually, of the United States.*

Linking Past to Present

Some experts believe that it takes a U.S. president two years to learn the job. John Fitzgerald Kennedy had not quite three years in office. Yet many of the domestic achievements of the 1960s, such as the Civil Rights Act of 1964, were begun by Kennedy. But his actions in foreign affairs were more debatable and some have been severely criticized.

Despite the triumphs and troubles, the main impression of the Kennedy presidency on many people was glamour. It was during the Kennedy years that politics seemed to become a kind of show business. Kennedy was handsome; his wife was beautiful; their children were appealing. And they seemed to live a storybook life of success and contentment. A popular musical at the time was called Camelot. It dealt with King Arthur and Queen Guinevere and their mythical court of Camelot. There, for "one brief shining moment" before it was destroyed, people developed their fullest potential for good.

Kennedy himself said something of the Camelot atmosphere was felt in America during the Kennedy years. It was a feeling, as one author wrote, as if the United States was being guided by "the brightest and the best" to new heights of achievement. But just as Camelot had a darker side, so did the Kennedy years. During them the world came close to a nuclear war, and they ended with the assassination of the young president.

1 A NEW KIND OF CANDIDATE WINS THE PRESIDENCY

It was clear, as the Eisenhower years drew to a close, that the Democrats stood a chance of regaining the White House. Democratic registrations were up. The popular Republican president was barred by the Twenty-second Amendment from running for a third term. And there was a restlessness among the voters, caused in part by an economic downturn beginning in 1957, that seemed to ask for change.

There were a number of strong contenders for the Democratic nomination that year. Senator Lyndon Baines Johnson of Texas was the powerful majority leader. Senator Hubert H. Humphrey of Minnesota had been a leading liberal legislator since 1948. Senator Stuart Symington of Missouri had been elected in 1952 after serving five years as the first secretary of the air force. And former candidate Adlai E. Stevenson had to be reckoned with. Why, then, did the Democratic party choose Massachusetts Senator John F. Kennedy?

Kennedy's Background

At first glance, Kennedy had distinct drawbacks when compared to the other contenders. Although he had served six years in the House of Representatives and eight years in the Senate, he had not been an outstanding legislator. His prolabor record attracted voters in the industrial Northeast. On the other hand, he had supported Senator Joseph McCarthy and criticized the United States government for "losing" China, which lessened his appeal to liberals. But perhaps his major drawbacks were his age, his family, and his faith.

Kennedy was only forty-three years old. If successful, he would be the youngest president ever elected. (Theodore Roosevelt had been younger when he entered the White House, but that had been following the assassination of President William McKinley.) Many people felt Kennedy was too youthful and inexperienced to lead the greatest nation in the world.

Then there was the candidate's father, Joseph P. Kennedy, who had been FDR's ambassador to Great Britain from 1935 to 1940. "Old Joe" Kennedy had favored Chamberlain's appeasement of Adolf Hitler. After World War II broke out, the older Kennedy took the position that Britain was doomed. The United States, he believed, should let England shift for itself and instead concentrate on building U.S. strength. When Britain continued fighting against the Nazis and America increased its aid to the Allies, the ambassador resigned.

The most negative factor was probably John Kennedy's faith. Ever since the defeat of Governor Alfred E. Smith in the 1928 presidential election, Democratic party leaders had been reluctant to risk a Catholic candidate. There was still considerable fear on the part of many Americans that having a Catholic in the White House would lead either to papal influence over American politics or to closer ties between church and state.

A Skillful Campaigner

Kennedy's campaign, first for the nomination and then for the presidency, turned his drawbacks into assets.

First, he presented his age as an advantage. His youthful vigor would help him withstand the long hours and heavy responsibilities of office. He was not restricted by outmoded ideas of the past but would bring a fresh and imaginative approach to problems. His strong voice and fine presence appealed to younger voters. And he had an outstanding war record. Although badly hurt while commanding a PT boat in the Pacific, he had succeeded in rescuing several of his crew.

Second, Kennedy received effective support from his family. His father was one of the wealthiest people in America, with a fortune estimated at $350 million. The Kennedy campaign was high-powered and heavily financed. In addition, Kennedy's numerous sisters and brothers, as well as his mother—all good-looking and energetic—campaigned widely. They shook hands with people in shopping centers, attended cocktail parties and sewing bees, and even rang doorbells asking for votes. The candidate's glamorous young wife, Jacqueline Kennedy, accompanied him on his visits to 25 states and stood beside him as he delivered more than 350 speeches before the convention was held.

Third, Kennedy caught the attention of many people by stating frankly that the future was dangerous but full of promise. He said "We stand today on the edge of a New Frontier." He said it was a "frontier of unknown opportunities and perils and a frontier of unfulfilled hopes and threats."

Kennedy also quieted the fears of many people by discussing the religious issue openly during a series of hard-fought primaries. His candor helped him win a significant victory against leading contender Humphrey in West Virginia, whose population was 97 percent Protestant. Kennedy finally laid the issue to rest after gaining a first-ballot nomination. On September 12 he spoke at a meeting of the Greater Houston Ministerial Association. He believed in the separation of church and state, he said. If there were ever a conflict between his conscience and his office, Kennedy told the ministers and the nation, he would resign the presidency.

The Television Debates

The presidential race of 1960 was the closest since 1884. Kennedy defeated the Republican candidate, Vice President Richard M. Nixon, by fewer than 113,000 votes out of more than 68,335,000. A shift of one vote every other precinct would have changed the outcome. Since less than two-tenths of 1 percent of the total popular vote separated the candidates, every event in the campaign could be seen as determining the result. Two, however, stand out. One was a series of four television debates.

The first debate, which was watched by 70 million people, took place on September 26, as the

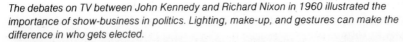

The debates on TV between John Kennedy and Richard Nixon in 1960 illustrated the importance of show-business in politics. Lighting, make-up, and gestures can make the difference in who gets elected.

Presidential Election of 1960

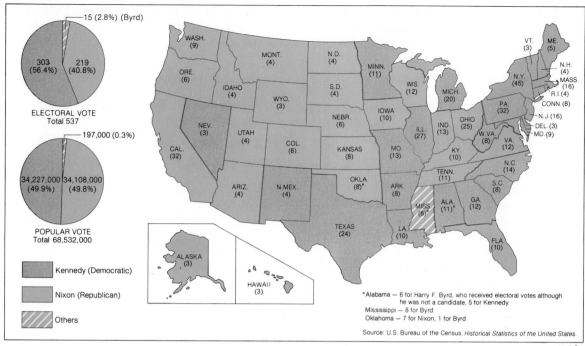

15 (2.8%) (Byrd)

303 (56.4%) | 219 (40.8%)

ELECTORAL VOTE
Total 537

197,000 (0.3%)

34,227,000 (49.9%) | 34,108,000 (49.8%)

POPULAR VOTE
Total 68,532,000

■ Kennedy (Democratic)

□ Nixon (Republican)

▨ Others

WASH. (9), ORE. (6), CAL. (32), NEV. (3), IDAHO (4), MONT. (4), UTAH (4), ARIZ. (4), WYO. (3), COL. (6), N.MEX. (4), N.D. (4), S.D. (4), NEBR. (6), KANSAS (8), OKLA. (8)*, TEXAS (24), MINN. (11), IOWA (10), MO. (13), ARK. (8), LA. (10), WIS. (12), ILL. (27), MICH. (20), IND. (13), OHIO (25), KY. (10), TENN. (11), MISS. (8)*, ALA. (11)*, GA. (12), FLA. (10), W.VA. (8), VA. (12), N.C. (14), S.C. (8), PA. (32), N.Y. (45), VT. (3), ME. (5), N.H. (4), MASS. (16), R.I. (4), CONN. (8), N.J. (16), DEL. (3), MD. (9)

ALASKA (3)

HAWAII (3)

*Alabama — 6 for Harry F. Byrd, who received electoral votes although he was not a candidate, 5 for Kennedy
Mississippi — 8 for Byrd
Oklahoma — 7 for Nixon, 1 for Byrd

Source: U.S. Bureau of the Census, *Historical Statistics of the United States.*

© ML & Co.

Map Skills *Kennedy, the Democrat, narrowly defeated Nixon, the Republican. What was Kennedy's victory margin in percentage of the popular votes? Who won your state?*

campaign was getting underway in earnest. Nixon, a public figure since the 1940s, was conceded to be the front runner. So, like Stephen Douglas in 1858, he had little to gain and much to lose by debating his opponent on a nationwide hookup. Why then did he agree to do so? Apparently because Nixon, himself an excellent debater, had watched his opponent's acceptance speech at the Democratic convention. Despite Kennedy's stirring pledge to get the country moving again and to carry the nation to "new frontiers," Nixon considered the speech a poor performance. Kennedy appeared nervous, spoke too quickly, and, in Nixon's view, expressed ideas beyond the understanding of most voters. The Republican candidate was sure he would win the debates.

Those who only heard the exchanges on radio or read them in the newspapers might have assumed that Nixon was in fact the winner. But the overwhelming majority of voters saw them on television. There, the way a candidate looks and speaks, the "TV image" presented, usually has more of an effect than what is said. Nixon lost the image battle. He had injured his knee early in the campaign and had spent time in the hospital with his leg in traction. Then he had caught a severe cold. On the TV tube, he appeared gaunt and underweight. His shirt collar seemed too large, his face was set, and he sweated visibly under his pancake makeup. By contrast, Kennedy looked tanned and trim and thoroughly at ease. Nixon's advantage of eight years of national executive experience evaporated into thin air. (Televised debates between presidential candidates were not held again for sixteen years, until 1976.)

The Courage of Conviction

A second major event of the 1960 campaign took place in October. Martin Luther King, Jr. and fifty-two other black demonstrators were arrested in an Atlanta department store for allegedly disturbing the peace by sitting at a lunch counter reserved for whites. Though the others were released, King was sentenced to four months at hard labor.

When Nixon was asked by newspaper reporters what he thought about the matter, the Republican candidate replied that he had no opinion. Privately, however, he called the Justice Depart-

737

ment and asked them to look into it. Nixon believed the incident violated King's constitutional rights. Eisenhower, however, refused to go along with an investigation, so nothing further was done.

The behavior of the Democratic candidate was different. Hearing of the arrest and sentence, Kennedy telephoned King's wife, Coretta, and offered his sympathy. Robert "Bobby" Kennedy, his brother and campaign manager, did more. He called the Georgia judge who had imposed the sentence on King and persuaded him to release the civil rights leader on bail, pending an appeal.

Politically, the Kennedys' actions were risky. Southern governors had warned that meddling with race issues might cost the Democrats the South on election day. But Kennedy stood firm. As Lyndon Johnson, Kennedy's running mate, remarked, "He's on the side of right."

News of the incident electrified America's black community. They swung behind the Democratic ticket, and their votes were enough to carry the key states of Michigan and Illinois.

Section 1 Review

COMPREHENSION   Developing Vocabulary

1. Explain these terms: TV image, New Frontier.

COMPREHENSION   Mastering Facts

1. What were three drawbacks many people thought Kennedy had as a presidential candidate?
2. How did Kennedy lay the question of his religion to rest?
3. What role did the television debates play in the 1960 election?
4. How did the Kennedy brothers react to the sentencing of Martin Luther King, Jr.?

2 KENNEDY ACHIEVES SUCCESS AT HOME

VOCABULARY   *Keynesian   depressed areas*

John F. Kennedy became the thirty-fifth president of the United States on a crisp and sparkling January day in 1961. Appearing without a coat in freezing weather, he gave the impression of a man ready and willing to fight, not even letting the elements stop him. His Inaugural Address was zestful and upbeat and it called for sacrifice.

❝ Let the word go forth . . . that the torch has been passed to a new generation of Americans . . . tempered by war, disciplined by a hard and bitter peace, proud of our ancient heritage. . . . Now the trumpet summons us again—not as a call to bear arms, though arms we need . . . but a call to bear the burden of a long twilight struggle year in and year out . . . a struggle against the common enemies of man: tyranny, poverty, disease and war itself. . . . And so, my fellow Americans, ask not what your country can do for you—ask what you can do for your country. **❞**

Kennedy's Style

The Kennedy years reminded many people of FDR's first term with the same heavy reliance on people from the academic world. The faculties of Harvard and Massachusetts Institute of Technology were raided for talent. One newspaper even asked who was left in Cambridge to teach the students. Among the president's circle of advisors were fifteen Rhodes scholars, including Secretary of State Dean Rusk; four professional historians; and a slew of former college teachers. But academics were balanced by such business leaders as Defense Secretary Robert McNamara of the Ford Motor Company, as well as by professional politicians Lawrence O'Brien and Kenneth O'Donnell. Most controversial of the president's appointments was that of his brother Robert Kennedy as attorney general. He was thought to be too young, too inexperienced, and too political for such a job.

In choosing people for administrative positions, the emphasis was on ability. Kennedy told one of his many talent scouts, "Now on those key jobs, I don't care if a man is a Democrat or an Igorot [a member of a Filipino tribe]. I want the best fellow I can get." However, they were, without exception, fellows. When longtime Washington correspondent May Craig reminded Kennedy of promises he had made to bring more women into government, she closed by asking, "And what have you done for women, Mr. President?" Kennedy replied, "Evidently, not enough, Miss Craig."

Kennedy ran the White House very differently from the way Eisenhower had done. As an activist president, Kennedy preferred to follow Franklin D. Roosevelt's pattern of dealing personally with assistants. Accordingly, Kennedy abolished both the position of presidential assistant and the staff system. Instead of simply approving or dis-

President and Mrs. Kennedy invited the leaders of business, science, and the arts, as well as the average voter, to some of the most glittering social events ever held in the White House.

approving decisions that were presented to him, Kennedy maintained close working relations with the various executive departments and officials. He was informed of problems as they arose and made decisions all along the line.

Kennedy's Economic Programs

During his campaign, Kennedy had pointed out various economic problems confronting the nation. Once in office, he moved ahead to try to solve them.

Kennedy was a Keynesian; that is, he accepted the ideas of English economist John Maynard Keynes. Keynes believed that a nation's economic growth depends on two things: (1) lowering taxes so as to leave companies and individuals with more money to invest and spend; and (2) at the same time, increasing public spending. In other words, a nation's government should run a deficit. However, to get the 5 percent annual growth Kennedy wanted meant having a budget $5 billion in the red each year. That could be politically disastrous, especially for a Democratic adminis-

tration, since the business community tended to see the party of FDR as habitual big spenders. Accordingly, Kennedy moved slowly and carefully.

Stimulating the Economy. Minimum wages were increased from one dollar to one dollar and twenty-five cents an hour. The Area Redevelopment Act of 1961 identified "depressed areas," or places where unemployment was higher than 6 percent of the labor force, and gave these areas money for retraining workers and building roads and other public works. The act also provided tax benefits for industries that would build new plants in depressed areas. The following year Congress passed the Manpower Development and Training Act of 1962. It set up three-year programs to retrain coal miners and others put out of work by technological changes.

Also designed to help the economy grow was the Trade Expansion Act of 1962. It gave the president the power to either raise or lower tariff rates 50 percent over a five-year period. If an industry was suffering because of foreign competition, the federal government could lend it money to change its product line. Workers in such an industry could receive money for retraining or relocating.

Other Kennedy spending proposals, however, were turned down by a congressional combination of Republicans and conservative Democrats. These proposals included federal aid for public school construction and teachers' salaries, medical care for the aged, and grants to encourage the rebuilding of city slums.

Spending on Space. One spending area where Kennedy had no trouble at all persuading Congress to go along was the exploration of space. Specifically, what Kennedy wanted was to put a man on the moon before the 1960s were over.

The reasons were psychological rather than either economic or military. There were other ways in which to spend public funds. And although Soviet rockets were larger than American ones, America's weapons systems were far superior. Yet the Russians had unquestionably achieved spectacular results in space. Not only had they been first in putting an unmanned satellite into orbit around the earth, they had also been first in sending a space probe to the moon and in orbiting Venus. The final blow to American prestige came in April 1961 when Soviet astronaut Yuri A. Gagarin soared 188 miles into the sky and circled the earth in 89 minutes.

So on May 25 Kennedy delivered a special message to Congress on "urgent national needs" in which he asked for some $9 billion over the next five years. The money was voted overwhelmingly, and work began immediately on launching facilities at Cape Canaveral, Florida, and on a mission control center in Houston.

The first pay-off came in February 1962 when Colonel John H. Glenn, Jr. orbited the earth three times. Like Charles Lindbergh, he received a hero's welcome both in the United States and abroad. By November 1963 the National Aeronautics and Space Administration (NASA) was ready to launch the first Saturn rocket. Six years later, it would win the "space race" by propelling Americans to the moon.

Cutting Taxes. In addition to higher spending, the Keynesian formula calls for tax cuts. But by 1963 the economy had been stimulated so much that the nation was no longer suffering from a recession. In fact, the gross national product was increasing by almost 6 percent a year, more than the planned 5 percent. Nevertheless, Kennedy asked Congress to lower taxes by $10 billion over a three-year period. The measure passed the House and was expected to do as well in the Senate.

Why did Kennedy want to stimulate the economy further? Because he wanted to have more federal funds available in order to help the country's hidden poor. He had been reading Michael Harrington's book *The Other America,* which shifted the problem of poverty from facts and figures to flesh-and-blood people. The president was so moved by the work that he decided to make a "war on poverty" the centerpiece of his 1964 program. To one of his advisors he said, "The time has come to organize a national assault on the cause of poverty. A comprehensive program, across the board."

Section 2 Review

COMPREHENSION   Developing Vocabulary
1.   Explain these terms: Keynesian, depressed areas.

COMPREHENSION   Mastering Facts
1.   How did Kennedy run the executive branch?
2.   In what two ways did Kennedy try to stimulate the economy?
3.   What was Kennedy's goal for the space program?
4.   What was the main problem Kennedy intended to attack in his 1964 program?

3   THE NATION COPES WITH PROBLEMS ABROAD

VOCABULARY   *Berlin Wall   strategic hamlet program   Alliance for Progress*

Despite their impressive qualifications, the Kennedy team ran into serious problems in foreign affairs. In fact, their first major venture couldn't have ended more badly. It concerned a land that had often been taken for granted.

In Cuba

Between 1933 and 1959 the island of Cuba was controlled by military dictator Fulgencio Batista. Although the position of president was held by different people, they took their orders from Batista. In 1956 a guerrilla movement led by Fidel Castro began a rebellion against the Batista regime. In 1959, with the help of Cuban businessmen and landowners, the revolt succeeded, and the Castro government was recognized by the United States.

Gradually, however, relations between the two nations deteriorated. First, Castro put on mass public trials and executions not only of Batista supporters but of others who might oppose his new regime. The United States denounced Cuba in the UN and accepted thousands of Cuban refugees who poured into Florida. Castro thereupon threatened the U.S. naval base at Guantánamo Bay and demanded reduction of the American embassy staff in Havana. Next, he signed an agreement to sell sugar to the Soviet Union and a few months later he seized business properties owned by U.S. citizens. President Eisenhower retaliated by cutting off Cuba's 1960 sugar quota. Castro responded by welcoming Soviet technicians and advisors. Finally, in January 1961 the United States broke diplomatic relations with Cuba.

The Bay of Pigs. Soon after his election, Kennedy was informed of a U.S. operation against Castro. At secret bases in Guatemala, the CIA was training Cuban refugees for an invasion of their homeland. This, it was hoped, would set off a general uprising of the Cuban people and bring down the Castro regime. The idea had been approved by Eisenhower and, Kennedy was told, had the full backing of the Joint Chiefs of Staff. Shortly after taking office, Kennedy, despite serious doubts, gave his consent for the plan to go ahead, insisting only that American troops should not be involved.

On the night of April 17, 1961, 1400 Cuban exiles landed on the island's south coast at Bahia de Conchinos, the Bay of Pigs. Nothing went right. Only 135 members of the invading group were trained soldiers. The rest were overage lawyers, bankers, doctors, teachers, and other professionals, and some of them did not even know how to fire a rifle. An air strike the day before the invasion by aged World War II bombers had failed to knock out the small Cuban air force, although the CIA reported that it had. None of the ammunition and supply ships got through to the attacking force. A small group that was supposed to make a separate landing to distract Castro, never got to shore. Most incredible of all, perhaps, it turned out that the chosen landing place was not a

swampy, deserted section of shoreline. Since the Cuban refugees had seen it, it had been made into a public park with buildings, blazing lights, and paved access roads.

Castro had no trouble surrounding the invaders with a force of 20,000 troops. Furthermore, there was no uprising in Cuba. The coded broadcast message that was supposed to give the signal to anti-Castro forces on the island never reached them. And even if it had, it would have made no difference. Warned by the ineffective air strike, Castro had rounded up several hundred thousand suspected opponents of his regime before the landing took place.

Kennedy was shattered. "How could I have been so stupid?" he kept asking. He was wondering why he had not questioned more closely the kind of invasion that had been planned and the many faulty assumptions on which it had been based. However, like early defeats in war, the Bay of Pigs fiasco served a purpose. It showed Kennedy how *not* to plan an operation.

In the meantime, Castro denounced the United States as an aggressor and soon after admitted that he was a Communist. He signed trade agreements with various Warsaw Pact nations and welcomed additonal Soviet technicians to the island.

The Cuban Missile Crisis. The summer of the following year, 1962, the CIA reported that the Soviet Union was up to something in Cuba. By now there were more than 5000 technicians on the island, and there had been a marked increase in shipping between the two nations. The CIA at first assumed that Cuba was getting surface to air missiles as a defense against another invasion attempt. But on October 16 the president received shocking news. Photographs taken by U-2 flights showed sixty-five sites that could only have been planned for offensive medium-range ballistic missiles. When they were installed, which according to the photographs would be in about ten days, the most heavily populated two-thirds of the United States would be within their reach. The warning time for an attack on the country would then be somewhere between two and three minutes.

Kennedy was anxious to avoid either of two extremes. One was making the kind of mistakes that had resulted in the Bay of Pigs fiasco. The other was setting off a chain of events that might end in nuclear war. At the same time, he had to force the USSR into removing this threat to American security.

Instead of the casual procedures followed in the Bay of Pigs affair, Kennedy set up a special committee to suggest action. The committee quickly decided there were only two possibilities: (1) bomb the missile sites, or (2) blockade Cuba and insist that the missiles be removed. Kennedy thereupon ordered a naval blockade of the island (although he used the word "quarantine" rather than "blockade" since a blockade is considered an act of war). Kennedy also warned that a missile attack from Cuba against any nation in the Western Hemisphere would be treated as if it were a Soviet attack against the United States. And he told the Soviets to dismantle the missile bases. Otherwise American planes would bomb them.

Meanwhile a dozen Soviet ships carrying weapons steamed steadily toward Cuba. For almost a week, the world was on the brink of nuclear war. At one tense moment Kennedy said, "This is the week I earn my salary." But the firm U.S. attitude worked. The Russian ships turned back before

reaching the American warships. Finally, in an exchange of letters with Kennedy, Soviet Premier Khrushchev agreed to dismantle the missiles under UN supervision in exchange for a promise by the United States not to invade Cuba. The threat of nuclear war had been averted; the war of nerves was over for the time being.

In Europe

The confrontation over the Cuban missiles was the second of two major disputes between the United States and the Soviet Union that took place during the Kennedy administration. The first had arisen in a grim conversation in Vienna between Kennedy and Khrushchev in the summer of 1961.

The Berlin Crisis. The two world leaders had met to discuss the question of Berlin. For fifteen years, the Soviets had been unhappy with the presence of Allied troops in the city. They were also unhappy because economic conditions in West Berlin were so much better than those in East Ber-

These photos convinced President Kennedy and his military advisers that there were Soviet missiles in Cuba which threatened the United States.

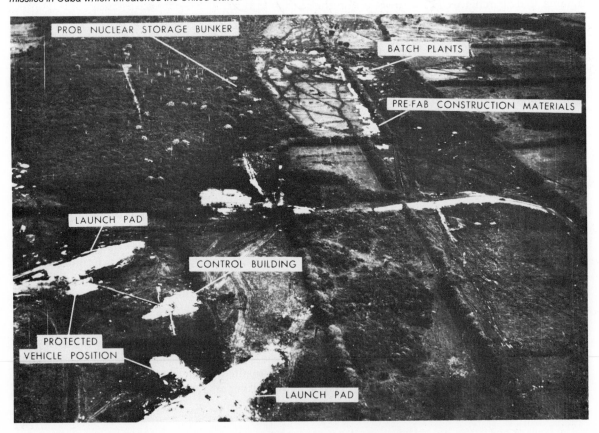

PROB NUCLEAR STORAGE BUNKER

BATCH PLANTS

PRE-FAB CONSTRUCTION MATERIALS

LAUNCH PAD

CONTROL BUILDING

PROTECTED VEHICLE POSITION

LAUNCH PAD

The Berlin Crisis   1961

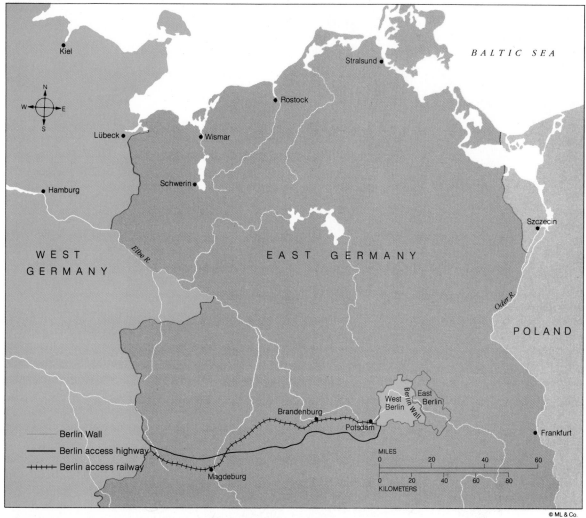

Map Skills   *What divides East Berlin and West Berlin? What is the highway distance from West Germany to West Berlin? What country lies to the east of East Germany?*

lin. This made it difficult to convince people that Communism was preferable to capitalism.

In 1957, when Sputnik I went up, Khrushchev had demanded that Berlin become a demilitarized "free city," part of neither West Germany nor East Germany. In 1961 the Russian premier not only repeated the demand. He said that unless this happened, the Soviet Union would sign a separate peace treaty with East Germany and "take firm measures." Khrushchev apparently believed, according to some historians, that after the Bay of Pigs disaster the young president could be intimidated. But Kennedy stood firm. He replied that the United States would not abandon the

people of West Berlin, and he asked Congress for an increase of 200,000 in the armed forces. He also asked for the reconditioning of ships and planes not ready for immediate military service.

In the meantime, alarmed over the dispute, thousands of East Germans moved into West Berlin. By early August almost 2000 refugees a day were flowing across the border. On August 12 the figure rose to more than 4000, most of them doctors, technicians, and other skilled workers. Shortly after midnight on August 13, Russian tanks and East German policemen took up positions along the twenty-five-mile border separating the two parts of the city. Four days later, a stone-and-

The Berlin Wall sliced a city in half, causing families and loved ones to be cruelly separated.

concrete wall topped by barbed wire cut off the stream of refugees.

By fall, however, it was clear to Khrushchev that the United States would not back down on Berlin. So he extended the deadline for withdrawal indefinitely, and the crisis faded away.

Trying to Ease Relations. Despite both the Berlin crisis and the Cuban missile crisis, relations between the United States and the Soviet Union improved in 1963.

In April of that year, the Soviets accepted a United States proposal for a hot line linking the White House and the Kremlin. This would enable leaders of the two nations to communicate at once should another crisis arise. The line went into operation at the end of August.

Speaking in June, Kennedy announced that the United States was suspending nuclear tests in the atmosphere, and he invited other atomic powers to do the same. The next month, talks were held in Moscow with the British and the Russians. The Nuclear Test Ban Treaty was completed that summer and ratified by the Senate in September. It ended all nuclear tests in the atmosphere, outer space, and underwater. It was a self-enforcing treaty; that is, modern science made it impossible for any nation to cheat on the ban without being found out.

In October Kennedy approved the sale to the USSR of $250 million worth of surplus American wheat. He described the transaction as "one more hopeful sign that a more peaceful world is both possible and beneficial to all."

In Vietnam

During the early 1960s, the position of the South Vietnamese government of Ngo Dinh Diem became increasingly unstable. The Vietcong were successfully taking over the South Vietnamese countryside. They would murder village chiefs, school teachers, and other educated persons and put in their own chiefs and tax collectors.

The Diem government fought back with its *strategic hamlet* program. The population of an entire village would be moved to a new area surrounded by walls and moats. Special teams were then organized to go from one hamlet to another to give medical assistance and advice on farming. But Vietnamese are very strongly attached to their ancestral homes. Also, they did not like living behind fences. The *strategic hamlet* program was a failure, and the Vietcong position in the countryside continued to be strong. Meanwhile, in the cities, the repressive policies and corruption of Diem's government turned more and more people against him.

In 1961 a special task force advised President Kennedy to send American combat troops to South Vietnam to assist the Diem regime. Kennedy, however, was torn between his belief in the domino theory and his belief that the only way the Diem government would win was by gaining the support of the Vietnamese people. So instead of sending in American soldiers, Kennedy simply increased the number of advisors who were helping train Diem's troops. He also supplied Diem's troops with helicopters. By the fall of 1963, there were about 17,000 American advisors in Vietnam.

Also by the fall of 1963, religious opposition to Diem had escalated. Following a series of demonstrations, the Diem regime imprisoned hundreds of Buddhist monks and destroyed numerous Buddhist pagodas, or temples. American officials tried to convince Diem to stop persecuting the Buddhists, who were a majority of the population, and to abolish the secret police headed by Diem's brother Nhu. When Diem refused, Kennedy ordered economic aid cut off. On November 1 a military coup overthrew the Diem regime and Diem and Nhu were executed. Soon after, Kennedy agreed to send American air-support combat troops to the new South Vietnamese government.

New Programs for Peace

Despite the setbacks and difficulties involved in American foreign policy, there were two creations of the New Frontier which had great success and influence for peace in the world.

The Alliance for Progress. Kennedy's desire to help the nations of Latin America was reinforced by the fear that Castro would export his revolutionary ideas to other nations in the Western Hemisphere. In March 1961 the president proposed a program of economic aid modeled on the Marshall Plan. It was approved in August by all the Latin American nations except Cuba.

The program called for spending $20 billion over a ten-year period. Half of this amount was to come from the United States, mostly from the government but about one-tenth from private in-

vestors. The rest of the funds were to be provided by the Latin American nations themselves. The money was to be used to build schools and houses, and to put in health and sanitation facilities. It was also to be used to break up large estates and give individual farmers land of their own, and to change the tax laws so that rich people paid their fair share. In other words, aid was to be combined with reforms.

The United States invested almost $12 billion in Latin America under the Alliance for Progress between 1961 and 1969. Then funds for the program were cut back drastically, partly because of a domestic recession and partly because of the costs of the Vietnam War.

The Peace Corps. A more imaginative program was the Peace Corps, established in March 1961. Peace Corps volunteers worked for two years in underdeveloped nations in Asia, Africa, and Latin America, and got just enough pay to sustain themselves. They served as agricultural advisors, teachers, health aides, or did whatever work the

The Peace Corps was one of the most idealistic programs of the Kennedy years. Here a volunteer explains agricultural techniques to people on an island in the Caribbean.

host country needed. The program was in the charge of Kennedy's brother-in-law, Sargent Shriver. Shriver made it his business to keep the Peace Corps out of diplomatic affairs and intelligence work. He apparently succeeded, although Communist governments attacked the new organization as a "nest of spies."

By 1968 there were 35,000 Peace Corps volunteers in sixty countries around the world. And several other nations had started similar programs of their own:

Section 3 Review

COMPREHENSION Developing Vocabulary

1. Explain these terms: Berlin Wall, strategic hamlet program, hot line.

COMPREHENSION Mastering Facts

1. What was the result of the Cuban missile crisis?
2. What led to the building of the Berlin Wall?
3. What led to the overthrow of the Diem regime in South Vietnam?
4. What were the aims of the Alliance for Progress?

4 AMERICANS ENDURE A NATIONAL TRAGEDY

VOCABULARY   sit-in   freedom ride

The year 1963 was the hundredth anniversary of the Emancipation Proclamation. President Lincoln's wartime action did not end slavery in the United States; it took the Thirteenth Amendment two years later to do that. But the proclamation had come to symbolize the end of slavery. Now its centennial served to remind the nation of how much remained to be accomplished in order for black Americans to have full equality.

New Tactics for Civil Rights

Beginning in 1955, the civil rights movement had begun shifting from court cases to direct non-violent action to bring about change. The shift grew stronger during the Kennedy years.

Sit-Ins. On February 1, 1960, Joseph McNeill and three fellow black college students walked into an F. W. Woolworth store in Greensboro, North Carolina. After buying a few items, they sat down at the lunch counter and ordered coffee. Since the store was segregated, the management ignored them. The four remained at the counter until the store closed. The next morning they returned, this time with five more blacks, and sat quietly all day long, ignoring the white youths who threw cigarette butts at them and dangled Confederate flags before their eyes. The next day they repeated the sit-in, and the day after that.

Within two weeks, the movement had spread throughout the South, not just to Woolworth stores but to other chain store lunch counters as well. Outside the South, blacks and white sympathizers picketed chains whose southern stores were segregated. From there, demonstrators began to use the sit-in tactics at other segregated facilities.

Within six months the lunch counter at the Woolworth store in Greensboro was desegregated. Hundreds of other facilities in the South were also.

Freedom Rides. In May of the following year, 1961, another direct but non-violent technique was used. It was sponsored by the Congress of Racial Equality (CORE) and it was called a freedom ride. A group of blacks and whites rode buses throughout the Deep South to see whether the 1950 Supreme Court decision outlawing segregation in interstate travel was being obeyed. In Alabama, mobs beat many of the freedom riders and firebombed one of the buses. The local police did little. When additional violence threatened, Attorney General Robert Kennedy sent 400 federal marshals into Montgomery. He then asked the Interstate Commerce Commission to order interstate trains, buses, airplanes, train depots, bus stations, and airports integrated. Within months, blacks could travel anywhere in the country without seeing "White" or "Colored" signs in waiting rooms.

The March on Washington. The direct non-violent campaign for civil rights reached its climax on August 28, 1963. About 200,000 persons, both white and black, gathered in the nation's capital. They covered the entire area between the Washington Monument and the Lincoln Memorial. Many carried signs reading "Freedom Now." What they wanted was federal civil rights legislation. It was the largest such demonstration ever held in the United States.

One hundred years after the Emancipation Proclamation, Dr. Martin Luther King Jr. gives his "I have a dream" speech from the Lincoln Memorial.

The crowd heard Dr. King deliver an inspiring and memorable address.

❝I have a dream that one day this nation will rise up and live out the true meaning of its creed: "We hold these truths to be self-evident, that all men are created equal." I have a dream that one day on the red hills of Georgia, the sons of former slaves and the sons of former slave-owners will be able to sit together at the table of brotherhood. . . . I have a dream that my four little children will not be judged by the color of their skin but by the content of their character. I have a dream.❞

Continuing Resistance

Unfortunately for Dr. King's dream, some white southerners stiffened their resistance to civil rights.

Confrontations at Universities. In 1962 a federal court ordered the University of Mississippi to admit James H. Meredith, a qualified black Air Force veteran. Governor Ross R. Barnett refused to allow Meredith to register. Standing at the school door, Barnett cited the doctrine of interposition, that is, putting himself between the federal government and the people of Mississippi. He announced that the state's laws on segregation

were superior to federal law. Attorney General Robert Kennedy then sent federal marshals to the campus and rioting broke out.

The marshals were forbidden to fire their guns. Their only weapon was tear gas. Most of the rioters were not students but members of the Ku Klux Klan and the National States' Rights Party from other southern states. They were armed with grenades, iron bars, bricks, and rifles. Two white spectators were killed, and more than a third of the marshals were injured. Finally, President Kennedy sent in federal troops to restore order. He also federalized the Mississippi National Guard.

The next day, Meredith registered for classes. He planned to major in political science.

In June of the following year, 1963, another university confrontation occurred, this time at the University of Alabama. A federal court ordered the school to admit two blacks, Vivian J. Malone and Jimmy A. Hood, to its summer session. Governor George Wallace, like Governor Barnett, stood in the doorway as the two students and their escort of federal marshals approached. But after being told that the National Guard had been federalized, the governor walked away. All seemed calm. However, that night, Medgar Evers, an official of

A rare time of relaxation in a tense period. This group of "freedom riders" includes clergymen, professors and students who rode buses in the South to test discrimination laws.

the NAACP, was gunned down by a sniper in Jackson, Mississippi.

Violence in Birmingham. The murder of Evers was only one in a series of events that would help bring about yet another change in the civil rights movement, a change from non-violent direct action to black militancy. Two of these events took place in Birmingham.

Blacks had been demonstrating against segregation in that city since early April. Almost every time King called for a march, police commissioner T. Eugene "Bull" Connor obtained an injunction forbidding it. The blacks marched anyway, were arrested and later released—and the process began again.

On May 2 some 500 blacks, most of them high school students, were arrested for marching in defiance of a court order. The next day other students marching in protest were hit by bottles and brickbats. On May 4 when about 2500 blacks marched in downtown Birmingham, the police turned fire hoses on them and loosed their dogs. Television cameras carried the scene into millions of living rooms with the evening news.

The sight of attack dogs and police brutalizing unresisting people was too much. Responsible local leaders realized that the situation was getting out of hand. With the help of federal officials, plus 3000 riot control troops, they succeeded in quieting things down. Some facilities were desegregated.

The resulting peace was short-lived. In September, passions flared again with the opening of school. And on September 15, a black church was bombed, resulting in the deaths of four young black girls who were attending Sunday school.

Federal Actions

President Kennedy, like Lincoln a hundred years earlier, approached the civil rights issue with caution. During his first two years in office, he tried to help blacks through executive action only.

In March 1961 he set up the Committee on Equal Employment Opportunity to encourage companies with government contracts to hire black employees. In 1962 he asked Congress to enable more blacks to vote by abolishing literacy tests and poll taxes. Congress passed the Twenty-fourth Amendment, which prohibits a state from requiring a citizen to pay a poll tax in order to vote in a federal election. The amendment was ratified in 1964. In November 1962 Kennedy issued an executive order prohibiting racial and religious discrimination in all housing either built or insured with federal money.

After the 1963 Birmingham disorders, Kennedy decided the time had come to seek new civil rights legislation. So he introduced what one historian called "the most sweeping legislation of its kind since Reconstruction." By October the bill had begun to move through Congress.

A Trip to Dallas

Party politics consumes a great deal of any president's time and energy. In November 1963 it brought John Kennedy to Texas to try to strengthen the position of the Democratic party before the upcoming election. On the evening of November 21, the president spoke in Houston, then flew on to Fort Worth. The next day's schedule called for a motorcade through downtown Dallas and a reception at the governor's mansion in Austin.

The reception was never held. On November 22, at 12:30 P.M. Dallas time, the car carrying the president, Texas Governor John Connally, and their wives passed a state building known as the Texas School Book Depository. Three shots rang out. The president pitched over. There was an immediate and frantic scurry of Secret Service men, a scream of sirens, and the official cars drove off at top speed toward Parkland Memorial Hospital. Less than one hour later John Kennedy was pronounced dead. Vice President Johnson, who had been riding two cars behind Kennedy, left Dallas with the body, being sworn in as president before the plane took off.

Later that afternoon a Dallas policeman was shot as he stopped a suspicious-looking young man for questioning. When caught, the gunman turned out to be Lee Harvey Oswald, a worker at the Texas School Book Depository. A rifle belonging to Oswald was found near a window that overlooked the motorcade route. Two days later, Oswald himself was shot by Jack Ruby, a Dallas nightclub owner, before the disbelieving eyes of millions of Americans who were watching live TV coverage of Oswald being moved to another jail. Ruby died of cancer before he could be tried.

The entire chain of events was so bizarre that there are still people who cannot accept it at face value. A commission presided over by Chief Justice Earl Warren made an extensive investigation that lasted 10 months and yielded 26 volumes of testimony. The Warren Commission concluded that Kennedy had been shot by Oswald—"a sorry little loser"—acting on his own. In 1978, however, a congressional committee that went over much of the same ground said it was theoretically possible that

Lyndon B. Johnson is sworn in as President of the United States on the plane bearing the body of John F. Kennedy back to Washington. Mrs. Johnson is on the left, Mrs. Kennedy on the right.

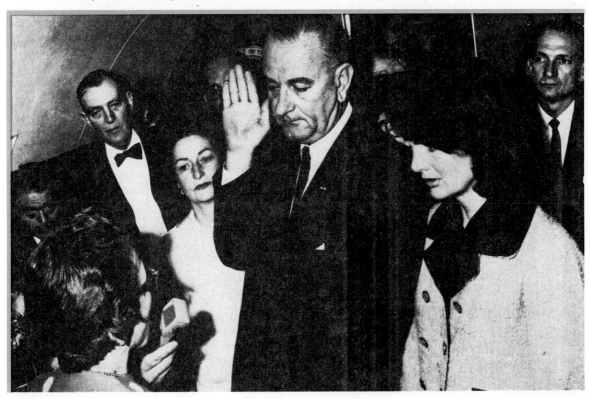

two persons had shot at Kennedy but that there was no proof. In between these two reports, numerous amateurs made their own investigations. Their explanations ranged all the way from a plot by anti-Castro Cubans to a communist conspiracy.

The assassination stunned the nation and the world. The three television networks stayed on the air providing live coverage for seventy-two consecutive hours until the president's body was laid to rest in Arlington Cemetery. Leaders from 92 nations attended the funeral. For weeks, hundreds of thousands of Americans wrote to Jacqueline Kennedy to express their sorrow. It was as if a member of their own family had died.

Section 4 Review

COMPREHENSION   Developing Vocabulary
1. Explain these terms: sit-in, freedom ride.

COMPREHENSION   Mastering Facts
1. What was the purpose of the 1963 march on Washington?
2. On what grounds did the governors of Mississippi and Alabama try to keep blacks from entering white schools?
3. How did the Twenty-fourth Amendment increase the number of potential voters?
4. What conclusion did the Warren Commission draw about Kennedy's assassination?

A grieving nation watches as its former president lies in state at the Rotunda of the Capitol in Washington, D.C.

Chapter Summary

After John F. Kennedy won the presidency in 1960, he tried to stimulate the economy and made a strong commitment to space exploration. Major foreign policy crises included the Bay of Pigs invasion and the tense Cuban missile crisis. In Europe, the Soviet Union and East Germany built a wall to divide Berlin and stop the flow of refugees to the West. Back in the United States, the civil rights movement began to use sit-ins and picketing to integrate public facilities. President Kennedy called for the most sweeping civil rights legislation since the days of Reconstruction. In November, 1963, Americans endured another national tragedy when John F. Kennedy was assassinated.

Questions for Critical Thinking

COMPREHENSION Summarizing Main Ideas

1. Describe the Kennedy image. Do you think Americans today would like a president with a similar image? What makes you think so?
2. What factors contributed to the failure of the Bay of Pigs landing?
3. What did Kennedy want to avoid in the Cuban missile crisis? What did he want to achieve? Was he successful?
4. Which events during the Kennedy administration increased the possibility of war between the United States and the Soviet Union? Which events decreased the possibility of war?
5. What personal qualities do you think were needed to take part in a sit-in?
6. How did Kennedy deal with the civil rights issue during his first two years in office? What new policy did he adopt in 1963? What made him change his attitude?

COMPREHENSION Interpreting Events

1. Why did the Democrats feel they could win the 1960 presidential election? List two events that influenced the final vote.

2. Why did Kennedy urge an intensive program of space exploration? Do you agree or disagree with his arguments?
3. Why did the Diem regime continue to lose ground in the Vietnamese countryside?
4. Why do you think sit-ins succeeded in eliminating segregation in many public facilities?

APPLICATION Using Skills To Infer Information

Reread the paragraph titled "Freedom Rides." Then indicate whether you can infer that the statements below are true or false, or whether the paragraph does not contain sufficient information for you to infer anything.

1. Direct non-violent techniques were first used in 1960.
2. A direct non-violent technique other than a freedom ride was used in 1960.
3. CORE was an organization that opposed segregation.
4. Many white southerners disagreed with the 1950 Supreme Court decision outlawing segregation in interstate travel.
5. Supreme Court decisions are not always obeyed.
6. Attorney General Robert Kennedy opposed racial segregation.
7. Attorney General Robert Kennedy believed that Supreme Court decisions should be obeyed.

EVALUATION Forming Generalizations

1. What are three issues over which the United States and the Soviet Union disagree today? Do you think we are closer to or further from peaceful relations with Communist nations than we were in the early 1960s? Explain your answer.
2. Have you ever watched a televised debate between presidential candidates? If you have, how did it affect you? Do you consider such debates desirable? Why or why not?
3. What is the present status of the Peace Corps?

Vietnam—From Past to Present

It is probably safe to assume that few Americans had ever heard of Vietnam before the 1950s. By the 1960s, however, most Americans knew a great deal about the tiny nation in Southeast Asia. Vietnam would eventually affect Americans and their nation's foreign and domestic policies in ways that are still felt today.

To understand the Vietnam War, it is important to know both the history and geography of Vietnam. This feature about those two subjects will explain why war began in that nation. The following chapter will show how the United States became involved, and what made fighting that war so difficult.

The land of Vietnam has had a long history of violence. Wars, revolts, and invasions have shaken that country periodically since its earliest days. Historians know very little about the origins of the Vietnamese people. It was the Chinese who first encountered them about 300 B.C. in the delta area of the Red River, in northern Vietnam. The Chinese group that moved south into the delta was called the Viets. The Viets gave their name to their southern neighbors but called them Viet Nam (Southern Viets).

In the year 111 B.C. the Chinese, under the Han dynasty, conquered Vietnam. They controlled it for 1000 years (to A.D. 939). During this time the Chi-

Trieu Au. One of the first of many Vietnamese women who fought for their nation's independence.

nese exploited the country. There were minerals and ivory in the great forests and there were pearls in the sea. In developing the country, the Chinese introduced the metal plow into Vietnam as well as the technique of using teams of animals to haul heavy loads. The Chinese built roads and improved the waterways and harbors of Vietnam. But the Chinese also taxed the people and recruited them into labor gangs. The Chinese language, the teachings of Confucius, and even Chinese clothes were forced on the Vietnamese people.

There were periodic revolts as the Vietnamese resisted these efforts to make them Chinese.

Finally, in 939 the Chinese forces were decisively defeated under the Vietnamese leader Ngo Quyen (no kwee-yen). From that year the Vietnamese date their independence. The capital was established in Hanoi, where it had been before the Chinese invaded the country.

But Vietnam had other enemies. The Vietnamese were but one of several powerful ethnic groups that inhabited the Indochina peninsula. The peninsula is called Indochina because the people there share a mixed culture that is part Indian and part Chinese. Indochina consists of two parts separated by a mountain backbone. On the east are the fertile and densely populated coastal plains. The Vietnamese at that time inhabited only the northern part of the plains around the Red River delta. West of the mountains are the people of Laos, who are related to the Thai people of Thailand farther west. The Cambodians are in the southwestern part of the peninsula. Their ancestors, a people called the Mon Khmer (ka *mear*), built a rich empire, the ruins of which can still be seen in such places as Angkor in Cambodia.

From about 1400 on, Vietnam, under energetic and able emperors, extended its territory south along the fertile coast. By 1550 Vietnamese farmers were tilling land as far south as Da Nang and by 1700, Saigon was Vietnamese.

By the beginning of the 1800s, however, the European influence was being felt throughout the Indochina peninsula. French merchants and missionaries had created in France a strong interest in the area. In 1857 Napoleon III of France decided to invade Vietnam. France needed markets overseas for its products. So, Napoleon III sent an army and naval force against Vietnam. The first two towns taken were Da Nang, near Hué (in 1858) and Saigon (in 1859). Despite fierce resistance, French influence gradually spread throughout the country.

For administrative purposes France split the country into various regions. North Vietnam became Tongking. The central section was called Annam and the southern section was named Cochin China.

The French tried to do as the Chinese had done. Paris introduced French style clothes, the French language, and French food into Indochina. Saigon became known as the "Paris of the East." But the Vietnamese had no more desire to become French than they did to become Chinese. They resisted the best way they could. They avoided open standing battles such as Europeans are accustomed to. They engaged in guerrilla warfare. That is, they

Ancient Vietnam

remained hidden, making quick surprise attacks from the forests and then quickly fading back into the jungle. They perfected this technique and used it with great effect against American troops years later.

The overthrow of the Manchu dynasty in Peking in 1911 inspired great hope in the Vietnamese. Like the Chinese, they believed the only way to achieve independence was to overthrow the monarchy and rid the country of foreign influence. In 1925 a Vietnamese man living in Canton formed the Revolutionary League of the Youth of Vietnam. This was the beginning of the Communist party in Vietnam. Its leader was Ho Chi Minh (hoh chee min).

During the 1930s the Communists in Vietnam, with aid from the Soviet Union and China, led attacks against the French. The guerrilla warfare was fierce. By the beginning of World War II there were many people who wanted independence but the group with the clearest military and political goals were the Communists. By the early 1940s their leader Ho Chi Minh had formed the Viet Minh (vee-yet min), a large coalition of all the Communist and some non-Communist groups throughout Vietnam. Other non-Communist patriots were simply overwhelmed by the more highly organized Communists. As you will read later, it was due to Ho Chi Minh that Vietnam became a united and independent nation. Many people both inside and outside Vietnam considered it unfortunate that the price of independence was control by the Communist party. They wondered if perhaps the Vietnamese had not simply exchanged a foreign tyranny for one of their own.

Understanding Geography

1. How does geography help explain the fact that both the Chinese and the French were interested in Vietnam?

2. Why did Napoleon III attack Vietnam?

3. How did the geography of Vietnam help make guerrilla warfare effective?

CHAPTER 38

War in Vietnam and Troubles at Home

1963–1968

People in the Chapter

Lyndon Baines Johnson—*the president whose political skill gets a great deal of legislation through Congress but whose Vietnam policy attracts increasing opposition.*

Barry Goldwater—*the Republican senator from Arizona whose conservative views attract many people who feel that the Republican party should move farther to the right.*

Betty Friedan—*the author of* The Feminine Mystique, *who helps start the women's rights movement of the 1960s.*

Linking Past to Present

The years between 1963 and 1968 were years of great public convulsion, anger, and what some called a "moral retreat." At the head of the nation was Lyndon B. Johnson, a leader noted for his ability to get people with different views to work out a compromise or agreement. Yet during his administration the United States was more divided than at any time since the Civil War.

Escalation of the war in Vietnam brought public opposition to American involvement. The increasing furor moved from demonstrations to the presidential primaries and persuaded Johnson not to seek reelection.

In domestic affairs, blacks and other minorities sought to gain full legal and social rights. Although many of their goals were realized under the Johnson administration, frustration sometimes erupted into violence. Also during this period, women began to feel increasing dissatisfaction with their position in American life.

1 JOHNSON TRIES TO BUILD A "GREAT SOCIETY"

VOCABULARY   *Great Society*   *Medicare*   *Appalachia*

The nation was still stunned by Kennedy's assassination as it watched and listened to President Lyndon B. Johnson address a joint session of Congress on the fifth day of his administration. The new leader began quietly by saying, "All I have I would have given gladly not to be standing here today." He reminded his audience how Kennedy had urged Americans to begin to solve national and world problems. Then he added his own statement, "Let us continue," and urged Congress to move ahead in such areas as civil rights, education, and lower taxes. Finally, he closed by asking the people to join with him in the spirit of Thanksgiving:

" America, America,
   God shed his grace on thee,
   And crown thy good
   With brotherhood
   From sea to shining sea. "

A Civil Rights Act is Passed

Johnson's domestic aims and achievements were later called the "Great Society." One of the cornerstones of the Great Society was the Civil Rights Act of 1964.

New Tactics. Johnson had spent some twenty-six years in Congress. From 1954 until becoming vice president, he had been the Democratic majority leader in the Senate. There he had enormous success in getting legislation adopted. He understood the legislative process of persuading people with different views to each give in just a little so that each could get part of what he or she wanted. Some people called this the art of "horsetrading."

On the issue of civil rights, though, Johnson decided to employ different tactics. He knew that senators who opposed the bill would threaten a *filibuster,* or a series of long speeches intended to delay passage. In return for not staging a filibuster, they would ask that certain parts of the bill be watered down. Since Johnson did not want to see this happen, he decided to go for a complete victory.

The battle raged for six months. Southern senators filibustered for eighty-three days, until the Senate cut off further debate. Johnson talked repeatedly with Republican leader Senator Everett Dirksen of Illinois, trying to convince him to support the legislation. Johnson also called on such black leaders as Roy Wilkins of the NAACP and Whitney Young of the Urban League for help. "When are you going to get down here and start civil-righting?" he asked them. He particularly wanted them to concentrate on Republican senators.

A Significant Law. The various tactics were successful. On July 2, 1964, President Johnson signed the most sweeping piece of civil rights legislation since Reconstruction.

The new law gave all citizens, regardless of race, the right to enter such public facilities as libraries, parks, and washrooms. It forbade discrimination in schools and gave the attorney general the power to file suit in court to help speed up desegregation. The law forbade discrimination in restaurants and theaters. It extended the power of the federal government to protect black voting rights. It set up an Equal Employment Opportunity Commission to help blacks to obtain fair treatment in businesses and unions. And it set up a Community Relations Service to help local officials deal with racial problems.

755

In addition to prohibiting discrimination because of race, color, religion, and national origin, the Civil Rights Act of 1964 prohibited discrimination because of sex. The word "sex" had been tacked on the bill by 81-year-old Representative Howard Smith of Virginia. An opponent of civil rights legislation, Smith hoped his action would result in the bill's being "laughed to death." But when the bill passed, it not only outlawed racial discrimination in many areas, it also made sex discrimination illegal. This accidental provision was to have far-reaching results.

Other Accomplishments

In response to Johnson's prodding, Congress in February 1964 passed Kennedy's tax reduction bill. A few months later, it set up a food-stamp plan for families on welfare, and also voted funds for public housing.

Office of Economic Opportunity. Having convinced Congress to carry out Kennedy's legislation, Johnson then moved ahead to propose measures of his own. He called for an unconditional "war on poverty" for those Americans who were living "on the outskirts of hope." In August 1964 Congress set up the Office of Economic Opportunity and voted it $1 billion to run ten antipoverty programs. One was the Job Corps, which was something like the Civilian Conservation Corps of the New Deal. But instead of paying unemployed youth to work on the land, it paid school drop-outs while they trained for industrial jobs. Another program was the so-called "domestic peace corps," officially known as VISTA (Volunteers in Service to America). VISTA volunteers worked in urban ghettos, depressed areas, and Indian reservations, teaching people there new skills. And then there was the Head Start educational program for preschool youngsters. In a Head Start center, children could learn how to distinguish colors, tell time, understand geographic directions, follow instructions, and do other things that would help them when they entered elementary school.

Congressional Reapportionment. In 1964 the Supreme Court acted to guarantee equal representation to all citizens in all states. This was a result of a long battle between the interests of rural areas and those of urban areas. Each congressional district elects one congressman. Before 1964, some

districts had fewer than 200,000 people. In many urban areas there were over 600,000 people in a district. Yet these 600,000 people were represented by only one congressman. The 200,000 in the rural district were also represented by one congressman. So, the voters in the rural areas had more representation (and thus more power) in government than those in the urban areas.

The Supreme Court, therefore, ruled that congressional district boundaries should be redrawn so that they would be equal in population "as nearly as practicable." The Court also ordered the states to redraw the state legislative districts to equalize the voting power of the different districts. In effect, this shifted the political power throughout the nation from rural areas to urban areas.

A Presidential Landslide

It is almost impossible to unseat an incumbent president who has made no serious mistakes. LBJ, as Johnson was called, had brought the nation through a difficult crisis and had enjoyed legislative success. True, many white southerners were unhappy about the Civil Rights Act, and Governor George C. Wallace of Alabama did well in several Democratic primaries. But by convention time, the Democratic party was united and enthusiastic for LBJ. For the Republicans to oust him would have been extremely difficult even had they put up a candidate with wide appeal. As it was, they nominated someone with very narrow appeal.

Goldwater Represents the Conservative Voice. Senator Barry Goldwater of Arizona was an attractive person of complete integrity who had successfully run a family business in Phoenix before entering politics. His experience in foreign affairs was limited, though generally his background was as good as Kennedy's had been when he entered the White House. But the senator represented the right wing of his party at a time when the country was moving in the opposite direction.

Goldwater's supporters, however, were convinced that there were a large number of Americans who favored "A Choice, Not An Echo," as their campaign literature put it. They believed the Republican candidates of the past twenty-four years had been mere carbon copies of the Democratic candidates. The only way to recapture the presidency, conservatives felt, was by offering a candidate people on the right could accept. Then

President Lyndon B. Johnson could exert a magnetic appeal among voters and nonvoters as well.

these people, who presumably had not voted for years, would come out and cast their ballots. The conservatives' slogan for Goldwater was, "In Your Heart You Know He's Right."

Issues in the Campaign. Probably most Americans agreed with some of Goldwater's criticisms. The federal bureaucracy had grown to about fifty times its original size during the twentieth century. Some public officials were undoubtedly rude or incompetent or both, and there was considerable waste and mismanagement.

On the other hand, some of Goldwater's ideas struck most people as unrealistic. Goldwater suggested selling the TVA for one dollar to private industry. He wanted Social Security to be voluntary and indicated that he would like to do away with other welfare measures. He had voted against the nuclear test ban treaty. And he had urged that NATO commanders be allowed to use nuclear weapons in the event of a crisis. The Democrats capitalized on people's fear of atomic warfare with a chilling television commercial. A picture of a little girl counting as she pulled the petals off a daisy turned into a picture of a mushroom cloud.

Events overseas probably helped strengthen Johnson's image as a man of peace. In the Soviet Union, Khrushchev was removed from office and replaced by two strongly anti-Western leaders, Leonid Brezhnev and Alexei Kosygin. The Chinese exploded an atomic bomb. When Goldwater said he would go all out to save South Vietnam from Communist aggression, Johnson presented himself as the "antiwar" candidate. "We don't want our American boys to do the fighting for Asian boys," he said in September. "We don't want to get involved . . . and get tied down in a land war in Asia." The following month he declared, "There can be, and will be, as long as I am President, peace for all Americans."

An Overwhelming Victory. Despite his enormous lead, LBJ ran as though his life depended on it. "Andy Jackson in a jetliner" a columnist in the *New York Times* called him.

On November 3, 1964, Johnson won his expected victory. More than 70 million Americans went to the polls, and 43 million of them, or 61 percent, voted Democratic. This was an even higher percentage than the previous record that FDR had set in 1936. The president carried forty-four states with 486 electoral votes to Goldwater's six states and 52 electoral votes. The Democrats also increased their majority in Congress enough so that, for the first time since 1938, a Democratic president did not need the votes of conservative southern Democrats in order to get laws passed.

The Great Society could now be launched in earnest.

The Great Society

When Lyndon Johnson left the White House in January 1969, Vice President Hubert H. Humphrey and the cabinet presented him with an engraved list titled "Landmark Laws of the Lyndon B. Johnson Administration." Beginning in 1963 and ending with 1968, it listed no fewer than 206 measures. Each one had been planned, drafted, and introduced under LBJ's guidance. And for most of them he had to battle as well.

Education. Johnson considered education "the key which can unlock the door to the Great Society." Elementary schools, high schools, and

Presidential Election of 1964

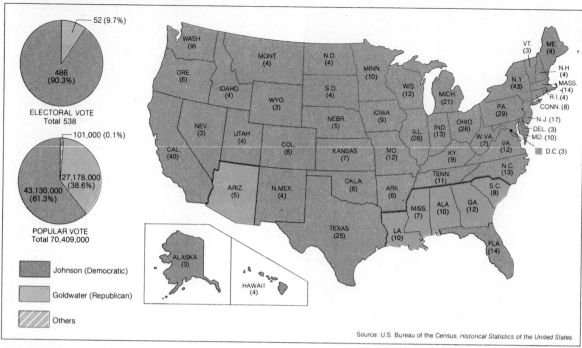

Map Skills   *Johnson overwhelmed Goldwater. How many electoral votes did Johnson get? What was his percentage of the popular vote? Which state won by Goldwater was not in the South?*

colleges were all given funds. However, the more poor families a school district had, the more money that district's elementary and high schools could receive. In order to receive funds, districts had to show that they were trying to eliminate racial discrimination.

Medicare.   The first major change in the Social Security system since it was adopted in 1935 was brought about through the establishment of Medicare. This program provides hospital insurance and some posthospital nursing care for almost every American once she or he reaches the age of sixty-five. It also provides low-cost insurance against doctor bills, laboratory tests, and other medical services and supplies.

Housing.   Congress appropriated money to build some 240,000 units of low-rent public housing. It also voted money to help low- and moderate-income families pay for better private housing. A new federal department, the Department of Housing and Urban Development (HUD), was established. It was headed by Robert C. Weaver, the nation's first black cabinet member.

The Model Cities program was likewise designed to direct federal assistance to urban areas that needed it most. About 75 cities were given funds to develop "model" plans for rebuilding their slums. People living in the slums were supposed to play a role in drawing up the plans.

Appalachia.   The Great Society attacked rural as well as urban poverty. The Appalachian Mountains run through eleven states from Pennsylvania to Georgia. The parts of the states that lie in the mountains are jointly called Appalachia. A beautiful area with many natural resources, it was relatively isolated from the rest of the country. Appalachia in the early 1960s was one of the most poverty-stricken parts of the country. So Congress provided money for building highways, setting up health centers, and otherwise developing the region.

Other Measures.   The Great Society did not restrict its fight against discrimination to civil rights. As you read in chapter 29, the National Origins Acts of 1924 and 1929 had established immigration quotas that discriminated strongly against Poles, Jews, Italians, and other "new immigrants."

In 1965 near the Statue of Liberty Johnson signed a bill abolishing the national origins system. However, an annual quota of 170,000 immigrants, including for the first time those from the Western Hemisphere, was set. Within this overall quota, no more than 20,000 persons from any one nation can enter the United States each year.

Other legislation had to do with improving the environment. Polluted waterways were to be restored. Smog-laden air was to be made cleaner. Only a limited number of advertising billboards could go up along new interstate highways. Safety standards for automobile manufacturers were to be established. And another federal department was created, the Department of Transportation.

Failures of the Great Society

Some of LBJ's programs worked well. Others fell apart. A variety of reasons may explain why, overall, the programs did not have greater effect.

First, although they improved conditions dramatically, they did not meet everyone's needs. Certain social problems were simply too big. Second, some of the programs were experimental and just did not work. Third, a number of the programs were designed to utilize existing local welfare, school, and health departments. But in many cities, the facilities of these departments were run-down and unable to handle the new tasks.

Most important of all, money ran out. President Johnson was trying to fight two wars at the same time. He began with a war against poverty, but gradually the war against communism in Asia became more important. Public funds went increasingly to the Vietnam struggle, and the Great Society, like the Johnson presidency, eventually became a casualty.

The life of Puerto Ricans in New York was the subject of a very popular musical called West Side Story. This is a scene from the movie.

Section 1 Review

COMPREHENSION   Developing Vocabulary

1. Explain these terms: Great Society, Medicare, Appalachia, filibuster.

COMPREHENSION   Mastering Facts

1. How had Lyndon Johnson, while a senator, been able to get legislation adopted?
2. What effect did the Civil Rights Act of 1964 have on Jim Crow?
3. What did the Supreme Court say in 1964 about the size of congressional districts? What effect did this decision have?
4. How did supporters of Senator Goldwater view the Republican presidential candidates of the previous twenty-four years?
5. What changes in immigration were made by the 1965 legislation?

2 THE UNITED STATES FIGHTS IN VIETNAM

VOCABULARY   *defoliants   credibility gap*

In 1947 President Truman announced the policy of containment: the United States would prevent any further advance of Communist power anywhere in the world. But by 1954 the French in Indochina had been defeated by Communist forces. The country was divided into a North and South Vietnam. The North was Communist. In 1954 President Eisenhower advanced the domino theory and approved direct economic and military aid to South Vietnam. President Kennedy sent 16,000 military advisors into South Vietnam and authorized U.S. helicopters to fly strafing missions against North Vietnam. President Johnson sent more than 500,000 American troops and spent about $25 billion a year in a futile effort to prevent a Communist government in South Vietnam.

Johnson's Dilemma

Despite the money and aid received by the regime of Ngo Dinh Diem, it had become increasingly unpopular and was overthrown by a military coup less than a month before Johnson became president. But the new South Vietnamese government turned out to be even more unstable and ineffective than the old government. Land reform still lagged; corruption went on; one general replaced another; and Vietcong influence grew steadily until it covered almost 80 percent of the countryside. In addition, some 30,000 North Vietnamese infiltrated South Vietnam and were providing military assistance to the estimated 150,000 Vietcong guerrillas.

Johnson had opposed the involvement of American combat troops when he had been vice-president. As a Democratic president, however, he faced certain political difficulties. He remembered how people criticized the government in 1949 when China became Communist. He was also afraid of seeming a weak president. He believed that other nations would lose respect for the United States if it did not live up to its anti-Communist policy. Moreover, the president's closest political and military advisors—Defense Secretary Robert McNamara, Secretary of State Dean Rusk, National Security Advisor McGeorge Bundy, General Maxwell Taylor, John Mc Cone of the CIA—assured him that it would take only a small investment of American troops and money to obtain a victory against the Vietcong.

The Gulf of Tonkin Resolution

On July 30, 1964, the Hanoi government of North Vietnam complained that South Vietnamese ships, protected by an American destroyer, had attacked two of their islands. On August 2, North Vietnamese patrol torpedo boats attacked the American destroyer *Maddox* in Tonkin Gulf but were driven off. Two days later, it was reported that the *Maddox* had been attacked again, as had another destroyer, the *Turner Joy*. The United States denied taking part in the attack on North Vietnam. North Vietnam denied the August 4 attack. (Several years later, the American government acknowledged that it had aided South Vietnamese ships to attack North Vietnam.)

Three days later, on August 7, Congress adopted what became known as the Gulf of Ton-

kin Resolution. It stated that the president could "take all necessary measures to repel any armed attack against armed forces of the United States and to prevent further aggression." The vote in the House was unanimous, 416 to 0. In the Senate, only Wayne Morse of Oregon and Ernest Gruening of Alaska voted "No." Morse, like Senator Robert A. Taft in 1950, believed the resolution gave the president power that rightfully belonged to Congress. Gruening called it "a predated declaration of war." The resolution signaled full-scale U.S. military aid to South Vietnam.

The Air War. Beginning in February 1965, the United States began bombing North Vietnam. The air attacks were designed to do two things: (1) slow down infiltration by North Vietnamese into South Vietnam; and (2) convince the Hanoi government that it could not resist the armed might of the United States and should reach a settlement with South Vietnam. The president himself chose the targets that American planes were to hit. By 1967, more bombs were being dropped on North Vietnam every week than had been dropped on Germany during all of World War II.

Now and again, the United States would halt the bombing in an effort to persuade North Vietnam to negotiate. In April 1965, Johnson also offered $1 billion in aid to the nations of Southeast Asia, including North Vietnam, if the fighting

Part of everyday life in Vietnam. Soldiers carry a wounded comrade to a waiting helicopter.

would stop. But each time the Hanoi government gave the same reply. The bombings must stop unconditionally and all American forces must leave Vietnam before peace negotiations could begin.

The Ground War. While American planes took to the air, American troops poured into Vietnam to assist the South Vietnamese army. A common tactic was the search-and-destroy mission. Helicopters would land troops in a village suspected of either supporting, or being controlled by, the Vietcong. The soldiers would spray the huts with machine guns, shoot the livestock, and then burn the village. Unfortunately, most of the casualties in this kind of fighting were old men, women, and children. The men of fighting age were usually hidden in the jungle.

One result was the creation of some 2 million refugees out of a total population of 16 million. They clogged the roads or crowded into special refugee camps or into the cities, where their need for food, shelter, and medical care added to the burden of the war.

Fighting the Vietcong guerrillas created yet another problem. In an effort to destroy the jungles that provided cover for the Vietcong, the United States sprayed huge quantities of toxic chemicals on the countryside. The defoliants, which caused leaves to drop off all plants, devastated about 20 percent of the landscape. Until 1967, South Vietnam had been a major exporter of rice. By 1968, it was importing rice in an effort to prevent mass starvation. The defoliants also led to birth defects in Vietnamese children and in the children of American servicemen, as well as to liver damage, muscular disorders, and other health problems for the adults who were exposed to the chemicals.

The Doves Against the Hawks

By 1965 many Americans were beginning to have serious doubts about the nation's growing involvement in Vietnam. And the more the United States became involved, the stronger and more widespread became the opposition. It took various forms. There were antiwar musical shows and stop-the-bombing marches. There were automobile bumper stickers that read "Make Love Not War" and posters stating that "War is not healthy for children and other living things." Young Americans burned their draft cards or picketed induction centers. Sit-ins and strikes erupted on college cam-

Demonstrations against the U.S. involvement in Vietnam increased in number and intensity during the late 1960s.

puses, especially after student draft deferments were abolished. By 1968 about 10,000 Americans had emigrated to Canada in order to avoid serving in what they considered an immoral war.

The arguments presented by the doves, as those who were against the war were called, varied. Probably the most common reason for opposition was the belief that the war was basically a civil war in which the Vietcong were trying to overcome a corrupt and inefficient government in Saigon. In trying to "save" South Vietnam from communism, these doves argued, the U.S. government was actually destroying an entire country and population. In addition, the critics pointed out, thousands of Americans were being killed and wounded, while the cost of the conflict was causing a serious inflation and forcing the nation to abandon the Great Society's social programs.

The hawks, people who supported the Vietnam War, agreed with President Johnson that Vietnam was vital to American security and that containing communism was a consideration more important than casualties or cost. Some hawks wanted to escalate the war even further. They believed there was "a light at the end of the tunnel" and that just one all-out military effort would bring about a complete victory. They pointed to the reports from U.S. diplomats and field commanders in Vietnam that the enemy was exhausted and at the brink of defeat.

The Tet Offensive

Tuesday evening, January 30, 1968, was the Vietnamese equivalent of New Year's Eve. The next day was Tet, the start of the lunar New Year. The streets of cities throughout South Vietnam were filling up with youngsters who were apparently arriving from the countryside to celebrate the holiday. There were also an unusually large number of funerals taking place, with the traditional firecrackers and flutes and, of course, coffins.

As it turned out, the coffins contained weapons, while the supposed farmers belonged to special Vietcong units. That night the enemy launched an overwhelming attack at about a hundred cities, including Saigon and some 26 provincial capitals. After less than a month of fighting, South Vietnamese and American troops regained control at a cost of 42,000 Vietcong casualties. But it was obvious even to President Johnson that the enemy was not at the brink of surrender and that the war was very far indeed from being won.

Johnson Decides Not To Run

On March 12 New Hampshire voters turned out for the presidential primary. Running against Johnson was Senator Eugene McCarthy of Minnesota, who had announced his candidacy the previous November. Although McCarthy had voted for the Tonkin Gulf Resolution, he had become increasingly dovish as the war went on. He was particularly bothered by the so-called "credibility gap," the difference between the optimistic statements of the Johnson administration and what was really happening in Vietnam. Helping McCarthy in his campaign were some 5000 young people from colleges throughout the Northeast. They poured into New Hampshire on their own, set up campaign centers, and talked to people about the need for a policy of peace in Washington.

When the ballots were counted, Johnson received 49 percent of the Democratic vote and McCarthy 42 percent. But enough Republicans wrote in McCarthy's name on their ballots to make his total almost the same as Johnson's. This was an amazing showing for an almost unknown

senator against an incumbent president, especially in a hawkish state.

Elated with the results, thousands of midwestern college students then poured into Wisconsin, where the next big presidential primary was scheduled for April 2. In the meantime, former attorney general Robert Kennedy, now a senator from New York, announced that he also would challenge Johnson. Kennedy had suggested an American withdrawal from Vietnam as early as August 1963, when his late brother had been president. In 1967 the younger Kennedy had criticized the administration's behavior. "We're killing innocent people . . . because [the Communists] are 12,000 miles away and they might get 11,000 miles away."

A shrewd politician, Johnson understood what was happening. On March 31, he addressed the nation on television. "I am taking the first step to de-escalate the conflict," he told the American people. "I have ordered our aircraft . . . to make no attacks on North Vietnam." Then, almost as an afterthought, he said, "There is division in the American house now. Accordingly, I shall not seek, and I will not accept, the nomination of my party for another term as your President." Four years before, LBJ had received the greatest majority of popular votes in the nation's history. Now he was calling an end to his political career.

The next month, preliminary peace talks began in Paris between representatives of Ho Chi Minh and the United States. Nevertheless, fighting continued. By the fall of 1968 the struggle in Vietnam had become the second longest war in American history, exceeded only by the Revolutionary War. Only the two world wars and the Civil War had resulted in more deaths.

Section 2 Review

COMPREHENSION   Developing Vocabulary

1. Explain these terms: credibility gap, defoliants, hawks, doves.

COMPREHENSION   Mastering Facts

1. What objection did Senator Wayne Morse make to the Gulf of Tonkin Resolution?
2. How did the use of defoliants affect Vietnam's economy?
3. What was the most commonly raised objection to American involvement in the Vietnam War?
4. What effect did the New Hampshire primary have on President Johnson?

VOCABULARY   *black power*

The Vietnam War was not the only issue that divided the nation during Johnson's administration. Another was the equally explosive question of race relations. Despite considerable progress in such areas as voting rights and housing, a new spirit of black militancy came to the fore.

A Drive for Voting Rights

In the summer of 1964, several thousand young black and white college students volunteered to go to Mississippi to help register that state's black voters. Before the summer was over, three of the volunteers—two whites, Michael H. Schwerner and Andrew Goodman, and one black, James E. Chaney—were murdered. (In 1967 an all-white jury convicted seven white defendants on charges of violating the civil rights of the three volunteers. The defendants, who included the deputy sheriff of the county where the murders had taken place, received jail sentences of up to ten years.) Three more volunteers were shot, eighty were beaten, more than a thousand were arrested, and dozens of homes and churches were bombed or burned.

In January of the following year, 1965, Dr. Martin Luther King launched a drive to register black voters in Alabama. At first there was little response. But in March a black would-be voter was murdered near the town of Selma. On March 7 about 700 of King's followers began a protest march from Selma to the state capital of Montgomery. State troopers and local police broke up the march with tear gas, billy clubs, and bullwhips in full sight of television cameras. Two weeks later, King led a second march. About 3200 blacks and whites, including ministers, priests, and rabbis from all over the country, left Selma on March 21. By the time the procession reached Montgomery four days later, it numbered 25,000.

The marchers were protected by the federalized Alabama National Guard, U.S. marshals, and two army battalions. Nevertheless, the night the march ended, Viola Gregg Liuzzo, a white housewife from Detroit, was shot by Ku Klux Klansmen. Earlier, a Boston minister and a New Hampshire seminary student had also been gunned down. Liuzzo's assailants were convicted, but the defendants in the two other trials were acquitted.

That same month, at President Johnson's request, Congress passed the Voting Rights Act of 1965. The act eliminated the literacy test and provided that federal examiners register qualified voters. The act also gave the attorney general the right to file suits against the use of the poll tax in state elections. In 1966, the Supreme Court ruled that all poll taxes were unconstitutional.

The Black Revolution

The Selma march and the passage of the Voting Rights Act were the high points of King's campaign of non-violence. From then on, a new mood emerged in the black community.

Population Changes. There were several reasons for this. One was the shift in the black population. In 1950 four out of six blacks lived in the South. By 1966 the proportion had dropped to three out of six. In 1950 about one-half of the black population lived in cities. By 1966 the proportion had risen to two-thirds. During the same period the black population grew by forty-three percent while the white population grew by twenty-six percent. In other words, by 1966 about one out of every two blacks was under eighteen years of age and the resident of an urban ghetto.

At the same time, facilities in the cities had usually not kept up with the population change. Housing was old and rundown. Schools were overcrowded and often lacked libraries and cafeterias. Many industries had relocated to the suburbs, which were often all-white. And even if blacks could find jobs in the suburbs, there was seldom any public transportation for them to use. The result was a black unemployment rate about double the rate for whites. Among black teen-agers, the unemployment rate was close to 25 percent. In addition, blacks tended to be concentrated in low-paying occupations. They also tended to receive lower wages than whites even when they were performing the same kind of work.

In 1964, black Congressman Adam Clayton Powell had predicted that the "black revolution" would consist of two parts. The first part, already underway, would take place in the South and would deal with "middle-class matters," such as sitting on buses and voting. The second part, he predicted, would take place in the North, where blacks already had the right to vote and to sit in the front of the bus. There, Powell said, the issue would be "who gets the money." Not only that; the second part of the revolution would be "rough." He was right.

Race Riots. Beginning in 1964 and for the next three years, more than 100 riots erupted in one major American city after another, from the Watts district of Los Angeles to Washington, D.C. The summer of 1967 was especially "hot," with 67 separate outbreaks, including one in Newark that took 25 lives and another in Detroit that took 43 lives. Property losses ran into hundreds of millions of dollars. In Detroit, it took federal troops in tanks to restore order.

In many cases, the riots were sparked by relatively minor incidents between white policemen and black youngsters. They seemed to reflect a widespread feeling among blacks that while civil rights legislation was well and good, government in general really did not care about the welfare of black citizens. Bayard Rustin recounts that a twenty-year-old black in Watts told him after the riot there, "We won." Rustin asked how he could say that when black homes and stores had been destroyed, blacks killed, and the entire area needed massive relief. "We won because we made the whole world pay attention to us," the youth replied. "The police chief never came here before; the mayor always stayed uptown. We made them come."

New Leaders and "Black Power." Among the blacks who were now beginning to attract attention were such individuals as Malcolm X. Born Malcolm Little, he changed his name because he did not want a last name that came from whites who had taken away his ancestral African name. He had been a minister of the Nation of Islam, or Black Muslims, for twelve years. Then he split and set up the Organization for Afro-American Unity. Malcolm X was impatient with King's non-violent approach. "The day of non-violent resistance is over," he asserted. "If they have the Ku Klux Klan non-violent, I'll be non-violent . . . . But as long as you've got somebody else not being non-violent, I don't want anybody coming to me talking any non-violent talk."

Malcolm X, and others like him, argued in favor of what they called "black power." Although the precise meaning of the phrase depended on who was talking, in general it included the following: (1) the development of black-owned businesses in black communities; (2) local control of schools in black communities; (3) the use of black police officers in black communities; (4) bloc voting to elect black representatives who would give priority to the needs of black communities; and (5) the development of a sense of pride in being black. Some black power advocates also favored the complete separation of blacks from whites.

The black power movement had varying results. Many black Americans were elected to public office. The number of black police officers increased. Middle-class blacks found more and more openings available in business and the professions. Blacks began appearing on the television screen and in newspaper advertisements. The number of black-owned businesses increased, and black community organizations of all kinds sprang up. And in 1968 Congress passed a new Civil Rights Act which prohibited discrimination in the sale or rental of all housing except for owner-occupied homes that were sold by the owner directly.

At the same time, public support for the civil rights movement began to diminish. Many whites who had supported the struggle were pushed out of organizations by blacks who considered it demeaning to accept white support.

Some areas saw a white backlash, with increased opposition to school integration. The violent statements and behavior of the more militant blacks, such as H. Rap Brown and Huey P. Newton of the Black Panther party, frightened or angered many white Americans. They felt that matters were getting out of hand and that respect for law and order was disappearing. Their feelings were to play a big part in the 1968 presidential election.

Section 3 Review

COMPREHENSION Developing Vocabulary

1. Explain these terms: black power, backlash.

COMPREHENSION Mastering Facts

1. What was the purpose of the Selma march?
2. What economic problems did urban black teen-agers face?
3. What was the major political difference between Malcolm X and Dr. Martin Luther King?
4. What did the Civil Rights Act of 1968 provide?

4 WOMEN SEEK TO IMPROVE THEIR STATUS

VOCABULARY   *Women's Liberation*

In the 1840s and 1850s, many women who were active in the abolitionist movement also became active in the struggle for woman suffrage. Similarly, in the 1960s, many of the women who protested against racial discrimination became active in the movement for women's rights, popularly known as Women's Liberation or Women's Lib.

Developments Since World War II

Between June and September of 1945, one out of every four employed women quit or was fired from her job, usually in a war plant, and was replaced by a returning serviceman. By 1947 the number of women in the work force had fallen by 5 million, and the annual birthrate had increased by 25 percent. Then the trend began to reverse. By 1960 more than one out of three women over the age of fourteen was working for pay. About half of these 22 million women either supported themselves or were the main breadwinner in their family. However, they were concentrated in low-paying clerical or service jobs.

Three additional trends could be observed during the fifties. First, women below age twenty-five in the work force declined. Second, women were marrying for the first time at a much younger age. One out of every two women was married before her twentieth birthday. Many started going steady in junior high school. Third, women's interest in higher education dropped. The proportion of women to men in college fell to 35 percent from almost 50 percent in 1920. And almost two out of three co-eds left college before graduation, either to marry or to "avoid becoming over-educated." Those who stayed felt considerable pressure not to major in math or science or to take up other "unfeminine" careers. Indeed, women who persisted in entering law, medicine, engineering, economics, architecture, or other non-traditional fields, had to meet higher standards than men. In return, they were usually offered inferior job opportunities.

Women's Social Role

The idea that a woman's place was in the home got lots of positive social reinforcement in romantic novels, films, and television shows. An editor of the *Ladies' Home Journal* once explained that "If we get an article about a woman who does anything adventurous, out of the way, something by herself, you know, we figure she must be terribly aggressive, neurotic." Such influential magazines as *Time* and *Life* ran numerous articles praising the glories of homemaking and encouraging women to find happiness only as wives and mothers. This was ironic, because Clare Boothe Luce, wife of the publisher, was a notable career woman of the decade. After divorcing her socialite first husband, she became managing editor of *Vanity Fair* magazine, wrote several Broadway plays, was elected to Congress from Connecticut, and served as ambassador to Italy during the Eisenhower administration.

Many corporations recognized the importance of the proper wife for their rising executives. Wives were often judged along with their husbands when promotions were being considered. Their behavior at company dinners and receptions was observed to be sure they possessed correct social skills. Some companies ran training programs in which wives were taught how to entertain and otherwise aid their husbands' careers.

Occasionally, however, there was some disagreement with the prevailing attitude. Anthropologist Margaret Mead attacked the belief that continual contact between mother and child is essential. She maintained that children are not necessarily damaged if their mothers work away from home. The quality of time a mother spends with her child, Mead believed, is more important than the quantity.

In 1956 *McCall's* published an article called "The Mother Who Ran Away." To the editor's amazement, it attracted more reader attention than any other article they had ever published. Another magazine edited for women readers, *Redbook*, printed "Why Mothers Feel Trapped." Twenty-four thousand women responded with letters saying that was exactly how they felt.

Then, in 1963, a significant event occurred.

The Feminine Mystique

Many people's feelings about slavery were brought to a head by *Uncle Tom's Cabin*. In the women's movement, too, a book by a woman author helped to crystalize attitudes. The author was

Percentage of Working Women

Age Group	1950	1960	1970	1980
16 and 17 years	30.1	28.6	34.6	45.8
18 and 19 years	51.3	51.0	53.4	62.9
20 to 24 years	46.1	46.1	57.5	69.1
25 to 34 years	34.0	35.8	44.8	63.8
35 to 44 years	39.1	43.1	50.9	63.6
45 to 54 years	38.0	49.3	54.0	58.4
55 to 64 years	27.0	36.7	42.5	41.9
65 years and over	9.7	10.5	9.2	8.3
Total 16 years and over	33.9	37.1	42.8	51.0

Which group had the top percentage in 1950 and 1960? 1970 and 1980?

Betty Friedan, a suburban housewife, and the book was called *The Feminine Mystique*. Here is Friedan's description of the problem to which the title refers.

“The problem lay buried, unspoken, for many years in the minds of American women. It was a strange stirring, a sense of dissatisfaction, a yearning that women suffered in the middle of the twentieth century in the United States. Each suburban wife struggled with it alone. As she made the beds, shopped for groceries, matched slipcover material, ate peanut butter sandwiches with her children, chauffeured Cub Scouts and Brownies . . . she was afraid to ask even of herself the silent question “Is this all?”

For over fifteen years there was no word of this yearning in the millions of words written about women, for women, in all the columns, books and articles by experts telling women their role was to seek fulfillment as wives and mothers. Over and over women heard in voices of tradition that they could desire no greater destiny than to glory in their own femininity. . . . They were taught to pity the neurotic, unfeminine, unhappy women who wanted to be poets or physicists or presidents. They learned that truly feminine women did not want careers, higher education, political rights—the independence and the opportunities that the old-fashioned feminists fought for. Some women, in their forties and fifties, still remembered painfully giving up those dreams, but most of the younger women no longer even thought about them. A thousand expert voices applauded their femininity, their adjustment, their new maturity. All they had to do was devote their lives from earliest girlhood to finding a husband and bearing children.”

The feminine mystique, according to Friedan, made the housewife-mother of the past, who of necessity had to confine herself to cooking, cleaning, washing, and bearing children, into the only role model for women today. No matter that the world had changed, that most women could now make use of dishwashers, washing machines, vacuum cleaners, frozen foods, diaper services, and other labor-saving conveniences. No matter that women's life expectancy was no longer forty years but at least seventy. The mystique taught that women were by nature passive and nurturing and subservient to men—and woe betide any woman who wanted to change her role.

The Beginnings of Change

The ideas expressed in *The Feminine Mystique* were reinforced that same year, 1963, by the publication of a report by the Commission on the Status of Women. The commission had been set up by President Kennedy, and it was the first government body to study the position of women in American society. The report showed that discrimination against women was widespread, and it made a few recommendations, including equal pay for equal work.

Federal Legislation. Later that year Congress did in fact pass the Equal Pay Act. But enforcing the law was something else again. Employers used a variety of tactics to avoid compliance. For example, they would give women different titles, such as "executive assistant," and then pay them different salaries from those paid men who were doing the same kind of work. And different always meant lower. In 1970 women high school graduates were earning only about 56 percent of the amount earned by men of equivalent age and education. Women college graduates did even worse; they earned only 55 percent of the amount earned by college-educated men.

The Civil Rights Act of 1964, to almost everyone's surprise, as you read earlier in the chapter, ended up including a prohibition against sex discrimination. Since then, hundreds of court cases have been filed, and changes are slowly being put into effect.

Women Start to Organize. In the meantime, many women felt the need for a political organization that would concern itself with women's rights. In 1966 Betty Friedan and others founded the National Organization For Women (NOW). Friedan became its first president. NOW advocated help for working parents, either free child-care centers or tax deductions for child-care expenses. It called for maternity leave benefits, and urged adoption of an Equal Rights Amendment (ERA) to the constitution. It wanted girls to be able to take the same courses in school as boys, and it wanted the amount of money spent on athletics for girls to be equal to the amount spent on athletics for boys. In general, the members of NOW believe in traditional methods of action such as legislative lobbying, peaceful demonstrations, the election of candidates favorable to women's rights, and court suits to end sex discrimination in employment.

Some NOW members, like militant blacks, did not agree with these traditional methods. They split off from NOW to form a variety of more radical groups. Most of these, however, no longer exist.

Section 4 Review

COMPREHENSION   Developing Vocabulary

1. Explain these terms: Women's Liberation, mystique.

COMPREHENSION   Mastering Facts

1. What percentage of women over fourteen were in the labor force by 1960?
2. What did most Americans in the early sixties believe to be the only proper role for women?
3. What effect did the Civil Rights Act of 1964 have on sex discrimination?
4. How did women's pay in 1970 compare with men's pay?

5   OTHER AMERICANS SEEK CHANGES

People's dissatisfaction with one or another aspect of American society expressed itself not only in political action but also in attempts to change lifestyles and challenge existing values. This was especially true of many young people between the ages of 16 and 30.

The Hippie Movement

A person wandering through certain sections of American cities in the mid-1960s would have found the streets filled with bushy-haired teenagers. Wearing blue jeans, fringed shirts, and brightly colored sneakers, with feathers on their hats and beads around their necks, they almost looked as if they were going to a costume party. Most of them worked at odd jobs, shared inexpensive living accommodations, and spent their considerable leisure time attending rock concerts or simply watching other people. Almost all of them smoked marijuana, and some used harder drugs such as LSD.

These people were known as "hippies." Most were youngsters who felt alienated from American society. They were bothered by the discrepancy between public statements that "All men are created equal" and the treatment of racial minorities. They found it difficult to understand the continuing existence of poverty and unemployment. Many came from middle-class families, and they questioned the amount of time and energy their parents devoted to earning a living and getting ahead. Not having experienced the Great Depression, they felt there were more important things to do than compete for material success.

Many hippies called themselves Flower Children or Gentle People. They believed the answer to social problems was love—a general feeling of brotherhood and a sharing of everything one owned. Some carried out their beliefs by organizing communes that resembled Brook Farm and other utopian communities of the nineteenth century. But other hippies, at least in the eyes of critics, simply dropped out of society. One critic wrote:

❝The pain threshold of today's youth is so much lower than it is for our generation. We can deal with problems—we did—that were very serious. We dealt with them because we had no choice. This generation seems to think it's got a choice. If it doesn't work out the way they want, they turn to drugs. They turn off. They're in their own world and it's a world of music and a world of . . . I don't know

... they think it's beauty and they always say, "We've got our heads together." But they are seriously getting into a psychological situation where instead of dealing with what life is, they just can't take it. They cop out. **"**

The Consumers' Champion

Most young people, however, did not cop out but continued to work for social and political change within the system. As you have read, they helped in the campaign to register blacks in the South and took an active part in opposing President Johnson in the 1968 primaries. Some of them joined the consumer movement.

On March 22, 1966, the president of General Motors publicly apologized to a young lawyer named Ralph Nader. He also gave Nader a check for $280,000 as settlement of a lawsuit against the company. The previous year, Nader had published *Unsafe at Any Speed*, a stinging, documented attack on the motor vehicle industry and its self-imposed safety standards.

In the book Nader charged that the industry was more interested in profit than human lives. General Motors thereupon hired detectives to investigate Nader. The kinds of questions they asked made it clear they were looking for information with which to embarrass or discredit him. The detectives found nothing. They were also so clumsy they were caught. Nader sued, the press had a field day, and GM quickly settled the case. The settlement money, like the royalties Nader received for the book, was used to lobby for auto safety legislation with teeth in it. That year Congress passed the National Traffic and Motor Vehicle Safety Act.

Nader continued his muckraking activities. He gathered a staff of eager young lawyers, soon known as "Nader's Raiders," and put them to work investigating problems in such areas as meat-packing, smoke pollution, and consumer credit.

The Singles Scene

Another social phenomenon that appeared during the sixties was the so-called singles subculture. As a result of the baby boom that followed World War II, there were more young people around than ever before. At the same time, the age at which people were marrying for the first time moved upward into the mid-twenties.

In 1962 a resort hotel in the Catskill Mountains of New York called Grossinger's ran a singles-only weekend. It drew some 1000 participants and was a resounding financial and matrimonial success. It was widely imitated by other resorts, and within a few years there were singles-only magazines and newspapers, singles-only tours, singles bars, and especially singles-only apartment houses. The latter featured swimming pools, tennis courts, gymnasiums, and lots of parties. Their tenants were mostly white-collar workers who tended to be uninterested in politics.

Older Americans

While Americans under 30 were attracting public attention, changes were also occurring among Americans over 65. First, there were many more of them. As of 1970, the average life expectancy was 75 years for women and 67 years for men. People in their eighties and nineties were not uncommon. Second, they were concentrated in such sunny resort states as Arizona, California, and Florida. Third, increasing numbers were living in so-called "retirement towns."

The first retirement town opened in 1960. Located in Arizona, it was the brainchild of businessman Del Webb, who felt that older people would appreciate homes "away from cities, children, grandchildren and cold weather." He was right. He sold almost 3000 houses the first weekend.

Since the 1960s the number of older Americans has continued to increase. This has forced Congress to seek new ways to fund Social Security and Medicare payments. In 1900 only 4 percent of the nation's residents were age 65 or older. By 1980 these senior citizens accounted for 11 percent of the population. As life expectancy keeps increasing, more ways will be needed to care for and effectively use the valuable talents of older Americans.

Section 5 Review

COMPREHENSION   Developing Vocabulary

1. Explain these terms: hippies, retirement towns.

COMPREHENSION   Mastering Facts

1. What caused many youngsters to become hippies?
2. What is a major criticism of the hippie movement?
3. What effect did *Unsafe at Any Speed* have on auto safety legislation?
4. Where are many retirement towns located?

CHAPTER 38 Review

Chapter Summary

President Lyndon Johnson tried to build a Great Society. Its cornerstones were the Civil Rights Act of 1964 and the war on poverty. Returned to office in 1964 by a landslide, Johnson continued to promote his Great Society program. However, domestic successes were eventually overshadowed by expansion of American involvement in Vietnam. Costly defeats on the battlefield and growing opposition to the war at home led Johnson not to seek reelection in 1968. The 1960s were a turbulent and violent decade, characterized by new militancy in the civil rights movement and race riots in a number of cities.

Questions for Critical Thinking

COMPREHENSION   Summarizing Main Ideas

1. Describe the legislative changes that occurred in each of the following areas under the Johnson administration: (a) civil rights for blacks and other minorities; (b) Social Security; (c) immigration; (d) civil rights for women.
2. Give three reasons why many people supported the Vietnam War. Give three reasons why many people opposed it.
3. Name some of the points usually included in a definition of "black power."
4. What are the arguments in favor of the feminine mystique? How did the idea receive positive social reinforcement during the 1950s and early 1960s?
5. List different ways in which young people in the 1960s reacted to social problems. Which approach or approaches would you have followed? Give reasons for your answer.

COMPREHENSION   Interpreting Events

1. If you had been a voter in 1964, whom would you have supported, Johnson or Goldwater? Give reasons for your choice.

2. Why was the Vietnam War so divisive of the American people?
3. If you had been President Johnson in 1968, would you have run for reelection? Why?
4. Why did many blacks shift tactics from nonviolence to militancy? Do you agree with the shift? Give reasons for your opinion.

APPLICATION   Using Skills To Infer Information

For each group of data below, indicate which is the most important and which is the least important.

1. Johnson defeated Goldwater in 1964 because
   a. he ran a more energetic campaign.
   b. he was an incumbent president who had not made serious mistakes.
   c. he had wider appeal.
2. The Great Society was not a great success because
   a. public funds went increasingly to the Vietnam War instead of to social programs.
   b. some of its programs had not been previously tested.
   c. certain social problems were simply too big to be solved within a few years.
3. Race riots were common in American cities between 1964 and 1967 because
   a. the black unemployment rate was double the rate for whites.
   b. many blacks felt that riots were the only way to get the government to pay attention to the needs of black communities.
   c. white policemen did not treat black youngsters fairly.

EVALUATION   Forming Generalizations

1. How do you think poverty in the United States can be ended? If you could make only one economic reform, what would it be? Explain.

2. Do most Americans today still believe that a woman's place is in the home? What do you believe? Why?

The Computer Revolution

Most people associate the word *revolution* with conflict, fighting, and perhaps the overthrow of a government. They do that with good reason, since the most common dictionary definition of revolution simply states: "a total and radical change."

There are, of course, many other types of revolutions besides political ones. For example, the Renaissance was a revolution in thought, and the Industrial Revolution marked a fundamental change in the production and distribution of goods. Electricity revolutionized peoples' lives, as did the automobile.

As you probably realize, Americans—and indeed the world—are right now in the midst of another such period of change: the computer revolution. This revolution also promises far-reaching consequences.

Computers are now so widely used that they have become part of everyday life. They are utilized to store, sort, and recall information. They are used to control and monitor complex operations. Indeed, it is difficult to imagine how modern transportation and communication systems, banks, business offices, hospitals, and factories could function without computers.

Early Computer History.
The idea of using machines as memory and information-processing aids is not new. The abacus, a manual computing device that uses beads to represent numbers, goes back to about 3000 B.C. Hole-punched cards were used by nineteenth-century weavers to control the patterns their looms made on cloth. Then, in the late 1880s, Herman Hollerith, an employee of the United States Bureau of the Census, developed a card which contained holes representing possible responses to questions. The cards were entered into a machine that counted the holes, and with this system the Census Bureau completed its population count in record time.

More Contributions.
The incredible speed and efficiency of modern computers owes much to a number of technical and scientific advances pioneered by Americans from about 1930. One major advance was the introduction of vacuum tubes into a new computer called the ENIAC (Electronic Numerical Integrator and Calculator). This was done in the mid-1940s. Since the ENIAC used electric current instead of moving gears and levers, it could perform calculations much faster than previous machines. However, its huge size (1500 square feet) and weight (30 tons) were disadvantages.

Developments since the 1950s have made possible a dramatic reduction in the size of computers. First was the introduction of the *transistor* to replace the vacuum tube. It is smaller, faster, easier to build, and uses much less electric power than a vacuum tube. In the mid-1960s the *integrated circuit* was introduced, which combined many electronic components into a single *chip* made of a common substance, silicon. The silicon chip measures only a quarter of an inch on a side, yet by the early 1970s it could do the work of 10,000 transistors.

A Continuing Revolution.
But what about the computer *revolution*? In what field can we find radical changes that have been brought about by computers? The answer lies in our nation's economy.

The computer has had an enormous effect on the American free enterprise system—with even more impact still to come. Computers have replaced thousands of American workers in all types of industries and businesses. The advantages of computers are obvious; in most cases they are faster, more accurate, and—in the long run—probably cheaper.

At the same time, computers have created thousands of new jobs in fields that were unheard of even a decade ago. The future seems brighter than ever for computer programmers, designers, systems analysts, and so on.

In businesses and factories, computers have changed the very nature of countless operations. Bookkeepers used to work days or even weeks keeping accurate records and accounts. Computer systems now do this work in a matter of minutes. Skilled typesetters used to carefully arrange the lines of metal type needed to print books, newspapers, and magazines; that process, which once took hours, also is now done by computers in a matter of minutes.

Criticism—and Questions. Like any radical departure from established practices, the computer revolution has its critics. Some are concerned with the tremendous possibility for invasion of privacy. Others resent the impersonality of dealing with computers rather than humans. In addition, educators worry that computers may undermine students' motivation to learn such basic skills as mathematics, spelling, penmanship, and creative writing.

Computer crime is still another area of great concern. Already billions of dollars are stolen each year through embezzlement and other "white collar" crimes—many of which are accomplished through the use of computers.

Where will the computer revolution lead the nation and the world during the mid-1980s and beyond? In what ways will family lifestyles change? How will our Constitution and democratic

Two computer operators sit before cathode-ray tube (CRT) display screens. The information they type can be stored on the reels of magnetic tape just above their heads. Information from the tapes can be called back to appear on the TV-like screens.

system adapt to the new challenges that will appear because of more amazing new technology? No one can answer these questions, but one thing is certain: just as it was once the American Revolution and the Industrial Revolution had started, there can now be no turning back from the computer revolution.

Understanding Free Enterprise

1. Name several jobs that did not exist during the early 1900s. Which of these are related to computers? How have computers both added and taken away jobs from the American economy?

2. Why is the word *revolution* used to describe the economic changes brought about by computers?

3. What negative aspects do critics of the computer revolution often point to? Do you agree with some of these criticisms? Explain.

4. How have you and your family been affected by the computer revolution so far? What further effects do you expect in the future?

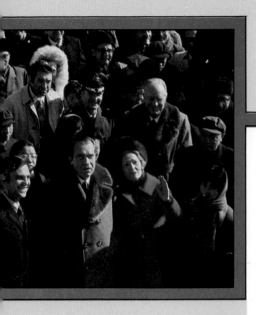

CHAPTER 39

The Nation Seeks New Directions

1968–1976

People in the Chapter

Richard Milhous Nixon—*U.S. president who ends the war in Vietnam but abuses his office to such an extent that he is forced to resign.*

Henry Kissinger—*secretary of state under Nixon who dramatically changes the foreign policy of the United States toward Communist China, Taiwan, and the Soviet Union.*

Spiro Agnew—*vice-president under Nixon who resigns rather than stand trial on charges of bribery and of filing a false tax return.*

Linking Past to Present

By the late 1960s the nation was weary of violence, demonstrations, and a war in Southeast Asia it apparently could neither win nor end. Events during the election year of 1968—the assassination of two political leaders, as well as one of the stormiest party conventions in U.S. history— deepened the national mood of fear and frustration. So Americans voted for a candidate who promised to unite the nation again.

Richard M. Nixon became president of the United States in January 1969. In 1972 he was reelected with a landslide majority. The Nixon administration turned American foreign policy around, reestablishing relations with Communist China and ending the nation's involvement in the Vietnam War. But with success and power came an increasing aloofness from the American people on Nixon's part. He also developed a tendency to behave as if the presidency were above the law. The results were tragic for the nation and for its leader. A constitutional crisis resulted in Nixon's becoming the first American president to resign his office. Although Nixon left office in 1974, his influence so dominated the brief administration of his successor, Gerald Ford, and the American consciousness, that the period up to the election of 1976 can be called the Nixon Years.

1 THE NATION ENDURES A TROUBLED YEAR

Some journalists have referred to 1968 as "the year everything went wrong." A number of violent events supported the characterization and led many to wonder what was happening to the American people and society.

Martin Luther King, Jr., Is Killed

On April 4 Martin Luther King, Jr. was in Memphis, Tennessee. He had been working on organizing a Poor People's March to Washington to emphasize the need for more jobs. But he had interrupted that work and come to Memphis to give what help and guidance he could to the city's garbage workers, mostly black, who had been on strike for two months. That evening, he was standing on the balcony outside his motel room talking to supporters below. There was the sharp crack of a gun, and King slumped to the floor. A single bullet had crashed through his neck, severing his spinal cord. He died instantly.

King had preached and practiced non-violence all his life. He had received the Nobel Peace Prize in 1964. It was ironic that his murder set off what one historian called "the worst outburst of arson, looting, and criminal activity in the nation's history." Fires and riots broke out in nearly 170 cities that night. Washington was hardest hit. The next day television screens showed clouds of smoke from burning buildings floating over the White House. Before the rioting was over, 2600 people had been arrested, another 22,000 injured, and 55,000 troops were needed to restore order.

Again, a saddened people, an estimated 120 million of them, watched a funeral on television. This one was held in a Baptist church in Atlanta. King's coffin rode to the cemetery on an old farmcart drawn by two mules. Behind the cart walked a crowd of 100,000 persons, including Vice President Hubert Humphrey and Democratic senators Robert Kennedy and Eugene McCarthy, as well as Republican Governor Nelson Rockefeller of New York. President Johnson ordered federal buildings to set their flags at half-mast in honor of King, and millions of whites turned their automobile headlights on all day as a sign of respect.

The killer was caught two months later. He had managed to reach London by way of Canada and Portugal, on two false names and a Canadian passport. But he had left his fingerprints all over the room from which the shot had been fired. They showed that he was James Earl Ray, a staunch racist and small-time thief who had escaped the previous year from a Missouri prison. Ray was never tried; he pleaded guilty and received a ninety-nine-year sentence. He escaped from prison in 1977 but was recaptured almost immediately. As yet, no one has discovered where he got the money to buy both the car in which he fled from Memphis and the plane ticket to Europe.

Robert Kennedy Is Killed

Since the end of March, when he declared his candidacy, Robert Kennedy had swept all the Democratic primaries except Oregon's, which he narrowly lost to McCarthy. On June 4 he all but assured his nomination with a resounding triumph in California.

Shortly after midnight, on the way from his Los Angeles hotel headquarters to a press conference, Kennedy walked through a crowded back passageway. He stopped for a moment to shake hands with a teen-aged busboy and to answer a question.

773

As he did so, eight shots rang out. Six men fell to the floor, five of them only slightly injured. The sixth, Kennedy, had a bullet in his brain. Despite almost immediate surgery, he died about twenty-five hours later.

The assassin, Sirhan Bishara Sirhan, was a young Jordanian Arab who was trying to make a political statement. June 4, 1968, was the first anniversary of the Six-Day War in which Israel had beaten its Arab neighbors, including Jordan. Kennedy had been a supporter of Israel.

Once again, the nation mourned a murdered leader. Funeral services were held in St. Patrick's Cathedral in New York City, and the body was then taken to Washington in a train pulled by two black engines. So many people lined the tracks along the way that the trip, which usually takes four hours, lasted more than eight hours. The senator's body was buried in Arlington National Cemetery near that of his brother, President John F. Kennedy.

Students Riot and Public Servants "Strike"

If Americans needed more evidence that the social fabric seemed to be unraveling, they had only to look at college campuses and at civil servants.

An Uprising at Columbia.   During the first six months of 1968, almost 40,000 students on more than a hundred campuses took part in 221 major demonstrations. The one that received the most publicity was the April uprising at Columbia University in New York City.

There had been considerable tension in the area for several years because the university, which owned a large number of Harlem tenements, was, in effect, a slumlord. The immediate spark was the university's publication of a plan for a new gymnasium to be built on nearby park land. The plan included a free gym and swimming pool on the ground floor which people living in the area could use. Unfortunately, the plan also included two entrances. The one that faced the university campus was large and imposing. The one that faced Harlem was small and plain.

Black leaders protested indignantly against the "separate but unequal facilities," and about one hundred and fifty students promptly marched to the campus shouting "Gym Crow must go." After tearing down a fence around the proposed site for the gymnasium, they seized the acting dean of Columbia College and two other officials and barricaded themselves in Hamilton Hall. The next day, some of them took over Low Library. By the end of the week, other students had seized three more halls. Supporters provided them with food and blankets.

On the sixth day, a thousand policemen arrived. At first some junior faculty members barred their way. Then the university's president ordered the police to clear the buildings by force. Students were clubbed, kicked, and thrown down concrete stairs. Several thousand spectators behind police barricades were likewise attacked by the police and beaten. In all, about 700 persons were arrested and 73 students were suspended for a year.

A commission that investigated the disorders stated that the students had behaved badly and damaged property. But the commission also charged the police with unnecessary brutality, and accused the university administration of paying little attention to student needs and grievances.

Some Public "Strikes."   There were other examples of disrespect for the law. The Taft-Hartley Act prohibited strikes by federal civil servants, and most states had similar laws. But in 1968 New York City's sanitation workers walked off the job after the mayor refused to grant them a pay raise. Within a few days, the stench of thousands of tons of garbage rotting in the streets was so bad that Governor Rockefeller agreed to give the workers the raise after all.

No sooner were the sanitation workers back on the job than policemen threw a picket line around City Hall and began calling in "sick" with imaginary illnesses. Next, the firemen stopped inspecting buildings and fire hydrants while their union bargained for more money. Then it was the turn of the city's teachers, who walked out three times during the fall of 1968.

A Chaotic Democratic Convention

The anger and frustration abroad in the land came to a climax during the Democratic convention in Chicago the last week of August 1968. Parts of the city were almost turned into an armed camp. The city had received reports that at least 100,000 students, hippies, and other antiwar activists would gather to protest the administration's Vietnam policies.

While some young people expressed their dissatisfaction with American politics, others broke away from mainstream society and formed communes such as this one in California.

Mayor Richard J. Daley ordered a seven-foot chain-link fence topped with barbed wire put up around the convention hall. Delegates, news reporters, and guests were searched on entering and at various times throughout the convention proceedings. The mayor also placed the city's 11,500 police on twelve-hour shifts and alerted 7500 National Guardsmen and 1000 FBI and Secret Service agents to stand by. The federal government had an additional 7500 troops ready to be airlifted in at a moment's notice.

Riots in the Streets. Actually, only 10,000 to 12,000 protesters showed up. Some of them had come for the purpose of creating violent confrontations. Mayor Daley refused to grant them permits to march peacefully or to hold a political rally. When several groups asked for permission to camp in the public parks, the mayor ordered an eleven o'clock curfew.

The results were predictable. For four nights in succession, police armed with clubs and tear gas drove curfew violators out of Lincoln Park and through the streets. More than twenty newspaper reporters observing the scene were slugged. Some of the protesters threw stones and bottles at the police but most just tried to walk away.

Wednesday, August 28, the protesters announced that they planned to march from Lincoln Park to the convention hall. They got as far as the intersection in front of the Conrad Hilton Hotel, where the three leading candidates for the Democratic nomination were headquartered. There, in full view of television cameras, they were beaten and gassed by the police for eighteen terrible minutes. No one was killed but hundreds were injured.

Fury in the Hall. Meanwhile, inside the convention hall a different kind of force was being displayed. Democrats opposed to the Vietnam War had captured 80 percent of the vote in the party primaries. But when their delegates entered the convention hall, they found pro-administration literature on every seat. When they tried to pass out antiwar literature of their own, they were prevented from doing so by the guards.

Presidential Election of 1968

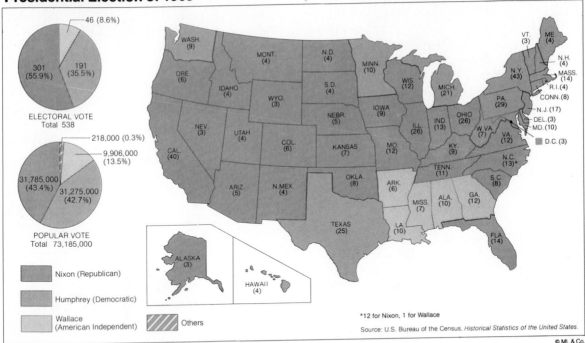

ELECTORAL VOTE
Total 538

- 46 (8.6%)
- 301 (55.9%)
- 191 (35.5%)

POPULAR VOTE
Total 73,185,000

- 218,000 (0.3%)
- 9,906,000 (13.5%)
- 31,785,000 (43.4%)
- 31,275,000 (42.7%)

Nixon (Republican)
Humphrey (Democratic)
Wallace (American Independent)
Others

*12 for Nixon, 1 for Wallace
Source: U.S. Bureau of the Census, *Historical Statistics of the United States.*
© ML & Co.

Map Skills *How many people voted for Nixon? for Humphrey? What percentage of the electoral vote did Nixon win? In what part of the country were the states won by Wallace?*

Tuesday evening, antiwar delegates sat in the galleries shouting "Stop the war!" The next night, the galleries were filled with city employees waving banners that read "We Love Daley." They had been allowed in despite their lack of proper credentials. At the same time, antiwar delegates were physically removed from the convention floor, supposedly because they refused to show their credentials to the guards. Some delegates accused Daley and his police of brutal and dictatorial behavior. The mayor answered back with obscenities.

All this confusion did not keep the delegates from nominating Vice President Hubert Humphrey on the first ballot, a decided victory for President Johnson. Among the four other nominees was the Reverend Channing E. Phillips of the District of Columbia, the first black to be nominated for the presidency at a national convention. But Humphrey's easy victory was apparently not enough for those in charge of the convention. Despite considerable opposition from the floor, they announced that the nomination was unanimous.

Humphrey chose as his running mate Senator Edmund S. Muskie of Maine. Then came a fight over the platform, which supported the administration's handling of the Vietnam War. After two days of sharp debate, it was approved by 1600 votes out of 2600.

A Close Election

With disappointed Eugene McCarthy followers refusing to help, the Democratic campaign began poorly. Crowds were small, hecklers were everywhere, and money was short. In addition, President Johnson did not try to hide the fact that he considered Humphrey weak, which did little to aid Humphrey's campaign.

The Republicans, on the other hand, had plenty of money and a smooth-running organization. Their presidential candidate, former vice-president Richard M. Nixon, promised to bring "peace with honor" in Vietnam, a vague promise that nevertheless had widespread appeal. The vice-presidential candidate, Governor Spiro T. Agnew of Maryland, emphasized the second major element in the Republican platform, namely, the need for measures that would bring about "law and order."

Minor Parties.　Two minor parties also entered the 1968 race. The Peace and Freedom party, organized by a combination of pacifists and black power supporters, nominated Black Panther leader Eldridge Cleaver for president. But the party was able to get on the ballot in only a few states. It fell apart because of internal arguments.

Far more significant was the American Independent party, which ran George C. Wallace, Alabama's former governor, and retired General Curtis LeMay. Wallace campaigned on a platform that combined the Democrats' support for the Vietnam War with the Republicans' support for law and order. Wallace appealed not only to southern whites but also to blue-collar workers in the North. Many of the latter belonged to "new immigrant" ethnic groups. Their parents had entered the United States and worked their way up without special help from the federal government. They did not see why they should pay taxes to help blacks. Nor did they see why they should support universities attended by young people who were demonstrating instead of studying.

Down to the Wire.　The campaign began with Nixon far ahead. Then, in late September, Humphrey moved away from the administration's position on Vietnam. He suggested that the United States stop bombing North Vietnam in order to encourage the Paris peace talks. On October 31, Johnson announced a halt in the bombing, and McCarthy announced he would vote for Humphrey. Liberals, city dwellers, and organized labor began returning to their traditional Democratic loyalties. In the meantime, Nixon began sounding overconfident. By election day, one opinion poll actually showed Humphrey ahead.

Even with modern electronic reporting, the outcome was in doubt until the day after the election. The lead changed hands several times during the night. In the end, Nixon received 31.8 million votes, or 43.4 percent, to Humphrey's 31.2 million, or 42.7 percent. Wallace got just under 10 million votes, or 13.5 percent. As always, the electoral vote showed a bigger spread: Nixon 301, Humphrey 191, and Wallace 46. Nixon thus entered the White House as a minority president.

Section 1 Review

COMPREHENSION　Developing Vocabulary

1. Explain these terms: Peace and Freedom party, American Independent party.

COMPREHENSION　Mastering Facts

1. What was the reaction to Martin Luther King's assassination?
2. What led to the student uprising at Columbia University?
3. What kind of force was displayed inside the Democratic convention hall in Chicago?
4. What were the two main elements in the Republican platform?

2　NIXON HEADS A LAW-AND-ORDER ADMINISTRATION

VOCABULARY　*right to counsel　revenue sharing*

Richard Nixon had spent most of his adult life working hard in politics. As vice-president under Eisenhower, he had been the first person in that office to make goodwill tours of foreign countries. Now, every vice-president makes them. Following his defeat by John F. Kennedy in 1960, he returned to California, where he ran for governor in 1962, but lost again. Declaring himself through with politics for good, he moved to New York City and soon after became a senior partner in a major law firm.

However, the former vice-president kept working for the Republican party. He proved an effective and tireless speaker at local fund raisers and rallies. And he loyally supported the Goldwater ticket in 1964 when many others deserted it. By 1968 he had paid enough political dues to claim the Republican nomination.

The Administration: Business-like and Conservative

Although Nixon had campaigned on a promise to "bring the nation together," his cabinet reflected primarily the business community. As one historian described its members, they were "all affluent, white, male, middle-class, and Republican."

The new administration had pledged to restore law and order. Nixon tried to do this in several ways. The Justice Department brought eight al-

President and Mrs. Nixon acknowledge applause after a 1968 speech he made in New York City.

sel. If he or she cannot afford an attorney, then the state should appoint one. The second decision was *Miranda* v. *Arizona* (1966), which stated that a person who is arrested must be told that she or he does not have to answer police questions and is entitled to have an attorney present. Critics of the Court felt these and similar decisions limited the powers of the police too much.

Nixon promised to appoint so-called "strict constructionists" to the Supreme Court. In 1969 Warren retired at the age of seventy-seven and Nixon chose Warren E. Burger of Minnesota to replace him. The Senate approved Burger. But then it balked at Nixon's next two nominees. Clement F. Haynesworth, Jr. of South Carolina was rejected because he had issued decisions favoring companies whose stock he owned. G. Harrold Carswell of Florida was rejected because of his racist views and because so many of his decisions were reversed on appeal for lack of knowledge about the law. Nixon reacted furiously, accusing the Senate of being antisouthern. His next nominee, approved unanimously, was Harry A. Blackmun of Minnesota. In 1971, however, Nixon nominated a respected and competent southerner, Lewis F. Powell of Virginia. Powell's nomination sailed through.

Revenue Sharing: No Strings Attached.   A major departure from previous practice was the revenue sharing program of 1972. Money had always gone from the federal government to state and local governments, but it had been earmarked for specific programs. Now the Nixon administration suggested that the federal government distribute more than $30 billion without any strings attached. This reflected the conservative view that Washington bureaucrats did not know what was best at the state and local levels.

A Push for Family Assistance.   Another interesting conservative idea was put forward by the Nixon administration in welfare reform. As of 1969, about 10 million Americans were receiving some form of welfare. Nixon believed this was one activity the federal government should take over from the states. He recommended a family assistance plan. It would set a minimum income that a family needed to stay above poverty level. Those families falling below the amount would receive direct supplemental payments from the federal government. Unemployed participants would have to take job training and accept any reasonable

leged leaders of the demonstrators at the Democratic convention to trial. Five of the eight were cleared of charges of actually inciting to riot but were convicted for crossing state lines with the intent to do so. (Three years later, the convictions were reversed by a higher court.) Laws against organized crime and drug abuse were tightened, and in 1970 Congress passed the Omnibus Crime Control Act, which increased the power of federal law-enforcement agencies.

Nixon believed that a major reason for the violence of the sixties was the federal government's attempts to enforce school desegregation. In particular, he questioned busing school children away from neighborhood schools in order to achieve racial balance. Accordingly, federal enforcement of civil rights legislation practically stopped. However, in 1971 the Supreme Court upheld the use of busing.

Seeking a More Conservative Court.   One controversial aspect of the sixties had been the record of the Warren Court (the Supreme Court while Earl Warren was chief justice). Many conservatives felt the Court had been too "permissive" with regard to the rights of accused persons.

The conservatives objected to two decisions in particular. One was *Gideon* v. *Wainwright* (1963), which said that a defendant has the right to coun-

Presidential Election of 1972

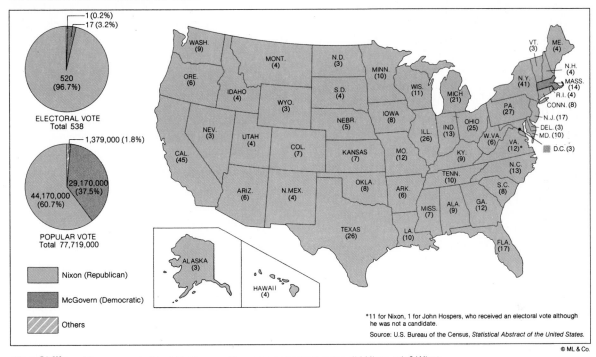

Map Skills *Nixon overwhelmed McGovern. How many electoral votes did Nixon win? What was his percentage of the popular vote? Where did McGovern win his 17 electoral votes?*

work offered to them. The proposal was passed by the House of Representatives but turned down in the Senate. Defeat came from both the right and the left. Some conservatives found the money too generous. Some liberals found the job and training requirements too difficult.

A Pledge Fulfilled

In 1961 President Kennedy had pledged to put a man on the moon and bring him back safely "before this decade is out." The pledge was fulfilled in 1969.

On July 20, as an estimated 600 million viewers all over the world watched on television, astronaut Neil A. Armstrong stepped cautiously out of the lunar module *Eagle* and stood on the moon's surface. As he did so, he radioed earthward: "I'm going to step off the LM now. That's one small step for a man, one giant leap for mankind." Twenty minutes later, Armstrong was followed by astronaut Edwin E. "Buzz" Aldrin, Jr. The two men set up scientific experiments and collected samples of rock and soil from the lunar surface. A third astronaut, Michael Collins, orbited above them in the command vessel *Columbia*. Less than an hour

later, President Nixon spoke from the White House to the men on the moon. "For every American, this has to be the proudest day of our lives."

The space program had cost more than $23 billion. Three astronauts had lost their lives in an accident at Cape Kennedy in 1967. Still, the moon landing was a triumph of science and courage, and a source of great national pride.

A Second Nixon Victory

At the Republican national convention in Miami Beach in August 1972, Nixon and Agnew won easy renomination. The Democrats had already met in the same city the month before. As a result of reforms adopted after the 1968 convention, their delegates included a large number of women, young people under thirty, and racial minorities. This was a decided change from the usual convention mixture of elected officials and party regulars. A striking example of the difference was a challenge to the Illinois delegation. The convention voted to replace Chicago Mayor Richard J. Daley and 58 other Chicago delegates on the ground that they had been chosen by procedures that did not meet the reform guidelines. Instead, the convention seated delegates led by Alderman William Singer and black activist Jesse Jackson.

The Democratic candidate was Senator George McGovern of South Dakota. He ran on a liberal domestic platform and a pledge for the "immediate and complete withdrawal of all U.S. forces" from Vietnam, where the war was still going on. McGovern took a worse beating than Goldwater had in 1964. The popular vote was 47 million to 29 million, the electoral vote 521 to 17. The Democratic ticket carried only Massachusetts and the District of Columbia (able to choose electors since 1961 under the Twenty-third Amendment).

One reason for McGovern's defeat was the public desire for conservative leadership at home. Another was widespread approval of many of Nixon's accomplishments in foreign affairs, about which you will read later in the chapter. A third reason was the shooting of George C. Wallace by a would-be assassin in the spring. Although Wallace survived the bullet, he was paralyzed from the waist down and did not take part in the presidential campaign. Most of his votes went to Nixon. Then, too, the president ran an extremely effective—and expensive—campaign.

Section 2 Review

COMPREHENSION   Developing Vocabulary

1. Explain these terms: right to counsel, revenue sharing, busing.

COMPREHENSION   Mastering Facts

1. What objections did many conservatives raise against decisions of the Warren Court regarding the rights of accused persons?
2. How did the revenue sharing program of 1972 differ from previous ones?
3. What caused the Senate to defeat Nixon's family assistance plan?
4. Give four reasons why Nixon was reelected in 1972.

3 THE UNITED STATES CHARTS A NEW FOREIGN POLICY

VOCABULARY   *détente   Vietnamization*

Soon after entering the White House, Nixon chose Henry Kissinger as his assistant for national security. After the 1972 election, Kissinger donned a second hat and became Nixon's secretary of state as well. Working closely together, the two men began to turn U.S. foreign policy around.

Kissinger, who was born in Germany, had come to the United States in 1938 when his family fled Hitler's persecutions. After serving with the army in World War II, he attended Harvard. He taught there during the fifties and became an authority on international relations and nuclear defense. Later he served as a consultant to the federal government and to private foundations.

A More Flexible Approach

In 1954 Kissinger published a book attacking the concept of massive retaliation against Communist countries advanced by Eisenhower's secretary of state, John Foster Dulles. Kissinger believed the main consideration should be power rather than ideology. If a nation were weak, it might be wiser for the United States to ignore a provocation, even if that nation were Communist. The weak nation could not do much damage. On the other hand, if a nation were strong and able to hurt the United States, then America must act to counter that nation.

Kissinger's approach was also a departure from the policy of containment, which aimed at keeping all Communist nations at arm's length. The new approach opened a number of possibilities. For example, mainland China need no longer be treated as though it did not exist just because it was Communist. After all, it contained at least one-fifth of the world's population. Furthermore, it was at odds with the Soviet Union. Among other matters, the two nations disagreed about their common border. It might be to America's advantage to balance one major Communist country against the other.

Recognizing Communist China. Since the takeover of mainland China by the Communists, the United States had not recognized that government. But, just as Roosevelt had finally recognized the Communist government of the Soviet Union in 1933, Nixon now decided the same recognition should be given to Communist China. Accordingly, in August 1971 President Nixon announced that he would visit mainland China within a year.

He did so in February 1972. After eight days of meetings, the two nations announced that neither would try to dominate the Pacific and that both would cooperate in settling disputes peacefully. They also agreed to open up trade and to improve scientific and cultural relations. The United States recognized that Taiwan was part of China and promised to eventually withdraw American forces from the island.

Nixon's statements regarding Taiwan were in line with a resolution the United States had introduced in the United Nations the previous October. The resolution recommended that mainland China be given Taiwan's permanent seat on the UN Security Council, but that Taiwan be allowed to continue as a member of the General Assembly. However, the UN vote went further than the United States wanted. It not only seated the People's Republic of China on the Security Council; it expelled Taiwan from the UN altogether.

In view of Nixon's strong record of anticommunism, the recognition of Red China came as a stunning surprise to the American people. Yet it was welcomed by most. Despite America's historic ties with the Nationalist Chinese on Taiwan, it seemed clear that the chances for peace in Asia were now much stronger. The visit to China helped Nixon win the election that year.

Détente with the Soviet Union. Nixon and Kissinger also adopted a more flexible approach to the Soviet Union. They tried to tone down the Cold War and its confrontations and to encourage *détente*, or the easing of tensions.

In 1971 the United States worked out an agreement with the Soviet Union about Berlin. The Soviets promised to guarantee access by the U.S., Britain, and France to West Berlin and to respect the city's independence. In return, the Western allies agreed to recognize East Germany. This agreement removed a major sore point in East-West relations.

In May 1972, three months after the summit meeting in Peking, Nixon took part in a summit meeting in Moscow. He and Soviet Premier Leonid Brezhnev agreed to increase trade and to cooperate on space exploration. They also signed two agreements on arms control based on the Strategic Arms Limitation Talks (SALT) that had been held earlier. The agreements limited the number of offensive missiles and defensive missile sites that each nation would build.

The Nixons atop the Great Wall of China. This 1972 visit signaled a dramatic change in U.S. foreign policy.

In June 1974 Nixon and Brezhnev held another summit meeting in Moscow. Again, agreements were reached on improved trade relations and greater cooperation in scientific matters. The U.S. and the Soviet Union also agreed not to test nuclear weapons underground. However, despite a strong warning from Kissinger about the dangers of nuclear warfare, the two nations failed to agree on a cutback in offensive missiles.

The Vietnam War Ends

In June 1969 President Nixon announced a program of "Vietnamization" of the war. This meant gradually withdrawing American ground troops and letting the South Vietnamese do their own fighting. By the end of August the first 25,000 U.S. troops had come home. At the same time Nixon stepped up air activity against North Vietnam. In addition, he secretly ordered U.S. planes to bomb Cambodia and Laos. Vietcong forces were using these two nations as sanctuaries. They would slip across the borders into South Vietnam and then return after attacking South Vietnamese strongholds.

Increased Antiwar Protests. Vietnamization was only partly successful. Although American soldiers began returning home in increasing numbers, the corrupt and inefficient regime of General Nguyen Van Thieu could not recruit enough South Vietnamese soldiers to take their place. In the meantime, public protests in the United States against the war grew. On May 15, 1969 hundreds of thousands of Americans wearing black armbands turned out to march throughout the nation. Another nationwide demonstration took place on October 15. On November 15 some 40,000 people took part in a March Against Death in Washington, D.C. They walked from Arlington National Cemetery four miles to the Capitol, and each person carried a card with the name of an American soldier who had died in Vietnam.

President Nixon did not see the march. He was in the White House watching a football game on television. He felt that an unconditional withdrawal from Vietnam would be humiliating and that the only way to secure "peace with honor" was through Vietnamization. A Gallup poll showed that three out of four Americans agreed with the president's view.

The Living Room War. Gradually, however, public opinion began to change. Television brought scenes of death and destruction directly into people's living rooms. Newspapers and magazines carried reports of such incidents as the American massacre of Vietnamese civilians in the village of My Lai (me *lie*). In the spring of 1970 Nixon announced that American troops had invaded Cambodia in order to clear out North Vietnam and Vietcong supply centers. Although the troops were withdrawn by June, the news led to the most massive antiwar demonstrations yet. Congress passed a resolution demanding that air activity over Cambodia stop by July.

The first general student strike in the nation's history broke out, and more than 400 campuses closed down. On the weekend of May 9–10, some 100,000 students protested before the White House. At first Nixon called them "bums." Later he tried to talk with them in a quiet and friendly manner. But instead of discussing the war, he spoke about football and surfing. As a newspaper reporter wrote, "The two Americas met and drifted apart in a state of mutual incomprehension." Neither could understand the other's point of view.

A Cease-Fire Agreement. Nevertheless, peace talks continued in Paris. On October 8, 1972, after much patient negotiation, Kissinger announced that a cease-fire with North Vietnam was about to be signed. "Peace is at hand." On October 23, he said the signing was being postponed. There were points to be "clarified." The South Vietnamese government, for one thing, would not accept the terms.

When clarification had not been achieved by December, Nixon ordered full-scale air attacks on North Vietnam. Unfortunately, most of the military barracks, warehouses, and factories that were the chief targets were located in heavily populated cities. Homes, schools, and hospitals were unintentionally hit, and civilian casualties were high.

At this point, even members of Congress who had previously supported Nixon's Vietnam policy urged an end. At the same time, Moscow and Peking told Hanoi it was time to get on with the peace. On January 27, 1973, the United States and North Vietnam finally signed a cease-fire agreement. The United States would withdraw its troops but would continue sending economic and military aid to South Vietnam. North Vietnam would release American prisoners of war.

Summing Up. The Vietnam War was the longest war in U.S. history. The direct cost to the nation was 58,000 battle deaths; 365,000 wounded; and a price tag of about $150 billion. A more intangible cost was divisiveness at home and a general feeling of unease. There seemed to be lessened respect for the federal government, which had concealed many of its activities from the public. There also seemed to be considerable confusion about the nation's role in world affairs. Americans agreed they did not want any more Vietnams, but they did not agree on what that meant. Should the United States turn isolationist again? Should it limit its interests to the Western Hemisphere? Should it try to contain communism, even if that meant supporting antidemocratic governments?

One specific result of the war was the setting of limits on the war-making powers of the president. In November 1973 Congress passed the War Powers Act. It said that a president who sent U.S. troops to a foreign country had to explain the action to Congress within 48 hours. Furthermore, Congress could order the troops withdrawn after 60 days. Nixon vetoed the measure, but it was repassed over his veto.

Section 3 Review

COMPREHENSION   Developing Vocabulary

1. Explain these terms: détente, Vietnamization.

COMPREHENSION   Mastering Facts

1. How did Nixon change U.S. policy toward Red China?
2. What effect did television have on people's opinions about the Vietnam War?
3. What were the terms of the cease-fire agreement between the United States and North Vietnam?
4. What did the War Powers Act of 1973 say?

4   THE NIXON ADMINISTRATION COLLAPSES

VOCABULARY   *executive privilege   plea bargain*

Historians will probably argue for years to come over the reasons for the events known collectively as Watergate. Some of the explanations advanced have little to do with Watergate but rather with Richard Nixon's personality. Others have to do with the changing role of the presidency.

The Imperial Presidency

Nixon always had to fight hard for what he achieved in life. Apparently this led him to regard the world as a permanent arena in which winning was the only thing that mattered. He seemed to view people who disagreed with him as more than opponents. They were enemies, threats to his authority, who had to be destroyed.

At the same time, the balance of power between the legislative, executive, and judicial branches of the federal government had shifted. It had done so in the past. Thomas Jefferson complained of the influence of Federalist judges. Andrew Johnson, many historians feel, successfully fought off Congress's efforts to wield too much power after the Civil War. By the time Nixon became president, the executive branch—as a result of the Great Depression, World War II, and the Cold War—had become, in many people's eyes, almost "imperial."

Nixon's Lifestyle.   Nixon lived, if not like an emperor, at least like a prince. He bought a $250,000 home in Key Biscayne, Florida, and another in San Clemente, California, which he dubbed the Western White House. The federal gov-

ernment spent $10.5 million on the two presidential estates, some of it for military and security equipment but a considerable amount for furniture and landscaping. Nixon installed a swimming pool, bowling alleys, and an archery range at Camp David, the presidential retreat near Washington. Sixteen planes and sixteen helicopters were kept at his disposal at all times. And his staff of butlers, maids, cooks, and chauffeurs—all paid for by the government—numbered well over one hundred.

Nixon's Manner.   Nixon believed, as he told a newspaper reporter in the fall of 1980, that "A President must not be one of the crowd. He must maintain a certain figure. People want him to be that way. They don't want him to be down there saying, 'Look, I'm the same as you.'" He reported that he always wore a coat and tie and that even his closest friends addressed him, never as Richard, but as Mr. Nixon or Mr. President. Many people found Nixon's manner cool and aloof. He relied on a sort of "palace guard" to supervise the executive branch and to protect him from the public.

Those he apparently listened to most were John Mitchell, formerly a law partner and now attorney general; Henry Kissinger; John Ehrlichman, his advisor on domestic affairs; and H. (for Harry) R. Haldeman, who served as his chief of staff. These people protected him from unwanted visitors. Government officials, congressmen, and members of Nixon's own cabinet found that to see the president they had to be cleared by Haldeman or Ehrlichman. Nixon allowed a protective wall to be built up around him. Press conferences were few, and important information was often withheld from the American people. For example, Nixon did not tell about the bombing of Cambodia for more than a year after it started.

Some people feared that the president was increasing his personal rule over government. For example, the president turned over many cabinet duties to his personal staff. Cabinet members have to be approved by the Senate. The president's staff were not subject to approval by the Senate and would do as he wished. Again, when the Senate refused to confirm Nixon's nomination of Carswell to the Supreme Court, the president accused the Senate of trying to take over executive rights. "What is centrally at issue in this nomination," he said, "is the constitutional responsibility of the President to appoint members of the Court." But it is likewise the constitutional responsibility of the Senate to approve or disapprove Supreme Court appointments.

Relations between the president and Congress were strained in other ways. On several occasions, Nixon vetoed bills calling for pollution controls and expanding social and medical services. When Congress overrode the vetoes, Nixon did not carry out the laws. Instead, somewhat like an absolute monarch, he impounded the funds. That is, he had them seized and held. He refused to spend the money that Congress appropriated.

The Pentagon Papers

The initial event that many historians believe led to Watergate took place on June 13, 1971. The *New York Times* began publishing a series of articles called "The Pentagon Papers." The articles, which were based on a study of how the United States got involved in Vietnam, were embarrassing. They showed that U.S. military intelligence was often inaccurate; that U.S. diplomats often sent back what they thought their superiors wanted to hear rather than what was actually going on; that President Johnson had ordered the Tonkin Gulf resolution drafted months before the Tonkin Gulf incident took place; and that the government had repeatedly withheld information from the American people.

The *New York Times* had obtained the Pentagon Papers from Daniel Ellsberg, a former employee of the Defense Department. But they were classified documents that were not supposed to be generally seen. So, although none of the informa-

tion was military, Attorney General Mitchell asked the courts to stop further publication of the Pentagon Papers on the grounds of national security. On June 30, 1971, the Supreme Court ruled against the Justice Department. Freedom of the press, the Court held, did not allow the government to censor historical information before it was published.

Later that year, the Justice Department indicted Ellsberg for theft, conspiracy, and espionage. But in 1973 the case was thrown out of court. The reason was the action taken by a group of special White House investigators known as the "Plumbers Unit." They had burglarized the office of Ellsberg's psychiatrist in a vain attempt to find damaging personal evidence against Ellsberg. Unfortunately for the Nixon administration, that was not the only burglary the Plumbers undertook.

The Watergate Break-in

Nixon had authorized creation of the Plumbers in 1971 after publication of the Pentagon Papers. Although the Papers stopped with 1968 and had nothing to do with him, he believed it was essential for a government to keep secrets, whether military or political. But the Plumbers were not used just to prevent government secrets from leaking to the media. They were also used to help ensure Nixon's reelection in 1972.

"A Third-Rate Burglary." On Saturday evening, June 17, 1972, five men were caught breaking into the headquarters of the Democratic National Committee. The headquarters were in a large apartment-office complex called Watergate, in Washington, D.C. The men had intended to photograph documents and to place wiretaps, or "bugs," on the telephones in the office.

The group's leader, James McCord, was a former CIA agent. He was also an official of the Committee to Re-Elect the President (CREEP), which was handling Nixon's campaign under the direction of John Mitchell, who had resigned as attorney general. Papers found in the pocket of one of the other burglars led to another ex-CIA agent, E. Howard Hunt, and to G. Gordon Liddy, also an employee of CREEP.

The Cover-up Begins. At that point, the White House might have disowned the entire operation and demanded the resignation of everyone involved. However, that would have meant getting rid of such people as Mitchell, Haldeman, and Ehrlichman, on whom Nixon depended so strongly in carrying the burdens of office. Instead, one step after another was taken to cover up the connection between the burglars and the White House.

Documents in CREEP's office were shredded. Other incriminating evidence was given for safekeeping to L. Patrick Gray, who had been acting director of the FBI since the death of J. Edgar Hoover. The president asked the CIA to urge the FBI to stop its investigation of the burglary on the grounds that national security was involved.

After the seven Watergate defendants were indicted in September, it was agreed to pay them "hush money" for their silence. Funds were no problem. CREEP was awash with millions of dollars that had been collected in great haste, sometimes from illegal sources, to beat an April 20th deadline. On that date, a new and much stricter campaign law went into effect limiting the size of contributions that individuals and firms could make. In all, about $500,000 was passed on to the defendants.

Through 1972 little was said about Watergate. A poll in early fall showed most voters had not heard of it. In October the *Washington Post* accused the White House and CREEP of wholesale "political spying and sabotage," but the charge was generally ignored. However, two *Post* reporters, Bob Woodward and Carl Bernstein, were assigned to keep digging for additional information. In November, Nixon was overwhelmingly reelected. In January 1973, the trial of the Watergate Seven was held. All the defendants pleaded guilty or were convicted, and it seemed as if that was that.

The Uncovering Begins

A number of people, however, believed there was more to Watergate than met the eye. One such person was Federal Judge John J. Sirica, who had presided over the burglary case. Accordingly, he imposed maximum sentences on the seven defendants and said he would review the sentences after three months. On March 23, 1973, he received a letter from burglar James McCord. In his letter, McCord admitted having lied under oath. There were indeed people other than the Watergate Seven involved in the break-in. Within days, McCord named John Dean, counsel to the president, and John Mitchell as two of the "others."

The next several months saw wholesale resignations and firings of White House aides, including Dean, Ehrlichman, and Haldeman. On April 30, President Nixon appeared on nationwide television. He told the American people that he had first learned about the attempt to cover up the scandal on March 21. He announced that he was appointing a new attorney general, Elliot Richardson, and authorizing him to appoint a Special Prosecutor to investigate Watergate. Richardson chose Archibald Cox, a professor of law at Harvard.

In the meantime, the Senate voted to set up a committee under Senator Sam Ervin of North Carolina to make its own investigation of Watergate. The committee began its hearings in May despite a major difference of opinion about its powers. Committee members wanted to question various presidential aides. The White House claimed the right of "executive privilege." As interpreted by Nixon, it meant that Congress could not question a single one of the 2.5 million employees of the executive branch, or any past employees either, about anything whatsoever without the president's approval. Many senators felt this violated the idea of checks and balances. How could Congress pass laws if it could not get information about official government acts? Furthermore, there was nothing in the Constitution about executive privilege. Some senators felt Nixon's position was a step down the road toward a secret government that would not be accountable to the people.

Senators Howard Baker of Tennessee (left) and Sam Ervin Jr. of North Carolina at the Watergate hearings.

The Senate hearings lasted three months. Millions of Americans watched them on television. In June they heard John Dean accuse the president of taking part in the cover-up. But it was one person's word against another's. Then in July they learned that most of Nixon's personal and telephone conversations in the White House and in the Executive Office Building had been secretly tape-recorded. Both the Ervin Committee and Prosecutor Cox immediately asked to hear those tapes that reportedly dealt with Watergate. Nixon refused. The committee and Cox issued subpoenas, Nixon rejected the subpoenas, and the issue went to court.

The Vice-President Resigns

During these months, Watergate drew so much public interest that a second political scandal got far less attention than it otherwise might have. In the midst of hearings, investigations, and almost daily revelations about spying on citizens and the harassment of media personnel by the president's men, Vice President Agnew resigned.

It seems that since 1967 Agnew, the administration's chief "law-and-order" spokesman, had accepted tens of thousands of dollars in bribes from Maryland engineering firms. Not only had he received payments while governor of Maryland, his accusers said. He had received them after being elected to the second highest office in the land.

In August 1973 the *Wall Street Journal* broke the story that the vice-president was under investigation for bribery, extortion, and tax evasion. At first Agnew called the reports "damned lies." But by October he had apparently decided that the best thing to do was to "plea bargain," that is, to plead guilty to a minor charge in exchange for a light sentence and protection against further prosecution.

Accordingly, on October 10, 1973, Agnew resigned as vice-president and pleaded no contest to one charge of tax evasion. The judge pointed out that the plea was the "full equivalent of a plea of guilty." Then he imposed a fine of $10,000 and placed Agnew on probation for three years without supervision. At the same time the Justice Department issued a detailed account of the illegal acts Agnew had been charged with.

Many people felt Agnew's sentence was much too lenient. But Attorney General Richardson defended it. An indictment and trial, he said, would leave "serious and permanent scars" on the nation. It was an argument that would be heard again some eleven months later.

On October 12, acting under the Twenty-fifth Amendment, Nixon nominated a new vice-president. He was the Republican House minority leader, Representative Gerald R. Ford of Michigan. Ford was confirmed by a majority of both Houses of Congress on December 6.

Impeachment Looms

Ten days after Agnew's resignation, another bombshell exploded. It became known as the Saturday Night Massacre. Nixon fired Cox and abolished the office of Special Prosecutor. Both Attorney General Richardson and Deputy Attorney General William Ruckelshaus resigned. They felt that Nixon was going back on his promise for a thorough investigation of Watergate. The American people agreed. Newspapers everywhere called for the president's resignation, and so many letters and telegrams of protest poured into the White House that Nixon made a complete about-face. He agreed to give Judge Sirica the subpoenaed tapes. And he appointed a new Special Prosecutor, Leon Jaworski.

By now, however, the House Judiciary Committee had decided to hold hearings to see if there were adequate grounds for impeaching the president. While the hearings were going on, more damaging incidents occurred. Some of the tapes could not be found. One tape contained an 18½-minute gap; apparently that portion of the tape had been erased.

"Operation Candor." Things went from bad to worse. News reports revealed that Nixon had taken questionable tax deductions. For example, he paid about $1000 tax on a $200,000 income in 1971 and 1972. One after another, medium-level figures in the Watergate affair pleaded guilty to lesser indictments in exchange for information on people higher up. In November the president set out on "Operation Candor," a barnstorming tour designed to gain popular support. At the tour's first stop, Disney World in Florida, Nixon said, "People have the right to know whether or not their President is a crook. Well, I am not a crook." Supporters cheered, but many Americans were heartsick and ashamed that their leader found it necessary to make such a statement.

In March 1974, Mitchell, Haldeman, Ehrlichman, and four other presidential aides were indicted on charges of conspiracy, obstruction of justice, and perjury. (All were eventually convicted.) Although no one knew it at the time, the grand jury had named Nixon as a co-conspirator. They had not indicted him because they had been told by Jaworski that such an action was probably not constitutional.

The Edited Tapes. On April 30, 1974, President Nixon made another nationwide speech over television. He announced that instead of additional tapes, he was releasing 1254 pages of edited transcripts of White House conversations about Watergate. The president hoped this would convince everyone of his truthfulness and leadership.

If anything, the transcripts only increased people's dismay. It was not that the language was extremely vulgar. It was the president's attitude. Senator Hugh Scott of Pennsylvania, the Republican minority leader, characterized it as "shabby." Alfred M. Landon, the 1936 Republican presidential candidate, observed that Nixon was concerned only about public relations—what Watergate looked like, rather than cleaning it up. Emmet John Hughes, administrative assistant to President Eisenhower, was shocked that Nixon never once considered what might be good for the country or what a president's responsibilities were.

The President Resigns

After that, events proceeded swiftly. In May, Judge Sirica ordered the president to turn over 64 disputed tapes to Jaworski. Nixon refused. On July 24 the Supreme Court ruled unanimously that the president must turn over the tapes. The Court rejected Nixon's argument that doing so would violate national security. Evidence needed for a criminal trial could not be withheld, even by a president.

At the end of July the House Judiciary Committee adopted three articles of impeachment. They charged the president with obstructing justice, abusing his power, and failing to obey lawful subpoenas issued by the House of Representatives. He was accused of the following constitutional offenses: (1) using the Internal Revenue Service to harass political opponents and interfere with the electoral process; (2) using the FBI, the Secret Service, and private agents to spy on citizens and invade their rights; (3) interfering with the proper working of the Justice Department and the CIA; and (4) failing to "take care" that his aides obeyed the law. Finally, the committee said:

" In all of this Richard M. Nixon has acted in a manner contrary to his trust as President and subversive of constitutional government, to the great prejudice of the cause of law and justice and to the manifest injury of the people of the United States. Wherefore, Richard M. Nixon, by such conduct, warrants (deserves) impeachment and trial, and removal from office. "

On August 5 Nixon made public three more tapes. They revealed what most people had come to realize: the president had been involved in the Watergate cover-up almost from the first day. He had lied to the American people, the House of Representatives, and even his own lawyers. On August 7, three Republican leaders, Senator Barry Goldwater, Senator Hugh Scott, and House minority leader John Rhodes of Ohio, advised the president that he would probably be impeached and convicted.

On August 9, 1974, Nixon resigned his office and left Washington with his family. He did not admit any guilt. He merely said that some of his judgments "were wrong" and that he had lost his "political base in the Congress."

That same day Gerald R. Ford was sworn in as thirty-eighth president of the United States. He declared, "I believe that truth is the glue that holds governments together. . . . That bond, though strained, is unbroken. . . . My fellow Americans, our long national nightmare is over. Our Constitution works. Our great republic is a government of laws and not of men."

Section 4 Review

COMPREHENSION   Developing Vocabulary

1. Explain these terms: executive privilege, plea bargain, impounded, wiretaps.

COMPREHENSION   Mastering Facts

1. What did the Pentagon Papers contain?
2. What effects did James McCord's letter to Judge Sirica have on the Watergate affair?
3. Why did Vice President Spiro Agnew resign from office?
4. What constitutional offenses did the House Judiciary Committee accuse Nixon of committing?

VOCABULARY   *OPEC*   *cartel*

Gerald Ford had been a member of the House of Representatives since 1949. He was a hardworking, straightforward, good-natured, and unpretentious person. His first month in the White House created a welcome feeling of openness and goodwill. But then Ford did something that almost destroyed that feeling.

Pardon for a President

On September 8, 1974, without any warning, Ford issued a blanket pardon to Nixon for all crimes he "had committed or may have committed" as president. In accepting the pardon, Nixon did not admit any guilt. He simply said that he could understand how his "mistakes and misjudgments" might have led some people to think that his behavior during the Watergate investigation had been "self-serving and illegal."

Many people agreed with the pardon. They felt Nixon had been punished enough by being forced to resign in disgrace. Other people were stunned by the action. It seemed that there were two standards of justice. A former president was living in luxury at taxpayers' expense: $150,000 a year for pension and expenses in addition to a travel allowance of $40,000, a miscellaneous allowance of $209,000, and a transition allowance of $450,000. In the meantime, almost forty underlings who had carried out his orders either sat in prison or were awaiting trial. As one commentator said, "Mercy without justice is favoritism."

President Ford explained his reason for the pardon. Without it, there would have been a long public trial of a former president. Did the nation really want to put itself through such an ordeal? A growing number of Americans began to feel that, all things considered, perhaps Ford had done the right thing.

Economic and Diplomatic Problems

Economically, Ford found both inflation and unemployment on the increase. He proceeded cautiously, cutting taxes a bit, holding down spending for social problems, and vetoing bills he considered inflationary. With regard to one item, however, he was unable to influence the price.

The new president, Gerald Ford, and his family. Attractive and unpretentious, they helped the American public get over the tragedy of the Nixon Administration's last days.

Oil Prices Rise. In October 1973, a new conflict broke out between Israel and its Arab neighbors. Because the United States and other Western nations were giving aid to Israel, certain Arab states placed an embargo on oil shipments to the West. Long lines developed at many U.S. gas stations, and there was a shortage of home heating oil. For the first time many Americans were shocked to realize that they were dependent on foreign nations for more than a third of their yearly supply of oil, much of it from Arab countries.

Shortly after the embargo, the Organization of Petroleum Exporting Countries (OPEC)—which includes thirteen nations in the Middle East, Africa, and South America, as well as Indonesia—began to fix prices. This is what a *cartel*, or an organization that controls enough of a commodity to set the world price, always does. The OPEC countries hiked the price of crude oil, which in turn drove the price of gasoline and heating oil in the United States upward.

As oil prices rose so did the public's temper. Some stations ran out of gas. Others sold it only in small amounts.

The Vietnam Takeover. In spite of the withdrawal of American troops, fighting continued in Vietnam, with both sides violating the cease-fire agreement. During 1973 South Vietnam, with $3.8 billion worth of aid from the U.S., increased the area it controlled. But in March 1975 the tables began to turn. Within six weeks, a major offensive from North Vietnam swept through South Vietnam. The South Vietnamese army collapsed. On April 30 the North Vietnamese army entered Saigon.

Meanwhile the United States officials in Saigon were evacuating as rapidly as possible some 1000 Americans and 5000 Vietnamese. Up until the last moment helicopters took off from the roof of the United States Embassy in Saigon carrying people to U.S. ships waiting offshore. The U.S. Ambassador was one of the last to leave the embassy roof and shortly afterwards the North Vietnamese troops entered the embassy. Within a few days the entire country was under the control of the Communist government in Hanoi. The reunification of the country was declared official in July, twenty-one years after the 1954 Geneva Agreement that followed the French defeat at Dien Bien Phu.

The Mayaguez Episode. At about the same time, a Communist government took over Cambodia. Shortly after coming to power, the new government seized the American freighter *Mayaguez* and a crew of thirty-nine in the Gulf of Siam. The United States called it an act of piracy. The Cambodians claimed the ship was in their territorial waters. The United States sent a force of marines on a rescue mission. Fifteen were killed, and about twice that number were wounded. But Cambodia surrendered the ship and crew.

The Bicentennial

The nation approached its two hundredth birthday in a relatively quiet mood. The boundless faith in its own future that had marked the 1876 celebration was missing. The nation had gone through some trying times, and trust in the government had decreased considerably. Yet people generally had a good time.

Those nations that still had great sailing vessels (mostly for training purposes) sent them to the United States. The parade of "tall ships" in New York and other east coast harbors was a beautiful and impressive sight. Queen Elizabeth II of England came to help celebrate the independence that had been declared against her great-great-great-grandfather, King George III. Millions of citizens put aside their cares for a time to relax, watch fireworks, and enjoy themselves.

With near perfect timing, on July 20 and September 3, 1976, *Viking I* and *II* touched down on

The nation celebrated its 200th birthday with many events. One of the most beautiful was the fleet of great sailing vessels sent by many foreign nations to express their best wishes.

the surface of Mars. These unmanned spacecraft were soon sending back excellent pictures of the red planet's rocky soil and pale blue sky. It was a fitting climax to a hundred years of technological advance since the Centennial Exposition of 1876.

Section 5 Review

COMPREHENSION   Developing Vocabulary

1. Explain these terms: OPEC, cartel, favoritism.

COMPREHENSION   Mastering Facts

1. Why did many people object to Ford's pardon of Nixon?
2. What reason did Ford give for his action?
3. What did OPEC do that affected inflation in the United States?
4. What was the eventual outcome of the Vietnam War?

CHAPTER 39   Review

Chapter Summary

Violence at the 1968 Democratic National Convention and the assassinations of Dr. Martin Luther King, Jr., and Robert Kennedy preceded the election to the presidency of Richard Nixon. A new foreign policy—including improved relations with China—served as the highlight of the Nixon administration. But soon after his landslide reelection in 1972, the Watergate scandal was exposed to a stunned American public. In 1974 Nixon became the first president to resign. Gerald Ford then tried to reunite the nation, but he achieved only limited success.

Questions for Critical Thinking

COMPREHENSION   Summarizing Main Ideas

1. In what ways did the Democratic convention of 1972 differ from that of 1968? Do you think the changes were an improvement? Defend your opinion.
2. What were the arguments in favor of U.S. recognition of Red China? What were the arguments against it?
3. In what ways did President Nixon increase the powers of the executive branch?
4. For what two purposes was the "Plumbers Unit" used? Do you believe that a president should maintain private spies? Why?
5. Explain what role each of the following played in uncovering the Watergate scandal: (a) Judge John J. Sirica; (b) the *Washington Post*; (c) the Ervin Committee; (d) the Supreme Court.

COMPREHENSION   Interpreting Events

1. What do you think might have happened in the 1968 election if Martin Luther King, Jr., had not been assassinated? What do you think might have happened if Senator Robert F. Kennedy had not been assassinated? Explain your answers.
2. If you had been Mayor Richard J. Daley, what steps would you have taken to maintain order in Chicago during the Democratic convention in 1968?
3. How did President Nixon try to restore law and order? Was he successful? Explain.

4. Why do you think it took the United States so many years to pull out of Vietnam despite the lack of military success?
5. What did Gerald Ford mean when he said that "Our great republic is a government of laws and not of men"? Do you agree? Explain.

APPLICATION   Using Skills To Distinguish Fact from Opinion

For each of the statements below, indicate whether it is a fact or an opinion.

1. Nixon appointed Henry Kissinger as secretary of state.
2. Most Americans supported the Vietnam War.
3. In 1971 the United States worked out an agreement with the Soviet Union concerning access to Berlin.
4. Nixon visited mainland China in 1972.
5. Daley's actions in 1968 did not affect what took place at the Democratic convention.
6. Ford stated in 1974 that the nation's "long nightmare" was over.
7. United Nations officials were pleased to expel Taiwan from the General Assembly.
8. The United States recognized Red China.
9. Brezhnev did not really want to achieve peaceful relations with the United States.
10. Revenue sharing returned billions in federal funds to state and local governments.

EVALUATION   Forming Generalizations

1. What scientific accomplishments has the space program achieved since 1969?
2. What is the current status of relations between the United States and Red China? Between the United States and Taiwan?
3. Is the United States still following a policy of détente with the Soviet Union? Explain.
4. Compare the constitutional issues raised in the impeachment proceedings against President Nixon with those raised in the impeachment of President Andrew Johnson.
5. About what percentage of its yearly oil supply does the United States import today? How does this compare with the figure in 1973?
6. What has OPEC done about oil prices since 1973?

OPEC and the Energy Crisis

Before the Civil War, petroleum could be found in many areas of western Pennsylvania, where it surfaced in brooks and wells. At that time, however, no one knew exactly what to do with it. But soon the possibilities of using refined petroleum—oil—as a lubricant and energy source became apparent, and in 1859 the first oil well was drilled near Titusville, Pennsylvania. Barely a decade later, United States oil production stood at twenty million barrels per year. The great oil rush had begun.

Since those early days of discovery, the United States has always been one of the leading producers and consumers of oil. For decades the nation was able to satisfy its own growing petroleum needs. But by World War II, American energy demands had expanded so much that the nation began to rely on foreign sources of oil. That is why the Middle East—a region that contains the greatest oil reserves of any area in the world—has attracted increased attention from the United States and other large consumers of oil since the 1940s. Oil has become the lifeblood of all industrial nations.

Today the United States still ranks as one of the top producers of petroleum. Nevertheless, because of its huge energy appetite, the nation must still import about 40 percent of the petroleum it requires. The largest

OPEC (Organization of Petroleum Exporting Countries)

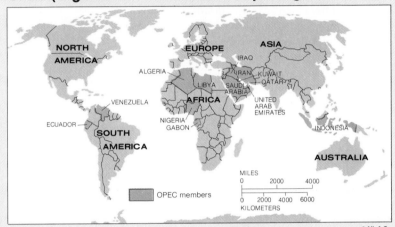

© ML & Co.

volume of oil comes from the Middle Eastern Arab nations, of which Saudi Arabia is the leading supplier.

Until the 1970s most oil production in the Middle East, as well as oil distribution, was controlled by seven great multinational corporations known as the Seven Sisters. Five of these corporations—Exxon, Gulf, Mobil, Standard Oil of California, and Texaco—are based in the United States. The other two are British Petroleum and, largest of all, Royal Dutch/Shell. In general, these companies paid a *royalty* (sum of money) to the oil-producing nations for each barrel of oil they pumped out of the ground.

The Rise of OPEC. Beginning in 1950 the oil producing countries began demanding more money for their oil. First

their royalties were increased sharply. Then, in 1960 the oil-producing nations throughout the world formed a *cartel* known as OPEC, or Organization of Petroleum Exporting Countries. A cartel is a combination of industrial businesses often from different countries, which is organized to control the price, production, and sales of a commodity—in this case, oil.

During the 1960s, OPEC raised the price of crude oil only gradually and by small amounts. Then, beginning in 1970, OPEC nations changed their policy.

First, they either nationalized foreign-owned oil companies, or insisted on so-called "participation agreements" under which they received a 51 to 65 percent share of company ownership. Second, almost all the Middle Eastern OPEC nations either froze the amount of oil being produced or cut oil production back by at least one-third. They argued that this was necessary in order to conserve dwindling supplies.

Then in 1973 the Yom Kippur War broke out between Israel and Egypt. Since the United States had long been a friend of Israel, the Arab nations showed their resentment by cutting off U.S. oil shipments. Then the OPEC nations raised the price of oil four times. The Arab embargo ended in March 1974. So many millions of dollars, pounds, yen, and other currencies poured into OPEC treasuries that most of the nations were unable to spend their income. Nevertheless, since the money earned kept losing value because of inflation, OPEC had to charge higher prices each year.

America's Response. A major reason for the inflation that has taken place in the United States during the 1970s and early 1980s has been the increase in the cost of gasoline, heating oil, and fertilizers and other petroleum-based products. The government and the private sector have attempted to handle the situation in several ways.

During the mid-1970s, automobile manufacturers began concentrating on producing smaller cars that would use less gasoline. The Alaska pipeline began operations. Highway speed limits were reduced to 55 miles per hour. And many Americans lowered the thermostats in their homes. These ac-

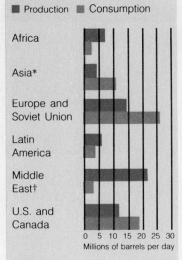

tions helped reduce our heavy reliance on foreign oil.

In 1979, the Carter administration urged a four-point program: (1) limit oil imports; (2) decontrol oil prices; (3) place an excess profits tax on the "windfall" profits oil companies would earn when prices were decontrolled; and (4) use the increased tax revenues to help low-income families pay for their higher energy costs. President Carter also wanted the federal government to encourage the development of liquid fuel substitutes for oil. These might come from coal, oil shale, tar sands, and biomass (organic materials such as corn cobs, leaves, and the like). One promising substitute seemed to be gasohol, a fuel that is 10 percent alcohol, and 90 percent gasoline.

In January 1981, President Reagan lifted all price controls on oil. Economists hoped that higher prices would reduce consumption and also enable oil companies to explore for new oil fields. In addition, companies were exploring other sources of energy, including solar, to supplement oil and coal.

As the graph on this page shows, most industrialized areas of the world use more oil than they produce. Nations in the Middle East, however, produce nearly twelve times as much oil as they consume. For that reason, the Middle East will continue to be an area of vital concern to the United States and the world as long as oil is needed to run machines—or until the Middle East oil wells run dry.

Understanding Free Enterprise

1. According to the graph, about how many barrels of oil do the United States and Canada produce daily? consume daily? What are the comparative figures for the Middle East? Which other areas produce more oil than they consume?

2. What effect has the increased price of oil had on the American economy?

3. How has the United States tried to solve problems caused by the oil shortage? What other measures do you think should be taken?

4. Use the map on page 792 to compile a list of the thirteen members of OPEC.

CHAPTER 40

Toward Another Century

Since 1976

People in the Chapter

James Earl Carter Jr.—*the former governor of Georgia who becomes president. Preferring to be known as Jimmy Carter, he appealed to many voters with his moral earnestness and down-to-earth manner.*

Mohammed Pahlevi—*the shah of Iran and perhaps the strongest ally of the United States in the Middle East, whose dictatorial rule is finally overthrown. The shah flees, and after an exile of several months he dies of cancer in Egypt.*

Ruhollah Khomeini—*one of the many Iranian Muslim holy men who hold the title of ayatollah ("reflection of God"). The Ayatollah Khomeini, a radical Muslim, masterminds the overthrow of the shah and takes control of Iran. His aim is to make Iran into a more traditional religious society.*

Ronald Reagan—*a former movie star and governor of California is elected president in a Republican sweep that sees that party capture control of the United States Senate for the first time since 1954.*

Linking Past to Present

In the last half of the 1970s, many people in the United States felt a rising sense of unease and frustration. At home they felt increasingly squeezed by spiraling inflation. Their standards of living were declining. Some 8 million people looked for jobs and couldn't find them. Then a large number of immigrants from Asia and Latin America entered the country and began competing for the already scarce jobs.

The situation overseas was no better. In the opinion of many, the United States was losing its prestige and power. The nation seemed to lack direction and force in foreign matters. The country watched as a series of revolutions broke out in Central America. In the Middle East the Soviet Union invaded Afghanistan and the United States could only make futile protests. Nor could the United States do any better when a mob of Muslims invaded the United States Embassy in Teheran and held Americans hostage for nearly a year and a half.

Concern over inflation and national pride contributed most to the defeat of Democratic President Jimmy Carter in 1980. Americans turned to a Republican, Ronald Reagan, who promised to reduce inflation by slicing the federal budget and reducing income taxes. He also promised to strengthen the nation's military power. In January 1981 President Reagan took the oath of office, and urged the American people to join him in "a new beginning."

Chapter Outline

1 THE 1976 ELECTION BRINGS A CHANGE
2 CARTER FACES ECONOMIC AND SOCIAL PROBLEMS
3 WORLDWIDE CONFLICTS DIM HOPES FOR PEACE
4 REPUBLICANS REGAIN THE WHITE HOUSE
5 AMERICANS FACE THE FUTURE

1 THE 1976 ELECTION BRINGS A CHANGE

Ever since 1960 there had been a decline in the number of people who voted in the national elections. In 1960, 63 percent of the voting age population voted. This was the highest percentage since the earliest days of the twentieth century. But thereafter, with every presidential and congressional race, the proportion of those who voted sank lower and lower. By the election of 1976 it was down to 54.3 percent. In 1980 it was 52.3 percent, the lowest since the election of 1948.

Disillusion and Distrust

Some students of elections blamed this small turnout on voter apathy. But more observers attributed it to the disillusionment and distrust of government that was left over from the Vietnam War and Watergate. Much public disillusionment with government undoubtedly was due to the Vietnam era when the government had not been successful in winning full popular support for its war policies. Until the Watergate scandal many Americans had not believed that the national political leadership would commit illegal acts. Yet week after week, the Congress, the courts, and the news media spread before the voters a shameful record of official wrongdoing.

During Gerald Ford's administration, investigators turned up the disquieting facts that the FBI had had thousands of Americans, including some prominent citizens, under surveillance for nearly twenty-five years. This surveillance was carried on with very questionable legal justification. Further, it was revealed that the Central Intelligence Agency (CIA) had also spied on American citizens, which is contrary to its charter. It was also charged that the CIA had hired members of the underworld to assassinate the Cuban premier, Fidel Castro, and had engineered the overthrow of the Chilean government in 1973. These disclosures and hints of illegal activity caused many citizens to demand stricter control over the activities of the FBI and CIA.

Most people regarded Ford as a "decent and honorable" man but critics wondered if he was big enough for the job. He suffered from the fact that he had been Nixon's vice-president and had succeeded to the presidency when Nixon resigned rather than by being elected.

A Fight Among Republicans. In the 1976 election Ford was anxious to win the office in his own right but he faced a strong challenge from within his own party. Ronald Reagan, the ex-governor of California, had a large following, especially among the more conservative Republicans. As a former Hollywood actor and TV personality, Reagan was well known. He was considered to have given the nation's most populous state an able and efficient administration. That gave him a claim to his party's consideration for president. Reagan went on to do well in some of the early primaries which caused deep concern in the Ford camp. Reagan lost the Republican nomination to Ford but only by 57 delegate votes out of more than 2000. It was clear that Reagan had become a powerful figure in the Republican party's more conservative wing. Ford selected Senator Robert Dole of Kansas, a conservative Republican, as his running mate.

A Throng of Democratic Hopefuls. On the Democratic side there was an assortment of representatives, senators, and former White House officials seeking the nomination. Senator Henry M. Jackson of Washington, Representative Morris K. Udall of Arizona, Sargent Shriver (brother-in-law of the late President Kennedy and first director of the Peace Corps), Senator Birch Bayh of Indiana, Senator Frank Church of Idaho, and Senator Philip A. Hart of Michigan were among them. For a brief time, so was Edmund G. ("Jerry") Brown, Jr., the young governor of California.

Senator Edward M. Kennedy of Massachusetts seemed the favorite of a large number of Democrats, but he consistently refused to run. He was the last surviving Kennedy brother. He had to be a father not only to his own children, but to a host of young nieces and nephews. Such family responsibilities made his reluctance to run understandable. When finally convinced that Kennedy would not be a candidate, one group of party leaders turned to Senator Hubert H. Humphrey of Minnesota. But by that time the race had been all but won by the most complete "outsider" of them all, former Governor James Earl Carter Jr. of Georgia.

The Peanut Farmer from Georgia

"Jimmy" Carter, as he preferred to be called, had been a career naval officer. On graduating from Annapolis, he entered the navy's nuclear submarine program. That brought him under the eye of the program's taskmaster, Admiral Hyman Rickover. Not everyone could take Rickover's mixture of faint praise and stern criticism, but the young officer adapted readily to it. Carter's naval career was well launched in 1953 when his father unexpectedly died of cancer. Carter left the navy, and at the age of twenty-nine returned to Plains, Georgia, to take over the family business.

The business of the Carter family was peanut farming, but it involved a lot more than planting and harvesting. Like many modern agricultural operations, it was a complex of producing, warehousing, partial processing, and marketing. In a few years Carter had mastered all of it sufficiently to make himself a millionaire and at the same time launch a career in Georgia politics. First he won a seat on the Sumter County School Board. Then he was elected to the Georgia state senate, and in 1966 ran for and lost the Georgia governorship. In 1970 he ran again and won that position.

As governor he had an opportunity to meet many top Washington political officials. This led him to think that he could do at least as well as some of those officials were doing. So he decided to run for the office of president.

This seemed truly an impossible dream. No one from the Deep South had won the presidency since Zachary Taylor in 1848. But Carter had an

The Carters, as this picture indicates, brought the warm friendliness of a small Southern town into the White House.

Presidential Election of 1976

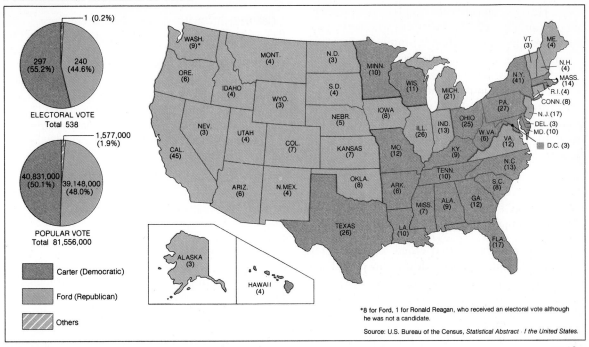

1 (0.2%)

297 (55.2%) 240 (44.6%)

ELECTORAL VOTE
Total 538

1,577,000 (1.9%)

40,831,000 (50.1%) 39,148,000 (48.0%)

POPULAR VOTE
Total 81,556,000

Carter (Democratic)

Ford (Republican)

Others

WASH. (9)*
MONT. (4)
N.D. (3)
MINN. (10)
ORE. (6)
IDAHO (4)
S.D. (4)
WIS. (11)
MICH. (21)
N.Y. (41)
VT. (3)
ME. (4)
N.H. (4)
MASS. (14)
R.I. (4)
WYO. (3)
NEV. (3)
UTAH (4)
NEBR. (5)
IOWA (8)
ILL. (26)
IND. (13)
OHIO (25)
PA. (27)
CONN. (8)
N.J. (17)
CAL. (45)
COL. (7)
KANSAS (7)
MO. (12)
KY. (9)
W.VA. (6)
VA. (12)
DEL. (3)
MD. (10)
D.C. (3)
ARIZ. (6)
N.MEX. (4)
OKLA. (8)
ARK. (6)
TENN. (10)
N.C. (13)
S.C. (8)
TEXAS (26)
MISS. (7)
ALA. (9)
GA. (12)
LA. (10)
FLA. (17)

ALASKA (3)

HAWAII (4)

*8 for Ford, 1 for Ronald Reagan, who received an electoral vote although he was not a candidate.

Source: U.S. Bureau of the Census, *Statistical Abstract · f the United States.*

© ML & Co.

Map Skills   *By what percentage of the popular vote did Carter defeat Ford? Which candidate won most of the South? Which state had the most electoral votes? Who won it?*

unfaltering ambition. Also he was not connected with the Washington scene in any way. He had not been part of any unpopular national policies. In fact, he ran against the politics-as-usual idea. He was not part of the Washington "establishment." He was an outsider, and was proud of it.

His record on civil rights measures while he was governor won him the support of black voters. In fact, the black vote may have been the key to Carter's winning the Democratic nomination. Organized labor also gave Carter its support.

Carter benefited indirectly by the tragedy involving George Wallace of Alabama. In 1972 Wallace, as you read in the last chapter, had been partially paralyzed by an assassination attempt and had been forced to withdraw from the campaign. The 1976 election was his last effort, though by then he had to campaign in a wheelchair. But some Democratic leaders became uneasy. Wallace obviously was not in the best physical condition. Could he campaign effectively even if he won the nomination? Also his campaign, which, as usual, was based primarily on his appeal for white voters, did not seem to generate much excitement. Since 1968 Wallace had seemed to be the spokesman for many southern whites. But when Wallace and

Carter came head-to-head in the Florida primary, Carter won. This convinced many Democratic politicians. If the Democrats wished to capture the presidency, they would have to do it with someone other than Wallace. Carter might be the man. So by the late spring of 1976 a man most of the country had never heard of a few months earlier was the frontrunner. He arrived at the 1976 convention with more committed delegates' votes than were needed for the nomination. Carter won easily in a convention that had no surprises. For his running mate, he chose a good-natured liberal, Senator Walter F. Mondale of Minnesota.

A Close Election

President Ford began the 1976 campaign far behind his opponent. Later, he caught up, much as Harry Truman had in 1948, but he did not gain enough. The main campaign issues were inflation, energy, and unemployment. But Carter's popularity did not seem to come from his views on those subjects. It came, rather, from his personality and manner. He had a direct and warm campaign style. He would walk up to a stranger on the street, smile, and stick out his hand. "Hello; I'm Jimmy

Carter and I'm running for President. I'd like your vote." He had a sincerity that contrasted sharply in people's minds with the politicans who had made the "mess in Washington." Jimmy Carter told them often: "I will never lie to you."

Nevertheless the vote was close. Carter won with a bare 40.8 million votes to Ford's 39.1 million votes. The electoral vote, usually lopsided even in close elections, was 297 for Carter to 240 for Ford. It was a smaller spread than in any election since 1916.

Section 1 Review

COMPREHENSION   Developing Vocabulary
1. Explain these terms: apathy, CIA.

COMPREHENSION   Mastering Facts
1. Why did some Republicans prefer Ronald Reagan in the Republican convention of 1976?
2. Why was Carter called a political "outsider"?
3. Why did many Democrats prefer Jimmy Carter to George Wallace as the Democratic candidate in the 1976 election?

2 CARTER FACES ECONOMIC AND SOCIAL PROBLEMS

VOCABULARY   *stagflation   double-digit inflation*

Carter faced problems that called for action. His administration did not lack ideas for meeting these issues, but every solution it put forward required sacrifice on someone's part. The president and his advisors could not muster in Congress, among the American people, or from the news media, a willingness to accept short-term burdens for the long-range general good. Political leadership in a democracy, however, depends on a president's ability to do just that. Carter's shortcomings in this area are perhaps nowhere better illustrated than in his struggle with the continuing energy problem.

The Continuing Energy Crisis

The nation's petroleum shortage was a key issue because it touched so many others: inflation, unemployment, and the troubled Middle East. Early in 1977, the Carter administration sent an energy bill to Congress. It was a complicated piece of legislation. Among other things, it called for a high sales tax on big, heavy cars (called "gas guzzlers") that were burning up so much of the fuel supply. The bill would give the president standby powers to raise gas prices and also to start rationing if a greater shortage threatened.

Fireside Appeals. To build support for his energy program, Mr. Carter appeared on television to speak directly to the American people. His address was billed as a "fireside chat," a term borrowed from the Franklin Roosevelt era (page 609). Unlike Roosevelt, Carter appeared sitting beside a handsome fireplace in the White House, warmed by a cheery blaze and wearing a sweater as he asked Americans to lower their thermostats.

Special Interests Interfere. These theatrics did little good so far as Congress was concerned. Some of the president's energy program got through the House of Representatives, but very little survived the powerful interest groups in the Senate. Automobile manufacturers were not happy at the idea of a tax on gas guzzlers, for that would adversely affect the sale of cars. The oil and gas lobby did not want gas rationing. Thus, as the 1980 election approached, there was no national energy program worthy of the name.

Some Successes. Some steps were taken by administrative action, however. A cabinet level Department of Energy was established in 1977. Controls were removed from newly discovered gas and oil and an excess profits tax was levied to soak up some of the "windfall" profits that oil companies might earn as a result of rising prices. The search for new petroleum deposits was encouraged, and a government-funded corporation, the Synthetic Fuels Corporation, was launched to develop synthetic fuels from coal, shale, oil, and alcohol. The same bill established a solar energy bank to harness and develop energy from the sun's rays.

Meanwhile, if United States dependence on foreign oil did not decline, at least it was no longer growing. This turnaround was attributed to several causes—conservation measures, a lucky succession of mild winters, more miles-to-the-gallon in the newer cars, and a decline in general business activity.

Rising Cost of Oil. Rising supplies of oil brought no drop in prices. Gasoline that had gone from thirty cents a gallon to over sixty cents during the Arab boycott of 1973 and 1974 now doubled again. A barrel of oil that sold for $1.20 in 1969 cost $10 in 1974. By 1978, the price of a barrel of oil soared to $30. This rise could be blamed on the ending of oil price controls in the United States, the higher cost of imports from the Organization of Petroleum Exporting Countries (OPEC) and a cutback in Saudi Arabian oil production.

Setback for Nuclear Power. Nuclear power, which had been counted on to replace imported oil for generating electricity, suffered a setback early in 1979. On March 28 of that year a reactor on Three Mile Island, in the Susquehanna River, near Harrisburg, Pennsylvania, developed a malfunction. Its cooling system failed, the reactor became dangerously overheated, and several of its fuel rods were damaged. There was a danger that deadly radiation would escape and spread over the countryside. Two days later, low-level radiation actually escaped from the plant's crippled cooling system. The governor of Pennsylvania ordered schools in the area closed. He also urged that preschool children be kept at least five miles from the island. On April 9, the Nuclear Regulatory Commission (NRC) announced that the danger was over. However, small amounts of radiation continued to leak from the plant. This added to the anxiety of people who lived in the area. For a while it seemed that the neighborhood would be permanently contaminated.

The events at Three Mile Island gave a new edge to an argument between the friends and foes of nuclear power. Those who favored it were embarrassed by some of the findings of the extensive investigation that followed. It was found that training of plant maintenance personnel was deficient, and certain precautions at the plant were lax. The advocates of nuclear power made much of the fact that no one had been killed or seriously injured in the mishap. Their opponents countered by saying that chance alone had averted a tragedy. They demanded that the government call a halt to the construction of nuclear power plants, and urged the gradual shutdown of existing nuclear facilities. A poll taken two weeks after the accident showed that among the American people, support for nuclear power had dropped from 69 to 46 percent. Yet a year and a half later, a referendum in Maine showed that citizens there overwhelmingly favored continued operation of the state's sole nuclear plant.

Inflation Rises

Adding to President Carter's energy woes was the problem of inflation. The recession that had helped the Democrats to defeat President Ford in 1976 soon subsided, but inflation did not.

The causes of inflation are numerous and complicated. The rising cost of oil certainly was one cause; high government spending another. Increased social security taxes were cited as a contributory factor. As inflation went up, so did monthly social security payments. And, since more people were living longer, more people were applying for social security pension benefits. The government programs to aid the sick, the unemployed, and the poor also contributed to inflation. In addition there was a huge increase in the cost of defense. The cost of military hardware, in particular, had skyrocketed. One of the controversial elements in the U.S. defense was the MX missile system—an advanced form of the intercontinental ballistic missile (ICBM) which was estimated in 1980 at $33.8 billion.

As the government continued to spend money to stimulate business, provide more social welfare, and improve its military defenses, the economy did not respond in the expected manner. The economy was not stimulated; rather, the United States experienced what economists had dubbed *stagflation*, that is, a stagnation in production accompanied by a rise in prices and increased unemployment.

Carter made a determined effort to cut down on expenses. He sent Congress a "lean" budget in January 1979. This meant that all spending was carefully controlled. But again groups representing special interests complained. Arms expenditures were kept down and this worried those who feared the United States was not strong enough militarily. At the same time the budget, which tried to cut back on certain social programs, angered some liberals. But a growing number of people were determined to slow down government spending even more.

In 1978 California voters, by a 65 percent majority, passed "Proposition 13," which drastically cut property taxes. This reflected a growing sentiment that government spending must be reduced, regardless of the effect of such reduction on social services and welfare programs.

Nevertheless, in spite of the austere budget, credit controls, and other efforts, the cost of living kept rising. Early in 1979 it reached "double-digit" levels. That is, it was high enough in certain months to indicate an annual rate of 10 percent or more for the year. Such a rate had not been seen since the mid-1970s. Unemployment kept rising too, in spite of a 3.5 million increase in the number of jobs. The work force was growing faster than the job supply.

In London, Paris, Berlin, and Tokyo, fears about the United States economy led banks and individuals to shift their holdings from dollars to gold. In times of economic uncertainty many people prefer gold. For a few weeks in 1980 the metal sold for over $800 an ounce—ten times its price in the years of America's greatest power.

Immigration Increases

Throughout the 1970s, the number of immigrants entering the United States continued to rise. By the end of the decade it had reached almost half a million a year. But fewer of them came from Europe.

Mexicans. From 1971 to 1977 Mexico led all other American countries, with 438,500 immigrants to the United States. These were legal immigrants. Some unofficial reports put the number of Mexicans entering the United States legally and otherwise as high as a million a year.

Asians. The Philippines sent 235,300 immigrants—more than any other Asian country. Then, in the 1970s, a new group came from Southeast Asia. An estimated 300,000 fled from their homelands to escape the Vietnam War and its aftermath. Half of that number found their way to the United States.

Cubans. Refugees from Cuba made a great change in the social structure of southern Florida. Soon after Fidel Castro took over the country in 1959, Cubans began coming to the United States. In all, 800,000 arrived during the 1970s, and half of them settled in the Miami area. By the end of the decade they made up 25 percent of the population of Dade County, where Miami is located.

The earliest Cuban refugees had among them a number of middle and upper income people. They tended to be well educated, and quickly established themselves in businesses and the professions. In a few years they had transformed Miami from a resort city and haven for retirees to a bustling Latin commercial center. A number of multinational companies set up offices there, and Miami became the focal point for trade with Latin America.

In 1980 Castro unexpectedly announced that any Cubans still wishing to move to the United States were free to do so. The floodgates opened, and in a few months 183,390 fled north. They came in small, leaky overcrowded boats that were totally unsuited for ocean travel. Many were the families and friends of Cubans already in the United States, but among the refugees were some undesirable elements that Castro had been eager to be rid of. Some, it was said, had been released from jails and some from mental hospitals. At military bases in Florida, Arkansas, and Pennsylvania, where refugees were temporarily housed awaiting resettlement, riots broke out among impatient younger men. As United States taxpayers were spending hundreds of millions caring for the refugees, these actions were not well received. Not surprisingly, a survey showed that a majority of black and non-Hispanic whites in the Miami area thought the coming of these additional Cubans would be disruptive to the economy and the social structure. Their feelings were based on fear that the newcomers would compete with them for already scarce jobs.

Haitians. At the same time as the later Cubans, another Caribbean people began to enter the United States in considerable numbers—the Haitians. These people were from the island country of Haiti. They, too, were refugees, fleeing from famine, poverty, and from the regime of dictator Jean-Claude Duvalier. Like the Vietnamese and Cubans, the Haitians were "boat people." They came by water on anything that would float. Often they were victimized by unscrupulous ship captains or by pirates. At first the Haitians were not accepted as refugees, since the United States had nominally friendly relations with the government of their native land. But later in 1980, the Haitians also began to receive some assistance in relocating and adjusting to a new life in the United States. The Haitians, like the Cubans, were not warmly welcomed by some groups in Florida because they were perceived as an economic threat. They competed for jobs and accepted jobs for less pay than other workers. This usually happens with new U.S. immigrants.

Shift of Political Power to the Sunbelt 1970–1980

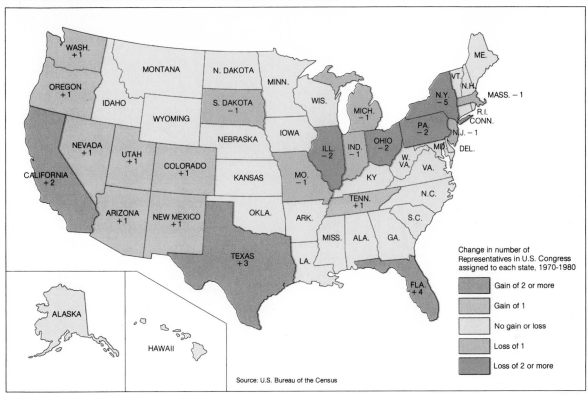

Source: U.S. Bureau of the Census

© ML & Co.

Map Skills *Which part of the country gained in Congress? Which part lost? Why did this shift in Congress occur? Did your state gain or lose? If so, by how much?*

Population Shifts. At the same time that there was an influx of Spanish-speaking people into the United States, there was another movement going on within the country, namely, a gradual shift of population from the so-called "frost belt" to the "sunbelt." Florida, California, and Texas were especially popular. This shift brought more English speakers into contact with those new Spanish-speaking immigrants. (See the map above.) Figures released for the 1980 census confirmed this trend that had been going on for some twenty years.

One reason for the shift was the increased cost of heating for homes and businesses in the North. Another was the attraction of lower living costs and milder weather in the South. There were other reasons that had nothing to do with climate. These had to do with business. The percentage of the country's largest corporations which located in the South nearly doubled between 1965 and 1975. The move continued into 1980 because of the lure of cheaper non-union labor and lower taxes.

The Equal Rights Amendment

President Carter was a strong supporter of equal rights for women and appointed two women to cabinet positions. Yet the struggle to get an equal rights amendment into the Constitution was still not resolved as the nation entered the 1980s.

Betty Friedan and others had organized in 1966 (see chapter 38) the National Organization for Women (NOW). The organization began to push for an amendment to the Constitution to guarantee women "full equal partnership with men" in American life. In 1972 Congress passed, by a two-thirds majority, the Equal Rights Amendment (ERA) and sent it, as the Constitution requires, to the states for ratification. The amendment read in part: "Equality of rights . . . shall not be denied or abridged by the United States or by any state on account of sex."

Many people welcomed the proposed amendment. Few doubted that women in the work force should be given the same pay for doing the same

801

This group of marchers, parading through Washington D.C. in 1978, was part of the intensified activity to get the Equal Rights Amendment ratified by the states.

work as men. However, it was realized that if women were to have equal rights, they would also have equal responsibilities and duties. Some critics of ERA saw this as tampering with traditional female roles. They feared, for example, that if ERA passed, women would have to serve with men in combat. (Interestingly, the U.S. Supreme Court in June 1981 ruled that Congress has the constitutional right to pass an all-male draft.) Others said ERA would cause the death of the traditional family unit. So, opposition to ERA mounted.

The Constitution requires that three-fourths of the states ratify an amendment before it can become law. In 1979 the ERA was still three states short of the required number. Congress, therefore, extended the deadline for ratification until June 30, 1982. But that date also passed without any more states giving their approval. Undaunted, ERA supporters vowed to begin the entire process again.

Section 2 Review

COMPREHENSION   Developing Vocabulary

1. Explain these terms: stagflation, double-digit inflation, boat people.

COMPREHENSION   Mastering Facts

1. Why did the Carter administration have trouble getting its energy program through Congress?
2. How did the antinuclear forces receive unexpected help in 1979?
3. What was the purpose of Proposition 13?
4. What changes in U.S. population were going on during the late 1970s and early 1980s?

3   WORLDWIDE CONFLICTS DIM HOPES FOR PEACE

VOCABULARY   *PLO*

Despite the nation's many domestic problems, the president and his administration began to spend more of their time and energy on foreign problems. Modern transportation and communication have brought all parts of the globe close together. And because of the possibility of a nuclear confrontation, political and social developments had to be watched very carefully. As President Carter said: "Next to the possibility of nuclear war, everything else pales in comparison."

802

Latin America

Two of Carter's international policies improved American popularity in Latin America, where the United States often was characterized as a powerful giant, insensitive to the needs and desires of the hemisphere's poorer people.

The Panama Canal Treaties. In 1904 the United States got the right to use and control the Panama Canal forever (chapter 25). But over the years a resentment built up among the Panamanians. It angered them to see within their nation a zone controlled by a foreign country. In 1964 the resentment boiled over into bloody riots. President Johnson began exploratory talks with Panama for a new treaty. The talks continued, off and on, into the Carter administration.

In August 1977, two treaties were drawn up. In one, the United States agreed to give Panama all of the Canal Zone, except certain military and naval installations, six months after the treaty was passed, but to keep control of the canal itself until December 31, 1999. The second treaty gave the United States the right to defend the canal against any attack. Meanwhile until 1991 the canal would be run jointly by the United States and Panama.

This gesture by the United States government disturbed some Americans. It seemed to be another sign of weakness, of retreat from the great days of the nation's power. After all, they said, the United States had built the canal, and paid for it. Why, they wondered, should it be given to Panama? Nevertheless, Carter fought hard to get the treaty through Congress and, despite strong opposition, he succeeded. In April 1978, the treaty was passed. The treaty helped create a warmer relationship between the United States and the countries of Latin America.

Revolt in Nicaragua. In July 1979, the largest country in Central America, Nicaragua, erupted into civil war. The dictator, Anastasio Somoza, was overthrown by Marxist rebels supported by Cuba and some other Central American countries. Somoza's father had been helped to power by the United States Marines in 1933, and then had run the country as if it were his private property. He was undoubtedly a dictator, but he stabilized the country and was regarded as a bulwark against communism in the area. But the younger Somoza did not have his father's skill as a leader and also,

in the 1970s, opposition to the Somoza regime grew steadily until in 1979 it turned into civil war. In July of that year Somoza was toppled and went into exile. A new government was set up along socialist lines, but with a private sector. Independent political opinions were allowed. The United States recognized the new government.

El Salvador. Early in 1980 the tiny Central American country of El Salvador was rocked by political violence following the establishment of a joint military-civilian government. The much admired Roman Catholic archbishop Oscar Romero was assassinated while officiating at a mass. Then in December of 1980 six Americans, including some nurses who were nuns, were killed. Some reporters charged that the assassins were in the pay of the Salvadoran regime; others charged that leftist guerrillas were responsible. The Carter administration demanded an investigation and temporarily withheld American aid.

The Middle East

Ever since the end of World War II the Middle East has been one of the world's trouble spots. It is an area of many ethnic, religious, and economic conflicts. Yet it is in this area that President Carter achieved one of his greatest diplomatic triumphs.

The independent state of Israel was proclaimed in 1948 with the backing of the United States and by a general resolution of the United Nations. Israel's Arab neighbors, however, refused to recognize Israel's right to exist. They claimed the nation had been created out of land that belonged to the Arabs. Between 1948 and 1972 there were four wars fought between the Arab nations and Israel. Much of the Arab manpower and material came from Egypt. But in November 1977, Egypt's president, Anwar Sadat made a bold move to establish relations with his old enemy. He flew to Israel and met with the Israeli prime minister, Menachem Begin, to discuss peace. This was the first high level meeting between the two governments since Israel had been established.

Camp David Accord. Desiring to build on this attempt at Israeli-Arab goodwill, President Carter invited Sadat and Begin to the presidential retreat at Camp David in the Maryland hills for peace talks. Bringing these two leaders under the same roof was an accomplishment; getting them to

Israel and the Middle East 1967–1980

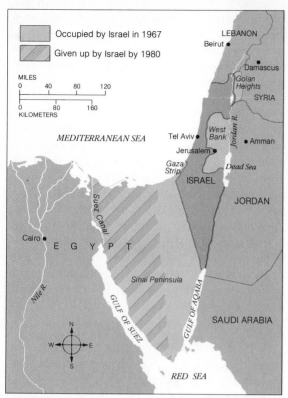

Occupied by Israel in 1967

Given up by Israel by 1980

MILES
0 40 80 120

0 80 160
KILOMETERS

LEBANON
Beirut ●
● Damascus
Golan Heights
SYRIA
MEDITERRANEAN SEA
Tel Aviv ●
West Bank
Jerusalem ●
Jordan R.
● Amman
Gaza Strip
Dead Sea
ISRAEL
JORDAN
Cairo ●
E G Y P T
Suez Canal
Sinai Peninsula
GULF OF SUEZ
GULF OF AQABA
SAUDI ARABIA
Nile R.
N W E S
RED SEA

© ML & Co.

Map Skills *What part of Egypt did Israel occupy in 1967? On what river is the West Bank? On what sea?*

agree to any kind of peace treaty was a triumph. After thirteen days of intensive discussions, however, the three leaders emerged to meet the world press. They announced they had reached an agreement in principle. In March 1979, a peace treaty was signed in the East Room of the White House before a national television audience. The treaty also provided for Egypt's recognition of Israel.

Palestinian Reaction. Many people were cheered by the news, but the Arab nations felt that Sadat had broken faith with them. The peace treaty did not deal with the status of Jerusalem or with the claims of the Palestinians—those Arabs whose land had been taken over by Israel during the wars. The Palestinian Liberation Front (PLO) continued its acts of terrorism against Israel. Israel's neighbor, Lebanon, was torn apart by warring factions that differed in their stance on Israel. Because Lebanon harbored significant numbers of the PLO, it was bombed repeatedly by Israeli war planes.

804

The policy of the United States in all this was to provide support for Israel while also trying to find a solution to the Palestinian issue. Meanwhile a revolution broke out in a Middle East country that the United States had always considered a staunch friend.

The Iranian Revolution. Iran had special importance to the United States. It supplied about 5 percent of the nation's petroleum. In addition, throughout the Cold War, the United States and its allies had seen Iran as the chief obstacle to Soviet expansion in the Persian Gulf. In 1952 there had been an uprising in the country that threatened the government of the young shah, Mohammed Pahlevi. At that time the United States secretly intervened to put down the revolution, fearing that political weakness there might pave the way for Soviet intervention. Thereafter, the United States openly provided the shah with military supplies and technical assistance. For his part, the shah used the oil wealth of his nation to push his people towards a Western way of life. He encouraged Western dress. He sent Iranian youths to school in America. He improved public health and the status of women. But in his haste to make Iran a modern nation the shah's government offended the strict Islamic religious beliefs of some of his people. Nor did his officials respect the human rights of those who opposed his regime. Instances of torture, as well as of imprisonment and execution without trial, were many and well documented.

Late in 1978, partly as a result of the shah's repression, there was widespread unrest throughout Iran. The shah's government attempted to stem the tide of opposition by declaring martial law and invoking even harsher measures than had been used before. Public demonstrations and violence continued in the capital city of Teheran and Iranian students demonstrated in the major cities of the United States. In Iran demonstrations led to the injury and death of hundreds. The United States ordered the dependents of Americans living or working in Iran to leave the country.

In January 1979, the shah fled the country for Egypt, Morocco, the Bahamas, and then Mexico. A Muslim religious leader, the Ayatollah (an Islamic religious title meaning "reflection of God") Ruhollah Khomeini (hoe-may-*nee*), who lived in exile for fifteen years, returned to Iran. The ayatollah called for the establishment of an Islamic re-

The Ayatollah Khomeini, leader of the Iranian revolution, surrounded by his devoted followers.

public to replace the shah. There followed a chaotic period during which a provisional government supposedly ran the country. However, real power was in the hands of the ayatollah and a revolutionary council in Teheran, dominated by Muslim clergy and militant revolutionaries.

American Diplomatic Personnel Become Hostages. The deposed shah had, meanwhile, fallen ill of cancer, and the United States government allowed him to come to New York for treatment. This seemingly humane act infuriated the revolutionaries in Iran. In the fall of 1979, they seized the United States Embassy in Teheran and with it a group of Americans who happened to be working in or visiting the embassy. Most of the women and blacks were released after a short period. The remaining 53 Americans were held as hostages pending the return of the shah and the shah's wealth, which the Iranians charged he had stolen from Iran with the aid of the United States. The militants at the embassy announced that they intended to put the shah on trial.

President Carter rejected at once the demand for the return of the shah. The United States began, however, to put diplomatic and economic pressure on Iran for the release of the hostages.

As months went by and the Iranians refused to return the hostages, the United States mounted a commando-like raid to rescue them. Because of faulty equipment, however, the plan failed and eight Americans lost their lives. Neither these efforts, nor the death of the shah in 1980, nor the condemnation of Iran by the United Nations seemed to have any effect on the status of the hostages.

Afghanistan Is Invaded. The Middle East suffered yet another shock when, on Christmas morning, 1979, wave after wave of Soviet transport planes landed at the airport of Kabul, capital of Afghanistan. This mountainous country is about twice the size of Texas and is situated between Iran and Pakistan, along the southern border of the Soviet Union. Men, equipment, and armored vehicles poured from the planes. Two days later, President Amin of Afghanistan was executed along with members of his family. A new president, Babrak Karmal, a great admirer of the Soviet Union, was installed.

As soon as he got the news President Carter picked up the seldom-used White House-Kremlin hot line. He protested to Soviet Premier Brezhnev that the Soviet invasion was a "gross interference in the internal affairs of Afghanistan." Critics of Carter's foreign policy say that the Soviets acted because the United States seemed unable to free its hostages in Iran. Another explanation was that religious unrest in the Islamic world—including Afghanistan—had spilled over into the Islamic regions within the Soviet Union and posed a threat to Soviet authority within its own homeland. Gaining control over Afghanistan was one way of quelling the unrest.

But by 1985 the Soviets were still having a hard time imposing their will on the rugged and independent people of Afghanistan. Soviet troops were being killed in large numbers by guerrilla tribesmen who struck suddenly and then retreated into the mountain wilderness of that country.

To show United States disapproval of the Soviet action, the House of Representatives voted 386 to 12 against American participation in the 1980 summer Olympics scheduled to be held in Moscow. Many other countries followed suit, although not as many as Carter had hoped. Nevertheless, their absence from the games was conspicuous and a blow to the prestige of the Soviet Union.

President Carter made it clear to the Soviet Union that any aggression by the Soviets toward the oil fields of the Persian Gulf would be resisted. He declared in a speech:

“ Any attempt by any outside force to gain control of the Persian Gulf region will be regarded as an assault on the vital interests of the United States of America. And such an assault will be repelled by any means necessary, including military force. **”**

But the next crisis in the Middle East came not from any "outside" force, but from nations within the Persian Gulf region.

Iraq Invades Iran. Apparently believing that the revolution in Iran had left its people confused, its government divided and its defenses weak, Iraq's president Saddam Hussein launched an invasion of Iran. Late in 1980, war broke out between Iraq and Iran. Although the United States and most of the other big powers adopted a neutral position towards the belligerents, there was great concern lest this conflict expand into a wider war. Moreover, since the war was fought around strategic Iranian oil fields, the supply of oil from that area was further threatened.

SALT Negotiations Stall

In 1972 the Strategic Arms Limitation Treaty (SALT) between the United States and the Soviet Union was signed. It attempted to halt the costly and dangerous nuclear arms race between the United States and the Soviet Union by restricting the type and number of warheads and missiles that each country could make. For example, both countries agreed to set up only two antiballistic missile (ABM) defense sites. They further agreed to build no more intercontinental ballistic missiles (ICBMs).

When President Carter took office, talks continued with the Soviet Union about reducing arms. In July 1977 he met with Soviet Premier Leonid Brezhnev in Vienna and signed a second treaty called SALT II. But the Senate refused to ratify the treaty. Senators opposed to it argued that the treaty would put the United States at a military disadvantage. Some people outside Congress, however, felt that the treaty was too technical and that few of the legislators had enough technical and scientific background to make intelligent decisions on these matters. Many were also unwilling to accept the judgments of technical experts within the State Department and the armed services. As late as 1981 the future of SALT II was still in doubt and many people feared that the world was moving closer to nuclear disaster.

Section 3 Review

COMPREHENSION   Developing Vocabulary

1. Explain these terms: PLO, Ayatollah, Camp David Accord.

COMPREHENSION   Mastering Facts

1. What event apparently caused the Iranians to seize the U.S. Embassy and its personnel in Teheran?
2. How did the U.S. government show its disapproval of the Soviet invasion of Afghanistan?
3. Why were some people against the SALT II treaty?

4 REPUBLICANS REGAIN THE WHITE HOUSE

VOCABULARY   *conservatives   space shuttle*

The 1980 campaign for the presidency began in late 1979, a full year before the election. Like Lyndon Johnson in 1968, President Carter faced a serious challenge from within his own party. It was an unusual development for an incumbent president. But polls showed Carter's popularity was slipping. Continuing inflation, the president's inability to maintain momentum in the Egypt-Israeli negotiations, and a general view that he was not up to the demands of his office contributed to Carter's low job rating.

Choosing Candidates

A few of the same Democrats who had run in 1976 lofted trial balloons for 1980, but all interest soon centered on Senator Edward M. Kennedy of Massachusetts, who this time seemed willing to make the run. Senator Kennedy had long been the favorite of many Democrats. Many saw him as the ideal or "dream" candidate; yet soon after he made his announcement, his popularity in the polls dropped alarmingly.

Carter Defeats Kennedy in the Primaries. Three factors appeared to contribute to Kennedy's decline. First, any challenger's popularity peaks at the moment of announcement. Now people take a closer look and usually find things to criticize. Second, the senator made a poor showing in some television interviews. He appeared ill at ease and poorly prepared. And in early platform appearances he seemed to shout at his audiences and so came across to some people as insincere. A third factor in Kennedy's failure was the Iran crisis. The first instinct of Americans in time of crisis is to close ranks around their leaders. Whatever misgivings they had about Carter, he was the president, and it made them uneasy to see him under attack. Then early in the Iran crisis Kennedy made an ill-timed speech in which he criticized the United States government because it had backed someone like the shah. Some Americans interpreted this as suggesting the United States was indirectly responsible for the Iranian action. The senator's popularity plummeted. President Carter and Vice President Mondale were easily renominated.

The Republicans Pick Reagan. On the Republican side a host of contenders claimed that former governor Ronald Reagan of California was too old or too conservative to be elected. (He was sixty-nine and the favorite of the party's more conservative wing.) But, one after another, their hopes fell by the wayside, leaving the field to Reagan. He selected his former opponent, George Bush, as his running mate. Bush was from Texas, but had a strong New England background.

Anderson Runs as Independent. An interesting development of the 1980 campaign was the emergence of Representative John B. Anderson of Illinois as an independent candidate. Anderson was a middle-of-the-road Republican who had served in Congress for twenty years. He presented himself in 1980 as a moderate, hoping to be more acceptable to independent voters than Reagan. Though he won not a single primary, Anderson appealed to a number of disenchanted citizens unwilling to accept either Carter or Reagan. To no one's surprise, before either convention had taken place, Anderson declared himself an independent candidate for president. He selected former governor and former ambassador Patrick Lucey of Wisconsin as his vice-presidential running mate. Lucey had once been a Democrat and a Carter appointee, and he had campaigned for Edward Kennedy earlier in the campaign.

Testing the National Mood

Never have the American voters been so closely questioned by the pollsters. Polls were taken each month, each week and, as the election day approached, almost every day. Nearly every candidate had a pollster (or a team of them) that reported the slightest change in voter reaction to issues and to the candidate personally. The pollsters reported that the American voting public was undergoing some changes.

A Growing Conservatism. The trend toward conservatism first showed up in the midterm congressional elections of 1978. Its effects were clearly seen in the Senate races. Of the fifteen senators seeking reelection that year, ten were defeated. Among them were several leading liberal Democrats of national standing like Dick Clark of Iowa and Thomas J. McIntyre of New Hampshire.

Conservatives usually give lower priority to government spending for social programs than do liberals. They are for giving incentives to private enterprise, and for a strong defense establishment. And they usually want to cut taxes and reduce the size and influence of the federal government in many areas.

"Single-Issue" Groups. "Single-issue" organizations—voter groups who supported or opposed a candidate on the basis of the candidate's stand on one particular issue—first showed their political power during the 1960s. At that time, like the majority of American voters, they tended to be liberal. They were likely to be antiwar, procivil rights, and feminists. To demonstrate their political power they sometimes targeted a candidate (either Republican or Democrat) whose record they found weak on one or another issue and often caused that candidate's defeat. Now, however, pollsters discovered that groups favoring what are generally seen as conservative positions were doing the same thing. There were groups against gun controls, against abortion, and against ERA. Still other groups favored a constitutional amendment to permit prayers in the public schools.

Single-issue voters are credited with defeating a number of liberals in 1978. Even more impressive

Presidential Election of 1980

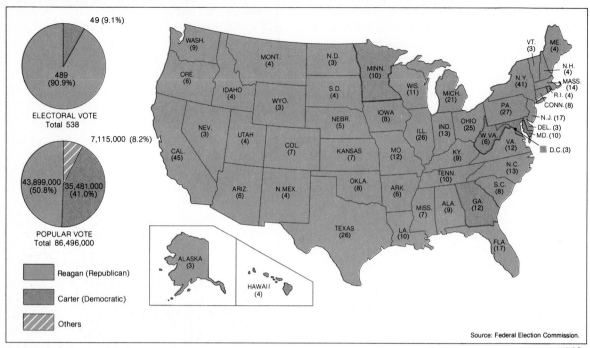

Map Skills *What percentage of the popular vote was won by Reagan? by Carter? How many votes were for neither Reagan nor Carter? Where did Carter win his 49 electoral votes?*

was their success in putting through rigid ceilings on state and local taxes in California and other states. Such activity of either liberals or conservatives clearly indicated that in the 1980 election the established political parties were losing their hold on the minds and loyalties of voters.

Too Close To Call?

Almost all the pollsters thought that the election would be very close. The Democrats tried to picture Ronald Reagan as too old, too conservative and likely to "shoot from the hip." That meant, they said, that he would be likely to get the nation into a shooting war with the Soviet Union. The Republicans tried to picture Carter as an inept bungler who had not been able to curb inflation, which was then running at about 11 percent. They said Carter had been unable to halt high unemployment, and they blamed him for what they said was the nation's weakening military power.

The two main candidates (and John Anderson, the Independent) crisscrossed the country many times during the final weeks of the campaign. They appeared in countless meetings and in tele-

vised commercials. The president and Ronald Reagan held a TV debate which many at the time called a draw. The general opinion, according to the pollsters, was that the American public liked neither of the main candidates and were unable to decide how to vote. But between the debate and voting day the public did decide.

Reagan Wins

The polls in the eastern part of the United States had only been closed for about two hours when pollsters began declaring Reagan the winner. They had come to this conclusion after interviewing people who had just voted. The results pointed to a Reagan victory. As the votes were counted the Reagan win became obvious. President Carter faced the inevitable and conceded defeat even before some people in the Pacific Time Zone had voted.

Reagan won 44 million votes (almost 51 percent of the popular vote) and carried 44 states with a total of 489 electoral votes. Carter carried six states and the District of Columbia with a total of 49 electoral votes. The Republicans also swept the

Senate. The new president's party now controlled that body for the first time since 1954. Republicans had gained 53 seats in the Senate to the Democrats' 46 (with one independent). Democrats kept control of the House (243 to 192 seats) but they lost 31 seats from their previous large majority. The number of Democratic governors also dropped from 31 to 27.

The small number of women and blacks in Congress increased by two each, however. In 1981 there were 21 women in Congress—two of them in the Senate. There were 18 blacks, all of them in the House.

What Did the Results Mean?

Some people talked of a long-term shift in American politics similar to the one that had occurred in the 1930s at the depth of the depression. The 1932 triumph of Franklin D. Roosevelt and the New Deal had made the federal government Democratic for almost half a century. For all but 16 of those 48 years the Democratic party also controlled the White House. In all but four of them there had been Democratic majorities in at least one house of Congress and more often than not the Democrats had controlled both houses.

But the 1980s were different from the 1930s. Political observers pointed out differences between the developments of 1932 and those of 1980. For one thing, the 1932 election took place at a time of increasing interest in politics and rising voter participation in elections. Second-generation immigrants, mostly city dwellers and workers in mass-production industries, were especially active in keeping the Democrats in power.

In 1980 there was a declining interest in politics and a falling off in voter participation, particularly among younger people. In addition, large numbers of industrial workers now saw themselves as members of the middle class. They no longer voted automatically for the Democratic party. They had voted Republican in the 1950s and in 1972, but they had not threatened Democratic control of Congress. Now they did.

The Hostages Are Freed

Despite the activity of an American political year, the Carter administration continued its quiet but intense efforts to get the 53 hostages in Iran released. In the fall of 1980 the negotiations speeded

The personnel of the U.S. Embassy in Teheran, Iran, reach freedom after being held as hostages.

up. The hostages had become a burden to Iran. That country was being hurt by the economic boycott imposed by the United States and other countries. Moreover, Iran had been invaded by Iraq and needed the military equipment which it had bought from the United States but was unable to receive because of the boycott. Iran was also becoming isolated from the international community because of its violation of international law.

An agreement on the release of the hostages was worked out between representatives of the United States government and those of the Ayatollah Khomeini. (Because the United States had no diplomatic relations with Iran, Algeria served as the go-between.) Among other things, the United States promised to transfer some $7.9 billion of Iranian assets from U.S. banks, where they had been frozen, back to Iran. Carter hoped to have the hostages freed while he was still in office. But because of last-minute delays and perhaps deliberate stalling by the Iranians, Carter did not get his wish. In fact, the hostages were not released until 33 minutes after President Reagan had taken the oath of office at 11 A.M. on January 20.

809

The inauguration of President Ronald Reagan. Observing are Mrs. Reagan (center), former president and Mrs. Carter (right), and former vice-president and Mrs. Walter Mondale (far right).

The long-awaited arrival of the ex-hostages in the United States after 444 days of captivity touched off a great burst of joy and patriotism. Millions of people watched on TV as the returnees were reunited with their loved ones. Thousands cheered them as their motorcade passed through Washington to a welcome at the White House by President and Mrs. Reagan.

Later, as the 52 people separated to return to their hometowns and to resume their former lives, the national mood was one of great relief. The long nightmare was over.

A New Beginning

President Reagan did not wait one day before telling the American people what he was going to do first. In his Inaugural Address he called for "a new beginning." He said that the nation's worst problem was inflation. Government spending had gotten out of control. He said that it sapped the nation's economic health causing hardship to young and old alike. He said that his job would be to reduce taxes and cut back on the power of the federal government.

Curbing Federal Power. The federal government, he said, had no power except that granted by the people. The power of such a government must be checked and reversed when it shows signs of having grown beyond the consent of the governed. Then, in a phrase reflecting one of the enduring ideas which surfaces periodically throughout American history, Reagan declared:

> **"** It will be my intention to curb the size and influence of the federal establishment and to demand recognition of the distinction between the powers granted to the federal government and those reserved to the states . . . . All of us need to be reminded that the federal government did not create the states: the states created the federal government. **"**

Many Republicans and Democrats agreed that inflation was the nation's major problem. Many of them (although fewer) also agreed that a budget cut was necessary for the nation's economic health. But that raised some questions: how much would be cut? Where? Whose programs would be eliminated? Some Republicans thought that cuts should be made in social services, and in the budgets of regulatory and environmental protection agencies. Some Democrats believed that savings should be made in military expenditures as well as in government subsidies to big business.

In Reagan's first economic report to the nation in February 1981 he startled many people by declaring that he wanted to cut some $41.4 billion out of the 1982 federal budget. Not since the beginning of the New Deal had any president advocated such slashes in the federal budget. Reagan chipped away at many popular social programs that had been untouched for years. No department was spared except the Department of Defense. Because of declining U.S. influence in a troubled world, Reagan declared that it was necessary to strengthen the nation's military might.

Relieving Taxpayers. The new president also repeated his campaign promise and recommended a 30 percent cut in income taxes over a three-year period. To those who worried that his economic cuts would fall unfairly on the poor, he replied that the "truly needy" would not suffer. The poor and the aged were not so sure, nor were the various interest groups concerned with public health and welfare.

As 1981 continued there were many objections in Congress to the president's cuts. Almost everyone had predicted that the president would not get everything he asked for. His requests had to be voted on by Congress. It is hard for a representative to vote for a budget cut that will cause economic hardship among his or her constituents. But Reagan and his administration seemed to believe that the majority of the people wanted a new attack on economic problems. The new administration declared that tax cuts were a part of the attack.

Breaking Precedent. During the presidential campaign Ronald Reagan promised that if an opening in the Supreme Court occurred, he would try to find a woman to fill the job. An opening did occur a few months later when Justice Potter Stewart retired. On July 7, 1981 President Reagan announced his choice to fill the new vacancy. He appointed Sandra Day O'Connor, a former Arizona state senator and a judge of the Arizona Court of Appeals. After confirmation by the Senate, Mrs. O'Connor would become the first woman in history to sit on the United States Supreme Court.

At a press conference at her home in Phoenix, Mrs. O'Connor introduced her husband, a lawyer,

and their three sons. She also said: "I will do my best to serve the Court and this nation."

An Assassination Attempt

Monday March 30, 1981 was a rainy day in Washington, D.C. It was also President Reagan's 70th day in office. That afternoon he made a speech at the Hilton Hotel during which he remarked, "violent crime has surged ten percent." It was a remark people soon had reason to remember.

After the speech the president left the hotel and was walking toward his car when some shots rang out. The president, two aides, and a policeman were wounded. Spectators and the police grabbed a young man with a gun in his hand and wrestled him to the ground. His name was John W. Hinckley, Jr., of Evergreen, Colorado. (In the summer of 1982 a jury found Hinckley not guilty by reason of insanity.)

Within two days the president was performing some of his duties even though he was in a hospital. The other wounded began to recover from the incident. Within a month the president was back in the White House on his regular schedule. Then came news that also lifted the nation's spirits.

Space Shuttle Success

On April 15, the world's first craft, which was built to take off like a rocket, orbit the earth like a spacecraft, and land like an airplane, made its first successful flight. The spaceship *Columbia* with astronauts John Young and Robert Crippen aboard had been shot into space three days before. After thirty-six orbits of the world, the space ship descended into the earth's atmosphere. At that point the ship became a glider. A few minutes later the astronauts brought the ship down to a perfect landing at Edwards Air Force Base in California.

Nearly a quarter of a million people at the airbase watched the event. Millions more around the world saw it on their television sets. As the media immediately reported: "A new era has begun." It was now possible for this first reusable manned spacecraft to shuttle between earth and space ferrying material and personnel. The next step, according to some space experts, would be to build one or more space stations and staff them with a permanent crew.

Three other shuttles were scheduled to be in use by 1985. Each craft is expected to make about 100

Astronauts John Young (left) and Robert Crippen at the controls of the Columbia.

trips into space. More than 400 shuttle flights are scheduled through 1992. Some important programs being planned are (1) the installation of a space telescope (2) the construction of huge solar power satellites that can collect energy from the sun and beam it to electrical generating stations on earth, and (3) a factory satellite to manufacture products such as computer crystals and medicines—which are best made in zero gravity.

Meanwhile, two historic shuttle flights took place in 1983. In June, Sally K. Ride became the first American female astronaut in space as a member of the *Challenger* crew. Two months later, Guion S. Bluford, Jr., became the first black American in space as he also completed a flight in *Challenger*. These and other shuttle missions attracted the attention of people everywhere.

The Falklands War

Even as fighting continued in Afghanistan, Lebanon, Iran, and Central America, the world saw another conflict erupt in early 1982. For ten weeks Britain and Argentina battled for control of the Falkland Islands, which lie off Argentina's Atlantic coast (see map on page 830). The two nations had negotiated for fifteen years over the disputed ownership of the islands before Argentina tried to take them by force on April 2, 1982. Soon the

two sides were fighting in freezing winter weather.

The United States, with its strong interest in the Western Hemisphere dating from the Monroe Doctrine, at first tried to mediate but then declared support for Britain. "Armed aggression of that kind (by Argentina) must not be allowed to succeed," said President Reagan. Finally, Argentine troops surrendered on June 14, 1982. Britain continued a naval presence around the Falklands.

Mid-Term Report Card

As the Congressional elections of 1982 approached, the American people had a chance to officially react to President Reagan's first two years in office. Some experts believed that the Republicans would lose some seats in Congress.

Reagan himself was still popular; the problem was economic. Inflation was down from 12.4% to about 7%. But many people complained that the overall interest rate (about 15%) and the unemployment rate (about 9.8%) were too high. They also pointed out that the national budget was expected to have the highest deficit in history—over $140 billion. Partly to offset this deficit, Congress passed sweeping new taxes in August 1982.

Republicans replied that there were no "quick fixes" to the economic woes. It had taken years for conditions to get so bad, and it would take more than two years for prosperity to return. They urged people to be patient a little longer.

It seemed to some in the fall of 1982 that neither the Democrats nor the Republicans were able to achieve the goal of low inflation with full employment. In that year's congressional elections, Americans did not endorse Republican policies. Democrats picked up twenty-six new House seats along with seven governorships. However, the Republican advantage in the Senate did not change.

Section 4 Review

COMPREHENSION   Developing Vocabulary
1. Explain these terms: conservatives, space shuttle.

COMPREHENSION   Mastering Facts
1. What were three reasons for Senator Edward Kennedy's defeat at the Democratic convention in 1980?
2. What is meant by single-issue groups? Give examples of such groups.
3. How did Democrats picture Ronald Reagan?
4. How did Republicans picture Jimmy Carter?

AMERICANS FACE THE FUTURE
VOCABULARY   *Reagonomics*

Following the 1982 election, the president continued to push ahead with *Reaganomics*, the name given by the press and public to his broad economic package. By 1983 many people did begin to see solid signs of recovery. Unemployment began to drop noticeably while inflation, which had been in double digits just a few years earlier, was less than 4 percent for all of 1983. Still, the growing national debt continued to be a major concern.

Old Problems Continue

While the economic picture brightened, a number of complex and stubborn problems remained. Two of these concerned education and a growing crime rate.

Education.   During the 1980s, more people became concerned about the quality of public education in the United States. Several international comparisons found American students significantly behind those in other industrial nations—especially in math and science. President Reagan and others called for excellence in education, stressing more discipline in schools and a return to more traditional teaching methods.

Crime.   As violent crime continued to increase in many areas of the United States, Americans debated whether possession of certain types of handguns should be made illegal. A few communities banned possession of handguns within their borders.

While violent crime statistics rose, so did those for "white-collar" crimes such as fraud and embezzlement. In addition, authorities continued to pursue those dealing in illegal drugs and tried to fight organized crime. A new kind of criminal activity also appeared, as more companies and organizations reported electronic break-ins of their computer systems by people who had cracked secret codes.

Meanwhile, as a response to increased worldwide terrorist activities, barricades and defensive missiles were installed around the White House and other buildings in Washington during late 1983. The defenses became a somber sign of the troubled times.

An Unsettled International Scene

Tension between the superpowers continued into the mid-1980s. In addition, smaller conflicts flared into warfare at several spots around the globe.

Relations with Soviets Worsen.   In late September 1983, Soviet pilots shot down a South Korean commercial airliner when the plane strayed over Russian territory. All two hundred forty passengers and twenty-nine crew members died. Some of the passengers were Americans. Nations everywhere condemned the Soviet action.

This incident increased tensions in a world becoming more concerned about the possibility of nuclear war. As relations between the United States and the Soviet Union became more hostile, many people called for a face-to-face meeting between President Reagan and the new leader of the Soviet Union, Mikhail S. Gorbachev. Gorbachev succeeded Konstantin U. Chernenko, who died in March, 1985. Chernenko had replaced Yuri Andropov, who died in 1984 after replacing Leonid Brezhnev in late 1982.

More Trouble in the Middle East.   In the volatile Middle East, American troops arrived in Lebanon in 1982 as part of a peacekeeping force. Soldiers from Britain, France, and Italy were also stationed in Lebanon. Their goal was to stabilize a nation torn by fighting between Christians and Moslems. They also helped evacuate Palestine Liberation Organization (PLO) forces. For years the PLO had staged terrorist attacks on Israel from bases in Lebanon.

The peacekeeping troops stayed in Lebanon about a year without major casualties. Then in October 1983, a truck filled with explosives crashed into the American compound near the Beirut airport, killing two hundred thirty-nine Americans. Some French and Israeli soldiers were killed in similar attacks.

A Moslem terrorist group, with ties to Iran and Soviet-backed Syria, was believed responsible for the attack. Some Americans pressured President Reagan to bring American troops back home, but for several months he chose to keep the marines in Lebanon while seeking a long-term solution to stability in the Middle East. Finally, in late February 1984, the American troops were removed from their land-based positions. The situation in Lebanon, however, remained far from settled.

Invasion of Grenada.   Just after the tragic bombing in Beirut, American marines and a small force from six Caribbean island nations invaded Grenada (see map on page 830) on October 25, 1983. Several small islands near Grenada had asked the United

States to help restore law and order after the Grenadian government had been overthrown and the prime minister killed.

Congress and the American public were stunned by news of the invasion. Many spoke out against the action. President Reagan defended the move, saying it was vital to American security and for the protection of Americans on the island. Many people agreed with Reagan that the successful mission was a "welcome change in foreign policy."

The Defense Department reported finding several hundred Cubans on Grenada. When the fighting ended, they were sent back to Cuba. United States forces also reported discovering warehouses of Soviet-made arms and ammunition, communications equipment, and secret Cuban documents.

As soon as an interim government was formed, the United States kept its promise and moved virtually all of its troops out of Grenada.

Central America. Reagan's firm policy against Soviet expansion extended into Central America. As early as February 1981, Reagan said he would not let Soviet expansion into weaker countries continue. He backed his words by sending military advisers to the tiny nation of El Salvador, where guerrilla tactics and Soviet influence were evident. Confrontations between United States-supported and Soviet-backed groups continued into the mid-1980s, especially in the nations of El Salvador and Nicaragua.

The Election of 1984

President Ronald Reagan sought reelection in 1984. He won his party's nomination without challenge and hoped to become the first president in twenty-three years to serve two complete terms.

Eight Democratic candidates competed for their party's nomination. Former Vice-President Walter Mondale eventually gained the nomination, with Senator Gary Hart of Colorado and the Reverend Jesse Jackson of Chicago as his closest challengers. Jackson, a well-known civil rights leader, was the first black presidential candidate. As part of his campaign, Jackson worked to increase black voter registration throughout the nation. Mondale chose New York Congresswoman Geraldine Ferraro as his vice-presidential running mate. Mondale and Ferraro campaigned hard, but Reagan was reelected in a landslide. He received 525 out of the 538 electoral votes and about 58 percent of the popular vote.

Presidential Election of 1984

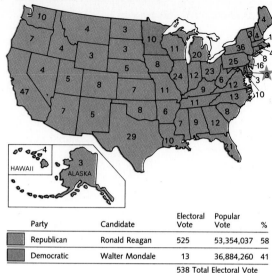

Party	Candidate	Electoral Vote	Popular Vote	%
Republican	Ronald Reagan	525	53,354,037	58
Democratic	Walter Mondale	13	36,884,260	41

538 Total Electoral Vote
©ML & Co.

Anticipating the Future

Many historians say that there is one basic belief which all Americans have shared throughout the nation's history. It is the belief that they are taking part in a great, unique, still-developing experiment: the creation of a freer, more just society. As Thomas Paine said: "We can recreate the world."

Issues raised during previous decades will continue to demand attention in the 1980s and beyond. Economic policies, social progress, foreign affairs, the energy crisis, and national security remain important issues for all Americans. Decisions must be made wisely; the consequences will affect people in all parts of the world for years to come.

The twentieth century brought new ways of both destroying and saving lives. What will the twenty-first century bring for Americans and for the world? What will history books then say about today?

Section 5 Review

COMPREHENSION   Developing Vocabulary
1. Explain these terms: Reaganomics, Grenada, "white-collar" crimes.

COMPREHENSION   Mastering Facts
1. How did the economy improve in 1983?
2. What new kind of criminal activity began to appear in the 1980s?
3. Why did the president send troops to Grenada?
4. Name several problems that continue to concern Americans in the mid-1980s.

814

Chapter Summary

In 1976 Americans turned to a political outsider, Democrat Jimmy Carter, as their new president. Carter achieved some foreign policy successes. Carter, however, could not control inflation, and he did not deal effectively with Iranian terrorists who took over the American embassy in Teheran. Americans elected Republican Ronald Reagan as president in 1980. Reagan vowed to reduce the size of government and increase U.S. defenses. By 1983 the nation's economy showed solid improvement. However, many frustrating national and world problems still confronted Americans.

Questions for Critical Thinking

COMPREHENSION   Summarizing Main Ideas

1. What were some causes of voter apathy and distrust of government during the 1970s?
2. What were some causes of inflation during the 1970s? What measures might Ford and Carter have taken to lower inflation? Why do you think they did not take them?
3. What were the arguments used by those against the Equal Rights Amendment? What were the arguments used for ERA? Do you think ERA should be passed? Explain your opinion.

COMPREHENSION   Interpreting Events

1. Why did many Americans oppose immigrants from Cuba and Haiti? Should the United States take in all who wish to come here? Explain your answer.
2. In Nicaragua and Iran, two undemocratic governments friendly to the United States were overthrown. Should our country support any friendly government or only those which are democratic? Defend your position.
3. Why is the Middle East considered such an explosive area? What could be done to reduce tension there?
4. It has been said that world war is inevitable unless there is some sort of nuclear treaty such as SALT II. Do you agree? Defend your answer.
5. Should one nation invade a neighboring country to put down political discord that could spread and threaten that nation? Why or why not? Has the United States taken such action? If so, when and where? Has the Soviet Union ever taken such action? If so, when and where?

APPLICATION   Using Skills To Infer Information

Drawing inference from data is an important skill in critical thinking. Reread the first five paragraphs under "Inflation Rises" in section 2 of this chapter. Then indicate whether you can infer that the statements below are true or whether the paragraphs do not contain sufficient information for you to infer anything.

1. Unemployment and prices do not always rise and fall together.
2. Government programs to the poor are the main cause of inflation.
3. It is difficult to get budget cuts through Congress.
4. The more a government spends on defense, the bigger will be the budget.
5. Stagflation is an inevitable result of our system of government.
6. Credit controls are the best way to reduce inflation.
7. The U.S. government has not yet found a cure for inflation.
8. The U.S. system of taxation is the most just in the world.

EVALUATION   Comparing Past to Present

1. How did the Carter administration's reaction to the revolt in Nicaragua in 1980 differ from the Theodore Roosevelt administration's reaction to the revolt in Panama in 1903? Which reaction do you think is preferable? Give reasons for your answer.
2. In 1952 the Republicans under General Eisenhower were swept into power with a large majority vote. In 1980 the Republicans did it again under Ronald Reagan. Are there any similarities between the two Republican leaders? Are there any great differences? Were the conditions that produced a Republican victory in 1952 about the same as, or different from, the conditions that produced the victory in 1980? Defend your answers.

Americans Work for Change

Americans live in a nation that is always changing. Many changes have been brought about by people working to improve their lives and serve their country. Also, government often plays a key role in bringing about significant change.

John Adams, Frederick Douglass, and Eleanor Roosevelt were three Americans whose collective life span extended over 225 years. Each witnessed many changes and each worked to make changes that improved American society.

John Adams. John Adams, born a British colonist in 1735, became an ardent patriot. As the nation's second president, Adams sacrificed his personal popularity to keep the nation out of war with France. When John Adams died on July 4, 1826, the United States had a stronger political system because of this dedicated public servant.

Frederick Douglass.
Frederick Douglass was only nine years old when John Adams died. Born a slave, Douglass escaped when he was twenty-one. Soon he started a newspaper, became a leading abolitionist, and used his excellent speaking talents to condemn all forms of discrimination. When Frederick Douglass died in 1895, many people realized that he had given the United States a stronger conscience.

Eleanor Roosevelt.
Eleanor Roosevelt was eleven when Frederick Douglass died. During and after the time her husband served as president, she worked tirelessly to further education, social reform, and the rights of minorities. Until she died in 1962, Eleanor Roosevelt served the nation and the world as an active humanitarian. Like Adams and Douglass, she also saw many changes during her lifetime.

Modern Challenges. Today's Americans face a world that includes many bewildering and rapid changes. But just as Americans in the past worked to change their society by improving it, so do Americans today.

Only one thing is obviously true about history: ever and always, things change. The challenge for our nation's government—and therefore the challenge for all Americans—is to work to insure that future changes reflect progress for all people.

Understanding Government

1. How did Adams, Douglass, and Roosevelt each work to improve American society?

2. Does our nation have a heritage of change? Explain your answer.

3. In your opinion, how can our nation's government prepare now to deal effectively with future changes?

UNIT 10 Review

Understanding Social Studies Concepts

History

1. What danger did the world face during the Cuban missile crisis? How was the situation finally resolved?

2. Explain the meaning of the phrase *Great Society*. Why was President Johnson unable to realize his goals?

3. What changes did President Nixon make in the direction of American foreign policy? What was President Carter's greatest foreign policy accomplishment?

4. Why do most Americans now realize that the United States can probably never again become an isolationist nation?

5. Why has 1968 been described by some as "the year everything went wrong"?

Economics

1. Explain the meanings of the terms *stagflation* and *Reaganomics*.

2. What effect did the Arab oil embargo have on the world economy during the mid-1970s?

Government

1. Why does the Watergate scandal rank as the greatest crisis in the history of our federal government? Have any of the effects been lasting? Explain your answer.

2. During the 1980 campaign, what changes did Ronald Reagan pledge to make concerning the power of the federal government? Did he make any of these changes?

3. In what ways have television and other forms of nearly instant news reporting become factors in American elections? Is too much emphasis now placed on a candidate's "image"? Explain.

Sociology

1. In what ways did the Vietnam War divide American society?

2. What population shifts have become evident in the United States during the 1970s and 1980s? Which are the fastest growing minority groups in the nation?

Extending Map, Chart, Picture Skills

1. Study the charts and graphs on pages 838–841. Write general descriptions of the trends since 1960 in these areas: unemployment; federal expenditures; women in the labor force; American petroleum imports; inflation; union membership; gross national product.

2. Study the unit opening picture on pages 732–733. What other picture would you have chosen to illustrate the present? Why?

Understanding Current Events

1. Which constitutional amendments have been ratified since 1960? Which directly affect you? What amendment could be approved next?

2. Is the Cold War still continuing between the United States and the Soviet Union? How has this struggle between the two superpowers changed during the 1970s and 1980s?

3. Is the Monroe Doctrine still an important part of American foreign policy? Explain.

Developing Effective Citizenship

1. The Vietnam War years ushered in a new era of protest. In what ways can citizens show their displeasure with certain policies? Which methods of protest are usually most effective?

2. Using the criteria on page 314, rate the men who have served as president in your lifetime.

3. Make a list of the most important problems facing the United States during the next decade. What steps should the nation take in meeting these challenges? What steps can you take as an individual citizen in helping to solve them?

Reference Section

Glossary of Social Studies Terms

This glossary explains many of the important words and ideas needed to understand history and the other social sciences. Each entry consists of a concise explanation and a page reference or references to where the term has been used in the text.

A

Abolitionist one who believed in the end of slavery either immediately or through a gradual process of emancipation (284–286).

Abrogated abolished, repealed, or annulled (507).

Absolute monarch ruler who exercises total power (53).

Adapted modified to suit new circumstances (19).

Admiralty courts special courts in which accused colonial smugglers were tried without local juries and sentenced by judges appointed by the Crown (85).

Afrika Korps General Erwin Rommel's German troops, who were defeated in North Africa by Allied forces in World War II (664).

Alliance for Progress President John F. Kennedy's proposals for assistance to Latin America, which combined economic aid with tax and land reforms (745).

Ally country or person joined with another for common purposes (685).

Amendment revision or addition to a bill, law, or constitution (183–184, 201–202).

Amnesty pardon, usually in reference to political offenses committed against a government (137, 359–360).

Anarchists people who oppose any form of government (580).

Anasazi ancestors of the Pueblo Indians, whose name meant "the ancient ones" (24).

Anesthetics any drug or gas which produces a temporary loss of feeling, especially one of pain (283).

Anschluss political or economic union, such as the one formed by Germany's annexation of Austria in 1938 (640).

Antifederalists opponents of the proposed Constitution who did not trust centralized government power and preferred greater authority for the states (166).

Appalachia region that includes states in the Appalachian Mountain range where many rural poor live (758).

Appomattox Court House site in Virginia where General Lee surrendered to General Grant on April 9, 1865 (353).

Arbitrate to hear both sides of a dispute and render a judgment (21).

Arbitration resolution of a dispute by a neutral third party (440).

Artifacts tools, utensils, furniture, or any objects made by people (42).

Artisans workers skilled in a particular craft (66–67).

Aryans Indo-European peoples; also, a term misused by Adolf Hitler to mean people of "pure" German blood (643).

Assembly line manufacture of a product by division of labor along a conveyor belt, with tasks arranged in sequence to maximize efficiency and increase output (588).

Assimilated absorbed, especially in reference to the incorporation of immigrants and other newcomers into American life (455–456).

B

Bank holidays temporary bank closings during the Great Depression, intended to prevent overwithdrawals and bank failures (606).

Bank notes paper money issued by a bank (204).

Bear Flag Republic independent government established by California settlers in 1848 (307).

Beringia narrow strip of land connecting Siberia and Alaska during the Ice Age which today lies under water (15).

Berlin Wall barricade built in 1961 by communist East Berlin to keep Germans from fleeing to free West Berlin (743–744).

Bessemer process steel-manufacturing technique which increased efficiency and reduced production costs (404).

Bicameral legislature having two houses, usually a Senate and House of Representatives (163).

Bill of Rights first ten amendments to the Constitution, which enumerate the rights of individual citizens (186–188, 201–202).

Bills of Credit paper money (165).

Bimetallism use of two metals, usually gold and silver, as a monetary standard, with a fixed ratio of value between the two (474).

Bipartisan having members of or support from both major political parties (608, 649).

Black codes laws passed in southern states to regulate the activities of former slaves after the Civil War (362).

Black power phrase referring in general to greater political representation, economic control, and racial pride among blacks (764).

Black Tuesday October 29, 1929, when stock prices fell drastically (594).

Blacklist list containing names of union members that is circulated among company owners who then refuse to hire those workers (443).

Blitzkrieg lightning war, the name given to Germany's quick and brutal invasion tactics used during World War II (646).

Blockade-running breaking through a naval blockade by using small, low boats; this tactic was used by the South during the Civil War (343, 347–348).

Boondoggle unnecessary government jobs or programs (616).

Bootleggers smugglers and other black marketers who sold illegal liquor during Prohibition (565).

Border states four slave states between the North and the South (Kentucky, Maryland, Delaware, and Missouri) which remained in the Union (338–339).

Boycott refusal to buy, sell, or use a good or service, an effective technique employed during the Revolution and the Civil Rights Movement (116–117, 721–722).

Brain trust group of professors and their associates who helped Franklin Roosevelt plan his New Deal programs (605, 607–608).

Breaker boys youngsters who broke coal in the mines before passage of child labor laws (437).

Bull Moose party Progressive party formed in 1912 by the supporters of Theodore Roosevelt, who ran for president as a third party candidate (532–533).

Bureaucrats government officials and workers (81).

Burgesses elected representatives in the House of Burgesses, colonial Virginia's lower legislative house (44).

Byelorussia one of the Soviet Union's fifteen republics, also known as White Russia (672).

C

Cabinet group composed of department heads within the nation's executive branch which meets regularly to advise the president (203).

Capital city which is the seat of government for a state or nation; also, wealth in the form of property, machinery, and other assets (216–217; 448–449).

Capitol Hill another name for the building where Congress meets (708).

Capital ship battleships and cruisers (583).

Capitalism economic system in which the means of production and distribution are privately owned and operated for profit, and decisions about what and how much to produce are determined by the demands of the marketplace (448–449).

Carpetbaggers northerners who moved south to take advantage of unsettled economic and political conditions for personal gain (367–368).

Cartel group organized for the establishment of a monopoly by price-fixing (789).

Caucus private meeting of leaders of a political party to decide on policy or pick candidates, especially before a regular meeting of the party (265).

Cease-and-desist order official order to stop a certain action or behavior (535).

Census official and regular record of population facts including age, sex, and so on; census information is used to determine the number of seats each state has in the House of Representatives (170–171, 801).

Charter official written permit granted by a ruler to a person, group, or corporation (39).

Chicanos Mexican-Americans (722–723).

Chinatowns segregated areas of cities where Chinese immigrants and their descendants often live (459–460).

Chivington massacre killing of Cheyenne Indians by the Colorado militia in 1864 (383).

Civil disobedience purposeful breaking of a law as part of an organized effort to get that law changed (719–720).

Civil rights constitutional rights guarantees to all Americans, including those enumerated in the Bill of Rights as well as Amendments 13, 14, 15, and 19 (719–722).

Civil war war between different regions or groups of the same nation; the Civil War in the United States was fought in 1861–1865 between the Northern and Southern states (336).

Classified government documents which are kept secret from the public to protect national security (690–691).

Closed shop agreement by which all workers employed by a company must belong to a union (529).

Coercion use of force to achieve results (227).

Cold War rivalry between the United States and the Soviet Union which involves conflict in diplomacy, economics, and smaller wars rather than all-out nuclear confrontation (725).

Collective security President Roosevelt's proposal in 1937 for cooperation among the western democracies to stop the aggressiveness of Italy, Germany, and Japan (640–645).

Colonialism system by which a nation maintains foreign colonies, especially for profit (58–59, 510–517).

Comintern international organization of communist parties, also called the Communist International, which advocated the overthrow of capitalism by worldwide revolution (579).

Commerce trade between buyers and sellers (241).

Committees of Correspondence communication network of groups within each colony which kept one another informed of British actions affecting American liberties (120).

Common Sense widely-read pamphlet written in 1776 by Thomas Paine which set forth persuasive arguments for American independence (131).

Commonwealth legal status of Puerto Rico, which governs itself but relies on the defense system of the United States (507).

Communism economic system characterized by common ownership of property, state control of the means of production and distribution, and decision-making by a dictator or government elite; in theory, a classless society with equal distribution of goods (448–449).

Compact agreement between individuals, groups, or nations (48).

Compromise solution to a deadlock in which each side gives up some demands (163–164, 309–312).

Conestoga wagons broad-wheeled covered wagons which pioneers used to cross the prairie (301).

Confederacy government established in 1861 by the seceding states of the South (331).

Confederation alliance of states or nations united for a common purpose (157).

Congress legislature of the United States consisting of the Senate and the House of Representatives (163–165, 169–177).

Conquistadors Spanish conquerors of the New World (29).

Conscription compulsory military service (346).

Consecrate to make holy or sacred (351).

Conservative believer in established tradition who politically tends to favor individual initiative, unfettered private enterprise, and a minimum of government social action (756–757, 778, 807).

Constitution written document ratified in 1788 which outlines the framework of the government of the United States and enumerates the rights of American citizens. The Constitution is the basic law of the land (162–166, 168–199).

Containment policy course of action advocated by George Kennan which required the United States to block Soviet attempts at expansion anywhere in the world (687–688).

Continentals Revolutionary War soldiers who served under George Washington in the Continental Army (135).

Contraband smuggled goods, often weapons and military supplies (543).

Convoy system protection of merchant ships from U-boat attacks which required travel with a large group of destroyers (550).

Copperheads northern Democrats who opposed the Civil War, sympathized with the South, and urged peace (338).

Corporation group of people who, through a charter, assume the legal powers, rights, and liabilities of a separate individual. A corporation can conduct business and buy or sell property (413–414, 652–653).

Cotton gin machine invented by Eli Whitney which removed seeds from cotton fibers and thus greatly increased cotton production (249).

Covenants agreements or compacts (553).

Craft unions associations of organized workers which restrict membership to those skilled in a particular craft (442).

Credibility gap public loss of trust in what government leaders claim is happening and what actually is happening; the term became popular during the Vietnam War (762).

Creditors lenders to whom money is owed (159).

Croix de guerre French military honor awarded for bravery in action (548).

Culture civilization of a particular group of people at a given period in history, including their ideas, habits, skills, beliefs, institutions, and so on (14, 22).

Culture shock various emotions such as loss, surprise, and alienation which a stranger first feels at coming into contact with people of different language, dress, and customs (455).

D

Dardanelles Turkish straits connecting the Black Sea to the Mediterranean (686).

Dark horse candidate nominee who is not a leading contender but receives unexpected support, often in response to a stalemate (302).

Debtors borrowers who owe money to others (159).

De facto segregation separation of races by tradition and custom rather than by law (423).

Defected deserted, as in leaving one's country to seek political asylum in another nation (690).

Defoliants toxic chemicals that cause leaves to drop off all plants (761).

Delegated powers rights exercised by the federal government which are specifically authorized in the Constitution (164).

Demobilized released from military service at the end of a war (679).

Democracy system of government in which the people hold the ruling power either directly or through elected representatives (423–433).

Democrats members of a political party that developed after Andrew Jackson's election as president in 1828. Today the Democrats and Republicans comprise the two major political parties in the United States (260).

Demokrashi democratic reforms instituted by General Douglas MacArthur during the American occupation of Japan after World War II (673).

Depressed areas as defined by the Area Redevelopment Act of 1961, regions of the United States where unemployment stood at higher than 6 percent (739).

Depression severe economic slump marked by high unemployment, falling prices, and a decline in overall business activity (270–271, 274–275, 599–604).

Détente easing of Cold War tensions between the United States and the Soviet Union (781).

Diplomacy skill in conducting relations between people or nations and reaching agreements (143–144, 517, 671–673).

Direct primary process of nominating political candidates by popular election rather than by machine bosses (527).

Discrimination to show partiality or prejudice in treatment, especially when directed against the welfare of minority groups (460).

Dissenters those who disagree with certain beliefs or opinions; Protestants who disagreed with the Anglican Church, England's established state religion (83).

Dixiecrats southern delegates at the 1948 Democratic convention who bolted the party and established the States' Rights Democratic party (682).

Dollar Diplomacy government policy of guaranteeing loans made by business investors to Latin American nations, which in the event of default was used as justification for United States military intervention (517).

Domino theory belief that if one nation in an area becomes communist, then neighboring nations will also fall under communist control (727).

Double-digit inflation annual rise in the cost of living of 10 percent or more (710–711, 799–800).

Dred Scott **decision** Supreme Court ruling in 1857 which excluded blacks from citizenship and legalized slavery in all territories (326–327).

Drought extended period without moisture or rain (389).

Due process of law part of the Fifth Amendment which guarantees to all American citizens a fair and orderly legal proceeding before life, liberty, or property can be taken away (187).

Dumbbell tenement overcrowded urban apartment building whose central air shaft became a breeding ground for disease and fires (423).

E

Eclectic choosing from a variety of systems, beliefs, or sources (486).

Economic multiplier effect on the nation's economy of a key industry whose needs are supplied by other industries which prosper as a result; the automobile was the first great economic multiplier (588).

Economics study of the production, distribution, and consumption of goods (108–109, 739).

Economy system of production, distribution, and consumption of goods and services (108–109).

Eisenhower Doctrine policy which stated that the United States would defend the Middle East against Soviet attack (726).

Elastic clause part of Article I, Section 8 of the Constitution which grants Congress the flexibility to exercise authority in matters not specifically mentioned elsewhere in the document (175, 204).

Elastic currency condition which permits the amount of money in circulation to increase or decrease, depending on the economy's needs (535).

Emancipation process of being set free from slavery (145, 346).

Emancipation Proclamation decree issued by Abraham Lincoln in 1863 which freed slaves in certain southern states (298).

Embargo government order closing a nation's ports to commercial shipping; used especially as a war measure (227).

Empire group of nations, colonies, or territories under one sovereign power (58–59).

Environment entire surroundings which affect an individual or group, including the social, political, economic, and geographical conditions (88).

Equal protection of the laws passage in the Fourteenth Amendment which requires states to apply the same laws to all citizens (189, 720).

Equal Rights Amendment proposed amendment which would require equality of rights regardless of sex (767, 801–802).

Era of Good Feelings period during Monroe's presidency when a new spirit of nationalism flourished (241).

Espionage practice of spying (691).

Evolution theory advanced by Charles Darwin which argued that human beings evolved from lower life forms (563–564).

Executive person or branch of government whose job is to enforce the laws and administer the government (164–165, 177).

Executive privilege precedent set by President Washington in 1796 which rejects the demands of congressional investigations by claiming that presidential communication with advisers is confidential (785).

Excise duty or sales tax on the manufacture, sale, or consumption of goods produced within a nation (205).

Exodusters blacks who moved from the post-Reconstruction South to Kansas (392).

Extraterritoriality exemption from the jurisdiction of local authority, such as the right enjoyed by an ambassador in a foreign country (510).

F

Farm bloc group of congressmen representing agricultural states (591).

Fascism system of government characterized by an absolute dictator; state precedence over individuals; and suppression of opponents to the government by force (636).

Federal Reserve System government-controlled, decentralized banking arrangement that manages the nation's money supply by controlling the rediscount rate (535).

Federalism system of government in which the nation and states share authority, with each having both shared and exclusive powers (163–164, 168).

Federalist one who supported adoption of the Constitution, a strong national government, and policies encouraging trade, manufacturing, and commerce; later, a member of the Federalist party (166, 206).

Filibuster extended speech in Congress with the purpose of holding the floor and preventing voting on a certain bill (570).

Fireside chats President Franklin Roosevelt's radio talks explaining his policies (609–610).

Flappers young women of the 1920s who shortened their hemlines and wore their hair short (567).

Floor price minimum price established by the government for an agricultural crop (591).

Free enterprise system economic system which encourages competition, allows individual corporations to earn profits, and lets the marketplace determine decisions of supply and demand (488–449).

Freedmen's Bureau federal agency instituted by President Lincoln to assist former slaves and poor whites after the Civil War (361).

Freedom ride   tactic of the civil rights movement whereby groups of whites and blacks forced integration of interstate transportation by riding together on buses throughout the South (746).

Freeport Doctrine   idea advanced by Stephen Douglas that slavery would not work in territories where voters refused to uphold it with supporting legislation (329).

Free-soil party   antislavery party of splinter Democrats whose 1848 platform favored abolition of slavery in the territories (308).

Frontier   edge of a settled area which borders on unpopulated wilderness (392).

Fugitive Slave Law   measure passed by Congress in 1850 which provided for the recovery of runaway slaves with the assistance of federal marshals (319).

Funding   payment of a debt by creating another debt through the issuing of bonds (203).

G

Gadsden Purchase   area in present-day New Mexico and Arizona purchased from Mexico for a southern railroad route (308).

Genocide   deliberate and systematic extermination of a group of people (646).

Geography   study of the earth, including landforms, climate, bodies of water, plants, animals, and so on (88).

G. I. Bill of Rights   legislation after World War II which established veterans' benefits in education, housing, employment, and health (680).

Gold standard   use of gold as the monetary basis by which currency is defined (474, 603).

Grand Old Party   nickname for the Republican party, also called the GOP (532).

Grandfather clause   voting requirement which allowed people to vote provided their fathers or grandfathers had been eligible to do so; such a rule virtually eliminated blacks from voting (373).

Great Awakening   series of religious revivals during the 1740s and 1750s which were sparked by the preaching of George Whitefield (96).

Great Society   name given to President Lyndon Johnson's overall domestic social program (757–759).

Greenbacks   paper money issued by the federal government (348).

Gullah   language composed of English and West African components which was spoken by many black slaves (68).

H

Hard money   gold, silver, or other such "hard" currency (268).

Harlem Renaissance   creative achievements of black Americans during the 1920s and 1930s, which were named for New York City's Harlem area (570–571).

Hartford Convention   meeting of New England states in 1814 which aired sectional grievances (232).

Head right system   homesteading plan whereby a settler immigrating to Virginia in the 1600s received fifty acres of free land for himself and for each person who accompanied him (43).

Heresy   opinion or belief which opposes an official view, especially concerning religious questions (50).

Hessians   German mercenaries who fought for the British during the American Revolution (135).

History   recorded events of the past (14).

Holding company   corporation organized to hold the stocks and bonds of other companies which it controls (413).

Homestead Act   congressional law which gave 160 acres of free land to any citizen who would settle and cultivate it for five years (348, 392, 399).

Hoovervilles   makeshift living areas, such as collections of tents or shacks, erected by the homeless during the Great Depression (603).

House of Representatives   lower branch of the legislature of the United States or of various individual states (163, 170–171).

Hypothesis   educated guess based on study, observation, and analysis which attempts to explain a certain event (17, 33).

Humanitarian   person devoted to helping others (603).

I

Immigration   entry into a new nation for the purpose of permanent residence (453).

Impeach   to charge a governmental official with a crime or other wrongdoing in office (165, 316–317, 724–725).

Imperialism   policy and practice of a nation to acquire an empire by controlling the economic and political affairs of weaker nations and territories (505–517).

Impressment   British practice of forcing men into involuntary military service, especially into its navy (226).

Incandescent light   light produced by a filament heated to a glow through use of an electric current (402).

Income tax   federal tax on citizens' incomes, as legalized by the Sixteenth Amendment (348, 535).

Indentured servants   immigrants who, in return for passage to the New World, contracted to work for someone, usually for seven years (44).

Indigo   violet-blue dye made from the leaves of certain pea plants; first made successful as a cash crop by Eliza Pinckney of South Carolina (61).

Industrial unionism   associations of organized workers which include both the skilled and unskilled workers of a particular industry (442).

Inflation   increase in prices accompanied by a decline in the purchasing power of money (710–711, 799–800).

Initiative   process of petitioning a legislature to introduce a bill (474, 527).

Injunction court order directing or commanding that a certain action be done (444).

Installment plan payment for the purchase of an item which is spread out over regular, timed intervals (278).

Interchangeable parts Eli Whitney's invention of standardized parts which could be used interchangeably and produced in mass quantities (251).

Interest group people with a common interest organized to achieve certain goals; often used to describe groups of lobbyists which attempt to influence representatives and the political process (539, 807–808).

Interest rates the cost, often stated as a percentage, of borrowing money (620).

Interlocking directorate system in which the directors of one firm also serve as directors of another, applying similar policies and practices to both (414).

Ironclads wooden ships built during the Civil War which were fortified with ironplate armor (341).

Isolationism belief that a nation should remain free of international alliances and refrain from intervention in the affairs of other nations (554–556, 638, 650).

J

Jim Crow laws laws which legitimized the practice of separation of the races in southern public facilities; these laws were upheld by the Supreme Court in 1896 but reversed in 1954 (373–374, 719–720).

Joint-stock companies businesses in which a group of people pool their money, receive shares of stock in proportion to their contributions, and thus share ownership jointly (39).

Judicial review judicial precedent established in *Marbury v. Madison* which gave the Supreme Court the power to judge the constitutionality of congressional legislation (195–196, 221).

Judiciary branch of government composed of courts and judges which upholds the law and decides punishments (165, 220–221).

K

Kamikaze Japanese suicide pilots who crashed bombladen planes into American ships during World War II (671).

Keynesian follower of the economist John M. Keynes, whose ideas about income determination and economic growth influenced politicians to lower taxes, promote investment, and increase public spending (739).

King Cotton main cash crop in the South during the early and mid-1800s (248).

Ku Klux Klan group formed to intimidate blacks, Jews, and other minorities (369–370, 580–581).

Know-Nothings nativists who sought to limit the political power of immigrants and supported native-born Protestants for public office (324, 457).

Kristallnacht Nazi destruction in 1938 of synagogues and Jewish homes and businesses which convinced many Jews to leave Germany (643).

L

Lafayette Escadrille unit of American fighter pilots who flew for the French before the United States entered World War I (550–551).

Legal immunity freedom from prosecution under the law (692).

Legislature branch of government composed of elected representatives who enact laws (162–165).

Lend-lease United States policy of loaning or renting military equipment to the Allied forces during World War II (655).

Libel any written, printed, or illustrated material which injures someone's reputation through damaging or false statements (101).

Liberal person whose political beliefs tend to favor experimentation and change, reform of inequalities, and an active role for the federal government (779, 797).

Lineage one's ancestors, family, and blood relatives (66).

Linsey-woolsey coarse cloth combining wool and linen or cotton (71).

Literacy test means of excluding blacks from voting in southern elections by testing their ability to read (373).

Lockout putting economic pressure on employees by closing a business temporarily so that workers will eventually yield to company demands (443).

Long March trek of 6000 miles made by the Chinese communists in 1934 to escape persecution by Chiang Kai-shek (697).

Longhorns breed of long-horned cattle originally found in Mexico which was well-suited to long cattle drives (388).

Loyalists opponents of American independence who remained loyal to the Crown during the Revolution (133–134).

Lyceum form of nineteenth century adult education in which management bureaus arranged lectures, debates, public information speakers, and popular entertainment for the public (487–488).

M

Mandates regions administered by victorious Allied nations after World War I as a first step toward eventual independence (553–554).

Manifest destiny belief that the United States was destined to expand westward across the entire continent (295).

Manifesto proclamation or declaration of a particular position (360).

Margin buying a stock with only part of the money to pay for it, hoping its price will then rise (592).

Massacre indiscriminate killing (118, 383–384).

Massive retaliation policy of John Foster Dulles stating American willingness to use nuclear weapons against an aggressor nation, which led to atomic stockpiling (725).

Mastodon shaggy, elephant-like mammal of the Ice Age (17).

Materialism belief that material goods and wealth are the most important values in life (574).

Matriarchal society social organization in which women exercise the most authority in family, government, and economic life (20).

Mechanization transformation from hand-made production to dependence on machines to perform work (600).

Mediate to act as a go-between in the settling of a dispute (698).

Medicare system of medical insurance for elderly Americans paid for through Social Security (758).

Medicine men priests and healers of North American Indian tribes (77).

Melodrama extravagant theatrical presentation especially popular during the late 1800s (493).

Melting pot the belief that the cultural heritages of many immigrant groups blended together as they all became Americans (450, 453).

Mercantilism economic theory which promised a nation power through the acquisition of wealth if a favorable balance of trade was maintained, especially with a nation's own colonies (58–59, 79).

Mercenaries hired soldiers who serve in a foreign army (134–135).

Merit system process of hiring people for government jobs on the basis of ability rather than patronage (469).

Metric system decimal (base 10) system of measurement for area, length, weight, and volume (10).

Middle colonies those colonies located south of New England and north of Virginia, including New York, Pennsylvania, Delaware, and New Jersey (56).

Midnight judges those judges appointed to the bench by John Adams during the last few days of his administration (195–196, 221).

Militarism excessive emphasis on aggressive attitudes, war policies, and military spirit in national life and government (72).

Minutemen special units of militia in colonial New England which were prepared to assemble at a moment's notice (122).

Missouri Compromise series of congressional measures which maintained a sectional balance in 1820 (247–248).

Moderate one who supports a middle-of-the-road political position and tends to avoid extremes (704).

Monopoly exclusive control of a certain product or service in a market; a monopoly makes price fixing possible and eliminates free competition (415).

Monroe Doctrine principles set forth in 1823 by President James Monroe warning Europe not to interfere in the New World and promising that the United States would not get involved in European affairs (246–247).

Moratorium authorized delay or postponement (603).

Mormons members of the Church of Jesus Christ of Latter-day Saints (303–304).

Muckrakers journalists of the early 1900s who reported on social injustices, especially in business practices (524).

Munitions military supplies, including weapons and ammunition (543).

N

National Association for the Advancement of Colored People (NAACP) black equal rights organization that was founded in 1909 by W. E. B. DuBois (569–570, 719–720).

National Grange association of farmers who organized political opposition to the railroads during the late 1800s (411–412).

National income total amount paid annually to producers of the nation's goods and services (600).

Nationalism feelings of loyalty, pride, and devotion to one's country; patriotism (240–241).

Nativism practice of favoring native-born Americans and placing restrictions on immigrants (324, 457, 584–585).

Natural rights God-given rights of life, liberty, and property, as explained by John Locke (94).

Naval stores supplies for ships, including masts, pitch, tar, turpentine, and so on (81).

Negotiate to discuss or bargain to achieve agreement (143–144).

Neutrality policy of not taking sides in a war and remaining at peace (207, 638–639, 645).

Niagara Movement national organization formed in 1905 to protest the treatment of blacks (569).

Nisei Americans of Japanese descent (659).

Non-aggression pact agreement between two nations not to fight one another; Germany and Russia signed such a pact in 1939 (645).

Non-importation agreement boycott of certain goods (116).

Normal school teacher training institute (486).

Northwest Ordinance law passed by Congress in 1787 establishing the process for lands in the old Northwest Territories to become states; these states eventually included Michigan, Ohio, Indiana, Illinois, Wisconsin, and Minnesota (158).

Nullification process whereby a state declares a federal law null and void and refuses to obey its provisions (213, 266–267).

O

Olive Branch Petition resolution adopted by the Second Continental Congress in 1775 which sought reconciliation with England (131).

Omnibus bill   legislative measure composed of several major provisions (312).

Open Door policy   proposal in 1900 by Secretary of State John Hay asking the colonial powers to give up their spheres of influence in China (510–512).

Operation Overlord   code name for the largest amphibious operation in history, the Allied invasion of France on D-Day, June 6, 1944 (666).

Organization of Petroleum Exporting Countries (OPEC)   cartel of oil-producing nations that sets a fixed world price for oil (789, 792–793).

P

Pacifists   people who reject the use of force, violence, or war (79, 541).

Palestine Liberation Organization (PLO)   coalition of groups dedicated to the establishment of a national Palestinian homeland and to the destruction of Israel; also Palestinian Liberation Front (804).

Panzer   German armored division (646).

Parity price   established fair market price of farm goods which equals the prices farmers received during certain base years (621).

Partisans   members of the underground resistance movement in Nazi-held countries (665).

Patronage   practice of rewarding political supporters with a job or other political appointment (467–469).

Perjury   lying in court while testifying under oath (691).

Petition   formal document, bearing the signatures of supporters, which makes a request from a group (287).

Philanthropy   strong desire to help people, as expressed through gifts and charitable deeds (426).

Photojournalism   recording of news events on film (489).

Piedmont   inland plateau region between the Atlantic Ocean and Appalachian Mountains which spans parts of Alabama, Georgia, the Carolinas, and Virginia (62).

Planned obsolescence   policy of producing goods which will soon wear out so consumers will have to replace them with new ones (589).

Plea bargain   agreeing to plead guilty to a lesser charge in exchange for having more serious charges dropped (786).

Pocket veto   Presidential rejection of a congressional measure by failure to sign it into law (174, 360).

Political machine   political party organization, especially a local one under strong control (426–428).

Political science   science of the principles, methods, and organization of government; political scientists also study politics and politicians (263, 467).

Poll tax   fee required of voters that was used as a means of excluding blacks from political participation in elections; abolished by Twenty-fourth Amendment (193, 373).

Pomanders   perforated bags or hollow clay balls containing scented spices (71).

Pool   business unit in which several similar companies function as one by informally agreeing to abide by jointly-made decisions (413–414).

Popular sovereignty   proposal advanced by Stephen A. Douglas in 1854 that settlers decide by election whether to allow slavery in their territory—as opposed to having Congress make the decision (321).

Populism   movement begun by farmers in the 1890s who wanted a number of economic and political reforms (470–474).

Porphyria   inherited disease which produces symptoms of insanity; it is believed that King George III suffered from this disease (111).

Pragmatist   person who believes that the value of an idea is whether or not it works (607).

Predestination   Puritan belief that God had decided everything, including the fate of people after death (46).

Prejudice   opinion formed without knowing all facts; an unreasonable or irrational bias directed toward people of another race, sex, religion, or background (457–460).

Price   amount of money required to buy a product or service (710–711).

Primary source material   direct or first-hand information about a past event, such as diaries, letters, documents, journals, and so on (132, 302, 684).

Primogeniture   system which entitled the eldest son to inherit his father's entire estate (62–63).

Proprietors   owners of a colony who were granted legal rights to the property by the English monarch (53, 55).

Privateers   owners of private ships commissioned by a government at war to attack enemy ships (135, 207).

Proclamation of 1763   royal decree which commanded colonists not to settle west of the Appalachian Mountains (113).

Profit   money gained in the sale of an item or service after costs are deducted (274–275).

Prohibition   period between 1920 and 1933 when it was illegal to manufacture, sell, or transport alcoholic beverages in the United States (190, 192, 564–565).

Propaganda   doctrines, information, or ideas (often deceptive and distorted) that are spread to further one's own cause or damage that of others (321, 637).

Protectorate   nation whose government and affairs are controlled by a stonger power (506).

Public utility   company which provides a service to a community such as water, gas, telephone, or electrical power (411).

Pueblo   Spanish word for village or town; also, name of a group of Indians living in the southwestern United States (24).

Pump-priming   government spending to stimulate a sluggish economy (618).

Puppet state   satellite nation whose government is controlled by another country (635).

Q

Quarantine   period of isolation to stop the spread of a disease (388, 640).

R

Radical supporting fundamental, rapid change rather than gradual reform, especially in government; used in the 1860s to describe extreme Republicans who favored harsh punishment for the former Confederate states (345, 362–365, 457–458).

Ranchero Spanish word meaning ranch (388).

Ratify to officially approve or confirm an agreement or course of action (23, 166, 184).

Rations specified food allotment, used especially in reference to military provisions for troops (504).

Reaganomics President Ronald Reagan's economic policies, which include tax cuts and increased defense spending (813).

Rebates partial refunds or deductions from bills (414).

Recall procedure whereby voters can remove elected officials from office before their terms are completed (474, 477).

Recession temporary decline in overall business activity, usually after a period of prosperity (274–275).

Reconstruction period of enormous social upheaval following the Civil War, which saw slavery end and federal troops occupy southern states; Reconstruction is generally considered as the period from 1865 to 1876 (358).

Rediscount rate interest rate which Federal Reserve banks charge member banks as a way of regulating the amount of currency in circulation (535).

Referendum process in which voters can approve or reject bills already passed by a legislature (474, 477).

Reparations compensation, especially by a defeated country for war damages suffered by the victors (583–584).

Republic state or nation in which power is held by voting citizens and administered by elected officials (183).

Republicans members of a political party led by Thomas Jefferson and James Madison; this party was a forerunner of the current Democratic party. The Republican party of today was organized in 1854 (206–207, 325).

Reservations areas of public land set aside for use by native Americans, especially as places to live (381–383, 386, 723).

Reserved powers rights exercised by state governments which are authorized in the Constitution (164).

Resources items or supplies which can meet important needs; natural resources include timber, soil, coal, oil, gas, water, and so on (530).

Revenue sharing Nixon administration policy of returning federal funds to states for spending on programs chosen by the states (778).

Revolution drastic change of any kind, especially the violent overthrow of a government and its replacement by a new system (129–146, 770–771).

Revues variety shows which include music, dancing, skits, magic, and other specialty acts (493).

Rhineland area in western Germany which Adolf Hitler rearmed in defiance of the Versailles Treaty (637).

Rigging manipulation of the stock market with inside information to make prices go up or down (620).

Right to counsel reference to a Supreme Court decision in 1963 (*Gideon v. Wainwright*) which said that a defendant has the right to a lawyer regardless of ability to pay (198, 778).

Roosevelt Corollary declaration by President Theodore Roosevelt in 1904 that the United States would use military intervention if necessary in the affairs of any Western Hemisphere nation (593).

Rough Riders volunteer cavalry regiment organized by Theodore Roosevelt which fought in Cuba during the Spanish-American War (504–505).

Row house middle class urban home which shared walls with houses on each side and used a minimum of land (422).

Rumbullion rum liquor distilled from molasses (68).

S

Sachems chiefs who governed the Indian League of Five Nations (21).

Sanctions various penalties, usually coercive measures undertaken by a group of nations to force another nation to change its actions (637).

Scabs workers who refuse to join a union, hire out for sub-union wages, or cross strike lines to work (443).

Scalawags scoundrels; a term specifically used to describe white Southerners who joined the Republican party after the Civil War (367).

Schutzstaffel one of Adolf Hitler's private protective armies, often called the SS (636).

Secession withdrawal of a state from the Union (267, 310, 331).

Second New Deal legislative reforms begun by Franklin Roosevelt in 1935 (618).

Secondary source material indirect information about a past event, usually obtained by interviewing people who were not actually present at the event or by interpreting primary source material about the event (226).

Sectionalism placing the interests of one region ahead of the welfare of the nation as a whole (211).

Sects small religious groups that have broken away from larger established churches (97).

Segregation practice of requiring races or groups to remain separate from each other, such as in living areas, schools, and so on (373, 719–722).

Self-determination belief in the right of national groups to decide for themselves what nation they want to be part of (553).

Senate upper branch of the legislature of the United States or of various individual states (163, 171).

Seniority status or privilege accorded to a person for length of service on the job (532).

Separatists persecuted Protestants who separated themselves entirely from the Anglican Church and formed their own independent congregations (47).

Settlement houses community centers, often in slum areas, where immigrants and poor people could obtain help from volunteer reformers (430).

Sharecropping southern agricultural arrangement that developed after the Civil War in which farm workers were loaned land, tools, and seed in exchange for giving a share of the harvest to the landowner (366).

Skyscrapers multistory urban buildings made possible by new construction techniques and the invention of the elevator (428).

Sit-down strike strike conducted within a place of business so that scabs cannot be brought in as strikebreakers (625).

Sit-in tactic of the civil rights movement whereby demonstrators occupied a public facility until it was desegregated (746).

Social gospel belief that churches should work to improve conditions for workers and the poor (523).

Socialism political system in which the government controls the means of production (rather then private individuals or companies) and makes major economic decisions (448–449, 525).

Socialist party political party founded in 1901 whose members favor, among other things, abolition of capitalism and state ownership of the means of production (525).

Sociology science of human society and of social relations, values, organizations, and changes (237, 817).

Soddy prairie home with walls made of turf strips chopped into blocks and stacked like bricks (394).

Sovereign supreme or superior to all others; monarch or ruler who possesses sovereign power (155).

Space shuttle reuseable vehicle designed to take off like a rocket, orbit the earth like a spacecraft, and land on earth like an airplane (811–812).

Speakeasies bars where liquor was sold illegally during Prohibition (565).

Specie gold and silver coin (270).

Speculation engagement in a risky business venture with the hope of substantial future profits (103).

Spheres of influence geographical areas in which a strong nation exercises power or can make its influence felt (510).

Spoils system practice whereby incoming political victors replace old appointees with their own bureaucratic choices (263, 467).

Sputnik I first unmanned space satellite launched in 1957 by the Soviet Union (728).

Square Deal phrase used by President Theodore Roosevelt to describe the motive underlying his basic programs (528–531).

Stagflation economic condition in which inflation accompanies sluggish business activity and increased unemployment (799).

Stalemate standoff or deadlock in which neither side gains a victory (703).

Staple crop chief or one of several important commodities regularly grown and sold in a particular area (54).

State interposition another name for nullification of a federal law by a state (720).

States' rights all powers not granted to the federal government by the Constitution nor denied to state governments; also, belief of some that states had the right to secede (260, 265–267, 682).

Status position or rank in society (288).

Steerage cargo holds of a ship, where poor immigrants often traveled during the ocean voyage to the United States (454).

Strategic hamlet program attempt in the early 1960s by the South Vietnamese government to relocate entire villages behind barriers safe from communist attacks (744).

Strategy overall plan, especially relating to a military operation (356–357).

Sturmabteilung one of Adolf Hitler's private armies, often called storm troopers (636).

Subpoena legal summons which orders a person to appear in court in order to testify (786).

Subsidiaries companies owned by another company (413).

Suburbia area consisting of outlying municipalities surrounding a city (715).

Subversive tending to overthrow or destroy the existing order (690).

Sudetenland mountainous region in Czechoslovakia bordering Germany which was annexed by Germany in 1938 (640–641).

Suffrage right to vote (191, 478, 566).

Sweatshop system manufacture of goods under difficult working conditions, usually in a crowded tenement room by employees paid by the piece (437–438, 445–446).

T

Tabloids small, easy-to-read newspapers which often feature sensational news items, bold headlines, and many pictures (572–573).

Tammany Hall Democratic political machine which controlled New York City's municipal government during the late nineteenth century (426–428).

Tariffs taxes on goods imported from foreign countries (469).

Tax required payment, often a percentage of income or property value, used to finance the operations of government (126–127).

Technology practical application of scientific knowledge (401, 730).

Telegraph communication device in which messages are transmitted by electric impulses in the form of coded signals (279, 401).

Tenant farming agricultural arrangement in which a worker farms another person's land as part of his rent payment (366).

Tenements   multi-family apartments in which urban poor often endure unsafe, unsanitary, and overcrowded conditions (422).

Tenochtitlan   ancient Aztec capital now known as Mexico City (29).

Theology   study of God and religious issues (50).

Tidewater   area of eastern Virginia that is located primarily along the James, Potomac, Rappahannock, and York rivers (48, 49).

Tierra   Spanish word for land (27).

Townshend Acts   series of revenue measures passed by Parliament in 1767 which taxed glass, lead, paints, paper, and tea that was imported into the American colonies (116–117).

Townsend Plan   scheme devised during the Great Depression to pay elderly people $200 a month (622–623).

Truman Doctrine   policy of giving economic and military aid to nations threatened by armed minorities or outside groups (686–687).

Trust   combination of corporations in the same industry whose stockholders entrust their stock to trustees in exchange for trust certificates and dividends, thus reducing competition (414).

Two-party system   practice of having candidates compete for office through the machinery of two rival political parties (260).

U

Underground railroad   system comprised of a network of people in various locations who sheltered runaway slaves and helped route them north to freedom (285).

Unicameral   legislature having only one house (56).

Union   association of workers to promote and protect the welfare, interests, and rights of its members (434, 438–446).

Unterseeboot   German word for submarine, also called a U-boat (543).

Urban   referring to a city or town with a population exceeding 2500 (421).

V

Vaqueros   Spanish word meaning people who work with cows; cowboys (388).

Veto   power of an executive to refuse to sign a bill, thus preventing it from becoming a law (174).

Victory gardens   name given to vegetable gardens grown by Americans during World War I so more food could be sent to people and troops in Europe (548–549).

Vietnamization   President Nixon's plan for gradually withdrawing American troops and letting the South Vietnamese do most of the fighting (781–782).

Virginia dynasty   phrase referring to the fact that four of the nation's first five presidents were Virginians (232).

Vocational education   courses designed to train students in practical job skills (486).

W

Waltham (Lowell) system   practice of providing chaperoned, boardinghouse accommodations for female mill workers during the early nineteenth century (252–253).

Whig party   originally a British political party, the Whig party emerged in the United States in opposition to the policies of Andrew Jackson. Eventually the Whig party in the United States disintegrated and was replaced by the Republican party (119, 272, 308).

Women's liberation   post World War II women's movement aimed primarily at greater economic and political equality (765).

Women's party   political party founded in 1914 whose members favored suffrage for women (565–566).

X

XYZ Affair   incident in 1797 in which three French agents demanded a bribe from three American envoys as a condition for negotiations. When made public, the affair led to an undeclared naval war with France (211–212).

Y

Yellow-dog contract   pledge required of new employees not to join a union (439).

Yellow journalism   practice of selling newspapers by overemphasizing sensational news events; first practiced during the Spanish-American War by Joseph Pulitzer and William Randolph Hearst (489–490).

Map of the World

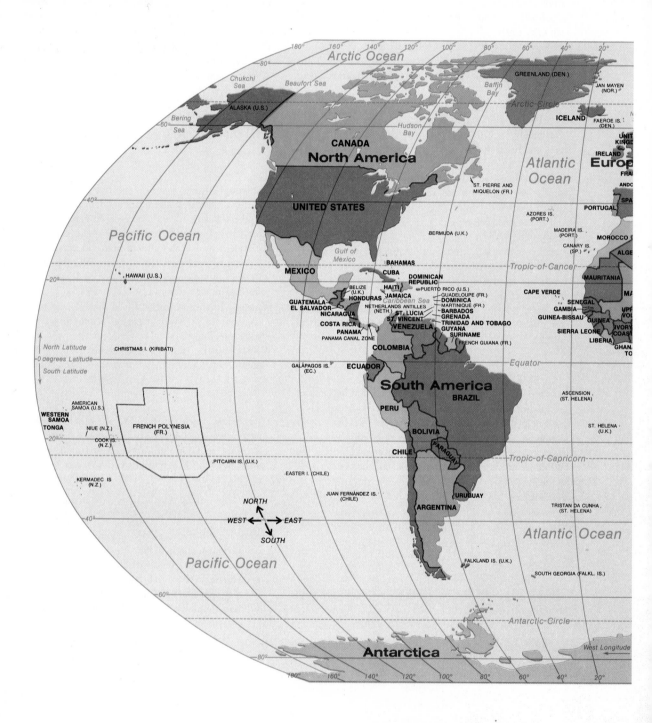

MAP LEGEND

CANADA   Country name (independent political unit)

GUAM (U.S.)   Other political name

AREA SCALE (AT EQUATOR)

This square shows area on map equal to 100,000 square kilometers (40,000 square miles)

1:120,000,000

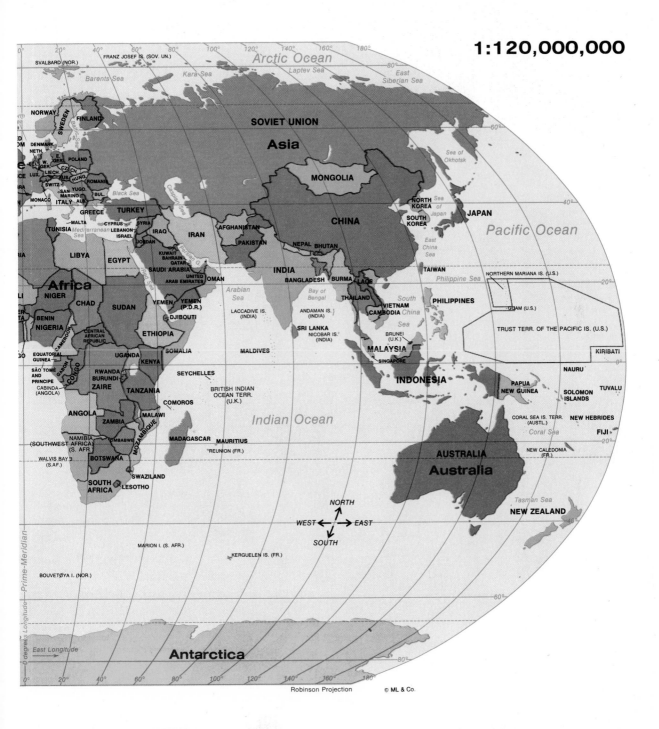

Robinson Projection   © ML & Co.

DISTANCE SCALE (AT EQUATOR)

0 Kilometers	2000	4000	6000	8000	10000	12000	14000	16000	18000
0 Miles		2000		4000		6000		8000	10000

Map of the United States

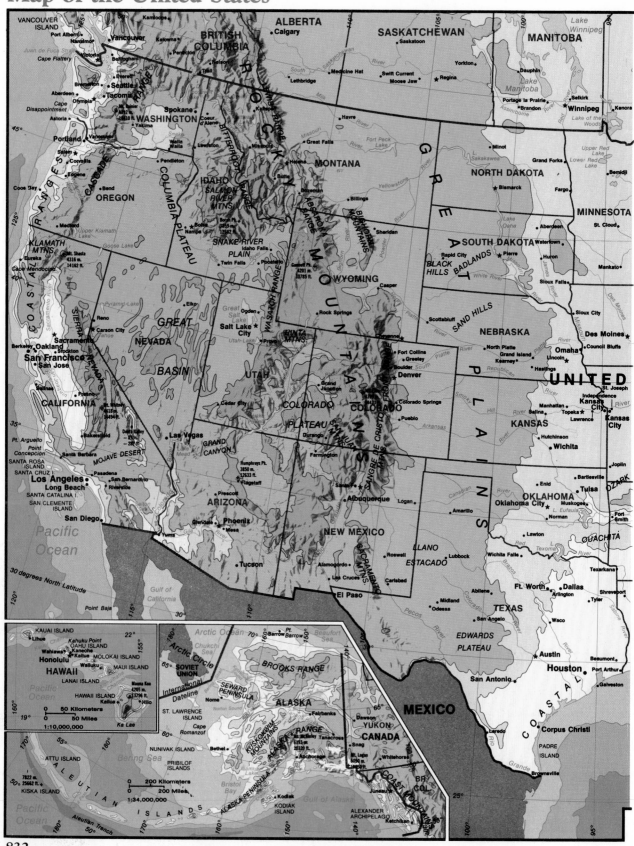

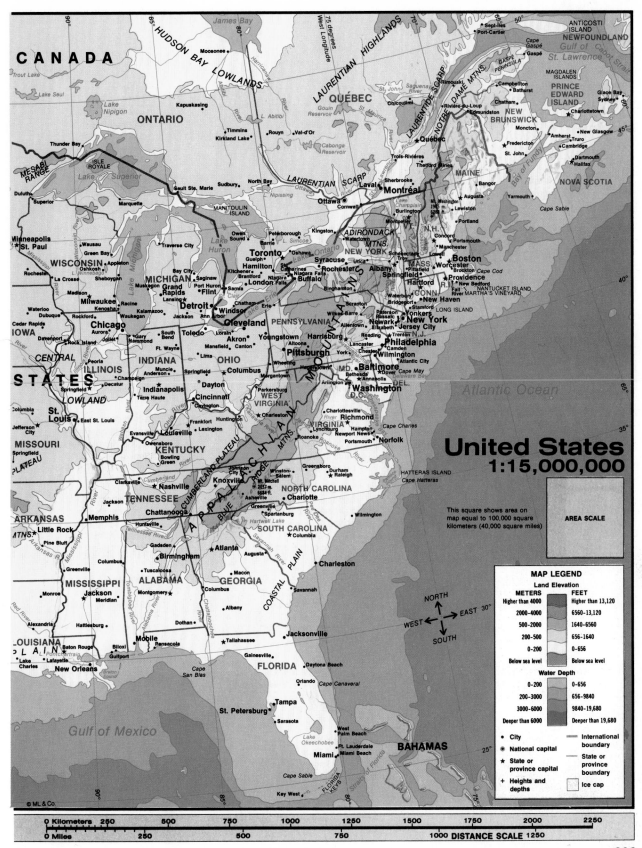

United States
1:15,000,000

This square shows area on
map equal to 100,000 square
kilometers (40,000 square miles)

AREA SCALE

MAP LEGEND

Land Elevation

METERS	FEET
Higher than 4000	Higher than 13,120
2000–4000	6560–13,120
500–2000	1640–6560
200–500	656–1640
0–200	0–656
Below sea level	Below sea level

Water Depth

0–200	0–656
200–3000	656–9840
3000–6000	9840–19,680
Deeper than 6000	Deeper than 19,680

- • City
- ◎ National capital
- ★ State or province capital
- + Heights and depths

- —— International boundary
- — State or province boundary
- ▢ Ice cap

NORTH
WEST — EAST 30°
SOUTH

© ML & Co.

0 Kilometers	250	500	750	1000	1250	1500	1750	2000	2250

0 Miles	250	500	750	1000 **DISTANCE SCALE** 1250

Facts About the States

1980 Census Figures

Alabama
Montgomery
3,890,061 people
51,609 square miles
Rank in Area: 29
Entered Union in 1819

Georgia
Atlanta
5,464,265 people
58,876 square miles
Rank in Area: 21
Entered Union in 1788

Maine
Augusta
1,124,660 people
33,215 square miles
Rank in Area: 39
Entered Union in 1820

Alaska
Juneau
400,481 people
589,757 square miles
Rank in Area: 1
Entered Union in 1959

Hawaii
Honolulu
965,000 people
6,450 square miles
Rank in Area: 47
Entered Union in 1959

Maryland
Annapolis
4,216,446 people
10,577 square miles
Rank in Area: 42
Entered Union in 1788

Arizona
Phoenix
2,717,866 people
113,909 square miles
Rank in Area: 6
Entered Union in 1912

Idaho
Boise
943,935 people
83,557 square miles
Rank in Area: 13
Entered Union in 1890

Massachusetts
Boston
5,737,037 people
8,257 square miles
Rank in Area: 45
Entered Union in 1788

Arkansas
Little Rock
2,285,513 people
53,104 square miles
Rank in Area: 27
Entered Union in 1836

Illinois
Springfield
11,418,461 people
56,400 square miles
Rank in Area: 24
Entered Union in 1818

Michigan
Lansing
9,258,344 people
58,216 square miles
Rank in Area: 23
Entered Union in 1837

California
Sacramento
23,668,562 people
158,693 square miles
Rank in Area: 3
Entered Union in 1850

Indiana
Indianapolis
5,490,179 people
36,291 square miles
Rank in Area: 38
Entered Union in 1816

Minnesota
St. Paul
4,077,148 people
84,068 square miles
Rank in Area: 12
Entered Union in 1858

Colorado
Denver
2,888,834 people
104,247 square miles
Rank in Area: 8
Entered Union in 1876

Iowa
Des Moines
2,913,387 people
56,290 square miles
Rank in Area: 25
Entered Union in 1846

Mississippi
Jackson
2,520,638 people
47,716 square miles
Rank in Area: 32
Entered Union in 1817

Connecticut
Hartford
3,107,576 people
5,009 square miles
Rank in Area: 48
Entered Union in 1788

Kansas
Topeka
2,363,208 people
82,264 square miles
Rank in Area: 14
Entered Union in 1861

Missouri
Jefferson City
4,917,444 people
69,686 square miles
Rank in Area: 19
Entered Union in 1821

Delaware
Dover
595,225 people
2,057 square miles
Rank in Area: 49
Entered Union in 1787

Kentucky
Frankfort
3,661,433 people
40,395 square miles
Rank in Area: 37
Entered Union in 1792

Montana
Helena
786,690 people
147,138 square miles
Rank in Area: 4
Entered Union in 1889

Florida
Tallahassee
9,739,992 people
58,560 square miles
Rank in Area: 22
Entered Union in 1845

Louisiana
Baton Rouge
4,203,972 people
48,523 square miles
Rank in Area: 31
Entered Union in 1812

Nebraska
Lincoln
1,570,006 people
77,227 square miles
Rank in Area: 15
Entered Union in 1867

Nevada
799,184 people
110,540 square miles
Rank in Area: 7
Entered Union in 1864

New Hampshire
920,610 people
9,304 square miles
Rank in Area: 44
Entered Union in 1788

New Jersey
7,364,158 people
7,836 square miles
Rank in Area: 46
Entered Union in 1787

New Mexico
1,299,968 people
121,666 square miles
Rank in Area: 5
Entered Union in 1912

New York
17,557,288 people
49,576 square miles
Rank in Area: 30
Entered Union in 1788

North Carolina
5,874,429 people
52,586 square miles
Rank in Area: 28
Entered Union in 1789

North Dakota
652,695 people
70,665 square miles
Rank in Area: 17
Entered Union in1889

Ohio
10,797,419 people
41,222 square miles
Rank in Area: 35
Entered Union in 1803

Oklahoma
3,025,266 people
69,919 square miles
Rank in Area: 18
Entered Union in 1907

Oregon
2,632,663 people
96,981 square miles
Rank in Area: 10
Entered Union in 1859

Pennsylvania
11,866,728 people
45,333 square miles
Rank in Area: 33
Entered Union in 1787

Rhode Island
947,154 people
1,214 square miles
Rank in Area: 50
Entered Union in 1790

South Carolina
3,119,208 people
31,055 square miles
Rank in Area: 40
Entered Union in 1788

South Dakota
690,178 people
77,047 square miles
Rank in Area: 16
Entered Union in 1889

Tennessee
4,590,750 people
42,244 square miles
Rank in Area: 34
Entered Union in 1796

Texas
14,228,383 people
267,336 square miles
Rank in Area: 2
Entered Union in 1845

Utah
1,461,037 people
84,916 square miles
Rank in Area: 11
Entered Union in 1896

Vermont
511,456 people
9,609 square miles
Rank in Area: 43
Entered Union in 1791

Virginia
5,346,279 people
40,817 square miles
Rank in Area: 36
Entered Union in 1788

Washington
4,130,163 people
68,192 square miles
Rank in Area: 20
Entered Union in 1889

West Virginia
1,949,644 people
24,181 square miles
Rank in Area: 41
Entered Union in 1863

Wisconsin
4,705,335 people
56,154 square miles
Rank in Area: 26
Entered Union in 1848

Wyoming
470 816 people
97,914 square miles
Rank in Area: 9
Entered Union in 1890

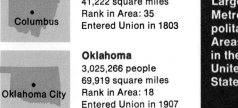

Largest Metropolitan Areas in the United States	Metropolitan Area	Population
	1. New York City, New York—New Jersey	9,119,737
	2. Los Angeles—Long Beach, California	7,477,657
	3. Chicago, Illinois	7,102.328
	4. Philadelphia, Pennsylvania—New Jersey	4,716,818
	5. Detroit, Michigan	4,352,762
	6. San Francisco—Oakland, California	3,252,721
	7. Washington, D.C.—Maryland—Virginia	3,060,240
	8. Dallas—Fort Worth, Texas	2,974,878
	9. Houston, Texas	2,905,350
	10. Boston, Massachusetts	2,763,357

Presents of the United States

1.
George Washington
1789–1797
No Political Party
Birthplace: Virginia
Born: February 22, 1732
Died: December 14, 1799

8.
Martin Van Buren
1837–1841
Democrat
Birthplace: New York
Born: December 5, 1782
Died: July 24, 1862

15.
James Buchanan
1857–1861
Democrat
Birthplace: Pennsylvania
Born: April 23, 1791
Died: June 1, 1868

2.
John Adams
1797–1801
Federalist
Birthplace: Massachusetts
Born: October 30, 1735
Died: July 4, 1826

9.
William H. Harrison
1841
Whig
Birthplace: Virginia
Born: February 9, 1773
Died: April 4, 1841

16.
Abraham Lincoln
1861–1865
Republican
Birthplace: Kentucky
Born: February 12, 1809
Died: April 15, 1865

3.
Thomas Jefferson
1801–1809
Democratic-Republican
Birthplace: Virginia
Born: April 13, 1743
Died: July 4, 1826

10.
John Tyler
1841–1845
Whig
Birthplace: Virginia
Born: March 29, 1790
Died: January 18, 1862

17.
Andrew Johnson
1865–1869
Democrat
Birthplace: North Carolina
Born: December 29, 1808
Died: July 31, 1875

4.
James Madison
1809–1817
Democratic-Republican
Birthplace: Virginia
Born: March 16, 1751
Died: June 28, 1836

11.
James K. Polk
1845–1849
Democrat
Birthplace: North Carolina
Born: November 2, 1795
Died: June 15, 1849

18.
Ulysses S. Grant
1869–1877
Republican
Birthplace: Ohio
Born: April 27, 1822
Died: July 23, 1885

5.
James Monroe
1817–1825
Democratic-Republican
Birthplace: Virginia
Born: April 28, 1758
Died: July 4, 1831

12.
Zachary Taylor
1849–1850
Whig
Birthplace: Virginia
Born: November 24, 1784
Died: July 9, 1850

19.
Rutherford B. Hayes
1877–1881
Republican
Birthplace: Ohio
Born: October 4, 1822
Died: January 17, 1893

6.
John Quincy Adams
1825–1829
Democratic-Republican
Birthplace: Massachusetts
Born: July 11, 1767
Died: February 23, 1848

13.
Millard Fillmore
1850–1853
Whig
Birthplace: New York
Born: January 7, 1800
Died: March 8, 1874

20.
James A. Garfield
1881
Republican
Birthplace: Ohio
Born: November 19, 1831
Died: September 19, 1881

7.
Andrew Jackson
1829–1837
Democrat
Birthplace: South Carolina
Born: March 15, 1767
Died: June 8, 1845

14.
Franklin Pierce
1853–1857
Democrat
Birthplace: New Hampshire
Born: November 23, 1804
Died: October 8, 1869

21.
Chester A. Arthur
1881–1885
Republican
Birthplace: Vermont
Born: October 5, 1829
Died: November 8, 1886

22, 24.
Grover Cleveland
1885–1889, 1893–1897
Democrat
Birthplace: New Jersey
Born: March 18, 1837
Died: June 24, 1908

23.
Benjamin Harrison
1889–1893
Republican
Birthplace: Ohio
Born: August 20, 1833
Died: March 13, 1901

25.
William McKinley
1897–1901
Republican
Birthplace: Ohio
Born: January 29, 1843
Died: September 14, 1901

26.
Theodore Roosevelt
1901–1909
Republican
Birthplace: New York
Born: October 27, 1858
Died: January 6, 1919

27.
William H. Taft
1909–1913
Republican
Birthplace: Ohio
Born: September 15, 1857
Died: March 8, 1930

28.
Woodrow Wilson
1913–1921
Democrat
Birthplace: Virginia
Born: December 29, 1856
Died: February 3, 1924

29.
Warren G. Harding
1921–1923
Republican
Birthplace: Ohio
Born: November 2, 1865
Died: August 2, 1923

30.
Calvin Coolidge
1923–1929
Republican
Birthplace: Vermont
Born: July 4, 1872
Died: January 5, 1933

31.
Herbert C. Hoover
1929–1933
Republican
Birthplace: Iowa
Born: August 10, 1874
Died: October 20, 1964

32.
Franklin D. Roosevelt
1933–1945
Democrat
Birthplace: New York
Born: January 30, 1882
Died: April 12, 1945

33.
Harry S Truman
1945–1953
Democrat
Birthplace: Missouri
Born: May 8, 1884
Died: December 26, 1972

34.
Dwight D. Eisenhower
1953–1961
Republican
Birthplace: Texas
Born: October 14, 1890
Died: March 28, 1969

35.
John F. Kennedy
1961–1963
Democrat
Birthplace: Massachusetts
Born: May 29, 1917
Died: November 22, 1963

36.
Lyndon B. Johnson
1963–1969
Democrat
Birthplace: Texas
Born: August 27, 1908
Died: January 22, 1973

37.
Richard M. Nixon
1969–1974
Republican
Birthplace: California
Born: January 9, 1913

38.
Gerald R. Ford
1974–1977
Republican
Birthplace: Nebraska
Born: July 14, 1913

39.
James E. Carter, Jr.
1977–1981
Democrat
Birthplace: Georgia
Born: October 1, 1924

40.
Ronald W. Reagan
1981–
Republican
Birthplace: Illinois
Born: February 6, 1911

Recent Statistical Trends in the United States

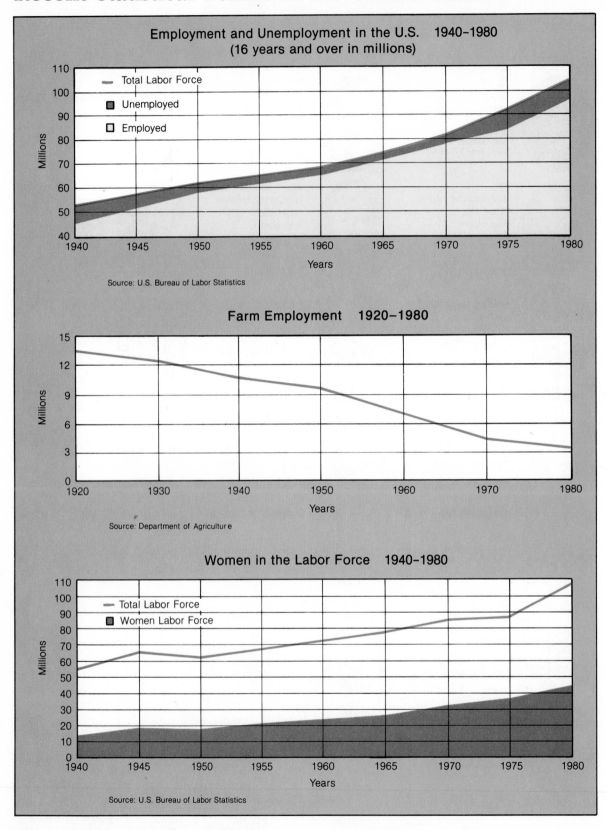

Employment and Unemployment in the U.S.   1940–1980
(16 years and over in millions)

- Total Labor Force
- Unemployed
- Employed

Millions

Years

Source: U.S. Bureau of Labor Statistics

Farm Employment   1920–1980

Millions

Years

Source: Department of Agriculture

Women in the Labor Force   1940–1980

- Total Labor Force
- Women Labor Force

Millions

Years

Source: U.S. Bureau of Labor Statistics

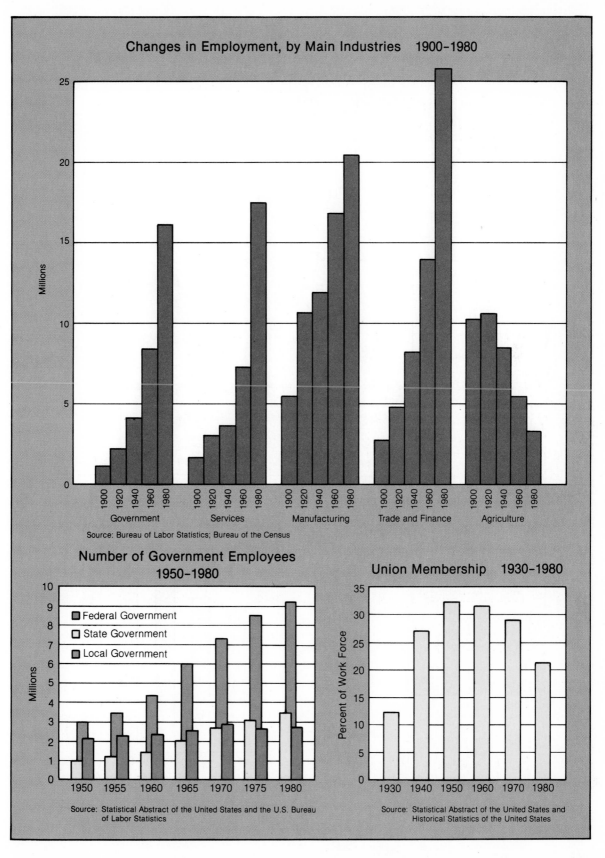

Changes in Employment, by Main Industries   1900–1980

Millions

Government   Services   Manufacturing   Trade and Finance   Agriculture

1900 1920 1940 1960 1980

Source: Bureau of Labor Statistics; Bureau of the Census

Number of Government Employees 1950–1980

Millions

■ Federal Government
□ State Government
■ Local Government

1950 1955 1960 1965 1970 1975 1980

Source: Statistical Abstract of the United States and the U.S. Bureau of Labor Statistics

Union Membership   1930–1980

Percent of Work Force

1930 1940 1950 1960 1970 1980

Source: Statistical Abstract of the United States and Historical Statistics of the United States

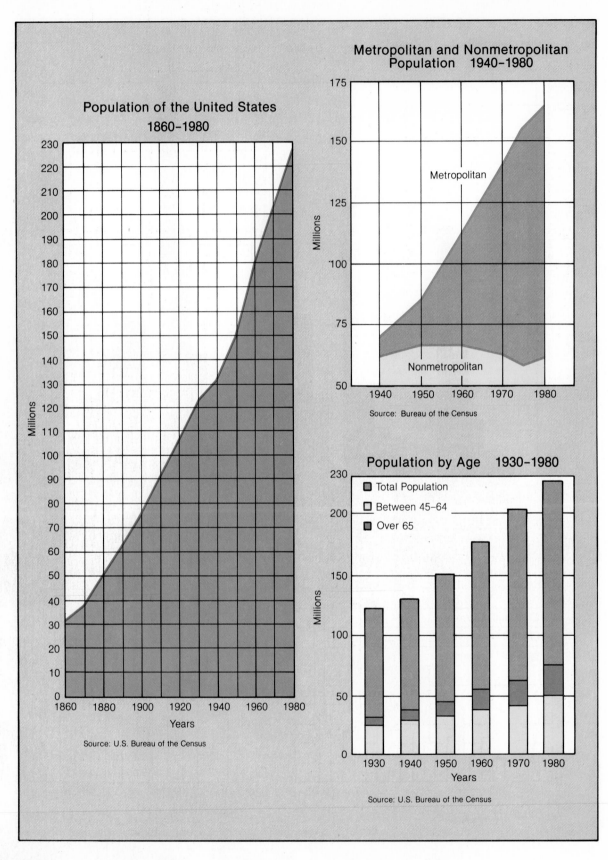

Population of the United States
1860–1980

Source: U.S. Bureau of the Census

Metropolitan and Nonmetropolitan
Population   1940–1980

Metropolitan

Nonmetropolitan

Source: Bureau of the Census

Population by Age   1930–1980

☐ Total Population
☐ Between 45–64
☐ Over 65

Source: U.S. Bureau of the Census

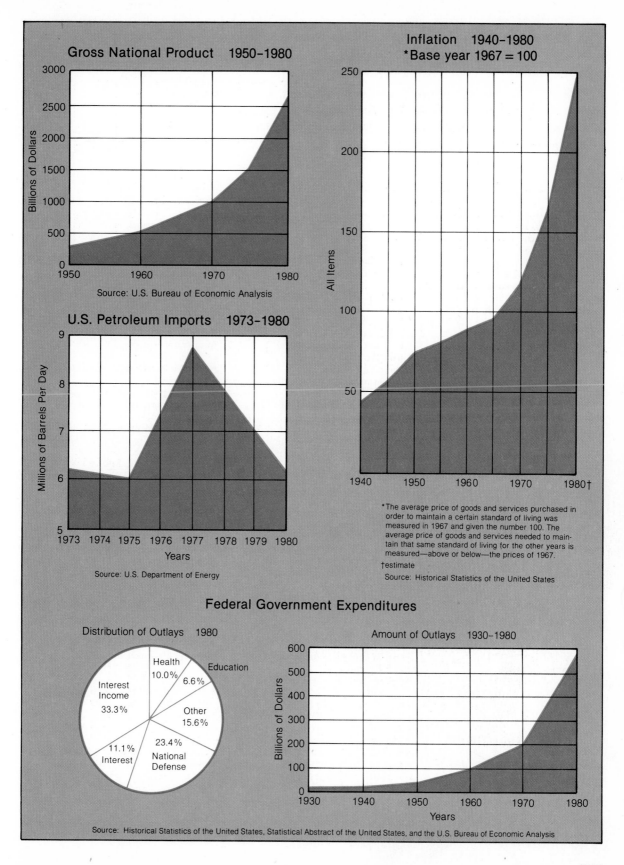

Gross National Product   1950–1980

Billions of Dollars

3000
2500
2000
1500
1000
500
0

1950   1960   1970   1980

Source: U.S. Bureau of Economic Analysis

U.S. Petroleum Imports   1973–1980

Millions of Barrels Per Day

9
8
7
6
5

1973 1974 1975 1976 1977 1978 1979 1980

Years

Source: U.S. Department of Energy

Inflation   1940–1980
*Base year 1967 = 100

All Items

250
200
150
100
50

1940   1950   1960   1970   1980†

*The average price of goods and services purchased in order to maintain a certain standard of living was measured in 1967 and given the number 100. The average price of goods and services needed to maintain that same standard of living for the other years is measured—above or below—the prices of 1967.

†estimate

Source: Historical Statistics of the United States

Federal Government Expenditures

Distribution of Outlays   1980

Health 10.0%
Education 6.6%
Interest Income 33.3%
Other 15.6%
Interest 11.1%
National Defense 23.4%

Amount of Outlays   1930–1980

Billions of Dollars

600
500
400
300
200
100
0

1930   1940   1950   1960   1970   1980

Years

Source: Historical Statistics of the United States, Statistical Abstract of the United States, and the U.S. Bureau of Economic Analysis

Index

An asterisk (*) indicates that there is a picture or photograph, and usually text information as well, on that page. When a word is defined in the text, the page number is underlined. An *m* or *c* following a page reference indicates a map or chart. References to other entries in the index are italicized.

A

Abolition movement, 283–285, 483
  opposition to, 286–287
Absolute monarch, 53
Acheson, Dean, 699
Adams, Abigail, 128, 132, 216
Adams, John, 128, 216, 816*, 836*
  and Second Continental Congress, 129, 132
  and 1783 Treaty of Paris, 143
  as first ambassador to Great Britain, 159
  as a nationalist, 161, 210–214, 212*
  death of, 259, 816
Adams, John Quincy, 232, 234, 245, 246, 258, 259–260, 836*
Adams, Samuel, 110, 117, 118, 120, 160
Adams, Sherman, 706
Adams–Onis, Treaty of, 233m, 234
Adapters, 14, 19m, 19–21
Addams, Jane, 37, 420, 430*
Administration of Justice Act (1774), 121
Admiralty court, 85, 114
Advertising, 278, 489, 589–590
Afghanistan, 830–831m
  Soviet invasion of, 805–806, 812
Africa, 830–831m
  as source of slaves for America, 64–68
  slave trade routes from, 65m
  slavery in, 66
  in World War II, 664
Age of Enlightenment, 92–95
Aged, 758, 768
Agnew, Spiro, 772, 786
Agriculture,
  "Dust Bowl," 399
  family farming, 69–70
  and Farmers' Alliance, 472
  and Farm Loan Act, 535
  and government price supports, 591, 707–708
  and Great Depression, 601
  inventions in, 277–278, 395–396
  and populist movement, 470–474
  sharecropping, 366
  tenant farming, 366
  during World War II, 661
Agriculture Act (1954), 707–708
Agriculture Adjustment Act (1933), 614, 616, 621
Aguinaldo, Emilio, 504, 509

Aix-la-Chapelle, Treaty of, 103
Alabama, 230, 249, 331, 573m, 763, 834mc
Alabama claims, 345
Alamo, Battle of, 297m, 297*–298
Alaska, 246, 247, 376m, 427, 499, 712, 760, 793, 834mc
Albany Congress, 104–105
Aldridge, Ira, 493
Alger, Horatio, Jr., 415–416*
Algonquin, 14, 21–23, 22*
  relations with early settlers, 40–41, 78
Alien and Sedition Acts (1798), 212–213
Alien Land Law (1913), 460
Aliens, *See Immigrants*
Alliance for Progress, 745
Amendments to the Constitution, 186–194
  Bill of Rights, 186–188, 201–202, 206, 432
  Fourteenth, 189–190, 363, 478
  Fifteenth, 190, 365, 478
  Sixteenth, 190, 535
  Seventeenth, 190, 527
  Eighteenth, 190–191, 566
  Nineteenth, 191, 566
  Twentieth, 191–192, 605–606
  Twenty-first, 192, 564–565
  Twenty-second, 192, 735
  Twenty-third, 192–193, 780
  Twenty-fifth, 193–194, 708
American Antislavery Society, 285
American Civil Liberties Union (ACLU), 564
American Colonization Society, 284
American Federation of Labor (AFL), 441–442, 446c
American Independent party, 777
American party, 324, 458
American Protective Association (APA), 458
American Railway Union (ARU), 442, 443–444
American Revolution, *See Revolutionary War*
Americans, Native, *See Indians*
American Stock Exchange (AMEX), 596
American Sugar Refining Company, 415
American System, 241–243
American Temperance Society, 283
Americas, 16m, 28m
Amnesty, 137, 359–360, 370, 819
Anarchists, 580
Anasazi, 23–24

Anderson, John B., 807, 808
Anderson, Marian, 626, 627*
Anderson, Robert, 337
Andropov, Yuri, 813
Andros, Sir Edmund, 76, 82*, 83
Anglican Church, *See Church of England*
Annapolis Convention, 161
Anthony, Susan B., 37, 466, 478–479*
Anti-Catholicism, 324, 458
Antietam, Battle of, 344, 344m, 345
Antifederalists, 166
Antilynching law, 569–570
Anti-Masonic party, 265
Antin, Mary, 485
Antipoverty programs, 739, 740, 756, 758, 778
Antislavery movement, *See Abolition movement*
Antitrust legislation, *See Trusts*
Antiwar protests, 761*, 774–776, 782
Apache, 19m, 24
Appalachian Mountains, 112m, 113, 221–222, 276, 356, 758, 822–823m
Appomattox Court House, 353*, 354m
Arbitration, 21, 440, 819
Architecture, 493–494
Area Redevelopment Act (1961), 739
Argentina, 812
Arizona, 29, 307m, 407, 754, 756, 768, 801m, 811, 834mc
Arkansas, 292, 338, 357m, 658–659*, 834mc
Armstrong, Neil A., 779
Arnold, Benedict, 128, 130–131, 138
Aroostook War, 301
Arthur, Chester A, 468–469, 836*
Articles of Confederation, 155, 157–158, 163
Artifacts, 42, 819
Artisans, 66–67, 819
Assembly line production, 588, 612
Astronauts, 740, 779, 811–812*
Asylums, 282–283
Atlantic Charter, 656
Atomic bomb, 662–663, 671
Atomic Energy Act (1954), 707
Atomic Energy Commission (AEC), 682, 686
Attucks, Crispus, 118
Austin, Stephen, 296, 388
Austria, 541, 555m, 558m, 640
Automobiles, 588–589, 730*
  American dependence on, 714
  attack on industry by Ralph Nadar, 768

E

F

Methodists, 97
Mexico, 16m, 29, 30m, 800
    French in, 516
    revolution in, 517–518
    and Texas, 296–298
    and war with U.S., 304–308, 305m
Mexican-Americans, 627, 722–723, 800
Meyers, Isaac, 434, 439
Miami Confederacy, 210
Michigan, 32, 158m, 231m, 242m, 589, 786, 834mc
Middle East, 813
    Cold War in, 726
    Egypt-Israeli peace negotiations, 803–804, 804m
    Iran-Iraq war, 806
    and OPEC, 792–793, 798–799
    revolution in Iran, 804–805
    Soviet invasion of Afghanistan, 805–806
Midway, Battle of, 669
Migration,
    of blacks to North, 568–569
    of early people, 14–18, 16m
    forced, of slaves, 250
    to suburbs, 713–714
    to "sun belt," 801
Miller, Elizabeth Smith, 288
Mills, See Factories
Mindszenty, Joseph Cardinal, 725
Miner, Myrtilla, 288
Mining industry, 405m, 405–406, 590
Minnesota, 292, 393m, 405, 405m, 411, 526, 797, 834mc
Minow, Newton, 717
Minutemen, 122
Miranda v. Arizona (1966), 198–199, 778
Mississippi, 19, 249, 331, 343m, 747–748, 834mc
Mississippi River, 20, 20m, 209, 232, 292–293*, 343m
Missouri, 247m, 248, 322, 338–339, 679, 834mc
Missouri Compromise, 247m, 248, 322
Mitchell, John, 784, 785, 787, See also Watergate
Mitchell, Margaret, 629
Model Cities program, 758
Molasses, 68
Moley, Raymond, 607
Molly Pitcher, 135*, 136
Molotov, V. M., 685
Mondale, Walter F., 797, 814
Monitor, 341–342
"Monkey trial," 563*–564
Monroe, James, 240, 241, 245–248, 836*
Monroe Doctrine, 246*–247, 555, 593, 812
    Roosevelt Corollary to, 516*, 593
Montana, 32, 385, 386m, 398, 399m, 834mc
Montcalm, Louis Joseph de, 106
Morgan, J. Pierpont, 475
Mormon Trail, 299m
Mormons, 303–304*

Morrill Act (1861), 348
Morrill Land Grant Act (1862), 348
Morris, Robert, 136
Morse, Samuel F. B., 279, 401
Mother Jones, See Jones, Mary Harris
Motion pictures, 390, 571–572, 717–718
Mott, Lucretia, 287, 289
Mound-building, 19–20, 22
Mount Holyoke Female Seminary, 288*
Mount St. Helens, 676, 677m
Muckrakers, 524–525
Mulberry Castle, 53
Mullaney, Kate, 439
Muller v. Oregon, 527
Multinational corporations, 652–653, 652m
Munich Pact, 642
Munn v. Illinois, 412
Murrow, Edward R., 642
Muskie, Edmund S., 776
Mussolini, Benito, 634, 636, 642, 664–665
My Lai, 782

N

Nader, Ralph, 768
Napoleon I, 223, 245
Napoleon III, 516
Narragansett Indians, 77, 78
Narvaez, Panfilo de, 29, 30m
Nasser, Gamal Abdel, 726
Nast, Thomas, 427
National Aeronautics and Space Administration (NASA), 740
National Association for the Advancement of Colored People (NAACP), 569, 570, 719
National Colored Labor Union (NCLU), 439
National Congress of American Indians, 729
National Gazette, 206
National Grange, 411–412, 523*
National Industrial Recovery Act (1933), 617, 621
National Labor Relations Act, See Wagner Act
National Labor Union (NLU), 438–439
National Organization for Women (NOW), 767, 801
National Origins Act (1924), 585, 758–759
National Peoples party, 472–473
National Recovery Administration (NRA), 617*–618
National Road, 242m, 243
National Security Council, 680
National Socialist German Workers' (Nazi) party, 635–636
National Union party, 353
National War Labor Board, 548, 660
Nationalism, 240, 241, 825
Nativism, 324, 452–460, 584–585
Natural resources, 88, 256, 292, 376, 398–399, 405–406, 405m, 730

conservation of, 530–531, 532
development of, 376, 616–617, 630, 792, 793, 798
Natural rights, laws of, 94
Natural selection, 415
Navajo, 19m, 24
Navigation Acts (1660, 1663), 81, 85
Nazi party, See National Socialist German Workers' party
Nebraska, 321–322, 386m, 398, 399m, 408, 834mc
Neutrality Acts (1935, 1936, 1937, 1939), 638–639, 645
Nevada, 405m, 491, 835mc
New Amsterdam, 52*–53, 52m
Newbold, Charles, 277
New Deal, 418, 607–610, 615–628, 622c
New England, 68–70, 71–72, 99, 227, 232, 243, 252–253, 282, 807
New Hampshire, 51, 55c, 244–245, 706, 835mc
New Harmony, 283
New Jersey, 55c, 72, 137m, 138, 245, 835mc
New Jersey Plan, 163
Newlands Reclamation Act, 530–531
New Mexico, 24*, 29, 299, 308, 386m, 405m, 520, 835mc
New Netherland, 51m
New Orleans, Battle of, 230–231, 231m
Newport, Christopher, 39
New Sweden, 51m
Newton, Sir Isaac, 93–94
New World civilizations, 18
New York, 51–52, 55c, 84, 136–137, 139m, 157, 245, 253–254, 423, 453, 768, 773, 835mc
New York City, 253–254*, 269–270, 427–428, 456, 573–574, 596–597
New York Stock Exchange, 596*–597, 597c
Ngo Dinh Diem, 727, 734, 744, 750
Niagara Movement, 569
Nicaragua, 517, 521, 803, 814
Nicholson, Francis, 84
Nimitz, Chester W., 670
Nine-Power Treaty, 583
Nisei, 659
Nixon, Richard M., 482, 690, 722, 837*
    and "Checkers speech," 704–705
    debates with Kennedy, 736–737
    pardoned by Ford, 788
    as president, 772, 776–787, 778*
    resignation of, 787
    visit to China, 780–781*
    and Watergate, 576, 784–787
Non-importation, 116
Non-Intercourse Act, 227
Norris, George W., 532
North, Lord, 119, 120, 121
North Africa, invasion of, in World War II, 664
North America,
    environments of, 88m
    French exploration of, 32m
    Spanish exploration of, 30m
North Atlantic Treaty Organization (NATO), 688

Presbyterians, 97
Presidency, 164–165, 177–181, 202–203
Presley, Elvis, 719
Press, freedom of, 100–101, 186, 576–577
Press gang, 226, 227
Prices, 274, 680, 710–711, 711c, 793, 799
Primogeniture, system of, 62–63
Printing, improvements in, 279, 488–489
Prison camps, Civil War, 349
Prisoners, as early colonists, 44
Privateers, 135, 207
Proclamation of Amnesty and Reconstruction, 360
Proclamation of 1763, 112m, 113
Productivity, and jobs, 612–613, 613c
Profit, 39, 59, 85, 227, 274, 414, 612, 613, 792, 826
Progressive movement, 418, 522–536, 539
Progressive party, 533
Prohibition, 190–191, 192, 564–565, 593, 594
Propaganda, 321, 334, 637, 826
Proposition 13, 799
Proprietary colony, 52–53
Protestants, 72
Public education, 496–497, See also Education
Public opinion, 334–335
Public Utility Holding Company Act (1935), 620
Public Works Administration (PWA), 618
Pueblo Bonito, 24
Pueblo Indians, 14, 19m, 24, 30, 626
Puerto Rico, 407, 504m, 505, 507
Pulaski, Casimir, 128, 139
Pulitzer, Joseph, 484, 489–490, 500
Pullman, George M., 410, 434, 438
Pure Food and Drugs Act (1906), 530
Puritans, 45–47, 50, 77–78, 95

Q

Quaker revival, 97–98
Quakers, 54–56, 79, 133
Quartering Acts (1765, 1774), 114, 121
Quebec, 106
Quebec Act (1774), 121
Queen Anne's War, 102c

R

Radicals, 345, 457–458, 827
and Reconstruction, 360–374
Radio, 627, 642, 717
Railroad Act (1864), 408
Railroads, 279, 280m, 322
and Crédit Mobilier scandal, 411
economic trouble of, 590

elevated, 424
impact of, 406–407
land grants, 408m
opposition to, by Grangers, 411–412
regulation of, 529
strikes against, 439, 440, 443–444
transcontinental, 308, 348, 393, 393m, 407–410*, 407m
Raleigh, Sir Walter, 33
Randolph, Edmund, 82, 85, 154, 162, 203
Randolph, John, 259
Rankin, Jeannette, 567
Raskob, John J., 596
Rauschenbusch, Walter, 523
Raw, William H., 451*
Ray, James Earl, 773
Reader, S. J., 322*
Reagan, Ronald, 520, 794, 795, 807, 808, 809–814, 810*, 837*
Reaganomics, 813
Reaper, invention of, 277–278
Recession, 274–275, 799, 827
Reciprocal Trade Agreement Act (1934), 637–638
Reconstruction, 358–374, 369mc
Reconstruction Act, 363
Reconstruction Finance Corporation (RFC), 602
Redemption, 370
Reed, Walter, 498, 507
Reform, in elections, 538–539
Religion,
anti-Catholicism, 458
effects of Revolutionary War on, 145–146
expansion of, 281
and immigrants, 452
influence of, on colonial life, 95–98
and reform movement, 523–524
and Scopes trial, 563–564
See also names of denominations
Remington, Frederic, 501
Republican party, 206–207
present-day, 325, 325c
and Reconstruction, 359–368, 370–372
split of, 533
See also Elections, presidential; Radicals
Reservations, 381–384, 386m
Restaurants, 429
Resumption Act (1875), 471
Retailing, 589
Retirement towns, 768
Reuther, Walter, 625
Revels, Hiram, 358, 367
Revenue Act (1935), 620
Revenue sharing, 778
Revere, Paul, 123
Revivalists, 97
Revolutionary War, 121c, 128–146
Battle of Bunker Hill, 129–130
Battles of Lexington and Concord, 123
effects of, on society, 145–146
in the middle states, 136–140, 137m
role of Indians in, 209
role of women in, 135–136

in the South, 140–141, 141m
surrender at Yorktown, 141–142, 143m
Treaty of Paris, 143–144, 144m
Rhee, Syngman, 696, 699
Rhode Island, 50, 55c, 120, 141, 161, 166, 835mc
Rice, 68
Richardson, Elliot, 785, 786, See also Watergate
Richmond, Virginia, 339–340, 340m, 342, 353, 359*
Riis, Jacob, 423
Riots, 764, 773, 774–775
Roanoke Island, 33, 33m
Robinson, Jackie, 678, 684*–685
"Rock and roll," 719
Rockefeller, John D., 400, 414
Rolfe, John, 41, 45
Rommel, Erwin, 664
Roosevelt, Eleanor, 598, 608–609, 626, 627*, 816*
Roosevelt, Franklin Delano, 314, 335, 598, 837*
death of, 674
during World War II, 635–672* passim
early presidency of, 606–628, 609*
in 1932 election, 603, 604–606
Roosevelt, Theodore, 498, 674, 694, 837*
and Corollary to Monroe Doctrine, 516*, 593
and Panama Canal, 514–516
as president, 502, 512*, 528*–531
in Spanish-American War, 504–505*
Rosenberg, Julius and Ethel, 691
Rough Riders, 505*, 528
Rubber, 278
Rumbullion, 68
Rush-Bagot agreement, 233
Rusk, Dean, 738
Russell, Charles, 382
Russia, See Soviet Union
Ruth, George Herman "Babe," 562, 573

S

Sacajawea, 225
Sacco-Vanzetti trial, 581–582*
Sadat, Anwar, 803, 804
St. Clair, Arthur, 210
St. Leger, Barry, 138
Salem witchcraft trials, 98
Salomon, Haym, 136
Samoset, 48
Sampson, William T., 504, 505
San Juan Hill, Battle of, 505*
Santa Anna, Antonio López de, 297–298, 307
Santa Fe Trail, 299m, 299–300
Santo Domingo, 223
Saratoga, Battle of, 138–139, 139m
Saudi Arabia, 792
Scabs, 443
Scalawags, 367

Twain, Mark, 292, 404, 490
Tweed, William Marcy, 427*–428, 433
Two-party system, 260
Tydings-McDuffie Act (1934), 510
Tyler, John, 272, 302, 836*
Typewriter, 404

U

Uncle Tom's Cabin (Stowe), 320–321, 765
Underground railroad, 285
Underwood-Simmons Tariff Act (1913), 535
Unemployment rate, 619c, 710–711
Unicameral legislature, 56
Unions,
    and AFL, 581
    and CIO, 625
    craft versus industrial, 442
    formation of, 253, 438–442
    membership, 446c, 839c
    United Mine Workers, 581
    See also Labor; Strikes
Unitarians, 281, 306
United Mine Workers, 581
United Nations, 672–673, 695*, 699–700
United States, 832–833m
    and acquisition of new
        territory, 307m, 511m
    and Bicentennial, 789–790*
    and Civil War, 336–354
    and Cold War, 725–728
    Constitution, 161–166, 168–199
    Declaration of Independence, 132, 148–150
    and Dollar Diplomacy, 517
    and Era of Good Feelings, 241
    and Great Depression, 598–610, 614–628
    and Korean War, 698–703
    and manifest destiny, 295–296, 498
    and Mexican War, 304–308
    and Reconstruction, 358–374
    Revolutionary War, 122–124, 128–146
    and Spanish-American War, 500–506
    and Vietnam War, 744–745, 759–762, 781–783
    and War of 1812, 226–234
    in World War I, 547–552
    in World War II, 656–671
Unity League, 723
Universal Negro Improvement
    Association (UNIA), 569
Unsafe at Any Speed (Nader), 768
Unterseeboots (U-boats), 543–544, 550, 665
Urbanization, *See Cities*
U'Ren, William S., 527
Utah, 300, 303–304, 307m, 393m, 478, 801m, 835mc
Utilities, public, 620
Utopian communities, 283, 448
U-2 incident, 725–726

V

Valley Forge, Pennsylvania, 139
Van Buren, Martin, 260*–261, 270–271, 298, 836*
Van Vorst, Maria, 437
Vergennes, Charles, 143
Vermont, 138, 230, 231m, 835mc
Verrazano, Giovanni da, 31, 32m
Versailles, Treaty of, 552–556, 558
Vespucci, Amerigo, 28m, 29
Vice-president, 177, 178c, 210, 213, 214, 528, 736, 749, 776, 786, 795, 797, 807
Vicksburg, Battle of, 343, 343m, 351, 356, 357m
Videotape, 717
Vietcong, 727, 746, 760, 761
Viet Minh, 727, 753
Vietnam, 726–728, 727m, 752*–753, 753m, 789
Vietnam War, 521, 744–745, 759–762, 781–783
    cease-fire agreement, 782
    Gulf of Tonkin Resolution, 760
    opposition to, 761*, 774–776, 782
    Tet offensive, 762
Vikings, voyages of, 28m
Villa, Francisco "Pancho," 517, 518*
Virginia, 55c, 143m, 163, 216, 219*, 232, 534, 835mc
    Bacon's Rebellion in, 62–64
    and Civil War, 338, 339–340, 344m, 350m, 353, 354m
    first laws established, 44
    founding of, 39–42
    head right system in, 39, 62
    House of Burgesses, 45, 63, 538
    and separation of church and state, 146
    slavery in, 44, 64–67
    supplies for newcomers to, 43c
Virginia Assembly of 1619, 48
Virginia Company, 39–40, 45
Virginia Plan, 163
Virginia Resolution, 213
Volcanoes, 676–677, 677m
Volunteers in Service to America
    (VISTA), 756
von Schlieffen, Alfred, 541
von Schuschnigg, Kurt, 640
von Steuben, Friedrich, 139
Voting restrictions, 373, 570
Voting Rights Act (1965), 763
Voyages, of early discovery and
    exploration, 26m, 28m

W

Wabash case, 412
Wade-Davis Bill, 360
Wagner, Robert F., Sr., 446
Wagner Act, 621
Wahunsonacock, *See Powhatan*
Wald, Lillian D., 430
Wall Street, 594, 596–597

Wallace, George C., 747, 756, 777, 780, 797
Wallace, Henry A., 687
Wallace, Henry C., 583
Wampanoag Indians, 78
Wampum, 21
Wanamaker, John, 402
War Hawks, 227–228, 229
War Industries Board (1917), 548
War of 1812, 217, 226–234, 230*, 231m
War of the Austrian Succession, *See King George's War*
War of the League of Augsburg, *See King William's War*
War of the Spanish Succession, *See Queen Anne's War*
War Powers Act (1978), 783
War Production Board (WPB), 661
Wars, British, 102c
Warsaw Treaty Organization, 688–689, 689m
Washington, 302m, 303, 407, 676, 677m, 835mc
Washington, Booker T., 361, 484, 486–487
Washington, D.C., 192–193, 204, 216–217, 219, 229–230*, 231m, 288, 309, 332, 340, 344m, 350m, 432, 583, 601, 657, 808, 835c
Washington, George, 92, 105, 106, 216, 217, 314, 836*
    as commander of Continental Army, 135, 136, 137–139, 140*, 144–145
    Farewell Address of, 210
    as first president, 200, 201–210 *passim*
    as nationalist, 160
    and ratification of Constitution, 166
    and Second Continental Congress, 129
Washington, Harold, 814
Washington Naval Disarmament
    Conference, 583
WASP, 295
Watergate, 576, 784–787, 788, 795
Waters, William, 598, 602
Watson, Thomas E., 473
Wayne, General Anthony, 210
Wealth of Nations (Smith), 108–109
Weapons,
    in Civil War, 341–342
    of early man, 17
    nuclear, 662–663, 671, 728, 799
    in Revolutionary War, 135
    in World War I, 543
    in World War II, 646, 658, 662–663
Webster, Daniel, 232, 267, 306, 311, 316*
Webster, Noah, 282
Webster-Ashburton Treaty, 300–301, 301m
Wedemeyer, Albert C., 698
Welfare reform, 778–779
West, American, movement to, 221–223, 295–296, 299–303, *See also Great Plains*
West Africans, 65–66
Western Land Claims, 156m, 157
West Indies, 68

List of Concepts and Skills

	Unit 1	Unit 2	Unit 3
Social Studies Concepts			
Understanding History	12, 13, 14, 38, 60, 76, 89	90, 91, 92, 110, 128, 151	152, 153, 154, 200, 218, 237
Understanding the Relation of History to Geography	88, 89	151	217
Understanding Economics and the Free Enterprise System	59, 89	109, 151	237
Understanding Government	89	127, 150, 151	185, 194, 237
Understanding Sociology			237
Understanding Our Nation's Heritage	37, 75		199, 236
Developing Effective Citizenship	89	151	185, 194, 199, 237
Comprehension Skills			
Developing Vocabulary and Mastering Facts	18, 24, 34, 42, 45, 49, 56, 64, 68, 70, 72, 79, 83, 86	95, 101, 106, 115, 117, 119, 124, 131, 134, 136, 142, 146	158, 162, 166, 185, 194, 199, 205, 207, 210, 214, 226, 229, 234
Summarizing Main Ideas	35, 57, 73, 87	107, 125, 147	167, 215, 235
Interpreting Events	35, 57, 73, 87	107, 125, 147	167, 215, 235
Recognizing Primary Source Material	20, 40, 62, 70	99, 100, 101, 113, 120, 132, 136, 142	161, 196, 197, 199, 222, 223, 226, 227, 228
Application Skills			
Evaluating Sources	35, 57, 73	107, 147	215
Distinguishing Fact from Opinion	87		
Recognizing Cause and Effect			235
Inferring Information			
Recognizing Similarities			
Understanding Time		125	167
Reading and Interpreting Maps	16, 19, 26, 28, 30, 32, 42, 48, 51, 56, 63, 65, 80, 88, 89	104, 112, 124, 137, 139, 141, 143, 144, 151	156, 224, 231, 233, 237
Interpreting Charts and Graphs	89		185
Evaluation Skills			
Comparing Past to Present	35, 57, 73, 87, 89	107, 125, 151	167, 185, 194, 199, 215, 235, 237
Forming Generalizations		147	

Unit 4	Unit 5	Unit 6	Unit 7
238, 239, 240, 258, 276, 294, 315	316, 317, 318, 336, 358, 377	378, 379, 380, 400, 420, 434, 450, 463	464, 465, 466, 484, 498, 522, 540, 559
293, 315	356, 357, 376	399, 463	558, 559
257, 275, 315	377	449, 463	559
314, 315	335, 377	419, 433, 463	521, 539, 559
315	377	463	
		462	483, 497
315	377	463	559
245, 248, 251, 254, 262, 265, 270, 272, 281, 283, 287, 290, 300, 304, 309, 312	321, 323, 326, 332, 340, 344, 347, 349, 354, 362, 365, 370, 374	384, 387, 391, 396, 406, 412, 416, 425, 428, 430, 438, 443, 446, 454, 457, 460	470, 474, 477, 480, 487, 490, 494, 501, 506, 510, 518, 527, 531, 533, 536, 546, 552, 556
255, 273, 291, 313	333, 355, 375	397, 417, 431, 447, 461	481, 495, 519, 537, 557
255, 273, 291, 313	333, 355, 375	397, 417, 431, 447, 461	481, 495, 519, 537, 557
247, 249, 250, 261, 264, 269, 270, 285, 295	327, 351	382, 383, 386, 387, 393, 394, 406, 415, 423, 425, 426, 427, 436, 442, 452, 453, 455, 456	470, 476, 479, 485, 486, 487, 488, 499, 503, 506, 514, 515, 525, 542, 543, 544, 545, 547, 548
291, 313		431	481, 519
		447	
			495
	355		537
273	333, 375		
		417	
242, 243, 247, 255, 280, 297, 299, 301, 302, 305, 307, 315	331, 338, 343, 344, 350, 352, 354, 356, 357, 365, 371, 376, 377	386, 393, 397, 405, 408, 463	475, 503, 504, 511, 512, 513, 533, 542, 545, 551, 555, 558
	377	461, 463	559
273, 291, 315	355, 377	397, 431, 447, 461, 463	495, 537, 559
255, 313	333, 375	417	481, 519, 557

List of Concepts and Skills, Continued

	Unit 8	Unit 9	Unit 10
Social Studies Concepts			
Understanding History	560, 561, 562, 578, 598, 614, 631	632, 633, 634, 654, 678, 696, 712, 731	732, 733, 734, 754, 772, 794, 817
Understanding the Relation of History to Geography	630	677	753
Understanding Economics and the Free Enterprise System	597, 613, 631	653, 711, 731	771, 793, 817
Understanding Government	631	731	816, 817
Understanding Sociology	631	731	817
Understanding Our Nation's Heritage	577	695, 730	
Developing Effective Citizenship	631	731	817
Comprehension Skills			
Developing Vocabulary and Mastering Facts	565, 568, 571, 574, 582, 586, 590, 592, 594, 602, 606, 610, 620, 625, 628	638, 642, 645, 650, 657, 663, 668, 671, 674, 682, 685, 689, 692, 700, 706, 716, 724, 728	740, 746, 750, 759, 762, 764, 767, 768, 777, 780, 783, 787, 790, 798, 802, 806, 812, 814
Summarizing Main Ideas	575, 595, 611, 629	651, 675, 693, 709, 729	751, 769, 791, 815
Interpreting Events	575, 595, 611, 629	651, 675, 693, 709, 729	751, 769, 791, 815
Recognizing Primary Source Material	566, 570, 601, 603, 604, 606, 609, 610, 616	647, 667, 668, 684, 700, 720	738, 755, 766, 787, 810
Application Skills			
Evaluating Sources	575, 611		
Distinguishing Fact from Opinion			791
Recognizing Cause and Effect			
Inferring Information		651, 675	751, 769, 815
Recognizing Similarities			
Understanding Time	629	709, 729	
Reading and Interpreting Maps	584, 587, 593, 595, 605, 624, 631	641, 644, 649, 658, 665, 667, 669, 689, 699, 701, 705, 727	737, 743, 758, 776, 779, 797, 801, 804, 808
Interpreting Charts and Graphs	597, 613, 631	693, 711	793, 817
Evaluation Skills			
Comparing Past to Present	595, 611, 629, 631	731	815, 817
Forming Generalizations	575	651, 675, 693, 709, 729	751, 769, 791

Acknowledgments of Quoted Material

UNIT ONE
Chapter 2: pages 40, 41, from *Discoverers of America* by Charles Norman. Copyright © 1968 by Charles Norman. Reprinted by permission of the author.

UNIT TWO
Chapter 7: page 136, Excerpt from *We Were There: The Story of Working Women in America* by Barbara Mayer Wertheimer. Copyright © 1977 by Barbara Mayer Wertheimer. Reprinted by permission of Pantheon Books. page 142, From *Diary of the American War* by Johann Ewald. Translated and edited by Joseph P. Tustin. Copyright © 1979 by Yale University. Reprinted by permission. page 143, From *Histoire de la Participation de la France à l'Establissement des États-Unis: d'Amerique* (Paris, 1888) III by Henry Doniol.

UNIT THREE
Chapter 10: page 222, Reprinted by permission of G. P. Putnam's Sons from LIFE IN THE NEW NATION 1787–1860 by Louis B. Wright & Elaine W. Fowler. Copyright © 1972 by Louis B. Wright & Elaine W. Fowler.

UNIT FOUR
Chapter 11: page 249, Excerpt from *For Jefferson and Liberty: The United States in War & Peace* 1800–1815 by Leonard Falkner. Copyright © 1972 by Leonard Falkner. Reprinted by permission of Alfred A. Knopf. **Chapter 12:** pages 269–270, Excerpt from *The Oxford History of the American People* by Samuel Eliot Morison. Copyright © 1965, 1972 by Samuel Eliot Morison. Reprinted by permission of Oxford University Press.

UNIT SIX
Chapter 18: pages 384, 389, Excerpt from *Once in the Saddle: The Cowboy's Frontier 1866–1896,* by Laurence I. Seidman. Copyright 1973 by Laurence I. Seidman. Reprinted by permission of the publisher, Alfred A. Knopf, Inc.; pages 386–387, From *Bury My Heart at Wounded Knee* by Dee Brown. Copyright © 1970 by Dee Brown. Reprinted by permission of Holt, Rinehart and Winston, Publishers, and Literistic, Ltd.; page 394, From *The Sod-House Frontier* by Everett Dick. Copyright, 1954, by Johnsen Publishing Company. Reprinted by permission of the Author; page 394, Adapted from "Nicodemus: Negro Haven on the Solomon" by Glen Schwendemann in Kansas Historical Quarterly, Vol. 34, No. 1 (Spring, 1958). By permission of Kansas State Historical Society; pages 393–394, "CIMMARON" by Edna Ferber. Copyright © 1929, 1930 by Edna Ferber. Copyright © Renewed 1957 by Edna Ferber. All Rights Reserved. **Chapter 19:** page 406, Excerpt from *Everyday Life in the Age of Enterprise 1865–1900* by Robert H. Walker © 1967 by Robert H. Walker. Reprinted by G. P. Putnam's Sons; page 415, From *Lost Men of American History* by Stewart H. Halbrook. Copyright 1946 by Stewart H. Halbrook, renewed 1974 by Sybil Halbrook Strahl. Reprinted by permission of Macmillan Publishing Co., Inc. **Chapter 20:** page 427, © 1970, 1971 by American Heritage Publishing Company. Reprinted by permission from THE AMERICAN HERITAGE HISTORY OF THE AMERICAN PEOPLE by Bernard A. Weisberger; page 426, Excerpt from *Happy Days* by H. S. Mencken. Copyright © 1939, 1940 by Alfred A. Knopf, Inc. By permission of Alfred A. Knopf, Inc. **Chapter 21:** page 436, Excerpt from *Bread and Roses: The Struggle of American Labor 1865–1915,* edited by Milton Meltzer. Copyright ©

1967 by Milton Meltzer. By permission of Alfred A. Knopf, Inc. page 445, Excerpt from *The Autobiography of Mother Jones* by Mary Harris Jones. Copyright 1974, Third Edition, Charles H. Kerr Publishing Company. **Chapter 22:** page 453, used by permission of Macmillan Publishing Co., Inc., From *The Melting Pot* by Israel Zangwill. Copyright 1909, 1914 by Macmillan Publishing Company, renewed 1937, 1942 by Edith A. Zangwill; page 454, From Issei: *A History of Japanese Immigrants in North America* by Kazuo Ito. Reprinted by permission of the author; page 456, Reprinted with the permission of Bernard Geis Associates from HARPO SPEAKS by Harpo Marx. © 1961 by Harpo Marx and Rowland Barber. page 456, Excerpt from *A Sunday Between Wars* by Ben Maddow. Copyright © 1979 by Ben Maddow. Reprinted by permission of W.W. Norton and Co., Inc. and the William Morris Agency.

UNIT SEVEN
Chapter 23: page 479, Excerpted from "The History of Woman Suffrage," by Susan Anthony, and Mathilda Joslyn Gage, vol. III (Rochester, New York, 1886). **Chapter 24:** page 485, *From The Promised Land*, 1969 edition, by Mary Antin. Copyright 1911 and 1912 by the Atlantic Monthly Company. Copyright 1912 by Houghton Mifflin Company. Copyright 1940 by Mary Antin. Reprinted by permission of Houghton Mifflin Company; pages 486–487, Excerpt from *From Slavery to Freedom: A History of Negro Americans,* Fourth Edition, by John Hope Franklin. Copyright 1947, © 1956, 1967, 1974 by Alfred A. Knopf, Inc. By permission of Alfred A. Knopf, Inc.; page 492, Quote from *Madame Sarah* by Cornelia Otis Skinner. Copyright © 1966 by Cornelia Otis Skinner. Reprinted by permission of Houghton Mifflin Co. and International Creative Management. **Chapter 25:** page 514, copyright © 1977 by David McCullough. Reprinted by permission of Simon & Schuster, a division of Gulf and Western Corporation. **Chapter 27:** page 545, Copyright © 1915, renewed 1943 Leo Feist, Inc. All rights reserved, used by permission. page 548, This Fabulous Century 1910–1920 by the Editors of Time-Life Books, © 1969 Time Inc.

UNIT EIGHT
Chapter 28: page 570, "Saturday's Child" from ON THESE I STAND by Countee Cullen. Copyright 1925 by Harper & Row, Publishers, Inc.; renewed 1953 by Ida M. Cullen. Reprinted by permission of the publisher. **Feature:** page 596, Reprinted by permission of Associated Press News Features; **Chapter 30:** page 601, Excerpt from *Hard Times: An Oral History of the Great Depression* by Studs Terkel. Copyright © 1970 by Studs Terkel. By permission of Random House, Inc., and Penguin Books, Ltd.; page 603, from AMERICA IN OUR TIME, 1896–1946 by Dwight Lowell Dumond. Copyright 1937, 1947, by Henry Holt and Company, Inc. Reprinted by permission of Holt, Rinehart and Winston.

UNIT NINE
Chapter 34: page 684, Harry S Truman, *Memoirs, Vol. II, Years of Trial and Hope,* Doubleday & Co., Inc., Publishers, 1955, used by permission of Harry S Truman Estate.

UNIT TEN
Chapter 38: page 766, From *The Feminine Mystique* by Betty Friedan. Copyright © 1963, 1974 by Betty Friedan. Reprinted by permission of W. W. Norton & Co., Inc.; pages 767–768, Columnist Art Buchwald.

Acknowledgments of Illustrative Material

Cover *George Washington* by Gilbert Stuart; oil on canvas; jointly owned by the Museum of Fine Arts, Boston, and the National Portrait Gallery, Smithsonian Institution, Washington, D.C. Courtesy, Museum of Fine Arts, Boston.

Table of Contents 3
Mike Mazzaschi/Stock Boston

UNIT ONE
Chapter 1 12–13 © Russ Kinne/Photo Researchers; 14 (detail) © Russ Kinne/Photo Researchers; 15 Ernest S. Carter/Museum of the American Indian, Heye Foundation; 17 Denver Museum of Natural History; 18 Victor Englebert/Photo Researchers; 20 © 1964 The Trustees of the British Museum/Photo courtesy of University of North Carolina Library at Chapel Hill; 21 © 1978 The Reader's Digest Association, Inc. Used by permission; 22 Courtesy of the American Museum of Natural History; 23 Courtesy of the American Museum of Natural History; 24 © George Gerster/Photo Researchers; 27 Library of Congress; 30 The Granger Collection; 31 Edward E. Ayer Collection, Newberry Library, Chicago; 33 North Carolina Collection, University of North Carolina at Chapel Hill; 37 Richard Sobal/Stock Boston.

Chapter 2 38 (detail) Courtesy of the Pilgrim Society, Plymouth, Massachusetts; 42 Richard Schlecht, © National Geographic Society; 44 The Bettmann Archive; 46 Courtesy of the Pilgrim Society, Plymouth, Massachusetts; 50 The Bettmann Archive; 51 The Bettmann Archive; 52 Rare Books and Manuscripts Division, The New York Public Library/Astor, Lenox and Tilden Foundations; 53 Carolina Art Association/Gibbes Art Gallery; 54 Courtesy of the Pennsylvania Academy of the Fine Arts, Joseph and Sarah Harrison Collection; 59 The Granger Collection.

Chapter 3 60 (detail) The Historical Society of Pennsylvania; 61 The Metropolitan Museum of Art, Gift of Edgar William and Bernice Chrysler Garbisch, 1963; 62 The Bettmann Archive; 66 Library of Congress; 67 Library of Congress; 69 The Bettmann Archive; 71 The Historical Society of Pennsylvania; 75 Margot Granitsas/Photo Researchers.

Chapter 4 76 (detail) The Bettmann Archive; 78 Rare Books and Manuscripts Division, The New York Public Library/Astor, Lenox and Tilden Foundations; 81 The Bettmann Archive; 82 The Bettmann Archive; 85 Culver Pictures.

UNIT TWO
Chapter 5 90–91 Library of Congress; 92 (detail), 93 The Bettmann Archive; 94 (detail) By courtesy of the National Portrait Gallery, London; 95 All rights reserved, The Metropolitan Museum of Art, gift of C. A. Munn; 96 Harper's Weekly, December 9, 1865, courtesy D. C. Heath and Company; 98 (top) Friends General Conference of the Religious Society of Friends; 98 (bottom) Courtesy of the Essex Institute, Salem, Mass.; 99 Courtesy of Massachusetts Historical Society; 100 Library of Congress; 101 Courtesy, American Antiquarian Society; 109 The Bettmann Archive.

Chapter 6 110 (detail) The Bettmann Archive; 111 By courtesy of the National Portrait Gallery, London; 114 Library of Congress; 116 The Bettmann Archive; 119 Library of Congress; 120 The Bettmann Archive; 122 Library of Congress; 123 The Connecticut Historical Society; 127 Delia Flynn/Stock Boston.

Chapter 7 128 (detail), 130 Delaware Art Museum, Howard Pyle Collection; 132 Library of Congress; 134 Library of Congress; 135 The Granger Collection; 138 Library of Congress, from original in Wadsworth Atheneum, Hartford, Conn.; 140 Courtesy of the Commonwealth of Pennsylvania; 142 Library of Congress.

UNIT THREE
Chapter 8 152–153, 154 (detail) Architect of the Capitol Collection; 157 The Bettmann Archive; 159 Brown Brothers; 160 Courtesy, American Antiquarian Society; 161 Library of Congress; 162 The Granger Collection; 165 The Granger Collection; 186 Museum of Art, Rhode Island School of Design; 191 American Antiquarian Society.

Chapter 9 200 (detail), 202 Library of Congress; 204 The Bettmann Archive; 205 The Granger Collection; 206 C. W. McAlpin Collection, Print Collection/Art, Prints and Photographs Division, The New York Public Library/Astor, Lenox and Tilden Foundations; 209 The Granger Collection; 211 By permission of The Huntington Library, San Marino, California; 212 All rights reserved, Museum of Fine Arts, Boston (Seth K. Sweetser Residuary Fund); 217 Library of Congress.

Chapter 10 218 (detail), 219 Collection of Lafayette College, Easton, Penn.; 220 (left and right) The Granger Collection; 222 The Bettmann Archive; 225 Library of Congress; 227 The Granger Collection; 228 Courtesy, Field Museum of Natural History, Chicago; 230 Library of Congress; 236 Museum of the Harry S Truman Library.

UNIT FOUR
Chapter 11 238–239 I. N. Phelps Stokes Collection/Art, Prints and Photograhs Division, The New York Public Library/Astor, Lenox and Tilden Foundations; 240 (detail) Courtesy of the New York Historical Society; 241 Culver Pictures; 244 National Portrait Gallery, Smithsonian Institution; 246 The Granger Collection; 249 (left) Yale University Art Gallery, Gift of George Hoadley, B.A. 1801; 249 (right) Smithsonian Institution Photo No. 73-11289; 250 The Granger Collection; 252 Trollope, *Michael Armstrong*, 1840, by courtesy of the Trustees of the Boston Public Library; 254 Courtesy of the New York Historical Society; 256 Library of Congress.

Chapter 12 258 (detail) Copyright by White House Historical Association/photograph by National Geographic Society; 261 (top and bottom) The Granger Collection; 262 Copyright by White House Historical Association/photograph by National Geographic Society; 264 Woolaroc Museum, Bartlesville, Oklahoma; 266 National Portrait Gallery, Smithsonian Institution; 268 Library of Congress; 271 Library of Congress; 275 AmeriTrust of Cleveland.

Chapter 13 276 (detail) The Bettmann Archive; 277 The Bettmann Archive; 278 The Bettmann Archive; 281 engraving by Cheney from painting by Washington Allston, in

Channing, *Memoirs*, 1848; **282** National Portrait Gallery, Smithsonian Institution; **284** Library of Congress; **286** The Sophia Smith Collection (Women's History Archive), Smith College, Northampton, Mass.; **288** Mount Holyoke College Library/Archives; **289** The Granger Collection; **293** Paolo Koch/Photo Researchers.

Chapter 14 **294** (detail) Library of Congress; **295** National Museum of American Art (formerly National Collection of Fine Arts), Smithsonian Institution, bequest of Sara Carr Upton; **297** Brass Door Galleries, Houston; **298** Library of Congress; **300** Butler Institute of American Art, Youngstown, Ohio; **304** Library of Congress; **306** Library of Congress; **309** Courtesy, the Bancroft Library, University of California, Berkeley; **311** City of Boston Art Commission; **314** O. Franken/Sygma.

UNIT FIVE
Chapter 15 **316–317** Courtesy Kenneth M. Newman, Old Print Shop, New York City/photo courtesy Time-Life Books, Inc.; **318** (detail) Library of Congress; **320** The Sophia Smith Collection (Women's History Archive), Smith College, Northampton, Mass.; **322** Kansas State Historical Society, Topeka; **326** Missouri Historical Society; **328** Library of Congress; **329** Courtesy of the Pennsylvania Academy of the Fine Arts; **330** Library of Congress; **335** Bohdan Hyrnewych/Stock Boston.

Chapter 16 **336** (detail) Chicago Historical Society; **337** Library of Congress; **341** National Gallery of Art, Washington (Gift of Edgar William and Bernice Chrysler Garbisch); **342** Chicago Historical Society; **346** Schomburg Center for Research in Black Culture, The New York Public Library/Astor, Lenox and Tilden Foundations; **349** The Bettmann Archive; **353** (left) J.L.G. Ferris, Archives of 76, Bay Village, Ohio; **353** (right) The Bettmann Archive.

Chapter 17 **358** (detail) The Bettmann Archive; **359** Library of Congress; **361** Library of Congress; **362** Library of Congress; **364** Library of Congress; **367** Library of Congress; **368** The Bettmann Archive; **372** (left and right) Culver Pictures.

UNIT SIX
Chapter 18 **378–379** Putnam County Historical Society, Cold Spring, New York; **380** (detail) Denver Public Library, Western History Department; **382** The Thomas Gilcrease Institute of American History and Art, Tulsa, Oklahoma; **383** Library of Congress; **385** Treasures of the West/Stella A. Foote, Billings, Montana; **389** Denver Public Library, Western History Department; **390** Schomburg Center for Research in Black Culture, The New York Public Library/Astor, Lenox and Tilden Foundations; **391** Library of Congress; **392** Library of Congress; **395** Nebraska State Historical Society; **398** John Running/Stock Boston.

Chapter 19 **400** (detail), **402** Courtesy of General Electric; **403** Reproduced with permission of AT & T Co.; **404** Library of Congress; **407** Library of Congress; **409** Smithsonian Institution Photo No. 3696; **410** The Oakland Museum History Department; **413** Library of Congress; **414** New York Daily News Photo; **416** International Museum of Photography at George Eastman House; **419** J. Rawle/Stock Boston.

Chapter 20 **420** (detail) Photo by Jacob A. Riis, Jacob A. Riis Collection, Museum of the City of New York; **421** Library of Congress; **423** Culver Pictures; **424** Photo by Jacob A. Riis, Jacob A. Riis Collection; Museum of the City of New York; **427** Library of Congress; **429** Courtesy of F. W. Woolworth Co.; **430** Wallace Kirkland/Life Magazine, © 1934 Time, Inc; **433** Bruce Roberts/Photo Researchers.

Chapter 21 **434** (detail) Library of Congress; **435** Brown Brothers; **437** Library of Congress; **440** Library of Congress; **441** Library of Congress; **445** The Archives of Labor and Urban Affairs, Wayne State University; **449** The Bettmann Archive.

Chapter 22 **450** (detail) Photograph by Jacob A. Riis, Jacob A. Riis Collection, Museum of the City of New York; **451** Library of Congress; **455** Photograph by Jacob A. Riis, Jacob A. Riis Collection, Museum of the City of New York; **458** Print Collection/Art, Prints and Photographs Division, The New York Public Library/Astor, Lenox and Tilden Foundations; **462** Donald Dietz/Stock Boston.

UNIT SEVEN
Chapter 23 **464–465** Culver Pictures; **466** (detail) Library of Congress; **468** Library of Congress; **471** Culver Pictures; **472** The Granger Collection; **473** Library of Congress; **476** Library of Congress; **479** Library of Congress; **483** W. Campbell/Free-lance Photographers.

Chapter 24 **484** (detail) Brown Brothers; **485** The Bettmann Archive; **487** The Bettmann Archive; **488** Brown Brothers; **491** Library of Congress; **492** Library of Congress; **493** Photo by Gurney/Theatre and Music Collection, Museum of the City of New York; **494** Missouri Historical Society; **497** Terry Quing/Free-lance Photographers.

Chapter 25 **498** (detail) Library of Congress; **501** Library of Congress; **502** The Bettmann Archive; **503** U.S. Department of the Navy; **505** Library of Congress; **508** Library of Congress; **509** The National Archives; **512** Library of Congress; **514** National Philatelic Collections, Smithsonian Institution; **515** The Bettmann Archive; **516** Culver pictures; **518** Library of Congress; **521** Sygma.

Chapter 26 **522** (detail) State Historical Society of Wisconsin; **523** Library of Congress; **524** The Bettmann Archive; **526** State Historical Society of Wisconsin; **528** Brown Brothers; **530** Brown Brothers; **531** Library of Congress; **534** Library of Congress; **539** New Jersey State Museum, gift of Mr. and Mrs. Michael Lewis.

Chapter 27 **540** (detail) United Press International; **542** United Press International; **543** Smithsonian Institution, War Department Collection/Photo courtesy of West Point Museum; **544** Culver Pictures; **547** The Bettmann Archive; **549** The National Archives; **550** National Air and Space Museum, Smithsonian Institution Photo No. A5403; **552** Brown Brothers; **554** United Press International.

UNIT EIGHT
Chapter 28 **560–561** New York Daily News Photo; **562** (detail) The Granger Collection; **563** United Press International; **564** The Bettmann Archive; **566** (top) Library of Congress; **566** (bottom) The Schlesinger Library, Radcliffe College; **567** (left and right) The Granger Collection; **569** National Portrait Gallery, Smithsonian Institution; **570** Theatre and Music Collection, Museum of the City of New York; **572** Paramount Pictures Corporation/photo courtesy of the Museum of Modern Art, Film Stills Archive; **574** (left, center, and right) The Bettmann Archive; **577** Randy Taylor/Sygma.

Chapter 29 **578** (detail) Library of Congress; **580** United Press International; **582** United Press International; **583** Library of Congress; **585** Library of Congress; **586** Library of Congress; **588** Ford Archives/Henry Ford Museum, Dearborn, Michigan USA; **591** Grant Wood, *Dinner for Threshers*. 1933. (right section). pencil on paper; 17¾ x 26¾ inches. Collection of Whitney Museum of American Art.; **592** The National Archives; **594** New York Daily News Photo; **596** © Jan Lukas/Photo Researchers.

Chapter 30 **598** (detail) New York Daily News Photo; **600** New York Daily News Photo; **604** Historical Pictures Service, Inc. Chicago; **607** Wide World Photos; **609** Wide World Photos.

Chapter 31 **614** (detail) The Bettmann Archive; **615** The National Archives, Forest Service Photo; **617** The Bettmann Archive; **619** The National Gallery of Fine Arts; **626** The Archives of Labor and Urban Affairs, Wayne State University; **627** Wide World Photos.

UNIT NINE
Chapter 32 **632–683** Walter Sanders, Life Magazine © 1947 Time, Inc.; **634** (detail) Wide World Photos; **636** Wide World Photos; **639** United Press International; **643** United Press International; **646** The National Archives; **650** United Press International.

Staff Credits

Director of Social Studies: Mercedes B. Bailey
Associate Editor: Daniel T. Kaye

Editor-in-Chief: Joseph F. Littell
Administrative Editor: Kathleen Laya
Managing Editor: Geraldine Macsai

Design and Production: The Quarasan Group, Inc.
Photo Research: Katherine Nolan